FOR THE 92ND CONGRESS

NUMBER OF REPRESENTATIVES BY STATES (U.S. TOTAL 435)

0 100 200 300 400 500 MILES

ALBERS EQUAL AREA PROJECTION – STANDARD PARALLELS $29\frac{1}{2}°$ and $45\frac{1}{2}°$
Scale 1:5,000,000

The following corrigenda record political events which occurred after the main body of the text was set by the printer. To appreciate their significance, the reader should consult the indicated pages.

ALABAMA (page 1). Postmaster General Winton Blount, a native of Birmingham, resigned from the Nixon Cabinet on October 29, 1971. He is expected to run as a Republican against Sen. John Sparkman in 1972.

ILLINOIS. An unanticipated redistricting plan approved by a federal court in September, 1971, appears to endanger the seats of Congressmen Abner Mikva (Illinois 2, page 197), George Collins (Illinois 6, page 204), Frank Annunzio (Illinois 7, 206), Philip Crane (Illinois 13, page 215), Leslie Arends (Illinois 17, page 222), and George Shipley (Illinois 23, page 231).

ILLINOIS 14 (page 217). Congresswoman Charlotte T. Reid resigned October 7, 1971, to become a member of the Federal Communications Commission.

INDIANA (page 234). Sen. Birch Bayh announced on October 12, 1971, that he would not seek the Democratic Presidential nomination.

INDIANA 4 (page 244). Democrat Ivan Lebamoff beat the incumbent Republican Mayor of Fort Wayne in the November, 1971, election.

KENTUCKY (page 282). Lt. Gov. Wendell Ford was elected Governor in the November, 1971, election. He defeated Republican Thomas Emberton, a protégé of incumbent Gov. Louie B. Nunn.

KENTUCKY 3 (page 289). Former Republican Congressman William O. Cowger died in September, 1971.

KENTUCKY 6 (page 294). Democratic Congressman John C. Watts died in September, 1971.

LOUISIANA 7 (page 310). Congressman Edwin W. Edwards, with 23% of the vote, led the field in the November 6, 1971, Democratic gubernatorial primary. He will face state Sen. J. Bennett Johnston in the December 18th runoff. The winner will face stiff competition from the Republican nominee, David Treen, in the February 1, 1972, general election. Treen, a conservative, ran strong races against Congressman Hale Boggs (Louisiana 2, page 302) in 1964 and 1968.

MASSACHUSETTS 9 (page 354). Congresswoman Louise Day Hicks was defeated in her second try for Mayor of Boston on November 2, 1971. Incumbent Mayor Kevin White, who had won a narrow victory over Hicks in 1967, trounced the Congresswoman, 62-38. The defeat, plus the redistricting plan that removes some of Hicks' stalwart neighborhoods, indicate that she will have a very difficult time keeping her seat in 1972.

MINNESOTA 4 (page 404). Congressman Joseph E. Karth was named to fill the vacancy on the House Ways and Means Committee created by the death of Congressman John C. Watts of Kentucky.

NEW JERSEY (page 470). Democrats gained at least a tie in the November, 1971, elections for the lower house of the New Jersey legislature. The results will prevent Republicans from exercising complete control of the redistricting process, unless Gov. William Cahill calls a special session before January, 1972.

OHIO 12 and 15 (pages 631 and 637). Four-term Mayor M. E. Sensenbrenner, a conservative Democrat, was defeated for reelection in November, 1971.

OKLAHOMA (page 654). Sen. Fred Harris withdrew as a candidate for the Democratic Presidential nomination on November 10, 1971. Harris, who was expected to face a tough fight for reelection, did not say at that time whether he would reenter the Oklahoma Senate contest.

PENNSYLVANIA 1-5 (pages 682-690). Former Police Commissioner Frank Rizzo was elected Mayor of Philadelphia, 53-47, over Republican W. Thatcher Longstreet, who sought black and white liberal support.

PENNSYLVANIA 18 (page 710). Republican H. John Heinz III, heir to the "57 Varieties" fortune, was elected November 2, 1971, to fill the vacancy caused by the death of Congressman Robert J. Corbett.

PENNSYLVANIA 27 (page 724). Congressman James G. Fulton died in October, 1971. A special election to fill the vacancy will be held on April 25, 1972. The 27th, however, is likely to be combined in redistricting with the 18th, currently represented by H. John Heinz III.

VIRGINIA (page 833). Liberal-populist state Sen. Harry Howell was elected Lieutenant Governor as an Independent. Howell filled the vacancy created by the death of J. Sergeant Reynolds. The Independent took 40% of the votes, the Democratic nominee won 37%, and the Republican 23%.

The ALMANAC *of* AMERICAN POLITICS

The Senators, the Representatives — their records, states and districts. 1972

Michael Barone
Grant Ujifusa
Douglas Matthews

GAMBIT

ACKNOWLEDGMENTS

We want to thank the senators and congressmen who responded to our queries with information and pictures, the state secretaries of state who furnished us with election data, and the personnel at various federal bureaus who sent along information used in the book.

We want to thank, in particular, Rob Lacy of Brookline, Massachusetts. Without his intelligence and industry the book would have been impossible.

We also gratefully acknowledge John Quincy Adams VI, Thomas B. Adams, Marie Andrews, R. Andrew Beyer, Jacob R. Brackman, Judy Brown, Elizabeth Deane, Steven and Susan Diamond, Theo Easter, Dan Fenn, Alan C. Feuer, Albert Frank III, Erlene Gilbert, Reuben and Helen Goodman, Dan and Martha Healy, Debbie Healy, Cathie Highiet, Joyce Hightower, Tony and Cathy Jackson, Kenny and Cindy Kaplan, Sara Lacy, Mary McLellan, Al Miano, Leanne Peters, Dan Rapoport, Julie Richmond, Greta Rigall, Richard B. Ruge, Joan Schneider, Michael Sorenson, Warren and Toshi Ujifusa, and Charlotte Young. And to the people at Gambit, Norman and Carol Wells, Ann Seamans, Alice Chludzinski, Kitty Dexter, and Lovell Thompson.

Special thanks go to Katherine Glover Ujifusa, John and Ruth Glover, Margaret Glover, and Tom and Mary Ujifusa.

None of these people, except for Mr. Lacy, should be held responsible for the errors of fact and judgment contained in the book.

For the history, if we may call it that, found in the Almanac we are indebted to Frederick Jackson Turner, John Hicks, Samuel Eliot Morison, Perry Miller, C. Vann Woodward, Clement Eaton, Richard Hofstadter, Henry Nash Smith, Arthur Schlesinger, Sr., Oscar Handlin, and many other students of our nation's remarkable past. The book also owes much to the political scientists, Arthur Bentley, V. O. Key, and Samuel Lubell.

This book is dedicated to the people of the United States of America

Library of Congress Catalog Card Number: 70–160417
International Standard Book Number: 0–87645–053–2
Printed in the United States of America
First Printing

CONTENTS

ABBREVIATIONS

ACA	Americans for Constitutional Action
ADA	Americans for Democratic Action
AEC	Atomic Energy Commission
AIP	American Independent Party
CFA	Consumer Federation of America
CHOB	Cannon House Office Building
CG	Coast Guard
Co.	County, Company
Com.	committee
Const.	Constitutional Party
COPE	Committee on Political Education
CSC	Civil Service Commission
D	Democrat
DFL	Democrat–Farmer–Labor Party
DOA	Department of Agriculture
DOC	Department of Commerce
DOD	Department of Defense
DOI	Department of the Interior
DOJ	Department of Justice
DOT	Department of Transportation
HEW	Department of Health, Education, and Welfare
HUD	Department of Housing and Urban Affairs
Ind.	Independent
Jt. Com.	Joint Committee
LCV	League of Conservation Voters
LHOB	Longworth House Office Building
Lib.	Liberal Party
NAB	National Association of Businessmen
NASA	National Aeronautics and Space Agency
NEL	Not Yet Elected
NFU	National Farmers' Union
NSI	National Security Index of the American Security Council
NSOB	New Senate Office Building
NREP	*New Republic* magazine Rating Index
OEO	Office of Economic Opportunity
OSOB	Old Senate Office Building
P.O.	Post Office
POD	Post Office Department
PF	Peace and Freedom Party
R	Republican
Rank. Mbr.	Ranking Member
Sub.	Subcommittee
Sel. Com.	Select Committee
Sp. Com.	Special Committee
SW	Socialist Worker Party
USAF	United States Air Force
USAFR	United States Air Force Reserve
USMC	United States Marine Corps
USMCR	United States Marine Corps Reserve

INTRODUCTION—A Capitol Hill Scorecard

You can't tell the players without a scorecard. This maxim is especially true when: (1) there are 535 of them; (2) the name of the game is power; (3) and the arena is Congress, the forum in which the economic and ideological conflicts of what remains the most powerful nation on earth are resolved—or at least sublimated into votes.

Up until now, however, there has been no single source to help the interested citizen make sense of the flux and confusion of Capitol Hill politics. All the information needed to prepare such a reference has been available; but it has been scattered through various arcane government publications, submerged in the media torrent, and locked in the frontal lobes of various insiders. Assembling even the most elementary information on legislators' performance has often required time-consuming and persistent effort by practiced researchers. The result has been not so much invisibility for our congressmen and senators as a dense smog shrouding them, from which one or another bobs up occasionally.

This book is an effort to clear away some of the vapors and enable Americans to keep at least rudimentary track of their legislators' performance in the high-stakes game of national government. Between these covers, you will find, for the first time, a systematic attempt to set down the essential politics of every nook and cranny of our vast land and to illuminate the behavior of each of the 535 men and women who represent them. The object is to convey enough information to enable you to take the measure of the men and women who run the legislative branch of the federal government. We like to think that making these judgments is a matter of some interest to all Americans, since the character and survival of the Republic depend to no small extent on our collective ability to do so.

If we have done our job well, a flip through these pages is the best way of understanding what we have produced. Nevertheless, some background explanation of the enterprise is necessary.

The *Almanac* was put together by a Democrat, an independent, and a Republican, all of us in our mid-twenties. Each of us has been involved in politics in some way or another—among other roles as campaign worker, fund raiser, political magazine editor, and even candidate—but none can be considered Congressional insiders, although we have drawn on some for guidance and assistance. We are neither radical nor reactionary, but on balance should be ranked more "liberal" than "conservative."

In order to minimize, or at least isolate, the effect of personal bias and maximize comprehensibility, we have divided the *Almanac* into two data and two prose sections. The first part of the data concerns the individual legislator. It provides a succinct biography of him, describes his relative position in the committee-seniority pecking order, names which lobby groups are his friends and which his foes, profiles his voting record, and tells how to get in touch with him. The other data section describes the legislator's constituency and lays out the political, economic, and demographic ABC's of his state or district. This last information is vital to any understanding of the behavior of *homo politicus.*

These two sections are as neutral as numbers can be. In contrast, the two prose sections are descriptive and analytical, and therefore neutral only to the degree attainable by human frailty, however sincerely intentioned and disciplined by professional standards. The first prose part provides a political overview of each state. It represents the conclusions of informed analysts about what are the most important elements of each state's politics, of what makes the state tick politically. Special attention is here given to the state's senatorial politics. These write-ups may suffer from some of the same defects of compression as do weekly newsmagazines and 30-page histories of China; but they are, we hope, the accurate distillations of extensive research. You will probably find it helpful to read the state write-up before proceeding to any individual district. These district write-ups, the second kind of prose commentary, take the same approach for each congressman and his district. Each write-up will tell you whence he came and by what route and assay his chances for political longevity. In all these analyses, we have circumscribed our perceptions only by the standards of responsible journalism, a profession which remains the first love of each of us.

One important point. There are without doubt errors—some of them glaring—in a work of this size, despite the immense amount of time spent checking, cross-checking, and re-checking the manuscript. It is our fervent hope and somewhat arrogant faith, however, that they are errors of detail rather than of conception. To be sure, our way of looking at things can be honestly attacked; but we feel that they can likewise be defended. Whatever the case, we are especially eager to hear about any kind of mistake we have made. This is because we will be revising and updating this book with every two-year session of Congress. We hope, then, to keep an eye on Congress for some time and also hope to improve our vision with practice.

We believe this is a unique book—a candid civics scorecard to be used with the realization that in the voters' hands is the power to keep or shift the line-up as they judge fit. We hope it proves of value to the American people in making that judgment, and that it conveys the drama, comedy, and excitement of the extraordinary game of politics to all who read it.

Following are specific instructions for decoding each section of the format.

I. THE LEGISLATOR—A Basic Dossier

This section gives you an insight into the politician's background, position, ideology, and voting record. It is composed of five parts.

A. Biography and Career—The Bare Bones

Here the following items of data are provided: date first elected; when seat is up (for senators); date and place of birth; residence; education and military service; family and children; religion. Also a brief outline of the legislator's career and his Washington and home office addresses and telephone.

B. Committees—The Back Rooms of Congress

Lawyers and pollsters know that the power to shape the question is, by and large, the power to determine the answer. Congressional committees, by hammering out the legislation which the Congress at large passes or rejects, do just that. Although bills in most—but not all—cases may be amended on the floor, what comes out of committee remains the point of departure. Moreover, there is a reluctance among senators and congressmen to alienate powerful committee and subcommittee chairmen by voting against their wishes either in the smaller units or on the floor. In the words of the late Speaker Sam Rayburn, "To get along, you have to go along." Committee chambers, then, are literally the back rooms where the decisions of Congress are shaped. So important are committee assignments—especially in the House where congressmen serve on only one or two committees and seldom switch—that it might be more useful to think of your vote as electing a man to a committee rather than to the Congress at large.

Technically, committee assignments are made by the entire Senate and House. In fact, they are determined by each party's Committee on Committees, which are usually dominated by senior and orthodox members. Probably the most important such committee consists of the Democratic members of the House Ways and Means Committee, which, when it isn't busy writing our tax laws, determines all House Democrats' committee assignments. Freshmen members—and junior members wishing to change assignments or win a seat on an additional committee—submit their preferences and attempt to muster support; then the committee in its wisdom may decide that the newly elected congressman from the Bronx should sit on the Agriculture Committee. Once on a committee, a senator or congressman often stays there for the rest of his congressional career, which may last 50 years. A switch can be made only if the appropriate Committee on Committees approves.

Inextricably enmeshed in the committee system is the seniority system. As far as the committee pecking order goes, first in time, first in line. Preference in committee assignments and accession to powerful committee chairmanships is determined, in practice and in theory, solely by consecutive time served on that particular committee. Thus Wilbur Mills became chairman of Ways and Means rather than another member with more seniority in the House, because Mills was the first to win assignment to the committee. (Freshmen are seldom assigned to the House Ways and Means, Appropriations, and Rules committees and the Senate Appropriations and Finance committees.) Two complicating fillips of the system are that a legislator's seniority is calculated only with respect to other members of his own party, and only members of the majority party—

Democrats in both houses since the 1954 elections—may hold committee and subcommittee chairmanships.

These chairmanship positions are prized in proportion to their power, which is great indeed. Chairmen schedule meetings at opportune or inopportune times and draw up agendas that may or may not have one's pet bill listed. They decide which bills deserve hearings—a valuable source of publicity for politicians who, after the phrase of the late Earl Long, love publicity like a pig loves slop. On another level, chairmen have a say in such things as who gets to go on the juicy junkets, and they generally do the staff hiring—an important source of patronage and power. In this latter regard, the minority party has a piece of the patronage pie also. It is controlled by the ranking minority member; that is, the Republican with the most seniority on the committee.

The result of this system is that Congress is essentially a gerontocracy where the old hum the tune and the young—that is, those in their 40's, 50's, and even 60's—dance and undergo varieties of rites of passage. There is much moaning about the committee system and vigorous agitation for change among the younger members. The critics point out that the American Congress is the only parliamentary body in the free world run on a strict seniority system. But despite a chance to do so in the Senate (see Key Votes section, "seniority"), not enough legislators seem to want to bell the cat, especially after they have gained a few years of seniority themselves. The system endures.

In the Committee section, we have listed each member's committee assignments and in parenthesis his seniority on the committee. Subcommittees of which the legislator is chairman have been listed first. Ranking Republicans are so indicated. In the case of Joint Committees, which are made up of representatives and senators, and the chairmanships of which rotate between the senior Democrat from each house, seniority has been calculated with respect to both party and branch of Congress. In the Appendix, we have indicated the full membership of all standing committees and subcommittees.

The following is a list of the committees of both branches with a short description of the types of bills each considers. Jurisdictional boundaries are often fuzzy, so there will be occasional overlapping. More complete descriptions of important committees' ways of doing business are provided in the Political Background sections under the districts of committee chairmen and, sometimes, under those of ranking minority members.

Standing Committees of the Senate

Aeronautics and Space Science—aerospace activities and science (except military), NASA.

Agriculture—agriculture, meat inspection, forestry, nutrition and anti-hunger programs, rural electrification.

Appropriations—all federal appropriations. Since the Appropriations Committee passes on federal spending for all departments and agencies, its subcommittees with jurisdiction over a given segment of the federal government are often as important in making policy as the Standing Committee with power over the same agency.

Armed Services—defense, naval petroleum reserves.

Banking, Housing, and Urban Affairs—banking and currency, public and private housing, controls of prices, of commodities, rents, and services, financial aid to industry except when under another committee's jurisdiction.

Commerce—interstate and foreign commerce, including transportation (railroads, buses, trucks, gas pipelines), communications (telephone, telegraph, radio, television), civil aeronautics, merchant marine and navigation, Coast Guard, fisheries and wildlife, Bureau of Standards.

District of Columbia—all lawmaking for the District of Columbia except appropriations.

Finance—taxation, including customs, tariffs, and import quotas, reciprocal trade agreements, social security, veterans' pensions and compensation.

Foreign Relations—foreign affairs, including consideration of all treaties.

Government Operations—structure of the federal government, including reorganizations, the budgetary process, and intergovernmental relations. The main function of the committee and its subcommittees is to investigate the efficiency of federal agencies; this has on occasion involved searing scrutiny of federal policies and operations in varied areas, as the decision surrounding the TFX, corruption in labor unions, and drug prices.

Interior and Insular Affairs—public lands and the minerals thereon, forest reserves and national parks, island possessions of the U.S., irrigation and reclamation, mining, oil conservation, Indians.

Judiciary—the federal judiciary and prison system, constitutional amendments and revision of statutes, antitrust, immigration and naturalization, bankruptcy, espionage, counterfeit, patent, copyright, and trademark law.

Labor and Public Welfare—education, labor, welfare, including the various antipoverty programs.

Post Office and Civil Service—civil service and post office, Census Bureau, National Archives.

Public Works—rivers and harbors, bridges and dams, navigation (on internal waterways) and flood control, water power, water pollution, federal buildings, highways.

Rules—credentials and election of Senators, corrupt practices, internal housekeeping matters.

The Select Committees on Small Business, Aging, and Nutrition and Human Needs do not report legislation; they simply study the problems in their jurisdiction and make reports of their findings to the Senate and appropriate standing committees.

Standing Committees of the House

Agriculture—agriculture, meat inspection, forestry, nutrition and anti-hunger programs, rural electrification.

Appropriations—all federal appropriations. Since the Appropriations Committee passes on federal spending for all departments and agencies, its subcommittees with jurisdiction over a given segment of the federal government are often as important in making policy as the Standing Committee with power over the same agency.

Armed Services—defense, naval petroleum reserves.

Banking and Currency—banking and currency, public and private housing, controls of prices of commodities, rents and services, and financial aid to industry except when under another committee's jurisdiction.

District of Columbia—all lawmaking for the District of Columbia except for appropriations.

Education and Labor—education, labor, welfare, including the various antipoverty programs.

Foreign Affairs—foreign affairs. The House Committee on Foreign Affairs is generally considered less important than the Senate Committee on Foreign Relations because, *inter alia,* the Senate but not the House has the responsibility of approving or disapproving treaties and appointments to ambassadorships and other foreign-policy posts.

Government Operations—structure of the federal government, including reorganizations and the budgetary process, and intergovernmental relations. The main function of the committee and its subcommittees is to investigate the efficiency of federal agencies; this can involve close scrutiny of federal policies and operations in many areas. Until recently the House Committee (in contrast to its Senate counterpart) has been considered moribund; under its new chairman, Chet Holifield of California, it is expected to be more active.

House Administration—internal housekeeping matters.

Interior and Insular Affairs—public lands and the minerals thereon, forest reserves and national parks, island possessions of the U.S., irrigation and reclamation, mining, oil conservation, Indians.

Internal Security—legislation and investigations pertaining to communists and other subversives. Formerly the House Un-American Affairs Committee (HUAC), this body has been attacked by House liberals for reporting out precious little legislation and for conducting McCarthy-like investigations. The liberals, however, have been unsuccessful in trying to cut its appropriations or rescind its status as a standing committee.

Interstate and Foreign Commerce—interstate and foreign commerce, including transportation (railroads, buses, trucks, gas pipelines), communications (telephone, telegraph, radio, television), civil aeronautics, securities and power regulation, railroad labor and retirement, inland waterways.

Judiciary—federal judiciary and prison system, constitutional amendments and revision of statutes, antitrust, immigration and naturalization, bankruptcy, espionage, counterfeit, patent, copyright, and trademark law.

Merchant Marine and Fisheries—merchant marine, navigation, water-borne common carriers except those under the jurisdiction of the Interstate Commerce Commission, Coast Guard, fisheries, and wildlife.

Post Office and Civil Service—civil service and Post Office, Census Bureau, National Archives.

Public Works—rivers and harbors, bridges and dams, navigation (on internal waterways) and flood control, water power, water pollution, federal buildings, highways.

Rules—conduct of House business. The Rules Committee is responsible for setting a "rule" for each bill which comes before the entire House. The "rule" sets the terms of debate and amendment; accordingly, a Rules Committee hostile to a particular piece of legislation can often prevent its passage by granting an unfavorable "rule" or, on occasion, no "rule" at all. This power was used with great skill by ultraconservative Chairman Howard W. Smith of Virginia until his defeat in a Democratic primary in 1966.

Ways and Means—taxation, including customs, tariffs, and import quotas, reciprocal trade agreements, social security. The Constitutional provision requiring all revenue bills to originate in the House and the canny leadership of Ways and Means Chairman (since 1958) Wilbur Mills have made Ways and Means one of the most important committees in either legislative branch. The Democratic members of Ways and Means also determine committee assignments for all House Democrats.

Joint Committees are made up of members from both houses, with the chairmanship rotating between senior House and Senate members of the majority party (since 1954, the Democrats). The Joint Committees on Congressional Operations, Defense Production, the Library, Navaho-Hopi Indian administration, Printing, and Reduction of Federal Expenditures handle their indicated subject matter without appreciable controversy, and so membership on these bodies has not been indicated. The Joint Committee on Internal Revenue Taxation is made up of members of the House Ways and Means and the Senate Finance committees: since these bodies do the actual legislating on tax matters, we also pass over this Joint Committee. That leaves two Joint Committees worthy of special attention.

Joint Committee on Atomic Energy—all matters relating to atomic energy and the Atomic Energy Commission. This committee by common consent has a very high degree of expertise in its field, and it is allowed access to internal (and often classified) information in a manner highly unusual for a congressional committee. It works very closely with the AEC.

Joint Economic Committee—set up under the Full Employment Act of 1946, it reviews the Economic Report of the president and makes recommendations and studies concerning the national economy.

C. Group Ratings—A Legislator's Report Card

You can tell a lot about a person from knowing who his friends and enemies are. Legislators are no exception, which is why we have compiled this section. The "rating groups," abbreviated ADA, COPE, NREP, etc., are all political interest groups of one kind or another. Some base their judgments on general ideology, liberal or conservative; others focus on the economic interests of the particular group they represent, such as farmers or small businessmen; still others are concerned with a single issue, such as environment or consumer protection. In most cases, the groups engage in various Washington lobbying activities for the causes they champion.

What they all have in common is sufficient interest in how congressmen and senators vote on certain issues to "grade" them on their performance. These ratings as a whole, then, constitute a very informative legislative report card on each man in Congress. Instead of marks on the three R's, we have an indication of the member's acceptability to unions, environmentalists, farmers, consumer advocates, miiltary-spending advocates, and civil liberties groups, among others. The resulting pattern is a revealing and statistically valid shorthand composite of a legislator's ideology and concerns. Many lobby groups, of course, do not issue ratings. We have covered some of their activities in the individual write-ups; the oil lobby, for example, is especially powerful in Texas politics as the prose devoted to that state shows.

For quick comprehension, we have arranged the ratings in a rough pattern, with "liberal" groups on the left, "conservative" ones on the right, and single issue groups in the middle. What the numbers represent specifically is the percentage of votes in favor of the group's position on a number of congressional votes it has singled out. This percentage is calculated by simply dividing the number "correct" by the total number of votes chosen, ignoring absences. In some cases, the groups themselves publish the ratings as a percentage and we have transcribed them directly; in others, only the "rights" and "wrongs" are indicated, in which case we have calculated the percentages ourselves with the permission of the group.

There are blanks for 1968 and/or 1969 under certain groups. This is because not all the groups have issued ratings every year. Some do so only at the end of each session of Congress, which lasts two years; others just this year began issuing ratings.

To interpret the ratings, of course, it is necessary to have a general idea of the groups, their orientation, and what issues and votes their ratings are based on. Here, then, is a descriptive list of the rating groups and what they stand for.

1. ADA—Americans for Democratic Action, 1424 16th St. NW, Washington, D.C. 20036, 202-265-5771.

ADA is synonymous with a certain brand of liberalism deemed at once too radical for conservatives and too conservative for radicals. High in the ADA pantheon are such figures as Joseph Rauh, John Kenneth Galbraith, Arthur Schlesinger, Jr., and Allard Lowenstein. These veterans of liberal politics continue to push for New Deal–Great Society legislation and against rising defense spending and encroachments on civil liberties.

Orientation. FOR: Social welfare legislation, cutting defense budget, voting rights, volunteer army, Adam Clayton Powell seating, cigarette labeling, right to picket the Pentagon, OEO funds, foodstamp funds, lower marijuana penalties, Philadelphia Plan, Cooper-Church.

AGAINST: ABM, AMSA bomber, House Un-American Activities Committee, surtax extension, Haynsworth and Carswell nominations, oil depletion allowance, no-knock, aid to Greece, D.C. Crime Bill, Nixon spending vetoes.

2. COPE—Committee on Political Action of the AFL-CIO, 815 16th St. NW, Washington, D.C. 20006, 202-293-5000.

As the political arm of the powerful AFL-CIO, COPE keeps an alert and New Dealish eye on who is voting for what it perceives to be the interests of the unionized and unionizeable working man. In its selection of votes, it has consistently avoided defense spending, civil liberties, environmental, consumer, and Vietnam war issues, but the traditionally Rooseveltian Democratic bread-and-butter issues are all there.

Orientation. FOR: Social welfare funding, voting rights, urban programs, increased personal tax exemptions, OEO legal services, desegregation.

AGAINST: Carswell and Haynsworth nominations, open shop legislation, filibusters, retaining Electoral College, Nixon appropriation vetoes.

3. NREP—*The New Republic* magazine, 1244 19th St. NW, Washington, D.C. 20036, 202-338-2494.

The New Republic, "a journal of politics and the arts," has provided a forum for a long list of social commentators ranging from Walter Lippmann in the early decades of the century to Ralph Nader today. As the '70's open, the magazine continues its mission as a vigilant civil libertarian member of the fourth estate and adheres to its reformist, lawyer-liberal point of view.

Orientation. FOR: Social welfare legislation, civil liberties, civil rights, voting rights, environmental programs, poverty programs, congressional reform.

AGAINST: Vietnam war, large weapons systems, Haynsworth and Carswell nominations, oil depletion allowance, current farm subsidy level.

4. NFU—National Farmers' Union, Suite 1200, 1012 14th St. NW, Washington, D.C. 20005, 202-628-9774.

NFU represents the interests of small-to-medium-sized farmers. Its rating vote selections are about equally divided between farm and non-farm issues and reflect a '70's version of the organization's heritage of midwest, agrarian populism.

Orientation. FOR: Social welfare spending, agricultural supports, arms control, foreign aid, voting rights, education funds, food inspection, government insurance guarantees, poverty programs, investment credits.
AGAINST: Filibusters, Carswell nomination, Nixon spending vetoes.

5. LCV—League of Conservation Voters, 917 15th St. NW, Washington, D.C. 20005, 202-638-2525.

LCV is a campaign committee that solicits money from those interested in conservation issues and channels them to candidates it considers friends of the environment. Since the votes chosen go back to the early sixties when much less emphasis was placed on this issue, the rating represents a particularly complete analysis for activists of groups like the Sierra Club.

Orientation. FOR: clean water and air funds, wilderness areas, mass transportation, strict auto pollution standards.
AGAINST: SST, timbering in national forests, Army Corps of Engineers canal and dam construction, Vietnam defoliation, billboards.

6. CFA—The Consumer Federation of America, 1012 14th St. NW, Washington, D.C. 20005, 202-737-3732.

CFA is a group spawned in the mid-sixties as a pro-consumer counterweight to various business-oriented lobbies felt to be all too successful in their efforts to load the market odds. The group lobbies for various pro-consumer activities and attempts to serve a clearing-house function for various consumer allies. Its vote selection comprises about 40 House and Senate votes from 1967 to the present.

Orientation. FOR: auto, toy, and other product safety, OEO legal services, right to sue states, strict gas pipeline standards, strict meat inspection, government mortgage funds, strong cigarette warnings, Railpax, public TV funds.
AGAINST: SST, newspaper antitrust exemption, unsolicited credit cards, high interest loans.

7. NAB—National Association of Businessmen, 1000 Connecticut Ave. Bldg., Washington, D.C. 20036, 202-296-5773.

Each year, NAB presents to high-NAB-vote-scoring members of Congress a small golden bulldog, its "Watchdog of the Treasury Award," which pretty well sums up its point of view. NAB's "economy voting record" measures a legislator's espousal of economy in government as reflected in his votes against funding for many types of legislation involving spending, which NAB feels to have less long-run beneficial effect than would a cut in spending.

Orientation. FOR: surtax extension, foreign aid cuts, NASA cuts, military spending cuts, Nixon spending vetoes, social welfare spending cuts, etc.
AGAINST: National Debt limit increases, poverty program supplements, social security increases, federal salary increases, food stamp allowance increases, more congressional employees, etc.

8. NSI—National Security Index of the American Security Council, 1101 17th St. NW, Washington, D.C. 20036, 202-296-4587.

Founded in 1955, NSI feels that American security is best served by vigorous support for anti-Communist countries around the world and continued increases in monies for the maintenance and development of large weapons systems. The Council enjoys the support of a number of individuals prominent in the military and in business, as well as a base of about 1700 companies who contribute dues based on the number of employees. The rating index, which covers 1969 and 1970, lists 20 major votes in various military and internal control issues; the rating singles out congressmen and senators active in "Members of Congress for Peace through Law," a group which favors a lower level of defense spending. The group's special notation has not been retained by us.

Orientation. FOR: ABM, C-5A transport plane, AMSA bomber, aid to South Korea and Taiwan, Subversive Activities Control Board funding, House Un-American Activities Committee funds, more power to classify information.
AGAINST: Cooper-Church, Pentagon picketing right, exports to Communist countries.

9. ACA—Americans for Constitutional Action, 955 L'Enfant Plaza North SW, Suite 1000, Washington, D.C. 20024, 202-484-5525.

ACA is "firmly convinced that if a significant number of dedicated and determined constitutional conservatives are elected to the Congress of the United States, they will retard, and eventually reverse, the massive movement of our Nation into Socialism and a regimented society," and rates legislators accordingly. ACA describes its rating index as being for individual rights, sound money, fiscal integrity, the private market, local self-government, and strengthening of national sovereignty, while being against group morality, a socialized economy, inflation, price controls, central government intervention in local affairs, coercion of individuals through government regulation, and any surrender of control of foreign or domestic affairs to any other nation or to any international organization.

Orientation. FOR: No-knock, right-to-work laws, farm subsidy limits, Nixon spending vetoes, Subversive Activities Control Board funds.

AGAINST: Social welfare legislation, busing, federal school lunch program increases, 18-year-old vote, increase in education funds, national debt limit increase, Cooper-Church, Hatfield-McGovern, urban renewal funds, foreign aid, Family Assistance Plan.

D. Key Votes—"When the Chips Are Down . . ."

Not all the bucks stop at the oval office of the White House. Quite a few of them come to rest on the floors of the House and the Senate. The question this section attempts to answer for you is which side of an important or revealing issue a legislator chose when presented with a clear choice for or against it. In other words, what did he do when the chips were down?

It is, of course, a matter of considerable responsibility—and temerity—to condense the substance of a vote into a little headline squib as we have done then translate a "yea" or "nay" on the vote into "for" or "against" what is sometimes a broader issue. Almost every vote on the floor of either branch reflects a complicated tug of war among some combination of the myriad interests trying to pry some goody out of Congress. The process of condensing months of debate, amendment, pressure, persuasion, and compromise into a 15-letter description tends to lose detail, to say the least.

Nor are oversimplification and author prejudice the only sources of possible distortion. How a congressman or senator votes on the floor is only one of the many components of his complex and endless job. Unfortunately, the others tend to be non-quantifiable or unavailable. Indeed, a record vote may be positively misleading. Many are the stories of legislators eviscerating some reform in the privacy of committee chambers and then trumpeting glowing support for the now-hollow measure in public. Or promising some lobbyist their vote on an issue if the vote is close, abstaining from the first roll call, then voting the opposite way for the record if the fate of the measure does not hinge on a few votes. Luckily, these souls are the exception rather than the rule. In cases like these, however, the only comfort to the concerned citizen is a belief in eternal damnation.

Despite these and other imperfections, a legislator's voting record remains the best single objective indicator of his position on a specific issue and of his general ideological persuasion. And most of the headlines in the "Key Votes" section are straightforward, non-interpretive descriptions of the issue, such as ABM, SST, 18-year-old vote, etc. You are either for them or against them. In other cases, we feel justified in generalizing a man's position on a broad issue from a relatively narrow but carefully selected vote.

A good example of the latter is Senate vote #17, labeled "consumer protection." Every politician is going to try to wrap himself in the flag of consumerism. What sane office holder is going to describe himself as "against" consumer protection? Yet, before passing by overwhelming voice-vote a bill to set federal standards for warranties covering goods costing over five dollars, the Senate considered several amendments that would have watered down the bill. One of them was vote #17, which would have raised the minimum cost of items protected to $25. Perhaps there are good reasons for voting in favor of this amendment, but they are not pro-consumer reasons. Therefore, when the Senate was confronted with a clear-cut and meaningful choice on the broad issue of consumer protection, we feel that those who voted for the minimum increase voted against consumer protection. And that's how we have labeled the vote.

To summarize our methodology, we have tried to choose hotly contested, revealing "key votes" on important and illustrative issues of 1969, 1970, and 1971 that demonstrated what decision a legislator made when the chips were down. And we have tried to present these choices in a convenient shorthand that minimizes the distortion of condensation.

Two technical points. The "for-against" notation conveys the legislator's relationship to the basic concept of the bill. Depending on how the legislation is phrased, he can be for a bill and against the concept or vice-versa. For example, a yes vote on House #3 is against the Philadelphia Plan. A second detail is our interpretation of paired votes. When a legislator wants to vote on a bill but finds it inconvenient or impossible to attend the vote, he will sometimes call up a colleague taking an opposite position and ask him to refrain from voting. Thus they form a "pair" with each on record but with zero net result. These pairs are recorded, but only some specify which way each man stood on the issue. In the case of specified pairs, we have listed the result just like a regular "for" or "against" vote. When the pairs are unspecified, we have listed the legislators "absent."

Here are the vital statistics on and a brief explanation of each of the 21 Senate and 15 House key votes:

SENATE

1) *ABM*—Safeguard anti-ballistic missile system, S-2546, Dept. of Defense appropriations, Roll Call Vote #65, Aug. 6, 1969.

The first and most fateful vote on the controversial ABM issue was on an amendment to delete funds for further research, development, and procurement of the Nixon administration's Safeguard system. This was the first major confrontation between the Senate and the Nixon administration. Defeated 50–50, with a tie-breaking vote cast by Vice-President Agnew. Yea = AGAINST ABM, Nay = FOR ABM.

2) *SST*—Supersonic transport plane, HJRes 468, Continuing Dept. of Transportation appropriations, Roll Call Vote #30, March 24, 1971.

An amendment to a bill providing continuing appropriations for the Dept. of Transportation for fiscal 1971 providing $289 million for further development of the supersonic transport plane. A particularly bitter and heavily lobbied fight. Defeated 46–51. Yea = FOR SST, Nay = AGAINST SST.

3) *Busing*—Use of federal funds to force school districts to bus students if necessary to achieve racial balance, HR 16916, Office of Education appropriations, Roll Call Vote #171, June 24, 1970.

An amendment to delete language in a House-passed version of the bill which would have prevented the use of federal funds to force desegregated school districts to institute busing plans. Passed 47–33. Yea = FOR busing, Nay = AGAINST busing.

4) *Tob Sub*—Tobacco support funds, HR 17923, Dept. of Agriculture appropriations, Roll Call Vote #226, July 8, 1970.

Amendment to prohibit use of fiscal 1971 agriculture appropriations to support tobacco prices and promote the use of tobacco. Defeated 15–52. Yea = FOR tobacco subsidies, Nay = AGAINST tobacco subsidies.

5) *Carswell*—Supreme Court nomination, Roll Call Vote #122, April 8, 1970.

President Nixon's nomination of G. Harrold Carswell as an associate justice of the Supreme Court. Debate centered around his judicial and ethical qualifications, which many felt were thin. Defeated, 45–51. Yea = FOR Carswell, Nay = AGAINST Carswell.

6) *No-Knock*—Police search authority, S 3246, Controlled Dangerous Substances Act, Roll Call Vote #12, Jan. 27, 1970.

Vote to delete controversial "no-knock" section of Controlled Dangerous Substances Act which would allow police to obtain a search warrant giving them power to enter a dwelling without notice if they believe giving notice would endanger officers or lead to the destruction of evidence. Defeated 35–50. Yea = AGAINST no-knock, Nay = FOR no-knock.

7) *Seniorty*—HR 17654, Congressional Reform Bill, Roll Call Vote #355, Oct. 6, 1970.

Vote to amend Congressional Reform Act to provide that the chairman and ranking minority members of Senate committees be chosen by majority vote of the members of their own party on the committee. Committee chairmen, who wield enormous power, are now chosen purely by the length of service without regard to any other qualifications. Although this does keep peace in the congressional family, it often entrenches men unrepresentative of the electorate at large and even out of line with the sentiments of their own party. Many feel that the seniority system is the biggest obstacle to meaningful and much needed congressional reform. Defeated, 22–46. Yea = FOR seniority, Nay = AGAINST seniority.

8) *Phil Pln*—Philadelphia Plan, HR 15209, supplemental appropriations bill, Roll Call Vote #274, Dec. 22, 1969.

A motion to delete rider amendment to a supplemental appropriations bill which would have killed the Nixon Administration's Philadelphia Plan. The plan gives the federal government power to force the hiring of minority workers on federally financed construction projects. This proposal was not enthusiastically embraced by the various construction unions, which are overwhelmingly white. Passed, 39–29. Yea = FOR Philadelphia Plan, Nay = AGAINST Philadelphia Plan.

9) *Vol Army*—Fund for volunteer army, HR 17123, Dept. of Defense appropriations, Roll Call Vote #272, Aug. 26, 1970.

Amendment to raise military pay scales to a level that would attract enough volunteers to make the draft unnecessary after mid-1971. Opposed by Nixon Administration, which in the past had repeatedly professed ideological support for it, on grounds that the draft was still needed for Vietnam and proposed reform would be inflationary. Defeated, 35–52. Yea = FOR volunteer army, Nay = AGAINST volunteer army.

10) *Prison* $—Prison construction funds, HR 17525, Dept. of Justice appropriations, Roll Call Vote #269, Aug. 24, 1970.

Amendment to increase from $22,350,000 to $26,155,000 the appropriations for Federal Bureau of Prisons facilities construction. The additional funds were to be used to design a new prison in San Francisco and to build a women's prison in Arizona. Defeated, 27–41. Yea = FOR prison construction funds, Nay = AGAINST prison construction funds.

11) *Cut Mil* $—Military spending limit, HR 17123, Dept. of Defense appropriations, Roll Call Vote #276, Aug. 28, 1970.

Amendment to limit all Dept. of Defense appropriations to a $66 billion ceiling in fiscal 1971. This amounted to a $5.2 billion cut in the proposed $71.2 billion budget. Defeated, 31–42. Yea = FOR cutting military budget, Nay = AGAINST cutting military budget.

12) *Defoliatn*—Use of plant killing chemicals in Vietnam, HR 17123, Dept. of Defense procurement appropriations, Roll Call Vote #272, Aug. 26, 1970.

Amendment to prohibit use of any funds for military operations involving "anti-plant chemicals." Specifically aimed at the vast Vietnam defoliation program, the bill sought to stop what many feel is permanent damage to the ecology caused by the use of herbicides to destroy food supplies believed used by the enemy and to clear trails. Defeated, 22–62. Yea = AGAINST defoliation, Nay = FOR defoliation.

13) *18-Yr-Vote*—18-year-old franchise, HR 4249, Voting Rights bill, Roll Call Vote #96, March 11, 1970.

Motion to strike amendment to Voting Rights bill prohibiting denial of right to vote in all elections to anyone 18 years old or over if the person is otherwise qualified. Defeated, 21–62. Yea = AGAINST 18-year-old vote. Nay = FOR 18-year-old vote.

14) *Pentg PR*—Pentagon public relations funds, HR 19590, Dept. of Defense appropriations, Roll Call #416, Dec. 8, 1970.

Amendment to reduce funds for Dept. of Defense public relations from $30.4 million to $20 million. This amendment was considered before the running of the controversial CBS expose on Pentagon public relations, "The Selling of the Pentagon." That and the closeness of the vote make this in our opinion one of the most interesting and revealing votes of 1970. Defeated, 44–46. Yea = AGAINST Pentagon PR, Nay = FOR Pentagon PR.

15) *Coop-Church*—Cooper-Church amendment to limit Presidential authority to conduct Cambodia military operations, HR 15628, Foreign Military Sales bill, Roll Call Vote #195, June 30, 1970.

Amendment by Senators Cooper and Church to Foreign Military Sales portion of Dept. of Defense appropriations, which prohibited the use of funds without specific congressional authorization after June 30, 1970, for retaining U.S. troops in Cambodia, for supporting U.S. personnel who furnish military instruction or combat support for Cambodian forces, for implementing any contract or agreement to provide such instruction or support, or for conducting air activity in direct support of Cambodian forces. This bill was introduced as part of the reaction to the Cambodian invasion. Passed, 58–37. Yea = FOR Cooper-Church, Nay = AGAINST Cooper-Church.

16) *Cut Oil Dpltn*—Reduction of proposed 23% depletion allowance on oil and gas to 20%, HR 13270, Tax Reform bill, Roll Call #162, Dec. 1, 1969.

Amendment to Tax Reform bill to reduce depletion allowance on oil and gas from 23% to 20% per year. Opposed by the very powerful oil lobby, naturally enough. Defeated, 38–52. Yea = FOR cutting oil depletion allowance, Nay = AGAINST cutting oil depletion allowance.

17) *Consumer Prot*—Consumer protection, S 3074, Warranty Regulation bill, Roll Call Vote #210, July 1, 1970.

Motion to table amendment to bill setting federal standards for warranties covering all goods that cost $5.00 or more which would have raised the minimum cost covered to $25. Passage of this amendment would have diluted the measures effectiveness considerably. Motion to table passed 47–26. Yea = FOR consumer protection, Nay = AGAINST consumer protection.

18) *Farm Sub Limit*—Farm subsidies limit, HR 17923, Dept. of Agriculture appropriations, Roll Call Vote #221, July 8, 1970.

Amendment to Dept. of Agriculture appropriations to limit price support payments made from funds appropriated by the bill to a maximum of $20,000 per producer per year. Some individuals were receiving six-figure bonanzas for not growing crops. Passed 40–35. Yea = FOR farm subsidy limits. Nay = AGAINST farm subsidy limits.

19) *Comp Bid Sales*—Mandatory competitive bidding on disposals of commodities from national stockpile, HR 16291, Disposals from stockpile, Roll Call Vote #112, April 2, 1970.

Amendment to bill authorizing disposal of corundum from national stockpile. The General Services Administration, which supervises such sales, wished to retain authority to use non-bid selling procedures. Approval of this clause for corundum disposal paved the way for its inclusion in similar bills for other commodities. Passed, 34–33. Yea = FOR competitive bidding, Nay = AGAINST competitive bidding.

20) *Pre-Prod Tests*—Pre-production tests of military hardware, HR 17123, Dept. of Defense procurement, Roll Call Vote #258, Aug. 17, 1970.

Amendment to Dept. of Defense procurement bill to require the Pentagon to implement a "fly-before-you-buy" policy recommended by a blue-ribbon commission studying the department and endorsed by Secretary of Defense Laird. The amendment required the department to report to the Armed Services Committee that certain pre-production conditions had been met before funds could be authorized or appropriated for production of weapons systems. Defeated, 22–43. Yea = FOR pre-production testing, Nay = AGAINST pre-production testing.

21) *Cut Marjna Pen*—Reduction of penalties for possession and certain sales of marijuana, S 3246, Dangerous Drugs Act, Roll Call Vote #20, Jan. 28, 1970.

Amendment to Dangerous Drugs Act reducing the bill's penalties for possession of marijuana; for second offenses by small distributors for no profit; and for large-scale distribution. Defeated 24–58. Yea = FOR marijuana penalty reduction, Nay = AGAINST marijuana penalty reduction.

HOUSE

1) *ABM*—Safeguard anti-ballistic missile system, HR 14000, Defense Procurement Authorization, Roll Call Vote #199, Oct. 3, 1969.

Motion to recommit bill to Armed Services Committee with instructions to delete $345.5 million for procurement and $400.9 million for research in the bill for the ABM. Defeated 92–271. Yea = AGAINST ABM, Nay = FOR ABM.

2) *SST*—Supersonic transport plane, HR 8190, Second Supplemental Appropriations bill, Roll Call Vote # 90, May 12, 1971.

Amendment providing that $85.3 million contained in the bill for termination of SST be used for continuing construction of two prototypes instead. A reconsideration of previous SST termination vote after a massive lobbying campaign by pro-SST forces. Passed, 201–197. Yea = FOR SST, Nay = AGAINST SST.

3) *Phil Pln*—Philadelphia Plan, HR 15209, supplemental appropriations bill, Roll Call Vote #353, Dec. 22, 1969.

Amendment to Housing and Urban Affairs Department supplemental appropriations bill to cut off the Nixon Administration's Philadelphia plan, which gave the federal government the power essentially to force the hiring of minority workers on federally financed construction projects. This proposal was not enthusiastically embraced by the various construction unions, which are overwhelmingly white. Defeated, 156–208. Yea = AGAINST Philadelphia plan, Nay = FOR Philadelphia plan.

4) *No-Knock*—Police Search Authority, HR 16196, D.C. Crime bill, Roll Call Vote #56, March 19, 1970.

A bill to provide a separate, local court system for the District of Columbia and to make substantial revisions in D.C. criminal procedures. The most controversial and debated feature of the bill was the "no-knock" clause, roundly opposed by civil libertarians. It gives police the authority to obtain a search warrant giving them the power to enter a building without notice if they believe giving notice would endanger officers or lead to the destruction of evidence. Passed, 294–47. Yea = FOR no-knock, Nay = AGAINST no-knock.

5) *Cmutr Tax*—Commuter tax, HR 2076, City Tax Withholdling, Roll Call Vote #252, Aug. 3, 1970.

Bill to allow federal agencies in cities of over 60,000 to withhold municipal taxes from the wages of their employees. One of the greatest headaches of cities with a municipal tax is the difficulties of collecting it. Proponents of this measure said that it would provide a convenient way for federal employees to pay taxes they already owe. Opponents argued that the bill would pave the way for "commuter taxes" across this country, and it was around this contention that the debate on the bill centered. Defeated, 145–184. Yea = FOR Commuter tax, Nay = AGAINST Commuter tax.

6) *18-Yr-Vote*—18-year-old franchise, HR Res 914, Voting Rights Act ratification, Roll Call Vote #176, June 17, 1970.

Resolution agreeing to the Senate amendments to HR 4249 authorizing 18-year-olds to vote in all elections. Passed 272–132. Yea = FOR 18-year-old vote, Nay = AGAINST 18-year-old vote.

7) *Farm Sub Lmt*—Farm subsidies limit, HR 11612, Dept. of Agriculture appropriations, Roll Call Vote #212, Oct. 9, 1969.

Motion to table motion to instruct House conferees on the Dept. of Agriculture appropriations bill to insist on a $20,000 ceiling on individual farm subsidy payments. Some individuals were receiving six-figure bonanzas for not growing crops. Passed, 181–177. Yea = AGAINST limiting farm subsidies, Nay = FOR limiting farm subsidies.

8) *Coop-Church*—Cooper-Church amendment to limit presidential authority to conduct Cambodia military operations, HR 15628, Foreign Military Sales bill, Roll Call Vote #208, July 9, 1970.

Motion to instruct House conferees to agree to the Senate Cooper-Church amendment, which prohibited the use of funds without specific congressional authorization after June 30, 1970, for retaining U.S. troops in Cambodia, for supporting U.S. personnel who furnish military instruction or combat support for Cambodian forces, for implementing any contract or agreement to provide such instruction or support, or for conducting air activities in direct support of Cambodian forces. This bill was introduced as part of the reaction to the Cambodian invasion. Defeated 237–153. Yea = AGAINST Cooper-Church, Nay = FOR Cooper-Church.

9) *Family Asst*—Family Assistance Plan, HR 16311, Welfare Reform bill, Roll Call Vote #83, April 16, 1970.

Bill to abolish the present welfare system—the Aid to Families with Dependent Children Program—with its wide variations in state standards and payments and replace it with a national minimum payment of $1600 a year. Passed, 243–155. Yea = FOR Family Assistance Plan, Nay = AGAINST Family Assistance Plan.

10) *Work Stamps*—Food Stamp work clause, HR 18582, Food Stamps, Roll Call Vote #454, Dec. 30, 1970.

Bill to authorize continuation of the food stamp program. The bill contained a provision denying food stamps to any adult who refused to accept an offer of any job, which many commentators found unfair and drastic. The procedural vote which allowed the measure to be brought to the floor prevented amendments to strike the clause. Passed 148–126. Yea = FOR work clause, Nay = AGAINST work clause.

11) *Clean Water* $—Funds to fight water pollution, HR 14159, Public Works Atomic Energy Commission appropriations, Roll Call Vote #209, Oct. 8, 1969.

Procedural motion moving the previous question on the bill, thereby cutting off further amendments. Conservationists had prepared an amendment providing for over a billion dollars to be devoted to assuring clean water. Passed 215–187. Yea = AGAINST clean water funds, Nay = FOR clean water funds.

12) *Mig Wrkrs Comp*—Unemployment compensation for migrant workers, HR 14705, Unemployment Compensation, Roll Call Vote #231, July 23, 1970.

Motion to recommit a House-Senate Conference report on a bill to expand coverage of the federal-state unemployment compensation program with instructions that the conferees add a Senate provision extending coverage to farm laborers employed by persons who employ eight or more workers for 26 or more weeks of the calendar year. Defeated, 170–219. Yea = FOR migrant workers compensation, Nay = AGAINST migrant workers compensation.

13) *Jets to Chiang*—Funds for a new squadron of F-4D jet aircraft for Nationalist China, HR 14580, foreign aid authorization, Roll Call Vote #284, Nov. 20, 1969.

Amendment increasing military assistance in the Foreign Aid bill by $54.5 million and earmarking the funds for a squadron of F-4D jets for the Republic of China. Passed, 175–169. Yea = FOR jets to Chiang, Nay = AGAINST jets to Chiang.

14) *State OEO Veto*—Veto power for governors over the poverty program activities in their state, HR 12321, Office of Economic Opportunity Authorization, Roll Call Vote #320, Dec. 12, 1969.

Motion to recommit the bill to extend the Office of Economic Opportunity for two years. The motion would have given state officials far-reaching powers over the poverty program, whose vigor in such activities as bringing test cases against state bureaucracies had been disturbing such governors as California's Ronald Reagan. Defeated, 163–231. Yea = FOR state OEO veto, Nay = AGAINST state OEO veto.

15) *Park Logging*—intensified timber cutting in national forests, HR 12025, Timber Cutting bill, Roll Call Vote #34, Feb. 26, 1970.

Motion for floor action on a bill allowing intensified commercial logging in national forests. The bill horrified conservationists but was strongly pushed by the timber industry. Defeated 150–229. Yea = FOR park logging, Nay = AGAINST park logging.

E. Election Results—Running Scared or Sitting Pretty?

A politician can do nothing without first getting elected. And in Congress one can't accomplish much without getting reelected—thereby accumulating seniority. This section gives you the raw facts on how many votes each senator and representative received and how soundly (or narrowly) he beat his opponents. We have included not only general election statistics, but also the results of primary elections. Most constituencies are considered one-party states or districts; winning the Democratic or Republican primary is thus tantamount to victory in the general election. In 1970, for example, almost as many incumbent House members were beaten in their party's primaries as in the general election.

Also included are 1964 and 1968 presidential election results for each state and the 1968 results for the congressional district. These give you a chance to assess the reaction of every constituency to the same set of candidates. Also worth noting is whether the incumbent senator or representative is running far ahead of his party (most are these days) or is coming in on other candidates' coattails. In the political background sections we draw heavily on these and other election statistics to analyze just how each member gets elected and reelected. But we have also provided the statistics, so you can draw your own conclusions if you want.

Obviously, a senator or a congressman from a "safe" state or district will behave somewhat differently on Capitol Hill than one who must scramble to win reelection every two or six years. Generally, a "safe" seat is defined as one in which the incumbent won 55% of the vote or more in the past election. Inspection of the figures will show that most senators and congressmen do have "safe" seats under this definition. In fact, in recent elections incumbency has proved to be a keen advantage. Twenty-four of the 31 Senators (77%) who sought reelection in 1970 won, as did 87% of all incumbent House members. But comb through the figures yourself; reading election returns shrewdly is one of the key skills to understanding American politics.

Many of these incumbents have constituencies which on paper would seem quite hostile, yet they go on winning by comfortable margins year after year. The explanation for this phenomenon lies in the advertising benefits of the franking privilege and the good will built up by the ombudsman role of a Congressman. Most congressmen make generous use of the frank—Congress' free mailing privileges—to send their constituents thousands of newsletters, pamphlets, and flags that have flown over the Capitol. (To generate a sufficient supply of such flags, there is a man who runs Old Glory up and down the Capitol flagpole all day long.) It has been estimated that diligent and astute use of the congressional frank allows a congressman to send out about $100,000 worth of "non-political" material—most with his name and face prominently displayed.

Most members of Congress also spend much of their time interceding with federal bureaucracies on behalf of constituents. Helping farmers with hassles at the Department of Agriculture, old people with delays in Social Security checks, young men with the draft, and so on not only lends an element of humanity to the massive government machine, it produces votes and leads to re-election.

II. THE DISTRICT—The Politician's Reality Principle

Talking about a congressman without taking his district into account is like talking about Roosevelt without mentioning the Depression, or Henry VIII without his wives. A vital dimension is lost. To understand the behavior of the political animal, you must understand his habitat. The political and economic demography of the legislator's home state is his political reality principle.

A. Census Data—What's Happening Out There

Together with voting figures, census results are perhaps the hardest kind of data available for analysis of states and congressional districts. Fortunately, most of the 1970 census results are in, so the data is relatively fresh—that won't be true again until 1980, unless proposals for a more frequent census are enacted by Congress. Figures presented here show the population of the state or district and the percentage of population change in the 1960's. The percentage of the population contained in Census Bureau-designated metropolitan areas (SMSAs, as they are called) and central cities is indicated—a fairly good indication of the urban-suburban-rural breakdown of the constituency. Each district's percentage deviation from the state's average congressional district size is indicated. This is important, since most district lines must be redrawn by state legislatures—with the governor usually having a veto, and therefore a certain amount of leverage in the process. A district with a population below the state average will have to be expanded, while one with a higher than average population will be reduced in size. Obviously, this can have important political effects, and we have tried to predict them, as accurately as possible, in the political background sections. In addition, the number of seats allotted to each state—its apportionment—is determined by a mathematical formula from the 1970 census results. Thus in 1972, California will elect 43 congressmen, as against 38 in 1970; New York will have 39, as against 41 at present. Sometimes it is easy to predict what will happen. California, with a Republican governor and a Democratic legislature, will probably provide all incumbents with safe seats, and draw two new Democratic and two new Republican districts, with one up for grabs. In New York, where Republicans control the governor's office and the legislature, there will be a concerted effort to retire several Democratic congressmen. Other results are not so easy to predict. The new district lines in Ohio will depend on the bargaining skill of the Democratic governor and the Republican legislative leaders, and few observers venture to predict what the Georgia legislature might do.

Even when a redistricting plan is enacted, disgruntled citizens may still take it to court; this may well happen in Texas, where the legislature carefully protected the seats of aging rural congressmen. If the state has lost representation and has failed to redistrict, all its congressmen must be elected at large (this happened in Alabama in 1962); if it has gained a district or more, the new seats must be filled by at-large elections (Michigan in 1962, Ohio in 1962 and 1964). And courts may require at-large elections if an equal-population redistricting plan is not enacted. This possibility horrifies many congressmen. House Republican Leader Gerald Ford, for example, would surely not be happy running at large in the usually Democratic state of Michigan.

The census data section also includes the state's percentage of the total U.S. population—a useful figure for comparison with its share of the tax burden and federal expenditures. It also indicates the state's per capita income, and its ranking in number of people considered "poor" by the Office of Economic Opportunity. The ranking of the 50 states include the District of Columbia and Puerto Rico. Some states, therefore, are ranked 51st or 52nd in some categories.

B. Federal Outlays and Tax Burden—Bringing Home the Bacon

Politicians like to boast of how much money they can bring into their states or districts. The late Mendel Rivers, for example, as chairman of the House Armed Services Committee, claimed, with apparent justice, that he was responsible for 35% of the payrolls in his district: the voters reelected him almost automatically, usually without opposition. But politicians' claims are not always known for their reliability, and so we have attempted to ascertain just how much federal money goes into each state and district. Outlays listed usually remain stable from one fiscal year to the next.

The 1970 share of federal tax burden is derived from figures provided by the Tax Foundation, Inc., of New York, a nonprofit, nonpartisan agency whose credentials are beyond reproach. The 1970 shares of federal outlays were derived from the Federal Outlays volume published annually by the Office of Economic Opportunity. This report shows more than 1,000 expenditure items by agency, program, and appropriation, broken down by individual counties and by cities over 25,000.

Although a rough comparison of federal tax burden and outlay is permissible, a simple input-output relationship should not be forced upon the data. An overly simple reading here would violate the many complex accounting problems involved in collating the data—some so complex that nobody in the government seems to know how to explain them. An additional caveat: many congressional districts cut across county lines, so the data is not perfectly congruent with individual districts. Where only an insignificant part of a county is in district A, we have included its outlays in district B. In metropolitan areas, where there are often several districts wholly or partially within a county, we have taken the whole county figures and indicated the average expenditure per district. This is more sensible than it seems at first glance. Take the NASA Center near Houston, the legacy of the late Congressman Albert Thomas. Though it is situated in only one of Harris County's three districts, whatever economic benefits it confers flow to all parts of the metropolitan area.

Limitations on space have, unfortunately, forced us to use the barbaric acronyms which pass for English in official Washington to indicate outlays for each department. The key is as follows:

DOD	Department of Defense	HEW	Department of Health, Education, and Welfare
AEC	Atomic Energy Commission	HUD	Department of Housing and Urban Development
NASA	National Aeronautic and Space Agency	OEO	Office of Economic Opportunity
DOT	Department of Transportation	DOA	Department of Agriculture
DOC	Department of Commerce	POD	Post Office Department
DOI	Department of the Interior	VA	Veterans' Administration
DOJ	Department of Justice	CSC	Civil Service Commission

For each state we have indicated the percentage of total U.S. outlays for each department, which finds its way back into the state and its rank order of money received. The "other" category includes money spent by all departments and agencies in the state or district not specifically listed. Please check the Appendix for the national summary of total federal outlays by department and agency for the fiscal years 1968, 1969, and 1970. The percentages of the total given the statistical sections of the states were computed from the totals for fiscal 1970. The percentages were calculated from totals somewhat lower than the ones found in the Appendix because the outlays for our trusts, territories, and possessions—except for those of Puerto Rico—were subtracted out.

Obviously, the lion's share of the money goes to the Defense Department. Accordingly, we have tried to indicate just how that money is spent. For each congressional district we have listed the Major Defense Installations and Leading Defense Contractors. The installations include those operated by NASA and the AEC as well as by the Army, Navy, and Air Force. CIA data, of course, is impossible to obtain; impressionistic evidence leads us to believe that the CIA has offices throughout the country, in addition to its large headquarters in Langley, Virginia, just down the road from the Pentagon.

Under Leading Defense Contractors we list by congressional district all firms which received over $5,000,000 in prime contract awards from DOD, NASA, and AEC for material, services, and research and development in fiscal year 1970. The specific amount awarded to a specific firm in a given fiscal year is, we feel, an interesting piece of information in itself. The information takes on greater significance if it is remembered that the amount awarded remains fairly stable from year to year. Chances are, a firm doing 500 million dollars worth of business with the Pentagon in fiscal 1970 will not be getting much less than that in fiscal 1971. Like any other business concern, a defense industry has to have a predictable amount of money coming in annually.

Only DOD contractors doing military work are listed in the book. Those providing goods or services for the civil functions of the Army Corp of Engineers, for example, are not included. There are also, of course, thousands of contractors doing less than $5,000,000 worth of work for the military. For the names of these concerns, we refer you to thc Controller's Office, the Pentagon. Following the amount awarded to the firm listed, we have given a brief description of what the money paid for. If you want more information about the goods and services purchased, we refer you again to the Controller's Office, the Pentagon. Or you might write to the individual firms themselves for the information. In the Appendix, we have included the names of the 50 largest defense contractors for fiscal 1970.

C. Economic Base—"The Senator from Boeing"

Throughout the 19th century, a major issue in American politics was the tariff, and an observer could predict how most senators and representatives would vote by examining the economic underpinnings of their constituencies. Today, it is still so; the tariff remains a major, if generally unreported, issue. Usually free-trade congressmen from New England, for example, are lobbying for import quotas on shoes, and South Carolina's Strom Thurmond is at this writing still smarting from the Nixon Administration's inability to extract textile import quotas from Wilbur Mills' House Ways and Means Committee. But the basis of the economy of a state or district illuminates a lot more than its representative's position on the tariff issue. It tells us something about the area's economic health, its prospects for growth, the jobs its citizens and voters hold, and the sources of wealth of its big money men.

In this section, we list the most important manufacturing, agricultural, and mining activities of the state and district. The classifications are derived from the Census Bureau's Standard Industrial Code (SIC). In some instances we include items like "higher education" and "banking," when it is clear that these services contribute greatly to the economy; but wholesaling, retailing, transportation, construction and other service industries are not included. Service industries are pretty much evenly spread across the nation; there is, for example, no district with a sizably disproportionate number of truck drivers or real estate salesmen.

Production activities are classified according to the SIC code and the sectors indicated in the *SIC Manual*. An effort has been made to be as specific as possible and to indicate by "esp." cases when one type of production is important but not all-dominant. Production activity is ranked in importance according to number of people employed. We chose to use this criterion—rather than value of plant, value added, total value of goods and services, etc.—since it seems most likely to be directly related to political activity and voter behavior. In the state of Washington, for example, Henry Jackson has earned the nickname of "The Senator from Boeing." The Senator has not hidden his devotion to the interests of the aircraft company, which happens to be one of the state's major employers.

Where a congressional district contains or is contained in a city which is the site of banks possessing combined assets greater than 500 million dollars, "banking" is listed. "Insurance" is listed when one of the hundred largest North American insurance companies, of which eighty-seven are in the United States, is based in the city. Any state in which more than 100,000 students are enrolled, or any congressional district in which a single university enrolls more than 10,000 students, has "higher education" in the service industry description. "Tourism" and "medicine" are listed according to the judgment of the authors.

Of course no one state, let alone a congressional district, exists as an isolated unit in the complex economy of our nation. Geographical divisions are necessarily artificial, and never more so than in the metropolitan areas where so many congressional districts are situated. A man living in one congressional district may well work in one 20 miles away; and so we have compiled the economic base sections in metropolitan districts according to individual formulas which seem most appropriate to the area.

D. Political Lineup—Who's in Charge?

This is very simple—the governor, the senators, the House delegation, and the state legislatures, by party. Some voters' guides provide this information only—and little else.

E. The Voters—The Basic Blocs

You don't really know why who gets elected until you know who votes—and why. We like to think of the American voter as a one-man civics class, gravely weighing the issues and measuring the mettle of competing candidates. But we know this is not so. Voters like to talk about being for the man, not the party; but as Harry Truman is supposed to have said, "I vote for the better man. He is the Democrat." And when people do actually "vote for the man," it is often for the only man in the race they've heard of—which in congressional races is usually the incumbent.

Political scientists have shown that more often than not people have inherited their partisan preferences, and that in most elections they remain the same. Accordingly, it makes sense to analyze the electorate by blocs. One source of division is economic status. We have provided a basic Employment Profile, showing the breakdown in each state and district between white-collar and blue-collar jobholders; this division, rather than any particular income level, seems to be a determinant of voter behavior. It should be noted, however, that rural areas are usually more blue-collar than even the factory precincts of most metropolitan areas. At the same time, rural people tend to have more conservative voting habits. In American politics, not all rich people vote Republican and poor people Democratic.

It is the conviction of the authors that ethnic divisions are more likely to correlate with political attitudes and behavior than economic disparities. This is, perhaps, a result of our widely varied ethnic backgrounds; our own ancestors, going back one or more generations, have been Italian, Irish, Scotch, Japanese, Portuguese, and French Canadian. But the conviction is also a product of considerable research in American voting patterns present and past. Therefore, we think that the Ethnic Groups section is an excellent beginning to an understanding of the political behavior and flavor of a particular state or district. The percentages are calculated from Census Bureau publications. Percentages for blacks are from the 1970 census; there have been significant changes since 1960, particularly in large metropolitan areas. One Chicago district, for example, went from 20% black to 50% black.

The figures for ethnic groups other than black are from the 1960 census; 1970 results, at this writing, are not available. This may well be more of an advantage than a drawback. Because of our restrictive laws, there has been relatively little immigration in recent years, and as older people die, the percentage of foreign stock—that is, first and second generation ethnic people—goes down. Ethnic consciousness lingers, however, and consequently even the 1960 figures understate the number of people with some kind of ethnic consciousness, who consider themselves "Irish" or "Italian" or whatever. The more distant in time the great bulk of immigration of a particular group, the greater the understatement; thus the figures indicate perhaps only a third of the people who "think Irish." Because figures in this section of the data have been rounded, discrepancies in the category "Total foreign stock" may occur from time to time.

A few caveats. Some ethnic groups are more ethnic than others. There are still substantial Italian ethnic communities in this country, but few cohesive neighborhoods made up of British or English-speaking Canadian immigrants. Therefore, the percentages of the latter ethnic groups have less political relevance than the former. The census figures do not distinguish between English-speaking Canadians and French-speaking Canadians; most of the Canadians in New England and eastern Upstate New York are of French-speaking stock and form an important ethnic group. Moreover the Census Bureau cannot qualify what we consider perhaps the most important "ethnic" cleavage —the division between Union and Confederate sympathizers from the Civil War era. Much of rural southern Ohio, Indiana, and Illinois, as well as most of Missouri, retain a Democratic sentiment from those days, while eastern Tennessee and the hills of North Carolina retain a sturdy Republicanism from the days they opposed secession. In many ways, these cleavages—between southern drawls and northern accents, hill farmers and lowland planters—are "ethnic," and they carry over into politics with great regularity.

The divisions are described with greater specificity in the appropriate sections of Political Background.

III. POLITICAL BACKGROUND—How the Pieces Fit

This is the guts of the book—our interpretation of how the pieces fit together. What kind of men or women are your senators and representatives? What do they accomplish on the Hill? How do they get elected, and what are their prospects for reelection? What are the local issues, and local attitudes on national issues?

These are the questions the Political Background sections seek to answer. We emphasize that this is *our interpretation*—as accurate and perceptive and objective as we could make it.

A. State Overview—Wide Angle Lens

American politics, for better or worse, is still the politics of 50 American states. There are signs that the influence of the national media have begun to homogenize our politics, to eliminate the local irregularities and to reproduce conflicts of roughly the same ideologies in various parts of the country. But even the most contemporary politics is the outgrowth of history, and for 180 years American politics has been a thing of incredible diversity. Each state is a little political arena all its own. Even in contests for President of the entire country, the winner in each state takes all its electoral votes; in 1968 Richard Nixon won Tennessee's 11 electoral votes with less than 38% of its votes. Most states have well-developed traditions of political conflict: New York City vs. Upstate New York, Chicago vs. Downstate Illinois, eastern Tennessee vs. middle Tennessee vs. western Tennessee. Some of these are changing; others remain rigidly fixed. We have tried to present them in their historical context and to explain what they mean today.

Each state also has its own political flavor, an ambience about its politicians and the voting behavior of its residents that is not found elsewhere. Connecticut, with its straight-ticket voting habits, lies next to Massachusetts, which splits its tickets on a massive scale. Illinois is a land of fabled political corruption and cronyism; Wisconsin is as clean as a hound's tooth and has nothing resembling Richard J. Daley's Machine. Southeastern Kansas is one of the most Democratic parts of that state; southwestern Missouri, right next door and settled by roughly the same kind of people, is the most Republican part of that state. The political patterns grow in response to local ground rules, pressures, and personal initiatives; the voting public responds in various ways, and a political culture is born. We have attempted to impart something of the ambience of the 50 political cultures which make up our Republic.

B. Congressional Districts—History and Prospects

There has been a great deal of writing on the politics of the various states, but very little on the politics of individual congressional districts. (Please see the maps in the Appendix; the ideal arrangement would be to have the *Almanac* laid out next to the maps in any standard road atlas.) One reason for the dearth of information about congressional districts is that they, unlike the states, usually do not have a political culture of their own. Each one is just a piece of culture that exists statewide, and each is often made up of disparate elements. The trend toward heterogeneity has been increased by the Supreme Court's one-man-one-vote decision, *Wesberry v. Sanders.* Today, the districts are pretty much equal in size under the 1960 census, and that will probably be the case under the 1970 census. The population requirement laid down by the Court, however, has produced some odd combinations. For example, the 200,000-population old Texas fourth district of Sam Rayburn was a compact, homogeneous unit; so was the 900,000-population district which included Dallas. Now Rayburn's successor has some of Dallas County in his district, making a description of the politics of the current 4th a more complicated affair.

Nevertheless, we have tried to describe and analyze the politics of each district, and to give some information as to the impact its congressmen make on Capitol Hill. In fact, we have devoted more space to some obscure representatives than to some freshmen senators. This is so because information about senators is more commonly available to the citizen than information about most congressmen.

What were our sources? Newspapers, periodicals, books, interviews with knowledgeable observers of Capitol Hill and various parts of the country, data compiled by government agencies, funds of political and historical miscellany, and the *Congressional Record*. But the most important source, perhaps, was election figures. We examined election results going back to at least 1964 in more detail than has been feasible to reprint. We did this to determine who voted for whom, and how congressman X or senator Y got elected. Election returns are probably the most precise kind of data available in the social sciences; millions of dollars are spent to verify their accuracy, both by disinterested officials and by very interested political adversaries. The results, we believe, are almost without exception very accurate, although certain Chicago Republicans may quarrel with our conclusion. Intelligently read, these figures give us the best insight obtainable into the attitudes of Americans on issues of the day. In the book, only those candidates who received 0.5% of the vote or more in the elections were listed.

Two apologies-in-advance must be entered. We have often used the terms "liberal," "conservative," and "moderate," in describing various political figures. They are meant to mean what they in fact mean to most ordinary intelligent observers of American politics today, whatever the historical derivation. Thus George McGovern is a "liberal," and Adam Smith, whatever economist Milton Friedman might argue, is not. We thought at one time that we might be able to avoid the jargon, but found in practice we could not; they are an irreplaceable form of shorthand. Some members of Congress will probably feel mislabelled, and to them we apologize. Those who feel the labeling might hurt them with their constituents can point to their performance in the Key Votes section.

As for the other apology. We said before that ethnic differences lie at the heart of American political divisions. Accordingly, our analyses in the Political Background section makes frequent references to the ethnic composition of states and congressional districts. In making the references, we have tried to use terms that will not be offensive; we have, for example, used "black" to the near exclusion of the word "Negro." Sometimes we say "Italian-American", sometimes "Italian." In our prose, they of course mean the same thing.

The history of the United States is a history of ethnic diversity. That fact is something to be recognized and appreciated. By noting differences we do not by any means imply that anyone or any group is "inferior" or "superior" to any other. Nor do we want to imply that any ethnic group behaves, politically or otherwise, as a complete monolith. Nevertheless, some people may be offended by ethnic references, and to them we also apologize in advance, and seek their criticism and suggestions.

If we may repeat some earlier statements, that final plea stands for the book as a whole. Our intention was to create something that the American public would find useful. Our readers' opinions of our success—or lack of it—we eagerly solicit. We hope to continue publishing a book of this format for each successive Congress, and any suggestions, criticisms, or corrections can only improve future editions.

Michael Barone

Grant Ujifusa

Douglas Matthews

ALABAMA

Political Background

George Corley Wallace is the big man in Alabama politics. Back in 1958, after the young lawyer was beaten in a primary election, he swore that he would never again be "out-segged." Wallace has kept his word. As a result, he has done what no other Southern politician has been able to do since Huey Long: (1) maintain his hold on the governor's chair (through his wife Lurleen) despite the traditional one-term limitation common in the South; (2) stamp his personal political imprint solidly on his state; (3) make himself into a more or less bona fide presidential candidate.

One source of Wallace's appeal has been his pugnacious rhetoric. In 1962, he promised to stand in the schoolhouse door; but in 1963, he stepped aside and let the federal marshals integrate the schools. By 1970, the Governor was reduced to extolling the merits of freedom-of-choice school desegregation plans; but now that the Supreme Court has made it quite plain that freedom-of-choice plans will not do, Wallace will undoubtedly preside over the massive integration of Alabama's school system. Wallace, the public speaker, has a Southern evangelist's gift for words, but like his oft-repeated 1968 threat to have his car driven over street demonstrators, much of his talk comes to little more than just talk.

The other source of the Governor's appeal—both in Alabama and his periodic forays into presidential politics—has been the long-standing formula of Alabama populism: big spending programs (often, oddly enough, federally funded) for the little man. It was this rough-edged economic liberalism, as well as his strident racism, that won Wallace big votes in Gary and East Baltimore in 1964 and 1968. And it was the same combination, with an emphasis on the anti-integration planks of his platform, that brought about his come-from-behind victory in the 1970 runoff Democratic primary against Gov. Albert Brewer, the man who had succeeded to the office after Lurleen Wallace's death in 1969.

Southern populism is an old tradition in Alabama—and a politically successful one going back to the days when Hugo Black, now of the Supreme Court, was elected to the Senate over the opposition of the railroads and banks in 1926. For 40 years New-Deal-style populists controlled Alabama's congressional delegation. The group took the obligatory stands against civil rights but were more interested in housing, hospitals, and roads. Today, only two of this breed—Sen. John Sparkman and Rep. Robert Jones—remain in the Congress. The others—Reps. Albert Rains, Kenneth Roberts, and Carl Elliott—succumbed, not to Wallace Democrats, but to Goldwater Republicans in the Arizonan's local 1964 landslide. In that election, we will note, Alabama lost a total of 87 years' seniority in the House. Finally, the grand old man of Alabama populism, Lister Hill, whose name remains on the Hill-Burton hospital construction law, retired in 1968 at age 74 after more than 30 years in the Senate and after a near defeat in 1962 by a conservative Republican.

Presently Wallace's control over the state's congressional delegation is still far from complete. Two Wallace supporters regained Republican seats in 1966, and in 1968 Wallace ally James B. Allen was elected to Hill's Senate Seat. But three of the Goldwater beneficiaries have held on to their offices, and Sen. John Sparkman won reelection without difficulty in 1966. There was speculation before that election that Wallace would challenge Sparkman and speculation now that he might in 1972. It seems, though, that the Governor prefers to be king of the roost in Alabama and a Montgomery-based presidential candidate rather than a junior member of the hurly-burly U.S. Senate. But whatever the rumors of a direct Wallace confrontation, Sparkman's voting record has become decidedly more conservative during the Wallace years, and it jars the memory to recall that in 1952 the Alabama Senator was considered an appropriate running mate for Adlai Stevenson. Sparkman remains chairman of the Senate Banking, Housing, and Urban Affairs Committee. Should he be reelected in 1972, he will have the option of becoming chairman of Foreign Relations if J. William Fulbright decides to retire in 1974.

Nor does Wallace enjoy a hegemony in the rest of Alabama political life. The state's Democratic party is in the hands of moderates who have denied Wallace the use of the traditional rooster emblem on his 1972 presidential ballot. And despite Wallace, the state has more black elected officials (110) than any other but Michigan, with the predominantly black National Democratic party of Alabama having run scores of candidates in many locales and having compiled respectable totals in statewide races. Blacks now have control of some local government in some Black Belt counties, and for the first time since Reconstruction black members sit in the Alabama legislature who, ironically, represent Wallace's home county.

But Alabama congressional politics is an affair for whites only. Blacks did win the ballot in the 1965 Voting Rights Act. Throughout the '60's, however, the state's black population dropped steadily, from 30% in 1960 to 26% in 1970. Moreover, the heavily Negro Black Belt counties in the middle of the state are carved up among several congressional districts, to prevent a black majority—or even a black-based coalition—from controlling an election. Those political units that the blacks do control are economically destitute, population-losing, rural enclaves. And in some rural counties, blacks are still intimidated from voting at all.

The 1970 census showed very little population gain overall for Alabama during the Wallace years. So the state will lose one of its eight House seats. With Wallace and a Democratic legislature in control of the redistricting process, the likely victim will be one of the state's three Goldwater Republicans.

Electoral Votes 9

Census Data 1970 pop. 3,444,165; 1.67% of U.S. total, 21st largest; change 1960–70, +5.4%. Metro. 52.3%, 25.6% central city. 1970 per capita income $2,828, 49th highest. 10th in number of poor.

1970 Share of Federal Tax Burden $2,166,060,000; 1.11% of U.S. total, 24th largest.

1970 Share of Federal Outlays $2,974,620,564; 1.57% of U.S. total, 22nd largest. Per capita federal spending, $864.

DOD	$892,008,000	19th (1.55%)	HEW	$847,548,960	21st (1.62%)
AEC	$110,090	44th (0.04%)	HUD	$40,085,415	18th (2.06%)
NASA	$275,963,933	5th (7.50%)	OEO	$13,668,799	18th (1.80%)
DOT	$125,059,373	23rd (1.75%)	DOA	$186,005,882	27th (1.45%)
DOC	$9,598,692	26th (0.83%)	POD	$79,980,524	28th (1.10%)
DOI	$8,063,615	45th (0.35%)	VA	$176,735,397	20th (2.39%)
DOJ	$6,211,947	27th (1.08%)	CSC	$49,140,487	17th (1.22%)
			Other	$215,409,053	

Economic Base Cotton, livestock, and poultry; primary metal industries, esp. blast furnaces, steel works, and rolling and finishing mills; textile mill products, esp. broad woven cotton fabric mills; apparel and other finished products made from fabrics, esp. men's, youths', and boys' furnishings, work clothing, and allied garments; food and kindred products, esp. meat products; lumber and wood products other than furniture, esp. sawmills and planing mills; transportation equipment, esp. aircraft and parts; fabricated metal products, esp. fabricated structural metal products; paper and allied products, esp. paper mills other than building paper mills.

Political Line-up Governor, George C. Wallace (D); seat up, 1974. Senators, John Sparkman (D) and James B. Allen (D). Representatives, 8 (5 D and 3 R). State Senate (35 D and 0 R); State House (104 D and 2 R).

The Voters

Registration 1,625,911 total. No party registration.

Employment profile White collar, 34%. Blue collar, 66%.

Ethnic groups Black, 26%. Total foreign stock, 2%. All groups less than 0.5%.

Presidential vote

1968	Humphrey (D)	142,435	(15%)
	Nixon (R)	146,923	(15%)
	Wallace (AIP)	691,425	(71%)

1964	Johnson (D)	*	
	Goldwater (R)	479,085	(70%)
1960	Kennedy (D)	318,303	(57%)
	Nixon (R)	237,918	(43%)

** 210,733 votes were cast for Democratic electors not pledged to Johnson.*

Senator

John J. Sparkman (D) Elected 1946, seat up 1972; b. Dec. 20, 1899, near Hartselle; home, Huntsville; U. of Ala., B.A., 1921, LL.B., 1923, M.A., 1924; Student Army Training Corps, 1918; Colonel USAR (Ret.); married, one child; Methodist.

Career Practicing atty., 1925–36; U.S. House of Reps., 1937–46; Majority Whip; Democratic candidate for V.P., 1952; Instructor, Huntsville Col., 1925–28.

Offices 3203 NSOB, 202-225-4124. Also P.O. Bldg., Huntsville 35801, and 1800 Fifth Ave. N., Rm. 208, Birmingham 35203, 205-325-3883.

Committees

Banking, Housing, and Urban Affairs (Chm.); Subs. (1) Chm., Housing and Urban Affairs, (2) Financial Institutions, (3) International Finance, (4) Production and Stabilization, (5) Small Business.

Foreign Relations (2nd); Subs. (1) Chm., European Affairs, (2) Far Eastern Affairs, (3) U.S. Security Agreements and Commitments Abroad, (4) Western Hemisphere Affairs.

Sel. Com. on Small Business (2nd); Subs. (1) Chm., Financing and Investment, (2) Government Procurement, (3) Monopoly.

Jt. Com. on Defense Production, Vice-Chm.

Jt. Economic Com. (2nd); Subs. (1) Chm., Inter-American Economic Relationships, (2) Foreign Economic Policy, (3) Priorities and Economy in Government.

Group Ratings

	ADA	COPE	NREP	NFU	LCV	NAB	NSI	ACA
1970	13	25	9	43	10	57	100	80
1969	11	—	—	53	—	—	—	64
1968	0	20	—	46	—	0	—	39

Key Votes

(1) ABM	FOR	(8) Phil Pln	AGN	(15) Coop-Church	AGN
(2) SST	FOR	(9) Vol Army	AGN	(16) Cut Oil Dpltn	AGN
(3) Busing	AGN	(10) Prison $	AGN	(17) Consumer Prot	FOR
(4) Tob Sub	FOR	(11) Cut Mil $	AGN	(18) Farm Sub Limit	AGN
(5) Carswell	FOR	(12) Defoliatn	FOR	(19) Comp Bid Sales	ABS
(6) No-Knock	AGN	(13) 18-Yr-Vote	AGN	(20) Pre-Prod Tests	AGN
(7) Seniorty	ABS	(14) Pentgn PR	ABS	(21) Cut Marjna Pen	FOR

Election Results

1966 general:	John Sparkman (D)	482,138	(60%)
	John Grenier (R)	313,018	(40%)
1966 primary:	John Sparkman (D)	378,295	(57%)
	Frank E. Dickson (D)	133,139	(20%)
	John Crommelin (D)	114,622	(17%)
	Mrs. Frank R. Stewart (D)	37,889	(6%)
1960 general:	John Sparkman (D)	389,196	(70%)
	Julian Elgin (R)	164,868	(30%)

Senator

James Browning Allen (D) Elected 1968, seat up 1974; b. Dec. 28, 1912, Gadsden; home, Gadsden; U. of Ala., U. of Ala. Law School; Navy, WWII; married, four children; Church of Christ.

Career Practicing atty., 1935–68; Lt. Governor of Ala., 1951–55, 1963–67; Ala. State Senate, 1946–50; Ala. House of Reps., 1938–42.

Offices 6313 NSOB, 202–225–5744. Also 227 Broad St., Gadsden 35902, 202-546-4258; 414 Van Antwert Bldg., Mobile 36602, 205-438-2635; and Frank Nelson Bldg., Birmingham 35203, 205-251-1874.

Committees

Agriculture and Forestry (6th); Subs. (1) Chm., Agricultural Research and Gen. Legislation, (2) Agricultural Credit and Rural Electrification, (3) Rural Development.

Government Operations (8th); Subs. (1) Executive Reorganization, (2) Permanent Sub. on Investigations.

Rules and Administration (5th); Subs. (1) Chm., Restaurant, (2) Printing. *Jt. Com. on Printing.* (2nd).

Group Ratings

	ADA	COPE	NREP	NFU	LCV	NAB	NSI	ACA
1970	16	18	20	36	40	60	100	83
1969	11	—	—	38	—	—	—	93

Key Votes

(1) ABM	FOR	(8) Phil Pln	AGN	(15) Coop-Church	AGN
(2) SST	AGN	(9) Vol Army	AGN	(16) Cut Oil Dpltn	AGN
(3) Busing	AGN	(10) Prison $	AGN	(17) Consumer Prot	FOR
(4) Tob Sub	FOR	(11) Cut Mil $	AGN	(18) Farm Sub Limit	AGN
(5) Carswell	FOR	(12) Defoliatn	FOR	(19) Comp Bid Sales	FOR
(6) No-Knock	AGN	(13) 18-Yr-Vote	AGN	(20) Pre-Prod Tests	AGN
(7) Seniorty	ABS	(14) Pentgn PR	FOR	(21) Cut Marjna Pen	AGN

Election Results

1966 general:	Jim Allen (D)	638,774	(70%)
	Perry Hooper (R)	201,227	(22%)
	Robert P. Schwenn (NDPA)	72,699	(8%)
1968 primary runoff:	Jim Allen (D)	196,511	(51%)
	Armistead Selden (R)	192,446	(49%)
1968 primary:	Jim Allen (D)	224,483	(40%)
	John Crommelin (D)	10,926	(2%)
	Jim Folsom (D)	32,004	(6%)
	Armistead Selden (D)	190,283	(34%)
	Mrs. Frank Stewart (D)	5,368	(1%)
	Bob Smith (D)	92,928	(17%)

FIRST DISTRICT Political Background

Alabama 1 reaches up from the Gulf Coast to Alabama's Black Belt, an area so named for its fertile black soil (ideal for growing cotton) and not for its coincidentally large black population. The geography of the district is deceiving. Although most of its land lies in the Black Belt, most of its people live in and around Mobile (pop. 190,000), the terminal city of the proposed Tennessee-Tombigbee Waterway and the largest port on the Gulf between New Orleans and Tampa. Since Mobile County cast close to 80% of the district's vote in the 1968 presidential election, any 1st-district politician can safely ignore the rest of the terrain.

Mobile is a blue-collar town with a smaller percentage of blacks than other large Alabama cities further inland. Most of the best jobs in a city dominated by shipping, shipbuilding, and other heavy industries go to whites, of course. And the white blue-collar worker has always been one of the main sources of George Wallace's political strength. In the 1970 Democratic primary, Mobile was the only large city-county won by the Governor.

The congressman from the 1st, however, is a Republican, W. Jack Edwards, a beneficiary of the 1964 Alabama Goldwater landslide. Edwards is a thoroughgoing, though not strident, conservative. His standing in the Republican Caucus is witnessed by his winning of a seat on the House Appropriations Committee and his narrow (85–82) defeat in his effort to become vice-chairman of the House Republican Conference. Very popular in Mobile, Edwards has won reelection by solid margins against various Democrats. Since the 1st occupies the southwest corner of the state, Edwards cannot be hurt by redistricting and can be expected to remain in the House for some time.

Census Data 1970 pop. 414,048; deviation from current state average, –3.8%; change 1960–70, –0.1%. Metro. 76.6%, 45.9% central city.

1970 Share of Federal Outlays $257,941,648

DOD	$67,804,000	HEW	$82,869,007
AEC	$000	HUD	$7,337,189
NASA	$10,616	OEO	$287,038
DOT	$25,051,835	DOA	$14,094,616
		Other	$60,487,347

Federal Military-Industrial Commitments

DOD Contractors Alabama Drydock Shipbuilding (Mobile), $10.510m: ship repair. Continental Motors Div., Teledyne Inc. (Mobile), $9.053m: overhaul of 5-ton-truck engines.

Economic Base Paper and allied products; shipbuilding and repair; cotton and livestock; fisheries; chemicals and allied products. Also, banking.

The Voters

Registration 180,854 total. No party registration.

Employment profile White collar, 38%. Blue collar, 62%.

Ethnic groups Black, 36%. Total foreign stock, 2%. All groups less than 0.5%.

Presidential vote

1968	Humphrey (D)	26,206	(21%)
	Nixon (R)	11,985	(10%)
	Wallace (AIP)	84,364	(69%)

Representative

W. Jack Edwards (R) Elected 1964; b. Sept. 20, 1928, Birmingham; home, Mobile; U. of Ala., B.S., 1952, LL.B., 1954; USMC, 1946–48, 1950–51; married, two children; Presbyterian.

Career Practicing atty., 1954–64.

Offices 137 CHOB, 202-225-4931. Also 319 Fed. Bldg., Mobile 36601, 205-433-9743.

Committees

Appropriations (18th); Subs. (1) Transportation, (2) Treasury, Post Office, and Gen. Government.

Group Ratings

	ADA	COPE	NREP	NFU	LCV	CFA	NAB	NSI	ACA
1970	4	0	0	31	0	44	90	100	83
1969	7	—	—	28	—	—	—	—	86
1968	0	0	—	29	—	—	100	—	100

Key Votes

(1) ABM	FOR	(6) 18-Yr-Vote	AGN	(11) Clean Water $	AGN
(2) SST	FOR	(7) Farm Sub Lmt	ABS	(12) Mig Wrkrs Comp	AGN
(3) Phil Pln	FOR	(8) Coop-Church	AGN	(13) Jets to Chiang	ABS
(4) No-Knock	FOR	(9) Family Asst	AGN	(14) State OEO Veto	FOR
(5) Cmutr Tax	AGN	(10) Work Stamps	FOR	(15) Park Logging	FOR

Election Results

1970 general:	Jack Edwards (R)	63,457	(61%)
	John Tyson (D)	27,457	(26%)
	Noble Beasley (NDPA)	13,789	(13%)
1970 primary:	Jack Edwards (R), unopposed		
1968 general:	Jack Edwards (R)	60,318	(57%)
	Arnold Debrow (D)	40,593	(38%)
	Noble Beasley (NDPA)	4,679	(4%)

SECOND DISTRICT Political Background

Alabama 2 contains the city of Montgomery, Alabama's capital, which was once the "Cradle of the Confederacy" and more recently the site of George Wallace's presidential campaign headquarters. The city was also the scene of the bus boycott of 1956, which resulted in the integration of Montgomery's public transit system and launched the national civil rights movement and the career of Martin Luther King, Jr. The 2nd also includes most of the route of the 1965 Selma-to-Montgomery march, including Lowndes County, where Viola Liuzzo was gunned down while driving two black marchers home.

Thanks to the Voting Rights Act of 1965, which was passed soon after the march, Lowndes County now has a black sheriff, while blacks in other Black Belt counties have also been able to elect several local officials. But not all of the 2nd is in the Black Belt; the district is also made up of several "piney woods" counties, where there are few blacks and the whites are enthusiastic supporters of George Wallace. The "piney woods" counties cast as many as 90% of their votes for Wallace in 1968, heavily outweighing the black votes from Montgomery and the Black Belt.

William L. Dickinson, a conservative Republican, has represented the 2nd since the Goldwater landslide of 1964, when he beat 28-year-veteran Rep. George Grant. Nationally, Dickinson is best known for his charge that the Selma marchers engaged in obscene practices—charges which he promised to document with photographs, but never did. Dickinson is 2nd ranking Republican on the House Administration Committee and also sits on Armed Services, as befits a man whose district includes a large air force base. On the latter committee, he has been known to pepper military officials with critical questions, but the Congressman can also be counted upon to vote with the committee's hawkish majority.

Alabama must lose a congressional seat as a result of the 1970 census, and Dickinson's is the prime candidate for political extinction. The indications are that the legislature will divide the district up among its neighbors, with a few counties in the southwest going to the 1st, the city of Montgomery to the 4th, and the remainder to the 3rd. Dickinson will then be faced with the choice of retiring from Congress (perhaps to an Administration job, if President Nixon is reelected), or running against Democrats George Andrews of the 3rd or Bill Nichols of the 4th—long-shot races at best. Or, just possibly, he may decide to make the Senate race against John Sparkman—another long shot, but with greater rewards if Dickinson should win.

Census Data 1970 pop. 384,932; deviation from current state average, −10.6%; change 1960–70, −0.3%. Metro. 59.0%, 34.7% central city.

1970 Share of Federal Outlays $362,285,895

DOD	$108,112,000	HEW	$121,385,758
AEC	$000	HUD	$3,368,840
NASA	$000	OEO	$2,825,818
DOT	$17,963,810	DOA	$32,029,064
		Other	$76,600,605

Federal Military-Industrial Commitments

DOD Installations Gunter AFB (Montgomery). Maxwell AFB (Montgomery).

Economic Base Livestock and cotton; lumber and wood products other than furniture; apparel and other finished products made from fabrics and similar materials.

The Voters

Registration 193,304 total. No party registration.

Employment profile White collar, 35%. Blue collar, 65%.

Ethnic groups Black, 33%. Total foreign stock, 2%. All groups less than 0.5%.

Presidential vote

1968	Humphrey (D)	22,001	(19%)
	Nixon (R)	12,198	(10%)
	Wallace (AIP)	83,064	(71%)

Representative

William L. Dickinson (R) Elected 1964; b. June 5, 1925, Opelika; home, Montgomery; U. of Ala., B.A., 1948, LL.B., 1950; Navy, WWII; married, four children; Methodist.

Career Practicing atty., 1950–; Judge, Opelika City Ct., 2 yrs., Lee County Ct. of Common Pleas and Juv. Ct., 4 yrs., Fifth Jud. Circuit of Ala., 4 yrs.; Asst. V.P. Southern Railway System, 18 mos.

Offices 404 CHOB, 202-225-2901. Also 401 P.O. Bldg., Montgomery 36104, 205-265-5611, ext. 453, and 111 Hoyle Ave., Bay Minette 36507, 205-937-8818.

Committees

Armed Services (11th); Subs. (1) Sub. No. 3, (2) Armed Services Investigating.

House Administration (2nd); Subs. (1) Accounts, (2) Sp. Sub. on Electrical and Mechanical Office Equipment, (3) Sp. Sub. on Police.

Group Ratings

	ADA	COPE	NREP	NFU	LCV	CFA	NAB	NSI	ACA
1970	4	0	0	62	0	44	90	100	79
1969	0	—	—	36	—	—	—	—	69
1968	0	0	—	50	—	—	100	—	96

Key Votes

(1) ABM	FOR	(6) 18-Yr-Vote	AGN	(11) Clean Water $	AGN
(2) SST	FOR	(7) Farm Sub Lmt	AGN	(12) Mig Wrkrs Comp	AGN
(3) Phil Pln	FOR	(8) Coop-Church	AGN	(13) Jets to Chiang	ABS
(4) No-Knock	FOR	(9) Family Asst	AGN	(14) State OEO Veto	FOR
(5) Cmutr Tax	AGN	(10) Work Stamps	FOR	(15) Park Logging	ABS

Election Results

1970 general:	William L. Dickinson (R)	62,316	(62%)
	Jack Winfield (D)	25,966	(26%)
	Percy Smith, Jr. (NDPA)	13,281	(13%)
1970 primary:	William L. Dickinson (R), unopposed		
1968 general:	William L. Dickinson (R)	60,743	(55%)
	Robert F. Whaley (D)	37,533	(34%)
	Richard Boone (NDPA)	11,446	(10%)

THIRD DISTRICT Political Background

Alabama 3 is the southeast corner of the state, a district that has been something of a breeding ground for Alabama politicians. George Wallace is from small (Pop. 22,000) Barbour County. His predecessor in office and the man who "out-segged" him in the 1958 Democratic primary was John Patterson, from just up the Chattahoochee River in Phenix City, a one-time "sin city" whose cleanup made Patterson's political career. The district is also home to Wallace's current lieutenant governor and to Richmond Flowers, of Dothan, who challenged Wallace's late wife Lurleen in the 1966 gubernatorial primary.

In addition to politicians, the 3rd has produced large amounts of cotton, and despite heavy migration to the North, the district still possesses a large black population (32% in 1970). Alabama's two black state legislators come from the 3rd, having their political power base in Macon County, site of Booker T. Washington's Tuskegee Institute. But since the Black Belt neatly bifurcates the district, the heavily white counties to the north and south insure that its total vote stays safely in the conservative column.

Since a 1944 special election, the congressman from the 3rd has been George W. Andrews, a conservative Democrat. A gravelly voiced, old-style orator, Andrews is one of those Southerners who has insisted that we should "win or get out" of Vietnam and has ended up supporting Administration policies that seem to do neither. With more than a quarter century of seniority, Andrews is an important man in the House. He holds the number three position on the House Appropriation's Legislative Subcommittee, which decides *how much* money the House will have to run its affairs and, accordingly, often has a lot to say on *how* they will be run. He is not a man to be crossed lightly by fledgling committee chairmen.

Andrews was lucky in 1964. Barry Goldwater won a landslide victory in Alabama and swept five Republican congressmen in with him. But for some reason the Republicans did not put up a candidate in the 3rd. If they had, Andrews would have probably lost. With Goldwater gone, however, the Alabama Democratic rooster is once again supreme in the district, and it seems unlikely that Andrews can be defeated. As a result of redistricting, he might be forced into a race with Republican William Dickinson, now of the 2nd district. In the event of a contest, Andrews will have the advantage of having represented most of the new district and can be expected to win fairly easily.

Census Data 1970 pop. 415,628; deviation from current state average, —3.5%; change 1960–70, +8.3%. Metro. 10.9%, 0.0% central city.

1970 Share of Federal Outlays $421,160,862

DOD	$221,176,000	HEW	$95,314,589
AEC	$83,790	HUD	$2,789,757
NASA	$561,581	OEO	$2,659,907
DOT	$2,312,383	DOA	$36,640,638
		Other	$59,622,217

Federal Military-Industrial Commitments

DOD Contractors Page Aircraft Maintenance (Ft. Rucker), $49.734m: helicopter and airplane maintenance. Hayes Holding Div., City Investing (Dothan), $5.285m: airplane maintenance.

DOD Installations Ft. Rucker (Ozark).

Economic Base Cotton and livestock; textile mill products; apparel and other finished products made from fabrics and similar materials. Also, higher education (Auburn U.).

The Voters

Registration 188,951 total. No party registration.

Employment profile White collar, 27%. Blue collar, 73%.

Ethnic groups Black, 32%. Total foreign stock, 1%. All groups less than 0.5%.

Presidential vote

1968	Humphrey (D)	21,267	(19%)
	Nixon (R)	8,821	(8%)
	Wallace (AIP)	84,474	(74%)

Representative

George William Andrews (D) Elected 1944; b. Dec. 12, 1906, Clayton; home, Union Springs; U. of Ala., LL.B., 1928; Navy, WWII; married, two children; Baptist.

Career Circuit solicitor, Third Jud. Circuit of Ala., 1931–43.

Offices 2466 RHOB, 202-225-4422. Also P.O. Bldg., Ozark 36360, 205-774-6417, and 325 N. Prairie, Union Springs 36089, 205-738-3142.

Committees

Appropriations (3rd); Subs. (1) Chm., Legislative, (2) Defense, (3) Public Works.

Group Ratings

	ADA	COPE	NREP	NFU	LCV	CFA	NAB	NSI	ACA
1970	8	36	20	23	22	44	73	100	78
1969	7	—	—	31	—	—	—	—	93
1968	0	0	—	27	—	—	60	—	89

Key Votes

(1) ABM	FOR	(6) 18-Yr-Vote	AGN	(11) Clean Water $	AGN
(2) SST	AGN	(7) Farm Sub Lmt	AGN	(12) Mig Wrkrs Comp	AGN
(3) Phil Pln	AGN	(8) Coop-Church	AGN	(13) Jets to Chiang	FOR
(4) No-Knock	FOR	(9) Family Asst	AGN	(14) State OEO Veto	FOR
(5) Cmutr Tax	AGN	(10) Work Stamps	FOR	(15) Park Logging	FOR

Election Results

1970 general:	George Andrews (D)	70,015	(89%)
	Detroit Lee (NDPA)	8,537	(11%)
1970 primary:	George Andrews (D), unopposed		
1968 general:	George Andrews (D)	86,796	(91%)
	Wilbur Johnston (NDPA)	8,031	(8%)
	Ralph Price (Ind)	763	(1%)

FOURTH DISTRICT Political Background

Alabama 4 is shaped like a top-heavy "S." At the southern tip are the Black Belt counties of Dallas and Autauga, including the now famous city of Selma, site of the 1965 civil rights demonstrations that led to the enactment of the Voting Rights Act. These two counties, however, are cut off from the rest of central Alabama's Black Belt, to preclude the possibility that black voters might elect a black congressman or hold the balance of power in a Democratic primary. In the north is the industrial city of Anniston (pop. 31,000) and, adjacent to it, Fort McClellan. This area is one of the few parts of the district to show significant population growth in the '60's; in fact, virtually all Southern counties with substantial population increases are those with military installations. The northwest part of the district includes a sizable portion (pop. 50,000) of Jefferson County (suburban Birmingham). Except for the two Black Belt counties, the district is heavily white, and the bulk of its population lives in small industrial cities and poor rural hill country.

National politics in Alabama has become a matter of blacks vs. whites. In the 1968 presidential election, for example, virtually all the black voters went for Humphrey and almost as large a percentage of the whites voted for Wallace. Nixon was a poor 3rd, with most of his votes coming from urban conservative whites turned off by Wallace's stridency. Thus, since the 4th district is one of the least black districts in the state, Wallace got a full 72% of its votes, as against 17% for Humphrey and 11% for Nixon. In congressional elections, the choice has been a little different. Longtime (1950–64) moderate incumbent Kenneth Roberts was ousted by a Goldwater Republican in 1964, and he in turn was beaten by the current representative, Bill Nichols, in 1966. Nichols, who was a Wallace floor leader in the Alabama Senate, has gone on to win reelection by majorities in the neighborhood of 80%. Black voters, faced with a choice between two arch-conservatives, seem to have been giving the Democrat something of a margin.

Because of its unusual shape, the 4th might appear to be a prime candidate for elimination by redistricting. But the political realities suggest otherwise. Gov. Wallace no doubt wishes to see Nichols remain in Congress, so the district's boundaries will probably be revised only slightly; a few counties will be added to the south and subtracted in the north. This will increase the black percentage in the district slightly, but in light of recent election results the change will not affect Nichols' chances for reelection.

Census Data 1970 pop. 432,199; deviation from current state average, +0.4%; change 1960–70, +7.0%. Metro. 23.9%, 0.2% central city.

1970 Share of Federal Outlays $297,522,000 (average outlay per district Alabama 4–6)

DOD	$72,435,000	HEW	$115,945,000
AEC	$9,000	HUD	$2,480,000
NASA	$836,000	OEO	$1,621,000
DOT	$17,628,000	DOA	$14,077,000
		Other	$72,491,000

Federal Military-Industrial Commitments (See Alabama 5 for greater Birmingham listing.)

Economic Base Cotton; textile mill products, especially broad woven cotton fabric mills; industrial inorganic and organic chemicals.

The Voters

Registration 209,253 total. No party registration.

Employment profile White collar, 29%. Blue collar, 71%.

Ethnic groups Black, 24%. Total foreign stock, 1%. All groups less than 0.5%.

Presidential vote

1968	Humphrey (D)	21,381	(17%)
	Nixon (R)	14,174	(11%)
	Wallace (AIP)	93,179	(72%)

Representative

William Nichols (D) Elected 1966; b. Oct. 18, 1916, near Becker, Miss.; home, Sylacauga; Auburn U., B.S., 1939, M.S., 1941; Army, WWII; married, three children; Methodist.

Career Ala. House of Reps., 1959; Ala. State Senate, 1963; V.P. Parker Fertilizer Co., Pres. Parker Gin Co., 1947–66.

Offices 1037 LHOB, 202-225-3261. Also Fed. Bldg. P.O. Box 2042, Anniston 36201, 205-236-9720, and Fed. Bldg. P.O. Box 953, Selma 36705, 205-872-2684.

Committees

Armed Services (18th); Sub. No. 4.

Group Ratings

	ADA	COPE	NREP	NFU	LCV	CFA	NAB	NSI	ACA
1970	8	34	9	33	50	63	50	100	73
1969	7	—	—	43	—	—	—	—	82
1968	0	8	—	30	—	—	100	—	86

Key Votes

(1) ABM	FOR	(6) 18-Yr-Vote	AGN	(11) Clean Water $	AGN
(2) SST	FOR	(7) Farm Sub Lmt	AGN	(12) Mig Wrkrs Comp	AGN
(3) Phil Pln	AGN	(8) Coop-Church	AGN	(13) Jets to Chiang	FOR
(4) No-Knock	ABS	(9) Family Asst	AGN	(14) State OEO Veto	FOR
(5) Cmutr Tax	AGN	(10) Work Stamps	FOR	(15) Park Logging	AGN

Election Results

1970 general:	Bill Nichols (D)	77,701	(84%)
	Glenn Andrews (R)	13,217	(14%)
	Wilpha Harrel, Jr. (NDPA)	1,903	(2%)
1970 primary:	Bill Nichols (D), unopposed		
1968 general:	Bill Nichols (D)	94,726	(81%)
	Robert M. Kerr (R)	12,427	(11%)
	T. J. Clemons (NDPA)	9,248	(8%)

FIFTH DISTRICT Political Background

Alabama 5 has the largest percentage of blacks (36%) of any of Alabama's districts. Greene County, in the southern portion of the 5th, where blacks outnumber whites by about 3:1, shows why black political gains in local county courthouses are not about to be repeated in the congressional elections of the rural South. Blacks have finally taken over all the county offices in Greene, after sharp resistance. The white probate judge there refused to put black candidates' names on the ballot; he has since been found guilty of civil and criminal contempt by a federal court.

But these hard-won gains were made in an extremely poor, almost entirely rural county with a 1970 population of only 10,650, down from 13,600 in 1960. The five black-majority counties in the 5th, taken together, have less than a quarter of the district's population. They cast even a smaller percentage of its votes. If the Voting Rights Act had been passed—and enforced—50 years ago, before the great black migrations northward, the 5th might have elected a black congressman. But it will not today, and, given the way Alabama politics works, black voters have little or no chance of influencing the outcome of congressional elections here.

Most of the voters in the district are in and around the city of Tuscaloosa (site of the University of Alabama and of Bear Byrant's football teams) and in the industrial suburbs of Birmingham like Bessemer and Fairfield. Overall, the 5th is less pro-Wallace than any other district in the state, being the only one in which Wallace got less than 50% of the vote in 1968. But the 5th can be considered liberal only by Alabama standards. The current congressman, conservative Democrat Walter Flowers, was first elected in 1968 when veteran Rep. (1952–68) Armistead Selden stepped down to challenge, unsuccessfully, George Wallace's choice for the Senate seat vacated by Lister Hill. (Selden has since become Principal Deputy Assistant Secretary of Defense for International Security Affairs.) Flowers has not had significant opposition since his lone opponent in 1970, T. Y. Rogers, a candidate of the predominantly black National Democratic party of Alabama, received only 21% of the votes. Flowers can be expected to remain in the House for many years to come.

Census Data 1970 pop. 435,232; deviation from current state average, +0.4%; change 1960–70, less than +0.5%. Metro. 67.4%, 15.1% central city.

1970 Share of Federal Outlays $297,522,000 (average outlay per district Alabama 4–6)

DOD	$72,435,000	HEW	$115,945,000
AEC	$9,000	HUD	$2,480,000
NASA	$836,000	OEO	$1,621,000
DOT	$17,628,000	DOA	$14,077,000
		Other	$72,491,000

Federal Military-Industrial Commitments

DOD Contractors Hayes Holding Div., City Investing (Birmingham), $41.587m: airplane maintenance; components for 2.75-inch rocket warheads. National Metals Mfg. (Sylacauga), $12.659m: 155-m projectile components.

DOD Installations Anniston Army Depot (Anniston). Craig AFB (Selma). Ft. McClellan (Anniston).

Economic Base Primary metal industries, especially blast furnaces, steel works, and rolling and finishing mills; cotton and livestock; food and kindred products; lumber and wood products other than furniture. Also, higher education (U. of Ala.).

The Voters

Registration 186,640 total. No party registration.

Employment profile White collar, 28%. Blue collar, 72%.

Ethnic groups Black, 36%. Total foreign stock, 1%. All groups less than 0.5%.

Presidential vote

1968	Humphrey (D)	36,229	(28%)
	Nixon (R)	13,344	(10%)
	Wallace (AIP)	80,260	(62%)

Representative

Walter Flowers (D) Elected 1968; b. April 12, 1933, Greenville; home, Tuscaloosa; U. of Ala., B.A., 1955, LL.B., 1957; Army 1958–59, USAR 1959–64; married, three children; Episcopalian.

Career Practicing atty., 1959–69.

Offices 327 CHOB, 202-225-2665. Also 204 Fed. Bldg., Tuscaloosa 35401, 205-752-3578, and Bessemer Ct. House, Bessemer 35020, 205-425-5031.

Committees

Judiciary (15th); Sub. No. 2.

Science and Astronautics (11th); Subs. (1) Manned Space Flight, (2) *NASA* Oversight.

Group Ratings

	ADA	COPE	NREP	NFU	LCV	CFA	NAB	NSI	ACA
1970	8	28	9	31	0	71	44	100	75
1969	13	—	—	40	—	—	—	—	75

Key Votes

(1) ABM	FOR	(6) 18-Yr-Vote	AGN	(11) Clean Water $	AGN
(2) SST	FOR	(7) Farm Sub Lmt	AGN	(12) Mig Wrkrs Comp	AGN
(3) Phil Pln	AGN	(8) Coop-Church	AGN	(13) Jets to Chiang	FOR
(4) No-Knock	FOR	(9) Family Asst	AGN	(14) State OEO Veto	FOR
(5) Cmutr Tax	FOR	(10) Work Stamps	FOR	(15) Park Logging	FOR

Election Results

1970 general:	Walter Flowers (D)	78,368	(76%)
	T. Y. Rogers (NDPA)	24,863	(24%)
1970 primary:	Walter Flowers (D), unopposed		
1968 general:	Walter Flowers (D)	69,110	(56%)
	Frank Donaldsen (R)	14,582	(12%)
	W. M. Branch (NDPA)	28,040	(23%)
	Mike Simpson (Ind)	9,429	(8%)
	W. C. Gibbs (CN)	1,226	(1%)

SIXTH DISTRICT Political Background

Alabama 6 comprises Birmingham and some of its suburbs including posh Mountain Brook and Vestavia Hills, where most of the city's white establishment lives. Birmingham was not on the map at the time of the Civil War; it was founded later as a steel-mill town and despite considerable growth has remained one ever since. In the early '60's it was famous as the home of Eugene "Bull" Connor, then police commissioner and Democratic National Committeeman, who set dogs and fire hoses against civil rights demonstrators. Blacks have made considerable progress since those days, but Birmingham remains a white-majority city. The steel town's large white working class has always supported George Wallace—a foreshadowing of his later successes in the Garys and Baltimores of the North.

Birmingham civic leaders, like those of most Southern cities, try to create a progressive, dynamic image and talk up the New South. But the 1970 census tells another story. In the last 10 years, a period roughly coinciding with Wallace's dominance in Alabama politics, Birmingham's population declined 10%, and the population of Jefferson County as a whole increased only 1.6%. The woes of the steel industry has something to do with this, but it is a fact that all of Alabama's cities, except Huntsville with its Redstone Arsenal, have lost population—in contrast to most cities in other Southern states. The Birmingham business establishment opposed Wallace in the 1970 gubernatorial primary, because it felt his kind of politics had been repelling Northern capital and industry. With Wallace back in, no sign of an economic upturn has appeared. It seems that the Governor thrives politically on the frustrations and resentments produced by economic stagnation.

In many Northern cities, economic adversity has turned voters against local Republican officeholders. This has not happened in Birmingham, at least on the congressional level. Rep. John H. Buchanan, Jr., was a beneficiary of the local Goldwater landslide in 1964 and has managed to remain in office with little difficulty since. Buchanan is a Baptist minister, and from his record in the House it seems safe to conclude that his theology is fundamentalist. He is a staunch and dependable conservative, although he did surprise some observers by denouncing the Ku Klux Klan when he was a member of the old House Un-American Activities Committee. Redistricting will probably produce another Birmingham-centered district which should give Buchanan very little trouble in future elections.

Census Data 1970 pop. 435,907; deviation from current state average, +1.3%; change 1960–70, −1.5%. Metro. 100%, 68.8% central city.

1970 Share of Federal Outlays $297,522,000 (average outlay per district Alabama 4–6)

DOD	$72,435,000	HEW	$115,945,000
AEC	$9,000	HUD	$2,480,000
NASA	$836,000	OEO	$1,621,000
DOT	$17,628,000	DOA	$14,077,000
		Other	$72,491,000

Federal Military-Industrial Commitments (See Alabama 5 for greater Birmingham listing.)

Economic Base Primary metal industries, especially blast furnaces, steel works, and rolling and finishing mills; fabricated metal products, especially fabricated structural metal products; printing, publishing, and allied industries. Also, banking.

The Voters

Registration 192,627 total. No party registration.

Employment profile White collar, 46%. Blue collar, 54%.

Ethnic groups Black, 33%. Total foreign stock, 4%. UK, 1%; Italy, 1%; others, 1%.

Presidential vote

1968	Humphrey (D)	39,495	(29%)
	Nixon (R)	32,467	(24%)
	Wallace (AIP)	66,373	(48%)

Representative

John Hall Buchanan, Jr. (R) Elected 1964; b. March 19, 1928, Paris, Tenn.; home, Birmingham; Southern Theological Sem., Samford U. (formerly Howard U.) 1949; LL.D., 1967; Navy, WWII; married, two children; Baptist.

Career Pastor, 1953–62; Finance Director, Ala. Republican Party, 1962–64.

Offices 1212 LHOB, 202-225-4921. Also 108 Fed. Bldg., 1800 Fifth Ave. N., Birmingham 35203, 205-325-3861.

Committees

Foreign Affairs (11th); Subs. (1) State Department Organization and Foreign Operations, (2) Europe, (3) Near East.

Government Operations (10th); Subs. (1) Government Activities, (2) Intergovernmental relations.

Group Ratings

	ADA	COPE	NREP	NFU	LCV	CFA	NAB	NSI	ACA
1970	4	9	0	62	0	43	90	100	79
1969	0	—	—	40	—	—	—	—	75
1968	0	8	—	19	—	—	100	—	100

Key Votes

(1) ABM	FOR	(6) 18-Yr-Vote	AGN	(11) Clean Water $	AGN
(2) SST	FOR	(7) Farm Sub Lmt	AGN	(12) Mig Wrkrs Comp	AGN
(3) Phil Pln	FOR	(8) Coop-Church	AGN	(13) Jets to Chiang	ABS
(4) No-Knock	FOR	(9) Family Asst	AGN	(14) State OEO Veto	FOR
(5) Cmutr Tax	AGN	(10) Work Stamps	FOR	(15) Park Logging	FOR

Election Results

1970 general:	John H. Buchanan, Jr. (R)	50,060	(60%)
	John C. Schmarkey (D)	31,378	(38%)
	Dan Moore (C)	1,900	(2%)
1970 primary:	John H. Buchanan, Jr. (R), unopposed		
1968 general:	John H. Buchanan, Jr. (R)	69,445	(59%)
	Quinton R. Bowers (D)	34,608	(30%)
	Thomas Wrenn (NDPA)	12,976	(11%)

SEVENTH DISTRICT Political Background

Alabama 7 is a political unit that demonstrates the changes wrought by the civil rights revolution in Alabama politics. As recently as a decade ago, the 7th was considered one of the two most liberal districts in the state. The local congressman Carl Elliott was thought sufficiently liberal by the Kennedy Administration to be one of the two members added to the House Rules Committee when it was enlarged in 1961. And organized labor in the district was strong enough to play some part in its politics. The working men from industrial towns like Gadsden, Japser, and Cullman and the leather-handed farmers of the northern Alabama hills consistently supported economic liberals like Lister Hill, John Sparkman, and ex-Gov. "Kissin' Jim" Folsom against conservative candidates backed by the business interests and the whites of the Black Belt.

But times have changed. The relevant factor today is not that the voters of the 7th are predominantly working class, but that they are almost entirely white. Only 7% are black. In politics where the only cleavages are racial, that makes the 7th a very conservative district.

The first man to take advantage of the changes in the political leanings of the district was Jim Martin, the conservative Republican who came within a hair's-breadth of defeating Sen. Lister Hill in 1962. Since no statewide office was up in 1964, Martin became the Republican candidate in the 7th. The four other Alabama Republicans elected to Congress in that year were clearly swept in on Barry Goldwater's coattails.

But Martin himself was so popular that he ran less than 1% behind the Arizonan and would have won, coattails or not.

As the congressman from the 7th, Martin continued to harbor ambitions for statewide office. These ambitions may have clouded his political judgment. He entered the 1966 governor's race, apparently figuring that Wallace's ploy of running his wife to succeed him would irritate the voters. Martin was dead wrong. The voters wanted Wallace again and were happy to go along with his explicit charade. Martin was defeated by a 2:1 margin in the general election, and that was pretty much the end of his political career as well as the end of the Republican party as a statewide political force in Alabama.

Martin's successor in Congress was Tom Bevill, a Wallace floor leader in the Alabama House. Bevill won handily in 1966 and has won by overwhelming margins in succeeding elections. He is unlikely to be defeated in the foreseeable future.

Census Data 1970 pop. 436,448; deviation from current state average, +1.4%; change 1960–70, +4.7%. Metro. 34.5%, 12.4% central city.

1970 Share of Federal Outlays $243,161,934

DOD	$42,061,000	HEW	$108,822,966
AEC	$000	HUD	$3,527,217
NASA	$72,887	OEO	$1,514,239
DOT	$4,746,391	DOA	$29,230,939
		Other	$53,186,295

Federal Military-Industrial Commitments

DOD Contractors Etowah Mfg. (Gadsden), $5.448m: rocket-booster components. Brads Machine Products (Gadsden), $5.271m: rocket-booster components.

Economic Base Cotton, poultry, and livestock; apparel and other finished products made from fabrics and similar materials; food and kindred products, especially meat products.

The Voters

Registration 255,833 total. No party registration.

Employment profile White collar, 28%. Blue collar, 72%.

Ethnic groups Black, 7%. Total foreign stock, 1%. All groups less than 0.5%.

Presidential vote

1968	Humphrey (D)	12,910	(9%)
	Nixon (R)	29,719	(20%)
	Wallace (AIP)	104,358	(71%)

Representative

Tom Bevill (D) Elected 1966; b. March 27, 1921, Townley; home, Jasper; U. of Ala., B.S., 1943, LL.B., 1948; Army, WWII, Lt. Col. USAR; married, three children; Baptist.

Career Practicing atty., 1949–67; Ala. House of Reps., 1958–66.

Offices 1207 LHOB, 202-225-4876. Also 600 Broad St., Gadsden 35901, 205-546-0201; 104 Cullman County Courthouse, Cullman 35055, 205-734-6043; and P.O. Box 685, Jasper 35501, 205-387-7213.

Committees

Banking and Currency (15th); Subs. (1) International Trade, (2) Small Business, (3) Bank Supervision and Insurance.

Post Office and Civil Service (14th); Subs. (1) Manpower and Civil Service, (2) Census and Statistics, (3) Postal Facilities and Mail.

Group Ratings

	ADA	COPE	NREP	NFU	LCV	CFA	NAB	NSI	ACA
1970	20	42	17	46	25	50	56	100	56
1969	7	—	—	46	—	—	—	—	69
1968	8	15	—	43	—	—	83	—	64

Key Votes

(1) ABM	FOR	(6) 18-Yr-Vote	AGN	(11) Clean Water $	AGN
(2) SST	AGN	(7) Farm Sub Lmt	AGN	(12) Mig Wrkrs Comp	AGN
(3) Phil Pln	FOR	(8) Coop-Church	AGN	(13) Jets to Chiang	ABS
(4) No-Knock	FOR	(9) Family Asst	AGN	(14) State OEO Veto	FOR
(5) Cmutr Tax	AGN	(10) Work Stamps	FOR	(15) Park Logging	AGN

Election Results

1970 general:	Tom Bevill (D), unopposed		
1970 primary:	Tom Bevill (D)	115,108	(88%)
	Mrs. Frank Stewart (D)	15,824	(12%)
1968 general:	Tom Bevill (D)	106,132	(76%)
	Jodie Connell (R)	29,923	(22%)
	James Bains (NDPA)	2,258	(2%)
	A. V. Stone (AIA)	1,132	(1%)

EIGHTH DISTRICT Political Background

In 1950, Huntsville, Alabama, was a sleepy hill-town of 14,000 people, famed chiefly as the home of Sen. John Sparkman. He had represented the area in the House for 10 years before taking his Senate seat in 1946. Today Huntsville has a population of 114,000—the fastest-growing city in Alabama. The principal agent of the change is the Redstone Missile Arsenal, home of Werner von Braun and other NASA and ABM technicians. Like most Deep South cities which have shown substantial growth in the last 20 years, Huntsville is a beneficiary of the military-industrial complex.

In the North, military installations tend to make a community more conservative; in the South, they sometimes have the opposite effect. The Redstone Arsenal has brought Northern and European technicians and administrators to Huntsville. These outlanders have not been attracted by the Deep South accents of George Wallace and find nothing entertaining in his country-music-singing campaign entourage. But neither are they Northern-style liberals; in 1968, Nixon outpolled Humphrey in Huntsville.

The Huntsville influx—and the George Wallace phenomenon—have changed the political leanings of the 8th, which 10 or 20 years ago could have been summed up in three letters: TVA. The Tennessee River runs through every county in the district, and through most of its length its level has been raised by the dams that have provided cheap power to the farmers and businessmen of the area.

The changes in the 8th district have been reflected in the voting record of Congressman Robert Jones, who succeeded Sparkman in the House in 1946. At one time Jones was one of the leading TVA-oriented Southern liberals, though he was always, of course, a segregationist. As late as 1961, he was one of the leading Southern supporters of the Kennedy Administration's move to expand the size of the then conservative House Rules Committee. Since Wallace's rise, Jones has seldom supported bills of Democratic administrations, but he does remain a member in good standing of the House establishment. Jones's course has been well calculated to please his constituency: the best the Republicans have been able to do against him was an 18% performance in 1966. He has had no serious opposition in the Democratic primary, and his age is such (60 in 1972) that he is likely to remain in the House for another decade or two.

Census Data 1970 pop. 489,771; deviation from current state average, +13.8%; change 1960–70, +27.7%. Metro. 46.6%, 28.1% central city.

1970 Share of Federal Outlays $797,502,882

DOD	$235,549,000	HEW	$91,321,648
AEC	$000	HUD	$15,621,859

NASA	$272,809,961	OEO	$1,269,633
DOT	$22,099,806	DOA	$31,780,643
		Other	$127,050,332

Federal Military-Industrial Commitments

DOD Contractors Genesco Inc. (Huntsville), $13.107m: men's oxford dress shoes. Thiokol Chemical (Huntsville), $11.019m: rocket motors and igniters.

DOD Installations Redstone Army Arsenal (Huntsville). Safeguard ABM System Command (Huntsville).

NASA Contractors IBM (Huntsville), $39.718m: Saturn, Apollo, and nuclear rocket instrument units. General Electric (Huntsville), $29.750m: various services to Apollo, Saturn rockets, and to the Mississippi Test Facility. Boeing (Huntsville), $18.208m: lunar roving vehicles for Apollo spacecraft. Sperry Rand (Huntsville), $9.865m: support of Saturn rocket. Brown Engineering Div., Teledyne Inc. (Huntsville), $8.469m: support of Saturn rocket. Computer Sciences (Huntsville), $7.179m: support for Saturn rocket.

NASA Installations Marshall Space Flight Center (Huntsville).

Economic Base Cotton; ordnance and accessories; primary metal industries; chemicals and allied products. Also, banking.

The Voters

Registration 210,829 total. No party registration.

Employment profile White collar, 36%. Blue collar, 64%.

Ethnic groups Black, 13%. Total foreign stock, 2%. Germany, 1%; others, 1%.

Presidential vote

1968	Humphrey (D)	16,900	(13%)
	Nixon (R)	23,576	(17%)
	Wallace (AIP)	94,659	(70%)

Representative

Robert E. Jones (D) Elected 1946; b. June 12, 1912, Scottsboro; home, Scottsboro; U. of Ala., LL.B., 1937; Navy, WWII; married, one child; Methodist.

Career Practicing atty., 1937–40; Judge, Jackson County Ct., 1940–43.

Offices 2426 RHOB, 202-225-4801. Also P.O. Bldg., Scottsboro 35768, 205-574-2618.

Committees

Government Operations (4th); Subs. (1) Government Activities, (2) Intergovernmental Relations.

Public Works (2nd); Subs. (1) Chm., Flood Control and Internal Dev., (2) Investigations and Oversight, (3) Public Buildings and Grounds, (4) Roads.

Group Ratings

	ADA	COPE	NREP	NFU	LCV	CFA	NAB	NSI	ACA
1970	24	50	27	67	63	89	17	70	26
1969	13	—	—	80	—	—	—	—	20
1968	42	54	—	87	—	—	—	—	13

Key Votes

(1) ABM	FOR	(6) 18-Yr-Vote	FOR	(11) Clean Water $	AGN
(2) SST	FOR	(7) Farm Sub Lmt	AGN	(12) Mig Wrkrs Comp	AGN
(3) Phil Pln	AGN	(8) Coop-Church	AGN	(13) Jets to Chiang	AGN
(4) No-Knock	FOR	(9) Family Asst	AGN	(14) State OEO Veto	AGN
(5) Cmutr Tax	FOR	(10) Work Stamps	FOR	(15) Park Logging	AGN

Election Results

1970 general:	Robert E. Jones (D)	76,413	(85%)
	Thornton Stanley (NDPA)	4,846	(5%)
	Ken Hearn (Cn)	7,599	(8%)
	Thomas Lee Harris (Ind)	1,200	(1%)
1970 primary:	Robert E. Jones (D), unopposed		
1968 general:	Robert E. Jones (D)	85,528	(76%)
	Ken Hearn (Cn)	16,900	(15%)
	Charlie Burgess (NDPA)	7,140	(6%)
	Richard J. Pella (AIA)	2,880	(3%)

ALASKA

Political Background

Alaska, the nation's largest state in area (550,000 square miles), is its smallest in population (302,000)—the land of the midnight sun, of the tallest mountains in North America, and of thousands of miles of rugged seacoast. It is also the land of the North Slope oil boom, so far worth $900 million to the state, and of desperately poor Eskimo and Indian villages. More than twice the size of Texas, Alaska's geographical expanse is hard to comprehend, having within it, like the entire continental United States, no less than four time zones. Distances in the state make the airplane the only practical means of transportation between most of its cities.

"People call themselves Republicans or Democrats, but the definitions don't appear to mean the same things in Alaska as they do elsewhere in the United States," writes one observer. Physical remoteness is one explanation for the anomaly; it is about as far from Anchorage to Seattle as it is from Seattle to Chicago. A related explanation is that Alaska is still a frontier state, in the old sense of the word. Hunters and trappers can range around and get lost; and some men, through perseverance and maybe a lucky break, will no doubt make fortunes from the state's largely untapped resources. Most important, Alaska is still a political frontier: political decisions remain to be made, in Juneau and Washington, which will shape the state's future as much as the Northwest Ordinance shaped Ohio's or the Homestead Act Nebraska's.

The decision about what to do with all that money from the oil companies will be made largely in the state by the rough-and-ready part-time politicians in the state legislature. But the crucial decision about Alaska's oil will be made in Washington: whether to allow an oil consortium to build the Trans Alaska Pipeline System (TAPS) from the Arctic oil fields to the warm-water port of Valdez (1970 pop. 1,005). Ecologists claim that the pipeline will melt the permafrost, the layer of permanently frozen ground just below the surface, and thereby change the ecology of the entire region which TAPS traverses. They also argue that a break in the pipeline is entirely possible in earthquake-prone Alaska and further contend that the waters around Valdez are so treacherous that some tanker will inevitably break up in them and spill thousands of barrels of oil into the Pacific. Oil men and other "boomers" discount such claims and argue that the state, with a 13% unemployment rate (25% in inland Fairbanks), must have the jobs and money the pipeline will bring.

Former Alaska Gov. (1966–68) Walter Hickel, as Interior Secretary, held up the pipeline permit. At this writing his successor is investigating the possibility of a trans-Canada pipeline along a route which would avoid much of the permafrost and the earthquake zone. Meanwhile, business analysts have come to doubt whether the North Slope oil strike was as big a bonanza as first thought. Real estate values around Valdez have doubtless plummeted.

A second great issue, that of the native land claims, will also be decided in Washington. The natives, Eskimos and Indians, claim title to virtually all of Alaska by aboriginal right. Their claims were left unaffected by the purchase of Alaska in 1867 (Seward's Folly) and the Statehood Act of 1959. In 1970 the Senate passed a bill giving the natives $1.10 billion. Sen. Fred Harris of Oklahoma, whose wife is a full-blooded Indian, opposed the measure, contending the Alaskan natives deserved more. The House failed to act, leaving the 92nd Congress faced with the issue.

Pending settlement of the native claims, the Interior Department imposed a land freeze. The freeze, one of the last acts of Secretary Stewart Udall, prevents the state from choosing, as it is entitled to do under the Statehood Act, which 100 million of the state's 350 million acres it wants title to. That 100 million acres will then become available for sale to private parties. Since the state had designated only 6 million acres before the freeze, real estate developers and other Alaskan boomers are coming down with a bad case of claustrophobia.

Alaskan voting habits are hard to understand in conventional political terms; voters are not tied to the patterns of the Lower 48. In 1970 Alaskans gave 60% of their votes to Republican Sen. Ted Stevens, while at the same time electing a Democratic governor, William Egan, and a Democratic congressman-at-large, Nick Begich. Egan was governor once before, from statehood in 1959 to 1966, and Begich was a state legislator. In 1968, Richard Nixon carried the state with 45% of the votes, while Democrat Mike Gravel, beneficiary of a high-powered TV campaign, received the same percentage in the Senate race. Both men won because third candidates took sizable hunks of the vote. George Wallace got 12%, a figure significantly higher than in most other western states, and incumbent Sen. Ernest Gruening, beaten by Gravel in the Democratic primary, got 17% as a write-in—an unheard-of percentage for a write-in candidacy in most other states.

In the ideological terms usually employed, these results make little sense. Liberal candidates received 62% of the votes in the 1968 Senate race and only 40% in the 1970 race for the same office. Meanwhile, conservatives had 57% for President in 1968 and only 40% for the House in 1970. Personal popularity seems to account for many of the discrepancies in vote totals. Then, too, stands on the great national issues are of less interest to Alaskans than positions on the questions which will determine the economic and ecological future of the state.

Those issues, as noted, will be resolved primarily in Washington, but Alaska's delegation will probably have relatively little to say about them. Currently Alaska has less seniority in the Congress than any other state. Until 1968, only two men had ever represented Alaska in the Senate. But Gruening, who was one of the two senators to vote against the Tonkin Gulf resolution in 1964, was beaten in the 1968 primary, and Sen. E. L. (Bob) Bartlett died early in 1969. Their successors have shown signs of the independence which is, to an increasing degree, characterizing the Senate. Gravel, one of the leaders in the movement to abolish the draft, has opposed the Vietnam war almost as vigorously as Gruening, the man he beat. Stevens is more in the conventional conservative Republican mold, having once chided Ralph Nader for doubting the good faith of Detroit car-makers. But Stevens has been heard to warn the Administration that its Vietnam policy will create trouble for Republican candidates in 1972. Because he is filling an unexpired term, the Republican Senator will have to stand for reelection in 1972 once more.

Not surprisingly, all of Alaska's elected representatives—Gravel and Stevens in the Senate and Begich in the House—serve on the Interior committee, which exercises a great deal of influence in this undeveloped state.

Electoral Votes 3

Census Data 1970 pop. 302,173; 0.15% of U.S. total, 52nd largest; change 1960–70, +33.6%. Metro. 0.0%, 0.0% central city. 1970 per capita income, $4,676, 4th highest. 52nd in number of poor.

1970 Share of Federal Tax Burden $273,200,000; 0.14% of U.S. total, 51st largest.

1970 Share of Federal Outlays $728,659,375; 0.39% of U.S. total, 45th largest. Per capita federal spending, $2,411.

DOD	$281,439,000	44th (0.49%)	HEW	$51,002,963	52nd (0.10%)
AEC	$21,673,298	19th (0.83%)	HUD	$4,320,024	47th (0.22%)
NASA	$302,098	42nd (0.08%)	OEO	$4,518,330	37th (0.59%)
DOT	$145,621,422	16th (2.04%)	DOA	$38,953,674	44th (0.30%)

DOC	$10,068,782	24th (0.87%)		POD	$20,899,661	45th (0.29%)
DOI	$86,873,070	8th (3.76%)		VA	$10,858,131	52nd (0.14%)
DOJ	$1,538,209	48th (0.27%)		CSC	$4,555,782	51st (0.11%)
				Other	$46,034,931	

Federal Military-Industrial Commitments

DOD Contractors RCA (Anchorage), $15.283m: unspecified communication services. Federal Electric Div., IT&T (Anchorage), $11.261m: unspecified communication services. General Electric (Shemya AF Station), $9.204m: support of military space satellites. Tensoro-Alaskan Petroleum (Kenai Village), $5.108m: petroleum products.

DOD Installations Ft. Richardson AB (Anchorage). Ft. Wainwright AB (Fairbanks). Ft. Greely AB (Big Delta). Naval Communication Station (Adak). Naval Communication Station (Kodiak). Naval Station (Adak). Naval Station (Kodiak). Eielson AFB (Fairbanks). Elmendorf AFB (Anchorage). Galena Airport (Galena). King Salmon Airport (King Salmon). Shemya AF Station (Shemya).

AEC Operations Holmes and Narver (Amchitka Island), $20.499m: support of ABM research in underground test facilities.

Economic Base Fisheries; crude petroleum and natural gas; lumber and wood products other than furniture.

Political Line-up Governor William A. Egan (D); seat up, 1974. Senators, Mike Gravel (D) and Ted Stevens (R). Representatives, 1 D, At Large. State Senate (10 D and 10 R); State House (27 D and 9 R).

The Voters

Registration 111,257 total. 32,394 D(29%); 19,098 R (17%); 58,409 Ind. (53%); 1,356 other (1%).

Employment profile White collar, 48%. Blue collar, 52%.

Ethnic groups Black, 3%. Total foreign stock, 14%. Canada, 3%; Germany, Norway, UK, 2% each; Sweden, Italy, USSR, 1% each; others, 3%.

Presidential vote

1968	Humphrey (D)	35,411	(43%)
	Nixon (R)	37,600	(45%)
	Wallace (AIP)	10,024	(12%)
1964	Johnson (D)	44,329	(66%)
	Goldwater (R)	22,930	(34%)
1960	Kennedy (D)	29,809	(49%)
	Nixon (R)	30,953	(51%)

Senator

Mike Gravel (D) Elected 1968, seat up 1974; b. May 13, 1930, Springfield, Mass.; home, Anchorage; Columbia U., B.S., 1956; married, two children; Unitarian.

Career Real estate developer; Alaska House of Reps., 1962–66; Speaker, 1965.

Offices 1251 NSOB, 202-225-6665. Also P.O. Box 2283, Anchorage 99501, 907-272-0713.

Committees

Interior and Insular Affairs (9th); Subs. (1) Indian Affairs, (2) Minerals, Materials, and Fuels, (3) Public Lands.

Public Works (7th); Subs. (1) Chm., Public Buildings and Grounds, (2) Economic Development, (3) Public Roads. *Jt. Com. on Congressional Operations* (2nd)

Group Ratings

	ADA	COPE	NREP	NFU	LCV	NAB	NSI	ACA
1970	72	83	91	94	27	14	10	0
1969	28	—	—	80	—	—	—	0

Key Votes

(1) ABM	AGN	(8) Phil Pln	FOR	(15) Coop-Church	FOR
(2) SST	FOR	(9) Vol Army	ABS	(16) Cut Oil Dpltn	AGN
(3) Busing	FOR	(10) Prison $	ABS	(17) Consumer Prot	FOR
(4) Tob Sub	ABS	(11) Cut Mil $	FOR	(18) Farm Sub Limit	ABS
(5) Carswell	AGN	(12) Defoliatn	AGN	(19) Comp Bid Sales	AGN
(6) No-Knock	AGN	(13) 18-Yr-Vote	FOR	(20) Pre-Prod Tests	FOR
(7) Seniorty	ABS	(14) Pentgn PR	AGN	(21) Cut Marjna Pen	ABS

Election Results

1968 general:	Mike Gravel (D)	36,527	(45%)
	Elmer Rasmuson (R)	30,286	(37%)
	Ernest Gruening (write-in)	14,188	(17%)
1968 primary:	Mike Gravel (D)	17,971	(53%)
	Ernest Gruening (D)	16,015	(47%)

Senator

Ted Stevens (R) Elected 1970, seat up 1976; b. Nov. 18, 1923, Indianapolis, Ind.; home, Anchorage; Oreg. State Col., Mont. State Col., UCLA, B.A., 1947; Harvard, LL.B., 1950; Army Air Corps, WWII; married, five children; Episcopalian.

Career Practicing atty., 1950–53, 1961–68; U.S. Dept. of Interior, 1956–61, Solicitor, 1960; Alaska House of Reps., 1964–68.

Offices 304 OSOB, 202-225-3004. Also 250 Fed. Bldg., Anchorage 99501, 907-272-9561.

Committees

Commerce (8th); Subs. (1) Aviation, (2) Communications, (3) Consumer, (4) Merchant Marine, (5) Oceans and Atmosphere, (6) Foreign Commerce and Tourism, (7) Sp. Sub. to Study Transportation on the Great Lakes and St. Lawrence Seaway.

Interior and Insular Affairs (6th); Subs. (1) Indian Affairs, (2) Minerals, Materials, and Fuels, (3) Territories and Insular Affairs.

Post Office and Civil Service (3rd); Subs. (1) Compensation and Employment Benefits, (2) Civil Service Policies and Practice.

Veterans Affairs (4th); Subs. (1) Housing and Insurance, (2) Readjustment, Education, and Employment.

(*Note: The following ratings and notes cover Sen. Stevens record in the House of Representatives where he served prior to his election in 1970.*)

Group Ratings

	ADA	COPE	NREP	NFU	LCV	NAB	NSI	ACA
1970	25	64	30	67	0	38	89	19
1969	28	—	—	56	—	—	—	17

Key Votes

(1) ABM	FOR	(8) Phil Pln	ABS	(15) Coop-Church	FOR
(2) SST	FOR	(9) Vol Army	FOR	(16) Cut Oil Dpltn	AGN
(3) Busing	FOR	(10) Prison $	ABS	(17) Consumer Prot	FOR
(4) Tob Sub	ABS	(11) Cut Mil $	AGN	(18) Farm Sub Limit	ABS
(5) Carswell	FOR	(12) Defoliatn	ABS	(19) Comp Bid Sales	AGN
(6) No-Knock	ABS	(13) 18-Yr-Vote	FOR	(20) Pre-Prod Tests	ABS
(7) Seniorty	FOR	(14) Pentgn PR	FOR	(21) Cut Marjna Pen	AGN

Election Results

1970 general:	Ted Stevens (R)	47,908	(59%)
	Wendell P. Kay (D)	32,636	(41%)

1970 primary:	Ted Stevens (R)	39,061	(97%)
	Fritz Singer (R)	1,359	(3%)

* *Appointed successor to Sen E. L. Bartlett in 1969.*

Representative

Nicholas J. Begich (D) Elected 1970; b. April 6, 1932, Eveleth, Minn.; home, Anchorage; St. Cloud, Minn., State Col., B.A., 1952; U. of Minn., M.A.; U. of Colo., U. of N. Dak., graduate studies; married, six children; Catholic.

Career Instructor at U. of Alaska, 1958–68; Supt., Ft. Richardson Public Schools, 1963–68; Alaska State Senate, 1963–70.

Offices 1210 LHOB, 202-225-5765. Also Fed. Bldg., Anchorage 99501, 907-279-2410.

Committees

Interior and Insular Affairs (22nd); Subs. (1) Indian Affairs, (2) National Parks and Recreation, (3) Public Lands, (4) Territorial and Insular Affairs.

Public Works (19th); Subs. (1) Flood Control and Internal Dev., (2) Rivers and Harbors, (3) Watershed Dev., (4) Economic Dev. Programs.

Group Ratings, Key Votes: Newly elected.

Election Results

1970 general:	Nick Begich (D)	44,137	(55%)
	Frank Murkowski (R)	35,947	(45%)
1970 primary:	Nick Begich (D), unopposed		

ARIZONA

Political Background

To most Americans, Arizona brings to mind scenic shots of the Grand Canyon and the Painted Desert laid out in *Arizona Highways.* But the political analyst's attention is focused almost entirely on Phoenix and Tucson. More than half of the state's voters live in and around Phoenix, and another quarter are residents of the Tucson area. Most of these people are newcomers to Arizona. In 1940 the state had a population of 550,000; today the figure is 1,750,000. This influx, in the years since World War II, has completely transformed the state's politics.

The change is best illustrated by contrasting the careers of Arizona's two best known politicians: ex-Rep. (1912–26) and Sen. (1926–68) Carl Hayden and Sen. (1952–64, 1968–) Barry Goldwater. Hayden began his political career as a town councilman in Tempe, formerly Hayden's Crossing, in 1902 when Phoenix was a sleepy station stop on the Southern Pacific Railroad. Hayden was a Democrat, and a rather conservative one—and so were all of Arizona's successful politicians up through the 1950's. The state had a Democratic heritage that was the result of the Southern origin of most of its early settlers and the Mexican origin of many others. Although Arizona sometimes went Republican in presidential races (never supporting a loser until 1960), Hayden and his fellow Democrats rarely had any difficulty with the voters. The longtime Senator's main legacy to the state was the Central Arizona Project—a giant water-diversion program which, ironically, made possible the huge growth that made his kind of politics obsolete.

One of the first to recognize the Republican party's postwar potential was Barry Goldwater, then proprietor of his family's Phoenix department store. Goldwater won election to the Phoenix City Council in 1949. He helped Republican radio announcer Howard Pyle win the governorship in 1950 and in 1952 himself defeated veteran (1940–52) Ernest MacFarland, who was then Senate Majority Leader. (MacFarland's departure set the stage for Lyndon Johnson's ascent to the Senate Democratic leadership.) Goldwater won reelection in 1958, again beating MacFarland, who had become governor in the interim. Following the '58 election, Goldwater attracted national attention as an outspoken conservative, particularly since he was one of the few who won in that recession year.

From that time on, things have been very good for Arizona Republicans. They have lost only one major statewide race in the last 12 years, the governorship in 1964, and that was regained two years later. As retirees keep pouring in from Chicago Tribuneland and points east, continued Republican dominance seems assured. Only the declining mine towns and the significant Mexican-American community in the southern part of the state remain dependably Democratic in national elections. But Democratic sheriffs and clerks—remnants of a once powerful Haydenesque establishment—do manage to keep winning in most of the smaller counties.

The 1970 elections saw a spirited, but unsuccessful, challenge of the new Arizona Republican establishment. Democrat Raul Castro, a former judge and ambassador to Bolivia and El Salvador, just missed unseating Gov. and ex-TV-newsman Jack Williams. Likewise, shopping center magnate and TV announcer Sam Grossman, a recent emigrant from California, ran a strong race against incumbent Sen. Paul Fannin. Grossman's lead in the preelection polls vanished when Fannin supporters charged that he had signed legal documents as a resident of California after the date Grossman claimed to have moved to Arizona. Curiously, Arizona voters, most of whom are migrants from other states themselves, resented Grossman's presumed California signature. By contrast, the state of New York, whose voters are mostly natives, has sent two nonresidents, Robert Kennedy and James Buckley, to the Senate. At any rate, Arizona Democrats have shown that they have the potential of winning occasional elections, and with candidates more in line with the liberal image of the national Democratic party than with the more conservative men in the tradition of Carl Hayden.

Goldwater and Fannin are about as conservative as any state's Senate delegation. Goldwater, a Brigadier General in the Air Force Reserve, seems primarily interested in military matters. He sits on the Senate Armed Services Committee, where he almost always supports the military. In line with his libertarian philosophy, however, he is one of the leading congressional opponents of the draft. Goldwater looks simply unbeatable in Arizona, the only non-Southern state he carried in his 1964 Presidential race. He can probably remain in the Senate as long as Carl Hayden, who retired at age 91. Sen. Fannin, as the 1970 election results show, may be somewhat more vulnerable and may retire at the expiration of his current term, when he will be 69.

Arizona has gained one congressional seat in each of the last two censuses, and in the 93rd Congress the state will have four representatives in the House. Redistricting is not hard to predict. Maricopa County (Phoenix and suburbs) will get two seats, one of which will return Congressman John J. Rhodes and the other another like-minded conservative Republican. The other two seats will be split between the northern and southern halves of the state, much as they are now.

Electoral Votes 6

Census Data 1970 pop. 1,772,482; 0.86% of U.S. total, 34th largest; change 1960–70, +36.1%. Metro. 74.5%, 47.7% central city. 1970 per capita income, $3,542, 30th highest. 31st in number of poor.

1970 Share of Federal Tax Burden $1,346,470,000; 0.69% of U.S. total, 31st largest.

1970 Share of Federal Outlays $1,832,153,705; 0.97% of U.S. total, 32nd largest. Per capita federal spending, $1,034.

DOD	$613,016,000	28th	(1.07%)	HEW	$415,088,100	35th	(0.79%)
AEC	$503,039	39th	(0.02%)	HUD	$13,654,519	36th	(0.70%)
NASA	$6,718,250	23rd	(0.18%)	OEO	$15,954,284	15th	(2.10%)
DOT	$65,819,984	37th	(0.92%)	DOA	$135,632,735	34th	(1.06%)
DOC	$11,116,993	21st	(0.96%)	POD	$48,548,034	35th	(0.67%)
DOI	$239,312,689	1st	(10.36%)	VA	$101,596,561	35th	(1.38%)
DOJ	$7,446,178	24th	(1.30%)	CSC	$35,731,728	26th	(0.89%)
				Other	$122,014,611		

Economic Base Livestock and cotton; electrical machinery, equipment, and supplies; metal mining, especially copper and molybdenum; nonelectrical machinery; food and kindred products; primary metal industries; printing, publishing, and allied industries. Also, tourism.

Political Line-up Governor, Jack Williams (R); seat up, 1974. Senators, Paul J. Fannin (R) and Barry Goldwater (R). Representatives, 3 (1 D and 2 R). State Senate (12 D and 18 R); State House (26 D and 34 R).

The Voters

Registration 749,785 total. 397,931 D (53%); 319,706 R (43%); 23,148 Other (3%).

Employment profile White collar, 43%. Blue collar, 57%.

Ethnic groups Black, 3%. Spanish surname, 15%. Total foreign stock, 18%. Mexico, 9%; Germany, 2%; Canada, UK, Italy, USSR, and Poland, 1% each. Others, 4%.

Presidential vote

1968	Humphrey (D)	170,514	(36%)
	Nixon (R)	266,721	(55%)
	Wallace (AIP)	46,573	(10%)
1964	Johnson (D)	237,753	(50%)
	Goldwater (R)	242,535	(50%)
1960	Kennedy (D)	176,782	(44%)
	Nixon (R)	221,241	(56%)

Senator

Paul Jones Fannin (R) Elected 1964, seat up 1976; b. Jan. 29, 1907, Ashland, Ky.; home, Phoenix; U. of Ariz., Stanford, B.A., 1930; married, four children; Methodist.

Career Former partner in Fannin Brothers, industrial firm marketing petroleum; three-term Governor of Ariz.

Offices 140 OSOB, 202-225-4521. Also 3417 Fed. Bldg., Phoenix 85025, 602-261-4486, and 326 Fed. Bldg., Tucson 85702, 602-792-6336.

Committees

Finance (5th).

Interior and Insular Affairs (3rd); Subs. (1) Indian Affairs, (2) Parks and Recreation, (3) Public Lands, (4) Water and Power Resources.

Sp. Com. on Aging (5th); Subs. (1) Health, (2) Housing, (3) Long-Term Care, (4) Employment and Retirement Incomes.

Group Ratings

	ADA	COPE	NREP	NFU	LCV	NAB	NSI	ACA
1970	3	8	0	30	0	75	100	90
1969	0	—	—	25	—	—	—	86
1968	7	0	—	30	—	60	—	86

Key Votes

(1) ABM	FOR	(8) Phil Pln	AGN	(15) Coop-Church	AGN
(2) SST	FOR	(9) Vol Army	FOR	(16) Cut Oil Dpltn	AGN
(3) Busing	ABS	(10) Prison $	AGN	(17) Consumer Prot	ABS
(4) Tob Sub	ABS	(11) Cut Mil $	AGN	(18) Farm Sub Limit	AGN
(5) Carswell	FOR	(12) Defoliatn	FOR	(19) Comp Bid Sales	FOR
(6) No-Knock	FOR	(13) 18-Yr-Vote	AGN	(20) Pre-Prod Tests	AGN
(7) Seniorty	ABS	(14) Pentgn PR	FOR	(21) Cut Marjna Pen	AGN

Election Results

1970 general:	Paul Fannin (R)	228,284	(56%)
	Sam Grossman (D)	179,512	(44%)
1970 primary:	Paul Fannin (R), unopposed		
1964 general:	Paul Fannin (R)	241,089	(51%)
	Roy Elson (D)	227,712	(49%)

Senator

Barry M. Goldwater (R) Elected 1968, seat up 1974; b. Jan. 1, 1909, Phoenix; home, Phoenix; U. of Ariz., 1928; Army Air Corps, WWII; married, four children; Episcopalian.

Career Brigadier Gen. USAFR (Ret.), 1937–67; Pres., Goldwater's Inc., 1929; Chm. Bd., 1937–53; Phoenix City Council, 1949–51; U.S. Senate, 1952–64; Republican candidate for Pres. 1964.

Offices 440 OSOB, 202-225-2235. Also 5420 Fed. Bldg., Phoenix 85025, 602-261-4086, and P.O. Bldg., Scott and Broadway, Tucson 85701, 602-792-6334.

Committees

Aeronautical and Space Sciences (3rd).

Armed Services (5th) Subs. (1) CIA, (2) National Stockpile and Naval Petroleum Reserves, (3) Preparedness Investigating, (4) Ad Hoc Sub. on Research and Dev., (5) Ad Hoc Sub. on Tactical Air Power.

Group Ratings

	ADA	COPE	NREP	NFU	LCV	NAB	NSI	ACA
1970	3	9	0	18	1	71	100	92
1969	0	0	—	14	—	—	—	90

Key Votes

(1) ABM	FOR	(8) Phil Pln	ABS	(15) Coop-Church	AGN
(2) SST	FOR	(9) Vol Army	FOR	(16) Cut Oil Dpltn	ABS
(3) Busing	ABS	(10) Prison $	ABS	(17) Consumer Prot	ABS
(4) Tob Sub	ABS	(11) Cut Mil $	ABS	(18) Farm Sub Limit	AGN
(5) Carswell	FOR	(12) Defoliatn	FOR	(19) Comp Bid Sales	ABS
(6) No-Knock	ABS	(13) 18-Yr-Vote	ABS	(20) Pre-Prod Tests	AGN
(7) Seniorty	FOR	(14) Pentgn PR	FOR	(21) Cut Marjna Pen	AGN

Election Results

1968 general:	Barry Goldwater (R)	274,607	(57%)
	Roy Elson (D)	205,338	(43%)
1968 primary:	Barry Goldwater (R), unopposed		

FIRST DISTRICT Political Background

Arizona 1 is the eastern portion of Maricopa County, including most of the city of Phoenix. This is the fastest growing part of Arizona: in 1950, Phoenix had 106,000 residents; by 1970, 581,000. The state capitol has always been considered Arizona's Republican city, with Tucson traditionally Democratic. But migrants to Phoenix have greatly strengthened the Republican party here. Mostly from the Midwest and South, they have brought with them conservative attitudes and a firm desire to hold fast to traditional values in a new and rootless environment. And because Phoenix is a city with few minorities and relatively few holders of blue-collar jobs, the usual Democratic voting blocs have little power to counter the growing strength of often affluent and staunchly Republican retirees.

Since 1952—the year of the Eisenhower-Goldwater landslide in Arizona—John J. Rhodes, a conservative Republican, has been the congressman from the 1st district. Rhodes is now chairman of the House Republican Policy Committee, a senior member of the Appropriations Committee, and ranking Republican on its Public Works Subcommittee—in short, a key member of the House Republican leadership team. Rhodes is an effective campaigner, but his days of worrying about reelection are long past. He should remain a power in the House for many years.

Census Data 1970 pop. 601,610; deviation from current state average, +1.8%; change 1960–70, +40.7%. Metro. 100%, 56.0% central city.

1970 Share of Federal Outlays $609,840,000 (average outlay per district Arizona 1–3)

DOD	$179,620,000	HEW	$151,071,000
AEC	$4,000	HUD	$2,587,000
NASA	$2,377,000	OEO	$6,804,000
DOT	$24,811,000	DOA	$50,817,000
		Other	$191,709,000

Federal Military-Industrial Commitments (Greater Phoenix listing, Arizona 1–3)

DOD Contractors Garrett Corp (Phoenix), $41.225m: turbo-prop aircraft engines. Motorola (Scottsdale), $33.094m: artillery and bomb fuses; electronic components for ABM system. Lockheed (Phoenix), $13.170m: aircraft maintenance. Talley Industries (Mesa), $9.638m: illumination projectile components. Goodyear Aerospace Div., Goodyear Tire (Litchfield Park), $8.336m: all-weather radar mapping systems. Sperry Rand (Phoenix), $6.864m: gyro-magnetic compass sets.

DOD Installations Navajo Army Depot, reserve status (Flagstaff). Gila Bend AF Auxiliary Field (Gila Bend). Luke AFB (Phoenix). Williams AFB (Chandler).

Economic Base Cotton, dairy, and livestock; electrical machinery, equipment, and supplies; nonelectric machinery; food and kindred products. Also, higher education (Ariz. State U.), tourism and banking.

The Voters

Registration 226,862 total. 105,287 D (46%); 114,592 R (51%); 6,983 Other (3%).

Employment profile White collar, 48%. Blue collar, 52%.

Ethnic groups Black, 4%. Spanish surname, 11%. Total foreign stock, 18%. Mexico, 5%; Germany, Canada, 2% each; UK, Italy, USSR, Poland, Sweden, 1% each. Others, 5%.

Presidential vote

1968	Humphrey (D)	61,413	(30%)
	Nixon (R)	123,796	(61%)
	Wallace (AIP)	16,592	(8%)

Representative

John J. Rhodes (R) Elected 1952; b. Sept. 18, 1916, Council Grove, Kans.; home, Mesa; Kans. State Col., B.S., 1938; Harvard Law School, LL.B., 1941; Army Air Corps, WWII; married, four children; Methodist.

Career Practicing atty., 1946–53; V.P. Farm & Home Life Ins. Co.; V. Chm. Ariz. Pub. Welfare Bd., 1951–52.

Offices 2312 RHOB, 202-225-2635. Also 6081 Fed. Bldg., Phoenix 85025, 602-261-3181.

Committees

Appropriations (4th); Subs. (1) Defense, (2) Legislative, (3) Public Works.

Group Ratings

	ADA	COPE	NREP	NFU	LCV	CFA	NAB	NSI	ACA
1970	24	91	18	50	11	53	100	100	72
1969	0	—	—	40	—	—	—	—	69
1968	8	0	—	38	—	—	83	—	75

Key Votes

(1) ABM	ABS	(6) 18-Yr-Vote	FOR	(11) Clean Water $	AGN
(2) SST	AGN	(7) Farm Sub Lmt	AGN	(12) Mig Wrkrs Comp	AGN
(3) Phil Pln	FOR	(8) Coop-Church	AGN	(13) Jets to Chiang	FOR
(4) No-Knock	FOR	(9) Family Asst	FOR	(14) State OEO Veto	FOR
(5) Cmutr Tax	AGN	(10) Work Stamps	FOR	(15) Park Logging	FOR

Election Results

1970 general:	John J. Rhodes (R)	99,706	(68%)
	Gerald A. Pollock (D)	45,870	(32%)
1968 primary:	John J. Rhodes (R), unopposed		
1968 general:	John J. Rhodes (R)	137,761	(72%)
	Robert E. Miller (D)	54,594	(28%)

SECOND DISTRICT Political Background

Arizona 2 is the southern part of the state, dominated by the city of Tucson, which possesses half of the district's residents. Traditionally, Tucson has been Arizona's Democratic city, but in recent national elections it appears to be trending conservative. The district also includes old mining towns like Tombstone and Bisbee, the town of Yuma, and vast stretches of Arizona desert. The 2nd has the largest Mexican-American population in the state, about 21%, and substantial numbers of Indians.

Udall is an old respected political name in Arizona. Since statehood, there has usually been a Udall on the state Supreme Court, and often in other offices as well. The current representative from the 2nd, Morris Udall, succeeded his brother Stewart in Congress when the latter became Secretary of the Interior in 1961. Since then Congressman Udall has become one of the leaders of the liberal bloc in the House. But a few of his votes—positions reflecting the conservatism of his constituency—have been looked upon with disfavor by organized labor. Udall is an imposing man (6′6″ tall) who is well liked by most of his colleagues, one reason being his effective management of the most recent congressional pay-raise bill.

In 1969, Udall challenged John McCormack for the Speakership. Though he received fewer votes than expected, the bid propelled him into further consideration for leadership positions. Two years later he was one of the liberals who opposed Hale Boggs of Louisiana for the post of Majority Leader. Udall finished a fairly strong second, 88 votes on the second ballot. He did far better than James O'Hara of Michigan, in large part because of his strong stand against the Vietnam war.

The next leadership contest in the House may not occur for some time. Carl Albert has announced that he will serve as Speaker until 1978 when he will become 70. At that time, Udall may win one of the top posts. In any event, he will not likely lose an election in the 2nd. In 1970, against the incumbent state treasurer, he received 69% of the votes—far ahead of the usual Democratic showing in the district.

Census Data 1970 pop. 556,949; deviation from current state average, −4.0%; change 1960–70, +26.5%. Metro. 63.2%, 47.3% central city.

1970 Share of Federal Outlays $612,473,596

DOD	$253,775,000	HEW	$112,945,777
AEC	$415,510	HUD	$8,481,486
NASA	$1,964,149	OEO	$2,346,436
DOT	$16,197,847	DOA	$33,989,672
		Other	$182,357,719

Federal Military-Industrial Commitments

DOD Contractors Hughes Aircraft (Tucson), $92.073m: TOW missiles. Forsberg and Gregory (Davis-Monthan AFB), $5.362m: construction of housing units.

DOD Installations Ft. Huachuca AB (Douglas). Yuma Army Proving Ground (Yuma). Davis-Monthan AFB (Tucson).

Economic Base Metal mining, especially copper; livestock and cotton. Also, higher education (U. of Ariz.), tourism (Tucson), and banking.

The Voters

Registration 189,578 total. 115,575 D (61%); 67,090 R (35%); 6,913 Other (4%).
Employment profile White collar, 42%. Blue collar, 58%.
Ethnic groups Black, 3%. Spanish surname, 21%. Total foreign stock, 23%. Mexico, 13%; Germany, UK, 2% each; Canada, Italy, USSR, 1% each; others, 4%.

Presidential vote

1968	Humphrey (D)	61,119	(42%)
	Nixon (R)	72,539	(49%)
	Wallace (AIP)	13,666	(9%)

Representative

Morris K. Udall (D) Elected May 2, 1961; b. June 15, 1922, St. Johns; home, Tucson; U. of Ariz., LL.B., 1949; Army Air Corps, WWII; divorced, two children; Church of Jesus Christ of Latter Day Saints.
Career Practicing atty., 1949–61; county atty. Pima County (Tucson), 1952–54; Co-founder and Dir. of Bank of Tucson and Catalina Savings and Loan Assn.
Offices 119 CHOB, 202-225-4065. Also 232 Fed. Bldg., Tucson 85702, 602-792-6404.

Committees

Interior and Insular Affairs (7th); Subs. (1) Public Lands, (2) National Parks, (3) Irrigation and Reclamation, (4) Environment.
Post Office and Civil Service (3rd); Subs. (1) Chm., Postal Service, (2) Employee Benefits, (3) Census and Statistics.

Group Ratings

	ADA	COPE	NREP	NFU	LCV	CFA	NAB	NSI	ACA
1970	76	82	75	100	86	94	9	44	0
1969	67	—	—	93	—	—	—	—	0
1968	92	100	—	100	—	—	0	—	0

Key Votes

(1) ABM	AGN	(6) 18-Yr-Vote	FOR	(11) Clean Water $	FOR
(2) SST	AGN	(7) Farm Sub Lmt	AGN	(12) Mig Wrkrs Comp	FOR
(3) Phil Pln	FOR	(8) Coop-Church	FOR	(13) Jets to Chiang	AGN
(4) No-Knock	ABS	(9) Family Asst	FOR	(14) State OEO Veto	AGN
(5) Cmutr Tax	FOR	(10) Work Stamps	AGN	(15) Park Logging	AGN

Election Results

1970 general:	Morris Udall (D)	86,760	(69%)
	Morris Herring (R)	37,561	(30%)
	Cliff Thomallo (AIP)	1,357	(1%)
1970 primary:	Morris Udall (D), unopposed		
1968 general:	Morris Udall (D)	102,301	(70%)
	G. A. McGinnis (R)	43,235	(30%)

THIRD DISTRICT Political Background

Arizona 3 is currently an amalgam: one-third of the district is part of metropolitan Phoenix and the remainder is the sparsely populated northern and central portions of the state. The latter includes most of the tourist's Arizona—the Grand Canyon, the Painted Desert, and the Petrified Forest. It also includes most of the state's Indian reservations, the most notable of which is the giant Navajo Reservation in the northeast corner of the state. To the south are the old mining towns of Globe and Morenci, which are still heavily Democratic. But most of the voters of the 3rd are conservatives who live in and around Phoenix and the small cities in the Arizona mountains and deserts: Prescott, Flagstaff (which is supposed to have had the last completely pure air in the United States), Winslow, and Kingman.

By 1972, the district lines will have to be redrawn. Most of the 3rd's portion of Maricopa County will go to form a new district, and some southern counties (probably Pinal and Cochise), currently in the 2nd, will have to be added. The redistricting should make the 3rd the most politically marginal of Arizona's House seats. The current representative, conservative Republican Sam Steiger, won with a comfortable 63% of the votes in 1970. But his biggest margins were in Maricopa County precincts—most of which will not be in the district in 1972—while Pinal and Cochise counties, which will be appended, usually produce Democratic margins. In his next race, Steiger will not enjoy many of the usual advantages of incumbents.

Steiger has a reputation for being something of a maverick in the House. The notion probably stems from a talk-show comment, early in his first term, in which he intimated that many of his colleagues were drunks. The remark cost him at least one project for his district that would have ordinarily gone through easily. Since then Steiger has been kept outside the inner circles of the House. Nevertheless, he has continued to rise on the seniority ladder, and is now chairman of the Interior Committee's Indian Affairs Subcommittee—a post of substantial importance to the district.

Census Data 1970 pop. 613,923; deviation from current state average, +3.9%; change 1960–70, 41.4%. Metro. 59.7%, 39.9% central city.

1970 Share of Federal Outlays $609,840,000 (average outlay per district Arizona 1–3)

DOD	$179,620,000	HEW	$151,071,000
AEC	$4,000	HUD	$2,587,000
NASA	$2,377,000	OEO	$6,804,000
DOT	$24,811,000	DOA	$50,817,000
		Other	$191,709,000

Federal Military-Industrial Commitments (See Arizona 1 for greater Phoenix listing)

Economic Base Cotton and livestock; metal mining, especially copper. Also, tourism (Grand Canyon).

The Voters

Registration 324,345 total. 177,069 D (55%); 138,024 R (43%); 9,252 Other (3%).

Employment profile White collar, 37%. Blue collar, 63%.

Ethnic groups Black, 2%. Spanish surname, 14%. Total foreign stock, 14%. Mexico, 8%; Canada, Germany, UK, Italy, 1% each; others, 2%.

Presidential vote

1968	Humphrey (D)	47,487	(36%)
	Nixon (R)	68,471	(52%)
	Wallace (AIP)	16,094	(12%)

Representative

Sam Steiger (R) Elected 1966; b. March 10, 1929, New York City; home, Prescott; Cornell U., 1946–48; Colorado A & M, B.S., 1950; Army, 1951–53; married, three children; Jewish.

Career Rancher and horse breeder.

Offices 126 CHOB, 202-225-4576. Also 5015 Fed. Bldg., Phoenix 85025, 602-261-4041.

Committees

Government Operations (11th); Subs. (1) Legal and Monetary Affairs, (2) Conservation and Natural Resources.

Interior and Insular Affairs (5th); Subs. (1) Indian Affairs, (2) Environment, (3) Mines, (4) Public Lands.

Sel. Com. on Crime (2nd).

Group Ratings

	ADA	COPE	NREP	NFU	LCV	CFA	NAB	NSI	ACA
1970	12	0	0	31	0	35	100	100	94
1969	0	—	—	21	—	—	—	—	94
1968	0	0	—	31	—	—	83	—	81

Key Votes

(1) ABM	FOR	(6) 18-Yr-Vote	AGN	(11) Clean Water $	AGN
(2) SST	AGN	(7) Farm Sub Lmt	AGN	(12) Mig Wrkrs Comp	AGN
(3) Phil Pln	AGN	(8) Coop-Church	AGN	(13) Jets to Chiang	FOR
(4) No-Knock	ABS	(9) Family Asst	AGN	(14) State OEO Veto	FOR
(5) Cmutr Tax	AGN	(10) Work Stamps	FOR	(15) Park Logging	FOR

Election Results

1970 general:	Sam Steiger (R)	81,239	(62%)
	Orren Beaty (D)	49,626	(38%)
1970 primary:	Sam Steiger (R), unopposed		
1968 general:	Sam Steiger (R)	79,667	(63%)
	Ralph Watkins (D)	46,072	(37%)

ARKANSAS

Political Background

For some 10 years after federal troops were sent in to integrate Little Rock's Central High School, Arkansas was known politically as the segregationist home of Gov. Orval Faubus. But that reputation was not entirely deserved. It is generally thought now that Faubus, who is from the almost all-white mountains in the northern part of the state, engineered the crisis in order to win an unprecedented third term as governor. Assuming he did, he was successful, having won reelection until his voluntary retirement in 1966.

Before the sensational events in Little Rock, it was already clear that Arkansas politics was not going the way of Alabama's or Mississippi's. Arkansas is a different kind of state. Less than half of it—the southern part of the state along the Louisiana border and the cottonfields lying just west of the Mississippi River—is really part of the Deep South. The Ozark area in the northwest part of Arkansas is traditionally Republican and not overly concerned with the racial issues which have traditionally structured Southern politics. And Little Rock, the capital and largest city, soon drew back from the segregationist's knee-jerk reactions that followed the Central High incidents. Finally, even before the Voting Rights Act of 1965, blacks were able to register and vote in Arkansas cities, and today black registration is high even in the rural counties across the river from Mississippi.

While it is true that Arkansas cast its electoral votes for George Wallace in 1968, the Alabaman was a minority winner in a rather close three-way race. Recent state election results suggest that Wallace may not be able to duplicate this showing in 1972. But the important political development occurred in 1966, the year Faubus retired and Winthrop Rockefeller—the only truly liberal Republican who has won office in the South—was elected governor. He won again in 1968 against a Faubus protégé. Rockefeller did have particularly strong support in the Republican Ozark counties and black areas, but he carried almost every other part of the state as well. His advocacy of equal opportunity for blacks seems not to have been an electoral detriment.

Rockefeller was beaten in 1970. The man who did it, however, was the first Democratic nominee in years not in the Faubus image. In fact, country lawyer and now Governor Dale Bumpers beat Faubus himself in the Democratic primary. Bumpers, like Rockefeller, is a racial moderate, having made considerable efforts during the campaign to win the black vote, even though he knew it was already solidly in Rockefeller's corner. Bumpers' huge victory was not so much a repudiation of Rockefeller as it was an indication that the politics he had helped to create had become firmly established.

The tone of the Bumpers-Rockefeller election should have been no real surprise to observers of Arkansas's congressional delegations over the years. Traditionally, most of its members have been distinct moderates, always voting against civil rights measures but never leading the opposition to them. At the same time, they often supported liberal social and economic measures. The best known of these, of course, is J. William Fulbright, who remains the state's junior senator though he was first elected in 1944. Fulbright's chief interest is foreign policy, having chaired the Senate Foreign Relations Committee since the 1950's. Under his leadership, the committee has become the leading national forum for opposition to the Vietnam war and for a reduction of American commitments abroad. Fulbright, who was once president of the University of Arkansas, is a contemplative man, and one seemingly out of tune with the temper of his state. But he knows how to mend political fences back home and won reelection by a very comfortable margin in 1968. In the Democratic primary of that year, Fulbright beat an arch-segregationist by better than 2:1. The former Rhodes Scholar has always voted against civil rights measures, but in 1970 was one of four Southern senators to vote against the Carswell nomination. Rumors have it that Fulbright will not seek reelection in 1974 when he will be 69. Should he choose to run, however, he will almost certainly win another term.

Arkansas's senior senator is John McClellan, a stern and austere conservative who was first elected to the Senate in 1942. McClellan is chairman of the Government Operations Committee and of its Permanent Subcommittee on Investigations. He has lead the subcommittee's widely publicized inquiries into such varied matters as labor union corruption in the late 1950's and the TFX (F-111) contract in the mid-1960's. McClellan has not faced a serious electoral challenge in almost 30 years, but 1972 promises to be different. Congressman David Pryor has indicated an interest in the Democratic nomination. Young (38 in 1972) Pryor will be able to campaign vigorously against McClellan (76 in 1972). At this writing, there appears to be some of that traditional jockeying for position which occurs when a challenger promises to take on an aging Southern senator. It is possible that McClellan, like Walter George of Georgia when challenged by Herman Talmadge in 1956, will choose to retire.

Not so many years ago, the Arkansas House delegation had an average seniority greater than that of any other state in the country. In 1966 its four members had served a total of 104 years in the House and each held an important committee post. Since then, one, James W. Trimble of the 3rd district, member of Rules, has been defeated; another, Oren Harris of the 4th, chairman of Interstate and Foreign Commerce, resigned to accept a federal judgeship; and a third, E. C. Gathings of the 1st, chairman of Agriculture's Cotton Subcommittee, has retired. Wilbur Mills, of course, stays on, and as chairman of Ways and Means, whose Democratic members determine their party's committee assignments, has seen to it that these veterans' successors received the places they wanted. It seems certain that the Arkansas delegation will continue to wield a disproportionate share of clout, if only because of Mills. Since redistricting has not changed the composition of Arkansas's districts appreciably, no one in the delegation appears to be in any danger.

Electoral Votes 6

Census Data 1970 pop. 1,923,295; 0.93% of U.S. total, 33rd largest; change 1960–70, +7.7%. Metro. 30.9%, 17.4% central city. 1970 per capita income, $2,742, 50th highest. 23rd in number of poor.

1970 Share of Federal Tax Burden $1,151,330,000; 0.59% of U.S. total, 34th largest.

1970 Share of Federal Outlays $1,575,125,429; 0.83% of U.S. total, 34th largest. Per capita federal spending, $819.

DOD	$244,321,000	40th (0.43%)	HEW	$497,753,834	33rd (0.95%)
AEC	$2,038,160	33rd (0.01%)	HUD	$23,975,869	27th (1.23%)
NASA	$70,006	48th (—)	OEO	$9,324,764	29th (1.23%)
DOT	$41,676,175	40th (0.58%)	DOA	$375,511,037	11th (2.92%)

DOC	$10,419,806	23rd (0.90%)		POD	$49,873,680	34th (0.68%)
DOI	$8,384,386	43rd (0.36%)		VA	$135,776,334	26th (1.84%)
DOJ	$3,084,080	38th (0.54%)		CSC	$23,851,664	33rd (0.59%)
				Other	$149,064,634	

Economic Base Cotton, poultry, and livestock; food and kindred products, esp. meat packing; lumber and wood products other than furniture, esp. sawmills and planing mills; electrical machinery, equipment, and supplies; apparel and other finished products made from fabrics and similar materials; furniture and fixtures; paper and allied products; printing, publishing, and allied industries; chemicals and allied products.

Political Line-up Governor, Dale Bumpers (D); seat up, 1972. Senators, John L. McClellan (D) and J. William Fulbright (D). Representatives, 4 (3 D and 1 R). State Senate (34 D and 1 R); State House (98 D and 2 R).

The Voters

Registration 881,403 total. No party registration.

Employment profile White collar, 33%. Blue collar, 67%.

Ethnic groups Black, 18%. Total foreign stock, 2%. Germany, 1%; others, 1%.

Presidential vote

1968	Humphrey (D)	188,228	(30%)
	Nixon (R)	190,759	(31%)
	Wallace (AIP)	240,982	(39%)
1964	Johnson (D)	314,197	(56%)
	Goldwater (R)	243,264	(44%)
1960	Kennedy (D)	215,049	(54%)
	Nixon (R)	184,508	(46%)

Senator

John L. McClellan (D) Elected 1942, seat up 1972; b. Feb. 25, 1896, Sheridan; home, Little Rock; admitted to Ark. bar by special act of legislature in 1913 after studying law in father's office; Army, WWII; married; Baptist.

Career Practicing atty., 1913–17, 1919–35, 1939–42; prosecuting atty., 7th Jud. Dist. of Ark., 1927–30.

Offices 3241 NSOB, 202-225-2353. Also 3030 Fed. Bldg., Little Rock 72201, 501-372-4361, ext. 5705.

Committees

Government Operations (Chm.) Subs. (1) Chm., Investigations, (2) Intergovernmental Relations.

Appropriations (2nd); Subs. (1) Chm., State, Justice, Commerce, Judiciary, and Related Agencies, (2) Defense and Intelligence, (3) Interior and Related Agencies, (4) Foreign Operations, (5) Public Works.

Judiciary (2nd); Subs. (1) Chm., Patents, Trademarks, and Copyrights, (2) Chm., Criminal Laws and Procedures, (3) Antitrust and Monopoly, (4) Constitutional Rights, (5) Federal Charters, Holidays, and Celebrations, (6) Immigration and Nationalization, (7) Improvements in Judicial Machinery, (8) Internal Security, (9) Refugees and Escapees, (10) Separation of Powers.

Sel. Com. on Equal Educational Opportunity (2nd).

Jt. Com. on Reduction of Federal Expenditures (3rd).

Group Ratings

	ADA	COPE	NREP	NFU	LCV	NAB	NSI	ACA
1970	0	18	0	33	27	64	100	89
1969	11	—	—	50	—	—	—	79
1968	0	10	—	25	—	40	—	73

Key Votes

(1) ABM	FOR	(8) Phil Pln	AGN	(15) Coop-Church	AGN
(2) SST	FOR	(9) Vol Army	AGN	(16) Cut Oil Dpltn	AGN
(3) Busing	AGN	(10) Prison $	AGN	(17) Consumer Prot	AGN
(4) Tob Sub	FOR	(11) Cut Mil $	AGN	(18) Farm Sub Limit	AGN
(5) Carswell	FOR	(12) Defoliatn	FOR	(19) Comp Bid Sales	ABS
(6) No-Knock	FOR	(13) 18-Yr-Vote	AGN	(20) Pre-Prod Tests	AGN
(7) Seniorty	AGN	(14) Pentgn PR	FOR	(21) Cut Marjna Pen	AGN

Election Results

1966 general:	John McClellan (D), unopposed		
1966 primary:	John McClellan (D)	310,526	(77%)
	Foster Johnson (D)	91,746	(23%)
1960 general:	John McClellan (D), unopposed		

Senator

J. William Fulbright (D) Elected 1944, seat up 1974; b. April 9, 1905, Summer, Mo.; home, Fayetteville; U. of Ark., B.A., 1925; Oxford U., Rhodes Scholar, B.A., 1928, M.A., 1931; George Washington U., LL.B., 1934; married, two children; Disciples of Christ Church.

Career Atty., Dept. of Justice, 1934–35; Instructor in law, George Washington U., 1935–36, Lecturer in law, 1936–39; President, U. of Ark., 1939–41; Delegate 9th General Assembly of U.N., 1954; U.S. House of Reps., 1943–45.

Offices 1215 NSOB, 202-225-4843. Also 2331 New Fed. Bldg., Little Rock 72203, 501-372-4361, ext. 5503.

Committees

Foreign Relations (Chm.); Sub. U.S. Security Agreements and Commitments Abroad.

Finance (5th).

Jt. Economic Com. (3rd); Subs. (1) Economic Progress, (2) Economic Statistics, (3) Foreign Economic Policy, (4) Inter-American Economic Relationships.

Group Ratings

	ADA	COPE	NREP	NFU	LCV	NAB	NSI	ACA
1970	66	36	90	75	47	20	0	22
1969	67	—	—	75	—	—	—	29
1968	14	36	—	38	—	50	—	63

Key Votes

(1) ABM	AGN	(8) Phil Pln	AGN	(15) Coop-Church	FOR
(2) SST	AGN	(9) Vol Army	AGN	(16) Cut Oil Dpltn	AGN
(3) Busing	ABS	(10) Prison $	AGN	(17) Consumer Prot	ABS
(4) Tob Sub	AGN	(11) Cut Mil $	FOR	(18) Farm Sub Limit	AGN
(5) Carswell	AGN	(12) Defoliatn	ABS	(19) Comp Bid Sales	FOR
(6) No-Knock	FOR	(13) 18-Yr-Vote	FOR	(20) Pre-Prod Tests	FOR
(7) Seniorty	AGN	(14) Pentgn PR	AGN	(21) Cut Marjna Pen	ABS

Election Results

1968 general:	J. William Fulbright (D)	349,965	(59%)
	Charles T. Bernard (R)	241,731	(41%)
1968 primary:	J. William Fulbright (D)	220,684	(53%)
	Bob Hayes (D)	52,906	(13%)
	Jim Johnson (D)	132,038	(32%)
	Foster Johnson (D)	11,395	(3%)

FIRST DISTRICT Political Background

Arkansas 1 is situated on the flat fertile plains just west of the Mississippi River. This is one of the nation's foremost cotton-producing areas, its vast farms interrupted only now and then by market towns like Jonesboro (pop. 27,000), Blytheville (pop. 24,000), and West Memphis (pop. 25,000). Like most cotton country, the farmlands of the 1st have historically been thickly populated, particularly by blacks. But migration to Memphis and the North has lowered the district's black population, which is today only 26%.

For 30 years, the representative from the 1st was E. C. Gathings, who never won much of a national reputation but rose diligently on the seniority ladder to become chairman of the Agriculture Committee's Subcommittee on Cotton. Gathings retired in 1968, and his successor, W. V. (Bill) Alexander, is a man in much the same mold. Consistently conservative on most issues, his main interest seems to be local: agriculture and river improvements. Thanks to Wilbur Mills, Alexander was placed on the Agriculture Committee in his 1st term, and now also sits on Government Operations.

Most rural Southern districts have a tradition of electing a young man to the House and then reelecting him for 20 or 30 years. He can thereby accumulate seniority and bring various benefits back to the district. This is the pattern in the 1st. Gathings was 35 when he won his first election in 1938, and Alexander was 34 when he won in 1968. All signs indicate that the 1st will continue to support Alexander and that, in a decade or so, he will succeed to an important subcommittee (or even committee) chairmanship. Redistricting has added several hill counties to the 1st, but that should not change its political behavior appreciably.

Census Data 1970 pop. 418,744; deviation from current state average, —12.9%; change 1960–70, —5.7%. Metro. 11.5%, 0.0% central city.

1970 Share of Federal Outlays $363,359,029

DOD	$49,242,000	HEW	$100,778,876
AEC	$000	HUD	$3,763,675
NASA	$25,006	OEO	$2,129,967
DOT	$3,441,843	DOA	$132,010,946
		Other	$71,966,716

Federal Military-Industrial Commitments

DOD Installations Blytheville AFB (Blytheville).

Economic Base Cotton; leather and leather products; electrical machinery, equipment, and supplies.

The Voters

Registration 179,843 total. No party registration.

Employment profile White collar, 26%. Blue collar, 74%.

Ethnic groups Black, 26%. Total foreign stock, 1%. All groups less than 0.5%.

Presidential vote

1968	Humphrey (D)	37,835	(31%)
	Nixon (R)	30,778	(25%)
	Wallace (AIP)	52,510	(43%)

Representative

William Vollie (Bill) Alexander, Jr. (D) Elected 1968; b. Jan. 16, 1934, Memphis, Tenn.; home, Osceola; U. of Ark., Southwestern at Memphis, Tenn., B.A., 1957; Vanderbilt U., LL.B., 1960; Army, Korean War; married, one child; Episcopalian.

Career Practicing atty., 1960–69.

Offices 116 CHOB, 202-225-4076. Also Drawer FFF, Ark. State U., Jonesboro 72467, 501-972-2135.

Committees

Agriculture (12th); Subs. (1) Oilseeds and Rice, (2) Conservation and Credit.

Government Operations (22nd); Subs. (1) Intergovernmental Relations, (2) Foreign Operations and Government Information.

Group Ratings

	ADA	COPE	NREP	NFU	LCV	CFA	NAB	NSI	ACA
1970	20	40	33	73	0	67	13	100	50
1969	13	—	—	67	—	—	—	—	27

Key Votes

(1) ABM	FOR	(6) 18-Yr-Vote	AGN	(11) Clean Water $	AGN
(2) SST	AGN	(7) Farm Sub Lmt	AGN	(12) Mig Wrkrs Comp	AGN
(3) Phil Pln	FOR	(8) Coop-Church	FOR	(13) Jets to Chiang	ABS
(4) No-Knock	FOR	(9) Family Asst	AGN	(14) State OEO Veto	AGN
(5) Cmutr Tax	FOR	(10) Work Stamps	FOR	(15) Park Logging	FOR

Election Results

1970 general:	W. V. Alexander (D), unopposed		
1970 primary:	W. V. Alexander (D), unopposed		
1968 general:	W. V. Alexander (D)	80,293	(69%)
	Guy Newcomb (R)	36,284	(31%)

SECOND DISTRICT Political Background

Arkansas 2 extends from the hills of the Ozarks down through Little Rock and almost reaches the Mississippi River in the east. It spans the geopolitical spectrum of Arkansas, from the Republican-leaning mountaineers of the north to the Deep South counties where race has always been the primary political issue. On paper, the district looks close to marginal politically, since there are Republican votes not only in the north but also in many of the city precincts of Little Rock where Nixon, Humphrey, and Wallace ran a near perfect three-way tie in 1968.

But in congressional elections the 2nd is not marginal and never will be, as long as Wilbur Mills is alive and running. Mills has represented the district and its predecessors since 1938 and has been chairman of the House Ways and Means Committee since 1958. Through his vast knowledge of the nation's tax laws, and his ability to elucidate them to his colleagues, Mills has become one of the most powerful men in the United States. The Harvard Law graduate from Kensett, Arkansas, has authority in tax matters—social security, welfare, medical care, tariffs, and import quotas—second only to that of the President.

And sometimes it is not second. At this writing, it appears that Mills will be able to block President Nixon's revenue-sharing program and enact his own program requiring the federal government to underwrite all welfare expenditures. Mills, however, is not one of those committee chairmen who impose their will singlehandedly on a hostile House. Sometimes the opposite criticism is heard: that he bends this way or that, depending on the mood of the majority. Certainly Mills cherishes his reputation for being able to steer legislation through the House. He was one of the co-sponsors of the Kerr-Mills medical care program in the early 1960's, but when the 1964 election changed the balance of power in the House, he switched to support of the Medicare program.

More recently, Mills shepherded an import quota measure through the House in 1970, only to oppose the Nixon Administration's import quota program in 1971. In the interim, he reportedly persuaded the Japanese to limit their textile exports voluntarily—and that fact is a sign of his prestige not only in this country but abroad.

Mills is also powerful because the Democratic members of Ways and Means constitute their party's Committee on Committees. This gives Mills and his colleagues on the committee an almost life-and-death power over the careers of Democratic congressmen. A good committee assignment—one which will give the congressman a chance to do things for his district—can mean the difference between defeat and reelection. And promotion to the committees on which few freshmen serve—Appropriations, Rules, Ways and Means—can give a middle-seniority congressman much power. Mills himself was spotted by Sam Rayburn and given a seat on Ways and Means early in his career; such being the case, he outranked on the committee men who had been in the House several years longer.

There is talk now that Mills will run for President or Vice-President in 1972, which probably means that he will be at least a favorite son of the Arkansas delegation. But most likely Mills, who is given to delphic pronouncements upon occasions, wants the move to give him and other moderate Southerners more of a say at the convention. The 1972 elections will doubtless see Mills as the sole candidate for Congress from the 2nd district of Arkansas, just as it has been in every election in the past eight years. And whoever is elected President will still have to deal with Wilbur Mills.

Census Data 1970 pop. 518,840; deviation from current state average, +7.9%; change 1960–70, +16.9%. Metro. 55.4%, 37.1% central city.

1970 Share of Federal Outlays $567,316,226

DOD	$102,262,000	HEW	$141,905,375
AEC	$15,000	HUD	$13,061,566
NASA	$45,000	OEO	$3,590,758
DOT	$17,690,554	DOA	$151,714,269
		Other	$137,031,704

Federal Military-Industrial Commitments

DOD Contractors Batesville Mfg. Div., General Tire (Batesville), $12.715m: bomb fuses; rocket launchers. Pace Corp. (Camden), $5.057m: parachute dropped illuminating flares.

DOD Installations Little Rock AFB (Little Rock).

Economic Base Cotton, livestock, and dairy; food and kindred products; electrical machinery, equipment, and supplies; printing, publishing, and allied industries. Also, banking.

The Voters

Registration 236,115 total. No party registration.

Employment profile White collar, 38%. Blue collar, 62%.

Ethnic groups Black, 15%. Total foreign stock, 3%. Germany, 1%. Others, 1%.

Presidential vote

1968	Humphrey (D)	51,786	(32%)
	Nixon (R)	52,012	(32%)
	Wallace (AIP)	58,345	(36%)

Representative

Wilbur D. Mills (D) Elected 1938; b. May 24, 1909, Kensett; home, Kensett; Hendrix Col., A.B., 1930; Harvard Law School, LL.B., 1933; married, two children; Methodist.

Career County and Probate Judge of White County, Ark., 1934–38.

Offices 1136 LHOB, 202-225-2506. Also 1527 New Fed. Bldg., Little Rock 72201, 501-372-4361, ext. 5522, and P.O. Bldg., Searcy 72143, 501-268-3989.

Committees

Ways and Means (Chm.).

Jt. Com. on Internal Revenue Taxation (Chm.).

Jt. Com. on Reduction of Federal Expenditures (2nd).

Group Ratings

	ADA	COPE	NREP	NFU	LCV	CFA	NAB	NSI	ACA
1970	12	42	27	50	20	43	60	84	59
1969	13	—	—	64	—	—	—	—	36
1968	8	17	—	50	—	—	50	—	77

Key Votes

(1) ABM	ABS	(6) 18-Yr-Vote	AGN	(11) Clean Water $	AGN
(2) SST	FOR	(7) Farm Sub Lmt	AGN	(12) Mig Wrkrs Comp	AGN
(3) Phil Pln	ABS	(8) Coop-Church	AGN	(13) Jets to Chiang	ABS
(4) No-Knock	ABS	(9) Family Asst	FOR	(14) State OEO Veto	AGN
(5) Cmutr Tax	FOR	(10) Work Stamps	FOR	(15) Park Logging	FOR

Election Results

1970 general:	Wilbur Mills (D), unopposed
1970 primary:	Wilbur Mills (D), unopposed
1968 general:	Wilbur Mills (D), unopposed

THIRD DISTRICT Political Background

Arkansas 3 is the western and northwestern portion of the state. It contains Fort Smith, the state's second largest city; Fayetteville, the home of the University of Arkansas and of Sen. J. William Fulbright; and Hot Springs, the onetime gambling resort. It also contains most of the state's reliably Republican territory, the mountain counties in the north which have consistently backed the Grand Old Party since the Civil War. In the south, the district stretches into thoroughly Confederate territory, nearly all the way to Texarkana.

The 3rd is the closest thing to a swing district in Arkansas; in fact, it is the only district where there has been a two-party battle in more than one of the past four congressional elections. In 1966, the 3rd surprised practically everyone by ousting longtime Rep. James W. Trimble, then 72 and a member of the House Rules Committee, and electing John Paul Hammerschmidt, then the Arkansas Republican State Chairman. Hammerschmidt carried the Republican counties in the north by large margins and generally profited from Winthrop Rockefeller's strong victory in the gubernatorial contest of that year.

Since then Hammerschmidt, who has a decidedly conservative voting record, has had little trouble winning reelection. He received more than 60% of the votes in 1968 and 1970. The strong showing of Democratic Gov. Dale Bumpers, who carried almost every county in the state, made little difference to Republican Hammerschmidt in the 3rd. The Congressman's prospects for continued reelection look very good.

Census Data 1970 pop. 530,325; deviation from current state average, +10.3%: change 1960–70, +19.2%. Metro. 19.8%, 11.8% central city.

1970 Share of Federal Outlays $348,701,099

DOD	$46,772,000	HEW	$143,611,216
AEC	$2,023,160	HUD	$6,850,628
NASA	$000	OEO	$2,325,960
DOT	$13,395,726	DOA	$36,659,319
		Other	$97,063,090

Federal Military-Industrial Commitments

None.

Economic Base Livestock, poultry, and dairy; food and kindred products, especially meat packing; electrical machinery, equipment, and supplies, especially electrical industrial apparatus. Also, higher education (U. of Ark.).

The Voters

Registration 253,246 total. No party registration.

Employment profile White collar, 33%. Blue collar, 67%.

Ethnic groups Black, 5%. Total foreign stock, 3%. Germany, 1%. Others, 1%.

Presidential vote

1968	Humphrey (D)	50,450	(27%)
	Nixon (R)	76,320	(41%)
	Wallace (AIP)	59,443	(32%)

Representative

John Paul Hammerschmidt (R) Elected 1966; b. May 4, 1922, Harrison; home, Harrison; The Citadel; Oklahoma A & M Col.; U. of Ark.; Army Air Corps WWII; Major, USAFR; married, one child; Presbyterian.

Career Pres. Hammerschmidt Lumber Co., Pres. Construction Products Co., Dir. First National Bank and Harrison Fed. Savings and Loan Assn.; Chm., Ark. Republican State Central Com., 1964.

Offices 437 CHOB, 202-225-4301. Also Rm. 209 Main P.O. Bldg., Harrison 72601, 501-365-6900, and Fed. Bldg., Hot Springs 72901, 501-623-4537.

Committees

Public Works (9th); Subs. (1) Rivers and Harbors, (2) Flood Control and Internal Development, (3) Investigations and Oversight, (4) Roads, (5) Sp. Sub. on Economic Development Programs.

Veterans' Affairs (3rd); Subs. (1) Compensation and Pension, (2) Hospitals, (3) Housing.

Group Ratings

	ADA	COPE	NREP	NFU	LCV	CFA	NAB	NSI	ACA
1970	16	17	0	38	0	43	82	100	84
1969	0	—	—	31	—	—	—	—	60
1968	0	0	—	44	—	—	100	—	87

Key Votes

(1) ABM	FOR	(6) 18-Yr-Vote	AGN	(11) Clean Water $	AGN
(2) SST	FOR	(7) Farm Sub Lmt	AGN	(12) Mig Wrkrs Comp	AGN
(3) Phil Pln	ABS	(8) Coop-Church	AGN	(13) Jets to Chiang	FOR
(4) No-Knock	FOR	(9) Family Asst	AGN	(14) State OEO Veto	FOR
(5) Cmutr Tax	AGN	(10) Work Stamps	FOR	(15) Park Logging	FOR

Election Results

1970 general:	John Paul Hammerschmidt (R)	115,532	(67%)
	Donald Poe (D)	57,679	(33%)
1970 primary:	John Paul Hammerschmidt (R), unopposed		
1968 general:	John Paul Hammerschmidt (R)	121,771	(67%)
	Hardy Croxton (D)	59,638	(33%)

FOURTH DISTRICT Political Background

Arkansas 4 is part of the Deep South. Its farmlands stretch across the southern half of the state, punctuated occasionally by towns like El Dorado (pop. 25,000), Camden (pop. 15,000), and Arkadelphia (pop. 9,000). Its largest city is Pine Bluff (pop. 57,000), the girlhood home of Martha Mitchell and the place where she feels compelled to return periodically either in person or by telephone. The 4th gave George Wallace his best showing in Arkansas in 1968 (47%); most of its white residents retain the same attitudes on national issues as their neighbors in northern Louisiana and Mississippi. Black residents of the district constitute 31% of the population, and, because of the 1965 Voting Rights Act, they now form a significant political bloc in the district.

Somewhat surprisingly, the 4th has had a rather moderate political tradition—at least in congressional elections. From 1940 through 1968 it was represented by Oren

Harris, who rose to become chairman of the House Interstate and Foreign Commerce Committee and was then appointed a federal judge by President Johnson. After Harris's resignation, there was some difficulty filling the seat. The legislature had redrawn the district lines since the previous election, leaving it unclear whether the new congressman should come from the old or new district.

As it turned out, the seat was not filled until the 1968 general election when David Pryor, a young (then 34) state legislator, was chosen to succeed Harris. Pryor has made a surprisingly liberal record for his district. Though he has not strayed from the Southern fold on civil rights questions, he has made a name for himself investigating abuses in Medicare-financed nursing homes. For eight weekends Pryor worked incognito as an attendant in Washington-area nursing homes. Since then he has held hearings on the subject and proposed legislation to curb the almost unbelievable abuses he encountered.

It has been reported that Pryor intends to challenge John McClellan for his Senate seat in the 1972 Democratic primary. The race will make a nice contrast. Although they are both from the same part of the state, McClellan will be twice Pryor's age that year. McClellan has not had strong opposition in years, while Pryor, who had a tough primary fight in 1968, is used to campaigning. Pryor's record is significantly more liberal than McClellan's, though just about as conservative as Wilbur Mills's. It is possible that McClellan will decide to retire, or that Pryor, who holds a seat on Appropriations, will choose to remain in the House and wait for a Senate vacancy to occur.

Census Data 1970 pop. 455,386; deviation from current state average, —5.3%; change 1960–70, +0.4%. Metro. 34.0%, 17.4% central city.

1970 Share of Federal Outlays $295,749,075

DOD	$46,045,000	HEW	$111,458,367
AEC	$000	HUD	$300,000
NASA	$000	OEO	$1,278,079
DOT	$7,148,052	DOA	$55,126,503
		Other	$74,393,074

Federal Military-Industrial Commitments

DOD Installations Pine Bluff Army Arsenal (Pine Bluff).

Economic Base Cotton and livestock; lumber and wood products other than furniture; paper and allied products.

The Voters

Registration 211,389 total. No party registration.

Employment profile White collar, 31%. Blue collar, 69%.

Ethnic groups Black, 31%. Total foreign stock, 1%. All groups less than 0.5%.

Presidential vote

1968	Humphrey (D)	48,157	(32%)
	Nixon (R)	31,649	(21%)
	Wallace (AIP)	70,684	(47%)

Representative

David Pryor (D) Elected 1966; b. Aug. 29, 1934, Camden; home, Camden; Henderson State Col., 1952–53; U. of Ark., B.A., 1957, LL.B., 1964; married, three children; Presbyterian.

Career Practicing atty., 1964–66; publisher, *Ouachita Citizen*, 1957–61; State Rep. of Ouachita County in Ark. General Assembly, 1961–66.

Offices 307 CHOB, 202-225-3772. Also Fed. Bldg., Pine Bluff 71601, 501-536-1180, and Fed. Bldg., Camden 71701, 501-836-3441.

Committees

Appropriations (25th); Subs. (1) D.C., (2) HUD, Space, and Science.

Group Ratings

	ADA	COPE	NREP	NFU	LCV	CFA	NAB	NSI	ACA
1970	48	55	45	83	25	82	44	90	27
1969	27	—	—	80	—	—	—	—	31
1968	42	39	—	73	—	—	33	—	26

Key Votes

(1) ABM	FOR	(6) 18-Yr-Vote	FOR	(11) Clean Water $	AGN
(2) SST	AGN	(7) Farm Sub Lmt	AGN	(12) Mig Wrkrs Comp	AGN
(3) Phil Pln	AGN	(8) Coop-Church	ABS	(13) Jets to Chiang	AGN
(4) No-Knock	FOR	(9) Family Asst	FOR	(14) State OEO Veto	AGN
(5) Cmutr Tax	FOR	(10) Work Stamps	AGN	(15) Park Logging	FOR

Election Results

1970 general: David Pryor (D), unopposed
1970 primary: David Pryor (D), unopposed
1968 primary: David Pryor (D), unopposed

CALIFORNIA

Political Background

Irony and contradiction are the two words that best sum up the country's most populous state: it is one of the most urbanized states and yet the home of a vast system of agribusiness; one of the most beautiful and scenic and yet the most smoggy and pollution-ridden; one where the peace movement first made an impact and yet where the economy would collapse if the Pentagon stopped sending checks to its contractors and installations. In fiscal 1970 alone, the military spent some $9.8 billion in California, the 1st-ranked state in Defense Department expenditures. Texas, ranked 2nd, got about half as much in the same period.

California is isolated from the other heavily populated parts of the nation. Nevertheless it has been able to anticipate many national trends—in suburban development, in popular music, and in politics. It was here that the politics of John Mitchell and Kevin Phillips—the unyoung, unblack, and unpoor's hatred and fear of the young, black, and poor—first proved to be a winner. And it is also here that the first signs of the failure of this kind of politics are appearing.

Not so long ago, when everybody took it on faith that Republicans had to support liberal programs to win elections, arch-conservative Republicans were already beating liberal Democrats in California. The first such victory came in 1962 when Max Rafferty was elected state Superintendent of Public Instruction. In the following year, two conservative Republicans won off-year congressional elections in districts which were considered safe Democratic seats (the 1st and the 23rd). After that, in 1964, George Murphy, the Yale man who danced in the movies, won surprise election to the Senate; at the same time, California voters approved anti-open-housing Proposition 14 and elected another Republican in another supposedly safe Democratic congressional district (the 27th). Outside the South, only four House districts that had elected Democrats in 1962 voted for Republicans in 1964, and three of them were in California.

Then in 1966 Ronald Reagan beat Gov. Pat Brown by 993,000 votes (58%). Suddenly everybody was saying that California was really a very conservative state. What happened? Reagan, like the earlier conservative winners, mined the anti-student and anti-Negro sentiments of the great mass of middle-class California homeowners. Berkeley in 1964 and Watts in 1965 brought the antagonisms out for all to see. The Governor and other like-minded politicians skillfully attuned themselves to generational and racial fears, fears which possessed no spokesmen in the liberal California politics of the '50's and early '60's. The Reaganites were thereby able to redefine completely the issues that had traditionally structured the state's political alignments. And so California, which had been among the most liberal states in the early '60's—it rejected Richard Nixon's bid for the governorship in 1962—became one of the most conservative.

Reagan's kind of Republicanism had its beginnings in southern California's rootless subdivisions, among parents worried about the status of their neighborhood and about the increasingly wayward habits of their children. Few observers noticed that in 1964 southern California gave Lyndon Johnson only 55% of its votes—far below his 64% in northern California and similar percentages in other large industrial states. But in 1966 southern Californians, particularly in fast-growing conservative areas like Orange and San Diego counties, turned out in record numbers to elect Ronald Reagan. In fact, conservatives like Reagan rise to power in California politics because the conservative south dominates the state's Republican primary. Reagan won the lion's share of his huge 1966 primary margin in the south, as did ex-Sen. George Murphy in 1964. The 1968 Senate primary was an even more clear-cut case of the south against the rest of the state. Sen. Thomas Kuchel, a leading Republican moderate, had a solid 153,000-vote lead outside the six southern counties, but Max Rafferty, the ultraconservative challenger, carried the six counties by 223,000 votes.

Rafferty, as it turned out, was not the strongest candidate the Republicans could have put up. A newspaperman, noting that Rafferty had nothing but harsh words for draft resisters, checked out the candidate's war record. The investigator found that Rafferty sat out World War II with an alleged injury and, reportedly, threw away his cane on V-J Day. The revelation was enough to give the Democratic candidate, former state controller Alan Cranston, a 52–48 victory. Thus conservative California elected a senator who opposes the Vietnam war, large military expenditures, and most of the domestic policies of the Nixon Administration.

Nor did the conservatives do very well in the 1970 Senate election. Early in the year, Sen. George Murphy looked like a sure bet for reelection. But then it was learned that Technicolor Incorporated had been giving the Senator $20,000 a year, rent on a Washington apartment, and use of a credit card. In the fall election, Congressman John Tunney, the Democratic candidate, carried both southern and northern California. He surprised many of the pundits, winning by a larger margin than Gov. Reagan's. Other conservatives in the state also ran into trouble. Because of a local scandal, the Republicans lost an important Assembly seat and the district attorney's office in San Diego; and Max Rafferty, the man who had begun the conservative surge in California eight years earlier, was himself defeated by Wilson Riles, a Negro and formerly Rafferty's deputy.

So now California has two Democratic senators for the first time since the 1860's. Both Cranston and Tunney are members of the Senate's liberal block, opposed to the war in Vietnam and large defense spending at home, except perhaps in California. Neither has the kind of seniority that confers certain kinds of clout in the Senate, but they can both take some satisfaction in having been elected with more votes than any other senators in history. Neither can look forward to automatic reelection. Generally, the voters have been hard on California senators. They have not reelected a senator since 1962; in fact, Californians have returned the incumbent in only three of nine Senate elections since World War II.

The reasons behind the recent conservatives' reverses in the state lie mainly in the inevitable price of victory. The Reaganites could not very well abandon their heroes Rafferty and Murphy even though both were in trouble. And scandal always hurts the ins, since no one bothers to bribe the outs. Finally, when you've been in office for four years, it becomes increasingly difficult to blame student riots, black unrest, and higher government spending on your opponents.

We can also note that as the conservative regime became more familiar, the traditional divergence in the political behavior of northern and southern California grew smaller. In 1964, the regions had been 9% apart; in the 1970 governor's race, the difference was only 4%. Northern Californians soon learned that Reagan, though not their man, was less radically conservative than they had expected. And in the south, many suburbanites showed signs of disenchantment with Reagan, who simply couldn't be as conservative as he promised to be.

Nevertheless, the conservatives retain the edge in California politics. Gov. Reagan did win 54–46 in 1970 over former Assembly Speaker Jess Unruh. Though Reagan's margin was nowhere near the 1,000,000 votes predicted by his supporters and Eastern columnists, he remains the most likely Republican presidential candidate if Richard Nixon decides, like his predecessor, to step down. Reagan has said that he will not again run for governor. But he may well run for the Senate in 1974 against Alan Cranston. If Reagan does, he must, at this point, be considered the favorite. Meanwhile, the Republicans will probably retain the governorship, unless a bitter primary fight develops between ex-HEW Secretary Robert Finch and conservative Lt. Gov. Ed Reinecke. But whatever else happens, the state will surely be the scene of fierce campaigning during the 1972 presidential election.

For the last 20 years, the California legislature has had more power to determine the composition of future Congresses than any group of men in the country. The power stems from the state's growing population, which has given it many new congressional districts: seven new seats after the 1950 census, eight in 1960, and five more in 1970. The party in control of the legislature can draw boundaries, particularly in Los Angeles County, so as to insure control of the majority of the districts. The Republicans did exactly this in 1951, and the Democrats did it in 1961. Since the Republicans controlled the legislature after the 1968 elections, most people thought that the Reaganites could completely transform the California House delegation—then made up of 21 Democrats and 17 Republicans. But, surprisingly, the Democrats regained control of both California houses in 1970. As a result, the Republicans will be prevented from gaining the 10 to 15 congressional seats they wanted and expected.

With Reagan in the governor's chair, the redistricting is likely to be a compromise, much like the one in 1967. At that time, the legislators, forced to redraw the lines to meet the one-man-one-vote requirement, simply strengthened all the incumbents. The 1970 census figures indicate that the five new seats will go to Orange, San Diego, and Santa Clara counties, with two others to be inserted somewhere in the Los Angeles area and in the Central Valley. The Orange and San Diego seats will be Republican. Two of the three other seats will probably be Democratic, depending on the bargaining finesse of the Governor and the legislative leadership.

Electoral Votes 45

Census Data 1970 pop. 19,953,134; 9.69% of U.S. total, 1st largest; change 1960–70, +27.0%. Metro. 92.7%, 36.3% central city. 1970 per capita income, $4,469, 9th highest. 1st in number of poor.

1970 Share of Federal Tax Burden $22,285,060,000; 11.42% of U.S. total, 2nd largest.

1970 Share of Federal Outlays $22,417,268,005; 11.86% of U.S. total, 1st largest. Per capita federal spending, $1,123.

DOD	$9,808,393,000	1st	(17.09%)	HEW	$5,800,308,365	1st	(11.10%)
AEC	$326,396,231	2nd	(12.56%)	HUD	$149,740,763	3rd	(7.68%)
NASA	$1,108,336,121	1st	(30.11%)	OEO	$73,832,548	2nd	(9.72%)
DOT	$608,232,820	1st	(8.52%)	DOA	$632,626,162	4th	(4.92%)
DOC	$109,918,737	4th	(9.50%)	POD	$783,838,626	2nd	(10.75%)
DOI	$178,550,025	2nd	(7.73%)	VA	$922,618,467	1st	(12.50%)
DOJ	$60,021,644	2nd	(10.45%)	CSC	$332,729,661	3rd	(8.27%)
				Other	$1,521,724,835		

Economic Base Livestock, dairy, and poultry; transportation equipment, esp. aircraft and parts; electrical machinery, equipment, and supplies, esp. communication equipment; ordnance and accessories; nonelectrical machinery, esp. office, computing, and accounting machines; food and kindred products, esp. canned, frozen, and preserved fruits, vegetables, and seafood; printing, publishing, and allied industries, esp. newspapers; fabricated metal products, esp. fabricated structural metal products; primary metal products, esp. blast furnaces, steel works, and rolling and finishing mills; lumber and wood products other than furniture, esp. sawmills and planing mills; stone, clay, glass, and concrete products, esp. concrete, gypsum, and plastic products. Also, higher education and banking.

Political Line-up Governor, Ronald Reagan (R); seat up, 1974. Senators, Alan Cranston (D) and John V. Tunney (D). Representatives, 38 (20 D and 18 R). State Senate (21 D and 19 R); State Assembly (43 D and 37 R).

The Voters

Registration 8,053,389 total. 4,388,052 D (55%); 3,274,967 R (41%); 71,570 AIP (1%); 36,487 PF (less than 0.5%); 4,029 other (less than 0.5%).

Employment profile White collar, 47%. Blue collar, 53%.

Ethnic groups Black, 7%. Spanish surname, 9%. Oriental, 2%. Total foreign stock, 25%. Mexico, 4%; Germany, 2%; Canada, 2%; UK, 2%; Italy, 2%; Ireland, Poland, Sweden, and USSR, all 1% each; others, 6%.

Presidential vote

1968	Humphrey (D)	3,186,270	(44%)
	Nixon (R)	3,407,851	(48%)
	Wallace (AIP)	481,665	(7%)
1964	Johnson (D)	4,171,877	(59%)
	Goldwater (R)	2,879,108	(41%)
1960	Kennedy (D)	3,244,099	(50%)
	Nixon (R)	3,259,722	(50%)

Senator

Alan Cranston (D) Elected 1968, seat up 1974; b. June 19, 1914, Palo Alto; home, Los Angeles; Pomona Col., 1932–33; U. of Mexico, summer 1935; Stanford U., B.A., 1936; Army, WWII; married, two children; Protestant.

Career Newspaperman, Intl. News Svc., 1937–38; Chief Foreign Language Div., Office War Info., 1940–44; businessman, land investment and home construction; Founder, Pres., Calif. Dem. Council, 1953–58; Controller, State of Calif., 1958–66.

Offices 2102 NSOB, 202-225-3553. Also 13220 Fed. Bldg., 11000 Wilshire Blvd., Los Angeles 90024, 213-824-7641, and 450 Golden Gate, San Francisco 94102, 415-556-8441.

Committees

Banking, Housing, and Urban Affairs (6th); Subs. (1) Chm., Production and Stabilization, (2) Financial Institutions, (3) Housing and Urban Affairs, (4) International Finance.

Labor and Public Welfare (8th); Subs. (1) Chm., Railroad Retirement, (2) Chm., Sp. Sub. on Human Resources, (3) Aging, (4) Alcoholism and Narcotics, (5) Children and Youth, (6) Education, (7) Employment, Manpower, and Poverty, (8) Handicapped Workers, (9) Health, (10) Sp. Sub. on National Science Foundation.

Veterans' Affairs (5th); Subs. (1) Chm., Health and Hospitals, (2) Housing and Insurance, (3) Readjustment, Education, and Employment.

Group Ratings

	ADA	COPE	NREP	NFU	LCV	NAB	NSI	ACA
1970	91	100	100	100	97	11	10	0
1969	72	—	—	92	—	—	—	0

Key Votes

(1) ABM	AGN	(8) Phil Pln	FOR	(15) Coop-Church	FOR
(2) SST	AGN	(9) Vol Army	FOR	(16) Cut Oil Dpltn	AGN
(3) Busing	FOR	(10) Prison $	FOR	(17) Consumer Prot	FOR
(4) Tob Sub	AGN	(11) Cut Mil $	FOR	(18) Farm Sub Limit	AGN
(5) Carswell	AGN	(12) Defoliatn	AGN	(19) Comp Bid Sales	AGN
(6) No-Knock	AGN	(13) 18-Yr-Vote	FOR	(20) Pre-Prod Tests	AGN
(7) Seniorty	FOR	(14) Pentgn PR	AGN	(21) Cut Marjna Pen	ABS

Election Results

1968 general:	Alan Cranston (D)	3,680,352	(52%)
	Max Rafferty (R)	3,329,148	(47%)
	Paul Jacobs (PF)	91,254	(1%)
1968 primary:	Alan Cranston (D)	1,681,825	(59%)
	Anthony C. Beilenson (D)	644,844	(23%)
	Walter R. Buchanan (D)	227,798	(8%)
	William M. Bennett (D)	207,720	(7%)
	Charles Crail (D)	89,023	(3%)

Senator

John Varick Tunney (D) Elected 1970, seat up 1976; b. June 26, 1934, New York City; home, Riverside; Yale U., B.A., 1956; Academy in Intl. Law at The Hague, Netherlands, 1957; U. of Va., LL.B., 1959; USAF, 1960–63; married, three children; Catholic.

Career Practicing atty., 1959–70; Business Law Lecturer, U. of Calif., 1961–62.

Offices 6237 NSOB, 202-225-3841. Also 500 Rotunda, Mission Inn, Riverside 92501, 714-682-0232.

Committees

District of Columbia (4th); Subs. (1) Chm., Public Health, Education, Welfare, and Safety, (2) Business, Commerce, and Judiciary.

Judiciary (9th); Subs. (1) Administrative Practice and Procedure, (2) Antitrust and Monopoly Legislation, (3) Constitutional Amendments, (4) Constitutional Rights.

Public Works (8th); Subs. (1) Air and Water Pollution, (2) Economic Development, (3) Environmental Science and Technology, (4) Flood Control—Rivers and Harbors, (5) Public Buildings and Grounds, (6) Public Roads.

(*Note: The following ratings and votes cover Sen. Tunney's record in the House of Representatives where he served prior to his election in 1970.*)

Group Ratings

	ADA	COPE	NREP	NFU	LCV	CFA	NAB	NSI	ACA
1970	60	100	75	100	100	100	0	0	0
1969	80	—	—	100	—	—	—	—	0
1968	92	100	—	87	—	—	25	—	5

Key Votes

(1) ABM	ABS	(6) 18-Yr-Vote	FOR	(11) Clean Water $	ABS
(2) SST	AGN*	(7) Farm Sub Lmt	FOR	(12) Mig Wrkrs Comp	FOR
(3) Phil Pln	FOR	(8) Coop-Church	FOR	(13) Jets to Chiang	ABS
(4) No-Knock	ABS	(9) Family Asst	ABS	(14) State OEO Veto	AGN
(5) Cmutr Tax	ABS	(10) Work Stamps	AGN	(15) Park Logging	ABS

* *As senator.*

Election Results

1970 general:	John Tunney (D)	3,496,558	(54%)
	George Murphy (R-Inc.)	2,877,617	(44%)
	Charles Ripley (AIP)	61,251	(1%)
	Robert Scheer (PF)	56,731	(1%)
1968 primary:	John Tunney (D)	1,010,812	(42%)
	George Brown, Jr. (D)	812,463	(33%)
	Kenneth Hahn (D)	417,970	(17%)
	Eileen Anderson (D)	60,977	(2%)
	Arthur Bell, Jr. (D)	48,878	(2%)
	Leonard Kurland (D)	43,923	(2%)
	Louis Di Salvo (D)	35,829	(1%)

FIRST DISTRICT Political Background

California 1 stretches for 300 miles along the Pacific coast from the Oregon border to Marin County, just north of San Francisco. The northern counties are famous for their redwood groves—the new Redwoods National Park is here in the 1st—and for their often foggy shoreline scenery. This area tends to vote Democratic, as does mountain-locked, wine-producing Napa County in the south. The district's Republican strength lies in its portion of Marin County and in Sonoma County, just to the north. The latter is rolling hill country, with small but growing cities like Santa Rosa (pop. 50,000), where one can see vestiges of early Russian attempts at colonization in California. Presently, the gentle climate and open spaces of Sonoma and Mendocio counties have attracted former residents of San Francisco's Haight-Ashbury. The commune people, however, have upset local officials, who are working very energetically to drive them out.

The current congressman from the 1st is conservative Republican Don Clausen. He first won the seat in a 1963 special election after Rep. Clement Miller was killed in an airplane crash during the 1962 campaign. Miller was an unusually sensitive congressman who authored the book *Member of the House.* California conservatives scored one of their first breakthroughs with Clausen's victory. In the ensuing years, the congressman has managed to win reelection easily, although Sens. Cranston and Tunney both carried the district.

Since redistricting is unlikely to affect the political balance of the 1st, Clausen will probably advance to more senior positions on the Interior and Insular Affairs and Public Works committees during the '70's. If Clausen is not a candidate, however, the 1st could go to either party.

Census Data 1970 pop. 494,079; deviation from current state average, —5.9%; change 1960–70, +19.7%. Metro. 66.5%, 17.4% central city.

1970 Share of Federal Outlays $276,348,218

DOD	$31,693,000	HEW	$156,193,045
AEC	$10,000	HUD	$2,219,000
NASA	$32,746	OEO	$1,021,618
DOT	$5,254,669	DOA	$12,640,242
		Other	$67,283,898

Federal Military-Industrial Commitments

DOD Installations Two Rock Ranch Station AB (Petaluma). Naval Security Group Activity (Sonoma). Klamath AF Station (Requa). Point Arena AF Station (Point Arena).

Economic Base Dairy and poultry; lumber and wood products other than furniture, esp. sawmills and planing mills; food and kindred products. Also, tourism (Redwoods).

The Voters

Registration 210,285 total. 112,749 D (54%); 88,686 R (42%); 1,261 AIP (1%); 1,196 PF (1%); 6,493 other (3%).

Employment profile White collar, 45%. Blue collar, 55%.

Ethnic groups Black, 1%. Spanish surname, 3%. Oriental, 2%. Total foreign stock, 22%. Italy, Germany, Canada, 3% each; UK, 2%; Ireland, Norway, Sweden, USSR, Mexico, 1% each; others, 7%.

Presidential vote

1968	Humphrey (D)	80,311	(44%)
	Nixon (R)	86,230	(48%)
	Wallace (AIP)	14,989	(8%)

Representative

Don H. Clausen (R) Elected 1962; b. April 27, 1923, Ferndale; home, Crescent City; San Jose State Col., Calif. Polytechnic, Weber Col., St. Mary's Col.; Navy, WWII; married, two children; Lutheran.

Career Businesses: Clausen Flying Service, Air Ambulance Service, and Clausen Assoc. (insurance).

Offices 1035 LHOB, 202-225-3311. Also 475 H St., Crescent City 95531, 707-464-3241, and 206 Rosenberg Bldg., Santa Rosa 95401, 707-545-8844.

Committees

Interior and Insular Affairs (7th); Subs. (1) Irrigation and Reclamation, (2) National Parks and Recreation, (3) Public Lands, (4) Territorial and Insular Affairs.

Public Works (4th); Subs. (1) Flood Control and Internal Dev., (2) Investments and Oversight, (3) Rivers and Harbors, (4) Roads, (5) Sp. Sub. on Economic Dev. Programs.

Group Ratings

	ADA	COPE	NREP	NFU	LCV	CFA	NAB	NSI	ACA
1970	16	17	17	54	13	43	75	100	72
1969	7	—	—	46	—	—	—	—	56
1968	0	9	—	63	—	—	67	—	82

Key Votes

(1) ABM	FOR	(6) 18-Yr-Vote	FOR	(11) Clean Water $	AGN
(2) SST	FOR	(7) Farm Sub Lmt	AGN	(12) Mig Wrkrs Comp	AGN
(3) Phil Pln	AGN	(8) Coop-Church	AGN	(13) Jets to Chiang	FOR
(4) No-Knock	FOR	(9) Family Asst	FOR	(14) State OEO Veto	FOR
(5) Cmutr Tax	AGN	(10) Work Stamps	FOR	(15) Park Logging	FOR

Election Results

1970 general:	Don Clausen (R-Inc.)	108,358	(63%)
	William Kortum (D)	62,688	(37%)
1970 primary:	Don Clausen (R), unopposed		
1968 general:	Don Clausen (R)	133,597	(75%)
	Don Graham (D)	37,756	(21%)
	Adolph Hofmann (PF)	3,379	(2%)
	Gladys O'Neal (AIP)	2,883	(2%)

SECOND DISTRICT Political Background

Geographically, California 2 is the state's largest district. It extends from the Oregon border near the Pacific Ocean in the north to Mount Whitney and Death Valley (the highest and lowest points in the continental United States) in the south. The district, most of which is mountainous, includes some of the areas most heavily prospected in the Gold Rush of 1849. One such place was Calaveras County, where the jumping frog contests first reported by Mark Twain are still held; another is Alpine County, which is now left with so few voters (384) that San Francisco's Gay Liberation Front has discussed sending in 500 members to take over the local government. The bulk of the 2nd's people live in the northern Sacramento River Valley, principally in (heavily Democratic) Shasta and (heavily Republican) Butte counties and in Placer County just a few miles from Sacramento.

California 2 has been a traditionally Democratic congressional district. Its current representative is Democrat Harold T. (Bizz) Johnson, who was first elected in 1958 when his predecessor, Clair Engle, went to the Senate. Since then Johnson has not had a tough election. In 1970, for example, the Congressman won 77% of the vote and carried every county in the district. In the House, Johnson is a senior member of the Public Works and Interior and Insular Affairs committees, and chairman of the latter's Irrigation and Reclamation Subcommittee. Known to be a generally loyal follower of the Democratic leadership, Johnson devotes most of his attention to the needs of his district. Redistricting will cost the 2nd some of its conservative southern counties, an excision which will only strengthen Johnson's already secure standing in the district.

Census Data 1970 pop. 549,132; deviation from current state average, +4.6%; change 1960–70, +22.9%. Metro. 14.1%, 0.0% central city.

1970 Share of Federal Outlays $455,627,420

DOD	$28,685,000	HEW	$199,770,199
AEC	$000	HUD	$137,000
NASA	$13,825	OEO	$2,374,297
DOT	$19,459,124	DOA	$79,436,014
		Other	$125,751,961

Federal Military-Industrial Commitments

DOD Installations Sierra Army Depot (Herlong).

Economic Base Livestock; lumber and wood products other than furniture. Also, tourism (Yosemite).

The Voters

Registration 245,539 total. 138,733 D (57%); 99,317 R (40%); 1,715 AIP (1%); 174 PF (—); 5,600 other (2%).

Employment profile White collar, 40%. Blue collar, 60%.

Ethnic groups Black, 1%. Spanish surname, 4%. Oriental, 2%. Total foreign stock, 16%. Germany, Italy, UK, Canada, 2% each; Ireland, Norway, Sweden, Mexico, 1% each; others, 4%.

Presidential vote

1968	Humphrey (D)	91,548	(43%)
	Nixon (R)	102,158	(48%)
	Wallace (AIP)	20,860	(10%)

Representative

Harold T. (Bizz) Johnson (D) Elected 1958; b. Dec. 2, 1907, Yolo County; home, Roseville; U. of Nevada; married, two children; Presbyterian.

Career Supervisor, Pacific Fruit Express Co.; Dist. Chm., Brotherhood of Railway Clerks; Mayor of Roseville, 1941–49; Calif. State Senate, 1948–58.

Offices 2347 RHOB, 202-225-3076. Also U.S. P.O. Bldg., Roseville 95678, 916-783-8845.

Committees

Interior and Insular Affairs (6th); Subs. (1) Chm., Irrigation and Reclamation, (2) Environment, (3) Public Lands, (4) National Parks and Recreation.

Public Works (8th); Subs. (1) Flood Control and Internal Dev., (2) Investment and Oversight, (3) Public Buildings and Grounds, (4) Rivers and Harbors, (5) Sp. Sub. on Economic Dev. Programs.

Group Ratings

	ADA	COPE	NREP	NFU	LCV	CFA	NAB	NSI	ACA
1970	56	100	67	100	44	78	0	70	6
1969	67	—	—	100	—	—	—	—	13
1968	67	100	—	87	—	—	17	—	6

Key Votes

(1) ABM	FOR	(6) 18-Yr-Vote	FOR	(11) Clean Water $	FOR
(2) SST	FOR	(7) Farm Sub Lmt	AGN	(12) Mig Wrkrs Comp	FOR
(3) Phil Pln	AGN	(8) Coop-Church	FOR	(13) Jets to Chiang	FOR
(4) No-Knock	FOR	(9) Family Asst	FOR	(14) State OEO Veto	AGN
(5) Cmutr Tax	FOR	(10) Work Stamps	AGN	(15) Park Logging	FOR

Election Results

1970 general:	Bizz Johnson (D)	151,070	(78%)
	Lloyd Gilbert (R)	37,223	(19%)
	Jack Carrigg (AIP)	5,681	(3%)
1970 primary:	Bizz Johnson (D), unopposed		
1968 general:	Bizz Johnson (D)	127,744	(61%)
	Osmer Dunaway (R)	78,986	(38%)
	Paul Huft (AIP)	3,574	(2%)

THIRD DISTRICT Political Background

California 3 is the city and some of the suburbs of Sacramento, the state capital. Ever since the Gold Rush, Sacramento has been a heavily Democratic city, and, despite large population influxes in recent years, remains so today. Even Ronald Reagan, a very popular politician in California, has never been able to carry the city. Since 1952, the district's congressman has been John E. Moss, a liberal Democrat best known for sponsoring the Freedom of Information Act. The measure, which Moss began to push as a junior member of the Government Operations Committee, is designed to open up government files to the public unless there is some compelling (i.e., military) reason for them to be kept secret. After years of a rather lonely struggle—the legislation was unpopular with federal bureaucrats and was not part of the usual liberal agenda—Moss finally managed to steer it through. But procedures for getting information remain cumbersome, and the press, which hailed the act's passage, has not been particularly eager to delve into the material contained in the files. Nevertheless, the law has made some difference, if only because it has facilitated some of Ralph Nader's investigations.

With nearly 20 years in the House, Moss has built up considerable seniority. He is currently chairman of the Commerce Committee's Subcommittee on Commerce and Finance, where he often leads the fights for pro-consumer legislation. He is also a high-ranking member of Government Operations, formerly chairman of its Foreign Operations and Government Operations subcommittee. In that capacity he earned high marks as an investigator, making forays into the foreign aid program and land reform in Vietnam.

Moss has a reputation for being abrasively self-righteous. For that reason, perhaps, nobody considered him a candidate for leadership posts after the 1970 elections. He was once Deputy Whip. None of this causes him any trouble back in the 3rd district, however, and his continuing reelection is assured.

Census Data 1970 pop. 506,234; deviation from current state average, −3.6%; change 1960–70, +20.8%. Metro. 100%, 48.7% central city.

1970 Share of Federal Outlays $960,977,000 (average outlay per district, California 3–4)

DOD	$480,208,000	HEW	$196,533,000
AEC	$1,885,000	HUD	$2,985,000
NASA	$31,153,000	OEO	$2,869,000
DOT	$29,884,000	DOA	$23,862,000
		Other	$191,599,000

Federal Military-Industrial Commitments (California 3–4, greater Sacramento listing)

DOD Contractors Aerojet General Div., General Tire (Sacramento), $116.925m: Titan, Minuteman, and Hawk missile engines.

DOD Installations Sierra Army Depot (Sacramento). Mather AFB (Sacramento). McClellan AFB (Sacramento). Naval Schools Command (Vallejo). Mare Island Naval Shipyard (Vallejo). Beale AFB (Marysville). Travis AFB (Fairfield).

NASA Contractors Aerojet General Div., General Tire (Sacramento), $53.651m: development of nuclear-powered rocket engine.

Economic Base Food and kindred products; dairy and livestock; printing, publishing, and allied industries, esp. newspapers. Also, higher education (Sacramento State).

The Voters

Registration 218,832 total. 132,533 D (61%); 78,992 R (36%); 1,738 AIP (1%); 387 PF (—); 5,182 other (2%).

Employment profile White collar, 53%. Blue collar, 47%.

Ethnic groups Black, 7%. Spanish surname, 6%. Oriental, 4%. Total foreign stock, 21%. Mexico, 3%; Germany, UK, Canada, 2% each; Ireland, Sweden, USSR, 1% each; others, 8%.

Presidential vote

1968	Humphrey (D)	100,361	(52%)
	Nixon (R)	80,516	(42%)
	Wallace (AIP)	12,494	(7%)

Representative

John Emerson Moss (D) Elected 1952; b. April 13, 1913, Carbon County, Utah; home, Sacramento; Sacramento City Col., 1931–33; Navy, WWII; married, two children; Protestant.

Career Businessman and real estate broker; Calif. Assembly 1948–52; Asst. Democratic Floor Leader of Assembly, 1949–52.

Offices 2185 RHOB, 202-225-7163. Also 8056 Fed. Bldg., 650 Capitol Mall, Sacramento 95814, 916-449-3543.

Committees

Government Operations (6th); Subs. (1) Conservation and Natural Resources, (2) Foreign Operations and Government Information.

Interstate and Foreign Commerce (4th); Chm., Sub. on Commerce and Finance.

Group Ratings

	ADA	COPE	NREP	NFU	LCV	CFA	NAB	NSI	ACA
1970	72	91	100	91	0	100	0	20	7
1969	87	—	—	93	—	—	—	—	13
1968	100	100	—	93	—	—	0	—	0

Key Votes

(1) ABM	AGN	(6) 18-Yr-Vote	FOR	(11) Clean Water $	FOR
(2) SST	AGN	(7) Farm Sub Lmt	FOR	(12) Mig Wrkrs Comp	FOR
(3) Phil Pln	ABS	(8) Coop-Church	FOR	(13) Jets to Chiang	AGN
(4) No-Knock	AGN	(9) Family Asst	FOR	(14) State OEO Veto	AGN
(5) Cmutr Tax	AGN	(10) Work Stamps	AGN	(15) Park Logging	ABS

Election Results

1970 general:	John Moss (D-Inc.)	117,496	(62%)
	Elmore Duffy (R)	69,811	(36%)
	Allen Priest (AIP)	3,554	(2%)
1970 primary:	John Moss (D), unopposed		
1968 general:	John Moss (D)	107,446	(56%)
	Elmore Duffy (R)	80,193	(42%)
	James Slaughter (AIP)	4,234	(2%)

FOURTH DISTRICT Political Background

California 4 stretches across the low, flat lands of the lower Sacramento Valley where the Sacramento and San Joaquin rivers empty into San Francisco Bay. The southern part of the district—Vallejo and Solano County—is industrial and heavily Democratic. That same political inclination is shared by the Sacramento suburbs in Yolo and Sacramento counties. The counties to the north are predominantly agricultural and decidedly more conservative. But since they make up only about a quarter of the district's population, the 4th can usually be counted in the Democratic column.

The 4th district was created after the 1960 census. Its first and only congressman has been a former state assemblyman, Robert L. Leggett, a man who is a comparative rarity —a liberal, antiwar member of the House Armed Services Committee. Although his district includes two air force bases, an arsenal, and a naval shipyard, Leggett has taken a stand against high defense expenditures (except on shipbuilding). And he has been so strident that the late Chairman Mendel Rivers once took to the floor to threaten revenge on Leggett and California 4. He nevertheless remains a member of the committee's now-growing antiwar minority.

Leggett has always won reelection by comfortable majorities. As for the future, the partisan division between Gov. Reagan and the Democratic legislature seems to make certain that redistricting will not weaken him significantly.

Census Data 1970 pop. 523,163; deviation from current state average, —0.4%; change 1960–70, +32.6%. Metro. 74.0%, 14.2% central city.

1970 Share of Federal Outlays $960,977,000 (average outlay per district, California 3–4)

DOD	$480,208,000	HEW	$196,533,000
AEC	$1,885,000	HUD	$2,985,000
NASA	$31,153,000	OEO	$2,869,000
DOT	$29,884,000	DOA	$23,862,000
		Other	$191,599,000

Federal Military-Industrial Commitments (See California 3 for greater Sacramento listing.)

Economic Base Cash grain, livestock, and dairy; food and kindred products. Also, higher education (U. Calif. Davis).

The Voters

Registration 189,545 total. 114,541 D (60%); 68,509 R (36%); 1,549 AIP (1%); 309 PF (—); 4,637 other (3%).

Employment profile White collar, 39%. Blue collar, 61%.

Ethnic groups Black, 4%. Spanish surname, 7%. Oriental, 3%. Total foreign stock, 19%. Mexico, 3%; Germany, UK, Canada, 2% each; Ireland, Italy, Sweden, USSR, 1% each; others, 7%.

Presidential vote

1968	Humphrey (D)	75,698	(47%)
	Nixon (R)	70,176	(44%)
	Wallace (AIP)	15,841	(10%)

Representative

Robert L. Leggett (D) Elected 1962; b. July 26, 1926, Richmond; home, Vallejo; U. of Calif., B.A., 1947, LL.B., 1950; Navy, WWII; married, three children; Catholic.

Career Practicing atty., 1952–64; Calif. State Assembly, 1960–62.

Offices 2263 RHOB, 202-225-5716. Also 1520 Tenn. St., Vallejo 94590, 707-691-0720; 540 Second St., Yuba City 95991, 916-673-3515; and 650 Capitol Mall, Sacramento 95814, 916-449-3535.

Committees

Armed Services (4th); Sub. No. 1.

Merchant Marine and Fisheries (14th); Subs. (1) Fisheries and Wildlife Conservation, (2) Merchant Marine, (3) Oceanography.

Group Ratings

	ADA	COPE	NREP	NFU	LCV	CFA	NAB	NSI	ACA
1970	84	91	83	83	84	100	9.1	30	17
1969	87	—	—	100	—	—	—	—	14
1968	63	100	—	94	—	—	100	—	0

Key Votes

(1) ABM	ABS	(6) 18-Yr-Vote	FOR	(11) Clean Water $	FOR
(2) SST	FOR	(7) Farm Sub Lmt	AGN	(12) Mig Wrkrs Comp	FOR
(3) Phil Pln	FOR	(8) Coop-Church	ABS	(13) Jets to Chiang	ABS
(4) No-Knock	AGN	(9) Family Asst	FOR	(14) State OEO Veto	AGN
(5) Cmutr Tax	ABS	(10) Work Stamps	AGN	(15) Park Logging	ABS

Election Results

1970 general:	Robert Leggett (D-Inc.)	103,485	(68%)
	Andrew Gyorke (R)	48,783	(32%)
1970 primary:	Robert Leggett (D-Inc.), unopposed		
1968 general:	Robert Leggett (D)	90,126	(56%)
	James Schumway (R)	67,225	(42%)
	Gene Clark (AIP)	4,670	(3%)

FIFTH DISTRICT Political Background

California 5 is the eastern half of the city of San Francisco, the part with all the familiar landmarks—Chinatown, Telegraph Hill, North Beach, Fisherman's Wharf, and the Top of the Mark. Of more significance politically are the city's poorer residents, most of whom live in the 5th: not only the Chinese, but also a large number of blacks, Mexicans, and whites who have not been able to climb the economic ladder. Another factor contributes to San Francisco's tradition of radical politics. The city possesses a distinctive sociological make-up; aside from the poor, many San Franciscans are single, or not at least living within the conventional family unit. Moreover, there is an attitude of noblesse oblige among the city's rich. The poor, the single, and the rich combine to produce an ambience of toleration for all kinds of deviant types. They also produce a district unsympathetic to Ronald Reagan's kind of conservatism.

The 5th has always voted Democratic and probably always will. Its current congressman is Phillip Burton, one of the most politically savvy of the House's ultraliberals. Burton moved into the seat when ex-Rep. John Shelley was elected mayor in 1963. Currently Burton and his brother John, a state assemblyman, are deeply involved in local political struggles with Mayor Joseph Alioto. It is possible that one of the Burtons will eventually become mayor of the city. Meanwhile, no one doubts that Congressman Phillip Burton can keep winning reelection as long as he chooses.

Census Data 1970 pop. 418,218; deviation from current state average, —20.4%; change 1960–70, –3.5%. Metro. 100%, 100% central city.

1970 Share of Federal Outlays $646,879,000 (average outlay per district, California 5–11, 14)

DOD	$282,253,000	HEW	$151,992,000
AEC	$33,646,000	HUD	$6,914,000
NASA	$11,711,000	OEO	$2,698,000
DOT	$11,106,000	DOA	$12,187,000
		Other	$134,373,000

Federal Military-Industrial Commitments (See California 9 for San Francisco Bay area listing.)

Economic Base Printing, publishing, and allied industries, esp. commercial printing; food and kindred products; fabricated metal products; apparel and other finished products made from fabrics and similar materials, especially women's, misses', and juniors' outerwear. Also, tourism (San Francisco) and banking.

The Voters

Registration 166,066 total. 113,146 D (68%); 39,763 R (24%); 695 AIP (—); 4,811 PF (3%); 7,651 other (5%).

Employment profile White collar, 44%. Blue collar, 56%.

Ethnic groups Black, 19%. Spanish surname, 8%. Oriental, 14%. Total foreign stock, 42%. Italy, 4%; Mexico, Germany, 3% each; Ireland, UK, USSR, Canada, 2% each; Austria, Norway, Poland, Sweden, 1% each; others, 21%.

Presidential vote

1968	Humphrey (D)	91,233	(67%)
	Nixon (R)	36,298	(27%)
	Wallace (AIP)	8,508	(6%)

Representative

Phillip Burton (D) Elected Feb., 1964; b. June 2, 1927, Cincinnati, Ohio; home, San Francisco; U. of Southern Calif., B.A., 1947; Golden Gate Law School, LL.B., 1952; Navy, WWII and Korean War; married, one child; Unitarian.

Career Practicing atty., 1952–64; Calif. Assembly, 1956–64.

Offices 339 CHOB, 202-225-4965. Also Rm. 11152 Fed. Ofc. Bldg., 450 Golden Gate Ave., San Francisco 94102, 415-556-4862.

Committees

Education and Labor (14th); Subs. (1) Gen. Sub. on Labor, (2) Sp. Sub. on Education, (3) Sel. Sub. on Labor.

Interior and Insular Affairs (8th); Subs. (1) Chm., Territorial and Insular Affairs, (2) Mines and Mining, (3) Public Lands.

Group Ratings

	ADA	COPE	NREP	NFU	LCV	CFA	NAB	NSI	ACA
1970	96	100	91	91	100	100	0	10	6
1969	93	—	—	86	—	—	—	—	6
1968	100	100	—	100	—	—	0	—	0

Key Votes

(1) ABM	AGN	(6) 18-Yr-Vote	FOR	(11) Clean Water $	FOR
(2) SST	AGN	(7) Farm Sub Lmt	AGN	(12) Mig Wrkrs Comp	FOR
(3) Phil Pln	FOR	(8) Coop-Church	FOR	(13) Jets to Chiang	AGN
(4) No-Knock	AGN	(9) Family Asst	FOR	(14) State OEO Veto	AGN
(5) Cmutr Tax	FOR	(10) Work Stamps	AGN	(15) Park Logging	AGN

Election Results

1970 general:	Phillip Burton (D-Inc.)	76,567	(71%)
	John Parks (R)	31,570	(29%)
1970 primary:	Phillip Burton (D-Inc.), unopposed		
1968 general:	Phillip Burton (D)	95,630	(73%)
	Waldo Velasquez (R)	31,157	(24%)
	Marvin Garson (PF)	4,607	(4%)

SIXTH DISTRICT Political Background

California 6 takes in the western half of San Francisco and most of Marin County, just across the Golden Gate Bridge. The San Francisco portion includes most of the more conventional residential neighborhoods of the city, where the middle-class descendants of Italian and Irish immigrants live in long blocks of houses sloping to the ocean. Also here are the city's wealthy precincts—Nob Hill, the Marina, and Pacific Heights. Marin County is physically quite different: fashionable high-income suburbs nestling between rugged mountains and San Francisco Bay. It's the kind of place where people wearing $80 sweaters go shopping barefooted. Marin, one of the few parts of California that still has large numbers of liberal Republicans, votes more Democratic than its party registration. In 1968 and 1970, the county supported Sens. Cranston and Tunney against their conservative opponents. And in 1964, Marin and San Francisco came as close as any large California counties to supporting open housing in the Proposition 14 referendum.

Since 1952 the district's congressman has been Republican William S. Mailliard, a wealthy member of an old California family. For many years Mailliard had a generally liberal voting record. He had no trouble at the polls, winning elections by large majorities in what is, by a small margin at least, a Democratic district. More recently, Mailliard seems caught between the increasing conservatism of the state's Republican party and the increasing liberalism of his constituency.

After Reagan's victory, Mailliard's voting record became noticeably more conservative. Because of this, he has been spared the tough conservative primary opposition that Paul McCloskey has confronted in the 11th. But Mailliard's move to the right has not gone unnoticed in the 6th district. In 1968 he received 73% of the vote, but in 1970 he won only 53%—a highly unusual drop for an incumbent of such long standing. Much of the difference must be attributed to the war issue. San Francisco and Marin are both antiwar strongholds; but Mailliard, who is the ranking Republican on the House Foreign Affairs Committee, has supported the Nixon Administration's war policy. In the 6th district, at least, that position is a sure vote-loser.

The outcome of the 1972 race will depend largely on the progress of the war. If, as Nixon strategists insist, the war is no longer an issue, then Mailliard will probably be reelected easily. Redistricting should help him marginally; the district will lose some Democratic territory to the 5th and probably gain some Republican areas in Marin County. But if the war is still on the minds of San Francisco area voters in 1972, the congressional contest in the 6th could be a very close one. Mailliard may have to run hard to win.

Census Data 1970 pop. 458,816; deviation from current state average, —12.6%; change 1960–70, +7.1%. Metro. 100%, 64.8% central city.

1970 Share of Federal Outlays $646,879,000 (average outlay per district, California 5–11, 14)

DOD	$282,253,000	HEW	$151,992,000
AEC	$33,646,000	HUD	$6,914,000
NASA	$11,711,000	OEO	$2,698,000
DOT	$11,106,000	DOA	$12,187,000
		Other	$134,373,000

Federal Military-Industrial Commitments (See California 9 for San Francisco Bay area listing.)

Economic Base Printing, publishing, and allied industries, esp. commercial printing; food and kindred products; fabricated metal products; apparel and other finished products made from fabrics and similar materials, esp. women's, misses', and juniors' outerwear. Also, tourism (San Francisco) and higher education (San Francisco State).

The Voters

Registration 248,058 total. 133,498 D (54%); 102,029 R (41%); 582 AIP (—); 2,511 PF (1%); 9,438 other (4%).

Employment profile White collar, 58%. Blue collar, 42%.

Ethnic groups Black, 5%. Spanish surname, 6%. Oriental, 4%. Total foreign stock, 44%. Italy, 7%; Germany, 5%; Ireland, 4%; UK, USSR, Canada, 3% each; Mexico, 2%; Austria, Norway, Poland, Sweden, 1% each; others, 14%.

Presidential vote

1968	Humphrey (D)	108,269	(52%)
	Nixon (R)	91,258	(43%)
	Wallace (AIP)	10,673	(5%)

Representative

William S. Mailliard (R) Elected 1952; b. June 10, 1917, Belvedere; home, San Francisco; Yale U., B.A., 1939; Navy, WWII; Rear Admiral, USNR; married, seven children; Protestant.

Career With American Trust Co. of S.F., 1940–41, 1946; Asst. to Dir., Calif. Academy of Sciences, 1951–52; Asst. to Dir. Calif. Youth Authority, 1947; Sec. to Gov. Earl Warren, 1949–51; Delegate, 18th Session UN General Assembly, 1963.

Offices 2336 RHOB, 202-225-5161. Also Rm. 11104 New Fed. Bldg., 450 Golden Gate Ave., San Francisco 94102, 415-556-1333.

Committees

Foreign Affairs (Ranking Mbr.); Sp. Sub. on Review on Foreign Aid.

Merchant Marine and Fisheries (2nd); Subs. (1) Fisheries and Wildlife Conservation, (2) Merchant Marine, (3) Oceanography.

Group Ratings

	ADA	COPE	NREP	NFU	LCV	CFA	NAB	NSI	ACA
1970	32	64	40	82	44	53	60	100	47
1969	13	—	—	28	—	—	—	—	29
1968	0	31	—	50	—	—	67	—	48

Key Votes

(1) ABM	FOR	(6) 18-Yr-Vote	FOR	(11) Clean Water $	AGN
(2) SST	FOR	(7) Farm Sub Lmt	FOR	(12) Mig Wrkrs Comp	ABS
(3) Phil Pln	FOR	(8) Coop-Church	AGN	(13) Jets to Chiang	FOR
(4) No-Knock	FOR	(9) Family Asst	FOR	(14) State OEO Veto	AGN
(5) Cmutr Tax	AGN	(10) Work Stamps	FOR	(15) Park Logging	AGN

Election Results

1970 general:	William Mailliard (R-Inc.)	96,393	(53%)
	Russell Miller (D)	84,255	(47%)
1970 primary:	William Mailliard (R-Inc.), unopposed		
1968 general:	William Mailliard (R)	151,336	(73%)
	Phillip Drath (D)	54,928	(27%)

SEVENTH DISTRICT Political Background

California 7 is Berkeley and north Oakland—the nation's most radical congressional district. Berkeley is of course the home of the University of California, where the Free Speech Movement of 1964 was the first of hundreds of campus reform movements that swept across the country. The university sits on the slope of a mountain; above it are the comfortable homes of academics; below, along San Francisco Bay, a large black community. The students in Berkeley, having registered to vote in record numbers, helped to provide the margins of victory for the so-called radical slate that won control of the city government in 1971. Oakland is Berkeley without the university. Well-off people (considerably more conservative than their Berkeley counterparts) reside in the hills, while the blacks live in the flat lands along the Bay.

The mix of people in the 7th has produced a yeasty politics. For one thing, the Oakland ghetto spawned the Black Panther Party; for another, in 1966, the district was the scene of one of the first major congressional primaries fought out on the Vietnam war issue. In that primary, *Ramparts* editor Robert Scheer challenged—and nearly beat—liberal incumbent Jeffery Cohelan. After the election, Cohelan, whose political career began in the labor movement, tried to counter accusations that he was only a lukewarm opponent of the war. But apparently Cohelan could not convince the voters of his sincerity. In 1970 Ronald V. Dellums, a Berkeley councilman and a black, challenged him in the primary and won, 43,000 to 35,000. Dellums did very well among the students and among high-income antiwar voters. Soon Spiro Agnew accused Dellums of sympathizing with Black Panthers and student rioters. In fact, as Dellums readily admitted, he did find himself agreeing with some Panther ideas, and he did object to what he considered illegal treatment of some of the student protesters.

In the general election, Dellums' Republican opponent was a 25-year-old Vietnam veteran and former Household Finance loan officer. The veteran took up Agnew's line and pushed it in his campaign and, as a result, cut into some working-class areas which ordinarily vote Democratic. Dellums won only 56% of the ballots, as against Cohelan's 63% in 1968. Meanwhile, Jess Unruh carried the district 64–36 over Ronald Reagan. But 56% gave Dellums enough confidence to flash the clenched-fist victory salute on election night. The Californian is now one of two blacks representing white-majority districts in the House.

Dellums is one of the most militant liberals in Congress. Presently he sits on Foreign Affairs and District of Columbia, holding positions on both far down the pecking order. Nevertheless, he has had no trouble making himself heard, having already chaired an unofficial inquiry into war crimes in Vietnam. 1972 will probably give Dellums no problems. Dellums has already won his first election and that is usually the toughest one for any congressman. Nor will redistricting lessen his chances. The 7th lost population in the '60's, which means territory must be added to it; but most of the areas that surround the 7th are safely Democratic. Moreover, the 18-year-old vote will make an enormous impact in student-filled Berkeley. And this vote will go almost entirely to Dellums.

Census Data 1970 pop. 388,415; deviation from current state average, −26.0%; change 1960–70, −2.0%. Metro. 100%, 62.7% central city.

1970 Share of Federal Outlays $646,879,000 (average outlay per district, California 5–11, 14)

DOD	$282,253,000	HEW	$151,992,000
AEC	$33,646,000	HUD	$6,914,000
NASA	$11,711,000	OEO	$2,698,000
DOT	$11,106,000	DOA	$12,187,000
		Other	$134,373,000

Federal Military-Industrial Commitments (See California 9 for San Francisco Bay area listing.)

Economic Base Motor vehicles and motor vehicle equipment, and other transportation equipment; food and kindred products; fabricated metal products, esp. fabricated structural metal products and metal cans; nonelectrical machinery, esp. office, computing, and accounting machines. Also, higher education (U. Calif. Berkeley).

The Voters

Registration 205,341 total. 130,155 D (63%); 62,464 R (30%); 533 AIP (—); 4,556 PF (2%); 7,633 other (6%).

Employment profile White collar, 53%. Blue collar, 47%.

Ethnic groups Black, 26%. Spanish surname, 4%. Oriental, 5%. Total foreign stock, 28%. Italy, Germany, UK, 3% each; Canada and Mexico, 2% each; Ireland, Norway, Poland, Sweden, USSR, 1% each; others, 10%.

Presidential vote

1968	Humphrey (D)	95,700	(61%)
	Nixon (R)	54,799	(35%)
	Wallace (AIP)	6,933	(4%)

Representative

Ronald V. Dellums (D) Elected 1970; b. Nov. 24, 1935, Oakland; home, Oakland; San Francisco State Col., B.A., 1961; U. of Calif., M.A., 1962; Marine Corps, 1954–56; married, five children; Protestant.

Career Psychiatric Social Worker, Dept. Mental Hygiene, 1962–64; Program Dir. Bayview Community Center, 1964–65; Assoc. Dir. and Dir., Hunter's Point Bayview Youth Opportunity Center, 1965–66; Dir., Concentrated Empl. Program, 1967–68; Berkeley City Council, 1967– ; Sr. Consultant, Social Dynamics, 1968– .

Offices 1417 LHOB, 202-225-2661. Also P.O. Bldg., Civic Center Div., 13th and Alice Streets, Oakland 94607, 415-763-0370.

Committees

District of Columbia (14th); Subs. (1) Housing and Youth Affairs, (2) Public Health and Welfare.

Foreign Affairs (21st); Subs. (1) Africa, (2) Inter-American Affairs, (3) International Organizations.

Group Ratings, Key Votes: Newly elected.

Election Results

1970 general:	Ronald Dellums (D)	89,784	(57%)
	John Healy (R)	64,691	(42%)
	Sarah Scahill (PF)	2,156	(1%)
1970 primary:	Ronald Dellums (D)	42,778	(55%)
	Jeffery Cohelan (D-Inc.)	35,223	(45%)

EIGHTH DISTRICT Political Background

California 8 comprises southern Oakland, several of the city's suburbs, and part of rural Alameda County. Most of the district's voters come from white blue-collar families who usually vote Democratic but who do not find the liberal issue-positions as attractive as voters in the 7th district to the north. The number of blacks in the Oakland portion of the 8th is growing. They do not, however, constitute the dominant political force in the district. In the foothills that rise several miles from San Francisco Bay, there are substantial pockets of conservative Republicans. The political preferences of the people here match those of ex-Sen. (1946–58) William Knowland, an arch-conservative who still publishes his family's *Oakland Tribune*. Inland, over the Diablo Range, lies the beginning of the Central Valley, within which one finds conservative towns like Livermore (site of a large AEC facility) and Pleasanton. On balance, the blue-collar voters in Oakland, San Leandro, and Castro Valley usually keep the district Democratic. But in 1966 it went for Ronald Reagan and almost did so again in 1970.

One of the senior members of the California delegation, Democrat George P. Miller, represents the 8th in the House. Miller has been congressman long enough (since 1944) to be chairman of the House Science and Astronautics Committee. Although his age (79 in 1970) has slowed him down, he still takes great pride in rising on the floor to announce the latest American space triumph. Miller is one of NASA's most ardent backers in the House.

Whatever limitations age may place on Miller's activities in the House, he is not about to lose an election in the 8th district. Apparently his middle-of-the-road stance on most issues suits his constituents nicely; he has beaten both primary and general election opponents with ease. If Miller's seat had become vacant a few years ago, the Republicans, with Reaganism at full tilt, might have won it. But in 1970, Democrats ran well along the East Bay, ousting a Republican state senator. The next congressman from the 8th will probably be one of several well-established legislators from the area—state Sen. Nicholas Petris (who sponsored the bill to ban the internal combustion engine in California) or Assemblyman Carlos Bee or Robert Crown.

Census Data 1970 pop. 464,710; deviation from current state average, −11.5%; change 1960–70, +19.2%. Metro. 100%, 25.4% central city.

1970 Share of Federal Outlays $646,879,000 (average outlay per district, California 5–11, 14)

DOD	$282,253,000	HEW	$151,992,000
AEC	$33,646,000	HUD	$6,914,000
NASA	$11,711,000	OEO	$2,698,000
DOT	$11,106,000	DOA	$12,187,000
		Other	$134,373,000

Federal Military-Industrial Commitments (See California 9 for San Francisco Bay area listing.)

Economic Base Motor vehicles and motor vehicle equipment, and other transportation equipment; food and kindred products; fabricated metal products, esp. fabricated structural metal products and metal cans; nonelectrical machinery, esp. office, computing, and accounting machines.

The Voters

Registration 188,956 total. 115,733 D (61%); 65,402 R (35%); 999 AIP (1%); 713 PF (—); 6,293 other (4%).

Employment profile White collar, 46%. Blue collar, 54%.

Ethnic groups Black, 13%. Spanish surname, 8%. Oriental, 3%. Total foreign stock, 27%. Germany, Italy, UK, Canada, 3% each; Mexico, 2%; Ireland, Norway, Sweden, USSR, 1% each; others, 10%.

Presidential vote

1968	Humphrey (D)	85,485	(52%)
	Nixon (R)	66,032	(40%)
	Wallace (AIP)	13,954	(8%)

Representative

George P. Miller (D) Elected 1944; b. Jan. 15, 1891, San Francisco; home, Alameda; St. Mary's Col., B.S., 1912; Army, WWI; married, one child; Catholic.

Career Calif. State Assembly, 1937–41; Exec. Secy., Calif., Div. of Fish and Game, 1941–44; Sp. Adviser to U.S. Ambassador to UN on Peaceful Uses of Outer Space.

Offices 2365 RHOB, 202-225-5065. Also 1516 Oak St., Alameda 94501, 415-523-0200.

Committees

Science and Astronautics (Chm.).

Group Ratings

	ADA	COPE	NREP	NFU	LCV	CFA	NAB	NSI	ACA
1970	56	92	55	100	84	100	0	70	11
1969	47	—	—	93	—	—	—	—	8
1968	75	100	—	81	—	—	0	—	0

Key Votes

(1) ABM	FOR	(6) 18-Yr-Vote	FOR	(11) Clean Water $	AGN
(2) SST	FOR	(7) Farm Sub Lmt	ABS	(12) Mig Wrkrs Comp	FOR
(3) Phil Pln	ABS	(8) Coop-Church	AGN	(13) Jets to Chiang	FOR
(4) No-Knock	FOR	(9) Family Asst	FOR	(14) State OEO Veto	AGN
(5) Cmutr Tax	FOR	(10) Work Stamps	AGN	(15) Park Logging	FOR

Election Results

1970 general:	George Miller (D-Inc.)	104,331	(69%)
	Michael Crane (R)	46,872	(31%)

1970 primary:	George Miller (D-Inc.)	42,916 (73%)
	John Burton (D)	6,130 (10%)
	Clarence Davis, Jr. (D)	10,073 (17%)

NINTH DISTRICT Political Background

California 9 is a creation of the '50's and '60's: 20 years ago its population was only about a quarter of its present figure. In 1950 San Jose (pop. 95,000) was primarily a market center for the agricultural Santa Clara Valley; in 1970 San Jose (pop. 445,000) was the center of the fastest-growing urban area in northern California. The eastern part of San Jose, which has a very large Mexican-American community, lies in the 9th. Also in the district are the equally fast-growing blue-collar urban sprawl cities of Hayward (pop. 93,000) and Fremont (pop. 100,000) in Alameda County, south of Oakland. The 9th is now a land of freeways, shopping centers, drive-in restaurants, and quickly built subdivisions. The flatlands around the shore of the bay are studded with large factories, the most notable of which is the Lockheed Sunnyvale plant. The Lockheed operation here is one of the nation's largest consumers of Department of Defense money, some $650 million in fiscal 1970. Most of the money went into Poseidon missile production.

The 9th is ordinarily Democratic (exception: the 1966 governor's race), due in large part to the skillful legislative line-drawing which placed most of the blue-collar and Mexican-American areas around San Jose in the district. Since its creation in 1962, the 9th's congressman has been W. Don Edwards—a former FBI agent and title-company owner, an outspoken liberal, early opponent of the Vietnam war, and former national chairman of Americans for Democratic Action. Edwards is a member of an informal group of antiwar liberal congressmen who often act jointly on a wide range of issues and who pool research efforts.

Generally speaking, Edwards has had little difficulty at the polls. In 1968, though, at the height of Reagan's influence, his percentage dipped to 56%. After that election, he reportedly considered retiring. But his term as ADA Chairman expired, he decided to run again and apparently spent more time cultivating the district. The result of his decision was a striking 69% of the vote in 1970—an indication that he can probably remain in the House as long as he chooses. He is just at the point where seniority starts to pay off, 7th ranking Democrat on the Judiciary Committee and a subcommittee chairmanship.

Because of its startling population growth (up from 642,000 in 1960 to 1,064,000 in 1970), Santa Clara County (San Jose and vicinity) should gain a new congressional seat before the 1972 election. Part of that new district will come out of what is presently in the 9th. Odds are the new political unit will consist of a string of cities between the Bayshore and Junipero Serra freeways: Santa Clara, Sunnyvale, Mountain View, and part of San Jose. In all likelihood, such an arrangement will produce another Democratic congressman, probably one of the state legislators from the area. Candidates include state Sen. Alfred Alquist (the 1970 Democratic candidate for lieutenant governor) or Assemblyman John Vasconcellos. These developments will not affect Edwards' chances for reelection very greatly.

Census Data 1970 pop. 673,201; deviation from current state average, +28.2%; change 1960–70, +67.7%. Metro. 100%, 37.3% central city.

1970 Share of Federal Outlays $646,879,463 (average outlay per district, California 5–11, 14)

DOD	$282,253,000	HEW	$151,992,000
AEC	$33,646,000	HUD	$6,914,000
NASA	$11,711,000	OEO	$2,698,000
DOT	$11,106,000	DOA	$12,187,000
		Other	$134,373,000

Federal Military-Industrial Commitments (California 5–11, 14, San Francisco Bay area listing)

DOD Contractors Lockheed Aircraft (Sunnyvale), $650.709m: Poseidon missiles; YO-3 aircraft; ABM development; Hudson Moon event support. Philco-Ford Div., Ford Motor Co. (Palo Alto), $75.371m: military space satellite support. FMC Corp. (San Jose), $49.624m: armored personnel carriers; amphibious landing craft; Chaparral missile carriers.

United Aircraft (Sunnyvale), $38.718m: Titan missile rocket motors. Westinghouse Electric (Sunnyvale), $38.241m: Poseidon missile launchers. World Airways (Oakland), $33.880m: air cargo transport. Phillips Petroleum (Avon), $32.778m: petroleum products. Sylvania Electric Div., General Telephone (Mountain View), $32.430m: electronic warfare development and production.

American President Lines (San Francisco), $24.504m: surface cargo transport. Stanford Research Institute (Menlo Park), $24.357m: ABM development. Trans International Airlines (Oakland), $23.551m: air cargo transport. Pacific Gas & Electric (San Francisco), $20.390m: utilities. Standard Oil of Calif. (San Francisco), $14.890m: petroleum products. Physics International (San Leandro), $14.890m: flash X-ray machine. States Steamship (San Francisco), $17.502m: surface cargo transport. Itek (Sunnyvale), $12.139m: aircraft radar assemblies. Saturn Airways (Oakland), $10.572m: air cargo transport. Stanford University (Palo Alto), $10.566m: research in computers and nuclear physics.

Matson Navigation (San Francisco), $9.069m: surface cargo transport. California Stevedore & Ballast (Oakland), $9.050m: stevedoring. Ampex Corp. (Redwood City), $6.714m: unspecified. Matson Terminals (Oakland), $5.687m: stevedoring. Durham Meat (San Jose), $5.060m: foodstuffs.

DOD Installations Oakland AB (Oakland). Ft. Barry AB (Sausalito). Ft. Baker AB (San Francisco). Presidio of San Francisco (San Francisco). Naval Air Rework Facility (San Francisco). Naval Air Station (Moffett Field, Mountain View). Naval Hospital (Oakland). Treasure Island Naval Schools Command (San Francisco). Treasure Island Naval Station (San Francisco). Naval Weapons Station (Concord). Naval Air Station (Alameda). Hunters Point Naval Shipyard (San Francisco). Naval Supply Center (Oakland). Almaden AF Station (Almaden). Hamilton AFB (San Rafael). Mill Valley AF Station (Mill Valley).

AEC Operations Lawrence Radiation Labs. (Berkeley), $37.762m. Sandia Corp. (Livermore), $31.723m: Lawrence Radiation Labs. Stanford U. (Menlo Park), $23.853m: research. General Electric (San Jose), $6.458m: unspecified. EG&G Inc. (San Ramon), $5.280m: unspecified.

NASA Installations Ames Research Center (Moffett Field).

Economic Base Electrical machinery, equipment, and supplies, esp. electronic components and accessories; ordnance and accessories; nonelectrical machinery, esp. office, computing, and accounting machines; food and kindred products. Also, higher education (San Jose State) and banking.

The Voters

Registration 212,567 total. 133,990 D (63%); 67,305 R (32%); 1,330 AIP (1%); 713 PF (—); 9,229 other (5%).

Employment profile White collar, 41%. Blue collar, 59%.

Ethnic groups Black, 4%. Spanish surname, 17%. Oriental, 3%. Total foreign stock, 27%. Mexico, 7%; Italy, 4%; Germany, UK, Canada, 2% each; Ireland, Sweden, 1% each; others, 9%.

Presidential vote

1968	Humphrey (D)	101,698	(55%)
	Nixon (R)	68,593	(37%)
	Wallace (AIP)	13,836	(8%)

Representative

Don Edwards (D) Elected 1962; b. Jan. 6, 1915, San Jose; home, San Jose; Stanford U., Stanford U. Law School, 1936–38; Navy, WWII; unmarried; Unitarian.

Career Sp. Agent, FBI, 1940–41; Pres., Valley Title Co.

Offices 2422 RHOB, 202-225-3072. Also 1961 Alameda, San Jose 95126, 408-296-7456.

Committees

Judiciary (7th); Chm., Sub. No. 4.

Veterans' Affairs (10th); Subs. (1) Education and Training, (2) Hospitals.

Group Ratings

	ADA	COPE	NREP	NFU	LCV	CFA	NAB	NSI	ACA
1970	88	100	91	91	80	100	0	0	12
1969	100	—	—	77	—	—	—	—	17
1968	100	100	—	92	—	—	0	—	5

Key Votes

(1) ABM	AGN	(6) 18-Yr-Vote	FOR	(11) Clean Water $	FOR
(2) SST	AGN	(7) Farm Sub Lmt	AGN	(12) Mig Wrkrs Comp	FOR
(3) Phil Pln	ABS	(8) Coop-Church	FOR	(13) Jets to Chiang	AGN
(4) No-Knock	AGN	(9) Family Asst	FOR	(14) State OEO Veto	AGN
(5) Cmutr Tax	FOR	(10) Work Stamps	AGN	(15) Park Logging	AGN

Election Results

1970 general:	Don Edwards (D-Inc.)	120,041	(69%)
	Mark Guerra (R)	49,556	(29%)
	Edmond Kaiser (AIP)	4,009	(2%)
1970 primary:	Don Edwards (D-Inc.), unopposed		
1968 general:	Don Edwards (D)	101,329	(57%)
	Larry Fargher (R)	77,847	(43%)

TENTH DISTRICT Political Background

Twenty years ago, what is now California 10 consisted, for the most part, of Stanford University and acres of vineyards growing along the mountainsides of the Coast Range above San Jose. Since then, the university and the surrounding areas have both grown considerably. The vineyards are now almost all gone, their owners having prudently recultivated the grapes in more remote places and sold the land for subdivisions. So great has been the population growth in the Santa Clara Valley that even the non-ecologically minded among the local residents wonder where the next wave of newcomers to the Valley plan to live.

The 10th extends along the western half of Santa Clara County. It includes part of the sprawling city-suburb of San Jose as well as the still agricultural and lightly populated (18,000) San Benito County to the south. The general rule in California is that the richer—and hence usually more conservative—the person is, the higher up the person lives. Accordingly, in the 10th, the foothill suburbs of Los Altos, Los Gatos, and Saratoga are the most Republican parts of the district. The larger towns in the valley—Mountain View and Sunnyvale—are politically marginal, generally supporting the winner of any statewide election. Palo Alto, the home of Stanford, is something of a cross between a prosperous suburb and a university town: it registers Republican, but often crosses lines when the Republicans put up a conservative.

Santa Clara County first got its own congressman after the 1950 census. Since that time, all or part of it has been represented in the House by conservative Republican Charles S. Gubser, a pro-Pentagon, senior member of the House Armed Services Committee. For some time, most political analysts have considered Gubser's seat a "safe" one. Nevertheless, in 1970, peace activists, noting the presence of Stanford in the district, decided to make a run at Gubser. But their candidate, Stuart McLean, a minister and teacher at Santa Clara University, succeeded only in reducing the incumbent's percentage 5 points to 62%.

For a man with nearly 20 years' seniority, Gubser is still comparatively young (54 in 1970). And although Democratic Sens. Cranston and Tunney both carried the district, the Republican Congressman seems likely to continue winning. Already entrenched in the 10th, Gubser stands to be strengthened even further by redistricting. The Democratic state legislators will no doubt want to create a second Democratic House seat in Santa Clara County. But to do this they will have to excise from the present 10th its most strongly Democratic territory, leaving Gubser less vulnerable in the future.

Census Data 1970 pop. 648,210; deviation from current state average, +23.4%; change 1960–70, +64.5%. Metro. 97.2%, 29.8% central city.

1970 Share of Federal Outlays $767,879,000 (average outlay per district, California 5–11, 14)

DOD	$282,253,000	HEW	$151,992,000
AEC	$33,646,000	HUD	$6,914,000
NASA	$11,711,000	OEO	$2,698,000
DOT	$11,106,000	DOA	$12,187,000
		Other	$134,373,000

Federal Military-Industrial Commitments (See California 9 for San Francisco Bay area listing.)

Economic Base Electrical machinery, equipment, and supplies, esp. electronic components and accessories; ordnance and accessories; livestock and cash grain. Also higher education (Stanford U.).

The Voters

Registration 268,579 total. 128,702 D (48%); 125,781 (47%); 933 AIP (—); 709 PF (—); 12,454 other (5%).

Employment profile White collar, 55%. Blue collar, 45%.

Ethnic groups Black, 1%. Spanish surname, 8%. Oriental, 2%. Total foreign stock, 25%. Mexico, Italy, Canada, 3% each; Germany, UK, 2% each; Ireland, Norway, Sweden, USSR, 1% each; others, 8%.

Presidential vote

1968	Humphrey (D)	109,522	(45%)
	Nixon (R)	121,967	(50%)
	Wallace (AIP)	11,639	(5%)

Representative

Charles S. Gubser (R) Elected 1952; b. Feb. 1, 1916, Gilroy; home, Gilroy; U. of Calif., B.A., 1937–38; married, one child; Episcopalian.

Career High school teacher; farmer; Calif. State Assembly, 1950–52.

Offices 2373 RHOB, 202-225-2631. Also 361 Town and Country Village, San Jose 95128, 408-246-1122.

Committees

Armed Services (5th); Subs. (1) Sub. No. 4, (2) Armed Services Investigating.

Group Ratings

	ADA	COPE	NREP	NFU	LCV	CFA	NAB	NSI	ACA
1970	20	25	17	70	13	44	64	100	50
1969	7	—	—	46	—	—	—	—	40
1968	8	17	—	58	—	—	83	—	74

Key Votes

(1) ABM	FOR	(6) 18-Yr-Vote	FOR	(11) Clean Water $	AGN
(2) SST	FOR	(7) Farm Sub Lmt	AGN	(12) Mig Wrkrs Comp	AGN
(3) Phil Pln	FOR	(8) Coop-Church	FOR	(13) Jets to Chiang	FOR
(4) No-Knock	FOR	(9) Family Asst	FOR	(14) State OEO Veto	FOR
(5) Cmutr Tax	AGN	(10) Work Stamps	FOR	(15) Park Logging	FOR

Election Results

1970 general:	Charles Gubser (R-Inc.)	135,864	(62%)
	Stuart McLean (D)	80,530	(37%)
	Joyce Stancliffe (AIP)	2,651	(1%)

1970 primary:	Charles Gubser (R-Inc.), unopposed		
1968 general:	Charles Gubser (R)	160,653	(67%)
	Grayson Taketa (D)	73,720	(31%)
	Martin Primack (PF)	4,320	(2%)

ELEVENTH DISTRICT Political Background

California 11 is virtually all of San Mateo County, or the Peninsula, as it is called, directly south of San Francisco. The northern towns—South San Francisco, Daly City, Pacifica—are direct outgrowths of the city itself and vote about as heavily Democratic. To the south, between the San Andreas Fault and San Francisco Bay, lies a series of towns strung out along the Southern Pacific commuter line. These suburbs are filled with middle-class white-collar people who work in San Francisco or, more often of late, on the Peninsula itself. Politically, the towns behave more like the upper-income suburbs of Boston or New York than the arch-conservative suburbs around Los Angeles. A few of the wealthy, higher altitude towns (e.g., Hillsborough, the home of Shirley Temple Black) are staunchly Republican. But most of the territory between the foothills and the Bayshore flats is prime ticket-splitting country.

As in Marin County north of San Francisco, the Peninsula has large numbers of liberal Republicans who react with a kind of frontlash against conservative Republican candidates. The war issue here has made reluctant Democratic voters out of well-meaning Republicans. San Mateo went for Humphrey in 1968, though it had gone for Nixon eight years before; in 1970 it gave Sen. John Tunney a bigger margin than Gov. Ronald Reagan. Also in 1970, to everyone's surprise, San Mateo elected a liberal Democrat to the state Senate. The candidate campaigned on an ecology platform and, by winning, kept the redistricting process from falling entirely into Republican hands.

The 11th is represented by Paul N. (Pete) McCloskey, who at this writing seems certain to challenge Nixon in the 1972 Republican primaries. Presidential candidates are made quickly these days, it seems. As late as 1967, when Spiro Agnew, another product of suburban politics, had just been elected Governor of Maryland, McCloskey was still a lawyer in Menlo Park. He was a man known locally for his military record (Marine hero in Korea), for his meticulous handling of legal cases even when non-paying, and for his dabblings in local Republican politics. He was, in short, the kind of man his neighbors would be happy to elect county judge or prosecutor.

Instead, McCloskey decided to run for Congress. The seat was vacant, because the incumbent, conservative Republican J. Arthur Younger, had died. A group of McCloskey's friends thought the ex-Marine would make a good Republican candidate. The main problem was the opposition—none other than Shirley Temple Black, a wealthy housewife and political friend of the newly installed and very popular Gov. Reagan. Moreover, Mrs. Black had no trouble getting all kinds of national publicity. But if all the newspaper reporters wanted to follow Shirley, the Menlo Park lawyer had hundreds of less obtrusive friends in the district. Pete's locally oriented campaign, as someone put it, wound up sinking the good ship Lollipop. The general election was an anti-climax, and Pete McCloskey went to Congress.

In Washington, the Californian soon developed a reputation for being one of the more liberal Republicans, particularly on issues like ecology and the war. His antiwar positions have been made distinctive by his record in the Marine Corps. But local Democratic officials did not think that was good enough or his record in general liberal enough to win their endorsement. McCloskey's performance in Congress did, however, inspire conservative opposition. In 1968 he won only 53% of the votes in a primary fight against Robert R. Barry, a roving ex-congressman who represented the 25th district of New York from 1958 to 1964 and who had run in the 38th district of California in 1966. In 1970, an even more concerted effort was thrown up against McCloskey, reportedly one of the main targets of Harry Salvatori, Reagan kitchen-cabinet member and oil millionaire. This time McCloskey took 60% of the primary vote.

General elections have always been easier than primaries for the Congressman, because most of the conservative Republicans return to the fold and the Democrats vote for him in droves. In both 1968 and 1970 he received 79% of the votes in the general election—in both cases one of the four best Republican showings in the nation.

McCloskey has promised that he will run against Nixon unless the President changes his war policies. This probably means that he will no longer be a candidate in the 11th.

The conservatives are out to get him now more than ever. The local Republican party has repudiated him and will probably nominate a conservative candidate in 1972. In that case, the likely winner in 1972 will be the Democratic candidate, possibly the 1970 surprise winner of a state Senate seat, Arlen Gregorio.

Census Data 1970 pop. 537,822; deviation from current state average, +2.4%; change 1960–70, 25.4%. Metro. 100%, 0.0% central city.

1970 Share of Federal Outlays $646,879,000 (average outlay per district, California 5–11, 14)

DOD	$282,253,000	HEW	$151,992,000
AEC	$33,646,000	HUD	$6,914,000
NASA	$11,711,000	OEO	$2,698,000
DOT	$11,106,000	DOA	$12,187,000
		Other	$134,373,000

Federal Military-Industrial Commitments (See California 9 for San Francisco Bay area listing.)

Economic Base Electrical machinery, equipment, and supplies, esp. communication equipment; fabricated metal products, esp. fabricated structural metal products; non-electrical machinery; food and kindred products. Also, extensive commuting to California 5 (San Francisco).

The Voters

Registration 235,119 total. 124,898 D (52%); 99,729 R (42%); 1,301 AIP (1%); 729 PF (—); 8,462 other (4%).

Employment profile White collar, 55%. Blue collar, 45%.

Ethnic groups Black, 3%. Spanish surname, 4%. Oriental, 2%. Total foreign stock, 30%. Italy, 5%; Germany, UK, Canada, 3% each; Austria, Ireland, Norway, Poland, Sweden, USSR, Mexico, 1% each; others, 8%.

Presidential vote

1968	Humphrey (D)	102,699	(48%)
	Nixon (R)	97,590	(45%)
	Wallace (AIP)	14,590	(7%)

Representative

Paul N. (Pete) McCloskey, Jr. (R) Elected 1966; b. Sept. 29, 1927, San Bernardino; home, San Mateo; Occidental Col. and Calif. Inst. of Tech., 1945–46; Stanford U., B.A., 1950, LL.B., 1953; Navy, 1945–47; USMC, Korean War; USMCR, 1952–60; married, four children; Presbyterian.

Career Practicing atty., 1953–67; Deputy Dist. Atty., Alameda County, 1953–54; Lecturer, Santa Clara and Stanford Law Schools, 1964–67.

Offices 1511 LHOB, 202-225-5411. Also 141 Borel Ave., San Mateo 94402, 415-341-3418.

Committees

Government Operations (9th); Subs. (1) Conservation and Natural Resources, (2) Foreign Operations and Government Information.

Merchant Marine and Fisheries (9th); Subs. (1) Fisheries and Wildlife Conservation, (2) Merchant Marine, (3) Sp. Sub. on Maritime Education and Training.

Group Ratings

	ADA	COPE	NREP	NFU	LCV	CFA	NAB	NSI	ACA
1970	64	42	75	62	100	82	70	22	59
1969	67	—	—	77	—	—	—	—	18
1968	33	75	—	44	—	—	80	—	43

Key Votes

(1) ABM	AGN	(6) 18-Yr-Vote	FOR	(11) Clean Water $	FOR
(2) SST	AGN	(7) Farm Sub Lmt	FOR	(12) Mig Wrkrs Comp	AGN
(3) Phil Pln	FOR	(8) Coop-Church	FOR	(13) Jets to Chiang	AGN
(4) No-Knock	FOR	(9) Family Asst	FOR	(14) State OEO Veto	AGN
(5) Cmutr Tax	AGN	(10) Work Stamps	FOR	(15) Park Logging	AGN

Election Results

1970 general:	Paul McCloskey, Jr. (R-Inc.)	144,500	(78%)
	Robert Gomperts (D)	39,188	(21%)
	Jack Wilson (R)	2,786	(1%)
1970 primary:	Paul McCloskey, Jr. (R-Inc.)	38,830	(60%)
	Forden Athearn (R)	25,907	(40%)

TWELFTH DISTRICT Political Background

California 12 contains some of the most spectacular scenery in the nation, from the Monterey cypresses at Carmel's Pebble Beach, through the mountainous, wild Big Sur coast, to William Randolph Hearst's San Simeon. It also includes some of the nation's richest farmlands: the lettuce fields in the Salinas Valley (where Cesar Chavez has been organizing farm workers) and the artichoke fields around Watsonville. All of the district lies between the Coast Range and the ocean, except for Kings County, a staunchly Democratic part of the Central Valley. Appended to satisfy the equal-population doctrine, Kings is totally unlike the rest of the district. In fact, to drive from Kings over the mountains to the rest of the district, the traveler must follow a road that leaves the 13th completely before returning to it.

The coast counties are politically marginal. Landowners around Salinas and retirees in Santa Cruz and the Monterey Peninsula tend to be conservative, while the district's sizable Mexican-American minority and its artists and writers tend to be liberal Democrats. The decisive middle of the electorate is equivocal: it prefers Republicans, but bridles at accepting those that it considers too conservative—e.g., ex-Sen. George Murphy, ex-Superintendent of Public Instruction Max Rafferty. Nevertheless, the district's Republican congressman, Burt L. Talcott, seems safely entrenched. Talcott had no Democratic opponent in 1968 and won 64% in 1970.

The Congressman from the 12th is a steadfast conservative whose concern for dress and decorum—he once chided his colleagues for wearing sports coats on the floor of the House—would make a suburban school principal wince. He has been slowly climbing the seniority ladder on the House Appropriations Committee, and, some day soon, Talcott will no doubt be the ranking Republican on one of its subcommittees. Redistricting will only aid his chances for reelection. The 1970 census figures indicate that Kings County, which was added to the district in 1968 to satisfy the population requirement, must now be subtracted for the same reason.

Census Data 1970 pop. 544,161; deviation from current state average, +3.6%; change 1960–70, +31.6%. Metro. 46.0%, 15.7% central city.

1970 Share of Federal Outlays $578,153,854

DOD	$287,774,000	HEW	$163,827,515
AEC	$133,662	HUD	$2,964,846
NASA	$96,608	OEO	$2,676,979
DOT	$20,727,364	DOA	$35,974,054
		Other	$63,978,826

Federal Military-Industrial Commitments

DOD Installations Presidio of Monterey AB (Monterey). Ft. Ord (Monterey). Naval Postgraduate School (Monterey). Naval Air Station (Lemoore).

Economic Base Livestock and cash grain; food and kindred products, esp. fresh produce; rubber and miscellaneous plastics products. Also, higher education (Calif. State Polytech.) and tourism (Monterey, Big Sur).

The Voters

Registration 196,833 total. 101,554 D (52%); 86,270 R (44%); 1,436 AIP (1%); 866 PF (—); 6,707 other (3%).

Employment profile White collar, 40%. Blue collar, 60%.

Ethnic groups Black, 3%. Spanish surname, 10%. Oriental, 4%. Total foreign stock, 26%. Mexico, 5%; Germany, Italy, UK, Canada, 2% each; Ireland, Sweden, 1% each; others, 9%.

Presidential vote

1968	Humphrey (D)	73,224	(43%)
	Nixon (R)	86,251	(50%)
	Wallace (AIP)	12,321	(7%)

Representative

Burt L. Talcott (R) Elected 1962; b. Feb. 22, 1920, Billings, Mont.; home, Salinas; Stanford U., B.A., 1942, LL.B., 1946; Army Air Corps, WWII; married, one child; Methodist.

Career Atty., Commissioner of Athletics, Coast Counties Athletic League, 1954–58; Monterey County Supervisor, 1954–62.

Offices 1524 LHOB, 202-225-2861. Also U.S. P.O. Bldg., Salinas 93901, 408-424-6447; Monterey City, 408-373-5402; Hanford, 109-582-3626; Lemoore, 209-924-5926; Paso Robles, 805-238-5447; San Luis Obispo, 805-543-1619; Watsonville, 408-722-6557.

Committees

Appropriations (14th); Subs. (1) HUD, Space and Science, (2) Military Construction.

Group Ratings

	ADA	COPE	NREP	NFU	LCV	CFA	NAB	NSI	ACA
1970	24	25	17	38	0	42	82	22	74
1969	7	—	—	43	—	—	—	—	47
1968	9	8	—	40	—	—	100	—	77

Key Votes

(1) ABM	ABS	(6) 18-Yr-Vote	AGN	(11) Clean Water $	AGN
(2) SST	AGN	(7) Farm Sub Lmt	AGN	(12) Mig Wrkrs Comp	AGN
(3) Phil Pln	FOR	(8) Coop-Church	AGN	(13) Jets to Chiang	ABS
(4) No-Knock	FOR	(9) Family Asst	FOR	(14) State OEO Veto	FOR
(5) Cmutr Tax	AGN	(10) Work Stamps	ABS	(15) Park Logging	FOR

Election Results

1970 general:	Burt Talcott (R-Inc.)	95,549	(64%)
	O'Brien Riordan (D)	50,942	(34%)
	Herbert Foster, Jr. (PF)	3,682	(2%)
1970 primary:	Burt Talcott (R-Inc.), unopposed		
1968 general:	Burt Talcott (R-D)	143,222	(93%)
	Ann Holliday (AIP)	7,705	(5%)
	Simon Lakritz (write-in)	3,784	(2%)

THIRTEENTH DISTRICT Political Background

California 13 runs along the southern part of California's Pacific coast, from Vandenberg Air Force Base north of Santa Barbara down to Malibu Beach and the Los Angeles city limits. Santa Barbara is, of course, the site of the famous 1969 oil slick and of the burning of the Bank of America office at the local branch of the University of California. Once considered ultraconservative, with a large colony of wealthy retirees, the city came alive with protest when oil began coating its beaches. Today it is one of the best places in America to run an ecology-oriented campaign. Vandenberg, in the northern part of Santa Barbara County, is a huge missile-launching complex, and the area around it is heavily dependent on military spending.

Ventura County, the other major portion of the district, is an interesting mix. Since large numbers of Mexican-Americans live in the cities of Oxnard (pop. 71,000) and Ventura (pop. 55,000), the county often went Democratic. But in the '60's there was a large population influx from Los Angeles' San Fernando Valley into the Simi Valley and Thousand Oaks areas. The migration contained a disproportionate number of conservative Republicans. This, together with the rise of Ronald Reagan, has given the county a much more conservative cast in recent elections.

Malibu, a strip of beach between the ocean and the mountains, contains the famous beach hideaways of many movie stars and is also the site of one of Gov. Reagan's ranches. Despite the liberalness of some of its show biz residents, Malibu leans heavily to the conservative side. Its votes, however, are not a significant part of the district's total.

The 13th's longtime (since 1954) representative is quiet, dignified Charles M. Teague, a conservative Republican. Teague has picked his committee spots well and will become a committee chairman if the Republicans ever gain control of the House. He is currently ranking minority member on the House Veterans' Affairs Committee (the chairman, oddly enough, is Texas' Olin E. "Tiger" Teague), and number two Republican on the House Agriculture Committee. The California Congressman has had little difficulty winning reelection in the past. But in 1970 he was the target of a vigorous and well-publicized challenge from a 27-year-old McCarthy campaign veteran, Gary Hart. Hart stressed the peace and ecology issues and reduced Teague's victory percentage from 66% to 59%. The young man made his biggest gains in the Santa Barbara area—a sign that the oil slick, as well as the war issue, worries high-income voters.

Redistricting will reduce the size of the 13th significantly. The new lines will probably place Malibu and eastern Ventura County (Simi Valley, Thousand Oaks) in another district with the more conservative part of the San Fernando Valley. Since the areas to be removed are solidly Republican, Teague will find the going a little tougher. He may well face a vigorous opponent in 1972.

Census Data 1970 pop. 699,237; deviation from current state average, +33.2%; change 1960–70, +77.8%. Metro. 100%, 32.2% central city.

1970 Share of Federal Outlays $675,559,019

DOD	$406,152,000	HEW	$141,881,132
AEC	$3,264,111	HUD	$4,848,417
NASA	$6,100,331	OEO	$820,009
DOT	$23,086,419	DOA	$11,289,984
		Other	$78,116,616

Federal Military-Industrial Commitments

DOD Contractors Federal Electric Div., IT&T (Lompoc), $28.732m: operation of AF Western Test Range technical facilities. McDonnell Douglas (Lompoc), $20.596m: ABM development. Lockheed Aircraft (Lompoc), $11.422m: unspecified. Boeing (Vandenberg AFB), $10.400m: unspecified. General Motors (Goleta), $8.523m: Mk 48 torpedo warheads. General Research Corp. (Santa Barbara), $6.752m: ABM development. Western Electric Div., AT&T (Lompoc), $6.469m: ABM development. Raytheon (Goleta), $5.156m: services to F-4 aircraft weapons system.

DOD Installations Naval Air Station (Point Mugu). Naval Construction Batallion Center (Port Heuneme). Navy Pacific Missile Range (Point Mugu). Vandenberg AFB (Lompoc).

Economic Base Livestock and poultry; electrical machinery, equipment, and supplies, esp. communication equipment; aircraft and parts and other transportation equipment. Also, higher education (U. Calif. Santa Barbara) and tourism (Santa Barbara).

The Voters

Registration 261,810 total. 128,184 D (49%); 121,732 R (47%); 1,743 AIP (1%); 1,052 PF (—); 9,099 other (4%).

Employment profile White collar, 43%. Blue collar, 57%.

Ethnic groups Black, 2%. Spanish surname, 15%. Oriental, 2%. Total foreign stock, 24%. Mexico, 9%; Germany, UK, Canada, 2% each; Ireland, Italy, Sweden, 1% each; others, 5%.

Presidential vote

1968	Humphrey (D)	93,614	(41%)
	Nixon (R)	123,437	(53%)
	Wallace (AIP)	14,223	(6%)

Representative

Charles M. Teague (R) Elected 1954; b. Sept. 18, 1909, Santa Paula; home, Ojai; Stanford U., B.A., 1931, LL.B., 1934; Army Air Corps, WWII; married, three children; Protestant.

Career Practicing atty., 1934–54.

Offices 1414 LHOB, 202-225-3601. Also 616 E. Main St., P.O. Box 1785, Ventura 93001, 805-643-5401.

Committees

Agriculture (2nd); Subs. (1) Conservation and Credit, (2) Forests.

Veterans' Affairs (Ranking Mbr.).

Group Ratings

	ADA	COPE	NREP	NFU	LCV	CFA	NAB	NSI	ACA
1970	8	11	22	63	14	42	50	100	62
1969	0	—	—	43	—	—	—	—	50
1968	0	0	—	31	—	—	100	—	83

Key Votes

(1) ABM	FOR	(6) 18-Yr-Vote	FOR	(11) Clean Water $	AGN
(2) SST	FOR	(7) Farm Sub Lmt	ABS	(12) Mig Wrkrs Comp	AGN
(3) Phil Pln	FOR	(8) Coop-Church	AGN	(13) Jets to Chiang	FOR
(4) No-Knock	FOR	(9) Family Asst	ABS	(14) State OEO Veto	FOR
(5) Cmutr Tax	FOR	(10) Work Stamps	FOR	(15) Park Logging	ABS

Election Results

1970 general:	Charles Teague (R)	127,507	(59%)
	Gary Hart (D)	87,980	(40%)
	Maude Jordet (AIP)	2,339	(1%)
1970 primary:	Charles Teague (R), unopposed		
1968 general:	Charles Teague (R)	151,608	(66%)
	Stanley Sheinbaum (D)	78,628	(34%)

FOURTEENTH DISTRICT Political Background

California 14 is Contra Costa County, the only California district consisting wholly of a single county unit. On a non-topographical map, the district looks compact—a parcel of suburban land across the bay from San Francisco. But actually the 14th is carved into several distinct parts by massive mountains. On the west, facing the Golden Gate, is Richmond, a working-class and heavily Democratic city with a large black population. Along the north side of the county, on the arm of the bay that leads to the Sacramento and San Joaquin rivers, lie the industrial towns of Martinez, Pittsburg, and Antioch—more Democratic bastions. Inland, surrounded by mountains, is the fastest-growing part of the county, middle-class suburbs like Concord and Pleasant Hill and Republican high-income strongholds like Walnut Creek and Lafayette.

The voting behavior of the county as a whole has a blue-collar cast to it, in contrast to the white-collar counties of San Mateo and Marin across the bay. Historically, Contra Costa has been Democratic, but it supported Ronald Reagan in both 1966 and 1970. It also heavily (65%) opposed open housing in the 1964 Proposition 14 referendum. Even as the war and ecology issues drive the liberal Republicans of San Mateo and Marin to the Democrats, so the crime and disorder issues raised by Ronald Reagan and Richard Nixon have driven the blue-collar voters of Contra Costa to the Republicans.

For more than 10 years (1954–66) the congressman from the 14th was John F. Baldwin, a liberal Republican who died unexpectedly in 1966. His successor is Jerome F. Waldie, a former Democratic assemblyman, who is well known in the district and has never had trouble winning elections. Waldie's experience as floor leader in the California Assembly—usually considered the best organized and staffed of all state legislatures—left him temperamentally unfit to cope with the tradition-bound ways of the House. In 1969, he spoke the unspeakable and called on John McCormack to step down. Waldie infuriated many elder members and also irritated the older reformers who felt they could achieve their ends soon enough if no one rocked the boat. Events vindicated Waldie. In 1970 McCormack announced he would retire. But the Californian remained on the outs, and none of his colleagues even suggested that impertinent Waldie be put up for a leadership post.

So Waldie remains a rather junior member of the Judiciary and Post Office and Civil Service committees, and chairman of the latter's Subcommittee on Retirement, Insurance, and Health Benefits. But whatever his standing with the House establishment, he is assured of reelection at home. Redistricting, which will reduce the size of his district considerably, should give him no problems.

Census Data 1970 pop. 558,389; deviation from current state average, +6.3%; change 1960–70, +36.5%. Metro. 100%, 0.0% central city.

1970 Share of Federal Outlays $646,879,000 (average outlay per district, California 5–11, 14)

DOD	$282,253,000	HEW	$151,992,000
AEC	$33,646,000	HUD	$6,914,000
NASA	$11,711,000	OEO	$2,698,000
DOT	$11,106,000	DOA	$12,187,000
		Other	$134,373,000

Federal Military-Industrial Commitments (See California 9 for San Francisco Bay area listing.)

Economic Base Petroleum refining and related industries; chemicals and allied products, esp. industrial inorganic and organic chemicals; primary metal industries, esp. blast furnaces, steel works, and rolling and finishing mills; fabricated metal products, esp. fabricated structural metal products and metal shipping barrels, drums, kegs, and pails.

The Voters

Registration 241,023 total. 134,086 D (56%); 97,027 R (40%); 1,893 AIP (1%); 804 PF (—); 7,213 other (3%).

Employment profile White collar, 48%. Blue collar, 52%.

Ethnic groups Black, 8%. Spanish surname, 6%. Oriental, 1%. Total foreign stock, 21%. Italy, 3%; Mexico, Germany, UK, Canada, 2% each; Ireland, Norway, Sweden, 1% each; others, 6%.

Presidential vote

1968	Humphrey (D)	101,668	(47%)
	Nixon (R)	97,486	(45%)
	Wallace (AIP)	18,330	(8%)

Representative

Jerome R. Waldie (D) Elected 1966; b. Feb. 15, 1925, Antioch; home, Antioch; U. of Calif., B.A., 1950, LL.B., 1953; Army, WWII; married, three children; religion unspecified.

Career Practicing atty., 1953–66; Calif. Assembly, 1955–66; Majority Leader, 1961–66.

Offices 408 CHOB, 202-225-5511. Also Civic Center, Box 864, Concord 94520, 415-687-1200, and 3915 Macdonald Ave., Richmond 94805, 415-233-4425.

Committees

Judiciary (13th); Subs. (1) Sub. No. 2, (2) Sub. No. 4.

Post Office and Civil Service (8th); Subs. (1) Chm., Retirement, Insurance, and Health Benefits, (2) Postal Service.

Group Ratings

	ADA	COPE	NREP	NFU	LCV	CFA	NAB	NSI	ACA
1970	96	91	93	75	100	100	0	0	19
1969	87	—	—	86	—	—	—	—	6
1968	92	92	—	60	—	—	33	—	9

Key Votes

(1) ABM	AGN	(6) 18-Yr-Vote	FOR	(11) Clean Water $	FOR
(2) SST	AGN	(7) Farm Sub Lmt	AGN	(12) Mig Wrkrs Comp	FOR
(3) Phil Pln	FOR	(8) Coop-Church	FOR	(13) Jets to Chiang	AGN
(4) No-Knock	AGN	(9) Family Asst	FOR	(14) State OEO Veto	AGN
(5) Cmutr Tax	FOR	(10) Work Stamps	AGN	(15) Park Logging	AGN

Election Results

1970 general:	Jerome Waldie (D-Inc.)	148,655	(75%)
	Byron Athan (R)	50,750	(25%)
1970 primary:	Jerome Waldie (D-Inc.), unopposed		
1968 general:	Jerome Waldie (D)	152,847	(72%)
	David Schuh (R)	56,730	(27%)
	Luis Hamilton (AIP)	3,952	(2%)

FIFTEENTH DISTRICT Political Background

California 15 is part of California's Central Valley, probably the richest farmland in the country. Between the Coast Range and the Sierra Nevada are vast, flat plains, heavily irrigated and often cultivated by Mexican-American migrant laborers. In the north, the Valley extends along the Sacramento River to a point near the Oregon border; in the south it parallels the San Joaquin River to the Tehachapi Mountains less than 100 miles from Los Angeles. The Tehachapi mark the traditional boundary between northern and southern California. Situated in the near middle of the Valley is the 15th district, San Joaquin and Stanislaus counties and part of Merced. Although the district contains significant cities—Stockton (pop. 107,000) and Modesto (pop. 61,000)—its economy is dependent mainly on agriculture.

Traditionally, the Valley has been Democratic, a political preference strengthened by the great wave of migration here from the Dust Bowl during the 1930's. But lately, as the region has grown prosperous and as that prosperity has been threatened by striking Mexican farm workers, the 15th and the districts around it have become increasingly conservative. Gov. Reagan made big gains here among nominal Democrats. Moreover, a carefully planned Republican campaign to win control of the state legislature met with its greatest successes here. In 1964, three of seven San Joaquin Valley Assembly districts elected Republican legislators; in 1970, the figure was six of seven.

But the 15th still retains its Democratic congressman, John J. McFall, who was first elected in 1956. In the House McFall has always been a part of the less liberal, more tradition-oriented wing of the Democratic party. As a result, he was long ago rewarded with a seat on the House Appropriations Committee. There he usually lines up with the conservative majority led by Chairman George Mahon and favors low spending on almost all federal programs except defense. McFall is now the chairman of the Transportation Subcommittee, in which capacity he led the unsuccessful floor fight for the SST in 1971.

Recent political trends in the Valley have put McFall's seat into the marginal category; in 1966 he won only 57% of the vote, and in 1968 even less, 54%. He rebounded in 1970 (63%), but so did most California Democrats. In the future, McFall will have to work his district harder than most congressmen with comparable seniority. The Republicans have two particularly strong candidates in the area, though neither seems likely to run unless there is a vacancy: former Assembly Speaker Bob Monagan and HEW Undersecretary (and former Assemblyman) John Veneman.

Census Data 1970 pop. 510,653; deviation from current state average, —2.7%; change 1960–70, +18.5%. Metro. 94.9%, 33.2% central city.

1970 Share of Federal Outlays $422,546,711

DOD	$134,100,000	HEW	$172,131,256
AEC	$000	HUD	$1,740,585
NASA	$299,922	OEO	$1,372,432
DOT	$23,811,473	DOA	$14,991,073
		Other	$74,099,970

Federal Military-Industrial Commitments

DOD Contractors Norris Industries (Riverbank), $14.831m: 105-mm cartridge cases; 81-mm mortal shells.

DOD Installations Sharpe Army Depot (Lathrop). Naval Communication Station (Stockton). Castle AFB (Merced).

Economic Base Dairy, livestock, and poultry; food and kindred products, esp. canned and preserved fruits and vegetables; stone, clay, glass, and concrete products, esp. flat glass; nonelectrical machinery, esp. special industry machinery other than metalworking machinery.

The Voters

Registration 190,356 total. 110,837 D (58%); 72,769 R (38%); 1,232 AIP (1%); 114 PF (—); 5,413 other (3%).

Employment profile White collar, 37%. Blue collar, 63%.

Ethnic groups Black, 4%. Spanish surname, 10%. Oriental, 3%. Total foreign stock, 25%. Mexico, 4%; Italy, 3%; Germany, USSR, 2% each; Sweden, UK, Canada, 1% each; others, 9%.

Presidential vote

1968	Humphrey (D)	75,579	(45%)
	Nixon (R)	78,983	(47%)
	Wallace (AIP)	13,428	(8%)

Representative

John J. McFall (D) Elected 1956; b. Feb. 20, 1918, Buffalo, N.Y.; home, Manteca; Modesto Jr. Col., A.A., 1936; U. of Calif., B.A., 1938, LL.B., 1941; Army, WWII; married, three children; Catholic.

Career Practicing atty., 1948–56; Mayor of Manteca, 1948–50; Calif. Assembly, 1951–56.

Offices 2346 RHOB, 202-225-2511. Also 146 N. Grant, Manteca 95336, 209-823-1112.

Committees

Appropriations (19th); Subs. (1) Chm., Transportation, (2) Defense.

Group Ratings

	ADA	COPE	NREP	NFU	LCV	CFA	NAB	NSI	ACA
1970	52	92	50	92	50	89	0	50	12
1969	53	—	—	100	—	—	—	—	12
1968	83	100	—	94	—	—	17	—	4

Key Votes

(1) ABM	FOR	(6) 18-Yr-Vote	FOR	(11) Clean Water $	AGN
(2) SST	FOR	(7) Farm Sub Lmt	AGN	(12) Mig Wrkrs Comp	FOR
(3) Phil Pln	AGN	(8) Coop-Church	AGN	(13) Jets to Chiang	AGN
(4) No-Knock	FOR	(9) Family Asst	FOR	(14) State OEO Veto	AGN
(5) Cmutr Tax	FOR	(10) Work Stamps	AGN	(15) Park Logging	FOR

Election Results

1970 general:	John McFall (D-Inc.)	98,442	(63%)
	Sam Van Dyken (R)	55,546	(36%)
	Francis Gillings (AIP)	1,994	(1%)
1970 primary:	John McFall (D-Inc.)	50,670	(86%)
	Albert Culhane (D)	8,410	(14%)
1968 general:	John McFall (D)	86,386	(54%)
	Sam Van Dyken (R)	74,058	(46%)

SIXTEENTH DISTRICT Political Background

California 16 is another San Joaquin Valley district, dominated by the city of Fresno (pop. 165,000). The 16th has the largest Mexican-American population of any Valley district. Accordingly, it has remained the most Democratic of them, despite the general conservative trend among most California voters. Many of its residents are descendants of the original "Okies," the people who left the dried-out fields of Oklahoma, Kansas, and Texas in the '30's for the promised land of California. Here, as John Steinbeck chronicled in *The Grapes of Wrath,* they did backbreaking work in the steamy-hot fields for next to nothing and lived in miserable migrant camps. Ironically, though perhaps not surprisingly, the sons and daughters of the Okies are not particularly sympathetic—are often even hostile—to the very similar plight of the Mexican-Americans in those same fields today.

The congressman from the 16th district is himself a transplant from the Dust Bowl. B. F. (Bernie) Sisk grew up on the dusty plains of central Texas and moved to the Valley in 1937. Some 17 years later he upset a Republican congressman, and, ever since, his ingratiating personality has helped him to win reelection. For his first 10 years or so in the House, Sisk was regarded as a typical northern Democrat. But in the mid-'60's, when the Reagan tide began running in, he became noticeably more conservative. In 1966 his vote in the House Rules Committee killed home rule for the District of Columbia. Around that time the Johnson Administration head-counters stopped regarding him as an automatic vote.

Sisk's conservative record—and, no doubt, his Southern origin—commended him to some of the more conservative Southern Democrats. In late 1970 he became a candidate for Majority Leader, reportedly at the behest of men like William Colmer of Mississippi, Omar Burleson of Texas, and Bob Sikes of Florida. For a while, Sisk's campaign made inroads in the California and the Southern delegations, endangering Hale Boggs's candidacy. But a chasm developed too wide to straddle: Sisk's voting record, organized labor said, was not acceptable. So most of the Southerners returned to Boggs, who was after all one of their own. Sisk got only 41 votes in the Democratic Caucus of January 1971, which means that he will most likely never hold a leadership post. But his seat on Rules—and his capable management of the Congressional Reorganization Bill—still gives him some power. He remains an important figure in the House.

The redistricting picture in the Central Valley is far from clear. From the 1970 census figures the area stands to gain a congressional district. As nearly as can be determined, it will be sandwiched between John McFall's 15th and Bernie Sisk's 16th. Such a district would be extremely marginal and could elect almost any kind of congressman. At this writing, however, the necessary bargaining between Democratic legislators and Gov. Reagan has not taken place, and so no firm predictions can be made.

Census Data 1970 pop. 491,743; deviation from current state average, −6.3%; change 1960–70, +13.7%. Metro. 84.0%, 33.8% central city.

1970 Share of Federal Outlays $458,208,055

DOD	$70,211,000	HEW	$181,161,136
AEC	$000	HUD	$10,977,927
NASA	$000	OEO	$1,291,438
DOT	$22,649,014	DOA	$76,803,391
		Other	$95,114,149

Federal Military-Industrial Commitments

DOD Installations Castle AFB (Merced).

Economic Base Cotton and dairy; food and kindred products, esp. canned and preserved fruits and vegetables; nonelectrical machinery, esp. office, computing, and accounting machinery; lumber and wood products other than furniture, esp. wooden containers. Also, higher education (Fresno State).

The Voters

Registration 180,544 total. 112,436 D (62%); 60,834 R (34%); 2,873 AIP (2%); 111 PF (—); 4,290 other (2%).

Employment profile White collar, 38%. Blue collar, 62%.

Ethnic groups Black, 5%. Spanish surname, 16%. Oriental, 3%. Total foreign stock, 25%. Mexico, 9%; USSR, 3%; Italy, 2%; Germany, Sweden, UK, Canada, 1% each; others, 7%.

Presidential vote

1968	Humphrey (D)	76,817	(49%)
	Nixon (R)	68,544	(43%)
	Wallace (AIP)	12,830	(8%)

Representative

B. F. Sisk (D) Elected 1954; b. Dec. 14, 1910, Montague, Texas; home, Fresno; Abilene Christian Col., 1929–31; married, two children; Church of Christ.

Career Day laborer, refrigerator salesman, orchard worker, 1937–45; tire company shipping clerk, service mgr., dept. mgr., asst. gen. mgr., 1946–54.

Offices 2242 RHOB, 202-225-6131. Also 1130 O St., Fresno 93721, 209-485-5000, ext. 261.

Committees

Agriculture (11th); Subs. (1) Cotton, (2) Domestic Marketing and Consumer Relations, (3) Livestock and Grains.

Group Ratings

	ADA	COPE	NREP	NFU	LCV	CFA	NAB	NSI	ACA
1970	44	89	60	92	44	94	0	90	7
1969	40	—	—	100	—	—	—	—	8
1968	75	100	—	81	—	—	20	—	4

Key Votes

(1) ABM	FOR	(6) 18-Yr-Vote	FOR	(11) Clean Water $	AGN
(2) SST	AGN	(7) Farm Sub Lmt	AGN	(12) Mig Wrkrs Comp	FOR
(3) Phil Pln	ABS	(8) Coop-Church	ABS	(13) Jets to Chiang	FOR
(4) No-Knock	ABS	(9) Family Asst	FOR	(14) State OEO Veto	AGN
(5) Cmutr Tax	FOR	(10) Work Stamps	AGN	(15) Park Logging	FOR

Election Results

1970 general:	B. F. Sisk (D-Inc.)	95,118	(66%)
	Phillip Sanchez (R)	43,843	(31%)
	James Scott (AIP)	4,237	(3%)
1970 primary:	B. F. Sisk (D-Inc.), unopposed		
1968 general:	B. F. Sisk (D)	97,476	(63%)
	David Harris (R)	55,188	(35%)
	John Carroll (AIP)	3,392	(2%)

SEVENTEENTH DISTRICT Political Background

California 17 is one of fifteen districts entirely within or primarily within Los Angeles County. The focus of the 17th lies in the busy port area of Los Angeles—San Pedro and Wilmington—in the adjoining working-class suburbs of Carson, Compton, Gardena, and Lawndale, and in the more white-collar towns of Torrance and Redondo Beach. Many of the district's residents work in Los Angeles' huge aircraft plants, in the port, or in the factories that are located in the industrial corridor to the east. An increasing percentage of the 17th's residents are black, moving into Carson from Compton and Watts to the north.

Most of the residents of the district are traditional Democrats, working people who supported the programs of Franklin D. Roosevelt and John F. Kennedy, but who feel threatened by social trends not to their liking. In 1966, the district violated its tradition and gave a substantial margin to Gov. Ronald Reagan. But its conservative ardor seems to have passed; Jess Unruh and his populist-style campaign carried the district in 1970.

For many years (1942–68), the 17th routinely reelected Democrat Congressman Cecil King, the co-sponsor of the Medicare act. When King retired in 1968, a real set-to followed between Democrat Glenn Anderson and Republican Joseph Blatchford. Anderson was lieutenant governor under Pat Brown and was unlucky enough to have been acting chief executive when the Watts riot broke out. Afterward people accused Anderson of having waited too long before dispatching the National Guard. He was then beaten badly by Robert Finch for reelection in 1966. In the 1968 congressional election he just squeaked by Blatchford with 51%. The loser went on to become Director of the Peace Corps and now of the consolidated version of the youth service agencies. Here he probably wields more power than a junior congressman anyway.

As befits a representative with a major port in his district, Anderson is a member of the Merchant Marine and Fisheries and Public Works committees. In the familiar pattern, after a tough initial election fight he won reelection with comparative ease. Anderson can be expected to continue winning in the future.

Census Data 1970 pop. 514,074; deviation from current state average, —2.1%; change 1960–70, +32.3%. Metro. 100%, 27.8% central city.

1970 Share of Federal Outlays $516,711,000 (average outlay per district, California 17, 19–32)

DOD	$209,052,000	HEW	$134,513,000
AEC	$2,555,000	HUD	$3,261,000
NASA	$58,761,000	OEO	$1,759,000
DOT	$12,454,000	DOA	$5,532,000
		Other	$88,823,858

Federal Military-Industrial Commitments (See California 28 for Los Angeles County listing.)

Economic Base Aircraft and parts, and other transportation equipment; electrical machinery, equipment, and supplies, esp. communication equipment, and electronic components and accessories; nonelectrical machinery, esp. office, computing, and accounting machines; ordnance and accessories.

The Voters

Registration 172,731 total. 108,294 D (63%); 53,743 R (31%); 3,649 AIP (2%); 334 PF (—); 6,711 other (4%).

Employment profile White collar, 37%. Blue collar, 63%.

Ethnic groups Black, 9%. Spanish surname, 10%. Oriental, 4%. Total foreign stock, 23%. Mexico, 5%; Germany, Italy, UK, Canada, 2% each; Norway, Poland, Sweden, USSR, 1% each; others, 7%.

Presidential vote

1968	Humphrey (D)	72,905	(48%)
	Nixon (R)	63,742	(42%)
	Wallace (AIP)	14,093	(9%)

Representative

Glenn M. Anderson (D) Elected 1968; b. Feb. 21, 1913, Hawthorne; home, Harbor City; UCLA, B.A., 1936; Army, WWII; married, three children; Protestant.

Career Mayor of Hawthorne, 1940–43; Calif. Assembly, 1943–51; Lt. Governor Calif., 1959–67; Regent, U. of Calif., 1959–66; Trustee, Calif. State Colleges, 1961–66.

Offices 1132 LHOB, 202-225-6676. Also 255 W. 5th St., San Pedro, 213-833-3547.

Committees

Merchant Marine and Fisheries (18th); Subs. (1) Fisheries and Wildlife Conservation, (2) Oceanography, (3) Sp. Sub. on Maritime Education and Training.

Public Works (14th); Subs. (1) Flood Control and Internal Dev., (2) Public Buildings and Grounds, (3) Rivers and Harbors, (4) Roads, (5) Watershed Dev.

Group Ratings

	ADA	COPE	NREP	NFU	LCV	CFA	NAB	NSI	ACA
1970	84	100	75	92	67	86	0	38	12
1969	87	—	—	93	—	—	—	—	18

Key Votes

(1) ABM	AGN	(6) 18-Yr-Vote	FOR	(11) Clean Water $	FOR
(2) SST	FOR	(7) Farm Sub Lmt	FOR	(12) Mig Wrkrs Comp	FOR
(3) Phil Pln	FOR	(8) Coop-Church	FOR	(13) Jets to Chiang	FOR
(4) No-Knock	FOR	(9) Family Asst	FOR	(14) State OEO Veto	AGN
(5) Cmutr Tax	FOR	(10) Work Stamps	AGN	(15) Park Logging	AGN

Election Results

1970 general:	Glenn Anderson (D-Inc.)	83,739	(62%)
	Michael Donaldson (R)	47,778	(36%)
	Robert Copeland (AIP)	1,724	(1%)
	Thomas Mathews (PF)	1,292	(1%)
1970 primary:	Glenn Anderson (D-Inc.), unopposed		
1968 general:	Glenn Anderson (D)	77,250	(51%)
	Joseph Blatchford (R)	73,351	(48%)
	Ben Dobbs (PF)	1,764	(1%)

EIGHTEENTH DISTRICT Political Background

California 18 is the southernmost—and most conservative—of the Central Valley districts, consisting of all of Tulare County and most of Kern. The most widely known town in the district is Delano, where Cesar Chavez led the four-year strike against the table-grape growers. The strike succeeded. But the polarization brought on by "La Huelga" seems to have broken up a rather uneasy Okie-chicano Democratic coalition. For the most part, the whites supported their own kind against the farm workers. And they were doubtless repelled by the support Chavez's group received from the Johnson Administration, which cut down the number of strikebreakers that could be imported from Mexico. Neither did the growers and their allies feel kindly toward organized labor or liberal political figures like Robert Kennedy. The animus against Kennedy showed up in the 1968 presidential primary totals: the late Senator from New York, who possessed great strength among working-class voters, carried most of the Valley, but lost Kern and Tulare counties.

The principal beneficiary of the old Democratic coalition was Congressman Harlen Hagen, who represented the district from 1952 to 1966. Hagen was one of the few non-Southerners on the Democratic side of the Agriculture Committee and there generally favored the interests of the large growers. But in the 1966 elections the conservative backlash in the district swept him aside.

The winner was a man whose name was probably as well known in the district as Hagen's: former Olympic decathlon champion Bob Mathias. Mathias is a foresquare conservative, usually unobtrusive in the Republican ranks, who has strenuously backed the big growers in the 18th. Since his election to the House, he has been joined on the Republican side of the aisle by such former sports heroes as Jackie Kemp of New York (Buffalo Bisons quarterback) and Wilmer "Vinegar Bend" Mizell of North Carolina (pitcher for several major league teams). Mathias now seems thoroughly entrenched among the voters; and redistricting is unlikely to affect his hold on the district.

Census Data 1970 pop. 472,496; deviation from current state average, −10.0%; change 1960–70, +11.5%. Metro. 60.1%, 14.7% central city.

1970 Share of Federal Outlays $450,702,332

DOD	$57,400,000	HEW	$181,022,422
AEC	$000	HUD	$1,030,095
NASA	$14,069,329	OEO	$4,179,087
DOT	$9,422,865	DOA	$110,465,193
		Other	$73,113,341

Federal Military-Industrial Commitments

None.

Economic Base Cotton; crude petroleum and natural gas; food and kindred products, esp. produce.

The Voters

Registration 170,299 total. 97,511 D (57%); 66,125 R (39%); 3,350 AIP (2%); 98 PF (—); 3,215 other (2%).

Employment profile White collar, 36%. Blue collar, 64%.

Ethnic groups Black, 4%. Spanish surname, 13%. Oriental, 2%. Total foreign stock, 17%. Mexico, 7%; Germany, Italy, UK, USSR, Canada, 1% each; others, 4%.

Presidential vote

1968	Humphrey (D)	66,932	(42%)
	Nixon (R)	77,615	(49%)
	Wallace (AIP)	14,959	(9%)

Representative

Robert B. Mathias (R) Elected 1966; b. Nov. 17, 1930, Tulare; home, Visalia; Stanford U., B.S., 1953; USMC, 1954–56; Capt. USMCR (Ret.); married, three children; First Methodist Church.

Career Olympic Decathlon winner, 1948 and 1952; Pres. Eisenhower's Rep. to 1956 Olympics; covered 1964 Olympics for *Sports Illustrated*; Bd. of Dir., Mid-State Savings and Loan; Sports Advisory Com., Sears Roebuck & Co.

Offices 1024 LHOB, 202-225-3341. Also Rm. 302, 800 Truxtun Ave., Bakersfield 93301, 805-323-8323.

Committees

Agriculture (6th); Subs. (1) Department Operations, (2) Domestic Marketing and Consumer Relations, (3) Family Farms and Rural Dev., (4) Oilseeds and Rice, (5) Tobacco.

Group Ratings

	ADA	COPE	NREP	NFU	LCV	CFA	NAB	NSI	ACA
1970	20	42	9	77	0	56	64	100	61
1969	0	—	—	50	—	—	—	—	47
1968	0	9	—	43	—	—	83	—	65

Key Votes

(1) ABM	ABS	(6) 18-Yr-Vote	FOR	(11) Clean Water $	AGN
(2) SST	FOR	(7) Farm Sub Lmt	AGN	(12) Mig Wrkrs Comp	FOR
(3) Phil Pln	FOR	(8) Coop-Church	AGN	(13) Jets to Chiang	ABS
(4) No-Knock	FOR	(9) Family Asst	AGN	(14) State OEO Veto	FOR
(5) Cmutr Tax	ABS	(10) Work Stamps	ABS	(15) Park Logging	FOR

Election Results

1970 general:	Bob Mathias (R-Inc.)	86,071	(63%)
	Milton Miller (D)	48,415	(36%)
	Nora Hensley (AIP)	1,709	(1%)
1970 primary:	Bob Mathias (R-Inc.), unopposed		
1968 general:	Bob Mathias (R)	100,115	(65%)
	Harlan Hagen (D)	51,373	(33%)
	Edwards Williams (AIP)	2,116	(1%)

NINETEENTH DISTRICT Political Background

California 19 is a predominantly blue-collar district in Los Angeles County, situated south and east of downtown Los Angeles. This area is a relatively old section of the nation's largest urban sprawl. Most of its residents live in slightly worn neighborhoods between the freeways and factories and strip commercial developments that characterize the district. There are virtually no blacks here (897 out of 487,000 in 1970 to be exact). But the district does have a large Mexican-American community, which begins in the slums of East Los Angeles and grows increasingly more comfortable as the neighborhoods spread southward. The 19th also contains the heavily Republican town of Whittier, boyhood home of Richard Nixon.

The California species of Republican conservatism made some of its greatest initial gains in areas like the 19th. Although 60% of its voters are registered Democrats, 61% voted for Ronald Reagan in 1966, and 48%, a plurality, went for Richard Nixon in 1968. But in 1970, the district seemed to bounce back, as the Democratic candidate for governor, Jess Unruh, stressed the wealth and privilege of Reagan's biggest backers. Unruh didn't carry the 19th, but he came close. His campaign suggests that concerns over rioting blacks and students are really less important to the voters of the 19th than unemployment and other pocketbook issues.

Despite the Republican successes here, the Democrats have managed to hold on to the House seat without difficulty. This is due to the popularity of Congressman Chet Holifield, in Congress since 1942 and dean of the California delegation. Some years back, when Holifield was chairman of the liberal Democratic Study Group, he was among the more intransigent of House liberals. But seniority and age have mellowed him, and today he is more at home with his fellow committee chairmen than with young insurgents.

For some time, Holifield was chairman of the Joint Committee on Atomic Energy. And it was his position on this body that alienated him most severely from the liberals. The Joint Committee legislates for the Atomic Energy Commission. The congressional unit and the bureaucracy have been able to work together with considerable expertise, much more than is common in other such legislative and bureaucratic pairings. And because Holifield, like most members of the Joint Committee, is a believer in the workings of our quasi-military and military agencies, the differences between him and younger liberals have grown in the years since 1965.

At the beginning of the 92nd Congress, Holifield became chairman of the Government Operations Committee, which, under the octogenarian chairmanship of William Dawson, had reached a rather somnolent state. Holifield will no doubt try to invigorate matters. Back home, Holifield is unlikely to face much trouble from either the voters, who gave him a 70–30 margin in 1970, or the redistricters.

Census Data 1970 pop. 487,644; deviation from current state average, –7.1%; change 1960–70, +19.3%. Metro. 100%, 0.0% central city.

1970 Share of Federal Outlays $516,711,000 (average outlay per district, California 17, 19–32)

DOD	$209,052,000	HEW	$134,513,000
AEC	$2,555,000	HUD	$3,261,000
NASA	$58,761,000	OEO	$1,759,000
DOT	$12,454,000	DOA	$5,532,000
		Other	$88,824,000

Federal Military-Industrial Commitments (See California 28 for Los Angeles County listing.)

Economic Base Transportation equipment, esp. aircraft and parts and motor vehicles and motor vehicle equipment; electrical machinery, equipment, and supplies, esp. communication equipment and electronic components and accessories; nonelectrical machinery, esp. office, computing, and accounting machines; ordnance and accessories.

The Voters

Registration 174,788 total. 105,624 D (60%); 61,777 R (35%); 2,717 AIP (2%); 200 PF (—); 4,470 other (3%).

Employment profile White collar, 44%. Blue collar, 56%.

Ethnic groups Black, less than 0.5%. Spanish surname, 18%. Oriental, 1%. Total foreign stock, 25%. Mexico, 9%; Germany, Italy, UK, Canada, 2% each; Poland, Sweden, USSR, 1% each; others, 5%.

Presidential vote

1968	Humphrey (D)	69,873	(45%)
	Nixon (R)	75,306	(48%)
	Wallace (AIP)	10,828	(7%)

Representative

Chet Holifield (D) Elected 1942; b. Dec. 3, 1903, Mayfield, Ky.; home, Montebello; married, four children; Disciples of Christ.

Career Mfg., selling men's apparel 38 yrs.; Mbr. Hoover Commission; V. Chm., President's Commission on Gov. Procurement; Rep. at Intl. Atomic Energy Meeting, Vienna, 1967; Cong. Advisor, U.S. Delegations, Int. Conf. on Peaceful Uses of Atomic Energy, Geneva, 1955; Conf. on Discontinuance of Nuclear Weapons Tests, Geneva, 1959; Genl. Conf. of Intl. Atomic Energy Agcy., 1959–63–65–68–69; Disarmament Conf., Geneva, 1967–70.

Offices 2469 RHOB, 202-225-3976. Also 9125 E. Whittier Blvd., Pico-Rivera 90660, 213-723-6561, 213-692-2242.

Committees

Government Operations (Chm.); Chm., Sub. on Legislation and Military Operation.

Standards of Official Conduct (6th).

Jt. Com. on Atomic Energy (2nd); Subs. (1) Chm., Agreements for Cooperation, (2) Legislation, (3) Military Applications, (4) Raw Materials, (5) Research, Dev., and Radiation.

Group Ratings

	ADA	COPE	NREP	NFU	LCV	CFA	NAB	NSI	ACA
1970	60	100	73	100	57	94	0	50	0
1969	53	—	—	—	—	—	—	—	15
1968	83	100	—	100	—	—	0	—	0

Key Votes

(1) ABM	FOR	(6) 18-Yr-Vote	FOR	(11) Clean Water $	AGN
(2) SST	FOR	(7) Farm Sub Lmt	FOR	(12) Mig Wrkrs Comp	FOR
(3) Phil Pln	AGN	(8) Coop-Church	ABS	(13) Jets to Chiang	AGN
(4) No-Knock	AGN	(9) Family Asst	FOR	(14) State OEO Veto	AGN
(5) Cmutr Tax	AGN	(10) Work Stamps	AGN	(15) Park Logging	FOR

Election Results

1970 general:	Chet Holifield (D-Inc.)	98,578	(70%)
	Bill Jones (R)	41,462	(30%)
1970 primary:	Chet Holifield (D-Inc.), unopposed		
1968 general:	Chet Holifield (D)	99,069	(63%)
	Bill Jones (R)	53,842	(34%)
	Wayne Cook (AIP)	4,101	(3%)

TWENTIETH DISTRICT Political Background

California 20, situated between and beneath the massive mountains just north of Los Angeles, is as profoundly conservative a district as any in the country. Here the Spanish-style bungalows of Glendale and Pasadena shelter conservative bankers, businessmen, and widows living off comfortable estates. The 20th is one of California's oldest districts, with a voter's median age of 46.8. And that median is significant in a state where generational divisions are so much a part of politics. The 20th dips down into the city of Los Angeles to include a few shabby neighborhoods, and Pasadena does have a large black community. But for the most part, the district is preeminently unyoung, unpoor, and unblack.

The 20th, of course, is one of California's most Republican areas; it has not supported a Democratic candidate in a major statewide race in years. In presidential politics, Goldwater took 60% of the votes in 1964 and Richard Nixon won 62% four years later. The congressman from the 20th since 1956 has been former FBI agent and conservative Republican, H. Allen Smith. Smith has climbed the seniority ladder rather quickly and is currently the ranking Republican on the House Rules Committee. There he can be depended upon to oppose any and all liberal legislation. Occasionally he and his fellow Republicans on Rules can still manage to join forces with enough conservative Democrats to block consideration of such legislation on the floor. Rules also sets the guidelines for amendments and debate—which can often be decisive in the lawmaking process. Smith shows no signs of retiring and will be reelected until he does.

Census Data 1970 pop. 429,953; deviation from current state average, −18.1%; change 1960–70, +4.9%. Metro. 100%, 17.4% central city.

1970 Share of Federal Outlays $516,711,000 (average outlay per district, California 17, 19–32)

DOD	$209,052,000	HEW	$134,513,000
AEC	$2,555,000	HUD	$3,261,000
NASA	$58,761,000	OEO	$1,759,000
DOT	$12,454,000	DOA	$5,532,000
		Other	$88,824,000

Federal Military-Industrial Commitments (See California 28 for Los Angeles County listing.)

Economic Base Aircraft and parts, and other transportation equipment; electrical machinery, equipment, and supplies, esp. communication equipment and electronic components and accessories; nonelectrical machinery, esp. office, computing, and accounting machines; ordnance and accessories. Also, tourism (Los Angeles, Pasadena).

The Voters

Registration 218,500 total. 84,942 D (39%); 123,199 R (56%); 1,592 AIP (1%); 1,021 PF (1%); 7,746 other (4%).

Employment profile White collar, 59%. Blue collar, 41%.

Ethnic groups Black, 7%. Spanish surname, 4%. Oriental, 1%. Total foreign stock, 29%. UK, Canada, 4%; Germany, 3%; Italy, USSR, Mexico, 2% each; Austria, Hungary, Ireland, Norway, Poland, Sweden, all 1% each; others, 6%.

Presidential vote

1968	Humphrey (D)	63,447	(33%)
	Nixon (R)	119,172	(62%)
	Wallace (AIP)	8,570	(5%)

Representative

H. Allen Smith (R) Elected 1956; b. Oct. 8, 1909, Dixon, Ill.; home, Glendale; UCLA, 1927–30; U. of Southern Calif., B.A., 1930, LL.B., 1933; married, two children; Methodist.

Career Practicing atty., 1934–35; Sp. agent FBI, 1935–42; Mgr. plant protection Lockheed Aircraft Corp., 1942–44; Calif. Assembly, 1948–56.

Offices 2433 RHOB, 202-225-4176. Also Box 1, P.O. Bldg., Glendale 91209, 213-241-2182.

Committees

Rules (Ranking Mbr.)

Group Ratings

	ADA	COPE	NREP	NFU	LCV	CFA	NAB	NSI	ACA
1970	12	9	17	23	33	50	92	90	89
1969	0	—	—	20	—	—	—	—	93
1968	0	0	—	13	—	—	100	—	87

Key Votes

(1) ABM	FOR	(6) 18-Yr-Vote	AGN	(11) Clean Water $	AGN
(2) SST	AGN	(7) Farm Sub Lmt	FOR	(12) Mig Wrkrs Comp	AGN
(3) Phil Pln	ABS	(8) Coop-Church	AGN	(13) Jets to Chiang	AGN
(4) No-Knock	FOR	(9) Family Asst	AGN	(14) State OEO Veto	FOR
(5) Cmutr Tax	AGN	(10) Work Stamps	FOR	(15) Park Logging	AGN

Election Results

1970 general:	H. Allen Smith (R-Inc.)	116,437	(69%)
	Michael Stolzberg (D)	50,033	(30%)
	Earl Harper (AIP)	2,100	(1%)
1970 primary:	H. Allen Smith (R-Inc.), unopposed		
1968 general:	H. Allen Smith (R)	136,238	(69%)
	Don White (D)	57,064	(29%)
	Robert Clarke (PF)	3,095	(2%)

TWENTY-FIRST DISTRICT Political Background

California 21 is Watts and the adjacent black ghetto, California's only black-majority district. The 21st begins just south of downtown Los Angeles and extends south along the Harbor Freeway to the black-majority suburb of Compton. The district's eastern boundary is Alameda Street, across which are many of Los Angeles's large factories and the all-white suburbs of Huntington Park, Lynwood, and South Gate. Most of the district itself is largely residential. Even today, however, there is still some evidence of the 1965 riot, which changed so many things, everything except the conditions that surround the people who live here.

The 1970 census showed that the district is 76% black; its Democratic registration runs even higher, usually over 90%. The House seat, a creation of the 1961 legislation, has had only one incumbent, Augustus F. Hawkins, a man who had represented the area in the California Assembly for 28 years. Hawkins, who was 67 in 1970, is not among the more militant members of the House's Black Caucus, but he is capable of sounding off when moved to do so. Like most black representatives, he has been a consistent opponent of the Vietnam war. It was Hawkins, along with Congressman William Anderson of Tennessee, who discovered the infamous Con San tiger cages during a Vietnam inspection tour.

Hawkins now enjoys the 9th ranking seat on the Education and Labor Committee, and, having spent nearly 30 years in Sacramento and Washington, the black Congressman's legislative experience is far greater than that of most House members.

Hawkins has had nuisance primary opposition in the past, but will be reelected for as long as he chooses to run. If he should retire, his successor is likely to be one of the black state legislators from the Watts area, probably state Sen. Mervin Dymally.

Census Data 1970 pop. 378,852; deviation from current state average, —27.8%; change 1960–70, —5.5%. Metro. 100%, 73.9% central city.

1970 Share of Federal Outlays $516,711,000 (average outlay per district, California 17, 19–32)

DOD	$209,052,000	HEW	$134,513,000
AEC	$2,555,000	HUD	$3,261,000
NASA	$58,761,000	OEO	$1,759,000
DOT	$12,454,000	DOA	$5,532,000
		Other	$88,824,000

Federal Military-Industrial Commitments (See California 28 for Los Angeles County listing.)

Economic Base Aircraft and parts, and other transportation equipment; electrical machinery, equipment, and supplies, esp. communication equipment, and electronic components and accessories; nonelectrical machinery, esp. office, computing, and accounting machines; ordnance and accessories. Also, higher education (U. Southern Calif.).

The Voters

Registration 12,071 total. 108,410 D (90%); 9,796 R (8%); 227 AIP (—); 351 PF (—); 2,287 other (2%).

Employment profile White collar, 22%. Blue collar, 78%.

Ethnic groups Black, 76%. Spanish surname, 13%. Oriental, 2%. Total foreign stock, 16%. Mexico, 8%; Germany, Italy, UK, Canada, 1% each; others, 4%.

Presidential vote

1968	Humphrey (D)	95,865	(92%)
	Nixon (R)	6,819	(7%)
	Wallace (AIP)	1,103	(1%)

Representative

Augustus F. Hawkins (D) Elected 1962; b. Aug. 31, 1907, Shreveport, La.; home, Los Angeles; UCLA, B.A., 1931; widowed; Methodist.

Career Instr. of Gov., U. of Southern Calif.; Real estate business, 1945– ; Calif. Assembly, 1935–62; founding member, Southeast Los Angeles Improvement Action Council.

Offices 1124 LHOB, 202-225-2201. Also 8563 S. Broadway, Suite 206, Los Angeles 90003, 213-750-0260.

Committees

Education and Labor (9th); Subs. (1) Gen. Sub. on Education, (2) Gen. Sub. on Labor, (3) Sel. Sub. on Labor.

House Administration (8th); Subs. (1) Chm., Sp. Sub. on Contracts, (2) Sp. Sub. on Police, (3) Accounts.

Group Ratings

	ADA	COPE	NREP	NFU	LCV	CFA	NAB	NSI	ACA
1970	84	100	93	73	80	94	0	0	0
1969	100	—	—	85	—	—	—	—	7
1968	83	100	—	89	—	—	0	—	0

Key Votes

(1) ABM	AGN	(6) 18-Yr-Vote	FOR	(11) Clean Water $	FOR
(2) SST	FOR	(7) Farm Sub Lmt	FOR	(12) Mig Wrkrs Comp	FOR
(3) Phil Pln	FOR	(8) Coop-Church	FOR	(13) Jets to Chiang	AGN
(4) No-Knock	AGN	(9) Family Asst	FOR	(14) State OEO Veto	AGN
(5) Cmutr Tax	FOR	(10) Work Stamps	AGN	(15) Park Logging	AGN

Election Results

1970 general:	Augustus Hawkins (D-Inc.)	75,127	(95%)
	Southey Johnson (R)	4,349	(5%)
1970 primary:	Augustus Hawkins (D-Inc.)	46,124	(89%)
	Louis Brooks (D)	5,434	(11%)
1968 general:	Augustus Hawkins (D)	89,536	(92%)
	Rayfield Lundy (R)	8,244	(8%)

TWENTY-SECOND DISTRICT Political Background

California 22 is the heart of the San Fernando Valley, the suburban-like area north of Los Angeles, across the mountains. The city annexed the area many years ago. The current shape of the district—neat and compact—was designed to protect the seat of Democratic Congressman James Corman, who was first elected in an upset when the district included the entire Valley. After the 1960 census, the 22nd's boundaries were redrawn to take in only the western half of the Valley, which includes the Republican areas of Woodland Hills, Reseda, and Northridge. These towns, as well as the entire San Fernando region, are heavily dependent on the aircraft and defense industries and are all white. But in the early '60's, Corman, because of his interest in civil rights legislation, insisted upon switching from a defense-oriented committee to Judiciary. This move and the conservative trends at work generally in California politics nearly cost Corman his seat; he won only 50.5% in 1964 and 53% in 1966.

When the Democratic legislature got the chance to redraw the district lines in 1968, it shifted the 22nd to the eastern half of the Valley, bringing in Democratic areas like North Hollywood (which has a large Jewish population) and Van Nuys. The district presently extends as far north as the Sylmar and Olive View areas, where the worst of the 1971 earthquake damage occurred. Thus fortified, Corman won with 57% and 59% in 1968 and 1970, running ahead of statewide Democratic candidates in the district. He has switched committees again, too, winning a seat on Ways and Means. The fact that he received the honor probably indicates that the House elders think that Corman now has a safe seat, and they are probably right.

Census Data 1970 pop. 501,866; deviation from current state average, —4.4%; change 1960–70, +17.2%. Metro. 100%, 97.7% central city.

1970 Share of Federal Outlays $516,711,000 (average outlay per district, California 17, 19–32)

DOD	$209,052,000	HEW	$134,513,000
AEC	$2,555,000	HUD	$3,261,000
NASA	$58,761,000	OEO	$1,759,000
DOT	$12,454,000	DOA	$5,532,000
		Other	$88,824,000

Federal Military-Industrial Commitments (See California 28 for Los Angeles County listing.)

Economic Base Aircraft and parts, and other transportation equipment; electrical machinery, equipment, and supplies, esp. communication equipment and electronic components and accessories; nonelectrical machinery, esp. office, computing, and accounting machines; ordnance and accessories.

The Voters

Registration 204,011 total. 117,225 D (58%); 76,506 R (38%); 1,853 AIP (1%); 1,024 PF (1%); 7,403 other (4%).

Employment profile White collar, 48%. Blue collar, 52%.

Ethnic groups Black, 3%. Spanish surname, 8%. Oriental, 1%. Total foreign stock, 24%. Mexico, 4%; UK, Canada, 3% each; Germany, Italy, USSR, 2% each; Austria, Poland, Sweden, 1% each; others, 4%.

Presidential vote

1968	Humphrey (D)	84,190	(47%)
	Nixon (R)	83,993	(47%)
	Wallace (AIP)	10,214	(6%)

Representative

James C. Corman (D) Elected 1960; b. Oct. 20, 1920, Galena, Kans.; home, Van Nuys; UCLA, B.A., 1942; U. of Southern Calif., LL.B., 1948; USMC, WWII and Korean War; married, two children; Methodist.

Career Practicing atty., 1949– ; Los Angeles City Council, 1957–61; Natl. Advisory Commission on Civil Disorders, 1967.

Offices 203 CHOB, 202-225-5811. Also 14422 Victory Blvd., Van Nuys 91401; 213-787-1766 and 9038 Woodley Ave., Sepulveda 91343, 213-893-1501, 213-893-3002.

Committees

Way and Means (11th).

Sel. Com. on Small Business (7th); Subs. (1) Chm., Government Procurement, (2) Minority Small Business Enterprise, (3) Small Business, Problems in Smaller Towns and Urban Areas.

Group Ratings

	ADA	COPE	NREP	NFU	LCV	CFA	NAB	NSI	ACA
1970	88	92	83	100	50	92	0	22	7
1969	87	—	—	86	—	—	—	—	0
1968	75	92	—	91	—	—	0	—	0

Key Votes

(1) ABM	AGN	(6) 18-Yr-Vote	FOR	(11) Clean Water $	FOR
(2) SST	FOR	(7) Farm Sub Lmt	ABS	(12) Mig Wrkrs Comp	FOR
(3) Phil Pln	FOR	(8) Coop-Church	FOR	(13) Jets to Chiang	ABS
(4) No-Knock	AGN	(9) Family Asst	FOR	(14) State OEO Veto	AGN
(5) Cmutr Tax	FOR	(10) Work Stamps	AGN	(15) Park Logging	FOR

Election Results

1970 general:	James Corman (D-Inc.)	95,256	(59%)
	Tom Hayden (R)	63,297	(39%)
	Callis Johnson (AIP)	1,880	(2%)
1970 primary:	James Corman (D-Inc.)	55,662	(88%)
	George Tabet (D)	7,618	(12%)
1968 general:	James Corman (D)	103,695	(57%)
	Joe Holt (R)	75,457	(41%)
	Hugh Manes (PF)	3,116	(2%)

TWENTY-THIRD DISTRICT Political Background

California 23 is a clear example of why party registration figures—so often used by political analysts—are often completely meaningless. On paper, the 23rd is a solidly Democratic district: 59% of its votes are registered Democrats and only 35% are Republicans. The near 2:1 edge in registration should produce automatic Democratic majorities. But it does not. The only major Democratic candidate to carry the district since Lyndon Johnson in 1964 was Sen. John Tunney in 1970. But Tunney got only 53% of the vote, and that was far less than the 62% Gov. Ronald Reagan won here in 1966.

Simple geography, not the registration figures, explains the political behavior of the 23rd. The district lies just east of the Watts ghetto, separated from the ghetto and from the 21st district by Alameda Street—the boundary between black and white neighborhoods since the 1920's. The 23rd is for the most part white working-class, made up of suburbs like South Gate, Lynwood, Huntington Park, and Bell Gardens. These neighborhoods were built up hastily in the years around World War II to house the workers in aircraft and other defense factories located in the industrial zone at the eastern end of the current district. Since then, the 23rd has not grown much, and the people, many of them from the South, have been paying off mortgages on small frame and stucco houses. As they make payments, they worry about whether the blacks will begin to move across Alameda and render their only investments, their homes, worthless.

Sometime in the early '60's the whites here stopped thinking of themselves as workers and started thinking of themselves as taxpayers. They began to resent the welfare mothers whom they felt they had been supporting. And they were horrified by the goings-on at the state universities which they also felt they were supporting and which most of their children would never attend. But college or no college, the parents of the 23rd hardly wanted their children (or grandchildren) to turn into the kind of impudent freaks seen on TV: the white blue-collar worker and his wife figured they had played by the rules and wanted to be respected for what they have accomplished, however little that might seem to some people. And if they could not receive that respect from the college-educated or from the long-hairs of one variety or another, they would get it from their kind of politician.

Ronald Reagan, George Murphy, and Max Rafferty all knew how disgruntled and threatened the typical voter of the 23rd felt, and that is why all of them did so well among the registered Democrats of the district. But as early as 1963, when Reagan was still the host of "Death Valley Days," a conservative Republican in this district won a surprise victory in a special congressional election. That election anticipated what was later to become an important part of the Reaganite strategy: win crossover Democratic votes not from the liberal and minority groups (the people Eastern Republicans like Rockefeller cultivate), but from discontented blue-collar families.

The special election was occasioned by the death of Congressman Clyde Doyle, a rather conservative Democrat who had served briefly as chairman of the House Un-American Activities Committee. It was held in June 1963, just after the bombings and police dog incidents in Birmingham. President Kennedy was then preparing to submit a civil rights bill to Congress and Martin Luther King, Jr., was beginning to plan the great march on Washington. In the 23rd, several Democrats were making a bid, the only serious Republican candidate being Del Clawson, the conservative mayor of Compton. (Compton was then a sharply divided city racially, but today, somewhat ironically, it has a large black majority—the only significant concentration of black votes in the district.) After an energetic campaign and a respectable turnout, Clawson took 53% of the votes. Then under a unique California statute he became a congressman without having won a general election.

Ever since, Clawson has won with great ease (over 60% of the votes in 1968 and 1970). His brand of conservatism, now called Reaganism—opposition to civil rights legislation, hawkish support of the Vietnam war, and stern disapproval of student rioters—has suited his working-class constituency. So what the Democratic legislature of 1961 intended to be a solid Democratic district has turned out to be a solid Republican one. And the voters of the 23rd, who still think of themselves as Democrats and who would probably brook no criticism of Franklin D. Roosevelt, come out for Republicans election after election.

Census Data 1970 pop. 440,094; deviation from current state average, –16.2%; change 1960–70, +12.7%. Metro. 100%, 0.0% central city.

1970 Share of Federal Outlays $516,711,000 (average outlay per district, California 17, 19–32)

DOD	$209,052,000	HEW	$134,513,000
AEC	$2,555,000	HUD	$3,261,000
NASA	$58,761,000	OEO	$1,759,000
DOT	$12,454,000	DOA	$5,532,000
		Other	$88,824,000

Federal Military-Industrial Commitments (See California 28 for Los Angeles County listing.)

Economic Base Aircraft and parts, and other transportation equipment; electrical machinery, equipment, and supplies, esp. communication equipment and electronic components and accessories; nonelectrical machinery, esp. office, computing, and accounting machines; ordnance and accessories.

The Voters

Registration 165,182 total. 97,478 D (59%); 57,797 R (35%); 5,027 AIP (3%); 645 PF (—); 4,675 other (3%).

Employment profile White collar, 40%. Blue collar, 60%.

Ethnic groups Black, 4%. Spanish surname, 7%. Oriental, 1%. Total foreign stock, 20%. Mexico, 4%; Germany, Italy, UK, 2% each; Poland, Sweden, USSR, 1% each; others, 4%.

Presidential vote

1968	Humphrey (D)	61,086	(41%)
	Nixon (R)	70,781	(48%)
	Wallace (AIP)	15,979	(11%)

Representative

Delwin (Del) Morgan Clawson (R) Elected 1962; b. Jan. 11, 1914, Thatcher, Ariz.; home, Downey; Ariz. Gila Col.; married, two children; Church of Jesus Christ of Latter Day Saints.

Career Salesman and bookkeeper, 1934–41; U.S. Employment Svc., Fed. Pub. Housing Auth., 1941–47; Mgr., Mutual Housing Assn. of Compton, 1947–63; Compton City Council, 1953–57; Mayor of Compton, 1957–63; Dir., Los Angeles County Sanitation Dists. 1, 2, 8, 1957–63.

Offices 227 CHOB, 202-225-3576. Also 10241 S. Paramount Blvd., Downey 90240, 213-923-9206.

Committees

Appropriations (19th); Subs. (1) HUD, Space, and Science. (2) Interior and Related Agencies.

Group Ratings

	ADA	COPE	NREP	NFU	LCV	CFA	NAB	NSI	ACA
1970	8	34	9	91	14	29	90	100	89
1969	13	—	—	21	—	—	—	—	94
1968	0	15	—	7	—	—	100	—	90

Key Votes

(1) ABM	ABS	(6) 18-Yr-Vote	AGN	(11) Clean Water $	AGN
(2) SST	FOR	(7) Farm Sub Lmt	FOR	(12) Mig Wrkrs Comp	AGN
(3) Phil Pln	AGN	(8) Coop-Church	AGN	(13) Jets to Chiang	ABS
(4) No-Knock	FOR	(9) Family Asst	AGN	(14) State OEO Veto	FOR
(5) Cmutr Tax	AGN	(10) Work Stamps	FOR	(15) Park Logging	AGN

Election Results

1970 general:	Del Clawson (R-Inc.)	77,346	(63%)
	G. L. Chapman (D)	44,767	(37%)
1970 primary:	Del Clawson (R-Inc.), unopposed		
1968 general:	Del Clawson (R)	97,232	(65%)
	Jim Sperrazo (D)	52,202	(35%)

THE TWENTY-FOURTH DISTRICT Political Background

California 24 is one of those Los Angeles area districts whose peculiar shape is the result of political history. Originally, the district was based in the Eagle Rock section of Los Angeles, a dependably conservative part of the city. Through successive redistrictings, it has spread eastward to land once given over entirely to orange groves. Today, it is made up of three distinct areas, connected mainly by the uninhabited San Gabriel mountains to the north. In the east are the marginal-to-Republican towns of Pomona and Claremont; to the west is a string of suburbs in the foothills of the mountains—Arcadia, Monrovia, and Azusa—like most foothill suburbs in California, heavily Republican. The Los Angeles portion of the district is connected to the rest by the small suburbs of South Pasadena and San Marino; the latter is the residence of some of Los Angeles' wealthiest, most powerful, and most conservative citizens.

The 1961 Democratic legislature happily conceded these heavily Republican areas to Congressman Glenard P. Lipscomb, who first won in a 1953 special election. In fact, the legislature wanted to package for Lipscomb as much Republican terrain as it could, which it did and which accounts for the peculiar shape of the present district. The Republicans would thus be corralled in the 24th, keeping them out of the adjoining 25th district. Here it was hoped that a young assemblyman could oust John Birch Republican—and then freshman Congressman—John Rousselot.

Initially, the strategy worked. Rousselot was defeated in 1962 and seemed out of electoral politics. But redistricters often fail to achieve their ends, especially if their decisions have to stand up over a ten-year period. The Republicans recaptured the 25th in 1966, and in 1970 Congressman Lipscomb died unexpectedly. His successor in the 24th was—who else?—the same John Rousselot, the politician supposedly gotten out of the way eight years before.

Rousselot, whose fierce drive and energy may derive à la Teddy Roosevelt from having been crippled since childhood, had a difficult time of it in the Republican primary. He faced two strong opponents and won by a scant 127 votes out of 187,000 cast. The choice in the general election was between Birch-organizer Rousselot and Mrs. Myrlie Evers, wife of the slain civil rights leader who had settled in Pomona. Mrs. Evers got the publicity, but Rousselot had the votes—65% of them. The legislature probably won't tamper too much with the district's boundaries, and, accordingly, Rousselot can expect to stay in the House for some time.

Census Data 1970 pop. 522,856; deviation from current state average, 0.4%; change 1960–70, 29.7%. Metro. 100%, 11.8% central city.

1970 Share of Federal Outlays $516,711,000 (average outlay per district, California 17, 19–32)

DOD	$209,052,000	HEW	$134,513,000
AEC	$2,555,000	HUD	$3,261,000
NASA	$58,761,000	OEO	$1,759,000
DOT	$12,454,000	DOA	$5,532,000
		Other	$88,824,000

Federal Military-Industrial Commitments (See California 28 for Los Angeles County listing.)

Economic Base Aircraft and parts and other transportation equipment; electrical machinery, equipment, and supplies, esp. communication equipment and electronic components and accessories; nonelectrical machinery, esp. office, computing, and accounting machines; ordnance and accessories.

The Voters

Registration 239,708 total. 95,710 D (40%); 133,594 R (56%); 2,076 AIP (1%); 668 PF (—); 7,660 other (3%).

Employment profile White collar, 59%. Blue collar, 41%.
Ethnic groups Black, 3%. Spanish surname, 5%. Oriental, less than 0.5%. Total foreign stock, 23%. Canada, 4%; Germany, UK, 3% each; Italy, Mexico, 2% each; Austria, Ireland, Norway, Poland, Sweden, USSR, 1% each; others, 4%.

Presidential vote

1968	Humphrey (D)	64,417	(31%)
	Nixon (R)	134,207	(64%)
	Wallace (AIP)	11,812	(6%)

Representative

John Harbin Rousselot (R) Elected July 1, 1970; b. Nov. 1, 1927, Los Angeles; home, San Gabriel; Principia Col., B.A., 1949; married, three children; First Church of Christ.

Career Pres. and owner, John H. Rousselot & Assoc., public relations consultants, 1954–58; Dir. Pub. Info., Fed. Housing Admin., 1958–60; Rep. Calif. 25th Congressional Dist., 1961–63; Management consultant, 1967–70.

Offices 1706 LHOB, 202-225-4206. Also 735 West Duarte Road, Arcadia 91006, 213-447-8125.

Committees

Banking and Currency (11th); Subs. (1) Bank Supervision and Insurance, (2) International Trade, (3) Small Business.

Post Office and Civil Service (8th); Subs. (1) Census and Statistics, (2) Manpower and Civil Service.

Group Ratings, Key Votes: Newly elected.

Election Results

1970 general:	John Rousselot (R)	124,071	(65%)
	Myrlie Evers (D)	61,777	(32%)
	Brian Sconlon (AIP)	3,018	(2%)
	Harold Kaplan (PF)	1,858	(1%)
1970 primary:	John Rousselot (R)	30,831	(34%)
	Bill McColl (R)	30,704	(34%)
	Patrick Hillings (R)	18,205	(21%)
	Jack Alex (R)	5,147	(6%)
	Ed Essertier (R)	823	(1%)
	James Booth (R)	787	(1%)
	Hugh Jenings (R)	588	(1%)

TWENTY-FIFTH DISTRICT Political Background

California 25 is the descendant, more or less, of a district once (1946–50) represented by a young Navy veteran named Richard Nixon. Its precise boundaries have changed several times (see California 24), but it remains essentially a valley district, covering a collection of suburbs about 20 miles east of downtown Los Angeles. In California, there is always a premium on high ground. The rich, Republican people, therefore, can be expected to live on hillsides and the not-so-rich, more often Democratic people, in the valleys. At one time people paid the premium for the view; nowadays, they pay to escape smog. The suburbs of the 25th include Democratic El Monte and Baldwin Park and Republican West Covina and Azusa. The 25th also contains a portion of Whittier, Nixon's hometown, to the west.

In 1961, the district lines were designed to enable Democratic Assemblyman Ronald Cameron to beat Birch Society Congressman Rousselot. Despite Rousselot's vigorous campaigning, he lost in 1962 by a narrow margin. Cameron won again two years later by a small margin. But in 1966 the Reagan tide proved too much for him, and the Republicans, in the person of Charles Wiggins, mayor of El Monte, won the seat. Since then the legislature has redrawn the boundaries to include Fullerton and

La Habra in conservative Orange County. Wiggins won by solid margins in 1968 and 1970 and seems destined for a long incumbency.

Census Data 1970 pop. 648,467; deviation from current state average, +23.5%; change 1960–70, 49.8%. Metro. 100%, 1.2% central city.

1970 Share of Federal Outlays $516,711,000 (average outlay per district, California 17, 19–32)

DOD	$209,052,000	HEW	$134,513,000
AEC	$2,555,000	HUD	$3,261,000
NASA	$58,761,000	OEO	$1,759,000
DOT	$12,454,000	DOA	$5,532,000
		Other	$88,824,000

Federal Military-Industrial Commitments (See California 28 for Los Angeles County listing.)

Economic Base Aircraft and parts, and other transportation equipment; electrical machinery, equipment, and supplies, esp. communication equipment and electronic components and accessories; nonelectrical machinery, esp. office, computing, and accounting machines; ordnance and accessories.

The Voters

Registration 235,987 total. 117,215 D (50%); 107,142 (45%); 3,178 AIP (1%); 310 PF (—); 8,142 other (4%).

Employment profile White collar, 41%. Blue collar, 59%.

Ethnic groups Black, 1%. Spanish surname, 11%. Oriental, 1%. Total foreign stock, 20%. Mexico, 6%; Canada, 3%; Germany, Italy, UK, 2% each; Poland, Sweden, USSR, 1% each; others, 3%.

Presidential vote

1968	Humphrey (D)	77,335	(37%)
	Nixon (R)	118,331	(56%)
	Wallace (AIP)	15,271	(7%)

Representative

Charles E. Wiggins (R) Elected 1966; b. Dec. 3, 1927, El Monte; home, El Monte; U. of So. Calif., B.A., 1953, LL.B., 1956; Army, WWII and Korean War; married, two children; Methodist.

Career Practicing atty., 1957–66; Chm., El Monte Planning Commission, 1954–60; Councilman, Mayor, El Monte, 1960–66; Party Whip of Calif. Repub. Delegation; Mbr., Repub. Task Force on Labor Law Reform.

Offices 229 CHOB, 202-225-4111. Also Suite 202, 11001 Valley Mall, El Monte 91731, 213-442-5726, and Suite 628 Brashears Center, 1400 N. Harbor Blvd., Fullerton 92632, 714-879-2542.

Committees

Judiciary (9th); Sub. No. 4.

Sel. Com. on Crime (Ranking Mbr.).

Group Ratings

	ADA	COPE	NREP	NFU	LCV	CFA	NAB	NSI	ACA
1970	16	0	8	27	0	35	80	90	71
1969	0	—	—	28	—	—	—	—	75
1968	8	8	—	0	—	—	100	—	87

Key Votes

(1) ABM	FOR	(6) 18-Yr-Vote	AGN	(11) Clean Water $	AGN
(2) SST	FOR	(7) Farm Sub Lmt	AGN	(12) Mig Wrkrs Comp	AGN
(3) Phil Pln	AGN	(8) Coop-Church	AGN	(13) Jets to Chiang	AGN
(4) No-Knock	FOR	(9) Family Asst	FOR	(14) State OEO Veto	FOR
(5) Cmutr Tax	FOR	(10) Work Stamps	FOR	(15) Park Logging	FOR

Election Results

1970 general:	Charles Wiggins (R-Inc.)	116,169	(63%)
	Leslie Craven (D)	64,386	(35%)
	Kevin Scanlon (AIP)	2,994	(2%)
1970 primary:	Charles Wiggins (R-Inc.), unopposed		
1968 general:	Charles Wiggins (R)	145,245	(69%)
	Keith Shirley (D)	66,263	(31%)

TWENTY-SIXTH DISTRICT Political Background

California 26 takes in many of the glamour spots of Los Angeles: the Sunset Strip, Beverly Hills, the Hollywood Bowl, Century City, and the new Los Angeles County Museum on the site of the La Brea tar pits. The district, heavily urbanized, extends from the Hollywood Hills almost to the ocean. Politically, it is consistently liberal and Democratic, mostly because it contains much of the city's large Jewish population and also its intellectual and show business communities. Some of the more conservative stars and ex-stars, John Wayne and Ronald Reagan, to name two, have moved to the more congenial surroundings of Orange County. Meanwhile, the superrich city of Beverly Hills remains, to most people's surprise, a staunch liberal Democratic stronghold. The 26th also has some solid middle-class areas and a growing number of blacks (13% in 1970). Most of the blacks reside in the integrated Crenshaw area.

The ideological liberal voters of the 26th, never much taken with the conservative appeal of Ronald Reagan, have always cast more than 60% of their votes for Democratic candidates for Congress. They have elected a series of prominent congressmen: Helen Gahagan Douglas (1944–50), who lost the 1950 Senate race to Richard Nixon; Samuel W. Yorty (1950–54), who went on to run for a number of offices, finally to become mayor of Los Angeles in 1961, and who is now rumored to be considering a hawkish bid for President; and James Roosevelt (1954–65), son of the President. Roosevelt was one of the leaders of the liberal bloc in the House and a power on the Education and Labor Committee. But he resigned in 1965 to become ambassador to UNESCO, and has since gone on to a number of other ventures. His successor is Thomas Rees, who in the pre-one-man days was state senator for all of Los Angeles County. Rees is generally with the antiwar congressmen and is particularly interested in reforming House procedures. There is no reason to doubt that Rees will continue to win reelection through the '70's.

Census Data 1970 pop. 442,181; deviation from current state average, −15.8%; change 1960–70, +5.4%. Metro. 100%, 78.7% central city.

1970 Share of Federal Outlays $516,711,000 (average outlay per district, California 17, 19–32)

DOD	$209,052,000	HEW	$134,513,000
AEC	$2,555,000	HUD	$3,261,000
NASA	$58,761,000	OEO	$1,759,000
DOT	$12,454,000	DOA	$5,532,000
		Other	$88,824,000

Federal Military-Industrial Commitments (See California 28 for Los Angeles County listing.)

Economic Base Aircraft and parts, and other transportation equipment; electrical machinery, equipment, and supplies, esp. communication equipment and electronic components and accessories; nonelectrical machinery, esp. office, computing, and accounting machines; ordnance and accessories. Also, tourism (Beverly Hills) and banking and insurance.

The Voters

Registration 237,839 total. 157,430 D (66%); 66,951 R (28%); 999 AIP (—); 2,398 (1%); 10,061 other (4%).

Employment profile White collar, 61%. Blue collar, 39%.

Ethnic groups Black, 13%. Spanish surname, 4%. Oriental, 2%. Total foreign stock, 44%. USSR, 11%; Poland, 5%; Germany, UK, 3% each; Austria, 2%; Czech, Hungary, Ireland, Italy, Sweden, 1% each; others, 8%.

Presidential vote

1968	Humphrey (D)	132,992	(65%)
	Nixon (R)	66,470	(33%)
	Wallace (AIP)	5,040	(3%)

Representative

Thomas M. Rees (D) Elected 1964; b. Mar. 26, 1925, Los Angeles; home, Los Angeles; Occidental Col., B.A., 1950; Army, WWII; married, two children; Episcopal.

Career Calif. Assembly, 1954–62; Calif. Senate, 1962–65.

Offices 1113 LHOB, 202-225-5911. Also 816 S. Robertson Blvd., Los Angeles 90035, 213-652-4000.

Committees

Banking and Currency (14th); Subs. (1) Domestic Finance, (2) International Finance, (3) International Trade.

Group Ratings

	ADA	COPE	NREP	NFU	LCV	CFA	NAB	NSI	ACA
1970	88	100	100	100	100	100	8	0	0
1969	93	—	—	83	—	—	—	—	8
1968	92	100	—	86	—	—	0	—	5

Key Votes

(1) ABM	AGN	(6) 18-Yr-Vote	FOR	(11) Clean Water $	ABS
(2) SST	AGN	(7) Farm Sub Lmt	ABS	(12) Mig Wrkrs Comp	FOR
(3) Phil Pln	ABS	(8) Coop-Church	FOR	(13) Jets to Chiang	AGN
(4) No-Knock	AGN	(9) Family Asst	FOR	(14) State OEO Veto	AGN
(5) Cmutr Tax	FOR	(10) Work Stamps	AGN	(15) Park Logging	AGN

Election Results

1970 general:	Thomas Rees (D-Inc.)	130,499	(71%)
	Nathaniel Friedman (R)	47,260	(26%)
	Lewis McCammon (PF)	3,677	(2%)
	Howard E. Hallinan (AIP)	1,639	(1%)
1970 primary:	Thomas Rees (D-Inc.)	75,932	(86%)
	Russell Bostrom (D)	12,369	(14%)
1968 general:	Thomas Rees (D)	134,642	(65%)
	Irving Teichner (R)	64,505	(31%)
	Jack Weinberg (PF)	6,622	(3%)

TWENTY-SEVENTH DISTRICT Political Background

California 27 is the most grotesquely shaped congressional district in the nation. Originally (1961), the Democratic state legislators placed the district on the east side of the San Fernando Valley in order to oust Republican Congressman Edgar Hiestand, a member of the John Birch Society. A Democrat, Everett Burkhalter, did beat Hiestand in the next election. But Burkhalter, a veteran of the very efficient California Assembly, grew so disgusted with the ways of the House that he refused to run for reelection.

In 1964, the district surprised almost everyone by choosing Republican Ed Reinecke to replace Burkhalter—thus making it one of only four districts (three in California) outside the South to elect a Democrat in 1962 and a Republican in 1964, the year of LBJ. Subsequently, Reinecke was considered conservative enough to win Gov. Reagan's appointment as lieutenant governor when Bob Finch went off to become HEW Secretary in 1969. In the special election that followed, the winner was a young stockbroker with little previous experience, one Barry Goldwater, Jr.

Once the district was safely in Republican hands, it was sharply redistricted. Most of its Democratic territory was placed in the 22nd—where Congressman James Corman needed it badly—and much of the 22nd's Republican territory was placed in the 27th. But the line-drawing left the 27th looking like a horseshoe with a chimney, having for one arm the eastern third of the San Fernando Valley, and for another, the western third of the same Valley. The loop of the horseshoe consists of the unpopulated mountains north of Los Angeles. The chimney part is a slice of the Kern County desert, which, except for a couple of military installations, is pretty much today as it was when God first laid it out.

Young Goldwater, who was once seen dozing in the Senate gallery while his father was making a speech, has not complained about the shape of his district. That is not surprising, since he received 67% of this conglomerate's votes in 1970. What the 27th will look like after redistricting is anyone's guess. But it is a safe bet that there will be a Republican district somewhere in the vicinity of the San Fernando Valley that will reelect Barry Goldwater, Jr.

Census Data 1970 pop. 590,698; deviation from current state average, +12.5%; change 1960–70, +37.7%. Metro. 100%, 59.7% central city.

1970 Share of Federal Outlays $516,711,000 (average outlay per district, California 17, 19–32)

DOD	$209,052,000	HEW	$134,513,000
AEC	$2,555,000	HUD	$3,261,000
NASA	$58,761,000	OEO	$1,759,000
DOT	$12,454,000	DOA	$5,532,000
		Other	$88,824,000

Federal Military-Industrial Commitments (See California 28 for Los Angeles County listing.)

Economic Base Aircraft and parts, and other transportation equipment; electrical machinery, equipment, and supplies, esp. communication equipment and electronic components and accessories; nonelectrical machinery, esp. office, computing, and accounting machines; ordnance and accessories. Also, higher education (San Fernando State) and tourism (Hollywood Hills).

The Voters

Registration 258,062 total. 125,660 D (49%); 119,535 (46%); 2,802 AIP (1%); 949 PF (—); 9,116 other (4%).

Employment profile White collar, 51%. Blue collar, 49%.

Ethnic groups Black, 1%. Spanish surname, 5%. Oriental, 1%. Total foreign stock, 25%. UK, USSR, Canada, 3% each; Germany, Italy, Mexico, 2% each; Austria, Hungary, Ireland, Norway, Poland, Sweden, 1% each; others, 4%.

Presidential vote

1968	Humphrey (D)	84,116	(38%)
	Nixon (R)	123,347	(55%)
	Wallace (AIP)	15,807	(7%)

Representative

Barry M. Goldwater, Jr. (R) Elected 1968; b. July 15, 1938, Los Angeles; home, Burbank; Staunton Military Acad., U. of Colo., 1957–60; Ariz. State U., B.A., 1962; unmarried; Episcopalian.

Career Stock brokerage firm, 1962–69, partner, 1968–69.

Offices 1421 LHOB, 202-225-4461. Also Suite 404, 10850 Riverside Dr., North Hollywood 91602, 213-769-0727.

Committees

Government Operations (13th); Subs. (1) Government Activities, (2) Special Studies.

Science and Astronautics (9th); Subs. (1) Advanced Research and Technology, (2) NASA Oversight, (3) Space Science and Applications.

Group Ratings

	ADA	COPE	NREP	NFU	LCV	CFA	NAB	NSI	ACA
1970	0	9	0	25	50	50	91	100	88
1969	0	—	—	8	—	—	—	—	91

Key Votes

(1) ABM	FOR	(6) 18-Yr-Vote	AGN	(11) Clean Water $	AGN
(2) SST	FOR	(7) Farm Sub Lmt	AGN	(12) Mig Wrkrs Comp	AGN
(3) Phil Pln	ABS	(8) Coop-Church	AGN	(13) Jets to Chiang	FOR
(4) No-Knock	FOR	(9) Family Asst	AGN	(14) State OEO Veto	FOR
(5) Cmutr Tax	AGN	(10) Work Stamps	FOR	(15) Park Logging	AGN

Election Results

1970 general:	Barry Goldwater, Jr. (R-Inc.)	139,326	(67%)
	N. Toni Kimmel (D)	63,652	(30%)
	Edward Richer (PF)	3,306	(2%)
	John Hind (AIP)	2,642	(1%)
1970 primary:	Barry Goldwater, Jr. (R-Inc.), unopposed		

TWENTY-EIGHTH DISTRICT Political Background

California 28 wins the runner-up spot (behind California 27) in the nation's most-grotesquely-shaped-district contest. As in the 27th and in the 24th, the classic gerrymander theory explains the shape of the 28th: if you know you're going to lose a district, lose it big. Accordingly, the Democrats who designed the 28th put the wealthy and conservative Santa Monica Mountains, with their expensive hillside homes like the one in which Sharon Tate was murdered, in the same district with Santa Monica, with its conservative retirees. A mere block or two of oceanfront connected these two places with the conservative beach towns of Hermosa, Manhattan, and Redondo Beaches. (See the Los Angeles area map in the Appendix.) The beach towns, in turn, were linked to the high-income, conservative Palos Verdes Peninsula further south. Finally, Santa Catalina Island, 26 miles across the sea, was thrown in too.

The congressman from this Republican district is Alphonzo Bell, a wealthy oil heir; the industrial suburbs of Bell and Bell Gardens are named after his family. Since Bell first went to Congress, in 1960, he has been one of California's more liberal Republicans. The rise of Ronald Reagan, however, has prompted him to save his liberal votes for crucial roll calls. In 1969 Bell ran for mayor of Los Angeles and made a respectable showing; after being eliminated in the primary, he supported black Councilman Thomas Bradley. Bell's action reportedly aroused the wrath of Harry Salvatori and other well-heeled advisers, who had been none too happy with the Congressman's voting record anyway. In 1970 he ran into a well-financed conservative primary opponent, John La Follette. Bell managed to win the primary 56–44 over the conservative. But the race would have been much closer if three splinter candidates had stayed out: Bell won only 51% of the total vote. The Congressman has had no difficulty winning general elections, but he will doubtless keep a close eye on the redistricting process, which could well determine his fate in a 1972 primary.

Census Data 1970 pop. 550,414; deviation from current state average, +4.8%; change 1960–70, 26.9%. Metro. 100%, 46.8% central city.

1970 Share of Federal Outlays $516,711,000 (average outlay per district, California 17, 19–32)

DOD	$209,052,000	HEW	$134,513,000
AEC	$2,555,000	HUD	$3,261,000
NASA	$58,761,000	OEO	$1,759,000
DOT	$12,454,000	DOA	$5,532,000
		Other	$88,824,000

Federal Military-Industrial Commitments (California 17, 19–32, Los Angeles County listing)

DOD Contractors Hughes Aircraft and Hughes Tool (Culver City, Fullerton, El Segundo, Canoga Park, Los Angeles), $422.345m: Phoenix, TOW, Walleye, and Falcon missiles; Poseidon missile guidance assemblies; aircraft electronic warfare components; ship radar systems; repair of crash-damaged helicopters. Lockheed Aircraft (Burbank, Van Nuys), $268.345m: P-3 and S-3 aircraft and weapons systems. McDonnell Douglas (Santa Monica, Palmdale, Torrance, Huntington Park, Huntington Beach, Long Beach), $197.398m: A-4 aircraft, F-111 bomb ejection racks; Thor missile support; ABM development. General Dynamics (Pomona), $163.409m: ARM, Terrier, and Tartar missiles; Redeye missile warheads. TRW (Redondo Beach and Lawndale), $111.976m: military space satellite support; Hard Rock Silo support; Tactical Air Control System support. Northrop Corp. (Hawthorne, Palos Verde Estates), $104.845m: F-5 aircraft; T-38 aircraft modification; tiny-nail-filled rocket warheads. Aerojet General Div., General Tire (Azusa, Fullerton), $103.847m: aircraft electronic warfare systems.

Western Electric Div., AT&T (Santa Monica, Los Angeles), $91.245m: ABM development. Aerospace Corp. (El Segundo), $72.565m: unspecified research. Litton Systems (Woodland Hills, Van Nuys), $68.990m: aircraft and ship navigation systems. Norris Industries (Pico Rivera, Vernon, Los Angeles), $65.278m: 5-inch 38-cal. rocket warheads; rocket motor tubes; cartridge cases. North American Rockwell (Los Angeles, Canoga Park), $54.720m: CT-39 aircraft; Thor missile propulsion system. Mobil Oil (Torrance, Los Angeles), $51.393m: petroleum products. ITT Gilfillan (Van Nuys, Los Angeles), $42.487m: radar systems. Flying Tiger Line (Los Angeles), $39.578m: air cargo transport. Continental Airlines (Los Angeles), $36.318m: air cargo transport. Philco-Ford Div., Ford Motor Co. (Lawndale), $33.130m: aircraft gun systems. American Electric (La Miranda), $28.118m: 500- and 750-lb. bombs.

Golden Eagle Refining (Carson), $23.429m: petroleum products. Rand Corp. (Santa Monica), $19.537m: studies in military science. Garrett Corp. (Torrance), $17.499m: aircraft engines. Singer General Precision Div., Singer Co. (Glendale), $17.420m: Mk 48 torpedo launch system. Whittaker Corp. (Saugus), $17.052m: 2.75-inch rocket components; bomb racks; parachute flares. Harbor Boat Building (Terminal Island), $13.268m: minesweeper repair. Bendix (N. Hollywood), $12.918m: Mk 46 torpedo guidance system. Atlantic Richfield (Long Beach), $12.657m: petroleum products. Ralph M. Parsons Co. (Los Angeles), $12.024m: design of ABM base sites. RCA (Van Nuys), $11.837m: electronic voice warning systems. Gold Pak Meat (Los Angeles), $11.837m: foodstuffs. Luer Packing (Los Angeles), $11.025m: foodstuffs. Hoffman Electronics (El Monte), $10.996m: Tacon navigation system; fins and nozzles for 2.75-inch rocket. Physical Sciences Corp. (Arcadia), $10.910m: unspecified.

Electronic Resources (Los Angeles), $9.250m: aircraft camera and electronic sensor controls. Bechtel Corp. (Vernon), $9.204m: unspecified. Marine Terminals (Long Beach), $8.916m: stevedoring. Douglas Oil (Lakewood), $8.558m: petroleum products. MacMillan Ring Free Oil (Carson), $8.179m: petroleum products. Honeywell (West Covina), $7.532m: sonar operator trainers. Marquardt Corp. (Van Nuys), $6.856m: 66-mm rocket warheads. Harvey Aluminum Sales Div., Martin Marietta (Torrance), $6.661m: ammunition boxes. A. J. Industries (El Monte), $6.441m: unspecified. Xerox Corp. (Pasadena), $5.721m: TOW missile components. Todd Shipyards (San Pedro), $5.702m: ship repair. Bethlehem Steel (Terminal Island), $5.655m: ship repair. UCLA (Los Angeles), $5.442m: Thailand counterinsurgency research. Powerine Oil (Santa Fe Springs), $5.353m: petroleum products. Gulf Oil (Santa Fe Springs), $5.080m: petroleum products.

DOD Installations Ft. MacArthur AB (San Pedro). Long Beach Naval Shipyard (Long Beach). Naval Hospital (Long Beach). Naval Weapons Center (China Lake). Naval Station (Long Beach). Navy Fuel Depot (San Pedro). Air Force Plant 42 (Palmdale). Boron AF Station (Boron). Edwards AFB (Muroc). Los Angeles AF Station (Los Angeles).

AEC Operations North American Rockwell (Canoga Park), $22.833m: reactor and research facilities.

NASA Contractors North American Rockwell (Canoga Park and Downey), $474.512m: Apollo and Saturn support and hardware. California Institute of Technology, Jet Propulsion Laboratory (Pasadena), $168.805m: development of unmanned space exploration techniques. McDonnell Douglas (Santa Monica), $103.263m: Delta space vehicle and Saturn rocket, support and hardware. TRW Inc. (Redondo Beach), $16.900m: Pioneer spacecraft. California Institute of Technology (Pasadena), $11.022m: research.

NASA Installations Flight Research Center (Edwards).

Economic Base Aircraft and parts, and other transportation equipment; electrical machinery, equipment, and supplies, esp. communication equipment and electronic components and accessories; nonelectrical machinery, esp. office, computing, and accounting machines; ordnance and accessories. Also, higher education (UCLA) and tourism (Coastline).

The Voters

Registration 276,983 total. 123,541 D (45%); 137,696 R (50%); 1,784 AIP (1%); 2,282 PF (1%); 11,680 other (4%).

Employment profile White collar, 64%. Blue collar, 36%.

Ethnic groups Black, 1%. Spanish surname, 4%. Oriental, 1%. Total foreign stock, 29%. UK, USSR, Canada, 4% each; Germany, 3%; Italy, Poland, 2% each; Austria, Hungary, Ireland, Norway, Mexico, 1% each; others, 6%.

Presidential vote

1968	Humphrey (D)	91,279	(39%)
	Nixon (R)	133,767	(57%)
	Wallace (AIP)	9,581	(4%)

Representative

Alphonzo Bell (R) Elected 1960; b. Sept. 19, 1914, Los Angeles; home, Los Angeles; Occidental Col., B.A., 1938; Army Air Corps, WWII; married, nine children; Presbyterian.

Career Pres., Chm., Bell Petroleum Co., 1938– ; Chm., Calif. Repub. Central Com., 1956–58; Chm., Repub. Central Com. of Los Angeles County, 1958–60.

Offices 113 CHOB, 202-225-6451. Also Rm. 14220, New Fed. Bldg., 11000 Wilshire Blvd., Los Angeles 90024, 213-478-0111.

Committees

Education and Labor (3rd); Subs. (1) Gen. Sub. on Education, (2) Gen. Sub. on Labor, (3) Sel. Sub. on Education.

Science and Astronautics (3rd); Subs (1) International Cooperation in Science and Space, (2) Manned Space Flight, (3) Science, Research, and Dev.

Group Ratings

	ADA	COPE	NREP	NFU	LCV	CFA	NAB	NSI	ACA
1970	28	50	30	56	22	63	78	100	62
1969	20	—	—	60	—	—	—	—	33
1968	33	50	—	86	—	—	0	—	37

Key Votes

(1) ABM	ABS	(6) 18-Yr-Vote	FOR	(11) Clean Water $	AGN
(2) SST	FOR	(7) Farm Sub Lmt	AGN	(12) Mig Wrkrs Comp	FOR
(3) Phil Pln	FOR	(8) Coop-Church	ABS	(13) Jets to Chiang	ABS
(4) No-Knock	FOR	(9) Family Asst	FOR	(14) State OEO Veto	ABS
(5) Cmutr Tax	FOR	(10) Work Stamps	FOR	(15) Park Logging	AGN

Election Results

1970 general:	Alphonzo Bell (R-Inc.)	154,691	(67%)
	Don McLaughlin (D)	57,882	(26%)
	Derck Gordon (AIP)	5,759	(3%)
	Jane Gordon (PF)	4,971	(2%)
1970 primary:	Alphonzo Bell (R-Inc.)	46,160	(51%)
	John La Follette (R)	36,390	(40%)
	Donald Gallagher (R)	6,667	(7%)
	Bruce Fagan (R)	770	(1%)
	Carl Miciak (R)	485	(1%)
1968 general:	Alphonzo Bell (R)	173,680	(71%)
	John Pratt (D)	65,233	(27%)
	Sherman Pearl (PF)	4,725	(2%)

TWENTY-NINTH DISTRICT Political Background

California 29 has an interesting genesis. In the mid-'50's George E. Brown, Jr., a young industrial physicist, was serving on the City Council of Monterey Park (1970 pop. 49,000), a middle-income suburb several miles east of downtown Los Angeles. Apparently dissatisfied with the way government operated, Brown decided to run for the California Assembly and, in the 1958 Democratic landslide, won. There he found himself on the committee which drew the state's congressional district lines and allotted eight new districts to various parts of California. California 29 was created in the process, and from this district, in 1962, Brown was elected to the United States House of Representatives. The district he won extends west from Monterey Park toward downtown Los Angeles, where there are lots of Democratic votes in the Mexican-American ghettos of East Los Angeles and Boyle Heights. The 29th also has its share of upper-middle-class Anglos in suburbs like Alhambra and San Gabriel.

Perhaps because of his strong stand against the Vietnam war and in favor of peace issues generally, Congressman Brown never won by convincing margins. His best performance was in 1964 when he won 59% of the vote. In 1966 and 1968, Brown was opposed by a conservative Mexican and barely scraped through both times. In 1970 Brown ran for the Senate on an outspoken peace platform—using Barry Goldwater's line about extremism in the defense of liberty being no vice. The Democrat from the 29th district ran a very respectable second to the well-financed favorite, Congressman John Tunney. In fact, if 4% of the primary vote had swung Brown's way, he might well have continued his climb from the Monterey Park City Council all the way to the United States Senate.

Brown's successor in the House is former state Senator George Danielson. The new representative, more interested in ecological issues than in those of peace, lacks Brown's controversial outspokenness. But as a result, Danielson in 1970 ran better (63%) than Brown ever did. The only possible threat to the Congressman's tenure is the rising militancy of the Mexican-American community, which makes up nearly a third of the current district's population. Although Edward Roybal of the 30th district is of Mexican descent, California's chicanos have not had heavy representation in the state's legislative bodies. And, as Danielson knows, the 29th as currently constituted is California's most heavily Mexican congressional district.

Census Data 1970 pop. 453,984; deviation from current state average, −13.5%; change 1960–70, +12.2%. Metro. 100%, 44.5% central city.

1970 Share of Federal Outlays $516,711,000 (average outlay per district, California 17, 19–32)

DOD	$209,052,000	HEW	$134,513,000
AEC	$2,555,000	HUD	$3,261,000
NASA	$58,761,000	OEO	$1,759,000
DOT	$12,454,000	DOA	$5,532,000
		Other	$88,824,000

Federal Military-Industrial Commitments (See California 28 for Los Angeles County listing.)

Economic Base Aircraft and parts, and other transportation equipment; electrical machinery, equipment, and supplies, esp. communication equipment and electronic components and accessories; nonelectrical machinery, esp. office, computing, and accounting machines; ordnance and accessories.

The Voters

Registration 160,255 total. 100,200 D (63%); 51,152 R (32%); 1,328 AIP (1%); 1,177 PF (1%); 6,398 other (4%).

Employment profile White collar, 44%. Blue collar, 56%.

Ethnic groups Black, 1%. Spanish surname, 28%. Oriental, 3%. Total foreign stock, 40%. Mexico, 16%; Italy, 4%; Germany, 3%; UK, USSR, Canada, 2% each; Austria, Ireland, Poland, Sweden, 1% each; others, 7%.

Presidential vote

1968	Humphrey (D)	74,517	(52%)
	Nixon (R)	59,812	(42%)
	Wallace (AIP)	7,925	(6%)

Representative

George E. Danielson (D) Elected 1970; b. Feb. 20, 1915, Wausa, Nebr.; home, Los Angeles; U. of Nebr., B.A., 1937, J.D., 1939; Navy, WWII; Lt. USNR; married; Protestant.

Career Lawyer; Sp. agent, FBI, Asst. U.S. Atty. in So. Dist. of Calif., 1949–51; Assemblyman, 1962–66; State Senator, 1966–70.

Offices 1513 LHOB, 202-225-5464. Also 3255 Fed. Office Bldg., 300 N. Los Angeles St., Los Angeles 90012.

Committees

Judiciary (21st); Sub. No. 2.

Veterans' Affairs (14th); Subs. (1) Education and Training, (2) Hospitals.

Group Ratings, Key Votes: Newly elected.

Election Results

1970 general:	George Danielson (D)	71,308	(63%)
	Tom McMann (R)	42,620	(37%)
1970 primary:	George Danielson (D)	25,957	(47%)
	Richard Calderon (D)	23,690	(43%)
	Francis Stiles (D)	3,494	(6%)
	Isaac Ruiz, Jr. (D)	2,236	(4%)

THIRTIETH DISTRICT Political Background

California 30 is central Los Angeles, from Hollywood and Vine in the west, through MacArthur Park and adjacent senior-citizen neighborhoods, to the Mexican-American slums of Boyle Heights in the east. There is glitter on the main boulevards, but many of the district's side streets are lined with not-so-elegant apartments and shabby, small houses. A disproportionate number of the residents here are indigent retirees, existing quietly in the smoggy, run-down back streets of Hollywood and other neighborhoods. A little less than half of the population of the 30th is made up of minorities; the largest are the Mexican-Americans, followed by blacks and Orientals. These groups help to make it one of the most reliably Democratic districts in the Los Angeles area.

The 30th's congressman is Edward R. Roybal, one of three House members of Mexican descent. For years, Roybal, one of the most liberal members of the House, found himself frustrated by his committee assignments: Foreign Affairs (unlike its Senate counterpart, not very active) and Veterans' Affairs. At the beginning of the 92nd Congress, Roybal won a seat on Appropriations—the first arch-liberal in some time to do so. The assignment may not give him much national exposure, but in a few years he should have considerable say over some large hunks of the federal budget. Redistricting poses no problems, and Roybal can expect continued reelection without difficulty.

Census Data 1970 pop. 397,222; deviation from current state average, −24.4%; change 1960–70, +1.6%. Metro. 100%, 96.9% central city.

1970 Share of Federal Outlays $516,711,000 (average outlay per district, California 17, 19–32)

DOD	$202,052,000	HEW	$134,513,000
AEC	$2,555,000	HUD	$3,261,000
NASA	$58,761,000	OEO	$1,759,000
DOT	$12,454,000	DOA	$5,532,000
		Other	$88,824,000

Federal Military-Industrial Commitments (See California 28 for Los Angeles County listing.)

Economic Base Aircraft and parts, and other transportation equipment; electrical machinery, equipment, and supplies, esp. communication equipment and electronic components and accessories; nonelectrical machinery, esp. office, computing, and accounting machines; ordnance and accessories. Also, higher education (Calif. State Los Angeles) and tourism (Hollywood).

The Voters

Registration 136,851 total. 85,248 D (62%); 42,532 (31%); 906 AIP (1%); 921 PF (1%); 7,244 other (5%).

Employment profile White collar, 47%. Blue collar, 53%.

Ethnic groups Black, 16%. Spanish surname, 22%. Oriental, 8%. Total foreign stock, 41%. Mexico, 13%; Germany, USSR, 3% each; UK, Canada, 2% each; Austria, Hungary, Ireland, Italy, Poland, Sweden, 1% each; others, 12%.

Presidential vote

1968	Humphrey (D)	68,612	(60%)
	Nixon (R)	41,396	(36%)
	Wallace (AIP)	4,292	(4%)

Representative

Edward R. Roybal (D) Elected 1962; b. Feb. 10, 1916, Albuquerque, N.M.; home, Los Angeles; UCLA; Southwestern U.; Army, 1944–45; married, three children; Catholic.

Career Social worker, pub. health educator, Calif. Tuberculosis Assn., 1942–49; Dir. Health ed., Los Angeles County T.B. and Health Assn., 1945–49; L.A. City Council, 1949–62; Pres. Pro-Tempore, 1961–62; Chm. of Bd., Eastland Savings & Loan Assn.

Offices 504 CHOB, 202-225-6235. Also Rm. 7110 New Fed. Bldg., N. Los Angeles St., Los Angeles 90012, 213-688-4870.

Committees

Appropriations (28th); Subs. (1) Foreign Operations, (2) Treasury, Post Office, and Gen. Government.

Group Ratings

	ADA	COPE	NREP	NFU	LCV	CFA	NAB	NSI	ACA
1970	100	100	100	92	67	100	0	0	6
1969	100	—	—	86	—	—	—	—	7
1968	100	100	—	88	—	—	0	—	5

Key Votes

(1) ABM	AGN	(6) 18-Yr-Vote	FOR	(11) Clean Water $	FOR
(2) SST	AGN	(7) Farm Sub Lmt	FOR	(12) Mig Wrkrs Comp	FOR
(3) Phil Pln	FOR	(8) Coop-Church	FOR	(13) Jets to Chiang	AGN
(4) No-Knock	AGN	(9) Family Asst	FOR	(14) State OEO Veto	AGN
(5) Cmutr Tax	FOR	(10) Work Stamps	AGN	(15) Park Logging	AGN

Election Results

1970 general:	Edward Roybal (D-Inc.)	63,903	(68%)
	Samuel Cavnar (R)	28,038	(30%)
	Boris Belousov (AIP)	1,681	(2%)
1970 primary:	Edward Roybal (D-Inc.)	34,466	(85%)
	Blase Bonpane (D)	6,343	(15%)
1968 general:	Edward Roybal (D)	76,967	(67%)
	Samuel Cavnar (R)	37,234	(33%)

THIRTY-FIRST DISTRICT Political Background

California 31 is the southwest part of the city of Los Angeles and several adjacent suburbs, including Inglewood, Hawthorne, and Ladera Heights. The suburbs are typical of Los Angeles and southern California country: neat single-family houses, parcels of still-vacant land here and some new subdivisions there, gaudy boulevards with strip commercial development, and '60's-style shopping centers. The Los Angeles part of the district is a little poorer and, lying just west of Watts, was the area of the greatest racial change in Los Angeles during the '60's. In 1960, 16% of the residents of the 31st were black; by 1970, after 10 years of blockbusting, the black community had expanded to the city limits and beyond. Currently, 41% of the district is black.

Politically, the massive population shift has made the district increasingly more Democratic. Jess Unruh, a resident of Inglewood and Ronald Reagan's 1970 opponent, took 63% of the district's votes in 1970—a better showing than Lyndon Johnson made in the same area in 1964. And Sen. John Tunney did better here than either. The trend has made the seat safer for Democratic Congressman and former Assemblyman Charles H. Wilson in general elections. But the black migration may cause him trouble in future primaries. So far Wilson has beaten black challengers. Almost half of the district's Democratic registration is now black, however, and the percentage is bound to rise. Depending on how the district lines are drawn, a prominent black candidate—someone of the stature of state Sen. Mervin Dymally, or Assemblyman Yvonne Brathwaite, or ex-Councilman and 1969 mayoral candidate Thomas Bradley—could capture the seat.

Census Data 1970 pop. 442,514; deviation from current state average, —15.7%; change 1960–70, +9.6%. Metro. 100%, 48.8% central city.

1970 Share of Federal Outlays $516,711,000 (average outlay per district, California 17, 19–32)

DOD	$209,052,000	HEW	$134,513,000
AEC	$2,555,000	HUD	$3,261,000
NASA	$58,761,000	OEO	$1,759,000
DOT	$12,454,000	DOA	$5,532,000
		Other	$88,824,000

Federal Military-Industrial Commitments (See California 28 for Los Angeles County listing.)

Economic Base Aircraft and parts, and other transportation equipment; electrical machinery, equipment, and supplies, esp. communication equipment and electronic components and accessories; nonelectrical machinery, esp. office, computing, and accounting machines; ordnance and accessories.

The Voters

Registration 191,628 total. 129,255 D (67%); 53,731 R (28%); 2,136 AIP (1%); 604 PF (—); 5,902 other (3%).

Employment profile White collar, 49%. Blue collar, 51%.
Ethnic groups Black, 41%. Spanish surname, 6%. Oriental, 3%. Total foreign stock, 28%. Germany, UK, Canada, Mexico, 3% each; Italy, USSR, 2% each; Austria, Hungary, Ireland, Norway, Poland, Sweden, 1% each.

Presidential vote

1968	Humphrey (D)	98,940	(59%)
	Nixon (R)	60,291	(36%)
	Wallace (AIP)	8,638	(5%)

Representative

Charles H. Wilson (D) Elected 1962; b. Feb. 15, 1917, Magna, Utah; home, Los Angeles; Army, WWII; married, four children; United Church of Christ.

Career Founded Charles H. Wilson Insurance Co., 1945; Calif. Assembly, 1954–62.

Offices 104 CHOB, 202-225-5425. Also 2013 W. Florence Ave., Los Angeles 90043, 213-753-2521, and 300 E. Hillcrest, Inglewood 90301, 213-674-4343.

Committees

Armed Services (13th); Sub. No. 4.

Post Office and Civil Service (7th); Subs. (1) Chm., Census and Statistics, (2) Employee Benefits.

Group Ratings

	ADA	COPE	NREP	NFU	LCV	CFA	NAB	NSI	ACA
1970	68	100	82	100	80	86	0	66	13
1969	60	—	—	100	—	—	—	—	0
1968	83	100	—	86	—	—	0	—	5

Key Votes

(1) ABM	FOR	(6) 18-Yr-Vote	ABS	(11) Clean Water $	FOR
(2) SST	FOR	(7) Farm Sub Lmt	ABS	(12) Mig Wrkrs Comp	FOR
(3) Phil Pln	FOR	(8) Coop-Church	FOR	(13) Jets to Chiang	AGN
(4) No-Knock	ABS	(9) Family Asst	FOR	(14) State OEO Veto	AGN
(5) Cmutr Tax	ABS	(10) Work Stamps	AGN	(15) Park Logging	AGN

Election Results

1970 general:	Charles Wilson (D-Inc.)	102,071	(73%)
	Fred Casmir (R)	37,416	(27%)
1970 primary:	Charles Wilson (D-Inc.)	41,288	(62%)
	Nathan Holden (D)	25,102	(38%)
1968 general:	Charles Wilson (D)	97,855	(59%)
	James Dunn (R)	65,004	(39%)
	Stanley Schulte (AIP)	3,315	(2%)

THIRTY-SECOND DISTRICT Political Background

California 32 is dominated by the city of Long Beach (pop. 358,000), which contains about three-quarters of the district's population. Long Beach was one of the early meccas for Midwestern retirees, whose attachment to wild welfare schemes like the Townsend Plan and the Ham 'n Eggs movement gave California politics much of its zany character in the years up to World War II. Oldtimers can recall the Iowa picnics of the '30's, gatherings which used to draw 50,000 people to Long Beach. They may also remember that the falling-out between the Ham 'n Eggs leaders and liberal Democratic Gov. Culbert Olson led to the election of Earl Warren as governor in 1942. There are still many retirees living in Long Beach and in the small Orange County portion of the 32nd. But today these folk are more likely to be militant conservatives, concerned about the moral decay of our society, and sometimes, too, about the fluoridation of the water.

So the 32nd, as much as any district in California, is personified by the little old lady in tennis shoes. And the district's congressman, conservative Republican Craig Hosmer, is a man of kindred spirit. Hosmer, in the House since 1952, is the number two Republican on the House Interior and Insular Affairs Committee. But he devotes much of his time and thought to military and atomic energy policy. Several years ago, convinced that victory in Vietnam was possible, Hosmer proposed that the Air Force drop the Vietnamese equivalent of voodoo dolls on the Viet Cong. The dolls, Hosmer figured, would scare the enemy into surrendering. The Pentagon, however, did not act on his suggestion.

Hosmer will maintain an effective hold on the 32nd. In 1970 he won 72% of the vote, and he will no doubt do as well in future elections.

Census Data 1970 pop. 468,884; deviation from current state average, —10.7%; change 1960–70, +19.1%. Metro. 100%, 77.9% central city.

1970 Share of Federal Outlays $516,711,000 (average outlay per district, California 17, 19–32)

DOD	$209,052,000	HEW	$134,513,000
AEC	$2,555,000	HUD	$3,261,000
NASA	$58,761,000	OEO	$1,759,000
DOT	$12,454,000	DOA	$5,532,000
		Other	$88,824,000

Federal Military-Industrial Commitments (See California 28 for Los Angeles County listing.)

Economic Base Aircraft and parts, and other transportation equipment; electrical machinery, equipment, and supplies, esp. communication equipment and electronic components and accessories; ordnance and accessories; nonelectrical machinery, esp. office, computing, and accounting machines. Also, higher education (Calif. State, Long Beach).

The Voters

Registration 218,678 total. 106,975 D (49%); 100,538 R (46%); 2,401 AIP (1%); 667 PF (—); 8,097 other (4%).

Employment profile White collar, 49%. Blue Collar, 51%.

Ethnic groups Black, 4%. Spanish surname, 3%. Oriental, 1%. Total foreign stock, 20%. Canada, UK, 3% each; Germany, 2%; Ireland, Italy, Norway, Poland, Sweden, USSR, Mexico, 1% each; others, 5%.

Presidential vote

1968	Humphrey (D)	71,875	(38%)
	Nixon (R)	103,848	(55%)
	Wallace (AIP)	11,634	(6%)

Representative

Craig Hosmer (R) Elected 1952; b. May 6, 1915, Brea; home, Long Beach; U. of Calif., B.A., 1937; U. of Mich. Law School; U. of So. Calif. Law School, J.D., 1940; U.S. Naval Acad., 1941; Navy, WWII; Rear Adm., USNR; married, three children; Episcopalian.

Career Practicing atty., 1946–48; 1949– ; Atty. for Atomic Energy Commission, 1948; Sp. Asst. U.S. Dist. Atty. at Los Alamos, N. Mex., 1948.

Offices 2217 RHOB, 202-225-2415. Also 620 Security Bldg., Long Beach 90802, 213-436-4865, 213-426-4294.

Committees

Interior and Insular Affairs (2nd); Subs. (1) Environment, (2) Irrigation and Reclamation, (3) Mines and Mining, (4) Territorial and Insular Affairs.

Jt. Com. on Atomic Energy (Ranking Rep. House Mbr.); Subs. (1) Legislation, (2) Military Applications, (3) Research, Dev., and Radiation.

Group Ratings

	ADA	COPE	NREP	NFU	LCV	CFA	NAB	NSI	ACA
1970	24	27	25	64	0	38	91	100	76
1969	13	—	—	43	—	—	—	—	50
1968	17	23	—	44	—	—	100	—	70

Key Votes

(1) ABM	FOR	(6) 18-Yr-Vote	FOR	(11) Clean Water $	AGN
(2) SST	FOR	(7) Farm Sub Lmt	FOR	(12) Mig Wrkrs Comp	ABS
(3) Phil Pln	FOR	(8) Coop-Church	AGN	(13) Jets to Chiang	FOR
(4) No-Knock	FOR	(9) Family Asst	FOR	(14) State OEO Veto	FOR
(5) Cmutr Tax	AGN	(10) Work Stamps	FOR	(15) Park Logging	FOR

Election Results

1970 general:	Craig Hosmer (R-Inc.)	119,340	(72%)
	Walter Mallonee (D)	44,228	(26%)
	John Donohue (PF)	3,227	(2%)
1970 primary:	Craig Hosmer (R-Inc.), unopposed		
1968 general:	Craig Hosmer (R)	142,401	(74%)
	Arthur Gottlieb (D)	46,404	(24%)
	Richard Williams (AIP)	3,991	(2%)

THIRTY-THIRD DISTRICT Political Background

California 33 is most of San Bernardino County, geographically the largest county in the United States. It is about the size of the state of West Virginia, some 20,000 square miles. Most of the acreage, however, can be ignored in any political survey. It is taken up by the nation's most arid desert, one which is untouched by civilization except for gas station colonies on freeway interchanges and wisps of smog from Los Angeles. About 99% of San Bernardino's population is clustered in the county's southwest corner, a valley which is an eastward extension of the Los Angeles Basin. The center of the city of San Bernardino, a low-income Mexican district, was removed from the 33rd district and added to the 38th for political reasons. What is left is mostly Republican—solid middle-income towns like Redlands, Upland, and Ontario, and a blue-collar enclave around the Kaiser Steel plant in Fontana. The orange groves and vineyards on the hillsides near places like Cucamonga have been uprooted for subdivisions or wilted by smog.

For almost 30 years (1936–64) the congressman from San Bernardino was Harry Sheppard, an old-style middle-of-the-road Democrat. He was succeeded, in a familiar pattern, by his administrative assistant. In 1966, however, the district turned out the ex-aide and installed the present incumbent, Jerry Pettis. Pettis, the only Seventh-Day Adventist in Congress, has gained a solid hold on the district. In 1971 he won a seat on the House Ways and Means Committee. This is a sure sign that the Republican leadership considers Pettis safely ensconced and safely conservative. Because of its substantial population growth, the 33rd stands to lose about 100,000 residents in redistricting. The people remaining will probably make the district even more pro-Pettis than it is now.

Census Data 1970 pop. 576,765; deviation from current state average, +9.8%; change 1960–70, +38.7%. Metro. 100%, 21.5% central city.

1970 Share of Federal Outlays $691,127,203

DOD	$337,013,000	HEW	$205,223,546
AEC	$000	HUD	$2,138,678
NASA	$138,900	OEO	$658,075

DOT	$42,432,150	DOA	$12,342,037
		Other	$91,180,817

Federal Military-Industrial Commitments

DOD Contractors TRW (Norton AFB), $46.496m: support of Minuteman missile. Lockheed Aircraft (Ontario), $19.981m: C-130 aircraft modification. Kaiser Steel (Fontana), $8.481m: fence posts; ammunition boxes.

DOD Installations Marine Corps Supply Center (Barstow). George AFB (Victorville). Norton AFB (San Bernadino).

Economic Base Primary metal industries, esp. blast furnaces, steel works, and rolling and finishing mills; poultry and dairy; aircraft and parts, and other transportation equipment.

The Voters

Registration 207,942 total. 106,920 D (51%); 91,518 R (44%); 2,749 AIP (1%); 189 PF (—); 6,566 other (3%).

Employment profile White collar, 43%. Blue collar, 57%.

Ethnic groups Black, 4%. Spanish surname, 8%. Oriental, 1%. Total foreign stock, 18%. Mexico, 4%; Germany, UK, Canada, 2% each; Italy, Sweden, 1% each; others, 4%.

Presidential vote

1968	Humphrey (D)	72,897	(39%)
	Nixon (R)	97,790	(52%)
	Wallace (AIP)	18,299	(10%)

Representative

Jerry L. Pettis (R) Elected 1966; b. July 18, 1916, Phoenix, Ariz.; home, Loma Linda; Pacific Union Col., B.A., 1938; Air Transport Command pilot, WWII; married, three children; Seventh-Day Adventist Church.

Career Rancher (citrus-avocado); Sp. Asst. to Pres. United Air Lines, 1946–50; Founder, Magnetic Tape Duplicators, Audio-Digest Foundation; Professor of economics, 1948–64, Chm. Bd. of Councilors, 1960–67, V.P. for Development, 1960–64, Loma-Linda U.

Offices 427 CHOB, 202-225-5861. Also Calif. Hotel, San Bernadino 92401, 714-884-8818; 209 Emmons Walk Bldg., Ontario 91761, 714-984-5715, and 220 E. Mt. View, Barstow 92311, 714-256-4913.

Committees

Ways and Means (8th).

Group Ratings

	ADA	COPE	NREP	NFU	LCV	CFA	NAB	NSI	ACA
1970	28	42	27	73	50	56	67	100	59
1969	7	—	—	28	—	—	—	—	65
1968	0	31	—	44	—	—	100	—	78

Key Votes

(1) ABM	FOR	(6) 18-Yr-Vote	FOR	(11) Clean Water $	AGN
(2) SST	FOR	(7) Farm Sub Lmt	FOR	(12) Mig Wrkrs Comp	FOR
(3) Phil Pln	FOR	(8) Coop-Church	AGN	(13) Jets to Chiang	FOR
(4) No-Knock	FOR	(9) Family Asst	FOR	(14) State OEO Veto	FOR
(5) Cmutr Tax	AGN	(10) Work Stamps	FOR	(15) Park Logging	ABS

Election Results

1970 general:	Jerry Pettis (R-Inc.)	116,093	(72%)
	Chester Wright (D)	44,764	(28%)
1970 primary:	Jerry Pettis (R-Inc.), unopposed		
1968 general:	Jerry Pettis (R)	123,507	(66%)
	Al Ballard (D)	56,649	(32%)
	Earl Wallen (AIP)	3,174	(2%)

THIRTY-FOURTH DISTRICT Political Background

California 34 is part of Orange County, a strip of land which lies between the ocean and the mountains southeast of Los Angeles and which is one of the fastest-growing parts of the country. In 1950 Orange County was still largely devoted to the cultivation of oranges, having just 216,000 residents. In 1960, after a decade of feverish growth, there were 703,000; by 1970, 1,420,000. Orange County is, of course, known far and wide for its brand of fierce conservatism, and its reputation for that is, in most cases, deserved. Nevertheless, ever since the district was created in 1962, it has sent a fairly liberal Democrat to Congress.

The apparent anomaly is in part the result of careful redistricting. The 34th's jagged boundary, drawn in 1962 and revised in 1968 (when a sliver of Los Angeles County was added to the district), was designed to enclose the maximum number of Democratic voters. The 34th seems to weave at random through the Orange County metropolises of Santa Ana (pop. 156,000), Anaheim (pop. 166,000), Garden Grove (pop. 122,000), and Huntington Beach (pop. 115,000). Along the way it takes in such attractions as Disneyland, Knott's Berry Farm, and the California Angels baseball park. More important politically, it manages to pull in all of the county's few black and Mexican residents and most of its economically marginal blue-collar and retired whites.

The strategy of gerrymander in Orange has been successful only because of the vote-getting prowess of Congressman Richard T. Hanna. For six years, he represented the area in the California Assembly. Moreover, Hanna—a Kemmerer, Wyoming, native—is an accomplished teller of funny stories and a tireless campaigner. Only one statewide Democratic candidate, Lyndon Johnson, carried the 34th during the '60's, but the feisty Hanna has managed to scrape through every two years, with margins always less than 60% of the vote. In 1968, at the height of Gov. Reagan's popularity, the Congressman had his closest call. He would have lost if the district lines had not just recently been redrawn. Hanna won that election by only 1,000 votes in the Orange County portion of the district, as compared to a 3,000-vote margin in the much smaller Los Angeles County part of his constituency.

If the Republicans had retained control of the California legislature in 1970, something they were expected to do, Hanna would now be making plans for his post-congressional career. But the current Democratic legislature is likely to fight hard to preserve Hanna's seat. The district's population has grown to 643,000 and must be reduced to about 466,000. The obvious thing to do in these circumstances is to remove the more Republican parts of the present 34th and add them to the new district Orange County has won, which is going to produce a Republican winner anyway. If this happens, and it probably will, Orange County will continue to send a Democrat to the House through the '70's.

Census Data 1970 pop. 576,765; deviation from current state average, +22.6%; change 1960–70, +58.7%. Metro. 100%, 52.6% central city.

1970 Share of Federal Outlays $775,152,000 (average outlay per district, California 34–37.)

DOD	$496,071,000	HEW	$146,012,000
AEC	$2,845,000	HUD	$3,267,000
NASA	$12,532,000	OEO	$1,050,000
DOT	$17,503,000	DOA	$2,959,000
		Other	$92,912,000

Federal Military-Industrial Commitments (See California 35 for San Diego and Orange counties listing.)

Economic Base Aircraft and parts, and other transportation equipment; electrical machinery, equipment, and supplies, esp. radio and television transmitting, signaling, and detection equipment and apparatus; ordnance and accessories; fabricated metal products, esp. screw machine products, bolts, nuts, screws, rivets, and washers; nonelectrical machinery, esp. office, computing, and accounting machines. Also, tourism (Disneyland).

The Voters

Registration 231,885 total. 119,993 D (52%); 99,056 R (43%); 3,249 AIP (1%); 199 PF (—); 9,388 other (4%).
Employment profile White collar, 46%. Blue collar, 54%.
Ethnic groups Black, 1%. Spanish surname, 8%. Oriental, 1%. Total foreign stock, 18%. Mexico, 4%; Canada, 3%; Germany, UK, 2% each; Italy, Poland, USSR, 1% each; others, 4%.

Presidential vote

1968	Humphrey (D)	76,022	(37%)
	Nixon (R)	113,470	(55%)
	Wallace (AIP)	18,076	(9%)

Representative

Richard T. Hanna (D) Elected 1962; b. June 9, 1914, Kemmerer, Wyo.; home, Anaheim; Pasadena Jr. Col., A.A., U. of Calif., B.A., 1937; UCLA Law School, LL.B., 1952; Navy Air Corps, WWII; married, three children; Church of Jesus Christ of Latter Day Saints.
Career Practicing atty., 1952– ; Calif. Assembly, 1957–62.
Offices 213 CHOB, 202-225-2965. Also Suite 654, 1695 W. Crescent, Anaheim 92801, 714-776-6850.

Committees

Banking and Currency (12th); Subs. (1) Consumer Affairs, (2) Domestic Finance, (3) International Finance, (4) International Trade.
Science and Astronautics (10th); Subs. (1) Manned Space Flight, (2) Science, Research, and Dev.

Group Ratings

	ADA	COPE	NREP	NFU	LCV	CFA	NAB	NSI	ACA
1970	72	90	67	92	50	93	20	78	35
1969	54	—	—	93	—	—	—	—	17
1968	67	83	—	73	—	—	25	—	10

Key Votes

(1) ABM	FOR	(6) 18-Yr-Vote	FOR	(11) Clean Water $	AGN
(2) SST	FOR	(7) Farm Sub Lmt	AGN	(12) Mig Wrkrs Comp	FOR
(3) Phil Pln	FOR	(8) Coop-Church	FOR	(13) Jets to Chiang	ABS
(4) No-Knock	FOR	(9) Family Asst	FOR	(14) State OEO Veto	AGN
(5) Cmutr Tax	AGN	(10) Work Stamps	AGN	(15) Park Logging	AGN

Election Results

1970 general:	Richard Hanna (D-Inc.)	101,664	(54%)
	William Teague (R)	82,167	(44%)
	Lee Rayburn (AIP)	2,843	(2%)
1970 primary:	Richard Hanna (D-Inc.), unopposed		
1968 general:	Richard Hanna (D)	107,113	(51%)
	William Teague (R)	103,470	(49%)

THIRTY-FIFTH DISTRICT Political Background

California 35 is made up of parts of ultraconservative Orange and San Diego counties. It is today the nation's largest and fastest-growing congressional district, the only one to have more than doubled its population during the '60's. The 35th is dominated politically by the 570,000 residents of the heavily Republican parts of Orange County which were carefully excluded from the 34th district. The northern portion of San Diego County is characterized by seaside towns full of Navy wives and retired military personnel. Among the district's 871,000 citizens is Richard M. Nixon, who stands well to the left of the 35th's ideological median.

The extreme conservatism of Orange County is a peculiar political phenomenon. Since the time of the New Deal, it has been a working assumption among political sociologists that wealth produces conservatism. But that simple relationship does not help us to understand Orange. There are, to be sure, subdivisions of $250,000 homes going up in seaside Newport Beach. But some parts of Los Angeles County are, on the average, wealthier and less adamantly conservative than Orange County. Most of the people who make up the business and financial establishment of Southern California, the really wealthy people, live in the mountains near Beverly Hills, Glendale, or Pasadena. Norton Simon, for example, whose empire (Canada Dry and *McCall's* magazine, among other things) was headquartered in Orange County, lives in the Hancock section of Los Angeles. For the most part, Orange County is solid white upper-middle-class and middle-class America. The county features miles of large stucco houses laid out in neat subdivisions along the freeways and major crossroads. So the passion that fuels Orange County's conservatism is not a result of wealth or the lack of it.

It is, instead, a response to the sense of rootlessness and impermanence felt by the county's citizens. Orange has attracted a disproportionate share of conservatively inclined Midwestern refugees from the older, smoggier parts of Los Angeles in the west. The émigrés, looking for the stability of suburban life, have boosted the population of the county from 215,000 in 1950 to 1,420,000 in 1970. But their very numbers—Orange is the fastest growing part of California—have produced in the new surroundings little that conveys permanence. The district is full of subdivisions and shopping centers that did not exist ten years ago and which in another ten will be decaying.

Orange County has not been able to restore the old values of the Midwest, now left far behind, and the sense of rootlessness goes on. Orange Countians hoped to find a simple, uncomplicated life, but instead find themselves baffled by their own rebellious children, many of whom would rather smoke marijuana than drink and who prefer protest rallies to sock hops. Drugs, rallies, and other aspects of the youth culture come as a particularly rude shock to those who admire John Wayne. Furthermore the problems of the world outside Orange County affect the lives of the suburbanites to an extent much greater than expected: high taxes—which even Governor Reagan can't seem to control—continue to dog them, as do smog and pollution. Moreover, developers are building high-density apartment houses on the little open land that remains. The 80,000-acre Irvine Ranch, the most valuable piece of undeveloped real estate in the world, is soon to become a city of 430,000.

These beleaguered residents of Orange County and others like them are the bedrock of southern California conservatism. They are men and women who have achieved modest success by most standards. Now that success, if not their very integrity, has been attacked, sneered at, by outsiders and in many cases by their own children. Their response has been, in part, confusion and doubt. But the final response, among the people determined to find something to which they can hold fast, is hard-line Orange County conservatism. It is a kind of political persuasion that seeks not so much to conserve, in the strict sense of that word, as to restore a vague something that never existed.

In Ronald Reagan, therefore, these conservatives find the articulation of what seems to escape their lives. Reagan's manner is at once assured and assuring. A very pleasant and nice man, Reagan uplifts his many followers, telling them that they have nothing to be ashamed of, that they have built a great country, that nothing is wrong with America and Orange County except the radicals who find fault with them.

Yet Reagan's conservatism has disappointed some of his supporters. So far, the Governor has not been able to provide his constituency with the relief from modern frustrations that he has promised them. In the short run, Reagan and the California radicals feed on each other: each helps the other to win recruits. But in the long run, a politics that believes that stern parenthood can bring the children home is bound to fail. The same can be said for a policy of benign neglect, a course of non-action that simply will not restrain the black militants.

The experts felt that Ronald Reagan was going to win reelection in 1970 by a margin even more convincing than his smashing success of 1966. He did not. Jess Unruh cut the Governor's margin in half. Reagan suffered especially heavy losses in the working- and middle-class suburbs of Los Angeles and Orange counties. Reagan promised to reestablish traditional values. Unable to do so, he lost votes in 1970.

But despite losses in Orange County, the district still remains the strongest source of the Governor's support. With 7% of the state's population, the county produced 32% of his statewide margin. For its congressional representation, the 35th district continues to choose ultraconservatives. James B. Utt, who represented the district since 1952, died in 1970, and his successor in Congress is former state Sen. John G. Schmitz, a member of the John Birch Society. Schmitz, who won 67% of the vote in 1970, will undoubtedly be reelected in 1972. The new Orange County district won in the 1970 census will possess a congressman of the same ideological stripe, perhaps state Sen. Dennis Carpenter, currently the Republican State Chairman.

Census Data 1970 pop. 871,862; deviation from current state average, +66.0%; change 1960–70, +101.2%. Metro. 100%, 18.6% central city.

1970 Share of Federal Outlays $775,152,000 (average outlay per district, California 34–37)

DOD	$496,071,000	HEW	$146,012,000
AEC	$2,845,000	HUD	$3,267,000
NASA	$12,532,000	OEO	$1,050,000
DOT	$17,503,000	DOA	$2,959,000
		Other	$92,912,000

Federal Military-Industrial Commitments (California 34–37, San Diego and Orange counties listing)

DOD Contractors North American Rockwell (Anaheim), $500.069m: Minuteman missile guidance systems; Atlas missile propulsion systems; ships' guidance systems. Teledyne Ryan (San Diego), $98.356m: Firebee target missile drone. Philco-Ford Div., Ford Motor Co. (Newport Beach), $50.762m: Chaparral missile system; 25-mm and 30-mm aircraft gun systems.

General Dynamics (San Diego), $27.474m: design of aircraft radar system; Atlas booster production. Interstate Electronics (Anaheim), $18.776m: Poseidon missile evaluation equipment. Rohr Corp. (Chula Vista), $17.514m: amphibious landing craft; various aircraft and helicopter assemblies. International Harvester (San Diego), $15.566m: 10-kw turbo-alternators. Collins Radio (Newport Beach), $15.429m: VLF radio sets. Wells Marine Div., City Investing (Costa Mesa), $13.466m: 20-mm projectiles; machine gun belt links; artillery fuze delay plungers. Susquehanna Corp. (Costa Mesa), $10.343m: unspecified. U. of California (La Jolla), $7.912m: unspecified research. National Steel & Shipbuilding (San Diego), $7.348m: ship repair. Campbell Machine (San Diego), $6.536m: ship overhaul. Stromberg Datagraphics Div., General Dynamics (San Diego), $5.696m: tactical display groups. Cubic Corp. (San Diego), $5.587m: unspecified.

DOD Installations Fleet Anti-Submarine Warfare School (San Diego). Fleet Anti-Air Warfare Training Center (San Diego). Marine Corps Base (Camp Pendleton). Marine Corps Recruit Depot (San Diego). El Toro Marine Corps Air Station (Santa Ana). Marine Corps Air Facility (Santa Ana). Naval Air Rework Facility (San Diego). Naval Air Station (Miramar). North Island Naval Air Station (San Diego). Coronado Naval Amphibious Base (San Diego). Ream Field Naval Air Station (San Ysidro). Naval Undersea Warfare Center (San Diego). Naval Communication Station (San Diego). Naval Hospital (Camp Pendleton, Oceanside). Naval Hospital (San Diego). Naval Amphibious School (Coronado). Naval Public Works Center (San Diego). Naval Station (San Diego). Naval Supply Center (San Diego). Naval Training Center (San Diego). Naval Recruit Training Command (San Diego). Naval Electronics Laboratory (San Diego). Mt. Laguna AF Station (Mt. Laguna).

AEC Operations Gulf General Atomic (San Diego), $5.717m: research in isotopes and life sciences.

NASA Contractors General Dynamics (San Diego), $33.004m: Centaur program support and hardware.

Economic Base Electrical machinery, equipment, and supplies, esp. communication equipment; ordnance and accessories; aircraft and parts; poultry, livestock, and dairy.

The Voters

Registration 354,638 total. 122,635 D (35%); 213,026 R (60%); 2,980 AIP (1%); 990 PF (—); 15,007 other (4%).

Employment profile White collar, 50%. Blue collar, 50%.

Ethnic groups Black, 1%. Spanish surname, 6%. Oriental, 1%. Total foreign stock, 20%. Canada, Mexico, UK, 3% each; Germany, 2%; Ireland, Italy, Norway, Sweden, USSR, 1% each; others, 4%.

Presidential vote

1968	Humphrey (D)	79,687	(27%)
	Nixon (R)	198,569	(67%)
	Wallace (AIP)	17,311	(6%)

Representative

John G. Schmitz (R) Elected June 30, 1970; b. Aug. 12, 1930, Milwaukee, Wis.; home, Santa Ana; Marquette U., B.A., 1952; Long Beach State Col., M.A., 1960; USMC, Korean War; USMCR, 1952–60; married, seven children; Catholic.

Career Instr., philosophy, history, political science, Santa Ana Col., 1960– ; Calif. State Senate, 1964–70.

Offices 1208 LHOB, 202-225-5611. Also Suite 206, 4340 Campus Dr., Newport Beach 92660, 714-557-8335.

Committees

Internal Security (4th).

Interstate and Foreign Commerce (13th); Sub. on Public Health and Environment.

Group Ratings, Key Votes: Newly elected.

Election Results

1970 general:	John Schmitz (R)	192,765	(67%)
	Thomas Lenhart (D)	87,019	(30%)
	Francis Halpern (PF)	7,742	(3%)
1970 primary:	John Schmitz (R)	79,259	(60%)
	John Steiger (R)	25,081	(19%)
	William Wilcoxen (R)	21,660	(17%)
	John Ratterree (R)	5,206	(4%)

THIRTY-SIXTH DISTRICT Political Background

California 36 is the central portion of San Diego, a fast-growing (1950 pop. 334,000; 1970 pop. 696,000), sunny, conservative city. This is Navy country: Navy wives, Navy widows, Navy retirees, Navy officers who vote by absentee ballot, and, of course, huge naval bases. Most of the naval personnel live in the comfortable neighborhoods of the 36th—Mission Bay, Linda Vista, El Cajon, La Mesa—and their voting behavior, to judge from district-wide results, is very conservative. Conservatism is also the mark of the civilian middle-class residents of San Diego, some of whom were about to take vigilante action against Herbert Marcuse to remove him from a post at the La Jolla branch of the University of California.

Since 1952, the congressman from the 36th district has been Bob Wilson, an enthusiastically conservative Republican who recently concluded nine years of service as head of the Republican National Congressional Campaign Committee. Under his leadership, that body has been far more aggressive and effective than its Democratic counterpart. Wilson probably takes special pride in the 1966 campaign, when the Republicans turned out some 40 LBJ Democrats.

Wilson is a lieutenant colonel in the Marine Reserve and is also 4th ranking minority member of the House Armed Services Committee. Here he is a mainstay of the hawkish bipartisan majority. The political leanings of his home district have left him plenty of time to attend to his military and Campaign Committee duties. Wilson usually receives more than 70% of the votes of the 36th district.

Redistricting will convert the San Diego portion of the 35th district, together with part of the 36th, into a new House seat. The new district will undoubtedly elect a second conservative Republican congressman. Wilson, of course, will be reelected easily.

Census Data 1970 pop. 575,763; deviation from current state average, +9.7%; change 1960–70, +29.3%. Metro. 100%, 67.9% central city.

1970 Share of Federal Outlays $775,152,000 (average outlay per district, California 34–37)

DOD	$496,071,000	HEW	$146,012,000
AEC	$2,845,000	HUD	$3,267,000
NASA	$12,532,000	OEO	$1,050,000
DOT	$17,503,000	DOA	$2,959,000
		Other	$92,912,000

Federal Military-Industrial Commitments (See California 35 for San Diego and Orange counties listing.)

Economic Base Aircraft and parts; ordnance and accessories; nonelectrical machinery, esp. office, computing, and accounting machines. Also, higher education (San Diego State) and banking.

The Voters

Registration 234,262 total. 103,738 D (44%); 117,791 R (50%); 1,421 AIP (1%); 1,057 PF (1%); 10,255 other (4%).

Employment profile White collar, 56%. Blue collar, 44%.

Ethnic groups Black, 1%. Spanish surname, 4%. Oriental, 1%. Total foreign stock, 19%. Canada, UK, 3% each; Germany, Italy, Mexico, 2% each; Ireland, Norway, Poland, Sweden, USSR, 1% each; others, 4%.

Presidential vote

1968	Humphrey (D)	70,529	(27%)
	Nixon (R)	125,185	(67%)
	Wallace (AIP)	13,837	(6%)

Representative

Bob Wilson (R) Elected 1952; b. April 5, 1916, Calexico; home, San Diego; San Diego State Col., 1933–35; Otis Art Inst.; Army, WWII; Lt. Col., USMCR; married, two children; Presbyterian.

Career Adv. and pub. relations, V.P., Tolle Co.; Repub. Natl. Congressional Campaign Com., 1962–71.

Offices 2235 RHOB, 202-225-3201. Also Main P.O. Bldg., P.O. Box 469, San Diego 92112, 714-239-1307.

Committees

Armed Services (4th); Sub. No. 3.

Group Ratings

	ADA	COPE	NREP	NFU	LCV	CFA	NAB	NSI	ACA
1970	20	17	82	42	0	44	89	100	67
1969	0	—	—	40	—	—	—	—	54
1968	33	0	—	20	—	—	50	—	76

Key Votes

(1) ABM	FOR	(6) 18-Yr-Vote	FOR	(11) Clean Water $	AGN
(2) SST	FOR	(7) Farm Sub Lmt	FOR	(12) Mig Wrkrs Comp	AGN
(3) Phil Pln	FOR	(8) Coop-Church	AGN	(13) Jets to Chiang	AGN
(4) No-Knock	ABS	(9) Family Asst	FOR	(14) State OEO Veto	AGN
(5) Cmutr Tax	AGN	(10) Work Stamps	FOR	(15) Park Logging	AGN

Election Results

1970 general:	Bob Wilson (R-Inc.)	132,446	(72%)
	Daniel Hostetter (D)	44,841	(24%)
	Orville Davis (AIP)	2,723	(1%)
	Walter Koppelman (PF)	5,139	(3%)
1970 primary:	Bob Wilson (R-Inc.), unopposed		
1968 general:	Bob Wilson (R)	148,854	(72%)
	Don Lindgren (D)	59,011	(28%)

THIRTY-SEVENTH DISTRICT Political Background

California 37 is the southern part of San Diego and several of its dock-side suburbs —Chula Vista and National City. It also contains much of the outlying part of the county, a sparsely inhabited area with a few Indian reservations. This part of the district is somewhat less conservative than San Diego itself. But the 37th was drawn to be a Democratic district, and accordingly it has most of San Diego's blacks (who make up 10% of the district's population) and Mexican-Americans (about 9%).

These groups provide the base of electoral support for Democratic Congressman Lionel Van Deerlin, a former TV newscaster and assemblyman who was able to build a personal following in the district even as Democratic fortunes in the state were waning. In Washington Van Deerlin serves as a member of the usually outmaneuvered pro-consumer bloc on the Interstate and Foreign Commerce Committee.

Van Deerlin's most newsworthy act in the House was to begin the assault against Adam Clayton Powell before the opening of the 90th Congress. The action eventually resulted in Powell's expulsion from the House, his vindication in the Supreme Court, and his subsequent defeat at the hands of his own district's voters.

Van Deerlin's involvement in the Powell affair apparently did not hurt him with local black voters, and it probably helped him in the district generally. Although he won 71% of the vote in 1970, Van Deerlin might well have become an ex-congressman if the Republicans had retained control of the California legislature in 1970. They did not, and so it is likely that the boundaries of the 37th will remain virtually unchanged. This means that Van Deerlin will be reelected to many more terms.

Census Data 1970 pop. 481,126; deviation from current state average, −8.4%; change 1960–70, +21.5%. Metro. 100%, 53.4% central city.

1970 Share of Federal Outlays $775,152,000 (average outlay per district, California 34–37)

DOD	$496,071,000	HEW	$146,012,000
AEC	$2,845,000	HUD	$3,267,000
NASA	$12,532,000	OEO	$1,050,000
DOT	$17,503,000	DOA	$2,959,000
		Other	$92,912,000

Federal Military-Industrial Commitments (See California 35 for San Diego and Orange counties listing.)

Economic Base Aircraft and parts and ship and boat building and repairing; ordnance and accessories; nonelectrical machinery, esp. office, computing, and accounting machines.

The Voters

Registration 167,960 total. 95,565 D (57%); 63,125 R (38%); 1,438 AIP (1%); 875 PF (1%); 6,957 other (4%).

Employment profile White collar, 43%. Blue collar, 57%.
Ethnic groups Black, 10%. Spanish surname, 9%. Oriental, 2%. Total foreign stock, 21%. Mexico, 6%; Canada, Germany, UK, 2% each; Ireland, Italy, Sweden, 1% each; others, 5%.

Presidential vote

1968	Humphrey (D)	67,401	(45%)
	Nixon (R)	70,168	(47%)
	Wallace (AIP)	12,714	(9%)

Representative

Lionel Van Deerlin (D) Elected 1962; b. July 25, 1914, Los Angeles; home, San Diego; U. of So. Calif., B.A., 1937; Army, WWII; married, six children; Episcopalian.

Career Newspaperman, radio and tv news editor, analyst.

Offices 211 CHOB, 202-225-5672. Also 205 P.O. Bldg., San Diego 92112, 714-233-6267.

Committees

Interstate and Foreign Commerce (7th); Sub. on Communications and Power.

Group Ratings

	ADA	COPE	NREP	NFU	LCV	CFA	NAB	NSI	ACA
1970	84	92	75	85	86	95	8	33	13
1969	87	—	—	80	—	—	—	—	19
1968	75	92	—	83	—	—	17	—	10

Key Votes

(1) ABM	FOR	(6) 18-Yr-Vote	FOR	(11) Clean Water $	FOR
(2) SST	FOR	(7) Farm Sub Lmt	FOR	(12) Mig Wrkrs Comp	FOR
(3) Phil Pln	FOR	(8) Coop-Church	FOR	(13) Jets to Chiang	AGN
(4) No-Knock	FOR	(9) Family Asst	FOR	(14) State OEO Veto	AGN
(5) Cmutr Tax	ABS	(10) Work Stamps	AGN	(15) Park Logging	AGN

Election Results

1970 general:	Lionel Van Deerlin (D-Inc.)	93,952	(72%)
	James Kuhn (R)	31,968	(25%)
	Faye Brice (AIP)	2,962	(2%)
	Fritjof Thygeson (PF)	1,386	(1%)
1970 primary:	Lionel Van Deerlin (D-Inc.)	43,660	(87%)
	Donald Shepherd (D)	6,765	(13%)
1968 general:	Lionel Van Deerlin (D)	96,130	(65%)
	Mike Schaeffer (R)	52,547	(35%)

THIRTY-EIGHTH DISTRICT Political Background

California 38, unlike most southern California districts, is not so much a part of the Los Angeles megalopolis, but more like a little empire of its own. It includes the heavily Mexican-American and Democratic heart of San Bernardino—added to the district in 1968 to make the seat safer for then Rep. John Tunney. Also in the district, a few miles south of San Bernardino, is the city of Riverside (pop. 140,000), a fast-growing retirement haven and former orange-growing center. To the east, toward Arizona, is Palm Springs, the wealthy desert oasis where there are nearly as many swimming pools as people, and Palm Desert, where ex-President Eisenhower used to spend his winters. The eastern boundary of the district is the Colorado River (the Arizona boundary), where thermometers usually record the highest temperatures in the United States.

To the south is Imperial County, 40 years ago a barren desert, but now, thanks to irrigation water diverted from Hoover and Parker dams, one of the richest farming lands in the nation. Poetry has been written about making the desert bloom, but the story of the Imperial Valley is mostly a matter of economics. Despite the Reclamation Act's 160-acre limit on farms receiving diverted water, most of the Imperial Valley is owned in huge tracts. The owners of these tracts now receive giant windfalls from the low rates charged for government-provided irrigation water.

Local OEO-funded lawyers have attempted to get the 160-acre limit enforced. But so much money is at stake—the Valley land is said to be worth $700 million with water and very little without—that the limit will probably never become fact. Politically, the Imperial County landowners count for much more than the more numerous Mexican-Americans who tend their fields. So every congressman from the 38th—including John Tunney—has supported the position of the owners in the Reclamation Act controversy.

In the early '60's, John V. Tunney, son of the former heavyweight boxing champion and law school roommate of Ted Kennedy, served in the Judge Advocates' Corps at March Air Force Base near Riverside. He and his Dutch-born wife liked the area and decided to stay after his military hitch was up. As it turned out, Tunney spent most of his time in Washington. He ran for Congress in 1964 and was elected; his opponent, a Republican, had won two years earlier largely because the Democratic incumbent was gravely ill. Tunney was reelected in 1966, and, after downtown San Bernardino was added to the district, he won 63% of the vote in 1968. After that victory—unusual in a district which almost always goes Republican in statewide races—he began to think about bigger things. Anticipating George Murphy's vulnerability, he decided to run for the Senate, and he won.

Tunney left his administrative assistant, David Tunno (*sic*), to run for his old seat. But, while Tunney won big, Tunno lost by 3,000 votes to Republican Assemblyman Victor Veysey. Veysey is from Imperial County and can be expected, like his predecessor, to support the interests of the large growers.

The advantages of incumbency are such that a contest like the one here in 1970—in which a candidate wins by a mere 2% of the vote—usually determines the district's representation for the next 10 years. Gov. Reagan and the Democratic legislature will bargain over redistricting. After all is said and done, they will probably agree to strengthen all incumbents. This means that San Bernardino, the only part of the district where Veysey lost heavily in 1970, will be removed from the 38th. Then, using his congressional mailing privileges, Republican Veysey will no doubt be able to increase his margins over the years just like Democrat Tunney before him. Accordingly, Veysey can be expected to remain in the House for some time.

Census Data 1970 pop. 595,515; deviation from current state average, +13.4%; change 1960–70, +37.1%. Metro. 87.5%, 28.0% central city.

1970 Share of Federal Outlays $465,730,139

DOD	$121,855,000	HEW	$188,352,167
AEC	$348,410	HUD	$426,413
NASA	$39,662	OEO	$1,533,731
DOT	$34,264,050	DOA	$38,651,833
		Other	$80,258,873

Federal Military-Industrial Commitments

DOD Installations Naval Air Facility (El Centro). March AFB (Riverside). Point Arena AF Station (Point Arena).

Economic Base Poultry, livestock, and cotton; aircraft and parts; primary metal industries; electronic components and accessories, and other electrical machinery, equipment, and supplies.

The Voters

Registration 214,567 total. 112,738 D (53%); 92,028 R (43%); 1,895 AIP (1%); 397 PF (–); 7,509 other (4%).

Employment profile White collar, 40%. Blue collar, 60%.

Ethnic groups Black, 5%. Spanish surname, 18%. Oriental, 2%. Total foreign stock, 26%. Mexico, 13%; Canada, Germany, UK, 2% each; Italy, Sweden, USSR, 1% each; others, 4%.

Presidential vote

1968	Humphrey (D)	87,208	(41%)
	Nixon (R)	105,379	(50%)
	Wallace (AIP)	19,940	(9%)

Representative

Victor Vincent Veysey (R) Elected 1970; b. April 14, 1915, Los Angeles; home, Brawley; Calif. Inst. of Tech., B.A., 1936; Harvard U., M.B.A., 1938; married, four children; Presbyterian.

Career Rancher; Instr. in industrial relations and industrial management, Caltech, Stanford U.; Calif. State Assembly, 1962–70.

Offices 1227 LHOB, 202-225-2305.

Committees

Education and Labor (14th); Subs. (1) Agricultural Labor, (2) Gen. Sub. on Education, (3) Sel. Sub. on Labor.

Group Ratings, Key Votes: Newly elected.

Election Results

1970 general:	Victor Veysey (R)	87,479	(50%)
	David Tunno (D)	85,648	(49%)
	William Pasley (AIP)	2,481	(1%)
1970 primary:	Victor Veysey (R)	28,153	(47%)
	William Norris (R)	13,415	(23%)
	Norman Davis (R)	8,236	(14%)
	Richard Purviance (R)	6,226	(10%)
	Henry Munson (R)	3,623	(6%)

COLORADO

Political Background

To the tourist, Colorado means hiking in the Rockies, skiing at Aspen, or panning for gold in Central City. But the part of Colorado that matters most politically is the thin strip of land along the Rockies' Eastern Slope, where the arid plateau of eastern Colorado suddenly turns into mountains. Two-thirds of Colorado's voters live on this sliver of land running up and down the state, and the proportion is growing—Eastern Slope population was up 33% in the '60's compared with 10% for the rest of the state. Attracted by the temperate climate, nearby recreation areas, and economic prosperity, newcomers continue to arrive in metropolitan Denver (which contains more than half of the state's population) and other Eastern Slope cities like Colorado Springs, Boulder, Greeley, and Fort Collins.

With one major exception—the large Mexican-American population in Denver, Pueblo, and the southern part of the state—Colorado is a remarkably homogeneous place. It has no readily identifiable voting blocs that have traditionally pitted themselves against each other. The Republicans here have won the lion's share of recent elections, but they do not constitute an overwhelming political force. Moreover, the tactics of Reagan's kind of conservative Republicanism have not gone over well with the voters. In 1970, the Republican candidates for regents of the University of Colorado campaigned on a platform which called for a crackdown on student agitators. But the school's alumni, who felt there had been very little unrest on the university campus, took offense and the voters installed the Democratic candidates. Meanwhile the Republicans made a sweep of other state offices.

The Republican domination of Colorado politics dates from a determined push in 1962 which replaced two aging Democratic incumbents with Gov. John Love and Sen. Peter Dominick. Both of these men have been reelected ever since. Dominick, whose pace has been slowed by a recent heart attack, sits on the Armed Services and Labor and Public Welfare committees. A Stamford, Connecticut, native and Yale College man, Dominick is known as one of the more ideological of the Senate conservatives. The state's senior senator, Gordon Allott, an articulate conservative and Nixon Administration supporter, has been in the Senate since 1954. As ranking Republican on the Appropriations Committee's HUD-Space-Science Subcommittee, Allott has been a leading opponent of liberal moves to cut spending on programs like space exploration and the SST. Allott is also ranking minority member of the Interior and Insular Affairs Committee, a congressional unit which handles much legislation of great importance to Colorado. Finally, he is currently chairman of the Senate Republican Policy Committee. Allott is an important man in Washington.

Both Allott and Dominick have proven to be strong vote-getters in recent years. Allott, who is from eastern Colorado, runs especially well in the state's rural areas, while Dominick, who once (1960–62) represented the Denver suburbs in the House, does best in the Denver metropolitan area. Allott may face opposition in 1972 from ex-Lt. Gov. Mark Hogan, who held the traditional steppingstone office in Colorado politics and who in 1970 gave Gov. Love his stiffest test to date.

Colorado, like most western states, has something of an aversion to large federal spending in the abstract. It is, nevertheless, the beneficiary of much federal government activity. Denver, the largest city in the Rocky Mountains, is regional headquarters for the federal bureaucracies. There is also a host of military and Atomic Energy installations in the state. Recently, the latter have engendered some controversy. In 1969 there was a fire at the Rocky Mountain Flats AEC plant just north of Denver. After the fire, it was discovered that wind-blown radium tailings—sandlike wastes—were emitting dangerous levels of radioactivity in and around Denver. Earlier, radium tailings were thoughtlessly used in the construction of foundations for houses in the uranium-rich Grand Junction area. As a result of these incidents, the once sacrosanct AEC has been criticized by Colorado politicians. Nevertheless, the commission continues to spend money in the state, some $105 million in fiscal 1970. And while current reductions in military and quasi-military spending have hurt places like Washington and California, Colorado as yet appears unaffected. Nor has the state's booming economy been much affected by the recent recession.

Colorado's population rose 26% in the '60's. This was the 6th-highest growth rate in the country and will give the state an additional House seat. Census figures indicate that the new fifth district of Colorado will be situated in the rapidly growing Denver suburbs. Because the Republicans control the governor's chair and both houses of the legislature, the new district will undoubtedly elect a third Republican congressman.

Electoral Votes 7

Census Data 1970 pop. 2,207,259; 1.07% of U.S. total, 31st largest; change 1960–70, +25.8%. Metro. 71.7%, 33.9% central city. 1970 per capita income, $3,751, 21st highest. 26th in number of poor.

1970 Share of Federal Tax Burden $1,853,840,000; 0.95% of U.S. total, 28th largest.

1970 Share of Federal Outlays $2,388,631,470; 1.26% of U.S. total, 26th largest. Per capital federal spending, $1,082.

DOD	$774,787,000	23rd (1.35%)	HEW	$519,359,964	31st (0.99%)
AEC	$104,887,970	9th (4.04%)	HUD	$17,313,411	32nd (0.89%)
NASA	$119,581,126	7th (3.25%)	OEO	$13,018,549	21st (1.71%)
DOT	$71,994,483	33rd (1.01%)	DOA	$176,084,540	29th (1.37%)
DOC	$36,880,184	9th (3.19%)	POD	$77,191,769	29th (1.06%)
DOI	$111,964,744	5th (4.85%)	VA	$111,400,341	30th (1.53%)
DOJ	$6,816,710	26th (1.19%)	CSC	$39,761,585	20th (0.99%)
			Other	$207,589,094	

Economic Base Livestock and wheat; food and kindred products, esp. meat products, beverages, and bakery products; nonelectrical machinery; printing, publishing, and allied industries, esp. newspapers; electrical machinery, equipment, and supplies, esp. electric transmission and distribution equipment; primary metal industries; ordnance and accessories; rubber and miscellaneous plastics products; crude petroleum and natural gas. Also, tourism.

Political Line-up Governor, John A. Love (R); seat up, 1974. Senators, Gordon Allott (R) and Peter H. Dominick (R). Representatives, 4 (2 D and 2 R). State Senate (14 D and 21 R); State House (27 D and 38 R).

The Voters

Registration 903,395 total. 319,625 D (35%); 269,864 R (30%); 313,906 other (35%).

Employment profile White collar, 46%. Blue collar, 54%.

Ethnic groups Black, 3%. Spanish surname, 9%. Total foreign stock, 15%. Germany, USSR, UK, 2% each; Italy, Mexico, Canada, Sweden, Austria, Ireland, 1% each; others, 4%.

Presidential vote

1968	Humphrey (D)	331,063	(41%)
	Nixon (R)	409,345	(51%)
	Wallace (AIP)	60,813	(8%)
1964	Johnson (D)	476,024	(62%)
	Goldwater (R)	296,767	(38%)
1960	Kennedy (D)	330,629	(45%)
	Nixon (R)	402,242	(55%)

Senator

Gordon Llewellyn Allott (R) Elected 1954, seat up 1972; b. Jan. 2, 1907, Pueblo; U. of Colo., B.A., 1927, LL.B., 1929; Army Air Corps, WWII; married, two children; Episcopalian.

Career Practicing atty., 1969– ; Prowers County Atty., 1934, 1940–46; Dist. Atty., 1946–48; Lt. Governor, 1950–54; Chm., Young Repub. National Fed., 1941–46; Exec. Com. Young Repub. Natl. Fed., 1946–49; U.S. Delegate to General Assembly of UN, 1962; Chm., Senate Repub. Policy Com., 1969.

Offices 5229 NSOB, 202-225-5941. Also 18037 Fed. Office Bldg., Denver 80202, 303-837-3451.

Committees

Appropriations (5th); Subs. (1) Defense, (2) HUD, Space, and Science, (3) Public Works, (4) Transportation and Related Agencies, (5) Treasury, Post Office, and Gen. Government.

Interior and Insular Affairs (Ranking Mbr.); Subs. (1) Indian Affairs, (2) Minerals, Materials, and Fuels, (3) Public Lands, (4) Water and Power Resources, (5) Sp. Sub. on Legislative Oversight.

Group Ratings

	ADA	COPE	NREP	NFU	LCV	NAB	NSI	ACA
1970	3	8	0	20	11	83	100	91
1969	6	—	—	27	—	—	—	80
1968	14	42	—	38	—	80	—	86

Key Votes

(1) ABM	FOR	(8) Phil Pln	AGN	(15) Coop-Church	AGN
(2) SST	FOR	(9) Vol Army	AGN	(16) Cut Oil Dpltn	AGN
(3) Busing	AGN	(10) Prison $	AGN	(17) Consumer Prot	AGN
(4) Tob Sub	FOR	(11) Cut Mil $	AGN	(18) Farm Sub Limit	FOR
(5) Carswell	FOR	(12) Defoliatn	FOR	(19) Comp Bid Sales	FOR
(6) No-Knock	FOR	(13) 18-Yr-Vote	AGN	(20) Pre-Prod Tests	AGN
(7) Seniorty	AGN	(14) Pentgn PR	FOR	(21) Cut Marjna Pen	AGN

Election Results

1966 general:	Gordon Allott (R)	368,307	(58%)
	Roy Romer (D)	266,259	(42%)
1966 primary:	Gordon Allott (R), unopposed		
1960 general:	Gordon Allott (R)	389,428	(54%)
	Robert L. Knous (D)	334,854	(46%)

Senator

Peter H. Dominick (R) Elected 1962, seat up 1974; b. July 7, 1915, Stamford, Conn.; home, Englewood; Yale U., B.A., 1937, LL.B., 1940; Army Air Corps, WWII; Col. USAFR; married, four children; Episcopalian.

Career Practicing atty., 1946–61; Colo. House of Reps., 1956–60; Colo. Senate, 1960–62.

Offices 248 OSOB, 202-225-5852. Also Suite 15030 New Fed. Bldg., Denver 80202, 303-297-3195, and First Natl. Bank Bldg., Pueblo 81003, 303-544-5277.

Committees

Armed Services (4th); Subs. (1) CIA, (2) Gen. Legislation, (3) Military Construction Authorization, (4) National Stockpile and Naval Petroleum, (5) Sp. Sub. to Review Bomber Defense, (6) Ad Hoc Sub. on Research and Dev.

Labor and Public Welfare (3rd); Subs. (1) Alcoholism and Narcotics, (2) Education, (3) Employment, Manpower, and Poverty, (4) Health, (5) Sp. Sub. on International Health, Education, and Labor Programs, (6) Sp. Sub. on National Science Foundation.

Sel. Com. on Equal Educational Opportunity (3rd).

Sel. Com. on Small Business (2nd); Subs. (1) Financing and Investment, (2) Government Regulation, (3) Science and Technology.

Jt. Com. on Atomic Energy (2nd); Subs. (1) Agreements for Cooperation, (2) Raw Materials, (3) Research, Dev., and Radiation.

Group Ratings

	ADA	COPE	NREP	NFU	LCV	NAB	NSI	ACA
1970	13	15	8	38	6	73	90	76
1969	17	—	—	56	—	—	—	80
1968	29	42	—	46	—	100	—	83

Key Votes

(1) ABM	FOR	(8) Phil Pln	AGN	(15) Coop-Church	AGN
(2) SST	FOR	(9) Vol Army	AGN	(16) Cut Oil Dpltn	AGN
(3) Busing	FOR	(10) Prison $	AGN	(17) Consumer Prot	AGN
(4) Tob Sub	FOR	(11) Cut Mil $	AGN	(18) Farm Sub Limit	FOR
(5) Carswell	FOR	(12) Defoliatn	FOR	(19) Comp Bid Sales	FOR
(6) No-Knock	FOR	(13) 18-Yr-Vote	FOR	(20) Pre-Prod Tests	AGN
(7) Seniorty	AGN	(14) Pentgn PR	FOR	(21) Cut Marjna Pen	ABS

Election Results

1968 general:	Peter H. Dominick (R)	459,952	(59%)
	Stephen McNichols (D)	325,584	(41%)
1968 primary:	Peter H. Dominick (R), unopposed		
1962 general:	Peter H. Dominick (R)	328,655	(54%)
	John A. Carroll (D)	279,586	(46%)
	Charlotte Benson (SL)	3,546	(1%)

FIRST DISTRICT Political Background

Colorado 1 is the city and county of Denver, the part of the state which most nearly resembles an Easterner's image of a city. Most of Denver, though, has a suburban atmosphere; despite occasional smog, Denver is clean and neat, its streets typically lined with comfortable one- and two-story houses. The southeast quarter of the city is a middle- to high-income area and consistently votes Republican. In the western part of the city are Mexican neighborhoods, some of them slums, and north Denver has a Negro section. The black and chicano communities of approximately equal size, show little bond of common feeling. Disputes have flared between the two groups over control of the local poverty program and other matters as well.

Recently, this seemingly placid city has been in an uproar over school desegregation policies. A liberal school board began to transfer students in order to achieve racial balance; soon after this, members of the board were drummed out of office. The new board canceled the transfers. But local lawyers—veterans of the Kennedy-McCarthy group which took over the Denver Democratic apparatus in 1968—obtained an injunction reversing the decision. The bitter controversy, in a city which has always prided itself on its racial tolerance, is probably a taste of things to come in Northern urban politics during the '70's.

One of the lawyers fighting the conservative school board was Craig Barnes, who surprised most people when he became the Democratic nominee for Congress. Congressman Byron Rogers, a Democrat first elected in 1950, had apparently grown far more comfortable with his senior colleagues in the House than with Denver voters. His votes on peace, and especially on environment issues, were severely criticized by local Democrats. Barnes's well-financed, energetically run primary campaign won 27,218 votes to Rogers' 27,188—a margin of just 30 votes. Rogers spent much of the fall challenging the results, but without success.

Meanwhile, the Republicans were not idle. Their candidate was James D. (Mike) McKevitt, who had recently won an upset victory for district attorney. Though he was behind in the polls clear into November, McKevitt won by 10,000 votes (51%). A new Mexican-American party, La Raza Unida, won 5,000 votes, most of which would otherwise have gone to Barnes. McKevitt had solid majorities in the Republican sections of the city and edged Barnes in white, middle-income areas which usually vote Democratic. Barnes thus became the only peace-oriented candidate in 1970 to beat an incumbent in the primary and then lose the general election.

McKevitt can expect some help for his 1972 campaign from the Republican legislature. Since the size of the 1st district will have to be reduced, the legislators will probably place some of the district's heavily Democratic precincts in a Republican suburban district, strengthening McKevitt's chances for reelection to the House throughout the '70's.

Census Data 1970 pop. 514,678; deviation from current state average, –6.7%; change 1960–70, +4.2%. Metro. 100%, 100% central city.

1970 Share of Federal Outlays $676,349,000 (average outlay per district, Colorado 1 and 2)

DOD	$195,937,000	HEW	$144,232,000
AEC	$44,560,000	HUD	$7,587,000
NASA	$59,442,000	OEO	$4,729,000
DOT	$15,332,000	DOA	$15,369,000
		Other	$189,163,000

Federal Military-Industrial Commitmnts (Colorado 1 and 2, metropolitan Denver listing)

DOD Contractors Martin Marietta (Denver), $101.293m: Titan missile boosters. Cardinal Meat Co. (Denver), $9.841m: foodstuffs. FTS Corp. (Denver), $8.059m: 2.75-inch rocket components; wing assemblies for Sidewinder and Chaparral missiles. Ball Brothers Research Corp. (Boulder), $6.267m: unspecified research and development. Beech Aircraft Corp. (Boulder), $6.145m: unspecified.

DOD Installations Rocky Mountain Army Arsenal (Denver). Fitzsimmons Army Hospital (Denver). AF Accounting & Finance Center (Denver). Lowry AFB (Denver).

AEC Operations Dow Chemical Co. (Rocky Flats), $42.086m.

NASA Contractors Martin Marietta Corp. (Denver), $92.763m: Skylab and Saturn program support; Martian softlander support; Apollo telescope mount. Ball Brothers Research (Boulder), $7.000m: solar orbiting observatories.

Economic Base Food and kindred products; printing, publishing, and allied industries; nonelectrical machinery; electrical machinery, equipment, and supplies, esp. electric transmission and distribution equipment. Also, tourism (Denver).

The Voters

Registration 237,608 total. 108,797 D (46%); 66,442 R (28%); 62,369 other (26%).

Employment profile White collar, 47%. Blue collar, 53%.

Ethnic groups Black, 9%. Spanish surname, 9%. Total foreign stock, 19%. Germany, 3%; USSR, UK, Italy, 2% each; Sweden, Canada, Mexico, Ireland, Poland, Austria, 1% each; others, 5%.

Presidential vote

1968	Humphrey (D)	106,081	(51%)
	Nixon (R)	92,003	(44%)
	Wallace (AIP)	11,408	(5%)

Representative

James D. (Mike) McKevitt (R) Elected 1970; b. Oct. 26, 1928, Spokane, Wash.; home, Denver; U. of Idaho, B.A., 1951; U. of Denver Law School, LL.B., 1956; Air Force, 1951–53; married, two children; Episcopalian.

Career Asst. Atty. Gen. of Colo., trial lawyer; Denver Dist. Atty., 1967–68; Pres., Colo. Dist. Attys' Assn.; Dir. and V.P., Natl. Dist. Attys' Assn.

Offices 506 CHOB, 202-225-3331. Also 1026 Fed. Bldg., 1961 Stout St., Denver 80202, 303-837-3051.

Committees

Interior and Insular Affairs (14th); Subs. (1) Irrigation and Reclamation, (2) Mines and Mining, (3) National Parks and Recreation, (4) Territorial and Insular Affairs.

Judiciary (16th) Sub. No. 1.

Sel. Com. on Small Business (7th); Subs. (1) Environment Problems Affecting Small Business, (2) Taxation, Oil Imports, and Marketing.

Group Ratings, Key Votes: Newly elected.

Election Results

1970 general:	James D. McKevitt (R)	84,643	(52%)
	Craig S. Barnes (D)	74,444	(45%)
	Salvadore Carpio, Jr. (LRU)	5,257	(3%)
1970 primary:	James D. McKevitt (R), unopposed		

SECOND DISTRICT Political Background

Colorado 2 comprises the Denver suburbs, plus Boulder, home of the University of Colorado, and a couple of sparsely populated mountain counties. Most of this area is prosperous, Anglo, and Republican. The chief exceptions are the industrial suburbs in Adams County just north of Denver, which usually vote Democratic.

The congressman from the 2nd is Republican Donald G. Brotzman, a generally reliable supporter of the Nixon Administration. Brotzman first won the seat in 1962, when then-Congressman Peter Dominick ran for the Senate; Brotzman lost it by a narrow margin in the 1964 Johnson landslide and won it back in 1966. In 1970 a peace-oriented Democratic candidate waged a vigorous campaign but could not dent the incumbent's popularity. Brotzman won 63% of the votes. At the beginning of the 92nd Congress, Brotzman was awarded a seat on the House Ways and Means Committee, and all indications are that he will be there for a long time.

The 1970 census showed that the 2nd was one of the largest districts in the country, having some 718,000 residents. (The national average is about 460,000.) Redistricting will, roughly speaking, divide the 2nd into two districts, each with a little extra territory appended. One will probably include part of the city of Denver and the other a portion of the northern Eastern Slope. This will result in two solidly Republican districts, one for Brotzman and one for a newcomer, most likely of the same moderate conservative bent. It is possible, however, that the Democrats will put up a battle in the no-incumbent seat, particularly if it includes either the university community in Boulder or Adams County, or if it happens to include both.

Census Data 1970 pop. 718,942; deviation from current state average, +30.3%; change 1960–70, +63.8%. Metro. 99.2%, 0.0% central city.

1970 Share of Federal Outlays $676,349,000 (average outlay per district, Colorado 1 and 2)

DOD	$195,937,000	HEW	$144,232,000
AEC	$44,560,000	HUD	$7,587,000
NASA	$59,442,000	OEO	$4,729,000
DOT	$15,332,000	DOA	$15,369,000
		Other	$189,163,000

Federal Military-Industrial Commitments (See Colorado 1 for metropolitan Denver listing.)

Economic Base Transportation equipment, esp. motor vehicles and motor vehicle equipment and aircraft and parts; food and kindred products; livestock and wheat. Also education (University of Colorado), tourism (Rocky Mountains), and extensive commuting to Colorado 1 (Denver).

The Voters

Registration 279,822 total. 79,073 D (28%); 84,048 R (30%); 116,701 other (42%).

Employment profile White collar, 52%. Blue collar, 48%.

Ethnic groups Black, less than 0.5%. Spanish surname, 4%. Total foreign stock, 13%. Germany, UK, 2% each; USSR, Italy, Canada, Sweden, 1% each; others, 5%.

Presidential vote

1968	Humphrey (D)	93,431	(37%)
	Nixon (R)	137,942	(55%)
	Wallace (AIP)	19,201	(8%)

Representative

Donald G. Brotzman (R) Elected 1962–64 and 1966–present; b. June 28, 1922, Logan County; home, Boulder; Colo. U. Law and Business schools; Army, WWII; married, two children; Methodist.

Career Practicing atty., 1949–59; Colo. House of Reps., 1950–52, Senate, 1952–56; Repub. Caucus leader in Colo. Senate, 1956; Repub. candidate for governor of Colo., 1954, 1956; U.S. Atty. for Colo., 1959–60.

Offices 413 CHOB, 202-225-6135. Also Room 202 Bldg. 40, Denver Fed. Ctr., Denver 80225, 303-233-3611, ext. 6079.

Committees

Ways and Means (10th).

Group Ratings

	ADA	COPE	NREP	NFU	LCV	CFA	NAB	NSI	ACA
1970	24	34	33	62	50	58	75	100	67
1969	13	—	—	46	—	—	—	—	53
1968	8	25	—	50	—	—	67	—	73

Key Votes

(1) ABM	FOR	(6) 18-Yr-Vote	FOR	(11) Clean Water $	AGN
(2) SST	AGN	(7) Farm Sub Lmt	FOR	(12) Mig Wrkrs Comp	AGN
(3) Phil Pln	FOR	(8) Coop-Church	AGN	(13) Jets to Chiang	FOR
(4) No-Knock	FOR	(9) Family Asst	FOR	(14) State OEO Veto	FOR
(5) Cmutr Tax	ABS	(10) Work Stamps	FOR	(15) Park Logging	AGN

Election Results

1970 general:	Donald G. Brotzman (R)	125,274	(63%)
	Richard G. Gebhardt (D)	72,339	(37%)
1970 primary:	Donald G. Brotzman (R), unopposed		
1968 general:	Donald G. Brotzman (R)	152,153	(63%)
	Roy H. McVicker (D)	89,917	(37%)

THIRD DISTRICT Political Background

Colorado 3 is roughly the southeastern quarter of Colorado, dominated by the two very dissimilar cities of Colorado Springs and Pueblo. Colorado Springs (pop. 135,000) is a wealthy, growing community, chiefly noted for its military installations (Fort Carson and the Air Force Academy) and its tourist attractions (Pike's Peak and the Garden of the Gods). The city, a Rocky Mountain version of San Diego, is heavily conservative and Republican. Pueblo (pop. 97,000) is a blue-collar city dominated by a giant steel mill. It has not had significant population growth lately, and its voters, especially the large number of Mexican-Americans, are heavily Democratic. Most of the rest of the district, except for some irrigated farmland along the Arkansas River, is flat, arid, empty plateau, with a few sparsely populated crossroads towns. There is a significant Spanish-speaking and Democratic population in some of the southern counties along the New Mexico border.

Congressman Frank Evans of the 3rd district is a classic illustration of the advantages of incumbency in congressional elections. Before 1964, the district was considered to be safely in the hands of veteran (1940–48, 1950–64) Republican J. Edgar Chenoweth. In 1964, Evans, a little-known state legislator from Pueblo, squeaked through to a narrow victory in the Johnson landslide. During the next two years Evans enjoyed the use of the congressional frank and built up recognition of his name in the district. He was reelected despite a strong Republican effort. In 1970, after six years of Evans' incumbency, the Republicans could put up only weak opposition, even though they normally carry the district in other races; Evans won in a 66% landslide, carrying Colorado Springs for the first time.

Though the Republicans will be doing the redistricting in Colorado, Evans appears to be in good shape. The redistricters know that Republican chances of regaining the 3rd will be excellent if he doesn't run (he has been mentioned as a possible opponent for Sen. Gordon Allott in 1972), and nonexistent if he does. Accordingly, there will be no point in altering the 3rd's boundaries significantly, and Evans—now a junior member of the House Appropriations Committee—will probably continue winning reelection in the '70's.

Census Data 1970 pop. 501,242; deviation from current state average, –9.2%; change 1960–70, +20.7%. Metro. 70.7%, 46.4% central city.

1970 Share of Federal Outlays $651,547,970

DOD	$372,498,000	HEW	$111,744,722
AEC	$118	HUD	$1,290,075
NASA	$166,595	OEO	$2,251,306
DOT	$14,319,461	DOA	$64,067,612
		Other	$85,210,081

Federal Military-Industrial Commitments

DOD Contractors Hewlett Packard (Colorado Springs), $6.272m: unspecified electronic equipment. Oakland Construction (Colorado Springs), $5.713m: Fort Carson construction work. Kaman Corp. (Colorado Springs), $5.582m: ABM lethality and vulnerability studies.

DOD Installations Fort Carson AB (Colorado Springs). Pueblo Army Depot (Pueblo). Air Force Academy (Colorado Springs). Ent AFB (Colorado Springs). Peterson AF Field (Colorado Springs).

Economic Base Livestock and wheat; electrical machinery, equipment, and supplies; blast furnaces, steel works, and rolling and finishing mills; printing, publishing, and allied industries. Also, tourism (Colorado Springs).

The Voters

Registration 191,065 total. 73,345 D (38%); 53,891 R (28%); 63,829 other (33%).

Employment profile White collar, 40%. Blue collar, 60%.

Ethnic groups Black, 3%. Spanish surname, 14%. Total foreign stock, 14%. Germany, Italy, Mexico, 2% each; UK, Canada, Austria, USSR, Sweden, 1% each; others, 4%.

Presidential vote

1968	Humphrey (D)	74,305	(43%)
	Nixon (R)	81,612	(48%)
	Wallace (AIP)	15,799	(9%)

Representative

Frank Edwards Evans (D) Elected 1964; b. Sept. 8, 1923, Pueblo; home, Pueblo; Pomona Col., 1941–43; U. of Denver, B.A., 1947, LL.B., 1949; Navy, WWII; married, four children; Presbyterian.

Career Practicing atty., 1950–64; Colo. House of Reps., 1961–65; Democratic Whip, 1963–65.

Offices 127 CHOB, 202-225-4761. Also 209 P.O. Bldg., Colo. Springs 80901, 303-632-7661.

Committees

Appropriations (26th); Subs. (1) Agriculture, Environmental and Consumer Protection, (2) Legislative.

Group Ratings

	ADA	COPE	NREP	NFU	LCV	CFA	NAB	NSI	ACA
1970	84	92	75	91	50	90	9	30	21
1969	80	—	—	100	—	—	—	—	6
1968	75	92	—	87	—	—	33	—	22

Key Votes

(1) ABM	AGN	(6) 18-Yr-Vote	FOR	(11) Clean Water $	AGN
(2) SST	AGN	(7) Farm Sub Lmt	AGN	(12) Mig Wrkrs Comp	FOR
(3) Phil Pln	FOR	(8) Coop-Church	FOR	(13) Jets to Chiang	AGN
(4) No-Knock	FOR	(9) Family Asst	FOR	(14) State OEO Veto	AGN
(5) Cmutr Tax	AGN	(10) Work Stamps	AGN	(15) Park Logging	AGN

Election Results

1970 general:	Frank E. Evans (D)	87,000	(64%)
	John C. Mitchell, Jr. (R)	45,610	(33%)
	Martin P. Serna (LRU)	1,828	(1%)
	Walter N. Cranson (Peace)	1,598	(1%)
1970 primary:	Frank E. Evans (D), unopposed		
1968 general:	Frank E. Evans (D)	88,368	(52%)
	Paul Bradley (R)	81,173	(48%)

FOURTH DISTRICT Political Background

Colorado 4 comprises the Western Slope of the Rockies and several counties in the northeastern part of the state. The district contains most of Colorado's majestic mountains and the sites of many of the state's successive mining booms in gold, silver, and, more recently, uranium. The mountain areas are in general sparsely populated; the biggest city in the western part of the district is Grand Junction (pop. 20,000). Some of the valleys in the 4th, however, are being transformed by winter sports developments, like those in Aspen and Vail.

The political map of the Western Slope reflects the diverse origins of the first settlers, who passed down their preferences, usually without variation, to their descendants. The Eastern Slope counties, added in the 1964 redistricting, have almost come to dominate the geographically larger portion west of the Continental Divide. The Eastern Slope now contains 48% of the district's population and, since it is heavily Republican, would probably tip the district in that direction were it not for the presence of Democratic Congressman Wayne Aspinall.

First elected in 1948, Aspinall now serves as chairman of the House Interior and Insular Affairs Committee. His policies as chairman have been attacked by ecology-minded groups, but such attacks seem to have had little impact in the district. The voters of the 4th, like those in many mountain West areas rich in scenic beauty and untouched wilderness, seem more eager to exploit their environment than to protect it. Aspinall had primary opposition in 1970—his first since 1948—from a peace-oriented Eastern Slope candidate, but won with ease.

Theoretically, the 4th should elect a Republican congressman. A 1970 Republican poll showed the district to be the strongest in Colorado in its support of Nixon Administration policies. Encouraged, Republican candidate Bill Gossard waged an energetic campaign, but, as one of his supporters said, "It's awful tough to get to the right of old Wayne." "Old Wayne's" share of the votes was held down to 54%—low for him—only because he failed to carry Weld and Larimer counties on the Eastern Slope. It is likely that part of these counties will be added to one of the two suburban Denver districts by the Republican legislature, thus making Aspinall's hold on the 4th even more secure. At the same time, it is clear that if Aspinall (who was 74 in 1970) should step down, a Republican candidate would probably win the seat.

Census Data 1970 pop. 472,397; deviation from current state average, −14.4%; change 1960–70, +16.4%. Metro. 0.0%, 0.0% central city.

1970 Share of Federal Outlays $384,384,568

DOD	$10,416,000	HEW	$119,151,949
AEC	$15,768,442	HUD	$849,301
NASA	$530,033	OEO	$1,316,460
DOT	$27,011,911	DOA	$96,648,158
		Other	$112,692,314

Federal Military-Industrial Commitments

AEC Operations Union Carbide Corp. (Uravan), $11.507m.

Economic Base Livestock and wheat; metal mining. Also, tourism (Rocky Mountain National Park).

The Voters

Registration 194,900 total. 58,410 D (30.0%); 65,483 (33.6%); 71,007 other (36.4%).

Employment profile White collar, 37%. Blue collar, 63%.

Ethnic groups Black, 0%. Spanish surname, 10%. Total foreign stock, 13%. USSR, 3%; Germany 2%; Mexico, UK, Sweden, Italy, Canada, 1% each; other 4%.

Presidential vote

1968	Humphrey (D)	61,357	(35%)
	Nixon (R)	97,788	(56%)
	Wallace (AIP)	14,405	(8%)

Representative

Wayne Norviel Aspinall (D) Elected 1948; b. April 3, 1896, Middleburg, Ohio; home, Palisade; U. of Denver, B.A., 1919, LL.B., 1925; Army, WWI and WWII; married, four children; Methodist.

Career Schoolteacher, 1919, 1921, 1925–33; Pres., School Bd., 1920–22; Trustee, Palisade, 1926–34; practicing atty., 1925–48; Colo. House of Reps., 1931–38.

Offices 2313 RHOB, 202-225-4431. Also Fed. Bldg., P.O. Box 604, Grand Junction 81501, 303-243-1736.

Committees

Interior and Insular Affairs (Chm.).

Standards of Official Conduct (4th).

Jt. Com. on Atomic Energy (3rd); Subs. (1) Chm., Raw Materials, (2) Legislation.

Group Ratings

	ADA	COPE	NREP	NFU	LCV	CFA	NAB	NSI	ACA
1970	28	60	33	85	50	83	40	80	25
1969	13	—	—	80	—	—	—	—	27
1968	33	62	—	88	—	—	50	—	22

Key Votes

(1) ABM	ABS	(6) 18-Yr-Vote	FOR	(11) Clean Water $	AGN
(2) SST	FOR	(7) Farm Sub Lmt	AGN	(12) Mig Wrkrs Comp	AGN
(3) Phil Pln	ABS	(8) Coop-Church	FOR	(13) Jets to Chiang	AGN
(4) No-Knock	FOR	(9) Family Asst	AGN	(14) State OEO Veto	AGN
(5) Cmutr Tax	FOR	(10) Work Stamps	AGN	(15) Park Logging	AGN

Election Results

1970 general:	Wayne N. Aspinall (D)	76,244	(55%)
	Bill Gossard (R)	62,169	(45%)
1970 primary:	Wayne N. Aspinall (D)	19,224	(72%)
	Richard L. Perchlik (D)	7,544	(28%)
1968 general:	Wayne N. Aspinall (D)	92,680	(55%)
	Fred E. Anderson (R)	76,776	(45%)

CONNECTICUT

Political Background

Connecticut is the state of the straight party lever. For years, in order to vote for anyone, you had to pull the straight party lever; only after that could you adjust the pullers to vote for a candidate of another party. As a result, Connecticut has the lowest number of ticket-splitters in the nation. This means that strength at the top of the ticket—governor in off-years, President in presidential years—is all-important. In the 1956 Eisenhower landslide, for example, the state elected six Republican congressmen and no Democrats. Two years later, when Abe Ribicoff was reelected governor by a record margin, the state elected six Democrats and no Republicans.

It is no surprise, then, that Connecticut has traditionally had the strongest party machines in the nation. Party nominees are chosen by conventions, gatherings of political underlings whose glory (or financial gain) depends on identification with and loyalty to the machine. Under a Connecticut law, only a candidate with 20% of the convention votes can enter a primary. There were no statewide primaries whatever until 1970, which testifies to the monolithic character of both Connecticut political parties.

In many ways this system performed well, particularly for the Democratic party, which produced leaders like Sen. Abraham Ribicoff and controlled the governorship—top priority for the machine—for 16 years straight. The Democrats' success was in part due to that timeworn device, the balanced ticket. Connecticut, like most Northeastern states, is full of hyphenated Americans of every description. More than half the population is Catholic; about the same number retain some kind of ethnic consciousness. The most notable ethnic group is the Italians, who are especially numerous in the industrialized cities and their middle-class suburbs along Long Island Sound and in the Connecticut River Valley. The state also has sizable numbers of Irish, Poles, French-Canadians, and Jews.

The archetypal Connecticut Yankees, whose ancestors, upon the election of godless Thomas Jefferson, feared for the safety of their womenfolk, dominated the state's politics through the 1930's. They still exist in sparsely populated towns away from the cities, but even there the Yankees have been joined by significant numbers of relative newcomers. Most of the state's WASP voters are affluent suburbanites from the towns in Fairfield County. It is a political ritual these days for Connecticut office-seekers to ride the New Haven Railroad from Fairfield County into New York City to campaign among the commuters. These people help to keep the per capita income of Connecticut second only to that of Washington, D.C. The state also has blacks and Puerto Ricans living in Bridgeport, Hartford, and New Haven. But because of small numbers and low voter participation, neither group swings much political weight.

Up until 1970, the undisputed king of Connecticut politics was John M. Bailey, a Harvard-educated Irishman who has been Democratic State Chairman since 1946 and was his party's national chairman from 1961 to 1968. Bailey carefully balanced his tickets, groomed strong candidates like Ribicoff, and kept his organization well-fed by controlling the governorship. But Bailey has not been able to cope with the new politics arising from the Vietnam war issue. In 1967, he announced that Lyndon Johnson was going to be the Democratic candidate for President in 1968, and that was that. Meanwhile, insurgent forces were building strength across the state and found a leader in the Rev. Joseph Duffey, a McCarthy supporter who became national chairman of Americans for Democratic Action. Early on, Duffey indicated an intention to run for the Senate in 1970 against the late Thomas J. Dodd, whose censure by the Senate was assumed to have ended his career. Dodd had never been a particular favorite of Bailey's. The Senator had built up his own strong following during the '50's among anti-Communist Catholic Democrats. In 1958 Dodd had more or less forced Bailey to give him the Senate nomination. Not caring much for either Duffey or Dodd, Bailey decided to run a nonentity in the 1970 elections, Stamford businessman Alphonsus J. Donahue, whose presumed victory could be attributed to nothing other than loyal organization votes.

Bailey's plan didn't work. Dodd, stricken with a heart attack, withdrew from the race (temporarily, as it turned out), and Duffey and a third candidate got enough votes at the convention to force a primary. The primary exposed Bailey's clay-footed organization. While Duffey was consolidating peace-minded communities and winning union support, Bailey's old reliables relaxed over long lunches and discussed printing up slates for election day. Duffey beat Bailey's man by a solid 12,000 votes, cutting heavily into blue-collar areas and racking up solid majorities in white-collar suburbs.

The general election revealed even more starkly the impotence of the Bailey machine. The organization put up Hartford Congressman Emilio Daddario for the governorship, Bailey's prime concern. But Daddario proved to be a lackluster candidate, while the Republican nominee, Congressman Thomas Meskill, waged a strong campaign. Dodd, perhaps concerned over a possible Justice Department income tax indictment, decided to reenter the Senate race as an independent. With weakness at the top of the ticket, Duffey and Dodd split the usual Democratic vote formerly held together by the balanced ticket. Duffey won substantial margins in Hartford and New Haven, but Dodd carried several important blue-collar suburbs dominated by Italian and Polish-American voters. The Republican Senate candidate, Congressman Lowell P. Weicker, Jr.—the wealthy heir to the Squibb drug fortune—ran somewhat behind Meskill. But Weicker's 42% of the vote was enough to win.

The Administration immediately cited Weicker's victory as a source of support for its policies. The Senator-elect, however, was at pains to make clear he would not be an Administration rubber stamp; and he has voted against the Administration, for example, on the SST.

Connecticut's senior senator, Abraham Ribicoff, was reelected easily in 1968. Before that election, some observers thought his anti-Daley comments at the Chicago convention might cause him trouble. But Ribicoff now enjoys considerable seniority in the Senate, serving as chairman of an important Government Operations subcommittee. The congressional unit has, among other things, investigated corruption in army PX operations. Ribicoff has generally sided with the Senate liberals, but has dissented from them on one important issue, racial segregation. He argues that there is just as much segregation in the North, especially in the suburbs, as in the South. The Connecticut Senator has joined with Southerners and a growing number of Northern liberals in a move to impose the same requirements for metropolitan integration in Northern areas as in places like troubled Charlotte, North Carolina. His actions have jeopardized some aspects of the bipartisan civil rights consensus, but Ribicoff's position is obviously sincere. It is a clear political risk in a heavily suburban state like Connecticut to insist that Northern suburbs be integrated.

With a Republican in the governor's chair and the Democrats still in control of the legislature, it seems safe to predict that the congressional redistricting to be done will not work any revolutions. Only minor adjustments are needed to meet the one-man-one-vote standard. The shape of the congressional districts, of course, usually has little influence on the outcome of major statewide elections, of which, except for the 1972 presidential contest, there will be none until 1974. Odds are that the Bailey machine will continue to disintegrate and that the split in the Democratic ranks, symbolized by the contrast between Duffey and Dodd, will strengthen trends toward Republican dominance of statewide races.

Electoral Votes 8

Census Data 1970 pop. 3,032,217; 1.47% of U.S. total, 24th largest; change 1960–70, +19.6%. Metro. 82.6%, 35.21% central city. 1970 per capita income, $4,807, 2nd highest. 35th in number of poor.

1970 Share of Federal Tax Burden $4,117,470,000; 2.11% of U.S. total, 14th largest.

1970 Share of Federal Outlays $3,101,930,380; 1.64% of U.S. total, 21st largest. Per capita federal spending, $1,023.

DOD	$1,356,342,000	15th (2.36%)	HEW	$734,133,142	25th (1.40%)
AEC	$6,506,630	23rd (0.25%)	HUD	$72,629,129	7th (3.73%)
NASA	$26,207,997	18th (0.71%)	OEO	$5,869,884	36th (0.72%)
DOT	$85,800,969	35th (1.20%)	DOA	$17,869,539	48th (0.14%)
DOC	$2,874,235	43rd (0.25%)	POD	$106,935,291	22nd (1.47%)
DOI	$7,386,182	46th (0.32%)	VA	$108,691,991	33rd (1.47%)
DOJ	$7,547,338	21st (1.32%)	CSC	$168,467,728	7th (4.19%)
			Other	$394,641,325	

Economic Base Transportation equipment, esp. aircraft and parts; nonelectrical machinery, esp. metalworking machinery and equipment and general industrial machinery and equipment; electrical machinery, equipment, and supplies, esp. electrical components and accessories; fabricated metal products, esp. cutlery, hand tools, and general hardware; fabricated structural metal products and metal stampings; primary metal industries, esp. rolling, drawing, and extruding of nonferrous metals; rubber and miscellaneous plastics products; ordnance and accessories; apparel and other finished products made from fabrics and similar materials, esp. women's, misses', and juniors' outerwear; textile mill products, esp. yarn and thread mills.

Political Line-up Governor, Thomas J. Meskill (R); seat up, 1974. Senators, Abraham A. Ribicoff (D) and Lowell P. Weicker (R). Representatives, 6 (4 D and 2 R). State Senate (19 D and 17 R); State House (99 D and 78 R).

The Voters

Registration 1,388,184 total. 485,657 D (35%); 401,877 R (29%); 500,650 other (36%).

Employment profile White collar, 44%. Blue collar, 56%.

Ethnic groups Black, 6%. Puerto Rican, 1%. Total foreign stock, 39%. Italy, 9%; Canada, Poland, 5% each; UK, Ireland, Germany, 3% each; USSR, 2%; Sweden, Austria, Hungary, Czech., 1% each; others, 5%.

Presidential vote

1968	Humphrey (D)	621,561	(50%)
	Nixon (R)	556,721	(44%)
	Wallace (AIP)	76,650	(6%)
1964	Johnson (D)	826,629	(68%)
	Goldwater (R)	390,996	(32%)
1960	Kennedy (D)	657,055	(54%)
	Nixon (R)	565,813	(46%)

Senator

Abraham A. Ribicoff (D) Elected 1962, seat up 1974; b. April 9, 1910, New Britain; home, Hartford; New York U., U. of Chicago, LL.B., 1933; married, two children; Jewish.

Career Conn. General Assembly, 1938–42; Municipal Judge, Hartford, 1941–43, 1945–47; House of Reps., 1948–52; Governor of Conn., 1954–1961; Secy., Dept. of Health, Ed., and Welfare, 1961–62.

Offices 321 OSOB, 202-225-2823. Also 707 New Fed. Bldg., 450 Main St., Hartford 06103, 203-244-3713.

Committees

Finance (6th).

Government Operations (5th); Subs. (1) Chm., Executive Reorganization, (2) Permanent Investigations.

Jt. Economic Com. (4th); Subs. (1) Chm., Economic Statistics, (2) Fiscal Policy, (3) Foreign Economic Policy, (4) Inter-American Economic Relationships, (5) Urban Affairs.

Group Ratings

	ADA	COPE	NREP	NFU	LCV	NAB	NSI	ACA
1970	94	100	93	81	82	20	100	0
1969	89	—	—	75	—	—	—	0
1968	86	100	—	62	—	25	—	45

Key Votes

(1) ABM	AGN	(8) Phil Pln	FOR	(15) Coop-Church	FOR
(2) SST	AGN	(9) Vol Army	FOR	(16) Cut Oil Dpltn	FOR
(3) Busing	FOR	(10) Prison $	FOR	(17) Consumer Prot	FOR
(4) Tob Sub	ABS	(11) Cut Mil $	FOR	(18) Farm Sub Limit	FOR
(5) Carswell	AGN	(12) Defoliatn	AGN	(19) Comp Bid Sales	FOR
(6) No-Knock	AGN	(13) 18-Yr-Vote	FOR	(20) Pre-Prod Tests	FOR
(7) Seniorty	AGN	(14) Pentgn PR	AGN	(21) Cut Marjna Pen	FOR

Election Results

1968 general:	Abraham A. Ribicoff (D)	655,043	(54%)
	Edwin H. May, Jr. (R)	551,455	(46%)
1968 primary:	Abraham A. Ribicoff (D), unopposed		
1962 general:	Abraham A. Ribicoff (D)	527,522	(51%)
	Horace Seely-Brown, Jr. (R)	501,694	(49%)

Senator

Lowell P. Weicker, Jr. (R) Elected 1970, seat up 1976; b. May 16, 1931, Paris, France; home, Greenwich; Yale U., B.A., 1953; U. of Va., LL.B., 1958; Army, Korean War; Capt. USAR, 1959–64; married, two children; Episcopalian.

Career Atty., Conn. Assembly, 1962–68; First Selectman, Greenwich, 1963–1968; Legislative Consultant, Conn. Transport Auth., 1965; Secy., Conn. Tax Study Commission, 1966–67.

Offices 5313 NSOB, 202-225-4041. Also 1 Bank St., Stamford 06902, 203-325-3866, and Rm. 11-C Fed. Ct. Bldg., Lafayette Plaza, Bridgeport 06603, 203-335-0195.

Committees

Aeronautical and Space Sciences (4th).
District of Columbia (2nd); Sub. on Fiscal Affairs.
Public Works (7th); Subs. (1) Flood Control—Rivers and Harbors, (2) Public Buildings and Grounds.

(*Note: The following ratings and votes cover Sen. Weicker's record in the House of Representatives where he served prior to his election in 1970.*)

Group Ratings

	ADA	COPE	NREP	NFU	LCV	CFA	NAB	NSI	ACA
1970	40	64	75	82	100	35	30	80	41
1969	40	—	—	67	—	—	—	—	41

Key Votes

(1) ABM	AGN	(6) 18-Yr-Vote	FOR	(11) Clean Water $	FOR
(2) SST	AGN*	(7) Farm Sub Lmt	FOR	(12) Mig Wrkrs Comp	ABS
(3) Phil Pln	FOR	(8) Coop-Church	FOR	(13) Jets to Chiang	AGN
(4) No-Knock	FOR	(9) Family Asst	FOR	(14) State OEO Veto	AGN
(5) Cmutr Tax	ABS	(10) Work Stamps	ABS	(15) Park Logging	AGN

* *as Senator.*

Election Results

1970 general:	Lowell P. Weicker, Jr. (R)	443,008	(42%)
	Joseph P. Duffey (D)	360,094	(34%)
	Thomas J. Dodd (Ind)	260,264	(24%)
1970 primary:	Lowell P. Weicker, Jr. (R), unopposed		

FIRST DISTRICT Political Background

Connecticut 1 is Hartford and vicinity—the state's capital, the center of its great insurance industry, and the site of many of its defense plants—most notably, those of United Aircraft, producers of aircraft engines. The district is almost entirely urban, from the black and Italian low-income sections of Hartford to the industrial working-class suburbs of East Hartford and Windsor along the Connecticut River, to the high-income WASP and Jewish precincts of West Hartford and Bloomfield. Politically, the 1st is usually as heavily Democratic as any area in the state. Nowadays, even the onetime Republican stronghold of West Hartford has doubts about the Nixon brand of conservatism.

Events in 1970, however, disrupted politics as usual in the district. Six-term Congressman Emilio Daddario, a respected specialist in science programs, retired to make an unsuccessful bid for the governorship. The Democratic primary was vigorously contested —a rare happening in Connecticut. The winner, William Cotter, the anti-organization candidate, was then further dogged by a third-party candidate. The Republicans put up Ann Uccello, the mayor of Hartford (a largely ceremonial post), who enjoyed enthusiastic support in the district's Italian neighborhoods. Cotter won, but by a hair, carrying only three of the district's thirteen cities and towns. Cotter made his strongest showing in Miss Uccello's own Hartford, where the Democrat won 65% of the votes compared to the Republican's 32%.

With an incumbent Democratic congressman once again representing the district in Washington, the 1st will in all likelihood revert to its heavily Democratic voting patterns. Redistricting is unlikely to affect significantly the political make-up of the district.

Census Data 1970 pop. 483,938; deviation from current state average, —4.2%; change 1960–70, +14.5%. Metro. 99.4%, 32.7% central city.

1970 Share of Federal Outlays $666,865,000 (average outlay per district, Connecticut 1 and 6)

DOD	$359,441,000	HEW	$124,715,000
AEC	$1,413,000	HUD	$11,312,000
NASA	$10,094,000	OEO	$682,000
DOT	$6,831,000	DOA	$3,004,000
		Other	$149,374,000

Federal Military-Industrial Commitments (Connecticut 1 and 6, greater Hartford listing)

DOD Contractors United Aircraft Corp. (East Hartford and Windsor Locks), $572.627m: various aircraft engines and parts. Kaman Corp. (Bloomfield), $22.826m: helicopter design modification. Chandler Evans Inc. (West Hartford), $13.007m: helicopter engine overhaul. McGraw Edison (Bristol), $7.304m: detonating fuzes.

DOD Installations Bradley Field AF (Windsor Locks).

NASA Contractors United Aircraft Corp. (Windsor Locks), $12.411m: development of Apollo spacesuits.

Economic Base Aircraft and parts, esp. aircraft engines and engine parts; nonelectrical machinery, esp. metalworking machinery and equipment; fabricated metal products, esp. cutlery, hand tools, and general hardware; electrical machinery, equipment, and supplies. Also, insurance.

The Voters

Registration Total 223,283. 104,187 D (46.7%); 61,527 R (27.6%), 57,569 other (25.8%).

Employment profile White collar, 44%. Blue collar, 56%.

Ethnic groups Black, 4%. Puerto Rican, 1%. Total foreign stock, 39%. Italy, 9%; Canada, 5%; Poland, 4%; UK, Ireland, Germany, 3% each; USSR, 2%; Sweden, Austria, Hungary, Czech., 1% each; others, 5%.

Presidential vote

1968	Humphrey (D)	118,164	(57%)
	Nixon (R)	79,232	(38%)
	Wallace (AIP)	9,991	(5%)

Representative

William R. Cotter (D) Elected 1970; b. July 18, 1926, Hartford; home, Hartford; Trinity Col., B.A., 1949; unmarried; Catholic.

Career Mbr., Ct. of Common Council, Hartford, 1953; Aide to Governor Abraham A. Ribicoff, 1955–57; Deputy Insurance Commissioner, 1957–64; Insurance Commissioner, 1964–70.

Offices 514 CHOB, 202-225-2265. Also 450 Main St., Hartford 06114, 203-278-3156.

Committees

Banking and Currency (21st); Subs. (1) Bank Supervision and Insurance, (2) International Finance, (3) Small Business.

Science and Astronautics (14th); Subs. (1) Advanced Research and Technology, (2) International Cooperation in Science and Space.

Group Ratings, Key Votes: Newly elected.

Election Results

1970 general:	William R. Cotter (D)	88,374	(49%)
	Antonio P. Uccello (R)	87,209	(48%)
	Edward T. Coll (Public Party)	5,774	(3%)
1970 primary:	William R. Cotter (D)	21,751	(55%)
	Jay W. Jackson (D)	17,455	(45%)

SECOND DISTRICT Political Background

Connecticut 2 is made up of the four eastern counties in the state: Tolland, Windham, New London, and Middlesex. Yankee villages and high-income summer and retirement home settlements like Old Saybrook and Old Lyme on Long Island Sound take up most of the land space of the district. But the bulk of the votes are cast in small and middle-sized mill and industrial towns, the most important of which abut the Thames and Quinebaug rivers—New London, Norwich, Danielson, Putnam—all near the eastern border of the state. There is also a substantial number of blue-collar and immigrant-stock voters in and around Middletown, at the western edge of the district.

This mixture makes the 2nd a middle-of-the-road bellwether district, at least when an incumbent is not running; or when, as has happened, the race is between a congressman and an ex-congressman. William L. St. Onge (whose name reflects the French-Canadian origin of many residents of the mill towns) managed to put together a string of four consecutive victories. He could have probably won again, but he died suddenly in 1970. The Republican statewide surge was enough to provide a 53% victory (an unusually large percentage in this district) for the new Republican congressman, Robert H. Steele. Steele's father, a popular radio and TV personality in Connecticut for years, no doubt aided his son's campaign.

Because he had served as an officer in the CIA, Steele was assigned to the House Foreign Affairs Committee. That assignment is usually the road to oblivion, since the committee is not known to be particularly active. But in 1971 Steele and freshman Democrat Morgan Murphy of Illinois made a much-publicized tour of Vietnam in which they investigated drug use among American soldiers. The congressmen found that heroin was cheap and readily available and that neither the military nor the Veterans' Administration was doing much to cure addicted GI's.

A hot issue like this, which provoked a response from Nixon himself, should enhance Steele's possibilities for reelection in 1972. He seems likely to stay in the House for some time, barring a big, straight-ticket Democratic sweep in Connecticut.

Census Data 1970 pop. 533,627; deviation from current state average, +5.6%; change 1960–70, +29.5%. Metro. 50.9%, 13.7% central city.

1970 Share of Federal Outlays $425,722,730

DOD	$176,040,000	HEW	$112,444,778
AEC	$55,705	HUD	$18,211,368
NASA	$1,111,052	OEO	$748,972
DOT	$56,212,497	DOA	$4,338,327
		Other	$56,560,031

Federal Military-Industrial Commitments

DOD Contractors General Dynamics (Groton), $91.205m: conversion of various submarines to Poseidon missile system. Yardney Electric (Pawcatuck), $6.899m: batteries for torpedoes.

DOD Installations Naval Submarine Base (Groton). Naval Underseas Research and Development Center (New London). Naval Submarine School (New London).

Economic Base Textile mill products, esp. yarn and thread mills; dairy and poultry; transportation equipment, esp. aircraft and parts and motor vehicles and motor vehicle equipment. Also, higher education (University of Connecticut).

The Voters

Registration Total 231,871. 79,200 D (34%); 64,432 R (28%); 88,239 other (38%).

Employment profile White collar, 51%. Blue collar, 49%.

Ethnic groups Black, 7%. Puerto Rican, 1%. Total foreign stock, 41%. Italy, 8%; Canada, 6%; Poland, 5%; Ireland, UK, 4% each; USSR, 3%; Germany, Sweden, 2% each; Austria, 1%; others, 7%.

Presidential vote

1968	Humphrey (D)	102,339	(50%)
	Nixon (R)	89,943	(44%)
	Wallace (AIP)	10,883	(5%)

Representative

Robert H. Steele (R) Elected 1970; b. Nov. 3, 1938, Hartford; home, Vernon; Amherst Col., B.A., 1960; Columbia U., M.A., Cert. of Russian Inst., 1963; married, three children; Episcopalian.

Career Soviet Specialist for the Central Intelligence Agency, Latin America, 1963–68; securities analyst, The Travelers Insurance Company, 1968– .

Offices 1206 LHOB, 202-225-2076. Also Mail Box 1970, Vernon 06086, 203-872-9183.

Committees

Foreign Affairs (16th); Subs. (1) Foreign Economic Policy, (2) Inter-American Affairs.

Merchant Marine and Fisheries (12th); Subs. (1) Coast Guard, Coast Geodetic Survey, and Navigation, (2) Merchant Marine, (3) Oceanography.

Group Ratings, Key Votes: Newly elected.

Election Results

1970 general:	Robert H. Steele (R)	92,846	(53%)
	John F. Pickett (D)	81,492	(47%)
1970 primary:	Robert H. Steele (R), unopposed		

THIRD DISTRICT Political Background

Connecticut 3 is made up of New Haven and the surrounding towns, a heavily industrialized area where Italians are the most notable ethnic group. Yale University is there, too, but is not a significant factor in the district's congressional politics, and neither is New Haven's increasingly vociferous black community. Both Yale and the blacks, if anything, serve to focus antipathy for the rest of the district: people of generally immigrant stock who live in neat suburban New England houses—the people whose parents lived in what are now the black ghettos and whose children don't go to Yale. Only 137,000 of the 3rd's 462,000 residents still live in New Haven itself, in part because ex-mayor (1953–69) Richard Lee's famous urban renewal program destroyed more housing units than it built.

Since 1958 the district's representative has been Robert N. Giaimo. The congressman is a middle-seniority member of the House Appropriations Committee who has often attacked New Haven's poverty program. And his increasingly conservative voting record is probably an accurate reflection of his constituency's disenchantment with Great Society social legislation. Giaimo has been a political friend of New Haven Town Chairman Arthur Barbieri, a supporter of the late Sen. Dodd and an antagonist of state party chairman John Bailey. And Giaimo may emerge as one of the leaders of an ethnically oriented conservative wing of the Connecticut state Democratic party.

Since 1964, Giaimo has been winning reelection with about 55% of the votes, hardly an impressive figure for a longtime incumbent. The Congressman's showing is in part explained by third-party candidates (peace-oriented in 1966 and 1968, in 1970 a "Dodd Independent") and by the antipathy of the Yale and black communities toward Giaimo's positions on issues. The fact that Giaimo has held on probably indicates that the Republicans can't beat him. But if he were not a candidate, then splits within the Democratic Party—which are especially visible in the New Haven area—could conceivably bring about the election of a Republican congressman.

Census Data 1970 pop. 462,082; deviation from current state average, −8.6%; change 1960–70, +12.8%. Metro. 97.9%, 29.8% central city.

1970 Share of Federal Outlays $447,492,000 (average outlay per district, Connecticut 3, 4, and 5)

DOD	$153,381,000	HEW	$124,086,000
AEC	$1,209,000	HUD	$10,598,000
NASA	$1,723,000	OEO	$1,253,000
DOT	$5,309,000	DOA	$2,508,000
		Other	$147,427,000

Federal Military-Industrial Commitments (See Connecticut 4 for NYC–New Haven corridor listing.)

Economic Base Fabricated metal products, esp. cutlery, hand tools, and general hardware, and metal stampings; primary metal industries, esp. rolling, drawing, and extruding of nonferrous metals; electrical machinery, equipment, and supplies; professional, scientific, and controlling instruments, photographic and optical goods, watches and clocks; ordnance and accessories. Also, higher education (South Connecticut State College).

The Voters

Registration Total 220,627. 61,299 D (28%); 46,050 R (21%); 113,278 other (51%).

Employment profile White collar, 46%. Blue collar, 54%.

Ethnic groups Black, 2%. Puerto Rican, less than 1%. Total foreign stock, 33%. Canada, 8%; Italy, Poland, 5% each; UK, 3%; Germany, Ireland, USSR, 2% each; Sweden, 1%; others, 6%.

Presidential vote

1968	Humphrey (D)	94,258	(48%)
	Nixon (R)	88,904	(45%)
	Wallace (AIP)	15,017	(8%)

Representative

Robert N. Giaimo (D) Elected 1958; b. Oct. 15, 1919, New Haven; home, North Haven; Fordham Col., B.A., 1941; U. of Conn., LL.B., 1943; Army, WWII; Capt. USAR; married, one child; Catholic.

Career Chm., Conn. Personnel Appeals Bd., 1955–58; Third Selectman of North Haven, 1955–57; Bd. of Ed., 1949–55; Bd. of Finance, 1952–55.

Offices 2338 RHOB, 202-225-3661. Also 301 P.O. Bldg., New Haven 06510, 203-624-1308, 203-772-0800, ext. 6361, and P.O. Bldg., Stratford 06497, 203-378-8710.

Committees

Appropriations (16th); Subs. (1) D.C., (2) HUD, Space, and Science.
Jt. Com. on Congressional Operations (2nd).

Group Ratings

	ADA	COPE	NREP	NFU	LCV	CFA	NAB	NSI	ACA
1970	56	80	73	83	78	65	0	70	19
1969	40	—	—	73	—	—	—	—	38
1968	58	83	—	87	—	—	0	—	14

Key Votes

(1) ABM	FOR	(6) 18-Yr-Vote	FOR	(11) Clean Water $	AGN
(2) SST	FOR	(7) Farm Sub Lmt	FOR	(12) Mig Wrkrs Comp	FOR
(3) Phil Pln	AGN	(8) Coop-Church	FOR	(13) Jets to Chiang	FOR
(4) No-Knock	FOR	(9) Family Asst	FOR	(14) State OEO Veto	FOR
(5) Cmutr Tax	FOR	(10) Work Stamps	AGN	(15) Park Logging	AGN

Election Results

1970 general:	Robert Giaimo (D)	89,042	(55%)
	Robert J. Dunn (R)	69,048	(42%)
	Richard P. Antonetti (Dodd Ind.)	5,062	(3%)
1970 primary:	Robert Giaimo (D), unopposed		
1968 general:	Robert Giaimo (D)	102,636	(54%)
	Stelio Salmona (R)	80,696	(42%)
	Robert M. Cook (AI)	7,123	(4%)

FOURTH DISTRICT Political Background

Connecticut 4 is separated into two distinct parts: the industrial, predominantly blue-collar city of Bridgeport and the wealthy Fairfield County suburbs along Long Island Sound. But there are pockets of poverty even in towns like Stamford and Norwalk, and not all of Bridgeport is a smoggy slum. Sociologically, the two parts of the 4th have little in common—people in Westport do not shop in Bridgeport, and Bridgeport residents are rarely seen in Westport. The two would never have been joined together but for geographical happenstance. Greenwich, Stamford, et al. are part of a panhandle surrounded by New York and cannot feasibly be attached to any other part of the state. Ordinarily, the commuter towns vote Republican, though there are sizable Democratic contingents in Stamford, Norwalk, and artsy-craftsy Westport, while Bridgeport votes Democratic. Since the commuter towns have 390,000 people and Bridgeport 156,000, Republicans usually carry the 4th.

There have been exceptions, however. Democrat Donald J. Irwin won in 1958, 1964, and 1966. He was beaten in 1968 only when his hawkish views stimulated a third-party peace candidate whose presence allowed now-Senator Weicker to regain the seat for the Republicans. In 1970 the current congressman, Stewart McKinney, a former state legislator, won easily. McKinney even carried Bridgeport, as did Gov. Meskill and Sen. Weicker. These results have sometimes been ascribed to the Democrats' failure to slate an Irish Catholic. But more plausible explanations were the splits among Democrats like Duffey-Dodd, and the greater success of the Nixon-Agnew blue-collar appeal in areas within the New York City media orbit, like Bridgeport, than in those outside the orbit, like Hartford and New Haven.

The 4th, the largest of Connecticut's districts, is due for some paring down in the redistricting process. One compromise—removing part of Bridgeport from the 4th and placing it in the 3rd—would strengthen both incumbents. So this move will probably commend itself to the Democratic legislature and the Republican governor.

Census Data 1970 pop. 546,964; deviation from current state average, +8.2%; change 1960–70, +13.4%. Metro. 98.6%, 63.0% central city.

1970 Share of Federal Outlays $447,492,000 (average outlay per district, Connecticut 3, 4, and 5)

DOD	$153,381,000	HEW	$124,086,000
AEC	$1,209,000	HUD	$10,598,000
NASA	$1,773,000	OEO	$1,253,000
DOT	$5,309,000	DOA	$2,508,000
		Other	$147,427,000

Federal Military-Industrial Commitments (Connecticut 3, 4, and 5, NYC–New Haven corridor)

DOD Contractors Avco Corp. (Stratford), $149.550m: helicopter engines; ABM development. United Aircraft Corp. (Stratford), $129.672m: H-3 and H-53 helicopters. Dynamics Corp. of America (Bridgeport), $24.387m: diesel generators. Remington

Arms Co. (Bridgeport), $20.850m: production of NATO and M-16 rifle cartridges. Condec Corp. (Old Greenwich), $12.017m: engineering services for M561 (Gamma Goat) truck. Stelma Inc. (Stamford), $11.670m: unspecified. Olin Corp. (New Haven), $6.565m: production of M-16 rifle cartridges.

Economic Base Electrical machinery, equipment, and supplies, esp. communication equipment and electronic components and accessories; aircraft and parts, and other transportation equipment; nonelectrical machinery, esp. metalworking machinery equipment and special industrial machinery; fabricated metal products, esp. cutlery, hand tools, and general hardware. Also, extensive commuting to New York 17 and 19 (New York City).

The Voters

Registration Total, 252,774. 74,808 D. (29.6%); 93,891 R (37.1%); 84,075 other (33.3%).

Employment profile White collar, 47%. Blue collar, 53%.

Ethnic groups Black, 6%. Puerto Rican, 1%. Total foreign stock, 39%. Italy, 14%; Ireland, 4%; Poland, UK, USSR, Germany, 3% each; Czech., 1%; others, 7%.

Presidential vote

1968	Humphrey (D)	100,018	(43%)
	Nixon (R)	118,374	(51%)
	Wallace (AIP)	13,607	(6%)

Representative

Stewart B. McKinney (R) Elected 1970; b. Jan. 30, 1931, Pittsburgh, Pa.; home, Fairfield; Princeton U., 1949—51; Yale U., B.A., 1958; USAF, 1951–55; married, five children; Episcopalian.

Career Pres., CMF Tires; operated Lantern Point Real Estate Dev.; Conn. House of Reps., 1967–70; Minority Leader, 1969–70.

Offices 1007 LHOB, 202-225-5541. Also P.O. Box 543, Fairfield 06430, 203-259-7802; Fed. Bldg., LaFayette Blvd., Bridgeport 06603, 203-384-2286; and 1116 Summer St., Stamford 06905, 203-259-7802.

Committees

Banking and Currency (12th); Subs. (1) Consumer Affairs, (2) International Trade, (3) Small Business.

District of Columbia (10th); Subs. (1) Education, (2) Housing and Youth Affairs, (3) Public Health and Welfare.

Group Ratings, Key Votes: Newly elected.

Election Results

1970 general:	Stewart B. McKinney (R)	104,494	(57%)
	T. F. Gilroy Daly (D)	78,699	(43%)
	Eileen M. Emard (AIP)	1,428	(1%)
1970 primary:	Stewart B. McKinney (R), unopposed		

FIFTH DISTRICT Political Background

Connecticut 5 is an amalgam of some of Connecticut's less well-known cities and towns spread over the hills just north of Long Island Sound. It includes the industrial city of Waterbury and the decaying mill towns of the Naugatuck Valley to the south; the relatively prosperous working-class towns of Meriden and Wallingford in the east; and Danbury, the onetime hat-manufacturing center, in the west. All of these places tend to vote Democratic and together form a majority of the district. Between them are scattered archetypal Yankee towns with strong Republican traditions.

The 5th is generally considered safe Democratic territory and certainly has proved to be such for incumbent (since 1958) John S. Monagan. In 1970, Monagan defeated ex-Rep. Joseph Patterson (1946–58) from whom he had won the district 12 years before.

Monagan's margins are generally not large—he usually loses the Yankee small towns—but he has always piled up enough votes in Waterbury and the other industrial towns to win. There is no compelling reason to believe that he will not continue to do so. But the 5th, like all Connecticut districts, is likely to be the scene of a closely contested fight if there is no incumbent running and if the statewide ticket does not go lopsidedly in one direction or another.

In Washington, Monagan is slowly inching up the seniority ladder on the Government Operations and Foreign Affairs committees, and in a few years he should succeed to an important subcommittee chairmanship.

Census Data 1970 pop. 497,184; deviation from current state average, −1.6%; change 1960–70, +22.9%. Metro. 74.4%, 43.2% central city.

1970 Share of Federal Outlays $447,492,000 (average outlay per district, Connecticut 3, 4, and 5)

DOD	$153,381,000	HEW	$124,086,000
AEC	$1,209,000	HUD	$10,598,000
NASA	$1,723,000	OEO	$1,253,000
DOT	$5,309,000	DOA	$2,508,000
		Other	$147,427,000

Federal Military-Industrial Commitments (See Connecticut 4 for NYC–New Haven corridor listing.)

Economic Base Electrical machinery, equipment, and supplies, esp. communication equipment and electronic components and accessories; transportation equipment, esp. aircraft and parts; fabricated metal products, esp. cutlery, hand tools, and general hardware, and metal stampings; nonelectrical machinery, esp. metalworking machinery and equipment and special industrial machinery.

The Voters

Registration Total, 229,043. 78,060 D (34%); 56,895 R (25%); 94,086 other (41%).

Employment profile White collar, 39%. Blue collar, 61%.

Ethnic groups Black, 3%. Puerto Rican, 1%. Total foreign stock, 41%. Italy, 11%; Poland, 5%; Canada, Ireland, UK, Germany, 3% each; USSR, 2%; Austria, Czech., Hungary, Sweden, 1% each; others, 6%.

Presidential vote

1968	Humphrey (D)	100,841	(49%)
	Nixon (R)	89,015	(43%)
	Wallace (AIP)	16,054	(8%)

Representative

John Stephen Monagan (D) Elected 1958; b. Dec. 23, 1911, Waterbury; home, Waterbury; Dartmouth Col., B.A., 1933; Harvard Law School, LL.B., 1937; married, four children; Catholic.

Career Practicing atty., 1938–58; Alderman, Waterbury, 1940–43; Mayor, 1943–48; U.S. Delegate to American, British and Canadian Parliamentarians Conference; U.S. Delegate to Interparliamentary Union Conferences, 1965–69.

Offices 2331 RHOB, 202-225-3822. Also 11 E. Main St., Waterbury 06702, 203-754-2424.

Committees

Foreign Affairs (9th); Subs. (1) Europe, (2) Inter-American Affairs, (3) Near East.

Government Operations (9th); Subs. (1) Chm., Legal and Monetary Affairs, (2) Government Activities.

Group Ratings

	ADA	COPE	NREP	NFU	LCV	CFA	NAB	NSI	ACA
1970	68	64	75	90	88	69	36	78	31
1969	40	—	—	80	—	—	—	—	24
1968	58	83	—	94	—	—	33	—	17

Key Votes

(1) ABM	FOR	(6) 18-Yr-Vote	FOR	(11) Clean Water $	FOR
(2) SST	AGN	(7) Farm Sub Lmt	FOR	(12) Mig Wrkrs Comp	FOR
(3) Phil Pln	AGN	(8) Coop-Church	FOR	(13) Jets to Chiang	AGN
(4) No-Knock	FOR	(9) Family Asst	FOR	(14) State OEO Veto	AGN
(5) Cmutr Tax	AGN	(10) Work Stamps	AGN	(15) Park Logging	AGN

Election Results

1970 general:	John S. Monagan (D)	96,947	(55%)
	James T. Patterson (R)	78,414	(44%)
	Alphonse Avitabile (Common People)	1,727	(1%)
1970 primary:	John S. Monagan (D), unopposed		
1968 general:	John S. Monagan (D)	110,337	(56%)
	Gaetano A. Russo, Jr. (R)	85,591	(44%)

SIXTH DISTRICT Political Background

Connecticut 6 is one of those districts that consists of everything left over after everyone else has constructed his own safe little constituency. It was probably meant to elect a Democrat, but it has done so in only two of four elections. The areas of Democratic strength in the 6th are geographically dispersed and sociologically dissimilar. Enfield, where Jonathan Edwards once delivered a remarkable piece of Puritan hellfire, and Windsor Locks in the far northeast corner are now both predominantly Italian, and both are part of the Hartford-to-Springfield, Massachusetts, industrial corridor. In the southeast part of the district are Bristol and New Britain, the home of Gov. Thomas Meskill and the city with the state's largest concentration of Polish-Americans. In the north central part of the 6th are the mill towns of Torrington and Winstead, the latter the boyhood home of Ralph Nader. Separating these areas are the posh and Republican Hartford suburbs of Farmington, Avon, and Simsbury. The rest of the district is given over to Yankee towns nestled between gentle mountains—towns like Sharon, the home of New York's Senator James L. Buckley.

The intended beneficiary of this diversity, back in 1964 when the district lines were first drawn, was a man named Bernard Grabowski, who was then congressman-at-large from the state. Connecticut at that time had only five districts, and it was traditional that the congressman-at-large be of Polish descent. Grabowski was slated in 1962 when the incumbent had rebelled against the Bailey leadership. He won again in 1964, but lost two years later to Meskill, then mayor of New Britain. Meskill was easily reelected in 1968.

When Meskill ran for governor, Secretary of State Ella Grasso, a Democrat often considered a bridge between Bailey and the intellectual wing of the party, was considered the solid favorite. She was, anyway, until it became clear just how badly the top of the Democratic ticket was doing. Mrs. Grasso won because she ran 11% ahead of her party's gubernatorial candidate, her election thus depending on a degree of ticket-splitting highly unusual in Connecticut.

Despite the narrowness of her victory (52%), Mrs. Grasso seems destined for a long career in the House. She will have the advantages of incumbency and is unlikely to face a strong statewide Republican ticket in 1972.

Census Data 1970 pop. 508,422; deviation from current state average, +0.6%; change 1960–70, +25.8%. Metro. 76.8%, 27.3% central city.

1970 Share of Federal Outlays $666,865,000 (average outlay per district, Connecticut 1 and 6)

DOD	$359,441,000	HEW	$124,715,000
AEC	$1,413,000	HUD	$11,312,000
NASA	$10,094,000	OEO	$682,000
DOT	$6,831,000	DOA	$3,004,000
		Other	$149,374,000

Federal Military-Industrial Commitments (See Connecticut 1 for greater Hartford listing.)

Economic Base Nonelectrical machinery, esp. general industrial machinery, equipment; fabricated metal products; electrical machinery, equipment, and supplies. Also, higher education (Connecticut Central State College).

The Voters

Registration Total, 230,586. 88,103 D (38%); 79,082 R (34%); 63,401 other (28%).

Employment profile White collar, 39%. Blue collar, 61%.

Ethnic groups Black, 1%. Puerto Rican, less than 0.5%. Total foreign stock, 40%. Italy, 9%; Poland, 7%; Canada, 6%; UK, Germany, 3% each; Ireland, Sweden, 2% each; USSR, Austria, Czech., 1% each; others, 5%.

Presidential vote

1968	Humphrey (D)	105,941	(51%)
	Nixon (R)	91,253	(44%)
	Wallace (AIP)	11,098	(5%)

Representative

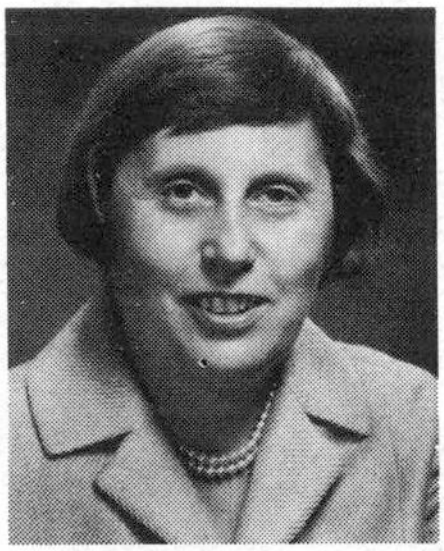

Ella T. Grasso (D) Elected 1970; b. May 10, 1919, Windsor Locks; home, Windsor Locks; Mount Holyoke Col., B.A., 1940, M.A., 1942; married, two children; Catholic.

Career War Manpower Commission of Conn., WWII; Conn. House of Reps., 1953–58; first woman Floor Leader, 1955–57; Conn. Sec. of State, 1958–70; Dem. State Platform Com., 1956–68; Platform Drafting Com., Dem. Natl. Convention, 1960.

Offices 513 CHOB, 202-225-4476. Also Court House Bldg., New Britain 06051, 203-223-3646.

Committees

Education and Labor (19th); Subs. (1) Agricultural Labor, (2) Sel. Sub. on Labor, (3) Sel. Sub. on Education.

Veterans' Affairs (15th); Subs. (1) Hospitals, (2) Insurance.

Group Ratings, Key Votes: Newly elected.

Election Results

1970 general:	Ella T. Grasso (D)	96,969	(52%)
	Richard C. Kilbourn (R)	92,906	(48%)
1970 primary:	Ella T. Grasso (D), unopposed		

DELAWARE

Political Background

Delaware's proudest boast is that it was the first state to ratify the Constitution. But since 1787 it has become most famous as the home of the duPont enterprises and, because of its liberal incorporation laws, as the technical home of most of the nation's giant business firms. Less often considered is the fact that Delaware, with about the same population as one average House district, wields as much power in the U.S. Senate as California or New York—and usually more, since Delaware, unlike the large states, ordinarily allows its senators to accumulate great seniority.

The political structure of this little state (second smallest in area) has seldom engaged the attention of national commentators. Historically Delaware has wavered between Democrats and Republicans, with duPont family members, corporation officers, and other retainers (the duPonts own the state's most important bank and the Wilmington newspapers) well entrenched in both parties. Lately the Republicans have gained a decisive edge, in large part because of the population growth in wealthy suburban Wilmington (New Castle County), which in 1970 cast 60% of the state's votes. Another factor is the increasing degree of attachment of the duPont establishment to the Republican party: a sizable percentage of top officials, most of them Republicans, hold public offices while on leave from jobs at the corporation.

The Democrats' weakness results from the dissimilarity of their two major sources of strength: the city of Wilmington with its substantial black and white blue-collar vote and the two southern counties (Delaware has only three counties) with their south-of-the-Mason-Dixon-line tradition. Hubert Humphrey nearly equaled Richard Nixon's vote in New Castle County in 1968, with a strong margin in Wilmington and a better than average showing in the suburbs. But Nixon beat Humphrey badly in the lower counties, with George Wallace taking 19% of the vote. In the 1970 Senate and House races—with no incumbents running—the opposite pattern emerged. Congressman William V. Roth, Republican Senate nominee, and Pierre S. duPont IV, the Republican House candidate, won by huge margins in the suburbs and made big inroads in Wilmington. Meanwhile, their Democratic opponents were making their strongest showings in the two southern counties.

In national races, Delaware must still be counted as marginal. Richard Nixon carried the state in 1968 by 7,200 votes (a 3% margin) and lost it in 1960 by 3,200 (2%). In state races, the Republicans have been better organized and better financed and now hold almost all the cards: the governorship, both Senate seats, and the House seat, all statewide offices but treasurer, and both houses of the state legislature. In the Senate and House races to come they will have the advantage of popular incumbents. Senior Senator J. Caleb Boggs was governor eight years before he went to the Senate in 1960. A generally steady and dependable conservative, Boggs is ranking minority member of Public Works' Air and Water Pollution Subcommittee. Sen. Roth, who now sits on the Banking, Housing, and Urban Affairs and Government Operations committees, wishes to follow in the footsteps of his predecessor, ex-Sen. (1946–70) John J. Williams, whose crusades against various evildoers earned him the title "Conscience of the Senate." Congressman duPont's family ties were thought to be a disadvantage in his 1970 race, but he seems to have overcome the problem by making speeches against the nation's corporate polluters.

Electoral Votes 3

Census Data 1970 pop. 548,104; 0.27% of U.S. total, 49th largest; change 1960–70, +22.8%. Metro. 70.4%, 14.7% central city. 1970 per capita income, $4,233, 12th highest. 43rd in number of poor.

1970 Share of Federal Tax Burden $702,510,000; 0.36% of U.S. total, 41st largest.

1970 Share of Federal Outlays $381,805,592; 0.20% of U.S. total, 50th largest. Per capita federal spending, $697.

DOD	$105,039,000	48th	(0.18%)	HEW	$112,293,846	49th	(0.21%)
AEC	$30,489	50th	(—)	HUD	$3,268,175	48th	(0.17%)
NASA	$13,434,035	20th	(0.36%)	OEO	$557,606	52nd	(0.07%)
DOT	$28,670,469	50th	(0.40%)	DOA	$10,672,200	51st	(0.08%)
DOC	$234,872	52nd	(0.02%)	POD	$16,261,235	50th	(0.22%)
DOI	$1,893,997	52nd	(0.08%)	VA	$22,076,572	49th	(0.30%)
DOJ	$1,204,410	51st	(0.21%)	CSC	$4,441,876	52nd	(0.11%)
				Other	$61,726,810		

Economic Base Chemicals and allied products, esp. plastics materials and synthetic resins, synthetic rubber, synthetic and other man-made fibers, except glass; food and kindred products, esp. meat products; poultry, corn, and dairy apparel and other finished products made from fabrics and similar materials; rubber and miscellaneous plastics products; primary metal industries, esp. blast furnaces, steel works, and rolling and finishing mills; leather and leather products.

Federal Military-Industrial Commitments

DOD Contractors Getty Oil (Delaware City), $6.631m: petroleum products. General Foods Corp. (Dover), $5.319m: instant rice packets.

DOD Installations Naval Facility (Lewes). Dover AFB (Dover).

NASA Contractors ILC Industries (Dover), $13.003m: Apollo space suit assemblies.

Political Line-up Governor, Russell W. Peterson (R); seat up, 1972. Senators, J. Caleb Boggs (R) and William V. Roth, Jr. (R). Representatives, 1 R, at large. State Senate (6 D and 13 R); State House (16 D and 23 R).

The Voters

Registration 245,945 total. 102,609 D (42%); 85,237 R (35%); 58,099 other (24%).

Employment profile White collar, 43%. Blue collar, 57%.

Ethnic groups Black, 14%. Total foreign stock, 13%. Italy, 3%; UK, Poland, 2% each; Germany, Ireland, USSR, Canada, 1% each; others, 3%.

Presidential vote

1968	Humphrey (D)	89,194	(42%)
	Nixon (R)	96,714	(45%)
	Wallace (AIP)	28,459	(13%)
1964	Johnson (D)	122,704	(61%)
	Goldwater (R)	78,078	(38%)
1960	Kennedy (D)	99,590	(51%)
	Nixon (R)	96,373	(49%)

Senator

James Caleb Boggs (R) Elected 1960, seat up 1972; b. May 15, 1909, Cheswood; U. of Del., B.A., 1931; Georgetown U., LL.B., 1937; Army Command and General Staff Col., 1942; Army, WWII; Col. USAR; Brigadier Gen. (Ret.) Del. Natl. Guard; married, two children; Protestant.

Career Judge, Family Ct., New Castle County, Del., 1946; House of Reps., 1946–52; Governor of Del., 1953–61; Chm., Natl. Governors' Conference, 1959; Pres., Council of State Governments, 1960.

Offices 3311 NSOB, 202-225-5042. No Delaware office.

Committees

Appropriations (9th); Subs. (1) Agriculture, Environmental and Consumer Protection, (2) Interior and Related Agencies, (3) Labor, HEW, and Related Agencies, (4) D.C., (5) Military Construction, (6) Treasury, Post Office, and Gen. Government.

Post Office and Civil Service (2nd); Subs. (1) Civil Service Policies and Practices, (2) Compensation and Employment Benefits, (3) Postal Operations.

Public Works (2nd); Subs. (1) Air and Water Pollution, (2) Public Buildings and Grounds, (3) Public Roads.

Group Ratings

	ADA	COPE	NREP	NFU	LCV	NAB	NSI	ACA
1970	31	39	25	47	51	67	90	57
1969	28	—	—	44	—	—	—	67
1968	43	60	—	46	—	80	—	63

Key Votes

(1) ABM	FOR	(8) Phil Pln	FOR	(15) Coop-Church	AGN
(2) SST	FOR	(9) Vol Army	FOR	(16) Cut Oil Dpltn	FOR
(3) Busing	FOR	(10) Prison $	AGN	(17) Consumer Prot	AGN
(4) Tob Sub	FOR	(11) Cut Mil $	AGN	(18) Farm Sub Limit	FOR
(5) Carswell	FOR	(12) Defoliatn	FOR	(19) Comp Bid Sales	FOR
(6) No-Knock	FOR	(13) 18-Yr-Vote	FOR	(20) Pre-Prod Tests	AGN
(7) Seniorty	AGN	(14) Pentgn PR	FOR	(21) Cut Marjna Pen	AGN

Election Results

1966 general:	J. Caleb Boggs (R)	97,268	(59%)
	James M. Tunnell (D)	67,263	(41%)
1966 primary:	Boggs nominated by the Republican State Convention. No primary elections held in Delaware at this time.		
1960 general:	J. Caleb Boggs (R)	98,874	(51%)
	J. Allen Frear, Jr. (D)	96,060	(49%)

Senator

William V. Roth, Jr. (R) Elected 1970, seat up 1976; b. July 22, 1921, Great Falls, Mont.; home, Wilmington; U. of Oregon, B.A., 1944; Harvard, M.B.A., 1947; Harvard Law School, LL.B., 1947; Army, WWII; married, two children; Episcopalian.

Career Chm., Del. Repub. State Com., 1961–64; Repub. Natl. Com., 1961–64; House of Reps., 1966–70.

Offices 3123 NSOB, 202-225-2441. Also 304 Fed. Bldg., Wilmington 19801, 302-658-6911, ext. 543, and 200 U.S. P.O. Bldg., Georgetown 19947, 302-856-7690.

Committees

Banking, Housing, and Urban Affairs (5th); Subs. (1) Housing and Urban Affairs, (2) International Finance, (3) Securities, (4) Small Business.

Government Operations (7th); Subs. (1) Executive Reorganization, (2) Intergovernmental Relations, (3) National Security and International Operations.

(*Note: The following ratings and votes cover Sen. Roth's record in the House of Representatives where he served prior to his election in 1970.*)

Group Ratings

	ADA	COPE	NREP	NFU	LCV	CFA	NAB	NSI	ACA
1970	20	17	25	62	75	57	75	90	79
1969	7	—	—	54	—	—	—	—	65
1968	8	9	—	57	—	—	100	—	96

Key Votes

(1) ABM	FOR	(6) 18-Yr-Vote	FOR	(11) Clean Water $	AGN
(2) SST	AGN*	(7) Farm Sub Lmt	FOR	(12) Mig Wrkrs Comp	AGN
(3) Phil Pln	FOR	(8) Coop-Church	AGN	(13) Jets to Chiang	AGN
(4) No-Knock	FOR	(9) Family Asst	AGN	(14) State OEO Veto	FOR
(5) Cmutr Tax	FOR	(10) Work Stamps	FOR	(15) Park Logging	AGN

* *as Senator.*

Election Results

1970 general:	William V. Roth (R)	96,021	(59%)
	Jacob W. Zimmerman (D)	64,835	(40%)
	Donald G. Gies (AIP)	2,183	(2%)
1970 primary:	Roth nominated by the Republican State Convention. No primary held because no other candidate received 35% of the votes of the convention.		

Representative

Pierre S. duPont IV (R) Elected 1970; b. Jan. 22, 1935, Wilmington; home, Rockland; Princeton U., B.S., 1952–56; Harvard Law School, LL.B., 1960–63; USNR, 1957–60; married, four children; Episcopalian.

Career Atty., marketing and plant control, DuPont Co., 1963–70; Del. House of Reps., 1968–70.

Offices 1209 LHOB, 202-225-4165. Also 506 Goldsborough Bldg., 1102 West Street, Wilmington 19801, 302-652-3933.

Committees

Foreign Affairs (17th); Subs. (1) Asian and Pacific Affairs, (2) Foreign Economic Policy.

Merchant Marine and Fisheries (14th); Subs. (1) Coast Guard, Coast and Geodetic Survey, and Navigation, (2) Merchant Marine, (3) Oceanography.

Group Ratings, Key Votes: Newly elected.

Election Results

1970 general:	Pierre S. duPont IV (R)	86,125	(54%)
	John D. Daniello (D)	71,429	(45%)
	Walter J. Hoey (AIP)	2,459	(2%)
1970 primary:	Dupont nominated by the Republican State Convention. No primary held because no other candidate received 35% of the votes of the convention.		

FLORIDA

Political Background

In the late 1940's, the eminent political scientist V. O. Key described Florida politics as "every man for himself." Now, despite the coming of age of the two-party system in the state, its politics are no more cohesive or disciplined than before. Hotly contested general elections since 1964 have not united the Florida Democratic party, but have left it even more fragmented. And since 1970, the Republicans—usually well organized in the South—have suffered from bitter intraparty feuding.

The chaotic state of Florida politics is nowhere better illustrated than in the political career of ex-Gov. Claude Kirk. In 1966 the Republican swept to victory, carrying all but 11 counties. His ebullient four years in office were highlighted by his third marriage and privately financed investigations of local Democratic politicians, for which Kirk reportedly still owes the Wackenhut detective agency $190,000. The Governor also made a last-minute switch to Nelson Rockefeller at the 1968 Republican convention; Kirk had vice-presidential ambitions, but was unable to carry even a single Florida delegate with him. In 1970, after surviving a runoff primary against a drugstore millionaire, Kirk went on to lose the general election by more than 200,000 votes, carrying only 10 counties.

In the late 1940's, Florida was considered a relatively small state, having less than 2,500,000 residents. Today it has more than 6,500,000. In the '60's alone, Florida added 1,837,000 to its population, an increase greater than that of any other state except California. In fact, most of the people now living in Florida were not born in the state, and only 4 of 14 men it sends to Congress are Florida natives.

The sharp growth has created many Floridas, politically and sociologically. The northern panhandle of the state remains a part of the Old South, much like the adjacent hill country of Alabama and Georgia. But southern sections of Florida reflect the various northern origins of their residents. The Miami area, for example, with its large Jewish population, tends to vote like New York City. Fort Lauderdale and Broward

County just to the north vote like the very conservative suburbs of Chicago, as do the Gulf Coast cities of Sarasota and Fort Meyers. St. Petersburg normally goes Republican, its numerous senior citizens voting here as they did when they lived in New Jersey or Minnesota or Ohio. Tampa, with a large Spanish-speaking community, has a significant liberal-labor vote, though George Wallace ran well in its white working-class precincts. Cape Kennedy, nearby Orlando, and Orange County, unlike other Republican centers in Florida, are less retirement colonies than Sun Belt boom towns. The politics here are like those in suburban Houston, Texas, or Orange County, California—very conservative. Jacksonville, however, is more like a present-day city in the Old South, with nearly equal numbers of liberal Democratic Negroes, white middle-class Nixon Republicans, and Wallace supporters.

It is against this background of diversity that the internal strife of the state's political parties and the rather surprising results of the 1970 election should be assessed. Before the 1970 elections, most political pros thought that Florida had become a bastion of Nixon Republicanism. There was much evidence to support this. In 1968 Nixon carried the state easily in a three-way race. At the same time, Republican Congressman Edward Gurney walloped Democratic ex-Gov. LeRoy Collins for the U.S. Senate seat vacated by George Smathers. Collins managed to carry only four counties, those containing Miami, Key West, Tampa, and the University of Florida. The well-financed Republicans came up with a sure-win tactic: because liberal voters in Miami and Tampa had come to dominate the Democratic primary, nominees of the party were labeled LBJ-style liberal hacks. And since the Florida Democratic candidates of 1968 were veterans of the political wars of the '50's and '60's, the Republicans were able to make the labels stick.

Florida Republicans eagerly anticipated the same scenario in 1970. Conservative Democrat Spessard Holland was retiring after 24 years in the Senate, and the Democrats were expected to put up party veterans Atty. Gen. Earl Faircloth and ex-Gov. Farris Bryant for governor and senator. But nothing seemed to go according to the Republicans' expectations. First, the Republicans had a bitter primary fight when Congressman William Cramer of St. Petersburg, a 16-year veteran of the House and Florida's first successful Republican officeholder, was unexpectedly confronted by the candidacy of Judge G. Harrold Carswell, who had just been denied the consent of the Senate for a Supreme Court seat. But Carswell's entry, engineered by Gov. Kirk and Sen. Gurney, failed: almost a quarter of the state's Republican primary voters lived in Cramer's own House district, while Carswell's strongest area was Dixie-oriented northern Florida where there are virtually no Republican voters. As it turned out, Cramer whipped Carswell statewide 220,000 to 120,000. The decision to give up a lifetime federal judgeship in order to challenge Cramer in this election was taken by many as a measure of Carswell's limited intellectual capacities.

Meanwhile, Kirk faced a runoff opponent in the primary, who, although not openly backed by Cramer, coincidentally came from Cramer's congressional district in the St. Petersburg area. In the general election, the Kirk-Cramer animosity continued to be costly to the Republicans. Kirk was unable to carry Cramer's Pinellas County (St. Petersburg), usually a Republican stronghold; and in the Kirk-Gurney combine's strongest area, around Orlando in central Florida, Cramer ran well behind Kirk.

The Republicans had a second problem. The state's Democrats did not nominate men the Republicans could depict as dried-up old liberal hacks. Instead, they gave the nomination for governor to 41-year-old State Sen. Reubin Askew of Pensacola, who campaigned and won on a platform of corporate income-tax reform; and the nomination for senator went to 40-year-old state Sen. Lawton Chiles of Lakeland. Chiles walked 1,003 miles down the state, from Pensacola to Miami, to demonstrate his inability to finance an expensive TV campaign. Although Chiles favored a specific date for withdrawal from Vietnam and also favored wage and price controls, Cramer was somehow unable to pin the liberal label on him. Chiles had the support of the conservative Sen. Holland, who is from the candidate's home county. And Chiles's open manner and his background as a small-town state legislator did not seem consistent with the image of a Washington-bound liberal, eager to tell Southerners how to run their affairs. Moreover, LBJ had retired, leaving the voters free to begin focusing their discontent on the Texan's successor. Even though Cramer's campaign featured his long-standing opposition to busing and a vigorous advocacy of capital punishment, it could not quell the enthusiasm generated by the "Walking Senator."

Both Chiles, who has taken antiwar and antidraft stands in the Senate, and Askew, who has gotten most of his complicated tax program enacted, seem like excellent prospects for reelection. So does Sen. Gurney, one of the most determined ideological conservatives in Congress. Gurney's seat is not up until 1974, at which time he should have little trouble unless Cramer decides to run against him in the primary. The state's House delegation remains Democratic and still predominantly conservative.

Florida will gain three new seats in the House as a result of the 1970 census, one in the Miami area and one each in the Atlantic and Gulf Coast retirement areas. The new seats probably will add one liberal (from Miami) and two conservatives—all of them likely to be Democrats, if only because the governorship as well as the legislature is in Democratic hands. The redistricting will jeopardize only one incumbent, 71-year-old conservative Democrat James Haley of Sarasota.

Florida will probably have a presidential primary in 1972, which should put in the national spotlight all the divisions and peculiarities of Florida politics.

Electoral Votes 15

Census Data 1970 pop. 6,789,443; 3.30% of U.S. total, 9th largest; change 1960–70, +37.1%. Metro. 68.6%, 28.7% central city. 1970 per capita income, $3,584, 29th highest. 5th in number of poor.

1970 Share of Federal Tax Burden $5,600,540,000; 2.87% of U.S. total, 10th largest.

1970 Share of Federal Outlays $5,791,865,948; 3.06% of U.S. total, 9th largest. Per capita federal spending, $853.

DOD	$1,907,588,000	7th (3.32%)	HEW	$2,001,002,896	8th (3.83%)
AEC	$20,973,873	20th (0.81%)	HUD	$51,914,828	11th (2.66%)
NASA	$357,277,889	3rd (9.71%)	OEO	$17,078,657	14th (2.25%)
DOT	$184,304,527	12th (2.58%)	DOA	$104,090,666	36th (0.81%)
DOC	$18,666,648	13th (1.61%)	POD	$192,130,018	11th (2.64%)
DOI	$27,142,347	28th (1.17%)	VA	$382,512,479	7th (5.18%)
DOJ	$20,020,375	7th (3.49%)	CSC	$173,442,625	5th (4.31%)
			Other	$350,520,120	

Economic Base Oranges, livestock, dairy; food and kindred products, esp. canned and preserved fruits, vegetables and seafood, and bakery products; printing, publishing, and allied industries, esp. newspapers and commercial printing; chemicals and allied products; apparel and other finished products made from fabrics and similar materials, esp. women's, misses', and juniors' outerwear; paper and allied products; ordnance and accessories; lumber and wood products, except furniture, esp. logging camps and logging contractors, and millwork, veneer, plywood, and prefabricated structural wood products. Also, tourism.

Political Line-up Governor, Reubin Askew (D); seat up, 1974. Senators, Edward J. Gurney (R) and Lawton Chiles (D). Representatives, 12 (9 D and 3 R). State Senate (34 D and 14 R); State House (81 D and 38 R).

The Voters

Registration 2,797,000 total. 2,024,387 D (72%); 711,090 R (25%); 61,523 other (3%).

Employment profile White collar, 42%. Blue collar, 58%.

Ethnic groups Black, 15%. Total foreign stock, 15%. Germany, UK, Canada, 2% each; Ireland, Italy, USSR, Poland, 1% each; others, 5%.

Presidential vote

1968	Humphrey (D)	676,794	(31%)
	Nixon (R)	886,794	(41%)
	Wallace (AIP)	624,207	(29%)
1964	Johnson (D)	948,540	(51%)
	Goldwater (R)	905,941	(49%)
1960	Kennedy (D)	748,400	(49%)
	Nixon (R)	795,476	(51%)

Senator

Edward John Gurney (R) Elected 1968, seat up 1974; b. Jan. 12, 1914, Portland, Maine; home, Winter Park; Colby Col., B.S., 1935; Harvard Law School, LL.B., 1938; Duke U., LL.M., 1948; Army, WWII; married, two children; Congregational Christian.

Career City Commissioner, Winter Park, 1952–58; Mayor, Winter Park, 1961–62; House of Reps., 1962–68.

Offices 5105 NSOB, 202-225-3041. Also P.O. Box 1179, Winter Park 32799, 305-647-3636, and Main P.O., Miami 33101, 305-503-5110.

Committees

Government Operations (4th); Subs. (1) Intergovernmental Relations, (2) Permanent Investigations.

Judiciary (7th); Subs. (1) Administrative Practice and Procedure, (2) Antitrust and Monopoly Legislation, (3) Constitutional Amendments, (4) Improvements in Judicial Machinery, (5) Internal Security, (6) Separation of Powers.

Sel. Com. on Small Business (5th); Subs. (1) Government Procurement, (2) Government Regulation, (3) Monopoly.

Sp. Com. on Aging (6th); Subs. (1) Consumer Interests of the Elderly, (2) Employment and Retirement Incomes, (3) Housing for the Elderly, (4) Retirement and the Individual.

Group Ratings

	ADA	COPE	NREP	NFU	LCV	NAB	NSI	ACA
1970	6	9	0	30	0	80	100	85
1969	0	—	—	25	—	—	—	93

Key Votes

(1) ABM	FOR	(8) Phil Pln	AGN	(15) Coop-Church	AGN
(2) SST	FOR	(9) Vol Army	FOR	(16) Cut Oil Dpltn	AGN
(3) Busing	AGN	(10) Prison $	AGN	(17) Consumer Prot	AGN
(4) Tob Sub	FOR	(11) Cut Mil $	AGN	(18) Farm Sub Limit	AGN
(5) Carswell	FOR	(12) Defoliatn	FOR	(19) Comp Bid Sales	FOR
(6) No-Knock	FOR	(13) 18-Yr-Vote	AGN	(20) Pre-Prod Tests	AGN
(7) Seniorty	AGN	(14) Pentgn PR	FOR	(21) Cut Marjna Pen	AGN

Election Results

1968 general:	Edward J. Gurney (R)	1,131,499	(56%)
	LeRoy Collins (D)	892,637	(44%)
1968 primary:	Edward J. Gurney (R)	169,805	(80%)
	Herman W. Goldner (R)	42,347	(20%)

Senator

Lawton Mainor Chiles (D) Elected 1970, seat up 1976; b. April 3, 1930, Lakeland; home, Lakeland; U. of Fla., B.S., 1952, LL.B., 1955; Army, Korean War; married, four children; Presbyterian.

Career Practicing atty., 1955– ; Fla. House of Reps., 1958–66; Fla. Senate, 1966–70.

Offices 421 OSOB, 202-225-5274.

Committees

Agriculture and Forestry (8th); Subs. (1) Chm., Agricultural Exports, (2) Agricultural Research and Gen. Legislation, (3) Environment, Soil Conservation, and Forestry.

Government Operations (10th); Subs. (1) Intergovernmental Re-

lations, (2) National Security and International Operations.
Jt. Com. on Congressional Operations (3rd).

Group Ratings, Key Votes: Newly elected.

Election Results

1970 general:	Lawton Chiles (D)	902,438	(54%)
	William C. Cramer (R)	772,817	(46%)
1970 primary runoff:	Lawton Chiles (D)	474,420	(66%)
	Ferris Bryant (D)	247,211	(34%)
1970 primary:	Lawton Chiles (D)	188,300	(26%)
	Ferris Bryant (D)	240,222	(33%)
	Fred Schultz (D)	175,745	(24%)
	Al Hastings (D)	91,948	(13%)
	Jeel T. Daves III	33,939	(5%)

FIRST DISTRICT Political Background

Florida 1 lies in the western panhandle of Florida, a region that is closer—politically as well as geographically—to Montgomery, Alabama, than to Miami. This was solid Goldwater country in 1964 and Wallace country in 1968. Along the Gulf Coast are the cities of Pensacola and Panama City. Just to the north is the Piney Woods section, where there are relatively few blacks and conservative candidates pile up overwhelming majorities. The 1st's many military installations are its most notable feature. Pensacola has a sprawling complex of naval facilities, and nearby Elgin Air Force Base is the largest in the nation in area. As in tidewater South Carolina, the military is the economic mainstay of the district.

The presence of all the installations is no doubt related to the political career of the 1st district's congressman, Robert L. F. Sikes. In the House since 1940, he is one of the senior members of the Appropriations Committee and of its Defense Subcommittee, and chairman of its subcommittee on Military Construction. Sikes has been a dependable supporter of military spending. He also vigorously supported the Cross-Florida Barge Canal, a project which environmentalists attacked and which was canceled by the Nixon Administration in 1971.

The Congressman's positions are apparently popular in the district. He won 77% of the vote in the 1970 Democratic primary and 80% in the general election. Sikes has represented Florida in Congress longer than any other man, and because he is now only 64, young for a 30-year man, he will likely be around many years more. Redistricting will not be a problem; the census figures indicate that the district may lose one county, but this will not change anything politically.

Census Data 1970 pop. 489,335; deviation from current state average, —13.5%; change 1960–70, +17.8%. Metro. 49.7%, 12.2% central city.

1970 Share of Federal Outlay $642,249,864

DOD	$459,429,000	HEW	$88,573,406
AEC	$000	HUD	$1,255,375
NASA	$17,261	OEO	$402,190
DOT	$14,018,514	DOA	$12,527,374
		Other	$65,926,744

Federal Military-Industrial Commitments

DOD Contractors Vitro Corp. of America (Valparaiso), $11.862m: operation of armament development test center, Elgin AFB. Western Mechanical Contractors (Elgin AFB), $11.850m: unspecified. Allen Campbell Co. (Elgin AFB), $5.119m: construction.

DOD Installations Naval Air Station (Pensacola). Naval Air Rework Facility (Pensacola). Saufley Naval Air Station (Pensacola). Whiting Naval Air Station (Milton). Naval Aerospace Medical Center (Pensacola). Ellyson Naval Air Station (Pensacola). Navy Mine Defense Laboratory (Panama City). Naval Public Work Center (Pensacola). Elgin AF Field 2 (Niceville). Elgin AF Field 3 (Crestview). Elgin AF Field 9 (Fort Walton Beach). Elgin AFB (Valparaiso). Tydall AFB (Panama City).

Economic Base Livestock, paper and allied products; chemicals and allied products.

The Voters

Registration 196,392 total. 178,525 D (91%); 14,905 R (8%); 2,962 other (2%).
Employment profile White collar, 40%. Blue collar, 60%.
Ethnic groups Blacks, 15%. Total foreign stock, 5%. Canada, Germany, UK, 1% each.

Presidential vote

1968	Humphrey (D)	30,241	(19%)
	Nixon (R)	31,770	(20%)
	Wallace (AIP)	97,811	(61%)

Representative

Robert L. F. Sikes (D) Elected 1940; b. June 3, 1906, Isabella, Georgia; home, Crestview; U. of Ga., B.S., 1927; U. of Fla., M.S., 1929; Army, WWII; married, two children; Methodist.

Career Newspaper publisher, Chm., County Democratic Executive Com., 1934; Florida Legislature, 1936–38; Asst. to treasurer Democratic Natl. Com., 1936–40–44.

Offices 2269 RHOB, 202-225-4136. Also County Court House, Crestwood 32536, 904-682-3132.

Committees

Appropriations (5th); Subs. (1) Chm., Military Construction, (2) Defense, (3) State, Justice, Commerce, and Judiciary.

Group Ratings

	ADA	COPE	NREP	NFU	LCV	CFA	NAB	NSI	ACA
1970	12	17	17	25	22	67	46	100	59
1969	0	—	—	36	—	—	—	—	67
1968	25	9	—	67	—	—	50	—	52

Key Votes

(1) ABM	FOR	(6) 18-Yr-Vote	AGN	(11) Clean Water $	AGN
(2) SST	FOR	(7) Farm Sub Lmt	AGN	(12) Mig Wrkrs Comp	AGN
(3) Phil Pln	ABS	(8) Coop-Church	AGN	(13) Jets to Chiang	ABS
(4) No-Knock	FOR	(9) Family Asst	AGN	(14) State OEO Veto	FOR
(5) Cmutr Tax	AGN	(10) Work Stamps	FOR	(15) Park Logging	FOR

Election Results

1970 general:	Robert L. F. Sikes (D)	88,744	(80%)
	H. D. Shumake (R)	21,952	(20%)
1970 primary:	Robert L. F. Sikes (D)	66,182	(77%)
	Bill Davis (D)	19,355	(23%)
1968 general:	Robert L. F. Sikes (D)	116,215	(85%)
	John Dizazga (R)	21,063	(15%)

SECOND DISTRICT Political Background

Florida 2 is the north central part of the state, culturally part of the Deep South. Most of the district is rural, and virtually all of the Northerners seeking Florida sun move farther south. The district's only significant urban centers are Tallahassee (pop. 71,000), the state capital and home of ex-Judge and Senate candidate G. Harrold Carswell, and Gainesville (pop. 64,000), site of the University of Florida.

The congressman from the 2nd is Don Fuqua (an old Southern name, pronounced FOOkway). The conservative Democrat, first elected in 1962, is rising at the usual slow pace on the Science and Astronautics and Government Operations committees. He is a reliable member of the House's dominant conservative coalition. Fuqua's toughest race was in 1964, when redistricting threw him into the same district with the more senior (1952–64) and slightly more liberal congressman D. R. (Billy) Matthews. Fuqua won that primary and since 1966 has had no opposition in primary or general elections. He is likely to continue representing the 2nd for some time.

Census Data 1970 pop. 501,500; deviation from current state average, −11.4%; change 1960–70, +23.0%. Metro. 41.4%, 27.2% central city.

1970 Share of Federal Outlays $436,935,411

DOD	$34,634,000	HEW	$186,599,288
AEC	$1,599,515	HUD	$2,795,000
NASA	$951,316	OEO	$2,817,038
DOT	$57,810,582	DOA	$29,126,778
		Other	$120,601,864

Federal Military-Industrial Commitments

DOD Contractors Aero Corp. (Lake City), $8.811m: P-2 aircraft repair.

DOD Installations Jacksonville AF Station (Orange Park).

Economic Base Tobacco and livestock; paper and allied products; lumber and wood products other than furniture. Also, higher education (University of Florida and Florida State University).

The Voters

Registration 200,147 total. 179,152 D (90%); 18,530 R (9%); 2,465 other (1%).
Employment profile White collar, 37%. Blue collar, 63%.
Ethnic groups Black, 26%. Total foreign stock, 3%. All groups less than 0.5%.

Presidential vote

1968	Humphrey (D)	42,627	(28%)
	Nixon (R)	36,203	(24%)
	Wallace (AIP)	75,520	(49%)

Representative

Don Fuqua (D) Elected 1962; b. Aug. 20, 1933, Jacksonville; U. of Fla., B.S., 1957; Army, Korean War; married, two children; Presbyterian.

Career Fla. House of Reps., 1958–62.

Offices 434 CHOB, 202-225-5235. Also 308 P.O. Bldg., Tallahassee 32302, 904-224-7510, and 314 Fed. Bldg., Gainesville 32601, 904-376-4215.

Committees

Government Operations (20th); Subs. (1) Intergovernmental Relations, (2) Legislation and Military Operations.

Science and Astronautics (7th); Subs. (1) Chm., International Cooperation in Science and Space, (2) Manned Space Flight.

Group Ratings

	ADA	COPE	NREP	NFU	LCV	CFA	NAB	NSI	ACA
1970	16	27	8	31	14	55	46	100	63
1969	7	—	—	40	—	—	—	—	77
1968	17	8	—	56	—	—	33	—	57

Key Votes

(1) ABM	FOR	(6) 18-Yr-Vote	AGN	(11) Clean Water $	AGN
(2) SST	AGN	(7) Farm Sub Lmt	AGN	(12) Mig Wrkrs Comp	AGN
(3) Phil Pln	AGN	(8) Coop-Church	AGN	(13) Jets to Chiang	FOR
(4) No-Knock	FOR	(9) Family Asst	AGN	(14) State OEO Veto	FOR
(5) Cmutr Tax	AGN	(10) Work Stamps	FOR	(15) Park Logging	FOR

Election Results

1970 general: Don Fuqua (D), unopposed
1970 primary: Don Fuqua (D), unopposed
1968 general: Don Fuqua (D), unopposed

THIRD DISTRICT Political Background

Florida 3 comprises most of the racially troubled city of Jacksonville in northern Florida. Since the climate here is notably cooler than in southern Florida, Jacksonville is not a retirement mecca like other large Florida cities. It is, however, an important Atlantic port and a banking and insurance center. Politically, Jacksonville is a Southern city. In 1968, George Wallace carried the district, with Hubert Humphrey, thanks to a large black vote, coming in a close second, just ahead of Richard Nixon.

Charles E. Bennett, the 3rd's representative since 1948, enjoys a reputation for probity and attention to duty that is second to none in the House. He was stricken by polio in the army during World War II, and in his first campaign it was suggested that he was not physically capable of representing the district properly. In fact, Bennett has not missed a roll call vote since June 4, 1951—the longest such record in the history of the House.

Bennett is basically a conservative legislator, but his vote is less predictable than most. Although he is a senior member and a subcommittee chairman on the House Armed Services Committee and has usually supported its conservative majority, he voted for the Nedzi-Whalen Amendment (similar to Hatfield-McGovern) in 1971. Congressman Bennett is well respected in Jacksonville and should easily win reelection as long as he chooses to run.

Census Data 1970 pop. 471,473; deviation from current state average, −16.7%; change 1960–70, +12.6%. Metro. 100%, 98.1% central city.

1970 Share of Federal Outlays $454,464,608

DOD	$164,640,000	HEW	$137,172,856
AEC	$000	HUD	$6,703,801
NASA	$296,505	OEO	$1,769,008
DOT	$14,440,738	DOA	$4,806,970
		Other	$124,634,730

Federal Military-Industrial Commitments

DOD Installations Naval Air Station (Jacksonville). Naval Air Station, Cecil Field (Jacksonville). Naval Air Rework Facility (Jacksonville). Naval Hospital (Jacksonville). Naval Station (Mayport). Navy Fuel Depot (Jacksonville). Naval Air Technical Training Unit (Jacksonville). Jacksonville Air Station (Jacksonville).

Economic Base Food and kindred products, esp. bakery products; paper and allied products, esp. paperboard mills; ship and boat building and repairing and other transportation equipment; printing, publishing, and allied industries. Also, banking and insurance.

The Voters

Registration 106,830 total. 89,215 D (84%); 3,697 R (4%); 13,918 other (13%).

Employment profile White collar, 45%. Blue collar, 55%.

Ethnic groups Black, 24%. Total foreign stock, 6%. Canada, Germany, UK, 1% each; others, 2%.

Presidential vote

1968	Humphrey (D)	48,866	(35%)
	Nixon (R)	39,774	(28%)
	Wallace (AIP)	52,543	(37%)

Representative

Charles E. Bennett (D) Elected 1948; b. Dec. 2, 1910, Canton, New York; home, Jacksonville; U. of Fla., B.A., 1934, J.D.; Army, WWII; married, four children; Disciples of Christ Church.

Career Practicing atty., 1934–48; Fla. House of Reps., 1941.

Offices 2113 RHOB, 202-225-2501. Also Suite 352 Fed. Office Bldg., 400 W. Bay St., Jacksonville 32202, 904-791-2587.

Committees

Armed Services (4th); Subs. (1) Chm., Sp. Sub. on Real Estate, (2) Chm., Sub. No. 3.

Group Ratings

	ADA	COPE	NREP	NFU	LCV	CFA	NAB	NSI	ACA
1970	24	47	25	54	70	76	75	100	68
1969	20	—	—	40	—	—	—	—	82
1968	17	15	—	31	—	—	83	—	78

Key Votes

(1) ABM	FOR	(6) 18-Yr-Vote	FOR	(11) Clean Water $	AGN
(2) SST	AGN	(7) Farm Sub Lmt	FOR	(12) Mig Wrkrs Comp	FOR
(3) Phil Pln	AGN	(8) Coop-Church	AGN	(13) Jets to Chiang	FOR
(4) No-Knock	FOR	(9) Family Asst	AGN	(14) State OEO Veto	FOR
(5) Cmutr Tax	AGN	(10) Work Stamps	FOR	(15) Park Logging	AGN

Election Results

1970 general:	Charles E. Bennett (D), unopposed		
1970 primary:	Charles E. Bennett (D), unopposed		
1968 general:	Charles E. Bennett (D)	103,540	(79%)
	Bill Parsons (R)	27,696	(21%)

FOURTH DISTRICT Political Background

Florida 4 is a collar of land across the neck of the Florida peninsula. It includes acres of orange groves, the hard-sand beach at Daytona, and farming country around Ocala. The 4th district is transitional Florida: several of the smaller counties have traditional Dixie voting habits, while Northern émigrés make Seminole and Lake Counties, near Orlando, conservative Republican territory. The largest city here, Daytona Beach (pop. 45,000), has a substantial black population, but, on the whole, blacks are not an important factor in the district's voting patterns.

The 4th's representative is conservative Democrat William Chappell, a former state legislator. His margins have not been as large as one normally associates with Southern Democrats. In his first race in 1968, Chappell received 53% of the votes, and in 1970 58%. The 4th is thus one of two Florida districts (the other is the 7th) that can be called marginal. Redistricting will require some adjustment of the 4th's boundaries. The legislators will probably remove one or two of the Republican counties from the district to help their former colleague.

Census Data 1970 pop. 554,997; deviation from current state average, —1.9%; change 1960–70, +36.6%. Metro. 25.4%, 10.0% central city.

1970 Share of Federal Outlays $327,530,732

DOD	$54,973,000	HEW	$157,506,958
AEC	$000	HUD	$1,270,000
NASA	$19,296,471	OEO	$1,374,722
DOT	$9,851,034	DOA	$10,967,469
		Other	$72,291,078

Federal Military-Industrial Commitments

DOD Contractors Sparton Corp. (DeLeon Springs), $21.043m: sonar equipment. McDonnell Douglas (Titusville), $19.345m: unspecified.

NASA Contractors General Electric (Daytona Beach), $15.006m: Apollo support.

Economic Base Livestock and poultry; food and kindred products; ordnance and accessories. Also, tourism (Daytona Beach).

The Voters

Registration 94,805 total. 57,410 D (61%); 34,600 R (37%); 2,795 other (3%).
Employment profile White collar, 38%. Blue collar, 62%.
Ethnic groups Black, 16%. Total foreign stock, 11%. Canada, Germany, UK, 2% each; Italy, 1%; others, 2%.

Presidential vote

1968	Humphrey (D)	54,226	(28%)
	Nixon (R)	77,766	(40%)
	Wallace (AIP)	63,866	(33%)

Representative

William V. Chappell, Jr. (D) Elected 1968; b. Feb. 3, 1922, Kendrick; home, Ocala; U. of Fla., B.A., 1947, LL.B., 1949, J.D., 1967; Navy, WWII, Capt., USNR; married, four children; Methodist.

Career Marion County Prosecuting Atty., 1950–54; Fla. House of Reps., 1955–64, 1967–68; Speaker Fla. House of Reps., 1961–63.

Offices 1131 LHOB, 202-225-4035. Also Rm. 258 Fed. Bldg., Ocala 32670, 904-629-0039, and 523 N. Halifax Ave., Daytona Beach 32016, 904-253-7632.

Committees

Banking and Currency (19th); Subs. (1) Bank Supervision and Insurance, (2) Consumer Affairs, (3) Small Business.

Post Office and Civil Service (15th); Subs. (1) Census and Statistics, (2) Manpower and Civil Service, (3) Retirement, Insurance, and Health Benefits.

Group Ratings

	ADA	COPE	NREP	NFU	LCV	CFA	NAB	NSI	ACA
1970	8	25	0	23	33	57	67	100	83
1969	7	—	—	40	—	—	—	—	93

Key Votes

(1) ABM	FOR	(6) 18-Yr-Vote	AGN	(11) Clean Water $	AGN
(2) SST	FOR	(7) Farm Sub Lmt	AGN	(12) Mig Wrkrs Comp	AGN
(3) Phil Pln	AGN	(8) Coop-Church	AGN	(13) Jets to Chiang	FOR
(4) No-Knock	FOR	(9) Family Asst	AGN	(14) State OEO Veto	FOR
(5) Cmutr Tax	AGN	(10) Work Stamps	FOR	(15) Park Logging	AGN

Election Results

1970 general:	William V. Chappell (D)	75,673	(58%)
	Leonard V. Wood (R)	55,311	(42%)
1970 primary:	William V. Chappell (D), unopposed		
1968 general:	William V. Chappell (D)	86,251	(53%)
	W. F. Herlong, Jr. (R)	76,974	(47%)

FIFTH DISTRICT Political Background

Florida 5 is dominated by the aerospace business. The district contains the gigantic NASA installations at Cape Kennedy (which many Floridians would rather call Cape Canaveral) as well as the growing inland city of Orlando. The 5th is solidly Republican, the new home for conservative Northerners who brought their politics with them. But unlike most other southern Florida population centers, the district is not top-heavy with retirees. In its economics and sociology, the region is more like the booming suburbs of Orange County, California, than St. Petersburg just across the peninsula. The government-funded aerospace industry makes up the economic base of the two similar regions, and the Disneyland people of Orange County have opened Disneyland East near Orlando.

For six years, the 5th and its predecessors (Florida had three redistrictings in the 1960's) was represented by Edward J. Gurney, a conservative Yankee who came south to practice law and became a United States senator from Florida in 1968. The current congressman is Louis Frey, Jr., Gurney's former law partner, and, like him, a hard-line conservative. Gurney and Frey have managed to make the 5th one of the most Republican districts in the nation. The district is also the core of strength for the Gurney-Kirk faction in Florida Republican politics.

Redistricting will probably alter the 5th substantially. But the census figures indicate that there will continue to be a heavily Republican Florida district centered in and around Orlando.

Census Data 1970 pop. 615,705; deviation from current state average, −8.8%; change 1960–70, +51.7%. Metro. 55.9%, 16.1% central city.

1970 Share of Federal Outlays $1,092,440,340

DOD	$542,249,000	HEW	$125,613,604
AEC	$17,400	HUD	$1,000,000
NASA	$318,210,655	OEO	$468,400
DOT	$7,909,487	DOA	$5,332,724
		Other	$91,639,070

Federal Military-Industrial Commitments

DOD Contractors Pan American World Airways (Cocoa Beach), $96.016m: support of Eastern Test Range, Patrick AFB. Martin Marietta (Orlando), $77.645m: ABM development; Pershing missile system. Western Electric (Orlando), $57.766m: ABM development. Radiation Inc. Div., Harris Intertype (Palm Bay and Melbourne), $29.558m: aircraft communication equipment; ship radio antennae. Gulf and Western Industries (Orlando), $11.967m: detonating fuzes. Xerox Corp. (Patrick AFB), $5.373m: unspecified.

DOD Installations Naval Training Device Center (Orlando). Naval Training Center (Orlando). McCoy AFB (Orlando). Patrick AFB (Cocoa Beach).

NASA Contractors Trans World Airlines (Kennedy Space Center), $34.779m: general and administrative support at the facility. North American Rockwell (Kennedy Space Center), $33.213m: Apollo spacecraft testing and support. Boeing Co. (Kennedy Space Center), $32.190m: Saturn V systems support. Bendix Corp. (Kennedy Space Center), $28.337m: Apollo and Saturn launch support. Grumman Aerospace (Kennedy Space Center), $26.430m: development of Apollo lunar module. IBM (Kennedy Space Center), $22.736m: fabrication and support of Saturn V instrument units. Federal Electric Div., IT&T (Kennedy Space Center), $19.060m: communications support. McDonnell Douglas (Kennedy Space Center), $14.207m: Saturn V support. Catalytic-Dow Chemical joint venture (Kennedy Space Center), $6.139m: Surveyor and Apollo spacecraft support. Chrysler Corp. (Kennedy Space Center), $5.903m: unspecified.

NASA Installations Kennedy Space Center (Cape Kennedy).

Economic Base Ordnance and accessories; livestock and poultry; food and kindred products, esp. canned and preserved fruits, vegetables, and seafoods. Also, tourism (Disneyland East) and banking.

The Voters

Registration 688,886 total. 478,646 D (70%); 203,972 R (30%); 6,268 other (1%).

Employment profile White collar, 47%. Blue collar, 53%.
Ethnic groups Black, 12%. Total foreign stock, 10%. Canada, Germany, UK, 2% each; Italy, 1%; others, 2%.

Presidential vote

1968	Humphrey (D)	43,972	(23%)
	Nixon (R)	94,169	(50%)
	Wallace (AIP)	52,285	(28%)

Representative

Louis Frey, Jr. (R) Elected 1968; b. Jan. 11, 1934, Rutherford, New Jersey; home, Winter Park; Colgate U., B.A., 1955; U. of Mich., J.D., 1961; Navy, 1955–58, Cdr., USNR; married, four children; Lutheran.

Career Practicing atty., 1961–68; Asst. County Solicitor, 1963; Acting General Counsel, Fla. Turnpike Auth., 1966–67; Treas. Fla. Repub. Party, 1966–67.

Offices 1315 LHOB, 202-225-3671. Also Rm. 222, 1040 Woodcock Rd., Orlando 32803, 305-843-2210, and 210 Brevard Ave., Cocoa 32922, 305-636-8307.

Committees

Interstate and Foreign Commerce (15th); Sub. on Communications and Power.
Science and Astronautics (8th); Subs. (1) Manned Space Flight, (2) Science, Research, and Dev.

Group Ratings

	ADA	COPE	NREP	NFU	LCV	CFA	NAB	NSI	ACA
1970	4	0	8	17	0	43	100	90	88
1969	0	—	—	27	—	—	—	—	94

Key Votes

(1) ABM	FOR	(6) 18-Yr-Vote	AGN	(11) Clean Water $	AGN
(2) SST	FOR	(7) Farm Sub Lmt	FOR	(12) Mig Wrkrs Comp	AGN
(3) Phil Pln	AGN	(8) Coop-Church	AGN	(13) Jets to Chiang	FOR
(4) No-Knock	FOR	(9) Family Asst	AGN	(14) State OEO Veto	FOR
(5) Cmutr Tax	AGN	(10) Work Stamps	FOR	(15) Park Logging	ABS

Election Results

1970 general:	Louis Frey, Jr. (R)	110,841	(76%)
	Roy Girod (D)	35,398	(24%)
1970 primary:	Louis Frey, Jr. (R), unopposed		
1968 general:	Louis Frey, Jr. (R)	108,620	(62%)
	James C. Robinson (D)	67,505	(38%)

SIXTH DISTRICT Political Background

Florida 6 includes Hillsborough County, which contains the city of Tampa, and a sliver of Polk County to the east. Tampa, an industrial city in the midst of retirement communities, dominates the district. The city is famous for its cigar factories and for the large number of Cubans who work in them. Tampa also has a substantial white working-class population which usually votes Democratic, but went heavily for George Wallace in 1968. The Hillsborough County vote was almost equally divided among the three candidates in that race: 35% for Nixon, 34% for Wallace, and 31% for Humphrey. In state elections the Tampa area usually goes Democratic, even when the rest of the state does not. In the 1968 Senate race, for example, it was one of four counties that ex-Gov. LeRoy Collins carried over Edward Gurney.

Sam Gibbons has been the 6th's congressman since 1962. He has been active among the younger Democrats in the House who have sought to reform its procedures and revamp its leadership. Unlike most Florida congressmen, Gibbons has supported civil rights legislation and has a generally liberal record. He served for several terms on the Education and Labor Committee and now sits on the tax-writing Ways and Means Committee. Gibbons has had no difficulty winning reelection in the 6th (72% in the 1970 general election). In 1968, however, he did have something of a scare in the Democratic primary when a conservative opponent got 40% of the votes.

Because of the population gain recorded in the 1970 census, the size of the district will have to be reduced. This probably means detaching the portion of Polk County and a rural portion of Hillsborough. This would make the district safer for Gibbons, because most of the voters lost would be conservatives. But it is possible that the Florida legislature will employ an entirely different redistricting strategy (see Florida 7), which would force Gibbons to run in a far more rural, conservative district. If this happens, he could lose his seat in 1972.

Census Data 1970 pop. 518,018; deviation from current state average, −8.4%; change 1960–70, +24.4%. Metro. 94.6%, 53.6% central city.

1970 Share of Federal Outlays $460,888,000 (average outlay per district, Florida 6 and 8)

DOD	$80,878,000	HEW	$184,823,000
AEC	$9,493,000	HUD	$3,076,000
NASA	$4,388,000	OEO	$1,271,000
DOT	$12,327,000	DOA	$2,663,000
		Other	$161,959,000

Federal Military-Industrial Commitments (See Florida 8 for greater Tampa-St. Petersburg listing)

Economic Base Food and kindred products, esp. canned and preserved fruits, vegetables, and seafoods; chemicals and allied products; poultry, livestock, and dairy. Also, higher education (University of Southern Florida) and banking.

The Voters

Registration 229,916 total. 192,121 D (84%); 34,049 R (15%); 3,746 other (2%).

Employment profile White collar, 40%. Blue collar, 60%.

Ethnic groups Black, 13%. Total foreign stock, 15%. Italy, 2%; Canada, Germany, UK, 1% each; others, 6%.

Presidential vote

1968	Humphrey (D)	46,964	(31%)
	Nixon (R)	51,933	(35%)
	Wallace (AIP)	50,928	(34%)

Representative

Sam M. Gibbons (D) Elected 1962; b. Jan. 20, 1920, Tampa; home, Tampa; U. of Fla., LL.B., 1947; Army, WWII; married, two children; Presbyterian.

Career Practicing atty., 1947–62; Fla. House of Reps., 1952–58; Fla. Senate, 1958–62.

Offices 430 CHOB, 202-225-3376. Also 510 Fed. Bldg., 500 Zack St., Tampa 33602, 913-228-7711, ext. 336.

Committees

Ways and Means (13th).

Group Ratings

	ADA	COPE	NREP	NFU	LCV	CFA	NAB	NSI	ACA
1970	60	91	73	100	71	100	0	89	39
1969	47	—	—	86	—	—	—	—	19
1968	58	77	—	85	—	—	17	—	15

Key Votes

(1) ABM	ABS	(6) 18-Yr-Vote	FOR	(11) Clean Water $	FOR
(2) SST	AGN	(7) Farm Sub Lmt	FOR	(12) Mig Wrkrs Comp	FOR
(3) Phil Pln	FOR	(8) Coop-Church	FOR	(13) Jets to Chiang	ABS
(4) No-Knock	FOR	(9) Family Asst	ABS	(14) State OEO Veto	AGN
(5) Cmutr Tax	AGN	(10) Work Stamps	ABS	(15) Park Logging	FOR

Election Results

1970 general:	Sam M. Gibbons (D)	78,832	(72%)
	Robert A. Carter (R)	30,252	(28%)
1970 primary:	Sam M. Gibbons (D), unopposed		
1968 general:	Sam M. Gibbons (D)	84,193	(62%)
	Paul A. Saad (R)	51,637	(38%)

SEVENTH DISTRICT Political Background

Florida 7 is made up of two disparate areas. About half of its population—the faster-growing half—lives along the Gulf Coast in towns like Bradenton, Sarasota, and Fort Myers. The people here are retired Northerners, many of them well-to-do. Their voting behavior is very Republican and very conservative. These towns do not possess many backers of either George Wallace or the national Democratic party. The few who do vote in the Democratic primaries, however, tend to favor the more liberal candidates, much like their former neighbors in the high-income suburbs of Chicago and New York.

The other half of the district is old Florida rural and small-town—Polk County (Lakeland) and sparsely populated DeSoto and Hardee counties. The old-time Southerners here went heavily for Wallace in 1968. In state elections, they favor Democrats, except when the Democrat can be tagged as a liberal, something which happened in both 1966 and 1968. But the old Florida part of the 7th also has a streak of Southern populism. Lakeland is the home of Sen. Lawton Chiles, who served Polk County for 12 years in the state legislature and whose walking-man 1970 Senate campaign proved to be very successful.

By all odds, the 7th should have a conservative Republican congressman. But instead it has continued to reelect conservative Democrat James A. Haley, a former owner, through marriage, of the Ringling Brothers Barnum and Bailey Circus which is headquartered in Sarasota. Haley is now 2nd ranking Democrat on the House Interior and Insular Affairs Committee and chairman of its Indian Affairs Subcommittee; he is also a senior member of Veterans' Affairs.

The Congressman's percentages have been declining for the past decade—from 67% in 1962 to 53% in 1970. In 1968 and 1970, Haley failed to carry the coastal counties, which now cast twice as many votes as the inland counties. By habit, old-line Southern Democrats in Polk County often don't bother to vote in general elections.

The 7th may pose a difficult redistricting problem for the Democratic legislature and governor. The current district has a population of 577,000, which must be cut down to about 452,000. One possible solution is to remove Polk County (pop. 222,000) and add a Gulf Coast county or two, thereby creating a coast district. Polk would then become the center of a conservative Democratic district encircling the Tampa-St. Petersburg area. But Haley would doubtless protest; he has failed to carry the coastal portions of the district in the last two elections. And such a district would be certain to elect a Republican, no matter what; presently in the 7th, voters could very well elect a Republican but only in the event incumbent Haley does not run.

An alternative solution, one which would please Haley, would split Hillsborough County (Tampa) between a coast district and a Polk County district. But this move would no doubt be unacceptable to Democrat Sam Gibbons, who currently represents Tampa and the 6th district (see Florida 6). The Democratic legislature might also try splitting Pinellas County (St. Petersburg). But Haley would want none of that either, since it is heavily Republican. A solution is not in sight—unless Haley, who will be 73 in 1972, decides to retire.

Census Data 1970 pop. 577,721; deviation from current state average, +2.1%; change 1960–70, +39.7%. Metro. 0.0%, 0.0% central city.

1970 Share of Federal Outlays $326,513,078

DOD	$18,700,000	HEW	$211,492,004
AEC	$000	HUD	$556,000
NASA	$733,270	OEO	$1,072,369
DOT	$2,981,241	DOA	$7,900,688
		Other	$83,077,506

Federal Military-Industrial Commitments

None.

Economic Base Livestock and poultry, canned and preserved fruits, vegetables, and seafood, and other food and kindred products; agricultural chemicals and other chemicals and allied products. Also, tourism (Sarasota).

The Voters

Registration 252,200 total. 163,013 D (65%); 83,957 R (33%); 5,230 other (2%).

Employment profile White collar, 38%. Blue collar, 62%.

Ethnic groups Black, 13%. Total foreign stock, 10%. Germany, UK, 2% each; Canada, Italy, Sweden, 1% each; others, 2%.

Presidential vote

1968	Humphrey (D)	45,749	(23%)
	Nixon (R)	94,603	(48%)
	Wallace (AIP)	57,278	(29%)

Representative

James Andrew Haley (D) Elected 1952; b. Jan. 4, 1899, Jacksonville, Alabama; home, Sarasota; U. of Ala., 1919–22; Army, WWI; married; Methodist.

Career Accountant 1920–33; Genl. Mgr., John Ringling estate, 1933–43; V.P. Ringling Circus, 1943–45, Pres. and Dir. Ringling Bros. Barnum & Bailey Circus, 1946–48; Fla. House of Reps., 1948 and 1950; Delegate to Natl. Convention, 1952 and 1960.

Offices 1236 LHOB, 202-225-5015. Also Rm. 107 Smith Bldg., 2070 Main St., Fort Myers 33901, 813-334-7416, and 113 East Main, Bartow 33803, 813-533-2881.

Committees

Interior and Insular Affairs (2nd); Subs. (1) Chm., Indian Affairs, (2) Environment, (3) Irrigation and Reclamation, (4) Territorial and Insular Affairs.

Veteran's Affairs (3rd); Sub. on Hospitals.

Group Ratings

	ADA	COPE	NREP	NFU	LCV	CFA	NAB	NSI	ACA
1970	8	25	8	23	11	45	73	100	83
1969	7	—	—	33	—	—	—	—	94
1968	0	0	—	19	—	—	100	—	100

Key Votes

(1) ABM	FOR	(6) 18-Yr-Vote	AGN	(11) Clean Water $	AGN
(2) SST	AGN	(7) Farm Sub Lmt	AGN	(12) Mig Wrkrs Comp	AGN
(3) Phil Pln	AGN	(8) Coop-Church	AGN	(13) Jets to Chiang	FOR
(4) No-Knock	FOR	(9) Family Asst	AGN	(14) State OEO Veto	FOR
(5) Cmutr Tax	AGN	(10) Work Stamps	FOR	(15) Park Logging	AGN

Election Results

1970 general:	James A. Haley (D)	78,535 (53%)
	Joe Z. Lovingood (R)	68,646 (47%)
1970 primary:	James A. Haley (D), unopposed	
1968 general:	James A. Haley (D)	91,539 (55%)
	Joe Z. Lovingood (R)	74,896 (45%)

EIGHTH DISTRICT Political Background

Florida 8 is St. Petersburg, Clearwater, and suburbs—retirement land. The district's median age, almost 49, and the median voter age, over 60, are the highest in the country. Many but not all of St. Petersburg's retirees are wealthy; most of them are dependably Republican. But there was a notable exception. In 1964 when Barry Goldwater intimated that he might abolish social security, St. Petersburg gave Lyndon Johnson a handsome 55% majority.

Florida's Republican Party got its start in St. Petersburg when the city elected William Cramer to the state legislature in 1950 and to the U.S. House of Representatives in 1954. Cramer spent 16 years in the House, where he became the ranking Republican on the pork-barreling Public Works Committee. The Congressman was also known as a tireless and effective partisan: a sponsor of the no-busing proviso to the 1968 Civil Rights Act and of the so-called Rap Brown law on which the Chicago 7 were tried. In addition, Cramer was a strong advocate of capital punishment.

Cramer ran for the Senate in 1970. He beat ex-Judge G. Harrold Carswell handily in the Republican primary but came to grief at the hands of state Sen. Lawton Chiles (see Florida state write-up). Cramer was replaced in the House by Republican ex-state Sen. C. W. (Bill) Young. Because the 8th is so dependably conservative and Republican it is difficult to see how Young can avoid indefinite reelection. In his first general election, 1970, a bad Republican year in Florida, Young got 67% of the vote.

Redistricting will reduce the size of the 8th, but since the district is heavily Republican, Democratic legislators will probably leave it pretty much intact. To carve it up would place too many Republicans in adjacent Democratic districts.

Census Data 1970 pop. 598,284; deviation from current state average, +5.7%; change 1960–70, +45.4%. Metro. 87.3%, 36.1% central city.

1970 Share of Federal Outlays $460,888,000 (average outlay per district, Florida 6 and 8)

DOD	$80,878,000	HEW	$184,823,000
AEC	$9,493,000	HUD	$3,076,000
NASA	$4,388,000	OEO	$1,271,000
DOT	$12,327,000	DOA	$2,663,000
		Other	$161,959,000

Federal Military-Industrial Commitments (Florida 6 and 8, greater Tampa-St. Petersburg listing)

DOD Contractors Honeywell Inc. (St. Petersburg and Tampa), $77.515m: guidance components for Poseidon, Polaris, and Minuteman missiles; other electronic equipment. Jackson Products (Tampa), $6.465m: 2.75-inch rocket fin and nozzle assemblies. Consolidated Box (Tampa), $5.633m: fiber containers. Electronic Communications Inc. (St. Petersburg), $5.591m: telemetry transmitters.

DOD Installations MacDill AFB (Tampa).

AEC Operations General Electric (Clearwater), $15.625m: operation of Pinellas Plant.

Economic Base Electrical machinery, equipment, and supplies, esp. communication equipment; tranportation equipment, esp. trailer coaches; food and kindred products, esp. canned and preserved fruits, vegetables, and seafoods. Also, tourism (St. Petersburg) and banking.

The Voters

Registration 298,488 total. 148,544 D (50%); 142,236 R (48%); 7,708 other (3%).
Employment profile White collar, 48%. Blue collar, 52%.

Ethnic groups Black, 8%. Total foreign stock, 22%. UK, 5%; Germany, 4%; Canada, 3%; Austria, Ireland, Italy, Poland, Sweden, USSR, 1% each; others, 4%.

Presidential vote

1968	Humphrey (D)	74,501	(32%)
	Nixon (R)	118,978	(51%)
	Wallace (AIP)	40,780	(17%)

Representative

C. W. (Bill) Young (R) Elected 1970; b. Dec. 16, 1930, Harmarville, Pa.; home, Seminole; Fla. Natl. Guard, 1948–57; married, three children; Methodist.

Career Dist. asst., Rep. William C. Cramer, 1957–60; Fla. Senate, 1960–70; Minority Leader, 1966; Chm., Southern Highway Policy Com., 1966–68; Eighth Congressional Dist. Campaign Chm. for Nixon-Agnew.

Offices 1721 LHOB, 202-225-5961. Also 627 Fed. Bldg., 144 First Ave. South, St. Petersburg 33701, 813-393-3191.

Committees

Armed Services (16th); Sub. No. 2.

Post Office and Civil Service (11th); Subs. (1) Census and Statistics, (2) Postal Facilities and Mail.

Group Rating, Key Votes: Newly elected.

Election Results

1970 general:	C. W. Young (R)	120,466	(67%)
	Ted A. Bailey (D)	58,904	(33%)
1970 primary:	C. W. Young (R)	57,587	(77%)
	Don H. Stafford (R)	12,336	(16%)
	Robert Mick (R)	5,010	(7%)

NINTH DISTRICT Political Background

Florida 9 is Palm Beach County, a slice of Broward County to the south, and several sparsely populated swamp and Everglades counties to the west. More than three-quarters of the 9th district's residents live along the Atlantic Coast from just north of Fort Lauderdale to Fort Pierce. The core of the district is West Palm Beach, a much larger city than its more fashionable namesake. Many of the residents here are retired, and most of them are politically conservative, more often than not Republican. The 9th's small number of blacks and the migrant workers living in festering swamp camps do not form significant voting blocs.

Paul G. Rogers, the district's congressman, succeeded his father in the House in 1955. A generally conservative Democrat, Rogers, who seems to be very popular in the district, habitually wins reelection by large margins. Rogers wins even though his constituents vote Republican in other contests. The Congressman is currently a high ranking member of the Interstate and Foreign Commercial and Merchant Marine and Fisheries committees.

Redistricting will require a substantial reduction in the size of the 9th, probably confining it to the coastal area. But this should not endanger Rogers' incumbency.

Census Data 1970 pop. 658,992; deviation from current state average, +16.5%; change 1960–70, +64.2%. Metro. 73.7%, 10.8% central city.

1970 Share of Federal Outlays $409,068,018

DOD	$155,175,000	HEW	$153,835,438
AEC	$24,129	HUD	$207,012
NASA	$6,683,071	OEO	$305,688
DOT	$10,238,293	DOA	$14,241,569
		Other	$68,357,819

Federal Military-Industrial Commitments

DOD Contractors Grumman Corp and Grumman Aerospace (Stuart), $25.772m: A-6 aircraft modification.

Economic Base Livestock; electrical machinery, equipment, and supplies, esp. electronic components and accessories; food and kindred products. Also, tourism (Palm Beach).

The Voters

Registration 262,097 total. 157,987 D (60%); 96,137 R (37%); 7,973 other (3%).

Employment profile White collar, 38%. Blue collar, 62%.

Ethnic groups Black, 17%. Puerto Rican, 1%. Total foreign stock, 15%. Canada, Germany, UK, 2% each; Ireland, Italy, Sweden, 1% each; others, 4%.

Presidential vote

1968	Humphrey (D)	56,279	(26%)
	Nixon (R)	114,009	(53%)
	Wallace (AIP)	44,770	(21%)

Representative

Paul G. Rogers (D) Elected 1954; b. June 4, 1921, Ocilla, Ga.; home, West Palm Beach; U. of Fla., B.A., 1942, LL.B., 1948; Army, WWII; married, one child; Methodist.

Career Practicing atty., 1948–54.

Offices 2417 RHOB, 202-225-3001. Also 416 Harvey Bldg., West Palm Beach 33401, 305-832-6424.

Committees

Interstate and Foreign Commerce (6th); Chm., Sub. on Public Health and Environment.

Merchant Marine and Fisheries (9th); (1) Coast Guard, Coast and Geodetic Survey and Navigation, (2) Fisheries and Wildlife Conservation, (3) Merchant Marine, (4) Oceanography.

Group Ratings

	ADA	COPE	NREP	NFU	LCV	CFA	NAB	NSI	ACA
1970	24	17	8	38	50	83	67	100	68
1969	7	—	—	40	—	—	—	—	94
1968	8	15	—	38	—	—	100	—	91

Key Votes

(1) ABM	FOR	(6) 18-Yr-Vote	FOR	(11) Clean Water $	AGN
(2) SST	AGN	(7) Farm Sub Lmt	AGN	(12) Mig Wrkrs Comp	AGN
(3) Phil Pln	AGN	(8) Coop-Church	AGN	(13) Jets to Chiang	FOR
(4) No-Knock	FOR	(9) Family Asst	AGN	(14) State OEO Veto	FOR
(5) Cmutr Tax	AGN	(10) Work Stamps	FOR	(15) Park Logging	AGN

Election Results

1970 general:	Paul G. Rogers (D)	120,565	(71%)
	Emil F. Danciu (R)	50,146	(29%)
1970 primary:	Paul G. Rogers (D), unopposed		
1968 general:	Paul G. Rogers (D)	111,539	(56%)
	Robert W. Rust (R)	87,074	(44%)

TENTH DISTRICT Political Background

Florida 10 centers on Fort Lauderdale and includes most of surrounding Broward County and a slice of northern Dade County (Miami suburbs) to the south. The invisible line which separates the two counties also separates two very different kinds of voters. Fort Lauderdale, Hollywood, and adjacent cities in Broward County, north of the line, abound with WASPish retired persons from Midwestern and Eastern suburbs who have brought their conservative Republicanism with them. Dade County, in contrast, is heavily Democratic, with large numbers of Jews, blacks, and Cubans, and less affluent retired residents who have retained liberal Democratic voting habits. The Broward-Dade line, in short, separates readers of the Chicago *Tribune* from readers of the New York *Times*.

Rep. J. Herbert Burke, a conservative Republican of the Cramer faction, has never carried the Dade portion of the district, but, since the district's creation after the 1964 election, has always swept the larger Broward segment. Redistricting should produce a new district entirely within fast growing Broward (up 83% in the '60's), which will make Burke's safe seat even safer.

Census Data 1970 pop. 687,075; deviation from current state average, +21.4%; change 1960–70, +69.8%. Metro. 100.0%. 33.8% central city.

1970 Share of Federal Outlays $393,666,000 (average outlay per district, Florida 10, 11, and 12)

DOD	$76,158,000	HEW	$180,189,000
AEC	$124,000	HUD	$10,658,000
NASA	$771,000	OEO	$2,295,000
DOT	$14,234,000	DOA	$3,947,000
		Other	$105,290,000

Federal Military-Industrial Commitments (Florida 10, 11, and 12, greater Miami listing)

DOD Contractors Airlift International Inc. (Miami), $35.394m: air cargo transport. Aerodex (Miami), $15.135m: overhaul of various aircraft engines.

DOD Installations Naval Security Group Activities (Homestead). Naval Air Station (Key West). Navy Fleet Sonar School (Key West). Naval Hospital (Key West). Naval Station (Key West). Homestead AFB (Homestead). Richmond AF Station (Perrine).

Economic Base Livestock; electrical machinery, equipment, and supplies, esp. communication equipment; fabricated structural metal products and other fabricated metal products. Also, tourism (Fort Lauderdale).

The Voters

Registration 85,297 total. 69,880 D (82%); 13,967 R (16%); 1,450 other (2%).

Employment profile White collar, 46%. Blue collar, 54%.

Ethnic groups Black, 12%. Total foreign stock, 22%. Canada, Germany, Italy, UK, 3% each; Austria, Ireland, Hungary, Poland, Sweden, USSR, 1% each; others, 4%.

Presidential vote

1968	Humphrey (D)	74,637	(37%)
	Nixon (R)	93,160	(46%)
	Wallace (AIP)	35,299	(17%)

Representative

J. Herbert Burke (R) Elected 1966; b. Jan. 14, 1913, Chicago, Ill.; home, Hollywood; Chicago YMCA Col., A.A., 1936; Northwestern U. and Chicago Kent Col. of Law, LL.B., 1940; J.D., 1969; Army, WWII; married, two children; Catholic.

Career Practicing atty., 1940– ; Mgr. Broward County Com., 1952–68; Mbr. Fla. State Repub. Com., 1954–59; Delegate Repub. Natl. Com., 1968; Mbr., Repub. Platform Com., 1968.

Offices 1127 LHOB, 202-225-3001. Also 416 Harvey Bldg., West Palm Beach 33401, 305-832-6424.

Committees

Foreign Affairs (13th); Subs. (1) Asian and Pacific Affairs, (2) Europe, (3) Foreign Economic Policy.

Group Ratings

	ADA	COPE	NREP	NFU	LCV	CFA	NAB	NSI	ACA
1970	8	17	9	15	0	39	91	100	93
1969	7	—	—	27	—	—	—	—	88
1968	0	8	—	27	—	—	100	—	100

Key Votes

(1) ABM	FOR	(6) 18-Yr-Vote	AGN	(11) Clean Water $	AGN
(2) SST	AGN	(7) Farm Sub Lmt	FOR	(12) Mig Wrkrs Comp	AGN
(3) Phil Pln	FOR	(8) Coop-Church	AGN	(13) Jets to Chiang	FOR
(4) No-Knock	FOR	(9) Family Asst	AGN	(14) State OEO Veto	FOR
(5) Cmutr Tax	AGN	(10) Work Stamps	FOR	(15) Park Logging	AGN

Election Results

1970 general:	J. Herbert Burke (R)	81,170	(54%)
	James J. Ward, Jr. (D)	68,847	(46%)
1970 primary:	J. Herbert Burke (R)	24,144	(62%)
	Edward J. Stack (R)	15,091	(38%)
1968 general:	J. Herbert Burke (R)	99,844	(55%)
	E. J. Gissendanner (D)	82,138	(45%)

ELEVENTH DISTRICT Political Background

Florida 11 is the northern half of Dade County except for the portion currently in the 10th district. The 11th, which includes most of the cities of Miami and Miami Beach, is the bastion of Florida liberalism. Voters in the 11th behave more like voters in the Bronx than they do like those in the rest of the state, in part because many of the district's residents are Jews actually from the Bronx and other sections of New York City. The 11th also has a large number of black voters and a growing number of Cuban refugees who have been gaining citizenship and the franchise. The refugees include many staunch anti-Communists and may prove to be significantly more conservative and Republican than the district's Jews and blacks.

Congressman Claude Pepper of the 11th is the grand old man of Florida liberal politics. For 14 years, from 1936 to 1950, he was a United States senator from Florida. And while other Southerners soured on the New Deal, Pepper remained one of its strongest proponents. Defeated in a bitter primary by George Smathers in 1950, Pepper retired to a lucrative law practice in Miami. But when the 1960 census forced Florida to create an additional Miami House seat, Pepper was the logical choice to fill it. In 1962 he won an absolute majority in a four-man Democratic primary. Since then Pepper has won renomination and reelection without difficulty. In the House, his voting record is substantially the same as that of most Northern liberal Democrats. Pepper sits on the House Rules Committee and is also Chairman of the Select Committee on Crime.

The 1970 census indicates that Dade County will receive a third House seat. The presence of a new seat will virtually guarantee Pepper's reelection, and the Miami area will probably send another liberal Democrat—there is no shortage of aspirants in politician-glutted Miami—to the Congress.

Census Data 1970 pop. 546,431; deviation from current state average, −3.4%; change 1960–70, +21.6%. Metro. 100.0%, 30.7% central city.

1970 Share of Federal Outlays $393,666,000 (average outlay per district, Florida 10, 11, and 12)

DOD	$76,158,000	HEW	$180,189,000
AEC	$124,000	HUD	$10,658,000
NASA	$771,000	OEO	$2,295,000
DOT	$14,234,000	DOA	$3,957,000
		Other	$105,290,000

Federal Military-Industrial Commitments (See Florida 10 for greater Miami listing.)

Economic Base Apparel and other finished products made from fabrics and similar materials, esp. women's, misses', and juniors' outerwear; transportation equipment, esp. aircraft and parts and boat building and repairing; food and kindred products. Also, tourism (Miami) and banking.

The Voters

Registration 199,052 total. 169,188 D (85%); 26,591 R (13%); 3,273 other (2%).

Employment profile White collar, 40%. Blue collar, 60%.

Ethnic groups Black, 23%. Puerto Rican, 2%. Total foreign stock, 26%. Italy, USSR, 3% each; Canada, Germany, Poland, UK, 2% each; Austria, Hungary, Ireland, 1%; others, 9%.

Presidential vote

1968	Humphrey (D)	86,918	(58%)
	Nixon (R)	42,473	(29%)
	Wallace (AIP)	19,507	(13%)

Representative

Claude Denson Pepper (D) Elected 1962; b. Sept. 8, 1900, Dudleyville, Ala.; U. of Ala., B.A., 1921; Harvard Law School, LL.B., 1924; married; Baptist.

Career Instr. in law, U. of Ark., 1924–25; practicing atty., 1925–37, 1951– ; Fla. House of Reps., 1929; State Bd. of Pub. Welfare, 1931–32; State Bd. of Law Examiners, 1933.

Offices 432 CHOB, 202-225-3931. Also 823 Fed. Bldg., Miami 33310, 305-350-5565.

Committees

Internal Security (2nd).

Rules (8th).

Sel. Com. on Crime (Chm.).

Group Ratings

	ADA	COPE	NREP	NFU	LCV	CFA	NAB	NSI	ACA
1970	56	78	73	100	50	87	14	88	13
1969	47	—	—	92	—	—	—	—	9
1968	75	100	—	92	—	—	0	—	0

Key Votes

(1) ABM	FOR	(6) 18-Yr-Vote	FOR	(11) Clean Water $	AGN
(2) SST	FOR	(7) Farm Sub Lmt	ABS	(12) Mig Wrkrs Comp	FOR
(3) Phil Pln	AGN	(8) Coop-Church	FOR	(13) Jets to Chiang	ABS
(4) No-Knock	FOR	(9) Family Asst	FOR	(14) State OEO Veto	AGN
(5) Cmutr Tax	ABS	(10) Work Stamps	AGN	(15) Park Logging	ABS

Election Results

1970 general:	Claude Pepper (D), unopposed		
1970 primary:	Claude Pepper (D)	39,673	(85%)
	Kenneth F. Collier (D)	7,152	(15%)
1968 general:	Claude Pepper (D)	99,154	(77%)
	Ronald I. Strauss (R)	30,324	(23%)

TWELFTH DISTRICT Political Background

Florida 12 is the southern half of Dade County, which includes part of Miami, and Monroe County, which includes the Everglades National Park and Key West—Key West being where most of the county's votes are cast. The 12th is slightly more conservative than the 11th or the Dade portion of the 10th; this district has fewer blacks and Jews but more Spanish-speaking voters than the 11th. Nevertheless, the 12th is much more liberal in national political terms than any other part of Florida outside of the core of Miami and usually gives Democratic candidates healthy majorities in general elections. This is perhaps why Richard Nixon, who often vacations in Key Biscayne, did not establish his voting residence here but in San Clemente, California, which is represented in the House by a very conservative Republican (see California 35).

The 12th's representative, Dante B. Fascell, an émigré from the Northeast and a former state legislator, has represented all or part of Miami in Washington since 1954. Fascell is considered liberal, though less so than Claude Pepper of the adjacent 11th. Congressman Fascell looks unbeatable. He is currently a high-ranking member of the Foreign Affairs Committee and chairman of its subcommittee on Inter-American Affairs, a unit that is of considerable interest to many of his constituents.

Redistricting will probably modify the district's lines. If territory verging on central Miami is removed from the 12th, it will become more conservative, but Fascell's tenure is unlikely to be affected.

Census Data 1970 pop. 569,912; deviation from current state average, +0.7%; change 1960–70, +42.3%. Metro. 90.8%, 29.3% central city.

1970 Share of Federal Outlays $393,666,000 (average outlay per district, Florida 10, 11, and 12)

DOD	$76,158,000	HEW	$180,189,000
AEC	$124,000	HUD	$10,658,000
NASA	$771,000	OEO	$2,295,000
DOT	$14,234,000	DOA	$3,947,000
		Other	$105,290,000

Federal Military-Industrial Commitments (See Florida 10 for greater Miami listing.)

Economic Base Poultry; apparel and other finished products made from fabrics and similar materials; fabricated metal products. Also, higher education (University of Miami) and tourism (Miami, Key West).

The Voters

Registration 182,890 total. 140,706 D (77%); 38,449 R (21%); 3,735 other (2%).

Employment profile White collar, 52%. Blue collar, 48%.

Ethnic groups Black, 9%. Puerto Rican, 1%. Total foreign stock, 30%. USSR, 5%; Canada, Germany, Italy, Poland, UK, 2% each; Austria, Hungary, Ireland, 1% each; others, 9%.

Presidential vote

1968	Humphrey (D)	59,213	(39%)
	Nixon (R)	68,567	(45%)
	Wallace (AIP)	25,428	(17%)

Representative

Dante B. Fascell (D) Elected 1954; b. March 9, 1917, Bridgehampton, L.I., N.Y.; home, Miami; U. of Miami, LL.B., 1938; Army, WWII; married, three children; Protestant.

Career Practicing atty., 1938–54; Legal Attaché Dade County Legis. Delegation, 1947–50; Fla. House of Reps., 1950–54; Mbr. U.S. Delegation 24th Gen. Assembly, UN.

Offices 2160 RHOB, 202-225-4506. Also 920 Fed. Bldg., 51 S.W. First Ave., Miami 33130, 305-350-5301.

Committees

Foreign Affairs (5th); (1) Chm., Inter-American Affairs, (2) International Organizations and Movements, (3) State Department Organization and Foreign Operations.

Government Operations (7th); Subs. (1) Conservation and Natural Resources, (2) Legal and Monetary Affairs.

Group Ratings

	ADA	COPE	NREP	NFU	LCV	CFA	NAB	NSI	ACA
1970	56	82	64	100	78	100	20	88	17
1969	53	—	—	83	—	—	—	—	13
1968	75	77	—	94	—	—	33	—	4

Key Votes

(1) ABM	AGN	(6) 18-Yr-Vote	FOR	(11) Clean Water $	FOR
(2) SST	FOR	(7) Farm Sub Lmt	ABS	(12) Mig Wrkrs Comp	FOR
(3) Phil Pln	ABS	(8) Coop-Church	FOR	(13) Jets to Chiang	FOR
(4) No-Knock	FOR	(9) Family Asst	FOR	(14) State OEO Veto	AGN
(5) Cmutr Tax	AGN	(10) Work Stamps	AGN	(15) Park Logging	AGN

Election Results

1970 general:	Dante B. Fascell (D)	75,895	(72%)
	Robert A. Zinxell (R)	29,935	(28%)
1970 primary:	Dante B. Fascell (D), unopposed		
1968 general:	Dante B. Fascell (D)	82,362	(57%)
	Mike Thompson (R)	62,032	(43%)

GEORGIA

Political Background

On January 4, 1971, as the 92nd Congress convened, Sen. Richard B. Russell—President Pro Tempore of the Senate, chairman of its Appropriations Committee, and former chairman of its Armed Services Committee—died, and an era in Georgia politics ended. Russell's Senate career began in 1933 and spanned nearly 38 years, the second-longest term of service in the history of the upper house.

Russell, whose father was a well-known Georgia politician, was elected to the state legislature while still in his twenties and was elected governor and senator before he was 40. In the 1936 Senate Democratic primary, he beat the quasi-populist, race-baiting Gov. Eugene Talmadge (father of the state's current senior senator). After that, he never had an opponent in any election. The Senator was a model of the aristocratic Southern tradition of public service, a tradition that began with George Washington and Thomas Jefferson. Russell never married, saying that a politician had to be totally committed to his work. Every day he read every word in the *Congressional Record,* a formidable task.

From the mid-1940's to the late 1960's, Russell, as the unofficial leader of the Senate's Southern Democrats, directed that group's stand against civil rights legislation. In 1952, the Southern Senator sought his party's nomination for President; he was rebuffed and later declined the position of Senate minority leader, which went, at his urging, to a young Senator from Texas, Lyndon B. Johnson. Russell was always interested in the policies governing the nation's security, and he advocated military preparedness as early as the 1930's—an unusual position in those days. In the 1960's the Senator saw little hope for success in Vietnam, but once the troops were sent in he loyally supported the policies of the Johnson and Nixon administrations.

Georgia's one-party, whites-only politics produced Richard Russell and gave him security of tenure and seniority, and consequently immense power in the affairs of the nation. That kind of Old South political pattern no longer exists in Georgia. To be sure, Sen. Herman Talmadge, now chairman of the Senate Agriculture Committee, will not face serious opposition when he seeks reelection in 1974. And most members of the state's House delegation, conservative Democrats from predominantly rural districts, will win reelection with monotonous regularity. It is very unlikely, however, that the state can again put together a tandem like Sen. Russell and Rep. Carl Vinson, a man who served in the House for 50 years (1914–64). As chairman of the House Armed Services Committee, Vinson worked closely with Russell. And largely because of their seniority and committee posts, Georgia now has 15 military installations employing some 45,000 people. These installations, plus the Lockheed plant in Marietta, contribute nearly two billion dollars annually to the state's economy.

How the state's old political patterns will change is not yet clear. Recent statewide elections for President and governor have pitted the South's booming commercial center, Atlanta, and several smaller cities (Savannah, Augusta, and Athens)—all with large black populations—against the rest of the state. In every test so far, the rest of the state, predominantly agricultural and small-town, has prevailed. Rural Georgia elected Lester Maddox governor in 1966 and Jimmy Carter governor in 1970 and delivered the state's electoral votes to Barry Goldwater in 1964 and George Wallace in 1968.

Metropolitan Atlanta, which has about a quarter of the state's population, votes like a comparable urban center in the North. In 1969, for example, Atlanta elected a Jewish mayor and a black vice-mayor. In general, greater Atlanta voters support liberal candidates in statewide primaries and urban-based Republicans in statewide general elections. In 1968, George Wallace finished a poor third in metropolitan Atlanta, taking only 22%. But Wallace swept the rest of Georgia, in the end winning 43% of the state's votes, with the rest split about equally between Nixon and Humphrey.

In the 1970 gubernatorial election, it appeared that Atlanta lost again. State Sen. Jimmy Carter, a peanut farmer and former staff aide to Adm. Hyman Rickover, had rural Georgia solidly behind him, beating Atlanta-backed candidates in both the Democratic primary and the general election. But in his inaugural speech, Carter surprised Lester Maddox followers and sophisticated Atlantans alike. The new Governor, with Lester Maddox himself sitting on the platform, asked Georgians to end their resistance to desegregation and called for the equal treatment of all races.

The man Carter chose to fill Russell's Senate seat was one early test of the Governor's sincerity. Many expected him to appoint ex-Gov. S. Ernest Vandiver, Russell's nephew by marriage and a hard-line segregationist. Instead, Carter named the finance chairman of his campaign, David H. Gambrell, a 41-year-old scholarly Atlanta lawyer. Soon after his appointment, Gambrell told Georgians of his plan to break with tradition. "The passage of time has changed a lot of things," he said. "I think he [Russell] would expect a younger person, who's had a different experience in life, to have different ideas."

Whether most Georgia voters are now ready for different ideas remains to be seen. The 1972 Senate election will provide part of the answer. A good number of men should be attracted to the race for the Senate seat, quite a prize in Georgia, particularly since its voters have elected only three men to the U.S. Senate in the past 38 years. One sure candidate is ex-Gov., now Lt. Gov. Lester Maddox, the chicken restaurateur and law-and-order advocate whose resistance to court-ordered integration carried him all the way into the governor's chair. Other possible candidates include ex-Gov. Vandiver and two other former governors—conservative S. Marvin Griffin and moderate Carl Sanders; Sanders, however, lost badly to Jimmy Carter in the 1970 gubernatorial primary.

If the state's political past is any guide, odds are that any one of these men—all of them more conservative than Gambrell—could beat him in a two-man race, that is, in a runoff primary, which will occur if no candidate in the primary wins an outright majority. But other races in the South, notably Albert Brewer's strong showing against George Wallace in Alabama and Lawton Chiles's victory over Bill Cramer in Florida, indicate that Gambrell has a chance. Moreover, as an important member of Gov. Carter's campaign staff, he developed many contacts with rural Georgia politicians, and these political friendships could prove to be very useful.

The Republicans will probably put up more than token opposition. Even before Russell's death, Congressman Fletcher Thompson, an urban conservative from the Atlanta area, expressed interest in the seat. Such a race in Georgia would be striking evidence of the increasing homogenization of hitherto distinctive regional and state political patterns into the standard national format.

Georgia's senior senator, Herman Talmadge, like Russell Long of Louisiana, is the son of a famous father who won high office at an early age. Talmadge's first days in Georgia politics were turbulent. In 1946, after the death of his father—just elected governor for the fourth time—the legislature elected young (33) Herman to succeed him. Talmadge held the governor's office for 67 days against the claims of a rival, until the state Supreme Court declared his election illegal. He regained the office in the 1948 election and won a four-year term in 1950. Two years after leaving the governor's chair, he won election to the Senate, easing aside veteran (1922–56) Sen. Walter George, then chairman of the Foreign Relations Committee.

Since his election to the Senate, Talmadge has gained a polish and respectability his father never enjoyed. His conservative stands on most issues have won the support of Atlanta's financial establishment; among rural Georgians Talmadge, like his father, enjoys complete trust. The attitudes of the financial elite as well as of rural Georgians are probably reflected in Talmadge's announcement in June 1971 that he could no longer support the Nixon Administration's Vietnam policy. "The policy of Vietnamization is dragging," he said. "It is time to put an end to this cruel and unusual war which we have never declared and which is tearing at the basic fabric that holds this country together." He added that he could not on constitutional grounds vote for the McGovern-Hatfield amendment at that time, but he later voted for the Vietnam Disengagement Act, which set a withdrawal deadline of December 31, 1971, upon the release of U.S. prisoners of war.

In Washington, Talmadge serves as chairman of the Senate Agriculture Committee. Back home, he has never had serious opposition in any election and will no doubt be reelected easily in 1974.

Electoral Votes 12

Census Data 1970 pop. 4,589,575; 2.23% of U.S. total, 15th largest; change 1960–70, +16.4%. Metro. 48.5%, 22.3% central city. 1970 per capita income, $3,277, 35th highest. 9th in number of poor.

1970 Share of Federal Tax Burden $3,297,880,000; 1.69% of U.S. total, 19th largest.

1970 Share of Federal Outlays $4,284,305,606; 2.27% of U.S. total, 15th largest. Per capita federal spending, $933.

DOD	$1,979,877,000	6th (3.45%)	HEW	$1,002,610,264	16th (1.92%)
AEC	$1,194,174	35th (0.05%)	HUD	$81,112,020	5th (4.16%)
NASA	$3,602,306	30th (0.10%)	OEO	$21,315,307	9th (2.80%)
DOT	$139,399,828	20th (1.95%)	DOA	$290,154,612	16th (2.26%)
DOC	$16,150,787	15th (1.40%)	POD	$140,979,792	15th (1.93%)
DOI	$27,234,240	28th (1.18%)	VA	$201,595,809	14th (2.73%)
DOJ	$13,271,955	10th (2.31%)	CSC	$57,772,852	16th (1.44%)
			Other	$308,034,660	

Economic Base Cotton and tobacco; textile mill products, esp. broad woven cotton fabric mills, floor covering mills, and yarn and thread mills; apparel and other finished products made from fabrics and similar materials, esp. men's, youths', and boys' furnishings, work clothing, and allied garments; transportation equipment, esp. motor vehicles and motor vehicle equipment and aircraft and parts; food and kindred products, esp. meat products; paper and allied products; lumber and wood products other than furniture; fabricated metal products, esp. fabricated structural metal products; stone, clay, glass, and concrete products; printing, publishing, and allied industries. Also, banking and insurance.

Political Line-up Governor, Jimmy Carter (D); seat up, 1974. Senators, Herman E. Talmadge (D) and David H. Gambrell (D). Representatives, 10 (8 D and 2 R). State Senate (50 D and 6 R); State House (172 D and 22 R).

The Voters

Registration 1,960,436 total. No party registration.
Employment profile White collar, 35%. Blue collar, 65%.
Ethnic groups Black, 26%. Total foreign stock, 2%. All foreign groups, less than 0.5%.

Presidential vote

1968	Humphrey (D)	334,439	(27%)
	Nixon (R)	366,611	(30%)
	Wallace (AIP)	535,550	(43%)
1964	Johnson (D)	522,577	(46%)
	Goldwater (R)	616,600	(54%)
1960	Kennedy (D)	458,638	(63%)
	Nixon (R)	274,472	(37%)

Senator

Herman Eugene Talmadge (D) Elected 1956, seat up 1974; b. Aug. 9, 1913, McRae; home, Lovejoy; U. of Ga., 1936; Northwestern U., LL.B., 1942; Navy, WWII; married, two children; Baptist.

Career Atty., Governor of Ga., 1949–55; owns and operates two farms.

Offices 347 OSOB, 202-225-3643. Also Rm. 430, 275 Peachtree St., N.E., Atlanta 30303, 404-524-7738.

Committees

Agriculture and Forestry (Chm.).

Finance (3rd).

Veterans' Affairs (2nd); Subs. (1) Chm., Compensation and Pensions, (2) Housing and Insurance, (3) Readjustment, Education, Employment.

Sel. Com. on Nutrition and Human Needs (3rd).

Sel. Com. on Standards and Conduct (2nd).

Jt. Com. on Internal Revenue Taxation (3rd).

Group Ratings

	ADA	COPE	NREP	NFU	LCV	NAB	NSI	ACA
1970	3	25	0	38	24	73	100	86
1969	6	—	—	44	—	—	—	80
1968	0	0	—	11	—	25	—	79

Key Votes

(1) ABM	FOR	(8) Phil Pln	ABS	(15) Coop-Church	AGN
(2) SST	FOR	(9) Vol Army	AGN	(16) Cut Oil Dpltn	AGN
(3) Busing	AGN	(10) Prison $	AGN	(17) Consumer Prot	FOR
(4) Tob Sub	FOR	(11) Cut Mil $	AGN	(18) Farm Sub Limit	AGN
(5) Carswell	FOR	(12) Defoliatn	FOR	(19) Comp Bid Sales	AGN
(6) No-Knock	AGN	(13) 18-Yr-Vote	AGN	(20) Pre-Prod Tests	AGN
(7) Seniorty	AGN	(14) Pentgn PR	FOR	(21) Cut Marjna Pen	AGN

Election Results

1968 general:	Herman E. Talmadge (D)	885,093	(78%)
	E. Earl Patton, Jr. (R)	256,793	(22%)
1968 primary:	Herman E. Talmadge (D)	627,915	(75%)
	Maynard Jackson (D)	207,171	(25%)
1962 general:	Herman E. Talmadge (D), unopposed		

Senator

David Henry Gambrell (D) Appointed Feb. 2, 1971, seat up 1972; b. Dec. 20, 1929, Atlanta; home, Atlanta; Davidson Col., B.S., 1949; Harvard Law School, LL.B., 1952; USAR, 1949–57; married; four children.

Career Atty., 1952–71; pres. State Bar Assn., 1967–68; dir.. Nat. Legal Aid and Defender Assn., 1965–71.

Offices 460 OSOB, 202-225-3521.

Committees

Aeronautical and Space Sciences (6th).

Banking, Housing, and Urban Affairs (8th); Subs. (1) Housing and Urban Affairs, (2) International Finance, (3) Production and Stabilization, (4) Securities.

Sel. Com. on Small Business (9th); Subs. (1) Chm., Science and Technology, (2) Government Procurement, (3) Government Regulation.

Group Ratings, Key Votes: Newly elected.

Election Results

1966 general:	Richard B. Russell (D), unopposed		
1966 primary:	Richard B. Russell (D)	596,209	(91%)
	Harry L. Hyde (D)	61,922	(9%)
1960 general:	Richard B. Russell (D), unopposed		

FIRST DISTRICT Political Background

Georgia 1 is in the southeastern part of the state. Savannah (pop. 118,000), the district's largest city and the state's fourth largest, is a port and industrial center. The rest of the district is almost entirely agricultural, with its small towns dependent largely on the cotton crop. Savannah and surrounding Chatham County have a substantial number of black voters—Humphrey carried the county in 1968—as do several of the rural counties in the district. But rural white people cast the bulk of the votes, the same "wool hats" who provided the electoral margins for Eugene Talmadge time after time.

Since 1960, the 1st's congressman has been G. Elliott Hagan, a predictably conservative member of the House Armed Services and District of Columbia committees, and chairman of the latter's Public Health and Welfare Subcommittee. Hagan, like many congressmen, is not too well known outside his district. Within it, he has encountered several challenges in the Democratic primary. In 1966, for example, he won only 53% in the primary runoff. Hagan is especially weak around Savannah.

Perhaps his performance at the polls has led him to cultivate his district with increasing care. But past results indicate that Hagan is less likely than most Southern congressmen to enjoy an indefinite incumbency. Southern politicos seem to know by instinct when an incumbent is in trouble, and when a congressman attracts continued primary opposition, he is usually beaten sooner or later. Moreover, in this case, Hagan's problems will be compounded if Georgia 1 is redistricted to include substantial areas where Hagan will not enjoy the usual advantages of incumbency.

Census Data 1970 pop. 431,793; deviation from current state average, −5.9%; change 1960–70, +2.7%. Metro. 43.5%, 27.4% central city.

1970 Share of Federal Outlays $347,197,471

DOD	$113,532,000	HEW	$93,774,255
AEC	$52,993	HUD	$17,110,509
NASA	$000	OEO	$1,330,729
DOT	$17,148,541	DOA	$41,524,883
		Other	$62,724,561

Federal Military-Industrial Commitments

DOD Installations Hunter Army Airfield (Savannah). Fort Stewart AB (Savannah).

Economic Base Cotton and livestock; paper and allied products; transportation equipment; food and kindred products.

The Voters

Registration 200,948 total. No party registration.

Employment profile White collar, 32%. Blue collar, 68%.

Ethnic groups Black, 35%. Total foreign stock, 2%. All foreign groups less than 0.5%.

Presidential vote

1968	Humphrey (D)	37,733	(30%)
	Nixon (R)	34,175	(26%)
	Wallace (AIP)	58,658	(45%)

Representative

G. Elliott Hagan (D) Elected 1960; b. May 24, 1916, Sylvania; home, Sylvania; U. of Ga., Emory U., John Marshall Law School; Army, WWII; married, three children; Baptist.

Career Life insurance and estate planning and farming; Sec. Treasurer and Deputy Dir., State Bd. of Workmen's Compensation, 1946; Mbr., Natl. Council of State Governments; Dist. Dir., Office of Price Stabilization, 1951–52; Ga. House of Reps., five terms; Ga. Senate, one term.

Offices 2443 RHOB, 202-225-5831. Also P.O. Bldg., Drawer D., 103 E. Telephone St., Sylvania 30467, 912-564-7446.

Committees

Armed Services (12th); Sub. No. 2.

District of Columbia (5); Subs. (1) Chm., Public Health and Welfare, (2) Education.

Group Ratings

	ADA	COPE	NREP	NFU	LCV	CFA	NAB	NSI	ACA
1970	12	25	8	33	20	47	67	100	76
1969	7	—	—	47	—	—	—	—	81
1968	8	0	—	42	—	—	60	—	72

Key Votes

(1) ABM	FOR	(6) 18-Yr-Vote	AGN	(11) Clean Water $	AGN
(2) SST	FOR	(7) Farm Sub Lmt	AGN	(12) Mig Wrkrs Comp	AGN
(3) Phil Pln	AGN	(8) Coop-Church	AGN	(13) Jets to Chiang	FOR
(4) No-Knock	AGN	(9) Family Asst	AGN	(14) State OEO Veto	FOR
(5) Cmutr Tax	ABS	(10) Work Stamps	FOR	(15) Park Logging	ABS

Election Results

1970 general:	G. Elliott Hagan (D), unopposed		
1970 primary:	G. Elliott Hagan (D)	45,551	(67%)
	Max Lockwood (D)	22,464	(33%)
1968 general:	G. Elliott Hagan (D)	77,403	(68%)
	Joseph J. Tribble (R)	36,118	(32%)

SECOND DISTRICT Political Background

Georgia 2 is the southwest corner of the state, a predominantly agricultural area, the largest city being Albany (pop. 68,000)—the scene of racial troubles several years ago. The 2nd has the highest black population of any rural Georgia district (38%), but the district's voting figures suggest that the blacks here have not yet begun to participate in the political process as much as they have in Southern urban centers like Atlanta. The district, like much of central and southern Georgia, is cotton and textile country, and both industries—local residents say—are in trouble and need help in the form of textile import quotas. Since the 2nd's population has been declining, substantial changes in its boundaries are likely. But the political nucleus of the district will probably stay intact, if only because of its geographical position in the corner of the state.

The newly elected congressman from the 2nd is Dawson Mathis, a 30-year-old former television newscaster. The presence of the TV newsman in politics is worthy of some note here, since alumni of the profession include the current governor of Arizona as well as Mr. Mathis and numerous other congressmen. Mathis worked for six years as a newscaster on an Albany television station that reaches most of the 2nd district. He became one of southwestern Georgia's few local celebrities—someone whose name and face almost everybody in the 2nd district recognized. In fact, Mathis may have enjoyed better name and face identification in the 2nd than its incumbent congressman.

Mathis beat several seasoned politicians in the Democratic primaries, and his Republican opponent withdrew before the general election. Mathis' goal has long been typical of young Southern politicians elected to the House: "To stay in Congress and represent the 2nd district for as long as I can." Rural Georgia politics has changed considerably in the past ten years, but unless it changes drastically in the next ten, Mathis will stay in the House as long as he wants.

Census Data 1970 pop. 360,705; deviation from current state average, —21.4%; change 1960–70, +0.7%. Metro. 24.9%, 20.1% central city.

1970 Share of Federal Outlays $222,693,746

DOD	$42,849,000	HEW	$83,310,529
AEC	$22,186	HUD	$2,282,919
NASA	$000	OEO	$713,588
DOT	$2,213,118	DOA	$51,831,678
		Other	$38,470,728

Federal Military-Industrial Commitments

DOD Installations Marine Corps Supply Center (Albany). Naval Air Station (Albany).

Economic Base Tobacco and livestock; textile mill products; food and kindred products.

The Voters

Registration 265,536 total. No party registration.

Employment profile White collar, 30%. Blue collar, 70%.

Ethnic groups Black, 38%. Total foreign stock, 1%. All foreign groups less than 0.5%.

Presidential vote

1968	Humphrey (D)	21,651	(22%)
	Nixon (R)	18,413	(18%)
	Wallace (AIP)	60,162	(60%)

Representative

M. Dawson Mathis (D) Elected 1970; b. Nov. 30, 1940, Nashville; home, Albany; South Georgia Col.; married, four children; Baptist.

Career News Director WALB-TV, Albany, Georgia.

Offices 502 CHOB, 202-225-3631. Also P.O. Bldg., Drawer D, 103 E. Telephone St., Sylvania 30467, 912-564-7446.

Committees

Agriculture (6th); Subs. (1) Department Operations, (2) Domestic Marketing and Consumer Relations, (3) Family Farms and Rural Development, (4) Oilseeds and Rice, (5) Tobacco.

Group Ratings, Key Votes: Newly elected.

Election Results

1970 general:	Dawson Mathis (D)	59,994	(92%)
	Thomas Ragdale (R)	5,376	(8%)
1970 primary:	Dawson Mathis (D)	27,188	(41%)
	Harry Wingate (D)	14,326	(22%)
	Fred B. Hand, Jr. (D)	14,024	(21%)
	Thomas C. Chatman (D)	10,614	(16%)

THIRD DISTRICT Political Background

Georgia 3 is one of the state's many rural and small-town congressional districts. It contains one good-sized city, Columbus (pop. 154,000), and two huge military installations, dividends of Carl Vinson's and Richard Russell's tenure in Congress. In the west, just south of Columbus, is Fort Benning, one of the Army's largest bases. Army planners may have put Benning here figuring that the excruciatingly hot, humid Georgia climate would best condition soldiers for the strains of warfare. But students of the relationship between the Pentagon and the congressional Armed Services committees can think of other reasons. The Warner Robbins Air Material Area is in the east of the district. The counties in which the two installations lie are the only ones in the 3rd to have significant population growth in the '60's.

The 3rd has the distinction of having once elected a Republican congressman, textile family scion Howard (Bo) Calloway. Calloway won the House seat in Georgia's Goldwater landslide of 1964 and went on to run for governor in 1966. Although he won 3,000 more votes than his major opponent, Lester Maddox, he failed to secure an absolute majority because Ellis Arnall, a liberal Democrat defeated in the primary, received 50,000 write-in votes. The race was thrown into the state legislature, which elected Maddox. Since then, Calloway has been Richard Nixon's Southern Campaign chairman and has shown no desire to challenge the present congressman from the 3rd, Jack Brinkley.

Brinkley was first elected in 1966 and, not surprisingly, is a member of the House Armed Services Committee. He is a conservative Democrat representing a typical Southern conservative district whose many blacks have not yet been able to affect its politics. Brinkley has begun what will probably be a long congressional career.

Census Data 1970 pop. 403,924; deviation from current state average, −12.0%; change 1960–70, +13.1%. Metro. 63.4%, 38.2% central city.

1970 Share of Federal Outlays $695,698,811

DOD	$518,095,000	HEW	$72,872,511
AEC	$000	HUD	$8,429,478
NASA	$000	OEO	$1,020,979
DOT	$16,004,637	DOA	$35,945,305
		Other	$43,330,901

Federal Military-Industrial Commitments

DOD Contractors Brown Construction (Fort Benning).

DOD Installations Fort Benning (Columbus). Warner Robbins Air Material Area (Macon).

Economic Base Cotton and livestock; textile mill products, esp. broad woven cotton fabric mills; food and kindred products.

The Voters

Registration 140,927 total. No party registration.

Employment profile White collar, 34%. Blue collar, 66%.

Ethnic groups Black, 33%. Total foreign stock, 4%. Germany, 1%; others, 1%.

Presidential vote

1968	Humphrey (D)	22,248	(24%)
	Nixon (R)	23,524	(26%)
	Wallace (AIP)	45,687	(50%)

Representative

Jack Thomas Brinkley (D) Elected 1966; b. Dec. 22, 1930, Faceville; home, Columbus; U. of Ga. Law School, LL.B., 1959; USAF, 1951–56; married, two children; Baptist.

Career Teacher, Georgia public schools, 1949–51; practicing atty., 1958–65; Ga. House of Reps., 1965–66.

Offices 317 CHOB, 202-225-5901. Also P.O. Bldg., Americus 31709, 912-222-2054, and P.O. Bldg., Columbus 31902, 404-324-3091.

Committees

Armed Services (19th); Sub. No. 4.

Group Ratings

	ADA	COPE	NREP	NFU	LCV	CFA	NAB	NSI	ACA
1970	4	25	0	31	0	55	83	100	74
1969	7	—	—	40	—	—	—	—	82
1968	0	9	—	47	—	—	67	—	83

Key Votes

(1) ABM	FOR	(6) 18-Yr-Vote	AGN	(11) Clean Water $	AGN
(2) SST	FOR	(7) Farm Sub Lmt	AGN	(12) Mig Wrkrs Comp	AGN
(3) Phil Pln	AGN	(8) Coop-Church	AGN	(13) Jets to Chiang	FOR
(4) No-Knock	FOR	(9) Family Asst	AGN	(14) State OEO Veto	FOR
(5) Cmutr Tax	AGN	(10) Work Stamps	FOR	(15) Park Logging	FOR

Election Results

1970 general:	Jack Brinkley (D), unopposed
1970 primary:	Jack Brinkley (D), unopposed
1968 general:	Jack Brinkley (D), unopposed

FOURTH DISTRICT Political Background

Georgia 4 comprises the eastern part of Atlanta and the city's eastern suburbs. This is mostly a well-off white area; 80% of its population—and a larger percentage of its voters—are white. It is also a basically conservative district, but conservative as that term is used in Northern politics, not as it is used in the rest of Georgia. In most statewide elections, a majority of the 4th's voters are now Republican, both out of a general agreement with the policies pursued by politicians like Richard Nixon and out of a reaction against the image of the cracker South. Though there are many transplanted Northerners here, most of the 4th's residents are of Southern, often rural Southern, origin. For many of the latter, Republicanism is a step up, a move to respectability. So it is not hard to see why the voters of the district backed Ivy-League-dressed Bo Calloway over Lester Maddox or TV commentator and Ohio native Hal Suit over peanut farmer and ex-state Sen. Jimmy Carter in the state's gubernatorial elections of 1966 and 1970.

The 4th was first created in 1964 as a direct result of a landmark Supreme Court redistricting case. Shortly before the decision, the whole Atlanta area, with a population then of more than 800,000 people, had just one congressman. In the 1964 congressional election, the voters of the 4th elected a moderate to liberal Democrat, James Mackay; Goldwater, meanwhile, managed to carry the district by a slim margin. In 1966, Mackay was defeated by Republican Ben Blackburn, who has been reelected ever since. Blackburn, a strong supporter of the Nixon Administration, reportedly plans to follow an old tradition among Southern politicians—accumulating many years of seniority. No doubt he will; he has been winning reelection with convincing margins, and redistricting will not alter his district significantly.

Census Data 1970 pop. 564,253; deviation from current state average, +22.9%; change 1960–70, +34.9%. Metro. 96.8%, 31.4% central city.

1970 Share of Federal Outlays $446,810,000 (average outlay per district, Georgia 4 and 5)

DOD	$72,094,000	HEW	$146,608,000
AEC	$160,000	HUD	$17,514,000
NASA	$1,077,000	OEO	$6,133,000
DOT	$19,279,000	DOA	$2,344,000
		Other	$181,602,000

Federal Military-Industrial Commitments (See Georgia 5 for greater Atlanta listing.)

Economic Base Food and kindred products; printing, publishing, and allied industries; motor vehicles and motor vehicle equipment; paper and allied products; apparel and other finished goods made from fabrics and similar materials; textile mill products. Also, extensive commuting to Georgia 5 (Atlanta).

The Voters

Registration 224,026 total. No party registration.
Employment profile White collar, 54%. Blue collar, 46%.
Ethnic groups Black, 20%. Total foreign stock, 4%. UK, USSR, 1% each; other, 2%.

Presidential vote

1968	Humphrey (D)	44,835	(32%)
	Nixon (R)	62,507	(44%)
	Wallace (AIP)	34,825	(25%)

Representative

Ben B. Blackburn (R) Elected 1966; b. Feb. 14, 1927, Atlanta; home, Atlanta; U. of N.C., B.A., 1947; Emory U., LL.B., 1954; Navy, 1944–46, Korean War; Lt. Cdr. USNR, 1952–54; married, four children; Episcopal.

Career Ga. Atty. General's Office, 1952–54; practicing atty., 1954–66.

Offices 1019 LHOB, 202-225-4272. Also New Fed. Bldg., 141 Trinty Place, Decatur 30030, 404-524-1275.

Committees

Banking and Currency (5th); Subs. (1) Domestic Finance, (2) Housing, (3) International Trade.

Jt. Economic Com. (4th); Subs. (1) Economic Progress, (2) Economic Statistics, (3) Urban Affairs, (4) Inter-American Economic Relationships.

Group Ratings

	ADA	COPE	NREP	NFU	LCV	CFA	NAB	NSI	ACA
1970	0	9	0	17	0	36	91	100	87
1969	0	—	—	0	—	—	—	—	88
1968	0	17	—	50	—	—	100	—	95

Key Votes

(1) ABM	FOR	(6) 18-Yr-Vote	AGN	(11) Clean Water $	AGN
(2) SST	FOR	(7) Farm Sub Lmt	AGN	(12) Mig Wrkrs Comp	AGN
(3) Phil Pln	AGN	(8) Coop-Church	AGN	(13) Jets to Chiang	FOR
(4) No-Knock	FOR	(9) Family Asst	AGN	(14) State OEO Veto	FOR
(5) Cmutr Tax	AGN	(10) Work Stamps	FOR	(15) Park Logging	FOR

Election Results

1970 general:	Ben Blackburn (R)	85,848	(65%)
	Franklin Shumake (D)	45,908	(35%)

1970 primary:	Ben Blackburn (R), unopposed		
1968 general:	Ben Blackburn (R)	78,753	(58%)
	James A. Mackay (D)	58,154	(42%)

FIFTH DISTRICT Political Background

Georgia 5 is made up of the west side of Atlanta and some of the city's western and southern suburbs. Atlanta has become the South's first major city with a majority of black residents, and most of the city's black voters live in the 5th. But because the district extends into the suburbs and because part of Atlanta's central black ghetto lies in the 4th district, only 39.5% of the 5th's residents—and a lower percentage of its voters—are black. Many whites here, however, have voted for liberal candidates in the Atlanta city elections, making the 5th the closest thing to a liberal district in the Deep South.

The Atlanta civic establishment has traditionally supported liberal political figures—men like mayors William B. Hartsfield and Ivan Allen, who between them governed the city for 30 years. But this tradition has not necessarily carried over into congressional races. Until 1962, when the district consisted of the entire Atlanta metropolitan area, the 5th was represented by arch-conservative Democrat James C. Davis, whose politics were barely distinguishable from those of most Black Belt segregationists. In 1962, Davis was upset in the Democratic primary by Charles Longstreet Weltner, a young liberal lawyer, who later, as a member of the House, voted for the Civil Rights Act of 1964. Reelected in 1964, Weltner seemed headed for a long career in Congress. But he withdrew from the 1966 election, saying that he could not subscribe to the state party's loyalty oath as long as Lester Maddox was its candidate for governor. Some speculated that Weltner knew he was going to lose and simply made the best of a bad thing. In any event, the Republican candidate, Fletcher Thompson, did win, and though Weltner came back to challenge him, Thompson remains in the House today.

Weltner's loss in 1968 seemed to indicate that the racial issue had so polarized the Georgia electorate that no liberal could win, even in Atlanta. But in the 1969 Atlanta city elections, a liberal coalition did prevail. Sam Massell, a Jew, was elected mayor even though he did not have the support of much of the city's establishment, and Maynard Jackson, a black, was elected vice-mayor by a comfortable margin. The results prompted the Rev. Andrew Young, one of the leaders of the Southern Christian Leadership Conference, to run for Thompson's seat. Young won the Democratic primary easily and went into the general election with national news coverage and high hopes.

But the hopes were soon dashed. Thompson ran film clips of a Young interview on Atlanta TV, which, Thompson said, showed that Young did not really favor the continuation of Western civilization. Many of the white Atlantans who had supported Massell and Jackson in the city elections felt misgivings about voting for Young; meanwhile the nearly all-white suburbs, fearful and suspicious of what was happening in Atlanta politics, gave Thompson overwhelming majorities. Thompson won 57% of the ballots, with less than 20% of the whites voting for Young.

Reportedly, Thompson now wants to run for the Senate in 1972, but his campaign strategy must await the outcome of the Democratic primary. If Lester Maddox, who is now lieutenant governor, decides to enter and wins the primary, Thompson will aim for huge majorities in metropolitan Atlanta where Maddox has always run poorly, even among conservative suburbanites. The Republican candidate will also look for votes in the black community. But if Sen. David Gambrell wins the nomination, Thompson will have to depend on his Atlanta suburban base and attempt to make inroads among segregationist rural voters—still a difficult task for an Atlanta Republican.

Thompson may be considering the Senate try because congressional redistricting could create problems for him. Although it is unlikely that the legislature will draw a black-majority district—it can be done on paper—the black percentage in the 5th will continue to climb as long as it is based in west and central Atlanta. This means that a Republican cannot hold on to the seat indefinitely. Young is reportedly eager to run again in 1972. Of course, the legislature could change the district lines so radically that no black candidate, or Democrat, could carry the 5th. But today there is probably less resistance in the legislature—and certainly in the governor's office—to the idea of a black congressman than there was just a few years ago.

Census Data 1970 pop. 476,878; deviation from current state average, +3.9%; change 1960–70, +17.6%. Metro. 100.0%, 67.0% central city.

1970 Share of Federal Outlays $446,810,000 (average outlay per district, Georgia 4 and 5)

DOD	$72,094,000	HEW	$146,608,000
AEC	$160,000	HUD	$17,514,000
NASA	$1,077,000	OEO	$6,133,000
DOT	$19,279,000	DOA	$2,344,000
		Other	$181,602,000

Federal Military-Industrial Commitments (Georgia 4 and 5, greater Atlanta listing)

DOD Contractors B. P. Oil Corp. (Atlanta), $5.590m: petroleum products.

DOD Installations Fort McPherson (Atlanta).

Economic Base Food and kindred products; printing, publishing, and allied industries; motor vehicles and motor vehicle equipment; paper and allied products; apparel and other finished products made from fabrics and similar materials; textile mill products. Also, banking, finance, and insurance, and higher education (Georgia State University).

The Voters

Registration 236,328 total. No party registration.

Employment profile White collar, 46%. Blue collar, 54%.

Ethnic groups Black, 39%. Total foreign stock, 3%. All foreign groups less than 0.5%.

Presidential vote

1968	Humphrey (D)	61,820	(43%)
	Nixon (R)	54,878	(38%)
	Wallace (AIP)	28,157	(19%)

Representative

Fletcher Thompson (R) Elected 1966; b. Feb. 5, 1925, College Park; home, East Point; Emory U., B.A., 1948; Woodrow Wilson Col. of Law, LL.B., 1957; Army Medical and Air Corps, 1943–46; Army Air Corps, Air Rescue Svc., 1950–53; USAF, Korean War; married, two children; Methodist.

Career Participated in Nev. atomic testing and first H-bomb test in Pacific; past V.P., Natl. Aviation Trades Assn.; Dir. Lawyer Pilots Bar Assn.; Ga. Senate, 1965–66.

Offices 208 CHOB, 202-225-3801. Also 327 Old P.O. Bldg., Atlanta 30303, 404-524-1275.

Committees

Internal Security (2nd).

Interstate and Foreign Commerce (11th); Sub. on Transportation and Aeronautics.

Group Ratings

	ADA	COPE	NREP	NFU	LCV	CFA	NAB	NSI	ACA
1970	0	9	0	23	25	37	100	100	89
1969	0	—	—	36	—	—	—	—	71
1968	0	9	—	33	—	—	100	—	86

Key Votes

(1) ABM	FOR	(6) 18-Yr-Vote	AGN	(11) Clean Water $	AGN
(2) SST	FOR	(7) Farm Sub Lmt	AGN	(12) Mig Wrkrs Comp	AGN
(3) Phil Pln	AGN	(8) Coop-Church	AGN	(13) Jets to Chiang	FOR
(4) No-Knock	FOR	(9) Family Asst	AGN	(14) State OEO Veto	FOR
(5) Cmutr Tax	ABS	(10) Work Stamps	FOR	(15) Park Logging	FOR

Election Results

1970 general:	Fletcher Thompson (R)	78,540	(57%)
	Andrew Young (D)	58,394	(43%)
1970 primary:	Fletcher Thompson (R), unopposed		
1968 general:	Fletcher Thompson (R)	79,258	(56%)
	Charles L. Weltner (D)	63,183	(44%)

SIXTH DISTRICT Political Background

Georgia 6 is a collection of counties in central Georgia between Atlanta and Columbus. Exurban Atlanta is marching relentlessly into the district, as is shown by the skyrocketing population of Clayton County, up 111% in the '60's. In the southeast corner of the district is the good-sized city of Macon (pop. 122,000). The rest of the 6th—about half its population—is predominantly rural, with some textile mill towns here and there. Despite its proximity to Atlanta, the 6th, with the occasional exception of Macon, votes like the rest of Georgia. It went heavily for Goldwater and Wallace and for conservative Democrats in congressional and local races.

The district's congressman, John J. Flynt, Jr., has been accumulating seniority since he won a special election in 1954 and is now 14th among Democrats on the House Appropriations Committee. Flynt has had no serious opposition in recent years and seems destined for a long incumbency, perhaps even a shot at the chairmanship of Appropriations.

Ordinarily a member in good standing of the Southern conservative bloc, Flynt surprised observers in 1971 when he and Congressman Phil Landrum of the 9th district announced their opposition to the Vietnam policies of the Nixon Administration. Visiting his district shortly afterwards, Flynt found his formerly hawkish constituents eager to end the conflict and pleased with his new stand. Whether this indicates that antiwar candidates can carry portions of the rural South remains to be seen.

Because of the population growth in Clayton County, the size of the 6th district will have to be reduced before the 1972 elections. But Flynt will probably retain a safe seat.

Census Data 1970 pop. 538,336; deviation from current state average, +17.3%; change 1960–70, +18.2%. Metro. 44.9%, 22.7% central city.

1970 Share of Federal Outlays $269,908,177

DOD	$61,393,000	HEW	$107,004,973
AEC	$000	HUD	$2,203,344
NASA	$000	OEO	$958,323
DOT	$17,545,006	DOA	$12,872,981
		Other	$67,930,550

Federal Military-Industrial Commitments

DOD Contractors Maxson Electronic Corp. (Macon), $11.814m: 66-mm four round clips; 60-mm illuminating projectiles. Thioko Chemical (Woodbine), $7.130m: riot control agent; surface flares.

DOD Installations Atlanta Army Depot (Forest Park).

Economic Base Textile mill products, esp. broad woven cotton fabric mills and knitting mills; cotton and livestock; fabricated metal products.

The Voters

Registration 227,619 total. No party registration.

Employment profile White collar, 32%. Blue collar, 68%.

Ethnic groups Black, 27%. Total foreign stock, 1%. All foreign groups less than 0.5%.

Presidential vote

1968	Humphrey (D)	34,442	(23%)
	Nixon (R)	42,407	(29%)
	Wallace (AIP)	70,857	(48%)

Representative

John James Flynt, Jr. (D) Elected 1954; b. Nov. 8, 1914, Griffin; home, Griffin; U. of Ga., B.A., 1936; Emory U. Law School, 1937–38; George Washington U. Law School, LL.B., 1940; Army, WWII; married, three children; Methodist.

Career Ga. House of Reps., 1947–48; Solicitor Gen., Griffin Judicial Circuit, 1949–54; Pres., Solicitors Gen. Assn. of Ga., 1950–51.

Offices 2335 RHOB, 202-225-4501. Also P.O. Box. 103, Griffin 30227, 404-227-1621.

Committees

Appropriations (14th); Subs. (1) Interior, (2) State, Justice, Commerce, and the Judiciary.

Group Ratings

	ADA	COPE	NREP	NFU	LCV	CFA	NAB	NSI	ACA
1970	4	25	8	15	57	56	80	100	88
1969	13	—	—	39	—	—	—	—	86
1968	0	15	—	27	—	—	80	—	81

Key Votes

(1) ABM	FOR	(6) 18-Yr-Vote	AGN	(11) Clean Water $	AGN
(2) SST	FOR	(7) Farm Sub Lmt	AGN	(12) Mig Wrkrs Comp	AGN
(3) Phil Pln	AGN	(8) Coop-Church	AGN	(13) Jets to Chiang	ABS
(4) No-Knock	FOR	(9) Family Asst	AGN	(14) State OEO Veto	FOR
(5) Cmutr Tax	AGN	(10) Work Stamps	FOR	(15) Park Logging	AGN

Election Results

1970 general:	John J. Flynt (D), unopposed
1970 primary:	John J. Flynt (D), unopposed
1968 general:	John J. Flynt (D), unopposed

SEVENTH DISTRICT Political Background

Georgia 7 occupies the northwest corner of the state. The district touches the Atlanta city limits on the southeast; to the northwest, it extends to the boundaries of Chattanooga, Tennessee. The population of the 7th grew significantly during the '60's. Most of the growth occurred in Cobb County, outside Atlanta, and in the suburbs outside Chattanooga. Rome, in the middle of the district, is an industrial and textile city of some significance. But the 7th's most famous employer is financially ailing Lockheed Aircraft, which has a huge plant in Marietta, some 30 miles from downtown Atlanta. This is where the C-5A's are built and the cost overruns accumulated. Naturally, most voters in the district are not critics of heavy military spending.

The 7th is less preoccupied with the race issue than most of rural Georgia. One reason is that few blacks live here—only 7% of the district's population. Moreover, substantial parts of the district do not follow the usual Deep South, conservative Democrat, Goldwater-Wallace tradition. Cobb County in the 7th is one of the more conservative parts of the Atlanta metropolitan area and usually gives Republican candidates hefty majorities, whether against Southern rural or Northern urban Democrats. In the north part of the district, several counties are part of the traditional Republican South: that is, they were against secession in 1860 and have been Republican ever since. In 1964, however, there was less Goldwater strength here than there was in other Southern counties. These Georgia counties constitute the southern tip of Appalachia, with an accent and mores different from those in the Deep South below Atlanta.

Since 1960, the congressman from the 7th has been John W. Davis, a conservative-to-moderate member of the Southern bloc and a high-ranking member of the Science and Astronautics Committee. Of course, Davis vigorously supported the interests of Lockheed in its financial difficulties. The Congressman has generally been renominated and reelected without difficulty, though he did have a relatively close race in Goldwater year of 1964.

The 7th will require significant redistricting, because it is now the largest district in the state (596,000). It may lose some territory on the northeast to the underpopulated 9th or part of Cobb County (pop. 200,000) to an Atlanta district. In either case, the district would lose predominantly Republican territory which, theoretically at least, should make Davis' seat even more secure.

Census Data 1970 pop. 596,037; deviation from current state average, +29.9%; change 1960–70, +32.2%. Metro. 41.5%, 0.0% central city.

1970 Share of Federal Outlays $1,029,531,193

DOD	$841,474,000	HEW	$98,663,912
AEC	$93,960	HUD	$2,929,776
NASA	$1,404,369	OEO	$445,909
DOT	$4,675,286	DOA	$12,819,282
		Other	$67,024,699

Federal Military-Industrial Commitments

DOD Contractors Lockheed Aircraft (Marietta), $805.957m: production of C-5A aircraft and spare parts.

DOD Installations Naval Air Station (Marietta). Dobbins AFB (Marietta).

Economic Base Textile mill products, esp. floor covering mills and yarn and thread mills; aircraft and aircraft parts; cotton and poultry; apparel and other finished products made from fabrics and similar materials; lumber and wood products, other than furniture.

The Voters

Registration 246,839 total. No party registration.

Employment profile White collar, 32%. Blue collar, 68%.

Ethnic groups Black, 7%. Total foreign stock, 1%. All foreign groups less than 0.5%.

Presidential vote

1968	Humphrey (D)	29,053	(19%)
	Nixon (R)	49,497	(32%)
	Wallace (AIP)	76,001	(49%)

Representative

John William Davis (D) Elected 1960; b. Sept. 12, 1916, Rome; home, Summerville; U. of Ga., B.A., 1937, LL.B., 1939; Army, WWII; widowed, three children; Presbyterian.

Career Practicing atty., 1939–49; Solicitor Gen., Rome Circuit, 1950–53; Judge, Lookout Mt. Judicial Circuit, 1955–60.

Offices 1728 LHOB, 202-225-2931. Also Fed. Bldg., Rome 30161, 404-235-0127.

Committees

Foreign Affairs (19th); Subs. (1) Asian and Pacific Affairs, (2) Foreign Economic Policy, (3) National Security Policy and Scientific Developments.

Science and Astronautics (5th); Subs. (1) Chm., Science, Research, and Development, (2) Advanced Research and Technology, (3) International Cooperation in Science and Space.

Group Ratings

	ADA	COPE	NREP	NFU	LCV	CFA	NAB	NSI	ACA
1970	4	56	0	50	33	80	44	100	60
1969	7	—	—	67	—	—	—	—	44
1968	25	15	—	73	—	—	33	—	45

Key Votes

(1) ABM	FOR	(6) 18-Yr-Vote	AGN	(11) Clean Water $	AGN
(2) SST	FOR	(7) Farm Sub Lmt	AGN	(12) Mig Wrkrs Comp	ABS
(3) Phil Pln	AGN	(8) Coop-Church	AGN	(13) Jets to Chiang	FOR
(4) No-Knock	ABS	(9) Family Asst	AGN	(14) State OEO Veto	FOR
(5) Cmutr Tax	AGN	(10) Work Stamps	FOR	(15) Park Logging	FOR

Election Results

1970 general:	John W. Davis (D)	80,149	(73%)
	Dick Fullerton (R)	30,392	(27%)
1970 primary:	John W. Davis (D)	52,137	(64%)
	Sam Hensley (D)	29,152	(36%)
1968 general:	John W. Davis (D), unopposed		

EIGHTH DISTRICT Political Background

Georgia 8, part of the Deep South, reaches from central Georgia all the way down to the Okefenokee Swamp. The 8th is basically rural and agricultural, and it has shown very little population change one way or the other. The district has no cities over 30,000—the largest are Valdosta, Waycross, and Brunswick—and probably never will. Peanuts have begun to replace cotton here, because cotton has exhausted the Black Belt soil.

Some 26% of the district's residents are black, but so far black voters have been unable to influence the outcome of elections in any significant way. Southern rural blacks, generally, have not participated in the electoral process as much as the blacks in Southern cities. Moreover, black outmigration has greatly reduced the number of blacks living in small-town and rural areas of the South. Those that remain no doubt understand the informal sanctions against black participation in politics. All in all, the chances of affecting the results of an election are too small to justify the risk of going to the polls.

Since the blacks don't vote in the 8th, the district has delivered large majorities to candidates like Wallace, Maddox, and Goldwater. Its congressional politics, however, have been less predictable. In 1966, that relatively rare event occurred—an incumbent Southern congressman was ousted by a challenger. The incumbent was J. Russell Tuten, and the challenger in the Democratic primary W. S. (Bill) Stuckey, Jr. Stuckey is a member of the family that has put up pecan-candy and gift shops along the freeway interchanges throughout the Midwest and South. In Washington, the Congressman has been an active and conservative member of the Interstate and Foreign Commerce Committee. It appears that he will enjoy a long congressional career.

Census Data 1970 pop. 350,929; deviation from current state average, —23.5%; change 1960–70, +3.6%. Metro. 0.0%, 0.0% central city.

1970 Share of Federal Outlays $257,073,895

DOD	$79,188,000	HEW	$77,421,202
AEC	$000	HUD	$4,881,327
NASA	$000	OEO	$1,853,486
DOT	$12,550,803	DOA	$33,872,978
		Other	$47,306,099

Federal Military-Industrial Commitments

DOD Contractors Standard Container (Homerville), $6.690m: small caliber ammunition packing boxes.

DOD Installations Naval Air Station (Glynco). Naval Air Technical Training Center (Glynco). Moody AFB (Valdosta).

Economic Base Tobacco, livestock, and peanuts; fresh and frozen packaged fish and seafoods; chemicals and allied products. Also, tourism (Sea Island).

The Voters

Registration 178,840 total. No party registration.

Employment profile White collar, 29%. Blue collar, 71%.

Ethnic groups Black, 26%. Total foreign stock, 1%. All foreign groups less than 0.5%.

Presidential vote

1968	Humphrey (D)	20,941	(20%)
	Nixon (R)	21,232	(21%)
	Wallace (AIP)	61,168	(59%)

Representative

Williamson Sylvester Stuckey, Jr. (D) Elected 1966; b. May 25, 1935, Dodge County; home, Eastman; U. of Ga., B.A., LL.B., 1956; married, five children; Episcopalian.

Career Pres., Stuckey's Timberland, Inc., formerly Exec. V.P. Stuckey's Inc., Advisor, Stuckey's Inc., div. of Pet Milk Co.

Offices 223 CHOB, 202-225-6531. Also P.O. Box 310, Old Eastman Bank Bldg., Eastman 31023, 912-374-4366.

Committees

District of Columbia (11th); (1) Chm., Housing and Youth Affairs, (2) Judiciary, (3) Public Health and Welfare.

Interstate and Foreign Commerce (14th); Sub. on Commerce and Finance.

Group Ratings

	ADA	COPE	NREP	NFU	LCV	CFA	NAB	NSI	ACA
1970	8	36	9	50	0	50	50	100	56
1969	7	—	—	50	—	—	—	—	63
1968	8	15	—	57	—	—	50	—	71

Key Votes

(1) ABM	FOR	(6) 18-Yr-Vote	FOR	(11) Clean Water $	AGN
(2) SST	FOR	(7) Farm Sub Lmt	AGN	(12) Mig Wrkrs Comp	ABS
(3) Phil Pln	AGN	(8) Coop-Church	AGN	(13) Jets to Chiang	FOR
(4) No-Knock	FOR	(9) Family Asst	AGN	(14) State OEO Veto	FOR
(5) Cmutr Tax	ABS	(10) Work Stamps	FOR	(15) Park Logging	FOR

Election Results

1970 general:	W. S. Stuckey, Jr. (D), unopposed
1970 primary:	W. S. Stuckey, Jr. (D), unopposed
1968 general:	W. S. Stuckey, Jr. (D), unopposed

NINTH DISTRICT Political Background

Georgia 9 is the northeast corner of the state—the southwestern edge of Appalachia. Fannin, Towns, and Upson counties in the north, along the Tennessee and North Carolina border, have a Republican tradition dating back to the days when they stood against the rest of Georgia and opposed secession. The 9th is a district of small towns and hill country spotted with little settlements. The largest city here is Gainesville (pop. 15,000), a textile center. In the south end of the district, however, metropolitan Atlanta spreads into Gwinnett and Forsyth counties, the district's only area of significant population growth during the '60's.

Phil M. Landrum has represented this part of Georgia in the House since 1952. Considered a moderate, Landrum was a co-sponsor of the House version of the 1959 Landrum-Griffin Act, a major piece of labor legislation. Currently, Landrum sits on the House Ways and Means Committee, where he strenuously backs import quotas for textiles, an economic mainstay of the 9th district.

Landrum has had little trouble winning reelection in the '60's. In 1970 a young Republican waged a vigorous campaign against him, but Landrum still won 70% of the vote. Despite its pockets of Republican strength, the 9th seems likely to reelect Landrum indefinitely. And the Congressman's announcement that he could no longer support Nixon's Vietnam policy will only increase his popularity in the district, at one time a bastion of pro-war sentiment. It seems unlikely that the Georgia legislature will tamper unduly with the boundaries of a congressman like Landrum with 18 years' seniority and a seat on a vital committee.

Census Data 1970 pop. 396,670; deviation from current state average, −13.6%; change 1960–70, +20.3. Metro. 18.2%, 0.0% central city.

1970 Share of Federal Outlays $158,218,339

DOD	$10,024,000	HEW	$77,308,360
AEC	$000	HUD	$2,478,000
NASA	$000	OEO	$624,942
DOT	$5,524,802	DOA	$20,737,369
		Other	$41,520,866

Federal Military-Industrial Commitments

None.

Economic Base Poultry and cotton; meat packing; textile mill products.

The Voters

Registration 194,107 total. No party registration.

Employment profile White collar, 26%. Blue collar, 74%.

Ethnic groups Black, 9%. Total foreign stock, 1%. All foreign groups less than 0.5%.

Presidential vote

1968	Humphrey (D)	23,078	(20%)
	Nixon (R)	35,527	(31%)
	Wallace (AIP)	55,122	(49%)

Representative

Phillip Mitchell Landrum (D) Elected 1952; b. Sept. 10, 1909, Martin; home, Jasper; Mercer U., 1926–27; La. State U., 1932; Piedmont Col., B.A., 1939; Atlanta Law School, LL.B., 1941; Army Air Corps, WWII; married, two children; Baptist.

Career Practicing atty., 1949–52; Supt. Pub. Schools, Nelson, 1937–41; Asst. Atty. Gen., 1946–47; Exec. Secy., Governor of Ga., 1947–48.

Offices 2308 RHOB, 202-225-5211. Also Jasper 30143, 404-692-2022.

Committees

Ways and Means (7th).

Group Ratings

	ADA	COPE	NREP	NFU	LCV	CFA	NAB	NSI	ACA
1970	8	45	0	33	20	72	82	100	82
1969	7	—	—	60	—	—	—	—	43
1968	8	23	—	58	—	—	33	—	58

Key Votes

(1) ABM	FOR	(6) 18-Yr-Vote	AGN	(11) Clean Water $	AGN
(2) SST	FOR	(7) Farm Sub Lmt	AGN	(12) Mig Wrkrs Comp	AGN
(3) Phil Pln	ABS	(8) Coop-Church	AGN	(13) Jets to Chiang	FOR
(4) No-Knock	FOR	(9) Family Asst	AGN	(14) State OEO Veto	FOR
(5) Cmutr Tax	FOR	(10) Work Stamps	FOR	(15) Park Logging	FOR

Election Results

1970 general:	Phil M. Landrum (D)	64,603	(72%)
	Bob Cooper (R)	25,476	(28%)
1970 primary:	Phil M. Landrum (D), unopposed		
1968 general:	Phil M. Landrum (D), unopposed		

TENTH DISTRICT Political Background

Georgia 10 is a group of counties in central Georgia anchored by the cities of Athens (pop. 44,000) in the north and Augusta (pop. 59,000) in the east. Both Athens, the site of the University of Georgia, and Augusta, site of the Master's Golf Tournament, tend to vote like metropolitan Atlanta: substantial numbers of votes for both Republican and Democratic candidates for President and usually a plurality for urban-oriented conservative candidates of the state Republican party. Since Augusta has one of Georgia's best-organized black communities outside Atlanta, the black voters of Augusta provide a solid base of support for liberal or moderate-to-liberal candidates whenever they appear on the ballot.

The rest of the district, primarily rural and small-town Georgia, has entirely different voting patterns. Out here the Republicans get few votes, and national and liberal Democrats get virtually all of their support from black voters. Hancock County, in the middle of the district, has a black majority and a black-controlled county government. But like most Southern counties where blacks have managed to win control, Hancock is poor, its cotton fields exhausted, and its population declining—down from 10,000 in 1960 to 9,000 in 1970.

The bulk of the district's votes are cast by Civil War Democrats, Southern conservative Democrats who have been drawn first to Goldwater and then to Wallace. The 10th's representative is Robert G. Stephens, a Southern conservative Democrat. First elected in 1960, Stephens has been returned to office with little fuss every two years thereafter. He currently serves as chairman of Banking and Currency's Small Business Subcommittee. The Congressman's record at the polls shows he has little to worry about in the future. Redistricting is unlikely to produce any problems for him either.

Census Data 1970 pop. 470,050; deviation from current state average, +2.4%; change 1960–70, +15.0%. Metro. 34.6%, 12.7% central city.

1970 Share of Federal Outlays $410,363,418

DOD	$169,134,000	HEW	$99,078,639
AEC	$644,273	HUD	$5,771,418
NASA	$44,829	OEO	$2,101,342
DOT	$25,181,440	DOA	$33,670,144
		Other	$74,737,333

Federal Military-Industrial Commitments

DOD Installations Fort Gordon (Augusta). Navy Supply Corps School (Athens).

Economic Base Cotton; textile mill products; food and kindred products, esp. bakery goods; paper and allied products. Also, higher education (University of Georgia).

The Voters

Registration 186,325 total. No party registration.

Employment profile White collar, 31%. Blue collar, 69%.

Ethnic groups Black, 34%. Total foreign stock, 2%. All foreign groups less than 0.5%.

Presidential vote

1968	Humphrey (D)	38,436	(32%)
	Nixon (R)	37,503	(31%)
	Wallace (AIP)	44,731	(37%)

Representative

Robert Grier Stephens, Jr. (D) Elected 1960; b. Aug. 14, 1913, Atlanta; home, Athens; U. of Ga., B.A., 1935, M.A., 1937, LL.B., 1941; U. of Hamburg, 1935–36; Army, WWII; married, four children; Presbyterian.

Career Legal staff, Nuremberg trials, 1945; Staff, Dept. pol. sci. and history, U. of Ga., 1936–41, 1946; practicing atty., 1946–61; City Atty., Athens, 1947–50; Ga. Senate, 1951–53; Ga. House of Reps., 1953–59.

Offices 343 CHOB, 202-225-4101. Also Mutual Bldg., Athens 30601, 404-549-1421.

Committees

Banking and Currency (7th); Subs. (1) Chm., Small Business, (2) Housing, (3) Consumer Affairs.

Interior and Insular Affairs (18th); Subs. (1) Indian Affairs, (2) Irrigation and Reclamation, (3) National Parks and Recreation, (4) Territorial and Insular Affairs.

Group Ratings

	ADA	COPE	NREP	NFU	LCV	CFA	NAB	NSI	ACA
1970	8	36	9	38	33	37	100	100	63
1969	0	—	—	53	—	—	—	—	55
1968	33	31	—	64	—	—	18	—	36

Key Votes

(1) ABM	ABS	(6) 18-Yr-Vote	AGN	(11) Clean Water $	AGN
(2) SST	FOR	(7) Farm Sub Lmt	AGN	(12) Mig Wrkrs Comp	AGN
(3) Phil Pln	ABS	(8) Coop-Church	AGN	(13) Jets to Chiang	ABS
(4) No-Knock	ABS	(9) Family Asst	AGN	(14) State OEO Veto	FOR
(5) Cmutr Tax	ABS	(10) Work Stamps	FOR	(15) Park Logging	FOR

Election Results

1970 general:	Robert G. Stephens, Jr. (D), unopposed
1970 primary:	Robert G. Stephens, Jr. (D), unopposed
1969 general:	Robert G. Stephens, Jr. (D), unopposed

HAWAII

Political Background

Several thousand miles of Pacific Ocean separate Hawaii from the rest of the United States, and its politics, as might be expected, are different from the mainland's. Much of the difference can be explained by the Islands' unique ethnic composition. The Polynesians, the people Captain Cook found on the Islands in 1778 and whose royal family ruled Hawaii until 1898, are now a small minority, often intermixed with Oriental and Caucasian stock. Japanese-Americans make–up almost a third of Hawaii's population, and there are also large numbers of descendants of Chinese and Filipino immigrants. Hawaii is the only state where Caucasians are a distinct minority.

Naturally, Hawaiian voters are very sensitive to civil rights issues, and the posture of the Nixon-Agnew Administration toward these issues has not done the Republican party any good here. Republicans did win statewide elections following statehood; but Hawaii's admission occurred during the Eisenhower Administration and over the opposition of Southern Democrats. Today, there are only a few reliably Republican enclaves left in the state, mainly high-income Caucasian neighborhoods in and around Honolulu.

Popular novels set in the Islands have acquainted readers with the economic power wielded by a few WASP families and their large corporations. But at the polls, the International Longshoremen's Union, formerly headed by the controversial Harry Bridges, now overshadows that power. The ILWU's power is a fact of Hawaiian political life: certain areas are referred to as ILWU precincts. The union, which usually supports Democrats, has not suffered a major political defeat since statehood. It has always, however, backed Republican Sen. Hiram Fong, and it helped to reelect him and Democratic Gov. John Burns in 1970, a year of hotly contested elections in the state.

A wealthy businessman of Chinese descent, Fong was considered a Senate liberal in the late '50's and early '60's. But in recent years, particularly since the Nixon Administration took office, the Senator has been lining up regularly with Republican conservatives. In the 1970 election, Fong's Democratic opponent, TV-station owner and Island newcomer Cecil Heftel, attacked the Senator for supporting Nixon's policies on the war and military spending. Fong eventually won the election, but by a scant 7,000 votes (52%).

The state's junior senator is Daniel K. Inouye, a former congressman (1959–62) and a much-decorated war veteran who lost his arm fighting in Europe during World War II. Inouye is a highly respected member of the liberal bloc in the Senate, as witnessed by his seat on the Senate Appropriations Committee. His standing among Hawaiian voters is also high: in 1968 he was reelected with 83% of the vote.

Inouye is one of the principals in the state's Democratic party, which, except when opposed by the ILWU, now dominates Hawaiian politics. But party dominance preceding party disintegration is an old pattern in American politics, and the Democrats in Hawaii seem to be running true to form. In 1970, Gov. Burns, another architect of the Democratic organization, faced primary opposition from Lt. Gov. Thomas Gill. Gill's issue was that Hawaii had had too much economic development. Oahu, the island with 82% of the state's population, is not much bigger in area than the city of Los Angeles, and the prospect of its "Los Angelesization" unsettles many Hawaiians. Gill got 40% of the primary votes, a solid showing. The issues he raised in his campaign will no doubt become increasingly important in the state's politics.

In the 1970 elections, Hawaii was for the first time divided into two congressional districts. Before then, the House seats were held at large. Currently the 1st is most of the city of Honolulu, and the 2nd the remainder of Oahu and the Neighbor Islands. The political differences between the districts are slight. Voters on the Neighbor Islands have always resented the political and social influence of Oahu. And, having a relatively fewer number of Caucasians, the Neighbor Islands tend to be marginally more Democratic.

The state's two Democratic congressmen, Spark Matsunaga of the 1st and Patsy Mink of the 2nd, are generally considered unbeatable. Mrs. Mink was unopposed in 1970, while Matsunaga won 73% of the votes in his district. Both are of Japanese ancestry and both are antiwar liberals. Mrs. Mink, one of nine women in the House, is an ardent advocate of women's rights on the hill. Matsunaga, who has somewhat better relationships with the House leadership, has a seat on the Rules Committee; Mrs. Mink is a middle-ranking member of the Education and Labor and Insular Affairs committees.

Electoral Votes 4

Census Data 1970 pop. 769,913; 0.37% of U.S. total, 41st largest; change 1960–70, +21%. Metro. 81.8%, 42.2% central city. 1970 per capita income, $4,530, 7th highest. 49th in number of poor.

1970 Share of Federal Tax Burden $741,530,000; 0.38% of U.S. total, 38th largest.

1970 Share of Federal Outlays $958,260,537; 0.51% of U.S. total, 40th largest. Per capita federal spending, $1,245.

DOD	$524,474,000	30th (0.91%)	HEW	$144,671,237	47th (0.28%)
AEC	$3,629,762	29th (0.14%)	HUD	$12,648,641	38th (0.65%)
NASA	$3,979,595	28th (0.11%)	OEO	$2,707,035	45th (0.36%)
DOT	$120,182,718	25th (1.68%)	DOA	$20,511,577	47th (0.16%)

DOC	$3,337,703	37th (0.29%)	POD	$19,639,172	47th (0.27%)
DOI	$6,201,587	46th (0.27%)	VA	$20,767,442	50th (0.28%)
DOJ	$2,140,334	44th (0.37%)	CSC	$23,662,805	34th (0.59%)
			Other	$49,706,931	

Economic Base Sugarcane and livestock; food and kindred products, esp. canned and preserved fruits, vegetables, and seafood, and sugar; apparel and other finished products made from fabrics and similar materials, esp. women's, misses', and juniors' outerwear; printing, publishing, and allied industries, esp. newspapers; stone, clay, glass, and concrete products, esp. concrete, gypsum, and plaster products. Also, tourism.

Political Line-up Governor, John A. Burns (D); seat up, 1974. Senators, Hiram L. Fong (R) and Daniel K. Inouye (D). Representatives, 2 (2 D and 0 R). State Senate (16 D and 8 R); State House (33 D and 17 R).

The Voters

Registration 295,098 total. 131,205 D (45%); 37,068 R (13%); 126,825 other (44%).

Employment profile White collar, 42%. Blue collar, 58%.

Ethnic groups Black, 1%. Puerto Rican, 1%. Total foreign stock, 38%. Oriental (Japan, China, Philippines), 35%; Germany, UK, Canada, 1% each.

Presidential vote

1968	Humphrey (D)	141,324	(60%)
	Nixon (R)	91,425	(39%)
	Wallace (AIP)	3,469	(2%)
1964	Johnson (D)	163,249	(79%)
	Goldwater (R)	119,277	(21%)
1960	Kennedy (D)	92,410	(50%)
	Nixon (R)	92,295	(50%)

Senator

Hiram Leong Fong (R) Elected Aug. 21, 1959, seat up 1976; b. Oct. 1, 1907, Honolulu; home, Honolulu; U. of Hawaii, B.A., 1930; Harvard Law School, LL.B., 1935; Army Air Corps, WWII; Col. (Ret.) USAF; married, four children; Congregational Christian.

Career Atty. and businessman; Corp. Pres. of Finance Factors, Grand Pacific Life Insurance, Finance Realty, Finance Home Builders, Finance Investment, Finance Factors Bldg., Finance Factors Found., Market City; operates banana farm in Honolulu; Legislature of Territory of Hawaii, 1938–54; Speaker, 6 yrs., V. Speaker, 4 yrs., Delegate, Repub. Natl. Conventions, 1952, '56, '60, '64, '68; V.P., Territorial Constitutional Convention, 1950.

Offices 1313 NSOB, 202-225-6361. Also 702 Finance Factors Bldg., 195 S. King St., Honolulu 96813, 808-533-4441.

Committees

Appropriations (8th); Subs. (1) Agriculture, Environmental and Consumer Protection, (2) Interior, (3) Labor, HEW, and Related Agencies, (4) State, Justice, Commerce, the Judiciary, and Related Agencies, (5) Foreign Operations.

Judiciary (2nd); Subs. (1) Antitrust and Monopoly Legislation, (2) Constitutional Amendments, (3) Constitutional Rights, (4) Immigration and Naturalization, (5) Juvenile Delinquency, (6) Patents, Trademarks, and Copyrights, (7) Refugees and Escapees.

Group Ratings

	ADA	COPE	NREP	NFU	LCV	NAB	NSI	ACA
1970	38	77	40	77	18	46	100	39
1969	33	—	—	62	—	—	—	43
1968	43	55	—	33	—	17	—	43

Key Votes

(1) ABM	FOR	(8) Phil Pln	ABS	(15) Coop-Church	AGN
(2) SST	FOR	(9) Vol Army	FOR	(16) Cut Oil Dpltn	AGN
(3) Busing	FOR	(10) Prison $	AGN	(17) Consumer Prot	ABS
(4) Tob Sub	FOR	(11) Cut Mil $	ABS	(18) Farm Sub Limit	AGN
(5) Carswell	AGN	(12) Defoliatn	ABS	(19) Comp Bid Sales	FOR
(6) No-Knock	FOR	(13) 18-Yr-Vote	FOR	(20) Pre-Prod Tests	AGN
(7) Seniorty	ABS	(14) Pentgn PR	FOR	(21) Cut Marjna Pen	AGN

Election Results

1970 general:	Hiram L. Fong (R)	124,163	(52%)
	Cecil Heftel (D)	116,597	(48%)
1970 primary:	Hiram L. Fong (R), unopposed		
1964 general:	Hiram L. Fong (R)	110,747	(53%)
	Thomas P. Gill (D)	96,789	(46%)
	Lawrence Domine (Ind)	1,278	(1%)

Senator

Daniel Ken Inouye (D) Elected 1962, seat up 1974; b. Sept. 7, 1924, Honolulu; home, Honolulu; U. of Hawaii, B.A., 1950; George Washington U., J.D., 1952; Army, WWII; married, one child; Methodist.

Career Asst. Pub. Prosecutor, Honolulu, 1953–54; practicing atty., 1954–59; Majority Leader, Territorial House of Reps., 1954–58; Territorial Senate, 1958–59.

Offices 442 OSOB, 202-225-3934. Also 602 Capitol Investment Bldg., Honolulu 96813, 808-533-441.

Committees

Appropriations (12th); Subs. (1) Chm., District of Columbia, (2) Agriculture, Environmental and Consumer Protection, (3) Interior, (4) Legislative, (5) Treasury, Post Office, and General Government.

Commerce (9th); Subs. (1) Chm., Foreign Commerce and Tourism, (2) Aviation, (3) Consumer, (4) Merchant Marine, (5) Oceans and Atmosphere.

District of Columbia (2nd); Sub. on Fiscal Affairs.

Sel. Com. on Equal Educational Opportunity (5th).

Group Ratings

	ADA	COPE	NREP	NFU	LCV	NAB	NSI	ACA
1970	72	91	90	100	76	18	14	0
1969	72	—	—	86	—	—	—	0
1968	64	89	—	90	—	20	—	0

Key Votes

(1) ABM	AGN	(8) Phil Pln	FOR	(15) Coop-Church	FOR
(2) SST	FOR	(9) Vol Army	ABS	(16) Cut Oil Dpltn	FOR
(3) Busing	FOR	(10) Prison $	ABS	(17) Consumer Prot	ABS
(4) Tob Sub	FOR	(11) Cut Mil $	ABS	(18) Farm Sub Limit	AGN
(5) Carswell	AGN	(12) Defoliatn	ABS	(19) Comp Bid Sales	AGN
(6) No-Knock	AGN	(13) 18-Yr-Vote	ABS	(20) Pre-Prod Tests	AGN
(7) Seniorty	AGN	(14) Pentgn PR	AGN	(21) Cut Marjna Pen	FOR

Election Results

1968 general:	Daniel K. Inouye (D)	189,248	(83%)
	Wayne L. Thiessen (R)	34,008	(15%)
	Oliver M. Lee (PF)	3,671	(2%)
1968 primary:	Daniel K. Inouye (D)	82,319	(83%)
	William Lampard (D)	12,122	(12%)
	J. P. P. Petrowski (D)	982	(1%)

1962 general:	Daniel K. Inouye (D)	136,294	(69%)
	Ben F. Dillingham (R)	60,067	(31%)

First District

Census Data 1970 pop. 362,119; deviation from current state average, −5.9%; change 1960–70, +13.0%. Metro. 100%, 89.7% central city.

1970 Share of Federal Outlays $479,130,000 (average outlay per district, Hawaii 1 and 2)

DOD	$262,237,000	HEW	$72,336,000
AEC	$1,815,000	HUD	$6,324,000
NASA	$1,990,000	OEO	$1,154,000
DOT	$60,091,000	DOA	$10,255,000
		Other	$24,853,000

Federal Military-Industrial Commitments

DOD Contractors Hawaiian Telephone Co. (Honolulu), $9.531m: communication services. Control Data Corp. (Honolulu), $7.970m: support of Vietnam pacification program. Standard Oil of Calif. (Honolulu), $6.128m: petroleum products.

DOD Installations Fort Shafter Army Military Reservation (Honolulu). Schofield Barracks (Honolulu). Tripler Army Hospital (Honolulu). Marine Corps Camp H. M. Smith (Honolulu). Naval Air Station Barbers Point (Honolulu). Hickam AFB (Honolulu).

Economic Base Food and kindred products, esp. sugar; apparel and other finished products made from fabrics and similar materials, esp. women's, misses', and juniors' outerwear; printing, publishing, and allied industries, esp. newspapers; stone, clay, glass, and concrete products, esp. concrete, gypsum, and plaster products. Also, higher education (University of Hawaii) and tourism (Honolulu).

The Voters

Registration 149,969 total. 62,159 D (41%); 19,100 R (13%); 68,710 other (46%).
Employment profile Not available.
Ethnic groups Not available.

Presidential vote

1968	Humphrey (D)	69,715	(59%)
	Nixon (R)	46,842	(40%)
	Wallace (AIP)	1,460	(1%)

Representative

Spark Masayuki Matsunaga (D) Elected 1962; b. Oct. 8, 1916, Kukuiula; home, Honolulu; U. of Hawaii, B.Ed., 1941; Harvard Law School, LL.B., 1951; Army, WWII; Lt. Col. (Ret.) JAGC-USAR; married, five children; Episcopalian.

Career Vets. Counsellor, Dept. of Interior, 1945–47; Chief, Priority Div., War Assets Admin., 1947–48; Asst. Pub. Prosecutor, City and County of Honolulu, 1952–54; practicing atty., 1954–63; Hawaii House of Reps., 1954–59, Majority Leader, 1959.

Offices 442 CHOB, 202-225-2726. Also Rm. 218 Fed. Bldg., Honolulu 96813, 808-531-6407.

Committees

Rules (9th).

Group Ratings

	ADA	COPE	NREP	NFU	LCV	CFA	NAB	NSI	ACA
1970	88	100	83	100	100	100	0	50	0
1969	73	—	—	100	—	—	—	—	0
1968	92	92	—	100	—	—	0	—	0

Key Votes

(1) ABM	AGN	(6) 18-Yr-Vote	FOR	(11) Clean Water $	FOR
(2) SST	AGN	(7) Farm Sub Lmt	AGN	(12) Mig Wrkrs Comp	FOR
(3) Phil Pln	FOR	(8) Coop-Church	FOR	(13) Jets to Chiang	AGN
(4) No-Knock	AGN	(9) Family Asst	FOR	(14) State OEO Veto	ABS
(5) Cmutr Tax	FOR	(10) Work Stamps	AGN	(15) Park Logging	AGN

Election Results

1970 general:	Spark M. Matsunaga (D)	85,411	(73%)
	Richard K. Kockey (R)	31,764	(27%)
1970 primary:	Spark M. Matsunaga (D), unopposed		

(In 1968, both Hawaii congressmen were elected at large.)

Second District

Census Data 1970 pop. 407,794; deviation from current state average, +5.9%; change 1960–70, +30.6%. Metro. 65.7%, 0.0% central city.

1970 Share of Federal Outlays $479,130,000 (average outlay per district, Hawaii 1 and 2)

DOD	$262,237,000	HEW	$72,336,000
AEC	$1,815,000	HUD	$6,324,000
NASA	$1,990,000	OEO	$1,154,000
DOT	$60,091,000	DOA	$10,255,000
		Other	$24,853,000

Federal Military-Industrial Commitments

DOD Contractors E. E. Black Ltd. (Pearl Harbor), $6.943m: construction.

DOD Installations Fleet Operations Control Center (Kunia). Marine Corps Barracks (Pearl Harbor). Marine Corps Air Station (Kailua). Naval Communication Station (Wahiawa). Naval Ammunition Depot (Lualualei). Naval Station (Pearl Harbor). Naval Submarine Base (Pearl Harbor). Naval Supply Center (Pearl Harbor). Navy Public Works Center (Pearl Harbor). Pearl Harbor Naval Shipyard (Pearl Harbor). Wheeler AFB (Wahiawa).

Economic Base Sugarcane and livestock; food and kindred products. Also, tourism (Outer Islands).

The Voters

Registration 145,129 total. 69,046 D (48%); 17,968 R (12%); 58,115 other (40%).

Employment profile Not available.

Ethnic groups Not available.

Presidential vote

1968	Humphrey (D)	70,345	(61%)
	Nixon (R)	42,770	(37%)
	Wallace (AIP)	1,648	(1%)

Representative

Patsy Takemoto Mink (D) Elected 1964; b. Dec. 6, 1927, Paia; home, Waipahu; Wilson Col., 1946; U. of Nebraska, 1947; U. of Hawaii, B.A., 1948; U. of Chicago, J.D., 1951; married, one child; Protestant.

Career Lecturer, U. of Hawaii, 1952–56, 1959–62; atty., Territorial Legislature, 1955; Hawaii House of Reps., 1956, 1958; Hawaii Senate, 1958–59, 1962–64; Charter Pres., Young Democrats of Oahu, 1954; Delegate to Natl. Convention and Platform Com., 1960.

Offices 301 CHOB, 202-225-4906. Also 346 Fed. Office Bldg., Honolulu 96813, 808-531-4602.

Committees

Education and Labor (11th); Subs. (1) Gen. on Education, (2) Gen. on Labor, (3) Sel. on Education.

Interior and Insular Affairs (13th); Subs. (1) Indian Affairs, (2) National Parks and Recreation, (3) Territorial and Insular Affairs.

Group Ratings

	ADA	COPE	NREP	NFU	LCV	CFA	NAB	NSI	ACA
1970	96	100	83	92	100	100	0	33	5
1969	93	—	—	93	—	—	—	—	6
1968	100	100	—	94	—	—	0	—	0

Key Votes

(1) ABM	AGN	(6) 18-Yr-Vote	FOR	(11) Clean Water $	FOR
(2) SST	AGN	(7) Farm Sub Lmt	AGN	(12) Mig Wrkrs Comp	FOR
(3) Phil Pln	FOR	(8) Coop-Church	FOR	(13) Jets to Chiang	AGN
(4) No-Knock	AGN	(9) Family Asst	FOR	(14) State OEO Veto	AGN
(5) Cmutr Tax	FOR	(10) Work Stamps	AGN	(15) Park Logging	AGN

Election Results

1970 general: Patsy T. Mink (D), unopposed.
1970 primary: Patsy T. Mink (D), unopposed.
(In 1968, both Hawaii congressmen were elected at large.)

IDAHO

Political Background

Back when Populist William Jennings Bryan was urging Americans to abandon the gold standard for the unlimited coinage of silver, silver mines dominated Idaho's politics. But today the state's principal concern is agriculture. Potatoes, for which Idaho is famous, are grown in the rich farmlands in the panhandle region just east of Spokane, Washington, and along the Snake River Valley in the southern part of the state. Because Idaho is mostly farmland, its population is not concentrated in large urban areas as in Utah, Colorado, or the states along the Pacific coast. The relatively thin distribution of Idaho's residents is one factor in its distinctive kind of politics. Another, more important, factor is the state's large Mormon community in southern Idaho, the largest group of Mormons outside Utah.

In the recent past, Idaho's politics have swung from pole to pole. During the Eisenhower years, a controversy over the construction of a Hell's Canyon Dam on the Snake River benefited the Democrats, who favored the development of public power. They won most of the Senate and House elections. In 1960 John F. Kennedy, though an Easterner and a Catholic, won 46% of the state's votes—one of his better showings in the mountain states. But during the '60's, Idahoans became increasingly disenchanted with what they saw as a Democratic Administration dominated by the East Coast. In 1964, a strong conservative push led by the Mormons gave 49% of the state's votes to Barry Goldwater; meanwhile Idaho's 2nd district ousted its Democratic congressman for a conservative Republican—the only district outside the South to do this in the year of the LBJ landslide. In 1968, the state showed its emphatic dislike of liberals by giving Hubert Humphrey just 31% of its votes. Richard Nixon won 57%, while George Wallace took 13%, the Alabaman's best showing in the Western states. A kind of moral fundamentalism swept the state, converting the economic liberals of the '50's to social-issue conservatives of the '60's.

The tide may be turning again, however. As Idahoans rejected the candidacy of Hubert Humphrey, they reelected liberal Sen. Frank Church with a resounding 60% of the vote. The Republicans had assumed that Church's seat was theirs. After all, they reasoned, Church's credentials were hardly impressive. He got to the Senate at age 32 by beating a very controversial Republican candidate, and he was reelected by a narrow margin in 1962 before the Goldwater-conservative sentiment began to show itself. In 1967, the conservatives were so convinced that Church was not the man for Idaho that they started a recall campaign against him. The effort was reportedly financed by California millionaire Patrick Frawley, whose company, Technicolor, Inc., later figured in the defeat of Sen. George Murphy. But the recall attempt only won sympathy for the Senator, and gave him a chance to get an early start on his 1968 campaign.

Soon after his initial election to the Senate, Church won a seat on the Foreign Relations Committee, and he will eventually serve as its chairman for a decade or two. As a member of that committee, the Senator took an early stand against the Vietnam war —a stand not thought to be popular in Idaho. To counter Republican complaints about his views, Church invoked the memory of one of their own: Sen. William E. Borah, the progressive and isolationist Republican who served in the Senate from 1907 until his death in 1940. Sen. Borah, Church partisans argued, was always respected as an independent foreign policy critic and thereby elevated the stature of Idaho all over the country. The election thus became not so much a contest between Church and his opponent, Congressman George Hansen, as a referendum on whether Church was or was not a distinguished representative of the state. Most Idahoans, whatever their views on foreign policy, agreed that he was—and most likely they will continue to do so in future elections.

Idaho's junior senator is Len B. Jordan, a moderate-to-conservative Republican who has, on occasion, dissented from Nixon Administration policies. Although Jordan has been in Idaho politics a long time—he was governor from 1950 to 1954—he has not been a strong vote-getter. In 1962 he barely beat Congressman Gracie Pfost for the seat to which he had been appointed after the death of Sen. Henry Dworshak. In 1966 he was reelected by a not-so-impressive 55–45 margin. Jordan will be 73 in 1972 and has announced he will retire rather than seek reelection. Already numerous contenders from both parties are emerging, and the outcome of both the Republican primary and the general election should be close.

In 1970, Idaho ousted its conservative Republican governor, Don Samuelson, in favor of Democrat Cecil Andrus. A major issue in the campaign was Samuelson's support of mine companies' plans to extract molybdenum from the scenic White Clouds area in the Salmon River Mountains. Unlike many mountain state residents, Idahoans apparently favored protection of the state's environment over economic development. The conservative wing of the Idaho Republican party, typified by Gov. Samuelson, has lost support since the mid-'60's. And so it may be that new issues are once again reorienting Idaho politics.

Electoral Votes 4

Census Data 1970 pop. 713,008; 0.35% of U.S. total, 44th largest; change 1960–70, +6.9%. Metro. 15.7%, 10.5% central city. 1970 per capita income, $3,206, 39th highest. 46th in number of poor.

1970 Share of Federal Tax Burden $507,370,000; 0.26% of U.S. total, 46th largest.

1970 Share of Federal Outlays $843,545,769; 0.45% of U.S. total, 41st largest. Per capita federal spending, $1,183.

DOD	$100,148,000	49th (0.17%)	HEW	$160,855,502	45th (0.30%)
AEC	$97,102,723	13th (3.74%)	HUD	$11,419,777	39th (0.59%)
NASA	$150,325	45th (—)	OEO	$1,402,260	50th (0.02%)
DOT	$40,493,665	41st (0.57%)	DOA	$281,896,552	17th (2.19%)
DOC	$1,843,968	47th (0.16%)	POD	$19,550,793	48th (0.27%)
DOI	$24,750,057	31st (1.07%)	VA	$38,009,525	43rd (0.51%)
DOJ	$1,635,565	46th (0.28%)	CSC	$9,191,848	44th (0.23%)
			Other	$55,095,209	

Economic Base Livestock, dairy, potatoes, and cash grain; food and kindred products, esp. canned and preserved fruits and vegetables; lumber and wood products other than furniture, esp. sawmills and planing mills; metal mining, esp. silver ores and lead and zinc ores; industrial inorganic and organic chemicals and other chemicals and allied products; trailer coaches and other transportation equipment; printing, publishing, and allied industries, esp. newspapers; paper and allied products.

Political Line-up Governor, Cecil D. Andrus (D); seat up, 1974. Senators, Frank Church (D) and Len B. Jordan (R). Representatives, 2 (0 D and 2 R). State Senate (16 D and 19 R); State House (29 D and 41 R).

The Voters

Registration 364,992 total. No party registration.
Employment profile White collar, 37%. Blue collar, 63%.
Ethnic groups Black, less than 0.5%. Total foreign stock, 12%. UK, Germany, Canada, 2% each; Sweden, Norway, USSR, Mexico, 1% each; others, 4%.

Presidential vote

1968	Humphrey (D)	89,273	(31%)
	Nixon (R)	165,369	(57%)
	Wallace (AIP)	36,541	(13%)
1964	Johnson (D)	148,920	(51%)
	Goldwater (R)	143,557	(49%)
1960	Kennedy (D)	138,853	(46%)
	Nixon (R)	161,597	(54%)

Senator

Frank Church (D) Elected 1956, seat up 1974; b. July 25, 1924, Boise; home, Boise; Stanford U., B.A., 1947, LL.B., 1950; Harvard, 1948; Army, WWII; married, two children; Presbyterian.

Career Practicing atty., 1950–56; State Chm., Idaho Young Democrats, 1952–54; Keynoter, Democratic Natl. Convention, 1960; U.S. delegate to 21st UN General Assembly; Bd. of Governors, Col. of the Virgin Islands, 1968.

Offices 204 OSOB 202-225-6142. Also Rm. 304 Fed. Office Bldg., Boise 83702, 208-342-2711, ext. 363.

Committees

Foreign Relations (4th); Subs. (1) Chm., Western Hemisphere Affairs, (2) Chm., Genocide Convention, (3) Arms Control, International Law and Organization, (4) Oceans and International Environment.

Interior and Insular Affairs (4th); Subs. (1) Chm., Public Lands, (2) Parks and Recreation, (3) Water and Power Resources.

Sp. Com. on Aging (Chm.); Subs. (1) Chm., Consumer Interests of the Elderly, (2) Employment and Retirement Incomes, (3) Housing for the Elderly, (4) Long-Term Care.

Group Ratings

	ADA	COPE	NREP	NFU	LCV	NAB	NSI	ACA
1970	75	91	91	100	73	30	0	11
1969	78	—	—	75	—	—	—	29
1968	43	90	—	40	—	80	—	68

Key Votes

(1) ABM	AGN	(8) Phil Pln	FOR	(15) Coop-Church	FOR
(2) SST	AGN	(9) Vol Army	FOR	(16) Cut Oil Dpltn	AGN
(3) Busing	FOR	(10) Prison $	AGN	(17) Consumer Prot	FOR
(4) Tob Sub	FOR	(11) Cut Mil $	FOR	(18) Farm Sub Limit	FOR
(5) Carswell	AGN	(12) Defoliatn	FOR	(19) Comp Bid Sales	ABS
(6) No-Knock	FOR	(13) 18-Yr-Vote	FOR	(20) Pre-Prod Tests	AGN
(7) Seniorty	ABS	(14) Pentgn PR	AGN	(21) Cut Marjna Pen	FOR

Election Results

1968 general:	Frank Church (D)	173,482	(60%)
	George V. Hansen (R)	114,394	(40%)

1968 primary:	Frank Church (D), unopposed		
1962 general:	Frank Church (D)	141,657	(55%)
	Jack Hawley (R)	117,129	(45%)

Senator

Len B. Jordan (R) Elected Aug. 6, 1962, seat up 1972; b. May 15, 1899, Mount Pleasant, Utah; home, Boise; U. of Oregon, B.A., 1923; Army, WWI; married, three children; Methodist.

Career Rancher; businessman; Idaho legislature, 1947; Governor of Idaho, 1951–55; Intl. Jt. Commission on the St. Lawrence Seaway, 1955–57; Intl. Water Development Advisory Bd., 1958–59.

Offices 437 OSOB, 202-225-2752. Also 134 Old P.O. Bldg., P.O. Box 2753, Boise 83701, 208-342-2661, and P.O. Box 1217, Idaho Falls 83401, 208-523-9669.

Committees

Finance (4th).

Interior and Insular Affairs (2nd); Subs. (1) Minerals, Materials, and Fuels, (2) Territories and Insular Affairs, (3) Water and Power Resources.

Sel. Com. on Standards and Conduct (3rd).

Group Ratings

	ADA	COPE	NREP	NFU	LCV	NAB	NSI	ACA
1970	9	23	8	50	23	75	80	82
1969	17	—	—	40	—	—	—	67
1968	21	25	—	46	—	83	—	88

Key Votes

(1) ABM	FOR	(8) Phil Pln	AGN	(15) Coop-Church	AGN
(2) SST	AGN	(9) Vol Army	FOR	(16) Cut Oil Dpltn	AGN
(3) Busing	AGN	(10) Prison $	AGN	(17) Consumer Prot	AGN
(4) Tob Sub	FOR	(11) Cut Mil $	AGN	(18) Farm Sub Limit	FOR
(5) Carswell	FOR	(12) Defoliatn	FOR	(19) Comp Bid Sales	ABS
(6) No-Knock	FOR	(13) 18-Yr-Vote	FOR	(20) Pre-Prod Tests	AGN
(7) Seniorty	FOR	(14) Pentgn PR	FOR	(21) Cut Marjna Pen	AGN

Election Results

1966 general:	Len B. Jordan (R)	139,819	(55%)
	Ralph R. Harding (D)	112,637	(45%)
1966 primary:	Len B. Jordan (R), unopposed		
1962 special:	Len B. Jordan (R)	131,279	(51%)
	Gracie Pfost (D)	126,398	(49%)

FIRST DISTRICT Political Background

Idaho 1 is the western half of the state. The district is divided into two distinct portions by the Salmon River Mountains. The northern half is made up of the Idaho panhandle, which, economically and sociologically, is part of the adjacent "Inland Empire" of eastern Washington. Residents here have always supported public power developments on the Columbia River and its tributaries. Moreover, since many of the people are of Scandinavian and Irish descent, the panhandle is the most consistently Democratic part of Idaho.

The southern half of the 1st is dominated by Boise and the smaller cities of Nampa and Canyon along the Snake River. This area is part of the conservative heartland of southern Idaho. Boise, like many Western cities, is a Republican stronghold. Many of the people living in the southern portion of the 1st are Mormons, and the increasing conservatism of the Church during the '60's was undoubtedly a factor in the increasing political conservatism of Idaho voters.

The 1st's congressman, Republican James A. McClure, is the most conservative member of the Idaho delegation. McClure first won in 1966, unseating Compton I. White, Jr., a two-term incumbent whose father had represented the district for many years (1932–46, 1948–50). In 1970, the Democrats waged a strenuous campaign against McClure. They charged that the Congressman, as a member of the Interior and Insular Affairs Committee, had not voted with the rest of the state's delegation on ecological issues as well as on other important legislation. McClure won with 58% of the votes—a solid margin, but not really so impressive for a two-term incumbent running among the conservative voters of Idaho. McClure may face a real test in 1972. Redistricting has removed part of the city of Boise from the 1st. In the new district, figures indicate that McClure's 1970 margin would have been significantly lower.

Census Data 1970 pop. 400,309; deviation from current state average, +12.3%; change 1960–70, +9.7%. Metro. 28.0%, 18.7% central city.

1970 Share of Federal Outlays $389,224,354

DOD	$86,878,000	HEW	$101,369,930
AEC	$000	HUD	$11,308,777
NASA	$24,328	OEO	$1,091,637
DOT	$24,571,713	DOA	$72,033,936
		Other	$91,946,033

Federal Military-Industrial Commitments

DOD Installations Mountain Home AFB (Mountain Home).

Economic Base Livestock, dairy, potatoes, and cash grain; lumber and wood products other than furniture, esp. sawmills and planing mills; metal mining, esp. silver ore. Also, banking.

The Voters

Registration 205,454 total. No party registration.

Employment profile White collar, 38%. Blue collar, 62%.

Ethnic groups Black, less than 0.5%. Total foreign stock, 13%. Canada, Germany, UK, 2% each; Sweden, Norway, USSR, Mexico, 1% each; others, 4%.

Presidential vote

1968	Humphrey (D)	53,664	(33%)
	Nixon (R)	87,942	(55%)
	Wallace (AIP)	19,122	(12%)

Representative

James A. McClure (R) Elected 1966; b. Dec. 27, 1924, Payette; home, Payette; U. of Idaho, LL.B., 1950; married, three children; Methodist.

Career Practicing atty., 1950–66; Prosecuting Atty., Payette County, 1950–56; City Atty., Payette, 1953–66; Idaho Senate, 1960–66, Asst. Majority Leader, 1965–66.

Offices 1034 LHOB, 202-225-6611. Also Rm. 319, 805 Idaho St., Boise 83701, 208-343-1421, and 305 Fed. Bldg., Coeur d'Alene 83814, 208-664-3086.

Committees

Interior and Insular Affairs (6th); Subs. (1) Environment, (2) Irrigation and Reclamation, (3) Mines and Mining, (4) National Parks and Recreation.
Post Office and Civil Service (6th); Subs. (1) Census and Statistics, (2) Postal Facilities and Mail.

Group Ratings

	ADA	COPE	NREP	NFU	LCV	CFA	NAB	NSI	ACA
1970	12	9	0	31	33	33	100	100	83
1969	7	—	—	21	—	—	—	—	76
1968	0	0	—	38	—	—	80	—	91

Key Votes

(1) ABM	ABS	(6) 18-Yr-Vote	AGN	(11) Clean Water $	ABS
(2) SST	FOR	(7) Farm Sub Lmt	AGN	(12) Mig Wrkrs Comp	AGN
(3) Phil Pln	FOR	(8) Coop-Church	AGN	(13) Jets to Chiang	FOR
(4) No-Knock	FOR	(9) Family Asst	AGN	(14) State OEO Veto	FOR
(5) Cmutr Tax	FOR	(10) Work Stamps	FOR	(15) Park Logging	FOR

Election Results

1970 general:	James A. McClure (R)	77,515	(58%)
	William J. Brauner (D)	55,743	(42%)
1970 primary:	James A. McClure (R), unopposed		
1968 general:	James A. McClure (R)	90,870	(59%)
	Compton I. White, Jr. (D)	62,002	(41%)

SECOND DISTRICT Political Background

Idaho 2 is the eastern half of the state. It includes the Sawtooth Mountains, whose relatively temperate climate attracts skiers to Sun Valley and whose beauty brought Ernest Hemingway to his last home in nearby Ketchum. There are other scenic wonders within the 2nd's boundaries: the Craters of the Moon National Monument and a small slice of Yellowstone National Park. But most of the district's voters live in small towns along the Snake River. And most of Idaho's Mormons live in the 2nd; Salt Lake City is only an hour's drive from the southern border of the district. Except for the 2nd's largest city, Pocatello (pop. 40,000), which still votes Democratic occasionally, this is rock-hard conservative territory. In some counties along the Snake, George Wallace almost matched Hubert Humphrey's vote totals in 1968.

After a four-year Democratic interlude, the Republicans recaptured the 2nd in 1964—a result which shows the vitality of Goldwater Republicanism in southern Idaho. The current congressman, Orval Hansen, was first elected in 1968 when his predecessor, George Hansen, stepped aside to challenge Sen. Frank Church. Orval Hansen has beaten Democratic opponents by 2:1 margins and seems assured of reelection. The addition of a portion of the conservative city of Boise to the district will only strengthen his position.

Census Data 1970 pop. 312,699; deviation from current state average, —12.3%; change 1960–70, +3.5%. Metro. 0.0%, 0.0% central city.

1970 Share of Federal Outlays $454,321,415

DOD	$13,270,000	HEW	$59,485,572
AEC	$97,102,723	HUD	$111,000
NASA	$125,997	OEO	$310,623
DOT	$15,921,952	DOA	$209,862,616
		Other	$58,130,932

Federal Military-Industrial Commitments

DOD Installations Naval Nuclear Training Unit (Idaho Falls).

AEC Operations Idaho Nuclear Div. (Idaho Falls), $43.581m: operation of ten facilities. Westinghouse Electric (Idaho Falls), $14.020m: submarine, ship, and other reactor facilities. Argonne National Laboratories (Idaho Falls), $13.441m: reactor facilities.

Economic Base Livestock, dairy, potatoes, and cash grain; food and kindred products; chemicals and allied products. Also tourism (Sun Valley).

The Voters

Registration 159,538 total. No party registration.

Employment profile White collar, 36%. Blue collar, 64%.

Ethnic groups Black, less than 0.5%. Total foreign stock, 11%. UK, Germany, 2% each; Sweden, Canada, USSR, Mexico, 1% each; others, 4%.

Presidential vote

1968	Humphrey (D)	35,609	(27%)
	Nixon (R)	77,427	(59%)
	Wallace (AIP)	13,419	(13%)

Representative

Orval Hansen (R) Elected 1968; b. Aug. 3, 1926, Firth; home, Idaho Falls; U. of Idaho, B.A., 1950; George Washington U., J.D., 1954; U. of London, 1954–55; Navy, WWII; Major USAFR; married, seven children; Church of Latter Day Saints.

Career Practicing atty., 1956–68; Idaho House of Reps., 1956–62, 1964–66, House Majority Leader, 1961–62; Idaho Senate, 1966–68; Chm., Idaho Manpower Advisory Com., 1963–68; Idaho Legis. Council, 1965–67.

Offices 312 CHOB, 202-225-5531. Also First Security Bank Bldg., P.O. Box 396, Idaho Falls 83401, 208-523-1000, and Twin Falls Bank & Trust Bldg., P.O. Box 362, Twin Falls 83301, 208-734-2020.

Committees

Education and Labor (11th); Subs. (1) Gen. on Labor, (2) Sel. on Education.

House Administration (6th); Sub. on Printing.

Jt. Com. on Atomic Energy (1st); Subs. on (1) Communities, (2) Research, Development, and Radiation, (3) Security.

Group Ratings

	ADA	COPE	NREP	NFU	LCV	CFA	NAB	NSI	ACA
1970	32	60	27	83	0	60	75	89	47
1969	7	—	—	67	—	—	—	—	35
1968	0	9	—	17	—	—	100	—	100

Key Votes

(1) ABM	FOR	(6) 18-Yr-Vote	FOR	(11) Clean Water $	AGN
(2) SST	FOR	(7) Farm Sub Lmt	AGN	(12) Mig Wrkrs Comp	FOR
(3) Phil Pln	FOR	(8) Coop-Church	AGN	(13) Jets to Chiang	AGN
(4) No-Knock	FOR	(9) Family Asst	FOR	(14) State OEO Veto	AGN
(5) Cmutr Tax	FOR	(10) Work Stamps	FOR	(15) Park Logging	FOR

Election Results

1970 general:	Orval Hansen (R)	66,428	(66%)
	Marden Wells (D)	31,872	(32%)
	Joel Anderson (AIP)	2,625	(3%)
1970 primary:	Orval Hansen (R), unopposed		
1968 general:	Orval Hansen (R)	65,029	(53%)
	D. V. Manning (D)	54,256	(44%)
	Joel Anderson (AIP)	4,377	(4%)

ILLINOIS

Political Background

Illinois is the "land of Lincoln," as its license plates proclaim. It is also a land of tough, victory-minded politicians, best typified by Mayor Richard J. Daley of Chicago, and the land of the hard-nosed partisan politics of powerful Machine Democrats and conservative Republicans. Both parties have a tradition of slating blue ribbon candidates to win patronage-rich offices—a tradition that gave the nation Abraham Lincoln and Stephen Douglas in 1858 and, more recently, Adlai Stevenson and Paul Douglas in 1948 and senators Charles Percy and Adlai Stevenson III in 1966 and 1970.

Between elections, the rival party leaders manage to live together comfortably, usually dividing the political spoils. But these spoils have helped to make Illinois a state of fabled corruption. The Republican state auditor went to jail in the 1950's for stealing $150,000, and the Democratic secretary of state left $800,000 cash in shoeboxes in his Springfield hotel room when he died in 1970. In the same year three members of the state Supreme Court were forced to resign, and the Republican Superintendent of Public Instruction lost his bid for reelection after a newspaper charged that he had used money allocated for handicapped children to pay for publicity pictures of himself. And most Illinois Republicans still believe that Mayor Daley's Cook County Machine stole enough ballots to give the state's electoral votes, and the presidency, to John F. Kennedy in 1960.

Illinois elections are usually depicted as contests between the Democratic Chicago Machine and the Republican Downstate. The reality is not that simple. With the growth of the suburbs, Chicago now has only a third of the state's voters, and the Cook and Dupage county suburbs are as Republican as the city is Democratic. Downstate is not a monolith, either. There are substantial pockets of Democratic strength around East St. Louis and in the scattered counties which have large working-class populations, or where the Civil War anti-Republican tradition persists. As a result, Illinois is one of the most evenly divided states in the nation. Today Republicans hold exactly half of the statewide offices, including the governorship, and Democrats hold the other half. One of Illinois' senators is a Republican, the other a Democrat, and the state's House delegation is split 12–12. The state legislature is divided: Republicans hold the General Assembly 90–87, and the state Senate is Democratic only because of Lt. Gov. Paul Simon's tie-breaking vote.

Because of this division, each party will have a veto over redistricting plans, and so it is unlikely that the redrawing of district boundaries will affect the composition of Illinois' congressional delegation. If the Republicans had one more seat in the state Senate they would probably create a new district in suburban Cook County at the expense of Chicago, whose population is declining. Daley's Democrats, however, will undoubtedly insist on adding just a little suburban territory to most of Chicago's districts, to preserve their present voting patterns.

Illinois has not backed a loser in a presidential race since 1916. If it is still an index of national politics, the 1970 state elections show that Richard Nixon is in trouble. Democrats swept the state, winning the two elections for statewide office and gaining ten seats in the state Senate. The Democrats even prevailed in races for education offices, where Republicans stressed their opposition to student violence: they ousted the long-entrenched Superintendent of Public Instruction by 473,000 votes and won the races for four seats on the Board of Trustees of the University of Illinois. Although Democrats did not gain any House seats, their candidates improved on their 1968 percentages in 18 of the state's 24 congressional districts, chipping away at the advantage usually enjoyed by incumbents.

The prize in Illinois' biggest race of the year was the four years remaining in the term of the late Senator Everett McKinley Dirksen. Governor Richard Ogilvie had appointed Ralph Taylor Smith, veteran state legislator and typical Illinois Republican, to the seat. Meanwhile, Mayor Daley and state treasurer Adlai Stevenson III came to terms, making Stevenson the early favorite.

Smith's backers, particularly millionaire insurance-executive W. Clement Stone, decided to take the offensive. The premise of the campaign was simple. Most Illinois voters are conservative, as is Ralph Smith. If, therefore, they could convince the voters that Stevenson was a liberal, or even a radical, Smith would win. The Republicans' television campaign made the national news. One of the ads joined half of Stevenson's face to half of Jerry Rubin's while the soundtrack boomed, "Why doesn't he speak out against students who tear down our universities? What does Adlai have against the Chicago Police and the FBI?"

Stevenson responded by wearing an American flag pin on his lapel and hiring Chicago Seven prosecutor Thomas Foran as co-manager of his campaign. This reaction was probably unnecessary. Smith's ads backfired, particularly among well-educated, high-income voters, and Illinois voters in general could not believe the son of the former governor and presidential candidate sympathized with Jerry Rubin. Smith campaigned on the slogan "He speaks for the majority," but on election day he took only 42% of the vote. Stevenson's majority of 545,000 fell just behind his father's 1948 statewide record of 572,000.

Stevenson ran well in suburban areas, and in every one of the Downstate cities. He carried traditionally Republican Rockford, Peoria, Champaign-Urbana (site of the University of Illinois), and Danville, as well as Democratic cities like East St. Louis, Rock Island, and Moline. Smith did best in the solid Republican rural areas around Chicago and in the southern end of the state, an area with a Democratic tradition, but with a definite Dixie accent. In general, Smith's hard-line version of the Nixon-Agnew position on social issues repelled white-collar voters without making significant inroads into the blue-collar vote, except in entirely rural areas.

The Stevenson election indicates that the Democratic presidential candidate will have an excellent chance of carrying Illinois in 1972. Humphrey lost the state primarily because of a heavy Wallace vote among blue-collar workers and a weak showing in the Chicago suburbs, which now cast between 15% and 20% of the state's votes. High-income voters seem to be increasingly repelled by the anti-Negro and anti-student overtones of the Nixon-Agnew rhetoric. And while in 1968 blue-collar workers could show their dissatisfaction with the national administration by voting either for Nixon or for Wallace, the entire reaction vote will probably go to the Democrats in 1972.

The Daley Machine is in fine shape. In 1970 it recaptured the Cook County sheriff's office and held on to the County Board presidency and assessorship, all important patronage offices. In 1972, Republican Governor Ogilvie and Senator Percy will be up for reelection. Ogilvie is suffering from income tax increases, but Percy should be virtually unbeatable. He won in 1966 with strong showing in the suburbs and the outer fringes of the city of Chicago. His greatest threat is conservative opposition in the Republican primary. But Percy has been promised by the Nixon Administration that he will not become one of its targets like fellow liberal Republican, ex-Senator Charles Goodell of New York. Moreover, Illinois Republicans, like Illinois Democrats, would rather win than promote an ideology. So they will undoubtedly swallow Percy's opposition to the Vietnam war and his liberal social views in order to strengthen the ticket for Nixon, Ogilvie, and other Republican candidates.

Electoral Votes 26

Census Data 1970 pop. 11,113,976; 5.40% of U.S. total, 5th largest; change 1960–70, +10.2%. Metro. 80.1%, 36.7% central city. 1970 per capita income, $4,516, 8th highest. 8th in number of poor.

1970 Share of Federal Tax Burden $13,054,910,000; 6.69% of U.S. total, 3rd largest.

1970 Share of Federal Outlays $7,792,409,791; 4.12% of U.S. total, 5th largest. Per capita federal spending, $701.

DOD	$1,538,789,000	13th (2.68%)	HEW	$2,687,877,000	4th (5.14%)
AEC	$150,872,685	7th (5.81%)	HUD	$43,965,684	15th (2.26%)
NASA	$9,893,262	21st (0.27%)	OEO	$34,430,634	4th (4.53%)
DOT	$252,357,030	9th (3.53%)	DOA	$585,151,017	6th (4.55%)
DOC	$12,136,918	19th (1.05%)	POD	$502,988,650	3rd (6.90%)
DOI	$54,973,663	12th (2.38%)	VA	$415,979,520	6th (5.63%)
DOJ	$23,997,827	5th (4.18%)	CSC	$95,792,477	10th (2.38%)
			Other	$1,383,204,424	

Economic Base Nonelectrical machinery, esp. construction, mining, and material handling machinery and equipment, metalworking machinery and equipment, and general industrial machinery and equipment; electrical machinery, equipment, and supplies, esp. communication equipment, and radio and television receiving sets; cash grain and livestock; fabricated metal products, esp. fabricated structural metal products, bolts, nuts, screws, rivets, and washers, and metal stampings; food and kindred products, esp. meat products, grain mill products, and bakery products; primary metal industries, blast furnaces, steel works, and rolling and finishing mills, iron and steel foundries, and rolling, drawing, and extruding of nonferrous metals; printing, publishing, and allied industries, esp. commercial printing and newspapers; chemicals and allied products; transportation equipment, esp. motor vehicle equipment and aircraft and parts. Also, higher education, banking, and insurance.

Political Line-up Governor, Richard B. Ogilvie (R); seat up, 1972. Senators, Charles H. Percy (R) and Adlai E. Stevenson III (D). Representatives, 24 (12 D and 12 R). State Senate (29 D and 29 R); State Assembly (87 D and 90 R).

The Voters

Registration 5,337,692 total. No party registration.

Employment profile White collar, 42%. Blue collar, 58%.

Ethnic groups Black, 13%. Total foreign stock, 24.3%. Germany, Poland, 4% each; Italy, UK, 2% each; Sweden, USSR, Ireland, Czech., Canada, Austria, Mexico, 1% each.

Presidential vote

1968	Humphrey (D)	2,039,814	(44%)
	Nixon (R)	2,274,774	(47%)
	Wallace (AIP)	390,958	(9%)
1964	Johnson (D)	2,796,833	(60%)
	Goldwater (R)	1,905,946	(41%)
1960	Kennedy (D)	2,377,846	(50%)
	Nixon (R)	2,368,988	(50%)

Senator

Charles Harting Percy (R) Elected 1966, seat up 1972; b. Sept. 27, 1919, Pensacola, Fla.; home, Wilmette; U. of Chicago, B.A., 1941; Navy, WWII; married, five children; Christian Scientist.

Career Pres., Bell & Howell Co., 1949–61; Chief Exec. Office, 1961–63; Chm. of Bd., 1961–66; Pres., United Repub. Fund of Ill., 1955; Pres. Eisenhower's Rep. to pres. inaugurations in Peru and Bolivia, 1959; Head of Repub. Com. on Programs and Progress, 1960; Chm., Repub. Party's Platform Com., 1965; Repub. candidate for governor, 1964.

Offices 1200 NSOB, 202-225-2152. Also Suite 1860, 219 S. Dearborn, Chicago 60604, 312-353-4952, and Rm. 104, Old P.O. Bldg., Springfield 62706, 217-525-4442.

Committees

Appropriations (10th); Subs. (1) District of Columbia, (2) Interior, (3) Labor, HEW, and Related Agencies, (4) HUD, Space, and Science, (5) Military Construction, (6) Transportation.

Government Operations (3rd); Subs. (1) Executive Reorganization, (2) Permanent Investigations.

Jt. Economic Com. (3rd); Subs. on (1) Economic Progress, (2) Fiscal Policy, (3) Foreign Economic Policy, (4) International Exchange and Payments, (5) Priorities and Economy in Government, (6) Urban Affairs.

Sel. Com. on Nutrition and Human Needs (4th).

Sp. Com. on Aging (9th): Subs. (1) Consumer Interests of the Elderly, (2) Employment and Retirement Incomes, (3) Federal, State, and Community Services, (4) Health of the Elderly.

Group Ratings

	ADA	COPE	NREP	NFU	LCV	NAB	NSI	ACA
1970	18	91	75	73	61	43	60	31
1969	72	—	—	44	—	—	—	8
1968	79	64	—	69	—	0	—	31

Key Votes

(1) ABM	AGN	(8) Phil Pln	FOR	(15) Coop-Church	FOR
(2) SST	AGN	(9) Vol Army	FOR	(16) Cut Oil Dpltn	ABS
(3) Busing	FOR	(10) Prison $	FOR	(17) Consumer Prot	ABS
(4) Tob Sub	ABS	(11) Cut Mil $	AGN	(18) Farm Sub Limit	ABS
(5) Carswell	AGN	(12) Defoliatn	FOR	(19) Comp Bid Sales	ABS
(6) No-Knock	FOR	(13) 18-Yr-Vote	FOR	(20) Pre-Prod Tests	AGN
(7) Seniorty	AGN	(14) Pentgn PR	AGN	(21) Cut Marjna Pen	AGN

Election Results

1966 general:	Charles H. Percy (R)	2,100,449	(55%)
	Paul H. Douglas (D)	1,678,147	(44%)
	Robert Sabonigian (write-in)	41,965	(1%)
1966 primary:	Charles H. Percy (R)	605,815	(91%)
	Howard J. Doyle (R)	38,636	(6%)
	Lar "America First" Daly (R)	23,889	(4%)

Senator

Adlai E. Stevenson III (D) Elected 1970, seat up 1976; b. Oct. 10, 1930; home, Chicago; Harvard Col., B.A., 1952; Harvard Law School, LL.B., 1957; USMC, Korean War; married, four children; Unitarian.

Career Atty., Law Clerk to Ill. Supreme Ct. Justice, 1957–58; Past Dir., Com. on Ill. Gov., Chicago Crime Commission; Ill. Rep., 1965–67; Ill. State Treasurer, 1967–70.

Offices 107 OSOB, 202-225-2854. Also Rm. 1758, Fed. Bldg., 219 S. Dearborn St., 312-525-5420, and Rm. 14, P.O. Bldg., 6th and Monroe Sts., Springfield 217-525-4126.

Committees

Banking, Housing, and Urban Affairs (7th); Subs. (1) Housing and Urban Affairs, (2) International Finance, (3) Production and Stabilization, (4) Securities.

District of Columbia (3rd); Subs. (1) Chm., Business, Commerce, and Judiciary, (2) Public Health, Education, Welfare.

Labor and Public Welfare (10th); Subs. (1) Chm., Migratory Labor, (2) Aging, (3) Children and Youth, (4) Employment, Manpower, and Poverty, (5) Labor, (6) Railroad Retirement, (7) Sp. Sub. on Social Programs.

Group Ratings, Key Votes: Newly elected.

Election Results

1970 general:	Adlai E. Stevenson III (D)	2,065,054	(58%)
	Ralph Tyler Smith (R)	1,519,718	(42%)
1970 primary:	Adlai E. Stevenson III (D), unopposed		

FIRST DISTRICT Political Background

Illinois 1 is the South Side of Chicago, the heart of the largest black ghetto in the country. Some 96% of the district's residents are black, and less than 1% of those residents voted for Wallace in 1968—the Alabaman's worst showing in any congressional district. The 1st is a poor district, its poverty manifest in the miles of 20-story housing project high-rises that line the 14-lane Dan Ryan Expressway.

The district is, of course, heavily Democratic and is part of Chicago's Daley country. For 28 years, until his death in 1970, William L. Dawson, the nation's second Negro congressman since Reconstruction, represented the 1st—and the Democratic Machine. Dawson rose quietly in the House to become chairman of the Government Operations Committee. Back on the South Side, he was constantly accused of Uncle Tomism, but Dawson whipped every primary challenger by at least a 2:1 margin. The Negro Congressman always capitalized fully on the strength of the Machine, its ability to confer favors and to oil the wheels of otherwise unresponsive bureaucracies for people whose lives depend on them. Good-government advocates may argue that the Machine delivers only that to which the citizen is already entitled. But this line of argument has never been accepted in Richard J. Daley's Chicago.

Dawson's successor is Ralph H. Metcalfe, an Olympic sprinter in the '30's, a former alderman and a loyal follower of the Machine. Metcalfe won the 1970 Democratic primary more than 2:1 over Alderman A. A. (Sammy) Rayner, who fared better in the liberal press than in South Side ballot boxes. Metcalfe has been a much more vigorous congressman than Dawson, who was 84 when he died, and, unlike Dawson, he has been an active participant in the militant House Black Caucus.

The 1970 census shows that the South Side, like most black ghetto areas, lost population during the '60's. The loss can be attributed either to the blacks' desire to move to neighborhoods newly opened up farther out in the city, or to Census Bureau undercounting. Whatever the case, the 1st will have to add 80,000 residents in redistricting. Most of them will probably come from what is now the 3rd district, where the white Machine-backed incumbent had black primary opposition in 1970. The additional territory will not keep Congressman Metcalfe from enjoying, like his predecessor, a long career in the House.

Census Data 1970 pop. 381,139; deviation from current state average, −17.7; change 1960–70, −7.5. Metro. 100.0%, 100.0% central city.

1970 Share of Federal Outlays $316,167,000 (average outlay per district, Illinois 1–11, 13, 14)

DOD	$50,554,000	HEW	$113,043,000
AEC	$7,397,000	HUD	$1,860,000
NASA	$674,000	OEO	$2,280,000
DOT	$5,550,000	DOA	$13,384,000
		Other	$121,426,000

Federal Military-Industrial Commitments (See Illinois 5 for greater Chicago listing.)

Economic Base Electrical machinery, equipment, and supplies, esp. communication equipment, radio and television receiving sets other than communication types, and electronic components and accessories; fabricated metal products, esp. metal stampings; nonelectrical machinery, especially metalworking machinery and equipment; printing, publishing, and allied industries, esp. commercial printing.

The Voters

Registration Not available.

Employment profile White collar, 29%. Blue collar, 71%.

Ethnic groups Black, 96%. Total foreign stock, 6%. Ireland, Germany, Sweden, 1% each; others, 4%.

Presidential vote

1968	Humphrey (D)	38,835	(93%)
	Nixon (R)	10,081	(7%)
	Wallace (AIP)	1,010	(1%)

Representative

Ralph H. Metcalfe (D) Elected 1970; b. May 29, 1910, Atlanta, Ga.; home, Chicago; Marquette U., B.A., 1936; U. of So. Calif., M.A., 1939; Army, 1942–45; married, one child; Catholic.

Career Coach, Instr., Zavier U., New Orleans; Dir., Dept. of Civil Rights for Commission on Human Relations, 1945; Ill. Athletic Commissioner, 1949–52; Chicago Third Ward Committeeman, 1952– ; Alderman, 1955–70; Chicago City Council, 1955–69; Pres. Pro Tempore of Chicago City Council, 1969–70; Natl. A.A.U. and N.C.A.A. Sports Arbitration Bd.; Dir., U.S. Olympics Com.; Dir., Ill. Fed. Savings & Loan Assn.

Offices 1100 LHOB, 202-225-4372. Also 219 S. Dearborn St., Chicago 60604, 313-353-4105.

Committees

Interstate and Foreign Commerce (23rd); Sub. on Transportation and Aeronautics.

Group Ratings, Key Votes: Newly elected.

Election Results

1970 general:	Ralph H. Metcalfe (D)	93,272	(91%)
	Janet R. Jennings (R)	9,267	(9%)
1970 primary:	Ralph H. Metcalfe (D)	42,575	(71%)
	A. A. Rayner, Jr. (D)	17,346	(29%)

SECOND DISTRICT Political Background

Illinois 2 lies next to all-black Illinois 1, Chicago's black ghetto. The 2nd is technically part of Chicago's South Side; it is, however, quite another kind of district, carefully drawn to exclude the heart of the black South Side. The 2nd extends south along Lake Michigan starting from the integrated academic community of Hyde Park-Kenwood around the University of Chicago. It then passes through a portion of the South Side ghetto to the port and steel mills around Lake Calumet. The 1965 redistricting added the industrial suburbs of Calumet City, reputedly a vice center, and Dolton.

The southern part of the district resembles nearby Gary, Indiana; but Gary is black and this part of the 2nd is not. Most of the 2nd's residents are of East European descent and hold blue-collar jobs. The northern end is more white-collar; Hyde Park is one of the centers of the Independent Voters of Illinois, a liberal reform group which has had little success affecting the style or substance of Illinois politics.

Abner Mikva, the 2nd's congressman, manages to represent the interests of both ends of the district. He is a successful lawyer of Czech descent and a top vote-getter in the 1964 court-ordered statewide election to the Illinois General Assembly. In 1966, Mikva bucked the Machine and won about 40% of the votes in the Democratic primary against 20-year incumbent Barratt O'Hara. The incumbent was then 84 and the last Spanish-American War veteran to sit in Congress. In 1968, Mikva won the Machine's endorsement—probably because it figured he would win anyway—and beat O'Hara. As congressman, Mikva is known for his liberal and antiwar views. Mikva, along with Adlai Stevenson III and ex-Gov. Otto Kerner, was reportedly under Pentagon surveillance during 1968.

Redistricting will add suburban territory to the 2nd. But its Democratic proclivities are so strong that any change in party control is highly unlikely. And odds are the Machine, knowing Mikva's standing in the district, will leave him alone in the 1972 primary.

Census Data 1970 pop. 415,380; deviation from current state average, −10.3%; change 1960–70, −1.7%. Metro. 100.0%, 82.8% central city.

1970 Share of Federal Outlays $316,167,000 (average outlay per district, Illinois 1–11, 13, 14)

DOD	$50,554,000	HEW	$113,043,000
AEC	$7,397,000	HUD	$1,860,000
NASA	$674,000	OEO	$2,280,000

DOT	$5,550,000	DOA	$13,384,000
		Other	$121,426,000

Federal Military-Industrial Commitments (See Illinois 5 for greater Chicago listing.)

Economic Base Electrical machinery, equipment, and supplies, esp. communication equipment, radio and television sets other than communication types, and electronic components and accessories; fabricated metal products, esp. metal stampings; nonelectrical machinery, esp. nonmetalworking machinery and equipment; printing, publishing, and allied industries, esp. commercial printing. Also, higher education (University of Chicago).

The Voters

Registration Not available.

Employment profile White collar, 47%. Blue collar, 53%.

Ethnic groups Black, 33%. Puerto Rican, 1%. Total foreign stock, 36%. Poland, 8%; Germany, 4%; Italy, USSR, 3% each; Mexico, UK, Ireland, Sweden, 2% each; Canada, Austria, Hungary, Czech., 1% each; others, 7%.

Presidential vote

1968	Humphrey (D)	103,924	(59%)
	Nixon (R)	52,311	(30%)
	Wallace (AIP)	18,896	(11%)

Representative

Abner J. Mikva (D) Elected 1968; b. Jan. 21, 1926, Milwaukee, Wis.; home, Chicago; U. of Chicago Law School, J.D., 1951; Army Air Corps, WWII; married, three children; Jewish.

Career Law clerk to U.S. Supreme Ct. Justice Sherman Minton, 1951–52; practicing atty., 1952–68; Ill. House of Reps., 1955–66.

Offices 1527 LHOB, 202-225-4835. Also 219 S. Dearborn, Chicago 60604, 312-353-6148, and 8808 Commercial Ave., Chicago 60617, 312-731-8484.

Committees

District of Columbia (12th); Sub. (1) Business, Commerce, and Fiscal Affairs, (2) Housing and Youth Affairs, (3) Judiciary.

Judiciary (17th); Sub. (1) No. 3, (2) No. 5.

Group Ratings

	ADA	COPE	NREP	NFU	LCV	CFA	NAB	NSI	ACA
1970	100	100	100	92	100	100	0	0	22
1969	100	—	—	86	—	—	—	—	12

Key Votes

(1) ABM	AGN	(6) 18-Yr-Vote	FOR	(11) Clean Water $	FOR
(2) SST	AGN	(7) Farm Sub Lmt	FOR	(12) Mig Wrkrs Comp	FOR
(3) Phil Pln	FOR	(8) Coop-Church	FOR	(13) Jets to Chiang	AGN
(4) No-Knock	AGN	(9) Family Asst	FOR	(14) State OEO Veto	AGN
(5) Cmutr Tax	FOR	(10) Work Stamps	AGN	(15) Park Logging	AGN

Election Results

1970 general:	Abner J. Mikva (D)	88,252	(75%)
	Harold E. Marks (R)	29,853	(25%)
1970 primary:	Abner J. Mikva (D), unopposed		

1968 general:	Abner J. Mikva (D)	106,642	(65%)
	Thomas R. Ireland (R)	56,513	(35%)

THIRD DISTRICT Political Background

Illinois 3 is southwest Chicago and a few adjacent suburbs. During the 1960's, the district was the scene of one of the nation's greatest racial population shifts. In 1960, 80% of the 3rd's residents were white; by 1970, after 10 years of blockbusting, blacks had a thin majority. The whites who remain are mostly blue-collar workers of Irish Catholic and East European descent.

Historically, the 2nd has been a Democratic district. But the black migration and the furor attending Martin Luther King's Chicago marches inspired the Republicans to make major efforts to take the seat. They tried twice, in 1966 and 1968, and twice the aging, Machine-backed Congressman William T. Murphy won reelection by narrow margins. In 1970, Murphy retired and was replaced by another Murphy, Morgan Murphy, the son of a Commonwealth Edison executive and a socialite supporter of the Daley Administration. Morgan Murphy beat his black primary opponent, Augustus Savage, by a 2:1 margin, a margin which indicated that a significant number of blacks voted for the white machine candidate. Murphy went on to win the general election by a surprisingly large vote, 68%. In Washington, the Congressman soon made a name for himself, spotlighting the extent of heroin addiction among American soldiers in Vietnam.

Before the 1972 election, many of the 3rd's black precincts will probably be redistricted into the 1st district, and a significant portion of suburban territory, primarily the city of Oak Lawn, will be added to the district. But given Murphy's present electoral strength, the adjustment of the 3rd's lines will not change the results of his 1972 general election. Moreover, the district's new make-up should protect Murphy from black primary opponents.

Census Data 1970 pop. 452,535; deviation from current state average, −2.3%; change 1960–70, +6.3%. Metro. 100.0%, 94.4% central city.

1970 Share of Federal Outlays $316,167,000 (average outlay per district, Illinois 1–11, 13, 14)

DOD	$50,554,000	HEW	$113,043,000
AEC	$7,397,000	HUD	$1,860,000
NASA	$674,000	OEO	$2,280,000
DOT	$5,550,000	DOA	$13,384,000
		Other	$121,426,000

Federal Military-Industrial Commitments (See Illinois 5 for greater Chicago listing.)

Economic Base Electrical machinery, equipment, and supplies, esp. communication equipment, radio and television sets other than communication types, and electronic components and accessories; fabricated metal products, esp. metal stampings; non-electrical machinery, esp. metalworking machinery and equipment; printing, publishing, and allied industries, esp. commercial printing.

The Voters

Registration Not available.

Employment profile White collar, 45%. Blue collar, 55%.

Ethnic groups Black, 50%. Total foreign stock, 32%. Ireland, 6%; Germany, 4%; Poland, Italy, 3% each; UK, Sweden, 2% each; Austria, Canada, Czech., USSR, Hungary, 1% each; others, 9%.

Presidential vote

1968	Humphrey (D)	111,357	(56%)
	Nixon (R)	69,344	(35%)
	Wallace (AIP)	16,665	(8%)

Representative

Morgan Francis Murphy (D) Elected 1970; b. April 16, 1932, Chicago; home, Chicago; Northwestern U., B.S., 1955; DePaul U. School of Law, LL.B., 1962; USMC, 1955–8; married, three children; Catholic.

Career Practicing atty., 1962–70; Admin. Asst. to Clerk, Circuit Ct., 1958–61; Hearing Officer, Local Liquor Control Commission, 1969–70; Chm., Gov. Div. Crusade of Mercy, 1967– ; Mbr., Bd. of Assn. of Mercy Hospital.

Offices 1108 LHOB, 202-225-3406. Also Rm. 1640, Dirksen Bldg., 219 S. Dearborn St., Chicago 60604, 312-353-5390.

Committees

Foreign Affairs (20th); Subs. (1) Asian and Pacific Affairs, (2) Europe, (3) State Dept. Organization and Foreign Operations.

Science and Astronautics (16th); Subs. (1) International Cooperation in Science and Space, (2) Space Science and Applications.

Sel. Com. on Crime (5th).

Group Ratings

	ADA	COPE	NREP	NFU	LCV	CFA	NAB	NSI	ACA
1970	52	92	58	100	40	89	9	80	16
1969	47	—	—	93	—	—	—	—	18
1968	92	100	—	100	—	—	0	—	5

Key Votes

(1) ABM	FOR	(6) 18-Yr-Vote	FOR	(11) Clean Water $	FOR
(2) SST	AGN	(7) Farm Sub Lmt	FOR	(12) Mig Wrkrs Comp	FOR
(3) Phil Pln	AGN	(8) Coop-Church	AGN	(13) Jets to Chiang	FOR
(4) No-Knock	FOR	(9) Family Asst	FOR	(14) State OEO Veto	AGN
(5) Cmutr Tax	FOR	(10) Work Stamps	AGN	(15) Park Logging	AGN

Election Results

1970 general:	Morgan F. Murphy (D)	97,693	(69%)
	Robert P. Rowan (R)	44,013	(31%)
1970 primary:	Morgan F. Murphy (D)	43,080	(72%)
	Augustus A. Savage (D)	16,905	(28%)

FOURTH DISTRICT Political Background

Illinois 4 is the southwest suburbs of Chicago—some white-collar, some blue-collar, some WASPish, some dominated by descendants of East European immigrants, a few with black residents—towns like Chicago Heights, Park Forest, Homewood, Harvey, and Oak Lawn. South Holland, another suburb in the 4th, was where Judge Julius Hoffman, in a landmark case, ordered the school board to begin busing because of the town's racially discriminatory patterns of school attendance. The economic status and the ethnic composition of the 4th's residents are not much different from the white southwest side of Chicago (3rd district), from which many of its residents have fled in the past 10 or 20 years. The 4th is a little richer, definitely whiter, and a little more white-collar.

But the politics of the 4th are quite the reverse of those in adjoining Chicago. The district is Republican with a vengeance, even more Republican than the adjacent white parts of the city are Democratic. The Chicago city limits mark the difference: inside, the precincts usually go the way Mayor Daley's organization would have them; outside, the vote goes almost entirely against the Machine.

In the 4th, the 10th, and the 13th, the three suburban Cook County districts, the more conservative the Republican candidate, the better. These districts deliver sweeping majorities for Republican candidates running for countywide offices rich in patronage. In recent years the suburban precincts have often outvoted the much larger city, electing Republican sheriffs in 1962 and 1966 and a Republican County Board president in 1966. The former board president is now Gov. Richard Ogilvie. In 1970, a heavily Democratic year, the Cook County suburbs almost won these same countywide offices.

The political clout of the city's Democratic Machine is usually called upon to explain the sharp differences in voting behavior inside and outside Chicago. But another set of circumstances also figures in the pattern. In metropolitan Chicago, or anywhere else in the country for that matter, people who share political inclinations and also share corresponding attitudes on any number of other questions tend to settle in areas where the political atmosphere is thought to be congenial (see California 35). Thus Chicago area residents who happen to be Republicans gravitate to the suburbs, while those who are Democrats tend to remain in the city itself.

Whatever the reasons, the 4th is solidly Republican. It was one of the few congressional districts (60 of 435) which Barry Goldwater carried in 1964. Since 1958, its representative in the House, Edward J. Derwinski, has been a conservative in the Goldwater mold; since 1966, he has won reelection every two years by margins better than 2:1. Derwinski's comparative youth (44 in 1970) and the composition of the 4th district suggest that he will continue to serve in the House for the forseeable future. He is currently the 2nd ranking Republican on the Post Office and Civil Service Committee. And since the ranking Republican, H. R. Gross of Iowa, is over 70, Derwinski may become committee chairman, if the Republicans win control of the House in some future election.

Redistricting will not threaten the Congressman's tenure. Because the population of the 4th skyrocketed during the '60's, parts of it—thanks to Mayor Daley's interest in the redistricting process—will be absorbed into adjacent Democratic Chicago districts. That which remains, the new 4th, will be even more Republican than the current district.

Census Data 1970 pop. 606,524; deviation from current state average, +31.0%; change 1960–70, +43.5%. Metro. 100.0%, 0.0% central city.

1970 Share of Federal Outlays $316,167,000 (average outlay per district, Illinois 1–11, 13, 14)

DOD	$50,554,000	HEW	$113,043,000
AEC	$7,397,000	HUD	$1,860,000
NASA	$674,000	OEO	$2,280,000
DOT	$5,550,000	DOA	$13,384,000
		Other	$121,426,000

Federal Military-Industrial Commitments (See Illinois 5 for greater Chicago listing.)

Economic Base Electrical machinery, equipment, and supplies, esp. communication equipment, radio and television sets other than communication types, and electronic components and accessories; fabricated metal products, esp. metal stampings; nonelectrical machinery, esp. metalworking machinery and equipment; printing, publishing, and allied industries, esp. commercial printing.

The Voters

Registration Not available.

Employment profile White collar, 49%. Blue collar, 51%.

Ethnic groups Black, 8%. Total foreign stock, 23%. Germany, 4%; Poland, Italy, 3% each; UK, 2%; Sweden, Canada, Czech., Ireland, Austria, Mexico, USSR, 1% each; others, 6%.

Presidential vote

1968	Humphrey (D)	73,987	(32%)
	Nixon (R)	128,964	(56%)
	Wallace (AIP)	27,581	(12%)

Representative

Edward J. Derwinski (R) Elected 1958; b. Sept. 15, 1926, Chicago; home, South Holland; Loyola U., B.S., 1951; Army, WWII; Major USAR; married, one child; Catholic.

Career Ill. House of Reps., 1957–58; Pres., West Pullman Savings & Loan Assn.

Offices 1401 LHOB, 202-225-3961. Also P.O. Bldg., 2441 Vermont St., Blue Island 60406, 312-389-2440.

Committees

Foreign Affairs (6th); Subs. (1) Africa, (2) Foreign Economic Policy, (3) International Organizations and Movements.

Post Office and Civil Service (3rd); Subs. (1) Manpower and Civil Service, (2) Postal Service, (3) Postal Operations.

Group Ratings

	ADA	COPE	NREP	NFU	LCV	CFA	NAB	NSI	ACA
1970	20	0	8	23	38	42	100	90	89
1969	40	—	—	14	—	—	—	—	88
1968	17	9	—	19	—	—	83	—	73

Key Votes

(1) ABM	FOR	(6) 18-Yr-Vote	AGN	(11) Clean Water $	FOR
(2) SST	FOR	(7) Farm Sub Lmt	AGN	(12) Mig Wrkrs Comp	AGN
(3) Phil Pln	AGN	(8) Coop-Church	AGN	(13) Jets to Chiang	FOR
(4) No-Knock	ABS	(9) Family Asst	AGN	(14) State OEO Veto	FOR
(5) Cmutr Tax	AGN	(10) Work Stamps	FOR	(15) Park Logging	AGN

Election Results

1970 general:	Edward J. Derwinski (R)	117,590	(68%)
	Melvin W. Morgan (D)	55,328	(32%)
1970 primary:	Edward J. Derwinski (R), unopposed		
1968 general:	Edward J. Derwinski (R)	151,216	(68%)
	Robert E. Creighton (D)	70,145	(32%)

FIFTH DISTRICT Political Background

Illinois 5, the home district of Mayor Richard J. Daley, is a slice of central Chicago, plus some suburbs. The district begins at the railroad freight yards south of the Loop and extends toward the west to include the Stock Yards and the Bridgeport area, where Daley still lives, a neighborhood composed of Irish and East European voters fanatically loyal to the Machine. The 5th also encompasses the famed River Wards, with their reputation for political deliverability. Beyond the city limits lie the industrial suburbs of Stickney and Bedford Park and half of heavily Republican Lyons Township. The Chicago portion of the district has an especially large number of Polish and Czech voters, many of whom expressed their dislike of the Great Society social legislation by voting Republican or American Independent in 1966 and 1968. Humphrey barely managed to carry the traditionally Democratic 5th, winning by some 14,000 votes out of the 185,000 cast.

The congressman from the 5th is John C. Kluczynski, who first won the seat in 1950 after spending 18 years in the Illinois legislature. A loyal supporter of the Daley organization, Kluczynski's voting record, like those of most other Chicago congressmen, usually reflects the wishes of the Mayor. Kluczynski is currently chairman of the Public Works Committee's subcommittee on roads, and in that capacity he has been attacked by environmentalists for his devotion to the interstate highway program. But there is virtually no chance that the ecology people can convince the voters of the 5th to unseat their congressman.

For a man who enjoys the support of the Daley machine, Kluczynski made some poor showings in the general elections of 1966 and 1968. Both times he got only about

55% of the vote. But 1966 and 1968 were Republican years in Illinois, and in 1965 redistricting added some heavily Republican suburban territory to Kluczynski's district. In the Democratic year of 1970, Kluczynski bounced back with 69%.

Redistricting will add more suburban territory to the 5th, making things a bit more uncomfortable for Kluczynski. It is possible that the Congressman, who will be 76 in 1972, will retire, to be replaced by a younger Machine loyalist.

Census Data 1970 pop. 413,497; deviation from current state average, −10.7%; change 1960–70, +3.2%. Metro. 100.0%, 77.1% central city.

1970 Share of Federal Outlays $316,167,000 (average outlay per district, Illinois 1–11, 13, 14)

DOD	$50,554,000	HEW	$113,043,000
AEC	$7,397,000	HUD	$1,860,000
NASA	$674,000	OEO	$2,280,000
DOT	$5,550,000	DOA	$13,384,000
		Other	$121,426,000

Federal Military-Industrial Commitments (Illinois 1–11, 13, 14, greater Chicago listing)

DOD Contractors Uniroyal Inc. (Joliet), $104.374m: operation of Joliet Army Ammunition Plant; TNT; 102-mm cartridges; 155-mm and 175-mm projectiles; cluster bombs. United Airlines (Chicago), $22.502m: transport services. Borg Warner (Chicago), $21.629m: bomb bodies. Cenco Piping Corp. (Joliet), $20.928m: construction of TNT manufacturing facilities at the Army Ammunition Plant. Pettibone Corp. (Chicago), $15.441m: fork lift trucks. Hallicrafters Co. (Rolling Meadows), $14.998m: electronic warfare assemblies. American Oil Co. (Chicago), $13.757m: petroleum products. Teletype Corp. (Skokie), $12.350m: teletypewriter modification. Rulon Co. (Chicago), $10.228m: artillery fuzes. Allis Chalmers Mfg. Co., (Harvey), $8.731m: fork lift trucks. Hoechst Uhde Corp. (Joliet), $7.766m: unspecified. Admiral Corp. (Chicago), $7.613m: aircraft radio sets. Monsanto Enviro-Chem Systems (Joliet), $7.365m: construction of acid recovery facilities at the Army Ammunition Plant. Smith-Corona Corp. (Deerfield), $6.890m: teletypewriter development. IT&T Research (Chicago), $6.743m: unspecified. International Harvester (Chicago), $6.614m: tractors. Agar Packing (Chicago), $6.499m: foodstuffs. Bell and Howell (Evanston), $6.363m: grenade fuzes. Olin Corp. (Joliet), $5.622m: ammunition components. Zenith Radio Corp. (Chicago), $5.439m: 2.75-inch rocket fuzes. Stewart Warner Corp. (Chicago), $5.569m: aircraft radar components.

DOD Installations Electronics Supply Office (Great Lakes). Naval Air Station (Glenview). Naval Hospital (Great Lakes). Naval Training Center (Great Lakes). Naval Public Works Center (Great Lakes). Naval Recruit Training Command (Great Lakes).

AEC Operations University of Chicago (Argonne), $71.718m: Argonne National Laboratory.

Economic Base Electrical machinery, equipment, and supplies, esp. communication equipment, radio and television sets other than communication types, and electronic components and accessories; fabricated metal products, esp. metal stampings; nonelectrical machinery, esp. metalworking machinery and equipment; printing, publishing, and allied industries, esp. commercial printing.

The Voters

Registration Not available.

Employment profile White collar, 38%. Blue collar, 62%.

Ethnic groups Black, 5%. Total foreign stock, 43%. Poland, 14%; Germany, Czech., 4% each; Italy, Ireland, 3% each; Austria, UK, Mexico, USSR, Canada, Sweden, 1% each; others, 10%.

Presidential vote

1968	Humphrey (D)	84,599	(46%)
	Nixon (R)	70,469	(38%)
	Wallace (AIP)	28,385	(16%)

Representative

John C. Kluczynski (D) Elected 1950; b. Feb. 15, 1896, Chicago; home, Chicago; Army, WWI; married; Catholic.

Career Ill. House of Reps., 1933–50; owner, Syrena Restaurant, Chicago.

Offices 2302 RHOB, 202-225-5701. Also Rm. 1730, 219 S. Dearborn St., Chicago 60604, 312-353-7251, and 4270 Archer Ave., Chicago 60632, 312-927-0606.

Committees

Public Works (3rd); Subs. (1) Chm., Roads, (2) Investment and Oversight, (3) Public Buildings and Grounds, (4) Watershed Development.

Sel. Com. on Small Business (4th); Subs. (1) Chm., Small Business Problems in Smaller Towns and Urban Areas, (2) Taxation, Oil Imports, and Marketing.

Sel. Com. on House Restaurant (Chm.).

Group Ratings

	ADA	COPE	NREP	NFU	LCV	CFA	NAB	NSI	ACA
1970	40	90	58	100	67	87	9	75	13
1969	40	—	—	93	—	—	—	—	17
1968	83	92	—	100	—	—	0	—	5

Key Votes

(1) ABM	FOR	(6) 18-Yr-Vote	FOR	(11) Clean Water $	FOR
(2) SST	FOR	(7) Farm Sub Lmt	FOR	(12) Mig Wrkrs Comp	FOR
(3) Phil Pln	AGN	(8) Coop-Church	AGN	(13) Jets to Chiang	FOR
(4) No-Knock	FOR	(9) Family Asst	FOR	(14) State OEO Veto	AGN
(5) Cmutr Tax	FOR	(10) Work Stamps	AGN	(15) Park Logging	AGN

Election Results

1970 general:	John C. Kluczynski (D)	97,278	(69%)
	Edmund W. Ochenkowski (R)	44,049	(31%)
1970 primary:	John C. Kluczynski (D), unopposed		
1968 general:	John C. Kluczynski (D)	96,584	(55%)
	Joseph J. Krasowski (R)	77,887	(45%)

SIXTH DISTRICT Political Background

Illinois 6 is a district with two very separate and distinct parts. A little more than half of its voters live within the city of Chicago. The other half live in the two suburban cities of Cicero and Berwyn. The Chicago portion of the 6th was once predominantly Jewish, along with significant numbers of Czechs, Irish, Poles, and other ethnic groups. Today, most of it is part of the expanding West Side black ghetto. The Chicago portion of the 6th is one of the poorest and toughest parts of the city. As recently as 1964, Alderman Ben Lewis was found there murdered gangland style for reasons which are still unknown.

Cicero, on the other hand, has not changed much since the 1930's when it was a Syndicate stronghold. Built up to house Czech and other East European factory workers, the city retains an ethnic flavor. It also possesses an aversion to any form of integration; in the mid-'60's Cicero made national headlines when it resisted the efforts of Martin Luther King to integrate the city. An anachronism from the '20's dominates Cicero politics: a Republican machine based on East European ethnic votes. Berwyn, which lies next to Cicero, is less distinctly ethnic and is less Republican, but is also all white.

The 6th is, of course, a Chicago Machine district. But the Machine's control over matters here has slipped somewhat since 1965, when the one-man-one-vote ruling forced the legislature to include Cicero and Berwyn in the 6th's terrain. For almost 30 years, the district was represented by "Blind Tom" O'Brien who got his nickname in the early '40's during what many charged was an unenergetic term as Cook County sheriff.

The congressman today is George W. Collins, a black Machine loyalist who succeeded the slain Alderman Lewis on the Chicago City Council. Collins also served as Ward Committeeman for the all-black 24th ward, which has routinely produced huge Democratic majorities. In the 1968 congressional race, for example, the 24th ward went 15,684 to 359 (97.8%) for the Democratic nominee. To explain results like these Collins uses an old Machine adage, "Serve the people 365 days a year, and the votes take care of themselves."

With the Machine behind him, Collins won the congressional seat in 1970. It had been vacant since the death of Congressman Dan Ronan in 1969. Collins had no trouble winning the primary, and later he didn't bother to campaign in Cicero or Berwyn. His opponent in the general election, Alex Zabroski, a political neophyte from Berwyn, campaigned very little anywhere in the district. The result was foreordained. Collins carried the city very heavily, while Zabroski carried the suburbs by a somewhat smaller margin. The Democratic white voters did not defect in any appreciable numbers, and the Democratic black voters in Chicago, as might be expected, were even more loyal to the ticket. So Collins won, 60–40, and is headed for a long career in the House—provided that redistricting is done carefully. If too many white suburbs are included in the 6th, which lost population during the '60's, it could go Republican in 1972.

Census Data 1970 pop. 389,686; deviation from current state average, —15.8%; change 1960–70, —7.2%. Metro. 100.0%, 69.3% central city.

1970 Share of Federal Outlays $316,167,000 (average outlay per district, Illinois 1–11, 13, 14)

DOD	$50,554,000	HEW	$113,043,000
AEC	$7,397,000	HUD	$1,860,000
NASA	$674,000	OEO	$2,280,000
DOT	$5,550,000	DOA	$13,384,000
		Other	$121,426,000

Federal Military-Industrial Commitments (See Illinois 5 for greater Chicago listing.)

Economic Base Electrical machinery, equipment and supplies, esp. communication equipment, radio and television sets other than communication types, and electronic components and accessories; fabricated metal products, esp. metal stampings; non-electrical machinery, esp. metalworking machinery and equipment; printing, publishing, and allied industries, esp. commercial printing.

The Voters

Registration Not available.

Employment profile White collar, 39%. Blue collar, 61%.

Ethnic groups Black, 42%. Puerto Rican, 1%. Total foreign stock, 34%. Czech., 7%; Italy, 5%; Poland, 4%; Germany, Ireland, 3% each; UK, USSR, Austria, Canada, Sweden, Mexico, 1% each; others, 6%.

Presidential vote

1968	Humphrey (D)	92,206	(56%)
	Nixon (R)	57,423	(35%)
	Wallace (AIP)	16,549	(10%)

Representative

George W. Collins (D) Elected 1970; b. March 5, 1925, Chicago; home, Chicago; Northwestern U., 1957; Army, WWII; married, one child; Baptist.

Career Clerk, Municipal Ct., 1955–58; Cook County Dept. Sheriff, 1958–61; Admin. Asst., Health Commission, 1963; Secy., Alderman B. Lewis, 1962–63; Chicago City Council, 1964–70.

Offices 1004 LHOB, 202-225-5006. Also 3604 W. Roosevelt, Chicago 60624, 219-826-5133.

Committees

Interstate and Foreign Commerce (14th); Sub. on Communications and Power.

Group Ratings, Key Votes: Newly elected.

Election Results

1970 general:	George W. Collins (D)	68,182	(56%)
	Alex J. Zabroski (R)	53,240	(44%)
1970 primary:	George W. Collins (D)	36,350	(86%)
	Brenetta M. Howell (D)	5,940	(14%)

SEVENTH DISTRICT Political Background

Illinois 7 is the heart of Chicago, from the skyscrapers of the Loop to the West Side black ghetto. In between are Jane Addams' Hull House, the University of Illinois Chicago Circle campus and medical school, and an assortment of low-income neighborhoods. Almost half of the 7th's residents are black. There are also sizable Italian and Polish contingents, which include many old people living in the same ethnic neighborhoods in which they first settled. The district is overwhelmingly Democratic, nearly as Democratic as the virtually all-black 1st district, and it is very loyal to the Daley organization.

Some writers have charged that leaders of organized crime control the Democratic primary in the 7th. That allegation may or may not be true, but the district does have a tradition of electing a congressman of Italian descent. Since 1964, he has been Frank Annunzio, a longtime Chicago officeholder. Annunzio is considered a loyal follower of the Machine, as was his more colorful predecessor, Roland V. Libonati. Redistricting will require the addition of substantial amounts of territory to the district, whose population declined by 19% during the '60's. As a result, the new 7th may have even more blacks, but it is unlikely that the district will elect a black congressman in 1972 unless Mayor Daley decides that it should.

Census Data 1970 pop. 342,375; deviation from current state average, −26.1%; change 1960–70, −17.6%. Metro. 100.0%, 100.0% central city.

1970 Share of Federal Outlays $316,167,000 (average outlay per district, Illinois 1–11, 13, 14)

DOD	$50,554,000	HEW	$113,043,000
AEC	$7,397,000	HUD	$1,860,000
NASA	$674,000	OEO	$2,280,000
DOT	$5,550,000	DOA	$13,384,000
		Other	$121,426,000

Federal Military-Industrial Commitments (See Illinois 5 for greater Chicago listing.)

Economic Base Electrical machinery, equipment, and supplies, esp. communication equipment, radio and television sets other than communication types, and electrical components and accessories; fabricated metal products, esp. metal stampings; nonelectrical machinery, esp. metalworking machinery and equipment; printing, publishing, and allied industries, esp. commercial printing. Also, higher education (University of Illinois at Chicago Circle); banking and finance; and medicine.

The Voters

Registration Not available.

Employment profile White collar, 26%. Blue collar, 74%.

Ethnic groups Black, 44%. Puerto Rican, 3%. Total foreign stock, 33%. Poland, 9%; Italy, 7%; Mexico, 5%; Czech., Germany, 2% each; USSR, Ireland, Austria, UK, 1% each; others, 6%.

Presidential vote

1968	Humphrey (D)	86,195	(78%)
	Nixon (R)	18,615	(17%)
	Wallace (AIP)	6,185	(6%)

Representative

Frank Annunzio (D) Elected 1964; b. Jan. 12, 1915, Chicago; home, Chicago; DePaul U., B.S., 1940; married, three children; Catholic.

Career Taught civics and history, Harper High School, 1940–42; Legislative and ed. rep., United Steelworkers of America, 1943–48; Dir. of Labor, Ill., 1948–52; businessman, 1954–64.

Offices 1224 LHOB, 202-225-6661. Also Rm. 1626, U.S. Court House, 219 S. Dearborn St., Chicago 60604, 312-353-4618.

Committees

Banking and Currency (13th); Subs. (1) Bank Supervision and Insurance, (2) Consumer Affairs, (3) Domestic Finance.

House Administration (12th); Subs. (1) Accounts, (2) Sp. on Police.

Group Ratings

	ADA	COPE	NREP	NFU	LCV	CFA	NAB	NSI	ACA
1970	60	92	67	100	63	94	8	60	14
1969	40	—	—	93	—	—	—	—	7
1968	92	92	—	100	—	—	0	—	0

Key Votes

(1) ABM	ABS	(6) 18-Yr-Vote	FOR	(11) Clean Water $	FOR
(2) SST	FOR	(7) Farm Sub Lmt	FOR	(12) Mig Wrkrs Comp	FOR
(3) Phil Pln	FOR	(8) Coop-Church	FOR	(13) Jets to Chiang	FOR
(4) No-Knock	FOR	(9) Family Asst	FOR	(14) State OEO Veto	AGN
(5) Cmutr Tax	FOR	(10) Work Stamps	AGN	(15) Park Logging	FOR

Election Results

1970 general:	Frank Annunzio (D)	70,112	(87%)
	Thomas J. Lento (R)	10,235	(13%)
1970 primary:	Frank Annunzio (D), unopposed		
1968 general:	Frank Annunzio (D)	86,769	(83%)
	Thomas J. Lento (R)	17,594	(17%)

EIGHTH DISTRICT Political Background

Illinois 8 is a chunk of northwest Chicago. This is middle- and lower-middle-class country in decline, with few blacks (3%), strip commercial developments along the major streets, and neighborhoods of neat one- and two-family houses. The 8th is the kind of urban area that many young middle-Americans, in a rush to the curved streets and shopping centers of suburbs, are leaving behind. But the atmosphere here is still ethnic, the 8th being the most Polish and the most German of any of the Chicago congressional districts. Its residents, less prosperous than their cousins in the adjoining 11th, are closer to the old country and more dependent on their ward organizations. Consequentially, the voters of the 8th have not deserted the Democratic party in great numbers, remaining dependably Democratic even during the Republican years of 1966 and 1968.

Dan Rostenkowski has been the district's congressman since 1958. Though he is relatively young (42 in 1970), he is the ablest of the Mayor's loyalists and the leader of the Daley bloc in the House. Rostenkowski is a member of the important Ways and Means Committee and was formerly chairman of the House Democratic Caucus (1966–70). In late 1970, rumors had it that he was going to be the candidate of a city Machine–Southern coalition for Carl Albert's old post of House Minority Leader. But Rostenkowski never surfaced as a candidate. And then, in a real surprise, Olin Teague of Texas unseated him as Caucus chairman. Rostenkowski lost the post because he apparently figured no serious challenge was in the offing.

Though his colleagues stung Rostenkowski in 1971, the Congressman has a long and powerful future ahead of him in the House. His age and seniority give him a good chance of becoming chairman of the House Ways and Means Committee some day. Reelection is no problem, since he has not had less than 60% of the votes in recent elections (1970, 74%). Moreover, he can absorb some suburban territory—which redistricting will require—without political damage.

Census Data 1970 pop. 420,506; deviation from current state average, —9.2%; change 1960–70, —6.8%. Metro. 100.0%, 100.0% central city.

1970 Share of Federal Outlays $316,167,000 (average outlay per district, Illinois 1–11, 13, 14)

DOD	$50,554,000	HEW	$113,043,000
AEC	$7,397,000	HUD	$1,860,000
NASA	$674,000	OEO	$2,280,000
DOT	$5,550,000	DOA	$13,384,000
		Other	$121,426,000

Federal Military-Industrial Commitments (See Illinois 5 for greater Chicago listing.)

Economic Base Electrical machinery, equipment, and supplies, esp. communication equipment, radio and television sets other than communication types, and electrical components and accessories; fabricated metal products, esp. metal stampings; nonelectrical machinery, esp. metalworking machinery and equipment; printing, publishing, and allied industries, esp. commercial printing.

The Voters

Registration Not available.

Employment profile White collar, 39%. Blue collar, 61%.

Ethnic groups Black, 1%. Puerto Rican, 1%. Total foreign stock, 51%. Poland, 15%; Germany, 8%; Italy, 6%; USSR, 4%; Austria, Norway, UK, 2% each; Ireland, Sweden, Czech., Canada, Hungary, Mexico, 1% each; others, 7%.

Presidential vote

1968	Humphrey (D)	90,088	(51%)
	Nixon (R)	69,019	(39%)
	Wallace (AIP)	16,484	(9%)

Representative

Dan Rostenkowski (D) Elected 1958; b. Jan. 2, 1928, Chicago; home, Chicago; Loyola U., 1948–51; Army, 1946–48; married, four children; Catholic.

Career Ill. House of Reps., 1952–54; Ill. Senate, 1954–56.

Offices 2348 RHOB, 202-225-4061. Also 2148 N. Damen Ave., Chicago 60647, 312-353-4596.

Committees

Ways and Means (6th).

Group Ratings

	ADA	COPE	NREP	NFU	LCV	CFA	NAB	NSI	ACA
1970	52	75	67	92	63	88	11	78	14
1969	40	—	—	86	—	—	—	—	10
1968	83	92	—	100	—	—	0	—	0

Key Votes

(1) ABM	FOR	(6) 18-Yr-Vote	FOR	(11) Clean Water $	FOR
(2) SST	AGN*	(7) Farm Sub Lmt	FOR	(12) Mig Wrkrs Comp	AGN
(3) Phil Pln	ABS	(8) Coop-Church	FOR	(13) Jets to Chiang	ABS
(4) No-Knock	FOR	(9) Family Asst	FOR	(14) State OEO Veto	AGN
(5) Cmutr Tax	FOR	(10) Work Stamps	AGN	(15) Park Logging	FOR

* *Absent on previous vote on same issue.*

Election Results

1970 general:	Daniel D. Rostenkowski (D)	98,453	(74%)
	Henry S. Kaplinski (R)	34,841	(26%)
1970 primary:	Daniel D. Rostenkowski (D), unopposed		
1968 general:	Daniel D. Rostenkowski (D)	105,003	(63%)
	Henry S. Kaplinski (R)	62,254	(37%)

NINTH DISTRICT Political Background

Illinois 9 is the Lake Shore district, which stretches from the mouth of the Chicago River north to the Chicago city limits at Evanston. The 9th includes fashionable North Michigan Avenue, the Lincoln Park Zoo, the dazzling high-rise apartments of Lake Shore Drive, and polyglot precincts of the near North with its Appalachian, Italian, Mexican, and American Indian communities. It also has the largest Jewish population of any Chicago district, found mostly in the northern part of the 9th, just south of the suburbs. Like most city districts in Chicago, the 9th is heavily Democratic; but unlike most of them, it is not always loyal to the Machine. It has produced several rebel aldermen and a notably independent congressman.

Sidney Yates has represented the Lake Shore area since 1948, well before the rise of Mayor Daley. The Congressman's tenure, however, has not been continuous; he spent two years in enforced political retirement following an unsuccessful attempt to unseat Sen. Everett Dirksen in 1962. Yates's district, like Abner Mikva's, contains the only sizable concentrations of well-to-do liberals in the city. Consequently, both men are less dependent politically on the Mayor and less mindful of his wishes. But the Machine has a straightforward policy toward ideological liberals and their aspirations: treat the liberals like any other ethnic group, entitled, like all others, to their share of the congressional delegation once they come up with enough votes to make their strength felt. So the city of Chicago has a delegation composed of three Poles, two blacks, one Irishman, one Italian, and two ADA liberals.

Yates serves on the Appropriations Committee. But because his current tenure dates only from 1964, he is near the bottom of the committee in seniority. In 1970 and 1971, Yates was the leader of the movement in the House to cut off funds for the SST and has been among the minority in that body opposed to military spending. Back home, he has never had much difficulty getting reelected, and, as long as redistricting is handled as expected, he will not encounter any trouble during the rest of the '70's. The 9th may be extended to take in the heavily Republican suburb of Evanston, home of Northwestern University and the WCTU. But his strong Democratic margins in Chicago indicate that Evanston will not affect the outcome of any election in which Yates is the candidate.

Census Data 1970 pop. 439,652; deviation from current state average, –5.1%; change 1960–70, –2.5%. Metro. 100.0%, 100.0% central city.

1970 Share of Federal Outlays $316,167,000 (average outlay per district, Illinois 1–11, 13, 14)

DOD	$50,554,000	HEW	$113,043,000
AEC	$7,397,000	HUD	$1,860,000
NASA	$674,000	OEO	$2,280,000
DOT	$5,550,000	DOA	$13,384,000
		Other	$121,426,000

Federal Military-Industrial Commitments (See Illinois 5 for greater Chicago listing.)

Economic Base Electrical machinery, equipment, and supplies, esp. communication equipment, radios and television sets other than communication types, and electronic components and accessories; fabricated metal products, esp. metal stampings; non-electrical machinery, esp. metalworking machinery and equipment; printing, publishing, and allied industries, esp. commercial printing. Also, higher education (Loyola University).

The Voters

Registration Not available
Employment profile White collar, 52%. Blue collar, 48%.
Ethnic groups Black, 8%. Puerto Rican, 2%. Total foreign stock, 41%. USSR, 7%; Germany, 6%; Poland, 3%; Ireland, Italy, UK, Sweden, Austria, Canada, 2% each; Hungary, Czech., Mexico, Norway, 1% each; others, 1%.

Presidential vote

1968	Humphrey (D)	114,570	(60%)
	Nixon (R)	69,724	(36%)
	Wallace (AIP)	8,288	(4%)

Representative

Sidney R. Yates (D) Elected 1948; b. Aug. 27, 1909, Chicago; home, Chicago; U. of Chicago, Ph.B., 1931; J.D., 1933; Navy, WWII; married, one child; Jewish.

Career Practicing atty., 1933– ; Asst. Atty. Gen. attached to Ill. Commerce Commission as traction atty., 1937–40; U.S. Rep. to Trusteeship Council of UN, 1963–64.

Offices 2234 RHOB, 202-225-2111. Also 1826 Fed. Bldg., 219 S. Dearborn St., Chicago 60604, 312-353-4596.

Committees

Appropriations (23rd); Subs. (1) Interior, (2) Transportation.

Group Ratings

	ADA	COPE	NREP	NFU	LCV	CFA	NAB	NSI	ACA
1970	96	100	100	91	88	100	8	0	17
1969	100	—	—	86	—	—	—	—	12
1968	100	92	—	81	—	—	0	—	9

Key Votes

(1) ABM	AGN	(6) 18-Yr-Vote	FOR	(11) Clean Water $	FOR
(2) SST	AGN	(7) Farm Sub Lmt	FOR	(12) Mig Wrkrs Comp	FOR
(3) Phil Pln	FOR	(8) Coop-Church	FOR	(13) Jets to Chiang	AGN
(4) No-Knock	AGN	(9) Family Asst	FOR	(14) State OEO Veto	AGN
(5) Cmutr Tax	FOR	(10) Work Stamps	AGN	(15) Park Logging	AGN

Election Results

1970 general:	Sidney R. Yates (D)	111,955	(76%)
	Edward Wolbank (R)	35,795	(24%)
1970 primary:	Sidney R. Yates (D), unopposed		
1968 general:	Sidney R. Yates (D)	119,032	(64%)
	Edward U. Notz (R)	65,687	(36%)

TENTH DISTRICT Political Background

Illinois 10 is one of Cook County's three suburban congressional districts (see also Illinois 4 and 13). The 10th lies in the geographic center of this group of three and also represents the group's political center. Roughly speaking, the district consists of the western and northwestern suburbs of Chicago: places like Oak Park (the very middle-class boyhood home of Ernest Hemingway), Maywood, Des Plaines, and a whole host of other towns whose names are various combinations of the words "Park," "River," and "Forest," sometimes appended to slightly more distinctive names. O'Hare Airport, the nation's busiest and biggest, is also part of the district.

Almost all of this area is white-collar country, where the Chicago *Tribune* is a staple and where children are brought up to despise and fear the city Machine. The 10th votes solidly Republican and, unlike many of the nation's suburban communities, had no reservations about the Republican presidential candidate of 1964. Since 1956 the district's congressman has been a *Tribune* Republican, Harold R. Collier. He has a seat on the House Ways and Means Committee, which means, among other things, that his Republican orthodoxy is unquestioned.

Back home, Collier has never had trouble at the polls, always winning reelection wth more than 60% of the vote. The population of the 10th rose significantly during the '60's, though not so fast, it might be noted, as the other two suburban districts built up more recently. The 10th will lose some territory in redistricting. But that will help Collier, since congressmen from the adjacent population-losing Chicago districts will want to grab off only the district's least Republican neighborhoods.

Census Data 1970 pop. 506,996; deviation from current state average, +9.5%; change 1960–70, +17.0%. Metro. 100.0%, 0.2% central city.

1970 Share of Federal Outlays $316,167,000 (average outlay per district, Illinois 1–11, 13, 14)

DOD	$50,554,000	HEW	$113,043,000
AEC	$7,397,000	HUD	$1,860,000
NASA	$674,000	OEO	$2,280,000
DOT	$5,550,000	DOA	$13,384,000
		Other	$121,426,000

Federal Military-Industrial Commitments (See Illinois 5 for greater Chicago listing.)

Economic Base Electrical machinery, equipment, and supplies, esp. communication equipment, radio and television sets other than communication types, and electrical components and accessories; fabricated metal products, esp. metal stampings; nonelectrical machinery, esp. metalworking machinery and equipment; printing, publishing, and allied industries, esp. commercial printing. Also, extensive commuting to Illinois 7 (Chicago).

The Voters

Registration Not available.

Employment profile White collar, 56%. Blue collar, 43%.

Ethnic groups Black, 3%. Total foreign stock, 33%. Germany, Italy, 6% each; Poland, Czech., 3%; UK, Ireland, Sweden, Canada, 2% each; USSR, Austria, Norway, 1% each; others, 6%.

Presidential vote

1968	Humphrey (D)	79,314	(34%)
	Nixon (R)	136,834	(59%)
	Wallace (AIP)	17,615	(8%)

Representative

Harold R. Collier (R) Elected 1956; b. Dec. 12, 1915, Lansing, Mich.; home, Western Springs; Morton Jr. Col., 1932–33; Lake Forest Col., 1933–34, 1935–37; married, three children; Methodist.

Career Editor, Berwyn *Beacon,* 1938; columnist, Berwyn *Life,* 1938–40; Personnel Mgr., Match Corp. of America, 1940–52; Alderman, City of Berwyn, 1950–52; Secy.-Treas., Cook County Supervisors Assn., 1953–56; Chm., First Senatorial Dist. Repub. Com., Secy., Third Legislative Dist. Repub. Com.

Offices 1436 LHOB, 202-225-4561. Also 8909 Cermak Rd., North Riverside 60546, 312-447-2746.

Committees

Ways and Means (4).
Sel. Com. on House Restaurant (Ranking Mbr.).

Group Ratings

	ADA	COPE	NREP	NFU	LCV	CFA	NAB	NSI	ACA
1970	16	9	25	23	22	50	100	100	89
1969	0	—	—	14	—	—	—	—	91
1968	8	0	—	27	—	—	83	—	90

Key Votes

(1) ABM	FOR	(6) 18-Yr-Vote	AGN	(11) Clean Water $	AGN
(2) SST	ABS*	(7) Farm Sub Lmt	FOR	(12) Mig Wrkrs Comp	AGN
(3) Phil Pln	ABS	(8) Coop-Church	AGN	(13) Jets to Chiang	FOR
(4) No-Knock	FOR	(9) Family Asst	FOR	(14) State OEO Veto	FOR
(5) Cmutr Tax	AGN	(10) Work Stamps	FOR	(15) Park Logging	AGN

* *Voted "against" in previous vote on same issue.*

Election Results

1970 general:	Harold R. Collier (R)	107,416	(62%)
	R. G. Patrick Logan (D)	65,170	(38%)
1970 primary:	Harold R. Collier (R), unopposed		
1968 general:	Harold R. Collier (R)	148,398	(67%)
	Seymour C. Axelrod (D)	73,766	(33%)

ELEVENTH DISTRICT Political Background

Illinois 11 is the northwest corner of Chicago, together with a couple of small suburbs that are almost totally surrounded by the city. The 11th, made up largely of comfortable middle-class homes, is the richest of the city's districts, having a median income higher than that of the suburban 4th. It is Chicago's most white-collar district, and, except for the Lake Shore 9th, the best-educated. The largely intown 11th even managed to gain some population during the '50's and '60's. When second- and third-generation ethnics can afford to leave the old neighborhoods, they move here, knowing they would be less comfortable in the suburbs, which are WASP-dominated. Almost 50% of the district's residents are of foreign stock, with especially large groups of Poles, Germans, and Jews.

For the past 5 years or so, the people of the 11th have been caught up in what is sometimes called "*the* social issue." They are by training and inclination Democrats; but their neighborhoods are all-white, and they want them to stay that way. Moreover, the people here do not want their hard-earned money taxed away and spent on foolish schemes to help those too lazy to help themselves. These attitudes have been reflected in the career of the district's congressman, Roman C. Pucinski, first elected in 1958. In the intervening years (a relatively short time by standards used in the House), Pucinski has become the 5th ranking Democrat on the House Education and Labor Committee. In the early '60's, the Congressman, like the other Chicago Democrats, faithfully supported the economic and social programs of the Kennedy and Johnson administrations. But as the civil rights revolution flowed and ebbed, and as the urban riots began, the programs over which Pucinski's committee presided, particularly the war on poverty, became distinctly unpopular in the 11th district.

Sometime in 1966, Pucinski assumed a new role, that of gadfly to poverty administrators; he opposed the community action programs and voted to hold down their authorizations. At the same time, back in the 11th, conservative Republican Alderman John J. Hoellen started a vigorous campaign to unseat Pucinski. In the 1966 elections, Hoellen nearly beat Pucinski, losing by 3,752 votes (49%), as the Republicans captured several of the 11th's seats in the state legislature. The results must have scared both Pucinski and the Daley organization: no Republican had won a congressional election in Chicago since 1946. Hoellen tried again in 1968, but this time Pucinski, who had backed the Mayor and the Chicago Police during the Democratic Convention of that year, took 56% of the vote.

In 1970, Illinois Republicans concentrated their energies on Ralph T. Smith's efforts to maintain Everett Dirksen's old Senate seat. So Pucinski had less trouble than in 1966 or 1968, and the Congressman won with 72%. His prospects for continued re-election appear good. There is adjacent suburban territory that can be added to the 11th in redistricting, territory which is not much less Democratic than his current constituency. But the combination of a good Republican year and a vigorous Republican candidacy could defeat Pucinski if he fails to mind his district properly.

Census Data 1970 pop. 454,329; deviation from current state average, —1.9%; change 1960–70, +0.7%. Metro. 100.0%, 92.9% central city.

1970 Share of Federal Outlays $316,167,000 (average outlay per district, Illinois 1–11, 13, 14)

DOD	$50,554,000	HEW	$113,043,000
AEC	$7,397,000	HUD	$1,860,000
NASA	$674,000	OEO	$2,280,000
DOT	$5,550,000	DOA	$13,384,000
		Other	$121,426,000

Federal Military-Industrial Commitments (See Illinois 5 for greater Chicago listing.)

Economic Base Electrical machinery, equipment, and supplies, esp. communication equipment, radio and television sets other than communication types, and electronic components and accessories; fabricated metal products, esp. metal stampings; non-electrical machinery, esp. metalworking machinery and equipment; printing, publishing, and allied industries, esp. commercial printing.

The Voters

Registration Not available.

Employment profile White collar, 53%. Blue collar, 46%.

Ethnic groups Black, less than 0.5%. Total foreign stock, 49%. Poland, 10%; Germany, 9%; Italy, USSR, 5% each; Sweden, 3%; Ireland, Austria, UK, 2% each; Czech., Norway, Canada, Hungary, 1% each; others, 7%.

Presidential vote

1968	Humphrey (D)	104,352	(44%)
	Nixon (R)	113,712	(48%)
	Wallace (AIP)	18,755	(8%)

Representative

Roman C. Pucinski (D) Elected 1958; b. May 13, 1919, Buffalo, N.Y.; home, Chicago; Northwestern U., John Marshall Law School; Army Air Corps, WWII; married, two children; Catholic.

Career Staff reporter, writer, Chicago *Sun-Times,* 1938–58.

Offices 2104 RHOB, 202-225-4211. Also 6200 N. Milwaukee Ave., Chicago 60646, 312-763-7300.

Committees

Education and Labor (5th); Subs. (1) Chm., Gen. on Education, (2) Gen. on Labor, (3) Sp. on Education.

Group Ratings

	ADA	COPE	NREP	NFU	LCV	CFA	NAB	NSI	ACA
1970	48	92	82	100	78	95	9	75	26
1969	47	—	—	80	—	—	—	—	27
1968	67	83	—	88	—	—	0	—	11

Key Votes

(1) ABM	ABS	(6) 18-Yr-Vote	FOR	(11) Clean Water $	FOR
(2) SST	AGN	(7) Farm Sub Lmt	FOR	(12) Mig Wrkrs Comp	FOR
(3) Phil Pln	AGN	(8) Coop-Church	FOR	(13) Jets to Chiang	ABS
(4) No-Knock	FOR	(9) Family Asst	FOR	(14) State OEO Veto	AGN
(5) Cmutr Tax	FOR	(10) Work Stamps	AGN	(15) Park Logging	AGN

Election Results

1970 general:	Roman C. Pucinski (D)	137,090	(72%)
	James R. Mason (R)	53,461	(28%)
1970 primary:	Roman C. Pucinski (D), unopposed		
1968 general:	Roman C. Pucinski (D)	128,152	(56%)
	John J. Hoellen (R)	101,665	(44%)

TWELFTH DISTRICT Political Background

Illinois 12 is part of the further stretches of the Chicago metropolitan area, far beyond the power of Mayor Daley's organization, but still within easy reach of the Chicago *Tribune*. The 12th is made up of Lake and McHenry counties and the two far-northwest townships of Cook County, Hanover and Barrington. Most of this territory is exurban, except the industrial city of Waukegan (Jack Benny's home town) on the shores of Lake Michigan. Below Waukegan, on the lake, are the railroad commuter towns of Highland Park and Lake Forest, where one will find the estates of many of Chicago's financial and social elite. Further inland are subdivisions, going up quickly here and there, cornfields, and old-fashioned small towns, one of which is Libertyville, the Stevenson family's ancestral home. The 12th has been growing rapidly, up from 395,000 to 537,000 during the '60's; many of the district's new residents are conservative people seeking relief from the increasingly cramped conditions of the suburbs closer to Chicago.

Except for Waukegan—the only portion of the district that has not been growing—the terrain here belongs to the Republicans. In 1964, the 12th was part of the *Tribune* belt, spread 20 to 50 miles around Chicago, which went for Barry Goldwater. In contrast, virtually all of the suburbs of the other major Great Lakes cities—Detroit, Milwaukee, Cleveland, and Buffalo, none of which had a major newspaper supporting Goldwater—went for Johnson. The *Tribune,* in short, is a very powerful newspaper.

Robert McClory, a typical Illinois conservative Republican, is the 12th's congressman and will probably remain so for some time. He usually wins with about 70% of the votes. But in the Democratic surge of 1970, when rock-hard Republican McHenry County elected a Democratic sheriff and Lake County a Democratic clerk, McClory won only 62%. The result may show the politician's neglect of his constituency; in 1970, Congress did not recess until October. And most observers, perhaps including McClory himself, did not expect the Illinois Democrats to do as well as they did. The 59% margin will no doubt spur McClory to run a little harder in 1972 and thereby quash any small hopes the Democrats may now have for his seat.

Census Data 1970 pop. 537,798; deviation from current state average, +16.1%; change 1960–70, +36.3%. Metro. 100.0%, 0.0% central city.

1970 Share of Federal Outlays $423,836,000

DOD	$262,841,000	HEW	$75,102,000
AEC	$000	HUD	$000
NASA	$85,000	OEO	$119,000
DOT	$579,000	DOA	$4,680,000
		Other	$80,430,000

Federal Military-Industrial Commitments

DOD Contractors Bournes CAI Inc. (Barrington), $11.995m: unspecified.

DOD Installations Fort Sheridan AB (Highwood).

Economic Base Electrical machinery, equipment, and supplies, esp. radio and television sets other than communication types; nonelectrical machinery, esp. metalworking machinery and equipment; chemicals and allied products.

The Voters

Registration Not available.
Employment profile White collar, 44%. Blue collar, 56%.
Ethnic groups Black, 4%. Total foreign stock, 24%. Germany, 5%; UK, Italy, Poland, Sweden, 2% each; Canada, USSR, Czech., Ireland, Norway, Austria, 1% each; others, 6%.

Presidential vote

1968	Humphrey (D)	57,889	(33%)
	Nixon (R)	104,153	(60%)
	Wallace (AIP)	12,470	(7%)

Representative

Robert McClory (R) Elected 1962; b. Jan. 31, 1908, Riverside; home, Lake Bluff; Dartmouth Col., 1926–28; Chicago-Kent Col. of Law, LL.B., 1932; USMCR, 1933–37; widowed, remarried, three children; Protestant.
Career Practicing atty., 1932–62; Ill. House of Reps., 1951–53; Ill. Senate, 1953–62.
Offices 426 CHOB, 202-225-5221. Also 326 N. Genesee St., Waukegan 60085, 312-336-4554.

Committees

Judiciary (4th); Subs. (1) No. 4, (2) No. 5.

Group Ratings

	ADA	COPE	NREP	NFU	LCV	CFA	NAB	NSI	ACA
1970	24	50	42	69	57	47	58	100	58
1969	33	—	—	67	—	—	—	—	31
1968	25	23	—	53	—	—	100	—	65

Key Votes

(1) ABM	FOR	(6) 18-Yr-Vote	FOR	(11) Clean Water $	FOR
(2) SST	FOR	(7) Farm Sub Lmt	AGN	(12) Mig Wrkrs Comp	AGN
(3) Phil Pln	ABS	(8) Coop-Church	AGN	(13) Jets to Chiang	FOR
(4) No-Knock	FOR	(9) Family Asst	FOR	(14) State OEO Veto	AGN
(5) Cmutr Tax	AGN	(10) Work Stamps	FOR	(15) Park Logging	AGN

Election Results

1970 general:	Robert McClory (R)	84,356	(62%)
	James J. Cone (D)	51,499	(38%)
1970 primary:	Robert McClory (R), unopposed		
1968 general:	Robert McClory (R)	120,370	(70%)
	Albert S. Salvi (D)	50,525	(30%)

THIRTEENTH DISTRICT Political Background

Illinois 13 is one of the wealthiest congressional districts in the United States. From Lake Michigan it sweeps some 25 miles inland across northern Cook County. The suburbs along the North Shore are usually taken to typify the district's wealth: Evanston, Wilmette, Kenilworth, Winnetka, and Glencoe. All of them are wealthy (though Evanston does have a black ghetto) and WASPy (except Glencoe, which has a substantial number of Jews). The North Shore—which owes its existence to Chicago's surprisingly successful railroad commuter lines—claims a great share of Chicago's elite (Sen. Charles Percy is among them), and also possesses public school systems known across the nation for their excellence. The schools not only educate children but also keep property values very high. The wealthy suburbs of the district are, of course, heavily Republican, but these Republicans, unlike those in almost any other part of Illinois, tend to support the liberal wing of the GOP. The 13th was the only suburban Chcago district that Barry Goldwater failed to carry in 1964.

To the west of the North Shore towns are the suburbs of Skokie, Morton Grove, Niles, Glenview, and Northbrook, which came into being in the '50's. Products of Chicago's expressway system, these towns are very different from those along the shore. They are less wealthy, and Skokie, to name one town in particular, is predominantly Jewish and consistently votes Democratic. To the west, separated by land that is largely undeveloped, are suburbs built during the '60's: Arlington Heights, Mount Prospect, and Palatine, all three strung out along the Northwest Tollway and the Chicago & Northwest commuter line. Here is where most of the district's recent population increase has occurred (up from 407,000 in 1960 to 626,000 in 1970). The residents of the three suburbs are overwhelmingly Republican, but they do not practice the kind of genteel liberal Republicanism found on the North Shore. Nixon-Agnewism is more their kind of thing.

All in all, the 13th is a solid Republican district, not having sent a Democrat to the House since the days of Woodrow Wilson when the Bull Moosers split the Republican vote. From 1962 until 1969, the 13th's congressman was Ronald Rumsfeld, a young (38 in 1970) Princeton graduate who went on to become the director of the Office of Economic Opportunity and then Counselor to President Nixon. Rumsfeld's record was that of an Illinois conservative, but his image was young, open, and activist. He was a remarkable vote-getter in the district, winning 76% in 1966, 73% in 1968. Rumsfeld's closest election occurred in 1964, Barry Goldwater's year, when his percentage dropped to 58.

Rumsfeld's successor is Congressman Philip M. Crane, a former history professor at Peoria's Bradley University and an early supporter of Goldwater in 1964 and Reagan in 1968. Crane is a conservative intellectual, a type that has become an increasingly common feature of American political life. Sen. John Tower of Texas and Bill Buckley of the *National Review* are two other such conservatives.

After Rumsfeld resigned to take the Nixon appointment, Crane won a 7-man Republican off-year primary by a slim margin, finishing with far less than a majority. He went on to win in November 1969 with 59%—not very impressive for a Republican in the 13th. In the 1970 general election, against the same opponent, state Rep. Edward Warman, Crane got only 58% of the vote. So the Congressman's percentage was higher as a newcomer than as an incumbent, a sequence that is rare in American congressional politics.

Crane's militant conservatism has obviously weakened him in the district and has allowed the Democratic candidate to win some normally Republican votes. But militant or not, Crane could go on winning indefinitely in the 13th were the district to retain all of its present boundaries. So what happens in redistricting could make a real difference in the district's politics. Everything depends on what suburbs are removed from the 13th, which gained population and are attached to Chicago districts, which lost population. The 13th might lose Evanston to the 9th and lose some of its Republican territory around Arlington Heights to the 10th and end up keeping the Democratic town of Skokie. If this happens, Crane will find himself in a tough campaign with a liberal Democrat. But most likely the Daley organization, as it bargains with Republican redistricters, will probably grab off Skokie in order to protect one of the Machine's city incumbents; in which case Crane's chances for a long House career are very good indeed.

Census Data 1970 pop. 626,145; deviation from current state average, +35.2%; change 1960–70, +53.8%. Metro. 100.0%, 0.0% central city.

1970 Share of Federal Outlays $316,617,000 (average outlay per district, Illinois 1–11, 13, 14).

DOD	$50,554,000	HEW	$113,043,000
AEC	$7,397,000	HUD	$1,860,000
NASA	$674,000	OEO	$2,280,000
DOT	$5,550,000	DOA	$13,384,000
		Other	$121,426,000

Federal Military-Industrial Commitments (See Illinois 5 for greater Chicago listing.)

Economic Base Electrical machinery, equipment, and supplies, esp. communication equipment, radio and television receiving sets other than communication types; and electronic components and accessories; fabricated metal products, esp. metal stampings; nonelectrical machinery, esp. metalworking machinery and equipment; printing, publishing, and allied industries, esp. commercial printing. Also, extensive commuting to Illinois 7 (Chicago); higher education (Northwestern); and insurance.

The Voters

Registration Not available.

Employment profile White collar, 67%. Blue collar, 33%.

Ethnic groups Black, 2%. Total foreign stock, 29%. Germany, 5%; USSR, 4%; Poland, 3%; Sweden, UK, Canada, 2%; Italy, Austria, Ireland, Norway, Czech., Hungary, 1% each; others, 5%.

Presidential vote

1968	Humphrey (D)	98,305	(37%)
	Nixon (R)	156,088	(59%)
	Wallace (AIP)	9,476	(4%)

Representative

Philip M. Crane (R) Elected Dec. 1969; b. Nov. 3, 1930, Chicago; home, Winnetka; Indiana U., M.A., Ph.D., U. of Mich., U. of Vienna, Hillsdale Col., DePauw U.; Army, 1954–56; married, seven children; unspecified Protestant.

Career Teaching, Indiana U., Asst. Prof. of history, Bradley U., author, *Democrat's Dilemma,* 1964; employed by Repub. Party as public relations expert, 1964; Dir. of Research, Ill. Goldwater Organ., Advisor to Richard Nixon, 1964–68.

Offices 1407 LHOB, 202-225-3711. Also Suite 1, First Natl. Bank Bldg., Randhurst Center, Mt. Prospect 60056, 312-394-0790.

Committees

Banking and Currency (10th); Subs. (1) Bank Supervision and Insurance, (2) Domestic Finance, (3) International Finance.

House Administration (7th); Subs. (1) Accounts, (2) Sp. on Electrical and Mechanical Equipment.

Group Ratings

	ADA	COPE	NREP	NFU	LCV	CFA	NAB	NSI	ACA
1970	8	0	10	15	100	50	100	100	100

Key Votes

(1) ABM	NEL	(6) 18-Yr-Vote	AGN	(11) Clean Water $	NEL
(2) SST	ABS	(7) Farm Sub Lmt	NEL	(12) Mig Wrkrs Comp	AGN
(3) Phil Pln	AGN	(8) Coop-Church	AGN	(13) Jets to Chiang	NEL
(4) No-Knock	FOR	(9) Family Asst	AGN	(14) State OEO Veto	FOR
(5) Cmutr Tax	AGN	(10) Work Stamps	FOR	(15) Park Logging	AGN

Election Results

1970 general:	Philip M. Crane (R)	124,649	(58%)
	Edward A. Warman (D)	90,364	(42%)
1970 primary:	Philip M. Crane (R), unopposed		

FOURTEENTH DISTRICT Political Background

Illinois 14 is the most conservative district in Illinois, which makes it one of the most conservative in the nation. The district comprises nearly all of DuPage County and enough of Will County to take in the city of Joliet. Joliet usually goes Democratic, but its votes are buried in the Republican avalanche that regularly comes out of DuPage. DuPage is an extension, economically and sociologically, of the western suburbs of Cook County, but the extension is somewhat richer, less densely settled, and more conservative. It is appropriate then that Dupage County contains the estate of the late Col. Robert McCormick, longtime publisher of the conservative and isolationist Chicago *Tribune*.

The *Trib* still exerts a tremendous influence in the county's politics. In 1964, for example, DuPage gave 60% of its vote to the *Tribune*'s candidate, Barry Goldwater; in 1968 Richard Nixon took 67%, George Wallace another 7%, leaving only 26% for Hubert Humphrey. Rapidly growing DuPage, along with adjacent Kane County and the Cook County suburbs, has now supplanted Downstate Illinois as the heartland of the state's Republicanism. Accordingly, DuPage gave Sen. Ralph Smith his most convincing county plurality, and Nixon's plurality was some 17,000 less statewide than it was coming out of the Tribune belt counties—DuPage, Kane, Lake, McHenry, and Kendall. If the Cook County suburbs are thrown in, Nixon's Tribune belt plurality was 321,311 votes, more than 100,000 votes better than his 204,699-vote Downstate margin.

The 14th's Republican congressman is John N. Erlenborn, a conservative who has very few disagreements with the rest of the Illinois Republican delegation. First elected in 1964, Erlenborn has since beaten Democratic opponents by margins better than 2:1: 72% in 1966, 71% in 1968, and 66% in 1970. Because of the phenomenal growth of DuPage during the '60's, the district's size will have to be trimmed down before the 1972 elections. DuPage County alone is now slightly larger (491,000) than the average Illinois district (463,000). Presumably most of the county will continue to make up the 14th and will reelect Rep. Erlenborn as long as he chooses to run.

Census Data 1970 pop. 641,274; deviation from current state average, +38.5%; change 1960–70, +46.0%. Metro. 100.0%, 0.0% central city.

1970 Share of Federal Outlays $316,167,000 (average outlay per district, Illinois 1–11, 13, 14)

DOD	$50,554,000	HEW	$113,043,000
AEC	$7,397,000	HUD	$1,860,000
NASA	$674,000	OEO	$2,280,000
DOT	$5,550,000	DOA	$13,384,000
		Other	$121,426,000

Federal Military-Industrial Commitments (See Illinois 5 for greater Chicago listing.)

Economic Base Electrical machinery, equipment, and supplies, esp. electronic components and accessories; fabricated metal products; printing, publishing, and allied industries, esp. commercial printing; nonelectrical machinery, esp. general industrial machinery and equipment.

The Voters

Registration Not available.

Employment profile White collar, 52%. Blue collar, 47%.

Ethnic groups Black, 3%. Total foreign stock, 25%. Germany, 5%; Italy, UK, Poland, Czech., Sweden, 2% each; Canada, Austria, Ireland, Norway, USSR, 1% each; others, 5%.

Presidential vote

1968	Humphrey (D)	71,013	(30%)
	Nixon (R)	147,354	(62%)
	Wallace (AIP)	21,316	(9%)

Representative

John N. Erlenborn (R) Elected 1964; b. Feb. 8, 1927, Chicago; home, Elmhurst; U. of Notre Dame, 1944; Indiana State Teachers Col., 1944–55; U. of Ill., 1945–46; Loyola U., LL.B., 1949; Navy, WWII; USNR; married, three children; Catholic.

Career Practicing atty., 1949–64. Asst. State's Atty., 1950–52; Ill. House of Reps., 1956–64.

Offices 330 CHOB, 202-225-3515. Also 108 N. Main St., Wheaton 60187, 312-668-1417, and Rm. 207, 34 W. Van Buren, Joliet 60431, 815-723-4203.

Committees

Education and Labor (5th); Subs. (1) Sp. on Education, (2) Gen. on Labor.

Government Operations (4th); Subs. (1) Foreign Operations and Government Information, (2) Legislation and Military Operations.

Group Ratings

	ADA	COPE	NREP	NFU	LCV	CFA	NAB	NSI	ACA
1970	24	10	18	55	13	28	100	90	69
1969	0	—	—	40	—	—	—	—	76
1968	8	8	—	27	—	—	100	—	72

Key Votes

(1) ABM	FOR	(6) 18-Yr-Vote	ABS	(11) Clean Water $	AGN
(2) SST	FOR	(7) Farm Sub Lmt	FOR	(12) Mig Wrkrs Comp	AGN
(3) Phil Pln	FOR	(8) Coop-Church	AGN	(13) Jets to Chiang	AGN
(4) No-Knock	ABS	(9) Family Asst	ABS	(14) State OEO Veto	FOR
(5) Cmutr Tax	ABS	(10) Work Stamps	ABS	(15) Park Logging	FOR

Election Results

1970 general:	John N. Erlenborn (R)	122,115	(66%)
	William J. Adelman (D)	64,231	(34%)
1970 primary:	John N. Erlenborn (R), unopposed		
1968 general:	John N. Erlenborn (R)	163,332	(71%)
	Marc Karson (D)	66,293	(29%)

FIFTEENTH DISTRICT Political Background

Illinois 15 is the frontier between greater Chicago and the prairie. In the east, Kane and Kendall counties are part of the Chicago Standard Metropolitan Statistical Area. Kane in particular has begun to show signs of suburban growth—up from 208,000 in 1960 to 250,000 in 1970. Kane County is dominated by two roughly equal-sized cities along the Fox River, Elgin and Aurora. Both are quintessentially Midwestern small cities, with a couple of industrial plants, clean downtown areas, and, here and there, the beginnings of a shopping center culture. Both cities are almost entirely WASP and very conservative; in fact they are more homogeneous and conservative than most Downstate cities. And it may be that all of the people in and around Chicago who like life in a small town gravitate to Elgin and Aurora.

Kane County soon gives way to the cornfields of DeKalb, Grundy, and LaSalle counties. DeKalb is heavily Republican, though Adlai Stevenson III carried Grundy in 1970 by one vote; LaSalle, which contains the small factory towns of Pontiac, Ottawa, LaSalle, and Streator, often goes Democratic. The LaSalle County votes, however, are not enough to make the 15th significantly less Republican. Neither Stevenson in 1970 nor Johnson in 1964 could carry the 15th, though Johnson ran only 71 votes behind Goldwater.

For about as long as anyone can remember, the 15th has sent a conservative Republican to the House. For years (1936–62), its congressman was Noah M. Mason, a crusty isolationist who became ranking Republican on the Ways and Means Committee. His successor was Charlotte T. Reid, an orthodox Republican and a former vocalist on Don McNeill's Breakfast Club.

Redistricting will not affect the political contours of the 15th. It may remove all or part of LaSalle County, which will make the district even more Republican than it now is. Mrs. Reid or her successor—she has been mentioned as a possible Nixon appointee to a regulatory commission—can count on a safe seat well into the '70's.

Census Data 1970 pop. 486,977; deviation from current state average, +5.2%; change 1960–70, +18.6%. Metro. 51.5%, 0.0% central city.

1970 Share of Federal Outlays $287,026,362

DOD	$30,648,000	HEW	$93,198,657
AEC	$50,126,221	HUD	$984,472
NASA	$000	OEO	$203,639
DOT	$17,954,034	DOA	$24,382,359
		Other	$69,528,980

Federal Military-Industrial Commitments

AEC Operations Universities Research Association (Batavia), $6.597m: National Accelerator Laboratory.

Economic Base Nonelectrical machinery, esp. construction, mining, and material handling machinery and equipment; cash grain and livestock; electrical machinery, equipment, and supplies; stone, clay, glass, and concrete products. Also, higher education (Northern Illinois University).

The Voters

Registration Not available.

Employment profile White collar, 38%. Blue collar, 62%.

Ethnic groups Black, 2%. Total foreign stock, 21%. Germany, 5%; Sweden, UK, Italy, 2% each; Norway, Poland, Canada, Czech., Ireland, Austria, 1% each; others, 6%.

Presidential vote

1968	Humphrey (D)	62,158	(34%)
	Nixon (R)	108,524	(59%)
	Wallace (AIP)	12,033	(7%)

Representative

Charlotte T. Reid (R) Elected 1962; b. ca. 1912; home, Aurora; Ill. Col., 1930–32; married, four children, United Church of Christ.

Career Under name of Annette King, served as staff vocalist, NBC, and on Don McNeill's radio program for 3 yrs.

Offices 2350 RHOB, 202-225-3635. Also 411 W. Galena Blvd., Aurora 60506, 312-896-3114.

Committees

Appropriations (15th); Subs. (1) Foreign Operations, (2) Labor and HEW.

Standards of Official Conduct (6th).

Group Ratings

	ADA	COPE	NREP	NFU	LCV	CFA	NAB	NSI	ACA
1970	20	0	17	54	38	43	100	100	67
1969	0	—	—	27	—	—	—	—	82
1968	8	0	—	31	—	—	100	—	100

Key Votes

(1) ABM	FOR	(6) 18-Yr-Vote	FOR	(11) Clean Water $	AGN
(2) SST	FOR	(7) Farm Sub Lmt	AGN	(12) Mig Wrkrs Comp	AGN
(3) Phil Pln	FOR	(8) Coop-Church	AGN	(13) Jets to Chiang	FOR
(4) No-Knock	ABS	(9) Family Asst	FOR	(14) State OEO Veto	FOR
(5) Cmutr Tax	AGN	(10) Work Stamps	FOR	(15) Park Logging	AGN

Election Results

1970 general:	Charlotte T. Reid (R)	95,222	(69%)
	James E. Todd (D)	43,014	(31%)
1970 primary:	Charlotte T. Reid (R), unopposed		

1968 general:	Charlotte T. Reid (R)	121,432	(69%)
	Benjamin P. Aschuler (D)	55,291	(31%)

SIXTEENTH DISTRICT Political Background

Illinois 16, the northwest corner of the state, is dominated by Rockford. Rockford is Illinois' second-largest city, but its entire metropolitan area has only 250,000 residents. The typical Midwestern city has a variety of industries, along with banking and commercial facilities which serve the surrounding farmlands. The other counties in the 16th are predominately agricultural. Points of interest include Freeport, site of a famous Lincoln-Douglas debate, and Galena, the home of President Ulysses S. Grant, once a thriving commercial center and mining town, but now a Mississippi River backwater.

The district is usually solid Republican territory. But like most of the Midwest's farming country (and unlike Chicago's exurban *Tribune* belt), the 16th went for Johnson over Goldwater in 1964. Rockford and its suburbs are marginal, about 60–40 Republican, and the remaining counties, which cast about half of the district's votes, go about 70–30 Republican. Stevenson, however, ran ahead of the usual partisan vote here; he carried Rockford, and missed carrying the entire district by just 1,000 votes.

John B. Anderson has been the 16th's congressman since 1960. Anderson began his career in the House as an orthodox conservative. But from time to time in recent years, he has strayed from the Illinois Republican fold; for example, he supported Nixon's family assistance plan. While he was still reliably orthodox, the Congressman won a seat on the House Rules Committee; he also serves as chairman of the House Republican Conference. In 1971 Anderson managed to retain the Conference post by only 8 votes (89–81) when arch-conservative Samuel Devine of Ohio challenged him for the leadership.

Anderson has had less difficulty winning in the district. His margins indicate that his somewhat liberal voting record has brought in some normally Democratic votes; in 1970, Sen. Ralph Smith took only 51% of the 16th's votes, while Anderson received 67%. The only significant threat to the Congressman's tenure is a strong challenge in a Republican primary, but so far no such opposition has materialized.

Census Data 1970 pop. 442,780; deviation from current state average, –4.4%; change 1960–70, +12.2%. Metro. 61.4%, 33.3% central city.

1970 Share of Federal Outlays $225,028,270

DOD	$49,784,000	HEW	$87,673,087
AEC	$195,949	HUD	$000
NASA	$40,160	OEO	$232,771
DOT	$3,192,082	DOA	$19,198,457
		Other	$64,711,764

Federal Military-Industrial Commitments

DOD Contractors Sundstrand Corp. (Rockford), $17.845m: aircraft drive units and gear boxes.

DOD Installations Savanna Army Depot (Savanna).

Economic Base Fabricated metal products, esp. cutlery, hand tools, and general hardware, and fabricated structural metal products; cash grain, dairy, and livestock; nonelectrical machinery, esp. metalworking machinery and equipment.

The Voters

Registration Not available.

Employment profile White collar, 37%. Blue collar, 63%.

Ethnic groups Black, 4%. Total foreign stock, 18%. Sweden, 5%; Germany, 4%; Italy, 2%; UK, Norway, Canada, Poland, 1% each; others, 4%.

Presidential vote

1968	Humphrey (D)	61,455	(36%)
	Nixon (R)	98,077	(58%)
	Wallace (AIP)	11,041	(7%)

Representative

John B. Anderson (R) Elected 1960; b. Feb. 15, 1922, Rockford; home, Rockford; U. of Ill., B.A., J.D.; Harvard Law School, LL.M.; Army, WWII; married, four children; First Evangelical Free Church.

Career Practicing atty., 1946–60; U.S. State Dept.'s Diplomatic Svc., 1952; Advisor, U.S. High Commissioner for Germany, 1952–55; State's Atty., Winnebago County, 1956–60.

Offices 1101 LHOB, 202-225-5676. Also Rock River Savings Bldg., 401 W. State St., Rockford 61101, 815-962-8807.

Committees

Rules (2nd).

Atomic Energy (2nd); Subs. (1) Agreements for Cooperation, (2) Legislation.

Group Ratings

	ADA	COPE	NREP	NFU	LCV	CFA	NAB	NSI	ACA
1970	28	34	45	62	25	55	91	80	67
1969	33	—	—	67	—	—	—	—	40
1968	17	23	—	50	—	—	83	—	67

Key Votes

(1) ABM	FOR	(6) 18-Yr-Vote	FOR	(11) Clean Water $	AGN
(2) SST	FOR	(7) Farm Sub Lmt	ABS	(12) Mig Wrkrs Comp	AGN
(3) Phil Pln	FOR	(8) Coop-Church	ABS	(13) Jets to Chiang	ABS
(4) No-Knock	FOR	(9) Family Asst	FOR	(14) State OEO Veto	AGN
(5) Cmutr Tax	AGN	(10) Work Stamps	FOR	(15) Park Logging	FOR

Election Results

1970 general:	John B. Anderson (R)	83,296	(67%)
	John E. Devine, Jr. (D)	41,459	(33%)
1970 primary:	John B. Anderson (R), unopposed		
1968 general:	John B. Anderson (R)	111,037	(67%)
	Stan Major (D)	53,838	(33%)

SEVENTEENTH DISTRICT Political Background

Illinois 17, which lies just to the south of Chicago, is where Downstate Illinois begins. The district is predominantly rural and agricultural, although exurban Chicago has begun to spread into the 17th's portion of Will County to the north. Each corner of the district has a middle-sized city: Kankakee, Bloomington, and Danville, all of them decidedly Republican, but all of them carried in 1970 by Adlai Stevenson III.

Leslie C. Arends has represented the 17th since 1934, when he beat a Democrat, winning the seat on the strength of Roosevelt's 1932 landslide. Since Arends' initial victory, he has regularly won reelection with handsome margins. The Congressman has been in the House longer than any other Republican. He has been the Republican whip since 1943, at which time only one other Republican now in the House was there with him. And while Arends has been party whip for nearly three decades, other members of the Republican leadership in the House have come and gone—Joseph Martin was ousted in 1959 and Charles Halleck in 1961.

Redistricting may change the character of Arends' district. In 1972 the 17th may include all of Democratic-leaning Will County (Joliet) rather than just the rural portion of that county as is presently the case. This change, however, will not affect Arends' conservative voting record or his continued incumbency.

Census Data 1970 pop. 489,396; deviation from current state average, +5.7%; change 1960–70, +14.2%. Metro. 41.8%, 13.6% central city.

1970 Share of Federal Outlays $275,030,495

DOD	$17,439,000	HEW	$91,816,686
AEC	$000	HUD	$6,015,714
NASA	$000	OEO	$552,068
DOT	$17,909,257	DOA	$69,294,792
		Other	$72,002,978

Federal Military-Industrial Commitments

DOD Contractors Hyster Co. (Danville), $6.190m: fork lift trucks.

Economic Base Cash, grain and livestock; electrical machinery, equipment, and supplies; chemicals and allied products, esp. industrial inorganic and organic chemicals; nonelectrical machinery. Also, insurance.

The Voters

Registration Not available.

Employment profile White collar, 37%. Blue collar, 64%.

Ethnic groups Black, 4%. Total foreign stock, 12%. Germany, 3%; UK, Sweden, Poland, Italy, Canada, Ireland, 1% each; others, 5%.

Presidential vote

1968	Humphrey (D)	63,879	(33%)
	Nixon (R)	112,950	(58%)
	Wallace (AIP)	19,630	(10%)

Representative

Leslie C. Arends (R) Elected 1934; b. Sept. 27, 1895, Melvin; home, Melvin; Oberlin Col., Ill. Wesleyan U., LL.D.; Navy, WWI; married, one child; Methodist.

Career Farming and banking, 1920– ; Minority Whip, 1943–47, 1949–53, 1955–71; Majority Whip, 1947–49, 1953–55; U.S. Delegate to NATO Parliamentarians' Conference (North Atlantic Assembly), 1961–71; Trustee, Ill. Wesleyan U.

Offices 2306 RHOB, 202-225-2976.

Committees

Armed Services (Ranking Mbr.).

Group Ratings

	ADA	COPE	NREP	NFU	LCV	CFA	NAB	NSI	ACA
1970	20	9	17	54	0	45	100	100	68
1969	0	—	—	47	—	—	—	—	71
1968	8	0	—	20	—	—	100	—	87

Key Votes

(1) ABM	FOR	(6) 18-Yr-Vote	FOR	(11) Clean Water $	AGN
(2) SST	FOR*	(7) Farm Sub Lmt	AGN	(12) Mig Wrkrs Comp	AGN
(3) Phil Pln	FOR	(8) Coop-Church	AGN	(13) Jets to Chiang	FOR
(4) No-Knock	FOR	(9) Family Asst	FOR	(14) State OEO Veto	FOR
(5) Cmutr Tax	AGN	(10) Work Stamps	FOR	(15) Park Logging	FOR

* *Absent on previous vote on same issue.*

Election Results

1970 general:	Leslie C. Arends (R)	92,917	(62%)
	Lester A. Hawthorne (D)	56,340	(38%)
1970 primary:	Leslie C. Arends (R), unopposed		
1968 general:	Leslie C. Arends (R)	122,513	(65%)
	Lester A. Hawthorne (R)	65,192	(35%)

EIGHTEENTH DISTRICT Political Background

Whenever Nixon Administration political strategists want to brush aside a liberal program, they ask how it would go over in Peoria. Illinois 18 contains Peoria, the city that for Nixon people, and many others as well, epitomizes America. The district also includes Pekin, Everett McKinley Dirksen's home town, and several rural prairie counties.

But the 1970 election results in the 18th indicate that Nixon strategists may not know Peoria as well as they think. The Democrats did well here, even though Peoria, dominated by the Caterpillar tractor concern and other heavy industries, was not really hurt by unemployment in 1970. Peoria County voters provided a Democratic candidate for the state Senate with enough votes for an upset victory. That victory gave the Democrats enough seats in the state legislature to prevent the Republicans from controlling the all-important redistricting process. Moreover, the 18th as a whole preferred Adlai Stevenson III (52%) to Sen. Ralph Tyler Smith, Dirksen's appointed successor. Smith ran a hard-line, anti-student, anti-rioter campaign, precisely the sort of campaign one would expect to go over in Peoria and Illinois 18.

But even as the district has become more Democratic in statewide races, it has given increasely large margins to its Republican congressman, Robert H. Michel: from 54% in 1964 to 66% in 1970. Michel served as administrative assistant to his predecessor, Rep. Harold H. Velde (1948–56), who was famed chiefly for his work on the House Un-American Activities Committee. Before Velde the seat was occupied by Everett Dirksen, who retired in 1948 when he thought he was going blind. When he learned later that he was not, Dirksen ran for the Senate 1950 and beat then Majority Leader Scott Lucas.

Congressman Michel is now a senior member of the House Appropriations Committee and ranking Republican on its Labor-HEW subcommittee. Redistricting is unlikely to alter the shape of the 18th significantly. Michel should go on winning elections here. But if he is not the Republican candidate, the 18th could be the scene of a Democratic upset.

Census Data 1970 pop. 432,185; deviation from current state average, –6.7%; change 1960–70, +7.6%. Metro. 79.1%, 29.4% central city.

1970 Share of Federal Outlays $325,070,818

DOD	$56,099,000	HEW	$95,705,017
AEC	$000	HUD	$2,606,000
NASA	$74,604	OEO	$327,328
DOT	$15,219,426	DOA	$35,888,317
		Other	$119,151,126

Federal Military-Industrial Commitments

DOD Contractors Caterpillar Tractor (Peoria and Morton), $30.983m: high output engines; road graders; tractors.

Economic Base Livestock and cash grain; food and kindred products; nonelectrical machinery; primary metal industries.

The Voters

Registration Not available.

Employment profile White collar, 38%. Blue collar, 62%.

Ethnic groups Black, 4%. Total foreign stock, 13%. Germany, 4%; UK, Italy, Ireland, Sweden, 1% each; others, 4%.

Presidential vote

1968	Humphrey (D)	71,534	(40%)
	Nixon (R)	93,503	(52%)
	Wallace (AIP)	14,044	(8%)

Representative

Robert H. Michel (R) Elected 1956; b. March 2, 1923, Peoria; home, Peoria; Bradley U., B.S., 1948; Army, WWII; married, four children; Apostolic Christian.

Career Admin. Asst., Rep. Harold Velde, 1949–56; past Pres. Ill. State Society.

Offices 2112 RHOB, 202-225-6201. 1007 First Natl. Bank, Peoria 61602, 309-673-6358.

Committees

Appropriations (6th); Subs. (1) Agriculture, Environmental and Consumer Protection, (2) Labor and HEW.

Group Ratings

	ADA	COPE	NREP	NFU	LCV	CFA	NAB	NSI	ACA
1970	20	34	8	23	25	39	92	100	82
1969	7	—	—	33	—	—	—	—	75
1968	25	23	—	40	—	—	100	—	90

Key Votes

(1) ABM	FOR	(6) 18-Yr-Vote	AGN	(11) Clean Water $	AGN
(2) SST	ABS*	(7) Farm Sub Lmt	AGN	(12) Mig Wrkrs Comp	AGN
(3) Phil Pln	FOR	(8) Coop-Church	AGN	(13) Jets to Chiang	FOR
(4) No-Knock	ABS	(9) Family Asst	AGN	(14) State OEO Veto	FOR
(5) Cmutr Tax	AGN	(10) Work Stamps	ABS	(15) Park Logging	FOR

* *Voted "against" in previous vote on same issue.*

Election Results

1970 general:	Robert Michel (R)	84,864	(66%)
	Rosa Lee Fox (D)	43,601	(34%)
1970 primary:	Robert Michel (R), unopposed		
1968 general:	Robert Michel (R)	106,122	(61%)
	James G. Hatcher (D)	68,173	(39%)

NINETEENTH DISTRICT Political Background

Illinois 19 is centered on the Rock Island-Moline-Davenport, Iowa, metropolitan area—the largest between Chicago and Omaha. Rock Island County makes up nearly one-half of the district's population, with the rest in several rural–small city counties, including Knox (Galesburg, Carl Sandburg's hometown) and Fulton (Canton). Rock Island, where farm machinery is manufactured, has a large force of blue-collar workers and usually votes Democratic, as does Fulton, situated on the Illinois River below Peoria. The rest of the counties are staunchly Republican, leaving the parties closely divided in the district.

The 19th was the only Illinois district to change partisan hands during the '60's. In 1964, Democrat Gale Schisler, in a mildly surprising victory, won the House seat; he was defeated in 1966 and was subsequently elected to the state legislature. The winner in 1966 was Republican Tom Railsback, who now serves on the House Judiciary Committee. Railsback dissents occasionally from the orthodox conservative line; he was a strong proponent of the 18-year-old vote, for example. Nonetheless he is a promising young (38 in 1970) House Republican, who may some day become part of the leadership in that body. Since his first victory, Railsback has strengthened his hold on the 19th, winning 64% of the votes in 1968 and 68% in 1970, a Democratic year in Illinois. There is no reason to suppose that he will not continue to win reelection indefinitely.

Census Data 1970 pop. 433,338; deviation from current state average, −6.4%; change 1960–70, +5.6%. Metro. 50.8%, 22.2% central city.

1970 Share of Federal Outlays $334,803,162

DOD	$102,285,000	HEW	$110,094,756
AEC	$457,763	HUD	$1,375,626
NASA	$53,691	OEO	$122,663
DOT	$12,613,847	DOA	$31,936,755
		Other	$75,863,061

Federal Military-Industrial Commitments

DOD Installations Rock Island Army Arsenal (Rock Island).

Economic Base Nonelectrical machinery, esp. farm machinery and equipment; livestock and cash grain; fabricated metal products.

The Voters

Registration Not available.

Employment profile White collar, 36%. Blue collar, 64%.

Ethnic groups Black, 3%. Total foreign stock, 15%. Sweden, 4%; Germany, 3%; UK, Canada, Italy, 1% each; others, 4%.

Presidential vote

1968	Humphrey (D)	78,285	(42%)
	Nixon (R)	94,848	(51%)
	Wallace (AIP)	13,305	(7%)

Representative

Thomas F. Railsback (R) Elected 1966; b. Jan. 22, 1932, Moline; home, Moline; Grinnell Col., B.A., 1954; Northwestern U., J.D., 1957; Army, 1957–59; married, four children; First Congregational Church.

Career Practicing atty., 1957– ; Ill. State Legislature, 1962–66.

Offices 218 CHOB, 202-225-5905. Also Fed. Bldg., 211 19th St., Rock Island 61201, 309-794-9701, ext. 285.

Committees

Judiciary (7th); Subs. (1) No. 2, (2) No. 3.

Group Ratings

	ADA	COPE	NREP	NFU	LCV	CFA	NAB	NSI	ACA
1970	48	60	55	83	67	41	75	100	53
1969	40	—	—	60	—	—	—	—	29
1968	33	39	—	67	—	—	100	—	55

Key Votes

(1) ABM	FOR	(6) 18-Yr-Vote	FOR	(11) Clean Water $	FOR
(2) SST	AGN	(7) Farm Sub Lmt	FOR	(12) Mig Wrkrs Comp	FOR
(3) Phil Pln	FOR	(8) Coop-Church	AGN	(13) Jets to Chiang	ABS
(4) No-Knock	FOR	(9) Family Asst	FOR	(14) State OEO Veto	AGN
(5) Cmutr Tax	AGN	(10) Work Stamps	AGN	(15) Park Logging	AGN

Election Results

1970 general:	Tom Railsback (R)	92,247	(68%)
	James L. Shaw (D)	43,094	(32%)
1970 primary:	Tom Railsback (R), unopposed		
1968 general:	Tom Railsback (R)	114,948	(64%)
	Craig Lovitt (D)	66,135	(37%)

TWENTIETH DISTRICT Political Background

Illinois 20 is a descendant of the district that sent Abraham Lincoln, a local Whig politician, to the House in 1846. The current 20th takes in several Democratic rural counties along the Mississippi and lower Illinois rivers, plus Sangamon County, which includes Springfield, the state capital. Some 120 years ago, the western part of the district took many immigrants from the South, and these Southerners' Democratic voting habits are still reflected in present-day elections. In most respects the area has changed little since those times before the Civil War. It remains a land of fertile prairies, farm center towns, and courthouse cities. The river port of Quincy on the Mississippi has not grown much since the nineteenth century, and neither has the river town of Nauvoo, some 50 miles to the north. In the 1840's, Nauvoo expelled its colony of Mormons, who then followed Brigham Young to the promised land in Utah.

Springfield, in the eastern part of the 20th, is a typical state capital: a middle-sized city (pop. 90,000), with an old capitol building, several not-so-elegant hotels, a small black ghetto, a little bit of industry, and some shopping centers at the edge of town. The Lincoln tourist business is the city's mainstay.

The 20th is a politically marginal district. It usually gives Republican candidates respectable, but not large, margins and will go Democratic on occasion. The 20th is never as Republican as the Illinois Downstate districts farther north, a testament to its Southern Democratic heritage; Yankee-settled districts Downstate have backed the Republican Party in virtually every election since the party's founding.

The 1960 census cost Illinois one congressional seat. Two incumbents—a Republican and a Democrat—were forced to fight it out in the 20th district. Paul Findley, the Republican, won the 1962 election and still holds the seat today. Findley is a middle-ranking Republican on Foreign Relations where he is considered a maverick not identified with any of the usual schools of thought. His work on the committee has also led him to take great interest in the affairs of NATO, a rather unusual concern for an Illinois Republican. Whatever his views on foreign policy, Findley's standing in the 20th is high; he has won every election since 1964 with more than 60% of the vote. And unlike most Illinois Republicans, Findley's performance at the polls was better in 1970, a strong Democratic year in the state, than his showing in 1968. Redistricting will give him no problems.

Census Data 1970 pop. 423,070; deviation from current state average, −8.6%; change 1960–70, +5.3%. Metro. 38.1%, 21.7% central city.

1970 Share of Federal Outlays $407,772,036

DOD	$23,413,000	HEW	$175,141,398
AEC	$3,350	HUD	$1,732,143
NASA	$66,006	OEO	$539,899
DOT	$19,920,037	DOA	$45,883,196
		Other	$141,073,007

Federal Military-Industrial Commitments

None.

Economic Base Livestock and cash grain; nonelectrical machinery; food and kindred products. Also, higher education (Western Illinois University), and tourism (Springfield).

The Voters

Registration Not available.

Employment profile White collar, 40%. Blue collar, 60%.

Ethnic groups Black, 3%. Total foreign stock, 9%. Germany, 3%; UK, Italy, Ireland, 1% each; others, 3%.

Presidential vote

1968	Humphrey (D)	74,107	(39%)
	Nixon (R)	102,316	(53%)
	Wallace (AIP)	16,208	(8%)

Representative

Paul Findley (R) Elected 1960; b. June 23, 1921, Jacksonville; home, Pittsfield; Ill. Col., B.A., 1943; Lindenwood Col., D.H.L., 1969; Navy, WWII; married, two children; Congregational Church.

Career Publisher, Pike Press, Inc., 1947– ; author.

Offices 2162 RHOB, 202-225-5271. Also Rm. 205, Fed. Ct. Bldg., Springfield 62701, 217-525-4062, and 400 WCU Bldg., Quincy 62301, 217-233-5917.

Committees

Agriculture (12th); Subs. (1) Livestock and Grains, (2) Oilseeds and Rice.

Foreign Affairs (10th); Subs. (1) Europe, (2) International Organizations and Movements, (3) National Security Policy and Scientific Developments.

Group Ratings

	ADA	COPE	NREP	NFU	LCV	CFA	NAB	NSI	ACA
1970	28	27	55	58	13	44	90	89	54
1969	40	—	—	60	—	—	—	—	53
1968	17	15	—	33	—	—	83	—	81

Key Votes

(1) ABM	FOR	(6) 18-Yr-Vote	FOR	(11) Clean Water $	AGN
(2) SST	AGN	(7) Farm Sub Lmt	FOR	(12) Mig Wrkrs Comp	AGN
(3) Phil Pln	ABS	(8) Coop-Church	ABS	(13) Jets to Chiang	AGN
(4) No-Knock	ABS	(9) Family Asst	FOR	(14) State OEO Veto	AGN
(5) Cmutr Tax	AGN	(10) Work Stamps	FOR	(15) Park Logging	AGN

Election Results

1970 general:	Paul Findley (R)	103,485	(68%)
	Billie M. Cox (D)	49,727	(32%)
1970 primary:	Paul Findley (R)	33,675	(86%)
	Mel Jones (R)	5,609	(14%)
1968 general:	Paul Findley (R)	124,121	(66%)
	Donald L. Schilson (D)	63,412	(34%)

TWENTY-FIRST DISTRICT Political Background

Illinois 21 is the state's southernmost district. And most of the 21st, its residents like to point out, lies south of Richmond, Virginia. Dixie is manifested here in the people's accents, in the cotton fields in the Little Egypt area, and in the virtual state of war between blacks and whites in Cairo. The 21st is also a coal-mining district with towns like West Frankfort dominated by that declining industry. Southern Illinois University in Carbondale gives the region a share in the nation's fastest-growing industry, education. In recent years, thanks largely to the growth of SIU, Carbondale has become the district's largest city. There are reports, however, that town-gown relations are very bad in Carbondale and that hard-won faculty members, harassed by the local citizenry, are leaving the university.

The Southern origin of many of its first settlers and the economic interests of its coal miners have made the 21st a long-standing Democratic district. But the position of the Democratic party here has become considerably less secure in recent years. Local Democrats do not like the stance of the national party toward the blacks, nor do they like the increasing prominence in the party of intellectuals and antiwar activists. In 1970, the 21st, unlike other southern Downstate districts, preferred Sen. Ralph Smith's antiradicalism to Adlai Stevenson's Democratic candidacy. And since Harry Truman carried it in 1948, no Democratic candidate for President (except LBJ) has even come close to winning the district.

Nevertheless, the 21st continues to reelect Democratic Congressman Kenneth J. Gray, who has served in the House since 1954. Gray, of course, has a voting record less liberal than that of most northern Illinois Democrats. He is presently a high-ranking member of the Public Works Committee, a unit with jurisdiction over many traditional pork-barrel projects. The last few times out, Gray has won reelection by respectable, but by no means stunning, margins. Redistricting will add some territory to the north. This will probably not affect Gray's chances, but if he were not the Democratic candidate in the 21st, the Republicans would probably capture the seat.

Census Data 1970 pop. 420,639; deviation from current state average, –9.2%; change 1960–70, +0.7%. Metro. 0.0%, 0.0% central city.

1970 Share of Federal Outlays $324,579,797

DOD	$45,933,000	HEW	$143,249,785
AEC	$78,732	HUD	$3,976,316
NASA	$700	OEO	$620,214
DOT	$25,485,461	DOA	$36,688,247
		Other	$68,547,342

Federal Military-Industrial Commitments

DOD Contractors Olin Corp. (Marion), $27.413m: 81-mm mortar shells; 60-mm illuminating projectiles; M-15 bomb components.

Economic Base Cash grain and livestock; bituminous coal. Also, higher education (Southern Illinois University).

The Voters

Registration Not available.

Employment profile White collar, 33%. Blue collar, 67%.

Ethnic groups Black, 4%. Total foreign stock, 6%. Germany, 2%; Italy, UK, 1% each; others, 2%.

Presidential vote

1968	Humphrey (D)	84,105	(40%)
	Nixon (R)	105,992	(50%)
	Wallace (AIP)	21,291	(10%)

Representative

Kenneth J. Gray (D) Elected 1954; b. Nov. 14, 1924, West Frankfort; home, West Frankfort; Army, Air Force, WWII; married, three children; Baptist.

Career Owner, Gray Motors, 1942–54; licensed auctioneer, airplane and helicopter pilot, formerly airport operator; founder, Walking Dog Found. for the Blind.

Offices 2372 RHOB, 202-225-5201. Also 212 W. Main St., West Frankfort 62896, 618-932-2560.

Committees

House Administration (7th); Subs. (1) Chm., Sp. on Police, (2) Elections, (3) Library and Memorials, (4) Sp. on Electrical and Mechanical Office Equipment.

Public Works (5th); Subs. (1) Chm., Public Buildings and Grounds, (2) Flood Control and Internal Development, (3) Investment and Oversight, (4) Rivers and Harbors, (5) Sp. on Economic Development Programs.

Group Ratings

	ADA	COPE	NREP	NFU	LCV	CFA	NAB	NSI	ACA
1970	40	92	42	100	63	68	8	100	18
1969	47	—	—	93	—	—	—	—	31
1968	67	100	—	87	—	—	0	—	13

Key Votes

(1) ABM	FOR	(6) 18-Yr-Vote	FOR	(11) Clean Water $	FOR
(2) SST	FOR	(7) Farm Sub Lmt	AGN	(12) Mig Wrkrs Comp	FOR
(3) Phil Pln	AGN	(8) Coop-Church	AGN	(13) Jets to Chiang	FOR
(4) No-Knock	FOR	(9) Family Asst	FOR	(14) State OEO Veto	AGN
(5) Cmutr Tax	AGN	(10) Work Stamps	AGN	(15) Park Logging	AGN

Election Results

1970 general:	Kenneth J. Gray (D)	110,374	(62%)
	Fred Evans (R)	66,273	(38%)
1970 primary:	Kenneth J. Gray (D), unopposed		
1968 general:	Kenneth J. Gray (D)	111,425	(54%)
	Val Oshel (R)	94,363	(46%)

TWENTY-SECOND DISTRICT Political Background

Illinois 22 is a chunk of central Downstate Illinois. The 22nd contains two significant urban areas: Champaign-Urbana, site of the University of Illinois, which usually goes Republican, and Decatur, an industrial town just east of Springfield, which is usually staunchly Democratic. Charleston and Matton, in the southern part of the district, have old Democratic traditions that are usually quiescent, but which are revived when the party runs a strong ticket, as was the case in 1964 and 1970. The remainder of the 22nd is agricultural Illinois prairie, where political inclinations haven't changed much in the past century: the counties south of Decatur are marginal-to-Democratic, while those to the north are decidedly Republican.

The congressman from the 22nd is an orthodox Illinois Republican, William L. Springer. First elected in 1950, Springer is now the ranking Republican on the House Interstate and Foreign Commerce Committee and is also vice chairman of the House Republican Campaign Committee. The Congressman had an unusually close call in 1964 (53%), and in 1970 ran worse than usual (59%) against a peace-oriented Democrat who had strong backing from University of Illinois students. Even so, Springer carried every county in the district. But because Springer's Democratic opponent was a peace Democrat rather than the more conventional sort, the Republican ran better (59%) in industrial Macon County (Decatur) than in strongly Republican but still university-oriented Champaign County (57%). Sometime in the future when Springer is not the Republican candidate, a Democrat who could put together a university–blue-collar coalition might win the seat. Meanwhile, redistricting is unlikely to affect either the political contours of the district or Springer's incumbency.

Census Data 1970 pop. 481,967; deviation from current state average, +4.1%; change 1960–70, +9.2%. Metro. 59.8%, 37.3% central city.

1970 Share of Federal Outlays $470,795,330

DOD	$135,502,000	HEW	$114,178,521
AEC	$4,246,634	HUD	$1,000,000
NASA	$805,572	OEO	$640,329
DOT	$46,119,612	DOA	$82,913,948
		Other	$85,388,714

Federal Military-Industrial Commitments

DOD Contractors University of Illinois (Urbana), $11.755m: research in electronics and plasma technology. Magnavox Co. (Urbana), $9.713m: aircraft radio sets; components of M-18 howitzer computer sets.

DOD Installations Chanute AFB (Rantoul).

Economic Base Cash grain and livestock; food and kindred products; nonelectrical machinery. Also, higher education (University of Illinois).

The Voters

Registration Not available.

Employment profile White collar, 42%. Blue collar, 58%.

Ethnic groups Black, 5%. Total foreign stock, 7%. Germany, 2%; UK, Canada, 1% each; others, 3%.

Presidential vote

1968	Humphrey (D)	72,430	(39%)
	Nixon (R)	96,274	(52%)
	Wallace (AIP)	17,446	(9%)

Representative

William L. Springer (R) Elected 1950; b. April 12, 1909, Sullivan, Ind.; home, Champaign-Urbana; DePauw U., B.A., 1931; U. of Ill., LL.B., 1935; Navy, WWII; married, three children; Presbyterian.

Career Practicing atty., 1935– ; State's Atty. of Champaign County, 1940–42; County Judge, Champaign County, 1946–50.

Offices 2202 RHOB, 202-225-2371. Also 501 Church St., Champaign 61820, 217-356-8633.

Committees

District of Columbia (2nd); Sub. on Education.

Interstate and Foreign Commerce (Ranking Mbr.); Sp. Sub. on Investigations.

Group Ratings

	ADA	COPE	NREP	NFU	LCV	CFA	NAB	NSI	ACA
1970	16	25	20	62	50	55	100	100	63
1969	0	—	—	57	—	—	—	—	50
1968	17	15	—	63	—	—	100	—	74

Key Votes

(1) ABM	FOR	(6) 18-Yr-Vote	FOR	(11) Clean Water $	AGN
(2) SST	FOR	(7) Farm Sub Lmt	AGN	(12) Mig Wrkrs Comp	AGN
(3) Phil Pln	FOR	(8) Coop-Church	AGN	(13) Jets to Chiang	FOR
(4) No-Knock	FOR	(9) Family Asst	FOR	(14) State OEO Veto	FOR
(5) Cmutr Tax	AGN	(10) Work Stamps	FOR	(15) Park Logging	AGN

Election Results

1970 general:	William L. Springer (R)	83,131	(59%)
	Robert C. Miller (D)	57,781	(41%)
1970 primary:	William L. Springer (R), unopposed		
1968 general:	William L. Springer (R)	115,258	(64%)
	Carl Franklin Firley (D)	63,957	(36%)

TWENTY-THIRD DISTRICT Political Background

Illinois 23 is a collection of 14½ Downstate Illinois counties. The 14 whole counties are heavily agricultural, fairly conservative, and typically middle-American. The district's portion of industrial Madison County, just outside St. Louis, was added to the 23rd in the 1965 redistricting. The Madison portion, which contains the city of Alton, is strongly Democratic, but there are not enough votes here to explain the 23rd's congressional politics. Since 1958, the predominately agricultural Downstate Illinois has continued to reelect a Democratic congressman, George Shipley.

Part of the explanation lies in the history of the region. Settled largely by Southerners, the 23rd was Democratic territory throughout the nineteenth century, and voting habits have a way of being passed on from generation to generation regardless of what may happen to the ideologies of the parties. Yet the 23rd has responded negatively to the increasingly liberal, pro-civil-rights, and antiwar programs of the national Democratic party. As a result, local voters have usually given recent Republican statewide candidates healthy margins.

The Democrat Shipley, however, keeps on winning, though his percentages are always marginal and though his district is repeatedly found on the Republican list of target seats. The Congressman first won in 1958, beating the incumbent Charles W. Vursall (1942–58) by 187 votes. In 1960 Shipley squeaked through despite John F. Kennedy's weak showing in the district, and in 1962, in another surprise, he won again. His margins in succeeding elections have not been impressive: 55% in 1964; 56%, 1966; 54%, 1968; 54%, 1970. In the meantime, Shipley has risen to become the 12th ranking Democrat on the House Appropriations Committee.

The 1970 Republican candidate was the best-financed and the best-known the party has run in the district. She was Phyllis Schlafly, a nationally prominent conservative activist and author of *A Choice, Not an Echo,* a 1964 Goldwater tract. Mrs. Schlafly is from Alton, the most Democratic part of the 23rd; the home-town factor, her strategists figured, would neutralize Shipley's main source of strength and free the candidate to campaign all the way from the outskirts of St. Louis to the Indiana line. The issue, Mrs. Schlafly said, was that Shipley was a liberal—a lukewarm one, but still a liberal—and that she was a supporter of President Nixon, a man whom the 23rd had backed just two years before. But as in Sen. Smith's campaign (see Illinois state write-up), Schlafly's approach to the issues didn't work out, and she lost the election.

Shipley probably won't be able to hold off the Republicans indefinitely, but since his strength lies in familiarity in the district rather than in his voting record, the necessary adjustments of redistricting will hurt him in 1972. Nonetheless, a man who has been challenged so many times and has each time emerged the winner must be conceded some kind of edge, against Mrs. Schlafly or any other opponent.

Census Data 1970 pop. 416,916; deviation from current state average, −10.0%; change 1960–70, +1.0%. Metro. 18.5%, 0.0% central city.

1970 Share of Federal Outlays $228,032,000

DOD	$7,733,000	HEW	$98,735,000
AEC	$000	HUD	$132,000
NASA	$000	OEO	$124,000
DOT	$12,791,000	DOA	$49,396,000
		Other	$59,221,000

Federal Military-Industrial Commitments

None.

Economic Base Cash grain and livestock; primary metal industries; bituminous coal.

The Voters

Registration Not available.

Employment profile White collar, 32%. Blue collar, 68%.

Ethnic groups Black, 2%. Total foreign stock, 8%. Germany, 4%; UK, 2%; Italy, 1%; others, 2%.

Presidential vote

1968	Humphrey (D)	81,947	(41%)
	Nixon (R)	99,718	(50%)
	Wallace (AIP)	19,772	(9%)

Representative

George Edward Shipley (D) Elected 1958; b. April 21, 1927, Olney; home, Olney; USMC, WWII; married, five children; Baptist.

Career Deputy Sheriff, 1950–54; Sheriff, 1954–58, Richland County.

Offices 237 CHOB, 202-225-5001. Also 111 S. Boone St., Olney 62450, 618-395-2171.

Committees

Appropriations (12th); Subs. (1) Agriculture, Environmental, and Consumer Protection, (2) HUD, Space, and Science.

Group Ratings

	ADA	COPE	NREP	NFU	LCV	CFA	NAB	NSI	ACA
1970	64	67	58	77	50	72	25	89	44
1969	40	—	—	80	—	—	—	—	47
1968	50	77	—	81	—	—	50	—	48

Key Votes

(1) ABM	FOR	(6) 18-Yr-Vote	FOR	(11) Clean Water $	AGN
(2) SST	FOR	(7) Farm Sub Lmt	FOR	(12) Mig Wrkrs Comp	AGN
(3) Phil Pln	AGN	(8) Coop-Church	FOR	(13) Jets to Chiang	AGN
(4) No-Knock	FOR	(9) Family Asst	AGN	(14) State OEO Veto	AGN
(5) Cmutr Tax	FOR	(10) Work Stamps	AGN	(15) Park Logging	AGN

Election Results

1970 general:	George E. Shipley (D)	91,158	(54%)
	Phyllis Schlafly (R)	77,762	(46%)
1970 primary:	George E. Shipley (D), unopposed		
1968 general:	George E. Shipley (D)	104,349	(54%)
	Bert Hopper (R)	88,945	(46%)

TWENTY-FOURTH DISTRICT Political Background

Illinois 24 is the area around East St. Louis—St. Clair and part of Madison County. Although East St. Louis, Belleville, and Granite City lie just across the Mississippi from St. Louis, they are by no means conventional suburban towns; they are instead little industrial core cities with all the usual attendant problems: air pollution, racial friction, bad housing, a declining tax base, and so forth. The 24th district is poor. East St. Louis, a black majority city, is nearly broke. The rich people in greater St. Louis stay away from the Illinois side of the river.

Being industrial and poor, the 24th is as heavily Democratic as the city of Chicago Upstate. In 1968, however, the Democratic majorities here were smaller than usual; George Wallace ran well among the district's white blue-collar voters. Melvin Price, who served as secretary to former Congressman Edwin M. Schaefer (1933–43), has represented the 24th in the House since 1944. He has won reelection easily; since 1962 his vote totals have been in excess of 70%. Price is currently number-two man on the House Armed Services Committee. In that capacity he usually votes with the Mendel Rivers–Edward Hebert establishment. On domestic issues, he has a labor-liberal type of record. The Illinois Congressman is also chairman of the House Committee on Standards of Official Conduct, which is supposed to set guidelines for congressional behavior. Price's chances for continued reelection are excellent.

Census Data 1970 pop. 458,872; deviation from current state average, —0.9%; change 1960–70, +10.5%. Metro. 100.0%, 0.0% central city.

1970 Share of Federal Outlays $380,263,000

DOD	$149,906,000	HEW	$133,421,000
AEC	$143,000	HUD	$1,959,000
NASA	$000	OEO	$1,017,000
DOT	$7,966,000	DOA	$10,899,000
		Other	$74,952

Federal Military-Industrial Commitments

DOD Contractors Olin Mathieson (East Alton), $52.135m: rocket propellant, 81-mm mortars, M-16 and .45 caliber cartridges.

DOD Installations Scott AFB (Belleville).

Economic Base Primary metal industries, esp. blast furnaces, steel works, and rolling and finishing mills; food and kindred products; stone, clay, and concrete products.

The Voters

Registration Not available.
Employment profile White collar, 36%. Blue collar, 64%.
Ethnic groups Black, 15%. Total foreign stock, 10%. Germany, 3%; UK, Italy, Poland, Czech., 1% each; others, 4%.

Presidential vote

1968	Humphrey (D)	83,280	(50%)
	Nixon (R)	58,551	(35%)
	Wallace (AIP)	26,512	(16%)

Representative

Melvin Price (D) Elected 1944; b. Jan. 1, 1905, East St. Louis; home, East St. Louis; St. Louis U., 1923–25; Army, WWII; married, one child; Catholic.

Career Newspaper correspondent, E. St. Louis *Journal,* St. Louis *Globe Democrat,* S. St. Louis *News-Review;* St. Clair County Board Supervisors, 1929–31; Secy., Rep. Edwin M. Schaefer, 1933–43.

Offices 2468 RHOB, 202-225-5661. Also Fed. Bldg., 604 Missouri Ave., East St. Louis 62201, 618-397-0500.

Committees

Armed Services (2nd); Chm., Sub. No. 1.
Jt. Com. on Atomic Energy (Vice-Chm.); Subs. (1) Chm., Legislation, (2) Chm., Research, Development, and Radiation, (3) Agreements for Cooperation.

Group Ratings

	ADA	COPE	NREP	NFU	LCV	CFA	NAB	NSI	ACA
1970	56	100	67	100	70	90	0	80	17
1969	53	—	—	93	—	—	—	—	19
1968	83	100	—	94	—	—	0	—	4

Key Votes

(1) ABM	FOR	(6) 18-Yr-Vote	FOR	(11) Clean Water $	FOR
(2) SST	FOR	(7) Farm Sub Lmt	FOR	(12) Mig Wrkrs Comp	FOR
(3) Phil Pln	FOR	(8) Coop-Church	FOR	(13) Jets to Chiang	FOR
(4) No-Knock	FOR	(9) Family Asst	FOR	(14) State OEO Veto	AGN
(5) Cmutr Tax	AGN	(10) Work Stamps	AGN	(15) Park Logging	AGN

Election Results

1970 general:	Melvin Price (D)	88,637	(68%)
	Scott R. Randolph (R)	30,784	(32%)
1970 primary:	Melvin Price (D), unopposed		
1968 general:	Melvin Price (D)	113,507	(71%)
	John S. Guthrie (R)	45,649	(29%)

INDIANA

Political Background

The most powerful political machines still at work in the country are not to be found in any of the big cities on the East Coast, but operate instead in the heart of Middle America, Indiana. Practically every public office in the state, including the positions of judge and clerk of court, is partisan; and nearly every Indiana partisan official and each of his political appointees must kick in 2% of his salary to the party coffers. In few other parts of the country is this practice, redolent of turn-of-the-century politics, so stringently enforced. And since the mayor of Indianapolis alone makes some 2,000 patronage appointments, the 2% kickback keeps the parties rolling in money.

The kickback system does not, as one might expect, produce gross discrepancies in the financial status of the two parties; because of the state's voting patterns, the parties are nicely balanced. Indiana partisan preferences, particularly those in rural areas, have changed very little since the Civil War—which means that party politicians can count on maintaining control of a predictable number of the state's 92 courthouses. A sizeable number of Indiana rural counties nearly always go Democratic, while cities like Indianapolis and Richmond go Republican with the same frequency.

Another factor contributes to the strength of the party machines. Candidates for statewide office are chosen, not in primaries, but by party conventions. Primaries do determine nominees for House seats, but local party organizations, of course, have a lot to say about who gets what here, too. Once nominated, the party candidate and the well-oiled party machine usually get along handsomely. So the unorthodox candidate can rarely surface in Indiana politics; there is, for example, no Indiana Republican version of Illinois' Charles Percy.

One cause—or perhaps result—of the strength of the parties is that Indiana elections, except those for President, are traditionally very close. As a rule, Indiana voters have not gone along with the East Coast liberalism of the post–New Deal Democratic candidates for President. In 1964, the year of the landslide, Lyndon Johnson won only 56% of the state's votes; the only Democrat in the last 25 years to run well in Indiana was Harry Truman, old Midwestern populist.

But in state elections, where the parties are able to field candidates more congenial to Indiana voters, the results are typically close. Sen. Birch Bayh, first elected in 1962 over four-term veteran Homer Capehart, won by just 10,944 votes out of 1,800,000 cast. And despite his subsequent emergence as a national political figure, Bayh did not win reelection in any kind of convincing fashion in 1968. He beat William Ruckelshaus, now the Nixon Administration's chief pollution fighter, by 71,905 votes out of slightly more than 2,000,000 cast.

But *the* close race of the state's recent past was the one between Sen. Vance Hartke and Rep. Richard Roudebush in 1970. Hartke entered the campaign with liabilities. The Senator had been a strong opponent of the Vietnam war since 1966—a position which partisan Republicans considered unpopular in Indiana—while Roudebush was unabashedly hawkish, as befits a former national chairman of the Veterans of Foreign Wars. Hartke was also under fire for having accepted a $30,000 campaign contribution from the Spiegel mail-order house. But Roudebush had problems, too. The Congressman, some people whispered, had been married four times and had not recovered fully from the effects of a 1968 plane crash. Roudebush also suffered a split in his ranks between the Marion County (Indianapolis) Republican chairman and Gov. Edgar Whitcomb, who controlled the state party machinery.

The Roudebush campaign was the Nixon-Agnew pitch to Middle America. "Roudebush thinks the way you do" was one slogan, while a Roudebush television ad accused Hartke of supporting trade with Communist countries that supplied arms to the Viet Cong killing our boys in Vietnam. Hartke, unlike Eastern liberals, had nowhere to turn but that same Middle America; the tone of campaign, therefore, was classically Hoosier. "In step with Indiana" the Hartke ads proclaimed. The Senator also said that the economic policies of the Nixon Administration were responsible for the heavy unemployment in Indiana's industrial cities. During the campaign, some 35,000 GM workers were living on strike benefits in Anderson, Kokomo, Marion, Muncie, and Indianapolis. These workers, Indiana Middle-Americans, listened closely whenever Hartke talked about unemployment, a phenomenon that has been known to reduce greatly the appeal of Nixon-Agnewism.

The election turned out to be the closest Senate race of the year. Hartke finished with 870,990 votes; Roudebush, 866,707—a Democratic margin of 4,283. Roudebush threatened a recount. But the state treasurer, a member of the Governor's Republican faction who wanted the Senate nomination himself, insisted that the election was an honest one.

The election results, county by county, were a virtual repeat of Bayh's two close contests. Hartke carried the industrial cities of Gary and South Bend in the north and the GM belt around Anderson and Muncie northeast of Indianapolis. Indianapolis and Marion County, usually heavily Republican, gave Roudebush a relatively small majority (about 10,000 votes), while Hartke carried traditionally Democratic southern Indiana cities like Evansville (his home town), Terre Haute (Bayh's home town), New Albany, and Jeffersonville. Hartke also carried a few German-oriented rural counties in the northern part of the state as well as the traditionally Democratic rural counties in the south, which have supported the party against Mr. Lincoln's war for over a century. The Hartke and Bayh results, however, differed in Allen County (Fort Wayne), which Hartke carried and Bayh did not. Here the recession hurt the Republicans, and the local Democratic Party pulled itself together after 30 years of feuding.

In general, Hartke was slightly stronger than Bayh in the industrial areas and slightly weaker in the rural areas—an indication that the "social issue" strategy used by Roudebush in Indiana (and by ex-Sen. Ralph Smith in Illinois) was a winner only among rural people and failed to attract new Republican votes among blue-collar workers.

The political career of Birch Bayh, the state's junior senator, suggests that the Horatio Alger story still has some vitality. Bayh grew up on a farm near Terre Haute and got a degree in agriculture from Purdue. In 1954, when he was 26 and still in law school, Bayh was elected to the Indiana House. Since there were then few Democrats in the Indiana legislature, Bayh's gifts for oratory, hard work, and Hoosier-style conviviality brought him a leadership position. After the 1958 Democratic landslide, Bayh became the Speaker of the Indiana House (at age 30), and in 1962 he decided to run for the Senate against conservative Republican Homer Capehart.

But first Bayh had to win the Democratic nomination—not an easy task, since party leaders had another candidate in mind. But the young man crisscrossed Indiana, talking to courthouse politicians and collecting political debts, and upset the favorite at the state convention. Today he is doing almost the same thing for bigger stakes, the Democratic nomination for President. No political dinner is too small, no local politician who may control convention votes too local for Bayh's attention.

Bayh has shown the same kind of enthusiasm for his work in the Senate. His seat on the Senate Judiciary Committee and a hitherto unimportant subcommittee chairmanship—Constitutional Amendments—were all he needed to become a well-known national figure. He steered to passage two constitutional amendments, on presidential succession and the 18-year-old vote. And when the liberals wanted a senator to lead the confirmation fights against Haynsworth and then Carswell, Bayh volunteered—and handed the Nixon Administration two of its most serious defeats. Bayh is a long shot for the presidency, but his political savvy, his good standing among labor leaders, and his near Southern drawl have made him into a bona fide candidate. Whatever happens, Bayh's talents have brought him a long way from the farm in Terre Haute.

An Indiana congressman will probably never become Speaker of the House or even a committee chairman. The state's House delegation, like that of Connecticut, another strong party state, experiences a lot of turnover—Indiana residents vote straight tickets much more often than voters in surrounding states. In the Democratic year of 1958, for example, Indiana sent nine Democrats and two Republicans to the House; two years later, with the very un-Hoosier John F. Kennedy at the top of the Democratic ticket, the delegation consisted of four Democrats, one reelected by a 99-vote plurality, and seven Republicans. This kind of turnover makes it hard for any Indiana congressman to accumulate much seniority.

Furthermore, the state was redistricted no less than three times during the 1960's, with the 1961 and 1968 plans favoring the Republicans, and the 1965 plan the Democrats. Counties were shuffled around so much that some congressmen from the middle of the state found themselves with almost entirely new constituencies in successive elections. Since almost all Indiana congressional districts are marginal, the Democrats in 1970 put on a concerted drive to oust three incumbents. This made Indiana the only state (except New York, where a Republican redistricting had just been passed) where a party seriously challenged incumbents in that many seats. The Democrats took only one of the three seats, and that was won by a former House member—another testimony to the power of incumbency in House races.

The Republicans, who currently control the legislature and the governorship, have redrawn the district lines, making relatively few significant changes. An exception lies in the Indianapolis area, where the boundaries were altered substantially in an attempt to defeat Democratic Congressman Andrew Jacobs in 1972.

Electoral Votes 13

Census Data 1970 pop. 5,193,669; 2.52% of U.S. total, 11th largest; change 1960–70, +11.4%. Metro. 61.9%, 34.5% central city. 1970 per capita income, $3,773, 20th highest. 18th in number of poor.

1970 Share of Federal Tax Burden $4,780,940,000; 2.45% of U.S. total, 11th largest.

1970 Share of Federal Outlays $3,550,624,066; 1.88% of U.S. total, 16th largest. Per capita federal spending, $684.

DOD	$1,216,501,000	16th (2.12%)	HEW	$1,056,901,091	15th (2.02%)
AEC	$3,499,431	30th (0.13%)	HUD	$25,797,693	24th (1.32%)
NASA	$4,440,138	25th (0.12%)	OEO	$6,573,042	34th (0.86%)
DOT	$123,935,435	24th (1.73%)	DOA	$226,528,924	22nd (1.76%)
DOC	$12,953,706	17th (1.12%)	POD	$150,769,921	12th (2.00%)
DOI	$23,902,378	32nd (1.03%)	VA	$182,539,457	19th (2.47%)
DOJ	$11,265,114	15th (1.96%)	CSC	$37,411,376	22nd (0.93%)
			Other	$467,605,358	

Economic Base Electrical machinery, equipment, and supplies, esp. radio and television receiving sets other than communication types; livestock and corn; transportation equipment, esp. motor vehicles and motor vehicle equipment and aircraft and parts; primary metal industries, esp. blast furnaces, steel works, and rolling and finishing mills, and iron and steel foundries; nonelectrical machinery, esp. general industrial machinery and equipment; fabricated metal products, esp. fabricated structural metal products; food and kindred products; rubber and miscellaneous plastics products; printing, publishing, and allied industries; household furniture and other furniture and fixtures. Also, higher education.

Political Line-up Governor, Edgar D. Whitcomb (R); seat up, 1972. Senators, Vance Hartke (D) and Birch E. Bayh (D). Representatives, 11 (5 D and 6 R). State Senate (21 D and 29 R); State House (46 D and 54 R).

The Voters

Registration No statewide registration.

Employment profile White collar, 37%. Blue collar, 63%.

Ethnic groups Black, 7%. Total foreign stock, 8%. Germany, 2%; Poland, UK, 1% each; others, 2%.

Presidential vote

1968	Humphrey (D)	806,659	(39%)
	Nixon (R)	1,067,885	(50%)
	Wallace (AIP)	243,108	(12%)
1964	Johnson (D)	1,170,848	(56%)
	Goldwater (R)	259,730	(44%)
1960	Kennedy (D)	952,358	(45%)
	Nixon (R)	1,175,120	(55%)

Senator

Vance Hartke (D) Elected 1958, seat up 1976; b. May 31, 1919, Stendal; home, Evansville; Evansville Col., B.A., 1941; Ind. U. School of Law, J.D., 1948; Navy, WWII; USCGR; USNR; married, seven children; Lutheran.

Career Practicing atty., 1948–56; Deputy Prosecuting Atty., Vanderburgh County, 1950–51; Mayor, Evansville, 1956–58; Chm., Democratic Senatorial Campaign Com., 1961–62; V.P., Natl. Capital Democratic Club, 1960–62; Bd. Mbr., 1963–66.

Offices 451 OSOB, 202-225-4814. Also Rm. 824, 328 Ft. Wayne Ave., Indianapolis 46204, 317-633-7066.

Committees

Commerce (3rd); Subs. (1) Chm., Sp. on Freight Car Shortage, (2) Chm., Sp. to Study Transportation on the Great Lakes and St. Lawrence Seaway, (3) Chm., Surface Transportation, (4) Aviation, (5) Communications, (6) Consumer, (7) Foreign Commerce and Tourism.

Finance (4th).

Veterans' Affairs (Chm.); Chm., Sub. on Readjustment, Education, Employment.

Sp. Com. on Aging (9th); Subs. (1) Consumer Interests of the Elderly, (2) Employment and Retirement Incomes, (3) Federal, State, and Community Services, (4) Health of the Elderly, (5) Retirement and the Individual.

Group Ratings

	ADA	COPE	NREP	NFU	LCV	NAB	NSI	ACA
1970	72	100	100	100	50	33	10	21
1969	100	—	—	75	—	—	—	21
1968	50	78	—	45	—	40	—	41

Key Votes

(1) ABM	AGN	(8) Phil Pln	FOR	(15) Coop-Church	FOR
(2) SST	AGN	(9) Vol Army	FOR	(16) Cut Oil Dpltn	FOR
(3) Busing	ABS	(10) Prison $	FOR	(17) Consumer Prot	FOR
(4) Tob Sub	ABS	(11) Cut Mil $	ABS	(18) Farm Sub Limit	ABS
(5) Carswell	AGN	(12) Defoliatn	ABS	(19) Comp Bid Sales	FOR
(6) No-Knock	ABS	(13) 18-Yr-Vote	FOR	(20) Pre-Prod Tests	ABS
(7) Seniorty	ABS	(14) Pentgn PR	AGN	(21) Cut Marjna Pen	ABS

Election Results

1970 general:	R. Vance Hartke (D)	870,990	(50%)
	Richard L. Roudebush (R)	866,707	(50%)
1970 primary:	R. Vance Hartke (D), nominated at state Democratic Convention		
1964 general:	R. Vance Hartke (D)	1,128,505	(55%)
	D. Russell Bontrager (R)	941,519	(45%)

Senator

Birch Bayh (D) Elected 1962, seat up 1974; b. Jan. 22, 1928, Terre Haute; home, Terre Haute; Purdue U., B.S., 1951; Ind. State Col., 1953–60; Ind. U. School of Law, J.D., 1960; Army, 1945–46; married, one child; Lutheran.

Career Farming, 1952–57; Ind. House of Reps., 1954–62; Minority Leader, 1957–58, 1961–62, Speaker, 1959–60.

Offices 363 OSOB, 202-225-5623. Also Rm. 610, 320 N. Meridian Ave., Indianapolis 46204, 317-633-8640.

Committees

Judiciary (6th); Subs. (1) Chm., Constitutional Amendments, (2) Chm., Juvenile Delinquency, (3) Administrative Practice and Procedure, (4) Constitutional Rights, (5) Internal Security, (6) Penitentiaries.

Public Works (4th); Subs. (1) Chm., Public Roads, (2) Air and Water Pollution, (3) Flood Control—Rivers and Harbors.

Sel. Com. on Equal Educational Opportunity (6th).

Group Ratings

	ADA	COPE	NREP	NFU	LCV	NAB	NSI	ACA
1970	72	100	91	100	58	10	22	11
1969	78	—	—	94	—	—	—	7
1968	50	91	—	50	—	40	—	38

Key Votes

(1) ABM	AGN	(8) Phil Pln	FOR	(15) Coop-Church	FOR
(2) SST	ABS	(9) Vol Army	AGN	(16) Cut Oil Dpltn	FOR
(3) Busing	FOR	(10) Prison $	FOR	(17) Consumer Prot	FOR
(4) Tob Sub	FOR	(11) Cut Mil $	ABS	(18) Farm Sub Limit	FOR
(5) Carswell	AGN	(12) Defoliatn	AGN	(19) Comp Bid Sales	AGN
(6) No-Knock	FOR	(13) 18-Yr-Vote	FOR	(20) Pre-Prod Tests	FOR
(7) Seniorty	AGN	(14) Pentgn PR	AGN	(21) Cut Marjna Pen	AGN

Election Results

1968 general:	Birch E. Bayh, Jr. (D)	1,060,456	(52%)
	William D. Ruckelshaus (R)	988,571	(48%)
1968 primary:	Birch E. Bayh, Jr. (D), nominated at state Democratic Convention		
1962 general:	Birch E. Bayh, Jr. (D)	905,491	(50%)
	Homer E. Capehart (R)	894,547	(50%)

FIRST DISTRICT Political Background

Indiana 1 is the northwest corner of Indiana: the cities of Gary, Hammond, East Chicago, and Whiting, and adjacent suburban territory. This is heavy-industry country. Gary was founded by the U.S. Steel Corporation and is named after its first board chairman. Its location is ideal for steel-making: freighters can bring iron ore from the Lake Superior ranges into the huge man-made port at the southern end of Lake Michigan. Moreover, most of the major east-west rail lines run through the 1st and go right by the big mills. So no less than five of the great steel manufacturers have plants here which have brought many immigrants to Gary and vicinity—Irish, Poles, Czechs, Ukrainians, and, most recently, blacks from the American South.

These groups, as even the casual newspaper reader knows, live in uneasy proximity. The hostility between the East European ethnic group and the blacks produces turmoil in Gary and Lake County politics. In 1967, Richard Hatcher, a black, won the Democratic nomination and was elected mayor of Gary, now 53% black. Hatcher was re-elected in 1971. But the county party machinery has remained in the hands of John Krupa, an unreconstructed opponent of race-mixing and radical-liberal schemes.

The hostility between blacks and ethnic groups has cut into Lake County's and the 1st district's usually heavy Democratic majorities. Many white ethnic voters have identified the Democratic party with the blacks and have therefore switched parties. Meanwhile, relatively few blacks have bothered to turn out and vote except for Gary city elections. In 1964, George Wallace carried Lake County in the Democratic presidential primary, and four years later Wallace won 15% of the 1st's votes in the 1968 general election—his best showing in Indiana. The only political figure who could win the allegiance of both groups was the late Sen. Robert Kennedy, who won large majorities in both black and ethnic Lake County precincts in the 1968 presidential primary.

The 1st's congressman is Ray J. Madden, an octogenarian first elected in 1942. Madden is number two in seniority on the House Rules Committee, right behind fellow octogenarian William Colmer of Mississippi. The perils of mortality make it problematical whether Madden will ever succeed to the chairmanship. If he does, he will not possess the autocratic control over the flow of legislation to the floor that Colmer and his predecessor, Jude Howard Smith of Virginia, often enjoyed. Times have changed, and the Rules Committee is no longer as powerful as it once was.

Meanwhile Madden's standing in the district is anything but secure. For many years, Madden did not have to campaign very hard for his majorities in general elections. His recent showings (only 57% in 1968) indicate that the veteran congressman would have trouble winning in any district less solidly Democratic. Moreover, in the 1970 Democratic primary, Madden received only 21,500 votes out of 60,000 cast (36%), while his nearest rival, one Frank Stodola, received more than 17,000. In a future election, either with or without Madden running, a number of white ethnic candidates could split the white vote and allow a black to win the Democratic nomination. This would set the stage for a law-and-order Republican candidate who, with enough white backlash votes, could win in the 1st, on paper the most Democratic district in Indiana.

The 1970 census added more suburban territory to the district. The adjacent suburbs lean Republican, having many former residents of Gary or Hammond who left because of the rising black population. Still, if a vigorous candidate can win the support of both the blacks and the whites in the 1972 Democratic primary, the 1st will remain as strongly Democratic as ever.

Census Data 1970 pop. 436,249; deviation from current state average, —7.6%; change 1960–70, +2.1%, Metro. 100.0%, 75.6% central city.

1970 Share of Federal Outlays $205,496,000

DOD	$9,656,000	HEW	$97,636,000
AEC	$000	HUD	$3,961,000
NASA	$000	OEO	$1,560,000
DOT	$5,834,000	DOA	$585,000
		Other	$89,264,000

Federal Military-Industrial Commitments

None.

Economic Base Blast furnaces, steel works, and rolling mills, and other primary metal industries; fabricated metal products, esp. fabricated structural metal products; petroleum refining, transportation equipment; chemicals and allied products, esp. industrial organic and inorganic chemicals.

The Voters

Registration No district-wide registration.

Employment profile White collar, 32%. Blue collar, 68%.

Ethnic groups Black, 26%. Puerto Rican, 1%. Total foreign stock, 25%. Poland, 4%; Czech., Germany, Hungary, Mexico, 2% each; Austria, Canada, Italy, Sweden, UK, USSR, 1% each; others, 6%.

Presidential vote

1968	Humphrey (D)	89,136	(52%)
	Nixon (R)	57,122	(33%)
	Wallace (AIP)	25,608	(15%)

Representative

Ray J. Madden (D) Elected 1942; b. Feb. 25, 1892, Waseca, Minn.; home, Gary; Creighton U., LL.B., 1913; Navy, WWI; unmarried; Catholic.

Career Practicing atty., 1913–42; Municipal Judge, Omaha, Nebr., 1916; City Comptroller, Gary, 1935–58; Lake County Treas., 1938–42; V. Chm. Democratic Congressional Campaign Com.

Offices 2409 RHOB, 202-225-2461. Also Rm. 310, New P.O. Bldg., Hammond 46320, 219-931-8280, and Fed. Bldg., Gary 46402, 219-886-2411.

Committees

Rules (2nd).

Group Ratings

	ADA	COPE	NREP	NFU	LCV	CFA	NAB	NSI	ACA
1970	72	100	91	100	89	47	0	56	18
1969	73	—	—	86	—	—	—	—	12
1968	83	100	—	88	—	—	0	—	4

Key Votes

(1) ABM	AGN	(6) 18-Yr-Vote	FOR	(11) Clean Water $	FOR
(2) SST	AGN	(7) Farm Sub Lmt	FOR	(12) Mig Wrkrs Comp	FOR
(3) Phil Pln	FOR	(8) Coop-Church	FOR	(13) Jets to Chiang	AGN
(4) No-Knock	FOR	(9) Family Asst	FOR	(14) State OEO Veto	AGN
(5) Cmutr Tax	FOR	(10) Work Stamps	AGN	(15) Park Logging	AGN

Election Results

1970 general:	Ray J. Madden (D)	73,145	(66%)
	Eugene M. Kirtland (R)	38,294	(34%)
1970 primary:	Ray J. Madden (D)	21,531	(36%)
	Frank Stodola (D)	17,330	(29%)
	Eugene Bainbridge (D)	9,061	(15%)
	Zarko Sekerez (D)	7,760	(13%)
	George Roche (D)	2,546	(4%)
	Terry C. Gray (D)	1,867	(3%)
1968 general:	Ray J. Madden (D)	90,055	(57%)
	Donald E. Taylor (R)	68,318	(43%)

SECOND DISTRICT Political Background

Indiana 2 comprises 9 counties in northwestern Indiana and half of another, the suburban and rural portions of Lake County (Gary). This is vintage Republican territory: rich farmland, small towns, and the influence of the Chicago *Tribune* noticeable in election returns. The only two cities of any size are Lafayette, in the south, the site of Purdue University, and Michigan City, an industrial town on the shores of Lake Michigan and a miniature version of Gary. Starke County, with a large German population, has something of a Democratic tradition (it was carried by Birch Bayh in 1962 and 1968 and Vance Hartke in 1964 and 1970), but most of the rest of the district is WASPish.

The 2nd district is a traditional Republican stronghold. For many years (1934–68) it was represented by Charles A. Halleck, the conservative Republican "gut-fighter" who was House Minority Leader from 1959 to 1965. Halleck had an unusually close call in 1964 (52%) and decided to retire four years later. His successor was Earl Landgrebe, generally considered the most conservative member of the Indiana delegation. Landgrebe has had some difficulty in the district. In 1968 he won with only 55% of the vote, and in 1970 challenger Philip A. Sprague came within 1,204 votes of unseating him. Sprague's strength was in industrial LaPorte County (Michigan City) and in Tippecanoe County (Lafayette), where local Republicans were unhappy with Landgrebe. The Indiana legislature in redistricting removed LaPorte County from the 2nd district, making it safer for Landgrebe.

Census Data 1970 pop. 507,944; deviation from current state average, +7.6%; change 1960–70, +20.0%. Metro. 60.3%, 12.7% central city.

1970 Share of Federal Outlays $233,840,000

DOD	$21,284,000	HEW	$78,563,000
AEC	$1,604,000	HUD	$1,577,000
NASA	$737,000	OEO	$235,000
DOT	$15,565,000	DOA	$43,369,000
		Other	$68,906,000

Federal Military-Industrial Commitments

None.

Economic Base Corn and livestock; fabricated metal products; electrical machinery, equipment, and supplies; printing, publishing and allied industries.

The Voters

Registration No district-wide registration.

Employment profile White collar, 36%. Blue collar, 64%.

Ethnic groups Black, 2%. Total foreign stock, 9%. Germany, 2%; Canada, Poland, Sweden, UK, 1% each; others, 2%.

Presidential vote

1968	Humphrey (D)	64,165	(32%)
	Nixon (R)	107,535	(54%)
	Wallace (AIP)	26,833	(14%)

Representative

Earl F. Landgrebe (R) Elected 1968; b. Jan. 21, 1916, Porter County; home, Valparaiso; married, two children; Lutheran.

Career Owns International Harvester Agency and Landgrebe Motor Transport, Inc.; Indiana Senate, 1958–68; past Dir., Porter County Guidance Clinic; United Cerebral Palsy of Northwest Indiana.

Offices 1238 LHOB, 202-225-5777. Also 451 Lincolnway, Box 323, Valparaiso 46383, 219-462-8750, and 3637 Beaumont Ct., Lafayette 47905, 317-447-3070.

Committees

District of Columbia (9th); Subs. (1) Housing and Youth Affairs, (2) Judiciary, (3) Public Health and Welfare.

Education and Labor (10th); Subs. (1) Gen. on Labor, (2) Sel. on Education.

Group Ratings

	ADA	COPE	NREP	NFU	LCV	CFA	NAB	NSI	ACA
1970	12	9	8	17	33	40	100	100	100
1969	0	—	—	14	—	—	—	—	88

Key Votes

(1) ABM	FOR	(6) 18-Yr-Vote	AGN	(11) Clean Water $	AGN
(2) SST	FOR	(7) Farm Sub Lmt	AGN	(12) Mig Wrkrs Comp	AGN
(3) Phil Pln	FOR	(8) Coop-Church	AGN	(13) Jets to Chiang	FOR
(4) No-Knock	FOR	(9) Family Asst	AGN	(14) State OEO Veto	FOR
(5) Cmutr Tax	AGN	(10) Work Stamps	FOR	(15) Park Logging	FOR

Election Results

1970 general:	Earl F. Landgrebe (R)	79,163	(50%)
	Philip A. Sprague (D)	77,959	(50%)
1970 primary:	Earl F. Landgrebe (R)	27,205	(56%)
	Albert F. Harrigan (R)	10,954	(21%)
	Donald W. Blue (R)	10,005	(21%)
1968 general:	Earl F. Landgrebe (R)	104,238	(55%)
	Edward F. Kelley (D)	81,084	(45%)

THIRD DISTRICT Political Background

Indiana 3 is four counties around South Bend. St. Joseph County, which contains South Bend and Mishawaka, is the heart of the area—heavily industrial (former home of the Studebaker company) and blue-collar. St. Joseph contains more than half of the district's population and is a Democratic stronghold. Elkhart, the district's other predominantly urban county, is more Republican; though industrial, Elkhart is a high-income town. Of the two rural counties, Marshall is politically marginal and Kosciusko heavily Republican.

Technically the 3rd is a politically marginal district; in statewide elections, it usually supports the winner, whether Democrat or Republican. Locally, it is loyal to Congressman John Brademas, a Democrat first elected in 1958. Brademas is an anomalous figure: of Greek descent, he is a Harvard graduate and a Rhodes Scholar representing a district that includes Notre Dame University. Although his percentage dipped to 52 in 1968, he has usually won by solid margins. He is currently the number-eight Democrat on the House Education and Labor Committee, which reports out most social legislation; the Congressman stands some chance of becoming chairman, as the members are all somewhat older (at least 8 years) than he is. Brademas' local popularity has been high enough to enable him to survive earlier redistrictings, and his chances for reelection in 1972 are good.

Census Data 1970 pop. 454,687; deviation from current state average. −3.7%; change 1960–70, +8.7%. Metro. 61.6%, 27.6% central city.

1970 Share of Federal Outlays $479,069,916

DOD	$303,068,000	HEW	$92,942,139
AEC	$1,619,000	HUD	$1,314,867
NASA	$123,837	OEO	$349,355
DOT	$1,629,726	DOA	$13,180,465
		Other	$66,472,231

Federal Military-Industrial Commitments

DOD Contractors Jeep Div., American Motors (South Bend), $260.431m: 2½- and 5-ton trucks. Bendix Corp. (South Bend and Mishawaka), $16.007m: Talos missile telemetry systems.

Economic Base Nonelectrical machinery, esp. general industrial machinery and equipment; transportation equipment, esp. motor vehicles and motor vehicle equipment and aircraft and parts; fabricated metal products.

The Voters

Registration No district-wide registration.

Employment profile White collar, 40%. Blue collar, 60%.

Ethnic groups Black, 5%. Total foreign stock, 18%. Germany, Poland, 4% each; Hungary, 2%; Austria, Canada, Italy, Sweden, UK, 1% each; others, 3%.

Presidential vote

1968	Humphrey (D)	72,363	(39%)
	Nixon (R)	93,521	(51%)
	Wallace (AIP)	18,773	(10%)

Representative

John Brademas (D) Elected 1958; b. March 2, 1927, Mishawaka; home, South Bend; Harvard, B.A., 1949; Oxford U., D. Phil., 1954; Navy, WWII; unmarried; Methodist.

Career Asst. Prof. political science, St. Mary's Col., Notre Dame, Ind., 1945–46; Exec. Asst. to Adlai E. Stevenson, 1955–56; Legislative Asst. to Senator Pat McNamara of Mich., 1955; Admin. Asst. to Rep. Thomas L. Ashley of Ohio, 1955.

Offices 2134 RHOB, 202-225-3915. Also 301 Fed. Bldg., South Bend 46601, 219-234-8111.

Committees

Education and Labor (7th); Subs. (1) Chm., Sel. on Education, (2) Gen. on Labor, (3) Sp. on Education.

House Administration (6th); Subs. (1) Chm., Printing, (2) Library and Memorials, (3) Sp. on Electrical and Mechanical Office Equipment.

Jt. Com. on the Library (3rd).

Jt. Com. on Printing (3rd).

Group Ratings

	ADA	COPE	NREP	NFU	LCV	CFA	NAB	NSI	ACA
1970	92	100	93	92	89	100	0	33	22
1969	73	—	—	86	—	—	—	—	7
1968	92	100	—	100	—	—	0	—	5

Key Votes

(1) ABM	AGN	(6) 18-Yr-Vote	FOR	(11) Clean Water $	FOR
(2) SST	AGN	(7) Farm Sub Lmt	FOR	(12) Mig Wrkrs Comp	FOR
(3) Phil Pln	FOR	(8) Coop-Church	FOR	(13) Jets to Chiang	AGN
(4) No-Knock	FOR	(9) Family Asst	FOR	(14) State OEO Veto	AGN
(5) Cmutr Tax	FOR	(10) Work Stamps	AGN	(15) Park Logging	AGN

Election Results

1970 general:	John Brademas (D)	87,064	(58%)
	Don M. Newman (R)	64,249	(42%)
1970 primary:	John Brademas (D), unopposed		
1968 general:	John Brademas (D)	94,452	(52%)
	William W. Erwin (R)	86,354	(48%)

FOURTH DISTRICT Political Background

Indiana 4 centers on Fort Wayne, the state's second largest city; more than half of the district's votes are cast in Allen County, which contains that city. Fort Wayne is a medium-sized Midwestern industrial town with a small black ghetto, large numbers of nondescript frame houses belonging to white blue-collar workers, and a small neighborhood of substantial-looking mansions, where the men who own and run the town live in comfort and ease.

The surrounding counties are primarily agricultural flatland. Those to the south and west of Fort Wayne—Adams, Wells, Huntington, Whitley, and Noble—have a Democratic tradition, while those to the north—Steuben, DeKalb, and LaGrange—are heavily Republican. A detailed poll of the two blocs of rural counties would not disclose any major dissimilarities of opinion on issues; their political disagreements are largely a matter of upbringing and tradition, traceable ultimately to differences in ethnic settlement patterns and attitudes toward the Civil War. Returns from the 1868 presidential election—Republican Ulysses Grant versus Democrat Horatio Seymour—show configurations little different from those of the closely contested 1962, 1968, and 1970 Senate elections.

The composition of the 4th makes it prime marginal territory, and as this district goes, so goes most of Indiana. In 1968, the district gave only 37% of its votes to Hubert Humphrey (Nixon had 55%)—showing Humphrey's weakness in what his partisans like to call his home country, small-town industrial and rural mid-America. In statewide elections, the results have been closer. Senators Bayh and Hartke carried just over 50% of the votes in the district when they won elections in 1968 and 1970; also in 1968, Republican Gov. Edgar Whitcomb took 54% of the 4th's ballots.

Indiana 4 is one of those districts that was created for the benefit of one party and wound up in the hands of the other. The 1968 congressional race pitted two incumbents against each other in the 4th's terrain. E. Ross Adair, a member of the House since 1950 and senior Republican on the House Foreign Relations Committee, was given a clear advantage. Most of the new district's counties had been part of his old constituency. Democrat J. Edward Roush, on the other hand, lost most of his old constituency to the new 5th district and retained only Adams, Wells, and Huntington counties. Adair won in 1968 with 51%, and normally, one assumes, the power of incumbency would guarantee him later victories.

But Roush decided to run again in 1970 and this time improved his showing, as did most Indiana Democrats. Roush wound up with 52% of the votes and so ended Adair's 20-year career in the House, unless the Republican comes back and wins in 1972, when he will be 65. Allen County and Fort Wayne figured most prominently in the Roush victory. In 1968 Adair carried the county 55,500 to 50,500 (52%); in 1970 Roush won it 47,700 to 43,500 (52%). High unemployment, much of it due to the GM strike, undoubtedy helped Roush, as did the rejuvenation of the long-feuding Democratic organization. Oddly enough, Roush increased his percentages everywhere but in his home county of Huntington and nearby Adams County. Since both counties were part of his old district, Roush had enjoyed the advantages of incumbency in the 1968 election;

but by 1970 Adair had two years in which to flood Huntington and Adams with franked mail, a powerful political weapon.

The prospects for 1972 are uncertain. The Republican governor and legislature in redistricting placed Roush's home county in another district. Most likely Roush will move into and run in the reconstituted 4th. As the incumbent there, he will have an advantage, but the 1972 race in the district should be a close one.

Census Data 1970 pop. 492,780; deviation from current state average, +4.4%; change 1960–70, +16.3%. Metro. 56.9%, 36.1% central city.

1970 Share of Federal Outlays $362,778,121

DOD	$128,762,000	HEW	$108,076,148
AEC	$000	HUD	$1,486,000
NASA	$1,924,005	OEO	$180,499
DOT	$1,782,280	DOA	$24,118,926
		Other	$96,448,763

Federal Military-Industrial Commitments

DOD Contractors Magnavox Co. (Fort Wayne), $74.422m: airborne electronic equipment; sonabuoys. IT&T Corp. (Fort Wayne), $10.037m: missile electronic units. LTV Electrosystems (Huntington), $9.876m: radio sets.

Economic Base Electrical machinery, equipment, and supplies, esp. electrical industrial apparatus; transportation equipment, esp. trailer coaches; cash grain, livestock, and dairy; nonelectrical machinery, esp. metalworking machinery and equipment; fabricated metal products, esp. fabricated structural metal products.

The Voters

Registration No district-wide registration.

Employment profile White collar, 40%. Blue collar, 60%.

Ethnic groups Black, 3%. Total foreign stock, 8%. Germany, 3%, Canada, UK, 1% each; others, 2%.

Presidential vote

1968	Humphrey (D)	72,815	(37%)
	Nixon (R)	107,471	(55%)
	Wallace (AIP)	16,276	(8%)

Representative

J. Edward Roush (D) Elected 1970; b. Sept. 12, 1920, Barnsdall, Okla.; home, Huntington; Huntington Col., B.A., 1938; Ind. U. Law School, J.D., 1949; Army, 1942–46, 1950; married, four children; United Brethren in Christ.

Career Atty., Indiana Gen. Assembly, 1949–50; Huntington County Prosecuting Atty., 1955–59; U.S. House of Reps., 1959–69.

Offices 2400 RHOB, 202-225-4436. Also 204 Strauss Bldg., Fort Wayne 46802, 219-742-6250.

Committees

Appropriations (32nd); Subs. (1) HUD, Space, and Science, (2) Legislative.

Group Ratings, Key Votes: Newly elected.

Election Results

1970 general:	J. Edward Roush (D)	86,582	(52%)
	E. Ross Adair (R)	80,326	(48%)
1970 primary:	J. Edward Roush (D), unopposed		

1968 general:	E. Ross Adair (R)	98,977	(51%)
	J. Edward Roush (D)	93,515	(49%)

FIFTH DISTRICT Political Background

Indiana 5 is the heartland of Indiana, perhaps of the entire Great Lakes midwest. It lies almost smack in the center of the state and contains acres and acres of rich farmland. The 5th also has two middle-sized cities, Marion and Kokomo, which are part of the GM belt running northeast from Indianapolis. Mostly this is Republican territory, as one might expect. Only three of the farm counties—Cass and Carroll, which supported Birch Bayh in 1968, and Blackford, which almost always goes Democratic—still reflect any nineteenth-century Democratic leanings (see Indiana state write-up). Hamilton County, in the southern part of the district and just to the north of Indianapolis, is a fast-growing, exurban-suburban Republican bastion. Hamilton's votes are enough to offset any Democratic margins coming out of Kokomo and Marion, which, in any event, are not as Democratic as the other GM belt towns, Anderson and Muncie, in the 10th district. The 5th's post-1964 Democratic high mark was Birch Bayh's 48% in 1968.

In his successful bid for reelection in 1970, Vance Hartke's showing here sagged 6 percentage points to 42%. This happened mainly because Hartke's opponent was Rep. Richard Roudebush, who represented the 5th and, thanks to frequent redistrictings, two other districts covering some of the same territory for the past 10 years. Roudebush's conservative voting record will probably be continued by his successor, Elwood Hillis, who won 56% of the district's votes in 1970 and carried every county but tiny Blackford. In 1970, Indiana Democrats went all out for Hartke and for three congressional seats in the 4th, 8th, and 10th. Since the Democrats did not strenuously contest the election in the 5th, Hillis had a comparatively easy time winning.

Redistricting has made the district slightly less Republican. But it is unlikely to produce a close contest in 1972 unless Democratic Congressman J. Edward Roush, whose home town lies near the 5th, decides to run here rather than in the new 4th as expected.

Census Data 1970 pop. 465,613; deviation from current state average, −1.5%; change 1960–70, +10.9%. Metro. 18.3%, 0.0% central city.

1970 Share of Federal Outlays $250,115,365

DOD	$52,423,000	HEW	$85,646,476
AEC	$000	HUD	$1,355,000
NASA	$91,915	OEO	$000
DOT	$9,974,758	DOA	$9,974,758
		Other	$77,659,554

Federal Military-Industrial Commitments

DOD Contractors Firestone Tire (Noblesville), $5.886m: wheel assemblies for armored personnel carriers.

DOD Installations Grissom AFB (Peru).

Economic Base Primary metal industries; cash grain and livestock; stone, clay, glass, and concrete products, esp. glass containers; electrical machinery, equipment, and supplies, esp. communication equipment and electronic components and accessories.

The Voters

Registration No district-wide registration.

Employment profile White collar, 32%. Blue collar, 68%.

Ethnic groups Black, 2%. Total foreign stock, 4%. Germany, UK, 1% each; others, 1%.

Presidential vote

1968	Humphrey (D)	64,062	(34%)
	Nixon (R)	104,769	(56%)
	Wallace (AIP)	19,568	(10%)

Representative

Elwood Haynes Hillis (R) Elected 1970; b. March 6, 1926, Kokomo; home, Kokomo; Ind. U., B.S., 1949; Ind. U. Law School, J.D., 1952; Army, 1944–46; married, three children; Presbyterian.
Career Practicing atty., 1952– ; Indiana House of Reps., 1966–70; Kokomo Housing Authority Bd.
Offices 1510 LHOB, 202-225-5037. Also 504 Union Bank Bldg., Kokomo 46901, 317-453-6814.

Committees

Post Office and Civil Service (9th); Subs. (1) Employee Benefits, (2) Postal Service.
Veterans' Affairs (10th); (1) Hospitals, (2) Housing.

Group Ratings, Key Votes: Newly elected.

Election Results

1970 general:	Elwood H. Hillis (R)	86,199	(56%)
	Kathleen Z. Williams (D)	67,740	(44%)
1970 primary:	Richard L. Roudebush (R)	43,001	(90%)
	Harry R. Fawcett (R)	2,453	(5%)
	Gerald Brissman (R)	2,447	(5%)

SIXTH DISTRICT Political Background

Indiana 6 is the suburban and exurban Indianapolis district, taking in about half of that recently expanded city and five adjacent counties. Indianapolis, like Columbus, Ohio, is a profoundly conservative city, almost always Republican in national elections (Goldwater got almost 48% here) and invariably Republican in statewide contests. Only in local elections has the city gone Democratic; for many years Indianapolis had conservative Democratic mayors, as did Columbus, Ohio, which has one today.

But in 1967, a young Indianapolis Republican and ex-Rhodes Scholar, Richard Lugar, won the technically nonpartisan mayoralty and the 2,000 patronage jobs that go with it. Two years later he persuaded the legislature to allow the city of Indianapolis to absorb almost all of surrounding Marion County. As a result, the city is now the nation's 10th largest and, at the same time, forever Republican. Of the nine township blocs that make up the county and now the city, six are in the 6th district; and only one of these townships, Wayne, which contains the Indianapolis Speedway and the west-side industrial area, has any Democratic inclinations.

The rest of the city-county and the counties around it—Morgan, Johnson, Shelby, and Hancock—are part of what might be called the Indianapolis *Star* belt. The *Star*'s editorial policies are somewhere to the right of the Chicago *Tribune*'s; and just as there was a belt of suburban and exurban territory around Chicago that went for Barry Goldwater in 1964 (see Illinois 12), so there was an ultraconservative belt around Indianapolis. The 6th was the only one of Indiana's current districts that Goldwater carried.

So it is hardly surprising that the 6th has proved to be a safe district for conservative Republican William G. Bray. Bray, who received a healthy 61% of the votes in the Democratic year of 1970, has done even better in other years. First elected in 1950, the Congressman has risen to become the 2nd ranking Republican on the House Armed Services Committee, where he is not known to dissent from the bipartisan, hawkish committee consensus. Only advancing age (he was 67 in 1970) stands as a possible bar to his continued reelection.

Census Data 1970 pop. 562,127; deviation from current state average, +19.7%; change 1960–70, +32.0%. Metro. 96.4%, 59.9% central city.

1970 Share of Federal Outlays $445,703,400 (average outlay per district, Indiana 6, 11)

DOD	$192,762,800	HEW	$10,421,040
AEC	$8,500	HUD	$6,145,560
NASA	$527,288	OEO	$863,871

DOT	$26,075,620	DOA	$10,030,980
		Other	$106,139,600

Federal Military-Industrial Commitments (See Indiana 11 for greater Indianapolis listing.)

Economic Base Transportation equipment, esp. motor vehicles and motor vehicle equipment and aircraft and parts; electrical machinery, equipment, and supplies; livestock and cash grain; nonelectrical machinery, esp. general industrial machinery and equipment; food and kindred products, esp. bakery products; chemicals and allied products; printing, publishing, and allied industries. Also, banking and insurance; extensive commuting to Indiana 11 (Indianapolis).

The Voters

Registration No district-wide registration.

Employment profile White collar, 50%. Blue collar, 50%.

Ethnic groups Black, 5%. Total foreign stock, 5%. Germany, UK, 1% each; others, 1%

Presidential vote

1968	Humphrey (D)	66,488	(29%)
	Nixon (R)	134,885	(59%)
	Wallace (AIP)	26,499	(12%)

Representative

William Gilmer Bray (R) Elected 1950; b. June 17, 1903, Mooresville; home, Martinsville; Ind. U., LL.B., 1927; Army, WWII; Col. (Ret.) USAR, married, one child; Society of Friends.

Career Prosecuting Atty., 1926–30; practicing atty., 1927–51.

Offices 2204 RHOB, 202-225-2276. Also 3901 N. Meridian St., Indianapolis 46208, 317-633-7277.

Committees

Armed Services (3rd); Subs. (1) No. 2, (2) Sp. on Real Estate.

Merchant Marine and Fisheries (8th); Subs. (1) Coast Guard, Coast and Geodetic Survey and Navigation, (2) Merchant Marine, (3) Panama Canal.

Group Ratings

	ADA	COPE	NREP	NFU	LCV	CFA	NAB	NSI	ACA
1970	0	0	0	31	13	37	100	100	86
1969	0	—	—	27	—	—	—	—	87
1968	0	0	—	33	—	—	100	—	100

Key Votes

(1) ABM	FOR	(6) 18-Yr-Vote	FOR	(11) Clean Water $	AGN
(2) SST	FOR	(7) Farm Sub Lmt	AGN	(12) Mig Wrkrs Comp	AGN
(3) Phil Pln	AGN	(8) Coop-Church	AGN	(13) Jets to Chiang	FOR
(4) No-Knock	FOR	(9) Family Asst	AGN	(14) State OEO Veto	FOR
(5) Cmutr Tax	AGN	(10) Work Stamps	FOR	(15) Park Logging	AGN

Election Results

1970 general:	William G. Bray (R)	115,113	(61%)
	Terrence D. Straub (D)	74,599	(39%)
1970 primary:	William G. Bray (R)	40,285	(88%)
	Berryman S. Hurley (R)	2,749	(6%)
	Henry W. Holt (R)	2,726	(6%)
1968 general:	William G. Bray (R)	142,207	(65%)
	Phillip L. Bayt (D)	76,940	(35%)

SEVENTH DISTRICT Political Background

Indiana 7 is west central Indiana, rolling farmland stretching to the north and south of the old National Road (now U.S. 40 and Interstate 70). The two main towns in the district are Bloomington, site of Indiana University, and Terre Haute, a grimy industrial town and onetime sin city, and also the home of Sen. Birch Bayh. Like most of Indiana, the 7th is marginal politically. The northern counties tend toward Republicanism, while those in the south, though rural, are among the state's Democratic strongholds. Vigo County (Terre Haute) usually goes Democratic, and so lately has Monroe County (Bloomington). The influence of the peace-minded university community in Bloomington has affected Monroe's traditional Republican tendencies.

The current 7th is the result of several redistrictings. Its predecessor was expected to elect a Democrat to the House in 1966 when there was no incumbent in the district. But since 1966 turned out to be a Republican year, John T. Myers, a young (43 in 1970) farmer and banker from the northern part of the 7th, won by a convincing margin. Myers was not a target of the 1970 Democratic push, but like all the state's Republican congressional candidates, his 1970 percentage was down from 1968. In 1971, Myers won a seat on the House Appropriations Committee, on which he can look forward to years of service.

Census Data 1970 pop. 475,473; deviation from current state average, +0.7%; change 1960–70, +11.5%. Metro. 48.2%, 14.8% central city.

1970 Share of Federal Outlays $358,771,307

DOD	$113,257,000	HEW	$128,826,786
AEC	$259,228	HUD	$40,000
NASA	$508,672	OEO	$304,452
DOT	$2,713,689	DOA	$34,643,083
		Other	$78,218,397

Federal Military-Industrial Commitments

DOD Contractors General Energy Systems Corp. (Newport), $9.406m: construction of acid recovery and TNT manufacturing units. Cenco Piping Corp. (Newport), $6.298m: construction of TNT manufacturing units.

DOD Installations Naval Ammunition Depot (Crane).

Economic Base Cash grain and livestock; electrical machinery, equipment, and supplies; food and kindred products. Also, higher education (Indiana University).

The Voters

Registration No district-wide registration.

Employment profile White collar, 36%. Blue collar, 64%.

Ethnic groups Black, 2%. Total foreign stock, 5%. Germany, Italy, UK, 1% each; others, 1%.

Presidential vote

1968	Humphrey (D)	75,121	(38%)
	Nixon (R)	100,876	(50%)
	Wallace (AIP)	24,048	(12%)

Representative

John Thomas Myers (R) Elected 1966; b. Feb. 8, 1927, Covington; home, Covington; Ind. State U., B.S., 1951; Army, WWII; married, two children; Episcopalian.

Career Cashier, trust officer, Foundation Trust Co., 1954–66; owner-operator, livestock farm.

Offices 103 CHOB, 202-225-5805. Also 203 Fed. Bldg., Terre Haute 47808, 812-232-1652, and 110½ N. Walnut St., Bloomington 47401, 812-336-1002.

Committees

Appropriations (22nd); Subs. (1) District of Columbia, (2) Treasury, Post Office, and General Government.

Group Ratings

	ADA	COPE	NREP	NFU	LCV	CFA	NAB	NSI	ACA
1970	12	9	0	55	0	42	92	100	83
1969	0	—	—	33	—	—	—	—	88
1968	0	15	—	53	—	—	100	—	91

Key Votes

(1) ABM	FOR	(6) 18-Yr-Vote	FOR	(11) Clean Water $	AGN
(2) SST	FOR*	(7) Farm Sub Lmt	AGN	(12) Mig Wrkrs Comp	AGN
(3) Phil Pln	AGN	(8) Coop-Church	AGN	(13) Jets to Chiang	FOR
(4) No-Knock	FOR	(9) Family Asst	AGN	(14) State OEO Veto	FOR
(5) Cmutr Tax	AGN	(10) Work Stamps	FOR	(15) Park Logging	FOR

* *Voted "against" in previous vote on same issue.*

Election Results

1970 general:	John T. Myers (R)	97,152	(55%)
	William D. Roach (D)	73,042	(45%)
1970 primary:	John T. Myers (R), unopposed		
1968 general:	John T. Myers (R)	115,921	(60%)
	Elden C. Tipton (D)	78,045	(40%)

EIGHTH DISTRICT Political Background

Indiana 8 is the southwestern corner of the state. The district contains the city of Evansville on the Ohio River and several river counties that are hilly, even mountainous by standards used in the Midwest. This part of Indiana was the first to be settled by white men—Vincennes, now a small town on the Wabash River, once was the metropolis of Indiana. Today Evansville is a reasonably prosperous industrial city (the fourth largest in the state), but most of the rest of the district has suffered economically ever since railroads took the traffic away from the steamboats of the Ohio River.

During the Civil War, what is now the 8th (except for Evansville) was Copperhead country, friendly to the South and hostile to Mr. Lincoln's war and the Republican party. Kentucky, a slave state, lay just across the Ohio River. Today, though the issues have changed, the 8th is still generally Democratic—except in presidential elections when the Southern-accented Hoosiers here refuse to support liberal candidates nominated by the national Democratic party. Yet both senators Bayh and Hartke have always carried the district. In fact, Hartke is a native son, having prepared for the Senate by a two-year stint as deputy prosecuting attorney of Vanderburgh County and by serving for three years as mayor of Evansville.

For many years the 8th belonged to Congressman Winfield K. Denton, a middle-of-the-road Democrat. Thinking that Denton was invulnerable, the Democratic redistricters of 1965 transferred heavily Democratic Clark County (across the river from Louisville) to the 9th district. The transfer was designed to help then freshman Rep. Lee Hamilton. The result was not anticipated: in 1966 Hamilton won by a surprisingly large margin, while the veteran Denton was swept out of office by 4,000 votes. Figures show that Denton could have won in his old district, and Hamilton, as it turned out, didn't need Clark County to win.

Since 1966, the man who beat Denton, Rep. Roger H. Zion, has won reelection twice. In 1970 Democrat J. David Huber waged a strong campaign, but was unable to dent Zion's strength in his hometown of Evansville. Vanderburgh County, which contains Evansville, cast about one-third of the district's votes and provided Zion with more than half of his 9,000-vote margin. Meanwhile, favorite son Vance Hartke was carrying Vanderburgh by 3,000 votes. But despite Zion's strength in Evansville, the 8th must be considered a typically marginal Indiana district, with the incumbent vulnerable whenever public opinion shifts widely. Redistricting will help Zion somewhat in 1972.

Census Data 1970 pop. 441,924; deviation from current state average, −6.4%; change 1960–70, +4.0%. Metro. 44.5%, 31.4% central city.

1970 Share of Federal Outlays $245,655,567

DOD	$25,349,000	HEW	$101,527,359
AEC	$000	HUD	$1,183,722
NASA	$000	OEO	$761,244
DOT	$34,117,776	DOA	$25,273,352
		Other	$57,443,114

Federal Military-Industrial Commitments

DOD Contractors Superior Steel Ball Co. (Washington), $7.776m: components for anti-personnel bombs.

Economic Base Livestock and cash grain; food and kindred products; nonelectrical machinery; miscellaneous plastic products; fabricated metal products.

The Voters

Registration No district-wide registration.

Employment profile White collar, 36%. Blue collar, 64%.

Ethnic groups Black, 3%. Total foreign stock, 3%. Germany, 2%; others, 1%.

Presidential vote

1968	Humphrey (D)	84,111	(41%)
	Nixon (R)	101,042	(49%)
	Wallace (AIP)	21,191	(10%)

Representative

Roger H. Zion (R) Elected 1966; b. Sept. 17, 1921, Escanaba, Mich.; home, Evansville; U. of Wisconsin, B.A., 1943; Harvard Graduate School of Business Admin., 1944–45; Navy, WWII; married, three children; Congregationalist.

Career Sales rep., sales training mgr., dir. of training and professional relations, Mead & Johnson Co., 1946–65; author.

Offices 1226 LHOB, 202-225-4636. Also Rm. 128, U.S. Courthouse & Fed. Bldg., Evansville 47708, 812-423-6871.

Committees

Internal Security (2nd).

Public Works (7th); Subs. (1) Flood Control and Internal Development, (2) Investment and Oversight, (3) Rivers and Harbors, (4) Roads, (5) Watershed Development.

Group Ratings

	ADA	COPE	NREP	NFU	LCV	CFA	NAB	NSI	ACA
1970	12	18	0	31	50	45	91	100	89
1969	7	—	—	33	—	—	—	—	69
1968	0	17	—	31	—	—	100	—	96

Key Votes

(1) ABM	FOR	(6) 18-Yr-Vote	FOR	(11) Clean Water $	AGN
(2) SST	FOR	(7) Farm Sub Lmt	AGN	(12) Mig Wrkrs Comp	AGN
(3) Phil Pln	FOR	(8) Coop-Church	AGN	(13) Jets to Chiang	FOR
(4) No-Knock	FOR	(9) Family Asst	AGN	(14) State OEO Veto	FOR
(5) Cmutr Tax	AGN	(10) Work Stamps	FOR	(15) Park Logging	AGN

Election Results

1970 general:	Roger H. Zion (R)	93,088	(53%)
	J. David Huber (D)	83,911	(47%)
1970 primary:	Roger H. Zion (R)	30,661	(88%)
	Herbert William Lane (R)	4,140	(12%)

1968 general:	Roger H. Zion (R)	109,585	(55%)
	K. Wayne Kent (D)	91,642	(45%)

NINTH DISTRICT Political Background

Indiana 9 is the southeast corner of the state, 16 rural and agricultural counties between the Ohio River and Indianapolis. Down here, inherited family loyalties and home-town traditions are more important in politics than ideology or particular stands on issues. The counties along the river are for the most part Democratic, a political inclination that reflects the Southern origin of many of their residents. To the north, the trend is toward solid conservative Hoosier Republicanism. The only urban concentration of any size in the 9th lies in Floyd and Clark counties, across the Ohio River from Louisville, which contain the cities of New Albany and Jeffersonville. The 9th also contains the small but growing (27,000) city of Columbus, home of the Cummins Diesel Company and its president, J. Irwin Miller. *Esquire* magazine once suggested that Miller, a liberal Republican, would make a better President than any of the current, better-known crop of aspirants.

Columbus is also the home of Congressman Lee Hamilton, one of those Democrats who have Barry Goldwater to thank for making it to the House and their own hard work to thank for staying there. In 1964, Hamilton beat conservative Republican incumbent Earl Wilson by a surprising 12,000 votes and even carried his normally Republican home county. The Congressman has been winning by steadily increasing margins ever since. And he would have won without the help he has received from successive redistrictings; in 1964, neither Floyd nor Clark counties, both heavily Democratic, were in the 9th; by 1968, both were. In 1970, Hamilton received 63% of the votes, the second-best percentage among Indiana Democrats and 10% ahead of the statewide ticket in the district. Only the 1st district, heavily industrial Gary and vicinity, produced a larger Democratic margin.

Hamilton, who is now Chairman of the Foreign Affairs Near East Subcommittee, is one of those congressmen who has created a safe seat for himself in a district which, on paper, belongs to the other party.

Census Data 1970 pop. 469,687; deviation from current state average, −0.5%; change 1960–70, +10.4%. Metro. 34.3%, 0.0% central city.

1970 Share of Federal Outlays $364,909,565

DOD	$160,898,000	HEW	$90,137,233
AEC	$000	HUD	$92,391
NASA	$000	OEO	$606,790
DOT	$6,222,205	DOA	$23,627,093
		Other	$83,325,853

Federal Military-Industrial Commitments

DOD Contractors Olin Mathieson Corp. (Charlestown), $134.271m: operation of Indiana Army Ammunition Plant and production of rocket propellant and ammunition components.

DOD Installations Jefferson Army Proving Ground (Madison).

Economic Base Cash grain and livestock; general industrial machinery and other nonelectrical machinery; iron and steel foundries; electrical machinery, equipment, and supplies.

The Voters

Registration No district-wide registration.

Employment profile White collar, 32%. Blue collar, 68%.

Ethnic groups Black, 2%. Total foreign stock, 3%. Germany, 1%; others, less than 0.5%.

Presidential vote

1968	Humphrey (D)	75,907	(39%)
	Nixon (R)	95,289	(49%)
	Wallace (AIP)	25,442	(13%)

Representative

Lee Herbert Hamilton (D) Elected 1964; b. April 20, 1931, Daytona Beach, Fla.; home, Columbus; DePauw U., B.A., 1952; Goethe U., Germany, 1952–53; Ind. U. School of Law, J.D., 1956; married, three children; Methodist.

Career Practicing atty., 1956–64; Inst. in contracts and negotiables at American Banking Inst.; Treas., Bartholomew County Young Democrats, 1960–63, Pres., 1963–64.

Offices 224 CHOB, 202-225-5315. Also U.S. P.O., Columbus 47201, 812-372-2571, and 1201 E. 10th St., Jeffersonville 47274, 812-283-1261.

Committees

Foreign Affairs (13th); Subs. (1) Chm., Near East, (2) Asian and Pacific Affairs, (3) Europe.

Post Office and Civil Service (11th); Subs. (1) Chm., Employee Benefits, (2) Investigations, (3) Postal Service.

Group Ratings

	ADA	COPE	NREP	NFU	LCV	CFA	NAB	NSI	ACA
1970	80	73	83	100	86	90	11	78	13
1969	53	—	—	86	—	—	—	—	13
1968	58	77	—	88	—	—	33	—	22

Key Votes

(1) ABM	FOR	(6) 18-Yr-Vote	FOR	(11) Clean Water $	FOR
(2) SST	AGN	(7) Farm Sub Lmt	FOR	(12) Mig Wrkrs Comp	FOR
(3) Phil Pln	FOR	(8) Coop-Church	FOR	(13) Jets to Chiang	AGN
(4) No-Knock	FOR	(9) Family Asst	FOR	(14) State OEO Veto	AGN
(5) Cmutr Tax	FOR	(10) Work Stamps	AGN	(15) Park Logging	AGN

Election Results

1970 general:	Lee H. Hamilton (D)	104,599	(63%)
	Richard B. Wathen (R)	62,772	(37%)
1970 primary:	Lee H. Hamilton (D), unopposed		
1968 general:	Lee H. Hamilton (D)	102,707	(54%)
	Robert D. Garton (R)	86,012	(46%)

TENTH DISTRICT Political Background

Indiana 10 is the east central part of the state and includes Anderson and Muncie, the two largest cities in the GM belt that radiates from Indianapolis toward the northeast. The 10th also includes Richmond, another middle-sized city which still bears the imprint of its original Quaker settlers. Richmond's Quakers were Civil War Republicans, opposed to slavery before the War, and after the War not kindly disposed to the party of rum, Romanism, and rebellion. The city and the surrounding countryside, also originally Quaker, remain staunchly Republican despite the changes that have taken place within the party over the last 100 years.

Muncie and Anderson are very similar in most respects. Muncie was the subject of *Middletown,* a pioneering sociological study done in the 1930's by Robert and Helen Lynd. *Middletown* showed that this seemingly placid and homogeneous industrial town was actually sharply divided along class lines with local affairs firmly in the hands of a small elite. Since *Middletown* was first published, the GM and other plants around town have been unionized, blue-collar workers have been making a lot more money, and the power of the local elite has been reduced. Life-and-death economic power over places like Muncie and other small industrial towns now belongs to giant corporations and conglomerates. So the Ball family, the most prominent locally, turned to philanthropy, contributing much to the growth of Ball State University. But the family has thereby subsidized the creation of political force—the students—many of whom do not accept the political values of their benefactors.

However much Muncie and Anderson have changed since the 1930's, there is still an element of class warfare in the politics of the 10th district. Newly created as a result of the redistricting of 1968, the 10th elected David Dennis, a Republican lawyer from Richmond, as its first congressman. Dennis won by a narrow margin (54%). In 1970 Indiana Democrats made the 10th one of their target districts and provided money and volunteer support to the party candidate, Philip R. Sharp, a 28-year-old Ball State University government professor. Sharp won his primary with only 22% of the votes, but for the general elections had support not only from students but also strong backing from labor, particularly from the UAW, which was striking GM at the time. The GM strike, as well as the national recession, apparently put economic issues ahead of the Nixon-Agnew "social issue" in the minds of many voters, and the underdog Sharp lost by less than 3,000 votes (49%). Sharp carried Madison and Delaware counties (Anderson and Muncie) by a large margin, while losing Richmond's Wayne County by a margin equally large. Redistricting has removed Anderson from the district and has added some heavily Republican Indianapolis suburbs, thus substantially increasing Dennis' prospects for reelection.

Census Data 1970 pop. 458,454; deviation from current state average, —2.9%; change 1960–70, +9.9%. Metro. 58.4%, 30.5% central city.

1970 Share of Federal Outlays $221,861,366

DOD	$34,413,000	HEW	$92,826,317
AEC	$000	HUD	$2,496,607
NASA	$000	OEO	$492,627
DOT	$2,509,822	DOA	$13,084,864
		Other	$75,957,129

Federal Military-Industrial Commitments

DOD Contractors Muncie Gear Works (Muncie), $7.139m: nozzle and fin assemblies for 2.75-inch rockets.

Economic Base Livestock, cash grain, and dairy; motor vehicles and motor vehicle equipment; primary metal industries; fabricated metal products.

The Voters

Registration No district-wide registration.

Employment profile White collar, 37%. Blue collar, 63%.

Ethnic groups Black, 4%. Total foreign stock, 3%. Germany, Sweden, 1%; others, 1%.

Presidential vote

1968	Humphrey (D)	71,321	(38%)
	Nixon (R)	95,630	(51%)
	Wallace (AIP)	22,321	(12%)

Representative

David Worth Dennis (R) Elected 1968; b. June 7, 1912, Washington, D.C.; home, Richmond; Earlham Col., B.A., 1933; Harvard Law School, LL.B., 1936; Army, WWII; married, two children; Society of Friends.

Career Practicing atty., 1936– ; Prosecuting Atty., Wayne County, 1939–43; Ind. House of Reps., 1947–49, 1953–59.

Offices 1729 LHOB, 202-225-3021. Also 111 Westcott Hotel Bldg., Richmond 47374, 317-966-6125, and 201 Fed. Bldg., Anderson 46016, 317-642-1777.

Committees

Judiciary (10th); Sub. No. 1.

Group Ratings

	ADA	COPE	NREP	NFU	LCV	CFA	NAB	NSI	ACA
1970	12	9	25	31	50	43	100	90	84
1969	0	—	—	33	—	—	—	—	81

Key Votes

(1) ABM	FOR	(6) 18-Yr-Vote	AGN	(11) Clean Water $	AGN
(2) SST	AGN	(7) Farm Sub Lmt	FOR	(12) Mig Wrkrs Comp	AGN
(3) Phil Pln	FOR	(8) Coop-Church	AGN	(13) Jets to Chiang	AGN
(4) No-Knock	FOR	(9) Family Asst	AGN	(14) State OEO Veto	FOR
(5) Cmutr Tax	AGN	(10) Work Stamps	FOR	(15) Park Logging	AGN

Election Results

1970 general:	David W. Dennis (R)	81,439	(51%)
	Philip R. Sharp (D)	78,871	(49%)
1970 primary:	David W. Dennis (R)	39,069	(89%)
	Frank Clinton Waltz (R)	2,669	(6%)
	David W. Kamens (R)	1,989	(5%)
1968 general:	David W. Dennis (R)	98,090	(54%)
	William J. Norton (D)	83,981	(46%)

ELEVENTH DISTRICT Political Background

Indiana 11 is part of the newly enlarged city of Indianapolis (see Indiana 6), consisting of Center, Warren, and Lawrence townships. The latter two are suburban, while Center is what the name implies, the central portion of the city. Center Township contains virtually all of Indianapolis's 100,000 blacks and also much of its large Slavic and East European ethnic population; the blacks and the ethnics make-up the only Democratic voting blocs in the city. Indianapolis is industrial, but it is one of the most conservative and Republican cities in the Midwest. Part of the reason for this is the influence of the heavily conservative Indianapolis *Star,* the city's most important newspaper.

Still, Indianapolis has had a liberal Democratic congressman since 1964. Rep. Andrew Jacobs, Jr., whose father represented the district from 1948 to 1950, had the good fortune to be running for the seat when Barry Goldwater was running for President and when the then incumbent, ultraconservative Donald Bruce, decided not to seek reelection. Even at that, Jacobs managed to carry the district, which then included all of Marion County, by a scant 3,000 votes. Jacobs' reelection was made easier by redistricting, which removed several suburban townships from the 11th, and he has won since with increasing margins. Like Lee Hamilton of the 9th, Jacobs is young (38 in 1970) and is an active and strong campaigner. The legislature has significantly altered the district—removing much of Center Township and adding the wealthy, conservative north side of Indianapolis—but Jacobs' popularity makes him at least an even bet for reelection.

Census Data 1970 pop. 425,731; deviation from current state average, –9.8%; change 1960–70, –0.6%. Metro. 100.0%, 95.0% central city.

1970 Share of Federal Outlays $445,703,400 (average outlay per district, Indiana 6, 11)

DOD	$192,762,800	HEW	$10,421,040
AEC	$8,500	HUD	$6,145,560
NASA	$527,288	OEO	$863,871
DOT	$26,075,620	DOA	$10,030,980
		Other	$106,139,600

Federal Military-Industrial Commitments (Indiana 6, 11, greater Indianapolis listing)

DOD Contractors General Motors (Indianapolis), $198.565m: Sheridan tank assemblies; lightweight helicopter engines; turboprop aircraft engines. State of Indiana (Indianapolis), $13.450m: unspecified services.

DOD Installations Fort Benjamin Harrison AB (Indianapolis). Naval Avionics Facility (Indianapolis).

Economic Base Transportation equipment, esp. motor vehicles and motor vehicle equipment and aircraft and parts; electrical machinery, equipment, and supplies; non-electrical machinery, esp. general industrial machinery and equipment; food and kindred products, esp. bakery products; chemicals and allied products; printing, publishing, and allied industries. Also, banking and insurance.

The Voters

Registration No district-wide registration.

Employment profile White collar, 42%. Blue collar, 58%.

Ethnic groups Black, 26%. Total foreign stock, 5%. Germany, 2%; Ireland, UK, 1% each; others, 1%.

Presidential vote

1968	Humphrey (D)	71,170	(45%)
	Nixon (R)	69,745	(44%)
	Wallace (AIP)	16,549	(11%)

Representative

Andrew Jacobs, Jr. (D) Elected 1964; b. Feb. 24, 1932, Indianapolis; home, Indianapolis; Ind. U., B.S., 1955, LL.B., 1958; USMC, Korean War; unmarried; Catholic.

Career Practicing atty., 1958–64; Ind. House of Reps., 1959–60.

Offices 1535 LHOB, 202-225-4011. Also 601 Wulsin Bldg., 222 E. Ohio St., Indianapolis 46204, 317-633-7331.

Committees

District of Columbia (7th); Subs. (1) Education, (2) Housing and Youth Affairs, (3) Judiciary.

Judiciary (10th); Subs. (1) No. 4, (2) No. 5.

Group Ratings

	ADA	COPE	NREP	NFU	LCV	CFA	NAB	NSI	ACA
1970	84	100	83	100	100	100	9	56	32
1969	80	—	—	86	—	—	—	—	12
1968	92	100	—	86	—	—	0	—	5

Key Votes

(1) ABM	FOR	(6) 18-Yr-Vote	FOR	(11) Clean Water $	FOR
(2) SST	AGN	(7) Farm Sub Lmt	FOR	(12) Mig Wrkrs Comp	FOR
(3) Phil Pln	FOR	(8) Coop-Church	FOR	(13) Jets to Chiang	AGN
(4) No-Knock	FOR	(9) Family Asst	FOR	(14) State OEO Veto	AGN
(5) Cmutr Tax	FOR	(10) Work Stamps	AGN	(15) Park Logging	AGN

Election Results

1970 general:	Andrew Jacobs, Jr. (D)	71,329	(58%)
	Danny L. Burton (R)	50,990	(42%)
1970 primary:	Andrew Jacobs, Jr. (D)	16,331	(94%)
	Ivan Korunek (D)	1,053	(6%)
1968 general:	Andrew Jacobs, Jr. (D)	80,015	(53%)
	W. W. Hill, Jr. (R)	70,725	(47%)

IOWA

Political Background

Iowa brings to mind Middle America of the nineteenth century: Grant Wood's *American Gothic,* Main Streets and county fairs, and acres of cornfields. Indeed, to this day, many aspects of life in Iowa have not been affected by the twentieth century. Most of the state's residents, 98.5% of which are white, still live on farms or in small towns, not in large cities and their suburbs. Iowa has no major military installations and, aside from Collins Radio in Cedar Rapids, very little defense industry. The state's politics have no equivalent to the machine in Chicago or the right-wing extremist movement in southern California.

Iowa's economic base is also very much like it was at the turn of the century; it is the nation's largest state in which agriculture is the major industry. There are fewer actual farmers than ever, of course, but the livelihood of most Iowans still depends, directly or indirectly, on the corn and hog industry. This means that the state is, as it was in the past, an economic colony: its fate is largely determined by the price fluctuations of commodity futures at the Chicago Board of Trade and by decisions made by the Department of Agriculture and the congressional committees with which the department works.

Because Iowa is an agricultural state, it has not been growing. Almost all of the state's counties lost population during the '60's; Iowa's comparatively small metropolitan areas accounted for virtually all of the state's population increase, 2%. And since many young people leave Iowa, its median age is one of the highest in the country.

Iowa's first white residents were WASPs who were part of the migration of Protestants from New England, upstate New York, and Pennsylvania, to northern Ohio, Indiana, and Illinois. To this day, most Iowans are WASPs. Unlike its neighbor states to the north, Iowa has few Scandinavians; nor does it have many WASPs of Southern origin like southern Illinois or Missouri. This pattern of migration is the principal factor in Iowa's staunchly Republican reputation. The state has supported only one Democrat for President in the last 20 years—Lyndon Johnson. But the results of statewide contests have been less one-sided; in fact, during the same 20-year span, the Republicans have held the governorship for only 8 years. In Iowa, as elsewhere, the state's minority party has done an excellent job attuning itself to the concerns of local voters. As a result, local candidates put up by the minority party do much better than its presidential nominee.

If there is any pattern of response in Iowa to national issues, it is the Farm Belt's tendency to revolt against the Administration in Washington, of whatever party. It may be, as John Kenneth Galbraith says, that very few people actually understand the economics of the nation's farm programs. But the residents of Iowa apparently feel they do understand them and the national Administration does not. In the 1950's, the name of Ezra Taft Benson, Eisenhower's Secretary of Agriculture, came up repeatedly in Democratic oratory. Benson's policies helped to elect Democrat Herschel Loveless Governor of Iowa (1954–60). Moreover, Iowa, like most of the Farm Belt (and California) and unlike the rest of the country, cast a smaller percentage of its votes for Eisenhower in 1956 than in 1952.

In the 1960's, Iowa Democrats prospered mainly because of the Goldwater candidacy in 1964 and because of the extraordinary appeal of Gov. (1962–68) and Sen. (1968–) Harold Hughes. Hughes is a reformed alcoholic and a truck driver who formed his own small company, became dissatisfied with the way the state was regulating trucking, ran as a Democrat for the appropriate state commission, and won. Soon, to most people's surprise, he was governor, and a very popular one. In 1964 he won 68% of the state's votes, running ahead of Lyndon Johnson, and in 1966 he won a third term when most of the state's Democratic ticket was going under. In 1968, Hughes replaced the retiring Bourke Hickenlooper in the Senate. His election was more difficult than expected, because his Republican opponent spent huge sums (by Iowa standards) on television and other media advertising.

Hughes's popularity is due in part to his unusual frankness. He has never tried to cover up his bout with alcoholism, and, despite his own strong feelings on the subject, Hughes supported liquor by the glass in Iowa. The Senator was one of the first major political figures to say that he opposed Johnson's Vietnam policies and was among very few willing to say so to the President's face. Hughes also possesses a remarkably powerful evangelical speaking style, a talent which springs, perhaps, from being a devout Methodist.

The Iowa Senator gained national attention in 1968 when he nominated Eugene McCarthy at the Democratic National Convention, and when he pushed through a proposal to reform the convention delegate-selection process. In the Senate, he has been particularly interested in the problems of alcoholism and drug abuse and has generally voted with other antiwar liberals on major issues.

Until July 1971, Hughes was a dark-horse candidate for the Democratic presidential nomination. As a former truck driver and outspoken dove, the Senator had demonstrated a capacity to bridge many of the schisms within the Democratic party. His problem was lack of public recognition; among other things, many people confused his name, *Harold* Hughes, with that of Howard Hughes, the elusive millionaire. Although the Iowan dropped out of the 1972 run for president, he would no doubt be happy to become his party's vice-presidential nominee.

Iowa's senior senator, Jack Miller, is a Republican whose conservatism is more in line with the state's political traditions. Miller is the ranking Republican on the Senate Agriculture Committee, obviously an important position for an Iowa senator. But because some of the farm programs of the Nixon Administration are unpopular in Iowa, Miller may have some trouble in 1972, when his seat is up. Rumors have it that Democratic Congressman John Culver, a proven vote-getter in the 2nd district, may challenge the Republican Senator. Miller has run very well in the past, but a strong Culver campaign, combined with a Farm Belt revolt against the Republican party, could make it a close election. If Culver chooses to remain in the House, Sen. Miller will probably win easily.

The state's House delegation is currently made up of 5 Republicans and 2 Democrats —in fact, the same 5 Republicans and 2 Democrats who have represented the state since 1966. But that will change in 1972. Iowa will lose one congressional seat, and the loss will force Congressman Neal Smith, a Democrat, and Congressman John Kyl, a Republican, into the same district. Smith is the likely winner in 1972.

Electoral Votes 8

Census Data 1970 pop. 2,825,041; 1.37% of U.S. total, 25th largest; change 1960–70, 2.4%. Metro. 35.6%, 22.4% central city. 1970 per capita income, $3,714, 23rd highest. 25th in number of poor.

1970 Share of Federal Tax Burden $2,361,200,000; 1.21% of U.S. total, 23rd largest.

1970 Share of Federal Outlays $2,258,832,451; 1.20% of U.S. total, 30th largest. Per capita federal spending, $800.

DOD	$277,067,000	37th (4.81%)	HEW	$701,603,874	26th (1.34%)
AEC	$27,085,692	16th (1.04%)	HUD	$26,743,953	23rd (1.37%)
NASA	$4,049,748	27th (0.11%)	OEO	$6,430,176	35th (0.85%)
DOT	$69,910,542	35th (0.98%)	DOA	$617,793,631	5th (4.81%)
DOC	$3,308,449	38th (0.29%)	POD	$96,369,415	23rd (1.32%)
DOI	$8,102,390	43rd (0.35%)	VA	$126,164,857	27th (1.71%)
DOJ	$3,796,387	34th (0.66%)	CSC	$27,302,543	31st (0.68%)
			Other	$263,100,800	

Economic Base Livestock, cash grain, and dairy; food and kindred products, esp. grain mill products; nonelectrical machinery, esp. farm machinery and equipment, and construction, mining, and material handling machinery and equipment; electrical machinery, equipment, and supplies, esp. household appliances; printing, publishing, and allied industries, esp. newspapers; fabricated metal products, esp. fabricated structural products and valves and pipe fittings other than plumbers' brass goods; primary metal industries, esp. iron and steel foundries, rubber and miscellaneous plastic products; transportation equipment, esp. motor vehicles and motor vehicle equipment.

Political Line-up Governor, Robert Ray (R); seat up, 1972. Senators, Jack Miller (R) and Harold E. Hughes (D). Representatives, 7 (2 D and 5 R). State Senate (12 D and 38 R); State House (37 D and 63 R).

The Voters

Registration No statewide registration.

Employment profile White collar, 37%. Blue collar, 63%.

Ethnic groups 1% Black. Total foreign stock, 14%. Germany, 5%; Sweden, UK, Norway, Canada, Czech., Ireland, 1% each; others, 4%.

Presidential vote

1968	Humphrey (D)	476,699	(41%)
	Nixon (R)	619,106	(53%)
	Wallace (AIP)	66,422	(5%)
1964	Johnson (D)	733,030	(62%)
	Goldwater (R)	449,148	(38%)
1960	Kennedy (D)	550,565	(43%)
	Nixon (R)	772,381	(57%)

Senator

Jack Richard Miller (R) Elected 1960, seat up 1972; b. June 6, 1916, Chicago, Ill.; home, Sioux City; Creighton U., B.A., 1938; Catholic U., M.A., 1939; Columbia U., LL.B., 1946; Army Air Corps, WWII; Brig. Gen. USAFR; married, four children; Catholic.

Career Atty., I.R.S., 1947–48; Lecturer, George Washington U., 1948; Asst. Prof, of law, Notre Dame U., 1948–49; practicing tax atty., 1949–60; Iowa House of Reps., 1955–56; Iowa Senate, 1957–60.

Offices 4313 NSOB, 202-225-3254. Also 735 Fed. Bldg., Des Moines 50309, 515-284-4193.

Committees

Agriculture and Forestry (Ranking Mbr.); Subs. (1) Agricultural Credit and Rural Electrification, (2) Agricultural Exports, (3) Agricultural Production, Marketing, and Stabilization of Prices.

Com. on Finance (3rd).

Jt. Economic Com. (2nd); Subs. (1) Economic Statistics, (2) Fiscal Policy, (3) Foreign Economic Policy.

Sp. Com. on Aging (3rd); Subs. (1) Federal, State, and Community Services, (2) Long-term Care, (3) Retirement and the Individual.

Group Ratings

	ADA	COPE	NREP	NFU	LCV	NAB	NSI	ACA
1970	13	9	0	20	35	80	100	86
1969	17	—	—	44	—	—	—	67
1968	14	17	—	46	—	100	—	88

Key Votes

(1) ABM	FOR	(8) Phil Pln	FOR	(15) Coop-Church	AGN
(2) SST	AGN	(9) Vol Army	AGN	(16) Cut Oil Dpltn	AGN
(3) Busing	AGN	(10) Prison $	AGN	(17) Consumer Prot	AGN
(4) Tob Sub	FOR	(11) Cut Mil $	AGN	(18) Farm Sub Limit	AGN
(5) Carswell	FOR	(12) Defoliatn	FOR	(19) Comp Bid Sales	FOR
(6) No-Knock	FOR	(13) 18-Yr-Vote	AGN	(20) Pre-Prod Tests	AGN
(7) Seniorty	FOR	(14) Pentgn PR	ABS	(21) Cut Marjna Pen	AGN

Election Results

1966 general:	Jack Miller (R)	522,339	(62%)
	E. B. Smith (D)	324,114	(38%)
1966 primary:	Jack Miller (R)	141,141	(84%)
	Herbert H. Hoover (R)	27,007	(16%)
1960 general:	Jack Miller (R)	642,463	(52%)
	Herschel C. Loveless (D)	595,119	(48%)

Senator

Harold Everett Hughes (D) Elected 1968, seat up 1974; b. Feb. 10, 1922, near Ida Grove; home, Ida Grove; U. of Iowa, 1940–41; Army, WWII; married, three children; Methodist.

Career Motor transportation business; Iowa State Commerce Commission, 1959–63, Chm., 1959–60, 1961–62; Governor of Iowa, 1962–68; Mbr., Natl. Governors' Conference Exec. Com., 1965–67; Chm., Democratic Governors' Conference, 1966–68; Asst. Majority Whip, 1969–

Offices 1327 NSOB, 202-225-3744. Also 721 Fed. Bldg., Des Moines 50309, 515-284-4056.

Committees

Armed Services (8th); Subs. (1) General Legislation, (2) Strategic Arms Limitation Talks, (3) Ad Hoc on Tactical Air Power.

Labor and Public Welfare (9th); Subs. (1) Chm., Alcoholism and Narcotics, (2) Chm., Sp. on Interna. Health, Education, and Labor Programs, (3) Aging, (4) Employment, Manpower, and Poverty, (5) Health, (6) Labor, (7) Migratory Labor, (8) Railroad Retirement.

Veterans' Affairs (4th); Subs. (1) Chm., Housing and Insurance, (2) Compensation and Pension, (3) Health and Hospitals.

Sel. Com. on Equal Educational Opportunity (8th).

Group Ratings

	ADA	COPE	NREP	NFU	LCV	NAB	NSI	ACA
1970	97	100	100	100	100	22	0	10
1969	89	—	—	94	—	—	—	8

Key Votes

(1) ABM	AGN	(8) Phil Pln	FOR	(15) Coop-Church	FOR
(2) SST	AGN	(9) Vol Army	FOR	(16) Cut Oil Dpltn	FOR
(3) Busing	FOR	(10) Prison $	FOR	(17) Consumer Prot	FOR
(4) Tob Sub	FOR	(11) Cut Mil $	FOR	(18) Farm Sub Limit	FOR
(5) Carswell	AGN	(12) Defoliatn	AGN	(19) Comp Bid Sales	ABS
(6) No-Knock	AGN	(13) 18-Yr-Vote	FOR	(20) Pre-Prod Tests	FOR
(7) Seniorty	AGN	(14) Pentgn PR	AGN	(21) Cut Marjna Pen	FOR

Election Results

1968 general:	Harold E. Hughes (D)	574,884	(50%)
	David M. Stanley (R)	568,469	(50%)
1968 primary:	Harold E. Hughes (D)	103,936	(86%)
	Robert L. Neveim (D)	15,772	(14%)

FIRST DISTRICT Political Background

Iowa 1 is the southeast portion of the state, west of the Mississippi River and north of the Missouri border. Davenport, on the river, has nearly 100,000 people. There are also urban concentrations in Iowa City, site of the University of Iowa, and in the old river towns on the Mississippi—Burlington (which gave its name to a major east-west railroad), Fort Madison, and Keokuk. The rest of the district is, of course, farm country.

Iowa has had some unusually close elections recently and is one of the few consistently marginal districts in the nation. Democratic strength lies in Davenport, Burlington, and Iowa City, while most of the Republican votes are cast in the rural areas of the 1st. Rep. Fred Schwengel, a liberal Republican, at least by standards used in the Midwest, has been the district's congressman for all but two years since 1954. But since 1962, he has had no easy time winning reelection. In fact, he was beaten in 1964 by Democrat John Schmidhauser, a college professor. In 1966 Schwengel recaptured the seat from Schmidhauser with 51% of the vote; the Congressman beat the professor again in 1968 with 53%. In 1970, Schwengel had primary opposition from David Stanley, the young Republican state senator who nearly defeated Harold Hughes in the 1968 Senate race. Once again Schwengel had a close call for a longtime incumbent, winning by a 3:2 margin. In the 1970 general election, antiwar Democrat Edward Mezvinsky came even closer, losing by only 765 votes out of 120,000 cast.

Schwengel has hung on so far, but his percentages indicate that he won't be able to win indefinitely. Schwengel is also getting old, 65 in 1972. A Democrat will probably win the district sometime in the 1970's, perhaps as early as 1972. Redistricting has added two rural counties, which should help Schwengel a little.

Census Data 1970 pop. 447,227; deviation from current state average, +10.8%; change 1960–70, +11.0%. Metro. 31.9%, 21.8% central city.

1970 Share of Federal Outlays $343,583,293

DOD	$65,212,000	HEW	$107,583,549
AEC	$18,149,897	HUD	$10,385,608
NASA	$1,889,770	OEO	$924,292
DOT	$12,546,620	DOA	$43,461,677
		Other	$82,429,880

Federal Military-Industrial Commitments

DOD Contractors Mason and Hanger (Burlington), $41.607m: operation of Army Ammunition Plant and production of 155-mm projectile detonators; grenade fuzes. Bendix Corp. (Davenport), $6.276m: aircraft electronic components.

AEC Operations Mason and Hanger (Burlington), $11.499m: unspecified.

Eonomic Base Livestock and cash grain; food and kindred products, esp. meat products; nonelectrical machinery, esp. farm machinery and equipment; primary metal industries. Also, higher education (University of Iowa).

The Voters

Registration No district-wide registration.

Employment profile White collar, 38%. Blue collar, 62%.

Ethnic groups Black, 1%. Total foreign stock, 12%. Germany, 5%; Sweden, UK, Canada, Czech., 1% each; others, 4%.

Presidential vote

1968	Humphrey (D)	76,949	(44%)
	Nixon (R)	88,955	(50%)
	Wallace (AIP)	10,476	(66%)

Representative

Fred Schwengel (R) Elected 1954; b. May 28, 1907, Franklin County; home, Davenport; Northeast Mo. Teachers Col., B.S., 1930; U. of Iowa, 1933–35; married, two children; Baptist.

Career Teacher, 1930–37; insurance business, 1937–54; Iowa House of Reps., 1944–54; Pres., U.S. Capital Historical Society.

Offices 2229 RHOB, 202-225-6576. Also 422 Union Arcade, Davenport 52801, 319-324-3527.

Committees

House Administration (4th); Subs. (1) Library and Memorials, (2) Sp. on Electrical and Mechanical Office Equipment.

Public Works (5th); Subs. (1) Flood Control and Internal De-

velopment, (2) Public Buildings and Grounds, (3) Roads, (4) Watershed Development, (5) Sp. on Economic Development Programs.
Jt. Com. on the Library (Ranking Rep. House Mbr.).

Group Ratings

	ADA	COPE	NREP	NFU	LCV	CFA	NAB	NSI	ACA
1970	40	42	73	69	50	60	67	80	61
1969	40	—	—	60	—	—	—	—	35
1968	33	17	—	63	—	—	67	—	48

Key Votes

(1) ABM	FOR	(6) 18-Yr-Vote	FOR	(11) Clean Water $	AGN
(2) SST	AGN	(7) Farm Sub Lmt	FOR	(12) Mig Wrkrs Comp	AGN
(3) Phil Pln	FOR	(8) Coop-Church	FOR	(13) Jets to Chiang	AGN
(4) No-Knock	FOR	(9) Family Asst	FOR	(14) State OEO Veto	AGN
(5) Cmutr Tax	FOR	(10) Work Stamps	FOR	(15) Park Logging	AGN

Election Results

1970 general:	Fred Schwengel (R)	60,270	(50%)
	Edward Mezvinsky (D)	59,505	(49%)
	Lee E. Foster (AIP)	1,168	(1%)
1970 primary:	Fred Schwengel (R)	24,140	(56%)
	David Stanley (R)	18,677	(44%)
1968 general:	Fred Schwengel (R)	91,419	(53%)
	John Schmidhauser (D)	81,049	(47%)

SECOND DISTRICT Political Background

Iowa 2 is the northeast corner of the state, dominated by Cedar Rapids, Iowa's second largest city (pop. 163,213), and by two aging river towns about half that size, Dubuque and Clinton. Cedar Rapids is politically marginal—that is, somewhat more Democratic than Iowa as a whole. Dubuque, with a large Roman Catholic population, is heavily Democratic; and WASPish Clinton is heavily Republican. Agriculture is not as important in the 2nd as in some other Iowa districts. The knobby hills that flank the Mississippi are less suitable for corn, hogs, and wheat than are the rolling plains further west.

In 1962, the Republicans took all but one of Iowa's seven congressional districts. But the Goldwater nomination in 1964 brought an electoral upheaval, and every Iowa district but one (the 3rd) elected a Democrat. Things returned to normal in 1966 when only one of the Democratic class of '64 won reelection. That was Rep. John Culver of the 2nd. Culver has an unusual background for an Iowa congressman. He was a college roommate of Sen. Edward Kennedy and served in administrative capacities at Harvard and on Kennedy's staff. Sensing a Democratic year in 1964, Culver returned to Cedar Rapids, campaigned hard, and unseated the Republican incumbent with 51% of the votes.

Since then, the Congressman has cultivated his district effectively, winning reelection each time by increasing percentages. In 1970, he won a full 60% in a district which had once been considered solidly Republican. His 1970 victory was particularly notable for another reason. Vice President Spiro Agnew came to Iowa and campaigned vigorously for Culver's Republican opponent. Agnew hoped perhaps that the pall of Chappaquiddick would find its way to Kennedy's former roommate and close friend. The results of the election showed that it did not and also showed that the voters of northeastern Iowa did not take to the Vice President's hard-line conservatism.

Census Data 1970 pop. 476,024; deviation from current state average, +18.0%; change 1960–70, +7.6%. Metro. 53.3%, 36.3% central city.

1970 Share of Federal Outlays $345,120,919

DOD	$116,239,000	HEW	$99,566,310
AEC	$000	HUD	$1,073,118
NASA	$183,423	OEO	$534,676

DOT	$6,627,782	DOA	$42,937,974
		Other	$77,958,636

Federal Military-Industrial Commitments

DOD Contractors Collins Radio (Cedar Rapids), $98.952m: components for aircraft and submarine communication equipment.

Economic Base Livestock and dairy; food and kindred products, esp. grain mill products and meat products; nonelectrical machinery, esp. construction and mining and material handling machinery and equipment.

The Voters

Registration No district-wide registration.

Employment profile White collar, 35%. Blue collar, 65%.

Ethnic groups Black, 1%. Total foreign stock, 14%. Germany, 6%; Czech., 2%; Norway, UK, Ireland, Canada, 1% each; others, 3%.

Presidential vote

1968	Humphrey (D)	84,210	(44%)
	Nixon (R)	96,983	(51%)
	Wallace (AIP)	9,700	(5%)

Representative

John C. Culver (D) Elected 1964; b. Aug. 8, 1932, Rochester, Minn.; home, Marion; Harvard, B.A., 1954, LL.B., 1962; Cambridge U., Harvard Scholar, 1954–55; USMC, 1955–58; married, four children; Presbyterian.

Career Dean of Men, Harvard U. Summer School, 1960; Legis. Asst. to Senator Edward M. Kennedy, 1962–63.

Offices 107 CHOB, 202-225-2911. Also 205 Fed. Bldg., Cedar Rapids 52401, 319-366-2411.

Committees

Foreign Affairs (12th); Subs. (1) Chm., Foreign Economic Policy, (2) Africa, (3) Inter-American Affairs, (4) State Department Organization and Foreign Operations.

Government Operations (17th); Subs. (1) Government Activities, (2) Intergovernmental Relations.

Group Ratings

	ADA	COPE	NREP	NFU	LCV	CFA	NAB	NSI	ACA
1970	96	100	100	92	84	100	0	20	0
1969	87	—	—	93	—	—	—	—	6
1968	83	100	—	94	—	—	33	—	10

Key Votes

(1) ABM	AGN	(6) 18-Yr-Vote	ABS	(11) Clean Water $	FOR
(2) SST	AGN	(7) Farm Sub Lmt	FOR	(12) Mig Wrkrs Comp	FOR
(3) Phil Pln	FOR	(8) Coop-Church	FOR	(13) Jets to Chiang	AGN
(4) No-Knock	AGN	(9) Family Asst	FOR	(14) State OEO Veto	AGN
(5) Cmutr Tax	AGN	(10) Work Stamps	AGN	(15) Park Logging	AGN

Election Results

1970 general:	John C. Culver (D)	84,049	(60%)
	Cole McMartin (R)	54,932	(40%)
1970 primary:	John C. Culver (D), unopposed		
1968 general:	John C. Culver (D)	103,651	(55%)
	Tom Riley (R)	84,634	(45%)

THIRD DISTRICT Political Background

Iowa 3 is an almost perfectly square district in north central Iowa. Most of the district is given over to large farms, mostly well-run family enterprises, but also an increasing number of corporate variety. Here and there, grain elevator towns dot the landscape. As in most of the Midwest, the farmers of the 3rd often favor the Democrats, but their numbers are declining and their votes are swamped by those coming out of the heavily Republican small towns. The 3rd also has a couple of small cities: Waterloo, which has had racial trouble, and Mason City, Meredith Wilson's home town and model for River City of *The Music Man*.

This district is one of the most Republican of Iowa's seven, its congressman being the only Republican to survive the party's 1964 debacle. That was surely a blessing, at least to Washington writers, since H. R. Gross, who has represented the 3rd since 1948, is widely considered the House's leading curmudgeon. Rep. Gross, a classic Midwestern conservative, is known as a stickler for parliamentary detail and a gadfly-like opponent of what he considers unnecessary federal spending.

Except for 1964, when his margin of victory was only 419 votes, Gross has had no difficulty winning reelection in the 3rd. He will have none in the future either, unless he chooses to retire. Gross will be 73 in 1972.

Census Data 1970 pop. 401,907; deviation from current state average, —0.4%; change 1960–70, —0.4%. Metro. 33.1%, 18.6% central city.

1970 Share of Federal Outlays $329,111,020

DOD	$24,341,000	HEW	$96,918,748
AEC	$5,000	HUD	$1,931,323
NASA	$000	OEO	$1,180,242
DOT	$12,174,548	DOA	$127,055,169
		Other	$65,504,990

Federal Military-Industrial Commitments

DOD Contractors Chamberlain Mfg. Co. (Waterloo), $17.075m: components for 2.75-inch rocket warheads.

Economic Base Livestock, cash grain and dairy; food and kindred products, esp. meat products; nonelectrical machinery, esp. farm machinery and equipment and general industrial machinery and equipment.

The Voters

Registration No district-wide registration.

Employment profile White collar, 34%. Blue collar, 66%.

Ethnic groups Black, 2%. Total foreign stock, 17%. Germany, 8%; Norway, 2%; UK, Canada, Czech., 1% each; others, 4%.

Presidential vote

1968	Humphrey (D)	63,080	(38%)
	Nixon (R)	93,640	(57%)
	Wallace (AIP)	7,648	(5%)

Representative

H. R. Gross (R) Elected 1948; b. June 30, 1899, Arispe; home, Waterloo; U. of Mo. School of Journalism; American Expeditionary Forces, WWI; married, three children; Presbyterian.

Career Newspaper reporter, editor, 1921–35; radio news commentator, 1935–48.

Offices 2368 RHOB, 202-225-3301.

Committees

Foreign Affairs (5th); Subs. (1) Inter-American Affairs, (2) International Organizations and Movements, (3) Near East.

Post Office and Civil Service (2nd); Subs. (1) Investigations, (2) Manpower and Civil Service, (3) Postal Service.

Group Ratings

	ADA	COPE	NREP	NFU	LCV	CFA	NAB	NSI	ACA
1970	20	25	17	15	43	35	83	89	89
1969	13	—	—	20	—	—	—	—	100
1968	0	0	—	25	—	—	100	—	100

Key Votes

(1) ABM	FOR	(6) 18-Yr-Vote	AGN	(11) Clean Water $	AGN
(2) SST	AGN	(7) Farm Sub Lmt	FOR	(12) Mig Wrkrs Comp	AGN
(3) Phil Pln	AGN	(8) Coop-Church	AGN	(13) Jets to Chiang	AGN
(4) No-Knock	FOR	(9) Family Asst	AGN	(14) State OEO Veto	FOR
(5) Cmutr Tax	AGN	(10) Work Stamps	FOR	(15) Park Logging	AGN

Election Results

1970 general:	H. R. Gross (R)	66,087	(59%)
	Lyle D. Taylor (D)	45,958	(41%)
1970 primary:	H. R. Gross (R), unopposed		
1968 general:	H. R. Gross (R)	101,839	(64%)
	John E. Van Eschen (D)	57,164	(36%)

FOURTH DISTRICT Political Background

Iowa 4 is south central Iowa, an area dominated by the feed-grain and hog business. The district's only cities of any size are Ottumwa (pop. 29,000) and Marshalltown (pop. 26,000), childhood home of actress Jean Seberg. There is significant Democratic-leaning territory around Ottumwa and to the east of Des Moines, which lies just outside the 4th. But overall the district is Republican; since 1964 Harold Hughes has been the only Democrat of any consequence to carry it.

The congressman from the 4th is conservative Republican John Kyl. He has served from 1959, when he won a special election, to 1964, and from 1966 to the present. The interregnum resulted from the 1964 victory of a Democrat, Bert Bandstra, whom Kyl beat in both 1966 and 1968. Despite these victories, however, Kyl does not have a safe seat; he has not received more than 55% of the vote in any of the last four elections and has shown continuing weakness in the Democratic areas of the district.

The 1971 redistricting has made Kyl's prospects for reelection very poor. About half of the current 4th district has been combined with Polk County (Des Moines), where Democratic Congressman Neal Smith has been winning with huge pluralities. If one takes the total congressional vote cast in the new district in 1968 (a presidential year), the Democrats come out with a 57:43 edge. Kyl at this time is most likely a lame duck congressman.

Census Data 1970 pop. 358,776; deviation from current state average, –11.1%; change 1960–70, –2.0%. Metro. 0.0%, 0.0% central city.

1970 Share of Federal Outlays $255,627,618

DOD	$8,062,000	HEW	$97,936,188
AEC	$000	HUD	$4,621,262
NASA	$000	OEO	$859,658
DOT	$6,916,229	DOA	$68,509,247
		Other	$68,723,034

Federal Military-Industrial Commitments

None.

Economic Base Livestock, cash grain and dairy; food and kindred products; non-electrical machinery.

The Voters

Registration No district-wide registration.

Employment profile White collar, 32%. Blue collar, 68%.

Ethnic groups Black, less than 0.5%. Total foreign stock, 10%. Germany, 3%; UK, Czech., Sweden, 1% each; others, 5%.

Presidential vote

1968	Humphrey (D)	66,913	(42%)
	Nixon (R)	82,660	(52%)
	Wallace (AIP)	9,605	(6%)

Representative

John Henry Kyl (R) Elected 1959–64, 1966; b. May 9, 1919, Wisner; home, Bloomfield; Neb. State Teachers Col., B.A., 1940; U. of Neb., M.A., 1947; Drake U.; married, three children; Presbyterian.

Career Mgr. Wayne Chamber of Commerce, 1949–53; merchant, Bloomfield, 1953–59; newscaster.

Offices 1026 LHOB, 202-225-3906.

Committees

Agriculture (13th); Subs. (1) Family Farms and Rural Development, (2) Forests, (3) Livestock and Grains.

Interior and Insular Affairs (4th); Subs. (1) Environment, (2) Indian Affairs, (3) National Parks and Recreation, (4) Public Lands.

Group Ratings

	ADA	COPE	NREP	NFU	LCV	CFA	NAB	NSI	ACA
1970	28	34	18	33	67	44	70	100	82
1969	13	—	—	52	—	—	—	—	77
1968	0	8	—	44	—	—	83	—	86

Key Votes

(1) ABM	FOR	(6) 18-Yr-Vote	FOR	(11) Clean Water $	AGN
(2) SST	AGN	(7) Farm Sub Lmt	AGN	(12) Mig Wrkrs Comp	AGN
(3) Phil Pln	FOR	(8) Coop-Church	AGN	(13) Jets to Chiang	ABS
(4) No-Knock	FOR	(9) Family Asst	AGN	(14) State OEO Veto	FOR
(5) Cmutr Tax	AGN	(10) Work Stamps	FOR	(15) Park Logging	AGN

Election Results

1970 general:	John Kyl (R)	59,396	(55%)
	Roger Blobaum (D)	49,369	(45%)
1970 primary:	John Kyl (R), unopposed		
1968 general:	John Kyl (R)	83,259	(54%)
	Bert Bandstra (D)	71,134	(46%)

FIFTH DISTRICT Political Background

Iowa 5 is the only predominantly urban congressional district in Iowa. It sits right in the middle of the state and takes in the state's capital and largest city, Des Moines (pop. 200,000), as well as the middle-sized cities of Ames and Fort Dodge. Some 67% or 281,000 of the 5th's 417,000 residents live in Polk County, which includes Des Moines, where there are large numbers of state employees and blue-collar workers employed in plants that make agricultural machinery. After Dubuque, Des Moines is Iowa's most Democratic city. Other counties in the district—Boone, Story, and Webster—also lean Democratic. The 5th was the only Iowa district Humphrey came close to carrying in 1968.

Since the Democratic year of 1958, Democrat Neal Smith has represented this part of Iowa in the House. In that time he has managed to climb halfway up the seniority ladder on the House Appropriations Committee. He has also managed to consolidate his position in the district. Since 1964, Smith has always won more than 60% of the votes in general elections and has had no serious opposition in the primaries. Iowa

Republican redistricters have placed Polk County in the same district with about half of the old 4th. But past election results indicate that Smith's strength in Des Moines will prevail over any Republican advantage in the outlying rural counties.

Census Data 1970 pop. 423,745; deviation from current state average, +5.0%; change 1960–70, +8.2%. Metro. 67.5%, 47.3% central city.

1970 Share of Federal Outlays $337,360,428

DOD	$23,136,000	HEW	$115,202,781
AEC	$8,930,795	HUD	$7,281,048
NASA	$36,697	OEO	$2,179,263
DOT	$5,490,809	DOA	$63,064,751
		Other	$112,038,284

Federal Military-Industrial Commitments

AEC Operations Ames Research Laboratory (Ames), $7.715m: research and reactor facilities.

Economic Base Cash grain and livestock; nonelectrical machinery, esp. farm machinery and equipment; food and kindred products, esp. dairy products; printing, publishing, and allied industries, esp. newspapers. Also, higher education (Iowa State University) and insurance.

The Voters

Registration No district-wide registration.

Employment profile White collar, 50%. Blue collar, 50%.

Ethnic groups Black, 3%. Total foreign stock, 13%. Germany, Sweden, UK, 2% each; Norway, Italy, Canada, Ireland, 1% each; others, 4%.

Presidential vote

1968	Humphrey (D)	75,978	(45%)
	Nixon (R)	79,750	(48%)
	Wallace (AIP)	11,884	(7%)

Representative

Neal Smith (D) Elected 1958; b. March 23, 1920, Hedrick; home, Altoona; U. of Mo., 1945–46; Syracuse U., 1946–47; Drake U. Law School, LL.B., 1950; Army Air Corps, WWII; married, two children; Methodist.

Career Farm operator, 1937– ; practicing atty., 1950–58; Pres., Natl. Young Democrats, 1953–55; Chm., Polk County Board of Social Welfare; Asst. County Atty., Polk County, 1951.

Offices 2458 RHOB, 202-225-4426. Also 544 Insurance Exchange Bldg., Des Moines 50309, 515-284-4634.

Committees

Appropriations (15th); Subs. (1) Labor and HEW, (2) State, Justice, Commerce, and the Judiciary.

Sel. Com. on Small Business (6th); Subs. (1) Chm., Sp. on Small Business Problems, (2) Environment Problems Affecting Small Business, (3) Government Procurement.

Group Ratings

	ADA	COPE	NREP	NFU	LCV	CFA	NAB	NSI	ACA
1970	48	82	64	85	67	94	11	100	13
1969	60	—	—	93	—	—	—	—	18
1968	75	100	—	100	—	—	20	—	14

Key Votes

(1) ABM	FOR	(6) 18-Yr-Vote	FOR	(11) Clean Water $	AGN
(2) SST	AGN	(7) Farm Sub Lmt	AGN	(12) Mig Wrkrs Comp	FOR
(3) Phil Pln	AGN	(8) Coop-Church	FOR	(13) Jets to Chiang	AGN
(4) No-Knock	FOR	(9) Family Asst	FOR	(14) State OEO Veto	AGN
(5) Cmutr Tax	AGN	(10) Work Stamps	AGN	(15) Park Logging	FOR

Election Results

1970 general:	Neal Smith (D)	73,820	(65%)
	Don Mahon (R)	37,374	(33%)
	John H. Grant (AIP)	1,297	(1%)
	Roy E. Berger (Iowa New Party)	1,262	(1%)
1970 primary:	Neal Smith (D), unopposed		
1968 general:	Neal Smith (D)	99,586	(62%)
	Don Mahon (R)	60,710	(38%)

SIXTH DISTRICT Political Background

Iowa 6 is the northwestern portion of the state, where the trees begin to get scarcer and the sky seems to get bigger. Except for Sioux City (pop. 85,000), the 6th is almost entirely rural. The district is mostly Iowa Republican, but with some exceptions. Politically deviant counties dot the landscape in all of the Great Plains states; their variance from the dominant political mores stems from their having been settled by a particular ethnic group. A colony of German Catholics, for example, would send an encouraging word back to the old country, saying that they had their own community somewhere in Iowa, Kansas, or the Dakotas. Upon arriving, the new immigrants would find train fare waiting for them or be met at the boat by their former countrymen. The political inclinations of many rural Iowa counties that are heavily Republican (e.g., Sioux County) or heavily Democratic (e.g., Palo Alto County) can be explained by this pattern of settlement.

Palo Alto County in the 6th is particularly interesting for another reason. For as long as anyone can remember, the county has supported the winning presidential candidate. In the recent close elections of 1960 and 1968, Palo Alto supported John Kennedy and Richard Nixon respectively. In 1970, it backed Democratic candidates for statewide office and was the only county in the 6th district that incumbent Republican Congressman Wiley Mayne could not carry. The results in the bellwether county suggest that Iowa, and perhaps the entire country, may be trending Democratic for the 1972 presidential election.

Iowa 6 is the home district of both Iowa senators—Jack Miller is from Sioux City and Harold Hughes from Ida Grove. But neither man has represented the 6th in the House. For many years (1942–64), this part of the state was represented by Charles B. Hoeven, a pillar of the conservative Republican establishment. A Democrat ousted the aging Congressman in 1964. Then in 1966, the current incumbent, Wiley Mayne, recaptured the seat for the Republicans and has remained the district's congressman ever since. Redistricting has added the Democratic city of Fort Dodge, but the political balance of the 6th will remain unchanged in 1972, barring a major farm revolt against the Republican party.

Census Data 1970 pop. 378,301; deviation from current state average, —6.3%; change 1960–70, –4.9%. Metro. 27.2%, 22.7% central city.

1970 Share of Federal Outlays $325,483,643

DOD	$15,787,000	HEW	$98,111,297
AEC	$000	HUD	$1,480,000
NASA	$000	OEO	$402,495
DOT	$3,399,183	DOA	$142,485,528
		Other	$63,318,140

Federal Military-Industrial Commitments

DOD Contractors Needham Packing Co. (Sioux City), $7.950m: foodstuffs.

Economic Base Livestock and cash grain; food and kindred products, esp. meat products; nonelectrical machinery.

The Voters

Registration No district-wide registration.
Employment profile White collar, 34%. Blue collar, 66%.
Ethnic groups Black, less than 0.5%. Total foreign stock, 20%. Germany, 7%; Sweden, Norway, 2% each; UK, Canada, Ireland, 1% each; others, 7%.

Presidential vote

1968	Humphrey (D)	59,311	(37%)
	Nixon (R)	96,279	(59%)
	Wallace (AIP)	6,926	(4%)

Representative

Wiley Mayne (R) Elected 1966; b. Jan. 18, 1917, Sanborn; home, Sioux City; Harvard Col., B.S., 1938; Iowa Law School, J.D., 1941; USR, 1943–45; married, three children; Presbyterian.

Career Special Agent, FBI, 1941–43; trial lawyer, 1946–67; Pres., Iowa State Bar Assn., 1963–64; Chm., Grievance Commission of Iowa Supreme Ct., 1964–66; Commissioner of Uniform State Laws, 1956–60.

Offices 114 CHOB, 202-225-5476. Also 320 Fed. Bldg., Sioux City 51101, 712-252-4161, ext. 281.

Committees

Agriculture (7th); Subs. (1) Conservation and Credit, (2) Department Operations, (3) Livestock and Grains.
Judiciary (13th); Sub. No. 1.

Group Ratings

	ADA	COPE	NREP	NFU	LCV	CFA	NAB	NSI	ACA
1970	24	9	33	46	25	57	100	89	78
1969	7	—	—	40	—	—	—	—	65
1968	0	0	—	36	—	—	83	—	70

Key Votes

(1) ABM	FOR	(6) 18-Yr-Vote	AGN	(11) Clean Water $	AGN
(2) SST	ABS*	(7) Farm Sub Lmt	FOR	(12) Mig Wrkrs Comp	AGN
(3) Phil Pln	FOR	(8) Coop-Church	AGN	(13) Jets to Chiang	AGN
(4) No-Knock	FOR	(9) Family Asst	FOR	(14) State OEO Veto	FOR
(5) Cmutr Tax	AGN	(10) Work Stamps	FOR	(15) Park Logging	FOR

* *Voted "against" in previous vote on same issue.*

Election Results

1970 general:	Wiley Mayne (R)	57,285	(57%)
	Fred H. Moore (D)	43,257	(43%)
1970 primary:	Wiley Mayne (R), unopposed		
1968 general:	Wiley Mayne (R)	100,802	(65%)
	Jerry O'Sullivan (D)	54,171	(35%)

SEVENTH DISTRICT Political Background

Iowa 7, a largely rural district, occupies the southwest corner of the state. But the 7th does include the city of Council Bluffs, which lies across the Missouri River from Omaha, and also includes the part of Des Moines' exurban sprawl which extends into Dallas County. Dallas, along with a few counties in the 7th's northern tier (Carroll, Crawford, Monona), sometimes ends up in the Democratic column. But the district is best described as Iowa's most Republican; no major Democrat has carried it since 1964. Council Bluffs, a railroad and meatpacking center that has not grown like the rest of the Omaha metropolitan area, is a solidly Republican town, the most Republican of any Iowa city over 50,000.

The recent history of the 7th's congressional representation is similar to that of most other Iowa districts. From 1938 until 1964, Goldwater's year, its congressman was Ben Franklin Jensen, a staunchly conservative Republican. After a two-year Democratic interlude, the Republicans won again, in the person of William Scherle, a far younger but only slightly less conservative man than Rep. Jensen. Scherle, who now serves on the House Appropriations Committee, was treated gently by the Republican redistricters and should have no trouble winning reelection.

Census Data 1970 pop. 339,061; deviation from current state average, —16.0%; change 1960–70, —4.0%. Metro. 25.7%, 0.0% central city.

1970 Share of Federal Outlays $322,545,620

DOD	$24,290,000	HEW	$86,285,001
AEC	$000	HUD	$1,000
NASA	$000	OEO	$349,550
DOT	$22,755,371	DOA	$130,279,285
		Other	$58,585,413

Federal Military-Industrial Commitments

DOD Contractors World Wide Meats (Denison), $18.383m: foodstuffs.

Economic Base Livestock and cash grain; food and kindred products, esp. meat products.

The Voters

Registration No district-wide registration.

Employment profile White collar, 32%. Blue collar, 68%.

Ethnic groups Black, less than 0.5%. Total foreign stock, 13%. Germany, 5%; Sweden, UK, Canada, Ireland, 1% each; others, 5%.

Presidential vote

1968	Humphrey (D)	50,258	(36%)
	Nixon (R)	80,839	(57%)
	Wallace (AIP)	10,283	(7%)

Representative

William J. Scherle (R) Elected 1966; b. March 14, 1923, Little Falls, N.Y.; home, Henderson; So. Methodist U.; USNR, WWII; married, two children; Catholic.

Career Grain and livestock farmer; Asst. Div. Mgr., George D. Barnard Co., Dallas, Tex.; Iowa House of Reps., 1958–66.

Offices 512 CHOB, 202-225-3806. Also Fed. Bldg., P.O. Box S, Council Bluffs 51501, 712-323-3577.

Committees

Appropriations (20th); Subs. (1) Agriculture, Environmental and Consumer Protection, (2) District of Columbia.

Group Ratings

	ADA	COPE	NREP	NFU	LCV	CFA	NAB	NSI	ACA
1970	8	27	0	38	50	21	80	100	88
1969	7	—	—	23	—	—	—	—	94
1968	0	9	—	38	—	—	100	—	95

Key Votes

(1) ABM	FOR	(6) 18-Yr-Vote	AGN	(11) Clean Water $	AGN
(2) SST	AGN	(7) Farm Sub Lmt	AGN	(12) Mig Wrkrs Comp	AGN
(3) Phil Pln	AGN	(8) Coop-Church	AGN	(13) Jets to Chiang	ABS
(4) No-Knock	FOR	(9) Family Asst	AGN	(14) State OEO Veto	FOR
(5) Cmutr Tax	AGN	(10) Work Stamps	FOR	(15) Park Logging	ABS

Election Results

1970 general:	William J. Scherle (R)	53,084	(63%)
	Lou Galetich (D)	31,552	(37%)
1970 primary:	William J. Scherle (R), unopposed		
1968 general:	William J. Scherle (R)	87,212	(65%)
	Richard Oshlo (D)	46,774	(35%)

KANSAS

Political Background

The political history of Kansas began in the late 1850's when slave-holding Democrats from Missouri and points south waged a bloody struggle with free-soil Republicans and abolitionists from the upper Midwest and New England for control of the territorial government. The guerrilla war on the Kansas frontier, which the inept James Buchanan mishandled completely, so inflamed the nation's sectional animosities that it became the proximate cause of the Civil War. By that time, Kansas had been admitted to the Union as a free state with the Republican party in solid control. And there it has remained, with few exceptions, ever since.

The major exception to the pattern occurred during the depression of the 1890's with the Populist revolt. During the 10 or 15 years before the depression, years of unusually high rainfall on the Great Plains, Kansas attracted many new settlers, most of whom were Republicans from the upper Midwest. But soon the rainfall returned to normal—contrary to the slogan, the rain did not follow the plow. The climatic change, coupled with a worldwide drop in commodity prices, showed that the new Kansas farmland could not support all the migrants who had come to live on it. The state was boom and then bust, and many of those busted went home and are now forgotten by local historical societies. Some Kansas counties have never again reached the populations recorded in the 1890 census.

The economic crisis produced Kansas political leaders who forsook their ancestral Republicanism: among them, Mrs. Mary Ellen Lease ("What you farmers need to do is raise less corn and more hell") and "Sockless" Jerry Simpson, a Populist congressman from the state. Mary Ellen Lease, Jerry Simpson, and the simple farmers of the Populist party became the advocates of the complex doctrines of free silver and commodity credit programs. William Jennings Bryan, lion of the prairies, was their man, and he swept the state in 1896.

The period of Populist dominance—colorful, revivalistic, desperate—was soon over. Around 1900 the nation began to enjoy a decade or so of agricultural prosperity, and this along with the jingoism of the Spanish-American War and the Alaskan gold that loosened up the money market seemed to satisfy the farmers and killed their interest in Populistic radicalism and free silver. With the small-town Republicans and Rotarians back in control, Bryan could not carry Kansas in 1900 and 1908. This left William Allen White of the Emporia *Gazette* the state's resident radical; few other Kansans showed any kind of enthusiasm for the reforms of the Progressive era.

But echoes of the great farm revolt of the 1890's can still be heard in Kansas politics. As in most of the Great Plains states, fewer and fewer Kansans can make a living as farmers, even though the state's economy depends heavily on money generated by agriculture. Since the farmers never seem to have it very good, there is always discontent with the Administration in Washington and its farm program, and usually that Administration, whatever the party, suffers when Kansans go to the polls.

In 1970, therefore, it was not overly surprising to find the state's voters reelecting their Democratic governor, Robert Docking, to an unprecedented third term and also electing a Democratic attorney general. To be sure, these two Democrats would not pass muster on the upper West Side of New York: the Governor's proudest accomplishments were keeping state and local taxes down and taking a firm hand in campus disorders, while the Attorney General, a former sheriff of Sedgwick County (Wichita), campaigned on a law-and-order platform against a 32-year-old Harvard Law graduate.

Kansas Democrats, like their counterparts in other Midwestern farm states (see Iowa state write-up), have adapted themselves very nicely to the local political ethos. Their margins of victory come from the state's large cities—Wichita, Kansas City, and Topeka—and from assorted Democratic or marginal enclaves in various parts of the state. But these votes are not ordinarily available to candidates put up by the national Democratic party. Hubert Humphrey carried only 1 of the state's 105 counties in 1968, and John Kennedy only 2 in 1960. Even Lyndon Johnson in 1964 took just 55% of the state's votes.

The most surprising of the state's 1970 results was the election of a Democrat, Dr. William Roy, to Congress from the 2nd district. His election was the first Democratic victory in the district in 63 years and the first time any Kansas Democrat had been elected to the House since 1960.

The state's two Republican senators have little to worry about in Kansas general elections. Bob Dole, who was elected to the Senate in 1968 after eight years in the House, has become known widely as the spirited and self-appointed defender of the Nixon Administration. Dole was so ardent in his support of the President that the freshman senator has now become Republican National Chairman. The state's other Republican senator, James B. Pearson, is something of an apostate. First appointed to fill a vacancy in 1962, Pearson subsequently won elections in that year and in 1966. The Senator was reelected in 1966 after a primary fight with then-Congressman Robert Ellsworth, who campaigned as a Republican liberal. The roles are now reversed. Ellsworth, a key Nixon backer in 1968, is currently Permanent Representative to NATO, while Pearson voted against the Administration on the ABM and Haynsworth nomination and came very close to voting against Carswell.

In 1972 Pearson could himself be faced with conservative primary opposition. Whether he will or not depends on the White House and whether the Administration thinks it is getting the kind of support it deserves from a Kansas Republican. Since most Kansas Republican primary voters are staunchly Republican, the threat of opposition in the primary is a potent one. Beyond that, it seems unlikely that Pearson, or any other Republican candidate for the Senate, can be beaten in a Kansas general election. The last Democrat to win did so in 1932.

Electoral Votes 7

Census Data 1970 pop. 2,249,071; 1.09% of U.S. total, 29th largest; change 1960–70, +3.2%. Metro. 42.3%, 17.9% central city. 1970 per capita income, $3,804, 18th highest. 34th in number of poor.

1970 Share of Federal Tax Burden $1,990,430,000; 1.02% of U.S. total, 26th largest.

1970 Share of Federal Outlays $2,279,588,066; 1.21% of U.S. total, 29th largest. Per capita federal spending, $1,014.

DOD	$582,242,000	29th (1.01%)	HEW	$550,802,764	29th (1.05%)
AEC	$857,496	37th (0.03%)	HUD	$32,025,187	22nd (1.64%)
NASA	$1,101,623	37th (0.03%)	OEO	$3,994,989	38th (0.53%)
DOT	$60,038,647	38th (0.53%)	DOA	$563,960,448	7th (4.39%)
DOC	$3,980,575	36th (0.34%)	POD	$83,918,179	27th (1.15%)
DOI	$25,241,343	29th (1.09%)	VA	$114,173,861	28th (1.56%)
DOJ	$8,745,092	18th (1.52%)	CSC	$27,223,987	32nd (0.68%)
			Other	$484,564,912	

Economic Base Livestock and cash grain; aircraft and parts, and other transportation equipment; food and kindred products, esp. meat products; printing, publishing, and allied industries, esp. newspapers; chemicals and allied products, crude petroleum and natural gas; stone, clay, glass, and concrete products; fabricated metal products.

Political Line-up Governor, Robert Docking (D); seat up, 1972. Senators, James B. Pearson (R) and Bob Dole (R). Representatives, 5 (1 D and 4 R). State Senate (8 D and 32 R); State House (41 D and 84 R).

The Voters

Registration No statewide registration.

Employment profile White collar, 42%. Blue collar, 58%.

Ethnic groups Black, 5%. Total foreign stock, 9%. Germany, 3%; UK, USSR, Sweden, Mexico, Canada, 1% each; others, 2%.

Presidential vote

1968	Humphrey (D)	302,996	(35%)
	Nixon (R)	478,674	(55%)
	Wallace (AIP)	88,921	(10%)
1964	Johnson (D)	464,028	(55%)
	Goldwater (R)	386,579	(45%)
1960	Kennedy (D)	363,213	(39%)
	Nixon (R)	561,474	(61%)

Senator

James Blackwood Pearson (R) Elected Feb. 5, 1962, seat up 1974; b. May 7, 1920, Nashville, Tenn.; home, Prairie Village; Duke U., 1940–42; U. of Va. Law School, LL.B., 1950; Navy, WWII; married, four children; Presbyterian.

Career Practicing atty., 1950–62; Probate Judge, Johnson County, 1954–66; Kans. Senate, 1956–60; State Rep. Chm., 1960–61; Campaign Mgr. for Governor Anderson, 1960.

Offices 4327 NSOB, 202-225-4774. Also 600 Merchants' Natl. Bank Bldg., Topeka 66612, 913-357-4312, and 5410 W. 58th Terrace, Shawnee Mission 66205, 913-262-0002.

Committees

Commerce (3rd); Subs. (1) Aviation, (2) Consumer, (3) Environment, (4) Surface Transportation, (5) Sp. on Freight Car Shortage.

Foreign Relations (7th); Subs. (1) African Affairs, (2) Arms Control, International Law and Organization, (3) European Affairs, (4) Near Eastern and South Asian Affairs.

Jt. Economic Committee (4th); Subs. (1) Economic Progress, (2) Inter-American Economic Relationships, (3) Priorities and Economy in Government.

Group Ratings

	ADA	COPE	NREP	NFU	LCV	NAB	NSI	ACA
1970	28	46	42	60	14	80	80	56
1969	33	—	—	56	—	—	—	47
1968	21	34	—	62	—	60	—	72

Key Votes

(1) ABM	AGN	(8) Phil Pln	ABS	(15) Coop-Church	FOR
(2) SST	FOR	(9) Vol Army	FOR	(16) Cut Oil Dpltn	AGN
(3) Busing	FOR	(10) Prison $	AGN	(17) Consumer Prot	FOR
(4) Tob Sub	FOR	(11) Cut Mil $	FOR	(18) Farm Sub Limit	AGN
(5) Carswell	FOR	(12) Defoliatn	FOR	(19) Comp Bid Sales	FOR
(6) No-Knock	FOR	(13) 18-Yr-Vote	FOR	(20) Pre-Prod Tests	AGN
(7) Seniorty	AGN	(14) Pentgn PR	AGN	(21) Cut Marjna Pen	FOR

Election Results

1966 general:	James B. Pearson (R)	350,077	(52%)
	J. Floyd Breeding (D)	303,223	(45%)
	Earl F. Dodge (Prohib.)	9,364	(1%)
	George W. Snell (Cons.)	7,103	(1%)
1966 primary:	James B. Pearson (R)	101,523	(50%)
	Robert Ellsworth (R)	83,083	(41%)
	Ava V. Anderson (R)	10,095	(5%)
	William D. Tarrant (R)	7,222	(4%)
1962 special:	James B. Pearson (R)	344,689	(56%)
	Paul L. Aylward (D)	260,756	(39%)
	E. E. Cowen (Prohib.)	7,804	(1%)

Senator

Robert J. Dole (R) Elected 1968, seat up 1974; b. July 22, 1923, Russell; home, Russell; U. of Kans., 1941–43; Washburn Municipal U., B.A., 1952, LL.B., 1952; Army, 1943–48; married, one child; Methodist.

Career Kans. House of Reps., 1951–53; Russell County Atty., 1953–61; U.S. House of Reps., 1960–68; Repub. Natl. Com. Chm., 1971– .

Offices 2327 NSOB, 202-225-6521. Also 708 Central St., Dodge City 67801, 316-225-4322.

Committees

Agriculture and Forestry (5th); Subs. (1) Agricultural Credit and Rural Electrification, (2) Agricultural Research and General Legislation, (3) Rural Development.

Public Works (4th); Subs. (1) Air and Water Pollution, (2) Economic Development, (3) Flood Control—Rivers and Harbors.

Sel. Com. on Nutrition and Human Needs (Ranking Mbr.).

Sel. Com. on Small Business (4th); Subs. (1) Government Procurement, (2) Monopoly, (3) Retailing, Distribution, and Marketing Practices.

Group Ratings

	ADA	COPE	NREP	NFU	LCV	NAB	NSI	ACA
1970	13	15	33	43	20	91	89	76
1969	0	—	—	25	—	—	—	64

Key Votes

(1) ABM	FOR	(8) Phil Pln	AGN	(15) Coop-Church	FOR
(2) SST	FOR	(9) Vol Army	FOR	(16) Cut Oil Dpltn	AGN
(3) Busing	FOR	(10) Prison $	ABS	(17) Consumer Prot	AGN
(4) Tob Sub	FOR	(11) Cut Mil $	AGN	(18) Farm Sub Limit	AGN
(5) Carswell	FOR	(12) Defoliatn	FOR	(19) Comp Bid Sales	FOR
(6) No-Knock	FOR	(13) 18-Yr-Vote	FOR	(20) Pre-Prod Tests	AGN
(7) Seniorty	AGN	(14) Pentgn PR	FOR	(21) Cut Marjna Pen	AGN

Election Results

1968 general:	Bob Dole (R)	490,911	(60%)
	William I. Robinson (D)	315,911	(39%)
	Joseph F. Hyskell (Prohib.)	10,262	(1%)
1968 primary:	Bob Dole (R)	190,782	(68%)
	William H. Avery (R)	87,801	(32%)

FIRST DISTRICT Political Background

Kansas 1 is a wheat and livestock district which takes up more than half of the state geographically. About half of the 1st lies west of the 100th meridian, which was used in the early nineteenth century to mark the beginning of the Great American

Desert. The region between the meridian and the Rocky Mountains was supposed to be too arid for farming and suitable only for grazing. In some places irrigation has changed this, but here in the western part of the 1st district the landscape is desertlike —treeless, slightly rolling brown fields sectioned off here and there by barbed-wire fence. The small towns in the district, commercial centers for the farmers, have the usual grain elevators and main streets lined on both sides by Victorian storefronts. The towns include Salina, at 37,000 the largest in the district; Dodge City, Matt Dillon's town; Holcolm, made famous by Truman Capote's *In Cold Blood*; and Hays, a predominantly German Catholic enclave that usually votes heavily Democratic.

The 1st is a predominantly Republican district, but discontent among the farmers occasionally shows itself in the district's politics. Back in 1956, 1958, and 1960, the western half of the present district (Kansas then had six districts) elected Democrat J. Floyd Breeding to the House. After the 1960 census, his district was combined with that of then-Rep. Bob Dole. Dole, as the Republican state legislators expected, defeated Breeding in 1962. The Republican Congressman had a close race in 1964, winning with less than 51% of the votes, but did so well in 1966 (69%) that his election to the Senate two years later came as no surprise. He was succeeded by another conservative Republican, Keith Sebelius, who won in 1968 with only 52%. In 1970, having the advantages of two years' incumbency, Sebelius increased his margin to 57%. Yet by standards employed by Kansas Republicans, 57% is not a particularly strong showing. The 1st could produce an upset in 1972 if the farm revolt continues to gather momentum and the Democrats put up a strong candidate.

Census Data 1970 pop. 406,610; deviation from current state average, —9.6%; change 1960–70, —6.6%. Metro. 0.0%, 0.0% central city.

1970 Share of Federal Outlays $504,819,401

DOD	$8,837,000	HEW	$97,651,428
AEC	$000	HUD	$398,900
NASA	$000	OEO	$70,343
DOT	$11,813,420	DOA	$296,698,313
		Other	$189,347,562

Federal Military-Industrial Commitments

None.

Economic Base Cash grain and livestock; crude petroleum and natural gas; aircraft and parts.

The Voters

Registration No district-wide registration.

Employment profile White collar, 36%. Blue collar, 64%.

Ethnic groups Black, 1%. Total foreign stock, 11%. German, 3%; USSR, 2%; UK, Sweden, Czech., Canada, Austria, 1% each; others, 3%.

Presidential vote

1968	Humphrey (D)	55,355	(32%)
	Nixon (R)	102,106	(59%)
	Wallace (AIP)	14,932	(9%)

Representative

Keith G. Sebelius (R) Elected 1968; b. Sept. 10, 1916, Almena; home, Norton; Fort Hays Kans. State Col., B.A.; George Washington U. Law School, J.D., 1939; Army, WWII and Korean War; married, two children; Methodist.

Career Practicing atty., City Councilman, Mayor, City Atty., County Atty., Norton; Kans. State Senate, 1962–68; Legislative Council, 4 yrs.

Offices 1117 LHOB, 202-225-2715. Also P.O. Box 40, Hays 67601, 913-628-1313.

Committees

Agriculture (10th); Subs. (1) Department Operations, (2) Livestock and Grains.

Interior and Insular Affairs (13th); Subs. (1) Environment, (2) Indian Affairs, (3) National Parks and Recreation, (4) Territorial and Insular Affairs.

Group Ratings

	ADA	COPE	NREP	NFU	LCV	CFA	NAB	NSI	ACA
1970	8	9	0	25	0	50	92	100	82
1969	0	—	—	20	—	—	—	—	86

Key Votes

(1) ABM	ABS	(6) 18-Yr-Vote	AGN	(11) Clean Water $	AGN
(2) SST	FOR	(7) Farm Sub Lmt	AGN	(12) Mig Wrkrs Comp	AGN
(3) Phil Pln	FOR	(8) Coop-Church	AGN	(13) Jets to Chiang	FOR
(4) No-Knock	FOR	(9) Family Asst	AGN	(14) State OEO Veto	FOR
(5) Cmutr Tax	AGN	(10) Work Stamps	ABS	(15) Park Logging	FOR

Election Results

1970 general:	Keith G. Sebelius (R)	83,923	(57%)
	Billy D. Jellison (D)	63,791	(43%)
1970 primary:	Keith G. Sebelius (R), unopposed		
1968 general:	Keith G. Sebelius (R)	87,012	(52%)
	George W. Meeker (D)	82,102	(49%)

SECOND DISTRICT Political Background

Kansas 2, in the northeast corner of the state, is a district dominated by Topeka. The 2nd is not an undifferentiated rural area. The district includes the suburban portions of heavily Democratic Wyandot County outside Kansas City, the old Missouri River towns of Leavenworth and Atchison, which sometimes vote Democratic, and, to the west, the towns of Manhattan and Junction City, which flank the Army's huge Fort Riley. About a third of the district's votes are cast in Topeka and surrounding Shawnee County. These votes are usually in line with the prevailing Kansas trend—Republican in national elections and often Democratic in state contests.

The 2nd was the scene of Kansas' big political upset of 1970 when Dr. William Roy, a Democrat, ousted Rep. Chester Mize. In 1968, Mize was the top vote-getter in the all-Republican Kansas House delegation with 68% of the ballots. Two years later, he was the low man with 45%. The 21-point difference was not the result of Mize's performance in the House, where he was a low-seniority, conservative Republican, but rather the result of the campaign waged by his opponent. Dr. Roy, a Topeka gynecologist and lawyer, had been a registered Republican until he filed for the 1970 congressional election. He conducted an active and well-financed campaign, including a large volume of direct mail. One of his political assets was reportedly the support he received from many of his quondam gynecological patients.

The doctor-lawyer wound up carrying enough votes in the urban counties of the district for a convincing victory; particularly notable was his showing in Shawnee County, where he won 58% of the votes. Dr. Roy's victory shows that it is possible to unseat an incumbent even in a district where your party's presidential candidate received only 33% of the votes two years before. The Republican legislature has, if anything, strengthened Roy's chances for reelection by adding a portion of heavily Democratic Kansas City to the district.

Census Data 1970 pop. 479,599; deviation from current state average, +6.6%; change 1960–70, +6.4%. Metro. 39.7%, 26.1% central city.

1970 Share of Federal Outlays $601,808,361

DOD	$272,057,000	HEW	$119,830,215
AEC	$426,906	HUD	$6,627,279
NASA	$53,994	OEO	$654,192
DOT	$10,720,965	DOA	$69,656,163
		Other	$121,781,647

Federal Military-Industrial Commitments

DOD Contractors United States Justice Department (Leavenworth), $5.487m: legal services.

DOD Installations Fort Leavenworth AB (Leavenworth). Fort Riley (Junction City). Forbes AFB (Topeka).

Economic Base Livestock and cash grain; food and kindred products, esp. meat products; nonelectrical machinery. Also, higher education (Kansas State University).

The Voters

Registration No district-wide registration.

Employment profile White collar, 41%. Blue collar, 59%.

Ethnic groups Black, 6%. Total foreign stock, 11%. German, 4%; UK, Sweden, Canada, Mexico, 1% each; others, 4%.

Presidential vote

1968	Humphrey (D)	54,814	(33%)
	Nixon (R)	92,559	(56%)
	Wallace (AIP)	18,004	(11%)

Representative

William R. Roy, Sr. (D) Elected 1970; b. Feb. 23, 1926, Bloomington, Ill.; home, Topeka; Ill. Wesleyan U., B.S., 1945; Northwestern U., M.D., 1948; Washburn U. School of Law, J.D., 1970; USAF, 1953–55; married, six children; United Methodist Church.

Career Practicing physician, 1953–70; Delegate, White House Conference on Children and Youth, 1960; Pres., Shawnee County Medical Society, 1967; Delegate, five times, Kans. Med. Soc., V. Speaker, Kans. Med. Soc. House of Delegates, 1969.

Offices 1118 LHOB, 202-225-6601. Also 1100 Merchants Natl. Bank Bldg., Kansas City 66101, 913-621-0832.

Committees

Interstate and Foreign Commerce (25th); Sub. on Public Health and Environment.

Group Ratings, Key Votes: Newly elected.

Election Results

1970 general:	Dr. William R. Roy (D)	80,161	(52%)
	Chester L. Mize (R)	68,843	(45%)
	Fred Kilian (C)	4,145	(3%)
1970 primary:	Dr. William R. Roy (D), unopposed		

THIRD DISTRICT Political Background

Kansas 3 contains the most Democratic and the most Republican parts of the state, both of which lie in the Kansas City metropolitan area. Nearly 80% of the district's population live in either heavily Democratic Wyandot County (Kansas City, much smaller than its Missouri neighbor) or heavily Republican Johnson County (prosperous Kansas City suburbs, including Overland Park, Prairie Village, and Shawnee). A single street separates the Johnson County suburbs from Kansas City, Missouri, yet a disproportionate number of the city's wealthy, conservative citizens have chosen to live on the Kansas side of the line. The only political issue about which Johnson and Wyandot counties can agree is liquor by the glass; both supported it heavily in the 1970 referendum, though it was defeated statewide by a narrow margin.

Also included in the 3rd district are a couple of agricultural counties and the city of Lawrence, home of the radicalized University of Kansas. A large number of street people have come to Lawrence (known in the underground press as River City), reportedly because marijuana is easily grown in the surrounding fields. Lawrence has had several student-police confrontations, fully as bitter, if not as well publicized, as those on the East and West coasts.

The 3rd is therefore not a typical Kansas congressional district, and election results here differ significantly from those in the rest of the state. In 1968 Hubert Humphrey —and George Wallace—made their best Kansas showings in the 3rd; some white-collar voters in Johnson County moved away from the law-and-order Nixon-Agnew line and voted for Humphrey, while some blue-collar workers in Wyandot County deserted the Democrats for Wallace.

Ever since moderate Republican Robert Ellsworth retired from the House in 1966 to seek James Pearson's Senate seat, congressional races in the district have been close. In 1970 the Democrats made a strong bid, running Lt. Gov. James DeCoursey against the incumbent Republican Larry Winn, Jr. Winn took 53% of the votes, carrying Johnson County by nearly 15,000, while losing Wyandot by about 8,000. Douglas County (Lawrence) and the rural areas gave Winn a very slight edge.

The result was probably not too comfortable for the Republicans; Winn had won 63% two years before. The 1971 redistricters subtracted a portion of Kansas City from the 3rd and therefore made the district somewhat safer for Winn in 1972.

Census Data 1970 pop. 477,498; deviation from current state average, +6.2%; change 1960–70, +21.2%. Metro. 77.6%, 0.0% central city.

1970 Share of Federal Outlays $317,838,706

DOD	$66,371,000	HEW	$102,210,217
AEC	$407,659	HUD	$8,686,266
NASA	$515,062	OEO	$1,222,224
DOT	$15,948,582	DOA	$19,568,898
		Other	$102,908,798

Federal Military-Industrial Commitments

DOD Contractors Hercules, Inc. (Lawrence), $36.907m: operation of Sunflower Army Ammunition Plant and production of rocket propellant.

Economic Base Livestock and cash grain; food and kindred products, esp. meat products; stone, clay, glass, and concrete products; printing, publishing, and allied products. Also, higher education (University of Kansas).

The Voters

Registration No district-wide registration.

Employment profile White collar, 49%. Blue collar, 51%.

Ethnic groups Black, 8%. Total foreign stock, 9%. German, 2%; UK, Mexico, USSR, Canada, Poland, 1% each; others, 4%.

Presidential vote

1968	Humphrey (D)	71,328	(38%)
	Nixon (R)	96,711	(51%)
	Wallace (AIP)	21,403	(11%)

Representative

Larry Winn, Jr. (R) Elected 1966; b. Aug. 22, 1919, Kansas City, Mo.; home, Overland Park; U. of Kans., B.A., 1941; married, five children; Protestant.

Career Radio announcer, WHB; builder; Pub. Relations Dir., American Red Cross; V.P., Winn-Rau Corp., 1950– ; Natl. Dir., Home Builders Assn.; Past GOP Chm., 3rd Dist. Kansas; Mbr., Repub. State Exec. Com. of Kans.; Mbr., Kans. U. Development Com.; Dir., Southgate State Bank.

Offices 428 CHOB, 202-225-2865. Also 204 Fed. Bldg., Kansas City 66101, 913-621-0832.

Committees

Science and Astronautics (6th); Subs. (1) International Cooperation in Science and Space, (2) Manned Space Flight, (3) Space Sciences and Applications.

Veterans' Affairs (8th); (1) Education and Training, (2) Hospitals, (3) Housing.

Sel. Com. on Crime (3rd).

Group Ratings

	ADA	COPE	NREP	NFU	LCV	CFA	NAB	NSI	ACA
1970	4	17	0	25	0	33	75	100	72
1969	0	—	—	33	—	—	—	—	64
1968	0	9	—	38	—	—	100	—	83

Key Votes

(1) ABM	ABS	(6) 18-Yr-Vote	AGN	(11) Clean Water $	AGN
(2) SST	FOR	(7) Farm Sub Lmt	AGN	(12) Mig Wrkrs Comp	AGN
(3) Phil Pln	FOR	(8) Coop-Church	AGN	(13) Jets to Chiang	FOR
(4) No-Knock	FOR	(9) Family Asst	AGN	(14) State OEO Veto	FOR
(5) Cmutr Tax	AGN	(10) Work Stamps	ABS	(15) Park Logging	FOR

Election Results

1970 general:	Larry Winn, Jr. (R)	74,603	(53%)
	James H. DeCoursey, Jr. (D)	64,344	(46%)
	Warren E. Redding (C)	1,820	(1%)
1970 primary:	Larry Winn, Jr. (R)	33,138	(81%)
	A. O. Tetzlaff (R)	7,913	(19%)
1968 general:	Larry Winn, Jr. (R)	100,877	(63%)
	Newell A. George (D)	59,672	(37%)

FOURTH DISTRICT Political Background

Kansas 4 is the Wichita district. More than half of the district's voters live in the city, and about a quarter of the remainder live in that part of surrounding Sedgwick County within the 4th (part of Sedgwick lies in the 5th). Wichita, like all Kansas cities, is an agricultural service center, but it is also a manufacturing city, most notably of airplanes. Boeing, whose problems have been well publicized, has a large plant here. Cutbacks in the aircraft industry as well as specific cutbacks at the Wichita Boeing plant have shown themselves in the population figures for metropolitan Wichita—virtually no growth during the '60's.

Many of the people who streamed into Wichita during and after World War II to man the aircraft and other factories were from the South, particularly nearby Oklahoma and Arkansas. The influence of these migrants is reflected in the district's voting habits. In presidential elections, the 4th is steadfastly Republican conservative: Humphrey had only 37% of the votes here, while Nixon took 54%. But in statewide elections, the voters often go Democratic; in 1970, they turned in big margins for Gov. Robert Docking and new Attorney General Vern Miller, former Sedgwick County sheriff.

In congressional contests, Wichita and the 4th vote as they do in presidential elections and have since 1960 elected and reelected Rep. Garner E. Shriver (no relation to the Kennedy kin). Shriver's seat on the House Appropriations Committee, to which only orthodox Republicans are usually appointed, attests to the Congressman's conservatism. He serves as a middle-ranking Republican on the committee. Shriver has been a remarkably consistent vote-getter; in 1964, when many Kansas Republicans suffered from Goldwater's candidacy, Shriver still took 59% and in 1970, a normal year, 63%. His prospects for continued reelection are bright.

Census Data 1970 pop. 462,528; deviation from current state average, +2.8%; change 1960–70, –0.1%. Metro. 68.0%, 59.7% central city.

1970 Share of Federal Outlays $523,306,322

DOD	$190,126,000	HEW	$106,638,999
AEC	$22,931	HUD	$13,879,550
NASA	$530,132	OEO	$1,516,649

DOT	$17,497,733	DOA	$101,190,810
		Other	$91,903,518

Federal Military-Industrial Commitments

DOD Contractors Boeing (Wichita), $43.597m: B-52 weapons system development; modification of B-52 and C-135 aircraft. Cessna Aircraft (Wichita), $38.264m: H-37 aircraft and spare parts; maintenance of other aircraft. Beech Aircraft (Wichita), $24.185m: U-21 series utility aircraft.

DOD Installations McConnell AFB (Wichita).

Economic Base Cash grain and livestock; nonelectrical machinery, esp. farm machinery and equipment and general industrial machinery and equipment; food and kindred products; aircraft and parts. Also, higher education (Wichita State University).

The Voters

Registration No district-wide registration.

Employment profile White collar, 47%. Blue collar, 53%.

Ethnic groups Black, 6%. Total foreign stock, 8%. Germany, USSR, 2% each; UK, Mexico, Sweden, Canada, 1% each; others, 2%.

Presidential vote

1968	Humphrey (D)	60,339	(37%)
	Nixon (R)	87,658	(54%)
	Wallace (AIP)	14,278	(9%)

Representative

Garner E. Shriver (R) Elected 1960; b. July 6, 1912, Towanda; home, Wichita; U. of Wichita, B.A., 1934; U. of So. Calif., 1936; Washburn U. Law School, J.D., 1940; Navy, WWII; married, three children; Methodist.

Career English Speech Instr., 1936–37; practicing atty., 1940–60; Kans. House of Reps., 1947–51; Kans. Senate, 1953–60.

Offices 2439 RHOB, 202-225-6216. Also 830 N. Main, Wichita 62703, 316-265-7111, and 210 P.O. Bldg., Hutchinson 67501, 316-662-0737.

Committees

Appropriations (10th); Subs. (1) Foreign Operations, (2) Labor and HEW.

Group Ratings

	ADA	COPE	NREP	NFU	LCV	CFA	NAB	NSI	ACA
1970	12	34	18	54	0	41	83	100	67
1969	7	—	—	60	—	—	—	—	53
1968	0	15	—	50	—	—	100	—	82

Key Votes

(1) ABM	FOR	(6) 18-Yr-Vote	AGN	(11) Clean Water $	AGN
(2) SST	FOR	(7) Farm Sub Lmt	ABS	(12) Mig Wrkrs Comp	AGN
(3) Phil Pln	FOR	(8) Coop-Church	AGN	(13) Jets to Chiang	FOR
(4) No-Knock	FOR	(9) Family Asst	AGN	(14) State OEO Veto	AGN
(5) Cmutr Tax	ABS	(10) Work Stamps	FOR	(15) Park Logging	FOR

Election Results

1970 general:	Garner E. Shriver (R)	85,058	(63%)
	James C. (Jim) Juhnke (D)	47,004	(35%)
	George W. Snell (C)	2,452	(2%)
1970 primary:	Garner E. Shriver (R)	34,311	(93%)
	Dell Crozier (R)	2,567	(7%)

1968 general:	Garner E. Shriver (R)	101,991	(65%)
	Patrick F. Kelly (D)	55,621	(35%)

FIFTH DISTRICT Political Background

Kansas 5 is a predominantly rural district, with no urban concentrations except for a portion of Sedgwick County adjoining the city of Wichita. It is not all farming country, however; in the southeast corner, there is an old coal-mining area around Pittsburg which has a significant East European ethnic population. That area is now in economic decline, and the district as a whole lost population during the '60's. In this southeast corner and in the environs of Wichita, there are some Democratic-leaning counties; but the residents here are Kansas Democrats, basically conservative people (often of Southern origin) who have not approved of the liberal presidential candidates the party has been putting up for the past 30 or 40 years. Most of the district, and especially some of the heavily WASP counties, is strongly Republican and conservative.

The 5th's congressman is Joe Skubitz, a moderate-to-conservative Republican who has proved, since he was first elected in 1962, to be very popular in the district. In 1970, he led all Kansas Republican congressmen with 66% of the votes. There appears to be nothing to prevent him from winning reelection indefinitely.

Census Data 1970 pop. 422,836; deviation from current state average, —6.0%; change 1960–70, —3.0%. Metro. 17.7%, 0.1% central city.

1970 Share of Federal Outlays $331,815,276

DOD	$44,851,000	HEW	$124,471,905
AEC	$000	HUD	$2,433,193
NASA	$000	OEO	$531,581
DOT	$4,057,947	DOA	$76,846,264
		Other	$78,623,387

Federal Military-Industrial Commitments

DOD Contractors Day and Zimmerman (Parsons), $31.001m: operation of Army Ammunition Plant and production of ammunition components and projectiles.

Economic Base Livestock and cash grain; food and kindred products; aircraft and parts; fabricated metal products; ordnance and accessories.

The Voters

Registration No district-wide registration.

Employment profile White collar, 37%. Blue collar, 63%.

Ethnic groups Black, 2%. Total foreign stock, 7%. Germany, 2%; UK, Italy, Mexico, 1% each; others, 3%.

Presidential vote

1968	Humphrey (D)	59,057	(34%)
	Nixon (R)	96,034	(55%)
	Wallace (AIP)	19,504	(11%)

Representative

Joe Skubitz (R) Elected 1962; b. May 6, 1906, Frontenac, Kans.; home, Pittsburg; Kans. State Col., B.S., 1929, M.S., 1934; Washburn U. Law School, 1938; George Washington U. Law School, LL.B., 1946; married, one child; Methodist.

Career Admin. Asst. to senators Clyde M. Reed and Andrew F. Schoeppel, 1952–62.

Offices 2447 RHOB, 202-225-3911. Also Pittsburg 66762, 316-231-6200; 206 E. 9th, Winfield 67156, 316-221-2020; and 601-1/2 Commercial, Emporia 66801, 316-342-6464.

Committees

Interior and Insular Affairs (3rd); Subs. (1) Mines and Mining, (2) National Parks and Recreation, (3) Territorial and Insular Affairs.

Interstate and Foreign Commerce (10th); Sub. on Transportation and Aeronautics.

Group Ratings

	ADA	COPE	NREP	NFU	LCV	CFA	NAB	NSI	ACA
1970	4	25	17	38	25	50	83	89	67
1969	7	—	—	47	—	—	—	—	56
1968	0	8	—	60	—	—	100	—	80

Key Votes

(1) ABM	FOR	(6) 18-Yr-Vote	AGN	(11) Clean Water $	AGN
(2) SST	FOR	(7) Farm Sub Lmt	AGN	(12) Mig Wrkrs Comp	AGN
(3) Phil Pln	ABS	(8) Coop-Church	AGN	(13) Jets to Chiang	AGN
(4) No-Knock	FOR	(9) Family Asst	FOR	(14) State OEO Veto	AGN
(5) Cmutr Tax	AGN	(10) Work Stamps	FOR	(15) Park Logging	AGN

Election Results

1970 general:	Joe Skubitz (R)	94,837	(66%)
	T. D. Saar, Jr. (D)	48,688	(34%)
1970 primary:	Joe Skubitz (R), unopposed		
1968 general:	Joe Skubitz (R)	107,085	(65%)
	A. F. Bramble (D)	59,005	(36%)

KENTUCKY

Political Background

In 1775 Daniel Boone made his way through the Cumberland Gap in the Appalachian Mountains and found what we know today as Kentucky—a fertile, virgin land of gentle, rolling hills. After the Revolutionary War, streams of people from Virginia traveled Boone's Wilderness Road and settled in the hills and countryside around Lexington. It was the nation's first frontier boom and, up to that time, one of the most extensive mass migrations in human history. The census of 1790 recorded 73,000 Kentuckians; by 1820 there were 564,000, which made the state the sixth largest in the nation. In those days, Kentucky was a frontier, its communities full of opportunity and unburdened by the hierarchies that structured the societies of coastal America. Henry Clay, for example, came to Kentucky from Virginia as a penniless young man. But by the time he was thirty he had done well enough in the law to build a mansion with silver doorknobs and well enough in Whig politics to become a United States senator.

In many respects Kentucky hasn't changed much since Clay's times. It is still a largely rural state; less than 25% of its residents live in greater Louisville, its one large metropolitan center. And in the last few decades, the state hasn't grown; in recent years, many Kentuckians have moved to the industrial cities of the Midwest and to California and Texas. Meanwhile, the tobacco fields and thoroughbred horse farms in the Bluegrass Region around Lexington are today pretty much as they always were; to the west, toward the Mississippi River, the landscape is also largely unchanged. But coal mining has left the once green mountains and hillsides of eastern Kentucky barren and erose. After a steady 30-year decline, the strip-mining technique has lately rejuvenated the industry in the state.

Kentucky politics, like that of many states east of the Mississippi River, is still based in large part on the divisions produced by the Civil War. In general, the eastern hill country was pro-Union and Republican. Some changes took place here during the 1930's when many miners and their families became Democrats. But south central Kentucky remains as heavily Republican as any part of the country. The western part of the state, which in appearance and economics is part of the South, retains its nineteenth-century allegiance to the Democratic party.

Up through the 1950's, the Democratic counties almost always outvoted the Republican ones. Kentucky politics, therefore, was like that of most Southern states: the real battles occurred in the Democratic primary, and a victory here, as the journalists used to put it, was tantamount to election. The most famous figure to come out of this era was Alben W. Barkley, who was congressman from Paducah from 1912 to 1926, senator from 1926 to 1948 (Majority Leader 1937–47), Vice President under Harry Truman, and senator again until his death in 1956.

But time has changed Kentucky's political patterns. Barkley's Democrats have not been able to carry the state in four of the last five presidential elections, while two Republicans occupy Kentucky's Senate seats. In statewide contests, the Democratic party has become notably more liberal since 1959, when Bert Combs replaced Chandler as governor. And the Republican party, particularly during the tenure of Gov. Louie B. Nunn (1967–71), has taken on an ideological conservatism unlike the traditional Republicanism of the Cumberland Plateau and more in line with the pattern found nationally.

The finest example of that earlier Republicanism is Sen. John Sherman Cooper, of Pulaski County (and also of Harvard and Yale). Cooper has been in and out of the Senate since the '40's, having been elected to fill unexpired terms in 1946, 1952, and 1956, finally winning a full six-year term in 1960. The Senator's major interest is foreign affairs; his expertise in the field has been recognized by appointments made by Administrations of both parties. Between Senate terms, he once served as ambassador to India. A member of the Foreign Relations Committee, Cooper is one of the Senate's leading opponents of the Vietnam war; he co-sponsored the Cooper-Church amendment, which prohibits the use of American ground troops in Cambodia and Laos. The Senator was also one of the leaders in the unsuccessful attempt to stop the development of the ABM.

Cooper is one of the Senate's most respected men, and his standing back home is so high that he would have no trouble winning reelection in 1972. But he has announced that he will retire at that time (when he will be 71). There will doubtless be a scramble for the seat. Possible candidates include conservative Republican Gov. Louie Nunn and Happy Chandler, onetime Democratic governor (1935–39, 1955–59) and baseball commissioner (1945–47). Chandler is currently conducting an independent campaign for governor. The state's Democratic party will probably put up a strong liberal candidate.

In 1968, Kentucky's junior senator, Marlow Cook, moved from county judge (an administrative post) of Jefferson County (Louisville) to the United States Senate, winning his seat by a narrow 37,000-vote margin. Like Cooper, the Republican Cook has sometimes made trouble for the Nixon Administration. Despite a personal plea from the President himself, Cook cast the deciding vote against the confirmation of Judge G. Harrold Carswell. But that vote is not the mark of the man. Earlier the Senator was the floor leader in the fight to confirm Judge Haynsworth. Cook has become another one of an increasing number of independent and unpredictable senators who take positions on what they see as the merits of each case. Since Cook seems to be inheriting Cooper's reputation as nonpartisan, the junior Senator will probably be unbeatable when he comes up for reelection in 1972.

Despite the likelihood of a clear-cut conservative Republican–liberal Democrat confrontation in the 1972 Senate race, congressional politics in the state is structured along more traditional lines. Each of Kentucky's seven districts is more or less a distinct area, with its character expressed by its congressman. The 1970 census will require some redrawing of the district lines, but none of the seats, with the exception of the 3rd (Louisville), seems likely to be contested vigorously.

Electoral Votes 9

Census Data 1970 pop., 3,219,311; 1.28% of U.S. total, 23rd largest; change 1960–70, +6.0%. Metro. 40.0%, 17.1% central city. 1970 per capita income, $3,060, 43rd highest. 23rd in number of poor.

1970 Share of Federal Tax Burden $2,146,550,000; 1.10% of U.S. total, 25th largest.

1970 Share of Federal Outlays $2,346,254,921; 1.24% of U.S. total, 27th largest. Per capita federal spending, $729.

DOD	$494,887,000	32nd (0.86%)		HEW	$793,462,151	24th (1.52%)
AEC	$55,966,977	15th (2.15%)		HUD	$25,197,953	26th (1.29%)
NASA	$329,786	40th (0.01%)		OEO	$12,762,407	22nd (1.68%)
DOT	$115,255,126	26th (1.61%)		DOA	$240,996,625	20th (1.87%)
DOC	$8,865,557	28th (0.76%)		POD	$86,373,076	25th (1.18%)
DOI	$8,191,046	42nd (0.35%)		VA	$152,402,846	23rd (2.06%)
DOJ	$8,206,584	19th (1.43%)		CSC	$32,194,506	27th (0.80%)
				Other	$636,358,276	

Economic Base Tobacco, livestock, and dairy; electrical machinery, equipment, and supplies, esp. household appliances; apparel and other finished products made from fabrics and similar materials, esp. men's, youths', and boys' furnishings, work clothing, and allied garments; nonelectrical machinery; food and kindred products, esp. beverages; fabricated metal products; bituminous coal; primary metal industries, esp. blast furnaces, steel works, and rolling and finishing mills; tobacco manufactures, esp. cigarettes; chemicals and allied products.

Political Line-up Governor, Louie B. Nunn (R); seat up, 1971. Senators, John Sherman Cooper (R) and Marlow W. Cook (R). Representatives, 7 (5 D and 2 R). State Senate (23 D and 15 R); State House (72 D and 28 R).

The Voters

Registration 1,525,597 total. 987,625 D (65%); 504,187 R (34%); 33,786 other (2%).

Employment profile White collar, 34%. Blue collar, 66%.

Ethnic groups Black, 7%. Total foreign stock, 3%. German, 1%. All other groups, less than 0.5% each.

Presidential vote

1968	Humphrey (D)	397,541	(38%)
	Nixon (R)	462,411	(44%)
	Wallace (AIP)	193,098	(18%)
1964	Johnson (D)	669,659	(64%)
	Goldwater (R)	372,977	(36%)
1960	Kennedy (D)	521,855	(46%)
	Nixon (R)	602,607	(54%)

Senator

John Sherman Cooper (R) Elected 1956, seat up 1972; b. Aug. 23, 1901, Somerset; Centre Col., 1918–19; Yale Col., B.A., 1922; Harvard Law School, 1923–25; Army, WWII; married; Baptist.

Career Mbr., Lower House, Ky. Legislature, 1928–30; Judge, Pulaski County Court, 1930–38; Circuit Judge, 28th Dist., 1946–48, 1952–54, 1956–66, 1966–73; Delegate to UN Gen. Assembly, 1949–51; Ambassador to India and Nepal, 1955–56; Senate, 1946–48, 1952–54.

Offices 125 OSOB, 202-225-2542. Also Beecher Hotel, Somerset 42501, 606-678-5021.

Committees

Foreign Relations (4th); Subs. (1) Arms Control, International Law and Organization, (2) European Affairs, (3) Far Eastern Affairs, (4) Genocide Convention, (5) U.S. Security Agreements and Commitments.

Public Works (Ranking Mbr.); Subs. (1) Air and Water Pollution, (2) Economic Development, (3) Flood Control—Rivers and Harbors, (4) Public Roads.

Rules and Administration (2nd); Subs. (1) Smithsonian Institution, (2) Standing Rules of the Senate.

Sel. Com. on Standards and Conduct (2nd).

Jt. Com. on the Library (Ranking Rep. Sen.).

Group Ratings

	ADA	COPE	NREP	NFU	LCV	NAB	NSI	ACA
1970	47	34	55	79	38	75	44	43
1969	50	—	—	40	—	—	—	56
1968	71	73	—	85	—	80	—	28

Key Votes

(1) ABM	AGN	(8) Phil Pln	ABS	(15) Coop-Church	FOR
(2) SST	AGN	(9) Vol Army	AGN	(16) Cut Oil Dpltn	FOR
(3) Busing	FOR	(10) Prison $	FOR	(17) Consumer Prot	AGN
(4) Tob Sub	FOR	(11) Cut Mil $	FOR	(18) Farm Sub Limit	AGN
(5) Carswell	FOR	(12) Defoliatn	FOR	(19) Comp Bid Sales	FOR
(6) No-Knock	AGN	(13) 18-Yr-Vote	FOR	(20) Pre-Prod Tests	FOR
(7) Seniorty	AGN	(14) Pentgn PR	AGN	(21) Cut Marjna Pen	AGN

Election Results

1966 general:	John Sherman Cooper (R)	483,805	(65%)
	John Young Brown (D)	266,079	(35%)
1966 primary:	John Sherman Cooper (R)	65,023	(93%)
	Sam M. Ward (R)	2,927	(4%)
	Thurman J. Hamlin (R)	2,120	(3%)
1960 general:	John Sherman Cooper (R)	644,087	(59%)
	Keen Johnson (D)	444,830	(41%)

Senator

Marlow W. Cook (R) Elected 1968, seat up 1974; b. July 27, 1926, Akron, N.Y.; home, Louisville; U. of Louisville Law School, LL.B., 1950; Navy, WWII; married, five children; Catholic.

Career Ky. House of Reps., 1957–61; Judge, Jefferson County, 1961–68.

Offices 342 OSOB, 202-225-4343. Also Rm. 172-C New Fed. Office Bldg., 600 Fed. Place, Louisville 40202, 502-582-5986.

Committees

Commerce (6th); Subs. (1) Aviation, (2) Communications, (3) Consumer, (4) Environment, (5) Oceans and Atmosphere.

Judiciary (5th); Subs. (1) Constitutional Amendments, (2) Criminal Laws and Procedures, (3) Immigration and Naturalization, (4) Internal Security, (5) Juvenile Delinquency, (6) Penitentiaries.

Veterans' Affairs (3rd); Subs. (1) Housing and Insurance, (2) Readjustment, Education, Employment.

Sel. Com. on Equal Educational Opportunity (6th).

Sel. Com. on Nutrition and Human Needs (5th).

Group Ratings

	ADA	COPE	NREP	NFU	LCV	NAB	NSI	ACA
1970	41	75	73	79	47	38	70	67
1969	50	—	—	57	—	—	—	33

Key Votes

(1) ABM	AGN	(8) Phil Pln	ABS	(15) Coop-Church	AGN
(2) SST	FOR	(9) Vol Army	FOR	(16) Cut Oil Dpltn	AGN
(3) Busing	FOR	(10) Prison $	AGN	(17) Consumer Prot	AGN
(4) Tob Sub	FOR	(11) Cut Mil $	AGN	(18) Farm Sub Limit	ABS
(5) Carswell	AGN	(12) Defoliatn	FOR	(19) Comp Bid Sales	FOR
(6) No-Knock	FOR	(13) 18-Yr-Vote	FOR	(20) Pre-Prod Tests	AGN
(7) Seniorty	FOR	(14) Pentgn PR	ABS	(21) Cut Marjna Pen	AGN

Election Results

1968 general:	Marlow W. Cook (R)	484,260	(51%)
	Katherine Peden (D)	448,960	(48%)
	Duane F. Olsen (AIP)	9,645	(1%)
1968 primary:	Marlow W. Cook (R)	73,171	(62%)
	Eugene Siler (R)	39,743	(34%)
	E. W. Kemp (R)	3,104	(3%)
	Thurman J. Hamlin (R)	2,015	(2%)

FIRST DISTRICT Political Background

Kentucky 1, the western end of the state, fronts on the Mississippi, Ohio, and Tennessee rivers. This area is part of the Deep South, closer in topography and political tradition to the flat lands of western Tennessee and eastern Arkansas than to most of the rest of Kentucky. All five counties that George Wallace carried in the state are in the 1st; the Alabama Governor won 29% of the district's votes—his best showing in any congressional district outside the eleven states of the old Confederacy. But the 1st's long-standing Southern Democratic tradition possessed enough vitality to make Hubert Humphrey the 1968 winner in the district.

Most of the 1st is given over to agriculture, to cotton and crops commonly grown in the Midwest. The district's congressman, Frank A. Stubblefield, is now 5th ranking Democrat on the House Agriculture Committee, having accumulated considerable seniority since his first election in 1958. Stubblefield has had little difficulty staying in Congress. In the past eight years he has had Republican opposition only once, 1966, winning that year with 71% of the votes. The outlook is for continued reelection, and, in the event that Stubblefield is not a candidate, for another conservative Democrat to succeed him.

Census Data 1970 pop. 449,344; deviation from current state average, −2.3%; change 1960–70, +2.8%. Metro. 8.0%, 0.0% central city.

1970 Share of Federal Outlays $436,757,037

DOD	$106,068,000	HEW	$118,444,712
AEC	$55,871,538	HUD	$1,069,055
NASA	$000	OEO	$358,442
DOT	$20,308,364	DOA	$39,462,448
		Other	$95,172,478

Federal Military-Industrial Commitments

DOD Installations Fort Campbell AB (Clarksville).

AEC Operations Union Carbide (Paducah), $53.544m: feed material and diffusion facilities.

Economic Base Tobacco and livestock; bituminous coal; electrical machinery, equipment, and supplies.

The Voters

Registration 224,642 total. 189,873 D (85%); 33,172 R (19%); 1,597 other. (1%).

Employment profile White collar, 30%. Blue collar, 70%.

Ethnic groups Black, 9%. Total foreign stock, 3%. German, 1%; others, 1%.

Presidential vote

1968	Humphrey (D)	61,094	(39%)
	Nixon (R)	50,419	(32%)
	Wallace (AIP)	44,779	(29%)

Representative

Frank A. Stubblefield (D) Elected 1958; b. April 5, 1907, Murray; home, Murray; U. of Ariz., 1927; U. of Ky., B.S., 1932; USNR, WWII; married, three children; Methodist.

Career Retail druggist, 1933–58; City Council, Murray, 1939–43; Railroad Commission, 1951–58.

Offices 228 RHOB, 202-225-3115. Also 203 S. Fifth St., Murray 42071, 502-753-7102.

Committees

Agriculture (5th); Subs. (1) Chm., Dairy and Poultry, (2) Conservation and Credit, (3) Tobacco.

Merchant Marine and Fisheries (10th); Subs. (1) Coast Guard, Coast and Geodetic Survey and Navigation, (2) Merchant Marine, (3) Panama Canal.

Group Ratings

	ADA	COPE	NREP	NFU	LCV	CFA	NAB	NSI	ACA
1970	20	50	27	69	55	75	36	90	44
1969	20	—	—	71	—	—	—	—	41
1968	42	54	—	79	—	—	50	—	37

Key Votes

(1) ABM	FOR	(6) 18-Yr-Vote	FOR	(11) Clean Water $	AGN
(2) SST	AGN*	(7) Farm Sub Lmt	AGN	(12) Mig Wrkrs Comp	AGN
(3) Phil Pln	AGN	(8) Coop-Church	AGN	(13) Jets to Chiang	FOR
(4) No-Knock	ABS	(9) Family Asst	AGN	(14) State OEO Veto	AGN
(5) Cmutr Tax	FOR	(10) Work Stamps	FOR	(15) Park Logging	FOR

* *Voted "for" in previous vote on same issue.*

Election Results

1970 general:	Frank A. Stubblefield (D), unopposed		
1970 primary:	Frank A. Stubblefield (D)	20,401	(72%)
	Bobby Joe Sims (D)	7,999	(28%)
1968 general:	Frank A. Stubblefield (D), unopposed		

SECOND DISTRICT Political Background

Kentucky 2 is middle Kentucky and spans a region between Bowling Green, near the Tennessee border, and Owensboro, a prosperous industrial town on the Ohio River, to the Bluegrass Country just outside of Frankfort. Fort Knox, in the northern part of the district, lies about 20 miles south of Louisville. Most of the land in between is agricultural, spotted with small communities like Bardstown, a tourist attraction made famous by Stephen Foster's "My Old Kentucky Home."

Most of the 2nd was sympathetic to the South in the Civil War, and most of it still votes Democratic today, at least in local and state elections. An exception is a group of Republican counties at the center of the T-shaped district. In national elections, however, the conservatism of the district has shown itself in declining Democratic vote totals. In 1968 many of the conservatively inclined went for Wallace rather than Nixon, with the AIP's candidate getting a solid 21% of the votes, Nixon 44%, and Humphrey 35%.

Since 1953, William H. Natcher, a conservative Democrat, has represented the 2nd in the House. He now enjoys the position of 9th ranking Democrat on the House Appropriations Committee and chairman of its District of Columbia subcommittee. In that capacity Natcher has usually worked in tandem with the conservative Southerners who, to the chagrin of most of the district's residents, control the House D.C. committee. An example of Natcher's power was his insistence that an unwanted freeway and bridge be built before any money would be appropriated for a badly needed Washington mass transit system.

In 1970 Natcher faced no opposition in the general elections, but in the two preceding contests he did, and made only mediocre showings for a longtime incumbent: 56% in 1968 and 59% in 1966. An aggressive Republican candidate could beat Natcher, and if the incumbent were not the Democrat running, the Republicans would have an excellent chance to pick up the seat.

Census Data 1970 pop. 470,826; deviation from current state average, +2.4%; change 1960–70, +11.7%. Metro. 16.9%, 10.7% central city.

1970 Share of Federal Outlays $470,823,442

DOD	$229,946,000	HEW	$90,796,675
AEC	$000	HUD	$8,505,859
NASA	$50,384	OEO	$772,790
DOT	$6,124,642	DOA	$47,796,373
		Other	$86,830,737

Federal Military-Industrial Commitments

DOD Installations Fort Knox (West Point).

Economic Base Tobacco and livestock; electrical machinery, equipment, and supplies, esp. electronic components and accessories; food and kindred products. Also, higher education (Western Kentucky State University).

The Voters

Registration 214,130 total. 154,545 D (72%); 56,929 R (27%); 2,656 other (1%).

Employment profile White collar, 29%. Blue collar, 71%.

Ethnic groups Black, 6%. Total foreign stock, 1%. All groups less than 0.5%.

Presidential vote

1968	Humphrey (D)	48,772	(35%)
	Nixon (R)	61,542	(44%)
	Wallace (AIP)	28,956	(21%)

Representative

William H. Natcher (D) Elected Aug. 1, 1953; b. Sept. 11, 1909, Bowling Green; home, Bowling Green; Western Ky. State Col., B.A., 1930; Ohio State U., LL.B., 1933; Navy, WWII; married, two children; Baptist.

Career Practicing atty., 1934– ; Fed. Conciliation Commissioner, Western Dist. of Ky., 1936–37; County Atty., Warren County, 1937–49; Commonwealth Atty., 8th Jud. Dist., 1951–53.

Offices 2333 RHOB, 202-225-3501. Also 414 E. 10th St., Bowling Green 42101, 502-842-7376, and 50 Public Square, Elizabethtown 42701, 502-765-4360.

Committees

Appropriations (9th); Subs. (1) Chm., District of Columbia, (2) Agriculture, Environmental and Consumer Protection, (3) Labor and HEW.

Group Ratings

	ADA	COPE	NREP	NFU	LCV	CFA	NAB	NSI	ACA
1970	28	60	33	69	50	76	33	100	42
1969	27	—	—	67	—	—	—	—	59
1968	42	69	—	81	—	—	50	—	35

Key Votes

(1) ABM	FOR	(6) 18-Yr-Vote	FOR	(11) Clean Water $	AGN
(2) SST	FOR	(7) Farm Sub Lmt	AGN	(12) Mig Wrkrs Comp	AGN
(3) Phil Pln	AGN	(8) Coop-Church	AGN	(13) Jets to Chiang	FOR
(4) No-Knock	FOR	(9) Family Asst	FOR	(14) State OEO Veto	AGN
(5) Cmutr Tax	AGN	(10) Work Stamps	AGN	(15) Park Logging	FOR

Election Results

1970 general:	William H. Natcher (D), unopposed		
1970 primary:	William H. Natcher (D), unopposed		
1968 general:	William H. Natcher (D)	65,860	(56%)
	Robert D. Simmons (R)	50,904	(44%)

THIRD DISTRICT Political Background

Kentucky 3 is the city of Louisville, together with the blue-collar suburb of Shively and a few other suburban towns in Jefferson County. Louisville, despite the local accent (LOO-uh-vul), is not really a Southern town. Louisville is an old river city, like Cincinnati and St. Louis. The river cities had many citizens, particularly among their large German communities, who were hostile to slave-holding and to the politics of their Southern-leaning rural neighbors. Partially as a result of the German heritage, present-day Louisville, though it has a large black population (33%), is far more Republican than most similar industrial cities to the north.

The decade of the 1960's was an especially good one for the Republicans here. They had a tightly-knit, well-financed organization, and, with strong support from the black community, elected a mayor and a Jefferson County judge (an administrative post) in 1961. Both officials went on to bigger things. Mayor William Cowger became a congressman in 1966 and County Judge Marlow Cook was elected U.S. senator in 1968.

But the Jefferson County Republican organization has gone slack. Political success, as it often does, split the winners and made losers of them once again. In 1969, Democratic ex-Congressman Frank Burke (1958–62) was elected mayor, while another Democrat won Cook's old post. And as the Nixon Administration came into office, Congressman Cowger found himself feuding with Republican Gov. Louie Nunn and also found his popularity among black voters ebbing.

As the 1970 elections approached, most local observers felt Cowger was in political trouble. The Democratic primary fight was a tough one between Tom Ray, the relatively conservative 1968 nominee, and state Sen. Romano Mazzoli, a thoroughgoing liberal and strong opponent of the Vietnam war. Mazzoli won, 2:1, with strong backing in the black community, and went into the general election as the favorite. He ran an energetic campaign staffed with many young volunteers and appeared to be forging a considerable lead over Cowger until the incumbent became ill and was hospitalized, two weeks before the election.

The illness apparently sparked the battered Republican organization and generated some sympathy for the Congressman. When Cowger got out of the hospital, he launched a blistering attack on his opponent, accusing him of consorting with radical elements, and so on. For Cowger this was somewhat out of character and probably cost him some votes, particularly among the blacks. The final result produced the closest congressional race in the nation: Mazzoli had 50,102 votes, Cowger 49,891, a margin of 211 votes.

Cities like Philadelphia and Boston that have large Italian-American populations have never had a congressman of Italian descent. But Louisville, where fettucine will never replace fried chicken, now does. Moreover, an antiwar Democrat here proved that he could win where more conservative Democrats could not. But Mazzoli's tenure is far from secure, particularly since the 1970 census will require the inclusion of 35,000 more suburbanites in his district. But by 1972, the Congressman will have all of the advantages of incumbency plus a strong local Democratic organization behind him. As of this writing, Cowger has not indicated whether he will make a bid to recapture his old seat.

Census Data 1970 pop. 421,982; deviation from current state average, −8.2%; change 1960–70, −2.4%. Metro. 100.0%, 85.4% central city.

1970 Share of Federal Outlays $284,540,000 (average outlay per district, Kentucky 3 and 4)

DOD	$43,049,000	HEW	$100,462,000
AEC	$000	HUD	$4,700,000
NASA	$000	OEO	$2,324,000
DOT	$21,193,000	DOA	$8,114,000
		Other	$104,689,000

Federal Military-Industrial Commitments (Kentucky 3 and 4, greater Louisville listing)
DOD Installations Naval Ordnance Station (Louisville).

Economic Base Household appliances and other electrical machinery, equipment, and supplies; food and kindred products; cigarettes and other tobacco manufactures. Also, banking and insurance.

The Voters

Registration 147,476 total. 80,874 D (55%); 54,061 R (37%); 12,541 other (9%).
Employment profile White collar, 40%. Blue collar, 60%.
Ethnic groups Black, 21%. Total foreign stock, 5%. Germany, 2%; all other groups less than 0.5% each.

Presidential vote

1968	Humphrey (D)	64,272	(46%)
	Nixon (R)	54,960	(39%)
	Wallace (AIP)	20,488	(15%)

Representative

Romano L. Mazzoli (D) Elected 1970; b. Nov. 2, 1932, Louisville; home, Louisville; Notre Dame U., B.S., 1954; U. of Louisville Law School, J.D., 1960; Army, 1954–56; married, two children; Catholic.

Career Practicing atty., 1960–70; Law Dept., Louisville and Nashville Railroad Co., 1960–62; Lecturer, Bellarmine-Ursuline Col., 1963–67; Ky. Senate, 1967–70.

Offices 1017 LHOB, 202-225-5401. Also 414 E. 10th St., Bowling Green 42101, 502-842-7376.

Committees

Education and Labor (21st); Subs. (1) Gen. on Education, (2) Gen. on Labor, (3) Sel. on Education.

Group Ratings, Key Votes: Newly elected.

Election Results

1970 general:	Romano L. Mazzoli (D)	50,102	(49%)
	William O. Cowger (R)	49,891	(48%)
	Ronald W. Watson (AIP)	3,265	(3%)
1970 primary:	Romano L. Mazzoli (D)	8,642	(60%)
	Tom Ray (D)	4,717	(33%)
	Shirley Small (D)	864	(6%)
	Philip Vernon Baker (D)	193	(1%)
1968 general:	William O. Cowger (R)	70,318	(56%)
	Tom Ray (D)	55,366	(44%)

FOURTH DISTRICT Political Background

Kentucky 4 is a geographical monstrosity, the result of Kentucky's loss of a congressional seat after the 1960 census and of successive redistrictings. The 4th now consists of two approximately equal-sized suburban areas connected by a thin strip of rural Kentucky along the Ohio River. The first of the suburban areas is Jefferson County, excluding Louisville and the few suburbs that make up the 3rd district. This part of the district is prosperous and growing rapidly and, like most such areas, votes heavily Republican. The other suburban part of the 4th consists of the three counties just south of Cincinnati, Ohio—Campbell, Kenton, and Boone. Just under half the people here live in the old, decaying cities of Covington and Newport along the Ohio River—Newport being famous for many years (but, we are told, no more) as a vice and gambling center. But most of the voters in this part of the district live in comfortable and sometimes posh hilltop suburbs, making this second area a Republican stronghold as well.

The connecting counties, along the river, are part of old Kentucky, having some tobacco land but few inhabitants. Those who do live here are solidly Democratic, but these votes are swamped by those cast in the suburbs to the east and west.

Since 1966, when the district took on its present shape, the congressman from the 4th has been M. G. (Gene) Snyder, a hard-line ideological conservative. Snyder also represented the old 3rd district from 1962 to 1964, when he was swept out by the Johnson landslide. In his first election in the 4th, Snyder faced strong opposition in the Republican primary from Campbell County (Newport) reform sheriff George Ratterman (onetime quarterback for the Cleveland Browns) and in the general election from then Rep. Frank Chelf, who had intended to retire but was called back to run after the death in October of the Democratic candidate. Since then, Snyder has had no trouble at all. He won 65% in 1968 and took 67% in 1970, even though a peace candidate, ex-Mayor Charles Webster of Carrollton, waged an arduous seven-month campaign against the incumbent.

Snyder's impressive margins have started talk of a statewide race for the Congressman. Though he chose not to run for governor in 1971, he may very well seek John Sherman Cooper's Senate seat in 1972. If Snyder does, Kentucky voters may see their first Senate election featuring a conservative Republican and a liberal Democrat.

Because of Jefferson County's population growth during the '60's, the 4th is now Kentucky's largest district (pop. 576,000). Redistricting will probably remove Campbell County (Newport) and the two counties to the south and place them in the 6th district, which would in turn lose some of its counties to the population-losing 5th and 7th districts. The character of the present 4th would not change much in the process. If Snyder does make a Senate try in 1972, the district might have an interesting primary fight between one of Marlow Cook's Jefferson County moderates and a conservative of the Snyder stripe. Whatever happens, it is quite certain that the 4th will continue to be represented by a Republican.

Census Data 1970 pop. 576,527; deviation from current state average, +25.4%; change 1960–70, +26.0%. Metro. 90.9%, 0.2% central city.

1970 Share of Federal Outlays $284,540,000 (average outlay per district, Kentucky 3 and 4)

DOD	$43,049,000	HEW	$100,462,000
AEC	$000	HUD	$4,700,000
NASA	$000	OEO	$2,324,000
DOT	$21,193,000	DOA	$8,114,000
		Other	$104,689,000

Federal Military-Industrial Commitments (See Kentucky 3 for greater Louisville listing)

Economic Base Tobacco and livestock; electrical machinery, equipment, and supplies. Also, extensive commuting to Kentucky 3 (Louisville) and Ohio 1 and 2 (Cincinnati).

The Voters

Registration 210,437 total. 131,536 D (63%); 68,804 R (33%); 10,097 other (5%).
Employment profile White collar, 43%. Blue collar, 57%.
Ethnic groups Black, 3%. Total foreign stock, 5%. Germany, 2%; UK, 1%; others, 2%.

Presidential vote

1968	Humphrey (D)	60,317	(34%)
	Nixon (R)	82,454	(47%)
	Wallace (AIP)	33,537	(19%)

Representative

Marion Gene Snyder (R) Elected 1962–64, 1966; b. Jan. 26, 1928, Louisville; home, Jeffersontown; Jefferson School of Law, LL.B., 1951; U. of Louisville, J.D., 1969; married, one child; Protestant.

Career Practicing atty., 1950– ; City Atty., 1953–57; Magistrate, 1957–61; farmer, 1957– ; realtor, 1955–56; builder, 1958–62.

Offices 306 CHOB, 202-225-3465. Also 140 Chenoweth Lane, St. Matthews 40207, 502-582-5985, and 310 Fed. Bldg., Covington 41011, 513-684-2154.

Committees

Merchant Marine and Fisheries (11th); Subs. (1) Coast Guard, Coast and Geodetic Survey and Navigation, (2) Panama Canal, (3) Sp. on Maritime Education and Training.

Public Works (6th); Subs. (1) Flood Control and Internal Development, (2) Investigation and Oversight, (3) Public Buildings and Grounds, (4) Rivers and Harbors, (5) Watershed Development.

Group Ratings

	ADA	COPE	NREP	NFU	LCV	CFA	NAB	NSI	ACA
1970	8	27	0	46	33	38	64	100	76
1969	7	—	—	40	—	—	—	—	85
1968	0	15	—	43	—	—	100	—	95

Key Votes

(1) ABM	ABS	(6) 18-Yr-Vote	FOR	(11) Clean Water $	AGN
(2) SST	FOR	(7) Farm Sub Lmt	AGN	(12) Mig Wrkrs Comp	AGN
(3) Phil Pln	AGN	(8) Coop-Church	AGN	(13) Jets to Chiang	FOR
(4) No-Knock	FOR	(9) Family Asst	AGN	(14) State OEO Veto	FOR
(5) Cmutr Tax	FOR	(10) Work Stamps	FOR	(15) Park Logging	AGN

Election Results

1970 general:	M. Gene Snyder (R)	83,037	(67%)
	Charles W. Webster (D)	41,659	(33%)
1970 primary:	M. Gene Snyder (R)	11,582	(91%)
	William E. Bartley, Jr. (R)	1,170	(9%)
1968 general:	M. Gene Snyder (R)	103,793	(65%)
	Gus Sheehan, Jr. (D)	55,971	(35%)

FIFTH DISTRICT Political Background

Kentucky 5 is the Republican heartland of Kentucky, a group of 22 counties in the south central part of the state. The small farmers here were hostile to the slave-holding South and have remained staunchly Republican ever since. The district was so loyal to the party that it even supported the candidacy of Barry Goldwater, otherwise a big loser in the state, in 1964. Only on the western and eastern edges of the 5th are there any counties which Democrats can hope to carry. The most notable of these is Harlan, an Appalachian mining county (1930 pop. 64,000; 1970 pop. 36,000). During the 1930's mine owners and members of the United Mine Workers shot and killed each other in Harlan County. Most of the 5th, however, is not Democratic mining country, but just typical rural Kentucky. The district has no town larger than 12,000.

In the 5th, therefore, the Republican primary is tantamount to a general election. So when Congressman Eugene Siler retired in 1964, the Republican primary had no fewer than 15 entrants; the Democratic primary, by comparison, had two. The Republican winner was Dr. Tim Lee Carter, who got a remarkable 45% of the votes. He got that probably because 13 of the 14 other candidates were from the eastern end of the district, while Carter shared the rest of the district with one other, less popular, Republican aspirant. Carter went on to win the general election with a surprisingly small 53%, Goldwater holding down Carter's percentage. But in the years since, the Congressman has had no trouble. In 1970, he announced that he wanted to win with 90%; he fell short, but not by much, with 80%. There is little doubt that he can continue winning, with similar margins, indefinitely.

Census Data 1970 pop. 391,419; deviation from current state average, −14.9%; change 1960–70, −6.3%. Metro. 0.0%, 0.0% central city.

1970 Share of Federal Outlays $244,377,491

DOD	$7,247,000	HEW	$120,978,555
AEC	$000	HUD	$506,527
NASA	$000	OEO	$1,542,437
DOT	$9,252,340	DOA	$43,675,569
		Other	$61,175,063

Federal Military-Industrial Commitments

None.

Economic Base Tobacco and livestock; bituminous coal.

The Voters

Registration 246,831 total. 87,552 D (36%); 158,159 R (64%); 1,121 other (1%).

Employment profile White collar, 26%. Blue collar, 74%.

Ethnic groups Black, 3%. Total foreign stock, 1%. All groups less than 0.5% each.

Presidential vote

1968	Humphrey (D)	36,703	(26%)
	Nixon (R)	85,254	(60%)
	Wallace (AIP)	19,485	(14%)

Representative

Tim Lee Carter (R) Elected 1964; b. Sept. 2, 1910, Tompkinsville, W. Ky.; W. Ky. U., B.A., 1934; U. of Tenn., M.D., 1937; Army, WWII; married, one child; Baptist.

Career Practicing physician, 1937– .

Offices 1202 LHOB, 202-225-4601. Also Hotel Beecher, Somerset 42501, 606-679-2544, and 805 N. Main St., Tompkinsville 42167, 502-487-6121.

Committees

Interstate and Foreign Commerce (7th); Subs. (1) Public Health and Environment.

Group Ratings

	ADA	COPE	NREP	NFU	LCV	CFA	NAB	NSI	ACA
1970	16	25	27	31	14	63	91	90	72
1969	13	—	—	43	—	—	—	—	53
1968	17	25	—	54	—	63	100	—	73

Key Votes

(1) ABM	FOR	(6) 18-Yr-Vote	FOR	(11) Clean Water $	AGN
(2) SST	FOR	(7) Farm Sub Lmt	AGN	(12) Mig Wrkrs Comp	AGN
(3) Phil Pln	FOR	(8) Coop-Church	AGN	(13) Jets to Chiang	AGN
(4) No-Knock	FOR	(9) Family Asst	FOR	(14) State OEO Veto	AGN
(5) Cmutr Tax	AGN	(10) Work Stamps	AGN	(15) Park Logging	FOR

Election Results

1970 general:	Tim Lee Carter (R)	49,266	(80%)
	Lyle Leonard Willis (D)	11,977	(20%)
1970 primary:	Tim Lee Carter (R)	14,593	(93%)
	Granville Thomas (R)	987	(6%)
	Noel Chilton (R)	148	(1%)
1968 general:	Tim Lee Carter (R)	86,391	(73%)
	Thomas J. Roberts (D)	30,575	(26%)
	Charles P. Peace (AAC)	1,721	(1%)

SIXTH DISTRICT Political Background

Kentucky 6 is the picture-postcard part of the state: the posh horse farms in the rolling Bluegrass Country around Lexington, the great tobacco farms, and the imposing early-nineteenth-century mansions, one of which belonged to Sen. Henry Clay. The 6th was a slave-holding region up until the Civil War, and to this day the rural counties here retain an allegiance to the Democratic party. But the political pivot of the district is Fayette County (Lexington), the fastest-growing area in Kentucky outside the Louisville suburbs and one that has become more and more Republican in both national and statewide elections.

But so far the Republican trend has not affected the incumbency of Congressman John C. Watts, a Democrat who has represented the district since 1950. He is now the 2nd ranking Democrat on the House Ways and Means Committee, just behind Chairman Wilbur Mills. Watts, despite his 28 years as Jessamine County Democratic Chairman, has not been known to campaign very hard in recent elections. The veteran Congressman has usually won reelection with ease. The one exception, a 57% showing in 1968, apparently doesn't bother him much, though perhaps it should, since Watts lost Fayette County by 2,500 votes.

The demographic trend in the 6th district is working against Watts and the Democratic party. The small rural counties, which the party always carries, are either losing population or gaining only a little, while 86% of the district's 1960–70 population increase occurred in the Republican counties, 63% in Fayette alone. Moreover, redistricting will probably add normally Republican Campbell County (Newport and Fort Thomas, suburbs of Cincinnati) to the 6th. The county's presence in the district would improve the chances of a strong Republican candidate in a good Republican year—perhaps all he'd need for an upset. In any case, if Watts is for some reason not the candidate of the Democrats, the Republicans will probably pick up the seat.

Census Data 1970 pop. 498,195; deviation from current state average, +8.3%; change 1960–70, +16.6%. Metro. 35.0%, 21.7% central city.

1970 Share of Federal Outlays $370,054,477

DOD	$56,726,000	HEW	$136,493,145
AEC	$89,089	HUD	$3,145,267
NASA	$279,402	OEO	$2,349,119
DOT	$8,849,437	DOA	$63,636,548
		Other	$98,486,470

Federal Military-Industrial Commitments

DOD Installations Blue Grass Army Depot (Lexington).

Economic Base Tobacco and livestock; fabricated metal products; food and kindred products. Also, higher education (University of Kentucky).

The Voters

Registration 219,302 total. 171,855 D (78%); 43,422 R (20%); 4,025 other (2%).

Employment profile White collar, 36%. Blue collar, 64%.

Ethnic groups Black, 9%. Total foreign stock, 2%. All groups less than 0.5% each.

Presidential vote

1968	Humphrey (D)	58,723	(38%)
	Nixon (R)	66,424	(43%)
	Wallace (AIP)	30,461	(20%)

Representative

John Clarence Watts (D) Elected July 9, 1902, Nicholasville; home, Jessamine County; U. of Ky., B.A., 1925, LL.B., 1927; married, one child; Disciples of Christ.

Career Lawyer; farmer; banker; Police Judge, City of Nicholasville, 1929–33; County Atty., Jessamine County, 1933–45; Majority Leader, Ky. House of Reps., 1947–48; Commissioner, Motor Trans., 1948–51.

Offices 2411 RHOB, 202-225-4706. Also c/o Watts & Garrison, 200 W. Maple, Nicholasville 40356, 606-885-5958.

Committees

Ways and Means (2nd).

Jt. Com. Internal Revenue Taxation (2nd).

Jt. Com. Reduction of Federal Expenditures (3rd).

Group Ratings

	ADA	COPE	NREP	NFU	LCV	CFA	NAB	NSI	ACA
1970	20	42	27	77	43	72	50	90	56
1969	13	—	—	60	—	—	—	—	53
1968	8	34	—	87	—	—	50	—	50

Key Votes

(1) ABM	FOR	(6) 18-Yr-Vote	FOR	(11) Clean Water $	AGN
(2) SST	FOR	(7) Farm Sub Lmt	AGN	(12) Mig Wrkrs Comp	AGN
(3) Phil Pln	AGN	(8) Coop-Church	AGN	(13) Jets to Chiang	AGN
(4) No-Knock	FOR	(9) Family Asst	AGN	(14) State OEO Veto	AGN
(5) Cmutr Tax	FOR	(10) Work Stamps	FOR	(15) Park Logging	AGN

Election Results

1970 general:	John C. Watts (D)	44,322	(65%)
	Gerald G. Gregory (R)	23,971	(35%)
1970 primary:	John C. Watts (D)	14,816	(86%)
	Pete Brown (D)	2,413	(14%)
1968 general:	John C. Watts (D)	78,536	(57%)
	Russell G. Mobley (R)	58,905	(42%)
	J. Donald Graham (AIP)	1,535	(1%)

SEVENTH DISTRICT Political Background

Kentucky 7 is Appalachia, the poorest part of Kentucky, which only recently has begun to get the highways it has so desperately needed. The only city of any size here is Ashland (pop. 29,000) on the Ohio River near Huntington, West Virginia. But the rest of the district is probably the most thickly populated rural area in the nation; twenty years ago it was even more thickly settled. Since then the coal industry collapsed, and the district's young men and would-be miners moved away to work in the factories of Akron, Cleveland, Detroit, and Flint. During the 1930's, the 7th was the scene of many bitter struggles between mine owners and the miners of the UMW. Today the same sort of animosity has developed between new and growing strip-mining interests and the local environmentalists.

Appalachian Kentucky is the one area of the state whose political identity was established in the 1930's by the New Deal and the United Mine Workers, and not by loyalties created during the Civil War. In the 1930's, the miners became Democrats, and though the UMW is not as powerful here as it once was, its membership remains staunchly Democratic. Since western Kentucky has grown increasingly conservative, the 7th is now the state's most Democratic district, in national elections as well as local.

The voters of the 7th have been particularly devoted to Democratic Congressman Carl Perkins who has averaged nearly 70% of the ballots in his last four times at the polls. First elected in 1948, he is currently the senior member of the Kentucky delegation. Since Adam Clayton Powell's ouster in 1967, Perkins has been chairman of the House Education and Labor Committee. The committee has jurisdiction over the anti-poverty program, as well as over education and labor bills, and its chairman has consistently supported Great Society-type legislation. Perkins has also seen to it that some of the federal money over which his committee has authority makes its way to the 7th district, which probably needs it as much as any. Pikesville, Kentucky (pop. 4,576), for example, was one of the nation's first Model Cities.

Despite the 7th's 10% population loss during the '60's, redistricting will not alter it significantly, and Carl Perkins will continue to represent the 7th and chair his committee for some years to come.

Census Data 1970 pop. 411,018; deviation from current state average, —10.6%; change 1960–70, —7.6%. Metro. 12.8%, 7.1% central city.

1970 Share of Federal Outlays $255,162,474

DOD	$7,397,000	HEW	$110,407,728
AEC	$6,350	HUD	$2,571,220
NASA	$000	OEO	$3,086,317
DOT	$19,491,307	DOA	$26,878,024
		Other	$85,315,528

Federal Military-Industrial Commitments

None.

Economic Base Tobacco and livestock; bituminous coal; petroleum refining and related industries; primary metal industries.

The Voters

Registration 262,779 total. 171,390 D (65%); 89,649 R (34%); 1,749 other (1%).

Employment profile White collar, 30%. Blue collar, 70%.

Ethnic groups Black, 1%. Total foreign stock, 1%. All groups less than 0.5% each.

Presidential vote

1968	Humphrey (D)	67,660	(47%)
	Nixon (R)	61,358	(42%)
	Wallace (AIP)	15,392	(11%)

Representative

Carl D. Perkins (D) Elected 1948; b. Oct. 15, 1912, Hindman; home, Hindman; Caney Jr. Col., Jefferson School of Law, LL.B., 1935; Army, WWII; married, one child; Baptist.

Career Practicing atty., 1935–48; Commonwealth Atty., 1939; Ky. House of Reps., 1940; Knott County Atty., 1941–48; Counsel, Ky. Dept. of Highways, 1948.

Offices 2252 RHOB, 202-225-4935.

Committees

Education and Labor (Chm.)

Group Ratings

	ADA	COPE	NREP	NFU	LCV	CFA	NAB	NSI	ACA
1970	40	75	42	92	60	71	0	80	21
1969	40	—	—	93	—	—	—	—	18
1968	50	100	—	88	—	—	0	—	9

Key Votes

(1) ABM	FOR	(6) 18-Yr-Vote	FOR	(11) Clean Water $	AGN
(2) SST	FOR	(7) Farm Sub Lmt	AGN	(12) Mig Wrkrs Comp	AGN
(3) Phil Pln	AGN	(8) Coop-Church	AGN	(13) Jets to Chiang	AGN
(4) No-Knock	FOR	(9) Family Asst	FOR	(14) State OEO Veto	AGN
(5) Cmutr Tax	FOR	(10) Work Stamps	AGN	(15) Park Logging	AGN

Election Results

1970 general:	Carl D. Perkins (D)	50,672	(75%)
	Herbert E. Myers (R)	16,648	(25%)
1970 primary:	Carl D. Perkins (D), unopposed		
1968 general:	Carl D. Perkins (D)	82,594	(62%)
	James D. Nickell (R)	50,699	(38%)

LOUISIANA

Political Background

It's been almost 40 years now since Huey P. Long was shot down in the halls of the state capitol in Baton Rouge, but the Kingfish still seems to dominate the politics of Louisiana. Both the state's U.S. senators are part of Huey's legacy, as are the roads, Louisiana State University, and other public improvements that were built during his tenure as governor and senator. Sen. Allen J. Ellender, a Long political ally, won Huey's seat in 1936 just after the assassination, and Sen. Russell B. Long, the great man's son, won his in 1948 at age 30. Many other lesser known Long cousins and cronies abound in Louisiana politics. Huey Long's name is still good for a cheer at most political rallies in the state.

If one theme of the politics here is the influence of the Kingfish, another is the ancient split between the French Catholic population of southern Louisiana and the white Anglo-Saxon Protestant farmers in the northern part of the state. New Orleans, of course, retains a French and Creole ambience, in the iron grille balconies of its French Quarter, its mansions of the Garden District, as well as in its very un-Southern urbanity. No other Southern city has a liberal mayor like Moon Landrieu, or a Mafia organization like that of Carlo Marcello, or a district attorney like Jim Garrison.

In the bayous to the south and east of New Orleans, the French influence is even more pronounced. The back-country swamplands are populated with the descendants of the French Acadians. In the eighteenth century, the British expelled these people from Nova Scotia, a fate lamented by Longfellow's "Evangeline." A unique French is still spoken in the Cajun country, where almost everyone is Roman Catholic. Not many blacks live this far south in the state, and the Cajun parishes (the Louisiana French-derived name for counties), like the city of New Orleans, have been traditionally tolerant about race, as they have been toward the political machines that have dominated the region.

Northern Louisiana, where there are more blacks, is much more like the rest of the Deep South. Here the poor whites usually vote for the most ardent segregationist on the ticket. Long was from Winn Parish in the north, but, unlike Vardaman and Bilbo in neighboring Mississippi, Huey rarely exploited the race issue. He won support in both regions of the state by pushing big government-spending programs and by smashing the power of the old Louisiana political bosses. With few exceptions, the north has dominated the state's politics since Long's day. The north has also dominated the state's presidential elections; in 1964 and 1968, it put the state's electoral votes in the Goldwater and Wallace columns, even though Johnson ran well in southern Louisiana and Humphrey carried New Orleans. Only when the Catholics in the south provided huge margins for Kennedy and Eisenhower did this part of the state prevail. Louisiana, having a Catholic-Protestant split, is not a typical Deep South state. But since the Protestants outvote the Catholics, Deep South-type politicians dominate Louisiana politics.

The Voting Rights Act of 1965 significantly increased the number of the state's black voters; in New Orleans, the blacks saved Hale Boggs's seat in 1968. But the black vote has not affected the outcome of any elections held in the rural parishes or the northern cities.

Neither of the state's senators—who will have 60 years of collective seniority in 1972—has ever had much electoral trouble from any quarter, nor much reason to expect any. Russell Long, chairman of the Senate Finance Committee, combines his own brand of Southern populism (high social security benefits and larger income tax deductions) with a solicitude for the interest of the oil industry. Long has come under fire for investments in the industry, but has nevertheless remained a firm partisan of the depletion allowance and oil import quotas. But since the Constitution stipulates that revenue measures be initiated in the House, Long's power as chairman of Finance is limited; moreover, he has none of the personal authority wielded by Wilbur Mills of Ways and Means. In recent years, Washington insiders have considered Long's performance as a politician rather erratic, the main reason for this being his loss of the Majority Whip post to Edward Kennedy in 1969. Yet Long will be a power in the Senate for some time, his power guaranteed by the seniority system. Long will be only 54 in 1972, when he will have 24 years of seniority.

Sen. Ellender, who was 80 in 1970, is now the senior member of the Senate, its President Pro Tempore (4th in line for the Presidency), and chairman of the Senate Appropriations Committee. Ellender is widely known for his many trips abroad, designed, he says, to uncover unnecessary federal expenses overseas. He duly inserts voluminous reports on his travels in the *Congressional Record;* these are full of folk wisdom, common sense, and opinions about the ability of various Third World governments to manage their affairs. The last have occasionally precipitated diplomatic crises. Ellender, who can whip up a marvelous Creole sauce, generally votes with other conservative Southern Democrats. But from time to time the Senator is maverick; in 1969, for example, he opposed the ABM. Ellender will be up for reelection in 1972, and, unless he chooses to retire, will be returned to serve his seventh term without opposition.

Louisiana's House delegation, like that of most Southern states, specializes in the accumulation of seniority. That seniority has produced Hale Boggs, the House Majority Leader, F. Edward Hebert, chairman of the House Armed Services Committee, and Otto Passman, a senior member of the House Appropriations Committee. Louisiana Democrats will go on piling up seniority with little opposition from the state's Republicans, who have been uniformly unsuccessful of late. Since the heyday of the Goldwater years, the Republicans here have rarely challenged major officeholders and are fading from the political scene. As a result, Louisiana is now the nation's most solid one-party state.

Electoral Votes 10

Census Data 1970 pop. 3,643,180; 1.77% of U.S. total, 20th largest; change 1960–70, +11.9%. Metro. 54.8%, 31.4% central city. 1970 per capita income, $3,065, 42nd highest. 14th in number of poor.

1970 Share of Federal Tax Burden $2,653,910,000; 1.67% of U.S. total, 22nd largest.

1970 Share of Federal Outlays $2,627,782,610; 1.39% of U.S. total, 24th largest. Per capita federal spending, $721.

DOD	$255,237,332	19th (1.99%)		HEW	$804,478,386	23rd (1.54%)
AEC	$299,677	42nd (0.01%)		HUD	$22,983,008	28th (1.18%)
NASA	$109,088,539	10th (2.96%)		OEO	$14,405,561	16th (1.90%)
DOT	$148,965,401	15th (2.09%)		DOA	$255,237,332	19th (1.99%)
DOC	$47,237,294	5th (4.08%)		POD	$88,062,045	24th (1.21%)
DOI	$9,934,980	40th (0.43%)		VA	$163,145,601	22nd (2.21%)
DOJ	$7,852,368	20th (1.37%)		CSC	$28,681,202	30th (0.71%)
				Other	$218,610,216	

Economic Base Cotton, livestock, and rice; crude petroleum and natural gas; food and kindred products, esp. beverages and sugar; chemicals and allied products, esp. inorganic and organic chemicals; motor vehicles and motor vehicle equipment, and other transportation equipment; lumber and wood products other than furniture; paper and allied products, esp. paperboard mills; ordnance and accessories; petroleum refining and related industries; fabricated metal products, esp. fabricated structural metal products.

Political Line-up Governor, John J. McKeithen (D); seat up, 1972. Senators, Allen J. Ellender (D) and Russell B. Long (D). Representatives, 8 (8 D and 0 R). State Senate (38 D and 1 R); State House (104 D and 1 R).

The Voters

Registration 1,435,053 total. 1,137,739 white (79%); 297,314 black (21%). Party registration not available.

Employment profile White collar, 38%. Blue collar, 62%.

Ethnic groups Black, 29.8%. Total foreign stock, 4%. Italian, 1%; others, 1%.

Presidential vote

1968	Humphrey (D)	309,615	(28%)
	Nixon (R)	257,535	(24%)
	Wallace (AIP)	530,300	(48%)
1964	Johnson (D)	387,068	(43%)
	Goldwater (R)	509,225	(57%)
1960	Kennedy (D)	407,339	(64%)
	Nixon (R)	230,980	(36%)

Senator

Allen Joseph Ellender (D) Elected 1936, seat up 1972; b. Sept. 24, 1890, Montegut; home, Houma; St. Aloysius Col., Tulane U., M.A., LL.B., 1913; Army, WWI; widowed, one child; Presbyterian.

Career City Atty., Houma, 1913–15; Dist. Atty., Terrebonne Parish, 1915–16; La. House of Reps., 1924–36, Floor Leader, 1928–32, Speaker, 1932–36.

Offices 245 OSOB, 202-225-5824. Also 209 American Bank Bldg., Houma 70360, 504-872-9107.

Committees

Agriculture and Forestry (2nd); Subs. (1) Agriculture Credit and Rural Electrification, (2) Agricultural Production, Marketing and Stabilization of Prices, (3) Rural Development.

Appropriations (Chm.); Subs. (1) Chm., Defense and Intelligence, (2) Foreign Operations, (3) HUD, Space and Science, (4) Legislative Branch, (5) Public Works, (6) State, Justice, Commerce, the Judiciary, and Related Agencies, (7) Treasury, Post Office, and General Government.

Sel. Com. on Nutrition and Human Needs (2nd).

Jt. Com. on Reduction of Federal Expenditures (Ranking Dem. Sen.).

Group Ratings

	ADA	COPE	NREP	NFU	LCV	NAB	NSI	ACA
1970	16	15	17	33	28	75	60	78
1969	17	—	—	44	—	—	—	67
1968	7	27	—	30	—	50	—	61

Key Votes

(1) ABM	AGN	(8) Phil Pln	ABS	(15) Coop-Church	AGN
(2) SST	FOR	(9) Vol Army	AGN	(16) Cut Oil Dpltn	AGN
(3) Busing	AGN	(10) Prison $	AGN	(17) Consumer Prot	ABS
(4) Tob Sub	FOR	(11) Cut Mil $	AGN	(18) Farm Sub Limit	AGN
(5) Carswell	FOR	(12) Defoliatn	FOR	(19) Comp Bid Sales	FOR
(6) No-Knock	FOR	(13) 18-Yr-Vote	AGN	(20) Pre-Prod Tests	AGN
(7) Seniorty	FOR	(14) Pentgn PR	FOR	(21) Cut Marjna Pen	AGN

Election Results

1966 general:	Allen J. Ellender (D), unopposed		
1966 primary:	Allen J. Ellender (D)	494,519	(73%)
	J. D. DeBlieux (D)	94,154	(14%)
	Troyce E. Guice (D)	78,137	(12%)
1960 general:	Allen J. Ellender (D)	432,228	(80%)
	George W. Reese (R)	109,698	(20%)

Senator

Russell B. Long (D) Elected 1948, seat up 1974; b. Nov. 3, 1918, Shreveport; home, Shreveport; La. State U., B.A., 1941, LL.B., 1942; Navy, WWII; Lt. USNR; married, two children; Methodist.

Career Practicing atty., 1945–47; U.S. Senate, Asst. Majority Leader, 1965–68.

Offices 217 OSOB, 202-225-4623. Also 502 Union Fed. Bldg., Baton Rouge 70801, 504-343-7696.

Committees

Commerce (6th); Subs. (1) Chm., Merchant Marine, (2) Communications, (3) Environment, (4) Foreign Commerce and Tourism, (5) Oceans and Atmosphere, (6) Surface Transportation, (7) Sp. to Study Transportation on the Great Lakes and St. Lawrence Seaway.

Finance (Chm.).

Sel. Com. on Small Business (3rd); Subs. (1) Financing and Investment, (2) Government Procurement, (3) Monopoly.

Jt. Com. on Internal Revenue Taxation (Vice Chm.).

Jt. Com. on Reduction of Federal Expenditures (2nd).

Group Ratings

	ADA	COPE	NREP	NFU	LCV	NAB	NSI	ACA
1970	13	20	0	36	27	50	100	67
1969	0	—	—	50	—	—	—	67
1968	0	25	—	33	—	50	—	76

Key Votes

(1) ABM	FOR	(8) Phil Pln	AGN	(15) Coop-Church	AGN
(2) SST	FOR	(9) Vol Army	AGN	(16) Cut Oil Dpltn	AGN
(3) Busing	AGN	(10) Prison $	AGN	(17) Consumer Prot	FOR
(4) Tob Sub	FOR	(11) Cut Mil $	AGN	(18) Farm Sub Limit	AGN
(5) Carswell	FOR	(12) Defoliatn	FOR	(19) Comp Bid Sales	ABS
(6) No-Knock	FOR	(13) 18-Yr-Vote	AGN	(20) Pre-Prod Tests	AGN
(7) Seniorty	ABS	(14) Pentgn PR	AGN	(21) Cut Marjna Pen	AGN

Election Results

1968 general:	Russell B. Long (D), unopposed		
1968 primary:	Russell B. Long (D)	494,467	(87%)
	Maurice P. Blache (D)	73,791	(13%)
1962 general:	Russell B. Long (D)	318,838	(76%)
	Taylors Walters O'Hearn (R)	103,066	(24%)

FIRST DISTRICT Political Background

Louisiana 1 is the western and more conservative half of New Orleans and the Mississippi Delta parishes of St. Barnard and Plaquemines. Political bosses, particularly the late Leander Perez of Plaquemines, have made the Delta parishes famous; even after Perez's death, his machine continues to function: in the 1970 general election, for example, Congressman F. Edward Hebert received 4,025 votes in Plaquemines, while his opponent got 141. But the machine's notoriety is out of line with its real political power. Plaquemines is a small parish, while New Orleans contains more than 80% of the district's voters.

Since he was first elected in 1940, the 1st's Congressman Hebert (AY-bear) has been reelected without difficulty. After the death of Mendel Rivers and the electoral defeat of Philip J. Philbin (D-3rd Mass.), Hebert, always a staunch friend of the military, became chairman of the House Armed Services Committee. The new Chairman lacks Rivers' showmanship but makes up for it in political savvy. Hebert, who was 69 in 1970, has not been in good health and may retire after a term or two as chairman.

Census Data 1970 pop. 431,963; deviation from current state average, —5.1%; change 1960–70, +6.7%. Metro. 94.2%, 81.9% central city.

1970 Share of Federal Outlays $463,985,000 (average outlay per district, Louisiana 1–2)

DOD	$118,859,000	HEW	$110,614,000
AEC	$20,000	HUD	$8,065,000
NASA	$52,796,000	OEO	$1,900,000
DOT	$28,878,000	DOA	$31,497,000
		Other	$111,357,000

Federal Military-Industrial Commitments (See Louisiana 2 for greater New Orleans listing.)

Economic Base Crude petroleum and natural gas; food and kindred products, esp. beverages; apparel and other finished products made from fabrics and similar materials. Also, tourism (New Orleans) and banking and insurance.

The Voters

Registration 162,639 total. White, 76%; black, 24%. Party registration not available.

Employment profile White collar, 44%. Blue collar, 56%.

Ethnic groups Black, 36%. Total foreign stock, 8%. Italy, 3%; Germany, 1%; others, 3%.

Presidential vote

1968	Humphrey (D)	45,114	(33%)
	Nixon (R)	32,800	(24%)
	Wallace (AIP)	57,264	(42%)

Representative

F. Edward Hebert (D) Elected 1940; b. Oct. 12, 1901, New Orleans; home, New Orleans; Tulane U., 1920–24; married, one child; Catholic.

Career Newspaperman, 1917–40; City Editor, 1937–40.

Offices 2340 RHOB, 202-225-3015. Also 642 Fed. Bldg., South, New Orleans 70130, 504-527-2279.

Committees

Armed Services (Chm.); Chm., Armed Services Investigating.

Group Ratings

	ADA	COPE	NREP	NFU	LCV	CFA	NAB	NSI	ACA
1970	4	18	10	33	25	60	50	100	64
1969	7	—	—	33	—	—	—	—	64
1968	25	17	—	50	—	—	67	—	50

Key Votes

(1) ABM	FOR	(6) 18-Yr-Vote	AGN	(11) Clean Water $	AGN
(2) SST	FOR*	(7) Farm Sub Lmt	AGN	(12) Mig Wrkrs Comp	AGN
(3) Phil Pln	AGN	(8) Coop-Church	AGN	(13) Jets to Chiang	FOR
(4) No-Knock	FOR	(9) Family Asst	AGN	(14) State OEO Veto	FOR
(5) Cmutr Tax	FOR	(10) Work Stamps	FOR	(15) Park Logging	FOR

* *Voted "for" in previous vote on same issue.*

Election Results

1970 general:	F. Edward Hebert (D)	66,284	(87%)
	Luke J. Fontana (Ind)	9,602	(13%)
1970 primary:	F. Edward Hebert (D)	59,512	(90%)
	Florence Tye Jennison (D)	6,382	(10%)
	(Redistricted 1969)		

SECOND DISTRICT Political Background

Louisiana 2 is the eastern part of New Orleans, which has most of its tourist attractions, and a portion of suburban Jefferson Parish. New Orleans is unusually liberal for a Southern city. Its citizens have been traditionally tolerant of the city's East-Coast-style machine and have also been quite cosmopolitan in their attitudes toward race. Currently 45% of New Orleans' residents are black, and substantial portions of the city—the Garden District west of the French Quarter, for example—are comfortably integrated.

The 2nd district contains a great proportion of New Orleans' black and white liberal voters. But beyond the city limits, the political behavior of the voters changes radically. The suburbs of Jefferson Parish, especially those around Metairie, west of the city between the Mississippi River and Lake Pontchartrain, are almost entirely white and very conservative. Unlike the suburbs of Atlanta and other large Southern cities, however, Jefferson Parish has not been trending Republican in national elections. The parish remains typically Southern conservative—probably because it has absorbed few Northern immigrants and because no one here believes that a Republican like Nixon can carry the entire state of Louisiana. In 1968, Jefferson Parish went heavily for Wallace. Only in the races for the congressional seat have the suburbs leaned Republican, and then only because the Republicans have run ultraconservative candidates against House Majority Leader Hale Boggs.

When Boggs was first elected in 1940, he was the youngest member of the House at 26. The freshman Congressman was probably quite certain that general elections in the 2nd would give him little trouble. But the Democratic primary remained a problem, and in 1942 Boggs was beaten by the old-line Democrat he had ousted two years before. At that point he went off to the Navy for four years and then returned to the House in 1946, after which reelection became automatic. The still young Boggs soon obtained a seat on Ways and Means, and, some years later, in 1961 when John McCormack became Speaker, the Louisianan was made Majority Whip, the third highest House leadership position.

But in the past several years, things have not been going smoothly for Boggs. He has faced unexpected trouble both at home and in the House; yet the Congressman has managed to come through his difficulties and has emerged an even more powerful man.

Boggs, who has always supported liberal domestic legislation, voted for the Civil Rights Act of 1964, a decision which many voters of the 2nd found unsatisfactory. In the 1964 general elections that followed, conservative Republican David C. Treen challenged Boggs and won 45% of the votes. The results prompted some fence mending, and two years later, against another Republican, the Congressman received the kind of percentage to which he had become accustomed, 69%. But in 1968, in a slightly altered district, Treen ran again, reportedly with a campaign chest of $100,000. This time the challenger came very close, losing by less than 4,000 votes out of 159,000 cast (49%). For the first time, Boggs lost Jefferson Parish and lost it by 12,000 votes.

In 1969, Louisiana was again under orders to redistrict. The state legislature—controlled by Democrats sympathetic to Boggs despite his generally liberal record—decided to do something about the Congressman's difficulties in the 2nd district. The redistricters removed a large part of Jefferson Parish, including most of Metairie where Boggs lost badly, and put it into the 3rd, where, it was thought, the suburbs would do no harm. As a result, the Republicans put up only token opposition in 1970, and Boggs, with strong black and white working-class support, again took 69%.

Meanwhile, in Washington, Speaker McCormack announced his retirement. Since it was clear that Majority Leader Carl Albert would move up to the Speaker's chair, Boggs argued that he, in turn, should move to the Majority leadership. In the early going, the handicappers felt that Boggs didn't have a chance. For one thing, many House members had said that Boggs, as a man, was aloof and haughty and that his performance as Whip had been erratic. For another, Morris Udall of Arizona and James O'Hara of Michigan both wanted the post and both had labor and liberal support. Meantime Bernie Sisk of California reportedly had the full backing of his state's large delegation and was picking up support in the South as well.

But once again Boggs turned things around. Sisk's challenge faded, and Udall and O'Hara didn't have all the liberal votes they had counted on. Those Northern liberal votes eventually went to Boggs. As a House insider and as a member of Ways and Means, Boggs could promise a desirable committee seat to any wavering member, and he did just that. When the votes were counted, the Whip was way ahead on the first ballot (95 to Udall's next-best 69) and won an easy majority on the second.

Boggs's performance is one example of the way the congressional establishment maintains its power. After the Louisianan's victory, Ways and Means rewarded many liberals with choice assignments—some of which rankled senior committee chairmen like George Mahon of Appropriations and F. Edward Hebert of Armed Services. But with the Democratic caucus growing increasingly liberal, this kind of accommodation has become necessary if a border-state man like Albert or a Southern liberal like Boggs is to remain in control. Albert has announced that he will retire in 1978 when he becomes 70. Boggs will no doubt want his job, and from the looks of things now, he is as likely as anyone to get it.

Census Data 1970 pop. 428,750; deviation from current state average, −5.9%; change 1960–70, +5.0%. Metro. 94.2%, 81.9% central city.

1970 Share of Federal Outlays $463,985,000 (average outlay per district, Louisiana 1–2)

DOD	$118,859,000	HEW	$110,614,000
AEC	$20,000	HUD	$8,065,000
NASA	$52,796,000	OEO	$1,900,000
DOT	$28,878,000	DOA	$31,497,000
		Other	$111,357,000

Federal Military-Industrial Commitments (Louisiana 1–2, greater New Orleans listing)

DOD Contractors Central Gulf Steamship Corp. (New Orleans), $18.431m: cargo transport services. James Flanagan Shipping Corp. (New Orleans), $9.713m: cargo transport services. Avondale Shipyards (New Orleans), $8.529m: ship repair.

DOD Installations Naval Air Station (New Orleans). Naval Support Activity (New Orleans).

NASA Contractors Boeing (New Orleans), $86.557m: construction and support of S-1C stage of Saturn V rocket. Chrysler Corp. (New Orleans), $9.212m: construction and support of S-1B stage of Saturn rocket. Mason-Rust (New Orleans), $5.940m: support of MTR vehicle.

Economic Base Food and kindred products, esp. beverages and canned and preserved fruits, vegetables, and seafood; crude petroleum and natural gas; fabricated metal products, esp. fabricated structural metal products. Also, tourism (New Orleans).

The Voters

Registration 150,642 total. White, 74%; black, 27%. Party registration not available.

Employment profile White collar, 45%. Blue collar, 55%.

Ethnic groups Black, 37%. Total foreign stock, 7%. Ireland, 2%; Germany, 1%; others, 2%.

Presidential vote

1968	Humphrey (D)	46,656	(38%)
	Nixon (R)	31,152	(26%)
	Wallace (AIP)	44,479	(36%)

Representative

Hale Boggs (D) Elected 1940–42, 1946; b. Feb. 15, 1914, Long Beach, Miss.; home, New Orleans; Tulane U., B.A., 1935, LL.B., 1937; USNR, WWII; married, three children; Catholic.

Career U.S. House of Reps., 1940–42; Practicing atty., 1943–46; Chm., Platform Com., Democratic Natl. Convention, 1968; Democratic Whip, 1962– ; Majority Leader, 92nd Congress.

Offices 2207 RHOB, 202-225-6636. Also 638 Fed. Bldg., South, New Orleans 70130, 504-527-2274.

Committees

Jt. Economic Com. (3rd); Subs. (1) Chm., Foreign Economic Policy, (2) Fiscal Policy, (3) Inter-American Economic Relationships, (4) International Exchange and Payments.

Group Ratings

	ADA	COPE	NREP	NFU	LCV	CFA	NAB	NSI	ACA
1970	48	83	42	92	55	81	8	90	16
1969	27	—	—	80	—	—	—	—	19
1968	67	92	—	94	—	—	0	—	0

Key Votes

(1) ABM	ABS	(6) 18-Yr-Vote	FOR	(11) Clean Water $	AGN
(2) SST	FOR	(7) Farm Sub Lmt	AGN	(12) Mig Wrkrs Comp	AGN
(3) Phil Pln	FOR	(8) Coop-Church	AGN	(13) Jets to Chiang	FOR
(4) No-Knock	FOR	(9) Family Asst	FOR	(14) State OEO Veto	AGN
(5) Cmutr Tax	FOR	(10) Work Stamps	AGN	(15) Park Logging	AGN

Election Results

1970 general:	Hale Boggs (D)	51,812	(69%)
	Robert E. Lee (R)	19,703	(26%)
	Benjamin E. Smith (Ind)	3,279	(4%)
1970 primary:	Hale Boggs (D), unopposed		
	(Redistricted 1969)		

THIRD DISTRICT Political Background

Louisiana 3 is Cajun country, where French is still spoken in the towns and villages along the bayous and in the district's rice and sugar cane fields. Since there are fewer blacks here than in any other part of the state and since the Roman Catholic Cajuns have sometimes felt the sting of prejudice themselves, the 3rd is somewhat more liberal about race than northern Louisiana. But even as the use of French grows less common, the difference on this score between the two regions has become less evident. In 1960 the Acadian counties were loyal to fellow Catholic John F. Kennedy and in 1964 to fellow Democrat Lyndon Johnson. But in 1968 the counties abandoned the Democrats and supported Wallace—though he received smaller margins here than in most other parts of the state.

The 3rd also takes in a couple of urban areas: Lafayette (pop. 68,000), a predominantly Cajun industrial town, and a portion of suburban New Orleans in Jefferson Parish in the west. Jefferson casts about 20% of the district's votes in general elections, but it does not swing that much clout in the all-important Democratic primary, an election dominated by the heavily French and Democratic bayou counties.

Yet, oddly enough, in recent years the overwhelmingly Cajun 3rd has not had a congressman with a French name. Edwin E. Willis, a moderate-to-conservative Democrat, represented the district long enough to reach a high-seniority position on the Judiciary Committee and to become chairman of the since-renamed House Un-American Activities Committee (currently Internal Security). But as Willis grew older, opposition appeared, and in 1966, the Congressman barely avoided a runoff. Two years later he wasn't as lucky. State Rep. Patrick T. Caffery (whose grandfather was a U.S. senator at the turn of the century) made a strong showing in the initial primary and whipped Willis in the runoff 60:40. Caffery, a much younger man (38 in 1970), is now solidly entrenched; in the 1970 primary, he trounced a state senator and a perennial aspirant, both of whom had French names. And as is usually the case in Louisiana outside New Orleans, Caffery had no opposition in the general election that followed. Considered somewhat more moderate than most congressmen from the Deep South, the 3rd's Representative seems destined for a long career in the House.

Census Data 1970 pop. 562,425; deviation from current state average, +23.5%; change 1960–70, +37.2%. Metro. 45.8%, 12.3% central city.

1970 Share of Federal Outlays $136,211,163

DOD	$20,399,000	HEW	$60,220,535
AEC	$000	HUD	$1,898,000
NASA	$000	OEO	$656,283
DOT	$3,395,023	DOA	$12,083,246
		Other	$37,559,076

Federal Military-Industrial Commitments

DOD Contractors Good Hope Refineries (Good Hope), $10.010m: petroleum products.

Economic Base Cotton, cash grain, and other field crops; crude petroleum and natural gas; chemicals and allied products.

The Voters

Registration 219,083 total. White, 86%; black, 14%. Party registration not available.
Employment profile White collar, 32%. Blue collar, 68%.
Ethnic groups Black, 16%. Total foreign stock, 2%. Italy, 1%; other, 1%.

Presidential vote

1968	Humphrey (D)	39,857	(25%)
	Nixon (R)	50,740	(32%)
	Wallace (AIP)	6,996	(44%)

Representative

Patrick Thomson Caffery (D) Elected 1968; b. July 6, 1932, near Franklin; home, New Iberia; U. of Southwestern La., B.A., 1955; La. State U., J.D., 1956; married, three children; Catholic.

Career Practicing atty., 1956–68; Asst. Dist. Atty., 1958–62; La. House of Reps., 1964–68.

Offices 216 CHOB, 202-225-4031. Also 114 W. Washington St., New Iberia, 70560, 318-364-1816.

Committees

Public Works (15th); Subs. (1) Flood Control and Internal Development, (2) Investigation and Oversight, (3) Public Buildings and Grounds, (4) Rivers and Harbors, (5) Watershed Development.

Group Ratings

	ADA	COPE	NREP	NFU	LCV	CFA	NAB	NSI	ACA
1970	8	30	0	17	33	43	71	100	91
1969	7	—	—	40	—	—	—	—	88

Key Votes

(1) ABM	FOR	(6) 18-Yr-Vote	AGN	(11) Clean Water $	AGN
(2) SST	AGN	(7) Farm Sub Lmt	AGN	(12) Mig Wrkrs Comp	ABS
(3) Phil Pln	ABS	(8) Coop-Church	AGN	(13) Jets to Chiang	FOR
(4) No-Knock	FOR	(9) Family Asst	AGN	(14) State OEO Veto	FOR
(5) Cmutr Tax	ABS	(10) Work Stamps	FOR	(15) Park Logging	AGN

Election Results

1970 general:	Patrick T. Caffery (D), unopposed		
1970 primary:	Patrick T. Caffery (D)	75,394	(77%)
	Julles G. Mollere (D)	18,607	(19%)
	Warren J. Moity (D)	3,831	(4%)
	(Redistricted 1969)		

FOURTH DISTRICT Political Background

Louisiana 4, in the northwest corner of the state, is dominated by Shreveport, a commercial center for parts of Louisiana, Arkansas, Texas, and Oklahoma. Unlike southern Louisiana, the 4th is definitely part of the Deep South; it occupies a central portion of the old cotton belt as it extends into nearby Texas. The district, with nary a Cajun or white liberal, is very conservative. The enfranchisement of the large black population here has not affected the district's political character. In presidential elections, the vote total of the blacks has simply replaced that of the whites who once voted for liberal candidates, but who have since refused to support the liberals' attachment to the civil rights revolution. In local elections, the blacks have also been shut out; the district has few constituencies with black majorities, and any candidate with black support will receive few white votes.

The 4th's congressman, Joe D. Waggonner, Jr., from Plain Dealing, won the seat in a 1961 special election called after the death of the district's veteran congressman. Waggonner has been reelected easily ever since. In his first years in office, Waggonner had a reputation as a firebrand. But the arch-conservative Congressman has mellowed and is now the informal leader of the Southern Democratic bloc in the House. In 1971, he won a seat on Ways and Means, and his age (52 in 1970) and electoral security indicate that he will be an influential man in Congress for many years to come.

Census Data 1970 pop. 412,900; deviation from current state average, −9.3%; change 1960–70, +1.5%. Metro. 71.2%, 44.0% central city.

1970 Share of Federal Outlays $342,978,068

DOD	$162,343,000	HEW	$94,277,590
AEC	$000	HUD	$1,188,075
NASA	$6,220	OEO	$1,529,177
DOT	$8,573,678	DOA	$17,363,118
		Other	$57,697,210

Federal Military-Industrial Commitments

DOD Contractors Sperry Rand Corp. (Shreveport), $65.625m: operation of army ammunition plant and production of projectiles, pack demolition charges, and anti-personnel mines.

DOD Installations Barksdale AFB (Shreveport).

Economic Base Cotton and livestock, crude petroleum and natural gas; fabricated metal products; food and kindred products.

The Voters

Registration 153,065, total. White, 79%; black, 21%. Party registration not available.

Employment profile White collar, 39%. Blue collar, 61%.

Ethnic groups Black, 35%. Total foreign stock, 2%. All groups less than 0.5% each.

Presidential vote

1968	Humphrey (D)	32,540	(26%)
	Nixon (R)	31,525	(25%)
	Wallace (AIP)	63,402	(50%)

Representative

Joe D. Waggonner, Jr. (D) Elected Dec. 19, 1961; b. Sept. 7, 1918, Plain Dealing; home, Plain Dealing; La. Polytechnic Inst., B.A., 1941; Navy, WWII and Korean War; married, two children; Methodist.

Career Operator, petroleum distributor, 1952– ; Bossier Parish School Bd., 1954–61, Pres., 1956–57; La. Bd. of Ed., 1960–61; Pres., United School Commission of La., 1961.

Offices 221 CHOB, 202-225-2777. Also 210 P.O. Bldg., Shreveport 71101, 318-424-5379.

Committees

Ways and Means (15th).

Group Ratings

	ADA	COPE	NREP	NFU	LCV	CFA	NAB	NSI	ACA
1970	4	25	0	15	11	58	67	100	78
1969	7	—	—	47	—	—	—	—	82
1968	17	9	—	50	—	—	100	—	76

Key Votes

(1) ABM	FOR	(6) 18-Yr-Vote	AGN	(11) Clean Water $	AGN
(2) SST	FOR	(7) Farm Sub Lmt	AGN	(12) Mig Wrkrs Comp	AGN
(3) Phil Pln	AGN	(8) Coop-Church	AGN	(13) Jets to Chiang	FOR
(4) No-Knock	FOR	(9) Family Asst	AGN	(14) State OEO Veto	FOR
(5) Cmutr Tax	AGN	(10) Work Stamps	FOR	(15) Park Logging	FOR

Election Results

1970 general:	J. D. Waggonner, Jr. (D), unopposed
1970 primary:	J. D. Waggonner, Jr. (D), unopposed (Redistricted 1969)

FIFTH DISTRICT Political Background

Louisiana 5 is a geographic anomaly, the result of several redistrictings mandated by the one-man-one-vote decision. Before the decision, the 5th was made up of the northeast portion of the state. This is an economically declining part of the Mississippi Delta region, having a large black population (38% in 1970) and a soil exhausted by too many crops of cotton. Redistricting added some parishes, also poor, that lie just south of the state of Misssissippi, east of the river; the terrain gave the district its present L-shaped appearance. The 5th's major city is Monroe (pop. 56,000), a regional commercial center.

Since 1946, the district has been represented by Otto E. Passman, a forthright conservative and stern critic of government spending. Passman is now 6th ranking Democrat on the House Appropriations Committee and chairman of its Foreign Operations Subcommittee. In the latter capacity he won great fame: Passman has been a sturdy opponent of the foreign aid program since the Eisenhower years. As the foreign aid program has become less popular generally, Passman's role in the issue has become less pivotal. Moreover, there are now enough liberals on the Foreign Operations Subcommittee to prevent its chairman from completely controlling the appropriations process. But much of the credit (or blame) for the steady decline in foreign aid expenditures belongs to the Louisiana Democrat.

Census Data 1970 pop. 415,192; deviation from current state average, —8.8%; change 1960–70, +2.1%. Metro. 27.8%, 13.6% central city.

1970 Share of Federal Outlays $271,427,451

DOD	$14,293,000	HEW	$102,028,173
AEC	$5,500	HUD	$1,617,000
NASA	$26,980	OEO	$1,223,138
DOT	$24,739,880	DOA	$75,738,706
		Other	$51,755,074

Federal Military-Industrial Commitments

None.

Economic Base Cotton and livestock; paper and allied products.

The Voters

Registration 155,783 total. White, 79%; black, 21%. Party registration not available.
Employment profile White collar, 31%. Blue collar, 69%.
Ethnic groups Black, 38%. Total foreign stock, 1%. All groups less than 0.5% each.

Presidential vote

1968	Humphrey (D)	29,968	(24%)
	Nixon (R)	25,343	(20%)
	Wallace (AIP)	71,049	(56%)

Representative

Otto Ernest Passman (D) Elected 1946; b. June 27, 1900, near Franklinton; home, Monroe; Navy, WWII; married; Baptist.

Career Owner, Passman Investment Co.

Offices 2108 RHOB, 202-225-2376. Also P.O. Box 6000, New P.O. Bldg., Monroe 71201, 318-387-1800, and U.S. P.O. Bldg., P.O. Box 138, Clinton 70722, 318-683-8666.

Committees

Appropriations (6th); Subs. (1) Chm., Foreign Operations, (2) Treasury, Post Office, and General Government.

Group Ratings

	ADA	COPE	NREP	NFU	LCV	CFA	NAB	NSI	ACA
1970	0	27	0	23	14	40	50	100	71
1969	7	—	—	36	—	—	—	—	82
1968	25	0	—	40	—	—	50	—	68

Key Votes

(1) ABM	FOR	(6) 18-Yr-Vote	AGN	(11) Clean Water $	AGN
(2) SST	FOR	(7) Farm Sub Lmt	AGN	(12) Mig Wrkrs Comp	AGN
(3) Phil Pln	AGN	(8) Coop-Church	AGN	(13) Jets to Chiang	FOR
(4) No-Knock	FOR	(9) Family Asst	AGN	(14) State OEO Veto	FOR
(5) Cmutr Tax	AGN	(10) Work Stamps	FOR	(15) Park Logging	FOR

Election Results

1970 general:	Otto E. Passman (D), unopposed		
1970 primary:	Otto E. Passman (D)	47,172	(62%)
	Paul Henry Kidd (D)	15,391	(20%)
	David I. Patten (D)	13,855	(18%)
	(Redistricted 1969)		

SIXTH DISTRICT Political Background

Louisiana 6 covers east central Louisiana and includes the city of Baton Rouge. When Huey Long came to Baton Rouge as governor, it was a small, sleepy town;

today it is a bustling, growing city of 165,000, with a major university (Louisiana State) and a major industry (state government). But Baton Rouge is not the entire 6th, though it does cast about half of its votes. To the east there is lowland farming country, Bogalusa, a lumber mill town on the Mississippi border and the scene of racial disorders, and an exurban extension of New Orleans around Slidell in St. Tammany Parish. In recent years, the Klan has probably been as active as civil rights groups in the eastern half of the 6th. The district has also been the site of feverish campaigning in its Democratic congressional primary.

For 28 years (1938–66), the 6th was represented by Jimmy Morrison, a battle-scarred Louisiana political veteran who once (1940) challenged Earl Long, Huey's brother, for the governorship. By Louisiana standards, Morrison had a liberal voting record, though he never, of course, supported a civil rights bill. The Congressman got through an uncomfortably close primary in 1964 when he received only 55,000 of 105,000 votes cast in a field of nine and barely avoided a runoff primary.

The results naturally attracted more opposition two years later. Conservative Judge John Rarick of Baton Rouge resigned his post in order to challenge Morrison. In the first primary, Rarick ran a close second behind the incumbent. But there would have been no runoff primary had it not been for a third candidate, one James E. Morrison, whose 6,562 votes were probably meant for the Congressman. In the runoff, Rarick squeaked through, beating Morrison by 3,876 votes in East Baton Rouge Parish and by 124 votes in the rest of the district, for a margin of an even 4,000.

A former Yankee from Indiana, Rarick is the most rabidly conservative member of Congress. Some claim that he was once associated with the Klan; however that may be, Rarick habitually inserts almost any kind of right wing propaganda into the *Congressional Record*. Even Rarick's fellow Southern congressmen don't take him very seriously. Back home, his strident, voluble conservatism has induced similar misgivings in his home town, Baton Rouge, a city not known for its liberalism. His strength now lies in the rural and small-town parishes of the district. In 1968, the Congressman was forced into a runoff primary when three challengers took 36,000 votes in East Baton Rouge while Rarick won just 20,888; in a 1970 two-man primary, he lost that parish by 1,000 votes, though he did win the election district-wide with 59%.

Rarick's difficulties at the polls indicate that there is steady, strong opposition to him developing in the 6th. If the redistricting due under the 1970 census removes Washington Parish (Bogalusa), a Rarick stronghold, the Congressman could very well lose his seat in 1972.

Census Data 1970 pop. 510,266; deviation from current state average, +12.0%; change 1960–70, +25.0%. Metro. 68.3%, 32.5% central city.

1970 Share of Federal Outlays $324,376,665

DOD	$62,873,000	HEW	$132,690,587
AEC	$255,117	HUD	$577,954
NASA	$3,387,003	OEO	$2,510,811
DOT	$16,248,972	DOA	$14,251,961
		Other	$91,581,260

Federal Military-Industrial Commitments

DOD Contractors Humble Oil and Refining (Baton Rouge), $51.114m: petroleum products.

Economic Base Chemicals and allied products, esp. industrial inorganic and organic chemicals; dairy, livestock, and cash grain; food and kindred products, esp. bakery products. Also, higher education (Louisiana State University).

The Voters

Registration 207,895 total. White, 81%; black, 18%. Party registration not available.

Employment profile White collar, 40%. Blue collar, 60%.

Ethnic groups Black, 26%. Total foreign stock, 4%. Italy, 1%; others, 1%.

Presidential vote

1968	Humphrey (D)	36,625	(24%)
	Nixon (R)	32,642	(21%)
	Wallace (AIP)	83,087	(56%)

Representative

John R. Rarick (D) Elected 1966; b. Jan. 19, 1924, Goshen, Ind.; home, Baton Rouge; Ball State Teachers Col., 1942, 1945; La. State U., 1943–44; Tulane U. Law School, J.D., 1949; Army, WWII; married, three children; Protestant.

Career Atty., Judge, 20th Judicial Dist., 1961–66.

Offices 1525 LHOB, 202-225-3901. Also Rm. 236 New Fed. Bldg., Baton Rouge 70801, 504-344-7679.

Committees

Agriculture (14th); Subs. (1) Livestock and Grains, (2) Oilseeds and Rice.

Group Ratings

	ADA	COPE	NREP	NFU	LCV	CFA	NAB	NSI	ACA
1970	4	25	0	8	0	24	80	100	75
1969	20	—	—	27	—	—	—	—	94
1968	0	0	—	22	—	—	100	—	100

Key Votes

(1) ABM	FOR	(6) 18-Yr-Vote	AGN	(11) Clean Water $	AGN
(2) SST	FOR	(7) Farm Sub Lmt	AGN	(12) Mig Wrkrs Comp	AGN
(3) Phil Pln	AGN	(8) Coop-Church	AGN	(13) Jets to Chiang	FOR
(4) No-Knock	FOR	(9) Family Asst	AGN	(14) State OEO Veto	FOR
(5) Cmutr Tax	ABS	(10) Work Stamps	FOR	(15) Park Logging	FOR

Election Results

1970 general:	John R. Rarick (D), unopposed		
1970 primary:	John R. Rarick (D)	57,835	(59%)
	Jesse H. Bankston (D)	40,451	(41%)
	(Redistricted 1969)		

SEVENTH DISTRICT Political Background

Louisiana 7, southwest Louisiana, extends from the Cajun country to the Texas border. Like the 3rd, this district is heavily French and Catholic, but as one goes farther west, the landscape changes. Bayous give way to coastal flat lands teeming with oil derricks. The steel towers are especially numerous around the city of Lake Charles (pop. 77,000) and toward the Gulf of Mexico to the north. The 7th is the center of Louisiana's large oil industry and is in many ways similar to adjacent east Texas. Politically, the district is moderate by Louisiana standards: for Johnson in 1964 and Wallace in 1968.

The 7th has also chosen a moderate man, Edwin W. Edwards, to represent the district in Congress. In 1965, when Edwards was a local state senator, he won a special election for the seat. Since then, he has had no significant opposition. His popularity indicates that Louisiana voters prefer Edwards' kind of quiet moderation to the strident conservatism practiced by John Rarick of the 6th district, a politician who has consistently run into electoral problems. All indications are that Edwards will have a long congressional career.

Census Data 1970 pop. 412,528; deviation from current state average, –9.4%; change 1960–70, +2.2%. Metro. 35.0%, 18.9% central city.

1970 Share of Federal Outlays $197,956,195

DOD	$30,879,000	HEW	$87,125,746
AEC	$000	HUD	$900,000
NASA	$75,725	OEO	$1,375,600
DOT	$1,050,706	DOA	$31,786,149
		Other	$43,763,269

Federal Military-Industrial Commitments

DOD Contractors Cities Service Oil (Lake Charles), $13.523m: petroleum products.

Economic Base Cotton, cash grain, and livestock; crude petroleum and natural gas; chemicals and allied products.

The Voters

Registration 191,212 total. White, 80%; black, 20%. Party registration not available.

Employment profile White collar, 32%. Blue collar, 68%.

Ethnic groups Black, 35%. Total foreign stock, 2%. All groups less than 0.5% each.

Presidential vote

1968	Humphrey (D)	39,378	(30%)
	Nixon (R)	24,682	(19%)
	Wallace (AIP)	68,243	(52%)

Representative

Edwin W. Edwards (D) Elected Oct. 18, 1965; b. Aug. 7, 1927, Marksville; home, Crowley; La. State U., LL.B., 1949; Naval Air Corps, WWII; Major CAP; married, four children; Catholic.

Career Practicing atty., 1949–65; Crowley City Council, 1954–62; La. Senate, 1964–65.

Offices 425 CHOB, 202-225-2031. Also 125 E. Hutchinson, Crowley 70526, 318-783-3897; 2508 P.O. & Fed. Bldg., Lake Charles 70604, 318-433-1122, and 111 N. Court St., Opelousas, 318-942-2152.

Committees

Internal Security (3rd).

Judiciary (7th); Subs. (1) No. 4.

Group Ratings

	ADA	COPE	NREP	NFU	LCV	CFA	NAB	NSI	ACA
1970	12	45	10	45	40	83	25	90	60
1969	20	—	—	67	—	—	—	—	54
1968	33	42	—	85	—	—	60	—	39

Key Votes

(1) ABM	FOR	(6) 18-Yr-Vote	FOR	(11) Clean Water $	AGN
(2) SST	FOR	(7) Farm Sub Lmt	AGN	(12) Mig Wrkrs Comp	AGN
(3) Phil Pln	ABS	(8) Coop-Church	ABS	(13) Jets to Chiang	ABS
(4) No-Knock	AGN	(9) Family Asst	AGN	(14) State OEO Veto	AGN
(5) Cmutr Tax	ABS	(10) Work Stamps	FOR	(15) Park Logging	ABS

Election Results

1970 general:	Edwin W. Edwards (D), unopposed		
1970 primary:	Edwin W. Edwards (D)	57,277	(67%)
	Robert B. Thompson (D)	13,943	(16%)
	Sidney S. Sylvester (D)	6,221	(7%)
	Alexander S. Jaworsky (D)	5,471	(6%)
	Warren J. Moity (D)	2,592	(3%)
	Charles N. Washington (D)	429	(1%)
	(Redistricted 1969)		

EIGHTH DISTRICT Political Background

Louisiana 8 is the area that remained after Louisiana's seven other districts were carved out. The 8th, shaped something like a steam shovel, extends from the Texas border all the way to Lake Pontchartrain. The weird shape was produced by two re-districtings in the '60's. The district was originally a relatively square portion of west central Louisiana. But that district had been losing population and required the addition of more territory. The easiest way to accomplish this and, at same time, avoid riling the 8th's incumbent and the state's other congressmen was to take a few parishes from several other districts. And that is what the legislature decided to do. The new territory is slightly more French and slightly less conservative than the old 8th, but the character of the old district has remained intact.

The old 8th was Huey Long country *par excellence*. The Kingfish himself was from Winn Parish, which is typical of the area: small towns, poor white farmers on hard-scrabble land, and fewer blacks than in the Mississippi-like parishes to the north. So it is hardly surprising that the 8th has been represented by a succession of Longs to this day.

In 1960 the aging and addled ex-Gov. Earl Long, Huey's brother, beat Congressman Harold McSween in the district's Democratic primary. But Earl died before the general election of that year and, to the dismay of gallery-watchers, never made it to Congress. McSween lasted only one more term, however, as he was ignominiously beaten without a runoff in the 1962 primary by Gillis W. Long, a cousin of Sen. Russell Long.

Gillis Long's two-year record in the House was relatively liberal, which probably explains why he was beaten in the 1964 primary by his cousin, Speedy O. Long. Congressman Speedy Long has shown himself to be more in line with the Southern conservative tradition and has won reelection with relative ease. In the House, Long won a seat on the Armed Services Committee and quickly became a favorite of the late Chairman Mendel Rivers. On paper, the Congressman could easily be redistricted out of office before the 1972 elections. But the Louisiana legislature, forced to redraw district lines twice in the past four years, has each time provided Long with a constituency to his liking. The legislature will probably do so again.

Census Data 1970 pop. 469,186; deviation from current state average, +3.0%; change 1960–70, +14.7%. Metro. 0.0%, 0.0% central city.

1970 Share of Federal Outlays $426,862,696

DOD	$180,297,000	HEW	$106,908,399
AEC	$000	HUD	$672,000
NASA	$000	OEO	$3,512,256
DOT	$39,199,404	DOA	$39,022,779
		Other	$57,250,858

Federal Military-Industrial Commitments

DOD Installations England AFB (Alexandria).

Economic Base Cotton and livestock; lumber and wood products, esp. furniture; food and kindred products.

The Voters

Registration 194,735 total. White, 76%; black, 24%. Party registration not available.

Employment profile White collar, 32%. Blue collar, 68%.

Ethnic groups Black, 30%. Total foreign stock, 2%. Italy, 1%; others, 1%.

Presidential vote

1968	Humphrey (D)	41,471	(29%)
	Nixon (R)	28,693	(20%)
	Wallace (AIP)	72,780	(51%)

Representative

Speedy O. Long (D) Elected 1964; b. June 16, 1928, Tullos; home, Jena; Northwestern State Col., B.A., 1951; La. State U. Law School, J.D., 1959; Navy, 1946–48; USNR, 1951–52; married, two children; Baptist.

Career Practicing atty., 1959– ; La. Senate, 1956–64.

Offices 419 CHOB, 202-225-4926. Also 210-211 Fed. Bldg., Alexandria 71301, 318-442-5856, and Oak St., Jena 71342, 318-992-2767.

Committees

Armed Services (16th); Sub. Number 2.

Merchant Marine and Fisheries (15th); Subs. (1) Chm., Sp. on Maritime Education and Training, (2) Chm., Operations, (3) Panama Canal, (4) Fisheries and Wildlife Conservation.

Group Ratings

	ADA	COPE	NREP	NFU	LCV	CFA	NAB	NSI	ACA
1970	8	18	0	23	33	46	56	100	75
1969	7	—	—	43	—	—	—	—	94
1968	17	9	—	62	—	—	80	—	81

Key Votes

(1) ABM	FOR	(6) 18-Yr-Vote	AGN	(11) Clean Water $	AGN
(2) SST	FOR	(7) Farm Sub Lmt	AGN	(12) Mig Wrkrs Comp	AGN
(3) Phil Pln	AGN	(8) Coop-Church	AGN	(13) Jets to Chiang	FOR
(4) No-Knock	FOR	(9) Family Asst	AGN	(14) State OEO Veto	FOR
(5) Cmutr Tax	ABS	(10) Work Stamps	FOR	(15) Park Logging	FOR

Election Results

1970 general:	Speedy O. Long (D), unopposed		
1970 primary:	Speedy O. Long (D)	59,032	(71%)
	John K. Snyder (D)	24,112	(29%)
	(Redistricted 1969)		

MAINE

Political Background

Down East Maine, once the nation's most Republican state, is now dominated by the Democratic party. The transformation of the state's politics began in 1953 when a young lawyer from the town of Waterville, while convalescing from a broken back, decided to run for governor as a Democrat. The young lawyer was Edmund S. Muskie. In 1954 Muskie became governor with 54% of the vote and was reelected two years later with 59%. The voters of the state, one of poorest outside of the South, especially appreciated Muskie's efforts to attract new industry. In 1958 Muskie ran for the Senate and defeated incumbent Republican Frederick G. Payne with 61% of the vote. At the same time, Maine voters selected another Democrat to succeed Muskie and also chose Democrats to fill two of its three House seats. Muskie won reelection in 1964 with a very strong 67%, and so by 1966—a Republican year in most parts of country—the transformation of Maine politics was complete: Democrat Kenneth Curtis upset the Republican incumbent for the governorship, and the state, which lost a congressional seat in the 1960 census, sent two Democrats to the House of Representatives.

The Democratic takeover was a result of intelligent organization, attractive candidates, and the carelessness of the state's Republican party which had enjoyed too much easy success. The Democrats also benefited from Maine's changing demography. As young people left the economically depressed state, the proportion of Maine's traditionally ethnic Democratic voters increased—the Irish, French-Canadians, and Italians. These ethnic voters, in the mill towns like Lewiston, the state's second largest city, or in the potato country of northern Aroostook County, produced lopsided majorities for the strong Democratic ticket run by the party. Meanwhile, Muskie's serene and plain manner made enough converts of Yankee Republicans to assure Democratic control of the state.

Only the heavily Yankee areas along the coast east of Portland are still solidly Republican, and the last of the consistent winners among the Republicans is the state's senior senator, Margaret Chase Smith. Mrs. Smith succeeded her late husband in the House in 1939 and served there nine years before going to the Senate in 1948. She is now the 3rd ranking Republican on Appropriations and the senior Republican on Armed Services, where she usually supports the military but often opposes some of its pet projects.

Mrs. Smith's independence is well known. After the ABM debate, for example, she offered her own amendment, and only after it was defeated on a 50-50 tie did she cast a deciding vote for the Nixon Administration program. The Senator has had few qualms about opposing Republican schemes or politicians. As early as 1950, long before others dared, she attacked Sen. Joseph McCarthy on the floor of the Senate.

Mrs. Smith is also well known for never announcing in advance how she will vote on crucial issues. When the White House was lobbying for the Carswell nomination, one of Nixon's staff implied to the wavering Sen. Marlow Cook that his fellow Republican, Margaret Chase Smith, would vote for confirmation. When Sen. Smith learned of this, she sent the presumptuous lobbyist a terse note and later voted against confirmation.

The Maine Senator has not revealed her plans for 1972, when her current Senate term expires. Mrs. Smith has won reelection easily, but she might have some trouble in 1972 if Sen. Muskie is nominated for President and heads the national Democratic ticket. There are rumors that Democratic Congressman William D. Hathaway, a strong vote-getter in the 2nd district, is interested in running for the seat. It is possible that the Senate's only lady will retire, but no one will know exactly what her plans are until she chooses to disclose them.

In 1970 when Edmund Muskie was campaigning for reelection to the Senate, there was talk that his political ambitions were turning his attention away from the people back home. Most Maine voters disagreed with this assessment of the Senator. Moreover, they were proud of Ed Muskie, the state's first presidential prospect since James G. Blaine, a Republican who lost to Grover Cleveland back in 1884. Muskie won reelection with 62%, carrying all but three staunch Republican counties.

For many years Muskie led anti-pollution fights in the Senate. His efforts culminated in a bill passed in 1970 that will require auto-makers to clean up exhaust emissions by 1975, five years earlier than the target date set by the Nixon Administration. After the 1968 election Muskie became an opponent of the war. Even though the Maine Senator has become a prominent national political figure, he has remained attentive to the needs of his home. He has supported such measures as shoe import quotas and the Machiasport oil refinery, though these positions run counter to his advocacy of free trade and his concern for the environment.

How Muskie became a presidential candidate is interesting. Four years ago, he was a little-known senator from a small state; he was an admittedly able man but his speciality, concern for the environment, was an obscure one which received little national attention. But in 1968 Humphrey picked him for a running mate. Out of the mess at Chicago, where Muskie loyally supported the Johnson Administration's Vietnam plank, and out of the slipshod Democratic campaign that followed, Muskie emerged looking very good indeed. As it happened, many, if not most, Americans would have elected Muskie President in 1968—given the choice of Humphrey, Nixon, Agnew, and Wallace. As of this writing, the Maine Senator, who has occasionally run ahead of Nixon in opinion polls, is the favorite to win the Democratic presidential nomination in 1972.

If Muskie's seat is vacant in January 1973, Democratic Gov. Kenneth Curtis will probably appoint 2nd district Congressman William Hathaway, whose voting record is very much like that of Senator Muskie.

Electoral Votes 4

Census Data 1970 pop. 993,663; 0.48% of U.S. total, 39th largest; change 1960–70, +6.0%. Metro. 22.6%, 13.0% central city. 1970 per capita income, $3243, 37th highest. 37th in number of poor.

1970 Share of Federal Tax Burden $741,530,000; 0.38% of U.S. total, 40th largest.

1970 Share of Federal Outlays $668,093,231; 0.35% of U.S. total, 47th largest. Per capita federal spending, $672.

DOD	$134,648,000	46th (0.23%)	HEW	$267,455,306	39th (0.51%)
AEC	$82,549	46th (—)	HUD	$5,176,801	45th (0.27%)
NASA	$4,490,000	24th (0.12%)	OEO	$3,209,202	43rd (0.04%)
DOT	$37,511,758	46th (0.53%)	DOA	$26,514,420	46th (0.21%)
DOC	$2,464,478	45th (0.21%)	POD	$38,551,594	37th (0.53%)
DOI	$5,791,699	47th (0.25%)	VA	$56,585,333	39th (0.77%)
DOJ	$3,285,909	37th (0.57%)	CSC	$16,609,255	39th (0.41%)
			Other	$668,093,231	

Economic Base Footwear other than rubber, and other leather and leather products; paper mills, and other paper and allied products; poultry, potatoes, and dairy; food and kindred products, esp. canned and preserved fruits, vegetables, and seafoods; textile mill products, esp. broad woven cotton fabric mills and broad woven wool fabric mills, including dyeing and finishing; lumber and wood products, except furniture; ship and boat building and repairing, and other transportation equipment; electrical machinery, equipment, and supplies.

Political Line-up Governor, Kenneth M. Curtis (D); seat up, 1974. Senators, Margaret Chase Smith (R) and Edmund S. Muskie (D). Representatives, 2 (2 D and 0 R). State Senate (14 D and 18 R); State House (71 D and 80 R).

The Voters

Registration 393,639 total. 170,536 D (43%); 223,103 R (57%).

Employment profile White collar, 41%. Blue collar, 59%.

Ethnic groups Black, 1%. Total foreign stock, 26%. Germany, Sweden, Norway, 5% each; Canada, 2%; Poland, UK, Czech., USSR, Austria, 1% each; others, 6%.

Presidential vote

1968	Humphrey (D)	217,312	(55%)
	Nixon (R)	169,254	(43%)
	Wallace (AIP)	6,370	(2%)
1964	Johnson (D)	262,264	(69%)
	Goldwater (R)	118,701	(31%)
1960	Kennedy (D)	181,159	(43%)
	Nixon (R)	240,608	(57%)

Senator

Margaret Chase Smith (R) Elected 1948, seat up 1972; b. Dec. 14, 1897, Skowhegan, Maine; home, Skowhegan; widowed; Methodist.

Career Ind. reporter, 1919–28; Daniel E. Cummings Co., 1928–30; Treas., New England Process Co., Skowhegan, 1928–30; Candidate for Pres., Repub. Natl. Convention, 1964.

Offices 2121 NSOB, 202-225-2523.

Committees

Aeronautical and Space Agencies (2nd).

Appropriations (3rd); Subs. (1) Defense and Intelligence, (2) HUD, Space, and Science, (3) Public Works, (4) State, Justice, Commerce, the Judiciary, and Related Agencies, (5) Transportation.

Armed Services (Ranking Mbr.); Subs. (1) Nuclear Test Ban Treaty Safeguards.

Group Ratings

	ADA	COPE	NREP	NFU	LCV	NAB	NSI	ACA
1970	22	23	17	43	47	90	60	76
1969	33	—	—	50	—	—	—	69
1968	36	34	—	54	—	50	—	64

Key Votes

(1) ABM	AGN	(8) Phil Pln	AGN	(15) Coop-Church	AGN
(2) SST	AGN	(9) Vol Army	AGN	(16) Cut Oil Dpltn	FOR
(3) Busing	AGN	(10) Prison $	AGN	(17) Consumer Prot	FOR
(4) Tob Sub	AGN	(11) Cut Mil $	AGN	(18) Farm Sub Limit	ABS
(5) Carswell	AGN	(12) Defoliatn	FOR	(19) Comp Bid Sales	AGN
(6) No-Knock	FOR	(13) 18-Yr-Vote	FOR	(20) Pre-Prod Tests	FOR
(7) Seniorty	FOR	(14) Pentgn PR	FOR	(21) Cut Marjna Pen	AGN

Election Results

1966 general:	Margaret Chase Smith (R)	188,291	(59%)
	Elmer Violette (D)	131,136	(41%)
1966 primary:	Margaret Chase Smith (R), unopposed		
1960 general:	Margaret Chase Smith (R)	256,890	(62%)
	Lucia M. Comier (D)	159,809	(38%)

Senator

Edmund S. Muskie (D) Elected 1958, seat up 1976; b. March 28, 1914, Rumford; home, Waterville; Bates Col., B.A., 1936; Cornell U., LL.B., 1939; USNR, WWII; married, five children; Catholic.

Career Practicing atty., Waterville; Maine House of Reps., 1947–51; Floor Leader, 1949–51; Dem. V.P. candidate, 1969.

Offices 221 OSOB, 202-225-5344. Also 112 Main St., Waterville 04901, 207-873-3361.

Committees

Foreign Relations (8th); Subs. (1) Chm., Arms Control, International Law and Organization, (2) Far Eastern Affairs, (3) Western Hemisphere Affairs.

Government Operations (4th); Subs. (1) Chm., Intergovernmental Relations, (2) National Security and International Operations.

Public Works (2nd); Subs. (1) Chm., Air and Water Pollution, (2) Economic Development, (3) Public Roads.

Sp. Com. on Aging (5th); Subs. (1) Chm., Health of the Aging, (2) Consumer Interests of the Elderly, (3) Housing for the Elderly, (4) Long-Term Care.

Group Ratings

	ADA	COPE	NREP	NFU	LCV	NAB	NSI	ACA
1970	91	100	90	100	73	18	10	10
1969	94	—	—	86	—	—	—	0
1968	97	80	—	77	—	25	—	5

Key Votes

(1) ABM	AGN	(8) Phil Pln	FOR	(15) Coop-Church	FOR
(2) SST	AGN	(9) Vol Army	AGN	(16) Cut Oil Dpltn	FOR
(3) Busing	FOR	(10) Prison $	FOR	(17) Consumer Prot	FOR
(4) Tob Sub	FOR	(11) Cut Mil $	FOR	(18) Farm Sub Limit	FOR
(5) Carswell	AGN	(12) Defoliatn	AGN	(19) Comp Bid Sales	AGN
(6) No-Knock	AGN	(13) 18-Yr-Vote	FOR	(20) Pre-Prod Tests	ABS
(7) Seniorty	ABS	(14) Pentgn PR	AGN	(21) Cut Marjna Pen	FOR

Election Results

1970 general:	Edmund S. Muskie (D)	199,954	(62%)
	Neil S. Bishop (R)	123,906	(38%)
1970 primary:	Edmund S. Muskie (D), unopposed		
1964 general:	Edmund S. Muskie (D)	253,511	(67%)
	Clifford G. McIntire (R)	127,040	(33%)

FIRST DISTRICT Political Background

Maine 1 includes Portland, the state's largest city, and Augusta, its capital. The 1st also takes in most of the famed rocky Maine coast, which each summer is visited by more and more tourists. The 1st is less depressed economically than the 2nd district further north. Here in the 1st the outmigration of the young people is balanced by retirees converting their vacation homes to year-round residences. Voters of old Yankee stock still dominate the small towns of Lincoln, Knox, and Waldo counties in the east, but to the west the sons and daughters of Irish and French-Canadian immigrants give the district a clear Democratic stamp. The mill towns of Saco and Sanford and the city of Portland produce especially heavy Democratic majorities.

Before the emergence of Ed Muskie in Maine politics, the 1st was a Republican district, and even as late as 1964, a Republican, liberal Stanley Tupper, was elected to represent it in the House. But in 1966 Tupper decided to retire in order to accept an appointment from the Johnson Administration. He was succeeded by Democrat Peter Kyros who won a relatively easy victory in the general election. In the elections that have followed, the Congressman has increased his margins and now seems invulnerable in the 1st, except, perhaps, in a strong Republican year. Kyros, of Portland, is part of a contingent of Greek-American congressmen from rather improbable places—John Brademas, of South Bend, Indiana, and Nick Galifianakis, of Durham, North Carolina.

In the House, Kyros has usually taken liberal positions on both domestic and foreign issues. He has also shown that solicitude for local interests which the 1st district of Maine, like most others in the nation, expects of its congressmen. Kyros has supported import quotas for shoe companies and the people employed in them; he has insisted that the Portsmouth Navy Yard, across Piscataqua River in New Hampshire, stay open; and he complained bitterly when the Bath Iron Works lost a two-billion-dollar destroyer contract to a Mississippi firm.

Maine has no redistricting problems. In 1961, the Republican split the state's major industrial areas in half in an effort to create two Republican constituencies. But the Republican plan did not work out; Democrats now represent both congressional districts. And, in a peculiar development, the rather large population discrepancy between the districts under the 1960 census—40,000—has been virtually eliminated by a shift of population within the state. The 1970 census shows the 1st district has 495,681 people and the 2nd 497,982. The balance will make Maine one of the most perfectly districted states in the nation. As a result, there will be little tampering with district lines.

Census Data 1970 pop. 495,681; deviation from current state average, −0.2%; change 1960–70, +6.9%. Metro. 28.6%, 13.1% central city.

1970 Share of Federal Outlays $349,744,055

DOD	$70,984,000	HEW	$137,037,598
AEC	$000	HUD	$1,461,575
NASA	$000	OEO	$2,436,996
DOT	$27,992,951	DOA	$6,161,749
		Other	$103,669,186

Federal Military-Industrial Commitments

DOD Contractors Bath Industries (Bath), $20.404m: ship construction and repair. Maremont Corp. (Saco), $15.788m: 7.62-mm machine guns.

DOD Installations Naval Air Station (Brunswick).

Economic Base Footwear other than rubber, and other leather and leather products; food and kindred products, esp. canned and preserved fruits, vegetables, and seafoods; textile mill products; poultry and dairy. Also, tourism (Rocky Coast).

The Voters

Registration 195,450 total. 78,482 D (40%); 116,968 R (60%).

Employment profile White collar, 38%. Blue collar, 62%.

Ethnic groups Black, less than 0.5%. Total foreign stock, 23%. Canada, 15%; UK, 2%; Ireland, Italy, 1% each; others, 4%.

Presidential vote

1968	Humphrey (D)	112,843	(55%)
	Nixon (R)	88,406	(43%)
	Wallace (AIP)	3,390	(2%)

Representative

Peter N. Kyros (D) Elected 1966; b. July 11, 1925, Portland; home, Portland; M.I.T., 1943–44; U.S. Naval Academy, B.S., 1947; Harvard Law School, LL.B., 1957; Navy, 1944–53; married, two children; Greek Orthodox.

Career Practicing atty., 1957–66; Counsel, Maine Pub. Utilities Commission, 1957–59.

Offices 228 CHOB, 202-225-6116. Also 151 Forest Ave., Portland 04104, 207-775-3131, ext. 561.

Committees

Interstate and Foreign Commerce (15th); Sub. on Public Health and Environment.

Merchant Marine and Fisheries (20th); Subs. (1) Coast Guard, Coast and Geodetic Survey and Navigation, (2) Fisheries and Wildlife Conservation, (3) Sp. on Maritime Education and Training.

Group Ratings

	ADA	COPE	NREP	NFU	LCV	CFA	NAB	NSI	ACA
1970	72	100	75	92	100	100	0	78	26
1969	73	—	—	100	—	—	0	—	12
1968	67	100	—	100	—	—	0	—	5

Key Votes

(1) ABM	FOR	(6) 18-Yr-Vote	FOR	(11) Clean Water $	FOR
(2) SST	AGN	(7) Farm Sub Lmt	AGN	(12) Mig Wrkrs Comp	FOR
(3) Phil Pln	AGN	(8) Coop-Church	FOR	(13) Jets to Chiang	AGN
(4) No-Knock	FOR	(9) Family Asst	FOR	(14) State OEO Veto	AGN
(5) Cmutr Tax	FOR	(10) Work Stamps	AGN	(15) Park Logging	AGN

Election Results

1970 general:	Peter N. Kyros (D)	99,483	(59%)
	Ronald T. Speers (R)	68,671	(41%)
1970 primary:	Peter N. Kyros (D)	19,914	(83%)
	John D. Rigazio (D)	4,029	(17%)
1968 general:	Peter N. Kyros (D)	113,501	(57%)
	Horace A. Hildreth, Jr. (R)	86,949	(43%)

SECOND DISTRICT Political Background

Maine 2, the northern and eastern district, covers most of the state's land area. Within the 2nd are Maine's famous pine trees—87% of the state is forested and 52% of it is owned by lumber companies. Aroostook County, in the north, long famous for Maine potatoes, has recently been suffering from the emigration of its young people. Washington County, in the east on the New Brunswick line, is even poorer, the poorest part of Maine. Washington, where 60% of the housing units are substandard, has a substantial amount of employment. Because of its poverty, the county is the proposed site of the Machiasport oil refinery, which would operate free of import quota restrictions, and also the site of the proposed Dickey-Lincoln dam. So far, Maine and other New England congressmen have been unable to get money appropriated for construction of the dam. Both developments are aimed at reducing the cost of fuel and electricity in New England, where they are the highest in the country. Oil and coal interests have opposed both projects.

The western part of the district, the most Democratic part of Maine, is dominated by Androscoggin County and its twin cities of Lewiston and Auburn; in 1970, for example, Lewiston gave Sen. Muskie 13,330 votes and his opponent 1,868. In 1961, when the state was being redistricted, the Democrats objected to the inclusion of Androscoggin in the 2nd district; but today, since both the state's House seats are filled by Democrats, they are no doubt quite content with the arrangement.

In 1964, Republican Congressman Clifford McIntire vacated the post to make a futile bid for Muskie's Senate seat. McIntire was succeeded by a young (then 40) Democratic lawyer, William D. Hathaway. Hathaway, who votes liberal and devotes a great amount of attention to local problems, has won reelection easily ever since. The Congressman is so popular that he ran 1% ahead of Muskie in the district in 1970.

Although Hathaway now has a seat on the Appropriations Committee, he seems less interested in waiting 20 years for a subcommittee chairmanship than in moving up to the Senate. If, as rumored, he challenges Margaret Chase Smith in 1972, he may not win; but he would be the logical choice to succeed Sen. Smith or Sen. Muskie, should either seat become vacant in the next few years.

Census Data 1970 pop. 497,982; deviation from current state average, +0.2%; change 1960–70, −1.5%. Metro. 14.6%, 12.9% central city.

1970 Share of Federal Outlays $318,349,176

DOD	$63,664,000	HEW	$130,417,708
AEC	$82,549	HUD	$3,715,226
NASA	$4,490,000	OEO	$172,206
DOT	$9,518,807	DOA	$20,352,671
		Other	$85,936,009

Federal Military-Industrial Commitments

DOD Installations Naval Radio Station (East Machias). Naval Security Group Activity (Winter Harbor). Bucks Harbor AF Station (Bucks Harbor). Caswell AF Station (Presque Isle). Charleston AF Station (Charleston).

Economic Base Potatoes and dairy; lumber and wood products except furniture; footwear other than rubber and other leather and leather products. Also, higher education (University of Maine), and tourism (Rocky Coast and woods).

The Voters

Registration 198,189 total. 92,054 D (46%); 106,135 R (54%).

Employment profile White collar, 33%. Blue collar, 67%.

Ethnic groups Black, less than 0.5%. Total foreign stock, 24%. Canada, 19%; UK, 1%; others, 4%.

Presidential vote

1968	Humphrey (D)	104,469	(56%)
	Nixon (R)	80,848	(43%)
	Wallace (AIP)	2,980	(2%)

Representative

William Dodd Hathaway (D) Elected 1964; b. Feb. 21, 1924, Cambridge, Mass.; home, Auburn; Harvard U., B.A., 1949, LL.B., 1953; USAF, WWII; married, two children; Episcopalian.

Career Practicing atty., 1953–64; Asst. Atty., Androscoggin County, 1955–57; Hearing Examiner, State Liquor Commission, 1957–61.

Offices 329 CHOB, 202-225-6306. Also 40 Pine St., Lewiston 04240, 207-783-2049, and 235 Fed. Office Bldg., Bangor 04401, 207-942-8271, ext. 310.

Committees

Appropriations (29th); Subs. (1) Foreign Operations, (2) Legislative.

Group Ratings

	ADA	COPE	NREP	NFU	LCV	CFA	NAB	NSI	ACA
1970	88	100	83	92	88	100	0	22	0
1969	100	—	—	100	—	—	—	—	0
1968	92	100	—	100	—	—	0	—	0

Key Votes

(1) ABM	AGN	(6) 18-Yr-Vote	FOR	(11) Clean Water $	FOR
(2) SST	AGN	(7) Farm Sub Lmt	AGN	(12) Mig Wrkrs Comp	FOR
(3) Phil Pln	FOR	(8) Coop-Church	FOR	(13) Jets to Chiang	AGN
(4) No-Knock	AGN	(9) Family Asst	FOR	(14) State OEO Veto	AGN
(5) Cmutr Tax	FOR	(10) Work Stamps	AGN	(15) Park Logging	FOR

Election Results

1970 general:	William D. Hathaway (D)	96,235	(64%)
	Maynard G. Conners (R)	53,642	(36%)
1970 primary:	William D. Hathaway (D)	24,708	(89%)
	Albion D. Boodwin (R)	3,039	(11%)
1968 general:	William D. Hathaway (D)	102,369	(56%)
	Elden H. Shute, Jr. (R)	81,398	(44%)

MARYLAND

Political Background

Maryland, one of the nation's most diverse states, is part urban, part suburban, part rural Southern, and part Appalachian. The city of Baltimore, having large black, Jewish, Irish, Italian, and Greek communities, contains nearly a quarter of the state's people. But a great portion, nearly half, of Maryland's residents live in suburbs: Baltimore County, north of the city, and wealthy Montgomery and middle-class Prince Georges counties outside Washington, D.C. The remaining quarter inhabit the rural areas and small towns found in the Southern-oriented Eastern Shore and in the hill country of the Maryland panhandle.

Baltimore, like most Northern industrial cities, usually votes Democratic. The older Democratic tradition in the state, however, is Southern-oriented; Maryland, lying below the Mason-Dixon line, was once a slave state. Today, like many residents of the South, rural Marylanders register Democratic and vote conservative. George Wallace almost carried the state in the 1964 presidential primary, winning big margins in the rural counties and in the working-class sections of Baltimore. The state's suburbs hold the balance of political power. Affluent Montgomery County has become a liberal stronghold, while Prince Georges and Baltimore counties have reacted much more favorably to the Nixon-Agnew appeal. The Maryland political mix—urban, suburban, and rural—has produced some close presidential elections of late; in 1968, for example, Humphrey carried Maryland by a scant 19,000 votes. The Democrat lost all but two counties, Montgomery and rural Calvert, but won by virtue of a big margin—95,000 votes—in the city of Baltimore.

Four years ago, Maryland had two Democratic senators; today, it has two Republicans. The man most responsible for the change in the state's representation is not Spiro Agnew but the man who made Agnew's political career possible—George Mahoney, a 68-year-old contractor who has run for governor and senator eight times and never won an election. During the '50's Mahoney's independent candidacies accounted for the victories of Republican Sen. J. Glenn Beall, Sr. (1952) and John Marshall Butler (1956). In 1966, Mahoney decided to run for governor in the Democratic primary. He based his campaign on a single slogan, "Your home is your castle," which was meant to indicate his opposition to open housing legislation. Getting heavy margins in Maryland's rural areas, Mahoney managed to edge out two other Democrats in the primary. As a result, Spiro Agnew, the Republican candidate, suddenly inherited massive liberal and black support, particularly in the city of Baltimore and Montgomery, and won the general election. If the runner-up in the Democratic primary, liberal Congressman-at-Large Carlton Sickles, had received a few thousand more votes, Agnew would not have gotten the support of Maryland liberals and would not have become governor of the state and subsequently Vice President of the United States. But Carlton Sickles, in fact, lost the Democratic primary.

In 1968, Mahoney continued his career as perennial candidate, running as an independent for the U.S. Senate against Democratic incumbent Daniel Brewster and liberal Republican Representative Charles Mathias. Mahoney cut heavily into the normally Democratic blue-collar vote; meanwhile, Mathias, who opposed the war policies of the Johnson Administration, beat Brewster, who supported them, soundly in high-income areas like Montgomery County. The result was a 100,000-vote Mathias victory, with Mahoney winning 150,000 votes. Ex-Senator Brewster, the LBJ stand-in in the 1964 primary against George Wallace, has since fallen on hard times; the horsy-set millionaire, under indictment on bribery charges, is ill on his farm in Ireland.

In 1970, Mahoney returned to the Democratic primary to oppose Sen. Joseph D. Tydings, who was in trouble with the right for his support of gun-control legislation and with the left for his support of the District of Columbia crime bill and its no-knock provision; other, less ideological, Maryland voters felt that the Senator was cold and aloof. Mahoney, oddly enough, was against no-knock. If "your home is your castle," he explained, your home should be protected from warrantless searches. Despite Mahoney's position on no-knock, conservative, rural Marylanders—the kind of citizens who, further north, vote in the Republican primary—supported the maverick candidate with large margins. In the four-man field, Mahoney finished with 37% and Tydings 53%. The Senator's showing was a poor one for an incumbent who won his 1964 primary against a machine candidate by 123,000 and took the 1964 general election by 276,000 votes.

Tydings was in so much trouble that his opponent, Congressman J. Glenn Beall, Jr., the son of the man Tydings had defeated in 1964, was content to run a quiet, relaxed campaign. The anti-gun-control lobby, which had made Tydings its number-one target, was pouring in money to beat him. And during the campaign, *Life* magazine charged that Tydings used his influence for the benefit of a company in which he was the largest stockholder. John Mitchell's Justice Department, several weeks after the election, announced that Tydings' actions were strictly within the law.

Tydings lost the election by 22,000 votes out of 945,000 cast. The incumbent carried Montgomery County by a thin 20,000 votes and Prince Georges by 9,000—both figures far under his campaign staff's predictions. His margin in the city of Baltimore was only 61,000, the result of a poor turnout, some 20% lower than in the state as a whole. Beall carried the rest of Maryland by solid margins; in the Eastern Shore, for example, he received 69% of the votes.

But Beall's Republican victory can in no way be attributed to the Vice President's standing among Maryland voters. In the election for governor, Agnew's protégé, C.

Stanley Blair, was beaten badly (65–35) by Democrat Marvin Mandel, the state legislator who succeeded Agnew when the now-famous man left for Washington. The rest of the Democratic ticket, most of it backed by the old Baltimore machine, also swept into office easily.

The State House Democrats controlled the redistricting process and produced no surprises. Republican Lawrence J. Hogan of the present 5th district was seriously hurt by the new lines. Baltimore, which lost population, also lost a congressional seat, leaving liberal insurgent Paul Sarbanes, now of the 4th, in the same district with machine veteran Edward Garmatz, now of the 3rd. The net result of the redistricting gives the Democrats a chance to increase their 5:3 advantage in the state's House delegation to 6:2 in 1972.

Electoral Votes 10

Census Data 1970 pop. 3,953,698; 1.94% of U.S. total, 18th largest; change 1960–70, +27.5%. Metro. 25.9%, 24.7% central city. 1969 per capita income, $4,073, 10th highest. 22nd in number of poor.

1970 Share of Federal Tax Burden $4,293,090,000; 2.20% of U.S. total, 12th largest.

1970 Share of Federal Outlays $4,517,117,485; 2.39% of U.S. total, 14th largest. Per capita federal spending, $1,143.

DOD	$1,697,640,000	10th	(2.96%)	HEW	$1,222,363,005	12th	(2.34%)
AEC	$80,144,588	14th	(3.34%)	HUD	$39,848,117	19th	(2.04%)
NASA	$238,470,463	6th	(6.48%)	OEO	$13,037,081	20th	(1.72%)
DOT	$178,182,497	13th	(2.50%)	DOA	$97,485,443	38th	(0.75%)
DOC	$208,115,925	1st	(17.99%)	POD	$113,013,614	19th	(1.55%)
DOI	$34,550,145	22nd	(1.50%)	VA	$141,030,704	25th	(1.91%)
DOJ	$4,843,275	30th	(0.84%)	CSC	$195,244,025	4th	(4.85%)
				Other	$254,168,603		

Economic Base Blast furnaces, steel works and rolling and finishing mills, and other primary metal industries; food and kindred products, esp. meat products; communication equipment and other machinery, equipment, and supplies; transportation equipment, esp. ship and boat building and repairing, and motor vehicles and motor vehicle equipment; apparel and other finished products made from fabrics and similar materials, esp. men's, youths', and boys' suits, coats, and overcoats; printing, publishing, and allied industries, esp. commercial printing; nonelectrical machinery, chemicals and allied industries; fabricated metal products, esp. fabricated structural metal products; paper and allied products, esp. paperboard containers and boxes.

Political Line-up Governor, Marvin Mandel (D); seat up, 1974. Senators, Charles McC. Mathias (R) and J. Glenn Beall, Jr. (R). Representatives, 8 (5 D and 3 R). State Senate (33 D and 10 R); State House (122 D and 20 R).

The Voters

Registration 1,510,071 total. 1,065,242 D (70%); 401,764 R (27%); 43,065 other (3%).

Employment profile White collar, 46%. Blue collar, 54%.

Ethnic groups Black, 17%. Total foreign stock, 12%. Germany, 2%; Ireland, Italy, Poland, UK, USSR, Canada, 1% each; others, 4%.

Presidential vote

1968	Humphrey (D)	538,310	(44%)
	Nixon (R)	517,995	(42%)
	Wallace (AIP)	178,734	(14%)
1964	Johnson (D)	730,912	(66%)
	Goldwater (R)	385,495	(34%)
1960	Kennedy (D)	565,808	(54%)
	Nixon (R)	489,538	(46%)

Senator

Charles McC. Mathias, Jr. (R) Elected 1964, seat up 1976; b. July 24, 1922, Frederick; home, Frederick; Haverford College, B.A., 1944; Yale, 1943–44; U. of Md., LL.B., 1949; USNR, WWII; married, two children; Episcopalian.

Career Asst. Atty. Gen. 1953–54; City Atty., Frederick, 1954–59; Md. House of Delegates, 1958–60; U.S. House, 1960–68.

Offices 240 OSOB, 1-202-225-4654. Also Fed. Office Bldg., Baltimore 21201, 1-301-962-4850, and P.O. Bldg., Hagerstown 21740, 1-301-733-2710.

Committees

District of Columbia (Ranking Mbr.); Sub. on Business, Commerce, and Judiciary.

Government Operations (5th); Subs. (1) Executive Reorganization, (2) National Security and International Operations.

Judiciary (6th); Subs. (1) Administrative Practice and Procedure, (2) Juvenile Delinquency, (3) Penitentiaries, (4) Refugees and Escapees, (5) Separation of Powers.

Group Ratings

	ADA	COPE	NREP	NFU	LCV	NAB	NSI	ACA
1970	78	83	100	69	0	33	0	15
1969	78	—	—	54	—	—	—	7

Key Votes

(1) ABM	AGN	(8) Phil Pln	FOR	(15) Coop-Church	FOR
(2) SST	FOR	(9) Vol Army	ABS	(16) Cut Oil Dpltn	AGN
(3) Busing	FOR	(10) Prison $	FOR	(17) Consumer Prot	AGN
(4) Tob Sub	FOR	(11) Cut Mil $	FOR	(18) Farm Sub Limit	FOR
(5) Carswell	AGN	(12) Defoliatn	FOR	(19) Comp Bid Sales	ABS
(6) No-Knock	AGN	(13) 18-Yr-Vote	FOR	(20) Pre-Prod Tests	ABS
(7) Seniorty	AGN	(14) Pentgn PR	AGN	(21) Cut Marjna Pen	ABS

Election Results

1968 general:	Charles McC. Mathias, Jr. (R)	541,893	(48%)
	Daniel B. Brewster (D)	443,667	(39%)
	George P. Mahoney (Ind.)	148,467	(13%)
1968 primary:	Charles McC. Mathias, Jr. (R)	66,777	(80%)
	Frederick Harry Lee Simms (R)	11,927	(14%)
	Paul Wattay (R)	4,790	(6%)

Senator

J. Glenn Beall, Jr. (R) Elected 1970; b. June 19, 1927, Cumberland; home, Frostburg; Yale U., A.B., 1950; USN 1945–46; married, two children; Episcopalian.

Career Partner, Beall, Garner and Geare, Inc., Insurance, 1952; Md. House of Delegates, 1962–68; U.S. House of Representatives, 1968–70.

Offices 458 OSOB, 1-202-225-4524. Also 1518 Fed. Bldg., Baltimore 21201, 1-301-962-4850, and P.O. Bldg., Cumberland 21502, 1-301-722-4535, and P.O. Bldg., Hagerstown 21740, 1-301-733-2710.

Committees

Labor and Public Welfare (7th); Subs. (1) Aging. (2) Children and Youth, (3) Education, (4) Health, (5) Migratory Labor, (6) Railroad Retirement, (7) Spec. on Social Programs.

Public Works (5th); Subs. (1) Air and Water Pollution, (2) Economic Development, (3) Flood Control—Rivers and Harbors, (4) Spec. on Economic Development.

Sel. Com. on Small Business (7th); Subs. (1) Financing and Investment, (2) Government Procurement.

Note: Except for the SST vote, the following ratings and votes cover Senator Beall's record in the House of Representatives where he served prior to his election in 1970.

Group Ratings

	ADA	COPE	NREP	NFU	LCV	CFA	NAB	NSI	ACA
1970	20	42	33	77	33	43	91	100	63
1969	20	—	—	54	—	—	—	—	47

Key Votes

(1) ABM	FOR	(6) 18-Yr-Vote	FOR	(11) Clean Water $	FOR
(2) SST	FOR	(7) Farm Sub Lmt	FOR	(12) Mig Wrkrs Comp	AGN
(3) Phil Pln	FOR	(8) Coop-Church	AGN	(13) Jets to Chiang	FOR
(4) No-Knock	FOR	(9) Family Asst	FOR	(14) State OEO Veto	FOR
(5) Cmutr Tax	AGN	(10) Work Stamps	FOR	(15) Park Logging	FOR

Election Results

1970 general:	J. Glenn Beall, Jr. (R)	484,960	(51%)
	Joseph D. Tydings (D)	460,422	(48%)
	Harvey Wilder (AIP)	10,988	(1%)
1970 primary:	J. Glenn Beall, Jr. (R)	99,687	(83%)
	Wainwright Dawson, Jr. (R)	9,786	(8%)
	Frederick Harry Lee Simms (R)	9,927	(8%)

FIRST DISTRICT Political Background

Maryland 1 comprises the Eastern Shore and also much of the western shore of Chesapeake Bay. The nine counties of the Eastern Shore, slave-holding before the Civil War, are really part of the rural South; during the mid-'60's the town of Cambridge, in Dorchester County, was the scene of a great deal of civil rights activity. George Wallace carried the Eastern Shore in the 1964 presidential primary and ran well here again in 1968, nearly finishing second in some counties. The western shore is more conventionally conservative. This side of the bay is a fast-growing suburban and exurban area surrounding the city of Annapolis, the state's quaint eighteenth-century capital.

For nine years the 1st district belonged to Rogers C. B. Morton, now Walter Hickel's successor in the Cabinet as Secretary of the Interior; Morton was also Republican National Chairman during the first two years of the Nixon Administration.

An imposing 6′7″ aristocrat, he settled on the Eastern Shore some years ago and in 1962 won the House seat when the Democratic incumbent, Thomas Johnson, was indicted in a savings and loan scandal. Rogers' brother, Thurston, was also a politically powerful man, having served as an Assistant Secretary of State in the Eisenhower Administration, senator from Kentucky (1956–68), and Republican National Chairman during the 1960 campaign.

Rogers Morton won reelection by huge margins in the 1st—69% of the vote in 1970, for example. And Morton's popularity no doubt helped to elect his Republican successor and his former administrative assistant, William Mills. The Eastern Shore and Anne Arundel County traditionally elect conservative Democrats to the state legislature and local office, but Mills beat such an opponent, state Sen. Elroy Boyles, 54:46.

Redistricting has altered the district to the Democrats' advantage, removing Anne Arundel County and adding more marginal, less Republican, rural and suburban terrain. But if Mills has any of Morton's vote-getting prowess, the new Congressman should be able to overcome the handicap and win reelection without much trouble.

Census Data 1970 pop. 461,907; deviation from current state average, —5.8%; change 1960–70, +18.9%. Metro. 40.9%, 0.0% central city.

1970 Share of Federal Outlays $564,639,685 (average outlay per district, Maryland 1–8)

DOD	$212,205,000	HEW	$152,795,376
AEC	$10,018,074	HUD	$4,981,015
NASA	$29,808,808	OEO	$1,629,635
DOT	$22,272,812	DOA	$12,060,680
		Other	$118,688,293

Federal Military-Industrial Commitments

DOD Contractors Westinghouse Electric (Annapolis), $17.50m: aircraft electronic warfare system assemblies. Ordnance Products (North East), $8.29m: production of hand grenades. IT&T (Annapolis), $5.07m: unspecified computer services.

DOD Installations Naval Academy (Annapolis). Naval Air Test Center (Patuxent River). Naval Hospital (Annapolis). Naval Station (Annapolis). Naval Ship Research and Development Center (Annapolis).

Economic Base Food and kindred products, esp. canned and preserved fruits, vegetables, and seafoods, and meat products; electrical machinery, equipment, and supplies, esp. communication equipment; apparel and other finished products made from fabrics and similar materials, esp. men's, youths', and boys' furnishings, work clothing, and allied garments.

The Voters

Registration 169,533 total. 115,945 D (68%); 50,848 R (30%); 3,640 other (2%).

Employment profile White collar, 34%. Blue collar, 66%.

Ethnic groups Black, 23%. Total foreign stock, 6%. Germany, UK, Canada, 1% each; others, 3%.

Presidential vote

1968	Humphrey (D)	43,139	(31%)
	Nixon (R)	64,792	(47%)
	Wallace (AIP)	30,667	(22%)

Representative

William Oswald Mills (R) Elected, May 1971; b. Aug. 12, 1924, Bethlehem; home, Easton; Army, WWII; married, two children; Methodist.

Career Dist. mgr., Chesapeake and Potomac Tel. Co., 1946–50; commercial mgr., Talbot and Caroline County Tel. Co., 1950–62; Adm. Asst., U.S. Rep. Thurston C. B. Morton, 1962–71.

Offices 1004 LHOB, 202-225-5311. Also Loyola Fed. Bldg., Harrison and Goldsborough Streets, Easton 21601, 301-822-4300.

Committees

Merchant Marine and Fisheries (15th); Subs. (1) Merchant Marine, (2) Oceanography.

Post Office and Civil Service (11th); Subs. (1) Employee Benefits, (2) Manpower and Civil Service.

Group Ratings, Key Votes: Newly elected.

Election Results

1971 special:	William O. Mills (R)	31,510	(54%)
	Elroy G. Boyles (D)	26,661	(46%)
1971 primary:	William O. Mills (R)	6,551	(63%)
	Robert Bauman (R)	3,911	(27%)

SECOND DISTRICT Political Background

Maryland 2 is currently the greater portion of suburban Baltimore County and rural-exurban Harford County to the east. Baltimore County, though 97% white, is by no means sociologically homogeneous. It extends from rural, horse-farm country in the north, through comfortable WASPy suburbs like Towson north of the city, to the industrial suburbs of Dundalk and Sparrows Point between Baltimore and Chesapeake Bay. Sparrows Point, the site of one of the largest steel plants in the nation, is perhaps where Spiro Agnew, who was Baltimore County Executive from 1962 to 1966, first learned to communicate with blue-collar workers.

Clarence D. Long has been the congressman from the 2nd district since 1962. Long, a former professor of economics at Johns Hopkins and a liberal on most domestic issues, is one of the very few members of Congress whose son has served with the military in Vietnam. Until the Cambodian invasion of 1970, Long was a firm supporter of Johnson and Nixon policies in southeast Asia; since then, he has been a resolute dove.

The 2nd has shown a pronounced conservative bent recently, going heavily against Joseph Tydings in 1970 and Humphrey in 1968 when there were many Wallace votes cast in Dundalk and Sparrows Point. But Long has had no difficulty bucking the conservative trend and has won with convincing majorities: 69% in 1970, 59% in 1968, and 69% in 1966. These showings indicate that he is unbeatable; but if the incumbent were not the Democratic candidate, a Republican—perhaps one of Agnew's old friends—might very well take the seat. For the 1972 election, the legislature has removed Harford County from the 2nd and has made some slight changes in the district's boundaries in Baltimore County.

Census Data 1970 pop. 497,431; deviation from current state average, +1.5%; change 1960–70, +26.5%. Metro. 100.0%, 0.0% central city.

1970 Share of Federal Outlays $564,639,685 (average outlay per district, Maryland 1–8)

DOD	$212,205,000	HEW	$152,795,376
AEC	$10,018,074	HUD	$4,981,015
NASA	$29,808,808	OEO	$1,629,635
DOT	$22,272,812	DOA	$12,060,680
		Other	$118,688,293

Federal Military-Industrial Commitments (Maryland 2–4, 7; greater Baltimore)

DOD Contractors Westinghouse Electric (Baltimore and Cockeyville), $212.97m: aircraft radar and submarine sonar systems; air traffic control units. Bendix Corp. (Baltimore and Towson), $26.45m: aircraft radio sets; space vehicle tracking. AAI Corp. (Cockeyville), $20.58m: electronic warfare trainer units; Nike-Hercules missile simulators; 40-mm grenade launchers. Schenuit Industries (Baltimore), $7.06m: aircraft tires.

DOD Installations Aberdeen Army Proving Ground (Aberdeen). Edgewood Arsenal (Baltimore).

NASA Contractors Bendix Corp. (Owings Mills), $52.37m: operation of Manned Space Flight Network, and other tracking services. RCA (Baltimore), $5.77m: tracking services.

Economic Base Blast furnaces, steel works, and rolling and finishing mills; communication equipment, and other electrical machinery, equipment, and supplies; transportation equipment; nonelectrical machinery, esp. special industrial machinery other than metalworking machinery; beverages and other foods and kindred products. Also, extensive commuting to Maryland 3, 4, and 7 (Baltimore).

The Voters

Registration 193,908 total. 142,872 D (74%); 47,960 R (25%); 3,186 other (1%).
Employment profile White collar, 45%. Blue collar, 55%.
Ethnic groups Black, 5%. Total foreign stock, 11%. Germany, Italy, 2% each; Poland, UK, Canada, Ireland, Czech, 1% each; others, 3%.

Presidential vote

1968	Humphrey (D)	52,384	(33%)
	Nixon (R)	81,707	(52%)
	Wallace (AIP)	24,248	(15%)

Representative

Clarence D. Long (D) Elected 1962; b. Dec. 11, 1908, South Bend, Ind.; home, Ruxton; Washington and Jefferson College, B.A.; Princeton, Ph.D; USN, WWII; married, two children; Presbyterian.

Career Prof., Johns Hopkins Univ., 1946–63; Assoc. Task Force Dir., Hoover Commission, 1948; Sr. Staff Mbr., Council of Econ. Advisers, 1953–54, 1956–57; Acting Chm., Md. Democratic Central Comm., 1961–62.

Offices 1126 LHOB 1-202-225-3061. Also Rm. 200, P.O. Bldg., Towson 21204, 1-301-828-6616.

Committees

Appropriations (22nd); Subs. (1) Foreign Operations, (2) Military Construction.

Group Ratings

	ADA	COPE	NREP	NFU	LCV	CFA	NAB	NSI	ACA
1970	64	73	93	64	75	73	13	79	56
1969	53	—	—	73	—	—	—	—	35
1968	67	100	—	86	—	—	0	—	17

Key Votes

(1) ABM	FOR	(6) 18-Yr-Vote	FOR	(11) Clean Water $	AGN
(2) SST	AGN	(7) Farm Sub Lmt	FOR	(12) Mig Wrkrs Comp	FOR
(3) Phil Pln	AGN	(8) Coop-Church	FOR	(13) Jets to Chiang	FOR
(4) No-Knock	FOR	(9) Family Asst	AGN	(14) State OEO Veto	AGN
(5) Cmutr Tax	FOR	(10) Work Stamps	FOR	(15) Park Logging	AGN

Election Results

1970 general:	Clarence D. Long (D)	87,224	(69%)
	Ross Z. Pierpont (R)	40,177	(31%)
1970 primary:	Clarence D. Long (D), unopposed		
1968 general:	Clarence D. Long (D)	86,025	(59%)
	John E. Mudd (R)	59,635	(41%)

THIRD DISTRICT Political Background

Maryland 3 is the southern and eastern portions of the city of Baltimore and part of Anne Arundel County between Baltimore and Annapolis. The district contains a mixture of blacks from central Baltimore, white blue-collar workers from east Baltimore, and some relatively affluent and conservative suburbanites from Anne Arundel. Since three-quarters of the 3rd's residents live within the city, the district has been traditionally Democratic.

The congressman from the 3rd is Edward A. Garmatz, an aging veteran of Baltimore politics. He was first elected in 1947 when Congressman Thomas d'Alessandro resigned the seat to become mayor of Baltimore. (D'Alessandro's son is currently mayor, another example—the Tydingses and Bealls are two others—of the power of dynasties in Maryland politics.) Garmatz patiently climbed the seniority ladder on the Merchant Marine and Fisheries Committee and is now its chairman, an important post locally since Baltimore is one of the nation's major ports.

In 1968, the Baltimore districts sent three committee chairmen to the House, but George Fallon of Public Works and Samuel Friedel of House Administration were beaten in the 1970 Democratic primaries. Garmatz, however, has had curiously little opposition in recent years, going unchallenged in the 1970 primary and general elections. In 1968, the last time the Republicans put up a candidate, the Congressman received 82% of the votes.

Garmatz will have a much harder time in 1972. Because of Baltimore's population loss, the legislature reduced the city's number of House seats from 3 to 2 and thereby placed Garmatz and freshman Paul Sarbanes, currently of the 4th, in the same district. On paper, Garmatz has the edge; most of the residents of the new 3rd are presently his constituents. Moreover, the Congressman will also get plenty of help from the heavily regulated maritime industry as well as backing from the Baltimore Democratic organization. But Sarbanes is a tough, proven campaigner who toppled Chairman Fallon in 1970 with support from blacks, peace groups, and organized labor. Garmatz, who will be 69 in 1972, has not had to campaign very hard for many years. Odds are for Sarbanes to beat Garmatz by a comfortable margin.

Census Data 1970 pop. 384,287; deviation from current state average, —21.6%; change 1960–70, —0.2%. Metro. 100.0%, 68.0% central city.

1970 Share of Federal Outlays $564,639,685 (average outlay per district, Maryland 1–8)

DOD	$212,205,000	HEW	$152,795,376
AEC	$10,018,074	HUD	$4,981,015
NASA	$29,808,808	OEO	$1,629,635
DOT	$22,272,812	DOA	$12,060,680
		Other	$118,688,293

Federal Military-Industrial Commitments (See listings under Maryland 2.)

Economic Base Transportation equipment, esp. ship and boat building and repairing; food and kindred products; apparel and other finished products made from fabrics and similar materials, esp. men's, youths', and boys' suits, coats, and overcoats; printing, publishing, and allied industries, esp. commercial printing.

The Voters

Registration 152,252 total. 129,847 D (85%); 20,199 R (13%); 2,206 other (1%)

Employment profile White collar, 31%. Blue collar, 69%.

Ethnic groups Black, 26%. Total foreign stock, 14%. Poland, Germany, 3% each; Italy, 2%; UK, USSR, Czech., 1% each; others, 3%.

Presidential vote

1968	Humphrey (D)	56,078	(51%)
	Nixon (R)	31,373	(29%)
	Wallace (AIP)	21,423	(20%)

Representative

Edward A. Garmatz (D) Elected 1946; b. Feb. 7, 1903, Baltimore; home, Baltimore; Poly. Inst., 1916–17; married; United Church of Christ.

Career Electrical business, 1920–46; assoc. with Md. State Racing Commission, 1941–47; police magistrate, 1944–47.

Offices 2187 RHOB, 1-202-225-6161. Also 1112 Fed. Office Bldg., Baltimore 21201, 1-301-539-2995.

Committees

Government Operations (5th); Subs. (1) Legislation and Military Operations, (2) Special Studies.

Merchant Marine and Fisheries (Chm.); Chm., Sub. on Merchant Marine.

Group Ratings

	ADA	COPE	NREP	NFU	LCV	CFA	NAB	NSI	ACA
1970	52	92	67	100	55	83	0	90	11
1969	40	—	—	93	—	—	—	—	20
1968	75	100	—	94	—	—	0	—	5

Key Votes

(1) ABM	FOR	(6) 18-Yr-Vote	FOR	(11) Clean Water $	FOR
(2) SST	FOR	(7) Farm Sub Lmt	FOR	(12) Mig Wrkrs Comp	FOR
(3) Phil Pln	FOR	(8) Coop-Church	FOR	(13) Jets to Chiang	ABS
(4) No-Knock	FOR	(9) Family Asst	FOR	(14) State OEO Veto	AGN
(5) Cmutr Tax	FOR	(10) Work Stamps	AGN	(15) Park Logging	FOR

Election Results

1970 general:	Edward A. Garmatz (D), unopposed		
1970 primary:	Edward A. Garmatz (D), unopposed		
1968 general:	Edward A. Garmatz (D)	63,269	(82%)
	James E. Chew (R)	14,604	(18%)

FOURTH DISTRICT Political Background

Maryland 4 comprises the central and northeast portions of the city of Baltimore and a small slice (pop. 36,000) of suburban Baltimore County. The district ranges from the poor, typically Baltimore row-house neighborhoods near Johns Hopkins University to the prosperous all-white outskirts of the city. A large and growing proportion of the 4th's voters are black. On balance, however, this is the most middle class and conservative and least Democratic of the three districts dominated by the city of Baltimore. In 1968, Humphrey edged out Nixon in the 4th 47:42. Many of the residents here are descendants of Irish, Italian, and Greek immigrants, all of whom are determined to protect their neat and comfortable homes from outsiders.

From 1944 to 1970, the district's congressman was George H. Fallon, a politician who became accustomed to handsome majorities without having to work very hard for them. During the '50's, Fallon became Chairman of the Public Works Committee's subcommittee on roads, where he soon became a stalwart friend of the highway lobby. In 1964 he became chairman of the full committee and continued to support the increasingly controversial interstate highway program.

Fallon's record was liberal on domestic issues, but definitely hawkish on the war. A peace candidate, state Sen. J. Joseph Curran, challenged the congressman in the 1968 primary and lost by less than 1,000 votes. Convinced that Fallon (who was 68 and 1970) would retire soon enough, Curran decided to sit out the 1970 primary. But another insurgent, Paul Sarbanes, decided to make the race.

Sarbanes, like Agnew a Baltimore-area Greek-American, was a four-year veteran of the state House of Delegates. Earlier he was a friend and classmate of Ralph Nader at Princeton, as well as a Rhodes Scholar and a cum laude graduate of the Harvard Law School. Sarbanes had support from Nader as well as financial and volunteer backing from peace and ecology groups. More important, and a mark of the insurgent's political savvy, Sarbanes won the support of the AFL-CIO, the UAW, and the Teamsters—a considerable accomplishment, since organized labor rarely bucks the big city 68 in 1970) would retire soon enough, Curran decided to sit out the 1970 primary. victory, 51%; the Democratic candidate went on to take 70% of the votes in the general election, a percentage as good as most of Fallon's old showings.

Because Baltimore lost a congressional seat in the 1971 redistricting, Sarbanes will be forced to run against 25-year-incumbent Edward Garmatz in the new 3rd district. For a discussion of the upcoming contest, see the Maryland 3 write-up.

Census Data 1970 pop. 372,386; deviation from current state average, —24.0%; change 1960–70, —2.7%. Metro. 100.0%, 90.2% central city.

1970 Share of Federal Outlays $564,639,685 (average outlay per district, Maryland 1–8)

DOD	$212,205,000	HEW	$152,795,376
AEC	$10,018,074	HUD	$4,981,015
NASA	$29,808,808	OEO	$1,629,635
DOT	$22,272,812	DOA	$12,060,680
		Other	$118,688,293

Federal Military-Industrial Commitments (See listings under Maryland 2.)

Economic Base Food and kindred products; apparel and other finished products made from fabrics and similar materials, esp. men's, youths', and boys' suits, coats, and overcoats; transportation equipment; printing, publishing, and allied industries, esp. commercial printing and newspapers.

The Voters

Registration 184,106 total. 143,981 D (78%); 36,621 R (20%); 10,341 other (2%).

Employment profile White collar, 47%. Blue collar, 53%.

Ethnic groups Black, 27%. Total foreign stock, 13%. Germany, 3%; Italy, 2%; Ireland, Poland, UK, USSR, 1% each; others, 4%.

Presidential vote

1968	Humphrey (D)	59,866	(47%)
	Nixon (R)	53,272	(42%)
	Wallace (AIP)	14,517	(11%)

Representative

Paul S. Sarbanes (D) Elected 1970; b. Feb. 3, 1933, Salisbury; home, Baltimore; Princeton, A.B., 1954; Oxford, B.A., 1957; Harvard, LL.B., 1960; married, three children; Greek Orthodox.

Career Asst. to Walt W. Heller, Chm. of Council of Economic Advisors, 1962–63; Md. House of Delegates, 1966–70.

Offices 1507 LHOB, 1-202-225-4016. Also 1414 Fed. Office Bldg., Baltimore 21201, 1-301-962-4436.

Committees

Judiciary (18th).

Group Ratings, Key Votes: Newly elected.

Election Results

1970 general:	Paul S. Sarbanes (D)	54,936	(70%)
	David Fentress (R)	23,491	(30%)
1970 primary:	Paul S. Sarbanes (D)	22,863	(51%)
	George H. Fallon (D)	20,456	(45%)
	Michael J. James (D)	1,619	(4%)

FIFTH DISTRICT Political Background

Maryland 5—Prince Georges and Charles counties—is currently one of the largest (pop. 708,245) and fastest-growing (up 82% in the '60's) districts in the nation. Prince Georges is the eastern half of Maryland's portion of suburban Washington—somewhat less white-collar and poorer than Montgomery County to the west. On paper, Prince Georges is the more Democratic of the two counties. Registered Democrats outnumber registered Republicans by more than 2:1, and Democrats still control most of the local offices. But in recent statewide elections, Prince Georges residents, still upward-striving and insecure, have found the law-and-order platform of Nixon-Agnew Republicans more and more congenial. Sen. Tydings could carry only 54% of the country's vote in 1970, and two years earlier Humphrey lost it by a similar margin.

For four years, the 5th's congressman was a conservative Democrat, Hervey G. Machen, who apparently thought he had the district safely put away. He did not. In

1968, Machen was ousted by an ex-FBI agent, Republican Lawrence J. Hogan. Hogan quickly established himself as the most conservative member of the Maryland delegation; he received reams of publicity in the Washington papers as a man looking out for the interests of his suburban constituents. Hogan is a stern and untiring backer of the Nixon Administration anticrime bills and has also urged the resumption of the bombing of North Vietnam. In 1970, for the first time in years, the Democratic candidate in the 5th was an outspoken liberal, who waged a vigorous and sometimes bitter campaign against the incumbent. The district's voters, given a clear choice, preferred the conservative. Hogan won 61% of the votes.

Normally, that showing would mean that the Congressman could expect automatic reelection for some time to come. But the Democratic state legislature has presented Hogan with a dilemma. Prince Georges was divided between two districts, with the larger and somewhat more Democratic portion, the new 4th district, staked off for Secretary of State Fred Wineland. Most of the voters of the new 5th district live in Anne Arundel County (Annapolis), an increasingly conservative but traditionally Democratic area south of Baltimore, which Hogan has never represented. His likely opponent, if Hogan decides to run in the 5th, is state Sen. Edward Conroy, the chairman of the legislative task force on redistricting. Wherever Hogan chooses to run, he faces a tough election in 1972 against a Democratic opponent far less controversial and liberal than the one he beat in 1970.

Census Data 1970 pop. 708,245; deviation from current state average, +44.5%; change 1960–70, +81.6%. Metro. 93.3%, 0.07 central city.

1970 Share of Federal Outlays $564,639,685 (average outlay per district, Maryland 1–8)

DOD	$212,205,000	HEW	$152,795,376
AEC	$10,018,074	HUD	$4,981,015
NASA	$29,808,808	OEO	$1,629,635
DOT	$22,272,812	DOA	$12,060,680
		Other	$118,688,293

Federal Military-Industrial Commitments (Maryland 5, 8; suburban Washington, D.C.)

DOD Contractors Applied Physics Lab, Johns Hopkins University (Silver Spring), $58.36m: Navy surface missile system research. Vitro Corp. Div., Automation Industries (Silver Spring), $42.26m: anti-submarine warfare studies. IBM (Gaithersburg and Riverdale), $27.70 ABM research; computer components and services for various DOD programs. Control Data (Bethesda and Rockville), $15.01m: services for Poseidon and Polaris missiles. Singer General Precision (Silver Spring), $13.75m: aircraft flight simulators. Bunker Ramo (Silver Spring), $13.74m: aircraft electronic warfare units. Booz Allen Applied Research (Bethesda), $5.42m: support for Navy Project Mallard.

DOD Installations Fort Mead AB (Odenton). Naval Ship Research and Development Center (Carderock). National Naval Medical Center (Bethesda). Naval National Security Agency (Odenton). Naval Oceanographic Office (Suitland). Naval Reconnaissance Technical Support Center (Suitland). Naval Communication Station (Cheltenham). Naval Air Facility (Camp Springs). Naval Ordnance Station (Indian Head). Andrews AFB (Camp Springs).

AEC Operations AEC Headquarters (Germantown).

NASA Contractors IBM (Gaithersburg), $5.07m: tracking services.

NASA Installations Goddard Space Flight Center (Greenbelt). Space Nuclear Propulsion Office (joint NASA-AEC) (Germantown).

Economic Base Printing, publishing, and allied industries, esp. commercial printing and newspapers; food and kindred products; communication equipment, and other electrical machinery, equipment, and supplies; tobacco. Also, extensive commuting to Washington, D.C.

The Voters

Registration 207,892 total. 135,992 D (65%); 61,559 R (30%); 10,341 other (5%).

Employment profile White collar, 55%. Blue collar, 45%.

Ethnic groups Black, 11%. Total foreign stock, 12%. Germany, Italy, UK, 2% each; Ireland, Poland, Canada, USSR, 1% each; others, 2%.

Presidential vote

1968	Humphrey (D)	75,771	(40%)
	Nixon (R)	77,914	(41%)
	Wallace (AIP)	36,040	(19%)

Representative

Lawrence J. Hogan (R) Elected 1968; b. Sept. 30, 1928, Boston, Mass.; home, Landover; Georgetown U., B.A., 1949, J.D., 1954; American U., A.M., 1965; San Francisco State Col., 1956–57; U. of Md., 1966–67; married, two children; Catholic.

Career Atty, pub. rel. executive; teacher, U. of Md., 1960–68; FBI, 1948–58; member Governor's Commission on Law Enforcement and the Administration of Justice (Md.), 1967–68.

Offices 1027 LHOB, 1-202-225-4131. Also G120 Center Bldg., 3700 E. West Hwy., Hyattsville 20782, 1-301-779-3430.

Committees

Judiciary (14th).

Post Office and Civil Service (7th); Subs. (1) Employee Benefits, (2) Retirement, Insurance and Health Benefits.

Group Ratings

	ADA	COPE	NREP	NFU	LCV	CFA	NAB	NSI	ACA
1970	24	25	27	77	100	67	58	90	47
1969	20	—	—	40	—	—	—	—	65

Key Votes

(1) ABM	FOR	(6) 18-Yr-Vote	FOR	(11) Clean Water $	FOR
(2) SST	FOR	(7) Farm Sub Lmt	FOR	(12) Mig Wrkrs Comp	AGN
(3) Phil Pln	FOR	(8) Coop-Church	AGN	(13) Jets to Chiang	AGN
(4) No-Knock	FOR	(9) Family Asst	FOR	(14) State OEO Veto	FOR
(5) Cmutr Tax	FOR	(10) Work Stamps	FOR	(15) Park Logging	AGN

Election Results

1970 general:	Lawrence J. Hogan (R)	84,314	(61%)
	Royal Hart (D)	52,979	(39%)
1970 primary:	Lawrence J. Hogan (R), unopposed		
1968 general:	Lawrence J. Hogan (R)	89,073	(53%)
	Hervey G. Machen (D)	79,870	(47%)

SIXTH DISTRICT Political Background

Maryland 6, the western panhandle of the state, extends from the Appalachian Mountains around Cumberland to the suburban and exurban reaches of greater Baltimore and Washington. The 6th is a picturesque region of gently rolling hills and small, neat, antique cities like Frederick (where Barbara Fritchie reared her old gray head), Hagerstown, and Cumberland. Like most of rural Maryland, the district has a Democratic heritage and conservative Republican ideological leanings. It gives Republican candidates big margins in presidential and senatorial races, but the local congressional race is usually close.

In the last four years, two congressmen from the 6th have gone on to the Senate: liberal Republican Charles Mathias, who represented the district from 1960 to 1968, and conservative Republican J. Glenn Beall, Jr., who served the term that followed. Both Beall and the current congressional incumbent, Democrat Goodloe E. Byron, are members of Maryland political dynasties. Beall's father was U.S. Senator from 1952 to 1964, while Byron's father and mother both represented the 6th in the House back in the days of Franklin D. Roosevelt. In 1968, Byron faced Beall and got 47% of the votes; in 1970 Byron beat Judge George Hughes with 51%. Hughes did as well as he did only because of a strong (70%) showing in his home county of Allegany (Cumberland).

Byron faces as secure a future as any 51% winner can expect. The legislature has added parts of suburban Baltimore, Howard, and Montgomery counties to the district. But the additional territory will not change the 4th's politics, and if Byron uses the advantages of incumbency adeptly, he can improve greatly on his 51% 1970 showing.

Census Data 1970 pop. 467,584; deviation from current state average, –4.6%; change 1960–70, +21.5%. Metro. 37.1%, 0.0% central city.

1970 Share of Federal Outlays $564,639,685 (average outlay per district, Maryland 1–8)

DOD	$212,205,000	HEW	$152,795,376
AEC	$10,018,074	HUD	$4,981,015
NASA	$29,808,808	OEO	$1,629,635
DOT	$22,272,812	DOA	$12,060,680
		Other	$118,688,293

Federal Military-Industrial Commitments

DOD Contractors Baltimore Contractors (Frederick), $6.61m: construction of medical building, Fort Detrick.

DOD Installations Fort Detrick AB (Frederick). Fort Richie AB (Cascade).

Economic Base Dairy; food and kindred products, esp. meat products; nonelectrical machinery, esp. special industrial machinery other than metalworking machinery.

The Voters

Registration 184,774 total. 104,836 D (57%); 76,072 R (41%); 2,866 other (2%).
Employment profile White collar, 37%. Blue collar, 63%.
Ethnic groups Black, 4%. Total foreign stock, 5%. Germany, UK, Italy, 1% each; others, 2%.

Presidential vote

1968	Humphrey (D)	52,978	(34%)
	Nixon (R)	77,686	(50%)
	Wallace (AIP)	23,667	(15%)

Representative

Goodloe E. Byron (D) Elected 1970; b. June 22, 1929, Williamsport; home, Frederick; U. of Va., B.A., 1951; George Washington, U., J.D., 1954; Army, 1955–58; married, three children; Episcopalian.

Career Atty., Md. House of Delegates, 1962–66; Md. Senate, 1966–70.

Offices 1730 LHOB, 1-202-225-2721. Also P.O. Bldg., Hagerstown 21740, 1-301-797-6043.

Committees

Interstate and Foreign Commerce (24th); Sub. on Communication, Power.

Group Ratings, Key Votes: Newly elected.

Election Results

1970 general:	Goodloe E. Byron (D)	59,267	(51%)
	George R. Hughes, Jr. (R)	55,511	(48%)
	Audrey B. Carroll (AIP)	1,873	(1%)
1970 primary:	Goodloe E. Byron (D)	30,088	(80%)
	Thomas F. Conlon (D)	6,057	(16%)
	Charles Curtis McPeek (D)	1,256	(3%)

SEVENTH DISTRICT Political Background

Maryland 7, the third Baltimore district, includes most of the west side of the city, as well as a substantial portion of suburban Baltimore County. The 7th is the heartland of Baltimore's large Jewish population, once centered in the city but now found mostly in the suburbs. Blacks have moved into the former Jewish ghetto, converting synagogues into Baptist and African Methodist churches. The blacks are now a majority in the city portion of the 7th, but they are a minority district-wide, since the suburbs are almost entirely white.

From 1952, when the district was created, until 1970 the 7th was represented by Samuel N. Friedel, a loyal supporter of the Baltimore City Democratic organization. Friedel, the chairman of the House Administration Committee, seldom encountered opposition in the district, and when he did, he could count on the organization's ward captains to get the vote out. But Friedel's hold on the 7th was broken in 1970. Parren Mitchell once again entered the Democratic primary; he also ran in 1968, but lost by 5,000 votes, the same number taken by a white peace candidate in the race. Mitchell, a former professor at black Morgan State College, is a member of an illustrious Baltimore family; his brother Clarence Mitchell is the NAACP's canny Washington lobbyist, and his nephew, Clarence III, is a state senator.

In 1970, the white peace people decided to support Mitchell and campaigned hard for him, particularly in the Jewish areas. Meanwhile, Friedel's problems were compounded by the entry of a third candidate, state Sen. Carl Friedler, who claimed to represent the middle ground between the two other men. Friedler would cut into the white vote, and doubtless some voters would confuse his name with the Congressman's and pull the wrong lever.

Mitchell campaigned hard in both black and white areas; but the results showed that most of his votes came from the black community, with Friedel and Friedler splitting the rest. Friedel carried the Baltimore County portion of the district 11,851 to 2,095, but lost in the city 22,170 to 12,375. The totals produced a 38-vote Mitchell victory—24,265 to 24,227—the third-closest major congressional primary in the nation (the others were a 30-vote difference in Denver and a 3-vote margin in North Dakota). Friedler took 16,910 votes, almost 25% and obviously enough to beat Friedel.

The 7th district Republicans also had a busy year in 1970. Although the district always goes heavily Democratic—except when George "Your Home Is Your Castle" Mahoney ran for governor against Spiro Agnew in 1966—many Republicans sensed that a Mitchell victory in a bitter primary would give them a chance in the general election. Seven candidates entered the Republican primary, and the winner, Peter Parker, campaigned hard all the way into November. The result was unusually close for a 7th district race: Mitchell took 59% of the votes, 72% in the city and 31% in the suburbs. Many white suburbanites who ordinarily vote Democratic had obviously abandoned their party and voted for the white candidate.

In Washington, Mitchell is now the first black member of the House Banking and Currency Committee, a congressional unit which has jurisdiction over federal housing programs. Mitchell, despite his narrow victory in the primary, has a secure political future. The Democrats in control of the Maryland legislature, wary of Baltimore's large black community, redrew the district lines to exclude the suburbs and include more black areas in the city. Mitchell will therefore have a safe seat in upcoming elections.

Census Data 1970 pop. 432,278; deviation from current state average, —11.8%; change 1960–70, +11.3%. Metro. 100.0%, 71.4% central city.

1970 Share of Federal Outlays $564,639,685 (average outlay per district, Maryland 1–8)

DOD	$212,205,000	HEW	$152,795,376
AEC	$10,018,074	HUD	$4,981,015
NASA	$29,808,808	OEO	$1,629,635
DOT	$22,272,812	DOA	$12,060,680
		Other	$118,688,293

Federal Military-Industrial Commitments (See listings under Maryland 2.)

Economic Base Transportation and equipment; food and kindred products; apparel and other finished products made from fabrics and similar materials; printing, publishing, and allied industries, esp. commercial printing and newspapers.

The Voters

Registration 201,008 total. 164,169 D (82%); 33,590 R (17%); 3,249 other (2%)
Employment profile White collar, 48%. Blue collar, 52%.
Ethnic groups Black, 33%. Total foreign stock, 18%. USSR, 6%; Germany, 3%; Poland, 2%; UK, Ireland, Italy, Austria, 1% each; others, 6%.

Presidential vote

1968	Humphrey (D)	97,023	(68%)
	Nixon (R)	35,116	(25%)
	Wallace (AIP)	10,399	(7%)

Representative

Parren J. Mitchell (D) Elected 1970; b. April 29, 1922, Baltimore; home, Baltimore; Morgan State College, B.A., 1950; U. of Maryland, M.S., 1952; doctoral studies, U. of Conn., 1960; Army 1942–46; unmarried; Episcopalian.

Career Sociology prof., Morgan State; Exec. Sec. Maryland Commission on Interracial Problems and Relations, 1963–65; Dir., Baltimore Community Action Agency, 1965–68.

Offices 1228 LHOB, 1-202-225-4741. Also 1018 Fed. Bldg., 31 Hopkins Plaza, Baltimore 21201, 1-301-962-4436.

Committees

Banking and Currency (22); Subs. (1) Domestic Finance, (2) International Trade, (3) Small Business.

Sel. Com. on Small Business (12); Subs. (1) Foundations: Their Impact on Small Business, (2) Minority Small Business Enterprise.

Group Ratings, Key Votes: Newly elected.

Election Results

1970 general:	Parren J. Mitchell (D)	60,390	(59%)
	Peter Parker (R)	42,566	(41%)
1970 primary:	Parren J. Mitchell (D)	24,265	(35%)
	Walter T. Dixon (D)	3,504	(5%)
	Samuel N. Friedel (D)	24,227	(35%)
	Carl L. Friedler (D)	16,909	(25%)

EIGHTH DISTRICT Political Background

Maryland 8 is Montgomery County and small portions of exurban Howard and Anne Arundel counties to the north and east. Montgomery is everyone's image of the Washington suburb—neat, attractive, one-family homes, bustling shopping centers, and good schools. In the past few years, the county has even had some blacks from Washington venture into some of its suburbs. The typical resident of the 8th is a GS-15 or -16, a high-ranking civil servant who is vaguely liberal on issues, but is barred from active participation in politics by the Hatch Act. Because of the government personnel living here, Montgomery has one of the highest average incomes in the country. But not that many Montgomery people are really rich—an index of the peculiar economic base of Washington's wealth.

As befits a heavily white-collar district, both the local Democratic and Republican parties are the most liberal in the state. Since 1966 the 8th's congressman has been Gilbert Gude, an antiwar Republican with an ADA rating higher than that of most Maryland Democrats. Gude had a tough fight in his first race when he won only 54% of the vote. But since then he has been unbeatable, winning 61% in both 1968 and 1970. His most recent opponent was Thomas H. Boggs, Jr., the son of Hale Boggs, House Majority Leader.

Gude is one of the more liberal members of the District of Columbia Committee and also serves on Government Operations. Redistricting has reduced the size of this fast-growing district, but it will doubtless continue to reelect Gude for years to come.

Census Data 1970 pop. 598,281; deviation from current state average, +22.0%; change 1960–70, +54.4%. Metro. 100.0%, 0.0% central city.

1970 Share of Federal Outlays $564,639,685 (average outlay per district, Maryland 1–8)

DOD	$212,205,000	HEW	$152,795,376
AEC	$10,018,074	HUD	$4,981,015
NASA	$29,808,808	OEO	$1,629,635
DOT	$22,272,812	DOA	$12,060,680
		Other	$118,688,293

Federal Military-Industrial Commitments (See listings under Maryland 5.)

Economic Base Electrical machinery, equipment, and supplies, esp. radio and television transmitting, signaling, and detection equipment and apparatus; printing, publishing, and allied industries; nonelectrical machinery; dairy. Also, extensive commuting to Washington, D.C.

The Voters

Registration 216,498 total. 128,510 D (59%); 74,915 R (35%); 13,073 other (6%).

Employment profile White collar, 68%. Blue collar, 32%.

Ethnic groups Black 5%. Total foreign stock, 17%. Germany, UK, USSR, 2% each; Ireland, Italy, Poland, Canada, Austria, 1% each; others, 6%.

Presidential vote

1968	Humphrey (D)	96,344	(47%)
	Nixon (R)	90,507	(44%)
	Wallace (AIP)	16,989	(8%)

Representative

Gilbert Gude (R) Elected 1966; b. March 9, 1923, Washington, D.C.; home, Bethesda; U. of Md.; Cornell U., B.S., 1948; George Washington U., M.A., 1958; Army, WWII; married, five children; Catholic.

Career House of Delegates, Md., 1953–61; Senate 1962–66.

Offices 332 CHOB, 1-202-225-5341. Also 11141 Georgia Ave., Wheaton 20902, 1-301-933-3340, and 10227 Wincopin Cir., Columbia 21043, 1-301-737-6088.

Committees

District of Columbia (6th); Subs. (1) Business, Commerce and Fiscal Affairs, (2) Education, (3) Public Health and Welfare.

Government Operations (8th); Subs. (1) Conservation and Natural Resources, (2) Government Activities, (3) Legal and Monetary Affairs.

Group Ratings

	ADA	COPE	NREP	NFU	LCV	CFA	NAB	NSI	ACA
1970	80	82	93	92	50	67	18	60	33
1969	73	—	—	67	—	—	—	—	24
1968	67	83	—	75	—	—	40	—	20

Key Votes

(1) ABM	AGN	(6) 18-Yr-Vote	FOR	(11) Clean Water $	FOR
(2) SST	AGN	(7) Farm Sub Lmt	FOR	(12) Mig Wrkrs Comp	FOR
(3) Phil Pln	FOR	(8) Coop-Church	FOR	(13) Jets to Chiang	FOR
(4) No-Knock	FOR	(9) Family Asst	FOR	(14) State OEO Veto	AGN
(5) Cmutr Tax	AGN	(10) Work Stamps	AGN	(15) Park Logging	FOR

Election Results

1970 general:	Gilbert Gude (R)	104,647	(63%)
	Thomas Hale Boggs, Jr. (D)	60,453	(37%)
1970 primary:	Gilbert Gude (R), unopposed		
1968 general:	Gilbert Gude (R)	109,167	(61%)
	Margaret C. Schweinhaut (D)	70,109	(39%)

MASSACHUSETTS

Political Background

Massachusetts is the most liberal large state in the nation today. Its citizens consistently vote for candidates who oppose the Vietnam war and favor civil rights legislation and social welfare programs. In 1968 Humphrey carried all twelve of the state's congressional districts and won 63% of the statewide vote. Richard Nixon has little chance of carrying Massachusetts in 1972.

Historically, the politics of the Bay State featured bitter struggles between Yankee Republicans and Irish Democrats. The potato famine of the 1840's drove thousands of Irishmen to Boston. A period of quiescence followed the migration; but after the Civil War, the Irish, upon realizing the strength of their numbers, entered Massachusetts politics with a vengeance. After the turn of the century, the Yankee-Irish conflicts were complicated by the demands of the state's sizable bloc of Italian, French-Canadian, Portuguese, Polish, and black voters. These ethnic divisions still play a part in Massachusetts local politics, but the fabled days of James Michael Curley (hero of *The Last Hurrah,* five times mayor of Boston, once congressman, and twice jailed) and Leverett Saltonstall (governor and senator three times each) are gone. In national politics, at least, the kelly green Irishman and the flinty Yankee have found a common dislike for the Republicanism of Nixon and Agnew.

The new generations of hyphenated Americans in Massachusetts have lost most of their previously intense ethnic consciousness, but they have retained their ancestral Democratic voting habits. The influence of the Kennedys, as well as the depressed state of the traditional industries—textiles and shoes—are in large part responsible for this. Moreover, to the older voting stream has been added a large number of liberal WASPish immigrants from points west, employed in the electronics industries around Boston's Route 128 or in the state's many universities and colleges. The technologists and academics seem to find the ambience of Boston and Cambridge appealing. The presence of these groups helps to make the Republican party here the nation's most liberal; the state has no viable conservative movement like the one led by James Buckley in New York. And of course many of the Massachusetts Democrats are far more liberal than most of the state's Republicans.

Present political feeling in the Commonwealth is summed up by the voting records of the state's two senators, Edward M. Kennedy and Edward W. Brooke, one a liberal Democrat and the other a liberal Republican. With help from two brothers, the President and the Attorney General of the United States, the youngest Kennedy, at age thirty, rose from assistant district attorney of Suffolk County to U.S. senator in 1962. Teddy's candidacy was resented by many of the state's white-collar voters, but he was elected nonetheless with the overwhelming support of Massachusetts' Catholic majority.

Kennedy's steadfastly liberal record in the Senate—his strong opposition to the war, his attention to the plight of Vietnamese refugees, and his attempt to create a system of national medical care—has drawn the state's two major voting blocs together. The reverence of Catholic voters for Kennedy and for his family has prevented them from moving to the right as they have done in other Eastern states. The increasingly liberal WASPs here, meanwhile, have approved of the Senator's stands on the issues. Chappaquiddick, of course, and the loss of the Senate Whip post have hurt Kennedy's chances for the Presidency, but he is still quite popular in Massachusetts. His share of the vote in 1964 was a phenomenal 74%; in 1970, a solid 62%.

Edward Brooke is the first black to serve in the Senate since 1881 when Blanche K. Bruce was denied reelection by the Mississippi "home rule" legislature. Brooke, a native of Washington, D.C., rose steadily through the state's Republican party, from appointive positions to the Attorney General's office, and his election to replace Leverett Saltonstall in 1966 came as no surprise. Brooke is neither abrasive nor militant, but only in Massachusetts could he have made it as far as the Senate. Since Brooke regularly takes liberal positions in the Senate, he has been at odds with the Nixon Administration on most major issues, notably on the Haynsworth and Carswell nominations and school desegregation issues. Brooke, like Kennedy, is assured of reelection as long as he chooses to run.

The most striking thing about Massachusetts' congressional voting patterns is their stability. In the past 10 years, only 14 men and 2 women have occupied the Commonwealth's 12 seats in the House of Representatives. The rumor is that former Speaker McCormack, knowing the value of seniority, took great pains to assure the continued incumbency of the state's House delegation, Democrat and Republican alike, and persuaded the legislature to carve out safe (if grotesquely shaped) districts for each member. Since 1954, the only shift in party control of a seat occurred in 1969 when a 6th district Democrat won a special election after the death of the Republican incumbent. Outside of the 12th district, it is unlikely that redistricting will pose any significant threat to the continued incumbency of the present membership.

Electoral Votes 14

Census Data 1970 pop. 5,689,170; 2.76% of U.S. total, 10th largest; change 1960–70, +10.5%. Metro. 84.7%, 30.3% central city. 1970 per capita income, $4,294, 10th highest. 26th in number of poor.

1970 Share of Federal Tax Burden $6,205,470,000; 3.18% of U.S. total, 9th largest.

1970 Share of Federal Outlays $4,907,202,416; 2.60% of U.S. total, 10th largest. Per capita federal spending, $863.

DOD	$1,677,690,000	12th (2.92%)	HEW	$1,682,580,420	9th (3.22%)
AEC	$26,663,640	17th (1.03%)	HUD	$68,292,353	9th (3.50%)
NASA	$92,213,418	13th (2.50%)	OEO	$22,621,048	7th (2.98%)
DOT	$140,217,970	19th (1.96%)	DOA	$88,912,754	39th (0.69%)
DOC	$7,715,222	31st (0.67%)	POD	$259,610,211	9th (3.56%)
DOI	$33,569,688	23rd (1.45%)	VA	$306,586,598	9th (4.15%)
DOJ	$11,380,270	14th (1.98%)	CSC	$84,736,109	12th (2.11%)
			Other	$404,358,706	

Economic Base Electrical machinery, equipment, and supplies, esp. electronic components and accessories; nonelectrical machinery, esp. special industry machinery other than metalworking machinery; apparel and other finished products made from fabrics and similar materials, esp. women's, misses', and juniors' outerwear; printing, publishing, and allied industries, esp. commercial printing and newspapers; fabricated metal products, esp. cutlery, hand tools, and general hardware; leather and leather products, esp. footwear other than house slippers and rubber footwear. Also services: higher education, insurance, and medicine.

Political Line-up Governor, Francis W. Sargent (R); seat up, 1974. Senators, Edward M. Kennedy (D) and Edward W. Brooke (R). Representatives, 12 (8 D and 4R). State Senate (30 D and 10 R); State House (178 D and 62 R).

The Voters

Registration 2,628,581 total. 1,135,103 D (43%); $547,393 R (21%); 946,085 Ind (36%).

Employment profile White collar, 44%. Blue collar, 56%.

Ethnic groups Black, 3%. Total foreign stock, 40%. Canada, 11%; Italy, 6%; Ireland, 5%; UK, 4%; Poland, USSR, 3% each; Germany, Sweden, 1% each; others, 6%.

Presidential vote

1968	Humphrey (D)	1,469,218	(63%)
	Nixon (R)	766,844	(33%)
	Wallace (AIP)	87,088	(4%)
1964	Johnson (D)	1,786,422	(76%)
	Goldwater (R)	549,727	(24%)
1960	Kennedy (D)	1,487,174	(60%)
	Nixon (R)	976,750	(40%)

Senator

Edward M. Kennedy (D) Elected 1962, seat up, 1976; b. Feb. 22, 1932, Brookline; home, Boston; Milton Academy; Harvard, B.A., 1956; International Law School, The Hague, Holland, 1958; U. of Va., LL.B., 1959; Army, 1951–53; married, three children; Catholic.

Career Asst. District Atty., Suffolk Co., 1961–62; Asst. Senate Majority Leader, 1969; Democratic Whip, 1968–70.

Offices 431 OSOB, 202-225-4543. Also Rm. 2400A, Kennedy Fed. Bldg., Boston 02203, 617-223-2826.

Committees

Judiciary (5th); Subs. (1) Chm., Administrative Practice and Procedure, (2) Chm., Refugees and Escapees, (3) Constitutional Rights, (4) Criminal Laws and Procedures, (5) Immigration and Naturalization, (6) Juvenile Delinquency, (7) Antitrust and Monopoly Legislation.

Labor and Public Welfare (4th); Subs. (1) Chm., Health, (2) Chm., Sp. on National Science Foundation, (3) Aging, (4) Alcoholism and Narcotics, (5) Children and Youth, (6) Education, (7) Employment, Manpower, and Poverty, (8) Migratory Labor.

Sel. Com. on Nutrition and Human Needs (4th).

Sp. Com. on Aging (7th); Subs. (1) Chm., Federal, State, and Community Services, (2) Consumer Interests of the Elderly, (3) Health of the Elderly, (4) Housing for the Elderly, (5) Long-Term Care, (6) Retirement and the Individual.

Group Ratings

	ADA	COPE	NREP	NFU	LCV	NAB	NSI	ACA
1970	84	100	100	100	71	18	0	5
1969	100	—	—	94	—	—	—	9
1968	71	100	—	88	—	0	—	0

Key Votes

(1) ABM	AGN	(8) Phil Pln	FOR	(15) Coop-Church	FOR
(2) SST	AGN	(9) Vol Army	AGN	(16) Cut Oil Dpltn	FOR
(3) Busing	FOR	(10) Prison $	ABS	(17) Consumer Prot	FOR
(4) Tob Sub	FOR	(11) Cut Mil $	FOR	(18) Farm Sub Limit	FOR
(5) Carswell	AGN	(12) Defoliatn	FOR	(19) Comp Bid Sales	ABS
(6) No-Knock	AGN	(13) 18-Yr-Vote	FOR	(20) Pre-Prod Tests	ABS
(7) Seniorty	AGN	(14) Pentgn PR	AGN	(21) Cut Marjna Pen	ABS

Election Results

1970 general:	Edward M. Kennedy (D)	1,202,856	(62%)
	Josiah Spaulding (R)	715,978	(38%)
1970 primary:	Edward M. Kennedy (D), unopposed		
1964 general:	Edward M. Kennedy (D)	1,716,907	(74%)
	Howard Whitmore, Jr. (R)	587,663	(26%)
1962 special:	Edward M. Kennedy (D)	1,162,611	(56%)
	George C. Lodge (R)	877,669	(42%)
	H. Stuart Hughes (Ind)	50,013	(2%)

Senator

Edward W. Brooke (R) Elected 1966, seat up, 1972; b. Oct. 26, 1919, Washington, D.C.; home, Newton Centre; Howard U., B.S., 1940; Boston U., LL.B., 1948, LL.M., 1949; Army, WWII; married, two children; Episcopalian.

Career Chm., Boston Finance Commission, 1961–62; Atty. Gen. Mass., 1963–66.

Offices 232 OSOB, 202-225-2742. Also Rm. 2003H, Kennedy Fed. Bldg., Boston 02203, 617-223-7420; and 1421 Main St., Springfield 01103, 413-781-6700.

Committees

Appropriations (11th); Subs. (1) Labor, HEW, and Related Agencies, (2) Foreign Operations, (3) Legislative Branch, (4) Military Construction, (5) State, Justice, Commerce, the Judiciary, and Related Agencies.

Banking, Housing, and Urban Affairs (3rd); Subs. (1) Financial Institutions, (2) Housing and Urban Affairs, (3) International Finance, (4) Securities, (5) Small Business.

Sel. Com. on Equal Educational Opportunity (4th).

Sp. Com. on Aging (8th); Subs. (1) Consumer Interests of the Elderly, (2) Federal, State, and Community Services, (3) Health of the Elderly, (4) Housing of the Elderly, (5) Long-Term Care.

Group Ratings

	ADA	COPE	NREP	NFU	LCV	NAB	NSI	ACA
1970	88	92	83	93	83	18	20	9
1969	89	—	—	69	—	—	—	9
1968	71	100	—	77	—	0	—	0

Key Votes

(1) ABM	AGN	(8) Phil Pln	FOR	(15) Coop-Church	FOR
(2) SST	AGN	(9) Vol Army	FOR	(16) Cut Oil Dpltn	FOR
(3) Busing	FOR	(10) Prison $	FOR	(17) Consumer Prot	FOR
(4) Tob Sub	AGN	(11) Cut Mil $	AGN	(18) Farm Sub Limit	FOR
(5) Carswell	AGN	(12) Defoliatn	FOR	(19) Comp Bid Sales	FOR
(6) No-Knock	FOR	(13) 18-Yr-Vote	FOR	(20) Pre-Prod Tests	AGN
(7) Seniorty	FOR	(14) Pentgn PR	FOR	(21) Cut Marjna Pen	FOR

Election Results

1966 general:	Edward W. Brooke (R)	1,213,473	(61%)
	Endicott Peabody (D)	774,761	(39%)
1966 primary:	Edward W. Brooke (R), unopposed		

FIRST DISTRICT Political Background

Massachusetts 1 is the western part of the state: the Berkshire Mountains and much of the Connecticut River Valley. The Berkshires are famous as a summer resort area and for picturesque towns like Stockbridge, the scene of *Alice's Restaurant,* and Lenox, site of the Tanglewood music festival. More important politically are the old mill towns in the mountains, particularly Pittsfield, the district's largest city (pop. 57,000), and North Adams. Residents of the mill towns, Democrats of immigrant stock, outvote the small-town Republican Yankees by substantial pluralities.

The Connecticut Valley is politically similar to the Berkshires: small Republican towns offset by occasional Democratic mill centers. In the middle of the Valley are the college towns of Amherst, with Amherst College and the University of Massachusetts, and Northampton, the home of Smith College (which despite the presence of Julie and David Eisenhower went heavily Democratic in the 1968 presidential election). To the south, on the west bank of the Connecticut River, are the industrial suburbs of Springfield: Holyoke, West Springfield, and Westfield, all of which normally vote Democratic.

In national elections, the 1st votes liberal and Democratic, but in congressional races it is firmly committed to liberal Republican Silvio O. Conte. Conte served as state senator from Berkshire County for eight years before he went to the House, and he has been well entrenched in the district for some time. His most notable challenge came in 1958 from Williams College political scientist James McGregor Burns. Burns received some national publicity, but Conte got the votes locally. So Burns went on to finish his Roosevelt biography, while Conte returned to the House to become one of the five liberal Republicans on the Appropriations Committee.

Conte, who votes like most northern Democrats, has not been afraid to buck the party leadership on issues like school desegregation and military aid to Taiwan. The Congressman has also opposed the war and what he considers excessive and wasteful military spending. Back home, Conte has had no Democratic opponents in the last eight years. As in most of Massachusetts, redistricting will have little effect on the district's boundaries or political inclinations.

Census Data 1970 pop. 470,856; deviation from current state average, —0.7%; change 1960–70, +9.9%. Metro. 55.1%, 22.8% central city.

1970 Share of Federal Outlays $408,934,000 (average outlay per district, Massachusetts 1–12)

DOD	$139,808,000	HEW	$140,215,000
AEC	$2,222,000	HUD	$5,691,000
NASA	$7,684,000	OEO	$1,885,000
DOT	$11,689,000	DOA	$7,409,000
		Other	$92,330,000

Federal Military-Industrial Commitments

DOD Contractors General Electric (Pittsfield), $57.768m: Poseidon missile launch control and guidance systems.

Economic Base Electrical machinery, equipment, and supplies, esp. electric transmission and distribution equipment; paper and allied products, esp. converted paper and paperboard products other than containers and boxes; nonelectical machinery, esp. special industry machinery other than metalworking machinery. Also tourism (Berkshires) and higher education (U. Mass.).

The Voters

Registration 218,271 total. 75,929 D (35%); 45,444 R (21%); 96,898 Ind (44%).

Employment profile. White collar, 41%. Blue collar, 59%.

Ethnic groups Black, 1%. Total foreign stock, 33%. Canada, 8%; Poland, 6%; Ireland, Italy, 4% each; UK, 3%; Germany, 2%; USSR, Austria, 1% each; others, 4%.

Presidential vote

1968	Humphrey (D)	110,313	(58%)
	Nixon (R)	71,702	(38%)
	Wallace (AIP)	8,546	(4%)

Representative

Silvio O. Conte (R) Elected 1958; b. Nov. 9, 1921, Pittsfield; home, Pittsfield; Boston Col. and Boston Col. Law School, LL.B., 1949; married, four children; Catholic.

Career Practicing atty., 1949–58; State Senator, 1950–58.

Offices 239 CHOB, 202-225-5335. Also North St., Pittsfield 01201, 413-442-0946.

Committees

Appropriations (7th); Subs. (1) Labor and HEW, (2) Transportation.

Sel. Com. on Small Business (Ranking Mbr.).

Group Ratings

	ADA	COPE	NREP	NFU	LCV	CFA	NAB	NSI	ACA
1970	72	75	83	92	75	80	42	44	28
1969	67	—	—	73	—	—	—	—	35
1968	67	77	—	75	—	—	17	—	35

Key Votes

(1) ABM	AGN	(6) 18-Yr-Vote	FOR	(11) Clean Water $	AGN
(2) SST	AGN	(7) Farm Sub Lmt	FOR	(12) Mig Wrkrs Comp	FOR
(3) Phil Pln	FOR	(8) Coop-Church	FOR	(13) Jets to Chiang	AGN
(4) No-Knock	FOR	(9) Family Asst	FOR	(14) State OEO Veto	AGN
(5) Cmutr Tax	AGN	(10) Work Stamps	AGN	(15) Park Logging	AGN

Election Results

1970 general:	Silvio Conte (R), unopposed
1970 primary:	Silvio Conte (R), unopposed
1968 general:	Silvio Conte (R), unopposed

SECOND DISTRICT Political Background

Massachusetts 2 is the city of Springfield, most of its suburbs, and a collection of rural and small industrial towns to the east. Springfield (pop. 163,000) and Chicopee (pop. 66,000), just to the north, are the Democratic bastions of the district, though most of the rest of the towns here also give Democratic candidates solid margins. The exception to the pattern is in races for governor. Voters of the 2nd, as well as those in the rest of the Commonwealth, seem to believe that a Democrat cannot be trusted with the top post in state government. So while the state legislature has been dominated by Democrats, Massachusetts has elected only one Democratic governor, and then by a small margin, since 1958.

Springfield is the home town of a number of famous political pros. Lawrence O'Brien, the Democratic National Chairman and ex-Postmaster General, Joe Napolitan, the well-known campaign consultant, and Sen. Mike Gravel of Alaska all grew up in the city and learned their first lessons in its wards and precincts. Springfield currently sends another political pro to the House, Edward P. Boland. Boland manages to bridge some of the gaps that have developed between the old Northern Democratic regulars—the kind of politician who used to dominate the Massachusetts delegation—and the current crop of young liberal insurgents. The 2nd's Congressman is respectful of the House leadership, but nonetheless has an increasingly liberal and antiwar record. Considered knowledgeable and astute, Boland was mentioned as a candidate for Majority Leader, though he declined to run.

First elected in 1952, Boland now stands 8th among Democrats on the Appropriations Committee and is chairman of its HUD-Space-Science Subcommittee. He has had no problem whatever winning reelection; in the last eight years the Republicans have challenged him only once, and they came away with a meager 26% of the votes.

Census Data 1970 pop. 460,050; deviation from current state average, —3.0%; change 1960–70, +7.6%. Metro. 84.4%, 22.8% central city.

1970 Share of Federal Outlays $408,934,000 (average outlay per district, Massachusetts 1–12)

DOD	$139,808,000	HEW	$140,215,000
AEC	$2,222,000	HUD	$5,691,000
NASA	$7,684,000	OEO	$1,885,000
DOT	$11,689,000	DOA	$7,409,000
		Other	$92,330,000

Federal Military-Industrial Commitments

DOD Contractors General Instrument (Chicopee), $15,484m: production of bomb fuzes.

DOD Installations Westover AFB (Chicopee Falls).

Economic Base Nonelectrical machinery; fabricated metal products, esp. cutlery, hand tools, and general hardware; paper and allied products, esp. converted paper and paperboard products other than containers and boxes.

The Voters

Registration 205,109 total. 96,771 D (47%); 36,238 R (18%); 72,100 Ind (35%).

Employment profile White collar, 41%. Blue collar, 59%.

Ethnic groups Black, 5%. Total foreign stock, 37%. Canada, 10%; Poland, 7%; Italy, 5%; Ireland, 4%; UK, 3%; USSR, 2%; Germany, Sweden, 1% each; others, 4%.

Presidential vote

1968	Humphrey (D)	114,520	(64%)
	Nixon (R)	56,157	(31%)
	Wallace (AIP)	9,000	(5%)

Representative

Edward P. Boland (D) Elected 1952; b. Oct. 1, 1911, Springfield; home, Springfield; attended Boston Col. Law School; Army, WWII; unmarried; Catholic.

Career State Rep., 1935–40; Register of Deeds, Hampden Co., 1941–52.

Offices 2111 RHOB, 202-225-5601. Also 1883 Main St., Rm. 100, Springfield 01103, 413-733-4127.

Committees

Appropriations (8th); Subs. (1) Chm., HUD, Space, and Science, (2) Public Works, (3) Transportation.

Group Ratings

	ADA	COPE	NREP	NFU	LCV	CFA	NAB	NSI	ACA
1970	76	83	75	100	80	95	17	40	12
1969	80	—	—	93	—	—	—	—	13
1968	83	92	—	92	—	—	0	—	5

Key Votes

(1) ABM	AGN	(6) 18-Yr-Vote	FOR	(11) Clean Water $	AGN
(2) SST	FOR	(7) Farm Sub Lmt	FOR	(12) Mig Wrkrs Comp	FOR
(3) Phil Pln	FOR	(8) Coop-Church	FOR	(13) Jets to Chiang	AGN
(4) No-Knock	FOR	(9) Family Asst	FOR	(14) State OEO Veto	AGN
(5) Cmutr Tax	FOR	(10) Work Stamps	AGN	(15) Park Logging	AGN

Election Results

1970 general:	Edward P. Boland (D), unopposed		
1970 primary:	Edward P. Boland (D), unopposed		
1968 general:	Edward P. Boland (D)	126,485	(74%)
	Frederick M. Whitney, Jr. (R)	45,262	(26%)

THIRD DISTRICT Political Background

Massachusetts 3 is an odd assortment of cities and towns that stretches from the Boston city limits to a point near the Vermont line. The present district is the stepchild of quite another district, the old 3rd, which was a horseshoe around the city of Worcester. The 1967 redistricting created the present 3rd which includes the northern half of the old one—mainly small industrial towns like Fitchburg, Leominster, Clinton, and Marlborough—and a slice of suburban Boston to the east—wealthy Concord, Lincoln, and Weston; industrial Waltham and Watertown; and middle-class and predominately Jewish Newton.

The 1967 redistricting probably worried veteran Congressman Philip J. Philbin. First elected in 1942, Philbin was number two man on the House Armed Services Committee, behind the late Chairman Mendel Rivers, whose hawkish stands he usually supported. Philbin, Congressman Harold Donohue of nearby Worcester (4th district), and Speaker McCormack of Boston (9th district) formed a comfortable trio of aging Irishmen prone to reminisce about the old days. The group, many said, was tired and out of touch with the rest of the House.

After the 1967 redistricting, some 46% of the new 3rd's population and 53% of its registered Democrats were in the new, suburban portion. The altered constituency soon gave the veteran politician problems; indeed, Philbin ran into them in the first election after redistricting. In 1966, he had no primary opposition and won the general election with 71% of the votes. In 1968, Philbin encountered three primary opponents and barely managed to fight them off with 49%. The general election that followed was a three-man race which featured an independent, antiwar candidate, Chandler Stevens, who carried six of the district's towns and cities and ran second. Philbin won but was held down to 48%.

It was becoming increasingly clear that a candidate with strength in strongly antiwar Newton and capable of making inroads in the heavily Catholic mill towns—where Philbin was still strong—could win the Democratic primary. Such a candidate was Father Robert F. Drinan, Dean of the Boston College Law School and a vigorous opponent of the Vietnam war, who challenged Philbin in 1970. Drinan had energetic student and volunteer support and swept Newton, which has a quarter of the district's registered Democrats, by a 4:1 margin. The priest also carried Waltham and the high-income suburban towns. A third candidate, state Rep. Charles Ohanian of predominantly Armenian Watertown, carried his home city, but finished third. Drinan won 58% of the votes in the new portion of the 3rd and a respectable 30% in the rest, for an 8,000-vote victory (46% to Philbin's 36%).

When old regulars win primaries, they often lecture the defeated insurgents about the need for party unity and so on. Philbin was an old regular who lost and, rather than accept defeat, decided to enter the general election as an independent. Here he hoped to reverse the results of the primary and extend his 28-year stay in the House. At the same time, state Rep. John McGlennon of Concord, the Republican candidate, was waging an effective campaign, labeling Drinan an extremist in an effort to win over normally Democratic votes. Drinan cranked up his volunteer organization once again, and this time his margin of victory was even smaller: Drinan had 38%, McGlennon 36%, and Philbin 27%. As in the primary, Philbin carried most of his old district, while Newton produced Drinan's biggest majority.

By winning, Father Drinan became the first Roman Catholic priest to serve in the House of Representatives. Philbin was left with one reward for his many years of service. Mendel Rivers died in late December of 1970, and so Philbin became the chairman of the House Armed Services Committee for a few days, spanning two calender years. It is unlikely that he will run again; should he win, he would no longer have his seniority or his old friend, John McCormack. Drinan's chief problem will be redistricting. Some of the 3rd's eastern towns may be shifted to districts in Boston, which have been losing population. But without Philbin in the race, Drinan, simply because he is the incumbent and a Democrat, should be able to carry the old as well as the new portions of the 3rd in 1972.

Census Data 1970 pop. 495,076; deviation from current state average, +4.4%; change 1960–70, +14.6%. Metro. 68.8%, 53.9% central city.

1970 Share of Federal Outlays $408,934,000 (average outlay per district, Massachusetts 1–12)

DOD	$139,808,000	HEW	$140,215,000
AEC	$2,222,000	HUD	$5,691,000
NASA	$7,684,000	OEO	$1,885,000
DOT	$11,689,331	DOA	$7,409,000
		Other	$92,330,000

Federal Military-Industrial Commitments (See Massachusetts 5 for greater Boston listing.)

Economic Base Electrical machinery, equipment, and supplies, esp. communication equipment; nonelectrial machinery, esp. office, computing, and accounting machines and metalworking machinery and equipment; fabricated metal products; professional, scientific, and controlling instruments, photographic and optical goods, watches, and clocks. Also, higher education (Boston College).

The Voters

Registration 220,241 total. 79,900 D (36%); 44,808 R (20%); 95,533 Ind (44%).

Employment profile White collar, 39%. Blue collar, 61%.

Ethnic groups Black, 1%. Total foreign stock, 37%. Canada, 13%; Italy, 5%; Ireland, Poland, UK, USSR, 3% each; Germany, Sweden, 1% each; others, 5%.

Presidential vote

1968	Humphrey (D)	124,927	(63%)
	Nixon (R)	67,648	(34%)
	Wallace (AIP)	5,951	(4%)

Representative

Robert F. Drinan (D) Elected 1970; b. Nov. 15, 1920, Boston; home, Newton; Boston Col., B.A., 1942, M.A., 1947; Georgetown U. Law Center, LL.B., 1949, LL.M., 1950; Catholic.

Career Jesuit Priest; Dean of Boston Col. Law School, 1956–70.

Offices 509 CHOB, 202-225--5931. Also 76 Summer St., Fitchburg 01420, 617-342-8722, and 681 Main St., Waltham 02154, 617-891-9466.

Committees

Internal Security (5th).

Judiciary (22nd); Sub. No. 3.

Group Ratings, Key Votes: Newly elected.

Election Results

1970 general:	Robert F. Drinan (D)	63,942	(38%)
	John McGlennon (R)	60,575	(36%)
	Philip J. Philbin (Ind)	45,278	(27%)
1970 primary:	Robert F. Drinan (D)	28,605	(46%)
	Philip J. Philbin (D)	22,133	(36%)
	Charles Ohanian (D)	11,434	(18%)

FOURTH DISTRICT Political Background

Massachusetts 4 is the city of Worcester and several nearby cities and towns. There are high-income Republican suburbs to the north, and heavily Democratic mill towns along the southern edge of the district. The fastest-growing portion of the 4th is around Framingham (pop. 64,000), an exurban community about midway between Boston and Worcester. The 4th, like most Massachusetts districts, is overwhelmingly Democratic in national elections, though it sometimes supports Republican candidates in state contests.

In congressional elections, the district has been strongly Democratic for about as long as anyone can remember. Since 1946, it has regularly returned Rep. Harold D. Donohue to the House with strong majorities. Donohue is an aging (69 in 1970) bachelor who is currently the 3rd ranking Democrat on the House Judiciary Committee. Generally liberal on domestic issues, he has supported the war policies of the Johnson and Nixon administrations. However, since there is no strong antiwar vote base in the 4th, as there is in the adjoining 3rd district, Donohue has had little difficulty winning renomination and reelection.

The scuttlebutt is that Donohue will retire soon, in large part because of the retirement of his friend Speaker McCormack and the defeat of another friend, Philip J. Philbin of the 3rd, with whom he used to spend long afternoons dozing in front of the Speaker's podium. If Donohue does retire, the 4th will no doubt elect another Democrat, probably one of the area's state legislators, whose voting will not differ much from his predecessor's.

Census Data 1970 pop. 497,392; deviation from current state average, +4.9%; change 1960–70, +16.8%. Metro. 85.8%, 35.5% central city.

1970 Share of Federal Outlays $408,934,000 (average outlay per district, Massachusetts 1–12)

DOD	$139,808,000	HEW	$140,215,000
AEC	$2,222,000	HUD	$5,691,000
NASA	$7,684,000	OEO	$1,885,000
DOT	$11,689,000	DOA	$7,409,000
		Other	$92,330,000

Federal Military-Industrial Commitments

DOD Contractors Raytheon Corp. (Wayland and Sudbury), $26,804m: Poseidon and Polaris guidance systems; Sea Sparrow missile development.

Economic Base Nonelectrical machinery, esp. metalworking machinery; fabricated metal products, esp. cutlery, hand tools, and general hardware; rubber and miscellaneous plastic products; primary metal products, esp. blast furnaces, steel works, and rolling and finishing mills.

The Voters

Registration 228,172 total. 90,619 D (40%); 52,366 R (23%); 85,187 Ind (37%).
Employment profile White collar, 45%. Blue collar, 55%.
Ethnic groups Black, 1%. Total foreign stock, 42%. Canada, 11%; Italy, 7%; Ireland, 5%; UK, USSR, Sweden, 3% each; Poland, 2%; Germany, 1%; others, 7%.

Presidential vote

1968	Humphrey (D)	127,882	(63%)
	Nixon (R)	70,871	(34%)
	Wallace (AIP)	5,725	(3%)

Representative

Harold D. Donohue (D) Elected 1946; b. June 18, 1901, Worcester; home, Worcester; Northeastern U., 1925; Navy, WWII; unmarried; Catholic.

Career Atty., 1926– ; Alderman, acting Mayor, Worcester.

Offices 2265 RHOB, 202-225-6101. Also 390 Main St., Worcester 01608, 617-754-7264.

Committees

Judiciary (3rd); Chm., Sub. No. 2.

Group Ratings

	ADA	COPE	NREP	NFU	LCV	CFA	NAB	NSI	ACA
1970	72	100	83	92	88	80	0	90	17
1969	67	—	—	93	—	—	—	—	18
1968	75	100	—	87	—	—	0	—	10

Key Votes

(1) ABM	FOR	(6) 18-Yr-Vote	FOR	(11) Clean Water $	FOR
(2) SST	AGN	(7) Farm Sub Lmt	FOR	(12) Mig Wrkrs Comp	FOR
(3) Phil Pln	AGN	(8) Coop-Church	FOR	(13) Jets to Chiang	FOR
(4) No-Knock	FOR	(9) Family Asst	FOR	(14) State OEO Veto	AGN
(5) Cmutr Tax	FOR	(10) Work Stamps	AGN	(15) Park Logging	AGN

Election Results

1970 general:	Harold D. Donohue (D)	95,016	(54%)
	Howard A. Miller, Jr. (R)	79,870	(46%)
1970 primary:	Harold D. Donohue (D)	38,005	(83%)
	Stephanie A. Riopel (D)	7,992	(17%)
1968 general:	Harold D. Donohue (D)	121,211	(61%)
	Howard A. Miller, Jr. (R)	77,658	(39%)

FIFTH DISTRICT Political Background

Massachusetts 5 is a district dominated by a string of towns along Route 128, a superhighway which encircles much of greater Boston. The portion of the highway in the 5th district is lined with once booming, but now financially ailing electronic and light industrial firms. Raytheon, the state's largest defense contractor, has most of its plants in the 5th.

Many of the voters here are upper-middle-class WASPs, left-leaning Republicans—the kind of mellowed Republican who seems native to Massachusetts. Towns like Lexington, Bedford, Wilmington, Tewksbury, and Chelmsford regularly cast heavy majorities for the liberal Republicans at the top of the state ticket—Sen. Brooke, Gov. Francis X. Sargent, and ex-Gov. John Volpe. But in presidential elections, they recoil from the harsh Republicanism of men like Barry Goldwater and Richard Nixon and reluctantly vote Democratic. In 1968, the 5th, one of the most reliably Republican districts in state elections, gave 64% of its votes to Hubert Humphrey, who did better here than on the normally 2:1 Democratic west side of Cleveland, Ohio.

There is a less prosperous side of the 5th, the old Merrimack River mill towns of Lowell and Lawrence. These were planned cities, way back in the 1820's, laid out by paternalistic textile-mill owners for their workers and considered model urban centers in their time. The nineteenth-century Lowells, Lawrences, and Cabots were shocked at the conditions in which the English mill operatives lived, and they wanted to provide better conditions for their own workers, then mostly young Yankee girls from farms in the countryside. This kind of labor was soon replaced by the immigrant Irish, for whom the mill owners showed less concern.

But for many years now the once-important textile industry in New England has been on the decline, and Lowell and Lawrence have been losing population. The Democratic votes cast in the two cities were first nullified by the popularity of the local congressman and then by the growing Republicanism of the surrounding suburbs.

From 1924 to 1960, the 5th was represented by Mrs. Edith Nourse Rogers, a genteel Republican beloved by her constituents. She was succeeded by a young attorney and former assistant to Sen. Leverett Saltonstall, F. Bradford Morse. Morse's toughest election occurred in 1962 when redistricting forced him into a race with Rep. Thomas J. Lane, Democrat of Lawrence. Morse had the advantage of incumbency in most of the new district, if only for two years, and Lane had spent some time in jail on an income tax charge. Morse won handily, as he has ever since. Lately he has been getting decent margins in Lowell and in 1970 managed to carry Lawrence.

Morse began his congressional career as a conventional Republican, but has become more liberal on major issues in recent years, as has his district. He is an opponent of the war and of what he considers excessive spending by the military. But Morse has been rather quiet in opposition to the Administration, probably because he was an early supporter of Nixon's candidacy in 1968. Redistricting should be no problem; Morse can look forward to certain reelection.

Census Data 1970 pop. 524,809; deviation from current state average, +10.7%; change 1960–70, +21.9%. Metro. 97%, 30.7% central city.

1970 Share of Federal Outlays $408,934,000 (average outlay per district, Massachusetts 1–12)

DOD	$139,808,000	HEW	$140,215,000
AEC	$2,222,000	HUD	$5,691,000
NASA	$7,684,000	OEO	$1,885,000
DOT	$11,689,000	DOA	$7,409,000
		Other	$92,330,000

Federal Military-Industrial Commitments (Massachusetts 3, 5–11, greater Boston listing)

DOD Contractors Raytheon Corp. (Lowell, Bedford, Andover, Waltham, Burlington, North Dighton), $266.793m: Hawk, Sparrow, Sidewinder, Nike, Tartar, and SAM-D missile guidance systems; aircraft electronic warfare assemblies; radar site operation, other electronic ware. General Electric (West Lynn), $109.591m: various jet aircraft and helicopter engines. Western Electirc Div., AT&T (Bedford), $107.265m: ABM development; other research in electronic ware. MIT (Lexington and Cambridge), $96.360m: Poseidon and Minuteman missile guidance systems development; development of computer analysis in behavioral sciences.

RCA (Burlington), $57.952m: land combat support systems studies. Avco (Wilmington and Everett), $51.086m: development of reentry vehicles for ABM system. Sylvania Div., General Telephone (Needham Heights and Waltham), $44.024m: Minuteman launch system; ABM radar system maintenance; portable radio sets. Mitre Corp. (Bedford), $33.347m: information systems research.

Central Beef Co. (Boston), $15.457m: foodstuffs. General Dynamics (Quincy), $9.942m: ship repair. United Fruit (Boston), $10.875m: foodstuffs. Northrop Corp. (Norwood), $8.660m: Minuteman missile gyrocompasses. Keystone Mfg. Co. (Boston), $7.349m: production of bomb components.

DOD Installations Army Material and Mechanical Research Center (Watertown). Fort Devens AB (Ayer). Boston Naval Shipyard (Boston). Naval Hospital (Chelsea). Naval Station (Boston). Hanscom Field (Bedford). Natick Army Laboratories (Natick).

AEC Operations MIT (Cambridge), $8.811m: Research Facilities. Harvard University (Cambridge), $6.406m: Cambridge Accelerator. EG&G (Bedford), $5.054m: Test Facilities.

NASA Contractors MIT (Cambridge), $15.438m: Apollo and LEM guidance systems design. Harvard University (Cambridge), $6.183m: ultraviolet telescope and spectrometer system. Itek (Lexington), $5.100m: photographic analysis.

Economic Base Electrical machinery, equipment, and supplies, esp. communication equipment; nonelectrical machinery; professional, scientific, and controlling instruments, photographic and optical goods, watches and clocks; leather and leather products.

The Voters

Registration 237,239 total. 103,308 D (43%); 49,237 R (21%); 84,694 Ind (36%).

Employment profile White collar, 45%. Blue collar, 55%.

Ethnic groups Black, 1%. Total foreign stock, 38%. Canada, 13%; Ireland, Italy, UK, 5% each; Poland, 2%; Germany, Sweden, 1% each; others, 5%.

Presidential vote

1968	Humphrey (D)	134,795	(64%)
	Nixon (R)	70,760	(33%)
	Wallace (AIP)	6,869	(3%)

Representative

F. Bradford Morse (R) Elected 1960; b. Aug. 7, 1921, Lowell; home, Lowell; Boston U., B.S., 1948; Army, WWII; married; United Church of Christ.

Career Practicing atty; law clerk, Mass. Supreme Court, 1949; faculty, Boston U. School of Law, 1949–53; Lowell City Council, 1952–53; atty., Senate Armed Services Com., 1953–54.

Offices 2442 RHOB, 202-225-3411. Also 15 Kearney Square, Lowell 01852, 617-458-1221, and 447 Essex St., Lawrence 01840, 617-683-2831.

Committees

Foreign Affairs (7th); Subs. (1) Inter-American Affairs, (2) National Security Policy and Scientific Development, (3) State Department Organization and Foreign Operations.

Group Ratings

	ADA	COPE	NREP	NFU	LCV	CFA	NAB	NSI	ACA
1970	56	55	83	73	88	79	60	11	33
1969	67	—	—	67	—	—	—	—	21
1968	57	83	—	60	—	—	0	—	17

Key Votes

(1) ABM	AGN	(6) 18-Yr-Vote	FOR	(11) Clean Water $	FOR
(2) SST	AGN	(7) Farm Sub Lmt	FOR	(12) Mig Wrkrs Comp	FOR
(3) Phil Pln	ABS	(8) Coop-Church	FOR	(13) Jets to Chiang	AGN
(4) No-Knock	FOR	(9) Family Asst	FOR	(14) State OEO Veto	AGN
(5) Cmutr Tax	FOR	(10) Work Stamps	AGN	(15) Park Logging	AGN

Election Results

1970 general:	F. Bradford Morse (R)	116,666	(63%)
	Richard Williams (D)	67,646	(37%)
1970 primary:	F. Bradford Morse (R), unopposed		
1968 general:	F. Bradford Morse (R)	124,930	(60%)
	Robert C. Maguire (D)	81,875	(40%)

SIXTH DISTRICT Political Background

Massachusetts 6 is the northeast corner of the state, where it juts out into the Atlantic Ocean. Living in this varied district are some of Boston's oldest families, including the Henry Cabot Lodges. Only a few miles away are the fishermen of Gloucester, the textile-mill workers of Newburyport and Haverhill, and the artists in Rockport. To the south is Salem, where twenty witches were hanged and pressed to death and where Hawthorne's House of Seven Gables still stands. Also to the south is the boating suburb of Marblehead, which the Jews now share with the WASPs, and Lynn, whose shoe industry is in serious trouble. The shoe men would like to block stylish Italian imports in particular.

The rich towns of the North Shore have given the district a Republican reputation, one that is not really accurate; Democratic presidential candidates have carried the 6th easily. The image of the district was sustained by its conservative Republican congressman, William H. Bates, who carried the district with big majorities. Bates took office in 1950, succeeding his father, who had held the seat since 1936, and, like many Massachusetts incumbents, had no trouble winning votes even from people ideologically opposed to him.

Bates died unexpectedly in 1969. In the special election called to fill the vacancy, state Rep. Michael Harrington waged a vigorous and sophisticated campaign, using computers and a well-organized volunteer staff, to beat state Sen. William Saltonstall, 52:48. The race was a test of the popularity of the Nixon Administration's foreign and defense policies. Harrington was a strong opponent of the war and of the ABM, while Saltonstall, Leverett's son, supported the President on both.

In the 1970 election, Harrington had weaker opposition and took 61% of the votes. At the beginning of the 92nd Congress, he won assignment to the House Armed Services Committee over the opposition of Rep. James A. Burke, Massachusetts' man on Ways and Means, the committee which makes Democratic committee assignments. For some time to come, at least, he will be part of a small anti-military minority on the committee (see Michigan 14); the seniority system does not permit the turnover necessary to convert Armed Services from hawk to dove in any kind of hurry.

Harrington has been active in state Democratic politics and is said to be already running for Governor in 1974. Harrington, a strong McCarthy supporter in 1968, is the leader of the McCarthy wing of the party here, and the young Congressman's ambitions are reportedly resented by Sen. Edward Kennedy. Harrington should have no difficulty winning reelection in 1972, and even if he goes on to statewide office two years after that, chances are the 6th district will remain in Democratic hands.

Census Data 1970 pop. 486,711; deviation from current state average, +2.7%; change 1960–70, +12.3%. Metro. 81.7%, 9.5% central city.

1970 Share of Federal Outlays $408,934,000 (average outlay per district, Massachusetts 1–12)

DOD	$139,808,000	HEW	$140,215,000
AEC	$2,222,000	HUD	$5,691,000
NASA	$7,684,000	OEO	$1,885,000
DOT	$11,689,000	DOA	$7,409,000
		Other	$92,330,000

Federal Military-Industrial Commitments (See Massachusetts 5 for greater Boston listing.)

Economic Base Electrical machinery, equipment, and supplies; aircraft engines and components; leather and leather products, footwear other than rubber; textile mill products.

The Voters

Registration 246,799 total. 83,747 D (34%); 65,934 R (27%); 97,098 Ind (39%).

Employment profile White collar, 42%. Blue collar, 58%.

Ethnic groups Black, 1%. Total foreign stock, 38%. Canada, 13%; Italy, 5%; Ireland, UK, 4% each; Poland, 3%; USSR, 2%; Germany, Sweden, 1% each; others, 5%.

Presidential vote

1968	Humphrey (D)	128,141	(60%)
	Nixon (R)	79,134	(37%)
	Wallace (AIP)	6,734	(3%)

Representative

Michael J. Harrington (D) Elected Sept. 1969; b. Sept. 2, 1936, Salem; home, Beverly; Harvard Col., A.B., 1958; Harvard Law School, LL.B., 1961; Harvard Grad. School of Pub. Adm., 1962-3; married, four children; Catholic.

Career Salem City Council, 1960–63; State Rep., 1964–69; partner atty., Roman and Harrington, Salem, Mass., 1962– .

Offices 435 CHOB, 202-225-8020. Also Salem P.O. Bldg., Salem 01970, 617-745-5800.

Committees

Armed Services (23rd); Sub. No. 3.

Group Ratings

	ADA	COPE	NREP	NFU	LCV	CFA	NAB	NSI	ACA
1970	88	100	100	92	100	100	0	13	18
1969	100	—	—	78	—	—	—	—	22

Key Votes

(1) ABM	AGN	(6) 18-Yr-Vote	FOR	(11) Clean Water $	FOR
(2) SST	AGN	(7) Farm Sub Lmt	FOR	(12) Mig Wrkrs Comp	FOR
(3) Phil Pln	FOR	(8) Coop-Church	FOR	(13) Jets to Chiang	AGN
(4) No-Knock	AGN	(9) Family Asst	FOR	(14) State OEO Veto	AGN
(5) Cmutr Tax	FOR	(10) Work Stamps	AGN	(15) Park Logging	AGN

Election Results

1970 general:	Michael J. Harrington (D)	60,372	(61%)
	Howard Phillips (R)	38,179	(39%)
1970 primary:	Michael J. Harrington (D), unopposed		
1969 special:	Michael J. Harrington (D)	72,030	(52%)
	William L. Saltonstall (R)	65,454	(48%)

SEVENTH DISTRICT Political Background

Massachusetts 7 is a collection of suburbs just north of Boston, ranging from blue-collar (Chelsea) to WASPy and comfortable (Melrose). Most of the communities here are somewhere in between and contain many descendants of Irish and Italian immigrants who have become financially secure, if not affluent. The trend in the 7th illustrates the liberalization of the state's politics in the past ten years. In 1960, when Kennedy ran for president, he carried the district with what was considered a very strong Democratic showing, 61%. Yet Humphrey, who was not a native son, did significantly better in 1968, 67%. Between the two elections, Nixon's percentage declined from 39% to 30%. Shifts in issues—from the bread and butter issues of the late '50's to the concern with foreign policy, crime, and civil rights of the late '60's—have led many voters in this very middle-class district to believe that voting for the national Republican ticket is no longer respectable.

To attack a president's foreign policy would have been unthinkable in the 7th in 1960, but by 1968 and 1970 it was just common sense. To a considerable degree, the shift in opinion is the result of the Massachusetts Kennedys, particularly Sen. Edward Kennedy, who has become more and more liberal in the recent past. Since the Senator is a Kennedy and is still a presidential figure in the state, his positions on the issues can hardly be attacked as un-American. So the Irish, many of whom backed Joe McCarthy in the '50's, think nothing now of supporting an immediate withdrawal from the war.

One of the beneficiaries of this trend is Torbert M. Macdonald, a college roommate of John F. Kennedy, who has represented the 7th since 1954. Macdonald is generally considered a liberal, though he did have primary opposition from a peace candidate in 1968. The Congressman is currently the number two man on the House Interstate and Foreign Commerce Committee and stands a good chance of becoming its chairman, since he is 10 years younger than the current incumbent, Harley O. Staggers of West Virginia. Macdonald usually wins by healthy majorities in the 7th—67% in 1970—and should have little trouble in the future even if redistricting places one of the more Republican suburbs to the north in his district.

Census Data 1970 pop. 440,221; deviation from current state average, —7.1%; change 1960–70, +3.2%. Metro. 100%, 0.0% central city.

1970 Share of Federal Outlays $408,934,000 (average outlay per district, Massachusetts 1–12)

DOD	$139,808,000	HEW	$140,215,000
AEC	$2,222,000	HUD	$5,691,000
NASA	$7,684,000	OEO	$1,885,000
DOT	$11,689,000	DOA	$7,409,000
		Other	$92,330,000

Federal Military-Industrial Commitments (See Massachusetts 5, for greater Boston listing.)

Economic Base Electrical machinery, equipment, and supplies; nonelectrical machinery, esp. office, computing, and accounting machines; leather and leather products. Also, extensive commuting to Massachusetts 9 (Boston).

The Voters

Registration 227,363 total. 117,021 D (52%); 43,412 R (19%); 66,930 Ind (29%).

Employment profile White collar, 49%. Blue collar, 51%.

Ethnic groups Black, 1%. Total foreign stock, 46%. Italy, 13%; Canada, 11%; Ireland, 6%; USSR, 5%; UK, 3%; Poland, 2%; Germany, 1%; other, 4%.

Presidential vote

1968	Humphrey (D)	134,490	(67%)
	Nixon (R)	60,258	(30%)
	Wallace (AIP)	6,619	(3%)

Representative

Torbert H. Macdonald (D) Elected 1954; b. June 6, 1917, Boston; home, Malden; Harvard Col., A.B., 1940; Harvard Law School, LL.B., 1946; Navy, WWII; married, four children; Catholic.

Career Practicing atty., 1946– .

Offices 2470 RHOB, 202-225-2836. Also Rm. 2100A, Kennedy Fed. Bldg., Boston 02203, 617-223-2781.

Committees

Government Operations (10th); Subs. (1) Foreign Operations and Government Information, (2) Government Activities.

Interstate and Foreign Commerce (2nd); Chm., Sub. on Communications and Power.

Group Ratings

	ADA	COPE	NREP	NFU	LCV	CFA	NAB	NSI	ACA
1970	80	83	93	77	100	100	9	0	16
1969	87	—	—	93	—	—	—	—	27
1968	92	92	—	82	—	—	20	—	15

Key Votes

(1) ABM	AGN	(6) 18-Yr-Vote	FOR	(11) Clean Water $	FOR
(2) SST	AGN	(7) Farm Sub Lmt	FOR	(12) Mig Wrkrs Comp	FOR
(3) Phil Pln	AGN	(8) Coop-Church	FOR	(13) Jets to Chiang	AGN
(4) No-Knock	FOR	(9) Family Asst	FOR	(14) State OEO Veto	AGN
(5) Cmutr Tax	AGN	(10) Work Stamps	AGN	(15) Park Logging	AGN

Election Results

1970 general:	Torbert H. Macdonald (D)	107,770	(67%)
	Gordon F. Hughes (R)	52,290	(33%)
1970 primary:	Torbert H. Macdonald (D), unopposed		
1968 general:	Torbert H. Macdonald (D)	119,652	(63%)
	William S. Abbott (R)	71,689	(37%)

EIGHTH DISTRICT Political Background

Massachusetts 8 is the direct descendant of the district represented by John F. Kennedy from 1946 to 1952 and, before that, by the impish sometime Mayor of Boston, James Michael Curley. It includes the cities of Cambridge and Somerville, the town of Brookline, and six wards of the city of Boston. Most of the things that tourists come to Boston to see are in the 8th: Faneuil Hall, Paul Revere's house, Beacon Hill, and the Boston Common. Harvard and MIT, also tourist attractions, are both in Cambridge.

The district, despite the presence of the universities and a street culture matched only by the one in Berkeley, is not dominated politically by students and academics. Most of the votes are cast by descendants of Irish and Italian immigrants in East and North Cambridge, Somerville, Charlestown, East Boston, the North End, and by the large Jewish population in Brookline and the adjacent Brighton section of Boston. The white-collar areas, in Cambridge west of Harvard and in the Back Bay of Boston, are traditionally Republican, but today are more concerned with ending the war. The district as a whole is, of course, heavily Democratic.

When John F. Kennedy moved up to the Senate in 1952, Thomas P. (Tip) O'Neill, Jr., then the first Democratic Speaker of the Massachusetts House, became the 8th's congressman. By temperament and background, O'Neill is more comfortable with older men who are the products of big city politics, like the recently retired Speaker, John McCormack. But on issues, he is as often as not with the young liberals. In 1967, O'Neill wrote a letter to President Johnson telling him that he could no longer support the war. Since then O'Neill frequently voted against continuing the war as well as against controversial military spending projects. In spite of his stands on these issues, O'Neill remains a House insider, as can be seen by his appointment in 1971 to the post of Majority Whip, the number-three leadership position. The Congressman also retains his seat on the important Rules Committee.

Redistricting will expand the 8th somewhat, but that is unlikely to affect O'Neill's tenure. He has not had a Republican opponent in the past four elections and has beaten primary opponents easily.

Census Data 1970 pop. 411,630; deviation from current state average, —13.2%; change 1960–70, —3.9%. Metro. 100%, 39.7% central city.

1970 Share of Federal Outlays $408,934,000 (average outlay per district, Massachusetts 1—12)

DOD	$139,808,000	HEW	$140,215,000
AEC	$2,222,000	HUD	$5,691,000
NASA	$7,684,000	OEO	$1,885,000
DOT	$11,689,000	DOA	$7,409,000
		Other	$92,330,000

Federal Military-Industrial Commitments (See Massachusetts 5 for greater Boston listing.)

Economic Base Electrical machinery, equipment, and supplies; nonelectrical machinery; printing, publishing, and allied industries. Services: higher education; medicine. Also extensive commuting to Mass. 9 (Boston); and higher education (Harvard U., M.I.T., Boston U.).

The Voters

Registration 183,301 total. 108,781 D (59%); 22,392 R (12%); 52,128 Ind (29%).

Employment profile White collar, 48%. Blue collar, 52%.

Ethnic groups Black, 3%. Total foreign stock, 50%. Italy, 13%; Canada, 10%; Ireland, 9%; USSR, 5%; UK, 3%; Poland, 2%; Germany, 1%; others, 7%.

Presidential vote

1968	Humphrey (D)	119,205	(76%)
	Nixon (R)	32,246	(21%)
	Wallace (AIP)	5,547	(3%)

Representative

Thomas P. O'Neill, Jr. (D) Elected 1952; b. Dec. 9, 1912, Cambridge; home, Cambridge; Boston Col., A.B., 1936; married, five children; Catholic.

Career Insurance; Cambridge School Com., 1946–47; State Rep., 1936–52; Minority Leader, 1947–48; Speaker, 1948–52; U.S. House Dem. Whip, 1971– .

Offices 2231 RHOB, 202-225-5111. Also 2200 Kennedy Fed. Bldg., Boston 02203, 617-223-2784.

Committees

Rules (5th).

Group Ratings

	ADA	COPE	NREP	NFU	LCV	CFA	NAB	NSI	ACA
1970	76	100	93	92	67	79	0	30	6
1969	87	—	—	100	—	—	—	—	6
1968	83	100	—	100	—	—	0	—	5

Key Votes

(1) ABM	AGN	(6) 18-Yr-Vote	FOR	(11) Clean Water $	FOR
(2) SST	AGN	(7) Farm Sub Lmt	FOR	(12) Mig Wrkrs Comp	FOR
(3) Phil Pln	FOR	(8) Coop-Church	FOR	(13) Jets to Chiang	AGN
(4) No-Knock	FOR	(9) Family Asst	FOR	(14) State OEO Veto	AGN
(5) Cmutr Tax	FOR	(10) Work Stamps	AGN	(15) Park Logging	AGN

Election Results

1970 general:	Thomas P. O'Neill, Jr. (D), unopposed
1970 primary:	Thomas P. O'Neill, Jr. (D), unopposed
1968 general:	Thomas P. O'Neill, Jr. (D), unopposed

NINTH DISTRICT Political Background

Massachusetts 9, which lies in the heart of Boston, is the nation's most Irish congressional district. Since Boston's Italians, Jews, and WASPs all live in other sections of the city, only its relatively small number of blacks share the 9th with the Irish.

The Irish part of the 9th is made up of old neighborhoods where people live pretty much as they did in 1900 or 1910. The ethos of these neighborhoods was reflected in the former Speaker of the House, John W. McCormack, who represented the district from 1925 to 1970. The retired Congressman still lives in the 9th in a modest house on Columbia Road, in the Dorchester section of Boston. McCormack, a devoted family man, has not missed having dinner with his wife since they were married. He is, as well, deeply religious, a sort of Irish Puritan. McCormack was always loyal to his political friends and to the Democratic party. No one believes that he knowingly allowed the misuse of his office by his aide Martin Sweig and lobbyist Nathan Voloshen, but it was probably the discovery of that misuse, rather than the rising opposition of House liberals, that convinced him that he should retire. McCormack's final legacy to the nation was the 18-year-old vote, which he supported ardently and which could become *the* factor in the election of a Democratic President in 1972.

McCormack's successor is quite another kind of politician—Mrs. Louise Day Hicks. Mrs. Hicks, who is also Irish and from South Boston, made national headlines while serving on the Boston School Committee. There she was an outspoken advocate of the neighborhood school and an opponent of busing to achieve integration. In 1967, campaigning on the slogan "You know where I stand," the pugnacious Mrs. Hicks came within a few thousand votes of defeating liberal Democrat Kevin White for mayor.

In 1970 the lady lawyer ran for Congress from the 9th district. She won the Democratic primary with 39% of the vote as the anti-Hicks vote was split between state Sen. Joseph Moakley and black attorney David Nelson. In the general election she did poorly for a Democrat here, taking only 59% of the vote while antiwar independent Daniel Houton took 21%. It may seem strange that a district as liberal as the 9th in national elections (see data below) should send to Congress a representative whose political career is based solely on opposition to race-mixing. But Hicks' success is more a matter of personality than stands on the issues, and she has a devoted following in South Boston.

In 1971, Mrs. Hicks again set her sights on the mayor's office. She announced her candidacy saying, "It is not in my nature to remain on the sidelines, safe in my congressional seat, and witness the destruction and demise of Boston." Hicks is considered a very strong contender in the five-man race, and more than likely will survive the nonpartisan primary in September to face incumbent Kevin White, whose term as big-city mayor has won him more enemies than friends.

If Hicks loses, she will still have plenty of time to campaign for reelection to the House, should choose to run. But her chances will be weakened by her apparent lack of interest in the job and by redistricting. The legislature will add areas to the 9th in which she is far less popular than she is in the current district. If the black, WASP, and university communities, where feeling runs high against the woman, could unite behind a single strong candidate, she could be beaten in the Democratic primary. David Nelson has said that he is no longer interested in the seat, but Joseph Moakley might be such a candidate.

If Hicks does become mayor, the race in the 9th could be a wide open affair with a large field of candidates.

Census Data 1970 pop. 368,888; deviation from current state average, −22.2%; change 1960–70, −14.2%. Metro. 100%, 100% central city.

1970 Share of Federal Outlays $408,934,000 (average outlay per district, Massachusetts 1–12)

DOD	$139,808,000	HEW	$140,215,000
AEC	$2,222,000	HUD	$5,691,000
NASA	$7,684,000	OEO	$1,885,000
DOT	$11,689,000	DOA	$7,409,000
		Other	$92,330,000

Federal Military-Industrial Commitments (See Massachusetts 5 for greater Boston listing.)

Economic Base Printing, publishing, and allied industries, esp. newspapers and commercial printing; apparel and other finished products made from fabrics and similar materials, esp. women's, misses', and juniors' outerwear. Services: insurance; and higher education (Northeastern U.).

The Voters

Registration 147,264 total. 101,475 D (69%); 10,813 R (7%); 34,976 Ind (24%).

Employment profile White collar, 43%. Blue collar, 57%.

Ethnic groups Black, 27%. Total foreign stock, 48%. Ireland, 12%; Canada, 8%; Italy, USSR, 4% each; UK, 3%; Poland, 2%; Germany, Sweden, both 1% each; others, 8%.

Presidential vote

1968	Humphrey (D)	93,954	(78%)
	Nixon (R)	18,984	(16%)
	Wallace (AIP)	7,555	(6%)

Representative

Louise Day Hicks (D) Elected 1970; b. Oct. 16, 1919, Boston; home, Boston; Wheelock Teachers Col.; Boston U. School of Ed., B.S., 1955; Boston U. Law School, LL.B., 1958; widow, two children; Catholic.

Career Practicing atty.; Treasurer (1962–67) and Chairman (1963–65) of the Boston School Committee; Boston City Council, 1969–70.

Offices 1232 LHOB, 202-225-8273. Also 1907A Kennedy Fed. Bldg., Boston 02203, 617-223-8273.

Committees

Education and Labor (20th); Subs. (1) Gen. on Education, (2) Sp. on Labor, (3) Sel. on Labor.

Veterans' Affairs (13th); Subs. (1) Hospitals, (2) Insurance.

Group Ratings, Key Votes: Newly elected.

Election Results

1970 general:	Louise Day Hicks (D)	50,269	(59%)
	Daniel J. Houton (Ind.)	17,395	(21%)
	Laurence Curtis (R)	17,324	(20%)
1970 primary:	Louise Day Hicks (D)	24,886	(39%)
	John J. Moakley (D)	19,656	(31%)
	David S. Nelson (D)	18,552	(29%)

TENTH DISTRICT Political Background

Massachusetts 10 is really two districts. In the north are posh, WASPy Boston suburbs like Wellesley and Dover, where most of the voters are genteel liberal Republicans. In the south is the city of Fall River and other, smaller, aging mill towns. This end of the district is dominated by ethnically oriented citizens, particularly those of Portuguese, French-Canadian, and Italian descent, all of whom ordinarily vote Democratic. In the middle part of the district are sparsely populated towns spread out over rolling hills—places like Foxboro, site of Boston's new football stadium, and North Attleboro, the home of the 10th's longtime (1925–66) Congressman Joseph W. Martin, Jr.

For many years the district's boundaries were drawn to provide a safe seat for Martin, who was one of FDR's famous Republican trio of Martin, Barton, and Fish, and who was also Speaker of the House twice (1947–49 and 1953–55). But as Martin aged, he became more and more congenial with Speaker Sam Rayburn, to the disgust of many partisan Republican congressmen. In 1959 Martin was ousted from the Minority Leadership and in 1966 was beaten in the Republican primary by the 10th's current representative, Margaret Heckler of Wellesley, an attorney who was then the only Republican on that Massachusetts anachronism, the Governor's Council.

Seen in national terms, the 10th is a solidly liberal district. It gave Humphrey a significant majority in 1968, and more recently Mrs. Heckler's standing was strengthened by her votes for the Cooper-Church Amendment and against the ABM. The Congresswoman has survived strong challenges from Patrick Harrington in 1966 and Bertram Yaffe, a McCarthy supporter from Fall River, in 1970. In both cases, she beat the Democratic candidate by piling up large majorities in the north end of the district and holding her own in the mill towns of the south. The strength of Yaffe's challenge may have been due in part to the mini-midi controversy. Fall River is dominated by the garment industry, and the American woman's reluctance to buy the midi resulted in sizable unemployment in the city during 1970.

Since Massachusetts has a Republican governor and a Democratic legislature, there is unlikely to be any radical change in the 10th's boundaries for 1972. Mrs. Heckler must be considered the favorite for reelection, but should she retire or seek higher office (some Republicans urged her to run against Edward Kennedy in 1970), a Democrat would probably take the seat.

Census Data 1970 pop. 504,217; deviation from current state average, +6.4%; change 1960–70, +17.3%. Metro. 77.6%, 19.1% central city.

1970 Share of Federal Outlays $408,934,000 (average outlay per district, Massachusetts 1–12)

DOD	$139,808,000	HEW	$140,215,000
AEC	$2,222,000	HUD	$5,691,000
NASA	$7,684,000	OEO	$1,885,000
DOT	$11,689,000	DOA	$7,409,000
		Other	$92,330,000

Federal Military-Industrial Commitments (See Massachusetts 5 for greater Boston listing.)

Economic Base Apparel and other finished products made from fabrics and similar materials, esp. women's, misses', and juniors' outerwear; electrical machinery, equipment, and supplies, esp. electronic components and accessories; rubber and miscellaneous plastics products.

The Voters

Registration 295,995 total. 101,384 D (34%); 74,057 R (25%); 120,554 R (41%).

Employment profile White collar, 43%. Blue collar, 57%.

Ethnic groups Black, 1%. Total foreign stock, 39%. Canada, 11%; UK, 5%; Ireland, Italy, 4% each; Poland 2%; Germany, Sweden, USSR, 1% each; others, 10%.

Presidential vote

1968	Humphrey (D)	122,626	(59%)
	Nixon (R)	80,088	(37%)
	Wallace (AIP)	6,863	(3%)

Representative

Margaret M. Heckler (R) Elected 1966; b. June 21, 1931, Flushing, N.Y.; home, Wellesley; Albertus Magnus Col., A.B., 1953; Boston Col. Law Sch., LL.B., 1956; married, three children; Catholic.

Career Governor's Council, 1962–66.

Offices 318 CHOB, 202-225-4335. Also 217 P.O. Bldg., Fall River 02722, and 1 Washington St., Wellesley Hills 02162, 617-235-3350.

Committees

Banking and Currency (9th); Subs. (1) Consumer Affairs, (2) Housing, (3) Small Business.

Veterans' Affairs (5th); Subs. (1) Education and Training, (2) Hospitals, (3) Housing.

Group Ratings

	ADA	COPE	NREP	NFU	LCV	CFA	NAB	NSI	ACA
1970	72	70	27	85	100	76	40	50	38
1969	60	—	—	67	—	—	—	—	38
1968	58	69	—	69	—	—	67	—	39

Key Votes

(1) ABM	AGN	(6) 18-Yr-Vote	FOR	(11) Clean Water $	FOR
(2) SST	AGN	(7) Farm Sub Lmt	FOR	(12) Mig Wrkrs Comp	FOR
(3) Phil Pln	FOR	(8) Coop-Church	FOR	(13) Jets to Chiang	AGN
(4) No-Knock	FOR	(9) Family Asst	ABS	(14) State OEO Veto	AGN
(5) Cmutr Tax	FOR	(10) Work Stamps	AGN	(15) Park Logging	AGN

Election Results

1970 general:	Margaret Heckler (R)	102,895	(57%)
	Bertram A. Yaffe (D)	77,497	(43%)
1970 primary:	Margaret Heckler (R), unopposed		
1968 general:	Margaret Heckler (R)	138,220	(67%)
	Edmund Dinis (D)	66,949	(33%)

ELEVENTH DISTRICT Political Background

Massachusetts 11 is the southern suburbs of Boston, stretching from the Hyde Park neighborhood of the city itself to shoe-manufacturing Brockton. With a few exceptions, the towns here—like older Quincy and Braintree (the ancestral home of the Adams family) along the South Shore of Massachusetts Bay, and the new Canton, Stoughton, and Randolph inland—are filled with the sons and daughters and grandsons and granddaughters of Irish and Italian immigrants. Since most of the 11th's residents have followed their forebears' Democratic voting habits, the district as a whole is heavily Democratic. Its Yankee minority, whose ancestors sent John Quincy Adams to the House for the last sixteen years of his life, has been steadily abandoning the Republican Party, thereby adding to Democratic candidates' majorities.

Since 1958, the 11th has sent Democrat James A. Burke to the House. Burke won his seat on the Ways and Means Committee early in his career, doubtless with John McCormack's sponsorship, and is now the 4th ranking Democrat on the committee. The Massachusetts Congressman believes in the traditional ways of doing things in the House. And since Democrats on Ways and Means control their party's committee assignments, Burke's attitude is one of the reasons why insurgents have a hard time winning key positions under the seniority system. On issues, Burke is a Northern Democrat who supports liberal domestic legislation but is reluctant to oppose Administration foreign and defense policies.

Despite this, Burke has not attracted significant opposition from peace candidates and has usually been unopposed in general elections. He will probably continue to represent the 11th for as long as he likes.

Census Data 1970 pop. 490,242; deviation from current state average, +3.4%; change 1960–70, +15.5%. Metro. 100%, 40.3% central city.

1970 Share of Federal Outlays $408,934,000 (average outlay per district, Massachusetts 1–12)

DOD	$139,808,000	HEW	$140,215,000
AEC	$2,222,000	HUD	$5,691,000
NASA	$7,684,000	OEO	$1,885,000
DOT	$11,689,000	DOA	$7,409,000
		Other	$92,330,000

Federal Military-Industrial Commitments (See Massachusetts 5 for greater Boston listing.)

Economic Base Printing, publishing, and allied industries, esp. newspapers and commercial printing; electrical machinery, equipment, and supplies, esp. electronic components and accessories; professional, scientific, and controlling instruments, photographic and optical goods, watches and clocks. Also, extensive commuting to Mass. 9 (Boston).

The Voters

Registration 239,201 total. 127,532 D (53%); 44,009 R (19%); 67,660 Ind (28%).

Employment profile White collar, 50%. Blue colar, 50%.

Ethnic groups Black, 1%. Total foreign stock, 39%. Canada, 9%; Ireland, Italy, 7% each; UK, 4%; USSR, 3%; Sweden, 2%; Poland, Germany, 1% each; others, 5%.

Presidential vote

1968	Humphrey (D)	139,835	(66%)
	Nixon (R)	63,338	(29%)
	Wallace (AIP)	10,066	(5%)

Representative

James A. Burke (D) Elected 1958; b. March 30, 1910, Boston; home, Milton; Suffolk U.; Army, WWII; married; Catholic.

Career State Rep., 1954–58; Asst. Majority Leader, 1954–58; Vice-Chm. Mass. Dem. State Com., 4 yrs.

Offices 241 CHOB, 202-225-3215. Also Rm. 203, P.O. Bldg., 47 Washington St., Quincy 02169, 617-472-1314.

Committees

Ways and Means (4th).

Group Ratings

	ADA	COPE	NREP	NFU	LCV	CFA	NAB	NSI	ACA
1970	64	86	75	92	90	76	8	80	11
1969	53	90	—	86	—	—	—	—	18
1968	75	100	—	94	—	—	0	—	9

Key Votes

(1) ABM	FOR	(6) 18-Yr-Vote	FOR	(11) Clean Water $	FOR
(2) SST	AGN	(7) Farm Sub Lmt	FOR	(12) Mig Wrkrs Comp	AGN
(3) Phil Pln	AGN	(8) Coop-Church	FOR	(13) Jets to Chiang	FOR
(4) No-Knock	FOR	(9) Family Asst	FOR	(14) State OEO Veto	AGN
(5) Cmutr Tax	FOR	(10) Work Stamps	AGN	(15) Park Logging	AGN

Election Results

1970 general:	James A. Burke (D), unopposed
1970 primary:	James A. Burke (D), unopposed
1968 general:	James A. Burke (D), unopposed

TWELFTH DISTRICT Political Background

Massachusetts 12 is the state's most Republican district—that is, the one that comes closest to voting Republican in presidential elections. Actually, it hasn't given the Republican candidate a plurality since 1956 and probably won't for some time. The main Democratic strength in the 12th is the old whaling port of New Bedford, which despite its size (pop. 101,000) has most of the problems of large East Coast cities: racial animosity, poverty, and unemployment. The rest of the district is more pastoral: to the north are fast-growing South Shore suburbs of Boston, like Weymouth, Hingham, Cohasset, and Marshfield. Below them, tourist country begins: Plymouth, with its Rock, and Cape Cod, with its National Seashore, beaches, and ponds, and the Kennedy family compound at Hyannisport. The district also includes the islands of Martha's Vineyard and Nantucket, the latter the nineteenth-century port from which Herman Melville sailed in pursuit of Moby Dick and the ultimate Void. Both are now resort islands, and, like the Cape, staunchly Republican.

Hastings Keith, a conservative Republican, has been the district's representative since 1958. He is definitely the state's most conservative congressman on the war and Defense Department spending. Until 1970, he had little opposition in the district, but in that year he had to face strong challenges both in the Republican primary and the general election. The latter proved more difficult. Gerry Studds, a former campaign aide to Sen. Eugene McCarthy, worked diligently in both New Bedford and the South Shore towns. Even the usually diffident Senator McCarthy came in to help out. Studds' hard work. coupled with the peace and military-spending issues—issues which usually win votes for liberal candidates in affluent areas—made the race the state's closest. Keith finally won, 100,432 to 98,910. But the narrow margin and the fact redistricting will pare some Republican towns from the 12th suggest that Keith, unlike most Massachusetts congressmen, no longer has a safe seat. Odds are he will lose it in 1972.

Census Data 1970 pop. 539,078; deviation from current state average, +13.7%; change 1960–70, +24.7%. Metro. 71.9%, 18.9% central city.

1970 Share of Federal Outlays $408,934,000 (average outlay per district, Massachusetts 1–12)

DOD	$139,808,000	HEW	$140,215,000
AEC	$2,222,000	HUD	$5,691,000
NASA	$7,684,000	OEO	$1,885,000
DOT	$11,689,000	DOA	$7,409,000
		Other	$92,330,000

Federal Military-Industrial Commitments

DOD Contractors Chamberlain Mfg. (New Bedford), $21.814m: production of 155-mm rocket components.

DOD Installations Naval Air Station (South Weymouth). Naval Facility (Nantucket). Otis AFB (Falmouth). North Truro AF Station (North Truro).

Economic Base Leather and leather products, esp. footwear other than rubber; electrical machinery, equipment, and supplies; apparel and other finished products made from fabrics and similar materials; food and kindred products, esp. seafood. Also tourism (Cape Cod).

The Voters

Registration 254,995 total. 77,163 D (30%); 71,265 R (28%); 106,567 Ind (42%).

Employment profile White collar, 39%. Blue collar, 61%.

Ethnic groups Black, 2%. Total foreign stock, 37%. Canada, 9%; UK, 5%; Ireland, Italy, Poland, 2% each; Germany, Sweden, USSR, 1% each; others, 14%.

Presidential vote

1968	Humphrey (D)	118,184	(53%)
	Nixon (R)	95,259	(43%)
	Wallace (AIP)	8,504	(4%)

Representative

Hastings Keith (R) Elected 1958; b. Nov. 22, 1915, Brockton; home, West Bridgewater; U. of Vt., B.S., 1938; Army, WWII; married, two children; Congregationalist.

Career Life insurance underwriter; State Sen., 1953–56.

Offices 2344 RHOB, 202-225-3111. Also 233 P.O. Bldg., New Bedford 02740, 617-993-7393.

Committees

Interstate and Foreign Commerce (4th); Sub. on Communications and Power.

Merchant Marine and Fisheries (5th); Subs. (1) Coast Guard, Coast and Geodetic Survey and Navigation, (2) Fisheries and Wildlife Conservation, (3) Oceanography.

Group Ratings

	ADA	COPE	NREP	NFU	LCV	CFA	NAB	NSI	ACA
1970	40	20	55	75	55	62	67	100	56
1969	33	78	—	60	—	—	—	—	29
1968	33	75	—	63	—	—	67	—	61

Key Votes

(1) ABM	FOR	(6) 18-Yr-Vote	FOR	(11) Clean Water $	FOR
(2) SST	FOR	(7) Farm Sub Lmt	FOR	(12) Mig Wrkrs Comp	AGN
(3) Phil Pln	FOR	(8) Coop-Church	FOR	(13) Jets to Chiang	FOR
(4) No-Knock	FOR	(9) Family Asst	FOR	(14) State OEO Veto	AGN
(5) Cmutr Tax	FOR	(10) Work Stamps	FOR	(15) Park Logging	AGN

Election Results

1970 general:	Hastings Keith (R)	100,432	(50%)
	Gerry E. Studds (D)	98,910	(50%)
1970 primary:	Hastings Keith (R)	22,335	(55%)
	William Weeks (R)	18,603	(45%)
1968 general:	Hastings Keith (R), unopposed		

MICHIGAN

Political Background

Michigan is the Motor State, and most facets of life there, including the politics, depend on the condition of the automobile industry. Originally settled by New Englanders and upstate New York Yankees who veered off the usual paths of westward migration, Michigan was something of a backwater and a Republican bastion—before the car business found a home in the state. In fact, the state's attachment to the Republican party persisted well into the 1940's despite the influx of thousands of immigrants from Canada, Poland, Italy, Appalachia, and the Deep South.

From the late 1940's until very recently, Michigan politics has been dominated by party persisted well into the 1940's despite the influx of thousands of immigrants from 1948 to 1960, and Republican George Romney, who served from 1962 until he resigned in 1970 to become HUD secretary. Both were invincible in their time, but both have suffered defeats in recent years, Williams in person and Romney by proxy, and their days of preeminence are over. Williams, along with UAW and other labor officials and Neil Staebler—longtime Democratic state chairman and one-term congressman-at-large (1962–64)—put together a political organization which captured all statewide offices by the mid-'50's. The organization gave Michigan, for the first time since the 1840's, the reputation of being a Democratic state. The Williams-Staebler formula was a straight-ticket coalition of union members (almost 40% of the families in the state have at least one union member), East European ethnics, blacks, and liberal intellectuals.

After the 1960 elections, Mennen Williams left for Washington to become something less than he had hoped for, Assistant Secretary of State for African Affairs, and George Romney, then the hard-sell president of American Motors, entered the Michigan political picture. Romney's road to power was smoothed by a state constitutional convention, which was supposed to be above partisan politics, but which wrote a very Republican document. By a narrow margin, the voters of the state approved the new constitution. In 1962, also by a slim margin, the voters elected Romney governor. His opponent, incumbent John B. Swainson, was hurt when he refused to allow suburbanites exemption from Detroit's city income tax. Once in office, Romney found the going much easier. He survived the Johnson landslide in 1964 with 56% of the votes and won a solid 61% two years later.

Meanwhile, the state's Senate seats were filled by two Democrats who looked unbeatable, Pat McNamara and Philip A. Hart. When McNamara died in the spring of 1966, Romney appointed 9th district Congressman Robert Griffin to serve out the term, but it appeared that the appointee would lose his seat in the fall elections. Mennen Williams, just returned from Washington, won the Democratic Senate primary 60:40 over Detroit Mayor Jerome P. Cavanagh. Once again, Williams got heavy support from ethnics and blacks; to Soapy's enthusiasts, it seemed the good old days were about to return. But they did not.

The not-so-impressive primary victory should have alerted the Williams people that something was wrong. For one thing, the good-old-days atmosphere of the Williams campaign alienated many young people; and for another, many voters remembered the recession and payless paydays crises of Williams' last term as governor. Griffin waged a strong, well-financed campaign, capitalizing on the growing disillusionment with the Johnson Administration. The Republican beat Williams 56:44. In the '50's, Soapy never won with a margin so convincing.

Both Romney and Griffin won by eating into the rather thin Democratic margins of the '50's. They were particularly successful among the growing number of young and white-collar voters. But the Republicans could not sustain the trend for the 1968 elections. Nixon and Agnew failed to attract those segments of the electorate, winning only 42% of the state's votes and only 31% in the Detroit metropolitan area, which has almost half of the state's population. Another factor in the strong Democratic showing was the demoralization of the Michigan Republican party after its hero, George Romney, was laughed out of the presidential race for his "brainwashing" remark.

In 1970, the Democratic resurgence in Michigan persisted. The main event was the Senate race between Philip Hart and Lenore Romney, George's wife. Hart, a leader in the liberal bloc of the Senate, defended the Fortas nomination, opposed the ABM, sponsored the truth-in-packaging law. And though he backed Johnson's policies until 1968, he had since become a vigorous critic of the Vietnam war. Hart's greatest political asset is a reputation for a soft-spoken, tentative reasonableness, a reputation that won him thousands of outstate (outside the Detroit metropolitan area) Republican votes in 1964.

Mrs. Romney's 1970 campaign was a catalogue of mistakes. The crude way in which George engineered her into the race was her first problem; to some, it seemed that he was trying to preserve the option of running himself. Following this, Mrs. Romney just narrowly won the Republican primary over an unknown arch-conservative state senator. During the campaign for the general election, the lady habitually took platitudinous and often contradictory stands on the issues; when the two candidates debated, Senator Hart spent most of his time saving Mrs. Romney from undue embarrassment. After the election, her husband claimed she had saved the governorship for incumbent Republican William Milliken; that, however, seems implausible, since Lenore won only 33% of the votes. The results showed that by 1970 the Michigan voters had had enough of the Romneys, just as they had grown tired of Williams four years earlier. Michigan politics will now have to get along without a charismatic leader.

Since the '50's the political configurations of the state have undergone considerable change. In the Williams era, Michigan elections were a form of near class warfare, with heavily blue-collar Detroit supplying a huge Democratic margin to offset the heavily Republican outstate counties. But recently, statewide Republican candidates have made strong inroads into the Detroit vote, particularly in the white-collar areas. At the same time, the Democrats have been doing better outstate—one need only contrast Nixon's 60% outside metropolitan Detroit in 1960 with his 51% in 1968. The 1970 gubernatorial contest revolved around the issue of aid to parochial schools. The incumbent Governor Milliken, who supported "parochiaid," ran well in urban and suburban areas with large numbers of Catholics, but in the outstate regions, state Sen. Sander Levin, the Democratic candidate, made a remarkably strong, 45% showing. The pattern emerging is this: as the image of a big city- and labor-dominated Democratic party fades, and as the national Republican party becomes more strident in its search for white urban votes, the outstate Michigan cities and even the countryside seem more ready to vote Democratic. For the 1972 presidential election, the state must be counted as solidly Democratic, already written off by Nixon strategists.

Such is the scene as Senator Robert Griffin seeks reelection in 1972. It may appear strange that a loyal supporter of the Nixon Administration should have a chance in an anti-Nixon state. But Griffin manages to maintain a rather nonpartisan image at home, even though he is an effective and vigorous partisan in the Senate. Moreover, the Republican Whip has dissented from Administration positions on a few, well-publicized occasions: the Haynsworth nomination and the SST. A bitter primary fight for the Democratic nomination is also shaping up and should help Griffin's chances. Ex-Detroit Mayor Cavanagh, Attorney General Frank Kelley, Secretary of State Richard Austin, and Sander Levin all seem interested in the nomination. Odds are that the incumbent Griffin will win.

Electoral Votes 21

Census Data 1970 pop. 8,875,083; 4.31% of U.S. total, 7th largest; change 1960–70, +13.4%. Metro. 76.7%, 27.8% central city. 1970 per capita income, $4,043, 13th highest. 11th in number of poor.

1970 Share of Federal Tax Burden $9,327,721,000; 4.78% of U.S. total, 6th largest.

1970 Share of Federal Outlays $4,870,730,684; 2.58% of U.S. total, 11th largest. Per capita federal spending, $549.

DOD	$887,807,000	20th (1.58%)	HEW	$2,046,745,951	7th (3.92%)
AEC	$6,213,495	24th (0.24%)	HUD	$77,688,851	6th (3.99%)
NASA	$27,490,138	17th (0.75%)	OEO	$20,192,264	
DOT	$172,271,895	14th (2.41%)	DOA	$146,223,714	33rd (1.14%)
DOC	$8,731,146	29th (0.75%)	POD	$263,390,757	7th (3.61%)
DOI	$23,120,118	33rd (1.00%)	VA	$312,723,678	8th (4.29%)
DOJ	$18,555,897	8th (3.23%)	CSC	$45,150,621	18th (1.12%)
			Other	$814,425,159	

Economic Base Motor vehicles and motor vehicle equipment, and other transportation equipment; nonelectrical machinery, esp. metalworking machinery and equipment; fabricated metal products, esp. metal stampings; primary metal industries, esp. iron and steel foundries; dairy, cash grain, and livestock; food and kindred products, esp. bakery products; electrical machinery, equipment, and supplies; printing, publishing, and allied industries, esp. newspapers; chemicals and allied products, esp. industrial inorganic and organic chemicals; paper and allied products, esp. paperboard containers and boxes. Also, tourism and higher education.

Political Line-up Governor, William G. Milliken (R); seat up, 1974. Senators, Philip A. Hart (D) and Robert P. Griffin (R). Representatives, 19 (7 D and 12 R). State Senate (19 D and 19 R); State House (58 D and 52 R).

The Voters

Registration 4,059,807 total. No party registration.

Employment profile White collar, 40%. Blue collar, 60%.

Ethnic groups Black 11%. Total foreign stock, 24%. Canada, 5%; Poland, 3%; Germany, 3%; UK, 2%; Austria, Hungary, Sweden, USSR, 1% each; others, 7%.

Presidential vote

1968	Humphrey (D)	1,593,082	(48%)
	Nixon (R)	1,370,665	(42%)
	Wallace (AIP)	331,968	(10%)
1964	Johnson (D)	2,136,615	(67%)
	Goldwater (R)	1,060,152	(33%)
1960	Kennedy (D)	1,687,269	(51%)
	Nixon (R)	1,620,428	(49%)

Senator

Philip A. Hart (D) Elected 1958, seat up 1976; b. Dec. 10, 1912, Bryn Mawr, Pa.; home, Mackinac Island; Georgetown U., B.A., 1934; U. of Mich., J.D., 1937; Army, WWII; married, eight children; Catholic.

Career Mich. Corp. and Securities Comm., 1949–50; Dir. Office of Price Stabilization, 1951; U.S. Atty., E. Mich., 1952; legal adviser to Gov. Williams, 1953–54; Lt. Gov., 1955–58; Asst. Majority Whip, 1966–67.

Offices 253 OSOB, 202-225-4822. Also 438 Fed. Bldg., Detroit 48226, 313-226-3188.

Committees

Commerce (4th); Subs. (1) Chm., Environment, (2) Vice-Chm., Consumer, (3) Aviation, (4) Communications, (5) Oceans and Atmosphere, (6) Sp. to Study Transportation on the Great Lakes and St. Lawrence.

Judiciary (4th); Subs. (1) Chm., Antitrust and Monopoly Legislation, (2) Administrative Practice and Procedure, (3) Constitutional Rights, (4) Criminal Laws and Procedures, (5) Immigration and Naturalization, (6) Improvements in Judicial Machinery, (7) Juvenile Delinquency, (8) Patents, Trademarks, and Copyrights, (9) Penitentiaries, (10) Refugees and Escapees, (11) Revision and Codification.

Sel. Com. on Nutrition and Human Needs (7th).

Group Ratings

	ADA	COPE	NREP	NFU	LCV	NAB	NSI	ACA
1970	97	100	100	100	60	8	0	9
1969	100	—	—	88	—	—	—	7
1968	86	100	—	92	—	40	—	0

Key Votes

(1) ABM	AGN	(8) Phil Pln	FOR	(15) Coop-Church	FOR
(2) SST	AGN	(9) Vol Army	FOR	(16) Cut Oil Dpltn	FOR
(3) Busing	FOR	(10) Prison $	FOR	(17) Consumer Prot	FOR
(4) Tob Sub	AGN	(11) Cut Mil $	FOR	(18) Farm Sub Limit	FOR
(5) Carswell	AGN	(12) Defoliatn	AGN	(19) Comp Bid Sales	ABS
(6) No-Knock	AGN	(13) 18-Yr-Vote	FOR	(20) Pre-Prod Tests	FOR
(7) Seniorty	FOR	(14) Pentgn PR	AGN	(21) Cut Marjna Pen	FOR

Election Results

1970 general:	Philip A. Hart (D)	1,744,672	(67%)
	Lenore Romney (R)	858,438	(33%)

1970 primary:	Philip A. Hart (D), unopposed		
1964 general:	Philip A. Hart (D)	1,996,912	(64%)
	Elly M. Peterson (R)	1,096,272	(35%)

Senator

Robert P. Griffin (R) Elected 1966, seat up 1972; b. Nov. 6, 1923, Detroit; home, Traverse City; Central Mich. U., A.B., B.S., 1947; U. of Mich., J.D., 1950; Army, WWII; married, four children; United Church of Christ.

Career Practicing atty., 1950–56; U.S. House, Jan. 1957–May 16, 1966.

Offices 353 OSOB, 202-225-6221. Also 1039 Fed. Bldg., 321 Lafayette Blvd., Detroit 48226, 313-226-6020.

Committees

Commerce (4th); Subs. (1) Aviation, (2) Communications, (3) Foreign Commerce and Tourism, (4) Merchant Marine, (5) Oceans and Atmosphere, (6) Sp. to Study Transportation on the Great Lakes and St. Lawrence Seaway.

Finance (7th).

Rules and Administration (4th); Subs. (1) Printing, (2) Restaurant.

Jt. Com. on Printing (Ranking Rep. Sen.).

Group Ratings

	ADA	COPE	NREP	NFU	LCV	NAB	NSI	ACA
1970	28	40	36	38	24	78	100	74
1969	28	—	—	50	—	—	—	38
1968	43	91	—	38	—	80	—	47

Key Votes

(1) ABM	FOR	(8) Phil Pln	FOR	(15) Coop-Church	AGN
(2) SST	AGN	(9) Vol Army	AGN	(16) Cut Oil Dpltn	FOR
(3) Busing	FOR	(10) Prison $	FOR	(17) Consumer Prot	ABS
(4) Tob Sub	AGN	(11) Cut Mil $	AGN	(18) Farm Sub Limit	FOR
(5) Carswell	FOR	(12) Defoliatn	FOR	(19) Comp Bid Sales	FOR
(6) No-Knock	FOR	(13) 18-Yr-Vote	AGN	(20) Pre-Prod Tests	AGN
(7) Seniorty	AGN	(14) Pentgn PR	FOR	(21) Cut Marjna Pen	AGN

Election Results

1966 general:	Robert P. Griffin (R)	1,363,808	(56%)
	G. Mennen Williams (D)	1,070,484	(44%)
1966 primary:	Robert P. Griffin (R), unopposed		

FIRST DISTRICT Political Background

Michigan 1 is the heart of Detroit's large black community, the site of the worst of the 1967 riots and also of the wealthiest integrated and all-black neighborhoods in the city. Before 1964, Detroit's congressional districts were slivers of land from the Detroit River on the south to the city limits on the north. But the 1964 redistricters broke up the pattern in order to create the state's second black-majority district—the 1960 census showed the new 1st district had a black population slightly over 50%. Today the black percentage is much higher (76%), because many whites, particularly after the riot, fled to the suburbs.

The 1st is by no means a slum or a ghetto of the Harlem variety, though it does have its destitute pockets. The bulk of the people here are middle-class citizens with a great interest in politics. The remaining whites live in various neighborhoods at the edges of the district and do not form a coherent political bloc.

When John Conyers, Jr., the congressman from the 1st, was elected in 1964, there were only four other blacks in the House. Adam Clayton Powell was then still a congressman and chairman of the Education and Labor Committee, but was already headed for trouble. The senior member of the black delegation, William Dawson of Chicago, was never a man to rock any boats. From the beginning, Conyers was unlike either of these two members: outspoken, energetic, and ambitious, but unwilling to kowtow to the powers of the House. He became the first black member of the Judiciary Committee, a congressional unit that has jurisdiction over civil rights legislation. The Detroit congressman also was one of the first in the House to oppose the Vietnam war, working closely with antiwar liberal whites. Since 1964, he has been joined by other militant black representatives and is now a leader in the House's Black Caucus.

Like most congressmen, Conyers' first race was his toughest. He beat Richard Austin, his major opponent in the 1964 Democratic primary, by a scant 108 votes out of 60,000 cast. (In 1970 Austin became Secretary of State after a narrow defeat in the 1969 Detroit mayoralty elections; both times Austin had Conyers' support.) But the Congressman's recent elections have been very different. In 1970 Conyers won the primary 9:1 and the general election with nearly the same margin. Redistricting will add a portion of northwest Detroit, but since this area is also predominantly black, Conyers should have no trouble getting reelected.

Census Data 1970 pop. 391,361; deviation from current state average, —16.2; change 1960–70, —7.5%. Metro. 100%, 87.7% central city.

1970 Share of Federal Outlays $255,411,000 (average outlay per district, Michigan, 12–19)

DOD	$54,215,000	HEW	$100,226,000
AEC	$104,000	HUD	$3,520,000
NASA	$102,000	OEO	$1,290,000
DOT	$7,702,000	DOA	$156,000
		Other	$88,095,000

Federal Military-Industrial Commitments (See Michigan 12 for greater Detroit listing.)

Economic Base Motor vehicles and motor vehicle equipment, and other transportation equipment; nonelectrical machinery, esp. metalworking machinery and equipment; fabricated metal products, esp. metal stampings; primary metal industries, esp. blast furnaces, steel works, and rolling and finishing mills.

The Voters

Registration 193,719 total. No party registration.

Employment profile White collar, 37%. Blue collar, 63%.

Ethnic groups Black, 76%. Total foreign stock, 23%. Canada, 5%; Poland, 4%; Germany, UK, USSR, 2% each; Austria, Ireland, Italy, 1% each; others, 7%.

Presidential vote

1968	Humphrey (D)	134,437	(86%)
	Nixon (R)	16,655	(11%)
	Wallace (AIP)	5,743	(4%)

Representative

John Conyers, Jr. (D) Elected 1964; b. May 16, 1929, Detroit; home, Detroit; Wayne State U., B.A., 1957, LL.B., 1958; Army, Korean War; unmarried; Baptist.

Career Legis. Asst., Rep. John Dingell, 1958–61; Mich. Wrokingmen's Compensation Referee, 1961–63.

Offices 222 CHOB, 202-225-5126. Also 307 Fed. Bldg., 231 Lafayette St., Detroit 48226, 313-226-7022.

Committees

Government Operations (21st); Subs. (1) Conservation and Natural Resources, (2) Foreign Operations and Government Information.

Judiciary (9th); Subs. (1) No. 3, (2) No. 4, (3) Sp. on Submerged Lands.

Group Ratings

	ADA	COPE	NREP	NFU	LCV	CFA	NAB	NSI	ACA
1970	92	100	100	82	100	100	0	0	21
1969	100	—	—	73	—	—	—	—	29
1968	100	92	—	75	—	—	33	—	6

Key Votes

(1) ABM	AGN	(6) 18-Yr-Vote	ABS	(11) Clean Water $	FOR
(2) SST	AGN	(7) Farm Sub Lmt	FOR	(12) Mig Wrkrs Comp	FOR
(3) Phil Pln	ABS	(8) Coop-Church	FOR	(13) Jets to Chiang	AGN
(4) No-Knock	AGN	(9) Family Asst	FOR	(14) State OEO Veto	AGN
(5) Cmutr Tax	FOR	(10) Work Stamps	AGN	(15) Park Logging	AGN

Election Results

1970 general:	John Conyers, Jr. (D)	93,075	(88%)
	Howard L. Johnson (R)	11,876	(11%)
	Jacqueline Rice (SW)	617	(1%)
1970 primary:	John Conyers, Jr. (D)	33,923	(85%)
	Willie L. Baxter (D)	5,915	(15%)
1968 general:	John Conyers, Jr. (D), unopposed		

SECOND DISTRICT Political Background

Michigan 2 is a compact district, made up of several very different areas in the southeast part of the state. It includes two rural and small-town counties, Lenawee and Livingston, which are heavily Republican; an industrial county, Monroe, which is Democratic; and the Republican Detroit suburbs of Plymouth and Northville in Wayne County. The 2nd also contains Washtenaw County, the largest in the district, which is itself divisible into three very distinct parts: Ypsilanti, a blue-collar, Democratic enclave; the outer townships, rural and heavily Republican; and Ann Arbor, home of the University of Michigan, traditionally Republican but often willing to support liberal Democrats. Ann Arbor's Republicanism comes from its original German settlers and its liberalism from the presence of the university and the attendant community of academics and students. On balance the district is Republican, although statewide and presidential Democratic candidates have been running stronger here of late.

For many years the representative from the 2nd was an aging conservative Republican, George Meader. As George Romney's kind of Republicanism grew increasingly popular in the state, local Republicans became unhappy with Meader, who voted against the Civil Rights Act of 1964; they almost unseated him in the primary of that year. In the 1964 general election which followed, the Democrats did unseat the long-time incumbent. Weston Vivian, a local scientist-businessman, beat Meader by 1,526 votes and immediately began preparations for the 1966 election. In another year he might have won, but 1966 was a very Republican year in Michigan. With George Romney and Robert Griffin at the top of the ticket, the Republicans ousted five freshman Democratic congressmen. Of the five, Vivian came closest to keeping his seat, 2,669 votes. He carried Monroe, Ypsilanti, and the city of Ann Arbor, but his margins here were not good enough to overcome the rural Republican votes.

The victor was Marvin Esch, who, like all five Republicans who beat freshman Democrats, remains in the House today. Esch had a rematch with Vivian in 1968, but the advantages of incumbency proved decisive, and the Republican won 55:45. His latest victory was by a greater margin, 58:42, and it appears that he will remain in the House for some time. Esch is one of the most liberal Republicans in the Michigan delegation. Since he has opposed Administration policy on Vietnam and military-spending issues, he is unlikely to face a vigorous challenge from Ann Arbor's peace community. Redistricting will alter the district's boundaries somewhat, probably removing Republican Plymouth and Northville. But since control over the process is split between a Republican governor and a Democratic House, it is unlikely that the district will be altered substantially.

Census Data 1970 pop. 531,988; deviation from current state average, +13.9%; change 1960–70, +28.4%. Metro. 73.6%, 18.8% central city.

1970 Share of Federal Outlays $318,495,952

DOD	$73,560,000	HEW	$111,301,285
AEC	$3,016,876	HUD	$3,023,279
NASA	$25,424,478	OEO	$165,556
DOT	$2,300,842	DOA	$16,392,914
		Other	$83,310,722

Federal Military-Industrial Commitments

DOD Contractors General Motors (Ypsilanti), $23.098m: production of M-16 rifles.

NASA Contractors Bendix Aerospace (Ann Arbor), $16.207m: Apollo Lunar surface experiment. University of Michigan (Ann Arbor), $5.592m: unspecified research.

Economic Base Motor vehicles and motor vehicle equipment, and other transportation equipment; nonelectrical machinery; cash grain and livestock. Also, higher education (U. of Michigan and E. Michigan U.).

The Voters

Registration 219,217 total. No party registration.

Employment profile White collar, 42%. Blue collar, 58%.

Ethnic groups Black, 4%. Total foreign stock, 16%. Canada, Germany, 3% each; UK, 2%; Italy, Poland, USSR, 1% each; others, 5%.

Presidential vote

1968	Humphrey (D)	74,021	(42%)
	Nixon (R)	85,262	(48%)
	Wallace (AIP)	18,158	(10%)

Representative

Marvin L. Esch (R) Elected 1966; b. Aug. 4, 1927, Flinton, Pa.; home, Ann Arbor; U. of Mich., A.B., 1950, M.A., 1951, Ph.D., 1957; Maritime and Army, WWII; married, three children; Presbyterian.

Career Asst. prof. Wayne State U., 1953–55; lecturer, Inst. of Labor and Industrial Relations, Wayne State U., 1955–64; State Rep., 1965–66; lay preacher.

Offices 412 CHOB, 202-225-4401. Also 200 E. Huron, Ann Arbor 41808, 313-665-0618.

Committees

Education and Labor (7th); Subs. (1) Gen. on Labor, (2) Sp. on Education, (3) Sel. on Labor.

Science and Astronautics (10th); Subs. (1) Advanced Research and Technology, (2) Science, Research, and Development.

Group Ratings

	ADA	COPE	NREP	NFU	LCV	CFA	NAB	NSI	ACA
1970	52	60	67	70	67	70	63	77	38
1969	53	—	—	84	—	—	—	—	44
1968	58	31	—	87	—	—	50	—	32

Key Votes

(1) ABM	FOR	(6) 18-Yr-Vote	FOR	(11) Clean Water $	FOR
(2) SST	AGN	(7) Farm Sub Lmt	FOR	(12) Mig Wrkrs Comp	AGN
(3) Phil Pln	FOR	(8) Coop-Church	FOR	(13) Jets to Chiang	AGN
(4) No-Knock	ABS	(9) Family Asst	FOR	(14) State OEO Veto	AGN
(5) Cmutr Tax	ABS	(10) Work Stamps	ABS	(15) Park Logging	ABS

Election Results

1970 general:	Marvin L. Esch (R)	88,071	(58%)
	R. Michael Stillwagon (D)	52,782	(42%)
1970 primary:	Marvin L. Esch (R), unopposed		
1968 general:	Marvin L. Esch (R)	90,804	(55%)
	Weston Vivian (D)	75,045	(45%)

THIRD DISTRICT Political Background

Michigan 3 is a typical outstate Michigan district, with two medium-sized cities—Kalamazoo and Battle Creek—and three rural and small-town counties. Kalamazoo is mostly a white-collar Republican town, the headquarters of the Upjohn drug firm and the home of Western Michigan University, though the city also has a GM plant. Battle Creek is more blue-collar and more Democratic; its major industry is making a number of very well-advertised breakfast cereals. The rural counties, which one would expect to be heavily Republican, have pockets of Democratic strength.

The political scenario of the 3rd resembles that of the 2nd: an aging, conservative Republican, August Johansen (a member of the old House Un-American Activities Committee), beat back a strong primary challenge in 1964, but lost the general election to a liberal Democrat, Kalamazoo millionaire Paul Todd. Todd served just one term, in which he managed to get birth control projects included in the foreign aid program, and was then narrowly defeated (52:48) by a Republican state legislator in the Romney mold, Garry E. Brown. Since then, the district has reverted to its old Republican habits, although Brown's increasingly conservative record stimulated a strong challenge from liberal Democrat Richard Enslen in 1970. Enslen raised the Democratic percentage from 35 to 44. But despite inroads in normally Republican Kalamazoo and other areas in the 3rd with high unemployment, the Democrat could not get enough votes in the rural counties to win.

The fact that a Democrat tried hard and couldn't beat Brown probably indicates that he has a safe seat by now. The redistricters will no doubt keep Kalamazoo and Battle Creek together and maintain the present political character of the district.

Census Data 1970 pop. 482,493; deviation from current state average, +3.3%; change 1960–70, +15.8%. Metro. 62.7%, 18.0% central city.

1970 Share of Federal Outlays $248,432,000

DOD	$35,293,000	HEW	$99,777,000
AEC	$9,000	HUD	$162,000
NASA	$104,000	OEO	$332,000
DOT	$18,193,000	DOA	$12,513,000
		Other	$82,049,000

Federal Military-Industrial Commitments

None.

Economic Base Nonelectrical machinery; paper and allied products, esp. paper mills other than building paper mills, and paperboard containers and boxes; dairy and cash grain; transportation equipment, esp. motor vehicles and motor vehicle equipment. Also, higher education (W. Michigan U.).

The Voters

Registration 207,532 total. No party registration.

Employment profile White collar, 39%. Blue collar, 61%.

Ethnic groups Black, 5%. Total foreign stock, 13%. Canada, Germany, UK, 2% each; Poland, 1%; others, 7%.

Presidential vote

1968	Humphrey (D)	66,035	(37%)
	Nixon (R)	95,522	(53%)
	Wallace (AIP)	18,244	(10%)

Representative

Gary Brown (R) Elected 1966; b. Aug. 12, 1923, Schoolcraft; home, Schoolcraft; Mich. State U. (Kalamazoo Col.), B.A., 1951; George Washington U. Law School, LL.B., 1954; Army, 1946–47; married, four children; Presbyterian.

Career Comm. U.S. Dist. Court, Western Mich., 1957–62; State Sen., 1962–66; Minority Floor Leader.

Offices 404 CHOB, 202-225-5011. Also, Rm. 2-1-36 Fed. Center, 74 N. Washington St., Battle Creek, 49017, 616-962-1551.

Committees

Banking and Currency (6th); Subs. (1) Domestic Finance, (2) Housing, (3) International Trade.

Government Operations (12th); Subs. (1) Legislation and Military Operations, (2) Intergovernmental Relations, (3) Legal and Monetary Affairs, (4) Special Studies.

Jt. Com. on Defense Production (2nd).

Group Ratings

	ADA	COPE	NREP	NFU	LCV	CFA	NAB	NSI	ACA
1970	24	42	36	55	33	41	67	77	71
1969	40	—	—	54	—	—	—	—	47
1968	33	50	—	53	—	—	100	—	64

Key Votes

(1) ABM	FOR	(6) 18-Yr-Vote	FOR	(11) Clean Water $	FOR
(2) SST	AGN	(7) Farm Sub Lmt	AGN	(12) Mig Wrkrs Comp	AGN
(3) Phil Pln	FOR	(8) Coop-Church	AGN	(13) Jets to Chiang	AGN
(4) No-Knock	ABS	(9) Family Asst	FOR	(14) State OEO Veto	AGN
(5) Cmutr Tax	ABS	(10) Work Stamps	FOR	(15) Park Logging	FOR

Election Results

1970 general:	Garry Brown (R)	80,447	(56%)
	Richard A. Enslen (D)	62,530	(44%)
1970 primary:	Garry Brown (R), unopposed		
1968 general:	Garry Brown (R)	109,754	(65%)
	Thomas L. Keenan (D)	58,692	(35%)

FOURTH DISTRICT Political Background

Michigan 4, the state's most Republican district, consists of seven counties in the southwest corner of Michigan. The 4th is a region of small towns and still-prosperous farming country; the southern tier of counties is mostly homogeneous, WASP, and Republican. In the north, not far from Grand Rapids, Allegan County has a substantial Dutch population, which is very conservative and Republican. The largest urban concentration in the 4th is around Benton Harbor and St. Joseph, a metropolitan area of only about 60,000. Benton Harbor now has a black majority; southwest of that city, around Cassopolis and Dowagiac, there is also a substantial black community whose citizens are descendants of slaves who fled here to a station on the Underground Railroad. The area of Michigan that currently makes up the 4th was a hotbed of abolition in the 1860's, but 100 years later it is generally skeptical about civil rights activism.

The skepticism is shared by Rep. Edward Hutchinson, the most conservative member of the Michigan delegation. Hutchinson took his seat in 1962, and no Democrat has come close to beating him since the Goldwater year of 1964. In Washington, Hutchinson has been lucky playing the seniority game: after only eight years in the House, he is number three among Republicans on the Judiciary Committee. The ranking Republican, William McCulloch, of Ohio, is retiring, and the number two man, Richard Poff of Virginia, is rumored to be in line for a federal judgeship, possibly the Supreme Court.

Thus Hutchinson's chances of becoming ranking minority member or even chairman, if the Republicans ever win control of the House, are very good. If Hutchinson becomes either, the GOP's principal House spokesman on civil rights legislation will be a man who has opposed such legislation in the past.

Census Data 1970 pop. 452,404; deviation from current state average, —3.1%; change 1960–70, +11.7%. Metro. 0.0%, 0.0% central city.

1970 Share of Federal Outlays $201,059,147

DOD	$9,298,000	HEW	$109,635,833
AEC	$000	HUD	$2,004,129
NASA	$255,132	OEO	$379,128
DOT	$4,624,900	DOA	$15,105,220
		Other	$59,756,805

Federal Military-Industrial Commitments

None.

Economic Base Nonelectrical machinery; dairy, livestock, and cash grain; food and kindred products; primary metal industries.

The Voters

Registration 179,014 total. No party registration.

Employment profile White collar, 32%. Blue collar, 68%.

Ethnic groups Black, 6%. Total foreign stock, 15%. Germany, 4%; Canada, Poland, 2% each; Czech., Italy, Sweden, UK, USSR, 1% each; others, 4%.

Presidential vote

1968	Humphrey (D)	55,196	(33%)
	Nixon (R)	90,599	(55%)
	Wallace (AIP)	20,442	(12%)

Representative

Edward Hutchinson (R) Elected 1962; b. Oct. 13, 1914, Fennville; home, Fennville; U. of Mich., A.B., 1936, LL.B. and J.D., 1938; Army, WWII; married; Christian Scientist.

Career State Rep., 1946–50; State Sen., 1951–60; Delegate, Vice-Pres. Mich. Constitutional Convention of 1961–62.

Offices 2436 RHOB, 202-225-3761. Also 201 Fed. Bldg., Benton Harbor 49022, 616-925-7962.

Committees

Judiciary (3rd); Sub. No. 5.

Standards of Official Conduct (5th).

Group Rating

	ADA	COPE	NREP	NFU	LCV	CFA	NAB	NSI	ACA
1970	12	0	25	23	25	45	100	90	100
1969	20	—	—	27	—	—	—	—	82
1968	0	0	—	25	—	—	100	—	95

Key Votes

(1) ABM	FOR	(6) 18-Yr-Vote	AGN	(11) Clean Water $	FOR
(2) SST	AGN	(7) Farm Sub Lmt	FOR	(12) Mig Wrkrs Comp	AGN
(3) Phil Pln	FOR	(8) Coop-Church	AGN	(13) Jets to Chiang	AGN
(4) No-Knock	FOR	(9) Family Asst	AGN	(14) State OEO Veto	FOR
(5) Cmutr Tax	AGN	(10) Work Stamps	FOR	(15) Park Logging	FOR

Election Results

1970 general:	Edward Hutchinson (R)	74,471	(62%)
	David R. McCormack (D)	45,838	(38%)
1970 primary:	Edward Hutchinson (R), unopposed		
1968 general:	Edward Hutchinson (R)	100,128	(66%)
	John V. Martin (D)	52,441	(34%)

FIFTH DISTRICT Political Background

Michigan 5 is the district around Grand Rapids, the state's second largest city. Grand Rapids is probably best known as a furniture-manufacturing center. But the most salient fact about it politically is that a very large number of the people who live here are of Dutch descent, the largest such concentration in the United States. Almost 10% of the district's residents are first- or second-generation Dutch, and many more are descended from the Dutch immigrants who originally settled around Grand Rapids. Politically, Dutch-Americans are very conservative—a reflection of the stern Calvinism of their Christian Reformed Church. Grand Rapids is, therefore, a thoroughly Republican city. The only Democrats to carry it in recent years were Sen. Philip Hart and Lyndon Johnson. In 1964, Dutch voters took Barry Goldwater's profanity as the mark of a flamboyant man.

Gerald R. Ford, Jr., currently the House Minority Leader, is Grand Rapids' representative in Washington. Ford was a young lawyer and ex-football player in 1948 when he decided to run against the 5th's isolationist Republican, Bartel J. Jonkman. Ford won that primary and has been in Congress ever since. In 1965, seventeen years after his first election, Ford again found himself just to the left of the right-wingers in the GOP when he challenged the old conservative "gut-fighter" Charles Halleck for the House Republican leadership and won. Ford's theme at that time was that the Republican party needed a new image and a new kind of leadership, one which proposed constructive alternatives rather than blind opposition to Democratic legislation. However successful Ford may have been on that score, his leadership was more vigorous and aggressive than that of ex-Speaker McCormack on the Democratic side of the aisle. No one has challenged Ford for the Minority Leadership. But if the Republicans were to lose a large number of seats, someone might; the party's last two leaders were deposed after the disastrous elections of 1958 and 1964.

Back home in Grand Rapids, Ford is a household word. The best the Democrats have been able to do against him was 39% in 1964 and 1970. The trend in the 5th seems to be slightly leftward, however. In 1970 Ford sounded a little less Nixonian on the campaign trail than he usually does in Washington. But there is little reason to doubt that he will continue to win reelection.

Census Data 1970 pop. 456,892; deviation from current state average, —2.2%; change 1960–70, +12.4%. Metro. 90.0%, 43.3% central city.

1970 Share of Federal Outlays $218,880,042

DOD	$33,827,000	HEW	$103,237,092
AEC	$000	HUD	$10,797,754
NASA	$55,671	OEO	$831,424
DOT	$2,710,443	DOA	$4,881,341
		Other	$62,539,317

Federal Military-Industrial Commitments

DOD Contractors Lear Siegler (Grand Rapids), $19.213m: bomb release computer sets; F-4 aircraft navigation systems.

Economic Base Fabricated metal products, esp. cutlery, hand tools, and general hardware, and metal stamping; furniture and fixtures, esp. household furniture; nonelectrical machinery, esp. metalworking machinery and equipment.

The Voters

Registration 200,731 total. No party registration.

Employment profile White collar, 42%. Blue collar, 57%.

Ethnic groups Black, 5%. Total foreign stock, 23%. Germany, 4%; Canada, Poland, 2% each; UK, USSR, Italy, Czech., Sweden, 1% each; others, 4%.

Presidential vote

1968	Humphrey (D)	67,946	(39%)
	Nixon (R)	94,435	(54%)
	Wallace (AIP)	12,845	(7%)

Representative

Gerald R. Ford (R) Elected 1948; b. July 14, 1913; home, Grand Rapids; U. of Mich., B.A., 1935; Yale U., LL.B., 1941; Navy, WWII; married, four children; Episcopalian.

Career Practicing atty., 1941–48; House Minority Leader, 1965–present.

Offices H-230, Capitol, 202-225-3831. Also 425 Cherry St., SE, Grand Rapids 49502, 616-456-9747.

Committees

Minority Leader

Group Ratings

	ADA	COPE	NREP	NFU	LCV	CFA	NAB	NSI	ACA
1970	12	9	17	54	10	50	83	100	68
1969	7	—	—	40	—	—	—	—	53
1968	17	17	—	56	—	—	100	—	74

Key Votes

(1) ABM	FOR	(6) 18-Yr-Vote	FOR	(11) Clean Water $	AGN
(2) SST	FOR	(7) Farm Sub Lmt	AGN	(12) Mig Wrkrs Comp	AGN
(3) Phil Pln	FOR	(8) Coop-Church	AGN	(13) Jets to Chiang	FOR
(4) No-Knock	FOR	(9) Family Asst	FOR	(14) State OEO Veto	FOR
(5) Cmutr Tax	FOR	(10) Work Stamps	FOR	(15) Park Logging	FOR

Election Results

1970 general:	Gerald Ford (R)	88,208	(61%)
	Jean McKee (D)	55,337	(39%)
1970 primary:	Gerald Ford (R), unopposed		
1968 general:	Gerald Ford (R)	105,085	(63%)
	Laurence E. Howard (D)	62,219	(37%)

SIXTH DISTRICT Political Background

Michigan 6 comprises three outstate counties and a portion of a fourth. The district's population is centered in the cities of Jackson and Lansing. Jackson (pop. 45,000) is an aging industrial town and site of the state prison, one of the nation's largest. Lansing (pop. 130,000), the state capital, is a much more prosperous community because of the presence of two growth industries, state government and education. Michigan State University with 44,000 students is in adjacent East Lansing. The city is also the site of the main Oldsmobile plant—which means that there is a lot of unemployment in the 6th district whenever there is a recession or a UAW strike against General Motors. During the 1970 campaign the district had both.

Jackson and Lansing are both marginal politically, while the rural areas surrounding them are heavily Republican. The number of Democratic votes has been increasing in the northern part of the 6th—Shiawassee County, the city of Owosso, and the Lansing suburbs in Clinton County. But the Republicans still win a majority here.

The representative from the 6th is Charles E. Chamberlain, a conservative and often voluble Republican. Chamberlain had some difficult races in the '50's when the district included industrial Genesee County (Flint). In 1956 he ousted a Democratic incumbent and barely held on in the recession year of 1958. After the 1964 redistricting removed Flint from his district, Chamberlain's standing among the voters became more secure. In 1970, however, his margin was held down to 60%. Recently Chamberlain won a seat on the Ways and Means Committee, a sure sign that the Republican Committee on Committees considers him an orthodox conservative. From the looks of the election returns in the 6th, Chamberlain will be in the House for a long time.

Census Data 1970 pop. 483,958; deviation from current state average, +3.6%; change 1960–70, +18.6%. Metro. 87.0%, 36.3% central city.

1970 Share of Federal Outlays $327,458,000

DOD	$34,199,000	HEW	$164,777,000
AEC	$2,145,000	HUD	$2,838,000
NASA	$118,000	OEO	$1,248,000
DOT	$11,488,000	DOA	$17,242,000
		Other	$93,405,000

Federal Military-Industrial Commitments

DOD Contractors White Motor Corp. (Lansing), $11.051m: 2½-ton trucks. Sparton Corp. (Jackson), $7.829m: sonar equipment.

Economic Base Motor vehicles and motor vehicle equipment, and other transportation equipment; nonelectrical machinery; fabricated metal products, esp. cutlery, hand tools, and general hardware. Also, state government and higher education (Michigan State U.).

The Voters

Registration 200,450 total. No party registration.

Employment profile White collar, 44%. Blue collar, 56%.

Ethnic groups Black, 5%. Total foreign stock, 14%. Canada, 3%; Germany, UK, 2%; Poland, Czech., Italy, 1% each; others, 5%.

Presidential vote

1968	Humphrey (D)	66,322	(39%)
	Nixon (R)	88,645	(52%)
	Wallace (AIP)	15,113	(9%)

Representative

Charles E. Chamberlain (R) Elected 1956; b. July 22, 1917, Ingham County; home, East Lansing; U. of Va., B.S., 1941, LL.B., 1949; USCG, WWII; married, three children; religion unspecified.

Career Atty., 1950–56; Counsel, Mich. Senate Judiciary Com., 1953–54; Pros. Atty., Ingham Co., 1955–56.

Offices 2233 RHOB, 202-225-4872. Also 245 Fed Bldg., Lansing 48933, 517-489-6517

Committees

Ways and Means (7th).

Group Ratings

	ADA	COPE	NREP	NFU	LCV	CFA	NAB	NSI	ACA
1970	12	8	17	54	11	48	91	100	78
1969	20	—	—	47	—	—	—	—	63
1968	8	34	—	44	—	—	100	—	91

Key Votes

(1) ABM	FOR	(6) 18-Yr-Vote	FOR	(11) Clean Water $	FOR
(2) SST	FOR	(7) Farm Sub Lmt	ABS	(12) Mig Wrkrs Comp	AGN
(3) Phil Pln	FOR	(8) Coop-Church	AGN	(13) Jets to Chiang	FOR
(4) No-Knock	FOR	(9) Family Asst	FOR	(14) State OEO Veto	FOR
(5) Cmutr Tax	FOR	(10) Work Stamps	FOR	(15) Park Logging	FOR

Election Results

1970 general:	Charles E. Chamberlain (R)	84,276	(60%)
	John A. Cihon (D)	55,591	(40%)
1970 primary:	Charles E. Chamberlain (R), unopposed		
1968 general:	Charles E. Chamberlain (R)	103,423	(64%)
	James A. Harrison (D)	57,839	(36%)

SEVENTH DISTRICT Political Background

Michigan 7, Genesee and Lapeer counties, is dominated by the state's third largest city, Flint (pop. 193,000) and its suburbs. Flint, with five major General Motors plants, is probably the nation's largest one-company town: more than half of the families in Flint depend directly on GM for their paychecks. The 1970 GM strike, of course, hit this city very hard. The rich section of Flint, where the GM millionaires live, sits on a rise with a panoramic view of a Chevrolet plant.

Most factory workers here come from the rural South—whites from Appalachia and blacks from Alabama and Mississippi. The mixture is sometimes volatile. In 1968 George Wallace had the support of many white blue-collar workers and a few UAW locals. Only a concerted effort by the union held Wallace's share of the vote in the district down to 15%.

While GM's management personnel is decidedly Republican, Flint's blue-collar work force makes the city the largest source of Democratic strength outside metropolitan Detroit. And yet the 7th district is currently represented by a Republican, Donald W. Riegle, Jr. Riegle was working on a doctorate at the Harvard Business School in 1966 when some friends suggested that he return to Flint to run for Congress. Since the race looked like a long shot, the local Republican party was having a hard time finding a candidate. The incumbent, John Mackie, had been State Highway Commissioner when that was an elective post and had won 66% of the district's vote two years before. In retrospect it seems that Mackie was supremely overconfident, spending time on his Virginia farm contemplating past victories, which in fact were won against only token opposition. Riegle campaigned hard all over the 7th and came out with 54% of the vote, doing almost as well as Gov. George Romney in the district.

In Washington, Riegle quickly established himself as a maverick liberal in the Republican caucus. At the same time, however, he did manage, presumably with Gerald Ford's help, to win a seat on the House Appropriations Committee. Moreover, unlike most politicians, Riegle refused to hide his ambitions for higher political office, not only for statewide office in Michigan but even for the Presidency. Lately, the Congressman has gained national attention as a caustic critic of the Administration's war policy and has supported the efforts of Rep. Paul McCloskey of California to dump Nixon in 1972.

Riegle's activities have not been very popular among his fellow Republicans, but they certainly have helped him in the 7th district. In 1968 he won reelection with 61% of the vote, and in 1970, when Riegle took 69%, he received the support of the UAW, local peace groups, and the black community. The Congressman was the first Republican ever to win the support of any of these groups.

It is clear that Riegle, who was only 32 in 1970, can go on winning in the 7th as long as he likes, and someday he may become the ranking Republican on the House Appropriations Committee. But waiting patiently is not Riegle's style. He wanted the 1970 Republican senatorial nomination, but was squeezed out when George Romney forced his wife's candidacy on party leaders. And unfortunately for Riegle, all roads to higher political office appear to be blocked for the next few years. The Congressman could challenge Sen. Robert Griffin, a staunch Nixon supporter, in the 1972 Senate primary. But the voters in that primary, many of whom are committed Republicans, are not likely to find Riegle's kind of politics very appealing. Beyond 1972, there is no major statewide office up for grabs without a Republican incumbent until 1976, and that is Philip Hart's Senate seat, which will be difficult to win if Hart runs for reelection.

Riegle has another option. Once a man declares his candidacy and gathers some support, the media can make a political unknown into a viable presidential candidate, which is what happened in the 1968 McCarthy campaign. And current noises about possible McCloskey or Lindsay candidacies show that a serious presidential candidate doesn't have to be a senator or a governor. So in 1976, the first election in which he will be old enough, Riegle could run for President from his current office. Stranger things have happened in the past few years.

Census Data 1970 pop. 496,658; deviation from current state average, +6.3%; change 1960–70, +19.3%. Metro. 100%, 38.9% central city.

1970 Share of Federal Outlays $204,927,724

DOD	$6,640,000	HEW	$93,064,196
AEC	$000	HUD	$8,898,724
NASA	$000	OEO	$560,918
DOT	$28,657,332	DOA	$4,803,009
		Other	$62,303,548

Federal Military-Industrial Commitments

None.

Economic Base Motor vehicles and motor vehicle equipment, and other transportation equipment; fabricated metal products; food and kindred products.

The Voters

Registration 220,977 total. No party registration.

Employment profile White collar, 33%. Blue collar, 67%.

Ethnic groups Black, 12%. Total foreign stock, 17%. Canada, 5%; UK, Germany, 2% each; Poland, USSR, Hungary, Czech., Italy, 1% each; others, 4%.

Presidential vote

1968	Humphrey (D)	80,373	(45%)
	Nixon (R)	72,814	(40%)
	Wallace (AIP)	26,620	(15%)

Representative

Donald W. Riegle, Jr. (R) Elected 1966; b. Feb. 4, 1938, Flint; home, Flint; Flint Jr. College; Western Mich. U.; U. of Mich., B.A., 1960; Mich. State U., MBA, 1961; married, three children; Methodist.

Career IBM Corp., 1961–64, consultant; Harvard-MIT Joint Center on Urban Studies; faculty Mich. State U., Boston U., Harvard U.

Offices 1408 LHOB, 202-225-3611.

Committees

Appropriations (16th); Subs. (1) Foreign Operations, (2) Treasury, Post Office, General Government.

Group Ratings

	ADA	COPE	NREP	NFU	LCV	CFA	NAB	NSI	ACA
1970	80	82	90	75	50	68	44	63	35
1969	67	—	—	73	—	—	—	—	27
1968	50	46	—	75	—	—	100	—	45

Key Votes

(1) ABM	AGN	(6) 18-Yr-Vote	FOR	(11) Clean Water $	FOR
(2) SST	AGN	(7) Farm Sub Lmt	FOR	(12) Mig Wrkrs Comp	FOR
(3) Phil Pln	FOR	(8) Coop-Church	FOR	(13) Jets to Chiang	AGN
(4) No-Knock	FOR	(9) Family Asst	FOR	(14) State OEO Veto	AGN
(5) Cmutr Tax	ABS	(10) Work Stamps	AGN	(15) Park Logging	AGN

Election Results

1970 general:	Donald W. Riegle (R)	97,683	(69%)
	Richard J. Ruhala (D)	41,235	(29%)
	Eugene L. Mattison (AIP)	2,194	(2%)
1970 primary:	Donald W. Riegle (R)	19,719	(77%)
	John F. Supt (R)	5,922	(23%)
1968 general:	Donald W. Riegle (R)	104,502	(61%)
	William R. Blue (D)	67,779	(39%)

EIGHTH DISTRICT Political Background

Michigan 8 is most of the Thumb of the Lower Peninsula, plus Saginaw County to the west. The Thumb remains almost entirely agricultural except for the small industrial city of Port Huron, where the St. Clair River flows out of Lake Huron. The Thumb is very much what it was 100 years ago when it was settled by Yankee and German immigrants. It is still about as Republican as it ever was, too, especially Sanilac County, which turned in majorities for Barry Goldwater in 1964 and Lenore Romney in 1970. Saginaw is quite different: an industrial town with a couple of General Motors plants and a large black population. The rural townships usually keep Saginaw County as a whole in the Republican column, though the city and most of its suburbs are Democratic.

The 8th district was altered completely in the 1964 redistricting. Before that, it faced west from Saginaw, and included none of the Thumb counties. Afterward, only Saginaw County remained from the old district. The change caused Rep. James Harvey some difficulty in the 1964 election. The Goldwater candidacy and the opposition of a well-known State Treasurer compounded Harvey's problems. Nevertheless, Harvey won, with 55%, and has been winning ever since. In the House, the Congressman is a moderate-to-conservative Republican who causes his fellow Michigan Republican, Minority Leader Gerald Ford, relatively little trouble. Although Harvey's share of the votes declined slightly in 1970, as did that of most Michigan Republicans', he appears to have a firm hold on his constituency. The only possible threat to his tenure is redistricting, and that is likely to work out to his satisfaction.

Census Data 1970 pop. 457,493; deviation from current state average, —2.10%; change 1960–70, +12.2%. Metro. 48.0%, 20.1% central city.

1970 Share of Federal Outlays $222,428,120

DOD	$17,842,000	HEW	$102,048,537
AEC	$000	HUD	$8,342,213
NASA	$000	OEO	$490,101
DOT	$7,206,344	DOA	$20,998,746
		Other	$65,500,179

Federal Military-Industrial Commitments

DOD Installations Port Austin AF Station (Port Austin).

Economic Base Motor vehicles and motor vehicle equipment, and other transportation equipment; cash grain and dairy; nonelectrical machinery; fabricated metal products.

The Voters

Registration 192,913 total. No party registration.

Employment profile White collar, 35%. Blue collar, 65%.

Ethnic groups Black, 7%. Total foreign stock, 23%. Canada, 8%; Germany, 5%; Poland, UK, 2% each; USSR, Mexico, Hungary, Austria, Czech., all 1% each; others, 2%.

Presidential vote

1968	Humphrey (D)	60,015	(37%)
	Nixon (R)	87,375	(53%)
	Wallace (AIP)	16,719	(10%)

Representative

James Harvey (R) Elected 1960; b. July 4, 1922, Iron Mountain; home, Saginaw; U. of Mich., LL.B., 1948; USAF, WWII; married, two children; Presbyterian.

Career Atty., 1949–61; Asst. City Atty., 1949–53; City Councilman, 1955–57; County Supervisor, 1955–57; Mayor, 1957–59.

Offices 2352 RHOB, 202-225-2806. Also 10-11 Jefferson-Baum Ct., Saginaw 48607, 517-755-6565.

Committees

House Administration (5th); Subs. (1) Elections, (2) Library and Memorials, (3) Sp. on Electrical and Mechanical Equipment.

Interstate and Foreign Commerce (6th); Sub. on Transportation and Aeronautics.

Jt. Com. on the Library (2nd).

Group Ratings

	ADA	COPE	NREP	NFU	LCV	CFA	NAB	NSI	ACA
1970	20	34	40	50	25	53	91	89	78
1969	27	—	—	54	—	—	—	—	43
1968	25	46	—	67	—	—	83	—	61

Key Votes

(1) ABM	ABS	(6) 18-Yr-Vote	FOR	(11) Clean Water $	FOR
(2) SST	AGN	(7) Farm Sub Lmt	ABS	(12) Mig Wrkrs Comp	AGN
(3) Phil Pln	ABS	(8) Coop-Church	AGN	(13) Jets to Chiang	AGN
(4) No-Knock	FOR	(9) Family Asst	FOR	(14) State OEO Veto	AGN
(5) Cmutr Tax	FOR	(10) Work Stamps	FOR	(15) Park Logging	FOR

Election Results

1970 general:	James Harvey (R)	85,634	(66%)
	Richard E. Davies (D)	44,400	(34%)
1970 primary:	James Harvey (R), unopposed		
1968 general:	James Harvey (R)	105,238	(69%)
	Richard E. Davies (D)	47,639	(31%)

NINTH DISTRICT Political Background

Michigan 9 is a series of counties running along the western shore of Lake Michigan, the little finger of Michigan's Lower Peninsula. Muskegon and Ottawa counties, in the southern end of the 9th, contain more than 60% of the district's population. Ottawa is heavily Dutch (its largest city is Holland, where a tulip festival is held every spring), and, untrammeled by the effects of urbanization, is even more conservative than neighboring Grand Rapids. The city of Muskegon is industrial and heavily Democratic, but the local Dutch dilute the county's Democratic strength. So once all the votes from Ottawa and Muskegon counties are counted, Democratic candidates come out on the short end. Besides, the rest of the district, like most of western Michigan, regularly turns in strong Republican margins. Exceptions to the pattern in the 9th include the lumber mill towns in Mason and Manistee counties and rural Lake County, which has a significant black population. At the northern end of the district is Traverse City (pop. 18,000), a small town which not only is a Republican bastion, but has also produced Michigan's two top Republican officeholders—Sen. Robert Griffin and Gov. William Milliken.

The 9th is Sen. Griffin's old district, which he relinquished to take on the risks of the Senate race in 1966. Griffin always won the 9th with big majorities, his closest call being 57% in 1964. In 1958 when his sponsorship of the Landrum-Griffin Act was expected to cost him union votes in Muskegon, Griffin still won convincingly. His successor, Guy Vander Jagt, has done as well, winning every election by 2:1 margins. In his most difficult test, the 1966 Republican primary, Vander Jagt had all the bases covered, having been a state senator from the northern part of the district, and being of Dutch ancestry like so many of the voters in the 9th's southern counties.

Vander Jagt is one of the increasing number of ex–TV newsmen in politics. He also has other talents, holding a law degree from the University of Michigan and a divinity degree from Yale. As ranking minority member on the Government Operations subcommittee on Conservation and Natural Resources, he has shown great interest in ecological issues. He was in large part responsible for the creation of the Sleeping Bear Dunes National Park, which had been held up during Griffin's tenure in the 9th. Despite the strong Republicanism of his district, Vander Jagt has dissented from his party's position on a number of issues, including the 1970 Cooper-Church Amendment, the SST, and some military appropriations bills. This has not hurt him in the 9th, however, and Vander Jagt seems destined for continual reelection.

Census Data 1970 pop. 458,307; deviation from current state average, —1.9%; change 1960–70, +13.2%. Metro. 62.3%, 13.5% central city.

1970 Share of Federal Outlays $245,497,104

DOD	$47,188,000	HEW	$112,974,503
AEC	$000	HUD	$4,557,036
NASA	$588,143	OEO	$2,116,358
DOT	$6,558,180	DOA	$10,515,018
		Other	$60,999,866

Federal Military-Industrial Commitments

DOD Contractors Continental Motors Div., Teledyne Industries, (Muskegon), $17.843m: engine parts for 2½- and 5-ton trucks. Teledyne Industries (Muskegon), $5.194m: engine parts for M-60 and M-48 tanks.

DOD Installations Empire AF Station (Empire).

Economic Base Nonelectrical machinery; furniture and fixtures, esp. office furniture; iron and steel foundries and other primary metal industries; fruit. Also tourism (Lake Michigan).

The Voters

Registration 205,936 total. No party registration.

Employment profile White collar, 35%. Blue collar, 65%.

Ethnic groups Black, 4%. Total foreign stock, 20%. Germany, Canada, 3% each; Sweden, Poland, 2% each; UK, Czech., Norway, 1% each; others, 9%.

Presidential vote

1968	Humphrey (D)	61,539	(35%)
	Nixon (R)	100,798	(57%)
	Wallace (AIP)	14,763	(8%)

Representative

Guy Vander Jagt (R) Elected 1966; b. Aug. 26, 1931, Cadillac; home, Cadillac; Hope Col., B.A., 1953; Yale U., B.D., 1955; Bonn U., 1956; U. of Mich., LL.B., 1960; married, one child; Presbyterian.

Career Atty., 1960–64; State Sen., 1965–66.

Offices 1211 LHOB, 202-225-3511. Also 408 W. Western, Muskegon 49411, 616-722-3741.

Committees

Foreign Affairs (15th); Subs. (1) Africa, (2) Europe, (3) State Department Organization and Foreign Operations.

Government Operations (7th); Subs. (1) Conservation and Natural Resources, (2) Intergovernmental Relations.

Group Ratings

	ADA	COPE	NREP	NFU	LCV	CFA	NAB	NSI	ACA
1970	48	42	9	58	75	63	83	75	69
1969	27	—	—	64	—	—	—	—	42
1968	33	25	—	57	—	—	100	—	60

Key Votes

(1) ABM	FOR	(6) 18-Yr-Vote	FOR	(11) Clean Water $	FOR
(2) SST	AGN	(7) Farm Sub Lmt	ABS	(12) Mig Wrkrs Comp	AGN
(3) Phil Pln	FOR	(8) Coop-Church	AGN	(13) Jets to Chiang	AGN
(4) No-Knock	ABS	(9) Family Asst	FOR	(14) State OEO Veto	AGN
(5) Cmutr Tax	AGN	(10) Work Stamps	FOR	(15) Park Logging	FOR

Election Results

1970 general:	Guy A. Vander Jagt (R)	94,027	(64%)
	Charles A. Rogers (D)	51,223	(35%)
	Patrick V. Dillinger (AIP)	811	(1%)
1970 primary:	Guy A. Vander Jagt (R), unopposed		
1968 general:	Guy Vander Jagt (R)	111,774	(68%)
	Jay A. Wabeke (D)	53,886	(32%)

TENTH DISTRICT Political Background

Michigan 10, a region taken up primarily by forests, lakes, and ski resorts, comprises most of the northern portion of the state's Lower Peninsula. Most of the 10th's residents live in the southern part of the district: in and around Bay City, an aging industrial town with a large Polish community; or in Midland, the very middle-class home of the Dow Chemical Company; or in the predominantly agricultural counties to the west. The northern counties have very few people living in them, except during summer when they are filled with vacationers from Detroit and Ohio.

Most of the 10th is Republican, with the exception of Bay County, a longtime Democratic stronghold that is consistently outvoted by the rest of the district. Since 1952, the 10th's congressman has been Elford Cederberg, a conservative Republican from Bay City. Cederberg is now the number three Republican on the House Appropriations Committee. Since he is at least fourteen years younger than the two Republicans ahead of him, Cederberg may some day serve as the ranking minority member or even chairman of this important congressional unit.

The Congressman is unlikely to have much trouble winning reelection from the 10th, so long as it remains essentially intact. The only way he could lose his seat is if by some unlikely chance Bay City and Saginaw were placed in the same district. Cederberg would then have to take on Rep. James Harvey for the Republican nomination and face a strong Democratic challenge in the general election. But the 1970 census figures and political realities indicate that this will not happen.

Census Data 1970 pop. 478,784; deviation from current state average, +2.5%; change 1960–70, +18.7%. Metro. 24.5%, 10.3% central city.

1970 Share of Federal Outlays $275,319,648

DOD	$56,503,000	HEW	$121,036,830
AEC	$000	HUD	$1,504,000
NASA	$000	OEO	$1,178,421
DOT	$9,826,338	DOA	$18,405,273
		Other	$66,865,786

Federal Military-Industrial Commitments

DOD Installations Wurtsmith AFB (Oscoda).

Economic Base Dairy, cash grain, and livestock; transportation equipment; chemicals and allied products, esp. plastics materials and synthetic resins, synthetic rubber, synthetic and other man-made fibers, other than glass. Also, tourism (Lake Huron) and higher education (Cent. Michigan U.).

The Voters

Registration 204,479 total. No party registration.

Employment profile White collar, 36%. Blue collar, 64%.

Ethnic groups Black, 1%. Total foreign stock, 17%. Canada, 5%; Germany, 3%; Poland, 2%; UK, Sweden, 1% each; others, 5%.

Presidential vote

1968	Humphrey (D)	63,392	(37%)
	Nixon (R)	93,778	(55%)
	Wallace (AIP)	13,043	(8%)

Representative

Elford Cederberg (R) Elected 1953; b. March 6, 1918, Bay City; home, Bay City; Bay City College; Army, WWII; married; Evangelical church.

Career Mgr. Nelson Mfg. Company; Mayor, Bay City, 1949–52.

Offices 2303 RHOB, 202-225-3561. Also 318 Fed. Bldg., Bay City 48706, 517-893-9443.

Committees

Appropriations (3rd); Subs. (1) Legislative, (2) Military Construction, (3) State, Justice, Commerce, and Judiciary.

Group Ratings

	ADA	COPE	NREP	NFU	LCV	CFA	NAB	NSI	ACA
1970	16	18	17	54	13	67	100	100	65
1969	7	—	—	54	—	—	—	—	43
1968	0	0	—	33	—	—	100	—	84

Key Votes

(1) ABM	FOR	(6) 18-Yr-Vote	FOR	(11) Clean Water $	AGN
(2) SST	FOR	(7) Farm Sub Lmt	AGN	(12) Mig Wrkrs Comp	AGN
(3) Phil Pln	FOR	(8) Coop-Church	AGN	(13) Jets to Chiang	FOR
(4) No-Knock	ABS	(9) Family Asst	FOR	(14) State OEO Veto	FOR
(5) Cmutr Tax	FOR	(10) Work Stamps	FOR	(15) Park Logging	AGN

Election Results

1970 general:	Elford A. Cederberg (R)	82,528	(59%)
	Gerald J. Parent (D)	57,031	(41%)

1970 primary:	Elford A. Cederberg (R), unopposed		
1968 general:	Elford A. Cederberg (R)	104,791	(66%)
	Wayne Miller (D)	54,152	(34%)

ELEVENTH DISTRICT Political Background

Michigan 11 is the northern tip of the Lower Peninsula and all of the Upper Peninsula. The U.P., as it is called, is a political world of its own, isolated most of the year from the rest of Michigan by the elements, and during the remainder by exorbitant tolls on the Mackinac Straits Bridge. The Upper Peninsula was settled around the turn of the century, and when its copper and iron mines were booming, the place had a Wild West air to it. The influx into the U.P. was polyglot: Irish, Italians, Swedes, Norwegians, and Finns. While working the mines these immigrants picked up Democratic voting habits which their descendants still retain. Some time ago, however, the mines petered out, leaving the U.P.'s stagnant economy dependent on summer tourists and fall hunters. And since the young people of the Upper Peninsula have been moving to Detroit, Chicago, or the West Coast, its population has hovered around 300,000 for the past 30 years. Today its only reasonably prosperous locale lies around Marquette, the U.P.'s largest city (pop. 22,000).

The 11th's portion of the Lower Peninsula has been doing somewhat better, particularly the resort areas around Gaylord, Charlevoix, and Petroskey. This region is marginal-to-Republican and offsets to some extent the usual Democratic majorities north of the Bridge. The district, as a whole, leans Democratic, but it has sent a Democrat to the House only once in the past 20 years. Before the 1964 redistricting, there were two districts in what is now the 11th—a relic of the days when the Upper Peninsula contained a far larger percentage of the state's population than it does today. In 1964 two Republican incumbent congressmen were preparing to square off in the primary when the more liberal of the two, Rep. John Bennett, died suddenly, leaving Rep. Victor Knox the winner by default. But in 1964, Goldwater's year, the Republican nomination was not worth much. The Democratic candidate Raymond Clevenger won the election with 53% of the votes.

Clevenger, in turn, was one of the five Michigan freshmen House Democrats who was defeated in 1966, as Mennen Williams' unanticipated weakness hurt the whole Democratic ticket. Williams, once strong in the U.P. (the Governor built the Mackinac Bridge), failed to carry the 11th (45%), while Clevenger won 48%. The winner was Republican Philip Ruppe, scion of a wealthy Houghton family. As befits a Republican congressman from a basically Democratic district, Ruppe has a moderate-to-liberal voting record. In 1970, he voted against the SST appropriation, but was one of five House members to reverse himself when the issue came up again in 1971. Ruppe has run well in the district, having been the only one of five Michigan Republican congressional candidates to run better in 1970 than in 1968. Redistricting can only help the Congressman: the 11th gained virtually no population in the '60's, and areas to the south which must consequently be added to the district are all heavily Republican.

Census Data 1970 pop. 415,005; deviation from current state average, —11.2%; change 1960–70, +2.9%. Metro. 0.0%, 0.0% central city.

1970 Share of Federal Outlays $309,537,549

DOD	$86,124,000	HEW	$126,827,333
AEC	$110,081	HUD	$3,880,572
NASA	$000	OEO	$1,227,517
DOT	$11,386,325	DOA	$11,259,605
		Other	$68,672,116

Federal Military-Industrial Commitments

DOD Contractors Harnischfeger (Escanaba), $9.950m: 20-ton cranes.

DOD Installations Sawyer AFB (Marquette). Sault Ste. Marie AF Station (Sault Ste. Marie).

Economic Base Dairy; metal mining, esp. iron ores; nonelectrical machinery, esp. construction, mining, and material handling machinery and equipment. Also, tourism (Mackinac and U.P.).

The Voters

Registration 193,053 total. No party registration.

Employment profile White collar, 36%. Blue collar, 64%.

Ethnic groups Black, 1%. Total foreign stock, 32%. Canada, 7%; Sweden, Germany, 3% each; UK, Italy, Poland, 2% each; Norway, Austria, Czech., 1% each; others, 11%.

Presidential vote

1968	Humphrey (D)	79,327	(48%)
	Nixon (R)	78,025	(47%)
	Wallace (AIP)	9,241	(6%)

Representative

Philip E. Ruppe (R) Elected 1966; b. Sept. 29, 1926, Laurium; home, Houghton; Yale U., B.A., 1948; Navy, Korean War; married, five children; Catholic.

Career Pres., Bosch Brewing Co., 1955–1965; Dir. Houghton Natl. Bank and Commercial Natl. Bank of L'Anse.

Offices 124 CHOB, 202-225-4735. Also West Memorial Rd., Houghton 49931, 906-482-4041.

Committees

Interior and Insular Affairs (8th): Subs. (1) Environment, (2) National Parks and Recreation, (3) Public Lands, (4) Territorial and Insular Affairs.

Merchant Marine and Fisheries (6th); Subs. (1) Coast Guard, Coast and Geodetic Survey, (2) Fisheries and Wildlife Conservation, (3) Merchant Marine.

Group Ratings

	ADA	COPE	NREP	NFU	LCV	CFA	NAB	NSI	ACA
1970	56	60	70	85	33	63	75	89	53
1969	40	—	—	77	—	—	—	—	14
1968	33	67	—	79	—	—	67	—	45

Key Votes

(1) ABM	FOR	(6) 18-Yr-Vote	FOR	(11) Clean Water $	FOR
(2) SST	AGN	(7) Farm Sub Lmt	FOR	(12) Mig Wrkrs Comp	FOR
(3) Phil Pln	FOR	(8) Coop-Church	FOR	(13) Jets to Chiang	AGN
(4) No-Knock	FOR	(9) Family Asst	FOR	(14) State OEO Veto	AGN
(5) Cmutr Tax	ABS	(10) Work Stamps	ABS	(15) Park Logging	FOR

Election Results

1970 general:	Philip E. Ruppe (R)	85,323	(62%)
	Nino Green (D)	53,146	(38%)
1970 primary:	Philip E. Ruppe (R), unopposed		
1968 general:	Philip E. Ruppe (R)	94,513	(59%)
	Raymond F. Clevenger (D)	66,251	(41%)

TWELFTH DISTRICT Political Background

Michigan 12 is Macomb County—the northeast suburbs of Detroit plus a few blocks of the city itself. The district is one of those suburban areas of neat subdivisions with winding streets, modern thin-walled apartment house complexes, and gleaming new shopping centers. But unlike the new suburbs of California, Macomb has roots—in the east side of Detroit. Michigan 12 is where the sons and daughters of the Polish, Irish, and Italian immigrants who came to work in Detroit's factories are moving. And many of the factories, also suburbanizing, are following them. So despite the upward mobility of many of its residents and the changing patterns of Detroit's economy, Macomb is still a blue-collar county.

In 1970 Macomb received a great deal of national publicity because of the controversy in Warren (pop. 179,000) over urban renewal and integration. Like most of Macomb's cities, Warren is all white and intends to stay that way; citizens of Warren, therefore, greatly resented George Romney's attempt to make it a kind of national laboratory for suburban integration. Why, some of the city's working people asked, didn't Romney try to integrate his own very rich suburb of Bloomfield Hills? But despite the opposition to neighborhood integration and despite George Wallace's strong 14% showing here in 1968, most of the 12th's residents have retained their parents' Democratic voting habits.

The Warren controversy in 1970 couldn't have come at a worse time for Lenore Romney, who was in the midst of her campaign for the Senate and who in the end received only 23% of the vote in the 12th. With the whites upset about George Romney's plans for Warren, Lenore managed to alienate the black community with some critical comments about the late Martin Luther King's tactics of civil disobedience. All this aside, Warren usually produces 3:1 Democratic majorities anyway, with the rest of the county not far behind.

Such margins have become commonplace for Rep. James O'Hara, a Democrat who first won in 1958 when the district included the heavily Republican Thumb counties as well as Macomb. Since then, O'Hara has become one of the leaders of the liberal Democratic Study Group and was one of the candidates for Majority Leader in the 1971 Democratic Caucus. But despite strong labor support, he received only 25 votes on the first ballot—a poor showing, resulting in large part from his longtime refusal to take a stand against the Vietnam war. Now that his labor allies, at least in Michigan, have come around to an antiwar position, O'Hara has opposed the Nixon policies.

O'Hara has no worries about reelection. He will lose some of Michigan 12 in redistricting, with part probably going to the 14th district (east side Detroit), and part to the 18th district in Oakland County. Whatever remains is sure to reelect him in 1972.

Census Data 1970 pop. 630,466; deviation from current state average, +35.0%; change 1960–70, +53.4%. Metro. 100%, 0.8% central city.

1970 Share of Federal Outlays $225,411,000 (average outlay per district Michigan 1, 12–19)

DOD	$54,215,000	HEW	$100,226,000
AEC	$104,000	HUD	$3,520,000
NASA	$102,000	OEO	$1,290,000
DOT	$7,702,000	DOA	$156,000
		Other	$88,095,000

Federal Military-Industrial Commitments (Michigan 1, 12–19, greater Detroit listing)

DOD Contractors Chrysler (Detroit and Warren), $72,866m: M-60 tank production and repair; cargo trucks; ambulances. Ford (Highland Park), $67.831m: 5-ton and ¼-ton trucks. LTV Inc. and LTV Aerospace (Warren), 46.400m: unspecified research. General Motors (Detroit and Warren), $35.093m: trucks; ambulances; diesel engines for various Army vehicles. Dana Corp. (Trenton), $6.134m: production of steel combat helmets.

DOD Installations Detroit Army Arsenal (Warren).

Economic Base Motor vehicles and motor vehicle equipment, and other transportation equipment; nonelectrical machinery, esp. metalworking machinery and equipment; fabricated metal products, esp. metal stamping.

The Voters

Registration 206,061 total. No party registration.

Employment profile White collar, 41%. Blue collar, 59%.

Ethnic groups Black, 1%. Total foreign stock, 31%. Canada, 7%; Poland, Germany, Italy, 4% each; UK, 2%; Austria, USSR, Hungary, Czech., 1% each; others, 6%.

Presidential vote

1968	Humphrey (D)	115,903	(55%)
	Nixon (R)	63,837	(31%)
	Wallace (AIP)	29,634	(14%)

Representative

James G. O'Hara (D) Elected 1958; b. Nov. 8, 1925, Washington, D.C.; home, Utica; U. of Mich., B.A., 1954, LL.B., 1955; Army, WWII; married, seven children; Catholic.

Career Atty., 1955–58; U.S. House Democratic Whip for Upper Midwest.

Offices 2241 RHOB, 202-225-2106. Also 215 S. Gratiot, Mt. Clemens 48043, 313-465-0911, and 6768 Twelve Mile Rd., Warren 48092, 313-756-8228.

Committees

Education and Labor (8th); Subs. (1) Chm., Agricultural Labor, (2) Sp. on Labor, (3) Sel. on Education.

Interior and Insular Affairs (11th); (1) Environment, (2) National Parks and Recreation, (3) Public Lands.

Jt. Com. on Congressional Operations (3rd).

Group Ratings

	ADA	COPE	NREP	NFU	LCV	CFA	NAB	NSI	ACA
1970	92	92	100	92	89	100	10	38	17
1969	87	—	—	100	—	—	—	—	6
1968	83	100	—	100	—	—	0	—	0

Key Votes

(1) ABM	FOR	(6) 18-Yr-Vote	FOR	(11) Clean Water $	FOR
(2) SST	AGN	(7) Farm Sub Lmt	FOR	(12) Mig Wrkrs Comp	FOR
(3) Phil Pln	AGN	(8) Coop-Church	FOR	(13) Jets to Chiang	AGN
(4) No-Knock	AGN	(9) Family Asst	FOR	(14) State OEO Veto	AGN
(5) Cmutr Tax	AGN	(10) Work Stamps	AGN	(15) Park Logging	AGN

Election Results

1970 general:	James G. O'Hara (D)	129,287	(76%)
	Patrick Driscoll (R)	38,946	(23%)
	Milton E. Deschaine (AIP)	1,562	(1%)
1970 primary:	James G. O'Hara (D)	43,066	(87%)
	Joseph G. Savage (D)	6,204	(13%)
1968 general:	James G. O'Hara (D)	131,517	(70%)
	Max B. Harris, Jr. (R)	54,760	(30%)

THIRTEENTH DISTRICT Political Background

Michigan 13 is the inner city of Detroit and the lower part of its east side along the Detroit River—the poorer of Detroit's two predominantly black districts. In the 1960's, the 13th suffered the largest population loss of any district in the nation. This was in part due to land clearance for urban renewal and the building of giant freeways, most of which were named after auto magnates: Edsel B. Ford, Walter P. Chrysler, and the Fisher Brothers of General Motors. Perhaps even more important was the voluntary exodus of the black community itself. Particularly after the 1967 riots, many residents of the 13th moved to the more middle-class surroundings of the 1st district and northwest Detroit. What is left is a collection of poor neighborhoods—some of them the remnants of old-time white ethnic centers—plus a couple of integrated upper-income enclaves and the skyscrapers of downtown Detroit. The 13th, of course, is solidly Democratic, but the declining number of votes cast here is the district's most salient political fact.

With the death of William Dawson of South Side Chicago and the involuntary retirement of Adam Clayton Powell of Harlem in 1970, the 13th's congressman, Charles C. Diggs, Jr., became (at 48) the dean of the House's black delegation and chairman of the increasingly energetic Black Caucus. Diggs is by trade a mortician, like his father, who 20 years ago was the leading politician and one of the wealthiest men in Detroit's black community. Diggs, Sr., masterminded his son's first congressional race in 1954, when he beat an aging incumbent in the Democratic primary; Diggs, Jr., has been unbeatable in the district ever since. Some blacks feel that the Congressman is not militant enough, though his record is solidly liberal and antiwar. Serious opposition has never materialized, however, and, now that he has close to 20 years of seniority, probably never will.

In the House, Diggs is the 5th ranking Democrat (and 1st ranking dove) on the Foreign Affairs Committee, where he is chairman of the subcommittee on Africa. In that capacity he has waged a forceful campaign against South Africa and Rhodesia. The Congressman is also the 4th ranking Democrat (and 1st ranking liberal) on the House District of Columbia Committee, where he fights for the interests of Washington's black majority but usually loses. When the 92nd Congress convened, the Democratic Caucus tried to substitute Diggs for South Carolina's John McMillan as chairman of the D.C. Committee. Although the move failed by a large margin, it did serve notice to many conservative committee chairmen that they can no longer expect automatic reelection to their posts.

Redistricting will probably add the Detroit portion of the 16th to the 13th. This area has a substantial Polish and Hungarian population, but the 13th as a whole will still have a large black majority, and Diggs' chances for reelection will not be endangered.

Census Data 1970 pop. 321,066; deviation from current state average, —31.3%; change 1960–70, —22.9%. Metro. 100%, 100% central city.

1970 Share of Federal Outlays $255,411,000 (average outlay per district Michigan 1, 12–19)

DOD	$54,215,000	HEW	$100,226,000
AEC	$104,000	HUD	$3,520,000
NASA	$102,000	OEO	$1,290,000
DOT	$7,702,000	DOA	$156,000
		Other	$88,095,000

Federal Military-Industrial Commitments (See Michigan 12 for greater Detroit listing.)

Economic Base Motor vehicles and motor vehicle equipment, and other transportation equipment; nonelectrical machinery, esp. metalworking machinery and equipment; fabricated metal products, esp. metal stampings; primary metal industries, esp. blast furnaces, steel works, and rolling and finishing mills. Also higher education (Wayne St. U.).

The Voters

Registration 124,326 total. No party registration.

Employment profile White collar, 26%. Blue collar, 74%.

Ethnic groups Black, 73%. Total foreign stock, 17%. Canada, Poland, 3% each; Germany, Italy, 2% each; UK, Mexico, Ireland, 1% each; others, 5%.

Presidential vote

1968	Humphrey (D)	88,625	(84%)
	Nixon (R)	11,302	(11%)
	Wallace (AIP)	5,313	(5%)

Representative

Charles C. Diggs, Jr. (D) Elected 1954; b. Dec. 2, 1922, Detroit; home, Detroit; U. of Mich., 1940–42; Fisk U., 1942–43; Wayne U. Mortuary Sch., 1945–46; Detroit Col., 1951–52; Army, WWII; married, five children; Baptist.

Career State Sen., 1951–54.

Offices 2464 RHOB, 202-225-2261. Also, 1201 E. Grant River Blv., Detroit 48211, 313-925-8300.

Committees

District of Columbia (4th); Sub. on Housing and Youth Affairs.
Foreign Affairs (6th); Subs. (1) Chm., Africa, (2) Asian and Pacific Affairs.

Group Ratings

	ADA	COPE	NREP	NFU	LCV	CFA	NAB	NSI	ACA
1970	80	100	100	82	84	100	0	11	6
1969	100	—	—	75	—	—	—	—	15
1968	100	100	—	92	—	—	0	—	6

Key Votes

(1) ABM	AGN	(6) 18-Yr-Vote	FOR	(11) Clean Water $	FOR
(2) SST	AGN	(7) Farm Sub Lmt	FOR	(12) Mig Wrkrs Comp	FOR
(3) Phil Pln	FOR	(8) Coop-Church	FOR	(13) Jets to Chiang	AGN
(4) No-Knock	AGN	(9) Family Asst	ABS	(14) State OEO Veto	AGN
(5) Cmutr Tax	ABS	(10) Work Stamps	AGN	(15) Park Logging	ABS

Election Results

1970 general:	Charles C. Diggs (D)	56,872	(86%)
	Fred W. Engel (R)	9,141	(14%)
1970 primary:	Charles C. Diggs (D)	22,372	(84%)
	David Boston (D)	4,190	(16%)
1968 general:	Charles C. Diggs (D)	81,951	(86%)
	Eugene Beauregard (R)	12,873	(14%)

FOURTEENTH DISTRICT Political Background

Michigan 14 is a virtually all-white district that extends from Polish Hamtramck section of Detroit on the east to the five posh Grosse Pointe suburbs on the west. Most of the votes are cast in the poorer Detroit portion of the district by ethnic white residents who have not yet made it out of the city to the suburbs. Most of the 14th, therefore, still shows the influence of the various ethnic backgrounds of its people. In fact, of the nation's districts, only two in Chicago have more first- and second-generation Polish-Americans. The 14th also contains Italians, Germans, Irish, and the nation's largest concentration of Belgian-Americans. Like their parents, the residents of the poorer part of the district vote Democratic, though they are decidedly conservative on social issues. The rich WASPs and Catholics (often, the Kennedys notwithstanding, the most conservative of all) of the Grosse Pointes always vote Republican and manage to hold the district's Democratic percentage down between 60 and 70 percent.

The congressman from the 14th is Lucien N. Nedzi, a liberal Democrat of Polish descent. Nedzi is not quite as secure politically as Detroit's other Democrats, largely because he is the only one among them with a large Republican bloc of voters in his district. The 1964 redistricters gave Nedzi his toughest test, placing him in the 14th to fight it out with the somewhat more conservative congressman, Harold Ryan. Even though Ryan was better known in most of the newly created district, Nedzi, with labor, the Poles, and the newspapers behind him, managed to squeak out a 3,000-vote victory. Since then, his most serious challenge was a well-financed Republican effort in 1968, which did little aside from holding Nedzi's total down to 63%. Redistricting will probably add some of heavily Democratic Macomb County, which will only strengthen the Congressman's position.

Some years before it became popular among liberals, Nedzi took a seat on Mendel Rivers' Armed Services Committee. There he and a few other Northern liberals struggled in vain with the Southern Democrat–conservative Republican coalition which dominated the committee. In the 92nd Congress, Nedzi, who now ranks 9th among the committee's Democrats, has been joined by a couple of other liberals. In a few years the liberals might be able to take over a subcommittee chairmanship and its attendant staff resources. The Michigan Congressman, who plugged on during all the lonely years, is as responsible as any man for the cracks that have begun to appear in the once monolithic structure of the House Armed Services Committee.

Census Data 1970 pop. 394,461; deviation from current state average, –15.6%; change 1960–70, –5.6%. Metro. 100%, 73.1% central city.

1970 Share of Federal Outlays $255,411,000 (average outlay per district, Michigan 1, 12–19)

DOD	$54,215,000	HEW	$100,226,000
AEC	$104,000	HUD	$3,520,000
NASA	$102,000	OEO	$1,290,000
DOT	$7,702,000	DOA	$156,000
		Other	$88,095,000

Federal Military-Industrial Commitments (See Michigan 12 for greater Detroit listing.)

Economic Base Motor vehicles and motor vehicle equipment, and other transportation equipment; nonelectrical machinery, esp. metalworking machinery and equipment; fabricated metal products, esp. metal stampings; primary metal industries, esp. blast furnaces, steel works, and rolling and finishing mills.

The Voters

Registration 212,395 total. No party registration.

Employment profile White collar, 48%. Blue collar, 52%.

Ethnic groups Black, 10%. Total foreign stock, 46%; Poland, 12%; Canada, 7%; Italy, Germany, 6% each; UK, 3%; USSR, Austria, Ireland, Hungary, 1% each; others, 8%.

Presidential vote

1968	Humphrey (D)	96,737	(55%)
	Nixon (R)	59,930	(34%)
	Wallace (AIP)	20,717	(12%)

Representative

Lucien N. Nedzi (D) Elected Nov. 1961; b. May 28, 1925, Hamtramck; home, Detroit; U. of Mich., B.A., 1948, LL.B., 1951; WWII and Korea; married, five children; Catholic.

Career Atty., 1952–60; Wayne County Public Administrator, 1955.

Offices 1125 LHOB, 202-225-6275. Also 11498 Portland St., Detroit 48205, 313-521-4880.

Committees

Armed Services (9th); Sub. No. 2.

House Administration (5th); Subs. (1) Chm., Library and Memorials, (2) Sp. on Electrical and Mechanical Office Equipment.

Jt. Com. on the Library (2nd).

Group Ratings

	ADA	COPE	NREP	NFU	LCV	CFA	NAB	NSI	ACA
1970	92	100	100	100	67	94	0	20	13
1969	80	—	—	86	—	—	—	—	24
1968	83	100	—	88	—	—	0	—	5

Key Votes

(1) ABM	FOR	(6) 18-Yr-Vote	FOR	(11) Clean Water $	FOR
(2) SST	AGN	(7) Farm Sub Lmt	FOR	(12) Mig Wrkrs Comp	FOR
(3) Phil Pln	AGN	(8) Coop-Church	FOR	(13) Jets to Chiang	AGN
(4) No-Knock	AGN	(9) Family Asst	FOR	(14) State OEO Veto	AGN
(5) Cmutr Tax	FOR	(10) Work Stamps	AGN	(15) Park Logging	AGN

Election Results

1970 general:	Lucien N. Nedzi (D)	91,111	(70%)
	John L. Owen (R)	38,956	(30%)
1970 primary:	Lucien N. Nedzi (D), unopposed		
1968 general:	Lucien N. Nedzi (D)	101,961	(63%)
	Peter O'Rourke (R)	59,757	(37%)

FIFTEENTH DISTRICT Political Background

Michigan 15 comprises the western and southwestern suburbs of Detroit, not high-income WASP suburbs like Westchester County, but solid working-class communities. The towns of the 15th are new; Lincoln Park was established in the '40's, Taylor, Dearborn Heights in the '50's, and Westland in the '60's. Most of them are predominately blue-collar, and one of them, Inkster, has a near-majority black population. In addition to the usual Polish and Irish elements, most of whom are now thoroughly middle class, there are large numbers of immigrants from the Appalachian South and, as everywhere in Michigan, Canada. The large Canadian population in the Detroit area may account for its being significantly more Democratic than any other large metropolis except Boston. Immigrant Canadian WASPs are much more likely to be Democrats than their longtime American cousins.

The economy of the 15th is dominated by the Ford Motor Company and its politics, more often than not by UAW political operatives. The district's congressman, William D. Ford, not related to the auto magnates, is a young attorney who was active in local politics and jumped from the state Senate to the U.S. House in 1964 when the legislature split the old 16th district in two.

In Washington, Ford has compiled a solidly liberal voting record on both domestic and foreign issues, even though his district gave Wallace his best vote in Michigan (16%). In part, the Alabaman's showing expressed the voters opposition to racial integration. But it does not mean that the Democratic 15th is going conservative generally; Nixon got only 28% here. Wallace's total represented as much as anything a disgust with the Johnson-Humphrey Administration, an alienation from the general drift of the country. Many of the Wallace votes were cast by young male blue-collar workers, men who have not yet identified their interests with the Democratic party and therefore felt free to cast a protest vote.

Ford's performance in 1970 suggests that Wallace would not find the 15th as receptive to his appeal in 1972 as it was in 1968. In 1968 Ford won 71% of the vote; in 1970 he took 80%, showing a sharp increase in popularity. Ford's record as an opponent of Nixon's economic policy and the war make it probable that in 1970 he received the protest vote that went to Wallace two years before. If the 1972 Democratic presidential candidate is a suitable recipient of that protest vote, it is likely that the party will improve substantially on its 1968 showing in areas like the 15th.

Census Data 1970 pop. 511,538; deviation from current state average, +9.5%; change 1960–70, +23.7%. Metro. 100%, 0.0% central city.

1970 Share of Federal Outlays $255,411,000 (average outlay per district Michigan 1, 12–19)

DOD	$54,215,000	HEW	$100,226,000
AEC	$104,000	HUD	$3,520,000
NASA	$102,000	OEO	$1,290,000
DOT	$7,702,000	DOA	$156,000
		Other	$88,095,000

Federal Military-Industrial Commitments (See Michigan 12 for greater Detroit listing.)

Economic Base Motor vehicles and motor vehicle equipment, and other transportation equipment; nonelectrical machinery, esp. metalworking machinery and equipment; fabricated metal products, esp. metal stampings; primary metal industries, esp. blast furnaces, steel works, and rolling and finishing mills.

The Voters

Registration 205,647 total. No party registration.

Employment profile White collar, 39%. Blue collar, 61%.

Ethnic groups Black, 5%. Total foreign stock, 25%. Canada, 7%; Poland, 4%; UK, 3%; Germany, Italy, Hungary, 2% each; Austria, USSR, Czech., 1% each; others 5%

Presidential vote

1968	Humphrey (D)	93,045	(56%)
	Nixon (R)	47,202	(28%)
	Wallace (AIP)	27,022	(16%)

Representative

William David Ford (D) Elected 1964; b. Aug. 6, 1927, Detroit; home, Taylor; Neb. Teachers Col., 1946; Wayne State U., 1947–48; U. of Denver, B.S., 1949, LL.B., 1951; USNR, WWII; Lt., USAF, 1950–58; divorced, two children; United Church of Christ.

Career Atty., 1951– ; J.P. of Taylor Township, 1955–57; city atty., Melvindale, 1957–59; State Senator, 1962–64; Delegate, Mich. Const. Conv., 1961–62.

Offices 125 CHOB, 202-225-6261. Also, Wayne Fed. Bldg., Wayne 48184, 313-722-1411.

Committees

Education and Labor (10th); Subs. (1) Gen. on Education, (2) Gen. on Labor, (3) Sel. on Labor.

Post Office and Civil Service (10th); Subs. (1) Manpower and Civil Service, (2) Postal Service.

Group Ratings

	ADA	COPE	NREP	NFU	LCV	CFA	NAB	NSI	ACA
1970	92	100	100	100	100	100	0	11	6
1969	93	—	—	86	—	—	—	—	8
1968	92	100	—	86	—	—	0	—	6

Key Votes

(1) ABM	AGN	(6) 18-Yr-Vote	FOR	(11) Clean Water $	FOR
(2) SST	AGN	(7) Farm Sub Lmt	FOR	(12) Mig Wrkrs Comp	FOR
(3) Phil Pln	AGN	(8) Coop-Church	FOR	(13) Jets to Chiang	AGN
(4) No-Knock	AGN	(9) Family Asst	FOR	(14) State OEO Veto	AGN
(5) Cmutr Tax	ABS	(10) Work Stamps	AGN	(15) Park Logging	AGN

Election Results

1970 general:	William D. Ford (D)	101,018	(80%)
	Ernest C. Fackler (R)	25,340	(20%)
1970 primary:	William D. Ford (D), unopposed		
1968 general:	William D. Ford (D)	106,960	(71%)
	John F. Boyle (R)	43,582	(29%)

SIXTEENTH DISTRICT Political Background

Michigan 16 is a heavily industrial area containing the city of Dearborn and the southwest section and downriver suburbs of Detroit. Dearborn (pop. 104,000) is the most famous part of the district, because the Ford Motor Company has its headquarters and largest plant here and because of Orville Hubbard, the city's mayor. Hubbard has plastered the city with signs saying "Keep Dearborn Clean," a slogan that some say is a euphemism for the Mayor's foremost concern: keeping Dearborn white. Though Detroit's ghetto lies adjacent to Dearborn and though thousands of blacks work in Ford's vast Rouge plant, there are no blacks in Hubbard's city and there will likely be none in the near future. Oddly enough, Hubbard has also became widely known as an opponent of the Vietnam war. The Mayor placed the first referendum on the war on the city's ballot in 1966; his constituents voted against withdrawal then, but reversed themselves in 1968.

The rest of the district is predominantly blue-collar, with a large black concentration in southwest Detroit, River Rouge, and Ecorse. A substantial number of Polish- and Hungarian-Americans are scattered throughout the 16th. These groups are all overwhelmingly Democratic; the only areas of Republican strength here lie in wealthy west Dearborn and Grosse Ile.

In 1964, the Michigan legislature redrew district lines (see Michigan 1) and threw two incumbent Democrats together in the new 16th district, John Lesinski, Jr., and John Dingell, Jr. Both are of Polish descent, and both had succeeded their fathers in the House. Lesinski, who had represented most of new 16th in his old district, was one of the few Northern Democrats to vote against the Civil Rights Act of 1964.

Name familiarity and the newly discovered white backlash made Lesinski the early favorite. But Dingell campaigned hard and, with vigorous labor support, won 30,000 to 25,000. Since then Dingell has had few worries; he usually receives more than 70% of the votes in general elections. The Congressman is now 5th ranking Democrat on both Interstate and Foreign Commerce, where he often leads the pro-consumer minority, and Merchant Marine and Fisheries, where he has become a diligent conservationist. On foreign policy and social issues, Dingell has been conservative—more in line with his blue-collar constituency than some of his Detroit colleagues. He is particularly hostile to gun-control legislation. But if the Congressman's stand on the issues can be taken as an index of the feelings in his district, the 16th is trending left. In 1971, after many years of hawkishness, Dingell announced his opposition to the Administration's war policy.

Redistricting will move the 16th's boundaries to the west, putting most of its black voters in the 13th district. Dingell will have a safe seat through the '70's.

Census Data 1970 pop. 406,011; deviation from current state average, —14.8%; change 1960–70, —2.1%. Metro. 100%, 31.4% central city.

1970 Share of Federal Outlays $255,411,000 (average outlay per district Michigan 1, 12–19)

DOD	$54,215,000	HEW	$100,226,000
AEC	$104,000	HUD	$3,520,000
NASA	$102,000	OEO	$1,290,000
DOT	$7,702,000	DOA	$156,000
		Other	$88,095,000

Federal Military-Industrial Commitments (See Michigan 12 for greater Detroit listing.)

Economic Base Motor vehicles and motor vehicle equipment, and other transportation equipment; nonelectrical machinery, esp. metalworking machinery and equipment; fabricated metal products, esp. metal stampings; primary metal industries, esp. blast furnaces, steel works, and rolling and finishing mills.

The Voters

Registration 178,082 total. No party registration.

Employment profile White collar, 39%. Blue collar, 61%.

Ethnic groups Black, 10%. Total foreign stock, 34%. Poland, 9%; Canada, 6%; Germany, UK, Italy, 3% each; Hungary, 2%; USSR, Austria, Mexico, Czech., Ireland, 1% each; others, 5%.

Presidential vote

1968	Humphrey (D)	95,603	(60%)
	Nixon (R)	43,432	(27%)
	Wallace (AIP)	20,268	(13%)

Representative

John D. Dingell (D) Elected 1954; b. July 8, 1926, Colorado Springs, Colo.; home, Dearborn; Georgetown U., B.S., 1949, LL.B., 1952; Army, WWII; married, four children; Catholic.

Career Atty. 1952– ; Res. Asst. U.S. Dist. Judge Levin, 1952–53; Asst. Pros. Atty., Wayne Co., 1953–55.

Offices 2210 RHOB, 202-225-4071. Also 4917 Schaefer, Dearborn 48126, 313-846-1276.

Committees

Interstate and Foreign Commerce (5th); Sub. on Transportation and Aeronautics.

Merchant Marine and Fisheries (5th); Subs. (1) Chm., Fisheries and Wildlife Conservation, (2) Merchant Marine.

Sel. Com. on Small Business (5th) Subs. (1) Chm., Activities of Regulatory Agencies, (2) Taxation, Oil Imports, and Marketing.

Group Ratings

	ADA	COPE	NREP	NFU	LCV	CFA	NAB	NSI	ACA
1970	68	100	93	91	80	100	0	44	12
1969	80	—	—	86	—	—	—	—	25
1968	75	83	—	85	—	—	0	—	5

Key Votes

(1) ABM	FOR	(6) 18-Yr-Vote	FOR	(11) Clean Water $	FOR
(2) SST	AGN	(7) Farm Sub Lmt	FOR	(12) Mig Wrkrs Comp	FOR
(3) Phil Pln	AGN	(8) Coop-Church	FOR	(13) Jets to Chiang	AGN
(4) No-Knock	AGN	(9) Family Asst	FOR	(14) State OEO Veto	AGN
(5) Cmutr Tax	FOR	(10) Work Stamps	AGN	(15) Park Logging	AGN

Election Results

1970 general:	John D. Dingell (D)	90,540	(79%)
	William E. Rostron (R)	23,867	(21%)
1970 primary:	John D. Dingell (D), unopposed		
1968 general:	John D. Dingell (D)	105,690	(74%)
	Monte R. Bona (R)	37,000	(26%)

SEVENTEENTH DISTRICT Political Background

Michigan 17 is northwest Detroit, the most white-collar, most Protestant, and most Republican part of the city. Since Detroit's giant auto factories are all outside the district, it is almost entirely residential: neat one-family houses on straight, tree-shaded streets. Before 1954, the year of the first Mennen Williams landslide, the 17th was solidly Republican. Later it was counted as a politically marginal area, after it proved to be fertile ground for George Romney's kind of political evangelism. Recently the 17th has been trending Democratic, as blacks move into more of its comfortable neighborhoods, and whites—at least the more conservative of them—flee to the suburbs. The conservative Republicanism of Richard Nixon and Spiro Agnew has flopped here, and in 1970 the last Republican state legislator from the district was replaced by a Democrat.

In congressional elections, the 17th is the property of Martha Griffiths, who has been its congresswoman since 1954. Somewhat more conservative than most Michigan Democrats, Mrs. Griffiths has become phenomenally popular in her district. In 1964 she won 72% of the votes in the 17th, some 4% better than Lyndon Johnson. In

1970, against a Republican whose slogan "May the better man win" attracted some attention, she got a whopping 80% of the votes.

Mrs. Griffiths is now the 5th ranking member of the powerful House Ways and Means Committee, where she helps write tax and welfare legislation and doles out Democratic committee assignments. In the 91st Congress she steered the Women's Rights Amendment to passage in the House, only to see it die in the Senate. There have been some rumors that Rep. Griffiths, a lawyer who served briefly as a judge in Detroit, is being considered for a Supreme Court appointment by President Nixon. It might not be a bad political move: she is by no means a Warren Court follower on criminal law matters, and the appointment of a Democrat, and a woman, would be well received. It also might make it possible—but far from likely—for a Republican to win in the 17th district.

Census Data 1970 pop. 413,337; deviation from current state average, −11.5%; change 1960–70, −0.6%. Metro. 100%, 100% central city.

1970 Share of Federal Outlays $255,411,000 (average outlay per district Michigan 1, 12–19)

DOD	$54,215,000	HEW	$100,226,000
AEC	$104,000	HUD	$3,520,000
NASA	$102,000	OEO	$1,290,000
DOT	$7,702,000	DOA	$156,000
		Other	$88,095,000

Federal Military-Industrial Commitments (See Michigan 12 for greater Detroit listing.)

Economic Base Motor vehicles and motor vehicle equipment, and other transportation equipment; nonelectrical machinery, esp. metalworking machinery and equipment; fabricated metal products, esp. metal stampings; primary metal industries, esp. blast furnaces, steel works, and rolling and finishing mills.

The Voters

Registration 192,720 total. No party registration.

Employment profile White collar, 55%. Blue collar, 45%.

Ethnic groups Black, 24%. Total foreign stock, 43%. Canada, 10%; Poland, 6%; UK, 5%; USSR, Germany, 4% each; Italy, 2%; Austria, Hungary, Ireland, Czech., Sweden, 1% each; others, 7%.

Presidential vote

1968	Humphrey (D)	106,860	(60%)
	Nixon (R)	55,093	(31%)
	Wallace (AIP)	17,695	(10%)

Representative

Martha W. Griffiths (D) Elected 1954; b. Jan. 29, 1912, Pierce City, Mo.; home, Detroit; U. of Mo., B.A., 1934; U. of Mich., LL.B., 1940; married; Protestant.

Career State Rep., 1948–52; Judge and Recorder of Recorder's Court of Detroit, 1953.

Offices 1536 LHOB, 202-225-4961. Also 14615 Grand River, Detroit 48227, 313-273-6991.

Committees

Ways and Means (5th).

Jt. Economic Com. (5th); Subs. (1) Chm., Fiscal Policy, (2) Economic Progress, (3) Economic Statistics, (4) Inter-American Economic Relationships, (5) Priorities and Economy, (6) Urban Affairs.

Group Ratings

	ADA	COPE	NREP	NFU	LCV	CFA	NAB	NSI	ACA
1970	64	82	77	91	78	72	13	63	0
1969	53	—	—	86	—	—	—	—	8
1968	75	100	—	94	—	—	0	—	9

Key Votes

(1) ABM	ABS	(6) 18-Yr-Vote	FOR	(11) Clean Water $	FOR
(2) SST	AGN	(7) Farm Sub Lmt	FOR	(12) Mig Wrkrs Comp	AGN
(3) Phil Pln	ABS	(8) Coop-Church	FOR	(13) Jets to Chiang	AGN
(4) No-Knock	ABS	(9) Family Asst	ABS	(14) State OEO Veto	AGN
(5) Cmutr Tax	FOR	(10) Work Stamps	AGN	(15) Park Logging	AGN

Election Results

1970 general:	Martha W. Griffiths (D)	108,176	(80%)
	Thomas E. Klunzinger (R)	27,608	(20%)
1970 primary:	Martha W. Griffiths (D), unopposed		
1968 general:	Martha W. Griffiths (D)	123,376	(75%)
	John M. Siviter (R)	40,906	(25%)

EIGHTEENTH DISTRICT Political Background

Michigan 18, part of Oakland County, comprises the northwest suburbs of Detroit. The 18th has the highest per capita income and the highest proportion of white-collar workers of any district in the state. Its make-up, however, is far from homogeneous. The heavily Republican, high-income, WASPy suburbs of Birmingham and Bloomfield Hills are often thought to typify the district. But there is a substantial Jewish community in Oak Park and Southfield, which is just as heavily Democratic as Birmingham and Bloomfield Hills are Republican. The working-class suburbs on the east edge of the 18th also supply large Democratic margins. The political fulcrum of the district is its largest city, Royal Oak (pop. 85,000), where until recently Father Charles Coughlin, the populistic and, some said, pro-fascist radio priest of the '30's, had his church. Royal Oak, a middle-class, white-collar town, has usually gone Republican, but lately it has been trending Democratic. Thus in 1968, Humphrey carried the district, winning 47% of the votes, while Nixon got 46% and Wallace 8%. Most of the Wallace votes came from blue-collar areas.

Theoretically, the congressional election in the 18th is ready for a Democratic breakthrough, but incumbent (since 1956) William Broomfield has withstood every challenge so far without much trouble. His political secrets consist of an industrious use of the frank and a seat on the House Foreign Affairs Committee, where he is an ardent supporter of Israel. In every election, he has cut deeply into the normally Democratic Jewish vote and has at the same time maintained his strength in Birmingham-Bloomfield and his native Royal Oak. In 1970, Gus Scholle, leader of the state AFL-CIO, edged peace candidate Annetta Miller in a close primary to become the Democratic nominee; by this time Scholle, a 1968 hawk had also become a dove. The white-collar voters of the 18th, however, were apparently not ready to elect a labor leader to the House, and Broomfield won 65% of the votes.

Redistricting may well determine who represents the district in the '70's. Control over the process is split between the two parties: the Republicans have the governorship and the state Senate, while the Democrats control the state House. The census returns suggest that most of the current 18th will be combined with a part of heavily Democratic Macomb County to form a new district. If the Republicans allow such a plan to go through, Broomfield could have a very tough fight in 1972. Democratic possibilities include 1970 gubernatorial candidate Sander Levin or state Sen. Daniel Cooper.

Census Data 1970 pop. 527,262; deviation from current state average, +12.9%; change 1960–70, +26.5%. Metro. 100%, 0.0% central city.

1970 Share of Federal Outlays $255,411,000 (average outlay per district Michigan 1, 12–19)

DOD	$54,215,000	HEW	$100,226,000
AEC	$104,000	HUD	$3,520,000
NASA	$102,000	OEO	$1,290,000
DOT	$7,702,000	DOA	$156,000
		Other	$88,095,000

Federal Military-Industrial Commitments (See Michigan 12 for greater Detroit listing.)

Economic Base Nonelectrical machinery, esp. metalworking machinery and equipment; fabricated metal products, esp. fabricated structural metal products; motor vehicles and motor vehicle equipment, and other transportation equipment. Also, extensive commuting to Michigan 13 (Detroit central city).

The Voters

Registration 250,625 total. No party registration.

Employment profile White collar, 56%. Blue collar, 44%.

Ethnic groups Black, 1%. Total foreign stock, 30%. Canada, 9%; UK, 4%; Poland, Germany, 3% each; USSR, 2%; Italy, Austria, Sweden, Hungary, Ireland, 1% each; others, 5%.

Presidential vote

1968	Humphrey (D)	102,817	(47%)
	Nixon (R)	100,114	(46%)
	Wallace (AIP)	17,150	(8%)

Representative

William S. Broomfield (R) Elected 1957; b. April 28, 1922, Royal Oak; home, Royal Oak; Mich. State U., B.A., 1951; married, three children; Presbyterian.

Career State Rep., 1948–54; State Sen., 1954–56; U.S. Del. to 22nd UN General Assembly.

Offices 2435 RHOB, 202-225-6135. Also 1029 S. Washington, Royal Oak, 313-543-2400.

Committees

Foreign Affairs (3rd); Subs. (1) Africa, (2) Asian and Pacific Affairs, (3) National Security Policy and Scientific Development, (4) Sp. for Review of Foreign Aid.

Group Ratings

	ADA	COPE	NREP	NFU	LCV	CFA	NAB	NSI	ACA
1970	32	36	22	67	63	44	73	100	50
1969	13	—	—	60	—	—	—	—	44
1968	42	31	—	67	—	—	100	—	57

Key Votes

(1) ABM	FOR	(6) 18-Yr-Vote	FOR	(11) Clean Water $	FOR
(2) SST	AGN	(7) Farm Sub Lmt	FOR	(12) Mig Wrkrs Comp	AGN
(3) Phil Pln	FOR	(8) Coop-Church	ABS	(13) Jets to Chiang	FOR
(4) No-Knock	ABS	(9) Family Asst	FOR	(14) State OEO Veto	FOR
(5) Cmutr Tax	ABS	(10) Work Stamps	FOR	(15) Park Logging	AGN

Election Results

1970 general:	William S. Broomfield (R)	113,309	(65%)
	August Scholle (D)	62,081	(35%)
1970 primary:	William S. Broomfield (R), unopposed		
1968 general:	William S. Broomfield (R)	124,025	(60%)
	Allen Zemmol (D)	82,234	(40%)

NINETEENTH DISTRICT Political Background

Michigan 19 is an amalgam of several diverse suburban and exurban areas. In the southern part of the district are Redford Township (pop. 71,000) and Livonia (pop. 110,000), white-collar suburbs of Detroit. Both are politically marginal and usually reliable bellwethers of the statewide vote. In the north are Pontiac (pop. 85,000) and Waterford Township (pop. 58,000), economically dominated by General Motors (Pontiac and GMC Truck). Pontiac is more like Flint than Detroit: hostile black and Appalachian communities face each other from opposite sides of town, having in common only their Democratic voting allegiance. Waterford, somewhat more affluent and all-white, is more conservative, and was a Wallace stronghold in 1968. Except for the rapidly growing Republican suburbs of Farmington and Orchard Lake, the remainder of the 19th is a largely rural, politically marginal area with a slight Republican bias.

The 19th was a new district in 1964. Its first congressman was former state Auditor Billie S. Farnum, a Democrat with strong union backing. Farnum had the distinction of serving his freshman term on the House Appropriations Committee, but after the 1966 returns came in, it appeared that he had spent too much of his time on committee business and too little electioneering back home. Republican Jack McDonald of Redford was the winner and has been winning with just under 60% ever since. But he hasn't as yet been able to dent the Democratic strength in Pontiac.

Redistricting will probably make major alterations in the district, eliminating Redford and all or part of Livonia, and adding a heavily Republican portion of the 18th. Anticipating this, McDonald has moved his residence to Farmington. The odds are that he will be able to increase his margins in the new district.

Census Data 1970 pop. 565,599; deviation from current state average, +21.1%; change 1960–70, +36.5%. Metro. 100%, 0.0% central city.

1970 Share of Federal Outlays $255,411,000 (average outlay per district Michigan 1, 12–19)

DOD	$54,215,000	HEW	$100,226,000
AEC	$104,000	HUD	$3,520,000
NASA	$102,000	OEO	$1,290,000
DOT	$7,702,000	DOA	$156,000
		Other	$88,095,000

Federal Military-Industrial Commitments (See Michigan 12 for greater Detroit listing.)

Economic Base Nonelectrical machinery, esp. metalworking machinery and equipment; fabricated metal products, esp. fabricated structural metal products; motor vehicles and motor vehicle equipment, and other transportation equipment.

The Voters

Registration 217,930 total. No party registration.

Employment profile White collar, 44%. Blue collar, 55%.

Ethnic groups Black, 4%. Total foreign stock, 23%. Canada, 8%; UK, 4%; Germany, Poland, 2% each; Italy, USSR, Sweden, 1% each; others, 4%.

Presidential vote

1968	Humphrey (D)	84,889	(44%)
	Nixon (R)	85,847	(44%)
	Wallace (AIP)	23,238	(12%)

Representative

Jack H. McDonald (R) Elected 1966; b. June 28, 1932, Farmington; home, Redford Township; Wayne State U.; married, two children; Presbyterian.

Career Census supv., Wayne Co., 1960; supv., Redford Township, 1961–66; Chm., Wayne Co. Bd. of Supvs., 1965.

Offices 1204 LHOB, 202-225-2101. Also 23622 Farmington Rd., Farmington, 48024, 313-476-6220.

Committees

Merchant Marine and Fisheries (10th); Subs. (1) Coast Guard, Coast and Geodetic Survey and Navigation, (2) Fisheries and Wildlife Conservation, (3) Panama Canal.

Public Works (8th); Subs. (1) Flood Control and Internal Development, (2) Investigation and Oversight, (3) Public Buildings and Grounds, (4) Rivers and Harbors, (5) Roads.

Group Ratings

	ADA	COPE	NREP	NFU	LCV	CFA	NAB	NSI	ACA
1970	24	55	64	58	100	67	75	90	63
1969	40	—	—	50	—	—	—	—	56
1968	42	31	—	60	—	—	100	—	57

Key Votes

(1) ABM	FOR	(6) 18-Yr-Vote	FOR	(11) Clean Water $	FOR
(2) SST	AGN	(7) Farm Sub Lmt	FOR	(12) Mig Wrkrs Comp	AGN
(3) Phil Pln	AGN	(8) Coop-Church	ABS	(13) Jets to Chiang	AGN
(4) No-Knock	ABS	(9) Family Asst	FOR	(14) State OEO Veto	AGN
(5) Cmutr Tax	AGN	(10) Work Stamps	FOR	(15) Park Logging	ABS

Election Results

1970 general:	Jack McDonald (R)	91,763	(59%)
	Fred L. Harris (D)	63,175	(40%)
	Hector M. McGregor (AIP)	990	(1%)
1970 primary:	Jack McDonald (R), unopposed		
1968 general:	Jack McDonald (R)	104,057	(58%)
	Gary R. Frink (D)	75,250	(42%)

MINNESOTA

Political Background

Minnesota is a state which exports political talent: in recent years it has given the nation such diverse personalities as Hubert Humphrey and Eugene McCarthy, Supreme Court Justices Warren Burger and Harry Blackmun, and, to go back a few more years, Harold Stassen, who was once taken very seriously as a presidential candidate. These men all came out of a state whose politics seem, on the surface, quite ordinary, but which are unique and distinctive.

Set far north of the great paths of east-west migration (Minneapolis and St. Paul are about as far north as Portland, Maine), Minnesota grew as the hub of a northern economic empire. North and South Dakota and Montana, as well as the prairies and lakes of Minnesota itself, developed as economic tributaries of the grain-milling and railroad centers of Minneapolis–St. Paul. The Yankee and Midwestern immigrants who thronged to Iowa, Nebraska, and Kansas never made it up as far as Minnesota, leaving the state to the Norwegians and Swedes and Germans.

The state's ethnic history gave its politics a liberal, Scandinavian ambience. As in neighboring Wisconsin and North Dakota, a strong third party developed after the Populist era, and that organization, the Farmer-Labor party, dominated Minnesota politics into the 1930's. In the 1940's, after Harold Stassen swept the Republicans back into power, the Farmer-Labor movement waned. The group eventually joined forces with the heavily outnumbered Democrats to form the Democratic-Farmer-Labor party, which, under the leadership of young Minneapolis Mayor Hubert Humphrey, triumphed in the 1948 elections. The DFL—and Humphrey—have controlled the state politically ever since.

Since an ethnic map of Minnesota is also a political one, the ancestral origins of any community usually determine its political allegiance. One key to the map is that Norwegians, for some reason, are more Republican than the Swedes; the state's most heavily Norwegian county Otter Tail, remained loyal to the party in 1964 and went for Barry Goldwater. The pattern in the state's southern counties resembles the one in Iowa: WASP and German rural Republican counties and Democratic strongholds in some of the small cities like Austin and Albert Lea. The city of St. Paul, settled by Irish and German Catholics, has always been Democratic, while Minneapolis, founded by the Swedes, is somewhat less so. But the most Democratic part of Minnesota does not lie in the Twin Cities metropolitan area (which now contains almost half of the state's population) but in the north country, particularly around Duluth and the iron-bearing Mesabi Range. Here in the early days of settlement, the Swedes were joined by Finns, Poles, and other Eastern European ethnics—all of them with a strong attachment to the liberal programs of the Democratic party.

Without question, the most successful politician to come out of Minnesota is Hubert Humphrey. Despite his unpleasant 1968 experience, Humphrey is still a talkative man, in the Senate and on the campaign trail. His speech-making bubbles over with ideas for new policies, with slogans of past campaigns, with the inspirational, and with shameless clichés. The Senator has now changed his mind completely about Vietnam, admitting that he was wrong when he defended the policies of the Johnson Administration. The former Majority Whip (1961–64) has not given up entirely on another try for the White House, though he will not risk entering any presidential primaries. If he does declare, he can no doubt still count on the support of George Meany and the other aging warriors of the labor movement who constituted the bedrock of his strength in 1968.

The Senator has always been a strong vote-getter in Minnesota. In 1948 he trounced incumbent Republican Sen. Joseph Ball and subsequently won reelection easily in 1954 and 1960. In 1968, Humphrey, who did poorly almost everywhere else in the nation, carried his home state with a healthy 54% of the votes; and in 1970, when he decided to return to the Senate, he did even better, 58%, despite a strong effort by Republican Congressman Clark MacGregor. Humphrey carried all eight of the state's congressional districts and led the rest of the DFL ticket to its strongest showing since 1964. The party took the governorship, the state Senate, and captured one congressional seat while nearly winning over two others. Humphrey won small majorities in the conservative southern part of the state and a solid 60% in the Twin Cities area, but he was especially strong in the north country, where the recession accounted for very strong DFL showings. Another area of DFL strength was the fast-growing suburban territory west of Minneapolis. Here the party posted its biggest increases over its weak 1966 statewide performance and nearly elected a congressman.

The results of the 1970 elections in the state left the Republican party in rather sad shape. The Republicans ran a strong ticket in 1970, but the DFL ran a stronger one. And the state GOP is likely to face the same circumstances in upcoming elections. In 1972, Sen. Walter Mondale's seat is up, but few Republicans believe that this earnest, hard-working liberal can be beaten. Mondale was the state attorney general and already a remarkable vote-getter when he was appointed to take Humphrey's place in 1964. The Senator was reelected in 1966 with a solid 54% when the rest of the DFL ticket was going under. In Washington, Mondale sits on the Labor and Public Welfare and the Banking and the Housing and Urban Affairs committees; in both places he champions programs for the black and the poor. Mondale has been mentioned at times as a possible presidential candidate, but the Minnesota Senator, whose father was a minister, has a rather pious and pedestrian manner—a personal style unsuitable in the era of TV politics.

Because of setbacks in 1968 and 1970, Minnesota Republicans may change their tack and swing a bit to the right. Former Lt. Gov. James Goetz is the man who may try to lead the party in that direction; in 1970, he wanted the Republican gubernatorial nomination but lost out to the more liberal former Atty. Gen. Douglas Head. The Republicans still do have a piece of the redistricting action. The Minnesota legislature is technically nonpartisan but splits up into conservative and liberal caucuses, which correspond to the two major parties. Redistricters of both parties face a major problem that will require careful thought. The rapidly growing 3rd district (Minneapolis suburbs), now with a population of 680,236, has to be cut down to 475,634, the Minnesota district average. Part of the current 3rd will go to the politically marginal 6th. Depending on what is transferred, one of the two Republican incumbents in those two districts, both of whom won by narrow margins in 1970, will come up against a very tough race in 1972. Redistricting is unlikely to affect the chances of any of the state's other congressmen.

Electoral Votes 10

Census Data 1970 pop. 3,805,069; 1.85% of U.S. total, 19th largest; change 1960–70, +11.5%. Metro. 56.9%, 24.4% central city. 1970 per capita income, $3793; 19th highest. 27th in number of poor.

1970 Share of Federal Tax Burden $3,258,850,000; 1.67% of U.S. total, 20th largest.

1970 Share of Federal Outlays $3,259,153,333; 1.72% of U.S. total, 19th largest. Per capita federal spending, $857.

DOD	$707,971,000	25th (1.23%)	HEW	$950,175,184	17th (1.82%)
AEC	$3,669,734	28th (0.14%)	HUD	$9,993,566	13th (0.51%)
NASA	$30,669,602	16th (0.83%)	OEO	$9,375,347	6th (1.23%)
DOT	$143,587,058	17th (2.01%)	DOA	$637,992,065	3rd (4.96%)
DOC	$7,051,911	33rd (0.61%)	POD	$147,274,149	13th (2.02%)
DOI	$40,660,721	19th (1.76%)	VA	$200,914,663	16th (2.72%)
DOJ	$9,546,889	17th (1.66%)	CSC	$36,281,727	24th (0.90%)
			Other	$323,989,717	

Economic Base Livestock, dairy, and field crops; nonelectrical machinery, esp. office, computing, and accounting machines; food and kindred products, esp. meat products; printing, publishing, and allied industries, esp. commercial printing; ordnance and accessories; electrical machinery, equipment, and supplies; fabricated metal products, esp. fabricated structural metal products; paper and allied products, esp. converted paper and paperboard products other than containers and boxes, and paper mills other than building paper mills; professional, scientific, and controlling instruments, photographic and optical goods, watches and clocks, esp. engineering, laboratory, and scientific and research instruments and associated equipment; iron ore and other metal mining.

Political Line-up Governor, Wendell R. Anderson (D); seat up, 1974. Senators, Walter F. Mondale (D) and Hubert H. Humphrey (D). Representatives, 8 (4 D and 4 R). State Senate (67 nonpartisan senators); State House (135 nonpartisan representatives).

The Voters

Registration No statewide registration.

Employment profile White collar, 41%. Blue collar, 59%.

Ethnic groups Black, 1%. Total foreign stock, 26%. Germany, Sweden, Norway, 5% each; Canada, 2%; Poland, UK, Czech., USSR, Austria, 1% each; others, 6%.

Presidential vote

1968	Humphrey (D)	857,738	(54%)
	Nixon (R)	658,643	(42%)
	Wallace (AIP)	68,931	(4%)
1964	Johnson (D)	991,117	(64%)
	Goldwater (R)	559,624	(36%)
1960	Kennedy (D)	779,933	(51%)
	Nixon (R)	757,915	(49%)

Senator

Walter F. Mondale (D) Appt. to Sen., Dec. 1964, elected 1966, seat up 1972; b. Jan. 5, 1928, Ceylon, Minn.; home, Minneapolis; Macalester College, U. of Minn., B.A., 1951, LL.B., 1956; Army, 1951–53; married, three children; Presbyterian.

Career Atty. 1956–60; Minn. Atty. Gen. 1960–64.

Offices 443 OSOB, 1-202-225-5641. Also 170 Fed. Ctr. Bldg., Minneapolis 55401, 1-612-725-2041.

Committees

Banking, Housing, and Urban Affairs (5th); Subs. (1) Chm., International Finance, (2) Financial Institutions, (3) Housing and Urban Affairs, (4) Securities, (5) Small Business.

Labor and Public Welfare (6th); Subs. (1) Chm., Spec. on Social Programs, (2) Chm., Children and Youth, (3) Alcoholism and Narcotics, (4) Education, (5) Employment, Manpower, and Poverty, (6) Health, (7) Migratory Labor.

Sel. Com. on Equal Educational Opportunity (Chm.).

Sel. Com. on Nutrition and Human Needs (8th).

Sp. Com. on Aging (8th); Subs. (1) Chm., Retirement and the Individual, (2) Consumer Interests of the Elderly, (3) Employment and Retirement Incomes, (4) Health of the Elderly, (5) Housing for the Elderly.

Group Ratings

	ADA	COPE	NREP	NFU	LCV	NAB	NSI	ACA
1970	97	100	100	100	80	20	0	5
1969	94	—	—	94	—	—	—	7
1968	86	100	—	90	—	25	—	0

Key Votes

(1) ABM	AGN	(8) Phil Pln	FOR	(15) Coop-Church	FOR
(2) SST	AGN	(9) Vol Army	AGN	(16) Cut Oil Dpltn	FOR
(3) Busing	FOR	(10) Prison $	FOR	(17) Consumer Prot	FOR
(4) Tob Sub	ABS	(11) Cut Mil $	FOR	(18) Farm Sub Limit	FOR
(5) Carswell	AGN	(12) Defoliatn	AGN	(19) Comp Bid Sales	FOR
(6) No-Knock	AGN	(13) 18-Yr-Vote	FOR	(20) Pre-Prod Tests	ABS
(7) Seniorty	FOR	(14) Pentgn PR	AGN	(21) Cut Marjna Pen	FOR

Election Results

1966 general:	Walter F. Mondale (DFL)	685,840	(54%)
	Robert A. Forsythe (R)	574,868	(46%)
1966 primary:	Walter F. Mondale (DFL)	410,841	(91%)
	Ralph E. Franklin (DFL)	40,785	(9%)

Senator

Hubert Horatio Humphrey, Jr. (D) Elected 1970 (previously U.S. Senator, 1948–64); b. May 27, 1911, Wallace, S.D.; home, Minneapolis; Denver Col. of Pharmacy, 1932–33; U. Minn., A.B., 1939; U. La., A.M., 1940; U. Minn. graduate studies, 1940–41; married, four children; Protestant.

Career Adm. staff, WPA; Asst. State Supervisor, adult education, Minn.; war services div. chief, 1941–43; Asst. Dir. War Manpower Commission, 1943; vis. prof. of pol. science, Macalister Col., 1943–44; state campaign manager, Roosevelt-Truman campaign; Mayor, Minneapolis, 1945–48; U.S. Senate 1948–64, Majority Whip 1961–64; Vice Pres. 1965–69.

Offices 411 OSOB, 1-202-225-3244. Also 176 Fed. Bldg., Minneapolis 55401, 1-612-725-2533.

Committees

Agriculture and Forestry (7th); Subs. (1) Chm., Rural Development, (2) Agricultural Credit and Rural Electrification, (3) Agricultural Production and Marketing.

Government Operations (9th); Subs. (1) Executive Reorganization, (2) Nat'l. Security and Intl. Operations.

Joint Economic Committee (5th); Subs. (1) Fiscal Policy, (2) Foreign Economic Policy, (3) International Exchange and Payments, (4) Priorities and Economy in Government, (5) Urban Affairs.

Group Ratings, Key Votes: Newly elected.

Election Results

1970 general:	Hubert H. Humphrey (DFL)	788,256 (58%)
	Clark MacGregor (R)	568,025 (42%)
1970 primary:	Hubert H. Humphrey (DFL)	388,705 (79%)
	Earl D. Craig, Jr. (DFL)	88,709 (21%)

FIRST DISTRICT Political Background

Minnesota 1, the southeast corner of the state, is the Minnesota district that has most in common with the rest of the rural Midwest. The 1st, a region of farms, grain elevators, and small industrial cities, is much like Iowa in its ethnic and political traditions, WASP and Republican. The district's largest city is Rochester (pop. 53,000), the home of the Mayo Clinic and, until recently, of Supreme Court Justice Harry Blackmun. Rochester is a comparatively wealthy, idyllic, white-collar town; in 1970, Olmsted County, in which the town is located, was the largest county in the state that Humphrey could not carry.

The only discordant section of the district lies in Dakota County, just south of St. Paul, a predominantly blue-collar and Democratic suburban area—and also the 1st's fastest growing, up 78% in the '60's. Dakota has inched the district toward the DFL in recent statewide elections, but despite the trend, the 1st has continued to provide solid support for its Republican congressman, Albert Quie.

Quie, in the House since a 1958 special election, is now the ranking Republican on the Education and Labor Committee. On the committee, he, along with maverick Democrat Edith Green of Oregon, has helped to fashion much of the nation's educational and social legislation. The Minnesotan's views, like Mrs. Green's, tend to run somewhere between those of the most liberal Democrats and most conservative Republicans on Education and Labor. Only 47 in 1970, Quie will probably be the House Republicans' principal spokesman on this kind of legislation for some time to come.

Quie is very strong at the polls; he consistently runs ahead of his party's ticket, further ahead than any Minnesota congressman, Republican or DFL. In 1970, for example, he won with 69% of the votes, while Clark MacGregor could get only 47% against Hubert Humphrey in the 1st. Quie's only close call (55%) came in 1964, but as the years go on and as he sends out more franked mail, it is unlikely that the DFL will ever do so well again. Even if Quie were not the Republican candidate here, the district would remain a long shot for the DFL. The Minnesota liberals are usually content to concentrate their efforts on districts farther north and concede the 1st district to the Republicans.

Census Data 1970 pop. 523,177; deviation from current state average, +10.0%; change 1960–70, +19.2%. Metro. 42.8%, 10.3% central city.

1970 Share of Federal Outlays $269,806,617

DOD	$11,775,000	HEW	$105,247,471
AEC	$000	HUD	$1,850,000
NASA	$117,040	OEO	$329,434
DOT	$30,421,112	DOA	$57,531,007
		Other	$62,535,553

Federal Military-Industrial Commitments

None.

Economic Base Livestock, dairy, and field crops; food and kindred products, esp. meat products; nonelectrical machinery.

The Voters

Registration No district-wide registration.

Employment profile White collar, 36%. Blue collar, 64%.

Ethnic groups Black, less than 0.5%. Total foreign stock, 20%. Germany, 6%; Norway, 3%; Sweden, 2%; Canada, 1%; Czech., UK, Poland, 1%; others, 5%.

Presidential vote

1968	Humphrey (D)	102,299	(49%)
	Nixon (R)	98,996	(47%)
	Wallace (AIP)	8,056	(4%)

Representative

Albert Harold Quie (R) Elected 1958; b. Sept. 18, 1923, Dennison; home, Dennison; St. Olaf Col., B.A., 1950; USN, WWII; married, five children; Lutheran.

Career State Senator, 1954–57; Sec., Board of Supv. of Rice County Soil Conservation Dist.

Offices 2334 RHOB, 1-202-225-2271; Also Rm. 436, First Natl. Bank Bldg., Rochester 55901, 1-507-288-2384.

Committees

Education and Labor (Ranking Mbr.).

Group Ratings

	ADA	COPE	NREP	NFU	LCV	CFA	NAB	NSI	ACA
1970	40	34	42	67	43	62	73	90	53
1969	13	—	—	54	—	—	—	—	53
1968	17	25	—	63	—	—	100	—	70

Key Votes

(1) ABM	FOR	(6) 18-Yr-Vote	FOR	(11) Clean Water $	AGN
(2) SST	AGN	(7) Farm Sub Lmt	FOR	(12) Mig Wrkrs Comp	FOR
(3) Phil Pln	FOR	(8) Coop-Church	AGN	(13) Jets to Chiang	AGN
(4) No-Knock	FOR	(9) Family Asst	FOR	(14) State OEO Veto	FOR
(5) Cmutr Tax	AGN	(10) Work Stamps	FOR	(15) Park Logging	AGN

Election Results

1970 general:	Albert H. Quie (R)	121,802	(69%)
	B. A. Lundeen (DFL)	53,995	(31%)
1970 primary:	Albert H. Quie (R), unopposed		
1968 general:	Albert H. Quie (R)	138,400	(69%)
	George Daley (DFL)	62,916	(31%)

SECOND DISTRICT Political Background

Minnesota 2 is southwest Minnesota, the state's most Republican district. For the most part, the 2nd is a rural and agricultural district; its largest population concentrations lie in the old German and Scandinavian towns along the Minnesota River (St. Peter, Mankato, New Ulm) and in Carver and Scott counties, which are rapidly becoming part of the Minnesota–St. Paul urban area. Like the 1st, the 2nd is more WASP and German and less Scandinavian than the rest of Minnesota—a fact which explains its adherence to the Republican party.

Ancher Nelsen, the congressman from the district, is the most conservative member of the Minnesota delegation. After a long career in state politics and a post in the Eisenhower Administration, Nelsen entered the House in 1958. He has subsequently risen to become ranking minority member on the District of Columbia Committee and 3rd ranking member on Interstate and Foreign Commerce. Nelsen's conservative record seems to have prevented him from cutting the normal DFL vote as heavily as Albert Quie of the adjoining 1st district. But the Congressman has no real worries about reelection; only advancing age (66 in 1970) will endanger his career in the House.

Census Data 1970 pop. 395,564; deviation from current state average, −16.8%; change 1960–70, +5.4%. Metro. 0.0%, 0.0% central city.

1970 Share of Federal Outlays $309,078,347

DOD	$13,572,000	HEW	$93,566,593
AEC	$000	HUD	$2,849,633
NASA	$2,502,317	OEO	$598,242
DOT	$6,163,258	DOA	$134,854,935
		Other	$54,971,369

Federal Military-Industrial Commitments

None.

Economic Base Livestock and field crops; food and kindred products; electrical machinery, equipment, and supplies. Also, higher education (Mankato State College).

The Voters

Registration No district-wide registration.

Employment profile White collar, 31%. Blue collar, 69%.

Ethnic groups Black, less than 0.5%. Total foreign stock, 22%. Germany, 10%; Norway, 3%; Sweden, 2%; Czech., Canada, UK, USSR, Austria, 1% each; others, 4%.

Presidential vote

1968	Humphrey (D)	74,900	(44%)
	Nixon (R)	88,725	(52%)
	Wallace (AIP)	7,416	(4%)

Representative

Ancher Nelsen (R) Elected 1958; b. Oct. 11, 1904, Renville County; home, Hutchinson; married, three children; Lutheran.

Career State Senator, 1935–48; Lt. Gov., 1952; State Rep. Chm.

Offices 2329 RHOB, 1-202-225-2472. Also Citizens Bank Bldg., Hutchinson, 55350, 1-612-879-2002.

Committees

District of Columbia (Ranking Mbr.).

Interstate and Foreign Commerce (3rd); Sub. Number 4.

Group Ratings

	ADA	COPE	NREP	NFU	LCV	CFA	NAB	NSI	ACA
1970	16	0	17	46	11	44	90	100	72
1969	0	—	—	57	—	—	—	—	59
1968	8	9	—	25	—	—	100	—	85

Key Votes

(1) ABM	FOR	(6) 18-Yr-Vote	FOR	(11) Clean Water $	AGN
(2) SST	FOR	(7) Farm Sub Lmt	FOR	(12) Mig Wrkrs Comp	AGN
(3) Phil Pln	FOR	(8) Coop-Church	AGN	(13) Jets to Chiang	FOR
(4) No-Knock	FOR	(9) Family Asst	FOR	(14) State OEO Veto	FOR
(5) Cmutr Tax	AGN	(10) Work Stamps	FOR	(15) Park Logging	AGN

Election Results

1970 general:	Ancher Nelsen (R)	94,080	(63%)
	Clifford R. Adams (DFL)	54,498	(37%)
1970 primary:	Ancher Nelsen (R), unopposed		
1968 general:	Ancher Nelsen (R)	100,623	(60%)
	Jon Wefald (DFL)	68,528	(40%)

THIRD DISTRICT Political Background

Minnesota 3 is Anoka and Hennepin counties, except for that part of Hennepin that lies in the city of Minneapolis. The 3rd is the state's only entirely suburban congressional district. Like most suburban districts, it is not a sociological monolith: the general rule here seems to be that the closer any part of the 3rd is to St. Paul, the more Democratic it will be. Anoka, the smaller of the two counties (pop. 154,000) and the more industrial, has a large contingent of the Twin Cities blue-collar labor force living in communities like Columbia Heights, Fridely, and Coon Rapids. The Hennepin suburbs include Bloomington, predominantly Jewish St. Louis Park, and the wealthy towns of Edina, Golden Valley, Minnetonka, and Wayzata, the last four of which supply a disproportionate share of the 3rd's Republican votes.

From 1960 to 1970, the congressman from the 3rd was Clark MacGregor, who, despite his somewhat liberal voting record, was an early Nixon supporter in 1968. In 1970, he ran on the President's record in an unsuccessful bid for the Senate against Hubert Humphrey. Because Congressman MacGregor gave up sure reelection to make the 1970 race, which was a long shot at best, he was rewarded with the post of Counselor to the President for Legislative Liaison; that is, the White House's lobbyist. MacGregor received one of the highest-ranking jobs parceled out by the Administration to a defeated Republican candidate.

The race to succeed MacGregor, between Republican state Representative William Frenzel and DFL ex-TV-editorialist George Rice, was the state's closest. Frenzel, liberal Republican, carried Hennepin by 14,000 votes but lost Anoka to Rice by 11,000, making the totals: Frenzel 110,921, and Rice 108,141. The margin may well have resulted from Frenzel's well-publicized trip to Israel; a *Minneapolis Tribune* survey of the results showed the Republican running 31% ahead of Rice in a sample Jewish precinct—that figure represents almost enough votes in itself to make the difference.

The 3rd will be in the middle of the redistricting struggle between the Republican House and the DFL Governor. Because of heavy population growth in the '60's, the 3rd is now by far the largest Minnesota district—680,000, as against the statewide average of 475,000. One redistricting plan would place some 40,000 residents of the 3rd in the population-losing 5th (Minneapolis), which would then leave another 155,000 to take care of. As it happens, that is almost the exact population of Anoka County, which could be transferred to the rural 6th district. But heavily Democratic Anoka would endanger Republican John Zwach's hold on the 6th, and Zwach, who is a 32-year veteran of the state legislature and doubtless still has many friends there, would protest vigorously.

An alternative plan would place a marginal or Republican portion of Hennepin County in the 6th, a move that would hurt Frenzel's reelection chances. Predictions of the likely outcome of the 1972 races in these districts must await the passage of the redistricting plan.

Census Data 1970 pop. 680,236; deviation from current state average, +43.0%; change 1960–70, +52.6%. Metro. 100.0%, 0.0% central city.

1970 Share of Federal Outlays $600,389,000 (average outlay per district, Minnesota, 3–5)

DOD	$210,672,000	HEW	$138,326,000
AEC	$1,110,000	HUD	$10,944,000
NASA	$9,350,000	OEO	$707,000
DOT	$25,063,000	DOA	$73,007,000
		Other	$131,212,000

Federal Military-Industrial Commitments (See Minnesota 5 for greater Minneapolis–St. Paul listing.)

Economic Base Nonelectrical machinery, professional, scientific, and controlling instruments, photographic and optical goods, watches and clocks; printing, publishing, and allied industries, esp. commercial printing; electrical machinery, equipment, and supplies. Also, extensive commuting to Minnesota 4 and 5 (St. Paul and Minneapolis).

The Voters

Registration No district-wide registration.

Employment profile White collar, 55%. Blue collar, 45%.

Ethnic groups Black, less than 0.5%. Total foreign stock, 19%. Sweden, 4%; Norway, Germany, 3% each; Canada, 2%; UK, Poland, USSR, Czech., 1% each; others, 4%.

Presidential vote

1968	Humphrey (D)	136,013	(52%)
	Nixon (R)	116,344	(44%)
	Wallace (AIP)	10,277	(4%)

Representative

William E. Frenzel (R) Elected 1970; b. July 31, 1929, St. Paul; home, Golden Valley; Dartmouth Col., B.A., 1950, M.B.A., 1951; USNR 1951–54; married, three children; religion unspecified.

Career Minneapolis Terminal Warehouse Co., 1954–62, Pres. and Dir., 1960–62; State Rep., 1962–68.

Offices 1725 LHOB, 1-202-225-2871. Also 120 U.S. Courthouse, Minneapolis 55401, 1-612-725-2173, and 5219 Wayzata Blvd., St. Louis Park 55416, 1-612-546-2426.

Committees

Banking and Currency (15th); Subs. (1) Domestic Finance, (2) International Finance.

House Administration (10th); Subs. (1) Elections, (2) Library and Memorials.

Group Ratings, Key Votes: Newly elected.

Election Results

1970 general:	Bill Frenzel (R)	110,921	(51%)
	George Rice (DFL)	108,141	(49%)
1970 primary:	Bill Frenzel (R), unopposed		

FOURTH DISTRICT Political Background

Minnesota 4, Ramsey and Washington counties, is St. Paul and some of its suburbs. St. Paul, more than its twin Minneapolis, is an old river city, like St. Louis, Cincinnati, or Louisville farther down the Mississippi Valley. St. Paul was settled before Minneapolis and for a few years, as many more Irish and German Catholics came to live in it, was the larger of the two. St. Paul began as a transportation hub—a railroad center and a river port—while Minneapolis was from the beginning a mill town and is still the greatest grain-processing center in the nation. St. Paul's early immigrants gave it a Democratic stamp, long before the DFL was organized, and it remains a Democratic city to this day.

For ten years, before he went to the Senate in 1958, Eugene McCarthy was the 4th's congressman. While in the House, McCarthy, one of the founders of the liberal Democratic Study Group, was an energetic and busy man. He organized caucuses, wrote letters to constituents, and did all the other chores that most congressmen have to do—a rather difficult scene to imagine now, because McCarthy has since developed a rather deep antipathy to the hassle of day-to-day politics.

McCarthy's successor is Democratic Congressman Joseph E. Karth, a former labor union activist and state legislator. Karth's career in the House has been very different from that of his predecessor—a fact that is highlighted by his choice of committees, Merchant Marine and Fisheries and Science and Astronautics. On the latter, he ranks third in seniority behind two Democrats who are considerably older, and so one day Karth will probably become chairman of Science and Astronautics. Karth, unlike McCarthy, was not an early opponent of the Vietnam war; on questions of foreign policy the Congressman's views are pretty much in line with those of his longtime allies in the labor movement.

Karth's electoral performance in the 4th, considered a safe Democratic district, has usually been excellent. One exception to the pattern occurred in 1966, when Karth got only 53% of the vote; his showing was one example of the overconfidence which hurt many Democrats after the party's resounding success of 1964. But Karth has bounced back well, winning 74% in 1970. Redistricting will probably take Washington County out of the 4th and put it in the 8th district; currently Ramsey County, standing alone, has just 634 residents less than the average Minnesota district. If anything, the move will make Karth's safe seat slightly safer.

Census Data 1970 pop. 559,203; deviation from current state average, +17.6%; change 1960–70, +17.7%. Metro. 100.0%, 55.4% central city.

1970 Share of Federal Outlays $600,389,000 (average outlay per district, Minnesota 3–5)

DOD	$210,672,000	HEW	$138,326,000
AEC	$1,110,000	HUD	$10,944,000
NASA	$9,350,000	OEO	$707,000
DOT	$25,063,000	DOA	$73,007,000
		Other	$131,212,000

Federal Military-Industrial Commitments (See Minnesota 5 for greater Minneapolis–St. Paul listing.)

Economic Base Nonelectrical machinery, esp. office, computing, and accounting machines; ordnance and accessories; printing, publishing, and allied industries, esp. commercial printing. Also, banking and insurance.

The Voters

Registration No district-wide registration.

Employment profile White collar, 49%. Blue collar, 51%.

Ethnic groups Black, 2%. Total foreign stock, 25%. Germany, 5%; Sweden, 4%; Norway, Canada, 2%; Poland, Austria, UK, USSR, Ireland, Italy, Czech., 1% each.

Presidential vote

1968	Humphrey (D)	139,017	(62%)
	Nixon (R)	74,989	(34%)
	Wallace (AIP)	10,070	(5%)

Representative

Joseph E. Karth (D) Elected 1958; b. Aug. 26, 1922, New Brighton; home, St. Paul; U. of Neb.; Army, WWII; married, three children; Presbyterian.

Career Labor-management relations for oil, chemical and atomic workers, 1947–58; State Rep. 1950–58.

Offices 2432 RHOB, 1-202-225-6631. Also 124 Fed. Cts. Bldg., St. Paul 55101, 1-202-225-6631.

Committees

Merchant Marine and Fisheries (12th); Subs. (1) Fishing and Wildlife Conservation, (2) Merchant Marine, (3) Oceanography, (4) Panama Canal.

Science and Astronautics (3rd); Subs. (1) Chm., Space Sciences and Applications, (2) NASA Oversight.

Group Ratings

	ADA	COPE	NREP	NFU	LCV	CFA	NAB	NSI	ACA
1970	88	100	91	92	67	82	0	22	12
1969	87	—	—	100	—	—	—	—	21
1968	83	100	—	64	—	—	0	—	10

Key Votes

(1) ABM	FOR	(6) 18-Yr-Vote	FOR	(11) Clean Water $	FOR
(2) SST	AGN	(7) Farm Sub Lmt	ABS	(12) Mig Wrkrs Comp	FOR
(3) Phil Pln	AGN	(8) Coop-Church	FOR	(13) Jets to Chiang	AGN
(4) No-Knock	FOR	(9) Family Asst	FOR	(14) State OEO Veto	AGN
(5) Cmutr Tax	FOR	(10) Work Stamps	AGN	(15) Park Logging	AGN

Election Results

1970 general:	Joseph E. Karth (DFL)	131,263	(74%)
	Frank L. Loss (R)	45,680	(26%)
1970 primary:	Joseph E. Karth (DFL), unopposed		
1968 general:	Joseph E. Karth (DFL)	129,082	(61%)
	Emery Barrette (R)	81,392	(39%)

FIFTH DISTRICT Political Background

Minnesota 5 comprises the larger of the Twin Cities, Minneapolis, a grain-milling center. Pillsbury, General Mills, and Cream of Wheat have their headquarters here, and their machinery converts the wheat stored in grain elevators found all over western Minnesota, the Dakotas, and eastern Montana and Wyoming into flour and cereal. Two other Minnesota companies, Minneapolis Honeywell and Minnesota Mining and Manufacturing, are also headquartered in the 5th.

But the great business enterprises do not give the politics of Minneapolis its distinctiveness; that comes instead from the Swedish and other Scandinavian immigrants who have been coming to Minneapolis since the 1880's. The Scandinavians were probably attracted to Minneapolis and to the rest of the state for two reasons: first, because the north country looked and felt like home: hilly countrysides, thousands of lakes, and long cold winters; second, because there were economic opportunities here which native Americans, eager to head straight west out of Illinois and Missouri, missed completely. The Scandinavians have given Minneapolis, which is still virtually all white (96%), a liberal political tradition; the city has been hospitable to the Harold Stassens of the Republican party and the Hubert Humphreys of the DFL. Humphrey was mayor here from 1943 to 1948.

It was therefore a surprise when liberal academic Arthur Naftalin was succeeded as mayor of Minneapolis in 1969 by police detective Charles Stenvig, a law-and-order advocate. By big-city standards, Minneapolis is relatively placid; but Stenvig apparently touched on something in the make-up of the older, lower-income whites who stayed behind in the city and watched the great suburban exodus of the 1960's. And Minneapolis, of course, has no large black community which could have voted solidly against the law-and-order candidate. Another reason for Stenvig's victory was a split between the labor and peace-oriented elements in the DFL. The McCarthy people took over the party apparatus in 1968, but efforts to deliver votes for their candidates have failed dismally. And so, by 1971, the more disciplined labor troops, once opposed to Stenvig, wound up supporting him.

One local politician left uncomfortable by the split is Congressman Donald Fraser, a vigorous opponent of the war with longtime ties to the Humphrey and labor wings of the DFL. Fraser won his seat from veteran (1942–62) Republican Congressman Walter Judd after the 1962 redistricting. Judd, who keynoted his party's 1960 national convention, was especially noted for his devotion to the interests of Nationalist China. Fraser has won with solid, though not spectacular, majorities ever since—the 5th contains some Republican neighborhoods on the city's well-to-do south and west sides.

In 1970, the Stenvig victory apparently inspired some local politicians to challenge Fraser. The Congressman had conservative opposition in the DFL primary from city Alderman Joe Greenstein and in the general election from Republican Dick Enroth. Enroth had Stenvig's endorsement and won 42% of the votes—thus making the 5th one of only two Minnesota districts (the other was Albert Quie's 1st) where the DFL candidate failed to improve on his 1968 performance. Fraser was also the only one of the three incumbent Democratic congressmen to run behind Humphrey.

Fraser's performance indicates that the law-and-order appeal will still win votes in Minneapolis. The Congressman did not attempt to hide or camouflage his liberal stands on foreign and domestic policy (as has been advocated by Humphrey and Messrs. Scammon and Wattenberg). Part of Fraser's problem was the press of outside activities. He was chairman of the Democratic Study Group in the 91st Congress and succeeded Sen. George McGovern as head of the Democratic party's commission on reform of procedures used at the national convention. But in spite of this and the law-and-order candidacies, Fraser is still the congressman from the 5th district of Minnesota.

Redistricting will probably add a suburb or two to the district—which is likely to be somewhat more Republican than the city, but somewhat less susceptible to any appeal for law and order.

Census Data 1970 pop. 434,400; deviation from current state average, —8.7%; change 1960–70, —10.0%. Metro. 100.0%, 100.0% central city.

1970 Share of Federal Outlays $600,389,000 (average outlay per district, Minnesota 3–5)

DOD	$210,672,000	HEW	$138,326,000
AEC	$1,110,000	HUD	$10,944,000
NASA	$9,350,000	OEO	$707,000
DOT	$25,063,000	DOA	$73,007,000
		Other	$131,212,000

Federal Military-Industrial Commitments

DOD Contractors Honeywell, Inc. (St. Louis Park, Minneapolis, New Brighton, Hopkins), $272.671m: Rockeye bomb cluster components; fuel-air-explosive weapons system; Mk 46 torpedoes; grenade fuzes; bombs; development of Area Denial Artillery Munitions. FMC Corp. (Fridley and Minneapolis), $68.289m: M-13 guided missile launching systems; 54-caliber gun mounts. Federal Cartridge Corp. (Minneapolis), $63.470m: production of M-16 and 7.62-mm ammunition. Sperry Rand Corp. (St. Paul), $61.442m: computers for Tartar and Talos missile launch control systems. Northwest Airlines (St. Paul), $24.778m: cargo transport services. Donovan Construction (New Brighton), $24.760m: components for 155-mm projectiles. Control Data Corp. (Minneapolis), $17.057m: leasing of data-processing equipment to various DOD installations.

DOD Installations Minneapolis-St. Paul Airport AF (Minneapolis).

Economic Base Nonelectrical machinery; professional, scientific, and controlling instruments, photographic and optical goods, watches, and clocks; printing, publishing, and allied industries, esp. commercial printing. Also, higher education (University of Minnesota); insurance and banking.

The Voters

Registration No district-wide registration.

Employment profile White collar, 51%. Blue collar, 49%.

Ethnic groups Black, 4%. Total foreign stock, 31%. Sweden, 8%; Norway, 6%; Germany, 4%; Canada, Poland, USSR, 2% each; UK, Czech., Austria, Ireland, 1% each; others, 5%.

Presidential vote

1968	Humphrey (D)	114,721	(59%)
	Nixon (R)	70,016	(36%)
	Wallace (AIP)	8,455	(4%)

Representative

Donald M. Fraser (D) Elected 1963; b. Feb. 20, 1924, Minneapolis; home, Minneapolis; U. of Minn., B.A., 1944, LL.B., 1948; USNR, WWII; married, six children; religion unspecified.

Career Atty., 1948–62; State Senator, 1954–62.

Offices 1111 Cannon House Bldg., 1-202-225-4755. Also 180 Fed. Cts. Bldg., Minneapolis 55401, 1-612-725-2081.

Committees

District of Columbia (6th); Subs. (1) Business, Commerce, and Fiscal Affairs, (2) Education.

Group Ratings

	ADA	COPE	NREP	NFU	LCV	CFA	NAB	NSI	ACA
1970	96	100	100	85	100	100	0	0	12
1969	100	—	—	93	—	—	—	—	6
1968	92	92	—	100	—	—	0	—	0

Key Votes

(1) ABM	AGN	(6) 18-Yr-Vote	FOR	(11) Clean Water $	FOR
(2) SST	AGN	(7) Farm Sub Lmt	FOR	(12) Mig Wrkrs Comp	FOR
(3) Phil Pln	FOR	(8) Coop-Church	FOR	(13) Jets to Chiang	AGN
(4) No-Knock	ABS	(9) Family Asst	FOR	(14) State OEO Veto	AGN
(5) Cmutr Tax	ABS	(10) Work Stamps	AGN	(15) Park Logging	AGN

Election Results

1970 general:	Donald M. Fraser (DFL)	82,307	(57%)
	Dick Enroth (R)	61,682	(42%)
	Derrel Myers (SW)	783	(1%)
1970 primary:	Donald M. Fraser (DFL)	38,112	(74%)
	Joe Greenstein (DFL)	13,359	(26%)
1968 general:	Donald M. Fraser (DFL)	108,588	(58%)
	Harmon T. Ogdahl (R)	78,819	(42%)
	William C. Braatz (IG)	747	(1%)

SIXTH DISTRICT Political Background

Minnesota 6 is farm country, the beginnings of the great wheat-fields that sweep across the Dakotas and into Montana. Long freight-trains move through the landscape headed west toward the Pacific or east toward St. Paul and Chicago; almost every little crossroads town here has a grain elevator near the depot station. The voting patterns of the 6th, Minnesota's most marginal district, record the ethnic groups which settled in this part of the state: Republican Norwegians and WASPs, the Democratic Swedes, and ticket-switching German Catholics.

The German population is concentrated in Stearns County, the district's largest (pop. 95,000), which contains St. Cloud (pop. 39,000) and Sauk Centre (pop. 3,000). The latter was the boyhood home of Sinclair Lewis and the model for his *Main Street.* The Germans of Stearns were originally Democratic but have often supported Republicans. As Samuel Lubell pointed out in *The Future of American Politics,* German-Americans were the prototypical isolationists, against intervention in the days before World War II not for any abstract reason but because of a desire to avoid war with the old homeland. Though the Germans were the most intense isolationists, they were often joined by Scandinavians; the ethnic combination produced the nation's strongest isolationist voting bloc in Minnesota and its neighbors, Wisconsin and the Dakotas.

Recently the Germans of Stearns have become more and more Republican, unlike most of northern Minnesota, which is trending left. Apparently the German community has been less affected by the economic downturn in the nation and here in the district, and they are therefore more receptive to the Nixon-Agnew stand on social issues. In 1970, Humphrey barely managed to carry Stearns while he swept the rest of the 6th; in the same year, the county also played a pivotal role in the reelection victory of Republican Congressman John Zwach.

Zwach spent 32 years in the Minnesota legislature, the last eight (1958–66) as Senate Majority Leader. His decision to run for Congress in 1966 was a shrewd one; the DFL was having a bad year and the 6th's incumbent Alec Olson had won the preceding two elections by only narrow margins. Zwach defeated Olson with 51% of the vote and stretched his margin to 56% two years later. In 1970, the DFL put up a strong fight for the seat in the person of Terry Montgomery, the 32-year-old vice president of St. Cloud State College. Montgomery carried eight of the district's seventeen counties, but took only 44% of the votes in Stearns County; he lost Stearns by 3,606 votes and the district by 7,749 (47%). Zwach ran best in the southwest corner of the 6th, near the Republican 2nd and his own home town.

Redistricting will have a decisive effect on the political character of the district in the '70's, when the seat will become the clear possession of either the Republicans (see Minnesota 3), or the DFL. The loss of some of the southern counties to the 2nd, a very real possibility, would place Zwach in the 2nd with Republican incumbent Ancher Nelsen, in which case Zwach would probably choose to run in the 6th.

Census Data 1970 pop. 447,058; deviation from current state average, −6.0%; change 1960–70, +6.4%. Metro. 0.0%, 0.0% central city.

1970 Share of Federal Outlays $315,405,129

DOD	$9,108,000	HEW	$116,910,174
AEC	$340,900	HUD	$362,970
NASA	$000	OEO	$709,148
DOT	$4,801,445	DOA	$109,170,183
		Other	$74,002,409

Federal Military-Industrial Commitments

None.

Economic Base Dairy, livestock, and field crops; food and kindred products.

The Voters

Registration No district-wide registration.

Employment profile White collar, 30%. Blue collar, 70%.

Ethnic groups Black, less than 0.5%. Total foreign stock, 24%. Germany, 8%; Norway, 5%; Sweden, 4%; Canada, Poland, UK, 1% each; others, 5%.

Presidential vote

1968	Humphrey (D)	95,102	(51%)
	Nixon (R)	82,894	(44%)
	Wallace (AIP)	9,398	(5%)

Representative

John M. Zwach (R) Elected 1966; b. Feb. 8, 1907, Gales Township; home, Walnut Grove; U. of Minn., B.S., 1933; married, five children; Catholic.

Career State Rep., 1934–46; State Senator, 1946–66; Majority Leader, 1959–66.

Offices 1502 LHOB, 1-202-225-2331. Also 216 Federal Bldg., St. Cloud 56301, 1-612-251-2120.

Committees

Agriculture (8th); Subs. (1) Dairy and Poultry, (2) Domestic Marketing and Consumer Relations, (3) Livestock and Grains.

Veterans' Affairs (6th); Subs. (1) Education and Training, (2) Hospitals, (3) Insurance.

Group Ratings

	ADA	COPE	NREP	NFU	LCV	CFA	NAB	NSI	ACA
1970	44	50	36	82	67	68	64	89	56
1969	20	—	—	64	—	—	—	—	56
1968	8	42	—	69	—	—	100	—	77

Key Votes

(1) ABM	FOR	(6) 18-Yr-Vote	FOR	(11) Clean Water $	AGN
(2) SST	AGN	(7) Farm Sub Lmt	FOR	(12) Mig Wrkrs Comp	FOR
(3) Phil Pln	FOR	(8) Coop-Church	AGN	(13) Jets to Chiang	ABS
(4) No-Knock	FOR	(9) Family Asst	FOR	(14) State OEO Veto	FOR
(5) Cmutr Tax	AGN	(10) Work Stamps	FOR	(15) Park Logging	AGN

Election Results

1970 general:	John M. Zwach (R)	88,753	(52%)
	Terry Montgomery (DFL)	81,004	(47%)
	Richard Martin (Ind.)	1,625	(1%)
1970 primary:	John M. Zwach (R), unopposed		
1968 general:	John M. Zwach (R)	104,664	(56%)
	J. Buford Johnson (DFL)	81,578	(44%)

SEVENTH DISTRICT Political Background

Minnesota 7 is the northwest quarter of the state. The district is composed of lakes, forests, resorts, and, to the west near the North Dakota line, wheat fields. This is the legendary country of Paul Bunyan, whose statue can be found in Bemidji, in the heart of the lake area. Also here is Lake Itasca, the headwaters of the Mississippi.

The 7th, settled by hardy Swedish and Norwegian farmers and lumbermen, is one of Minnesota's prime marginal districts. Like the 6th, it votes for winners in statewide contests, and its congressional races are usually close, with the winner rarely receiving as much as 55% of the vote. The Republican stronghold here is Otter Tail County, heavily Norwegian; the DFL territory is more to the north, where the farmers of the once radical prairies were the backbone of the state's old Farmer-Labor party.

In the 1950's, the 7th district of Minnesota made news nationwide when DFL Rep. Coya Knutson's husband issued a public statement urging her to come home and mind the household. Male chauvinists in the 7th apparently sympathized with the husband, as Mrs. Knutson was defeated in the otherwise Democratic year of 1958. The Knutsons were divorced in 1962. The winner that year was state legislator Odin Langen, who spent six terms in the House; except for the Republican year of 1966, the Congressman barely managed to win each time out. Since Langen was one of Minnesota's more conservative Republicans, he was a prime DFL target for many years. In 1968, DFL candidate Bob Bergland came within 4,046 votes of taking the seat, and in 1970 he decided to try again.

Bergland spent time in Washington as an employee of the Department of Agriculture, but some years ago returned to his Roseau, Minnesota, farm. Bergland ran as a strong critic of the Nixon Administration's farm policy, while Langen bravely, though perhaps unwisely, defended the Administration. This was a thankless task in farm areas in 1970, as it was in the days of Ezra Taft Benson (whose name still crops up in Hubert Humphrey's oratory). The DFL's get-out-the-vote drive proved to be Bergland's strongest weapon. For the first time, the party used a statewide computer system to keep track of identified Democrats and to get them out on election day. The effort was particularly successful in the 7th, where the turnout dipped only 9% from the presidential year of 1968—the smallest such dip in the state. Bergland won handily, 79,378 to 67,296 (54%), one of the strongest showings against an incumbent in the entire nation. Bergland has taken a seat on the Agriculture Committee, where he will continue to criticize Administration farm policy. The Congressman will probably weather a Republican challenge and win reelection in 1972.

Census Data 1970 pop. 375,180; deviation from current state average, +21.1%; change 1960–70, –0.7%. Metro. 12.9%, 7.9% central city.

1970 Share of Federal Outlays $301,141,051

DOD	$7,274,000	HEW	$111,595,760
AEC	$000	HUD	$327,971
NASA	$000	OEO	$1,800,487
DOT	$8,869,916	DOA	$105,351,638
		Other	$65,921,279

Federal Military-Industrial Commitments

DOD Installations Baudette AF Station (Baudette).

Economic Base Dairy and field crops; food and kindred products; toys, amusement, sporting and athletic goods. Also, tourism (lakes).

The Voters

Registration No district-wide registration.

Employment profile White collar, 30%. Blue collar, 70%.

Ethnic groups Black, less than 0.5%. Total foreign stock, 28%. Norway, 10%; Germany, Sweden, 5% each; Canada, 2%; Czech., UK, Poland, 1% each; others, 3%.

Presidential vote

1968	Humphrey (D)	77,796	(48%)
	Nixon (R)	76,302	(47%)
	Wallace (AIP)	8,190	(5%)

Representative

Bob Bergland (D) Elected 1970; b. July 22, 1925, Roseau; home, Roseau; U. of Minn., 1946–48; married, seven children; Lutheran.

Career Farmer, Midwest area Dir. of Agric. Stabilization and Conservation Service, 1961–68; Sec. and Chm., Roseau County Democratic Farmer Labor Party of Minn., 1951–54.

Offices

1008 LHOB, 1-202-225-2165. Also 920 28th Ave. South, Moorehead 56560, 1-218-236-5050.

Committees

Agriculture (19th); Subs. (1) Conservation and Credit, (2) Livestock and Grains.

Group Ratings, Key Votes: Newly elected

Election Results

1970 general:	Bob Bergland (DFL)	79,378	(54%)
	Odin Langen (R)	67,296	(46%)
1970 primary:	Bob Bergland (DFL), unopposed		
1968 general:	Odin Langen (R)	83,113	(51%)
	Bob Bergland (DFL)	79,067	(49%)

EIGHTH DISTRICT Political Background

Minnesota 8 is the northeast corner of the state and centers on Duluth and the Mesabi Range. The 8th, rather than a district in Minneapolis-St. Paul, is Minnesota's most heavily Democratic; it usually turns in about 70% of its votes for statewide DFL candidates. The reasons lie in its economic and ethnic history. Like most of the area around Lake Superior, this is mining country, and the Mesabi Range, about 70 miles inland from Duluth, has long been the nation's leading source of iron ore. The ore comes by rail cars to Duluth, where it is loaded on huge Great Lakes freighters bound for Chicago, Gary, Detroit, Cleveland, and the overland route to Pittsburgh. The men who came to work the mines and the Duluth docks were mostly Swedes, Finns, Italians, Poles, and Yugoslavs; their hard economic lot and their ethnic background led them into the Democratic party. They voted heavily Democratic, as have their descendants. Now because the region is in economic decline—both Duluth and the Mesabi towns have lost population—the districts longstanding political bias has been intensified.

It is a measure of the 8th's Democratic strength that DFL Congressman John Blatnik was first elected to the House in 1947, the best Republican year since before the Great Depression. Blatnik has never had to worry about reelection (1970: 76%) and never will. With the enforced retirement of Baltimore's George Fallon, Blatnik became chairman of the House Public Works Committee. Since the Minnesotan has been strongly pro-conservation, the committee will most likely become less interested in building roads and canals and more interested in protecting the environment. Blatnik, one of the founders of the liberal Democratic Study Group, has a solid liberal record, though he is a less outspoken opponent of the war than many of the younger members.

Redistricting will probably add Washington County, just outside St. Paul, to the district, which will change nothing in the 8th's political balance.

Census Data 1970 pop. 390,251; deviation from current state average, —18.0%; change 1960–70, −1.9%. Metro. 56.6%, 25.8% central city.

1970 Share of Federal Outlays $262,554,376

DOD	$34,226,000	HEW	$107,850,621
AEC	$000	HUD	$11,749,554
NASA	$000	OEO	$792,063
DOT	$18,141,833	DOA	$12,064,428
		Other	$77,729,877

Federal Military-Industrial Commitments

DOD Installations Duluth Airport AF (Duluth). Finland AF Station (Finland).

Economic Base Iron and other metal mining; dairy; paper and allied products; food and kindred products. Also, tourism (lakes).

The Voters

Registration No district-wide registration.

Employment profile White collar, 36%. Blue collar, 64%.

Ethnic groups Black, less than 0.5%. Total foreign stock, 35%. Sweden, 8%; Norway, 4%; Canada, Germany, 3% each; Italy, 2%; Poland, UK, Austria, Czech., 1% each; others, 12%.

Presidential vote

1968	Humphrey (D)	117,890	(67%)
	Nixon (R)	50,377	(29%)
	Wallace (AIP)	7,069	(4%)

Representative

John A. Blatnick (D) Elected 1947; b. Aug. 17, 1911, Chisholm; home, Chisholm; Winona State Col., B.E., 1935; U. of Chicago; U. of Minn., 1941–42; Army Air Corps, WWII; married, three children; Catholic.

Career Teacher, school administration, 1932–40; State Senator, 1941–46.

Offices 2449 RHOB, 1-202-225-6211. Also 412 Federal Bldg., Duluth 55802, 1-218-727-7474.

Committees

Public Works (Chm.); Chm., Sub. on Economic Development Programs.

Group Ratings

	ADA	COPE	NREP	NFU	LCV	CFA	NAB	NSI	ACA
1970	76	92	90	91	88	100	0	44	7
1969	73	—	—	100	—	—	—	—	0
1968	75	100	—	94	—	—	0	—	0

Key Votes

(1) ABM	AGN	(6) 18-Yr-Vote	FOR	(11) Clean Water $	FOR
(2) SST	AGN	(7) Farm Sub Lmt	FOR	(12) Mig Wrkrs Comp	FOR
(3) Phil Pln	FOR	(8) Coop-Church	FOR	(13) Jets to Chiang	ABS
(4) No-Knock	ABS	(9) Family Asst	FOR	(14) State OEO Veto	AGN
(5) Cmutr Tax	FOR	(10) Work Stamps	AGN	(15) Park Logging	AGN

Election Results

1970 general:	John A. Blatnik (DFL)	118,149	(76%)
	Paul Reed (R)	38,369	(24%)
1970 primary:	John A. Blatnik (DFL)	57,343	(82%)
	John J. Perko (DFL)	12,248	(18%)
1968 general:	John A. Blatnik (DFL)	115,343	(68%)
	James A. Hennen (R)	55,209	(32%)

MISSISSIPPI

Political Background

Mississippi, a land of gentle hills and fertile river bottoms, was once the booming frontier of the American South. In the late 1820's, land-hungry Jacksonian farmers poured in from Tennessee and parts of North Carolina after the Chickasaws were cleared out of the central and northern parts of the state. These farmers and would-be planters (Faulkner's Thomas Sutpen was a farm boy who made it) eventually took control of the state away from a group of already established Whig planter-aristocrats who had settled around Natchez, to the south, at the turn of the eighteenth century. King Cotton is what brought both groups to Mississippi, and since cotton was then a labor-intensive crop, slaves were purchased in Virginia and the Carolinas and brought here by the thousands. In 1940, some seventy-five years after the Civil War, 49% of the state's population was black, and even today, after decades of black migration to Northern cities, Mississippi has the largest proportion of blacks of any state, 37%.

The presence of the black man has always been the central issue in Mississippi politics. From the end of Reconstruction in the 1880's to the mid-1960's, the franchise was a concern of whites only. But for some twenty years after Reconstruction, the black man was not completely shut out of the political process; he was a ward of the rich Delta planters, so-called "Bourbons," who had "redeemed" Mississippi from Northern carpetbaggers and who were then running the state. With slavery gone, the black man was the planter's cheapest source of tenant labor, and so the planter often defended his new economic interest, the ex-slaves. Shortly after the turn of the nineteenth century, the poor white farmers of the eastern hill country—descendants of the old Jacksonian boomers who failed to make good—worked another revolution in Mississippi politics and wrested control of the state's politics from the Bourbons. The political style of the poor whites, "rednecks" some called them, was a strange mix of buffoonery—the politician was first of all a yarn-swapper—of populistic humanitarianism—a poor white governor abolished the state's infamous convict-labor system—and, most important, of the most extreme form of race-baiting demagoguery imaginable. The rednecks feared and resented the wealth and social position of the Bourbons, and unlike the Bourbons, they were in no way dependent on the blacks, who were viewed as a threat, both economic and sexual. The poor whites' perception of the blacks accounted for the unmitigated fury of their racism. Faced with a new kind of Mississippi politics, the planter class soon tried to "outseg" the up-country politicians, but with little success—men like the notorious governor (1904–08) and U.S. senator (1913–19) James K. Vardaman and the equally notorious senator (1934–47) Theodore Bilbo were the absolute masters of Mississippi demagoguery.

Throughout the state's history, the moderating influence of urban life and, more particularly, of the businessman has been absent from Mississippi. Even today, it remains a rural state: Jackson, the capital and largest city, has just 153,000 residents, and Mississippi still exists as an economic colony of the cotton exchanges in Memphis and New Orleans.

In the 1960's, the central premise of the state's politics—the exclusion of the black man—was challenged. Hundreds of civil rights activists descended upon Mississippi and organized black voter-registration drives. Local black leaders began to emerge—Charles Evers, Aaron Henry, Fannie Lou Hamer, and so by the time federal registrars were sent into the state under the Voting Rights Act of 1965, Mississippi blacks were ready to register, and they did so by the thousands. Since that time, the classic sanctions against black participation—economic reprisals and physical violence—have still been used in many areas of the state. But in others, blacks were able to win control of local government; the most notable example of this was when Charles Evers was elected mayor of Fayette (pop. 1,725). In 1970 a black was elected to the state legislature, and in 1971, Evers announced that he was running as an independent for governor. No one expects him to beat Attorney William Waller (a moderate by white Mississippi standards), who will undoubtedly be the state's next governor. But in making a run at him, Evers hopes to poll a respectable percentage of the vote and to carry into office black local officials and state legislators.

The black voters, however, will never dominate the state politically, for the basic condition for black success—a split among the whites—is not present in Mississippi. The outmigration of blacks continues, and even if the registration figures of the remaining blacks were proportional to that of the whites, they would never make up more than 35% of the voting age population. Moreover, in 1970 the state legislature adopted a new set of voting laws designed to restrict black voter participation, and since Attorney General Mitchell's Justice department has approved this particular strategem, more of them will doubtless follow.

A minority can have plenty of political clout if the majority happens to be divided. But because the civil rights revolution put an end to the old Delta-versus-hills struggles of the whites, the Mississippi white majority has voted with near-perfect solidarity. In 1968, when black voters accounted for virtually all of Humphrey's 23% of the state's votes, Nixon was brushed aside with 14%, as the whites united behind Wallace, giving him 63%. The Republicans have also been a negligible force in state and local politics. This means that the Democrats do not have to cultivate the black vote, as they have been forced to do in Strom Thurmond's South Carolina. Since black voters in Mississippi can in no way deliver margins essential to Democratic victory, they have no bargaining strength. Moreover, the pockets of potential black voting majorities are shrinking. The nine counties carried by Humphrey in 1968 contain only 8% of the state's residents and declined 13% in population during the '60's.

So even as the integration of the state's school system continues, and as blacks win control of some local governments, the bulk of the political power here remains in white hands. The governorship and the legislature are still strongholds of segregationists and the conservative, anti-civil rights Mississippi congressional delegation continues to accumulate seniority with little fear of deposition.

Both of the state's senators have been in office since the '40's and both will be re-elected as long as they care to run. The senior senator, James O. Eastland, has been chairman of the Senate Judiciary Committee since the late '50's. There was a time when Eastland could—and did—bottle up civil rights legislation single-handedly. But those days are gone, because most of the Democrats and many of the Republicans now on his committee are Northern liberals. Eastland can still use the chairman's power, however, to schedule and delay to some effect, and his opposition to any measure is not to be taken lightly.

The state's junior senator, John C. Stennis, is the pro-Pentagon chairman of the Armed Services Committee. He was, for example, the Senate's chief backer of the ABM, and despite the close vote on that particular issue, Stennis is considered an able floor manager of legislation. The Senator and former judge also has a reputation for unshakable integrity, which resulted in his appointment as chairman of the Senate Select Committee on Standards and Conduct.

Stennis is not an unthinking Mississippi reactionary. Noting that Southern schools are now more fully integrated than those in the North, he has proposed legislation that would require all regions of the country to meet equal integration standards. Moreover, the chairman of Armed Services has begun to question, on constitutional grounds, the legitimacy of the Vietnam war and has sponsored a bill that would prevent future presidents from involving the nation in similar wars without congressional approval.

Today, as in the past, Mississippi's delegation in the House has a great deal of seniority. William Colmer of the 5th district is chairman of the Rules Committee; Jamie Whitten of the 2nd is the number two Democrat on Appropriations; and Thomas Abernethy of the 1st, a fifteen-term veteran, holds high-ranking positions on the Agriculture and District of Columbia committees. None of these men will ever face trouble at the polls. In 1966, after it became obvious that large numbers of blacks were going to be able to vote, the Mississippi legislature redrew the congressional district lines to prevent even the slightest possibility of a black victory. A similar kind of plan will no doubt be adopted in the future.

Electoral Votes 7

Census Data 1970 pop. 2,216,912; 1.08% of U.S. total, 30th largest; change 1960–70, +1.8%. Metro. 17.7%, 11.0% central city. 1970 per capita income, $2561; 51st highest. 13th in number of poor.

1970 Share of Federal Tax Burden $1,151,330,000; 0.59% of U.S. total, 35th largest.

1970 Share of Federal Outlays $2,322,530,463; 1.23% of U.S. total, 28th largest. Per capita federal spending, $1048.

DOD	$809,566,000	22nd (1.41%)	HEW	$549,622,946	30th (1.05%)
AEC	$72,676	47th (—)	HUD	$34,300,901	21st (1.76%)
NASA	$1,969,853	32nd (0.05%)	OEO	$13,061,984	19th (1.72%)
DOT	$92,980,183	29th (1.30%)	DOA	$372,261,953	12th (2.90%)
DOC	$37,890,682	7th (3.28%)	POD	$47,929,041	36th (0.66%)
DOI	$16,993,341	36th (0.74%)	VA	$114,690,799	29th (1.55%)
DOJ	$3,641,658	36th (0.63%)	CSC	$23,537,084	35th (0.58%)
			Other	$204,011,362	

Economic Base Cotton, livestock, and soybeans; primary metal industries, esp. iron and steel foundries; lumber and wood products other than furniture, esp. saw mills and planing mills; food and kindred products; transportation equipment, esp. ship and boat building and repairing; electrical machinery, equipment, and supplies; household furniture and other furniture and fixtures; fabricated metal products, esp. fabricated structural metal products; nonelectrical machinery; textile mill products, esp. knitting mills.

Political Line-up Governor, John Bell Williams (D); seat up, 1971. Senators, James O. Eastland (D) and John C. Stennis (D). Representatives, 5 (5 D and 0 R). State Senate (54 D and 2 R); State House (122 D, 1 R, and 1 Ind.)

The Voters

Registration No statewide registration.

Employment profile White collar, 29%. Blue collar, 71%.

Ethnic groups Black, 37%. Total foreign stock, 1%. All groups less than 0.5% each.

Presidential vote

1968	Humphrey (D)	150,644	(23%)
	Nixon (R)	88,516	(14%)
	Wallace (AIP)	415,349	(63%)
1964	Johnson (D)	52,618	(13%)
	Goldwater (R)	356,528	(87%)
1960	Kennedy (D)	108,362	(60%)
	Nixon (R)	73,561	(40%)

Senator

James O. Eastland (D) Elected 1942, seat up 1972; b. Nov. 28, 1904, Doddsville; home, Doddsville; U. of Miss.; Vanderbilt U.; U. of Ala.; married, four children; Methodist.

Career State Rep., 1928–32; practicing atty., 1932–41.

Offices 2241 NSOB, 1-202-225-5054. Also 532 P.O. Bldg., Jackson 39205, 1-601-352-6298, and Ruleville 38771, 1-601-756-4766.

Committees

Agriculture and Forestry (3rd); Subs. (1) Chm., Environment, Soil Conservation, Forestry, (2) Agricultural Production, Marketing, and Stabilization of Prices, (3) Agricultural Research and General Legislation.

Judiciary (Chm.); Subs. (1) Chm., Immigration and Naturalization, (2) Chm., Internal Security, (3) Constitutional Amendments, (4) Criminal Laws and Procedures.

Group Ratings

	ADA	COPE	NREP	NFU	LCV	NAB	NSI	ACA
1970	3	18	11	22	3	56	100	80
1969	0	—	—	47	—	—	—	78
1968	0	0	—	20	—	25	—	75

Key Votes

(1) ABM	FOR	(8) Phil Pln	ABS	(15) Coop-Church	AGN
(2) SST	FOR	(9) Vol Army	AGN	(16) Cut Oil Dpltn	AGN
(3) Busing	AGN	(10) Prison $	AGN	(17) Consumer Prot	ABS
(4) Tob Sub	FOR	(11) Cut Mil $	AGN	(18) Farm Sub Limit	AGN
(5) Carswell	FOR	(12) Defoliatn	FOR	(19) Comp Bid Sales	AGN
(6) No-Knock	AGN	(13) 18-Yr-Vote	AGN	(20) Pre-Prod Tests	ABS
(7) Seniorty	AGN	(14) Pentgn PR	FOR	(21) Cut Marjna Pen	AGN

Election Results

1966 general:	James O. Eastland (D)	258,248	(66%)
	Prentiss Walker (R)	105,150	(27%)
	Clifton R. Whitley (Ind.)	30,502	(8%)
1966 primary:	James O. Eastland (D)	240,171	(83%)
	Clifton Whitley (D)	34,323	(12%)
	Charles P. Mosby, Jr. (D)	14,591	(5%)
1960 general:	James O. Eastland (D)	244,341	(92%)
	Joe A. Moore (R)	21,807	(8%)

Senator

John C. Stennis (D) Elected 1947, seat up 1976; b. Aug. 3, 1901, Kemper County; home, De Kalb; Miss. State U., B.S., 1923; U. of Va., LL.B., 1928; married, two children; Presbyterian.

Career State Rep., 1928–32; dist. atty., 16th Judicial Dist., 1931–37; circuit judge, 1937–47.

Offices 209 OSOB, 1-202-225-6253. Also 303 P.O. Bldg., Jackson 39201, 1-601-353-5494.

Committees

Aeronautical and Space Sciences (4th).

Appropriations (4th); Subs. (1) Chm., Public Works, (2) Agriculture, Environmental and Consumer Protection, (3) Defense and Intelligence, (4) Labor and HEW and Related Agencies, (5) HUD, Space, and Science, (6) Transportation.

Armed Services (Chm.); Subs. (1) Chm., Central Intelligence Agency, (2) Chm., Preparedness Investigating, (3) Chm., Sp. to Review Bomber Defense, (4) Strategic Arms Limitation Talks.

Sel. Com. on Standards and Conduct (Chm.).

Group Ratings

	ADA	COPE	NREP	NFU	LCV	NAB	NSI	ACA
1970	9	17	8	29	22	70	100	80
1969	6	—	—	47	—	—	—	88
1968	0	9	—	25	—	33	—	68

Key Votes

(1) ABM	FOR	(8) Phil Pln	AGN	(15) Coop-Church	AGN
(2) SST	FOR	(9) Vol Army	AGN	(16) Cut Oil Dpltn	AGN
(3) Busing	AGN	(10) Prison $	AGN	(17) Consumer Prot	FOR
(4) Tob Sub	FOR	(11) Cut Mil $	AGN	(18) Farm Sub Limit	AGN
(5) Carswell	FOR	(12) Defoliatn	FOR	(19) Comp Bid Sales	AGN
(6) No-Knock	AGN	(13) 18-Yr-Vote	AGN	(20) Pre-Prod Tests	AGN
(7) Seniorty	AGN	(14) Pentgn PR	FOR	(21) Cut Marjna Pen	AGN

Election Results

1970 general:	John C. Stennis (D)	286,622	(88%)
	William R. Thompson (Ind.)	37,593	(12%)
1970 primary:	Results not consolidated by the Mississippi Secretary of State.		
1964 general:	John C. Stennis (D), unopposed		

FIRST DISTRICT Political Background

Mississippi 1 spans the north central section of the state, from the Mississippi River to the hill country along the Alabama border. The flat and incredibly fertile land in the east, between the great river and the smaller Yazoo, is the Delta, the most famous part of the state. The Delta was not developed fully until after the Civil War, but it soon became the region of the state's largest and most productive cotton plantations. As a result, it also became the part of Mississippi with the greatest concentrations of black people, and blacks still constitute a majority in most Delta counties. Since the rich Delta counties and the poor hill country of the east were traditional political enemies, they were never before placed in the same congressional district. But in 1966 the lines were redrawn to assure that blacks did not seize control of the old Delta district: the threat of black voting strength created by the Voting Rights Act of 1965 united the Delta and up-country whites.

In 1960, 51% of the 1st's population was black, but after another decade of black outmigration, the figure fell to 46% (1970). Still, the large minority would be expected to exert a considerable amount of political power. It does not. In the rural Delta counties, the whites still control the livelihoods of most blacks, and that, coupled with occasional threats of violence, keeps the Negro vote in its proper place. As it is, the seniority of the 1st's congressman, Thomas G. Abernethy, is preserved.

Abernethy has been in the House since 1942, and only the slightly greater seniority of W. R. Poage of Texas and John McMillan of South Carolina stands between him and the chairmanship of the powerful Agriculture Committee. But Abernethy has not been heard to complain about this, since he is presently chairman of Agriculture's Cotton subcommittee. That post gives him control over the price-support program, one of considerable importance to some of his constituents. Sen. James Eastland, for example, receives about $160,000 annually for not growing cotton on his plantations in Sunflower County. On the other hand, Abernethy is, of course, a stern foe of government handout programs, like those which distribute food to undernourished people.

Abernethy is also a ranking member of the House District of Columbia Committee, whose conservative majority governs the capitol in a fashion contrary to the wishes of most of its residents. Abernethy, who was 67 in 1970, will succeed John McMillan to the chairmanship of the District committee should McMillan retire or leave the District chairmanship to chair Agriculture, which may be vacated by the retirement of Bob Poage. It is also possible that both Poage and McMillan will retire in time to give Abernethy the chair in Agriculture. Thirty-odd years of congressional service open up such possibilities.

Census Data 1970 pop. 422,283; deviation from current state average, —4.8%; change 1960–70, −6.0%. Metro. 0.0%, 0.0% central city.

1970 Share of Federal Outlays $315,493,765

DOD	$43,026,000	HEW	$106,800,743
AEC	$000	HUD	$3,105,869
NASA	$389,636	OEO	$4,953,268

DOT	$4,151,687	DOA	$122,801,440
		Other	$66,265,122

Federal Military-Industrial Commitments

DOD Installations Columbus AFB (Columbus).

Economic Base Cotton and livestock; lumber and wood products other than furniture; apparel and other finished products made from fabric and similar materials, esp. men's, youths', and boys' separate trousers.

The Voters

Registration No district-wide registration.

Employment profile White collar, 26%. Blue collar, 74%.

Ethnic groups Black, 46%. Total foreign stock, 1%. All groups less than 0.5% each.

Presidential vote

1968	Humphrey (D)	29,392	(26%)
	Nixon (R)	15,273	(14%)
	Wallace (AIP)	68,020	(60%)

Representative

Thomas Gerstle Abernethy (D) Elected 1942; b. May 16, 1908, Europa; home, Okolona: U. of Ala.; Cumberland U., LL.B., 1924; U. of Miss.; married, three children; Methodist.

Career Atty., 1925–42; Mayor, Europa, 1927–29; dist. atty., 3rd Jud. Dist., 1936–42.

Offices 2371 RHOB, 1-202-225-5876. Also P.O. Bldg., Okolona 38660.

Committees

Agriculture (3rd); Subs. (1) Chm., Cotton, (2) Department Operations.

District of Columbia (2nd); Subs. (1) Business, Commerce, and Fiscal Affairs, (2) Judiciary.

Group Ratings

	ADA	COPE	NREP	NFU	LCV	CFA	NAB	NSI	ACA
1970	0	25	0	15	11	30	82	100	89
1969	7	—	—	21	—	—	—	—	87
1968	0	0	—	27	—	—	100	—	95

Key Votes

(1) ABM	FOR	(6) 18-Yr-Vote	AGN	(11) Clean Water $	AGN
(2) SST	FOR	(7) Farm Sub Lmt	AGN	(12) Mig Wrkrs Comp	AGN
(3) Phil Pln	AGN	(8) Coop-Church	AGN	(13) Jets to Chiang	ABS
(4) No-Knock	FOR	(9) Family Asst	AGN	(14) State OEO Veto	FOR
(5) Cmutr Tax	AGN	(10) Work Stamps	FOR	(15) Park Logging	FOR

Election Results

1970 general:	Thomas G. Abernethy (D), unopposed
1970 primary:	Thomas G. Abernethy (D), unopposed
1968 general:	Thomas G. Abernethy (D), unopposed

SECOND DISTRICT Political Background

Mississippi 2, the northernmost section of the state, spans the gamut of Mississippi's geopolitical terrain, running from the cotton-rich Delta to the Tennessee River in the state's northwest corner. The black majority in most of the Delta counties is becoming politically active, fighting the white establishment that has controlled the area since Reconstruction. As one moves east toward the hills, there are fewer and fewer blacks.

In the northeast corner is Tishomingo County, which had Union and Republican sympathies during the Civil War and which in 1968 was the only Mississippi county to give Richard Nixon a plurality of its votes. In the middle of the 2nd lies Oxford, site of Ole Miss and lifelong residence of William Faulkner.

The 2nd represents the median Mississippi congressional district. Its voting pattern in the 1968 presidential election was almost the same as the pattern statewide: white residents preferred Wallace to Nixon four to one—about the same margin they gave Goldwater over Johnson in 1964—while the blacks cast 23% of the district's votes for Humphrey.

Congressman Jamie Whitten has represented the 2nd district and its predecessors ever since he won a special election a month before Pearl Harbor; currently, only ten members of the House have been there longer. Whitten is a Delta man, from Tallahatchie County. Before the 1966 redistricting his constituency comprised nearly all of the Delta, which then had a voteless 59% black majority. Whitten has always been supported by rich Delta planters; the Congressman can do things for them as chairman of the Agriculture subcommittee of the Appropriations Committee. Like other members of the Mississippi delegation, Whitten backs large subsidies for owners of big cotton plantations and opposes programs to feed the poor.

Because he controls the pursestrings of the Department of Agriculture, he is able to promote his views effectively within that bureaucracy no matter which party happens to control the White House. Whitten, who was sixty in 1970 (young for a thirty-year veteran), is in line to succeed Texas' George Mahon, who is ten years older, as chairman of the Appropriations Committee. So, barring an audacious move by House liberals, Whitten will some day soon have vast power over the federal budget.

At the beginning of the 92nd Congress, Whitten's subcommittee was given jurisdiction over environmental programs, to the horror of ecology activists. These activists were surprisingly successful unseating congressmen not to their liking in the 1970 elections. But there is little they can do about Whitten. Blacks now make up only 34% of Whitten's constituency, and ecology will never replace race as the major concern of the district's white voters.

Census Data 1970 pop. 433,825; deviation from current state average, —2.2%; change 1960–70, +1.5%. Metro. 0.0%, 0.0% central city.

1970 Share of Federal Outlays $304,981,316

DOD	$19,403,000	HEW	$101,441,866
AEC	$72,676	HUD	$7,562,346
NASA	$000	OEO	$2,249,564
DOT	$6,812,985	DOA	$106,769,413
		Other	$60,669,466

Federal Military-Industrial Commitments

DOD Contractors Poloron Products Inc. (Batesville), $8.151m: fin assemblies for 500-pound bombs.

Economic Base Cotton and livestock; apparel and other finished products made from fabrics and similar materials, esp. men's, youths', and boys' furnishings, work clothing, and allied garments; food and kindred products.

The Voters

Registration No district-wide registration.

Employment profile White collar, 23%. Blue collar, 77%.

Ethnic groups Black, 34%. Total foreign stock, 1%. All groups less than 0.5% each.

Presidential vote

1968	Humphrey (D)	29,660	(23%)
	Nixon (R)	17,832	(14%)
	Wallace (AIP)	82,062	(63%)

Representative

Jamie L. Whitten (D) Elected 1940; b. April 18, 1910, Cascilla; home, Charleston; U. of Miss.; married, two children; Presbyterian.

Career State Rep., 1931; dist. atty., 1933.

Offices 2413 RHOB, 1-202-225-4306. Also P.O. Bldg., Charleston 38921, 1-601-647-2413.

Committees

Appropriations (2nd); Subs. (1) Chm., Agriculture, Environmental and Consumer Protection, (2) Defense, (3) Public Works. *Jt. Com. on Reduction of Federal Expenditures* (2nd).

Group Ratings

	ADA	COPE	NREP	NFU	LCV	CFA	NAB	NSI	ACA
1970	4	25	8	23	17	67	64	100	71
1969	13	—	—	33	—	—	—	—	88
1968	17	8	—	31	—	—	60	—	80

Key Votes

(1) ABM	ABS	(6) 18-Yr-Vote	AGN	(11) Clean Water $	AGN
(2) SST	FOR	(7) Farm Sub Lmt	AGN	(12) Mig Wrkrs Comp	AGN
(3) Phil Pln	AGN	(8) Coop-Church	AGN	(13) Jets to Chiang	FOR
(4) No-Knock	FOR	(9) Family Asst	AGN	(14) State OEO Veto	FOR
(5) Cmutr Tax	AGN	(10) Work Stamps	FOR	(15) Park Logging	FOR

Election Results

1970 general:	Jamie L. Whitten (D)	51,689	(86%)
	Eugene Carter (Ind.)	8,092	(14%)
1970 primary:	Jamie L. Whitten (D), unopposed		
1968 general:	Jamie L. Whitten (D), unopposed		

THIRD DISTRICT Political Background

Mississippi 3 includes Jackson, the state's capital and largest city (pop. 153,000); Jackson and surrounding Hinds County contain almost half of the 3rd's residents. Most of the rest live along the Mississippi River in the fabled towns of Vicksburg and Natchez and in the small black-majority counties of Wilkinson, Claiborne, and Jefferson.

The last of these is the home of Charles Evers, the brother of the slain civil rights leader and the present mayor of Fayette. In 1968 a special election was called to fill the vacancy created when the district's congressman, John Bell Williams, was elected governor. Evers finished first in the initial primary—leading to hopes (and fears) that he might became Mississippi's first black congressman since Reconstruction. It was not to be, of course. Charles Griffin, Williams' administrative assistant, took virtually all the white votes in the runoff and won with a solid majority. Griffin is considered a moderate by Mississippi standards, but by any other he is a staunch conservative.

John Bell Williams, for whom Griffin worked for almost twenty years, is one of the South's most outspoken segregationists. In 1965 the Democratic Caucus stripped the Congressman of his seniority because he had supported Goldwater the year before. In the normal course of things, Williams, who had been in the House since 1946, would have become chairman of Interstate and Foreign Commerce in 1966. And since he was not yet 50 at the time, he would have remained chairman for a quarter of a century. Reduced to freshman status in Washington and elevated to martyrdom at home, Williams ran for governor in 1967 and won easily.

Mississippi Republicans, who have had some limited success in the state's urban areas, picked the 3rd for a major effort in 1970. Dr. Ray Lee, the Republican candidate, campaigned hard, looking for Wallace votes, and in the process won the endorsement of

Mayor Evers. Nevertheless, Griffin cruised to an easy 64% victory; he carried every county and won particularly big majorities in those with large black populations. With Nixon and Mitchell running the Republican party, Mississippi blacks, like those in South Carolina, seem to prefer conservative Democrats to conservative Republicans. Griffin in the 2nd will no doubt be reelected during the '70's.

Census Data 1970 pop. 444,704; deviation from current state average, +0.3%; change 1960–70, +3.8%. Metro. 48.3%, 34.6% central city.

1970 Share of Federal Outlays $426,655,091

DOD	$52,232,000	HEW	$143,073,179
AEC	$000	HUD	$1,118,214
NASA	$22,000	OEO	$2,875,911
DOT	$35,319,200	DOA	$30,040,606
		Other	$161,973,981

Federal Military-Industrial Commitments

DOD Contractors Sperry Rand Corp. (Jackson), $5.462m: aircraft electronic components.

Economic Base Cotton and livestock; lumber and wood products other than furniture; nonelectrical machinery. Also, higher education (Jackson State College).

The Voters

Registration No district-wide registration.

Employment profile White collar, 38%. Blue collar, 62%.

Ethnic groups Black, 43%. Total foreign stock, 1%. All groups less than 0.5% each.

Presidential vote

1968	Humphrey (D)	41,696	(30%)
	Nixon (R)	22,236	(16%)
	Wallace (AIP)	77,047	(55%)

Representative

Charles H. Griffin (D) Elected Mar. 1968; b. May 9, 1926, Utica; home, Utica; Mississippi State U., B.S., 1949; USN 1944–46; married; Disciples of Christ Church.

Career Asst. U.S. Rep. John Bell Williams, 1949–68.

Offices 1330 LHOB, 1-202-225-5865. Also 1823 Deposit Guaranty Nat. Bank Bldg., Jackson 39201, 1-601-355-4242.

Committees

Banking and Currency (16th); Subs. (1) Bank Supervision and Insurance, (2) International Trade, (3) Small Business.

Merchant Marine and Fisheries (17th); Subs. (1) Coast Guard, Coast and Geodetic Survey and Navigation, (2) Oceanography.

Group Ratings

	ADA	COPE	NREP	NFU	LCV	CFA	NAB	NSI	ACA
1970	8	17	8	15	33	67	70	100	83
1969	7	—	—	46	—	—	—	—	86
1968	0	25	—	40	—	—	75	—	84

Key Votes

(1) ABM	FOR	(6) 18-Yr-Vote	AGN	(11) Clean Water $	AGN
(2) SST	FOR	(7) Farm Sub Lmt	AGN	(12) Mig Wrkrs Comp	AGN
(3) Phil Pln	AGN	(8) Coop-Church	AGN	(13) Jets to Chiang	ABS
(4) No-Knock	FOR	(9) Family Asst	AGN	(14) State OEO Veto	FOR
(5) Cmutr Tax	AGN	(10) Work Stamps	FOR	(15) Park Logging	FOR

Election Results

1970 general:	Charles H. Griffin (D)	50,527	(64%)
	Ray Lee (R)	28,847	(36%)
1970 primary:	Charles H. Griffin (D), unopposed		
1968 general:	Charles H. Griffin (D), unopposed		

FOURTH DISTRICT Political Background

Mississippi 4 is one of three districts that stretch from the heavily black Delta across the hills of central Mississippi to the Alabama border. Its contours, like those of the 1st and 2nd districts, were obviously designed to prevent black voters from controlling or influencing in any significant way the state's congressional elections. The 4th is predominantly agricultural with most of its voters living in or near little crossroads towns. Meridian (pop. 45,000) is the district's largest city, and its most famous is Philadelphia, where three civil rights workers were found murdered in 1964.

The longtime (since 1942) congressman from the 4th, W. Arthur Winstead—a Philadelphia native—was rudely surprised in 1964: a Republican, one Prentiss Walker, unseated him. Goldwater carried the state by a 7–1 margin, and Winstead was the only incumbent congressman unfortunate enough to have a Republican challenger that year. If the Republicans had run candidates in the other four districts, they too would have won. And that would have disposed of the 95 years of seniority accumulated by Thomas Abernethy, Jamie Whitten, John Bell Williams, and William Colmer. It is an interesting exercise to consider just how the House would function without these powerful conservatives.

In 1966, Walker, interpreting his Goldwater coattail victory as a sign of great personal popularity, undertook the hopeless task of unseating Sen. James Eastland. The Democrats then recaptured the 4th in the person of state Sen. G. V. (Sonny) Montgomery. The Congressman, an unabashed conservative, is a member of the Armed Services and Veterans' Affairs committees. The 1970 census indicates that his district needs some reshaping, but that is unlikely to give him any worries.

Census Data 1970 pop. 403,173; deviation from current state average, —9.1%; change 1960–70, —4.8%. Metro. 10.9%, 0.0% central city.

1970 Share of Federal Outlays $284,290,839

DOD	$37,197,000	HEW	$97,711,068
AEC	$000	HUD	$5,566,346
NASA	$000	OEO	$1,809,485
DOT	$7,180,584	DOA	$78,205,148
		Other	$56,621,208

Federal Military-Industrial Commitments

DOD Installations Naval Air Station (Meridian).

Economic Base Cotton and livestock; apparel and other finished products made from fabric and similar materials; lumber and wood products other than furniture.

The Voters

Registration No district-wide registration.

Employment profile White collar, 25%. Blue collar, 75%.

Ethnic groups Black, 41%. Total foreign stock, 1%. All groups less than 0.5% each.

Presidential vote

1968	Humphrey (D)	28,724	(23%)
	Nixon (R)	11,377	(9%)
	Wallace (AIP)	87,546	(69%)

Representative

Gillespie V. Montgomery (D) Elected 1966; b. Aug. 5, 1920, Meridian; home, Meridian; Miss. State U., B.S., 1943; Army, WWII, Korea; married, two children; Episcopalian.

Career Miss. Senate, 1956–66.

Offices 503 CHOB, 1-202-225-5031. Also Meridian 39301, 1-601-483-8153.

Committees

Armed Services (22nd); Sub. Number 1.

Veterans' Affairs (11th); Subs. (1) Chm., Insurance, (2) Compensation and Pension, (3) Hospitals.

Group Ratings

	ADA	COPE	NREP	NFU	LCV	CFA	NAB	NSI	ACA
1970	0	20	0	9	0	43	88	100	87
1969	7	—	—	27	—	—	—	—	86
1968	0	0	—	33	—	—	100	—	87

Key Votes

(1) ABM	FOR	(6) 18-Yr-Vote	AGN	(11) Clean Water $	AGN
(2) SST	FOR	(7) Farm Sub Lmt	AGN	(12) Mig Wrkrs Comp	AGN
(3) Phil Pln	AGN	(8) Coop-Church	AGN	(13) Jets to Chiang	ABS
(4) No-Knock	FOR	(9) Family Asst	AGN	(14) State OEO Veto	FOR
(5) Cmutr Tax	AGN	(10) Work Stamps	FOR	(15) Park Logging	FOR

Election Results

1970 general:	G. V. "Sonny" Montgomery (D), unopposed		
1970 primary:	G. V. "Sonny" Montgomery (D), unopposed		
1968 general:	G. V. "Sonny" Montgomery (D)	78,768	(70%)
	Prentiss Walker (R)	33,683	(30%)

FIFTH DISTRICT Political Background

Mississippi 5 is the state's Gulf Coast district, though it does extend toward the north to take in several small agricultural counties and the small cities of Hattiesburg and Laurel. Almost half of the 5th's people live in and around the Gulf Coast cities of Biloxi, Gulfport, and Pascagoula. This area, which experienced substantial population increase in the '60's, is the most prosperous in Mississippi. Its economic health is due in large part to the defense contracts won by the shipbuilding concerns here; in 1970, the Litton Pascagoula yards brought in some $423 million of Defense department money. This region of Mississippi is slightly less conservative and segregationist than the rest of the state. The comparative moderation is a function of its relatively large number of Northern immigrants and of its proximity to the cosmopolitan big city of New Orleans. The district also has the state's lowest percentage of blacks, 21%.

Since 1932, the 5th has sent William M. Colmer to the House of Representatives. Some thirty-four years after his first election, Colmer succeeded to the chairmanship of the Rules Committee as the Democratic voters of the 8th district of Virginia ended the congressional career of Chairman Howard Smith. Since 1961 neither chairman has had a reliable majority on the committee, one which controls the flow of almost all business to the House floor. In 1961, the newly inaugurated Kennedy Administration and the ailing Speaker Sam Rayburn, on a 217–212 vote, managed to increase the number of members on the committee. Even at that, Colmer, who is considered less adept at parliamentary maneuvering than his predecessor, can still pigeonhole liberal legislation from time to time. Colmer has the most success at this when one of the liberal members of the committee is absent.

As the 92nd Congress convened, liberals attempted to deny the Mississippi delegation membership in the Democratic caucus; the liberals argued that the delegation was not a legitimate part of the Democratic party since its members had refused to run on the ticket of the integrated National Democratic party of Mississippi, which had been seated as the state's delegation to the 1968 national convention. The move, designed to deprive Colmer *et al.* of their seniority and chairmanships, failed, but it failed by a smaller number of votes than expected. The Mississippians will face a much more formidable challenge if the Democrats once again score a success like the one of 1964 and bring to the House many liberals untutored in its traditional ways. At the moment, however, odds are that Colmer, who was 80 in 1970, will remain chairman for as long as he chooses.

Census Data 1970 pop. 512,927; deviation from current state average, +15.7%; change 1960–70, +14.1%. Metro. 26.2%, 17.4% central city.

1970 Share of Federal Outlays $955,379,452

DOD	$657,708,000	HEW	$100,643,190
AEC	$000	HUD	$16,948,126
NASA	$1,558,217	OEO	$885,713
DOT	$39,515,600	DOA	$36,445,346
		Other	$101,675,260

Federal Military-Industrial Commitments

DOD Contractors Litton Systems Inc. (Pascagoula), $432.472m: ship construction and overhaul.

DOD Installations Naval Construction Battalion Center (Gulfport). Keesler AFB (Biloxi).

NASA Installations Mississippi Test Facility (Bay St. Louis).

Economic Base Livestock and cotton; shipbuilding and repair; food and kindred products; apparel and other finished products made from fabrics and similar materials.

The Voters

Registration No district-wide registration.
Employment profile White collar, 34%. Blue collar, 66%.
Ethnic groups Black, 21%. Total foreign stock, 3%. All groups less than 0.5% each.

Presidential vote

1968	Humphrey (D)	21,172	(15%)
	Nixon (R)	21,798	(15%)
	Wallace (AIP)	100,674	(70%)

Representative

William M. Colmer (D) Elected 1932; b. Feb. 11, 1890, Moss Point; home, Pascagoula; Millsaps Col., A.B., 1910–14; Miss. bar, 1917; Army, WWI; married, three children; Presbyterian.

Career High school teacher, 1914–17; county atty., Jackson County, 1921–27; dist. atty., 2nd dist. Miss., 1928–33.

Offices 2307 RHOB, 1-202-225-5772. Also P.O. Box 100, Pascagoula, Miss., 39567, 1-601-762-1414.

Committees

Rules (Chm.).

Group Ratings

	ADA	COPE	NREP	NFU	LCV	CFA	NAB	NSI	ACA
1970	0	9	0	17	11	37	100	100	89
1969	0	—	—	14	—	—	—	—	93
1968	8	0	—	21	—	—	100	—	87

Key Votes

(1) ABM	ABS	(6) 18-Yr-Vote	AGN	(11) Clean Water $	AGN
(2) SST	FOR	(7) Farm Sub Lmt	AGN	(12) Mig Wrkrs Comp	AGN
(3) Phil Pln	ABS	(8) Coop-Church	AGN	(13) Jets to Chiang	ABS
(4) No-Knock	FOR	(9) Family Asst	AGN	(14) State OEO Veto	FOR
(5) Cmutr Tax	FOR	(10) Work Stamps	FOR	(15) Park Logging	FOR

Election Results

1970 general:	William M. Colmer (D)	58,546	(90%)
	Earnest J. Creel (Ind.)	6,225	(10%)
1970 primary:	William M. Colmer (D), unopposed		
1968 general:	William M. Colmer (D), unopposed		

MISSOURI

Political Background

A look at the voter registration figures shows that Missouri has the largest percentage of Democrats of any large state. But at the polls, Missouri is politically marginal and in recent national elections has been trending Republican. The discrepancy between voter preference and voter behavior is rooted in the state's history. Missouri was admitted to the Union as a slave state in 1821, and its residents, both urban and rural, have been, as a matter of tradition, part of the Southern wing of the Democratic party. Although the border state did not secede from the Union in 1861, many Missourians, including the uncle of the state's leading citizen, Harry S. Truman, fought in the Confederate Army. So it was hardly surprising that Truman, after going broke in his haberdashery, became active in Democratic politics. The former President's background—rural Southern and urban Kansas City—exemplifies the tensions within the Missouri Democratic party and also explains why Truman, who integrated the armed forces during his term as President, would later react negatively to the sit-in demonstrations of the early 1960's. Moreover, Truman's combination of liberalism on economic issues, a mixed response on social questions, and an affection for old political friends still characterizes the leaders of the Missouri Democrats. For Truman and for the party, the combination has produced many election-day victories. The Democrats ordinarily win large margins in the St. Louis and Kansas City areas and also carry pluralities in the Southern-oriented rural counties.

But the growing strength of the Republican party throughout the South has recently become an important factor in Missouri politics, and the GOP has cut into the state's traditional Democratic majority. Many rural counties are now going Republican with increasing frequency, and, statewide, Republican presidential candidates have consistently attracted the votes of many old Missouri Democrats. As a result, the presidential elections here—except for the one in 1964—in the last two decades have been very close, with no winning candidate's margin being more than 30,000 votes out of nearly 2,000,000 cast and none receiving more than 51% of the two-party vote. In 1968, Nixon managed to carry Illinois and Missouri by narrow margins—without them Humphrey would have become President. Until recently, Democratic senatorial candidates have run far ahead of the national ticket, but in 1968 and 1970 liberal Democrats Thomas Eagleton and Stuart Symington each won with 51% of the votes.

Eagleton's race in 1968 was expected to be close. In a bitter Democratic primary, he defeated incumbent Edward Long, who, according to *Life* magazine, had been on the payroll of one of Jimmy Hoffa's attorneys. In the general election, Eagleton faced Thomas R. Curtis, a Republican congressman from suburban St. Louis and a proven vote-getter. Nixon carried Missouri in 1968 by 20,000 votes, but Curtis lost by 35,000. In Washington, Eagleton is a member of the Senate's liberal, antiwar bloc; he sits on the Labor and Public Welfare and the Public Works committees, which together have jurisdiction over a great deal of economic and environmental legislation. And as chairman of District of Columbia—the youngest and least senior committee chairman in the Senate—he is a strong proponent of home rule for the capital city.

In 1970, Democratic Senator Stuart Symington expected little trouble winning re-election. Symington, who was then 69, had served three terms in the upper House, after holding a number of high administrative positions in the Truman Administration, including Secretary of the Air Force. During the '50's Symington won a reputation nationwide as an advocate of military preparedness and of the big bomber in particular. His position on these issues led to an unsuccessful bid for the 1960 Democratic presidential nomination. During the course of the Vietnam war, however, Symington became a committed dove, and he now uses his senior positions on Foreign Relations and Armed Services (the only senator to sit on both committees) to lead opposition to controversial military spending programs like the ABM. Back home, the Senator had become accustomed to big majorities; his 67% showing in 1964 was 3% better than Lyndon Johnson's in Missouri. As a result, his Republican challenger, young (34 in 1970) John Danforth, appeared to have little chance. Danforth, heir to the Ralston Purina fortune, took both law and divinity degrees at Yale before returning to enter Missouri politics in 1966. Two years later he was state Attorney General. He was the second youngest man, after Eagleton, ever to hold the post and the first Republican in forty years. Danforth ran a strong campaign, with a million-dollar TV budget and hundreds of youthful volunteers. Observers said that his speaking style was more like that of a preacher's than a politician's and that Danforth would keep his audiences in rapt silence, though the substance of his speeches was often nothing more than vague talk about the need to back the President and unify the country. Except for the Senator's support of the Hatfield-McGovern Amendment, Danforth did not attack Symington on the issues, but instead tried to link him with the old-crony ambience of the Missouri state Democratic party.

By October, it was clear that Danforth was picking up the bulk of the undecided votes. So Symington began to campaign harder, as hard as he did in 1952 when he first won the seat. The results produced a scant 37,000-vote, 51% victory for the Senator and dealt a temporary setback to Danforth's political career. Like Eagleton in 1968, the Democrat carried the city of St. Louis by a margin better than 2–1, ran even in suburban St. Louis County, and carried the Kansas City area. Except for the state's southeast corner and the Little Dixie section between Hannibal and Columbia, the rest of the state voted Republican, with the Ozarks producing especially heavy Republican margins.

The same patterns are likely to develop in future elections, including the one for governor in 1972. The incumbent Hearnes has come under fire from Danforth and his Republican colleague, state Auditor Christopher (Kit) Bond. Like Danforth, Bond received an Ivy League education before going home to run the family business and enter politics. He was 31 in 1970 when he teamed with Danforth in the elections of that year. Danforth, of course, lost, but Bond ousted the long-entrenched Democratic auditor by 195,000 votes, the largest margin in the state. Because of a few years of law practice in New York, Danforth is ineligible under Missouri's ten-year residency requirement to run for governor. So Bond will most likely be the Republican candidate for that office, with a likely Democratic choice being 8th district Congressman Richard Ichord. Danforth will probably challenge Senator Eagleton in 1974, which should make for an interesting race. Symington, meanwhile, will be 75 when his current term expires and may choose at that time to retire. If he does, the Senator's son, James Symington, is a likely successor; the younger Symington captured the previously Republican 2nd district congressional seat in 1968.

Missouri politics has come a long way from the days of Harry Truman. With all the rich people running things in the state—Danforth, Eagleton, Bond, and the Symingtons—there's little room left for any bankrupt haberdasher to maneuver. But in this respect, Missouri is little different from any place else in the country.

Electoral Votes 12

Census Data 1970 pop. 4,677,399; 2.27% of U.S. total, 13th largest; change 1960–70, +8.3%. Metro. 64.1%, 29.4% central city. 1970 per capita income, $3,659; 26th highest. 17th in number of poor.

1970 Share of Federal Tax Burden $4,273,580,000; 2.19% of U.S. total, 13th largest.

1970 Share of Federal Outlays $4,579,266,816; 2.42% of U.S. total, 13th largest. Per capita federal spending, $979.

DOD	$438,828,161	14th (3.41%)	HEW	$1,275,467,171	11th (2.44%)
AEC	$97,971,793	12th (3.77%)	HUD	$44,481,719	14th (2.28%)
NASA	$103,424,673	11th (2.81%)	OEO	$19,415,929	11th (2.55%)
DOT	$143,129,910	18th (2.00%)	DOA	$438,828,161	9th (3.41%)
DOC	$15,445,198	16th (1.34%)	POD	$202,882,467	10th (2.78%)
DOI	$28,832,328	25th (1.25%)	VA	$220,689,485	11th (2.99%)
DOJ	$412,953,075	11th (2.26%)	CSC	$63,025,476	15th (1.57%)
			Other	$497,012,431	

Economic Base Livestock, soybeans, and dairy; transportation equipment, esp. motor vehicles and motor vehicle equipment; food and kindred products, esp. meat products; electrical machinery, equipment, and supplies; printing, publishing, and allied industries, esp. commercial printing and newspapers; apparel and other finished products made from fabrics and similar materials, esp. men's, youths', and boys' furnishings, work clothing, and allied garments, and women's, misses', and juniors' outerwear; nonelectrical machinery; fabricated metal products, esp. fabricated structural metal products; chemicals and allied products, esp. industrial inorganic and organic chemicals; ordnance and accessories.

Political Line-up Governor, Warren E. Hearnes (D); seat up, 1972. Senators, Stuart Symington (D) and Thomas F. Eagleton (D). Representatives, 10 (9 D and 1 R). State Senate (25 D and 9 R); State House (112 D and 51 R).

The Voters

Registration No statewide registration.

Employment profile White collar, 40%. Blue collar, 60%.

Ethnic groups Black, 10%. Total foreign stock, 8%. Germany, 3%; Ireland, Italy, UK, USSR, 1% each; others, 1%.

Presidential vote

1968	Humphrey (D)	791,444	(44%)
	Nixon (R)	811,932	(45%)
	Wallace (AIP)	206,126	(11%)
1964	Johnson (D)	1,164,344	(64%)
	Goldwater (R)	653,535	(36%)
1960	Kennedy (D)	972,201	(50%)
	Nixon (R)	962,221	(50%)

Senator

Stuart Symington (D) Elected 1952, seat up 1976; b. June 26, 1901, Amherst, Mass.; home, St. Louis; Yale, A.B., 1923; Army, WWI; married, two children; Episcopalian.

Career Asst. Secy. of War for Air, 1946–47; Secy. of the AF, 1947–50; Chm., Natl. Security Resources Bd., 1950–51; Reconstruction Finance Corp. Administrator, 1951–52.

Offices 229 OSOB, 1-202-225-6154. Also 7730 Corondelet, Clayton 63111, 1-314-725-5860, and U.S. Courthouse, Kansas City 64106, 1-816-374-3068.

Committees

Aeronautical and Space Sciences (3rd).

Armed Services (2nd); Subs. (1) Chm., Military Construction Authorization, (2) Central Intelligence Agency, (3) National Stockpile and Naval Petroleum Reserves, (4) Nuclear Test Ban Treaty Safeguards, (5) Preparedness Investigating, (6) Strategic Arms Limitation Talks, (7) Ad Hoc Sub. on Tactical Air Power.

Foreign Relations (5th); Subs. (1) Chm., Near Eastern and South Asian Affairs, (2) Chm., U.S. Security Agreements and Commitments Abroad, (3) European Affairs, (4) Genocide Convention.

Jt. Com. on Atomic Energy (4th); Sub. on Military Applications.

Group Ratings

	ADA	COPE	NREP	NFU	LCV	NAB	NSI	ACA
1970	69	100	90	100	34	11	25	6
1969	89	—	—	86	—	—	—	18
1968	64	80	—	54	—	67	—	44

Key Votes

(1) ABM	AGN	(8) Phil Pln	ABS	(15) Coop-Church	FOR
(2) SST	FOR	(9) Vol Army	FOR	(16) Cut Oil Dpltn	FOR
(3) Busing	FOR	(10) Prison $	ABS	(17) Consumer Prot	FOR
(4) Tob Sub	FOR	(11) Cut Mil $	FOR	(18) Farm Sub Limit	AGN
(5) Carswell	AGN	(12) Defoliatn	FOR	(19) Comp Bid Sales	AGN
(6) No-Knock	FOR	(13) 18-Yr-Vote	ABS	(20) Pre-Prod Tests	ABS
(7) Seniorty	AGN	(14) Pentgn PR	FOR	(21) Cut Marjna Pen	AGN

Election Results

1970 general:	Stuart Symington (D)	654,831	(51%)
	John C. Danforth (R)	617,903	(48%)
	Gene Chapman (AIP)	10,065	(1%)
1970 primary:	Stuart Symington (D)	392,670	(89%)
	Douglas V. White (D)	15,187	(3%)
	William M. Thomas (D)	13,018	(3%)
	Lee C. Sutton (D)	11,105	(3%)
	Hershel V. Page (D)	7,843	(2%)
1964 general:	Stuart Symington (D)	1,186,666	(67%)
	Jean Paul Bradshaw (R)	596,377	(33%)

Senator

Thomas F. Eagleton (D) Elected 1968, seat up 1974; b. Sept. 4, 1929, St. Louis; home, St. Louis; Amherst College, B.A. cum laude, 1950; Harvard, LL.B., 1953; USN, 1948–49; married, two children; Catholic.

Career Circuit atty., 1956–60; Mo. Atty. Gen., 1960–64; Mo. Lt. Gov., 1964–68.

Offices 4102 NSOB, 1-202-225-5721. Also 4039 Fed. Bldg., St. Louis 63103, 1-314-622-5067.

Committees

District of Columbia (Chm.); Subs. (1) Chm., Fiscal Affairs.

Labor and Public Welfare (7th); Subs. (1) Chm., Aging, (2) Education, (3) Health, (4) Labor, (5) Sp. on Arts and Humanities, (6) Sp. on Social Programs, (7) Sp. on National Science Foundation.

Public Works (11th); Subs. (1) Chm., Environmental Science and Technology, (2) Economic Development, (3) Flood Control—Rivers and Harbors.

Sp. Com. on Aging (11th); Subs. (1) Federal, State, and Community Services, (2) Consumer Interests of the Elderly, (3) Health of the Elderly, (4) Long-Term Care, (5) Retirement and the Individual.

Group Ratings

	ADA	COPE	NREP	NFU	LCV	NAB	NSI	ACA
1970	91	100	93	100	80	18	0	4
1969	94	—	—	88	—	—	—	0

Key Votes

(1) ABM	AGN	(8) Phil Pln	FOR	(15) Coop-Church	FOR
(2) SST	AGN	(9) Vol Army	AGN	(16) Cut Oil Dpltn	FOR
(3) Busing	FOR	(10) Prison $	ABS	(17) Consumer Prot	FOR
(4) Tob Sub	FOR	(11) Cut Mil $	FOR	(18) Farm Sub Limit	AGN
(5) Carswell	AGN	(12) Defoliatn	AGN	(19) Comp Bid Sales	AGN
(6) No-Knock	FOR	(13) 18-Yr-Vote	FOR	(20) Pre-Prod Tests	ABS
(7) Seniorty	FOR	(14) Pentgn PR	AGN	(21) Cut Marjna Pen	AGN

Election Results

1968 general:	Thomas F. Eagleton (D)	880,113	(51%)
	Thomas R. Curtis (R)	845,144	(49%)
1968 primary:	Thomas F. Eagleton (D)	224,017	(37%)
	Edward V. Long (D)	198,901	(33%)
	True Davis (D)	178,961	(29%)
	William M. Thomas (D)	4,879	(1%)

FIRST DISTRICT Political Background

Missouri 1 comprises the north side of the city of St. Louis and a few suburbs in the separate county of St. Louis. Because of black migration and the transformation of neighborhood patterns within St. Louis, the north side is predominantly black, and in 1968 the fourth Missouri redistricting of the decade made the blacks a majority in the district. The suburban areas that lie at the edge of the city are mostly white, with blue-collar workers in the north (Jennings and Riverview) and white-collar workers to the south (Maplewood, Richmond Heights, and University City). The 1st also includes Washington University, just west of the city line, with an adjacent liberal academic community.

The 1st is the most consistently Democratic district in Missouri. For years it was represented by Democrat Frank Karsten, but in 1968 he lost the seat when redistricting removed some of the westernmost white middle-class suburbs and added part of the St. Louis ghetto. In 1968, he was defeated in the Democratic primary by former black alderman and civil rights activist, William Clay. In the general election, Clay took the city portion of the district 3–1, but polled only 39% in the normally Democratic white suburbs. He was reelected in 1970 with less trouble, winning with 91% of the votes. His only opponent was a candidate of the American party, and this time he carried the suburban section, which had again been altered by redistricting.

In the House, Clay has a seat on Education and Labor, a committee that handles most social legislation. He is also one of the leaders of the twelve-member Black Caucus, which, after repeated requests stretching over months and a boycott of the State of the Union address, finally gained an audience with President Nixon. But the militant Clay is used to this kind of treatment: in 1963 he was jailed for 105 days and fined $1,000 for participating in a St. Louis civil rights demonstration.

Since the 1970 census showed a large population loss in the district, more white suburbs will have to be added to the 1st. In the summer of 1971, Clay was fighting a move in the state legislature which would again make the 1st a white-majority district. If it succeeds, it will cost Missouri's first black congressman his seat. But chances are that Clay will end up with a district he can win.

Census Data 1970 pop. 377,097; deviation from current state average, −19.4%; change 1960–70, −14.3%. Metro. 100%, 77.5% central city.

1970 Share of Federal Outlays $606,130,000 (average outlay per district, Missouri 1–3)

DOD	$299,659,000	HEW	$127,159,000
AEC	$268,000	HUD	$6,049,000
NASA	$34,117,000	OEO	$2,126,000
DOT	$5,193,000	DOA	$12,223,000
		Other	$246,495,000

Federal Military-Industrial Commitments (See Missouri 3 for greater St. Louis listing.)

Economic Base Food and kindred products, esp. beverages and bakery products; fabricated metal products, esp. fabricated structural metal products; transportation equipment; printing, publishing, and allied industries, esp. commercial printing. Also, higher education (Washington University).

The Voters

Registration No district-wide registration.

Employment profile White collar, 39%. Blue collar, 61%.

Ethnic groups Black, 62%. Total foreign stock, 11%. Germany, 4%; Italy, 2%; Ireland, Poland, UK, 1% each; others, 1%.

Presidential vote

1968	Humphrey (D)	92,774	(68%)
	Nixon (R)	24,389	(18%)
	Wallace (AIP)	18,640	(14%)

Representative

William L. Clay (D) Elected 1968; b. April 30, 1931, St. Louis; home, St. Louis; St. Louis U., B.S., 1953; married, three children; Catholic.

Career Alderman, 26th Ward, St. Louis, 1959–64; business rep., city employees union, 1961–64; education coordinator, Steamfitters Local No. 562, 1966–67.

Offices 328 CHOB, 1-202-225-2406. Also 515A Delmar, St. Louis 63108, 1-314-367-0930.

Committees

Education and Labor (16th); Subs. (1) Gen. on Labor, (2) Sel. on Education, (3) Sp. on Labor.

Group Ratings

	ADA	COPE	NREP	NFU	LCV	CFA	NAB	NSI	ACA
1970	84	100	100	82	100	100	0	0	7
1969	100	—	—	73	—	—	—	—	15

Key Votes

(1) ABM	AGN	(6) 18-Yr-Vote	FOR	(11) Clean Water $	FOR
(2) SST	AGN	(7) Farm Sub Lmt	FOR	(12) Mig Wrkrs Comp	FOR
(3) Phil Pln	FOR	(8) Coop-Church	FOR	(13) Jets to Chiang	AGN
(4) No-Knock	AGN	(9) Family Asst	FOR	(14) State OEO Veto	AGN
(5) Cmutr Tax	FOR	(10) Work Stamps	AGN	(15) Park Logging	AGN

Election Results

1970 general:	William Clay (D)	58,082	(91%)
	Gerald G. Fischer (AIP)	6,078	(9%)
1970 primary:	William Clay (D), unopposed		
	(Redistricted 1969)		

SECOND DISTRICT Political Background

Missouri 2 lies in the heart of suburban St. Louis County, the largest and fastest growing county in the state. The 2nd is sociologically diverse. In the north are Ferguson, Berkeley, and Hazelwood, which are white working-class suburbs with a few small black enclaves; in the south are towns like Kirkwood and Webster Groves, which are upper-middle-class, WASPy, and Republican. Also here is University City, a community of liberal, upper-middle-class Jews. In the middle of the 2nd is Ladue, the home of wealthy members of the St. Louis establishment. In close statewide elections this mix produces a very even political balance, with the large Democratic pluralities in the north offset by big Republican margins in the south and west.

In congressional elections, however, the 2nd has been in the clear possession of first one party and then the other. Until 1968, the district was represented by conservative Republican Thomas B. Curtis, a senior member of the House Ways and Means Committee. He was regarded in Washington circles as one of the GOP's experts in economics and tax issues. After polling a very strong 66% in the 1966 election, Curtis decided to run for Edward Long's Senate seat in 1968. If Long, who was the target of sensational charges made by *Life* magazine, had won the Democratic primary, Curtis would have probably beaten the incumbent in the general election. But Lt. Gov. Thomas Eagleton defeated Long in the primary and then bested Curtis by 35,000 votes. The outcome might have been different again if the Congressman's performance in his old district had not dropped to 52%.

Curtis's successor is Democrat James W. Symington, son of Sen. Stuart Symington and grandson and namesake of James Wadsworth, New York Republican senator from 1914 to 1926. Rep. Symington, like his father, held a number of important offices in a Democratic national administration and then returned to Missouri to run for Congress. Prior to winning the seat in the 2nd district, he was Deputy Director of the Food for Peace Program under George McGovern, Administrative Assistant to Attorney General Robert Kennedy, Director of the President's Commission on Juvenile Delinquency (which developed the antipoverty program), and Chief of Protocol in the State Department.

Despite his wide range of administrative experience, Symington has played the role of a typically unobtrusive freshman congressman; he has been forced to do this by the workings of the seniority system. In the 2nd, Symington has had no more difficulty getting reelected than his Republican predecessor. In 1970, he won with 58% of the votes. The state legislature will most likely strengthen his position in the district, and Symington will probably remain in the House until he decides to run for statewide office, possibly in 1976 to succeed his father, who may retire at that time.

Census Data 1970 pop. 508,745; deviation from current state average, +8.8%; change 1960–70, −14.3%. Metro. 100%, 0% central city.

1970 Share of Federal Outlays $606,130,000 (average outlay per district, Missouri 1–3)

DOD	$299,659,000	HEW	$127,159,000
AEC	$268,000	HUD	$6,049,000
NASA	$34,117,000	OEO	$2,126,000
DOT	$5,193,000	DOA	$12,223,000
		Other	$246,495,000

Federal Military-Industrial Commitments (See Missouri 3 for greater St. Louis listing.)

Economic Base Motor vehicles and motor vehicle equipment, and other transportation equipment; chemicals and allied products; electrical machinery, equipment, and supplies. Also, extensive commuting to Missouri 1 and 3 (St. Louis).

The Voters

Registration No district-wide registration.

Employment profile White collar, 59%. Blue collar, 41%.

Ethnic groups Black, 5%. Total foreign stock, 17%. Germany, 5%; USSR, 3%; Austria, Hungary, Ireland, Italy, Poland, UK, Canada, 1% each; others, 3%.

Presidential vote

1968	Humphrey (D)	95,631	(44%)
	Nixon (R)	102,107	(47%)
	Wallace (AIP)	21,057	(10%)

Representative

James W. Symington (D) Elected 1968; b. Sept. 28, 1927, Rochester, N.Y.; home, Clayton; Yale, A.B., 1950; Columbia U., LL.B., 1954; USMCR, 1945–46; married, two children; Episcopalian.

Career Asst. city counselor, St. Louis, 1954–55; atty., 1955–58, 1960–61; U.S. Foreign Service, London, 1958–60; Deputy Dir., Food for Peace, 1961–62; Adm. Asst., Atty. Gen. Robert F. Kennedy, 1962–63; Dir., Pres. Comm. on Juv. Del., 1965–66; Consultant, Pres. Comm. on Law Enforcement, 1965–66; Chief of Protocol, Dept. of State, 1966–68.

Offices 1533 LHOB, 1-202-225-2561. Also 10 S. Brentwood, Clayton 63106, 314-726-1410.

Committees

Interstate and Foreign Commerce (21st); Sub. on Public Health and Environment.

Science and Astronautics (9th); Subs. (1) Science, Research, and Development, (2) Space Sciences and Applications.

Group Ratings

	ADA	COPE	NREP	NFU	LCV	CFA	NAB	NSI	ACA
1970	72	92	75	90	100	100	0	78	24
1969	73	—	—	100	—	—	—	—	7

Key Votes

(1) ABM	FOR	(6) 18-Yr-Vote	FOR	(11) Clean Water $	FOR
(2) SST	AGN	(7) Farm Sub Lmt	ABS	(12) Mig Wrkrs Comp	FOR
(3) Phil Pln	AGN	(8) Coop-Church	FOR	(13) Jets to Chiang	FOR
(4) No-Knock	FOR	(9) Family Asst	FOR	(14) State OEO Veto	AGN
(5) Cmutr Tax	ABS	(10) Work Stamps	AGN	(15) Park Logging	ABS

Election Results

1970 general:	James W. Symington (D)	93,294	(58%)
	Phil R. Hoffman (R)	66,503	(41%)
	Sterling E. Lacy (AIP)	2,206	(1%)
1970 primary:	James W. Symington (D), unopposed		
	(Redistricted 1969)		

THIRD DISTRICT Political Background

Missouri 3 comprises the south side of St. Louis and some adjacent suburban territory. Most of the residents here are white blue-collar workers employed by St. Louis' manufacturing concerns, the most notable of them being the huge McDonnell Douglas aircraft plant. The ethnic groups of the city, the largest of which is German, are centered in this district.

Like many of the women in the House, the 3rd's Leonor K. Sullivan won her seat following the death of the husband, Congressman John B. Sullivan, who represented the district from 1940 to 1942 and from 1944 to 1951. The special election called to fill the vacancy was won by a Republican, and he in turn was defeated by Mrs. Sullivan in 1952. Since then, she has had little difficulty winning reelection in this heavily Democratic district. Since she has gotten more than 70% of the votes in the last four elections, Mrs. Sullivan, a liberal Democrat, will no doubt continue to win as long as she chooses to run.

The Missouri Congresswoman is the 3rd ranking Democrat on the House Banking and Currency Committee and chairman of its subcommittee on Consumer Affairs. As chairman of that congressional subunit, she led the fight for the Truth-in-Lending law. She was also one of the chief proponents of the Truth-in-Packaging bill, and today she continues to be one of the leaders in the consumer movement.

Census Data 1970 pop. 376,211; deviation from current state average, −19.6%; change 1960–70, −11.9%. Metro. 100%, 87.7% central city.

1970 Share of Federal Outlays $606,130,000 (average outlay per district, Missouri 1–3)

DOD	$299,659,000	HEW	$127,159,000
AEC	$268,000	HUD	$6,049,000
NASA	$34,117,000	OEO	$2,126,000
DOT	$5,193,000	DOA	$12,223,000
		Other	$246,495,000

Federal Military-Industrial Commitments (Missouri 1–3, greater St. Louis listing)

DOD Contractors McDonnell Douglas Corp. (St. Louis and Robertson), $585.983m: production of F-4 Phantom jet aircraft. Emerson Electric (St. Louis), $19.902m: F-4 and F-111 electronic test equipment; repair parts of XM28 helicopter armament subsystem. Kisco Co. (St. Louis), $16.200m: metal parts for 105-mm cartridge cases. IBM Corp. (St. Louis), 9.715m: unspecified.

DOD Installations Aeronautical Chart and Information Center.

NASA Contractors McDonnell Douglas (St. Louis), $96.095m: Skylab program, shops and airlock modules; Saturn rocket support.

Economic Base Food and kindred products, esp. beverages and bakery products; fabricated metal products, esp. fabricated structural metal products; transportation equipment, esp. aircraft and parts; printing, publishing, and allied industries, esp. commercial printing. Also, higher education (St. Louis University); banking and insurance.

The Voters

Registration No district-wide registration.

Employment profile White collar, 40%. Blue collar, 60%.

Ethnic groups Black, 10%. Total foreign stock, 15%. German, 5%; Italy, 2%; Austria, Czech., Hungary, Ireland, Poland, UK, 1% each; others, 3%.

Presidential vote

1968	Humphrey (D)	74,642	(56%)
	Nixon (R)	51,497	(39%)
	Wallace (AIP)	6,504	(5%)

Representative

Leonor K. Sullivan (D) Elected Mar. 1951; b. ca. 1900, St. Louis; home, St. Louis; Washington U.; widowed; Catholic.

Career Teacher and Dir., St. Louis Comptometer Sch.; Adm. Asst., U.S. Rep. John B. Sullivan, 1942–51.

Offices 2221 RHOB, 1-202-225-2671. Also 2918 Fed. Bldg., 1520 Market St., St. Louis 63103, 1-314-622-4500.

Committees

Banking and Currency (3rd); Subs. (1) Chm., Consumer Affairs, (2) Housing, (3) Small Business.

Merchant Marine and Fisheries (2nd); Subs. (1) Coast Guard, Coast and Geodetic Survey and Navigation, (2) Merchant Marine, (3) Panama Canal.

Jt. Com. on Defense Production (3rd).

Group Ratings

	ADA	COPE	NREP	NFU	LCV	CFA	NAB	NSI	ACA
1970	68	92	64	92	89	95	17	70	22
1969	67	—	—	100	—	—	—	—	8
1968	75	100	—	100	—	—	0	—	5

Key Votes

(1) ABM	ABS	(6) 18-Yr-Vote	FOR	(11) Clean Water $	FOR
(2) SST	AGN	(7) Farm Sub Lmt	ABS	(12) Mig Wrkrs Comp	FOR
(3) Phil Pln	ABS	(8) Coop-Church	FOR	(13) Jets to Chiang	FOR
(4) No-Knock	FOR	(9) Family Asst	AGN	(14) State OEO Veto	AGN
(5) Cmutr Tax	FOR	(10) Work Stamps	AGN	(15) Park Logging	AGN

Election Results

1970 general:	Leonor K. Sullivan (D)	73,021	(75%)
	Dale F. Troske (R)	24,651	(25%)
1970 primary:	Leonor K. Sullivan (D), unopposed (Redistricted 1969)		

FOURTH DISTRICT Political Background

Missouri 4 contains part of Kansas City and nearly all of its suburbs, as well as a number of traditionally Democratic rural counties to the south and east. During the '20's and '30's the notorious Prendergast machine in Kansas City and Jackson County delivered huge Democratic majorities; these majorities embarrassed the machine only when the number of Democratic votes in some precincts exceeded the total number of residents living in them. Today Jackson County remains Democratic only because of the black vote, most of which is in the 5th district. The Democratic margins in the Kansas City area have been dropping slowly, even as they have been going up in greater St. Louis across the state.

In the other counties of the 4th, which include about half of the district's population, the swing to the Republicans has been even more pronounced. It was from these counties that pro-slavery Missouri men crossed into Kansas during the 1850's to battle abolitionists for control of the territorial government (see Kansas state write-up). Today, a new set of national issues has finally begun to eradicate the old Southern allegiance to the Democratic party; in 1968, Humphrey could win only 40% of the votes here in the 4th.

The congressman from the district is William J. Randall, a Democrat from Independence; from 1946 to 1959 he was Judge of Jackson County, an administrative post once held by Harry Truman. In 1959 Randall was elected to the House, but despite more than a decade of service, the Congressman holds only middle seniority positions on Armed Services and Government Operations. On major issues, Randall usually votes with the Southern Democrat and conservative Republican bloc in the House. In recent elections, he has had no serious opposition and generally wins reelection with about 60% of the votes.

Census Data 1970 pop. 537,990; deviation from current state average, +15.0%; change 1960–70, 21.8%. Metro. 58.5%, 11.3% central city.

1970 Share of Federal Outlays $530,035,000 (average outlay per district Missouri 4 and 5)

DOD	$131,460,000	HEW	$112,723,000
AEC	$48,645,000	HUD	$9,753,000
NASA	$303,000	OEO	$2,503,000
DOT	$15,352,000	DOA	$76,594,000
		Other	$132,702,000

Federal Military-Industrial Commitments (See Missouri 5 for greater Kansas City listing.)

Economic Base Livestock and cash grain; printing, publishing, and allied industries; electrical machinery, equipment, and supplies, esp. communication equipment; motor vehicles and motor vehicle equipment; and other transportation equipment. Also, higher education (Central Missiouri State University).

The Voters

Registration No district-wide registration.

Employment profile White collar, 38%. Blue collar, 62%.

Ethnic groups Black, 2%. Total foreign stock, 6%. Germany, 2%; UK, Canada, 1% each; others, 1%.

Presidential vote

1968	Humphrey (D)	77,044	(40%)
	Nixon (R)	91,360	(47%)
	Wallace (AIP)	25,985	(13%)

Representative

William J. Randall (D) Elected 1958; b. July 16, 1909, Independence; home, Independence; U. of Mo., A.B., 1931; U. of Kansas City, LL.B., 1936; Army, WWII; married, one child; Methodist.

Career Judge, Jackson Co. Ct., 1946–58.

Offices 2431 RHOB, 1-202-225-2876. Also 219 Fed. Bldg., 301 W. Lexington, Independence 64050, 1-816-252-7171.

Committees

Armed Services (11th); Subs. (1) No. 3, (2) Armed Services Investigations.

Government Operations (13th); Subs. (1) Chm., Special Studies, (2) Legal and Monetary Affairs.

Group Ratings

	ADA	COPE	NREP	NFU	LCV	CFA	NAB	NSI	ACA
1970	32	64	17	62	67	65	50	100	53
1969	27	—	—	57	—	—	—	—	59
1968	17	62	—	75	—	—	100	—	77

Key Votes

(1) ABM	FOR	(6) 18-Yr-Vote	AGN	(11) Clean Water $	FOR
(2) SST	FOR	(7) Farm Sub Lmt	AGN	(12) Mig Wrkrs Comp	FOR
(3) Phil Pln	AGN	(8) Coop-Church	AGN	(13) Jets to Chiang	FOR
(4) No-Knock	FOR	(9) Family Asst	AGN	(14) State OEO Veto	FOR
(5) Cmutr Tax	ABS	(10) Work Stamps	AGN	(15) Park Logging	AGN

Election Results

1970 general:	William J. Randall (D)	80,153	(60%)
	Leslie O. Olson (R)	53,204	(40%)
1970 primary:	William J. Randall (D)	43,622	(86%)
	William M. Hannay (D)	7,385	(14%)
	(Redistricted 1969)		

FIFTH DISTRICT Political Background

Missouri 5, the western portion of Kansas City, contains most of the city's numerous black residents as well as a large number of working-class whites. This is the core of the Kansas City metropolitan area, an important manufacturing center and the commercial hub for most of the farmlands of Missouri and Kansas. The 5th is heavily Democratic in both state and national elections—it was one of three in the state (the other two were in greater St. Louis) that Humphrey carried in 1968.

A distinguished young veteran of World War II, Richard Bolling, won the 5th's House seat in 1948. Bolling soon became one of Speaker Sam Rayburn's protégés, and the old Texan schooled him in the ways of the House. Bolling was a favorite of the House establishment and at the same time, as a congressman from urban Kansas City, maintained a solidly liberal voting record. He seemed destined to become Speaker of the House some day. After Rayburn's death, however, Bolling got only a seat on the Rules Committee. In the years that followed he wrote two books, *House out of Order* and *Power in the House,* both of which attacked many of the traditional ways of doing things on the Hill; he was not seriously considered for a leadership position when

Speaker McCormack retired in 1970. And that winter Bolling missed an important vote on the Rules Committee when he refused to fly back for it from a Caribbean vacation.

The inexorable workings of the seniority system may yet make Bolling chairman of Rules, where he is currently the 4th ranking Democrat. In 1970, the Congressman was 54, while the more senior committee members, Chairman William Colmer and Ray Madden, were nearing 80, and James Delaney was almost 70. Bolling was one of two Missouri Democrats whose share of the votes dipped between 1968 and 1970 from 65% to 61%, and redistricting may add some Republican suburbs to his district. But the Congressman should not have much more difficulty winning elections in the future than he has had in the past.

Census Data 1970 pop. 379,619; deviation from current state average, —18.8%; change 1960–70, —11.7%. Metro. 100.0%, 99.9% central city.

1970 Share of Federal Outlays $530,035,000 (average outlay per district, Missouri 4 and 5)

DOD	$131,460,000	HEW	$112,723,000
AEC	$48,645,000	HUD	$9,753,000
NASA	$303,000	OEO	$2,503,000
DOT	$15,352,000	DOA	$76,594,000
		Other	$132,702,000

Federal Military-Industrial Commitments (Missouri 4 and 5, greater Kansas City listing)

DOD Contractors Remington Arms Div., Du Pont E. I. De Nemours (Independence), $128.083m: 20-mm and 50-mm small arms ammunition and operation of the Lake City Army Ammunition plant. American Oil Co. (Sugar Creek), $8.373m: petroleum products.

DOD Installations Richards-Gebaur AFB (Grandview). Whiteman AFB (Knobnoster).

AEC Operations Bendix Corp. (Kansas City), $82.669m: unspecified.

Economic Base Printing, publishing, and allied industries; electrical machinery, equipment, and supplies, esp. communication equipment; motor vehicles and motor vehicle equipment, and other transportation equipment. Also, banking and insurance.

The Voters

Registration No district-wide registration.

Employment profile White collar, 48%. Blue collar, 52%.

Ethnic groups Black, 28%. Total foreign stock, 12%. Germany, Italy, 2% each; Ireland, Poland, Sweden, UK, USSR, Canada, Mexico, 1% each; others, 2%.

Presidential vote

1968	Humphrey (D)	72,425	(55%)
	Nixon (R)	47,300	(36%)
	Wallace (AIP)	12,997	(10%)

Representative

Richard Bolling (D) Elected 1948; b. May 17, 1916, New York; home, Kansas City; U. of the South, B.A., 1937, M.A., 1939; Vanderbilt U., 1939–40; Army, WWII; married, one child; Episcopalian.

Career Dir. student activities and vet affairs, U. of Kansas City, 1946–47; Midwest Dir. Americans for Democratic Action, 1947; Natl. Vice-Chm. Am. Vets. Comm., 1947–48.

Offices 2465 RHOB, 1-202-225-4535. Also 935 Fed. Ct. Bldg., 811 Grand Ave., Kansas City 64106, 1-816-VI2-4798.

Committees

Rules (4th).

Jt. Economic Com. (2nd); Subs. (1) Chm., Urban Affairs, (2) Economic Statistics, (3) Fiscal Policy.

Group Ratings

	ADA	COPE	NREP	NFU	LCV	CFA	NAB	NSI	ACA
1970	52	82	82	100	80	100	9	22	6
1969	73	—	—	90	—	—	—	—	0
1968	100	100	—	93	—	—	0	—	5

Key Votes

(1) ABM	FOR	(6) 18-Yr-Vote	FOR	(11) Clean Water $	FOR
(2) SST	AGN	(7) Farm Sub Lmt	AGN	(12) Mig Wrkrs Comp	FOR
(3) Phil Pln	ABS	(8) Coop-Church	AGN	(13) Jets to Chiang	AGN
(4) No-Knock	ABS	(9) Family Asst	FOR	(14) State OEO Veto	AGN
(5) Cmutr Tax	ABS	(10) Work Stamps	AGN	(15) Park Logging	AGN

Election Results

1970 general:	Richard Bolling (D)	51,668	(61%)
	Randall Vanet (R)	31,806	(38%)
	Jim E. Kernodle (AIP)	778	(1%)
1970 primary:	Richard Bolling (D), unopposed (Redistricted 1969)		

SIXTH DISTRICT Political Background

Missouri 6 is the northwest corner of the state. Half of the district's residents live in the declining city of St. Joseph, an old river town, and in rapidly growing suburban areas of Platte and Clay counties, which have been annexed by Kansas City. Once Democratic, the 6th is now politically marginal; most counties here regularly switch parties from one election to the next.

Since 1954, the district has been represented by conservative Democrat W. R. (Bill) Hull, who is currently 20th ranking Democrat on the Appropriations Committee. His share of the votes in the 6th has declined steadily since 1964, and in 1970 he encountered strong opposition from Republican Hugh Sprague. In 1968 Hull carried Buchanan County (St. Joseph) by 6,300 votes; in 1970, Sprague, who comes from Buchanan, carried the county by 54 votes. Sprague also reduced Hull's margin in the Kansas City area, where the Congressman has usually run best, by 2%. But Hull increased his margin in the rural counties by 4%, one index of the Nixon Administration's general weakness among the nation's farmers.

Since the population of the 6th is just 6,000 below the state congressional district average, the district's boundaries are unlikely to change significantly. But because of Hull's continuing electoral weakness, and his narrow 1970 victory in particular, the Republicans will probably wage a serious campaign to capture the seat in 1972. If they do not succeed at that time, it is entirely possible that they will some time during the 1970's.

Census Data 1970 pop. 462,024; deviation from current state average, −1.2%; change 1960–70, +6.9%. Metro. 52.5%, 29.1% central city.

1970 Share of Federal Outlays $365,858,000

DOD	$12,013,000	HEW	$149,892,000
AEC	$30,000	HUD	$2,000
NASA	$16,000	OEO	$3,536,000
DOT	$14,891,000	DOA	$80,949,000
		Other	$104,529,000

Federal Military-Industrial Commitments

None.

Economic Base Livestock and cash grain; food and kindred products; chemicals and allied products; fabricated metal products.

The Voters

Registration No district-wide registration.

Employment profile White collar, 36%. Blue collar, 64%.

Ethnic groups Black, 1%. Total foreign stock, 5%. Germany, 2%; UK, 1%; others, 1%.

Presidential vote

1968	Humphrey (D)	82,725	(42%)
	Nixon (R)	96,584	(48%)
	Wallace (AIP)	20,158	(10%)

Representative

W. R. Hull, Jr. (D) Elected 1954; b. Apr. 17, 1906, Weston; home, Weston; widowed, two children; Christian Church.

Career Mayor of Weston, 1939; Vice Pres. for Mo. of Nat'l. Rivers and Harbors Congress.

Offices 2349 RHOB, 1-202-225-7041. Also Platte City 64079, 1-816-431-2451.

Committees

Appropriations (20th); Subs. (1) Agriculture, Environmental and Consumer Protection, (2) Labor and HEW.

Group Ratings

	ADA	COPE	NREP	NFU	LCV	CFA	NAB	NSI	ACA
1970	8	34	9	54	22	47	67	100	71
1969	13	—	—	50	—	—	—	—	85
1968	8	31	—	57	—	—	60	—	80

Key Votes

(1) ABM	ABS	(6) 18-Yr-Vote	AGN	(11) Clean Water $	AGN
(2) SST	FOR	(7) Farm Sub Lmt	ABS	(12) Mig Wrkrs Comp	AGN
(3) Phil Pln	ABS	(8) Coop-Church	AGN	(13) Jets to Chiang	FOR
(4) No-Knock	FOR	(9) Family Asst	AGN	(14) State OEO Veto	FOR
(5) Cmutr Tax	FOR	(10) Work Stamps	ABS	(15) Park Logging	FOR

Election Results

1970 general:	W. R. Hull (D)	74,496	(54%)
	Hugh A. Sprague (R)	63,789	(46%)
1970 primary:	W. R. Hull (D)	39,850	(76%)
	William H. Ford (D)	8,168	(16%)
	Ronnie C. Radmer (D)	4,457	(8%)
	(Redistricted 1969)		

SEVENTH DISTRICT Political Background

Missouri 7 is the southwest corner of the state and the most Republican part of Missouri, except for a few high-income suburbs around St. Louis. It includes most of the Ozark Mountain region, the state's third largest city, Springfield (pop. 120,000), and Joplin (pop. 39,000). The 7th has had an allegiance to the Republican Party since the time of the Civil War. The people of the Ozarks did not share the Confederate sympathies of many central Missourians. The region's traditional Republicanism, reinforced by a distaste for the social programs initiated by the national Democratic party, is remarkably consistent: none of the counties in the 7th gave a plurality to Humphrey, Eagleton, or Symington in the close statewide races of 1968 and 1970.

The 7th is the only Missouri district to send a Republican to Congress. Durward G. Hall, first elected in 1960, ran unopposed in the general election of 1970 and in 1968 won 64% of the votes. Hall will continue to win as long as he chooses to run. Hall is one of the few physicians serving in the House (the others are Tim Lee Carter of Kentucky and Thomas Morgan of Pennsylvania), and he is also one of its most conservative members.

Census Data 1970 pop. 481,313; deviation from current state average, +2.9%; change 1960–70, +11.4%. Metro. 31.8%, 25.0% central city.

1970 Share of Federal Outlays $270,795,000

DOD	$27,314,000	HEW	$138,005,000
AEC	$000	HUD	$2,468,000
NASA	$238,000	OEO	$428,000
DOT	$3,358,000	DOA	$21,847,000
		Other	$77,138,000

Federal Military-Industrial Commitments

None.

Economic Base Dairy and livestock; food and kindred products; nonelectrical machinery; apparel and other finished products made from fabrics and similar materials, esp. men's, youths', and boys' furnishings, work clothing, and allied garments.

The Voters

Registration No district-wide registration.

Employment profile White collar, 35%. Blue collar, 65%.

Ethnic groups Black, 1%. Total foreign stock, 3%. Germany, UK, 1% each; others, 1%.

Presidential vote

1968	Humphrey (D)	64,721	(32%)
	Nixon (R)	115,434	(58%)
	Wallace (AIP)	20,346	(10%)

Representative

Durward Gorham Hall (R) Elected 1960; b. Sept. 14, 1910, Cassville; home, Springfield; Mo. State Col., 1926; Drury Col., A.B., 1930; Rush Med. Col., M.D., 1934; Army, WWII; married, one child; Baptist.

Career Chief surgeon with Smith-Glynn-Callaway Clinic, 1936; general practice, 1936–60.

Offices 2351 RHOB, 1-202-225-6536. Also 204 Wilhait Bldg., Springfield 65805, 1-417-862-4317.

Committees

Armed Services (7th); Subs., (1) No. 1, (2) Sp. on Armed Services Investigating.

Jt. Com. on Congressional Operations (Ranking Rep. House Mbr.).

Group Ratings

	ADA	COPE	NREP	NFU	LCV	CFA	NAB	NSI	ACA
1970	8	10	9	17	13	32	100	100	89
1969	0	—	—	23	—	—	—	—	100
1968	0	0	—	13	—	—	100	—	100

Key Votes

(1) ABM	FOR	(6) 18-Yr-Vote	AGN	(11) Clean Water $	AGN
(2) SST	FOR	(7) Farm Sub Lmt	FOR	(12) Mig Wrkrs Comp	AGN
(3) Phil Pln	ABS	(8) Coop-Church	AGN	(13) Jets to Chiang	FOR
(4) No-Knock	FOR	(9) Family Asst	AGN	(14) State OEO Veto	FOR
(5) Cmutr Tax	ABS	(10) Work Stamps	FOR	(15) Park Logging	AGN

Election Results

1970 general:	Durward G. Hall (R), unopposed		
1970 primary:	Durward G. Hall (R)	42,002	(72%)
	John H. Simmons (R)	16,526	(28%)
	(Redistricted 1969)		

EIGHTH DISTRICT Political Background

Missouri 8 is made up of everything left over after the state's other districts were drawn. Parts of the old 11th, which disappeared when Missouri lost a House seat after the 1960 census, were added to parts of the old 8th to produce a district which, after re-destricting in 1961, 1965, 1967, and 1969, looks something like a sling shot. The western arm contains the Democratic Little Dixie area, whose original settlers came from Kentucky and Virginia, and the city of Columbia, the home of the University of Missouri. The eastern arm contains a heavily Republican part of St. Louis County, outside the city of St. Louis; some 40% of the district's residents live in St. Louis County, in towns like Kirkwood and Concord. Just to the south is fast-growing suburban Jefferson County, which is heavily Democratic. Of the southern counties, Cole, which contains the state capital, Jefferson City, has been staunchly Republican since it was settled by German '48'ers, while Pulaski, site of Fort Leonard Wood, is usually Democratic. The rest of the counties are politically marginal.

The voters of the 8th range from Republican suburbanites to antiwar academics to Southern-oriented farmers, but they all seem to be united in their support of Congressman Richard H. Ichord. In 1970, Ichord carried every county in the district, winning 64% of the votes; he has done about as well in previous elections. Since the Congressman has demonstrated his ability to survive repeated redistrictings, he should have no trouble in the unlikely event that the 8th is substantially altered by the legislature. He has also withstood challenges in the Democratic primary, but because some 55% of the primary votes are cast in suburban St. Louis and Jefferson counties and Boone County, which includes the University of Missouri, a strong peace candidate stands a chance of beating him. Ichord has been mentioned as a possible candidate for governor in 1972.

Ichord seems to have broken the jinx on the chairmanship of the House Internal Securities Committee. One chairman of what was formerly the House Un-American Activities Committee later went to jail, and in the '60's, two chairmen, Francis Walter of Pennsylvania and Clyde Doyle of California, died in rapid succession, and a third, Edwin Willis of Louisiana, was defeated in a Democratic primary. Ichord, who was 40 in 1970 and has been in Congress since 1960, is currently the youngest committee chairman in the House.

A classic Missouri Democrat, Ichord is moderate to liberal on issues of domestic spending and conservation, a strong supporter of the military, and an aggressive opponent of communists, both foreign and domestic. Ichord believes that many of the recent campus disorders were the product of a nationwide conspiracy, and in spite of a federal court order he has circulated a list of sixty-five alleged subversives who have spoken at various universities. Ichord has also conducted an investigation of the Ku Klux Klan. Under him the committee still rarely reports out legislation, but it has less of a circus atmosphere than in the past. Ichord is also a hawkish member of the House Armed Services Committee.

Census Data 1970 pop. 604,525; deviation from current state average, +29.2%; change 1960–70, +42.5%. Metro. 61.4%; 97.3% central city.

1970 Share of Federal Outlays $432,113,000

DOD	$168,581,000	HEW	$126,695,000
AEC	$248,000	HUD	$1,134,000
NASA	$215,000	OEO	$2,025,000
DOT	$5,677,000	DOA	$29,946,000
		Other	$97,592,000

Federal Military-Industrial Commitments

DOD Installations Fort Leonard Wood AB (Waynesville).

Economic Base Livestock and dairy; chemicals and allied products; stone, clay, glass, and concrete products. Also, higher education (University of Missouri).

The Voters

Registration No district-wide registration.

Employment profile White collar, 35%. Blue collar, 65%.

Ethnic groups Black, 3%. Total foreign stock, 5%. Germany, 2%; UK, 1%; others, 1%.

Presidential vote

1968	Humphrey (D)	76,909	(38%)
	Nixon (R)	101,211	(50%)
	Wallace (AIP)	23,612	(12%)

Representative

Richard H. Ichord (D) Elected 1960; b. June 27, 1926, Licking; home, Houston; U. of Mo., B.S., 1949, LL.B., 1952; married, three children; Baptist.

Career State Rep., 1952–60, Speaker, 1959.

Offices 2429 RHOB, 1-202-225-5155. Also Houston 65483, 1-417-967-2270.

Committees *Armed Services* (8th); Sub. No. 1.
Internal Security (Chm.).

Group Ratings

	ADA	COPE	NREP	NFU	LCV	CFA	NAB	NSI	ACA
1970	12	45	25	64	40	53	46	100	63
1969	20	—	—	40	—	—	—	—	81
1968	8	17	—	64	—	—	83	—	86

Key Votes

(1) ABM	FOR	(6) 18-Yr-Vote	AGN	(11) Clean Water $	AGN
(2) SST	FOR	(7) Farm Sub Lmt	ABS	(12) Mig Wrkrs Comp	ABS
(3) Phil Pln	AGN	(8) Coop-Church	AGN	(13) Jets to Chiang	FOR
(4) No-Knock	ABS	(9) Family Asst	AGN	(14) State OEO Veto	FOR
(5) Cmutr Tax	ABS	(10) Work Stamps	FOR	(15) Park Logging	FOR

Election Results

1970 general:	Richard Ichord (D)	97,560	(64%)
	John L. Caskanett (R)	53,181	(35%)
	Charles H. Byford (Ind.)	879	(1%)
1970 primary:	Richard Ichord (D)	43,351	(76%)
	Clyde Wilson (D)	12,583	(22%)
	Joseph A. Schwan (D)	1,087	(2%)
	(Redistricted 1969)		

NINTH DISTRICT Political Background

Missouri 9, in the northeast corner of the state, is dominated politically by the Little Dixie region. These counties, which extend from near the Missouri River to just short of the northern border of the state, were originally settled by people from Virginia and Kentucky. Little Dixie, which contains Mark Twain's Hannibal, accounts for 40% of the current 9th's residents. The region has retained its Democratic voting habits, even in recent presidential elections. St. Charles County and the 9th's share of St. Louis County together account for another 40% of the district's population. St. Louis County contains Black Jack, a newly incorporated city that is being sued for excluding blacks, and the heavily Democratic town of Florissant. Just to the north, St. Charles County, which is growing rapidly as the St. Louis metropolitan area expands, is marginal to Democratic. The rest of the district is made up of several counties along the Missouri River. These were settled in the nineteenth century by German immigrants who have retained a strong identification with the Republican party over the years.

From the 1920's until his death in 1964, Clarence Cannon, chairman of the Appropriations Committee for more than 20 years, was the congressman from the 9th. Cannon, who was also Parliamentarian of the House, was a fiercely independent and conservative Democrat, who pigeonholed much of the Kennedy-Johnson legislative program.

His successor, William L. Hungate, generally votes with Northern liberals on domestic, defense, and war issues. Except for 1968, when Republican challenger Christopher Bond, now State Auditor, held his margin to 52%, Hungate has run well in the district. In 1970, he polled 63%. The 9th will have to be altered to meet the one-man-one-vote requirement, but Hungate should have no trouble winning reelection.

Census Data 1970 pop. 551,132; deviation from current state average, +17.8%; change 1960–70, 27.7%. Metro. 48.8%, 0.0% central city.

1970 Share of Federal Outlays $265,954,000

DOD	$33,113,000	HEW	$112,866,000
AEC	$1,000	HUD	$1,624,000
NASA	$000	OEO	$569,000
DOT	$4,800,000	DOA	$45,778,000
		Other	$67,202,000

Federal Military-Industrial Commitments

DOD Contractors Conductron Div., McDonnell Douglas (St. Charles), $20.917m: A-7 aircraft flight simulator trainers.

Economic Base Livestock and cash grain; footwear other than rubber, and other leather and leather products; stone, clay, glass, and concrete products, esp. structural clay products.

The Voters

Registration No district-wide registration.

Employment profile White collar, 32%. Blue collar, 68%.

Ethnic groups Black, 2%. Total foreign stock, 5%. Germany, 3%; UK, 1%; others, 1%.

Presidential vote

1968	Humphrey (D)	87,016	(41%)
	Nixon (R)	100,784	(47%)
	Wallace (AIP)	26,194	(12%)

Representative

William L. Hungate (D) Elected 1964; b. Dec. 14, 1922, Benton, Ill.; home, Troy; Mo. U., A.B., 1943; Harvard, LL.B., 1948; Army, WWII; married, two children; First Christian Church.

Career Practicing atty.; prosecuting atty. of Lincoln County; Special Asst. Atty. Gen. of Mo., 1958–64.

Offices 439 CHOB, 1-202-225-2956. Also 219 W. College St., Troy 63379, 1-314-528-7533.

Committees

District of Columbia (8th); Subs. (1) Chm., Judiciary, (2) Education.

Group Ratings

	ADA	COPE	NREP	NFU	LCV	CFA	NAB	NSI	ACA
1970	60	83	73	67	86	79	17	70	32
1969	67	—	—	73	—	—	—	—	47
1968	42	45	—	87	—	—	40	—	21

Key Votes

(1) ABM	FOR	(6) 18-Yr-Vote	FOR	(11) Clean Water $	FOR
(2) SST	AGN	(7) Farm Sub Lmt	FOR	(12) Mig Wrkrs Comp	FOR
(3) Phil Pln	AGN	(8) Coop-Church	FOR	(13) Jets to Chiang	AGN
(4) No-Knock	FOR	(9) Family Asst	AGN	(14) State OEO Veto	AGN
(5) Cmutr Tax	ABS	(10) Work Stamps	AGN	(15) Park Logging	AGN

Election Results

1970 general:	William L. Hungate (D)	100,988	(63%)
	Anthony C. Schroeder (R)	58,103	(36%)
	Orvil C. Hale (AIP)	1,198	(1%)
1970 primary:	William L. Hungate (D)	51,571	(90%)
	Vince Roth (D)	5,899	(10%)
	(Redistricted 1969)		

TENTH DISTRICT Political Background

Missouri 10, the southeast corner of the state, was originally settled by Southerners coming up the Mississippi in search of more cotton land. Cape Girardeau, on the river, is a Republican stronghold, and to the west the district extends a little way (Howell County) into the Republican Ozarks. But Democrats with a pronounced Southern orientation dominate the 10th, and its voting patterns resemble those in nearby Arkansas, Tennessee, Kentucky, and southern Illinois. In 1968, Wallace took 18% of the votes in the 10th, his best showing in any Missouri district.

Bill D. Burlison, formerly a county prosecutor in Cape Girardeau, was first elected congressman from the 10th in 1968. Burlison, who serves on the Agriculture and the Interior and Insular Affairs committees, has a middle-of-the-road voting record. The Republicans have made strong efforts to take the seat. Because their candidate received 46% of the vote in 1968, they had high hopes in 1970. They were disappointed that year with an ultraconservative who won just 44%. The 1970 election is another example of the power of incumbency, but Burlison might still be vulnerable in a strong Republican year. His chances of reelection would also be weakened by another round of civil rights legislation sponsored by the national Democratic party. But Burlison, like most of his constituents, usually opposes such legislation.

Census Data 1970 pop. 408,743; deviation from current state average, —12.6%; change 1960–70, —5.4%. Metro. 0.0%, 0.0% central city.

1970 Share of Federal Outlays $364,087,000

DOD	$12,791,000	HEW	$141,084,000
AEC	$000	HUD	$1,601,000
NASA	$000	OEO	$1,475,000
DOT	$67,131,000	DOA	$69,907,000
		Other	$70,098,000

Federal Military-Industrial Commitments

None.

Economic Base Cotton and livestock; leather and leather products; apparel and other finished products made from fabrics and similar materials.

The Voters

Registration No district-wide registration.

Employment profile White collar, 30%. Blue collar, 70%.

Ethnic groups Black, 6%. Total foreign stock, 2%. Germany, 1%; all other groups, less than 1%.

Presidential vote

1968	Humphrey (D)	59,797	(38%)
	Nixon (R)	70,098	(44%)
	Wallace (AIP)	29,122	(18%)

Representative

Bill D. Burlison (D) Elected 1968; b. March 15, 1931, Wardell; home, Cape Girardeau; Mo. State Col., B.A., 1953, B.S., 1959; U. of Mo., LL.B., 1956; M. Ed., 1964; USMC, 1956–59; married, three children; Baptist.

Career Atty., 1956–59; real estate broker, 1960–62; Pres. Cape Girardeau County Bd. of Ed., 1966; Asst. Atty. Gen. Mo., 1959–62; pros. atty. Cape Girardeau County, 1962–68.

Offices 1338 LHOB, 1-202-225-4404. Also New Fed. Bldg., Cape Girardeau 63701, 1-314-335-0101.

Committees

Agriculture (13th); Subs. (1) Cotton, (2) Forests, (3) Oilseeds and Rice.

Interior and Insular Affairs (17th); Subs. (1) Environment, (2) Mines and Mining, (3) National Parks and Recreation, (4) Territorial and Insular Affairs.

Group Ratings

	ADA	COPE	NREP	NFU	LCV	CFA	NAB	NSI	ACA
1970	48	60	50	67	67	75	59	80	53
1969	53	—	—	73	—	—	—	—	41

Key Votes

(1) ABM	AGN	(6) 18-Yr-Vote	FOR	(11) Clean Water $	FOR
(2) SST	AGN	(7) Farm Sub Lmt	AGN	(12) Mig Wrkrs Comp	AGN
(3) Phil Pln	AGN	(8) Coop-Church	FOR	(13) Jets to Chiang	AGN
(4) No-Knock	FOR	(9) Family Asst	FOR	(14) State OEO Veto	AGN
(5) Cmutr Tax	FOR	(10) Work Stamps	FOR	(15) Park Logging	FOR

Election Results

1970 general:	Bill D. Burlison (D)	62,764	(56%)
	Gary Rust (R)	49,355	(44%)
1970 primary:	Bill D. Burlison (D), unopposed		
	(Redistricted 1969)		

MONTANA

Political Background

Though Montana is the nation's fourth largest state in area, only seven states have fewer people living in them. In the Big Sky country, a land of vast and barren plains and rugged mountains, one can drive down a major highway for 40 miles without seeing another car. Most Montanans like it this way and prefer weekends of fishing, hunting, or boating to anything they might find in a big city. The state's largest metropolitan areas are Billings and Great Falls, each with only 60,000 people.

Montana's first settlers were miners, some of whom found large deposits of gold, silver, and copper in the mountains in the western part of the state. Later, cattlemen, dry-land wheat farmers, and sugar beet farmers using diverted irrigation water moved into the plains and river valleys of eastern Montana. Throughout the United States, miners seem to be Democrats and Montana miners are no exception. Butte and Anaconda, copper towns, are both losing population as the profitable ores are depleted, but both still cast 3–1 Democratic margins in nearly every election. Toward the east, around Billings, the state's fastest-growing area, the voters are mostly conservative Republicans. The general rule for the rest of the state is that the counties to the north are Democratic, and to the south, Republican. Montana voters, however, are not very predictable. It is not unusual to see a county switch parties to vote for the losers in two successive elections, a rather uncommon form of political behavior in other states.

The senior senator from Montana is Mike Mansfield, the Senate Majority Leader. Mansfield, born in Manhattan in 1903, was sent by his Irish immigrant parents to live with relatives in Montana. When he was fourteen, he enlisted in the Navy, and later served in the Army and the Marine Corps. After a few years of working the mines he went back to school, at his wife's insistence, and earned two college degrees. During the '30's Mansfield was a professor of Latin American and Far Eastern history at Montana University in Missoula. In 1942 he was elected to the House; ten years later, in a close race, he defeated incumbent Zales N. Ecton for a seat in the Senate. Since then, Mansfield has never received less than 60% of the votes in Montana.

Mansfield has been the Senate Majority Leader since 1961, when Lyndon Johnson became Vice President. The criticism he once drew for a lack of aggressiveness in that post subsided as the country became polarized and hot-tempered over Vietnam and the black revolution. The Montana Senator's fairness and humility are legendary in the Senate. His civility and respect for his opponents are as unflagging as his determination to make his own point. Mansfield is one of the few senators who has always been skeptical about the nation's involvement in Vietnam, and one of the few men in public life with the nerve to confront Johnson personally with the issue. In addition, Mansfield has for years crusaded for a reduction in the number of American troops stationed in Europe.

Mansfield is also attentive to the needs of his Montana constituency. When, for example, Railpax planned to cut off passenger service to the state's largest cities, the Majority Leader saw to it that service was restored. Mansfield is, of course, unbeatable in the state, but in 1970 one issue—support of gun-control legislation—affected his performance at the polls. In Montana, where the attitudes of the firearm buff resemble those of car buffs elsewhere, that support created some political enemies. In 1970, Mansfield's Republican opponent, a Missoula sporting goods dealer, based his campaign on the gun issue and a charge that the Senator was "soft on communism." The strategy gave the Republican 39% of the votes, the best anybody has been able to do against Mansfield since 1952.

Democrat Lee Metcalf won a House seat in 1952 and became the state's junior Senator in 1960. Like many Western politicians, Metcalf is especially interested in electric power—the Senator is a strong proponent of public power development and an equally vigorous critic of private utilities. Not as strong at the polls as Mansfield, Metcalf fought off a challenge by then Governor Tim Babcock in 1966 with only 53% of the votes. He will probably be reelected in 1972, if only because there is no well-known Republican to run against him. The outcome of that election, however, will depend largely on the popularity of the Nixon Administration. In 1968, Nixon carried Montana with 51%, with Humphrey getting 42% and Wallace 7%. But dissatisfaction with the Administration is growing, particularly in agricultural eastern Montana.

Electoral Votes 4

Census Data 1970 pop. 694,409; 0.34% of U.S. total, 45th largest; change 1960–70, +2.9%. Metro. 24.4%, 17.5% central city. 1970 per capita income, $3,381; 34th highest. 39th in number of poor.

1970 Share of Federal Tax Burden $546,390,000; 0.28% of U.S. total, 44th largest.

1970 Share of Federal Outlays $824,387,715; 43% of U.S. total, 42nd largest. Per capita federal spending, $1,187.

DOD	$143,048,000	43rd (0.36%)		HEW	$182,069,652	43rd (0.29%)
AEC	$11,888	52nd (—)		HUD	$7,867,580	42nd (0.40%)
NASA	$000			OEO	$3,938,300	39th (0.45%)
DOT	$92,874,215	30th (1.30%)		DOA	$206,009,779	24th (1.61%)
DOC	$3,231,289	40th (0.27%)		POD	$22,457,394	44th (0.31%)
DOI	$44,167,203	16th (1.91%)		VA	$35,618,978	44th (0.48%)
DOJ	$2,387,898	41st (0.42%)		CSC	$10,192,730	43rd (0.25%)
				Other	$70,512,269	

Economic Base Livestock and cash grain; lumber and wood products other than furniture, esp. saw mills and planing mills; primary metal industries, esp. smelting and refining of nonferrous metals; food and kindred products; metal mining, esp. copper, lead, and zinc, and gold and silver; crude petroleum and natural gas.

Political Line-up Governor, Forrest Anderson (D); seat up, 1972. Senators, Mike Mansfield (D) and Lee Metcalf (D). Representatives, 2 (1 D and 1 R). State Senate (30 D and 25 R); State House (49 D and 55 R).

The Voters

Registration 325,315 total. No party registration.

Employment profile White collar 39%. Blue collar, 61%.

Ethnic groups Black, less than 0.5%. Total foreign stock, 22%. Canada, 4%; Germany, Norway, 3% each; UK, USSR, 2% each; Sweden, Ireland, Italy, Austria, 1% each; others, 5%.

Presidential vote

1968	Humphrey (D)	114,117	(42%)
	Nixon (R)	138,835	(51%)
	Wallace (AIP)	20,015	(7%)
1964	Johnson (D)	164,246	(59%)
	Goldwater (R)	113,032	(41%)
1960	Kennedy (D)	134,891	(49%)
	Nixon (R)	141,841	(51%)

Senator

Michael J. Mansfield (D) Elected 1952, seat up 1976; b. March 16, 1903, New York City; home, Missoula; Mont. School of Mines, 1927–28; Mont. State U., B.A., 1933, M.A., 1934; U. of Calif., 1936–37; Navy, 1918–19; Army, 1919–20; USMC, 1920–22; married, one child; Catholic.

Career Miner, mining engineer, 1922–31; Prof., Mont. U., 1933–43; U.S. House of Reps., 1942–52; Asst. Majority Leader, U.S. Senate, 1957–61, Majority Leader, 1961– .

Offices 133 OSOB, 202-225-2644.

Committees

Appropriations (9th); Subs. (1) Chm., Military Construction, (2) Agriculture, Environmental and Consumer Protection, (3) Department of Defense, (4) Departments of State, Justice, Commerce, the Judiciary, and Related Agencies, (5) HUD, Space, and Science.

Foreign Relations (3rd); Subs. (1) Chm., Far Eastern Affairs, (2) Near Eastern and South Asian Affairs, (3) U.S. Security Agreements and Commitments Abroad, (4) Western Hemisphere Affairs.

Group Ratings

	ADA	COPE	NREP	NFU	LCV	NAB	NSI	ACA
1970	75	83	73	94	27	20	20	29
1969	72	—	—	73	—	—	—	17
1968	80	80	—	46	—	33	—	21

Key Votes

(1) ABM	AGN	(8) Phil Pln	FOR	(15) Coop-Church	FOR
(2) SST	AGN	(9) Vol Army	FOR	(16) Cut Oil Dpltn	AGN
(3) Busing	FOR	(10) Prison $	FOR	(17) Consumer Prot	FOR
(4) Tob Sub	FOR	(11) Cut Mil $	FOR	(18) Farm Sub Limit	FOR
(5) Carswell	AGN	(12) Defoliatn	AGN	(19) Comp Bid Sales	AGN
(6) No-Knock	AGN	(13) 18-Yr-Vote	FOR	(20) Pre-Prod Tests	ABS
(7) Seniorty	FOR	(14) Pentgn PR	AGN	(21) Cut Marjna Pen	FOR

Election Results

1970 general:	Mike Mansfield (D)	150,060	(61%)
	Harold E. Wallace (R)	97,809	(39%)
1970 primary:	Mike Mansfield (D)	68,146	(77%)
	Tom McDonald (D)	10,733	(12%)
	John W. Lawlor (D)	9,384	(11%)
1964 general:	Mike Mansfield (D)	180,643	(65%)
	Alex Blewett (R)	99,367	(35%)

Senator

Lee Metcalf (D) Elected 1960, seat up 1972; b. Jan. 28, 1911, Stevensville; home, Helena; Stanford U., B.A., 1936; Mont. State U., LL.B., 1936; Army, WWII; married, one child; Methodist.

Career Practicing atty., 1936–53; Mont. House of Reps., 1937; Asst. Atty. Gen., Mont., 1937–41; Assoc. Justice, Mont. Supreme Ct., 1946; U.S. House of Reps., 1952–60.

Offices 427 OSOB, 202-225-2651. Also Lalonde Bldg., 41½ N. Main St., Helena 59601, 406-442-4361, and 4439 Fed. Bldg., Billings 59101, 406-259-5966.

Committees

Government Operations (7th); Subs. (1) Executive Reorganization, (2) Intergovernmental Relations.

Interior and Insular Affairs (8th); Subs. (1) Indian Affairs, (2) Public Lands, (3) Territories and Insular Affairs, (4) Water and Power Resources.

Jt. Com. on Congressional Operations (Ranking Dem. Sen.).

Group Ratings

	ADA	COPE	NREP	NFU	LCV	NAB	NSI	ACA
1970	72	100	82	100	63	0	13	0
1969	89	—	—	94	—	—	—	0
1968	79	100	—	46	—	0	—	9

Key Votes

(1) ABM	AGN	(8) Phil Pln	FOR	(15) Coop-Church	FOR
(2) SST	AGN	(9) Vol Army	ABS	(16) Cut Oil Dpltn	FOR
(3) Busing	ABS	(10) Prison $	ABS	(17) Consumer Prot	AGN
(4) Tob Sub	ABS	(11) Cut Mil $	FOR	(18) Farm Sub Limit	AGN
(5) Carswell	AGN	(12) Defoliatn	AGN	(19) Comp Bid Sales	ABS
(6) No-Knock	AGN	(13) 18-Yr-Vote	FOR	(20) Pre-Prod Tests	FOR
(7) Seniorty	AGN	(14) Pentgn PR	AGN	(21) Cut Marjna Pen	FOR

Election Results

1966 general:	Lee Metcalf (D)	138,166	(53%)
	Tim Babcock (R)	121,697	(47%)
1966 primary:	Lee Metcalf (D), unopposed		
1960 general:	Lee Metcalf (D)	140,331	(51%)
	Orwin B. Fjare (R)	136,281	(49%)

FIRST DISTRICT Political Background

Montana 1 is the state's western congressional district. Most of the 1st's residents live in small towns nestled in the Rocky Mountains; the rest live in scattered ranches and mountain cabins or on Indian reservations. The district's largest city is Missoula (pop. 29,000), home of the University of Montana; followed by Butte, a mining town whose population today is barely half of what it was forty years ago. Anaconda, another mining town, lies to the west, and Kalispell, near Lake Flathead, to the north. Missoula is politically marginal, but Butte and Anaconda are sources of Democratic strength, as is the Blackfoot Indian Reservation which covers most of Glacier County, and the mountain counties in the northeast corner of the district. Republicans usually carry Helena, the state capital, and the sparsely populated counties near Yellowstone Park, to the south.

The 1st has consistently been one of the nation's most marginal districts, even though it sent only Democrats to Congress from the early '40's to 1970. Former Congressman Arnold Olsen, who succeeded Senator Metcalf in 1960, was never able to amass a solid majority. In 1970, after winning five successive elections with less than 55% of the votes. Olsen finally lost to the Republican mayor of Missoula, 64,388 to 63,175. Shoup's victory can be attributed to strength in his home county; outside of Missoula County he ran only 12 votes ahead of Olsen.

The Olsen loss was only one of two 1970 House races in the nation where a conservative Republican ousted an incumbent liberal Democrat; the other was Allard Lowenstein, who was redistricted out of his seat in New York. In Montana 1, the Republican trend could also be seen in the other races. For the first time in recent history, a major statewide Democratic candidate (Mansfield) did not do as well in the 1st as he did in the 2nd. The changing demography of the district probably accounts for the growing Republican strength here. As heavily Democratic Butte and Anaconda lose population and Missoula, which is politically marginal, gains, the balance shifts towards the Republicans. In 1966, the four heavily Democratic counties around Butte cast 39% of the votes in the 1st; in 1970, the figure was down to 37%. In most districts such a change would be trivial, but in the closely balanced 1st it may have been decisive.

Certainly the long-range population trends here favor the Republicans (redistricting will make minor changes, if any), and Shoup's odds in 1972, when he will have all the advantages of incumbency, are better than even. If the Congressman decides to run against Metcalf for the Senate seat, all that can be said is that the House race in the 1st will be a close one.

Census Data 1970 pop. 353,563; deviation from current state average, +1.8%; change 1960–70, +8.1%. Metro. 0.0%, 0.0% central city.

1970 Share of Federal Outlays $401,342,374

DOD	$63,579,000	HEW	$96,568,372
AEC	$11,888	HUD	$7,365,404
NASA	$000	OEO	$2,081,216
DOT	$39,328,510	DOA	$93,274,296
		Other	$99,133,688

Federal Military-Industrial Commitments

DOD Contractors Morrison-Knudsen and Assoc. (Libby), $22.900m: construction of Safeguard ABM sites.

DOD Installations Kalispell AF Station (Kalispell).

Economic Base Livestock and cash grain; lumber and wood products other than furniture, esp. saw mills and planing mills; metal mining. Also, tourism (Glacier National Park).

The Voters

Registration 325,315 total. No party registration.

Employment profile White collar, 39%. Blue collar, 61%.

Ethnic groups Black, less than 0.5%. Total foreign stock, 22%. Canada, 4%; UK, Germany, 3% each; Norway, Ireland, 2% each; Sweden, USSR, Austria, Italy, 1% each; others, 5%.

Presidential vote

1968	Humphrey (D)	60,338	(43%)
	Nixon (R)	67,386	(48%)
	Wallace (AIP)	11,406	(8%)

Representative

Richard G. Shoup (R) Elected 1970; b. Nov. 29, 1923, Salmon, Idaho; home, Missoula; U. of Mont., B.S., 1950; Army, WWII and Korean War; married, three children; Disciples of Christ.

Career Alderman; Missoula City Council, 1963–67, Pres., 1965–67; Mayor, Missoula, 1967–70; owner-operator, laundry and dry-cleaning business.

Offices 1724 LHOB, 202-225-3211. Also 1609 South Ave. West, Missoula 59801, 406-543-7882.

Committees

Interstate and Foreign Commerce (18th); Subs. (1) Sp. on Investigations.

Group Ratings, Key Votes: Newly elected.

Election Results

1970 general:	Richard G. Shoup (R)	64,388	(50%)
	Arnold Olsen (D)	63,175	(50%)
1970 primary:	Richard G. Shoup (D)	17,989	(61%)
	Thomas M. Mongar (D)	5,874	(20%)
	Tom Winsor (D)	5,801	(20%)
1968 general:	Arnold Olsen (D)	74,974	(54%)
	Richard Smiley (R)	64,862	(46%)

SECOND DISTRICT Political Background

Montana 2 is a region of vast ranches and, to east, of large farms and the state's two largest cities, Billings and Great Falls. These cities and their surrounding suburbs cast almost half of the district's votes. Great Falls is traditionally Democratic, while Billings is strongly conservative. The rest of the 2nd is Democratic along the Canadian border and Republican to the south. Like the 1st, this has been marginal country politically; but unlike the 1st, it elected congressmen during the '60's with margins far in excess of those usually won by their respective parties.

In 1969, Republican Congressman James F. Battin, accustomed to winning here by solid majorities (68% in 1968), resigned to become a federal judge. A special election was called, and as in several other such elections that year (e.g., Massachusetts 6 and Wisconsin 7), a Democrat captured a formerly Republican seat. Democratic state Sen. John Melcher put his opponent, state Rep. W. S. Mather, on the defensive by attacking the economic policies of the Nixon Administration, especially its farm programs. Mather responded, saying that he didn't think much of them either. Melcher also criticized Nixon's ABM policy, but did not stress the issue in his campaign. The attack was unpopular, since one of the nation's first ABM sites was then scheduled to become operational at Malstrom Air Force Base, outside of Great Falls. Melcher won a large enough margin in Great Falls to balance Mather's strength in Billings, and he carried the rest of the district for a 51% victory.

In 1970, the Republicans very much wanted to recapture the 2nd, and they seemed to have a strong candidate in Jack Rehberg, a popular Billings state Senator. Rehberg campaigned hard all over the district. He stressed the law-and-order issue and argued that because the country was going to have a Republican President for some time, the district needed a Republican congressman. Melcher responded with a vigorous campaign of his own; he spoke in favor of greater health and education outlays and a reduction of expenditures for the space program and the SST. Although Melcher had voted against the ABM in the House, he intimated on the campaign trail that he would now support it. Melcher also dealt with issues of parochial concern: he opposed the phasing out of the farm price-support system and advocated an import quota on foreign meat.

What was surprising about the result was not that Melcher won—after all, incumbents, even in marginal districts, usually do—but the size of the majority: 64% of the votes. Melcher even carried Yellowstone County (Billings), only the fourth Democratic House candidate in forty years to do so, by the remarkable margin of 5,066 votes. The Congressman outpolled Mansfield in Yellowstone and district-wide ran 3% ahead of the Senator.

Why the strong showing? One factor is the farm revolt. Farmers, ranchers, and the many others whose economic well-being depends upon the health of agriculture have, since the '50's, expressed dissatisfaction with the nation's farm programs by voting against whatever party happens to occupy the White House. Another factor was Melcher's strong, well-financed campaign, and his adroit use of the advantages of incumbency. And although Melcher supported liberal programs in Washington, back home on the campaign trail he spoke like a Montanan. He stressed the right of dissent, but quickly condemned the violence which the President encountered in San Jose. After his defeat, Rehberg conceded that his repeated use of the law-and-order issue was a mistake. That appeal, designed to attract blue-collar voters fearful of Negro incursions in places like Baltimore and Cleveland, did not go over with residents of small, well-ordered cities like Billings or with ranchers worried about the price of beef on the hoof. Melcher's convincing victory means that he can remain in the House for as long as he wishes. It also makes him a leading contender for the Senate if Mike Mansfield retires in 1976. The other man in the picture is former NBC newscaster Chet Huntley, a Montana native who has returned to the state. He is currently building a tourist development in the middle of what some environmental activists say should remain virgin wilderness. There is a national trend toward electing newscasters to Congress, and Huntley, one of the really big men in the field, would be an easy winner in a Montana race. The House may not be enough to tempt him away from his Big Sky promotions, but Mansfield's Senate seat probably could.

Census Data 1970 pop. 340,846; deviation from current state average, —1.8%; change 1960–70, –2.0%. Metro. 49.6%, 35.7% central city.

1970 Share of Federal Outlays $423,045,341

DOD	$79,469,000	HEW	$85,501,280
AEC	$000	HUD	$502,176
NASA	$000	OEO	$1,857,084
DOT	$53,545,705	DOA	$112,735,483
		Other	$89,434,613

Federal Military-Industrial Commitments

DOD Contractors Avco Economic Systems (Glasgow), $5.761m: ammunition components.

DOD Installations Malstrom AFB (Great Falls). Havre AF Station (Havre). Opheim AF Station (Opheim).

Economic Base Livestock and cash grain; food and kindred products; primary metal industries, esp. primary smelting and refining of nonferrous metals.

The Voters

Registration 158,708 total. No party registration.

Employment profile White collar, 40%. Blue collar, 60%.

Ethnic groups Black, less than 0.5%. Total foreign stock, 22%. Canada, Germany, Norway, USSR, 3% each; UK, 2%; Sweden, Czech., Italy, Ireland, Austria, 1% each; others, 4%.

Presidential vote

1968	Humphrey (D)	53,779	(40%)
	Nixon (R)	71,449	(53%)
	Wallace (AIP)	8,609	(6%)

Representative

John Melcher (D) Elected 1968; b. Sept. 6, 1924, Sioux City, Iowa; home, Forsyth; U. of Minn., 1942–43; Iowa State U., D.V.M., 1950; Army, WWII; married, five children; Catholic.

Career Veterinary; Alderman, Forsyth, 1953; Mayor, Forsyth, 1955–61; Mont. House of Reps., 1961–62, 1969; Mont. Senate, 1963–67.

Offices 1504 LHOB, 202-225-4415. Also 1016 Fed. Bldg., Billings 59102, 406-245-6644, and 9 Sixth St. N., Great Falls 59401, 406-761-3365.

Committees

Agriculture (16th); Subs. (1) Family Farms and Rural Development, (2) Livestock and Grains.

Interior and Insular Affairs (20th); Subs. (1) Environment, (2) Indian Affairs, (3) Mines and Mining, (4) National Parks and Recreation, (5) Public Lands.

Group Ratings

	ADA	COPE	NREP	NFU	LCV	CFA	NAB	NSI	ACA
1970	68	75	75	92	100	100	36	75	35
1969	78	—	—	91	—	—	—	—	29

Key Votes

(1) ABM	FOR	(6) 18-Yr-Vote	FOR	(11) Clean Water $	FOR
(2) SST	AGN	(7) Farm Sub Lmt	AGN	(12) Mig Wrkrs Comp	FOR
(3) Phil Pln	AGN	(8) Coop-Church	FOR	(13) Jets to Chiang	AGN
(4) No-Knock	FOR	(9) Family Asst	FOR	(14) State OEO Veto	AGN
(5) Cmutr Tax	FOR	(10) Work Stamps	AGN	(15) Park Logging	AGN

Election Results

1970 general:	John Melcher (D)	78,082	(64%)
	Jack Rehberg (R)	43,752	(36%)
1970 primary:	John Melcher (D), unopposed		

NEBRASKA

Political Background

Nebraska is the most Republican state in the country. Nixon got his best percentages here in both 1960 and 1968, and the state's congressional delegation has more often than not been entirely Republican. The origin of the state's Republicanism lies in the great land rush of the 1880's, which brought some 600,000 new residents to Nebraska mainly from the Republican Midwest. In 1880 Nebraska had a population of 452,000; ten years later it was 1,062,000—not far below the 1970 figure of 1,483,000. During the depression of the 1890's Nebraska produced the "Silver Tongue Orator of the Platte," William Jennings Bryan, and his populist prairie radicalism, but the state quickly reverted to its Republican voting habits, supporting McKinley over Bryan in 1900. Since then Nebraska's only notable lapse from conservative Republicanism was the long career enjoyed by George W. Norris (congressman 1902–12 and senator 1912–42). In the Progressive era, Norris led the House rebellion against Speaker Cannon in 1909, and during the 1930's he fathered the TVA and the Norris-LaGuardia Anti-Injunction Act.

Since 1900 most of Nebraska's growth has occurred in and around the state's two major cities, Omaha (pop. 347,000) and Lincoln (pop. 149,000), which between them contain about 40% of the state's population. Most of the immigrants to Omaha, a railroad, meat-packing, and manufacturing center, and Lincoln, the state capital and home of the University of Nebraska, come from the rural, Republican hinterlands. There is a sizable eastern European, especially Czech., community on the south side of Omaha, which votes Democratic, as do a few isolated German-Catholic rural counties. In 1960 and 1968 Nixon carried both Omaha and Lincoln and all but three or four counties in rural Nebraska.

But if the state is overwhelmingly Republican in national and congressional elections, it has achieved a kind of equilibrium in state contests. As in a number of states, Nebraska's minority party has made especially strong efforts to win state elections and has scored some surprising successes. Since 1960, Democrats have held the governorship for all but four years; in 1970 the Democratic candidate for governor, adapting himself to local political sentiments, won a 55% victory with the classic Republican approach—lower taxes and less government spending. The Democratic surge in the state was also part of the senatorial and congressional races and produced some near upsets.

As a matter of tradition, Nebraska has had one senator from Omaha and one from the rural outstate. Roman L. Hruska, Nebraska's senior senator, has held the Omaha seat since 1954. In 1970, Hruska was challenged by another veteran campaigner, Democrat Frank B. Morrison. Morrison was governor from 1960 to 1966. He had run against Hruska once before in 1958 and against junior Senator Carl Curtis in 1966; in 1968, the only election year since 1956 in which Morrison has not run for statewide office, his wife ran for Congress in the 2nd district. Hruska campaigned as a staunch conservative and supporter of the Nixon Administration, while Morrison tried to project a middle-of-the-road image and contrasted his record as governor with that of his unpopular Republican successor. The most highly charged issue in the campaign was Morrison's allegation that a chain of drive-in movie theaters, of which Hruska was half owner, a director, and the secretary, was showing movies like "The Blood Drinker," "Girl on a Chain Gang," "Easy Rider," and "Catch 22." No doubt Hruska was embarrassed by this since he has always been an outspoken critic of pornography and had objected just some months before to the report of the presidential commission on the subject. The Senator responded with an "I-didn't-do-it, but-if-I-did-it-wasn't-so-bad" defense. Hruska claimed that he did not run the firm while at the same time claiming credit for the fact that it was one of the few chains that refused to show X-rated movies.

The pornography issue was a factor in Morrison's strong 47% showing—Hruska's closest race in sixteen years. Morrison carried Omaha and nearly carried the 1st and 2nd congressional districts. Even in the 3rd (western Nebraska), where he said that he did not have the time or money to wage an effective campaign, he ran well ahead (45%) of most Democratic candidates. Out here Morrison was helped by the farmer's traditional antagonism toward the farm program of the incumbent national Administration.

Hruska, now fifth in seniority among all Senate Republicans, is the ranking minority member of the Senate Judiciary Committee, where it fell upon him to defend the President's nomination of Judge G. Harrold Carswell to the Supreme Court. Hruska's remarks in a radio interview inadvertently contributed to Carswell's rejection. "Even if he were mediocre," the Nebraska Senator said, "there are a lot of mediocre judges and people and lawyers. They are entitled to a little representation, aren't they, and a little chance? We can't have all Brandeises and Frankfurters and Cardozos and stuff like that there."

Nebraska's junior senator, Carl Curtis, first won his seat in 1954, after sixteen years in the House. Curtis, a staunch supporter of Goldwater's bid in 1964, is the ranking Republican on the Aeronautical and Space Sciences Committee, while serving as 4th ranking Republican on Agriculture. Curtis has always run well in Nebraska; in 1966, for example, he defeated Frank Morrison with 61% of the votes. The Senator has announced that he will seek reelection in 1972. He will win, unless he runs into a combination of two things: (1) Nebraskans turning against the Nixon Administration, and (2) a popular Democrat opponent with a strong, well-financed campaign.

Electoral Votes 5

Census Data 1970 pop. 1,483,791; 0.72% of U.S. total, 36th largest; change 1960–70, +5.1%. Metro. 42.8%, 33.5% central city. 1970 per capita income, $3,700; 24th highest. 38th in number of poor.

1970 Share of Federal Tax Burden $1,248,900,000; 0.64% of U.S. total, 32nd largest.

1970 Share of Federal Outlays $1,508,834,585; 0.80% of U.S. total, 35th largest. Per capita federal spending, $1,017.

DOD	$239,604,000	41st	(0.42%)	HEW	$367,836,620	36th	(0.70%)
AEC	$349,916	41st	(0.01%)	HUD	$2,958,343	49th	(0.15%)
NASA	$111,352	47th	(—)	OEO	$3,909,773	40th	(0.51%)
DOT	$39,493,231	42nd	(0.55%)	DOA	$451,908,131	8th	(3.51%)
DOC	$1,391,193	49th	(0.12%)	POD	$61,009,084	31st	(0.84%)
DOI	$21,223,281	35th	(0.98%)	VA	$72,278,729	37th	(0.98%)
DOJ	$2,525,199	40th	(0.43%)	CSC	$77,186	38th	(—)
				Other	$244,128,447		

Economic Base Livestock and cash grain; electrical machinery, equipment, and supplies, esp. electronic components and accessories; nonelectrical machinery, esp. farm machinery and equipment; printing, publishing, and allied industries, esp. newspapers; fabricated metal products, esp. fabricated structural metal products; transportation equipment, esp. motor vehicles and motor vehicle equipment; ordnance and accessories; professional, scientific, and controlling instruments; photographic and optical goods, watches and clocks; food and kindred products.

Political Line-up Governor, J. J. Exon (D); seat up, 1974. Senators, Roman L. Hruska (R) and Carl T. Curtis (R). Representatives, 3 (0 D and 3 R). State unicameral legislature (49 nonpartisan members).

The Voters

Registration 687,142, total. 306,225 D (45%); 358,654 R (52%); 22,263 other (3%).

Employment profile White collar, 39%. Blue collar, 61%.

Ethnic groups Black, 3%. Total foreign stock, 18%. Germany, 6%; Czech., Sweden, 2% each; Italy, UK, USSR, Canada, 1% each; others, 3%.

Presidential vote

1968	Humphrey (D)	170,784	(32%)
	Nixon (R)	321,163	(60%)
	Wallace (AIP)	44,904	(8%)
1964	Johnson (D)	307,307	(53%)
	Goldwater (R)	276,847	(47%)
1960	Kennedy (D)	232,542	(38%)
	Nixon (R)	380,553	(62%)

Senator

Roman Lee Hruska (R) Appointed Nov. 1954, seat up 1976; b. Aug. 16, 1904, David City; home, Omaha; U. of Omaha, 1923–25; U. of Chicago, 1927–28; Creighton U., J.D., 1929; married, three children; Unitarian.

Career Practicing atty., 1929–53; Commissioner, Douglas County, 1944–52; Regent, U. of Omaha, 1950–57; U.S. House of Reps., 1952–54.

Offices 313 OSOB, 202-225-6551. Also 8424 Fed. Office Bldg., 215 N. 17th St., Omaha 68102, 402-221-4791.

Committees

Appropriations (4th); Subs. (1) Agriculture, Environmental and Consumer Protection, (2) Defense, (3) HUD, Space, and Science, (4) Public Works, (5) State, Justice, Commerce, the Judiciary, and Related Agencies.

Judiciary (Ranking Mbr.); Subs. (1) Federal Charters, Holidays, and Celebrations, (2) Antitrust and Monopoly Legislation, (3) Constitutional Amendments, (4) Constitutional Rights, (5) Criminal Laws and Procedures, (6) Improvements in Judicial Machinery, (7) Juvenile Delinquency, (8) Penitentiaries.

Sel. Com. on Equal Educational Opportunity (Ranking Mbr.).

Group Ratings

	ADA	COPE	NREP	NFU	LCV	NAB	NSI	ACA
1970	0	0	0	20	0	83	100	87
1969	6	—	—	25	—	—	—	80
1968	7	9	—	36	—	75	—	100

Key Votes

(1) ABM	FOR	(8) Phil Pln	AGN	(15) Coop-Church	AGN
(2) SST	FOR	(9) Vol Army	AGN	(16) Cut Oil Dpltn	AGN
(3) Busing	AGN	(10) Prison $	AGN	(17) Consumer Prot	AGN
(4) Tob Sub	FOR	(11) Cut Mil $	AGN	(18) Farm Sub Limit	AGN
(5) Carswell	FOR	(12) Defoliatn	FOR	(19) Comp Bid Sales	ABS
(6) No-Knock	FOR	(13) 18-Yr-Vote	AGN	(20) Pre-Prod Tests	AGN
(7) Seniorty	AGN	(14) Pentgn PR	FOR	(21) Cut Marjna Pen	AGN

Election Results

1970 general:	Roman L. Hruska (R)	240,894	(53%)
	Frank B. Morrison (D)	217,681	(47%)
1970 primary:	Roman L. Hruska (R)	159,059	(86%)
	Otis Glebe (R)	26,627	(14%)
1964 general:	Roman L. Hruska (R)	345,772	(61%)
	Raymond Arnt (D)	217,605	(39%)

Senator

Carl T. Curtis (R) Elected 1954, seat up 1972; b. March 15, 1905, Minden; home, Minden; attended Neb. Wesleyan U., awarded LL.D., 1958; widowed, one child; Presbyterian.

Career Practicing atty., 1931–35; Kearney County Atty., 1931–35; U.S. House of Reps., 1938–54; Repub. Natl. Convention, 1964, Chm., Neb. Delegation, Floor Manager for Sen. Barry M. Goldwater.

Offices 2213 NSOB, 202-225-4224. Masonic Bldg., Minden 68959, 308-832-2670.

Committees

Aeronautical and Space Sciences (Ranking Mbr.).

Agriculture and Forestry (4th); Subs. (1) Agricultural Production, Marketing, and Stabilization of Prices, (2) Agricultural Research and General Legislation, (3) Rural Development.

Finance (3rd).

Jt. Com. on Internal Revenue Taxation (2nd).

Group Ratings

	ADA	COPE	NREP	NFU	LCV	NAB	NSI	ACA
1970	0	0	0	21	3	100	100	95
1969	0	—	—	25	—	—	—	87
1968	7	0	—	23	—	80	—	96

Key Votes

(1) ABM	FOR	(8) Phil Pln	AGN	(15) Coop-Church	AGN
(2) SST	FOR	(9) Vol Army	AGN	(16) Cut Oil Dpltn	AGN
(3) Busing	AGN	(10) Prison $	AGN	(17) Consumer Prot	AGN
(4) Tob Sub	FOR	(11) Cut Mil $	AGN	(18) Farm Sub Limit	AGN
(5) Carswell	FOR	(12) Defoliatn	FOR	(19) Comp Bid Sales	FOR
(6) No-Knock	FOR	(13) 18-Yr-Vote	AGN	(20) Pre-Prod Tests	AGN
(7) Seniorty	AGN	(14) Pentgn PR	FOR	(21) Cut Marjna Pen	AGN

Election Results

1966 general:	Carl T. Curtis (R)	296,116	(61%)
	Frank B. Morrison (D)	187,950	(39%)
1966 primary:	Carl T. Curtis (R), unopposed		
1960 general:	Carl T. Curtis (R)	352,748	(59%)
	Robert B. Conrad (D)	215,807	(41%)

FIRST DISTRICT Political Background

Nebraska 1 is a group of 27 counties in the east central section of the state. Outside of Lincoln, the district's largest city, the 1st's economy is based on agriculture. There are a number of rural counties with large Catholic populations in the middle of the district near the Platte River, and these are either Democratic or marginal. Lincoln, the state capital and home of the University of Nebraska, is traditionally Republican. But the city's large number of state employees have sometimes joined members of the university community to swing Lincoln into the Democratic column. That vote can also work against the Democrats. In 1970, for example, Democratic gubernatorial candidate J. J. Exon ran an anti-tax, anti-spending campaign. He carried most of the state including Omaha, but lost badly in Lincoln. State employees and academics are not fond of politicians who are eager to cut the budget.

For the past ten years, the 1st has been the state's most closely contested district. In 1964, it went Democratic, electing Clair A. Callan to the House with 51% of the votes. Callan took Lancaster County (Lincoln) 60:40 and just missed carrying the rest of the district. In 1966 and again in 1968 Callan lost close elections to conservative Republican Robert V. Denney. Because Denney knew he was to be appointed a federal judge, he did not run in 1970, and a curious three-man race to succeed him developed. This time Callan, who had been the Democratic nominee since 1962, failed to win his party's endorsement but ran anyway as an independent. As it turned out, Callan beat the Democrat, 26:23, but in the process split the vote and both lost to the Republican, Charles Thone, who took 51%.

Thone ran as a supporter of the Nixon Administration and with the backing of his political mentor, Sen. Carl Curtis. Thone's 51% was a surprisingly poor performance. No Republican has been able to carry Lancaster County since Callan began running, but Thone polled just 52% in the rest of the district, the weakest Republican showing there since 1964. This was another indication of Nixon's vulnerability in the farm belt.

Nonetheless, Thone will win reelection in 1972 unless the farm revolt continues to gain momentum and makes the Republican label a major liability. It is, of course, always easier to capture a seat when the incumbent is not running, and so the Democrats, by splitting the vote in 1970, lost an excellent chance to carry the 1st. Thone has been suggested as Sen. Carl Curtis's likely successor, but since Curtis will seek reelection in 1972, Thone will have to wait until 1978.

Census Data 1970 pop. 494,335; deviation from current state average, —0.1%; change 1960–70, +1.1%. Metro. 36.6%, 30.2% central city.

1970 Share of Federal Outlays $439,184,972

DOD	$25,662,000	HEW	$140,427,660
AEC	$349,916	HUD	$2,011,000
NASA	$111,352	OEO	$1,390,822
DOT	$8,970,213	DOA	$156,697,071
		Other	$103,564,938

Federal Military-Industrial Commitments

None.

Economic Base Livestock and cash grain; food and kindred products; printing, publishing, and allied industries. Also, higher education (University of Nebraska); insurance.

The Voters

Registration 231,815, total. 98,848 D (43%); 126,439 R (55%); 6,528 other (3%).

Employment profile White collar, 37%. Blue collar, 63%.

Ethnic groups Black, 1%. Total foreign stock, 19%. Germany, 8%; Czech., 3%; Sweden, 2%; UK, USSR, Canada, 1% each; others, 2%.

Presidential vote

1968	Humphrey (D)	61,274	(33%)
	Nixon (R)	110,909	(60%)
	Wallace (AIP)	11,633	(6%)

Representative

Charles Thone (R) Elected 1970; b. Jan. 4, 1925, Hartington; home, Lincoln; U. of Neb. Law School, J.D., 1950; Army, WWII; married, three children; Presbyterian.

Career Deputy Neb. Secy. of State, 1950–51; Asst. State Atty. Gen., 1951–52; Asst. U.S. Dist. Atty., 1952–54; Admin. Asst. to Sen. Roman L. Hruska, 1954–59; practicing atty., 1959–70.

Offices 1531 LHOB, 202-225-4806. Also 120 Anderson Bldg., Lincoln 68501, 402-432-8541.

Committees

Government Operations (16th); Subs. (1) Legal and Monetary Affairs.

Public Works (13th); Subs. (1) Investigation and Oversight, (2) Public Buildings and Grounds, (3) Rivers and Harbors, (4) Roads, (5) Sp. on Economic Dev. Programs.

Group Ratings, Key Votes: Newly elected.

Election Results

1970 general:	Charles Thone (R)	79,131	(51%)
	Clair A. Callan (Ind.)	40,919	(26%)
	George B. Borrows (D)	36,240	(23%)
1970 primary:	Charles Thone nominated by Republican caucus.		

SECOND DISTRICT Political Background

Nebraska 2 is metropolitan Omaha. The rest of the district is politically unimportant, because Omaha casts three-quarters of the votes in the 2nd and determines the winner of the House seat. Both of the industries for which the city is famous, railroading and meat packing, have had some difficult years; as a result, Omaha has shown very little growth recently. But it is still the commercial and industrial center for much of the Great Plains—the largest city between Chicago and Denver. Although Omaha does contain significant numbers of Democratic Czechs and blacks, the city tends to vote Republican, like the rest of Nebraska.

Until 1970, the 2nd was represented by Republican Glenn Cunningham, who sponsored the law that required any person receiving mail from communist countries to register with the post office. The legislation was designed to prevent subversives from getting written instructions from the Kremlin. It may have done that, but it has also irritated scholars and other subscribers to Soviet periodicals. Cunningham was not especially strong among the 2nd's voters, and in 1970 he was upset in the Republican primary by John Y. McCollister, an Omaha businessman and Nixon backer.

McCollister's Democratic opponent was former television newsman John Hlavacek. The close race was probably decided by a state issue, Amendment 12, a referendum that would have permitted government support of private and parochial schools. Though it was defeated statewide, the amendment was supported by the voters of Douglas County (Omaha); it was especially popular in the heavily Catholic precincts of the city. Hlavacek came out against the amendment, while McCollister took no position. Hlavacek still managed to run ahead of the Republican in Catholic neighborhoods, but his position on the issue undoubtedly cost him some votes. McCollister slipped by with a 52% win.

McCollister will have an easier race in 1972 and will probably go on winning for as long as he likes. The Congressman has been mentioned as a possible successor to the Senate seat traditionally held by an Omaha man, if Sen. Hruska, who will be 72 when his current term expires in 1976, decides to retire.

Census Data 1970 pop. 495,095; deviation from current state average, +0.1%; change 1960–70, +19.3%. Metro. 91.8%, 70.3% central city.

1970 Share of Federal Outlays $459,913,700

DOD	$183,989,000	HEW	$101,255,458
AEC	$000	HUD	$947,343
NASA	$000	OEO	$1,335,199
DOT	$12,482,230	DOA	$51,079,717
		Other	$108,824,753

Federal Military-Industrial Commitments

DOD Contractors Wilkinson Mfg. Co. (Fort Calhoun), $8.982m: 81-mm mortar fuzes; 60-mm projectile fin assemblies.

DOD Installations Offutt AFB (Omaha), headquarters of the Strategic Air Command.

Economic Base Food and kindred products, esp. meat products; cash grain and livestock; nonelectrical machinery, esp. farm machinery and equipment. Also, higher education (University of Nebraska at Omaha); banking and insurance.

The Voters

Registration 205,795, total. 107,469 D (52%); 89,221 R (43%); 9,105 other (4%).

Employment profile White collar, 47%. Blue collar, 53%.

Ethnic groups Black, 7%. Total foreign stock, 19%. Germany, 4%; Czech., 2%; Ireland, Italy, Poland, Sweden, UK, USSR, Canada, 1% each; others, 4%.

Presidential vote

1968	Humphrey (D)	59,078	(36%)
	Nixon (R)	84,690	(52%)
	Wallace (AIP)	19,044	(12%)

Representative

John Y. McCollister (R) Elected 1970; b. June 19, 1921, Iowa City, Iowa; home, Omaha; U. of Iowa, B.S., 1943; USNR, WWII; married, three children; Presbyterian.

Career IBM salesman; Pres., McCollister and Co., selling lubricants; Commissioner, Douglas County, 1964–68.

Offices 511 CHOB, 202-225-4155. Also 2313 Fed. Bldg., 215 N. 15th St., Omaha 68102, 402-221-3251.

Committees

Interstate and Foreign Commerce (17th); Subs. (1) Commerce and Finance.

Group Ratings, Key Votes: Newly elected.

Election Results

1970 general:	John Y. McCollister (R)	69,671	(52%)
	John Hlavacek (D)	64,520	(48%)
1970 primary:	John Y. McCollister (R)	25,911	(56%)
	Glenn Cunningham (R)	20,328	(44%)

THIRD DISTRICT Political Background

Nebraska 3 has one-third of the state's population spread out over the Western three-quarters of the state's land area. As one drives west through the district, the rolling cornfields and wheatlands give way to sand hills and cattle country, much of it devoid of any signs of human habitation for miles on end. This is the part of Nebraska to which settlers thronged in the land rush of the 1880's and which they and their descendants have been steadily abandoning ever since. Today most of the people here live along the Platte River, in and around towns like Grand Island (pop. 31,000), Hastings (pop. 23,000), Kearney (pop. 19,000), North Platte (pop. 19,000), and Scottsbluff (pop. 14,000).

The district is conservative on most issues, and except for a few counties with large ethnic populations like Greeley and Sherman, it is traditionally Republican. But the 3rd is always ready to vote against whatever party occupies the White House when farm prices drop. In the early '60's, the district's congressman, David T. Martin, had some close races. But as he accumulated seniority and became better known, his margins increased. The 1970 results, however, indicate that the dissatisfied farmers of western Nebraska are once again trending Democratic. Martin won reelection with 60%, but that percentage was far below his 68% in 1968 and 73% in 1966. In the House, Martin, who is one of the five Republicans on the important Rules Committee, votes with the conservative wing of his party.

The 3rd's population loss during the '60's actually helped to equalize Nebraska's three congressional districts, which were redrawn in 1968. According to the 1970 census, the difference between the largest and smallest is only 760 people. Martin is a safe bet for reelection in 1972.

Census Data 1970 pop. 494,361; deviation from current state average, 0.0%; change 1960–70, –2.6%. Metro. 0.0%, 0.0% central city.

1970 Share of Federal Outlays $609,735,913

DOD	$29,983,000	HEW	$126,153,502
AEC	$000	HUD	$000
NASA	$000	OEO	$1,183,752
DOT	$18,040,788	DOA	$244,131,343
		Other	$190,243,528

Federal Military-Industrial Commitments

DOD Contractors Mason and Hanger (Grand Island), $21.252m: operation of Cornhuskers Army Ammunition plant and production of various types of bombs and projectiles.

Economic Base Livestock and cash grain; food and kindred products; fabricated metal products.

The Voters

Registration 249,532, total. 99,908 D (40%); 142,994 R (57%); 6,630 other (3%).

Employment profile White collar, 33%. Blue collar, 67%.

Ethnic groups Black, less than 0.5%. Total foreign stock, 16%. Germany, 6%; Sweden, USSR, 2% each; Czech., Poland, UK, Canada, Mexico, 1% each; others, 2%.

Presidential vote

1968	Humphrey (D)	50,432	(27%)
	Nixon (R)	125,564	(66%)
	Wallace (AIP)	14,227	(8%)

Representative

David Thomas Martin (R) Elected 1960; b. July 9, 1907, Kearney; home, Kearney; Dartmouth Col., 1925–28; married, three children; Presbyterian.

Career Retail lumber business; Chm., Neb. State Repub. Com., 1949–54; Repub. Natl. Com., 1952–54.

Offices 2227 RHOB, 202-225-6435. Also Kearney 68847; 308-237-2155.

Committees

Rules (3rd).

Group Ratings

	ADA	COPE	NREP	NFU	LCV	CFA	NAB	NSI	ACA
1970	8	10	0	23	0	44	90	89	89
1969	0	—	—	23	—	—	—	—	93
1968	0	8	—	29	—	—	100	—	95

Key Votes

(1) ABM	FOR	(6) 18-Yr-Vote	AGN	(11) Clean Water $	AGN
(2) SST	FOR	(7) Farm Sub Lmt	AGN	(12) Mig Wrkrs Comp	AGN
(3) Phil Pln	ABS	(8) Coop-Church	AGN	(13) Jets to Chiang	AGN
(4) No-Knock	FOR	(9) Family Asst	AGN	(14) State OEO Veto	FOR
(5) Cmutr Tax	AGN	(10) Work Stamps	FOR	(15) Park Logging	FOR

Election Results

1970 general:	Dave Martin (R)	93,705	(60%)
	Donald Searcy (D)	63,698	(40%)
1970 primary:	Dave Martin (R), unopposed		
1968 general:	Dave Martin (R)	123,838	(68%)
	J. B. Dean (D)	58,728	(32%)

NEVADA

Political Background

After the discovery of the Comstock Lode in 1859, thousands of miners and other fortune-seekers poured into the deserts of Nevada, and in 1864 it became one of the first Western states to be admitted to the Union. But the veins of gold and silver soon petered out, and for decades the economy of the state languished. Then during the depression of the 1930's, Nevada legalized gambling and liberalized its divorce laws. The move brought in tourists, six-week residents, and eventually big (some said tainted) money.

The crucial event in modern Nevada history occurred in 1947 when Bugsy Siegel opened the Flamingo, the first big casino-hotel on the Las Vegas strip. At the same time, just outside the city, the Atomic Energy Commission established the Nuclear Test Facility, which is now the state's third largest employer. Since then, Las Vegas has grown from a small desert crossroads town into a major city. Clark County, which contains Las Vegas, the Strip, and Hoover Dam, now has 56% of the state's population. Washoe County and Reno have another 23%, leaving just 21% of people residents of Nevada's so-called "cow counties."

Today, Nevada is part of the Sun Belt, a swath of states in the southern regions of the nation. Drawing people who want to escape colder climates, the states of the Sun Belt are the most rapidly growing in the country. But Nevada's early settlers, like those in Arizona and New Mexico, came here from the South and brought with them their conservative Democratic voting habits. Like a Southern state, Nevada has elected conservative Democrats to the Senate and kept them there to accumulate seniority. In the '30's Key Pittman was the famous chairman of the Senate Foreign Relations Committee, and later, in the '50's, Nevada's conservative and influential Pat McCarran sponsored the largely unconstitutional McCarran-Walter Act designed to curb the activities of subversives. Today the state's senators are more moderate men out of the same tradition. Alan Bible, first elected in 1954, is now chairman of the Select Committee on Small Business and a senior member of Appropriations and Interior and Insular Affairs. Howard Cannon was first elected in 1958 and is a middle-ranking member on four committees, including Armed Services and Commerce. Both men have middle-of-the-road voting records, rather different from those of most Northern Democratic members of the Senate. Both are strong supporters of military, space, and atomic energy programs, though Cannon did vote against the ABM.

Bible has won reelection easily. In 1968 he ran 2% ahead of the combined Humphrey-Wallace percentage and carried most of the state. Cannon, on the other hand, has had some tough elections. In 1964, when Goldwater hurt many Republican candidates, the Democratic Senator barely managed a 48-vote victory over then Republican Lt. Gov. Paul Laxalt. In 1970, when Nevada Republicans and Richard Nixon hoped that he would again challenge Cannon, Laxalt, who had become governor in the interim, announced that he was retiring from politics and surprised most observers by doing just that.

Meanwhile, Cannon increased the number of times he took the long flight from Washington to Nevada, and in Las Vegas and Reno he reminded the voters that his seniority brought them post offices, water projects, and money from the AEC. Cannon's backers pointed out that the state had 28 years of seniority in the Senate and argued convincingly that with the seniority Nevada wielded more influence in that body than California and New York together. Spiro Agnew chose Cannon's Republican opponent. A phone call from the Vice President led William Raggio to make the race. Perhaps at Agnew's suggestion, Raggio ran a strong law-and-order campaign in which he stressed his opposition to pornography, narcotics, and student unrest. This was probably not the wisest strategy: Nevada has few students but lots of gambling, girlie shows, and, in some rural counties, legalized prostitution. The White House and Raggio had high hopes, but Cannon's campaigning and seniority prevailed with 58% of the votes, a better showing than Bible's two years before. Las Vegas was where Raggio had the most trouble. Cannon won 68% there, while Bible took 60% in 1968. Bible, the state's only congressman, and Raggio are all from Reno, and so Las Vegas wanted to keep at least one of its own men in Washington.

Nevada's congressman is Walter Baring, who, according to his billboards, is a "state's rights Democrat." He served in the House from 1948 to 1952, and then, after an absence of four years, returned to Washington, where he has been accumulating seniority ever since. Baring usually votes with the Southern Democrats and is easily the most conservative member of his party from any state outside the Deep South. Efforts to defeat him are concentrated in the Democratic primary; in 1970 a lone challenger took a meager 31%. In the general election Baring won with 83%, taking most of the state's Republican votes. Although Baring runs behind the ticket in the state's few liberal and black precincts, the *Las Vegas Sun*'s position on the election conveys the despair of Baring's political opponents: "We are not going to take a stand this year because every time we have opposed Walter Baring, he has been elected. Perhaps, if we ignore him, the voters will too." The chances for the Congressman's reelection in 1972 look good.

Electoral Votes 3

Census Data 1970 pop. 488,738; 0.24% of U.S. total, 49th largest; change 1960–70, +71.3%. Metro. 80.7%, 40.6% central city. 1970 per capita income, $4,544; 5th highest. 51st in number of poor.

1970 Share of Federal Tax Burden $526,880,000; 0.27% of U.S. total, 45th largest.

1970 Share of Federal Outlays $602,530,971; 0.32% of U.S. total, 48th largest. Per capita federal spending, $1,233.

DOD	$127,655,000	41st (0.22%)		HEW	$86,240,377	50th (0.16%)
AEC	$172,498,177	4th (6.64%)		HUD	$1,306,402	51st (0.07%)
NASA	$1,717,399	48th (0.05%)		OEO	$1,717,399	48th (0.23%)
DOT	$38,067,975	44th (0.53%)		DOA	$49,433,343	41st (0.38%)
DOC	$2,986,646	42nd (0.26%)		POD	$15,397,109	51st (0.21%)
DOI	$40,224,815	19th (1.74%)		VA	$20,172,355	51st (0.27%)
DOJ	$1,576,145	47th (0.25%)		CSC	$7,459,191	47th (0.19%)
				Other	$36,368,575	

Federal Military-Industrial Commitments

DOD Contractors Quiller Construction Co. (Nellis AFB), $5.364m: building construction.

DOD Installations Naval Ammunition Depot (Hawthorne). Naval Auxiliary Air Station (Fallon). Fallon AF Station (Fallon). Indian Springs Auxiliary Air Field (Indian Springs). Nellis AFB (Las Vegas).

AEC Operations Reynolds Electrical and Engineering (Mercury), $84.904m: Nevada Test Site. EG&G Inc. (Mercury), $17.134m: Test Facilities. Holmes and Narver (Nye County), $10.366m: unspecified. AEC Western Headquarters (Las Vegas), $5.408m: administrative. University of California (Las Vegas), $5.312m: unspecified.

Economic Base Livestock; metal mining, esp. copper ores; primary metal industries, esp. rolling, drawing, and extruding of nonferrous metals; printing, publishing, and allied industries, esp. newspapers; stone, clay, glass, and concrete products, esp. concrete, gypsum, and plaster products; food and kindred products, esp. dairy products; chemicals and allied industries, esp. industrial inorganic and organic chemicals. Also, tourism (Las Vegas, Reno, and Tahoe).

Political Line-up Governor, Mike O'Callaghan (D); seat up, 1974. Senators, Alan Bible (D) and Howard W. Cannon (D). Representatives, 1 D at large, State Senate (13 D and 7 R); State Assembly (19 D and 21 R).

The Voters

Registration 192,933, total. 112,246 D (58%); 67,713 R (35%); 12,972 other (7%).

Employment profile White collar, 41%. Blue collar, 59%.

Ethnic groups Black, 6%. Total foreign stock, 18%. Italy, 3%; UK, Canada, Germany, 2% each; Mexico, USSR, Ireland, Sweden, 1% each; others, 6%.

Presidential vote

1968	Humphrey (D)	60,598	(39%)
	Nixon (R)	73,188	(48%)
	Wallace (AIP)	20,432	(13%)
1964	Johnson (D)	79,339	(59%)
	Goldwater (R)	56,094	(41%)
1960	Kennedy (D)	54,880	(51%)
	Nixon (R)	52,387	(49%)

Senator

Alan Bible (D) Elected 1954, seat up 1974; b. Nov. 20, 1909, Lovelock; home, Reno; U. of Nev., B.A., 1930; Georgetown U. School of Law, LL.B., 1934; married, four children; Methodist.

Career Practicing atty., 1934–54; Dist. Atty., Storey County, 1935–37; Atty. Gen., Nev., 1938–42; Pres., Natl. Assn. of Atty. Gen., 1950.

Offices 145 OSOB, 202-225-3542. Also 2014 Fed. Bldg., Reno 89502, 702-784-5568, and 4626 Fed. Bldg., Las Vegas 89101, 702-385-6341.

Committees

Appropriations (6th); Subs. (1) Chm., Interior, (2) Defense, (3) Labor, HEW, and Related Agencies, (4) Public Works, (5) Transportation.

Interior and Insular Affairs (3rd); Subs. (1) Chm., Parks and Recreation, (2) Minerals, Materials and Fuels, (3) Public Lands.

Sel. Com. on Small Business (Chm.).

Sp. Com. on Aging (3rd); Subs. (1) Employment and Retirement Incomes, (2) Federal, State, and Community Services, (3) Retirement and the Individual.

Jt. Com. on Atomic Energy (5th); Subs. (1) Legislation, (2) Military Applications, (3) Research, Development, and Radiation.

Group Ratings

	ADA	COPE	NREP	NFU	LCV	NAB	NSI	ACA
1970	9	62	17	64	41	33	90	59
1969	33	—	—	67	—	—	—	57
1968	14	36	—	39	—	40	—	67

Key Votes

(1) ABM	FOR	(8) Phil Pln	AGN	(15) Coop-Church	FOR
(2) SST	FOR	(9) Vol Army	AGN	(16) Cut Oil Dpltn	AGN
(3) Busing	AGN	(10) Prison $	AGN	(17) Consumer Prot	FOR
(4) Tob Sub	FOR	(11) Cut Mil $	AGN	(18) Farm Sub Limit	FOR
(5) Carswell	FOR	(12) Defoliatn	FOR	(19) Comp Bid Sales	AGN
(6) No-Knock	FOR	(13) 18-Yr-Vote	FOR	(20) Pre-Prod Tests	ABS
(7) Seniorty	FOR	(14) Pentgn PR	FOR	(21) Cut Marjna Pen	AGN

Election Results

1968 general:	Alan Bible (D)	83,622	(55%)
	Ed Firke (R)	69,083	(45%)
1968 primary:	Alan Bible (D), unopposed		
1962 general:	Alan Bible (D)	63,443	(65%)
	William B. Wright (R)	33,749	(35%)

Senator

Howard Walter Cannon (D) Elected 1958, seat up 1970; b. Jan. 26, 1912, St. George, Utah; home, Las Vegas; Ariz. State Teachers Col., B.E., 1933; U. of Ariz., LL.B., 1937; Army Air Corps, WWII; Maj. Gen., USAAFR; married, two children; Church of Latter Day Saints.

Career Practicing atty., 1938– ; Atty., Utah Senate, 1939; Washington County Atty., 1940–41; City Atty., Las Vegas, 1949–58.

Offices 259 OSOB, 202-225-6244. Also 4602 Fed. Bldg., Las Vegas 89101, 702-385-6278, and 4024 Fed. Bldg., 300 Booth St., Reno 89502, 702-784-5544.

Committees

Aeronautical and Space Sciences (5th).

Armed Services (5th); Subs. (1) Chm., National Stockpile and Naval Petroleum, (2) Chm. Ad Hoc Sub. on Tactical Air Power, (3) Military Construction Authorization, (4) Preparedness Investigating.

Commerce (5th); Subs. (1) Chm., Aviation, (2) Communications, (3) Foreign Commerce and Tourism, (4) Surface Transportation, (5) Sp. on Freight Car Shortage.

Rules and Administration (2nd); Subs. (1) Chm., Privileges and Elections, (2) Computer Services, (3) Standing Rules of the Senate.

Jt. Com. on the Library (3rd).

Group Ratings

	ADA	COPE	NREP	NFU	LCV	NAB	NSI	ACA
1970	19	73	30	85	21	27	78	50
1969	50	—	—	80	—	—	—	54
1968	29	73	—	54	—	50	—	61

Key Votes

(1) ABM	AGN	(8) Phil Pln	AGN	(15) Coop-Church	FOR
(2) SST	FOR	(9) Vol Army	ABS	(16) Cut Oil Dpltn	AGN
(3) Busing	AGN	(10) Prison $	ABS	(17) Consumer Prot	ABS
(4) Tob Sub	AGN	(11) Cut Mil $	AGN	(18) Farm Sub Limit	FOR
(5) Carswell	AGN	(12) Defoliatn	ABS	(19) Comp Bid Sales	AGN
(6) No-Knock	FOR	(13) 18-Yr-Vote	FOR	(20) Pre-Prod Tests	AGN
(7) Seniorty	ABS	(14) Pentgn PR	FOR	(21) Cut Marjna Pen	AGN

Election Results

1970 general:	Howard W. Cannon (D)	85,187	(58%)
	William J. Raggio (R)	60,838	(41%)
	Harold G. De Sellem (AIP)	1,743	(1%)
1970 primary:	Howard W. Cannon (D)	54,320	(89%)
	Walter D. Duesenberg (D)	4,350	(7%)
	George R. Lill (D)	2,160	(4%)
1964 general:	Howard W. Cannon (D)	67,336	(50%)
	Paul Laxalt (R)	67,288	(50%)

Representative

Walter S. Baring (D) Elected 1948–52, 1956; b. Sept. 9, 1911, Goldfield; home, Reno; U. of Nev., B.A., B.S., 1934; Navy, WWII; married, four children; unspecified Protestant.

Career Furniture business; Chm., Dem. Central Com. of Washoe County, 1936; Nev. State Legislature, 1936–38; Councilman, Reno City Council, 1947–48.

Offices 2434 RHOB, 202-225-5965. Also 300 Booth St., Reno 89502, 702-786-3498, and Suite 4, 620 Fed. Bldg., 300 Las Vegas Blvd., South, Las Vegas 89101, 702-385-6222.

Committees

Interior and Insular Affairs (4th); Subs. (1) Chm., Public Lands, (2) Environment, (3) Irrigation and Reclamation, (4) Mines and Mining.

Veterans' Affairs (4th); Subs. (1) Education and Training, (2) Hospitals, (3) Housing.

Group Ratings

	ADA	COPE	NREP	NFU	LCV	CFA	NAB	NSI	ACA
1970	12	50	27	50	40	47	46	100	64
1969	7	—	—	14	—	—	—	—	93
1968	8	8	—	8	—	—	80	—	90

Key Votes

(1) ABM	FOR	(6) 18-Yr-Vote	AGN	(11) Clean Water $	AGN
(2) SST	FOR	(7) Farm Sub Lmt	FOR	(12) Mig Wrkrs Comp	ABS
(3) Phil Pln	AGN	(8) Coop-Church	AGN	(13) Jets to Chiang	FOR
(4) No-Knock	ABS	(9) Family Asst	AGN	(14) State OEO Veto	FOR
(5) Cmutr Tax	ABS	(10) Work Stamps	FOR	(15) Park Logging	ABS

Election Results

1970 general:	Walter S. Baring (D)	113,496	(83%)
	J. Robert Charles (R)	24,147	(17%)
1970 primary:	Walter S. Baring (D)	41,925	(69%)
	Otto Ravenholt (D)	19,086	(31%)
1968 general:	Walter S. Baring (D)	104,136	(72%)
	James Michael Slattery (R)	40,209	(28%)

NEW HAMPSHIRE

Political Background

Once every four years New Hampshire becomes the center of the nation's political attention. Presidential candidates trudge through the melting snow and mud of its industrial cities and small New England towns, wooing the votes of less than 100,000 people. New Hampshire's presidential primary, always the first in the country and therefore the most influential, brings the politicians to the state. (The primary is now held in early March, though the state legislature will move it up, if necessary, to keep it first.) The voters here have often surprised the political pundits. In 1964, for example, the New Hampshire Republicans rejected the candidacies of Barry Goldwater and Nelson Rockefeller, both of whom spent lots of money, and supported Henry Cabot Lodge in a last-minute write-in effort. And in 1968, Eugene McCarthy's surprisingly strong 42% among the Democrats shattered the myth that incumbent Presidents are unbeatable.

By the second week in March the presidential aspirants have left the state, and because New Hampshire has only four electoral votes, they very often never come back. Politics in the state then returns to normal, dominated as it is by fractious local politicians and by William Loeb, owner of the *Manchester Union Leader*. The newspaper reaches about a quarter of the state's households with Loeb's ardent conservatism, his opposition to pornography, campus unrest, civil rights legislation, and taxes of all kinds. The *Union Leader* is quite outspoken about whom it likes and dislikes in public life, and those whom it dislikes claim that Loeb slants not only its lengthy front-page editorials but its news columns against them.

Loeb has not been as successful in the recent past as he was during the '50's. Among the losers he has backed are Mrs. Styles Bridges, the late Senator's widow (Senate 1962); Barry Goldwater (presidential primary 1964); General Harrison Thyng (Senate 1966); and Emil Bussiere (governor 1968). In 1970 a Loeb man just missed winning the Republican gubernatorial primary, and the Democratic candidate whom he then supported was narrowly defeated in the general election. Still, most New Hampshire politicians feel that Loeb can swing 25,000 votes in a state where some 200,000 go to the polls in an off-year election. This makes Loeb a very powerful man.

The *Union Leader* has always supported New Hampshire's conservative senior senator, Republican Norris Cotton. First elected in 1954, Cotton serves on the powerful Appropriations Committee and the Commerce Committee, where he is the ranking Republican. Cotton will be 74 when his current term expires in 1974 and may retire at that time.

What could happen if he does retire is suggested by the election in which Thomas J. McIntyre, the state's junior senator, first won his seat. When Senator Styles Bridges, the grand old man of New Hampshire politics, died in 1961, McIntyre was living the comfortable life of a successful lawyer in Laconia. He had dabbled in Democratic politics, served a brief term as mayor of Laconia, and lost a race for Congress in 1954. The fight for the Republican nomination included Mrs. Bridges, both the state's congressmen Chester Merrow and Perkins Bass, and ex-Gov. Wesley Powell. The primary was a bitter one, so bitter that when Bass came out of it the winner, he was beaten by McIntyre. McIntyre was also helped by the coattails of John W. King, a Democrat who then won the first of his three terms as governor. In 1966 when the term expired, the Senator was expected to lose, but he won reelection with 54% against the conservative Loeb-backed General Thyng.

McIntyre is a Democrat who is liberal on domestic issues and usually conservative on questions of military spending and foreign policy. He was a loyal supporter of President Johnson in the 1968 presidential primary, but has since became more dovish about the war. In 1969, he was a crucial undecided on the ABM vote; he eventually came out against the program, though he has once again become undecided about the issue.

McIntyre will come up for reelection in 1972 with ten years of incumbency going for him. Louis C. Wyman, 1st district congressman, is the Senator's most likely opponent. Wyman is a hard-line conservative who has always had Loeb's enthusiastic support. A contest between the two men would be a classic one, between incumbency and ideology, with the odds favoring no one. The Republicans usually have an edge in statewide races, but the Democrats do have a solid electoral base in the state's largest cities, Manchester (pop. 87,000) and Nashua (pop. 55,000), as well as in the mill towns to the north of the state. Here the sons and daughters of Irish, French-Canadian, and Italian immigrants vote heavily Democratic and nearly balance the Republican margins in the small Yankee towns. The fastest growing part of the state lies along its southern edge, into which Boston-area commuters, in search of lower taxes, are moving (New Hampshire is the only state in the country with no sales or income tax). These voters, accustomed to the liberal politics of Massachusetts and unfamiliar with Loeb's kind of conservatism, will provide additional support for McIntyre.

Electoral Votes 4

Census Data 1970 pop. 737,681; 0.36% of U.S. total, 43rd largest; change 1960–70, +21.5%. Metro. 27.3%, 19.5% central city. 1970 per capita income, $3,608; 24th highest. 45th in number of poor.

1970 Share of Federal Tax Burden $682,990,000; 0.35% of U.S. total, 43rd largest.

1970 Share of Federal Outlays $590,476,617; 0.31% of U.S. total, 49th largest. Per capita federal spending, $800.

DOD	$246,805,000	39th (0.43%)	HEW	$168,477,276	44th (0.32%)
AEC	$350,173	40th (0.01%)	HUD	$5,874,023	44th (0.30%)
NASA	$3,644,900	29th (0.10%)	OEO	$1,422,585	49th (0.19%)
DOT	$31,267,372	49th (0.44%)	DOA	$15,733,854	49th (0.12%)
DOC	$1,953,869	46th (0.17%)	POD	$22,712,702	43rd (0.31%)
DOI	$4,995,727	49th (0.26%)	VA	$33,255,158	45th (0.45%)
DOJ	$1,293,497	50th (0.23%)	CSC	$14,737,927	40th (0.37%)
			Other	$37,952,554	

Economic Base Footwear other than rubber, and other leather and leather products; electrical machinery, equipment, and supplies, esp. communication equipment and electronic components and accessories; textile mill products, esp. broad-woven man-made fiber and silk fabric mills; nonelectrical machinery, esp. special industrial machinery other than metalworking machinery and general industrial machinery and equipment; dairy and poultry; rubber and miscellaneous plastics products; paper and allied products; lumber and wood products other than furniture; printing, publishing, and allied industries, esp. newspapers and commercial printing.

Political Line-up Governor, Walter Peterson (R); seat up, 1972. Senators Norris Cotton (R) and Thomas J. McIntyre (D). Representatives, 2 (0 D and 2 R). State Senate (9 D and 15 R); State House (148 D and 252 R).

The Voters

Registration 262,389 total. 100,473 D (38%); 161,916 R (62%).

Employment profile White collar, 36%. Blue collar, 64%.

Ethnic groups Black, less than 0.5%. Total foreign stock, 29%. Canada, 17%; Ireland, UK, 2% each; Germany, Italy, Poland, Sweden, USSR, 1% each; others, 3%.

Presidential vote

1968	Humphrey (D)	130,589	(44%)
	Nixon (R)	154,903	(52%)
	Wallace (AIP)	11,173	(4%)
1964	Johnson (D)	184,064	(64%)
	Goldwater (R)	104,029	(36%)

1960	Kennedy (D)	137,772	(47%)
	Nixon (R)	157,989	(53%)

Senator

Norris Cotton (R) Elected 1954, seat up 1974; b. May 11, 1900, Warren; home, Lebanon; Wesleyan U., 1919–21; Georgetown U. Law School, 1927; married; United Church of Christ.

Career N.H. Legislature, 1923, 1943–46; Secy., Senator George Moses, 1924–28; Grafton County Atty., 1933–39; Justice, Lebanon Municipal Ct., 1939–44; N.H. House of Reps., 1943, Speaker, 1945; U.S. House of Reps., 1946–54.

Offices 4121 NSOB, 202-225-3324. Also Fed. Bldg., Concord 03301, 603-224-4321.

Committees

Appropriations (6th); Subs. (1) Department of Defense, (2) Department of Labor, HEW, and Related Agencies, (3) Foreign Operations, (4) Legislative Branch, (5) Public Works.

Commerce (Ranking Mbr.); Subs. (1) Aviation, (2) Consumer.

Group Ratings

	ADA	COPE	NREP	NFU	LCV	NAB	NSI	ACA
1970	0	8	9	42	34	73	100	85
1969	17	—	—	38	—	—	—	92
1968	29	45	—	31	—	100	—	88

Key Votes

(1) ABM	FOR	(8) Phil Pln	ABS	(15) Coop-Church	AGN
(2) SST	FOR	(9) Vol Army	AGN	(16) Cut Oil Dpltn	AGN
(3) Busing	AGN	(10) Prison $	ABS	(17) Consumer Prot	AGN
(4) Tob Sub	FOR	(11) Cut Mil $	ABS	(18) Farm Sub Limit	FOR
(5) Carswell	FOR	(12) Defoliatn	FOR	(19) Comp Bid Sales	FOR
(6) No-Knock	FOR	(13) 18-Yr-Vote	FOR	(20) Pre-Prod Tests	AGN
(7) Seniorty	FOR	(14) Pentgn PR	FOR	(21) Cut Marjna Pen	AGN

Election Results

1968 general:	Norris Cotton (R)	170,163	(59%)
	John W. King (D)	116,816	(41%)
1968 primary:	Norris Cotton (R)	78,053	(93%)
	John Mongan (R)	6,279	(7%)
1962 general:	Norris Cotton (R)	190,444	(60%)
	Alfred Catalfa, Jr. (D)	134,035	(40%)

Senator

Thomas James McIntyre (D) Elected 1962, seat up 1972; b. Feb. 20, 1915, Laconia; home, Laconia; Dartmouth Col., 1937; Boston U. Law School, LL.B., 1940; Army, WWII; married, one child; Catholic.

Career Practicing atty., 1940– ; Mayor of Laconia, 1949–51; City Solicitor, 1953; Dir., Laconia Industrial Dev. Corp., 1962.

Offices 405 OSOB, 202-225-2841. Also 208 Fed. Bldg., Manchester 03103, 603-669-1232, and Fed. Bldg., Portsmouth 03001, 603-436-7720.

Committees

Armed Services (6th); Subs. (1) Chm., Ad Hoc on Research and Development, (2) General Legislation, (3) Preparedness Investigating, (4) Status of Forces, (5) Sp. to Review Bomber Defense.

Banking, Housing, and Urban Affairs (4th); Subs. (1) Chm., Small Business, (2) Financial Institutions, (3) Housing and Urban Affairs, (4) Production and Stabilization, (5) Securities.

Sel. Com. on Small Business (8th); Subs. (1) Chm., Government Regulation, (2) Financing and Investment, (3) Monopoly.

Group Ratings

	ADA	COPE	NREP	NFU	LCV	NAB	NSI	ACA
1970	50	100	55	100	54	10	60	39
1969	78	—	—	81	—	—	—	13
1968	50	91	—	70	—	20	—	23

Key Votes

(1) ABM	AGN	(8) Phil Pln	FOR	(15) Coop-Church	FOR
(2) SST	AGN	(9) Vol Army	AGN	(16) Cut Oil Dpltn	FOR
(3) Busing	FOR	(10) Prison $	AGN	(17) Consumer Prot	FOR
(4) Tob Sub	FOR	(11) Cut Mil $	AGN	(18) Farm Sub Limit	FOR
(5) Carswell	AGN	(12) Defoliatn	FOR	(19) Comp Bid Sales	ABS
(6) No-Knock	FOR	(13) 18-Yr-Vote	FOR	(20) Pre-Prod Tests	AGN
(7) Seniorty	FOR	(14) Pentgn PR	FOR	(21) Cut Marjna Pen	AGN

Election Results

1966 general:	Thomas J. McIntyre (D)	123,888	(54%)
	Harrison R. Thyng (R)	105,241	(46%)
1966 primary:	Thomas J. McIntyre (D), unopposed		
1962 special:	Thomas J. McIntyre (D)	117,612	(52%)
	Perkins Bass (R)	107,199	(48%)

FIRST DISTRICT Political Background

New Hampshire 1 is the eastern half of the state. New Hampshire's two congressional districts, slightly revised only once (1970) since 1881, were designed to split the Democratic strength found in the state's two largest cities; Manchester is in the 1st, and Nashua lies in the 2nd. The 1st also contains Portsmouth, with its large Naval Shipyard, and fast-growing Rockingham County, which has an increasing number of Boston commuters. New Hampshire's two districts are very similar in their response to national candidates; in local contests, the Manchester *Union Leader* has more influence in the 1st than in the 2nd.

Republican Louis C. Wyman was first elected to the House in 1962, but lost the seat, 51:49, in the Johnson landslide of 1964 to Democrat J. Oliva Huot. Wyman went back to Washington in 1966 and has been there since. As the state's attorney general in the '50's, he urged the adoption of some controversial anti-subversive laws which were passed by the state legislative but then found defective by the Supreme Court. The Congressman, a fierce opponent of communists foreign and domestic, was one of the leaders on the Hill in the move to impeach Supreme Court Justice William Douglas. Wyman is also a no-nonsense man in the home; he posted bail for his nineteen-year-old son, who was arrested on a marijuana charge in Virginia, only on the condition that he adopt conventional dress and visit the barber every ten days.

The Congressman has also protected the interests of his district. He convinced the Nixon Administration to hold off the planned shutdown of the Portsmouth Naval Shipyard in 1974. He was allowed to announce the decision of the Administration long before any other New Hampshire politician had the news. Republican Sen. Cotton was outraged. Wyman will probably give Sen. McIntyre a stiff challenge in 1972. With the help of Loeb's *Union Leader,* he can probably cut into the normally Democratic blue-collar vote in Manchester. Wyman is very popular in the 1st; in 1970 he won 67%, and in 1968, 63%. He could certainly hold his House seat indefinitely should he choose to do so.

Census Data 1970 pop. 359,900; deviation from current state average, —2.4%; change 1960–70, +17.7%. Metro. 32.0%, 24.4% central city.

1970 Share of Federal Outlays $245,238,000 (average outlay per district, New Hampshire 1 and 2)

DOD	$123,403,000	HEW	$84,239,000
AEC	$175,000	HUD	$2,937,000
NASA	$1,822,000	OEO	$711,000
DOT	$15,634,000	DOA	$7,867,000
		Other	$18,976,000

Federal Military-Industrial Commitments

DOD Contractors Simplex Wire and Cable Co. (Newington), $12.944m: ocean cable for ABM system.

DOD Installations Naval Disciplinary Command (Portsmouth). Naval Hospital (Portsmouth). Portsmouth Naval Shipyard (Portsmouth). Pease AFB (Portsmouth).

Economic Base Leather and leather products, esp. footwear other than rubber; nonelectrical machinery; electrical machinery, equipment, and supplies. Also, tourism (White Mountains).

The Voters

Registration 138,063 total. 56,395 D (41%); 81,668 R (59%).

Employment profile White collar, 36%. Blue collar, 64%.

Ethnic groups Black, 1%. Total foreign stock, 30%. Canada, 17%; UK, 3%; Ireland, Poland, 2% each; Germany, Italy, USSR, 1% each; others, 3%.

Presidential vote

1968	Humphrey (D)	63,097	(43%)
	Nixon (R)	77,568	(53%)
	Wallace (AIP)	6,197	(4%)

Representative

Louis Crosby Wyman (R) Elected 1962, 1966; b. March 16, 1917, Manchester; home, Manchester; U. of N.H., B.S., 1938; Harvard Law School, LL.B., 1941; USNR, WWII; married, two children; United Church of Christ.

Career Gen. Counsel, Senate Com. on Campaign Expenditures, 1946; Secy., Senator Styles Bridges, 1947; Atty. Gen., N.H., 1953–61; Pres., Natl. Assn. of Atty. Gen., 1957; Legislative Council, Governor of N.H., 1961; Chm., N.H. Commission on Interstate Cooperation, 1953–61; Commissioner, Uniform State for N.H., 1953–61.

Offices 410 CHOB, 202-225-5456. Rm. 217 P.O. Bldg., Manchester 03104, 603-669-7011, and Rm. 209, Fed. Bldg., Portsmouth 03801, 603-436-7720.

Committees

Appropriations (13th); Sub. on Defense.

Group Ratings

	ADA	COPE	NREP	NFU	LCV	CFA	NAB	NSI	ACA
1970	8	9	8	38	50	67	82	100	84
1969	13	—	—	33	—	—	—	—	75
1968	0	15	—	50	—	—	100	—	78

Key Votes

(1) ABM	FOR	(6) 18-Yr-Vote	AGN	(11) Clean Water $	FOR
(2) SST	FOR	(7) Farm Sub Lmt	FOR	(12) Mig Wrkrs Comp	AGN
(3) Phil Pln	FOR	(8) Coop-Church	AGN	(13) Jets to Chiang	FOR
(4) No-Knock	FOR	(9) Family Asst	AGN	(14) State OEO Veto	FOR
(5) Cmutr Tax	AGN	(10) Work Stamps	AGN	(15) Park Logging	AGN

Election Results

1970 general:	Louis C. Wyman (R)	72,170	(67%)
	Chester E. Merrow (D)	34,882	(33%)
1970 primary:	Louis C. Wyman (R), unopposed (Redistricted 1970)		

SECOND DISTRICT Political Background

New Hampshire 2, the western half of the state, includes the Merrimack Valley cities of Nashua, a textile-mill center, and Concord, the state capitol. The heavily French-Canadian lumber-mill town of Berlin lies in the north of the district. Like the 1st, the district is normally Republican, but it has backed Democrats at times. In 1966, for example, both Sen. Thomas McIntyre and then Gov. John W. King carried the 2nd. As in all of northern New England, the Catholic mill town voters are Democrats while the small town Yankees are Republican.

The district's congressman, Republican James C. Cleveland, has a somewhat less conservative voting record than that of the 1st's Louis Wyman. By a margin of 892 votes, Cleveland survived the 1964 Johnson landslide that interrupted Wyman's tenure, and so he now has greater seniority. He is the 3rd ranking Republican on the House Administration Committee and 3rd on Public Works. In recent years Cleveland has shown remarkable strength at the polls, winning every election since 1966 with about 70% of the votes. Since redistricting cannot hurt him, he will no doubt keep his seat in the House until he decides to leave it, perhaps to run for the Senate.

Census Data 1970 pop. 377,781; deviation from current state average, +2.4%; change 1960–70, 25.5%. Metro. 22.9%, 14.8% central city.

1970 Share of Federal Outlays $245,238,000 (average outlay per district, New Hampshire 1 and 2)

DOD	$123,403,000	HEW	$84,239,000
AEC	$175,000	HUD	$2,937,000
NASA	$1,822,000	OEO	$711,000
DOT	$15,634,000	DOA	$7,867,000
		Other	$18,976,000

Federal Military-Industrial Commitments

DOD Contractors Sanders Associates (Nashua), $59.667m: sonobuoys; electronic warfare equipment; Safeguard ABM development.

Economic Base Nonelectrical machinery, esp. special industrial machinery other than metalworking machinery; electrical machinery, equipment, and supplies, esp. electronic components and accessories; leather and leather products, esp. footwear other than rubber. Also, tourism (White Mountains).

The Voters

Registration 124,326, total. 44,078 D (36%); 80,248 R (65%).

Employment profile White collar, 36%. Blue collar, 64%.

Ethnic groups Black, less than 0.5%. Total foreign stock, 28%. Canada, 18%; UK, 2%; Germany, Ireland, Italy, Poland, Sweden, USSR, 1% each; others, 3%.

Presidential vote

1968	Humphrey (D)	67,492	(45%)
	Nixon (R)	77,335	(52%)
	Wallace (AIP)	4,976	(3%)

Representative

James C. Cleveland (R) Elected 1962; b. June 13, 1920, Montclair, N.J.; home, New London; Colgate U., B.A., 1941; Yale Law School, LL.B., 1948; Army, WWII and Korean War; married, five children; unspecified Protestant.

Career Practicing atty., 1949–62; N.H. Senate, 1950–62, Majority Floor Leader, 1952–55.

Offices 1112 LHOB, 202-225-5206. Also Fed. Bldg., 55 Pleasant St., Concord 03301, 603-224-4187, and 23 Temple St., Nashua 03060, 603-883-4225.

Committees

House Administration (3rd); Subs. (1) Accounts, (2) Printing, (3) Contracts.

Public Works (3rd); Subs. (1) Investigation and Oversight, (2) Public Buildings and Grounds, (3) Rivers and Harbors, (4) Roads, (5) Sp. on Economic Development Program.

Jt. Com. on Congressional Operations (2nd).

Group Ratings

	ADA	COPE	NREP	NFU	LCV	CFA	NAB	NSI	ACA
1970	44	34	33	46	63	67	83	90	84
1969	33	—	—	33	—	—	—	—	71
1968	17	25	—	64	—	—	100	—	68

Key Votes

(1) ABM	FOR	(6) 18-Yr-Vote	FOR	(11) Clean Water $	FOR
(2) SST	AGN	(7) Farm Sub Lmt	FOR	(12) Mig Wrkrs Comp	AGN
(3) Phil Pln	FOR	(8) Coop-Church	AGN	(13) Jets to Chiang	AGN
(4) No-Knock	FOR	(9) Family Asst	AGN	(14) State OEO Veto	FOR
(5) Cmutr Tax	AGN	(10) Work Stamps	AGN	(15) Park Logging	AGN

Election Results

1970 general:	James C. Cleveland (R)	74,219	(70%)
	Eugene S. Daniell, Jr. (D)	32,374	(30%)
1970 primary:	James C. Cleveland (R), unopposed (Redistricted 1970)		

NEW JERSEY

Political Background

New Jersey, the 8th most populous state in the nation, is a state without an identity. Sandwiched between New York City and Philadelphia, Jerseyites read out-of-state newspapers, watch out-of-state television stations, and follow out-of-state political contests. Although the residents of the state are among the nation's best educated and most affluent, local affairs do not seem to interest them, which makes for meager participation in local politics. This means that party machines dominate New Jersey politics.

The enterprise here is based on the county party organizations, which select the candidates for local offices, the state legislature, Congress, and the governorship. The last of these is most important to the machines, because the governor appoints the state attorney general and all the county prosecutors and so affects law enforcement or, what is more accurate in many cases, non-enforcement. The recent conviction of many New Jersey politicians on bribery charges, including ex-Mayor Hugh Addonizio of Newark and Mayor Thomas Whalen of Jersey City, surprised many cynical observers.

They suspected corruption but did not expect any New Jersey politician would be prosecuted.

Sociologically, New Jersey is a state made up of suburbs and medium-sized industrial cities. The suburbs range from the elegant horse farms of Morris and Somerset counties to the working-class subdivisions of Middlesex County. The cities include Newark, Jersey City, Camden, and Trenton, all of them with more than their share of urban problems. The state's presidential elections are usually close, the outcome depending on the vigor with which the county party machines support the candidate. In 1960, Nixon lost New Jersey by 22,000; in 1968, he carried it by 61,000. The performance of certain Democratic organizations accounted for most of the difference: in 1960, Hudson County produced a 60,000-vote Kennedy majority; in 1968, after local schisms, corruption, and George Wallace battered the organization, Hudson Democrats could manage only a 33,000-vote margin for Humphrey. Similarly, the blue-collar suburban county of Middlesex, home of one of the state's most powerful Democrats, David Willentz, went for Kennedy by 33,000 votes and for Humphrey by less than 7,000.

In 1960, New Jersey Democrats were a hungry group, united by a desire for some federal patronage positions. By 1968, they were weakened and divided by the infighting that comes from too much success. The Republican resurgence, both in New Jersey and nationally, was foreshadowed in 1967 when the state's voters, weary of the Johnson Administration, responded to the Republicans' campaign theme—an invitation to get rid of the Democrats a year early—by giving the Republicans a 2–1 majority in the state legislature.

By 1970, the Republicans had won four straight statewide elections, all but one by huge margins—1966 Senate, 1967 legislature, 1968 President, and 1969 governor. And in 1970 they expected to win the other Senate seat held by Democrat Harrison Williams. The Senator appeared to be in trouble. Though he won handily in 1958 and 1964, Williams was not very well known in the state. And Williams was once censured by the NAACP for showing up drunk for a breakfast speech; he was, as he later admitted, an alcoholic. And finally, New Jersey was the one big Eastern state Nixon carried in 1968.

Republican State Chairman Nelson Gross, once regarded as a liberal, launched an aggressive Nixon-style Senate campaign, complete with references to law-and-order and Williams' radical-liberalism. Williams, for the most part, ignored Gross. Just before the campaign started, he admitted that he was once an alcoholic but was now off the bottle, an announcement that probably got him more favorable publicity than the mass transit bill he had steered through Congress when times were better for the Democratic party. Williams refused to debate Gross and instead spoke of the serious unemployment in the state and stressed the value of his incumbency. In the spring, Ralph Yarborough was defeated in the Texas Democratic primary, which meant that Williams, if reelected, would become chairman of the Senate Labor and Public Welfare Committee. Knowing this, labor began to support Williams in a big way. In addition, Williams' opposition to the ABM and SST and his support of the Hatfield-McGovern and Cooper-Church amendments won him the backing of the New Jersey peace activists.

Nixon and Agnew both stumped the state for Gross. But Williams won in a landslide, 54% of the two-party vote and a 250,000-vote margin. The voters were most concerned about the economy and unemployment and did not want to turn out an incumbent they had no real reason to dislike. Despite Nixon's pitch to the hard-hat vote, Williams did well in blue-collar areas. He carried Middlesex, for example, by 36,000 votes. And he also carried Gross's home county, white-collar Bergen, by 34,000 votes.

After the election, the state's Republican Senator, Clifford P. Case, chided Gross, saying that he should have emphasized positive issues and avoided the hard-line Nixon-Agnew rhetoric. That is certainly what Case will do when he campaigns for reelection in 1972. The former Wall Street lawyer is one of the Senate's most liberal Republican members. His 88 ADA rating falls just short of Williams' 95. He currently sits on the Foreign Relations and the Appropriations committees. After serving in the House from 1944 to 1952, Case won a close race in the 1954 Republican primary against a conservative opponent. He has won every election since with ease; in his last race, in 1966, he polled 60%. Unlike liberal Republican Charles Goodell of New York, Case does not expect Republican or third party opposition in 1972, and no one doubts he will win reelection.

Despite the string of Republican victories during the late '60's, 9 of 15 in New Jersey's House delegation are Democrats. Reelection of liberal incumbents who first won in the Johnson landslide accounts for the Democratic majority. New Jersey redistricted four times in the '60's, but the redistricting which will precede the 1972 election will yield some important changes; for the first time in almost 20 years, both the governor and the legislature are Republican. Precisely how the lines will come out is, at this writing, impossible to predict. But the Republicans will probably try to make reelection tougher for Democrats Henry Helstoski of the 9th and James J. Howard of the 3rd and may eliminate the seat of Cornelius Gallagher of the 13th. The redistricters may also create a new Republican district in the central part of the state.

Electoral Votes 17

Census Data 1970 pop. 7,168,164; 3.48% of U.S. total, 8th largest; change 1960–70, +18.2%. Metro. 76.9%, 16.3% central city. 1970 per capita income, $4,539; 6th highest. 19th in number of poor.

1970 Share of Federal Tax Burden $8,332,500,000; 4.27% of U.S. total, 8th largest.

1970 Share of Federal Outlays $6,961,892,777; 3.68% of U.S. total, 8th largest. Per capita federal spending, $965.

DOD	$1,686,972,000	11th (2.94%)	HEW	$1,619,781,860	10th (3.10%)
AEC	$19,146,555	21st (0.74%)	HUD	$42,448,360	16th (2.18%)
NASA	$3,659,891	14th (0.10%)	OEO	$18,471,237	13th (2.43%)
DOT	$244,124,473	10th (3.42%)	DOA	$150,101,281	32nd (1.17%)
DOC	$42,411,687	6th (3.67%)	POD	$262,811,396	8th (3.61%)
DOI	$37,624,512	20th (1.63%)	VA	$250,938,185	10th (3.40%)
DOJ	$12,254,011	12th (2.13%)	CSC	$73,583,207	14th (1.83%)
			Other	$2,497,564,124	

Economic Base Electrical machinery, equipment, and supplies, esp. communication equipment; chemicals and allied products, esp. industrial inorganic and organic chemicals and drugs; apparel and other finished products made from fabrics and similar materials, esp. women's, juniors', and misses' outerwear; nonelectrical machinery; fabricated metal products, esp, fabricated structural metal products; food and kindred products, esp. bakery products and beverages; printing, publishing, and allied industries, esp. commercial printing and newspapers; stone, clay, glass, and concrete products, esp. glass and glassware, pressed and blown; primary metal industries, esp. rolling, drawing, and extruding of nonferrous metals; paper and allied products; transportation equipment; esp. motor vehicles and motor vehicle equipment and aircraft and parts.

Political Line-up Governor, William T. Cahill (R); seat up, 1973. Senators, Clifford P. Case (R) and Harrison A. Williams, Jr. (D). Representatives, 15 (9 D and 6 R). State Senate (9 D, 28 R, and 3 vacant); State Assembly (21 D and 59 R).

The Voters

Registration 3,167,532 total. No party registration.

Employment profile White collar, 45%. Blue collar, 55%.

Ethnic groups Black, 11%. Puerto Rico, 1%. Total foreign stock, 35%. Italy, 9%; Poland, Germany, 4% each; UK, USSR, 3% each; Ireland, 2%; Hungary, Austria, Czech., Canada, 1% each; others, 5%.

Presidential vote

1968	Humphrey (D)	1,264,206	(44%)
	Nixon (R)	1,325,467	(46%)
	Wallace (AIP)	262,187	(9%)
1964	Johnson (D)	1,867,671	(66%)
	Goldwater (R)	963,843	(34%)
1960	Kennedy (D)	1,385,415	(50%)
	Nixon (R)	1,363,324	(50%)

Senator

Clifford P. Case (R) Elected 1954, seat up 1972; b. April 16, 1904, Franklin Park; home, Rahway; Rutgers U., B.A., 1925; Columbia U., LL.B., 1928; married, three children; Presbyterian.

Career Practicing atty., N.Y.C., 1928–53; Rahway Common Council, 1938–42; N.J. House of Assembly, 1943–44; U.S. Delegate to 21st Gen. Assembly of UN; U.S. House of Reps., 1944–53.

Offices 315 OSOB, 202-225-3224.

Committees

Appropriations (7th); Subs. (1) Defense, (2) Labor, HEW, and Related Agencies, (3) HUD, Space, and Science, (4) Public Works, (5) Transportation.

Foreign Relations (3rd); Subs. (1) Arms Control, International Law and Organization, (2) European Affairs, (3) Oceans and International Environment, (4) U.S. Security Agreements and Commitments Abroad, (5) Western Hemisphere Affairs.

Jt. Com. on Congressional Operations (3rd).

Group Ratings

	ADA	COPE	NREP	NFU	LCV	NAB	NSI	ACA
1970	88	92	100	87	81	10	0	4
1969	100	—	—	60	—	—	—	7
1968	100	92	—	64	—	50	—	18

Key Votes

(1) ABM	AGN	(8) Phil Pln	ABS	(15) Coop-Church	FOR
(2) SST	AGN	(9) Vol Army	AGN	(16) Cut Oil Dpltn	FOR
(3) Busing	FOR	(10) Prison $	FOR	(17) Consumer Prot	FOR
(4) Tob Sub	AGN	(11) Cut Mil $	FOR	(18) Farm Sub Limit	FOR
(5) Carswell	AGN	(12) Defoliatn	AGN	(19) Comp Bid Sales	FOR
(6) No-Knock	AGN	(13) 18-Yr-Vote	FOR	(20) Pre-Prod Tests	FOR
(7) Seniorty	AGN	(14) Pentgn PR	AGN	(21) Cut Marjna Pen	FOR

Election Results

1966 general:	Clifford P. Case (R)	1,278,843	(60%)
	Warren W. Wilentz (D)	788,021	(37%)
	Robert Lee Schlachter (Con.)	53,606	(3%)
1966 primary:	Clifford P. Case (R), unopposed		
1960 general:	Clifford P. Case (R)	1,483,832	(56%)
	Thorn Lord (D)	1,151,385	(44%)

Senator

Harrison Arlington Williams, Jr. (D) Elected 1958, seat up 1976; b. Dec. 10, 1919, Plainfield; home, Westfield; Oberlin Col., B.A., 1941; Columbia Law School, LL.B., 1948; Georgetown Foreign Service School; USNR, WWII; married, five children; Unitarian.

Career Practicing atty., 1951– .

Offices 352 OSOB, 202-225-4744. Also Rm. 939A, Fed. Bldg., 970 Broad St., Newark 07102, 201-645-3030.

Committees

Banking, Housing, and Urban Affairs (3rd); Subs. (1) Chm., Securities, (2) Financial Institutions, (3) Housing and Urban Affairs, (4) International Finance, (5) Small Business.

Labor and Public Welfare (Chm.); Subs. (1) Chm., Labor, (2) Aging, (3) Alcoholism and Narcotics, (4) Children and Youth, (5) Education, (6) Handicapped Workers, (7) Health, (8) Migratory Labor, (9) Sp. on International Health, Education, and Labor Programs.

Sel. Com. on Small Business (4th); Subs. (1) Financing and Investments, (2) Retailing, Distribution, and Marketing Practices, (3) Science and Technology.

Sp. Com. on Aging (2nd); Subs. (1) Chm., Housing for the Elderly, (2) Health of the Elderly, (3) Long-Term Care.

Jt. Com. on Defense Production (3rd).

Group Ratings

	ADA	COPE	NREP	NFU	LCV	NAB	NSI	ACA
1970	94	100	93	94	68	10	0	5
1969	94	—	—	94	—	—	—	7
1968	86	100	—	83	—	33	—	8

Key Votes

(1) ABM	AGN	(8) Phil Pln	FOR	(15) Coop-Church	FOR
(2) SST	AGN	(9) Vol Army	FOR	(16) Cut Oil Dpltn	FOR
(3) Busing	FOR	(10) Prison $	ABS	(17) Consumer Prot	ABS
(4) Tob Sub	AGN	(11) Cut Mil $	FOR	(18) Farm Sub Limit	FOR
(5) Carswell	AGN	(12) Defoliatn	AGN	(19) Comp Bid Sales	AGN
(6) No-Knock	AGN	(13) 18-Yr-Vote	FOR	(20) Pre-Prod Tests	FOR
(7) Seniorty	AGN	(14) Pentgn PR	AGN	(21) Cut Marjna Pen	FOR

Election Results

1970 general:	Harrison A. Williams, Jr. (D)	1,157,074	(54%)
	Nelson G. Gross (R)	903,026	(42%)
	Four others	54,291	(3%)
1970 primary:	Harrison A. Williams, Jr. (D)	190,692	(66%)
	Frank J. Guarini (D)	100,045	(34%)
1964 general:	Harrison A. Williams, Jr. (D)	1,677,515	(62%)
	Bernard M. Shanley (R)	1,011,280	(38%)

FIRST DISTRICT Political Background

New Jersey 1 is suburban Philadelphia, most of Camden County and all of Gloucester County. Gloucester includes the town of Glassboro where President Johnson met Premier Kosygin in 1967; the county is experiencing rapid population growth as its vegetable truck farms are being replaced by new suburban developments. More densely settled Camden County contains the industrial city of Camden, just across the Delaware River from downtown Philadelphia. In general, the suburbs in the district along the river are industrial and Democratic, while those to the east, higher-income and Republican.

In theory, the 1st is a Democratic district; in 1968 it favored Humphrey over Nixon, 46–39. But the 1st and its predecessors have sent only Republicans to Congress since 1883. Liberal Republican William Cahill represented the district from 1958 to 1966 before leaving to capture the seat in the newly-created 6th; in 1970, Cahill became governor. The new 1st was designed by Democrats for a Democrat, but 1966 was a Republican year and conservative John E. Hunt won the seat and has held it ever since.

Hunt, a former sheriff and state senator, admires the attitudes of Frank Rizzo, the ex-Police Commissioner and law-and-order candidate for mayor of Philadelphia. Hunt, who supports heavy military spending, is one of the hard-core conservatives in the House; after the Cambodian invasion of 1970, the Congressman was the only one on the Hill to throw antiwar college students out of his office. His constituents, many of them Italian immigrants who had to work their way out of the South Philadelphia slums, seem to like Hunt's performance as congressman. His margins have been increasing steadily—52% in 1966, 58% in 1968, and 61% in 1970.

Because of its population increase, the Republican legislature will have to reduce the size of the 1st. A logical move would be to transfer some Republican suburbs to the 6th to strengthen Republican Edwin Forsythe, who has not run as strong there as Hunt has in the 1st. On paper, this would make the 1st more Democratic, but if past performance means anything, Hunt will go on winning.

Census Data 1970 pop. 483,518; deviation from current state average, +1.2%; change 1960–70, +15.6%. Metro. 100.0%, 0.0% central city.

1970 Share of Federal Outlays $348,204,575

DOD	$88,685,000	HEW	$124,440,861
AEC	$000	HUD	$1,352,377
NASA	$24,575,524	OEO	$1,159,327
DOT	$13,009,435	DOA	$2,479,869
		Other	$92,502,182

Federal Military-Industrial Commitments

DOD Contractors RCA Corp. (Camden), $28.979m: operation of Atlantic Fleet Range Support Facility; P-3C aircraft communication equipment.

DOD Installations Gibbsboro AF Station (Gibbsboro).

NASA Contractors RCA Corp. (Camden), $18.189m: tracking and data acquisition services.

Economic Base Electrical machinery, equipment, and supplies, esp. communication equipment; food and kindred products; chemicals and allied products, esp. industrial organic and inorganic chemicals. Also, banking.

The Voters

Registration 218,881 total. No party registration.

Employment profile White collar, 37%. Blue collar, 63%.

Ethnic groups Black, 13%. Puerto Rico, 1%. Total foreign stock, 22%. Italy, 7%; Germany, UK, 3% each; Poland, 2%; Austria, Ireland, USSR, Canada, 1% each; others, 2%.

Presidential vote

1968	Humphrey (D)	88,661	(46%)
	Nixon (R)	75,496	(39%)
	Wallace (AIP)	28,110	(15%)

Representative

John E. Hunt (R) Elected 1966; b. Nov. 25, 1908, Lambertville; home, Pitman; Newark Business School; N.J. State Police Academy; FBI National Academy; Harvard School of Police Science; U.S. Army Intelligence School; Army, WWII; Lt. Col. USAR; married, one child; Baptist.

Career Criminology Consultant, N.J. State Police, 1930–59; Sheriff, Gloucester County, 1960–64; N.J. Senate, 1964–66.

Offices 1440 LHOB, 202-225-6501. Also 114 N. 7th St., Camden 08102, 609-365-4442, and 67 Cooper St., Woodbury 08096, 609-845-0200.

Committees

Armed Services (13th); Subs. (1) Sub. No. 4, (2) Armed Services Investigating.

Group Ratings

	ADA	COPE	NREP	NFU	LCV	CFA	NAB	NSI	ACA
1970	8	17	17	31	50	50	82	100	89
1969	7	—	—	28	—	—	—	—	88
1968	0	23	—	44	—	—	100	—	91

Key Votes

(1) ABM	FOR	(6) 18-Yr-Vote	AGN	(11) Clean Water $	AGN
(2) SST	AGN	(7) Farm Sub Lmt	FOR	(12) Mig Wrkrs Comp	AGN
(3) Phil Pln	FOR	(8) Coop-Church	AGN	(13) Jets to Chiang	FOR
(4) No-Knock	FOR	(9) Family Asst	AGN	(14) State OEO Veto	FOR
(5) Cmutr Tax	AGN	(10) Work Stamps	FOR	(15) Park Logging	AGN

Election Results

1970 general:	John E. Hunt (R)	83,726	(61%)
	Salvatore T. Mansi (D)	25,567	(39%)
1970 primary:	John E. Hunt (R), unopposed		
1968 general:	John E. Hunt (R)	105,856	(58%)
	Thomas S. Higgins (D)	74,703	(41%)
	Raymond V. S. Miller (Abolish Port Authority)	1,072	(1%)

SECOND DISTRICT Political Background

New Jersey 2—Atlantic, Cape May, Cumberland, and Salem counties—spreads out across the flat, often swampy, coastal plain at the southern end of the state. Along the coast are the great, aging beach resorts of Atlantic City, Wildwood, and Cape May. Cumberland and Salem counties are filled with vegetable farms and conditions here in the migrant worker camps have prompted some controversy. The city of Vineland, in Cumberland County, is the fastest-growing part of the 2nd; many of the district's new residents are New York or Philadelphia retired people in search of sandy beaches and clean air. Along with the neighboring state of Delaware, Cumberland and Salem have a Southern ambience about them and the voting patterns here are traditionally Democratic. Cape May is a Republican bastion. Atlantic City, with most of the district's blacks, should be Democratic—Humphrey carried it in 1968. Atlantic City is also, however, the home of state Sen. Frank S. (Hap) Farley, one of the state's most powerful Republican county chairmen. His machine has been charged with corruption, but it still wins on election day.

The 2nd's conservative Republican congressman, Charles W. Sandman, Jr., first won the seat in 1966, when he defeated a Democrat elected on the strength of Johnson's landslide in 1964. Before that, Sandman was a powerful Republican state senator. He sought the Republican gubernatorial nomination in 1965 and again in 1969, when he almost defeated William Cahill in the primary.

Sandman's conservatism has not gone over as well in the 2nd as John Hunt's in the 1st. The 2nd is rural in Cape May and Salem counties and urban in Atlantic City, which is inhabited by many hotel service personnel. The Nixon-Agnew law-and-order rhetoric may not appeal to these voters as much as it does to the suburbanites of the 1st, many of whom have only recently escaped from life in the core city of Philadelphia. In 1968 Sandman was reelected with 55% of the vote, but in 1970 his percentage shrunk to 52%. His opponent that year, a former Cape May prosecutor and firm law-and-order man, increased the Democratic percentage 10% in rural Cape May and Salem counties. It appears that he attracted the votes of many of the Southern-oriented Democrats living in this part of New Jersey.

Redistricting will probably add a portion of Ocean County, with its many Republican retirees, to the 2nd. This will help Sandman, but the congressman is still vulnerable to a conservative Democratic challenge.

Census Data 1970 pop. 416,317; deviation from current state average, —12.9%; change 1960–70, +11.0%. Metro. 85.7%, 32.9% central city.

1970 Share of Federal Outlays $271,773,111

DOD	$35,476,000	HEW	$129,263,350
AEC	$000	HUD	$164,859
NASA	$125,200	OEO	$1,562,128
DOT	$46,213,641	DOA	$4,725,345
		Other	$54,242,588

Federal Military-Industrial Commitments

DOD Contractors Pembroke Inc. (Egg Harbor City), $5.861m: Army wool overcoats.

Economic Base Stone, clay, glass, and concrete products, esp. glass and glassware, pressed and blown; apparel and other finished products made from fabrics and similar materials, esp. men's, youths', and boys' suits, coats, and overcoats; poultry and dairy. Also, tourism (Atlantic City).

The Voters

Registration 196,207 total. No party registration.

Employment profile White collar, 35%. Blue collar, 65%.

Ethnic groups Black, 15%. Puerto Rico, 1%; Total foreign stock, 23%. Italy, 7%; Germany, UK, USSR, 3% each; Ireland, Poland, Canada, 1% each; others, 3%.

Presidential vote

1968	Humphrey (D)	78,078	(44%)
	Nixon (R)	77,572	(44%)
	Wallace (AIP)	20,029	(11%)

Representative

Charles W. Sandman, Jr. (R) Elected 1966; b. Oct. 23, 1921, Philadelphia, Pa.; home, Cape May; Temple U., 1940–42; Rutgers U., 1946–48; USAAF, WWII; married, six children; Catholic.

Career N.J. Senate, 1956–66, Majority Leader, 1962–63, Pres., 1964–65; Acting Governor, 1964–65.

Offices 115 CHOB, 202-225-6572. Also 421 Washington St., Cape May 08204, 608-884-8492, and Landis Ave., Vineland 08360.

Committees

Judiciary (6th); Subs., (1) Sub. No. 2, (2) Sub. No. 4.

Sel. Com. on Crime (4th).

Group Ratings

	ADA	COPE	NREP	NFU	LCV	CFA	NAB	NSI	ACA
1970	16	25	25	46	25	58	75	100	63
1969	13	—	—	39	—	—	—	—	47
1968	8	31	—	25	—	—	100	—	74

Key Votes

(1) ABM	FOR	(6) 18-Yr-Vote	AGN	(11) Clean Water $	AGN
(2) SST	FOR	(7) Farm Sub Lmt	FOR	(12) Mig Wrkrs Comp	AGN
(3) Phil Pln	FOR	(8) Coop-Church	AGN	(13) Jets to Chiang	FOR
(4) No-Knock	FOR	(9) Family Asst	FOR	(14) State OEO Veto	FOR
(5) Cmutr Tax	AGN	(10) Work Stamps	FOR	(15) Park Logging	AGN

Election Results

1970 general:	Charles W. Sandman, Jr. (R)	69,392	(52%)
	William J. Hughes (D)	64,882	(48%)
1970 primary:	Charles W. Sandman, Jr. (R), unopposed		
1968 general:	Charles W. Sandman, Jr. (R)	91,218	(55%)
	David Dichter (D)	73,361	(44%)

THIRD DISTRICT Political Background

New Jersey 3 comprises Monmouth County, the portion of Middlesex County around Madison Township, and part of Ocean County including Lakewood. This is the northern part of the Jersey Shore, with little cities like Long Branch. Asbury Park, and Neptune dotting the beaches along the coast. Subdivisions, advertised as an hour's commute from New York City, are going up inland in Madison Township and around Englishtown, Matawan, and Freehold. Monmouth is traditionally Republican, but as its population grows (up 37% in the '60's), the county has become increasingly marginal. In 1970, Democratic Sen. Harrison Williams carried Monmouth by 5,000 votes.

The 3rd would send a Republican to Washington were it not for the presence of the incumbent congressman, James J. Howard. Howard was lucky enough to be running as a Democrat in the LBJ year of 1964 and to be running when the veteran Republican James C. Auchincloss had decided to retire after 24 years in the House. The Democrat won a bare majority—1,740 votes—and has worked hard to strengthen his position ever since. For the most part he has succeeded, even though his record in Congress is liberal and antiwar. In 1970, however, former White House assistant William F. Dowd returned to the district to run as a Nixon man. Dowd reduced the incumbent's margin to 56%, down 2% from 1968. Dowd was no doubt helped by racial trouble in Asbury Park and Long Branch since the Republican percentage in Monmouth County rose some 3%. The 3rd was one of three New Jersey districts where the Republican House candidate fared better in 1970 than in 1968.

The Republican redistricters will try to make things even more difficult for Howard. Population changes, as well as the composition of the legislature, indicate that the district will be shifted to the south. The 3rd will lose Madison Township and much of Monmouth and pick up the larger part of Ocean County, the fastest-growing in the state. Here it is estimated that 40% of the new residents are retired people attracted to the beaches and quiet of the Jersey Shore; most of them are Republicans. If Howard can win these people over, like he did those of Monmouth County earlier, he can win reelection in 1972.

Census Data 1970 pop. 555,706; deviation from current state average, +16.3%; change 1960–70, +45.3%. Metro. 0.0%, 0.0% central city.

1970 Share of Federal Outlays $481,643,060

DOD	$217,315,000	HEW	$96,967,478
AEC	$53,000	HUD	$36,762
NASA	$1,019,465	OEO	$864,075
DOT	$1,810,913	DOA	$3,459,073
		Other	$160,117,294

Federal Military-Industrial Commitments

DOD Contractors Harvard Industries (Farmingdale), $5.861m: armament subsystems for Cobra helicopters.

DOD Installations Fort Monmouth (Oceanport). Naval Ammunition Depot (Earle).

Economic Base Electrical machinery, equipment, and supplies, esp. communication equipment and electronic components and accessories; apparel and other finished products made from fabrics and similar materials, especially women's, misses', and juniors' outerwear. Also, tourism (Jersey Shore).

The Voters

Registration 223,026 total. No party registration.

Employment profile White collar, 46%. Blue collar, 54%.

Ethnic groups Black, 8%. Total foreign stock, 29%. Italy, 6%; Germany, UK, 4% each; Poland, USSR, 3% each; Ireland, 2%; Austria, Czech., Hungary, Canada, 1% each; others, 4%.

Presidential vote

1968	Humphrey (D)	83,308	(41%)
	Nixon (R)	101,891	(51%)
	Wallace (AIP)	16,248	(8%)

Representative

James J. Howard (D) Elected 1964; b. July 24, 1927, Irvington; home, Wall Township; St. Bonaventure U., B.A., 1952; Rutgers U., M.Ed., 1958; Navy, WWII; married, three children; Catholic.

Career Teacher, principal, Wall Township, N.J., 1952–64; Pres., Monmouth County Ed. Assn., Mbr. Delegate Assembly of N.J. Ed. Assn.

Offices 131 CHOB, 202-225-4671. Also P.O. Bldg., 501 Main St., Asbury Park 07712, 201-774-1600.

Committees

Public Works (13th); Subs. (1) Investigation and Oversight, (2) Public Buildings and Grounds, (3) Rivers and Harbors, (4) Roads, (5) Sp. on Economic Development Programs.

Group Ratings

	ADA	COPE	NREP	NFU	LCV	CFA	NAB	NSI	ACA
1970	76	92	83	92	100	100	0	33	11
1969	80	—	—	85	—	—	—	—	8
1968	83	92	—	87	—	—	0	—	5

Key Votes

(1) ABM	AGN	(6) 18-Yr-Vote	FOR	(11) Clean Water $	FOR
(2) SST	AGN	(7) Farm Sub Lmt	FOR	(12) Mig Wrkrs Comp	FOR
(3) Phil Pln	FOR	(8) Coop-Church	FOR	(13) Jets to Chiang	AGN
(4) No-Knock	FOR	(9) Family Asst	FOR	(14) State OEO Veto	AGN
(5) Cmutr Tax	FOR	(10) Work Stamps	AGN	(15) Park Logging	AGN

Election Results

1970 general:	James J. Howard (D)	87,937	(56%)
	William F. Dowd (R)	68,675	(44%)
1970 primary:	James J. Howard (D), unopposed		
1968 general:	James J. Howard (D)	113,587	(58%)
	Richard R. Stout (R)	82,441	(42%)

FOURTH DISTRICT Political Background

New Jersey 4, in the northwest part of the state, comprises three predominantly rural counties—Hunterdon, Warren, and Sussex—and Mercer County, which contains the state capital, Trenton (pop. 104,000). Hunterdon and Sussex are heavily Republican; Warren, just across the Delaware River from Pennsylvania's industrial Lehigh valley, is politically marginal. Mercer County, except for the university town of Princeton, which is marginal, is heavily Democratic. Because Mercer contains 60% of the 4th's population, the district is reliably Democratic.

Frank Thompson, Jr., a leading House liberal, has been the congressman from the 4th since 1954. He is currently 3rd ranking Democrat on Education and Labor—a unit responsible for social and educational legislation. Thompson could become chairman of the committee since both Carl Perkins and Edith Green, who outrank him, are older. The New Jersey Congressman, a founder of the liberal Democratic Study Group, has always had strong support from organized labor, and his opposition to the Vietnam war has won him high regard among the students, especially those from Princeton.

In 1966, the 4th was altered drastically by redistricting; it lost Burlington County and gained Hunterdon, Warren, and Sussex. Thompson's performance at the polls since 1966 is a case study of how an incumbent congressman, out of line with his district's ideological persuasions, can become unbeatable. In 1966, Thompson carried Mercer by 23,000 votes and lost the three new counties by 4,600, winning reelection with 56% of the votes. He then survived a district-wide drop in his vote two years later. In 1970, the Congressman carried Mercer County by 20,000 votes and the rest of the district by 6,000, finishing with 58%. The drop in Mercer resulted from the attempt of his hard-line conservative opponent to exploit the racial unrest which had developed in

Trenton. But for four years Thompson had been making friends in Hunterdon, Warren, and Sussex, busy doing the kind of chores that congressmen do. In this case, Thompson concerned himself with the interests of dairy farmers at the Department of Agriculture. The results of his efforts were clear when the results came in from the 4th's northern counties.

The 1970 census may again alter the district drastically; it is quite possible that Thompson will lose his new friends in the rural areas and face a new group of voters in parts of Middlesex or Burlington counties. But as long as an undivided Mercer County remains in the district, Thompson is likely to win reelection, and even if the new portion of the district leans Republican, he will win them over, given time.

Census Data 1970 pop. 525,093; deviation from current state average, +9.9%; change 1960–70, +21.3%. Metro. 72%, 19.9% central city.

1970 Share of Federal Outlays $522,982,234

DOD	$82,589,000	HEW	$174,485,960
AEC	$15,557,331	HUD	$5,320,934
NASA	$17,012,428	OEO	$6,018,039
DOT	$35,713,874	DOA	$7,841,003
		Other	$178,443,665

Federal Military-Industrial Commitments

DOD Contractors RCA Corp. (Princeton), $14.892m: Navy navigation satellite program support. Delaval Turbine, Inc. (Trenton), $10.775m: ship fuel pumps. Trenton Textile Engineering (Trenton), $7.815m: Army ponchos. Plastoid Corp. (Hamburg), $5.034m: telephone cable.

DOD Installations Naval Air Propulsion Test Center (Trenton).

AEC Operations Princeton University (Princeton), $7.458m: Stellarator and Accelerator facilities.

NASA Contractors RCA Corp. (Princeton), $7.146m: Tiros M spacecraft development.

Economic Base Nonelectrical machinery; fabricated metal products; electrical machinery, equipment, and supplies, esp. electrical lighting and wiring equipment; dairy. Also, higher education (Trenton State College); banking.

The Voters

Registration 234,402 total. No party registration.

Employment profile White collar, 41%. Blue collar, 59%.

Ethnic groups Black, 10%. Total foreign stock, 28%. Italy, 7%; Germany, Poland, UK, 3% each; Hungary, 2%; Austria, Czech., Ireland, USSR, Canada, 1% each; others, 3%.

Presidential vote

1968	Humphrey (D)	93,120	(44%)
	Nixon (R)	93,198	(44%)
	Wallace (AIP)	23,887	(11%)

Representative

Frank Thompson, Jr. (D) Elected 1954; b. July 20, 1918, Trenton; home, Trenton; Wake Forest Col., LL.B., 1941; Navy, WWII; Cdr. USNR; married, two children; Catholic.

Career Practicing atty., 1948– ; N.J. Gen. Assembly, 1949–54, Asst. Minority Leader, 1950, Minority Leader, 1954; Chm., Natl. Voters Registration Com. for 1960 Pres. Campaign.

Offices 2246 RHOB, 202-225-3765. Also 383 W. State, Trenton 08618, 609-599-1619.

Committees

Education and Labor (3rd); Subs. (1) Chm., Sp. on Labor, (2) Agricultural Labor, (3) Sp. on Education.

House Administration (2nd); Subs. (1) Chm., Accounts, (2) Library and Memorials.

Group Ratings

	ADA	COPE	NREP	NFU	LCV	CFA	NAB	NSI	ACA
1970	92	100	100	92	100	100	0	0	0
1969	93	—	—	86	—	—	—	—	14
1968	92	100	—	100	—	—	0	—	0

Key Votes

(1) ABM	AGN	(6) 18-Yr-Vote	FOR	(11) Clean Water $	FOR
(2) SST	AGN	(7) Farm Sub Lmt	FOR	(12) Mig Wrkrs Comp	FOR
(3) Phil Pln	FOR	(8) Coop-Church	FOR	(13) Jets to Chiang	ABS
(4) No-Knock	AGN	(9) Family Asst	FOR	(14) State OEO Veto	AGN
(5) Cmutr Tax	AGN	(10) Work Stamps	AGN	(15) Park Logging	AGN

Election Results

1970 general:	Frank Thompson, Jr. (D)	91,670	(58%)
	Edward A. Costigan (R)	65,030	(42%)
1970 primary:	Frank Thompson, Jr. (D), unopposed		
1968 general:	Frank Thompson, Jr. (D)	106,504	(53%)
	Sydney S. Souter (R)	92,710	(46%)

FIFTH DISTRICT Political Background

New Jersey 5, Morris and Somerset counties in the northcentral part of the state, is the most Republican district in New Jersey. There is a great deal of wealth in the district. Old line WASP families hold large country estates here, especially around Morristown and in the horse country near Far Hills and Peapack. The suburbs at the southern and eastern edges of the district are not as opulent, more conventional, but far from uncomfortable. This part of the district grew rapidly during the '60's, as the suburbs and white-collar industries spread out toward the hilly reaches of Morris County.

The district is appropriately represented in the House by Peter H. B. Frelinghuysen. Frelinghuysen is a member of an old aristocratic family which has produced three New Jersey senators; the Congressman is himself a wealthy man who owns a 200-acre estate near Morristown. A moderate Republican, Frelinghuysen is not as conservative as most Midwestern and New Jersey Republicans and not as liberal as some of his New York GOP colleagues. In 1965, he was the liberal's candidate for chairman of the Republican Policy Committee and nearly defeated Melvin Laird for the post. Since then, the Congressman has not sought other positions of leadership and currently serves as the 2nd-ranking minority member of the House Foreign Affairs Committee.

Frelinghuysen has supported Nixon's Vietnam policy, and as a result, has faced opposition from Democratic peace candidates. In the 5th, as in most high-income areas, peace activists tend to dominate the local Democratic party. Recently, the Democrats have whittled down the Congressman's margins—evidence of the strength of the peace issue in high-income communities. But Frelinghuysen has little to worry about; he has won reelection easily since 1952. In 1964, he took 64% of the votes, which was one of the best Republican showings in the country.

Redistricting could alter the shape of the 5th considerably; it may place Morris County with Republican Sussex and make Somerset (pop. 198,000) the nucleus of another Republican district. Whatever happens Frelinghuysen will likely continue to win reelection by handsome margins.

Census Data 1970 pop. 581,826; deviation from current state average, +21.8%; change 1960–70, +43.5%. Metro. 65.9%, 0.0% central city.

1970 Share of Federal Outlays $598,014,545

DOD	$260,031,000	HEW	$79,396,354
AEC	$000	HUD	$1,668,622
NASA	$257,033	OEO	$331,346
DOT	$30,029,899	DOA	$2,559,323
		Other	$223,740,968

Federal Military-Industrial Commitments

DOD Contractors Western Electric Div., AT&T (Whippany and Morris Plains), $148.950m: Safeguard ABM guidance system research and development; aircraft navigation and radar systems.

DOD Installations Picatinny Arsenal (Dover).

Economic Base Electrical machinery, equipment, and supplies; chemicals and allied products; stone, clay, glass, and concrete products, esp. gaskets, packing, and asbestos insulation.

The Voters

Registration 245,892 total. No party registration.

Employment profile White collar, 50%. Blue collar, 50%.

Ethnic groups Black, 3%. Total foreign stock, 31%. Italy, 6%; Germany, UK, 4% each; Poland, 3%; Ireland, USSR, 2% each; Austria, Czech., Hungary, Norway, Sweden, Canada, 1% each; others, 4%.

Presidential vote

1968	Humphrey (D)	79,978	(36%)
	Nixon (R)	127,971	(57%)
	Wallace (AIP)	16,990	(8%)

Representative

Peter H. B. Frelinghuysen (R) Elected 1952; b. Jan. 17, 1916, New York City; home, Morristown; Princeton, B.A., 1938; Yale Law School, LL.B., 1941; USNR, WWII; married, five children; Episcopalian.

Career Businessman—investments; Dir., American Natl. Bank and Trust Co., Morristown; Bd. of Managers, Howard Savings Institution, Newark.

Offices 2110 RHOB, 202-225-7300. Also 3 Schuyler Place, Morristown 07960, 201-538-7267.

Committees

Foreign Affairs (2nd); Subs. (1) Europe, (2) Inter-American Affairs, (3) International Organizations, (4) Sp. for Review of Foreign Aid.

Group Ratings

	ADA	COPE	NREP	NFU	LCV	CFA	NAB	NSI	ACA
1970	40	34	50	69	38	61	80	55	53
1969	47	—	—	60	—	—	—	—	20
1968	33	31	—	73	—	—	40	—	28

Key Votes

(1) ABM	FOR	(6) 18-Yr-Vote	FOR	(11) Clean Water $	AGN
(2) SST	AGN	(7) Farm Sub Lmt	FOR	(12) Mig Wrkrs Comp	AGN
(3) Phil Pln	FOR	(8) Coop-Church	AGN	(13) Jets to Chiang	AGN
(4) No-Knock	FOR	(9) Family Asst	FOR	(14) State OEO Veto	AGN
(5) Cmutr Tax	AGN	(10) Work Stamps	FOR	(15) Park Logging	AGN

Election Results

1970 general:	Peter H. B. Frelinghuysen (R)	111,553	(68%)
	Ronald C. Eisele (D)	53,436	(32%)
1970 primary:	Peter H. B. Frelinghuysen (R), unopposed		
1968 general:	Peter H. B. Frelinghuysen (R)	143,963	(68%)
	Robert F. Allen (D)	63,208	(30%)
	Robert G. Wright (C)	3,926	(2%)

SIXTH DISTRICT Political Background

New Jersey 6 is a strip of land across the southcentral portion of the state. It stretches from the Philadelphia suburbs of Pennsauken, Collingswood, Willingboro,

Cherry Hills (home of Muhammed Ali), across the central flatland, to the seaside resorts and retirement homes of the Jersey Shore. Most of the territory is politically marginal-to-Republican.

William Cahill, congressman from the 6th since 1958, was elected governor in 1969. In the hard-fought contest to fill the seat in 1970, conservative Republican Edwin B. Forsythe, a 54-year-old state senator, defeated Democrat Charles Yates, a wealthy, 31-year-old owner of a local metals fabricating concern. The Republican won heavy margins in Camden and Ocean counties (to the east and west respectively), while losing Burlington County by 2,000 votes.

Forsythe should be able to take advantage of his incumbency to strengthen his position in the district. No doubt the Republican redistricters will try to help win reelection in 1972. But that may be a difficult task. Parts of Camden and Ocean counties may have to be moved to the 2nd, and even more Republican territory will have to be taken from the 6th if the legislators want to strengthen James Howard in the 3rd. The redistricting plan adopted will determine how hard it will be for Forsythe to win reelection in 1972.

Census Data 1970 pop. 629,444; deviation from current state average, +31.7%; change 1960–70, +51.3%. Metro. 74.4%, 0.0% central city.

1970 Share of Federal Outlays $610,608,335

DOD	$401,892,000	HEW	$112,675,097
AEC	$000	HUD	$646,280
NASA	$118,081	OEO	$372,967
DOT	$40,301,512	DOA	$4,492,767
		Other	$50,109,671

Federal Military-Industrial Commitments

DOD Contractors RCA Corp. (Moorestown), $71.777m: development of an advanced surface missile system; Marine Corps battlefield surveillance radar equipment. Chamberlain Mfg. (Burlington), $11.321m: 81-mm mortar shells. Delaware Valley Armaments (Cherry Hill), $6.495m: rocket booster components.

DOD Installations Fort Dix AB (Wrightstown). Naval Air Station (Lakehurst). McGuire AFB (Wrightstown).

Economic Base Communication equipment and other electrical machinery, equipment, and supplies; primary metal industries; ordnance and accessories; poultry and dairy. Also, tourism (Jersey Shore).

The Voters

Registration 262,227 total. No party registration.

Employment profile White collar, 50%. Blue collar, 50%.

Ethnic groups Black, 5%. Total foreign stock, 23%. Italy, 5%; Germany, 4%; UK, 3%; Ireland, 2%; Austria, Hungary, USSR, Canada, 1% each; others, 3%.

Presidential vote

1968	Humphrey (D)	87,786	(39%)
	Nixon (R)	113,906	(50%)
	Wallace (AIP)	24,283	(11%)

Representative

Edwin B. Forsythe (R) Elected 1970; b. Jan. 17, 1916, Westtown, Pa.; home, Moorestown; married, one child; Society of Friends.

Career Secy., Moorestown Bd. of Adjustment, 1948–52; Mayor of Moorestown, 1957–62; Moorestown Township Com., 1953–62; Chm., Moorestown Planning Bd., 1962–63; N.J. State Senate, 1964–71, Asst. Minority Leader, 1966, Minority Leader, 1967, Pres., 1968; acting Governor, 1968; Senate Pres. Pro Tempore, 1969.

Offices 331 CHOB, 202-225-4765. Also Third and Mill Streets, Moorestown 08057, 609-235-6622.

Committees

Education and Labor (13th); Sel. Sub. on Labor.

Merchant Marine and Fisheries (13th); Subs. (1) International Organizations, (2) National Security Policy and Scientific Developments, (3) Near East, (4) Sp. for Review of Foreign Aid Programs.

Government Operations (3rd); Sub. Chm., Intergovernmental Relations.

Group Ratings, Key Votes: Newly elected.

Election Results

1970 general:	Edwin B. Forsythe (R)	88,051	(55%)
	Charles B. Yates (D)	72,347	(45%)
1970 primary:	Edwin B. Forsythe (R)	18,953	(55%)
	Walter L. Smith, Jr. (R)	15,752	(45%)

SEVENTH DISTRICT Political Background

New Jersey 7 comprises most of Bergen County west of the Hackensack River and north of the Teterboro Airport. The northern part of the district contains some of the wealthiest and most Republican of New Jersey's New York City suburbs. These are sparsely settled, largely because of minimum-acreage zoning. Towards the south—East Paterson and Garfield, across the Pasaic River from Paterson, and to a lesser degree the county seat of Hackensack, are industrial blue-collar towns, all of which vote heavily Democratic.

Moderate-to-liberal Republican William B. Widnall has been the congressman from the 7th since a special election held in 1950. He serves as the senior Republican on both the Joint Economic Committee and the Banking and Currency Committee. The latter unit has jurisdiction over federal housing programs, and Widnall has managed to push through several pieces of housing legislation which have been opposed by more conservative members of his party.

The solid margins to which Widnall had become accustomed were reduced after the 1968 redistricting. Although he opposed the Cambodian invasion of 1970, Widnall has usually supported Nixon on Vietnam; as a result, an antiwar Democratic opponent held the Congressman down to 59% in 1970. The legislature could make the 7th safer for Widnall if it swapped some Democratic towns in the district for some Republican territory in the northern end of the adjoining 9th district. But since such a move would also strengthen the 9th's Democratic congressman, Henry Helstoski, the 7th's lines will likely remain pretty much as they are. Widnall looks like a good bet to win as long as he chooses to run.

Census Data 1970 pop. 465,716; deviation from current state average, —2.5%; change 1960–70, +19.4%. Metro. 100.0%, 0.0% central city.

1970 Share of Federal Outlays $383,046,000 (average outlay per district, New Jersey 7 and 9)

DOD	$201,790,000	HEW	$81,118,000
AEC	$20,000	HUD	$2,357,000
NASA	$4,082,000	OEO	$158,000
DOT	$1,874,000	DOA	$943,000
		Other	$90,710,000

Federal Military-Industrial Commitments (See New Jersey 9 listing.)

Economic Base Electrical machinery, equipment and supplies, esp. radio and television transmitting, signaling, and detection equipment and apparatus; nonelectrical machinery; fabricated metal products, esp. fabricated structural metal products; chemicals and allied products, esp. soaps, detergents, and cleaning preparations, perfumes, cosmetics, and other toilet preparations, and industrial inorganic and organic chemicals. Also, some commuting to New York 17 and 19 (New York City); banking.

The Voters

Registration 226,391 total. No party registration.

Employment profile White collar, 61%. Blue collar, 39%.

Ethnic groups Black, 2%. Total foreign stock, 39%. Italy, 8%; Germany, 6%; Poland, UK, 4% each; Ireland, 3%; Czech., USSR, 2% each; Austria, Hungary, Norway, Sweden, Canada, 1% each; others, 6%.

Presidential vote

1968	Humphrey (D)	79,234	(38%)
	Nixon (R)	118,424	(57%)
	Wallace (AIP)	11,634	(6%)

Representative

William Beck Widnall (R) Elected 1950; b. March 17, 1906, Hackensack; home, Saddle River; Brown U., Ph.B, 1926; N.J. Law School (now Rutgers), LL.B., 1931; married, two children; Episcopalian.

Career Practicing atty., 1932– ; N.J. Legislature, 1946–50.

Offices 2309 RHOB, 202-225-4465. Also 97 Farview Ave., Paramus 07652, 201-265-3550.

Committees

Banking and Currency (Ranking Min. Mbr.); Subs. (1) Domestic Finance, (2) Housing.

Jt. Com. on Defense Production (Ranking Rep. House Mbr.).

Jt. Economic Com. (Ranking Rep. House Mbr.); Subs. (1) Fiscal Policy, (2) Foreign Economic Policy, (3) International Exchange and Payments, (4) Urban Affairs.

Group Ratings

	ADA	COPE	NREP	NFU	LCV	CFA	NAB	NSI	ACA
1970	40	36	64	69	63	92	82	100	47
1969	20	—	—	60	—	—	—	—	31
1968	33	62	—	63	—	—	67	—	41

Key Votes

(1) ABM	FOR	(6) 18-Yr-Vote	FOR	(11) Clean Water $	AGN
(2) SST	AGN	(7) Farm Sub Lmt	FOR	(12) Mig Wrkrs Comp	AGN
(3) Phil Pln	FOR	(8) Coop-Church	FOR	(13) Jets to Chiang	ABS
(4) No-Knock	FOR	(9) Family Asst	FOR	(14) State OEO Veto	AGN
(5) Cmutr Tax	AGN	(10) Work Stamps	FOR	(15) Park Logging	FOR

Election Results

1970 general:	William B. Widnall (R)	90,410	(59%)
	Arthur J. Lesemann (D)	63,928	(41%)
1970 primary:	William B. Widnall (R), unopposed		
1968 general:	William B. Widnall (R)	120,523	(62%)
	Charles S. Gregg (D)	71,123	(37%)
	William Craig Kennedy (C)	2,186	(1%)

EIGHTH DISTRICT Political Background

New Jersey 8 is Passaic County, which can be divided into two sections: upcounty consists mostly of mountains, lakes, and small Republican suburban developments, while downcounty includes the cities of Paterson, Passaic, and Clifton. The Federalist Alexander Hamilton envisioned a major industrial development around Paterson, with the falls of the Passaic River furnishing the waterpower necessary to turn the wheels of 18th century machines. Hamilton's plans fell through, but sometime later this part of New Jersey did indeed became a center of industry. So much so that it led the local poet, William Carlos Williams, using Hamilton's prose for a start, to write a remarkable poem about not-so-poetic Paterson. Today, both Paterson and Passaic are industrial, blue-collar towns—sizable communities of black, Italian, Polish, and other ethnic groups; they are, of course, heavily Democratic. Clifton, which lies half way between them is more middle-class and less Democratic. West of Paterson is Wayne Township, a rapidly-growing upper-middle-class suburb, and the source of the district's Republican strength.

From 1960 to 1969, the congressman from the 8th was Charles S. Joelson, a liberal Democrat whose assiduous cultivation of the district brought him more than 60% of its votes in every election. Joelson retired from the House for the quieter life of a judge in 1969, a year when the Democrats were in trouble. In 1960, Kennedy carried Passaic County by 10,000 votes; four years later, Humphrey lost it by 6,000, the difference being the 16,000 votes that went to Wallace. The conservative tide was also running in state elections. Republican Congressman William Cahill was on the verge of winning the governorship by a record margin in 1969. The Democrats put up Richard Roe, the mayor of Wayne and state Commissioner of Conservation and Economic Development. The Republican candidate was a popular restaurant owner and political amateur, Gene Boyle. Roe had the support of the county Democratic organization, for what that was worth; but since the special election and the contest for state offices were scheduled for the same day, Roe was forced to buck the Republican strength of Cahill *et al.* Roe won the election by 960 votes.

In 1970, after just one year of incumbency, Roe defeated an Italian-American assemblyman with 61% of the votes—a margin as good as Joelson's old ones. Given Roe's 1970 performance, it appears that he could go on winning indefinitely. But the 8th will be redistricted before the 1972 elections. According to the 1970 census, Passaic County has a population very close to that of an average New Jersey district. Yet the Republican legislature may draw some lines which would allow the Republicans in adjacent counties to control the 8th. Just what the redistricters will do cannot be predicted at this writing.

Census Data 1970 pop. 460,782; deviation from current state average, −3.6%; change 1960–70, +13.3%. Metro. 100.0%, 61.3% central city.

1970 Share of Federal Outlays $420,517,282

DOD	$93,727,000	HEW	$106,818,323
AEC	$000	HUD	$2,285,422
NASA	$681,872	OEO	$1,094,003
DOT	$15,398,465	DOA	$681,872
		Other	$199,715,202

Federal Military-Industrial Commitments

DOD Contractors IT&T Corp. (Clifton), $24.037m: Army radio sets. Singer General Precision (Wayne), $9.162m: aircraft radar sets; Safeguard ABM development. REDM Corp. (Wayne), $7.846m: fuzes for 81-mm mortars and general purpose bombs.

Economic Base Electrical machinery, equipment, and supplies; apparel and other finished products made from fabrics and similar materials; esp. women's, misses', and juniors' outerwear; textile mill products, esp. dyeing and finishing textiles other than wool fabrics and knit goods.

The Voters

Registration 189,186 total. No party registration.

Employment profile White collar, 40%. Blue collar, 60%.

Ethnic groups Black, 11%. Puerto Rico, 2%. Total foreign stock, 45%. Italy, 12%; Poland, 6%; Germany, UK, 4% each; USSR, 3%; Austria, Hungary, Ireland, 2% each; Czech., Canada, 1% each; others, 8%.

Presidential vote

1968	Humphrey (D)	74,442	(44%)
	Nixon (R)	79,862	(47%)
	Wallace (AIP)	16,617	(10%)

Representative

Robert A. Roe (D) Elected Nov. 4, 1969; b. Feb. 28, 1924, Wayne; home, Wayne; Oregon State U.; Washington State U.; Army, WWII; unmarried; Catholic.

Career Chm., Bd. of Dir., Morris Canal & Banking Co.; Committeeman, Wayne Township, 1955–56; Mayor of Wayne, 1956–61; Mbr. of Passaic County Bd. of Freeholders, 1959–62, Dir., 1962–63; N.J. Commissioner, Conservation and Econ. Dev., 1963–69.

Offices 1009 LHOB, 202-225-5751. Also U.S. Post Office, 194 Ward St., Paterson 07510, 201-523-5152.

Committees

Public Works (16th); Subs. (1) Flood Control and Internal Development, (2) Investigations and Oversight, (3) Public Buildings and Grounds, (4) Rivers and Harbors, (5) Sp. on Economic Development Programs.

Science and Astronautics (12th); Subs. (1) International Cooperation in Science and Space, (2) Manned Space Flight.

Group Ratings

	ADA	COPE	NREP	NFU	LCV	CFA	NAB	NSI	ACA
1970	80	78	90	75	100	100	0	56	28
1969	75	—	—	71	—	—	—	—	29

Key Votes

(1) ABM	NEL	(6) 18-Yr-Vote	FOR	(11) Clean Water $	NEL
(2) SST	FOR	(7) Farm Sub Lmt	NEL	(12) Mig Wrkrs Comp	FOR
(3) Phil Pln	AGN	(8) Coop-Church	FOR	(13) Jets to Chiang	AGN
(4) No-Knock	FOR	(9) Family Asst	FOR	(14) State OEO Veto	AGN
(5) Cmutr Tax	AGN	(10) Work Stamps	AGN	(15) Park Logging	AGN

Election Results

1970 general:	Robert A. Roe (D)	75,056	(61%)
	Alfred E. Fontanella (R)	48,011	(39%)
1970 primary:	Robert A. Roe (D), unopposed		

NINTH DISTRICT Political Background

New Jersey 9, the eastern and southern half of Bergen County, is made up of high-income suburbs and pollution-ridden industrial towns. North of the George Washington Bridge and west of the Palisades that rise above the Hudson River, lie the wealthy, Republican parts of the 9th: Tenafly, Dumont, Closter, and Old Tappan. Near the Jersey end of the bridge, there are a number of predominantly Jewish suburbs, among them Teaneck (pop. 42,000). Many of the people who live here grew up on the Upper West Side of New York City and retain their liberal voting habits. Along the Palisades are huge apartment towers overlooking New York City; these are occupied by well-to-do and often liberal white-collar people employed in the City. They like a room with a view and also prefer to pay New Jersey rather than New York taxes.

The Jersey Meadows separates the southern portion of the 9th, with about one-fifth of its population, from the rest of the district. For the most part, the Meadows are a fetid swamp lining the Hackensack River, for which developers have great plans, but which today has only gas stations, oil tank farms, trucking terminals, and eight lanes of the New Jersey Turnpike. The 9th's southern towns are found along the Passaic River and are dominated by Italian and Polish working-class Democrats. This is the part of the district that produced the 9th's present congressman, Henry Helstoski.

From 1957 to 1964, Helstoski was the flamboyant mayor of East Rutherford (pop. 8,500). In 1964, Helstoski, for some reason, decided to challenge the 9th's veteran

(1938–42, 1950–64) Republican congressman, Frank C. Osmers, Jr. And in the Johnson landslide, Helstoski won, by 2,428 votes.

Helstoski, a liberal who even as early as 1964 opposed the war, was not expected to win reelection. In 1965, however, the Democratic state legislature redistricted the 9th to include the working-class towns of Garfield, East Paterson, and Hackensack, and in 1966, Helstoski won again, by 2,564 votes. But the 1965 redistricting plan did not meet the approval of the courts; and so, after the 1967 elections, Republican legislators redrew the lines for the benefit of one of their colleagues, Peter Moraites, who challenged Helstoski for the seat in 1968. The 9th lost the East Paterson area and picked up the Republican suburbs north of Teaneck.

Again it was assumed that the Congressman was finished. But again he won, by 2,334 votes. In 1970, after finishing a strong third in the 1969 gubernatorial election, the Congressman finally won a decent margin against a pro-Nixon law-and-order candidate, polling 57%.

The Republican legislature would like to weaken Helstoski for the 1972 elections. But they are limited in their options. All territory south of the current district is heavily Democratic and the addition of Republican terrain to the west can only be done at the expense of Republican William Widnall of the 7th. Since Helstoski has demonstrated an ability to win in spite of adverse redistricting, the legislators might just leave the 9th alone. Many expect the Congressman to seek higher office—the Senate in 1972 if Clifford Case retires, or the governorship in 1973. With Helstoski gone, the Republicans might then be able to recapture the 9th.

Census Data 1970 pop. 432,296; deviation from current state average, −9.5%; change 1960–70, +10.8%. Metro. 100.0%, 0.0% central city.

1970 Share of Federal Outlays $383,046,000 (average outlay per district, New Jersey 7 and 9)

DOD	$201,790,000	HEW	$81,118,000
AEC	$20,000	HUD	$2,357,000
NASA	$4,082,000	OEO	$158,000
DOT	$1,874,000	DOA	$943,000
		Other	$90,710,000

Federal Military-Industrial Commitments (New Jersey 7 and 9 listing)

DOD Contractors Curtis Wright Corp. (Wood Ridge), $67.827m: overhaul and spare parts for various aircraft engines. Bendix Corp. (Teterboro), $62.819m: modification of B-52 aircraft; computers for various aircraft. Seatrain Lines (Edgewater), $27.935m: cargo transport services. Eisen Metal Products (Lodi), $10.115m: 40-mm high explosive projectile components.

Economic Base Electrical machinery, equipment, and supplies, esp. radio and television transmitting, signaling, and detection equipment and apparatus; nonelectrical machinery; fabricated metal products, esp. fabricated structural metal products; chemicals and allied products, esp. soaps, detergents, and cleaning preparations, perfumes, cosmetics, and other toilet preparations and industrial inorganic and organic chemicals. Also, higher education (Earl Dickinson University); some commuting to New York 17 and 19 (New York City).

The Voters

Registration 225,231 total. No party registration.

Employment profile White collar, 49%. Blue collar, 51%.

Ethnic groups Black, 4%. Total foreign stock, 45%. Italy, 13%; Germany, 6%; Poland, UK, 3% each; Austria, Ireland, USSR, 2% each; Czech., Hungary, Canada, 1% each; others, 5%.

Presidential vote

1968	Humphrey (D)	82,948	(41%)
	Nixon (R)	106,487	(53%)
	Wallace (AIP)	12,029	(6%)

Representative

Henry Helstoski (D) Elected 1964; b. March 21, 1925, Wallington; home, East Rutherford; Paterson State Col., B.A., 1947; Montclair State Col., M.A., 1949; Army Air Corps, WWII; married, two children; Catholic.

Career Teacher; high school principal; Superintendent of Schools, 1949–62; Councilman, E. Rutherford, 1956, Mayor, 1957–64; Chm., Jt. Sewer Authority, 1957–64.

Offices 326 CHOB, 202-225-5061. Also 666 Paterson Ave., East Rutherford 07073, 201-939-9090.

Committees

Interstate and Foreign Commerce (20th); Sp. Sub. on Investigations.

Veterans' Affairs (8th); Subs. (1) Chm., Education and Training, (2) Housing.

Group Ratings

	ADA	COPE	NREP	NFU	LCV	CFA	NAB	NSI	ACA
1970	96	100	100	92	100	100	0	0	6
1969	93	—	—	77	—	—	—	—	12
1968	100	100	—	93	—	—	—	—	5

Key Votes

(1) ABM	AGN	(6) 18-Yr-Vote	FOR	(11) Clean Water $	FOR
(2) SST	AGN	(7) Farm Sub Lmt	FOR	(12) Mig Wrkrs Comp	FOR
(3) Phil Pln	FOR	(8) Coop-Church	FOR	(13) Jets to Chiang	AGN
(4) No-Knock	ABS	(9) Family Asst	FOR	(14) State OEO Veto	AGN
(5) Cmutr Tax	FOR	(10) Work Stamps	AGN	(15) Park Logging	AGN

Election Results

1970 general:	Henry Helstoski (D)	91,589	(57%)
	Henry L. Hoebel (R)	68,974	(43%)
1970 primary:	Henry Helstoski (D), unopposed		
1968 general:	Henry Helstoski (D)	97,599	(50%)
	Peter Moraites (R)	95,267	(49%)
	Hannibal Cundari (C)	1,582	(1%)
	Henry Koch (Ind.)	1,067	(1%)

TENTH DISTRICT Political Background

New Jersey 10 comprises most of Newark and a few suburban cities to the north, among them Belleville, Bloomfield, and Montclair. Newark's North Ward is the home of Anthony Imperiale, the militant anti-integrationist member of the City Council who ran a strong 3rd in the 1970 race for mayor of Newark. Imperiale's support comes from the city's large Italian-American community which is not economically much better off than Newark's black majority and which resents the attention given to the black ghetto.

Sociologists have noted that the Italians are usually the last ethnic group to leave the central city. They have a great attachment to close-knit neighborhoods where everyone knows everybody else, where nobody steals from anybody else, and where Italian is spoken on the streets and in the shops. The Italians of Newark fear what they regard as black crime and resist the movement of blacks into their neighborhoods. Since the Newark riot of 1967, the North Ward has been heavily armed, and Imperiale and others have organized neighborhood groups to patrol the streets.

However conservative the North Ward may be in city politics, its allegiance to the Democratic party in congressional elections has remained strong. The reason, perhaps, is that Congressman Peter W. Rodino, Jr., is himself of Italian descent and still lives in the North Ward. First elected in 1948, Rodino has consistently won by stunning margins ever since; in 1968, for example, a good Republican year in New Jersey, Rodino took 64% of the votes. In the House, Rodino is the 2nd-ranking Democrat on the Judiciary Committee; he will probably become chairman in a few years, since the current chairman, Emanuel Celler of New York, will be 86 in 1972 and by then will have served 50 years in the House. Rodino votes with liberals on civil rights legislation and with conservatives on anticrime measures such as the District of Columbia crime bill of 1970. Like many big city Democrats, the Congressman supported Nixon Vietnam policy until the Cambodian invasion then changed his mind.

Rodino is probably more liberal than most of his constituents. Recognizing this, the Republicans in 1970 made use of a New York advertising agency, a public relations firm, and ads in *Time* magazine in a vigorous and expensive campaign based on the Agnew-hard-hat appeal. But their candidate, Griffith Jones, a Harvard-educated lawyer from the wealthy suburb of Montclair, did not do very well in the Italian precincts along the Passaic. After less than an energetic campaign, Rodino took 70% of the district's votes.

The only threat to Rodino's tenure is redistricting by the Republican legislature. As a partisan group, the Republicans should make the entire city of Newark the nucleus of one district, which would probably elect a black congressman. The Essex County suburbs might then elect a Republican. If such a plan went through, both Rodino and the 11th district Democrat, Joseph Minish, would lose their seats. But both Rodino and Minish are of Italian descent, and New Jersey Republicans know full well that the state's Italian voters are responsible for the party's recent statewide gains. At this writing, the legislature is deadlocked, with no redistricting action due before 1972. Chances are that the increasingly militant Italian-American community, combined with the political clout of Rodino and Minish, will prevail and that both congressmen will keep a reasonably safe seat.

Census Data 1970 pop. 439,300; deviation from current state average, −8.1%; change 1960–70, +2.8%. Metro. 100.0%, 57.5% central city.

1970 Share of Federal Outlays $431,635,000 (average outlay per district, New Jersey 10–14)

DOD	$53,914,000	HEW	$107,982,000
AEC	$272,000	HUD	$5,151,000
NASA	$263,000	OEO	$1,199,000
DOT	$8,638,000	DOA	$23,859,000
		Other	$230,357,000

Federal Military-Industrial Commitments (See New Jersey 13 for listing.)

Economic Base Apparel and other finished products made from fabrics and similar materials, esp. women's, misses', and juniors' outerwear; electrical machinery, equipment, and supplies, esp. electric lamps, and electric transmission and distribution equipment; chemicals and allied products, esp. drugs; food and kindred products, esp. malt liquors. Also, banking and insurance.

The Voters

Registration 172,152 total. No party registration.

Employment profile White collar, 42%. Blue collar, 58%.

Ethnic groups Black, 31%. Puerto Rico, 2%. Total foreign stock, 39%. Italy, 13%; Poland, 4%; Germany, UK, USSR, 3% each; Austria, Ireland, 2% each; Czech., Hungary, Canada, 1% each; others, 5%.

Presidential vote

1968	Humphrey (D)	78,790	(52%)
	Nixon (R)	59,822	(39%)
	Wallace (AIP)	13,527	(9%)

Representative

Peter Wallace Rodino, Jr. (D) Elected 1948; b. June 7, 1909, Newark; home, Newark; N.J. Law School (now Rutgers), LL.B., 1937; Army, WWII; married, two children; Catholic.

Career Practicing atty., 1938; Senior Mbr., N.J. Congressional Delegation, 1971; Asst. Majority Whip.

Offices 2266 RHOB, 202-225-3436. Also Fed. Bldg., 970 Broad St., Newark 07102, 201-645-3213.

Committees

Judiciary (2nd); Chm., Sub. No. 1.

Group Ratings

	ADA	COPE	NREP	NFU	LCV	CFA	NAB	NSI	ACA
1970	84	100	82	100	89	84	0	60	16
1969	80	—	—	86	—	—	—	—	12
1968	75	100	—	94	—	—	—	—	9

Key Votes

(1) ABM	AGN	(6) 18-Yr-Vote	FOR	(11) Clean Water $	FOR
(2) SST	AGN	(7) Farm Sub Lmt	FOR	(12) Mig Wrkrs Comp	FOR
(3) Phil Pln	FOR	(8) Coop-Church	FOR	(13) Jets to Chiang	AGN
(4) No-Knock	FOR	(9) Family Asst	FOR	(14) State OEO Veto	AGN
(5) Cmutr Tax	AGN	(10) Work Stamps	AGN	(15) Park Logging	AGN

Election Results

1970 general:	Peter W. Rodino, Jr. (D)	71,003	(70%)
	Griffith H. Jones (R)	30,460	(30%)
1970 primary:	Peter W. Rodino, Jr. (D), unopposed		
1968 general:	Peter W. Rodino, Jr. (D)	89,109	(64%)
	Celestino Clemente (R)	47,989	(34%)
	Harry Press (SL)	1,440	(1%)
	William D. Tyus (Ind.)	735	(1%)

ELEVENTH DISTRICT Political Background

New Jersey 11 comprises the West and part of the Central Ward of Newark, and the suburbs of East, South, and West Orange, Orange, Maplewood, and Irvington. The Central Ward is the heart of Newark's black ghetto; the scene of most of the violence during the 1967 riot. The West Ward, where Philip Roth and Alexander Portnoy grew up, also has a substantial black population, which is growing as the whites continue to flee to the suburbs. East Orange and Orange are middle to lower-middle-class bedroom communities, again with growing black populations. South Orange, West Orange, and Maplewood are high-income suburbs with many prosperous Italian and Jewish residents. The Republican vote coming out of these three wealthy towns is swamped by the heavily Democratic majorities cast by the poorer and more populous areas of the 11th.

Hugh Addonizio was the district's congressman until 1962 when he resigned to become mayor of Newark. He has since been convicted on federal bribery charges and was then defeated in a bid for reelection by Newark's first black mayor, Kenneth Gibson. Addonizio was succeeded in the House by Joseph G. Minish, who was active in the labor movement prior to his election. In the years following Minish's first election, the blacks displaced the Italians as the major voting-bloc in the district. Recognizing this, the Republicans fielded a liberal candidate in 1970, who tried to appeal to both the blacks and the liberal suburbanites in the district. The Republican may have had some success in the suburbs, but Minish walked away with 68% of the votes.

According to the 1970 census, the 12th has the second smallest population of the state's 15 congressional districts. Unless the legislature drastically alters the districts in the Newark area (see New Jersey 10), parts of Republican Essex County will have to be added to the 12th. The addition would not change the partisan balance of the district. But Minish, who is of Italian descent, might have some trouble if a strong black candidate were to enter the Democratic primary. So far, Newark blacks have focused their efforts on winning City Hall, which has much more direct influence on their lives. But a black candidate will probably challenge Minish some time during the '70's, if the current urban and suburban migrations continue.

Census Data 1970 pop. 383,429; deviation from current state average, −19.8%; change 1960–70, −7.1%. Metro. 100.0%, 33.9% central city.

1970 Share of Federal Outlays $431,635,000 (average outlay per district, New Jersey 10–14)

DOD	$53,914,000	HEW	$107,982,000
AEC	$272,000	HUD	$5,151,000
NASA	$263,000	OEO	$1,199,000
DOT	$8,638,000	DOA	$23,859,000
		Other	$230,357,000

Federal Military-Industrial Commitments (See New Jersey 13 for listing.)

Economic Base Apparel and other products made from fabrics and similar materials, esp. women's, misses', and juniors' outerwear; electrical machinery, equipment, and supplies, esp. electric lamps and electric transmission and distribution equipment; chemicals and allied products, esp. drugs; food and kindred products, esp. malt liquors.

The Voters

Registration 163,057 total. No party registration.

Employment profile White collar, 44%. Blue collar, 56%.

Ethnic groups Black, 37%. Puerto Rico, 1%. Total foreign stock, 35%; Italy, 10%; Germany, 5%; USSR, 4%; Ireland, Poland, UK, 3% each; Austria, 2%; Czech., Hungary, Canada, 1% each; others, 4%.

Presidential vote

1968	Humphrey (D)	86,733	(58%)
	Nixon (R)	51,420	(35%)
	Wallace (AIP)	10,989	(7%)

Representative

Joseph George Minish (D) Elected 1962; b. Sept. 1, 1916, Throop, Pa.; home, West Orange; Army, WWII; married, three children; Catholic.

Career Pres., local 445 I.U.E. AFL-CIO, 1949–53; Political Action Dir., Dist. 4, 1953–54; Exec. Secy., Essex W. Hudson Labor Council, 1954–61, Exec. Secy. and Treas., 1961–62.

Offices 438 CHOB, 202-225-5035. Also 308 Main St., Orange 07050, 201-676-0827.

Committees

Banking and Currency (10th); Subs. (1) Consumer Affairs, (2) Domestic Finance, (3) Housing.

Group Ratings

	ADA	COPE	NREP	NFU	LCV	CFA	NAB	NSI	ACA
1970	84	100	83	92	100	84	0	60	21
1969	80	—	—	86	—	—	—	—	12
1968	75	100	—	—	93	—	0	—	9

Key Votes

(1) ABM	AGN	(6) 18-Yr-Vote	FOR	(11) Clean Water $	FOR
(2) SST	AGN	(7) Farm Sub Lmt	FOR	(12) Mig Wrkrs Comp	FOR
(3) Phil Pln	FOR	(8) Coop-Church	FOR	(13) Jets to Chiang	AGN
(4) No-Knock	FOR	(9) Family Asst	FOR	(14) State OEO Veto	AGN
(5) Cmutr Tax	AGN	(10) Work Stamps	AGN	(15) Park Logging	AGN

Election Results

1970 general:	Joseph G. Minish (D)	68,075	(68%)
	James W. Shue (R)	31,369	(32%)
1970 primary:	Joseph G. Minish (D), unopposed		
1968 general:	Joseph G. Minish (D)	91,496	(66%)
	George M. Wallhauser, Jr. (R)	46,426	(33%)
	William D. Murray (C)	1,329	(1%)

TWELFTH DISTRICT Political Background

New Jersey 12 comprises parts of Essex County, which contains Newark, and Union County, which contains Elizabeth; but the district takes in no part of either central city. The 12th is a classic suburban district, and like most of these districts, its towns and people are diverse. There are a few stereotype, affluent WASP suburbs like Millburn, Short Hills, and Summit, but more typical of the 12th are Livingston, Caldwell, Cranford, and Union, which are dominated by the newly prosperous sons and daughters of Italian, Polish, and German immigrants. Plainfield, which contains most of the district's blacks, as well as Roselle and Roselle Park, are blue-collar suburbs. The district is bisected by perhaps the most garish strip of highway in the East, U.S. 22; the frenetic neon signs that line the roadway suggest some of the energy latent in the leafy-green, placid suburbs through which it runs.

The 12th has been electing Republican Florence P. Dwyer to Congress with huge pluralities since 1956. The Democratic congressman she ousted that year was Harrison Williams, who went on to become a U.S. senator from the state. In the last decade, no Democrat has polled more than 40% against Mrs. Dwyer. Her popularity is due to an extensive use of ranking privileges and a liberal record; the Republican usually votes with the Northern Democrats. Vigorous campaigns waged by 12th district Democratic peace candidates in 1966, 1968, and 1970 have only reduced her share of the vote from 74% to 66%.

The Republican legislature might seriously change the character of the 12th, adding Elizabeth and Bayonne, and removing some western and northern suburbs. Though this would make the district more Democratic, it would also force Democrat Cornelius Gallagher of the 13th—who, according to *Life* magazine, is an agent of organized crime—into a fight with Mrs. Dwyer. The Congresswoman carried blue-collar Elizabeth when it was part of the 12th; and she has demonstrated a capacity to beat Democrats over the years. Chances are, Gallagher will lose to Mrs. Dwyer. But such a district would go Democratic if she were not the Republican candidate.

Census Data 1970 pop. 467,196; deviation from current state average, –2.2%; change 1960–70, +13.3%. Metro. 100.0%, 0.0% central city.

1970 Share of Federal Outlays $431,635,000 (average outlay per district, New Jersey 10–14)

DOD	$53,914,000	HEW	$107,982,000
AEC	$272,000	HUD	$5,151,000
NASA	$263,000	OEO	$1,199,000
DOT	$8,638,000	DOA	$23,859,000
		Other	$230,357,000

Federal Military-Industrial Commitments (See New Jersey 13 for listing.)

Economic Base Chemicals and allied products, esp. drugs; nonelectrical machinery, esp. general industrial machinery and equipment; electrical machinery, equipment, and supplies, esp. communication equipment; fabricated metal products. Also, extensive commuting to New York 17 and 19 (New York City) and New Jersey 10 (Newark).

The Voters

Registration 325,328 total. No party registration.
Employment profile White collar, 57%. Blue collar, 43%.
Ethnic groups Black, 8%. Total foreign stock, 36%. Italy, 7%; Germany, 5%; Poland, UK, 4% each; USSR, 3%; Austria, Ireland, 2% each; Czech., Hungary, Sweden, Canada, 1% each; others, 4%.

Presidential vote

1968	Humphrey (D)	90,462	(41%)
	Nixon (R)	114,175	(52%)
	Wallace (AIP)	14,040	(6%)

Representative

Florence P. Dwyer (R) Elected 1956; b. July 4, 1902, Reading, Pa.; home, Elizabeth; widowed, one child; Protestant.

Career N.J. Legislature, 1950–56.

Offices 2421 RHOB, 202-225-5361. Also Rm. 202, 40 Somerset St., Plainfield 07060, 201-754-6686.

Committees

Banking and Currency (2nd); Subs. (1) Consumer Affairs, (2) Housing.

Government Operations (Ranking Mbr.); Sub. on Intergovernmental Relations.

Group Ratings

	ADA	COPE	NREP	NFU	LCV	CFA	NAB	NSI	ACA
1970	52	75	58	83	78	79	58	78	53
1969	40	—	—	64	—	—	—	—	33
1968	50	67	—	67	—	—	40	—	43

Key Votes

(1) ABM	FOR	(6) 18-Yr-Vote	FOR	(11) Clean Water $	FOR
(2) SST	AGN	(7) Farm Sub Lmt	FOR	(12) Mig Wrkrs Comp	FOR
(3) Phil Pln	ABS	(8) Coop-Church	FOR	(13) Jets to Chiang	AGN
(4) No-Knock	ABS	(9) Family Asst	FOR	(14) State OEO Veto	AGN
(5) Cmutr Tax	AGN	(10) Work Stamps	AGN	(15) Park Logging	AGN

Election Results

1970 general:	Florence P. Dwyer (R)	109,537	(66%)
	Daniel F. Lundy (D)	55,930	(34%)
1970 primary:	Florence P. Dwyer (R), unopposed		
1968 general:	Florence P. Dwyer (R)	146,264	(72%)
	John B. Duff (D)	58,112	(28%)

THIRTEENTH DISTRICT Political Background

New Jersey 13 comprises Rahway, Linden, and Elizabeth in Union County; Bayonne, and the southern half of Jersey City in Hudson County. The Union County portion of the district was added in the 1966 redistricting; previously, it backed Republican Florence Dwyer of the 12th, but it is usually Democratic. Elizabeth is a typical central city with a substantial number of blacks and large, white, working-class neighborhoods. Linden is a newer, predominantly blue-collar suburb; Rahway, the home of Sen. Clifford Case, is more middle-class.

Hudson County, just across the river from Manhattan, has the highest population densities in the country. Italian, Polish, Irish, and Jewish immigrants, their children and grandchildren, live side by side in two and four family houses. There are significant black and Puerto Rican populations in Jersey City, but for the most part these new immigrants avoid the tightly-knit white ethnic neighborhoods of Hudson County and settle instead in Newark and New York City.

Urban political machines thrive in places like Hudson County, and over the years it has had one of the most famous machines. During the '30's, Jersey City mayor and boss, Frank Hague, proclaimed "I am the law," and in Hudson County, he was: CIO organizers who set foot in his county were thrown out bodily by the Jersey City police. It took a U.S. Supreme Court decision to force Hague to relent on the issue. Under Hague and his successors, patronage appointees supplied the kind of services New Deal bureaucracies are supposed to provide, and on election day the appointees supplied the votes. Lately, leaders of the Hudson County Democratic organization have been feuding; and what is more, the mayor and City Council president of Jersey City have been convicted on bribery charges. The machine is no longer what it once was. But in 1969, it was still able to deliver the Democratic county to the Republican candidate for governor, William Cahill, when the New Jersey Democrats nominated a man whom the Hudson bosses mistrusted.

Cornelius Gallagher was for some time one of the finest products of the Hudson County organization. A war hero, attorney, and congressman since 1958, Gallagher won reelection here by substantial, often 3–1, majorities. In Washington, he had a solidly liberal voting record and was chairman of a special subcommittee on privacy. Then in 1968, *Life* magazine charged that Gallagher had ties with organized crime in Hudson County. The Congressman vehemently denied the charge, went to the people of the 13th for vindication, and got it. He was reelected by 30,000 votes; his margin in 1970 was even larger.

Hudson County's declining population will allow the Republican legislature to eliminate the 13th as it now exists. To stay in the House, Gallagher will either have to defeat Dominick V. Daniels of the 14th in the Democratic primary, or the hitherto unbeatable Republican Florence Dwyer of the 12th. Since Daniels is almost twenty years older than Gallagher, he might retire and leave the 14th for Gallagher. Just what will happen depends on the redistricting plan adopted by the legislature.

Census Data 1970 pop. 392,821; deviation from current state average, −17.8%; change 1960–70, +1.0%. Metro. 100.0%, 34.9% central city.

1970 Share of Federal Outlays 431,635,000 (average outlay per district, New Jersey 10–14)

DOD	$53,914,000	HEW	$107,982,000
AEC	$272,000	HUD	$5,151,000
NASA	$263,000	OEO	$1,199,000
DOT	$8,628,000	DOA	$23,859,000
		Other	$230,357,000

Federal Military-Industrial Commitments (New Jersey 10–14 listing)

DOD Contractors Sea Land Div., R. J. Reynolds Industries (Elizabeth), $86.388m: cargo transport services. Singer General Precision (Little Falls), $35.410m: Poseidon missile guidance system components; aircraft radar systems. IT&T Corp. (Nutley), $15.870m: support for SAC automatic command control system; electronic warfare equipment. Lockheed Aircraft (Plainfield), $15.663m: computer oriented gunfire control systems. International Terminal Co. (Bayonne), $6.328m: stevedoring services. Krafteo Corp. (Hillside), $5.130m: unspecified.

Economic Base Apparel and other products made from fabrics and similar materials, esp. women's, misses', and juniors' outerwear; electrical machinery, equipment, and supplies; food and kindred products, esp. meat products; chemicals and allied products, esp. soaps, detergents, and cleaning preparations, perfumes, cosmetics, and other toilet preparations. Also, banking.

The Voters

Registration 172,995 total. No party registration.

Employment profile White collar, 41%. Blue collar, 59%.

Ethnic groups Black, 20%. Puerto Rico, 1%. Total foreign stock, 42%. Italy, 9%; Poland, 8%; Ireland, 5%; USSR, 4%; Germany, UK, 3% each; Austria, Czech., 2% each; Hungary, Canada, 1% each; others, 5%.

Presidential vote

1968	Humphrey (D)	89,058	(56%)
	Nixon (R)	53,426	(34%)
	Wallace (AIP)	16,243	(10%)

Representative

Cornelius E. Gallagher (D) Elected 1958; b. March 2, 1921, Bayonne; home, Bayonne; John Marshall Col., 1941, LL.B., 1947; N.Y.U., 1950; Army, WWII and Korean War; married, four children; Catholic.

Career Practicing atty., 1948; Hudson County Bd. of Freeholders, 1953; Commissioner, N.J. Turnpike Authority, 1955, Vice Chm., 1956–58; Dir. and Counsel, Broadway Natl. Bank.

Offices 235 CHOB, 202-225-5801. Also Suite 302, 520 Westfield Ave., Elizabeth 07204, 201-437-3611, and Post Office, Bayonne 07002, 201-339-3802.

Committees

Foreign Affairs (7th); Subs. (1) Chm., Asian and Pacific Affairs, (2) Europe, (3) International Organizations and Movements.

Government Operations (12th); Subs. (1) Legal and Monetary Affairs, (2) Special Studies.

Group Ratings

	ADA	COPE	NREP	NFU	LCV	CFA	NAB	NSI	ACA
1970	80	100	91	100	100	100	0	56	7
1969	67	—	—	83	—	—	—	—	15
1968	92	100	—	90	—	—	0	—	5

Key Votes

(1) ABM	ABS	(6) 18-Yr-Vote	FOR	(11) Clean Water $	FOR
(2) SST	AGN	(7) Farm Sub Lmt	FOR	(12) Mig Wrkrs Comp	FOR
(3) Phil Pln	FOR	(8) Coop-Church	FOR	(13) Jets to Chiang	FOR
(4) No-Knock	AGN	(9) Family Asst	FOR	(14) State OEO Veto	AGN
(5) Cmutr Tax	AGN	(10) Work Stamps	AGN	(15) Park Logging	AGN

Election Results

1970 general:	Cornelius E. Gallagher (D)	77,789	(71%)
	Raul E. L. Comesanas (R)	27,929	(26%)
	Everett C. Miller (Tax Reform)	3,675	(3%)
1970 primary:	Cornelius E. Gallagher (D)	28,736	(76%)
	David Wolf (D)	5,043	(13%)
	James I. Eagen (D)	4,182	(11%)
1968 general:	Cornelius E. Gallagher (D)	83,151	(56%)
	Marion D. Dwyer (R)	52,159	(35%)
	Jeremiah O'Callaghan (Voice of Independence)	9,399	(6%)
	Allen Zavadnick (No Additional Taxes)	5,012	(3%)

FOURTEENTH DISTRICT Political Background

New Jersey 14 comprises the northern two-thirds of Hudson County, including Hoboken (Frank Sinatra's home town), Union City, Weehawken (where Aaron Burr shot Alexander Hamilton), West New York, Secaucus, and half of Jersey City. Most of the people of the 14th live on a ridge which slopes down to the New York Harbor, and the view accentuates the urban problems, such as decaying housing, polluted air and water, which the district shares with much of the urban northeast. Inland are the marshy Jersey Meadows along the Hackensack River. The politics of Hudson County and its clannish white ethnic communities constitute a unique world (see New Jersey 13).

The 14th is most Italian of the state's districts; some 16% of its residents are first or second generation Italians and many more are of more distant Italian descent. These voters, who tend to remain in central cities long after other ethnic groups have fled to the suburbs, have begun to abandon a traditional allegiance to the Democratic party. They have grown disenchanted with the social policies of the national party, particularly its commitment to civil rights legislation. In 1968, Humphrey polled only 49% in the 14th, far below most Democrats in the past.

But if the district is any index of the success of the Nixon-Agnew attempt to exploit ethnic resentments, the 1970 elections here indicate that the great days of the so-called "social issue" are over. Senator Harrison Williams, against a fervent advocate of the Nixon Administration, carried the 14th better than 2–1. And Democratic Congressman Dominick Daniels, who is of Italian descent like so many of his constituents, improved on his 1968 showing. He then received 59% of the vote, with 7% going to third party candidates, but in 1970 took 71%.

Daniels was a judge before he was first elected to the House in 1958. He is the 6th ranking Democrat on the important Education and Labor Committee, and 4th ranking Democrat on Post Office and Civil Service. But because he was 62 in 1970, Daniels is unlikely to become a committee chairman. If redistricting were to put most of Hudson County into a single district, it is possible that he would retire or seek another judgeship and allow the 13th's Cornelius Gallagher to take his seat.

Census Data 1970 pop. 399,622; deviation from current state average, −16.4%; change 1960–70, +0.7%. Metro. 100.0%, 30.9% central city.

1970 Share of Federal Oulays $431,635,000 (average oulay per disrict, New Jersey 10–14)

DOD	$53,914,000	HEW	$107,982,000
AEC	$272,000	HUD	$5,151,000
NASA	$263,000	OEO	$1,199,000
DOT	$8,638,000	DOA	$23,859,000
		Other	$230,357,000

Federal Military-Industrial Commitments (See New Jersey 13 for listing.)

Economic Base Apparel and other finished products made from fabrics and similar materials, esp. women's, misses', and juniors' outerwear; electrical machinery, equipment, and supplies; food and kindred products, esp. meat products; chemicals and allied products, esp. soaps, detergents, and cleaning preparations, perfumes, cosmetics, and other toilet preparations.

The Voters

Registration 169,935 total. No party registration.

Employment profile White collar, 38%. Blue collar, 62%.

Ethnic groups Black, 3%. Puerto Rico, 3%. Total foreign stock, 47%. Italy, 16%; Germany, 6%; Poland, 5%; Ireland, UK, 4% each; Austria, USSR, 2% each; Czech., Canada, 1% each; others, 7%.

Presidential vote

1968	Humphrey (D)	74,700	(49%)
	Nixon (R)	62,537	(41%)
	Wallace (AIP)	15,103	(10%)

Representative

Dominick V. Daniels (D) Elected 1958; b. Oct. 18, 1908, Jersey City; home, Jersey City; Fordham U., 1925–26; Rutgers U. Law School, LL.B., 1929; married, two children; Catholic.

Career Practicing atty., 1930– ; Magistrate, Jersey City Municipal Ct., 1952–58.

Offices 2370 RHOB, 202-225-2765. Also Main Post Office, Union City 07087, 201-863-0015, and Kearney Post Office, Kearney 07032, 201-991-5100.

Committees

Education and Labor (6th); Subs. (1) Chm., Sel. on Labor, (2) Sp. on Education.

Post Office and Civil Service (4th); Subs. (1) Investigations, (2) Retirement, Insurance, and Health Benefits.

Group Ratings

	ADA	COPE	NREP	NFU	LCV	CFA	NAB	NSI	ACA
1970	72	100	75	100	86	95	0	78	20
1969	67	—	—	93	—	—	—	—	20
1968	83	100	—	94	—	—	0	—	4

Key Votes

(1) ABM	AGN	(6) 18-Yr-Vote	FOR	(11) Clean Water $	FOR
(2) SST	FOR	(7) Farm Sub Lmt	FOR	(12) Mig Wrkrs Comp	FOR
(3) Phil Pln	AGN	(8) Coop-Church	FOR	(13) Jets to Chiang	ABS
(4) No-Knock	FOR	(9) Family Asst	FOR	(14) State OEO Veto	AGN
(5) Cmutr Tax	AGN	(10) Work Stamps	AGN	(15) Park Logging	AGN

Election Results

1970 general:	Dominick V. Daniels (D)	77,771	(71%)
	Carlo N. DeGennaro (R)	31,161	(29%)
1970 primary:	Dominick V. Daniels (D)	34,488	(87%)
	John J. Hallanan, Jr. (D)	5,190	(13%)
1968 general:	Dominick V. Daniels (D)	87,187	(59%)
	Joseph Bartletta (R)	50,829	(34%)
	Mervin Murray (C)	7,634	(5%)
	Vincent L. Vendiramo (No Additional Taxes)	3,481	(2%)

FIFTEENTH DISTRICT Political Background

New Jersey 15 takes in almost all of Middlesex County, the state's fastest-growing Democratic area. The 15th has the largest concentration of Hungarians of any district in the nation, centered around New Brunswick; there are large numbers of Poles living in Woodbridge and Italians in Perth Amboy. From these substantial ethnic communities in the older cities, the population has spread into places like Edison Township (site of Thomas Edison's Menlo Park Laboratory), Piscataway Township, East and North Brunswick Townships and Sayreville. These towns, classic blue-collar suburbs, all had populations over 30,000 by 1970. Here the New Jersey countryside has been developed with subdivisions à la Levittown, and the sons and daughters of the immigrants have gone to live in settings which are pastoral when compared to the central cities of New Brunswick or Perth Amboy. The new suburban voters have not forgotten their Democratic heritage, though they are upset about high taxes, rebellious students, and black militants. The plurality that they gave Humphrey in 1968 was much smaller than Kennedy's in 1960.

The 15th's 1970 Democratic primary received national attention. The results of the primary were trumpeted by many pundits as an I-told-you-so failure of the peace-oriented student political movement. It was not that at all, but rather a testament to the district's specific kind of political culture and the Democratic organization that dominates that culture, one of New Jersey's most powerful county machines.

In the primary, peace candidate Lewis Kaden challenged the 15th's veteran incumbent, Congressman Edward J. Patten. Kaden, a 28-year-old native of Perth Amboy, was a staffer for both Robert Kennedy and New York labor mediator Theodore Keel. The Cambodian invasion seemed to come at a propitious time, and in the last month before the June 2nd primary, hundreds of students from Princeton and other colleges canvassed 100,000 of the district's voters on Kaden's behalf. Patten, a garrulous extrovert, has spent innumerable hours listening to the complaints and needs of his constituents; he mingles easily with ethnic working-class voters, who swing the political weight in the 15th. And though the Democratic organization appeared dormant, the machine got out the blue-collar vote and buried Kaden 24,000 to 12,000. That same year peace candidates won in Denver, Baltimore, and Boston.

In the general election that followed, Republican Peter P. Garibaldi, a bricklayer, ran a hard-hat campaign against Patten. He was no more successful among the blue-collar voters than Kaden. As Garibaldi said later, "Running against Ed Patten is like running against Santa Claus." Unless redistricting seriously alters the district, Ed Patten will go on winning, come peace candidate or hard-hat.

Census Data 1970 pop. 535,098; deviation from current state average, +12.0%; change 1960–70, +30.2%. Metro. 0.0%, 0.0% central city.

1970 Share of Federal Outlays $386,784,325

DOD	$34,109,000	HEW	$93,586,924
AEC	$2,138,374	HUD	$526,177
NASA	$284,624	OEO	$760,094
DOT	$14,706,608	DOA	$2,682,737
		Other	$237,989,787

Federal Military-Industrial Commitments

DOD Contractors Amerada Hess Corp. (Woodbridge), $7.089m: petroleum products.

Economic Base Primary metal industries, esp. primary smelting and refining of nonferrous metals; electrical machinery, equipment, and supplies, esp. electronic components and accessories; nonelectrical machinery, esp. special industrial machinery other than metalworking machinery; apparel and other finished products made from fabrics and similar materials, esp. women's, misses', and juniors' outerwear. Also, higher education (Rutgers University).

The Voters

Registration 232,572 total. No party registration.

Employment profile White collar, 42%. Blue collar, 58%.

Ethnic groups Black, 5%. Puerto Rico, 1%. Total foreign stock, 38%. Hungary, Italy, Poland, 6% each; Germany, USSR, 3% each; Austria, Czech., UK, 2% each; Ireland, Canada, 1% each; others, 4%.

Presidential vote

1968	Humphrey (D)	96,598	(46%)
	Nixon (R)	88,943	(43%)
	Wallace (AIP)	22,436	(11%)

Representative

Edward James Patten (D) Elected 1962; b. Aug. 22, 1905, Perth Amboy; home, Perth Amboy; Newark State Col.; Rutgers Law School, LL.B., 1926; Rutgers U., B.S.Ed., 1928; married, one child; Catholic.

Career Practicing atty., 1927– ; teacher, 1927–34; Mayor, Perth Amboy, 1934–40; Middlesex County Clerk, 1940–54; Campaign Mgr. for Gov. Robert B. Meyner, 1953, 1957; N.J. Secy. of State, 1954-62; Pres., Salvation Army Bd.

Offices 2332 RHOB, 202-225-6301. Also Natl. Bank Bldg., Perth Amboy 08861, 201-826-4610.

Committees

Appropriations (21st); Subs. (1) Labor and HEW, (2) Military Construction.

Group Ratings

	ADA	COPE	NREP	NFU	LCV	CFA	NAB	NSI	ACA
1970	80	100	73	92	67	89	10	70	16
1969	73	—	—	93	—	—	—	—	6
1968	83	100	—	100	—	—	0	—	9

Key Votes

(1) ABM	FOR	(6) 18-Yr-Vote	FOR	(11) Clean Water $	AGN
(2) SST	AGN	(7) Farm Sub Lmt	AGN	(12) Mig Wrkrs Comp	FOR
(3) Phil Pln	FOR	(8) Coop-Church	FOR	(13) Jets to Chiang	FOR
(4) No-Knock	FOR	(9) Family Asst	FOR	(14) State OEO Veto	AGN
(5) Cmutr Tax	AGN	(10) Work Stamps	AGN	(15) Park Logging	AGN

Election Results

1970 general:	Edward J. Patten (D)	94,772	(61%)
	Peter P. Garibaldi (R)	60,450	(39%)
1970 primary:	Edward J. Patten (D)	24,690	(66%)
	Lewis B. Kaden (D)	12,667	(34%)
1968 general:	Edward J. Patten (D)	107,316	(55%)
	George W. Luke (R)	88,043	(45%)
	Joseph J. Hischar (Independent's Choice)	1,314	(1%)

NEW MEXICO

NEW MEXICO Political Background

The politics of New Mexico prove again that the average is not necessarily the typical. Since it was admitted to the Union in 1912, New Mexico has backed the winning candidate in 15 consecutive presidential elections. It is the most reliable bellwether state in the country, but could hardly be less typical. For a start, nearly a third of its population is Spanish-speaking; few of them are recent immigrants from Mexico, most being descendents of the Spanish conquistadores and the Pueblo Indians. Before New Mexico absorbed heavy immigration after World War II, the Spanish-speaking community made up nearly half the state's population. The culture of these people is centered in northern New Mexico, in the mountains around Taos and Santa Fe. Santa Fe, which is now the state capital, was once the provincial capital of a Spanish colony and flourished long before the pilgrims ever saw Plymouth Rock.

The southeast part of the state, "Little Texas," with its small cities and vast ranches, is economically and politically similar to the adjacent plains of West Texas. There is some oil here, but more important to the area are its military installations. These include a number of Air Force bases and the White Sands Missile Range, near Alamogordo, where the first atomic bomb was detonated. Little Texas is traditionally Democratic and conservative; in recent years, more conservative than Democratic.

Albuquerque, in the middle of the state, changed from a small desert town into a booming Sun Belt city; booming at least, until recent cutbacks in defense spending. Albuquerque depends heavily on defense spending; there are two military bases within the city limits and its largest employer is Sandia Laboratories, an AEC contractor. Like most Sun Belt cities, Albuquerque has become a Republican bastion. The voters in the city and its suburbs, which contain nearly a third of New Mexico's population, hold the balance of power in the state's elections.

For many years, New Mexico politics was a somnolent business. Local bosses—first Republican, then Democratic—controlled the large Spanish vote, and state elections were often merely ratifications of their decisions. The most interesting feature of the politics was a balanced ticket: New Mexico usually had one Spanish and one Anglo senator, with the position of governor and lieutenant governor alternating between the two groups. Recently, as Albuquerque became a major political force and as Little Texas grew increasingly Republican, elections have tested political leaders' skill at assembling winning coalitions from three roughly equal-sized voting blocks—the Spanish, Little Texas, and Albuquerque.

The 1970 Senate election provided observers with an interesting example of the game. Republican strategists considered Sen. Joseph M. Montoya vulnerable, despite the fact that since first winning a seat in the state legislature at age 21, he had spent 34 successful years in New Mexico politics. Two models for an electoral strategy were at hand. One was based on Nixon's substantial (52–40–8) victory in the state in 1968. The conservative carried Little Texas and Albuquerque by heavy margins and just lost the Spanish counties. The other model was the one used by the liberal Republican Gov. David Cargo in 1966 and 1968. Cargo made strong inroads into the Spanish vote and did in well in Albuquerque, although his liberal stance repelled many of the voters in Little Texas.

Two men, Cargo himself and Anderson Carter, entered the Republican senatorial primary. Cargo, an immigrant from the Midwest, was barred from seeking a third term as governor; Carter, a wealthy rancher and a Goldwater and Reagan backer, had won 47% of the vote against Sen. Clinton Anderson in 1966. To the surprise of the national news media, which had always given Cargo excellent press, Carter won the primary by a 2–1 margin. The reason for the defeat was apparent. Spanish voters do not register Republican, and in Albuquerque and Little Texas, the Goldwater conservatives who do register gave Carter huge majorities.

As in so many 1970 contests pitting hard-line conservatives against liberal incumbents, Carter's campaign developed little momentum after the primary. While Carter attacked all federal spending except for the military, Montoya pointed out how much federal money he had succeeded in bringing to the state. Montoya polled 55% in the 1st congressional district, which contains most of the Spanish counties, and just over 50% in the 2nd. Statewide, Carter won 47%, just as he did against Clinton Anderson four years earlier. The state also elected a Democratic governor to succeed Cargo.

Though he has indicated that he will run for reelection in 1972, the state's senior senator, Clinton Anderson, will probably retire at that time. The Senator was 75 in 1970 and suffers from Parkinson's disease, diabetes, and a bad heart. After three years as Secretary of Agriculture and five years in the House, Anderson was elected to the Senate in 1948, where he soon became quite influential. He is currently chairman of the Senate Committee on Science and Astronautics and of the Joint Committee on Atomic Energy. As the state data sheet indicates, the AEC spends a good deal of money in New Mexico. In the '50's, Anderson lead the well-publicized fight to deny Lewis Strauss, a former head of the AEC, confirmation as Commerce Secretary. It was one of the few times in American history in which a Cabinet nominee was rejected by the Senate. In his heyday, Anderson was considered a flaming liberal; more recently, his support for large military and AEC budgets has won him a more middle-of-the road reputation.

If Anderson does retire, there will be plenty of contenders for his seat. Possible Democratic candidates include former Governor Jack Campbell and former Congressman Thomas Morris; David Cargo and Anderson Carter may again fight it out in the Republican primary.

Electoral Votes 4

Census Data 1970 pop. 1,016,000; 0.49% of U.S. total, 38th largest; change 1960–70, +6.8%. Metro. 31.1%, 24.0% central city. 1970 per capita income, $3,044; 45th highest. 36th in number of poor.

1970 Share of Federal Tax Burden $702,510,000; 0.36% of U.S. total, 42nd largest.

1970 Share of Federal Outlays $1,485,868,780; 0.79% of U.S. total, 36th largest. Per capita federal spending, $1,462.

DOD	$362,594,000	34th	(0.18%)	HEW	$246,440,096	40th	(0.47%)
AEC	$374,255,560	1st	(14.40%)	HUD	$14,000,411	35th	(0.72%)
NASA	$9,487,870	22nd	(0.26%)	OEO	$8,923,674	30th	(1.17%)
DOT	$70,464,518	34th	(0.99%)	DOA	$101,863,348	37th	(0.79%)
DOC	$8,882,280	27th	(0.77%)	POD	$25,324,711	42nd	(0.35%)
DOI	$107,992,651	7th	(4.67%)	VA	$61,329,300	38th	(0.83%)
DOJ	$2,585,998	39th	(0.45%)	CSC	$19,516,030	37th	(0.48%)
				Other	$75,208,333		

Economic Base Livestock and cotton; crude petroleum and natural gas; metal mining, esp. uranium-radium-vanadium ores; food and kindred products; mining and quarrying of nonmetallic minerals other than fuels; lumber and wood products other than furniture, esp. saw mills and planing mills; electrical machinery, equipment, and supplies, esp. electronic components and accessories, printing, publishing, and allied industries, esp. newspapers; concrete, gypsum, and plaster products, and other stone, clay, glass, and concrete products.

Political Line-up Governor, Bruce King (D); seat up, 1972. Senators, Clinton P. Anderson (D) and Joseph M. Montoya (D). Representatives, 2 (1 D and 1 R). State Senate (28 D and 14 R); State House (48 D and 22 R).

The Voters

Registration 387,982 total. 253,532 D (65%); 116,462 R (30%); 17,989 other (5%).

Employment profile White collar, 44%. Blue collar, 56%.

Ethnic groups Black, 2%. Spanish surname, 28%. Total foreign stock, 8%. Mexico, 4%; Germany, UK, Canada, 1% each; others, 1%.

Presidential vote

1968	Humphrey (D)	130,081	(40%)
	Nixon (R)	169,692	(52%)
	Wallace (AIP)	25,737	(8%)
1964	Johnson (D)	194,017	(59%)
	Goldwater (R)	131,838	(41%)
1960	Kennedy (D)	156,027	(50%)
	Nixon (R)	153,733	(50%)

Senator

Clinton P. Anderson (D) Elected 1948, seat up 1972; b. Oct. 23, 1895, Centerville, S.D.; home, Albuquerque; S. Dakota Wesleyan U., 1913–15; U. of Mich., 1915–16; married, two children; Presbyterian.

Career Reporter, editor, 1918–22; Mgr. Insurance Dept., N.M. Loan & Mortgage Co., 1922–24; owner, insurance business, 1925–63; Treas., State of N.M., 1933–34; Administrator, N.M. Relief Admin., 1935; Chm., Exec. Dir., Unemployment Compensation Commission of N.M., 1936–38; Secy. of Agriculture, 1945–48; U.S. House of Reps., 1940–June 30, 1945.

Offices 4215 NSOB, 202-225-6621. Also 10013 Fed. Bldg. and U.S. Ct. House, Albuquerque 87101, 505-843-2488.

Committees

Aeronautical and Space Sciences (Chm.).

Finance (2nd).

Interior and Insular Affairs (2nd); Subs. (1) Chm., Water and Power Resources, (2) Indian Affairs, (3) Parks and Recreation, (4) Sp. on Legislative Oversight.

Jt. Com. on Atomic Energy (2nd); Subs. (1) Chm., Security, (2) Agreements for Cooperation, (3) Military Applications, (4) Raw Materials.

Jt. Com. on Internal Revenue Taxation (2nd).

Jt. Com. on Reduction of Federal Expenditures (2nd).

Group Ratings

	ADA	COPE	NREP	NFU	LCV	NAB	NSI	ACA
1970	31	75	43	90	35	38	75	29
1969	44	—	—	80	—	—	—	20
1968	21	45	—	44	—	25	—	0

Key Votes

(1) ABM	FOR	(8) Phil Pln	ABS	(15) Coop-Church	FOR
(2) SST	AGN	(9) Vol Army	AGN	(16) Cut Oil Dpltn	AGN
(3) Busing	FOR	(10) Prison $	AGN	(17) Consumer Prot	ABS
(4) Tob Sub	ABS	(11) Cut Mil $	ABS	(18) Farm Sub Limit	ABS
(5) Carswell	ABS	(12) Defoliatn	FOR	(19) Comp Bid Sales	ABS
(6) No-Knock	FOR	(13) 18-Yr-Vote	FOR	(20) Pre-Prod Tests	AGN
(7) Seniorty	FOR	(14) Pentgn PR	FOR	(21) Cut Marjna Pen	ABS

Election Results

1966 general:	Clinton P. Anderson (D)	137,205	(53%)
	Anderson Carter (R)	120,988	(47%)
1966 primary:	Clinton P. Anderson (D), unopposed		
1960 general:	Clinton P. Anderson (D)	190,654	(63%)
	William Colwes (R)	109,897	(37%)

Senator

Joseph M. Montoya (D) Elected 1964, seat up 1976; b. Sept. 24, 1915, Pena Blanca; home, Santa Fe; Regis Col., 1931, 1933–34; Georgetown U. Law School, LL.B., 1938; married, three children; Catholic.

Career Practicing atty., 1939– ; N.M. House of Reps., 1936–40, Majority Floor Leader, 1939–40; N.M. Senate, 1940–46, Majority Whip, 1945–46; Lt. Governor, 1946–48, 1955–57; U.S. House of Reps., 1957–64.

Offices 4109 NSOB, 202-225-5521. Also New Fed. Bldg., Albuquerque 87101, 505-843-2551, and Rm. 221, Fed. Bldg., Santa Fe 87501, 505-982-3801, ext. 461.

Committees

Appropriations (11th); Subs. (1) Chm., Treasury, Post Office, and General Government, (2) Labor, HEW, and Related Agencies, (3) District of Columbia, (4) Interior, (5) Military Construction.

Public Works (5th); Subs. (1) Chm., Economic Development, (2) Air and Water Pollution, (3) Public Roads.

Sel. Com. on Small Business (6th); Subs. (1) Chm., Government Procurement, (2) Retailing, Distribution, and Marketing Practices, (3) Science and Technology.

Group Ratings

	ADA	COPE	NREP	NFU	LCV	NAB	NSI	ACA
1970	63	100	67	93	62	11	33	20
1969	72	—	—	75	—	—	—	7
1968	36	88	—	78	—	25	—	6

Key Votes

(1) ABM	AGN	(8) Phil Pln	FOR	(15) Coop-Church	FOR
(2) SST	AGN	(9) Vol Army	ABS	(16) Cut Oil Dpltn	AGN
(3) Busing	FOR	(10) Prison $	ABS	(17) Consumer Prot	FOR
(4) Tob Sub	FOR	(11) Cut Mil $	ABS	(18) Farm Sub Limit	AGN
(5) Carswell	AGN	(12) Defoliatn	ABS	(19) Comp Bid Sales	ABS
(6) No-Knock	FOR	(13) 18-Yr-Vote	FOR	(20) Pre-Prod Tests	ABS
(7) Seniorty	ABS	(14) Pentgn PR	AGN	(21) Cut Marjna Pen	FOR

Election Results

1970 general:	Joseph M. Montoya (D)	151,486	(52%)
	Anderson Carter (R)	135,004	(47%)
	William L. Higgs (AIP)	3,382	(1%)
1970 primary:	Joseph M. Montoya (D)	85,285	(73%)
	Richard B. Edwards (D)	31,381	(27%)
1964 general:	Joseph M. Montoya (D)	178,209	(55%)
	Edwin L. Mechem (R)	17,562	(45%)

FIRST DISTRICT Political Background

New Mexico 1 comprises the northeastern third of the state. It includes metropolitan Albuquerque, which casts about 60% of the votes, and most of the state's Spanish speaking counties, which cast most of the remaining 40%. Santa Fe is the center of the Spanish culture here; unlike Albuquerque, which has become a Sun Belt boom town, Santa Fe has retained an old world charm. The Sangre de Cristo Mountains around the city and Taos, farther north, have attracted many artists and writers. D. H. Lawrence was here during the '20's; currently Dennis Hopper of *Easy Rider* fame lives near Taos. And each summer the Santa Fe Opera brings in a fair number of jet-setters from both coasts.

Lately the Spanish-speaking Indians in the hills of northern New Mexico have suddenly become militant. Reportedly, there was an armed rebellion in Rio Arriba County, where the Taos Pueblo Indians agitated until they secured from Congress title to a mountain lake of religious significance to them. For some reason, Sen. Clinton Anderson opposed the interests of the Indians.

Traditionally, the Spanish-American people of northern New Mexico have been the state's staunchest liberal Democrats. But lately they have become increasingly dissatisfied with the Democratic politicians who have dominated the area for so long. The Spanish are trending Republican while the residents of the Sun Belt city of Albuquerque constitute the established Republican bastion of the state. So in 1968, the 1st broke with tradition and elected New Mexico's first Republican congressman in more than two decades. Congressman Manuel Lujan, Jr., was probably helped in Albuquerque by Nixon's strong showing there. But in the rest of the district, Lujan's Spanish name probably helped Nixon; Lujan's opponent was Anglo incumbent, Thomas Morris.

In Washington, Lujan has compiled the record of a moderate Republican; in the district, a quiet but effective campaigner. In 1970 Fabian Chavez, who had carried the 1st when he was narrowly defeated by David Cargo in the 1968 gubernatorial election, challenged Lujan for the House seat. Chavez's vigorous attack on the Nixon Administration did him little good; Lujan's incumbency, along with the Spanish disaffection with the state's Democrats, resulted in the Republican incumbent taking 58% of the vote. In a state with only two congressional districts, Lujan's success in the 1st might very well raise the possibility of running for statewide office. But as the 1970 Senate race showed (see state write up), the Republican primary in New Mexico is heavily weighted in favor of conservative candidates. Chances are, Lujan will remain content to occupy a safe seat in the House.

Census Data 1970 pop. 511,135; deviation from current state average, +0.6%; change 1960–70, +13.5%. Metro. 61.8%, 47.7% central city.

1970 Share of Federal Outlays $902,230,452

DOD	$141,480,000	HEW	$151,484,670
AEC	$345,518,137	HUD	$9,827,265
NASA	$671,918	OEO	$6,648,113
DOT	$45,816,788	DOA	$34,944,545
		Other	$165,839,016

Federal Military-Industrial Commitments

DOD Contractors EE&G Inc. (Albuquerque), $8.723m: unspecified.

DOD Installations Sandia Army Base (Albuquerque). Kirtland AFB (Albuquerque).

AEC Operations Sandia Corp. Div., AT&T (Albuquerque), $161.703m: Sandia Laboratory. University of California (Los Alamos), $96.302m: unspecified.

Economic Base Livestock; food and kindred products; lumber and wood products other than furniture, esp. millwork, veneer, plywood, and prefabricated structural wood products. Also, tourism (Santa Fe and Taos); higher education (University of New Mexico).

The Voters

Registration 209,288 total. 127,419 D (61%); 70,471 R (34%); 11,398 other (5%).

Employment profile White collar, 46%. Blue collar, 54%.

Ethnic groups Black, 1%. Spanish surname, 32%. Total foreign stock, 9%. Mexico, 4%; Germany, UK, Canada, 1% each; others, 1%.

Presidential vote

1968	Humphrey (D)	75,328	(43%)
	Nixon (R)	91,729	(52%)
	Wallace (AIP)	7,850	(5%)

Representative

Manuel Lujan (R) Elected 1968; b. May 12, 1928, San Ildefonso; home, Albuquerque; Col. of Santa Fe, B.S., 1950; married, four children; Catholic.

Career Businessman—insurance; Bernalillo County Crime Commission, 1967–68; Pres., N.M. Assn. Industrial Insurance Agents, 1968; Mbr., State Corp. Commission, Advisory Bd. on Insurance, 1965–68.

Offices 1323 LHOB, 202-225-6316. Also Rm. 1004 Fed. Bldg., 500 Gold Ave., S.W., Albuquerque 87103, 505-843-2538, and San Fidel Hotel, Las Vegas 87701, 505-425-6684.

Committees

Interior and Insular Affairs (10th); Subs. (1) Indian Affairs, (2) Irrigation and Reclamation, (3) Public Lands, (4) Territorial and Insular Affairs.

Sel. Com. on Small Business (6th); Subs. (1) Foundations: Their Impact on Small Business, (2) Minority Small Business Enterprise.

Group Ratings

	ADA	COPE	NREP	NFU	LCV	CFA	NAB	NSI	ACA
1970	36	30	42	25	100	40	100	100	69
1969	13	—	—	23	—	—	—	—	76

Key Votes

(1) ABM	FOR	(6) 18-Yr-Vote	FOR	(11) Clean Water $	FOR
(2) SST	FOR*	(7) Farm Sub Lmt	FOR	(12) Mig Wrkrs Comp	FOR
(3) Phil Pln	FOR	(8) Coop-Church	AGN	(13) Jets to Chiang	FOR
(4) No-Knock	ABS	(9) Family Asst	FOR	(14) State OEO Veto	AGN
(5) Cmutr Tax	AGN	(10) Work Stamps	ABS	(15) Park Logging	AGN

* *Voted "against" in previous vote on same issue.*

Election Results

1970 general:	Manuel Lujan, Jr. (R)	91,187	(58%)
	Fabian Chavez, Jr. (D)	64,598	(41%)
	Anita Montano (PCP)	1,763	(1%)
	Norbert J. McGovern (INM)	811	(1%)
1970 primary:	Manuel Lujan, Jr. (R), unopposed		
1968 general:	Manuel Lujan, Jr. (R)	88,517	(53%)
	Thomas G. Morris (D)	78,117	(47%)
	William Higgs (PC)	854	(1%)

SECOND DISTRICT Political Background

New Mexico 2 comprises two-thirds of the state, to the south and west. There are pockets of Spanish voting strength in the Rio Grande Valley and in the far southwest corner; in the north, around Gallup and Grants, the Navajo Indians form an important part of the electorate. Farmington, in the natural gas and uranium rich San Juan Basin of the Four Corners region, was a boom town during the '50's and is currently a conservative bastion.

The Little Texas area around Hobbs, Clovis, Carlsbad, and Roswell, contains almost half of the district's population and determines its political character. The conservative ranchers and townspeople here are strongly opposed to federal spending—except on military projects, in which case they strongly support the spending. What happened to Roswell illustrates how much the 2nd depends on Defense Department money. In 1960, Roswell was the state's second largest city with 39,000 residents. The Johnson Administration shut down nearby Walker Air Force Base in 1967; within a year, the city's population dropped to 32,000, and many of those were unemployed. Although defense-related industries have moved on to the vacated installation, the cutback lingers in the minds of the Roswell voters.

The base shutdown was one reason—Humphrey's weak showing (36%) in the 2nd was another—that Democratic Congressman E. S. (Johnny) Walker lost his seat in 1968. Until that election, New Mexico's congressmen were elected at large, and in 1966, Walker had won statewide because of the 54% he polled in what is now the 2nd district. In 1968, his percentage dropped to 49%—he lost Chaves County, which contains Roswell, by more votes than his total deficit district-wide.

The winner in that contest was conservative Republican Ed Foreman, who thereby gained the distinction of being the second person in this century to have been elected to the House from two different states. He had served the adjoining 16th district of Texas from 1962 to 1964. In 1970, Foreman gained the further distinction of being the first person in American political history to have been elected and then defeated in House contests in two different states. The man who beat him was state Sen. Harold Runnels, whose outlook is nearly as conservative as that of Foreman's. Runnels has a seat on the Armed Services Committee; the Congressman, by ideology and temperament, finds the committee's hawkish and pro-Pentagon majority quite agreeable. It remains to be seen whether he will have any more luck than his two predecessors retaining his seat.

Redistricting is no problem in New Mexico. Because the populations of the two districts differ by just 6,000 people, they could be equalized by moving one county from the 1st district to the 2nd. This should have little effect on the politics of either district.

Census Data 1970 pop. 504,865; deviation from current state average, –0.6%; change 1960–70, +0.8%. Metro. 0.0%, 0.0% central city.

1970 Share of Federal Outlays $583,637,328

DOD	$221,114,000	HEW	$94,955,426
AEC	$28,737,423	HUD	$4,173,146
NASA	$9,175,952	OEO	$2,275,561
DOT	$24,647,730	DOA	$66,918,803
		Other	$131,639,287

Federal Military-Industrial Commitments

DOD Contractors Dynaelectron Corp. (White Sands Missile Range), $7.285m: aircraft maintenance.

DOD Installations White Sands Army Missile Range (Las Cruces). Naval Ordnance Missile Test Facility (White Sands Missile Range). Cannon AFB (Clovis). Holloman AFB (Alamogordo).

AEC Operations Kerr-McGee (Grants), $9.118m: uranium concentrates. United Nuclear-Homestake Partners (Grants), $7.536m: uranium concentrates. Anaconda Co. (Grants), $6.784m: uranium concentrates. United Nuclear Corp. (Grants), $5.300m: uranium concentrates.

Economic Base Livestock and cotton; crude petroleum and natural gas; metal mining, esp. uranium-radium-vanadium ores; mining and quarrying of nonmetallic minerals other than fuels.

The Voters

Registration 178,695 total. 126,113 D (71%); 45,991 R (26%); 6,591 other (4%).
Employment profile White collar, 41%. Blue collar, 59%.
Ethnic groups Black, 2%. Spanish surname, 24%. Total foreign stock, 8%. Mexico, 5%; Germany, UK, 1% each; others, 1%.

Presidential vote

1968	Humphrey (D)	54,753	(36%)
	Nixon (R)	77,963	(52%)
	Wallace (AIP)	17,887	(12%)

Representative

Harold L. Runnels (D) Elected 1970; b. March 17, 1924, Dallas, Tex.; home, Lovington; Cameron State Agricultural Col., B.S., 1943; USAFR, WWII; married, four children; Baptist.

Career Owner and manager of two oil-drilling equipment companies; N.M. State Senate, 1960–70.

Offices 1726 LHOB, 202-225-2365. Also Suite D, McCrory Bldg., Lovington 88260, 505-396-2252, and Suite 1022, First Natl. Tower, Las Cruces 88001, 505-526-6156, and City Hall, Gallup 87301, 505-863-3400.

Committees

Armed Services (24th); Sub. No. 2.

Group Ratings, Key Votes: Newly elected.

Election Results

1970 general:	Harold Runnels (D)	64,518	(51%)
	Ed Foreman (R)	61,074	(48%)
	Julian A. Roybal (PCP)	1,388	(1%)
1970 primary:	Harold Runnels (D), unopposed		

NEW YORK

NEW YORK Political Background

In political discourse, "New York" is shorthand for the "Eastern liberal establishment" and for all the hopes and fears that the word "liberal" conjures up. But New York is not as liberal as all that. In 1969, the idea of a U.S. Senator from this state out of the Conservative party was laughable. It is not so today. And even the 1968 election results should have made the pundits question New York's political image. Humphrey's margin in that election looks impressive in raw figures—370,000 votes—but in percentage terms it was smaller than his margins in Massachusetts, Michigan, and Minnesota. Humphrey bested Nixon in the state by 7%.

Political analysts commonly divide New York into three parts: New York City, which casts about 40% of the state's votes and which is usually heavily Democratic; the suburbs, with about 20% of the votes—a share that is slowly increasing; and Upstate, by itself larger than all but eight states, which casts the remaining 40%. But an understanding of the complex politics of the Empire State requires a look beneath the City-suburb-Upstate trichotomy at the fissures and currents which lie below. As in most states, political alignments in New York grew from the antipathies of successive waves of its immigrants. Alexander Hamilton's Federalists opposed the rule of the Dutch Patroons, and the new-rich and the would-be rich of Aaron Burr's National Republican party challenged the hegemony of Hamilton's merchants and bankers. Later, when the Irish arrived and found the WASPs in control of the Whig party, the immigrants became Democrats and soon came to dominate the party. Later arrivals—the Italians, for example—tended to be more Republican than the Irish, since the Irish did not go out of their way to welcome them into the Democratic party. The most important ethnic antipathy, and one that continues to echo in various ways in New York politics to this day, was the one which developed between the Irish of Tammany Hall and the Jewish immigrants from Eastern Europe.

As everyone knows, the Jewish immigrants and their descendants have been much more successful, given the standards used by our society to measure success, than any other American ethnic group. But as the Jews rose in economic and social status, they retained their liberal political attitudes; in most states, the Jewish vote is heavily Democratic. In New York—where nearly half of the nation's Jews live—the Jewish voters' mistrust of Democratic Tammany led to the creation of third parties during the '30's and '40's; first the American Labor, then the Liberal party. With the third party on the ballot, one could vote for Roosevelt for president and for the anti-Tammany Republican LaGuardia for mayor. The power brokers of the Liberal party, primarily aging Jewish union leaders, skillfully used the promise of their line on the ballot to promote the nomination of liberal candidates by both major parties. Their most recent success was the reelection of Mayor Lindsay in 1969 on the Liberal line of the ballot after he had lost the Republican primary.

The same attitudes that led to the formation of the Liberal party explain the election of liberal Republicans like Gov. Nelson Rockefeller and Sens. Irving Ives, Kenneth Keating, and Jacob Javits. Up through the mid-'60's, Rockefeller and the others built on the traditional Republican voting base and won over Democrats who voted for the national ticket but were disgusted with the local Democratic machines. The Republicans were aided by the ineptitude and hamhandedness of Democratic leaders like Carmine De Sapio of Manhattan and Congressman Charles A. Buckley of the Bronx.

This pattern began to break up in the '60's. In 1962 the Conservative party fielded its first slate of candidates; its objective was to force Rockefeller and other Republicans either more to the right or out of office. Conservative party leaders were surprised when most of their votes came not from traditionally conservative Upstate, but from Brooklyn, Queens, and the Bronx; from ancestral Democrats upset with what they saw as the consequences of liberal policies.

Another development was scarcely noticed, coming as it did in the year of the massive and well-publicized LBJ landslide. That was the election of Sen. Robert F. Kennedy in 1964. Most observers were unimpressed by Kennedy's margin—almost twice as large as his brother's four years earlier—and attributed the younger Kennedy's showing to Johnson's coattails. They pointed out that Kennedy had suffered severe defection from upper-income liberals, particularly in Manhattan; these liberals resented what they saw as a Massachusetts carpetbagger running in New York and were also upset because Kennedy was nominated with the approval of Democratic party bosses. What the pundits missed was Kennedy's strong showing among the lower-income, predominantly Catholic voters of the outer boroughs of New York City, and his strength in the Upstate cities of Buffalo, Syracuse, Utica, and Albany. In many such working-class areas, Kennedy ran virtually even with Johnson, and there is no reason to believe that these voters were not perfectly capable of splitting their tickets. In the end, Kennedy lost the intellectuals and a significant percentage of the Jews, but he forged a new, populistic coalition of blacks, Puerto Ricans, and white Catholics. Many of the white Catholics would later vote for Buckley and support the Conservative party.

The press, however, was more interested in the coalition assembled by Mayor John V. Lindsay. In 1965, and then again to an even greater extent in 1969, Lindsay won the overwhelming support of affluent liberals in Manhattan and large margins in black and Puerto Rican areas. In both elections he won with less than a majority and lost the four boroughs outside Manhattan. But many found his victories quite satisfactory. These victories took City Hall patronage away from the Democratic machines and also made him a possible presidential candidate. Only in New York could a 42%-mayor be considered a promising presidential vote-getter, Democrat or Republican. The campaign in 1969, during which Lindsay was called a "limousine liberal," shows the extent to which cultural differences have replaced ethnic origins as the basis of the City's political alignments: the Beautiful People (and their poor allies) versus the dutiful people; Manhattan versus Queens; radical chic versus Joe. The battlelines were set for the 1970 senatorial election.

"Isn't it time *we* had a Senator?" was the way James Buckley's signs asked the question. "We" was the people who voted for Nixon but, with the success of the Liberal party, never had the chance to vote for a senator with similar views. "We" are the blue-collar workers, service employees, and civil servants who live in heavily mortgaged houses in Queens and Staten Island, struggling with high taxes and New York's outrageous cost of living—people, therefore, with little patience for the "welfare chiseler" and with the City's poor generally. "We" was disgusted by Leonard Bernstein's party for some of the City's Black Panthers.

Buckley's opponents were incumbent Republican Sen. Charles Goodell and Democratic Congressman Richard Ottinger. Goodell was an Upstate congressman appointed by Gov. Rockefeller to succeed Robert Kennedy in 1968; after his appointment, Goodell suddenly became one of the Senate's most outspoken liberals and doves. The views of Congressman Ottinger, a liberal who had won the Democratic primary with a saturation TV campaign, were virtually indistinguishable from Goodell's.

Goodell's strategy was modeled after Lindsay's, and had produced victories for the state's liberal Republicans. He expected to hold the normal Republican vote and win a plurality by attracting the antiwar support of both whites and blacks. The strategy didn't work. President Nixon and the increasingly conservative Gov. Rockefeller gave covert support to Buckley, whose views, after all, were far closer to theirs than Goodell's. Vice-President Agnew then attended a Buckley dinner in New York City. But even before these signals went out, Goodell's Republican support had collapsed; he ran third, usually a poor third, in every published poll. As it turned out, Goodell got only 29% of the votes Upstate—down from Sen. Javits' 54% in 1968—and only 17% in the New York City suburbs—down from Javits' 52%. The weakness of the old liberal Republican strategy came to the surface; most of the votes such candidates received were cast by people who did not share their views on the issues. Eventually, voters began to wonder when "we" are going to have a senator. Most Upstate WASP Republicans stayed with Goodell, but the switch to Buckley was massive among Upstate Catholic Republicans.

But thanks to Agnew and Buckley, Goodell succeeded in winning votes that no statewide Republican had ever won. Since Goodell was running poorly in the polls, Buckley strategists knew that Ottinger was the man to beat. So Agnew made a point of attacking Goodell; a "political Christine Jorgenson," was one memorable evaluation. The attacks were intended to draw liberal votes away from Ottinger and they succeeded. The votes went to Goodell.

As a matter of tradition, New York liberals have been very much taken by aloof, WASP politicians like Adlai Stevenson; the tradition was bred in the Tammany years, years of cigar-chomping Democratic-machine candidates. The New York liberal press works out of this heritage. Its columnists, therefore, plowed through Goodell's conservative House record to find evidence of the man's liberalism and then scanned Ottinger's liberal record to find, as one writer put, "feet of clay." The *New York Times* editorialized that voters should not be swayed by the polls in which Goodell, whom they had endorsed, was doing badly; as if the right of franchise obliges one to vote for a loser and against somebody who shares his views on the issues. In Manhattan, Goodell won 30% of the vote, as against 14% city-wide. If that 16% margin had gone to Ottinger, he would have won the election.

Ottinger's strategy was to assemble a coalition similar to Kennedy's. He of course took a forceful stand against the war. But in an attempt to reach the voters in the farther reaches of the City, in the suburbs, and in the cities Upstate, the candidate stressed his strong record as a pollution-fighter and his opposition to the economic policies of the Nixon Administration. To a considerable extent the Ottinger strategy worked; the Democrat held on to much more of his party's traditional base of support than did Goodell. Ottinger's weapon was television; the heir to a plywood fortune spent about a million dollars on TV advertising in the primary and general elections. Buckley's budget for the medium in the general election was also about a million dollars.

The candidate of the Conservative party ran best among Catholic voters, who probably cast a solid majority of his 39% plurality. He was especially strong in Suffolk County, one of the two to give him an absolute majority. Suffolk, at the eastern end of Long Island, is the fastest-growing part of the state—up from 666,000 to 1,116,000 during the '60's. This is where thousands of middle-class families from Queens and Brooklyn have settled in what are, by any comparison to the City, bucolic suburbs. Buckley's strength among the Catholics paralleled that of Gov. Rockefeller's. In 1970, the increasingly conservative governor sought out the City votes he needed to win in the Catholic areas of Queens and Brooklyn rather than in the liberal precincts of Manhattan, which is where he got votes in 1966.

Columnist Kevin Phillips has claimed that the growing conservatism of New York's Catholics is a harbinger of a nationwide trend. But Phillips' prediction is only typical of a kind of New York parochialism that assumes anything that happens here will soon happen everywhere else. In this case, it probably won't. The peculiarities of politics in New York explain why the state's Catholics vote conservative. In Massachusetts, Sen. Edward Kennedy is *the* man in the state's politics; Kennedy is very popular with the Catholic voters in Massachusetts and the Catholic vote there has become increasingly liberal in recent years. In metropolitan New York, Mayor Lindsay is the politician who gets the publicity. His name is mud in most Catholic neighborhoods and the City's Catholic vote has grown conservative. Political allegiance is a badge of cultural style in New York, and so long as liberal politics remains a plaything of the rich, liberal politicians will have a tough time winning elections in places like Suffolk County, Queens, and the blue-collar suburbs of Utica. In states where there is not such a voluble liberal elite, there is less likely to be a conservative reaction.

Because New York will have neither a senatorial nor a gubernatorial race in 1972, local political entrepreneurs have some time in which to plot strategy. Sen. Jacob Javits comes up for reelection in 1974. The Senator, who represented a heavily Democratic Manhattan district in the House, defeated Franklin D. Roosevelt, Jr., for attorney general in 1954 and then won election to the Senate in 1956. Because Javits is, perhaps, the Senate's most liberal Republican, he is theoretically vulnerable to the treatment Goodell got in 1970. But his popularity, especially among Jewish voters, is much more deeply rooted. Moreover, his opposition to the war and other policies of the Nixon Administration has been far less strident than was Goodell's. Goodell lost mainly because prominent Republicans spread the word to the faithful that it was O.K. to support Buckley; it is unlikely that they would dare do anything like that to Javits. This Republican has seniority and some clout in the Senate. He is the ranking Republican on the Labor and Public Welfare Committee and also sits on Government Operations and Foreign Relations.

Senator Buckley will probably have less trouble winning reelection in 1976 than some suggest. He has been inching toward the ideological center, mentioning with some frequency, for example, his concern for the environment; and his unabrasive manner makes it difficult for his opponents to label him a conservative extremist. In fact, he is probably more comfortable in the Senate Republican caucus than Javits; back home in 1976, the odds are that he will win the nomination of both the Republican and Conservative parties. The position Buckley takes in the 1974 campaign will be of some interest. If he supports Javits, or does nothing to oppose him, it will indicate that an accommodation has been reached between the liberal and conservative wings of the New York Republican party.

The House delegation is the only thing the Democrats still control in the state's politics. But the Republicans, who hold both the governorship and the state legislature, will have a free hand in redistricting. Census figures indicate that the two seats the state lost in the 1970 census will both come out of New York City, which means that there will be two fewer liberal Democrats in the delegation after 1972. The Republicans might be able to pick up even more than that, but despite great skill in redrawing the lines just before the 1970 elections, they were able to unseat just one Democratic incumbent. And because of the popularity of most Upstate and suburban Democrats within their districts, it is unlikely that the Republicans can do much better this time.

Electoral Votes 41

Census Data 1970 pop. 18,241,266; 8.84% of U.S. total, 2nd largest; change 1960–70, +8.7%. Metro. 86.5%, 51.1% central city. 1970 per capita income, $4,797; 3rd highest. 4th in number of poor.

1970 Share of Federal Tax Burden $22,909,510,000; 11.74% of U.S. total, 1st largest.

1970 Share of Federal Outlays $21,354,943,161; 11.30% of U.S. total, 2nd largest. Per capita federal spending, $1,174.

DOD	$3,775,485,000	3rd	(6.58%)	HEW	$5,602,016,228	2nd	(10.7%)
AEC	$157,732,528	6th	(6.07%)	HUD	$182,805,422	1st	(9.38%)
NASA	$299,831,410	4th	(8.14%)	OEO	$76,685,081	1st	(10.09%)
DOT	$395,576,419	2nd	(5.54%)	DOA	$915,368,679	2nd	(7.12%)
DOC	$142,347,489	2nd	(12.30%)	POD	$962,987,151	1st	(13.21%)
DOI	$72,095,319	10th	(3.12%)	VA	$747,391,603	2nd	(10.12%)
DOJ	$48,699,765	3rd	(8.48%)	CSC	$502,352,028	2nd	(12.48%)
				Other	$7,473,569,039		

Economic Base Apparel and other finished products made from fabrics and similar materials, esp. women's, misses', and juniors' outerwear; electrical machinery equipment and supplies, esp. electrical machinery, electronic components and accessories; printing, publishing, and allied industries, esp. commercial printing; nonelectrical machinery; dairy, poultry, and livestock; food and kindred products; transportation equipment, esp. aircraft and parts and motor vehicles and motor vehicle equipment; fabricated metal products, esp. fabricated structural metal products; professional, scientific, and controlling instruments, photographic and optical goods, watches and clocks, esp. photographic equipment and supplies; miscellaneous manufacturing industries, esp. toys, amusement, sporting, and athletic goods; primary metal industries, esp. blast furnaces, steel works, and rolling and finishing mills. Also, banking, stock brokerage, insurance, and higher education.

Political Line-up Governor, Nelson A. Rockefeller (R); seat up, 1974. Senators, Jacob K. Javits (R) and James L. Buckley (Conservative). Representatives, 41 (24 D and 17 R). State Senate (25 D and 32 R); State Assembly (71 D and 79 R).

The Voters

Registration 7,438,008 total. 3,566,252 D (48%); 2,957,908 R (40%); 109,311 L (1%); 107,372 C (1%); 697,165 other (9%).

Employment profile White collar, 47%. Blue collar, 53%.

Ethnic groups Black, 11.9%. Puerto Rico, 4%. Total foreign stock, 39%. Italy, 9%; Germany, Poland, USSR, 4% each; Ireland, UK, 3% each; Austria, Canada, 2% each; Czech., Hungary, 1% each; others, 6%.

Presidential vote

1968	Humphrey (D and L)	3,378,470	(58%)
	Nixon (R)	3,007,932	(40%)
	Wallace (AIP)	358,864	(3%)
1964	Johnson (D and L)	4,913,156	(69%)
	Goldwater (R)	2,243,559	(31%)
1960	Kennedy (D and L)	3,830,085	(53%)
	Nixon (R)	3,446,419	(47%)

Senator

Jacob K. Javits (R) Elected 1956, seat up 1974; b. May 18, 1904, New York City; home, New York City; N.Y.U. Law School, LL.B., 1926; Army, WWII; married, three children; Jewish.

Career Practicing atty., 1927– ; Sp. Asst. to the Chief of Chemical Warfare Service during WWII; Att. Gen. N.Y. State, 1955–57.

Offices 320 OSOB, 202-225-6542. Also 100 E. 45th St., New York City 10017, 212-687-7777, and Rm. 414, W.S. Courthouse, Buffalo 14202, 716-842-3690.

Committees

Foreign Relations (5th); Subs. (1) Arms Control, International Law and Organization, (2) European Affairs, (3) Genocide Convention, (4) U.S. Security Agreements and Commitments Abroad, (5) Western Hemisphere Affairs.

Government Operations (2nd); Subs. (1) Executive Reorganization, (2) Perm. Sub. on Investigations.

Labor and Public Welfare (Ranking Mbr.); Subs. (1) Alcoholism and Narcotics, (2) Children and Youth, (3) Education, (4) Employment, Manpower and Poverty, (5) Health, (6) Labor, (7) Migratory Labor, (8) Sp. on Arts and Humanities, (9) Sp. on Social Programs.

Sel. Com. on Equal Educational Opportunity (2nd).

Sel. Com. on Small Business (Ranking Mbr.).

Jt. Economic Com. (Ranking Rep. Sen.); Subs. (1) Fiscal Policy, (2) Foreign Economic Policy, (3) Inter-American Economic Relationships, (4) International Exchange and Payments, (5) Urban Affairs.

Group Ratings

	ADA	COPE	NREP	NFU	LCV	NAB	NSI	ACA
1970	75	92	100	93	48	25	10	0
1969	100	—	—	63	—	—	—	14
1968	86	92	—	75	—	40	—	13

Key Votes

(1) ABM	AGN	(8) Phil Pln	FOR	(15) Coop-Church	FOR
(2) SST	AGN	(9) Vol Army	AGN	(16) Cut Oil Dpltn	FOR
(3) Busing	FOR	(10) Prison $	FOR	(17) Consumer Prot	FOR
(4) Tob Sub	ABS	(11) Cut Mil $	FOR	(18) Farm Sub Limit	FOR
(5) Carswell	AGN	(12) Defoliatn	FOR	(19) Comp Bid Sales	FOR
(6) No-Knock	ABS	(13) 18-Yr-Vote	FOR	(20) Pre-Prod Tests	AGN
(7) Seniorty	ABS	(14) Pentgn PR	AGN	(21) Cut Marjna Pen	ABS

Election Results

1968 general:	Jacob K. Javits (R and L)	3,269,772	(50%)
	Paul D. Dwyer (D)	2,150,659	(33%)
	James L. Buckley (C)	1,139,402	(17%)
1968 primary:	Jacob K. Javits (R), unopposed		
1962 general:	Jacob K. Javits (R)	3,272,417	(58%)
	James B. Donovan (D)	2,289,323	(40%)
	Kieran O'Doherty (C)	116,151	(2%)

Senator

James Lane Buckley (Cons.) Elected 1970, seat up 1976; b. March 9, 1923, New York City; home, New York City; Yale, B.A., Oct. 1943, LL.B., 1949; Navy, WWII; married, six children; Catholic.

Career Businessman; Conservative Candidate for Senate, 1968.

Offices 452 OSOB, 202-225-4451. Also 110 E. 45th St., New York City 10022, 212-697-3000.

Committees

Aeronautical and Space Sciences (5th).

District of Columbia (3rd); Sub. on Public Health, Education, Welfare, and Safety.

Public Works (6th); Subs. (1) Air and Water Pollution, (2) Economic Development, (3) Environmental Science and Technology, (4) Public Roads.

Group Ratings, Key Votes: *Newly elected.*

Election Results

1970 general:	James L. Buckley (C and Ind. Alliance)	2,288,190	(39%)
	New York City	797,144	
	Outside New York City	1,491,046	

Richard L. Ottinger (D)	2,171,232	(37%)
New York City	979,328	
Outside New York City	1,191,904	
Charles E. Goodell (R and L)	1,434,472	(24%)
New York City	439,452	
Outside New York City	995,020	

1970 primary: James L. Buckley (C), unopposed

FIRST DISTRICT Political Background

New York 1 occupies the eastern end of Suffolk County on Long Island; the district's western boundary lies some 50 miles east of New York City. The best known part of the 1st consists of its extreme eastern tip, the Hamptons, Montauk Point, and Sag Harbor—fancy beach resort country. Elegant parties have been held in the Southampton "cottages" to benefit the migrant workers in California, but the plight of the vegetable workers around nearby Riverhead is fully as miserable. Most of the district's population live in middle-class subdivisions to the west, among them Islip, Brentwood, Smithtown, and Patchogue. The mood here is very conservative: people worry about crime and about the puzzling habits their children seem to be learning from somebody.

The importance of defense industries to the district's economy, including the Brookhaven National Laboratory (AEC) and the giant Grumman Aviation plant, strengthens the conservatism of its residents. The industries also explain why a Democrat, Congressman Otis G. Pike, consistently wins reelection in this very conservative district; Pike is the 7th ranking member of the House Armed Services Committee. His seat on the committee and his campaigning skill account for his strong showings on election day; in 1964, he won a resounding 65% of the votes. Lately, however, as the strength of the Conservative party has grown, Pike's margins have diminished. In 1970, when Conservative party Senate candidate James Buckley carried the district, the Congressman managed only 52%—his weakest outing since 1960.

The redistricting situation improves Pike's chances for reelection in 1972. The 1st, whose population jumped by 80% during the '60's, now has enough people for two congressional districts; so when it is split by redistricting, Pike will be able to choose the more Democratic of the two, and run there as the incumbent. Moreover, there will be no statewide races except the one for President in 1972; if the Republican party does what it did in 1968, it will not allow the Conservatives to run Richard Nixon on their line. As a result, Pike's Republican opponent in 1972 will not benefit from the straight Conservative vote.

If the conservative trend on Long Island continues, however, Pike may be defeated sometime during the '70's. The Congressman has toyed with the idea of running for statewide office. If he vacates the House seat, a conservative Republican is sure to win it.

Census Data 1970 pop. 745,134; deviation from current state average, +69.3%; change 1960–70, +82.1%. Metro. 100%, 0.0% central city.

1970 Share of Federal Outlays $602,511,000 (average outlay per district, New York 1–5)

DOD	$220,753,000	HEW	$96,802,000
AEC	$14,733,000	HUD	$1,585,000
NASA	$53,181,000	OEO	$534,000
DOT	$11,513,000	DOA	$2,051,000
		Other	$201,357,000

Federal Military-Industrial Commitments (New York 1–5, Long Island listing)

DOD Contractors Grumman Aerospace and Grumman Corp. (Bethpage), $634.757m: F-14A aircraft weapons system; E-2C aircraft; A-6A aircraft; modification of various other aircraft. Sperry Rand (Syosset), $50.445m: various ship and submarine navigation systems; Poseidon and Terrier missile guidance systems. PRD Electronics (Jericho and Syosset), $42.115m: aircraft communication systems. Fairchild Camera and Instrument Corp. (Copiague and Syosset), $31.420m: electric bomb fuzes; electronic warfare assemblies. Cutler-Hammer Inc. (Deer Park), $24.103m: airborne reconnaissance systems support. Fairchild Hiller Corp. (Farmingdale), $20.083m: unspecified. Hazeltine Corp. (Little Neck), $15.514m: acoustic-seismic electronic detection sets; airborne interrogator sets; various other electronic warfare equipment. American Machine and Foundry (Garden City), $14.006m: metal parts for 750-pound bombs. Bulova Watch Co. (Valley Stream), $11.002m: rocket and mortar detonating fuzes. Republic Electronics Corp. (Melville), $10.224m: aircraft navigation units. Dynamic Corp. of America (Garden City), $9.408m: repair of mobile ground communication units. Texaco Inc. (Long Island City), $7.642m: petroleum products. General Instrument Corp. (Hicksville), $7.320m: battlefield surveillance radar. Dynell Electronics Corp. (Melville), $6.597m: submarine acoustic-warfare sets.

DOD Installations Montauk AF Station (Montauk).

AEC Operations Associated Universities, Inc. (Upton), $49.485m: Brookhaven National Laboratory.

NASA Contractors Grumman Aerospace (Bethpage), $258.130m: Apollo Lunar module; astronomical orbiting observatory development; propulsion technology research.

Economic Base Electrical machinery, equipment, and supplies, esp. communication equipment; aircraft and parts and other transportation equipment; apparel and other finished products made from fabrics and similar materials, esp. women's, misses', and juniors' outerwear. Also, tourism (Hamptons).

The Voters

Registration 262,235 total. 77,258 D (30%); 138,041 R (53%); 1,763 L (1%); 8,360 C (3%); 36,831 other (14%).

Employment profile White collar, 41%. Blue collar, 59%.

Ethnic groups Black, 3%. Puerto Rico, 1%. Total foreign stock, 32%. Italy 7%; Germany, 5%; Ireland, Poland, UK, 3% each; Austria, Czech., Hungary, Norway, Sweden, USSR, Canada, 1% each; others, 4%.

Presidential vote

1968	Humphrey (D)	73,298	(31%)*
	Nixon (R)	141,652	(60%)
	Wallace (AIP)	21,863	(9%)

Representative

Otis G. Pike (D) Elected 1960; b. Aug. 31, 1921, Riverhead; home, Riverhead; Princeton U., B.A., 1943; Columbia U., J.D., 1948; USMC, WWII; married, three children; Congregationalist.

Career Practicing atty., 1953– ; Justice of Peace and Mbr. Town Bd., Riverhead, 1953–60; V.P., Long Island Home, Ltd., Past Dir., Central Suffolk.

Offices 2428 RHOB, 202-225-3826. Also 130 Ostrander Ave., Riverhead 11901, 516-727-2332.

Committees

Armed Services (7th); Subs. (1) Sub. No. 2, (2) Armed Services Investigating.

Group Ratings

	ADA	COPE	NREP	NFU	LCV	CFA	NAB	NSI	ACA
1970	84	67	75	92	90	74	25	40	37
1969	67	—	—	67	—	—	—	—	35
1968	50	83	—	69	—	—	50	—	32

Key Votes

(1) ABM	FOR	(6) 18-Yr-Vote	FOR	(11) Clean Water $	FOR
(2) SST	AGN	(7) Farm Sub Lmt	FOR	(12) Mig Wrkrs Comp	FOR
(3) Phil Pln	FOR	(8) Coop-Church	AGN	(13) Jets to Chiang	AGN
(4) No-Knock	FOR	(9) Family Asst	AGN	(14) State OEO Veto	AGN
(5) Cmutr Tax	FOR	(10) Work Stamps	AGN	(15) Park Logging	AGN

** These figures do not include votes Humphrey received on the Liberal line. His performance, therefore, is understated by one to five percent in each New York district.*

Election Results

1970 general:	Otis Pike (D and L)	108,746	(52%)
	Malcolm E. Smith, Jr. (R and C)	99,249	(48%)
1970 primary:	Otis Pike (D and L), unopposed (Redistricted 1970)		

SECOND DISTRICT Political Background

New York 2 comprises the towns of Babylon and Huntington at the western end of Suffolk County, and a portion of eastern Nassau County including three suburbs dating from the '50's: Hicksville, Plainview, and Farmingdale. The north shore, around Huntington, is white-collar; while the south shore, around Babylon, is blue-collar. All three areas are heavily conservative and gave big pluralities to Conservative Sen. James Buckley in 1970. Many of the people who moved out here from the City found work in the huge defense plants built during and after World War II; contractors like Grumman (see New York 1 data section) are still very important to the district.

Conservative Republican James R. Grover was first elected congressman in 1962. He has rapidly climbed the seniority ladder in the Public Works Committee, where he is now the 2nd-ranking Republican. He has won reelection with substantial margins since 1966, and should have no trouble in 1972.

Redistricting will alter the Long Island districts somewhat. Fast-growing Suffolk County will have two full districts, while Nassau County, which had little population growth in the '60's, will be divided into two full districts and parts of two others (see maps in appendix). Grover will presumably run in the western Suffolk County district unless it is chosen by incumbent Democrat Otis Pike, a proven vote-getter in the area. In any event, the Republican legislature will make sure that Grover has a safe House seat.

Census Data 1970 pop. 548,783; deviation from current state average, +23.3%; change 1960–70, +34.0%. Metro. 100%, 0.0% central city.

1970 Share of Federal Outlays $602,511,000 (average outlay per district, New York 1–5)

DOD	$220,753,000	HEW	$96,802,000
AEC	$14,733,000	HUD	$1,585,000
NASA	$53,181,000	OEO	$534,000
DOT	$11,513,000	DOA	$2,051,000
		Other	$201,357,000

Federal Military-Industrial Commitments (See New York 1 for Long Island listing.)

Economic Base Electrical machinery, equipment, and supplies, esp. communication equipment; aircraft and parts and other transportation equipment; apparel and other finished products made from fabrics and similar materials, esp. women's, misses', and juniors' outerwear. Also, extensive commuting to New York 17, 19 (New York City).

The Voters

Registration 502,570 total. 175,066 D (35%); 248,886 R (53%); 3,377 L (1%); 13,377 C (3%); 61,864 other (12%).

Employment profile White collar, 50%. Blue collar, 50%.

Ethnic groups Black, 5%. Total foreign stock, 33%. Italy, 8%; Germany, 5%; UK, 3%; Ireland, Poland, USSR, 2% each; Austria, Czech., Hungary, Norway, Sweden, Canada, 1% each; others, 4%.

Presidential vote

1968	Humphrey (D)	67,366	(35%)*
	Nixon (R)	112,403	(58%)
	Wallace (AIP)	13,606	(7%)

** These figures do not include votes Humphrey received on the Liberal line. His performance, therefore, is understated by one to five percent in each New York district.*

Representative

James R. Grover, Jr. (R) Elected 1962; b. March 5, 1919, Babylon; Hofstra Col., B.A., 1941; Columbia U., LL.B., 1949; Army Air Corps, WWII; married, four children; Catholic.

Career Practicing atty., 1951– ; N.Y. Assembly, 1957–62; Sp. Counsel, Babylon.

Offices 1234 LHOB, 202-225-3335. Also 1801 Argyle Square, Babylon 11702, 516-669-1028.

Committees

Merchant Marine and Fisheries (4th); Subs. (1) Coast Guard, Coast and Geodetic Survey and Navigation, (2) Merchant Marine, (3) Panama Canal.

Public Works (2nd); Subs. (1) Flood Control and Internal Development, (2) Investigation and Oversight, (3) Public Buildings and Grounds, (4) Rivers and Harbors, (5) Watershed Development.

Group Ratings

	ADA	COPE	NREP	NFU	LCV	CFA	NAB	NSI	ACA
1970	12	10	17	25	50	60	100	100	75
1969	13	—	—	15	—	—	—	—	81
1968	17	23	—	40	—	—	100	—	78

Key Votes

(1) ABM	FOR	(6) 18-Yr-Vote	AGN	(11) Clean Water $	AGN
(2) SST	FOR	(7) Farm Sub Lmt	FOR	(12) Mig Wrkrs Comp	AGN
(3) Phil Pln	AGN	(8) Coop-Church	AGN	(13) Jets to Chiang	ABS
(4) No-Knock	ABS	(9) Family Asst	AGN	(14) State OEO Veto	FOR
(5) Cmutr Tax	AGN	(10) Work Stamps	FOR	(15) Park Logging	AGN

Election Results

1970 general:	James R. Grover (R and C)	107,433	(66%)
	Harvey M. Sherman (D and L)	54,996	(34%)
1970 primary:	James R. Grover (R and C), unopposed (Redistricted 1970)		

THIRD DISTRICT Political Background

New York 3 comprises most of Long Island's North Shore in Nassau County, and part of adjacent Queens, in New York City. The North Shore is the wealthiest part of Long Island. There are huge estates in the WASP towns like Locust Valley, Old Westbury, and Theodore Roosevelt's Oyster Bay. The estate of one Jay Gatsby, so F. Scott Fitzgerald tells us, was also somewhere on the North Shore. The streets of WASP Manhasset and Jewish Great Neck are lined with comfortable homes. There are a few poor areas to the south, such as predominantly black New Cassel, but most of the rest of the district is solidly middle-class. The 3rd, unlike most of Long Island, has a significant liberal voting bloc. These are wealthy people with a sense of *noblesse oblige*. A liberal Democrat can run well among the rich, but a liberal Republican far better. Little Neck and Glen Oaks, in Queens, are middle-class and more conventionally Republican.

Democrat Lester L. Wolff of the 3rd is by far the most liberal of Long Island's congressmen. He has long opposed the Vietnam war. Wolff was a successful Great Neck businessman when, in 1964, he challenged the district's Steven B. Derounian, an arch-conservative who had been the district's congressman since 1952. As it turned out, Derounian was a conservative who was done in by the nomination of Barry Goldwater, a man the Congressman very much admired. Wolff won the election by 2,620 votes and survived Derounian's comeback attempt in 1966 by 837 votes. In both elections he had the support of many of the district's liberal Republicans. In 1968 and in 1970, the Republicans put up nominees who were more liberal, but they were weakened by separate Conservative party candidates. Both times the Conservatives took 8% of the votes, while Wolff won just over 50%.

Althought Wolff's pluralities look fairly substantial, the Congressman could be seriously hurt by redistricting. The 1970 census indicates that part of conservative Suffolk County will have to be added to one of Nassau County's districts, and much more of Queens', to another. If the Republican legislature adds either area to Wolff's district, he will face a group of voters far more conservative than those to which he has become accustomed. A challenger with the support of both the Republicans and Conservatives could beat Wolff in 1972.

Census Data 1970 pop. 447,780; deviation from current state average, +0.6%; change 1960–70, +10.6%. Metro. 100%, 19.2% central city.

1970 Share of Federal Outlays $602,511,000 (average outlay per district, New York 1–5)

DOD	$220,753,000	HEW	$96,802,000
AEC	$14,733,000	HUD	$1,585,000
NASA	$53,181,000	OEO	$534,000
DOT	$11,513,000	DOA	$2,051,000
		Other	$201,357,000

Federal Military-Industrial Commitments (See New York 1 for Long Island listing.)

Economic Base Electrical machinery, equipment, and supplies, esp. communication equipment; printing, publishing, and allied industries, esp. commercial printing; nonelectrical machinery; fabricated metal products, esp. fabricated structural metal products. Also, extensive commuting to New York 17, 19 (New York City).

The Voters

Registration 211,349 total. 84,377 D (40%); 92,442 R (44%); 2,247 L (1%); 2,829 C (1%); 29,454 other (14%).

Employment profile White collar, 59%. Blue collar, 41%.

Ethnic groups Black, 4%. Total foreign stock, 41%. Italy, 9%; Germany, USSR, 5% aech; Poland, UK, 4% each; Ireland, 3%; Austria, 2%; Czech., Hungary, Norway Sweden, Canada, 1% each; others, 5%.

Presidential vote

1968	Humphrey (D)	84,742	(45%)*
	Nixon (R)	96,635	(51%)
	Wallace (AIP)	7,655	(4%)

Representative

Lester Lionel Wolff (D) Elected 1964; b. Jan. 4, 1919, New York City; home, Great Neck; N.Y.U., 1939; Army Air Corps, WWII; married, two children; Jewish.

Career Head, Marketing Dept., Collegiate Inst., 1945–49; Chm. of Bd., Coordinated Marketing Agency, 1945–64; Bd. Mbr., Madison Life Insurance Co.; TV moderator, producer, "Between the Lines," 1948–60; Mbr., U.S. Trade Mission to Philippines, 1962, Malaysia and Hong Kong, 1963.

Offices 403 CHOB, 202-225-5956. Also 156 A Main St., Port Washington 11050, 516-767-4343.

Committees

Foreign Affairs (15th); Subs. (1) Asian and Pacific Affairs, (2) Foreign Economic Policy, (3) Near East.

Veterans' Affairs (16th); Subs. (1) Hospitals, (2) Insurance.

** These figures do not include votes Humphrey received on the Liberal line. His performance, therefore, is understated by one to five percent in each New York district.*

Group Ratings

	ADA	COPE	NREP	NFU	LCV	CFA	NAB	NSI	ACA
1970	84	92	93	92	100	69	0	10	27
1969	80	—	—	80	—	—	—	—	29
1968	75	83	—	81	—	—	50	—	17

Key Votes

(1) ABM	ABS	(6) 18-Yr-Vote	FOR	(11) Clean Water $	FOR
(2) SST	AGN	(7) Farm Sub Lmt	FOR	(12) Mig Wrkrs Comp	FOR
(3) Phil Pln	ABS	(8) Coop-Church	FOR	(13) Jets to Chiang	FOR
(4) No-Knock	FOR	(9) Family Asst	FOR	(14) State OEO Veto	AGN
(5) Cmutr Tax	FOR	(10) Work Stamps	AGN	(15) Park Logging	AGN

Election Results

1970 general:	Lester L. Wolff (D and L)	94,414	(54%)
	Raymond J. Rice (R and Environment)	66,196	(38%)
	Lola Camardi (C)	12,925	(8%)
1970 primary:	Lester L. Wolff (D and L), unopposed (Redistricted 1970)		

FOURTH DISTRICT Political Background

New York 4, a classic suburban district, stretches across the middle of Nassau County, taking in Garden City, Hempstead, Valley Stream, East Meadow, and Levittown. Most of these suburbs were laid out during the '30's, but had few people in them until after World War II. It was then that the great Nassau County population boom began. People who had grown up on the streets of Brooklyn and the Bronx moved out to subdivisions claimed from Long Island potato fields. And soon Levittown earned a spot beside Oshkosh as a place beneath the contempt of all good intellectuals. But Levittown, to people used to Brownsville or Jackson Heights, looked pretty good. The Nassau boom stopped in the early '60's; all the subdivisions were by then filled. The homeowners, with their mortgages paid off, built additions to their small houses.

The Nassau County phenomenon led sociologists to declare that people became Republicans the moment they became suburbanites. But these increasingly prosperous voters would have probably become Republican even if they had stayed in the City (see state write up). Today Nassau, whose population has become stable, is still Republican, but it is markedly less conservative than rapidly growing and changing Suffolk County farther out on Long Island.

John W. Wydler, a middle-of-the-road Republican, has represented the district since it was created in 1962. The importance of space-related defense industry in the 4th is reflected in Wydler's membership on the Science and Astronautics Committee. The Congressman seems to be well-known and well-liked in the district; he has had no trouble winning reelection, even in the Johnson landslide year of 1964. The 1970 redistricting increased the number of Democrats in the 4th, but he still won a solid 57% of the votes, while his Democratic opponent took 35% and the Conservative candidate, 8%. Republican redistricters will no doubt make sure that Wydler will continue to have a safe seat for the rest of the '70's.

Census Data 1970 pop. 426,676; deviation from current state average, 4.0%; change 1960–70, +3.2%. Metro. 100%, 0.0% central city.

1970 Share of Federal Outlays $602,511,000 (average outlay per district, New York 1–5)

DOD	$220,753,000	HEW	$96,802,000
AEC	$14,733,000	HUD	$1,585,000
NASA	$53,181,000	OEO	$534,000
DOT	$11,513,000	DOA	$2,051,000
		Other	$201,357,000

Federal Military-Industrial Commitments (See New York 1 for Long Island listing.)

Economic Base Electrical machinery, equipment, and supplies, esp. communication equipment; printing, publishing, and allied industries, esp. commercial printing; nonelectrical machinery; fabricated metal products, esp. fabricated structural metal products. Also, extensive commuting to New York 17, 19 (New York City); higher education (Hofstra University).

The Voters

Registration 195,503 total. 65,600 D (34%); 106,811 R (55%); 1,336 L (1%); 1,965 C (1%); 19,791 other (10%).

Employment profile White collar, 59%. Blue collar, 41%.

Ethnic groups Black, 5%. Total foreign stock, 40%. Italy, 9%; USSR, 6%; Germany, 5%; Ireland, Poland, UK, 3% each; Austria, 2%; Czech., Hungary, Norway, Sweden, Canada, 1% each; others, 5%.

Presidential vote

1968	Humphrey (D)	73,331	(40%)*
	Nixon (R)	101,605	(56%)
	Wallace (AIP)	9,553	(5%)

Representative

John W. Wydler (R) Elected 1962; b. June 9, 1924, Brooklyn; home, Garden City; Brown U., 1941–42, 1945–47; Harvard Law School, LL.B., 1950; Army, WWII; USAFR; married, three children; Episcopalian.

Career Practicing atty., 1950– ; U.S. Atty.'s Office, 1953–59; Mbr., N.Y. State Investigation Commission to probe N.Y.C. school construction irregularities, 1959–60.

Offices 2444 RHOB, 202-225-5516. Also 150 Old Country Rd., Mineola, Long Island 11501, 516-248-7676.

Committees

Government Operations (5th); Subs. (1) Legislation and Military Operations, (2) Special Studies.

Science and Astronautics (5th); Subs. (1) Advanced Research and Technology, (2) NASA Oversight.

Group Ratings

	ADA	COPE	NREP	NFU	LCV	CFA	NAB	NSI	ACA
1970	56	60	50	69	71	83	75	89	58
1969	47	—	—	60	—	—	—	—	64
1968	33	50	—	43	—	—	100	—	62

Key Votes

(1) ABM	FOR	(6) 18-Yr-Vote	FOR	(11) Clean Water $	FOR
(2) SST	AGN	(7) Farm Sub Lmt	FOR	(12) Mig Wrkrs Comp	FOR
(3) Phil Pln	FOR	(8) Coop-Church	AGN	(13) Jets to Chiang	FOR
(4) No-Knock	FOR	(9) Family Asst	FOR	(14) State OEO Veto	AGN
(5) Cmutr Tax	ABS	(10) Work Stamps	AGN	(15) Park Logging	AGN

Election Results

1970 general:	John W. Wydler (R)	91,787	(57%)
	Karen S. Burstein (D and L)	56,411	(35%)
	Donald A. Derham (C)	12,701	(8%)
1970 primary:	John W. Wydler (R), unopposed		
	(Redistricted 1970)		

* *These figures do not include votes Humphrey received on the Liberal line. His performance, therefore, is understated by one to five percent in each New York district.*

FIFTH DISTRICT Political Background

New York 5 is the South Shore of Long Island, a series of towns which lie along the Sunrise Highway—Lynbrook, Rockville Centre, Oceanside, Freeport, Merrick, Wantagh, Seaford, and Massapequa. The 5th also takes in a stretch of the Atlantic Coast, separated from the rest of the district by swampy Hempstead Bay, including Long Beach and Jones Beach, the huge state park built by Robert Moses in the '30's. The Sunrise Highway leads out of and into Brooklyn, and many of the residents of the 5th are Brooklyn natives, with the borough's many ethnic strains represented in the towns of the district. Most of the towns to the west have substantial Jewish populations, which cast most of the 5th's liberal Democratic vote. To the east there are more Italians and Irish, notably more conservative and Republican. Long Beach, across the causeway on the Atlantic, is heavily Jewish and Democratic.

From 1968 to 1970, the 5th's congressman was Allard Lowenstein, currently ADA Chairman, who has been an activist in many liberal causes for some time. During 1967, Lowenstein, who had many contacts in the universities and various liberal circles, helped to organize the country's antiwar groups. He then tried to persuade Sen. Robert F. Kennedy to run against Lyndon Johnson. When this failed, he helped to draw Sen. Eugene McCarthy into the race. Lowenstein was as responsible as anyone for Johnson's decision to step down.

In 1968, Lowenstein, a Manhattan resident, decided to run for Congress in the 5th district. Since the Democratic incumbent, wealthy businessman Herbert Tenzer, was retiring, the seat looked a good bet. With the help of student volunteers who canvassed practically the entire district, Lowenstein defeated the organization candidate in the Democratic primary. The Republican primary was won by a registered Conservative, Mason Hampton. So the general election became a fierce battle of ideological opposites, an election that Lowenstein won by 2,766 votes.

In 1970, the Republican legislature removed the heavily Jewish and Democratic five towns, near Queens, from the 5th, and added Massapequa, where many New York policemen live. Their objective was to unseat Lowenstein and they succeeded. He was one of two incumbent Democrats in the nation to lose to a Republican in 1970. The election results show that Lowenstein would have won in his old district, but in the district as it was redrawn, he took only 47%. The Congressman's defeat was hardly a repudiation of the peace movement, but no victory either.

Lowenstein's successor, Republican Norman Lent, made his political reputation in the state Senate where he sponsored a bill to prohibit busing to achieve racial balance in the state's schools. He is one of the more conservative Republicans in the New York House delegation. Since his old state Senate district includes the more Democratic portions of the 5th, he will probably run much better in 1972 than he did against Lowenstein in 1968. The Congressman will also get some help from the Republican redistricters who will alter the district lines to his liking.

Census Data 1970 pop. 474,533; deviation from current state average, +4.1%; change 1960–70, +15.9%. Metro. 100%, 0.0% central city.

1970 Share of Federal Outlays $602,511,000 (average outlay per district, New York 1–5)

DOD	$220,753,000	HEW	$96,802,000
AEC	$14,733,000	HUD	$1,585,000
NASA	$53,181,000	OEO	$534,000
DOT	$11,513,000	DOA	$2,051,000
		Other	$201,357,000

Federal Military-Industrial Commitments (See New York 1 for Long Island listing.)

Economic Base Electrical machinery, equipment, and supplies, esp. communication equipment; printing, publishing, and allied industries, esp. commercial printing; nonelectrical machinery; fabricated metal products, esp. fabricated structural metal products. Also, extensive commuting to New York 17, 19 (New York City).

The Voters

Registration 214,426 total. 81,491 D (38%); 104,339 R (49%); 1,609 L (1%); 3,958 C (2%); 32,029 other. (11%).

Employment profile White collar, 58%. Blue collar, 42%.
Ethnic groups Black, 6%. Total foreign stock, 38%. Italy, 8%; Germany, USSR, 5% each; Austria, Ireland, Poland, UK, 3% each; Hungary, Norway, Sweden, Canada, 1% each; others, 5%.
Presidential vote

1968	Humphrey (D)	82,551	(41%)*
	Nixon (R)	106,987	(53%)
	Wallace (AIP)	10,713	(5%)

Representative

Norman Frederick Lent (R) Elected 1970; b. March 23, 1931, Oceanside; home, East Rockaway; Hofstra Col., B.A., 1952; Cornell U. Law School, LL.B., 1957; USNR, 1952–54; married, three children; Methodist.

Career Practicing atty.; Asst. Police Justice, East Rockaway, N.Y., 1960–62; N.Y. State Senate, 1962–70.

Offices 1230 LHOB, 202-225-7896. Also County Fed. Savings and Loan Bldg., 53 North Park Ave., Rockville Centre 11572, 516-536-2121.

Committees

Banking and Currency (13th); Subs. (1) Bank Supervision and Insurance, (2) International Finance, (3) International Trade.

Group Ratings, Key Votes: Newly elected.

Election Results

1970 general:	Norman F. Lent (R and C)	93,824	(53%)
	Allard K. Lowenstein (D and L)	84,738	(47%)
1970 primary:	Norman F. Lent (R and C), unopposed (Redistricted 1970)		

SIXTH DISTRICT Political Background

New York 6 is part of Queens, long recognized as the most conservative of New York City's four large boroughs. The traditionally Republican residents of Queens—Irish, German, and Italian homeowners—have never had much regard for Manhattan, "the City" as it is known locally. But Queens has far fewer Republican voters now than it had before the great suburban migration took many of them to Long Island. The 6th does, however, continue to reelect liberal Republican Congressman Seymour Halpern. Former state Sen. Halpern had more than a little to do with the peculiar shape of the district, which manages to take in the rather widely separated Republican neighborhoods of Bayside, Flushing, Forest Hills, Hollis, and Queens Village.

Halpern was first elected to Congress in 1958. He is one of the most liberal Republicans in the House, but lately, with the growing strength of the Conservative party, he has not advertised his voting record with much vigor. In 1970, the Congressman stayed neutral in the race between James Buckley and his old colleague Charles Goodell. His own race was simplified by a deal made between Queens' Democratic and Republican organizations; his only opponent was a Conservative candidate who polled 23%.

Halpern got some headlines in 1969. The *Wall Street Journal* charged that he received loans totaling nearly $100,000 from various banks without collateral. Some suspected that this sort of thing occurs only when the borrower happens to be the 3rd-ranking Republican on the House Banking and Currency Committee. Halpern has since left Banking and Currency for a low seniority post on Foreign Affairs. The suspicions generated by the Congressman's financial dealings do not seem to have hurt him among the voters of the 6th. Halpern campaigns constantly and makes liberal use of congressional mailing privileges. Moreover, because Republican redistricters will treat Halpern kindly, the Congressman will remain in the House for many years to come.

Census Data 1970 pop. 414,804; deviation from current state average, —6.7%; change 1960–70, +1.8%. Metro. 100%, 100% central city.

* *These figures do not include votes Humphrey received on the Liberal line. His performance, therefore, is understated by one to five percent in each New York district.*

1970 Share of Federal Outlays $565,470,000 (average outlay per district, New York 6–24)

DOD	$76,898,000	HEW	$154,742,000
AEC	$739,000	HUD	$2,744,000
NASA	$921,000	OEO	$2,012,000
DOT	$6,423,000	DOA	$42,872,000
		Other	$334,666,000

Federal Military-Industrial Commitments (See New York 17 for New York City listing.)

Economic Base Electrical machinery, equipment, and supplies, esp. radio, transmitting, signaling, and detection equipment and apparatus; food and kindred products; apparel and other finished products made from fabrics and similar materials, esp. women's, misses', and juniors' outerwear; fabricated metal products. Also, higher education (CUNY, Queens, and St. John's University).

The Voters

Registration 202,384 total. 118,132 D (58%); 58,128 R (29%); 3,844 L (2%); 4,797 C (2%); 17,483 other (9%).

Employment profile White collar, 60%. Blue collar, 40%.

Ethnic groups Black, 5%. Puerto Rico, 1%. Total foreign stock, 50%. Italy, 9%; Germany, 8%; USSR, 6%; Ireland, Poland, 5% each; UK, 4%; Austria, 3%; Czech., Hungary, Sweden, Canada, 1% each; others, 7%.

Presidential vote

1968	Humphrey (D)	74,447	(47%)*
	Nixon (R)	76,226	(48%)
	Wallace (AIP)	9,043	(6%)

Representative

Seymour Halpern (R-Lib.) Elected 1958; b. Nov. 19, 1913, New York City; home, Jamaica; Columbia U., 1932–34; married; Jewish.

Career Insurance business; V.P., John C. Paige & Co., reporter, L.I. Daily Press, 1931–32; feature writer, Chicago Herald-Examiner, 1932–33; Staff Asst., Mayor Fiorello H. LaGuardia, 1937; Asst. to Pres., N.Y.C. Council, 1938–40, N.Y. Senate, 1941–54.

Offices 2236 RHOB, 202-225-2536. Also 89-31 161st St., Jamaica 11432, 212-658-0300.

Committees

Foreign Affairs (14th); Subs. (1) Asian and Pacific Affairs, (2) International Organizations, (3) Near East.

Group Ratings

	ADA	COPE	NREP	NFU	LCV	CFA	NAB	NSI	ACA
1970	76	82	93	100	80	94	9	30	22
1969	73	—	—	71	—	—	—	—	0
1968	83	92	—	87	—	—	17	—	9

Key Votes

(1) ABM	AGN	(6) 18-Yr-Vote	FOR	(11) Clean Water $	FOR
(2) SST	AGN	(7) Farm Sub Lmt	ABS	(12) Mig Wrkrs Comp	FOR
(3) Phil Pln	FOR	(8) Coop-Church	FOR	(13) Jets to Chiang	AGN
(4) No-Knock	ABS	(9) Family Asst	FOR	(14) State OEO Veto	AGN
(5) Cmutr Tax	ABS	(10) Work Stamps	AGN	(15) Park Logging	AGN

* *These figures do not include votes Humphrey received on the Liberal line. His performance, therefore, is understated by one to five percent in each New York district.*

Election Results

1970 general:	Seymour Halpern (R and L)	89,250	(77%)
	John J. Flynn (C)	26,244	(23%)
1970 primary:	Seymour Halpern (R and L), unopposed (Redistricted 1970)		

SEVENTH DISTRICT Political Background

New York 7, in southern Queens, comprises a series of neighborhoods of varying ethnic compositions. The homes here are one and two family houses. The 7th also includes the John F. Kennedy Airport and the Rockaway Peninsula south of Jamaica Bay. Blacks make up about 30% of the district's population; most of them live in the middle-class communities of South Jamaica, St. Albans, and South Ozone Park. There is a Jewish section in Laurelton, adjacent to Nassau County's five towns, and a fair number of Italians in Ozone Park, near the Brooklyn line. Most of the rest of the 7th is typical of Queens; neat neighborhoods of lower-middle-class Irish, Italians, and Germans.

While the 7th is probably more Democratic than Republican, it is also more conservative than liberal: Mayor Lindsay did poorly here in 1969 in spite of the large black population, and Sen. James Buckley proved to be quite popular. In congressional elections, the district has backed moderate-to-liberal Democrat Joseph P. Addabbo since 1960. Addabbo has combined a mild opposition to the Vietnam war with strong support for anticrime measures. The Congressman's vehement opposition to the SST came as a surprise to many, but it was undoubtedly shared by many of his constituents who own homes near Kennedy Airport. Addabbo's formula has won him more than 60% of the votes in the last four elections, and no matter how much the Republican legislature alters the 7th in redistricting, chances are Addabbo will win reelection through the '70's.

Census Data 1970 pop. 503,343; deviation from current state average, +13.1%; change 1960–70, 21.8%. Metro. 100%, 100% central city.

1970 Share of Federal Outlays $565,470,000 (average outlay per district, New York 6–24)

DOD	$76,898,000	HEW	$154,742,000
AEC	$739,000	HUD	-$2,744,000
NASA	$921,000	OEO	$2,012,000
DOT	$6,423,000	DOA	$42,872,000
		Other	$334,666,000

Federal Military-Industrial Commitments (See New York 17 for New York City listing.)

Economic Base Electrical machinery, equipment, and supplies, esp. radio and television transmitting, signaling, and detection equipment and apparatus; food and kindred products; apparel and other finished products made from fabrics and other similar materials, esp. women's, misses', and juniors' outerwear; fabricated metal products.

The Voters

Registration 199,292 total. 132,799 D (71%); 37,110 R (20%); 4,099 L (2%); 3,686 C (2%); 10,598 other (6%).

Employment profile White collar, 42%. Blue collar, 58%.

Ethnic groups Black, 37%. Puerto Rico, 1%. Total foreign stock, 41%. Italy, 11%; Germany, 9%; Ireland, Poland, 3% each; Austria, UK, USSR, 2% each; Hungary, Canada, 1% each; others, 7%.

Presidential vote

1968	Humphrey (D)	88,737	(58%)*
	Nixon (R)	54,829	(36%)
	Wallace (AIP)	9,148	(6%)

* *These figures do not include votes Humphrey received on the Liberal line. His performance, therefore, is understated by one to five percent in each New York district.*

Representative

Joseph P. Addabbo (D-Lib.) Elected 1960; b. March 17, 1925, Queens; home, Ozone Park; City Col. of N.Y., 1942–44; St. John's Law School, LL.B., 1946; married, three children; Catholic.

Career Practicing atty., 1946– .

Offices 2440 RHOB, 202-225-3461. Also 96-11 101st Ave., Ozone Park Office, 212-849-6625.

Committees

Appropriations (18th); Subs. (1) Defense, (2) Treasury, Post Office and General Government.

Sel. Com. on Small Business (8th); Subs. (1) Chm., Minority Small Business Enterprise, (2) Government Procurement, (3) Special Small Business Problems.

Group Ratings

	ADA	COPE	NREP	NFU	LCV	CFA	NAB	NSI	ACA
1970	80	92	83	100	78	89	8	33	12
1969	80	—	—	86	—	—	—	—	33
1968	75	100	—	94	—	—	33	—	17

Key Votes

(1) ABM	AGN	(6) 18-Yr-Vote	FOR	(11) Clean Water $	FOR
(2) SST	AGN	(7) Farm Sub Lmt	FOR	(12) Mig Wrkrs Comp	FOR
(3) Phil Pln	AGN	(8) Coop-Church	FOR	(13) Jets to Chiang	AGN
(4) No-Knock	AGN	(9) Family Asst	FOR	(14) State OEO Veto	AGN
(5) Cmutr Tax	FOR	(10) Work Stamps	AGN	(15) Park Logging	AGN

Election Results

1970 general:	Joseph P. Addabbo (R, D and L)	112,983	(91%)
	Christopher T. Acer (C)	11,515	(9%)
1970 primary:	Joseph P. Addabbo (R, D and L), unopposed (Redistricted 1970)		

EIGHTH DISTRICT Political Background

New York 8, in central Queens, owes its grotesque shape to the efforts of the Republican legislature to assure that the adjacent 6th district continues to elect a Republican congressman. The 8th takes in the old Irish neighborhoods of Whitestone and College Point on Long Island Sound; parts of Flushing, Elmhurst, Forest Hills, and predominantly black Corona; and, on the Brooklyn line to the south, the conservative neighborhoods of Glendale and Ridgewood. The district includes the major tourist attractions in Queens: Shea Stadium, home of the baseball Mets and the football Jets, and Flushing Meadow Park, site of the 1939 and 1964 World Fairs. There is a booming apartment and shopping center complex along Queens Boulevard. The 8th was one of the few districts in New York City to gain population during the '60's, largely because of the construction of huge new apartment complexes like Lefrak City, which holds 25,000 people.

The 8th has a larger Jewish population than any other district in Queens, centered around Flushing Meadow Park. It is consequently the most liberal district in the borough, in spite of the addition of conservative Glendale and Ridgewood in the 1970 redistricting. Liberal Democrat Benjamin S. Rosenthal, congressman from the 8th since 1962, took an impressive 63% in 1970.

Rosenthal is part of the minority on the House Foreign Affairs Committee that has opposed Nixon's Vietnam policies. He is also a member of the Government Operations Committee, where, as one of Washington's leading advocates of consumer legislation, the New Yorker finds himself frustrated by the way the House conducts its business. In 1970, his consumer bill was blocked by the House Rules Committee when Congressman Richard Bolling (see Missouri 5), on vacation in the Caribbean, refused to fly back to break a tie vote; and in 1971, Rosenthal lost his subcommittee position. The Congressman has hired student interns, known as Rosenthal's Roustabouts, to conduct Ralph Nader-style investigations.

In redistricting, the Republican legislature will probably devote itself to preserving Republican Seymour Halpern's seat in the 6th. This means that the 8th will remain strongly liberal and Democratic and that Rosenthal will continue to win reelection.

Census Data 1970 pop. 474,795; deviation from current state average, +6.7%; change 1960–70, +15.1%. Metro. 100%, 99.8% central city.

1970 Share of Federal Outlays $565,470,000 (average outlay per district, New York 6–24)

DOD	$76,898,000	HEW	$154,742,000
AEC	$739,000	HUD	$2,744,000
NASA	$921,000	OEO	$2,012,000
DOT	$6,423,000	DOA	$42,872,000
		Other	$334,666,000

Federal Military-Industrial Commitments (See New York 17 for New York City listing.)

Economic Base Electrical machinery, equipment, and supplies, esp. radio and television transmitting, signaling, and detection equipment and apparatus; food and kindred products; apparel and other finished products made from fabrics and similar materials, esp. women's, misses', and juniors' outerwear; fabricated metal products, esp. fabricated structural metal products.

The Voters

Registration 215,130 total. 142,922 D (66%); 444,641 R (21%); 4,622 L (2%); 4,321 C (2%); 18,624 other (9%).

Employment profile White collar, 57%. Blue collar, 43%.

Ethnic groups Black, 6%. Puerto Rico, 1%; Total foreign stock, 57%. Italy, USSR, 11% each; Poland, 7%; Germany, 6%; Austria, 4%; Ireland, 3%; Hungary, UK, 2% each; Czech., Canada, 1% each; others, 9%.

Presidential vote

1968	Humphrey (D)	94,085	(52%)*
	Nixon (R)	77,066	(42%)
	Wallace (AIP)	10,468	(6%)

Representative

Benjamin S. Rosenthal (D-Lib.) Elected 1962; b. June 8, 1923, New York City; home, Elmhurst, L.I.; Brooklyn Col., LL.B., 1949; New York U., LL.M., 1952; Army, WWII; married, two children; Jewish.

Career Practicing atty., 1949– .

Offices 2453 RHOB, 202-225-2601. Also GPO Bldg., 41-65 Main St., Flushing, L.I. 11351, 212-939-8200.

Committees

Foreign Affairs (11th); Subs. (1) Chm., Europe, (2) Inter-American Affairs, (3) International Organizations and Movements.

Government Operations (14th); Subs. (1) Intergovernmental Relations, (2) Legislation and Military Operations.

Group Ratings

	ADA	COPE	NREP	NFU	LCV	CFA	NAB	NSI	ACA
1970	96	100	100	92	88	100	0	0	17
1969	93	—	—	86	—	—	—	—	13
1968	100	100	—	82	—	—	0	—	6

* *These figures do not include votes Humphrey received on the Liberal line. His performance, therefore, is understated by one to five percent in each New York district.*

Key Votes

(1) ABM	AGN	(6) 18-Yr-Vote	FOR	(11) Clean Water $	FOR
(2) SST	AGN	(7) Farm Sub Lmt	FOR	(12) Mig Wrkrs Comp	FOR
(3) Phil Pln	FOR	(8) Coop-Church	FOR	(13) Jets to Chiang	AGN
(4) No-Knock	AGN	(9) Family Asst	FOR	(14) State OEO Veto	AGN
(5) Cmutr Tax	FOR	(10) Work Stamps	AGN	(15) Park Logging	ABS

Election Results

1970 general:	Benjamin Rosenthal (D and L)	93,666	(63%)
	Cosmo J. Di Tucci (R and C)	55,406	(37%)
1970 primary:	Benjamin Rosenthal (D and L), unopposed (Redistricted 1970)		

NINTH DISTRICT Political Background

New York 9, at the western end of Queens, is made up of lower-middle-class residential neighborhoods like Astoria and Jackson Heights, and industrial Long Island City and Maspeth. The 9th has more Irish than any other New York district, as well as large populations of Italians and Germans. It also contains more heavy industry than any other district in the city. The neighborhoods in the shadows of the giant factories suffer from many common urban problems—decaying housing, air pollution, and a rising crime rate. The residents of the traditionally Democratic 9th have responded by becoming increasingly conservative. This is in part due to the peculiarities of New York politics. Liberalism is personified, for these people, by Mayor Lindsay, a WASP from Manhattan's stylish Upper East Side, and by the blacks who support him. This combination of the oldest and the newest enemies of the white ethnic groups has had tremendous impact in the 9th.

The increasing conservatism of the people here is measured by the recent electoral performances of the Democrat who represents the district, James J. Delaney. Delaney polled just over 50% in the three- and four-candidate races of 1966 and 1968. And Delaney is hardly a raving liberal. Quite the contrary. As a member of the House Rules Committee, he held up federal aid to education in the early '60's because no provision was made to aid Catholic schools. More recently, the Congressman has opposed welfare and mass transit legislation.

In 1970, Delaney publicly endorsed Conservative party Senate candidate, James Buckley. The endorsement may have been part of a deal between the Republican and Democratic organizations in Queens, the terms of which left incumbents in three of the borough's four districts (New York 6, 7, and 9) without major party opposition. Delaney's only challenger was a Liberal party candidate who won just 8% of the votes. Delaney's endorsement of Buckley probably indicates that Republicans and Conservatives will not give the Democrat much trouble, so long as he maintains a conservative voting record. But the Congressman was 69 in 1970, and once he decides to retire or for some other reason is not the incumbent, a Republican-Conservative could carry the 9th. The Republican legislature will no doubt lay the groundwork for that victory in their redistricting efforts.

Census Data 1970 pop. 419,610; deviation from current state average, −6.29%; change 1960–70, +2.3%. Metro. 100%, 100% central city.

1970 Share of Federal Outlays $565,470,000 (average outlay per district, New York 6–24)

DOD	$76,898,000	HEW	$154,742,000
AEC	$739,000	HUD	$2,744,000
NASA	$921,000	OEO	$2,012,000
DOT	$6,423,000	DOA	$42,872,000
		Other	$334,666,000

Federal Military-Industrial Commitments (See New York 17 for New York City listing.)

Economic Base Electrical equipment, machinery, and supplies, esp. radio and television transmitting, signaling, and detection equipment and apparatus; food and kindred products; apparel and other finished products made from fabrics and similar materials, esp. women's, misses', and juniors' outerwear; fabricated metal products, esp. fabricated structural metal products.

The Voters

Registration 181,347 total. 112,255 D (62%); 45,853 R (25%); 5,556 L (3%); 4,882 C (3%); 12,801 other (7%).

Employment profile White collar, 51%. Blue collar, 49%.

Ethnic groups Black, 3%. Puerto Rico, 2%. Total foreign stock, 59%. Italy, 14%; Ireland, 8%; Germany, 6%; Poland, UK, USSR, 4% each; Austria, 3%; Czech., Hungary, 2% each; Canada, 1%; others, 11%.

Presidential vote

1968	Humphrey (D)	60,280	(41%)*
	Nixon (R)	73,002	(50%)
	Wallace (AIP)	12,029	(8%)

Representative

James J. Delaney (D) Elected 1945; b. March 19, 1901, New York City; home, Long Island City; St. John's U., LL.B., 1932; married, one son; Catholic.

Career Asst. Dist. Atty., Queens County, 1936–44.

Offices 2267 RHOB, 202-225-3965. Also 40-10 82nd St., Jackson Heights 11373, 212-898-5065.

Committees

Rules (3rd).

Group Ratings

	ADA	COPE	NREP	NFU	LCV	CFA	NAB	NSI	ACA
1970	40	75	40	85	72	82	27	75	47
1969	40	—	—	67	—	—	—	—	46
1968	50	83	—	94	—	—	50	—	36

Key Votes

(1) ABM	ABS	(6) 18-Yr-Vote	FOR	(11) Clean Water $	FOR
(2) SST	FOR	(7) Farm Sub Lmt	FOR	(12) Mig Wrkrs Comp	FOR
(3) Phil Pln	ABS	(8) Coop-Church	AGN	(13) Jets to Chiang	AGN
(4) No-Knock	FOR	(9) Family Asst	AGN	(14) State OEO Veto	AGN
(5) Cmutr Tax	FOR	(10) Work Stamps	AGN	(15) Park Logging	AGN

Election Results

1970 general:	James J. Delaney (R, D, and C)	102,205	(92%)
	Rose L. Rubin (L)	9,025	(8%)
1970 primary:	James J. Delaney (R, D, and C), unopposed (Redistricted 1970)		

TENTH DISTRICT Political Background

New York 10 is the heart of Brooklyn: Flatbush and East Flatbush. A glance at a roadmap will show how Queens and Long Island differ from Brooklyn. The newer suburban terrain is crisscrossed by freeways; Brooklyn has only one, running along its shore. Most of this borough was laid out and occupied before the automobile became a necessity: one and two family homes, miles of low-rise apartment houses, and

* These figures do not include votes Humphrey received on the Liberal line. His performance, therefore, is understated by one to five percent in each New York district.

clusters of retail stores at the major intersections. Brooklyn's population has grown little since the 1930 census.

In the 1910's and 1920's, the new neighborhoods of Flatbush attracted the increasingly prosperous Jews who had grown up in the ghettos of the Lower East Side. Today, Flatbush is still predominantly Jewish, though more and more blacks are moving in from Bedford-Stuyvesant and Crown Heights to the north. The average age here has been going up, as young people move to Long Island, Westchester, or the Upper East Side. Among the older people, there is a good deal of talk about crime. But despite these trends, Flatbush is still liberal and Democratic in its politics.

In the 1920 landslide for Warren Harding, the area which is now the 10th district elected a Republican congressman. Two years later, a young Jewish lawyer won the Democratic nomination and then unseated the incumbent by a slight majority. Since then, the Flatbush district has been altered many times by redistricting but it has always reelected Emanuel Celler as its congressman. In 1970, when Celler was 82, he had 6 more years seniority than anyone else.

Celler is the chairman of the House Judiciary Committee. In that role he reported all the civil rights legislation of the past two decades, along with many other bills including the Celler-Kefauver Anti-Merger Act of 1950. The Congressman is one of the still small number of liberal committee chairmen. He has, however, been less successful than many Southern chairmen as a floor manager. Celler, therefore, has less often gotten what he wanted.

The Congressman, who polled 73% in 1970, would have no trouble winning reelection in 1972, and thereby set an all-time record for years of service in the House. He may, however, retire to make room for a younger incumbent congressman if Brooklyn loses a seat in redistricting.

Census Data 1970 pop. 420,486; deviation from current state average, —5.5%; change 1960–70, 2.1%. Metro. 100%, 100% central city.

1970 Share of Federal Outlays $565,470,000 (average outlay per district, New York 6–24)

DOD	$76,898,000	HEW	$154,742,000
AEC	$739,000	HUD	$2,744,000
NASA	$921,000	OEO	$2,012,000
DOT	$6,423,000	DOA	$42,872,000
		Other	$334,666,000

Federal Military-Industrial Commitments (See New York 17 for New York City listing.)

Economic Base Apparel and other finished products made from fabrics and similar materials, esp. women's, misses', and juniors' outerwear; food and kindred products, esp. beverages; fabricated metal products; electrical machinery, equipment, and supplies, esp. electric lighting and wiring equipment.

The Voters

Registration 176,295 total. 130,598 D (74%); 26,955 R (15%); 5,063 L (3%); 2,671 C (2%); 176,295 other (6%).

Employment profile White collar, 41%. Blue collar, 59%.

Ethnic groups Black, 30%. Puerto Rico, 4%. Total foreign stock, 54%. USSR, 17%; Poland, 10%; Italy, 7%; Austria, 4%; Germany, Hungary, 2% each; Ireland, UK, 1% each; others, 10%.

Presidential vote

1968	Humphrey (D)	88,613	(66%)*
	Nixon (R)	41,616	(31%)
	Wallace (AIP)	4,530	(3%)

* *These figures do not include votes Humphrey received on the Liberal line. His performance, therefore, is understated by one to five percent in each New York district.*

Representative

Emanuel Celler (D-Lib.) Elected 1922; b. May 6, 1888, Brooklyn; home, Brooklyn; Columbia U., B.A., 1910, LL.B., 1912; widower, two children; Jewish.

Career Practicing atty., 1912–23.

Offices 2136 RHOB, 202-225-3531. Also 1501 Broadway, New York City 10036, 212-524-9700.

Committees

Judiciary (Chm.); Chm., Sub. No. 5.

Group Ratings

	ADA	COPE	NREP	NFU	LCV	CFA	NAB	NSI	ACA
1970	80	100	73	100	75	93	10	33	0
1969	80	—	—	86	—	—	—	—	7
1968	92	92	—	100	—	—	0	—	6

Key Votes

(1) ABM	FOR	(6) 18-Yr-Vote	FOR	(11) Clean Water $	FOR
(2) SST	AGN	(7) Farm Sub Lmt	AGN	(12) Mig Wrkrs Comp	FOR
(3) Phil Pln	FOR	(8) Coop-Church	FOR	(13) Jets to Chiang	AGN
(4) No-Knock	AGN	(9) Family Asst	FOR	(14) State OEO Veto	AGN
(5) Cmutr Tax	FOR	(10) Work Stamps	AGN	(15) Park Logging	AGN

Election Results

1970 general:	Emanuel Celler (D and L)	78,324	(73%)
	Frank J. Occhiogrosso (R and C)	29,012	(27%)
1970 primary:	Emanuel Celler (D and L), unopposed		
	(Redistricted 1970)		

ELEVENTH DISTRICT Political Background

New York 11 comprises the southeastern shore of Brooklyn, the area inland around East New York and Brownsville, and the tip of Rockaway Peninsula, in Queens. East New York is the most populous section of the district. This predominantly Italian middle-class area, lying between the slums of Brownsville and the Queens' border, is traditionally Democratic, but has become increasingly conservative; Vito P. Battista, the well-known gadfly of the United Taxpayers party, represents East New York in the state Assembly. The slums of Brownsville, the focus of the 1968 school decentralization dispute, are in such miserable condition that they are rapidly being abandoned completely. To the south, Canarsie, Flatlands, and Sheepshead Bay are all middle-income Italian and Jewish communities. These were developed on the swampy land along the shore some time after the rest of Brooklyn. In 1970, the borough's first suburban-style shopping center was opened here—an event that suggests how this area differs from the rest of Brooklyn (see New York 10).

In spite of East New York's increasing conservatism, the 11th remains heavily Democratic; it has consistently given 70% of its vote to liberal Democratic Congressman Frank J. Brasco. Brasco was first elected in 1966, when Eugene Keough, who was then just 59, retired after thirty years in the House. Keough was the 3rd ranking Democrat on the Ways and Means Committee; he might have left the House because he had no hope of ever succeeding to Wilbur Mills' chairmanship. Brasco is affiliated with the Brooklyn Democratic organization, but his liberal record and staunch opposition to the Vietnam war belies the contention of pundits who insist that the New York Democratic organization is a conservative monolith. For some reason the Liberal Party keeps running a candidate against him.

The Republican legislature could hurt Brasco badly in redistricting, with the new 11th including East New York and Canarsie; and, in Queens, the heavily conservative areas of Woodhaven, Glendale, and Ridgewood. The rest of what is now the 11th would then be divided among other Brooklyn districts. If such a district is drawn, it is a payoff to Assemblyman Battista, who, when he withdrew from the 1969 Republican mayoral primary, assured state Sen. John J. Marchi's victory over John Lindsay. Still, odds are that Brasco can win in any district the Republicans care to design; in Brooklyn, there are too many Brasco Democrats for any Republican to contend with.

Census Data 1970 pop. 442,345; deviation from current state average, —0.6%; change 1960–70, +8.9%. Metro. 100%, 100% central city.

1970 Share of Federal Outlays $565,470,000 (average outlay per district, New York 6–24)

DOD	$76,898,000	HEW	$154,742,000
AEC	$739,000	HUD	$2,744,000
NASA	$921,000	OEO	$2,012,000
DOT	$6,423,000	DOA	$42,872,000
		Other	$334,666,000

Federal Military-Industrial Commitments (See New York 17 for New York City listing.)

Economic Base Apparel and other finished products made from fabrics and similar materials, esp. women's, misses', and juniors' outerwear; food and kindred products, esp. beverages; fabricated metal products; electrical machinery, equipment, and supplies, esp. electric lighting and wiring equipment.

The Voters

Registration 154,757 total. 115,640 D (75%); 25,231 R (16%); 3,897 L (3%); 3,089 C (2%); 6,900 other (5%).

Employment profile White collar, 39%. Blue collar, 61%.

Ethnic groups Black, 28%. Puerto Rico, 8%. Total foreign stock, 46%. Italy, 14%; USSR, 10%; Poland, 6%; Austria, Germany, 3% each; Ireland, UK, 1% each; others, 8%.

Presidential vote

1968	Humphrey (D)	68,554	(60%)*
	Nixon (R)	39,466	(35%)
	Wallace (AIP)	5,784	(5%)

Representative

Frank James Brasco (D) Elected 1966; b. Oct., 15, 1932, Brooklyn; home, Brooklyn; Brooklyn Col., B.A., 1955, LL.B., 1957; Capt. USAR; married, four children; Catholic.

Career Staff Atty., Legal Aid Society, 1957–61; Asst. Dist. Atty., Rackets Bureau, Kings County, 1961–66; JAGC; 4th Judge Advocate General Corps; Athletic Director, Brownsville Boys Club.

Offices 405 CHOB, 202-225-5471. Also 1449 Rockaway Parkway, Brooklyn 11236, 212-649-0614.

Committees

Banking and Currency (18th); Subs. (1) Bank Supervision and Insurance, (2) Domestic Finance, (3) International Finance.

Post Office and Civil Service (12th); Subs. (1) Employee Benefits, (2) Retirement, Insurance, and Health Benefits.

Sel. Com. on Crime (3rd).

Group Ratings

	ADA	COPE	NREP	NFU	LCV	CFA	NAB	NSI	ACA
1970	84	100	100	100	75	100	0	0	6
1969	87	—	—	93	—	—	—	—	6
1968	92	100	—	100	—	—	0	—	0

** These figures do not include votes Humphrey received on the Liberal line. His performance, therefore, is understated by one to five percent in each New York district.*

Key Votes

(1) ABM	AGN	(6) 18-Yr-Vote	FOR	(11) Clean Water $	FOR
(2) SST	AGN	(7) Farm Sub Lmt	FOR	(12) Mig Wrkrs Comp	FOR
(3) Phil Pln	FOR	(8) Coop-Church	FOR	(13) Jets to Chiang	AGN
(4) No-Knock	AGN	(9) Family Asst	FOR	(14) State OEO Veto	AGN
(5) Cmutr Tax	FOR	(10) Work Stamps	AGN	(15) Park Logging	AGN

Election Results

1970 general:	Frank J. Brasco (D)	60,919	(79%)
	William Sampol (C)	9,462	(12%)
	Paul Meyrowitz (L)	7,156	(9%)
1970 primary:	Frank J. Brasco (D)	18,811	(80%)
	Dominick Barbarino (D)	4,641	(20%)
	(Redistricted 1970)		

TWELFTH DISTRICT Political Background

New York 12, designed as a black-majority district in 1968, comprises the Bushwick and Bedford-Stuyvesant sections of Brooklyn. Bushwick is an old Jewish and Italian neighborhood into which blacks have been moving. Bedford-Stuyvesant, Brooklyn's black ghetto, and now a larger ghetto than Manhattan's Harlem, was previously carved up among several districts to provide Democratic votes for Jewish and Irish congressmen. Like most ghettos, it is not completely homogeneous. There are, of course, blocks of dilapidated tenements that are inhabited, *inter alia,* by drug addicts; and to the north, there are some high-rise public housing projects. But Bedford-Stuyvesant also has some middle-class neighborhoods; some of the old brownstones here are being renovated by Robert Kennedy's development corporation and other such groups.

In 1968, the new seat attracted two major candidates: Assemblywoman Shirley Chisholm, who won the Democratic nomination, and the former director of CORE, James Farmer, with both the Liberal and Republican nominations. Farmer's campaign, which was well-financed, took a cue from the militants and stressed black masculine pride. Mrs. Chisholm's campaign relied on a forceful speaking style and on the corps of women volunteers whose help enabled her to defeat machine-backed candidates in other elections. Farmer's strategy was probably a mistake because a substantial majority of black voters, perhaps as many as 60%, are women. Moreover, in the 12th district, the Democratic line on the voting machines turned out to be far stronger than the Republican and Liberal lines put together. Mrs. Chisholm finished with 66% of the votes; Farmer with 26%; and the Conservative candidate with 7%, mostly from Bushwick.

Congresswoman Chisholm, who entitled her autobiography *Unbought and Unbossed,* was given the kind of committee assignment usually reserved for those who defy the congressional establishment—a seat on Veterans' Affairs. Nonetheless, her position as the first black woman in Congress, her unequivocal speaking manner, and her determination not to fall into the quiescent role assumed by most freshman congressmen, won her a national forum and a full schedule on the liberal speech-making circuit. In 1971, she was reassigned to Education and Labor, which handles most social legislation. This came, according to some reports, as a reward for having joined the rest of the Brooklyn delegation in supporting Hale Boggs for Majority Leader (see Louisiana 2).

Chisholm had no trouble in the 1970 elections, winning 82%. And though her district lost population during the '60's, she is unlikely to have trouble in the future. Even a conservative Republican legislature is not about to deny the black community congressional representation at this point in our political and social history.

Census Data 1970 pop. 402,036; deviation from current state average, —9.6%; change 1960–70, —2.0%. Metro. 100%, 100% central city.

1970 Share of Federal Outlays $565,470,000 (average outlay per district, New York 6–24)

DOD	$76,898,000	HEW	$154,742,000
AEC	$739,000	HUD	$2,744,000
NASA	$921,000	OEO	$2,012,000

DOT	$6,423,000	DOA	$42,872,000
		Other	$334,666,000

Federal Military-Industrial Commitments (See New York 19 for New York City listing.)

Economic Base Apparel and other finished products made from fabrics and similar materials, esp. women's, misses', and juniors' outerwear; food and kindred products, esp. beverages; fabricated metal products; electrical machinery, equipment, and supplies, esp. electric lighting, and wiring equipment.

The Voters

Registration 73,874 total. 56,627 D (77%); 10,963 R (15%); 2,103 L (3%); 517 C (0%); 3,664 other (5%).

Employment profile White collar, 36%. Blue collar, 64%.

Ethnic groups Black, 66%. Puerto Rico, 4%. Total foreign stock, 32%. Italy, USSR, 7% each; Poland, 4%; Ireland, 3%; Czech., Germany, Hungary, UK, Canada, 1% each; others, 5%.

Presidential vote

1968	Humphrey (D)	41,955	(78%)*
	Nixon (R)	10,165	(19%)
	Wallace (AIP)	1,742	(3%)

Representative

Shirley Anita Chisholm (D) Elected 1968; b. Nov. 30, 1924, Brooklyn; home, Brooklyn; Brooklyn Col., B.A., 1946; Columbia U., M.A., 1952; married; Methodist.

Career Nursery school teacher and dir., 1946–53; Dir., Hamilton-Madison Child Care Center, N.Y., 1953–59; Educational Consultant, Div. of Day Care, N.Y., 1959–64; N.Y. Legislature, 1964–68.

Offices 123 CHOB, 202-225-6231. Also 587 Eastern Parkway, Brooklyn 11216, 212-596-3500.

Committees

Education and Labor (17th); Subs. (1) Education, (2) Sel. on Education, (3) Agricultural Labor.

Group Ratings

	ADA	COPE	NREP	NFU	LCV	CFA	NAB	NSI	ACA
1970	80	100	91	83	100	100	0	0	25
1969	100	—	—	67	—	—	—	—	29

Key Votes

(1) ABM	AGN	(6) 18-Yr-Vote	ABS	(11) Clean Water $	FOR
(2) SST	AGN	(7) Farm Sub Lmt	FOR	(12) Mig Wrkrs Comp	FOR
(3) Phil Pln	FOR	(8) Coop-Church	FOR	(13) Jets to Chiang	AGN
(4) No-Knock	AGN	(9) Family Asst	AGN	(14) State OEO Veto	AGN
(5) Cmutr Tax	FOR	(10) Work Stamps	AGN	(15) Park Logging	ABS

Election Results

1970 general:	Shirley Chisholm (D and L)	31,500	(82%)
	John Coleman (R)	5,816	(15%)
	Martin S. Shepherd, Jr. (C)	1,204	(3%)
1970 primary:	Shirley Chisholm (D and L), unopposed		
	(Redistricted 1970)		

* *These figures do not include votes Humphrey received on the Liberal line. His performance, therefore, is understated by one to five percent in each New York district.*

THIRTEENTH DISTRICT Political Background

New York 13, in southcentral Brooklyn, might be called the Ocean Parkway district. The 13th takes in the terrain on both sides of that thoroughfare as it makes its way from Prospect Park to Coney Island. There is a large Italian community in Bensonhurst and Bath Beach along the western edge of the district; but most of the neighborhoods, from Midwood in the north to Gravesend, Sheepshead Bay, Brighton Beach, and Coney Island in the south, are predominately Jewish. Together with Flatbush, this is the heartland of liberal Jewish Brooklyn. The 13th is consistently and overwhelmingly Democratic, though it did cast a substantial plurality of its votes for John Lindsay in 1965 and 1969.

The congressman from the 13th is Bertram L. Podell, a former assemblyman, who since winning a special election in early 1968, has won easy reelection. The special election was heralded as a Johnson Administration victory because Podell's primary opponent was an outspoken peace candidate, and Podell himself had the support of the Brooklyn Democratic organization. But such an assessment was not really accurate. The Congressman did not campaign as a Johnson man; in fact, as it turned out, Podell became an opponent of both Johnson and Nixon over Vietnam.

Podell presents a nice contrast with his predecessor, Abraham Multer, who retired to a judgeship amid charges that he used his position on the Banking and Currency Committee to his own financial advantage. Liberal journalists continually attacked Multer as the man who demonstrated what was wrong with machine politics. Podell, after his initial campaign, has won good reviews from the New York press. He has not had strong primary opposition, though the Liberal party, perhaps out of habit, continues to run a candidate against the man out of the Brooklyn Democratic organization. In spite of this, Podell has had no trouble winning reelection with the sort of majorities a liberal Democrat can expect in the 13th: 68% in 1968 and 77% in 1970. It is unlikely that Republican redistricters can do anything to prevent the Congressman from winning reelection for at least another ten years.

Census Data 1970 pop. 425,040; deviation from current state average, —4.5%; change 1960–70, +3.8%. Metro. 100%, 100% central city.

1970 Share of Federal Outlays $565,470,000 (average outlay per district, New York 6–24)

DOD	$76,898,000	HEW	$154,742,000
AEC	$739,000	HUD	$2,744,000
NASA	$921,000	OEO	$2,012,000
DOT	$6,423,000	DOA	$42,872,000
		Other	$334,666,000

Federal Military-Industrial Commitments (See New York 17 for New York City listing.)

Economic Base Apparel and other finished products made from fabrics and similar materials, esp. women's, misses', and juniors' outerwear; food and kindred products, esp. beverages; fabricated metal products; electrical machinery, equipment, and supplies, esp. electric lighting and wiring equipment. Also, higher education (CUNY, Brooklyn).

The Voters

Registration 214,884 total. 167,107 D (79%); 26,240 R (12%); 6,398 L (3%); 2,620 C (1%); 12,519 other (6%).

Employment profile White collar, 54%. Blue collar, 46%.

Ethnic groups Black, 2%. Puerto Rico, 1%. Total foreign stock, 69%; Italy, 21%; USSR, 20%; Poland, 10%; Austria, 6%; Germany, Hungary, Ireland, UK, Canada, 1% each; others, 8%.

Presidential vote

1968	Humphrey (D)	110,841	(68%)*
	Nixon (R)	46,662	(29%)
	Wallace (AIP)	5,662	(3%)

** These figures do not include votes Humphrey received on the Liberal line. His performance, therefore, is understated by one to five percent in each New York district.*

Representative

Bertram L. Podell (D) Elected Feb. 20, 1968; b. Dec. 27, 1925, Brooklyn; home, Brooklyn; St. John's U., B.A., 1944; Brooklyn Law School, LL.B., 1950; Navy, WWII; married, three children; Jewish.

Career Atty., N.Y. Assembly, 1954–68.

Offices 1712 LHOB, 202-225-2361. Also 1507 Ave. M., Brooklyn 11230, 212-336-7575.

Committees

House Administration (11th); Subs. (1) Accounts, (2) Sp. on Electrical and Mechanical Office Equipment.

Interstate and Foreign Commerce (19th); Sub. on Transportation and Aeronautics.

Group Ratings

	ADA	COPE	NREP	NFU	LCV	CFA	NAB	NSI	ACA
1970	92	100	100	92	67	100	0	0	14
1969	87	—	—	86	—	—	—	—	0
1968	100	100	—	100	—	—	0	—	0

Key Votes

(1) ABM	AGN	(6) 18-Yr-Vote	FOR	(11) Clean Water $	FOR
(2) SST	AGN	(7) Farm Sub Lmt	FOR	(12) Mig Wrkrs Comp	FOR
(3) Phil Pln	FOR	(8) Coop-Church	FOR	(13) Jets to Chiang	AGN
(4) No-Knock	AGN	(9) Family Asst	FOR	(14) State OEO Veto	AGN
(5) Cmutr Tax	FOR	(10) Work Stamps	AGN	(15) Park Logging	AGN

Election Results

1970 general:	Bertram L. Podell (D)	102,247	(77%)
	George W. McKenzie (R)	20,550	(15%)
	Herbert Dicker (L)	9,925	(7%)
1970 primary:	Bertram L. Podell (D), unopposed (Redistricted 1970)		

FOURTEENTH DISTRICT Political Background

New York 14 extends along the Brooklyn waterfront, from Greenpoint on the Queens' border, to the Bush Terminal in the south, near the Verrazano Narrows Bridge. As its contorted shape suggests, the district is polyglot; its varied groups have in common only a tendency to vote Democratic. In the north, Greenpoint and Williamsburg are industrial areas with large Orthodox Jewish communities, as well as a number of Puerto Ricans. In Brooklyn Heights, and adjacent Cobble Hill and Boerum Hill, all lying in the middle of the 14th, picturesque brownstones are being restored by young affluent New Yorkers. Just to the south of Cobble Hill are the old Italian neighborhoods of South Brooklyn and Red Hook. The Fort Greene area to the east, next to Bedford-Stuyvesant, is predominantly black.

The district's congressman, John J. Rooney, in the House since 1944, is the 4th-ranking member of the Appropriations Committee. He chairs the subcommittee that determines how much money the State, Commerce, and Justice departments will get to run their affairs. In this capacity, Rooney has won the reputation of a penny-pincher, though few personnel in these bureaucracies dare say anything like this publicly. Until late in the 1970 campaign, Rooney vigorously supported the nation's involvement in Vietnam—a position which inspired electoral opposition.

In 1968 and again in 1970, the big political event in the 14th was the Democratic primary, as liberal, antiwar candidates tried to unseat Rooney. In 1968, wealthy manufacturer Frederick W. Richmond spent an estimated $200,000 in his primary campaign only to fall some 3,000 votes short of victory. Those votes were taken by a third candidate, Peter Eikenberry, who in turn became Rooney's liberal opponent in 1970. Eikenberry, then 36, ran a campaign staffed by hundreds of student volunteers who canvassed voters all over the district and then attempted to get their vote out on election day. Rooney, who was 67, waged the most strenuous campaign of his career, making frequent appearances before those ethnic voters, among whom he was most popular. By a narrow margin, Rooney again won and later had no trouble in the general election in which Eikenberry, as the candidate of the Liberal party, could win only 18%.

Rooney may have even more trouble winning reelection in 1972. The Republican legislature may force him into the same district with Hugh Carey, the incumbent in the 15th. Carey's record has become increasingly liberal; he has at the same time won the favor of the Irish and Italian voters in his district and strengthened himself within the House establishment. Some 20 years younger than Rooney, Carey can campaign far more energetically than the veteran Democrat and should defeat him in any election.

Census Data 1970 pop. 367,850; deviation from current state average, —17.3%; change 1960–70, —10.1%. Metro. 100%, 100% central city.

1970 Share of Federal Outlays $565,470,000 (average outlay per district, New York 6–24)

DOD	$76,898,000	HEW	$154,742,000
AEC	$739,000	HUD	$2,744,000
NASA	$921,000	OEO	$2,012,000
DOT	$6,423,000	DOA	$42,872,000
		Other	$334,666,000

Federal Military-Industrial Commitments (See New York 17 for New York City listing.)

Economic Base Apparel and other finished products made from fabrics and similar materials, esp. women's, misses', and juniors' outerwear; food and kindred products, esp. beverages; fabricated metal products; electrical machinery, equipment, and supplies, esp. electric lighting and wiring equipment.

The Voters

Registration 101,208 total. 73,339 D (72%); 18,094 R (18%); 2,612 L (3%); 1,547 C (2%); 5,616 other (6%).

Employment profile White collar, 30%. Blue collar, 70%.

Ethnic groups Black, 19%. Puerto Rico, 20%. Total foreign stock, 41%. Italy, 17%; Poland, 5%; Germany, Ireland, USSR, 2% each; Austria, Czech., Hungary, UK, Canada, 1% each; others, 6%.

Presidential vote

1968	Humphrey (D)	42,928	(57%)*
	Nixon (R)	26,664	(36%)
	Wallace (AIP)	5,067	(7%)

Representative

John J. Rooney (D) Elected June 6, 1944; b. Nov. 29, 1903, Brooklyn; home, Brooklyn; St. Francis Col., 1920–22; Fordham U., LL.B., 1925; married, five children; Catholic.

Career Practicing atty., 1926–40; Asst. Dist. Atty., 1940–44.

Offices 2268 RHOB, 202-225-5936. Also Suite 276, U.S. Ct. House, 225 Cadman Plaza East, Brooklyn 11201, 212-596-6910.

Committees

Appropriations (4th); Subs. (1) Chm., State, Justice, Commerce, and the Judiciary, (2) Foreign Operations.

** These figures do not include votes Humphrey received on the Liberal line. His performance, therefore, is understated by one to five percent in each New York district.*

Group Ratings

	ADA	COPE	NREP	NFU	LCV	CFA	NAB	NSI	ACA
1970	60	100	67	100	50	88	0	78	6
1969	47	—	—	93	—	—	—	—	14
1968	75	100	—	100	—	—	0	—	0

Key Votes

(1) ABM	FOR	(6) 18-Yr-Vote	FOR	(11) Clean Water $	FOR
(2) SST	FOR	(7) Farm Sub Lmt	AGN	(12) Mig Wrkrs Comp	FOR
(3) Phil Pln	FOR	(8) Coop-Church	FOR	(13) Jets to Chiang	FOR
(4) No-Knock	FOR	(9) Family Asst	FOR	(14) State OEO Veto	AGN
(5) Cmutr Tax	AGN	(10) Work Stamps	AGN	(15) Park Logging	AGN

Election Results

1970 general:	John J. Rooney (D)	31,586	(55%)
	John F. Jacobs (R and C)	15,222	(27%)
	Peter Eikenberry (L)	10,452	(18%)
1970 primary:	John J. Rooney (D)	12,244	(50%)
	Peter Eikenberry (D)	10,621	(44%)
	Irving Gross (D)	1,392	(6%)
	(Redistricted 1970)		

FIFTEENTH DISTRICT Political Background

New York 15 extends to the north and southwest of Prospect Park, in western Brooklyn. To the north, Fort Greene and Park Slope have a significant black population, and an increasing number of affluent New Yorkers who are renovating the picturesque town-houses in the area. The neighborhoods to the south are middle- to lower-middle-class. Sunset Park has the nation's largest community of Norwegians outside of Minnesota and the Great Plains; Borough Park, which is predominantly Irish, is less affluent, as is New Utrecht, an Italian and Irish neighborhood. The Norwegians are traditionally Republican, but the other groups are Democratic. Of late, however, the Catholic areas in the south have been trending toward the Conservative party.

Until 1960, the 15th was Brooklyn's Republican stronghold; the district at that time included conservative Bay Ridge, now in the 16th. In that year, Democrat Hugh Carey, a 39-year-old Irish lawyer, captured the 15th's House seat from the eight-year veteran, Francis E. Dorn. In 1962, despite the efforts of Republican redistricters, Carey won again by 383 votes. An indefatigable campaigner, the Congressman has been reelected by increasing margins ever since; in 1970, after a Republican redistricting conceded him the district, he won 65% of the votes.

Carey, who became a dove before the 1968 elections, is one of the few remaining New York politicians who can win Irish working-class votes and who at the same time possesses a liberal voting record. His success at the polls indicates that Robert Kennedy's coalition of New York's blacks, Puerto Ricans, and white Catholic lower-middle-class, is still viable (see state write-up). In 1969, like so many other Democrats, he declared his candidacy for mayor of New York; he later chose to run for the number two position, City Council President, on ex-Mayor Robert F. Wagner's slate. In a crowded field, Carey finished a very close second to the candidate slated by Proccaccino—it was the nearest thing to a liberal victory in that Democratic primary.

In 1971, Carey led the Brooklyn delegation's support of Hale Boggs in the Louisianan's bid to become House Majority Leader. Since Boggs was successful, Carey moved from Education and Labor, where he had less seniority than some younger liberals, to Ways and Means, a powerful committee. Not only does this committee handle all tax and social security legislation, its Democratic members control their party's committee assignments. Carey has sold his house in Brooklyn and moved his family, which includes twelve children, to the Washington area. This suggests that the Congressman has abandoned plans he may have had for political office in New York City, and has decided in favor of a long career in the House. The Republican legislature, however, could force Carey into a rough primary fight in 1972. For a discussion of this, see New York 14.

Census Data 1970 pop. 388,540; deviation from current state average, —12.7%; change 1960–70, —5.5%. Metro. 100%, 100% central city.

1970 Share of Federal Outlays $565,470,000 (average outlay per district, New York 6–24).

DOD	$76,898,000	HEW	$154,742,000
AEC	$739,000	HUD	$2,744,000
NASA	$921,000	OEO	$2,012,000
DOT	$6,423,000	DOA	$42,872,000
		Other	$334,666,000

Federal Military-Industrial Commitments (See New York 17 for New York City listing.)

Economic Base Apparel and other finished products made from fabrics and similar materials, esp. women's, misses', and juniors' outerwear; food and kindred products, esp. beverages; fabricated metal products; electrical machinery, equipment, and supplies, esp. electric lighting and wiring equipment.

The Voters

Registration 134,615 total. 95,834 D (71%); 25,503 R (19%); 3,149 L (2%); 2,582 C (2%); 7,547 other (6%).

Employment profile White collar, 51%. Blue collar, 49%.

Ethnic groups Black, 15%. Puerto Rico, 4%. Total foreign stock, 52%. Italy, 18%; Ireland, 6%; Norway, 5%; Germany, Poland, UK, 3% each; USSR, Canada, 2% each; Austria, Sweden, 1% each; others, 8%.

Presidential vote

1968	Humphrey (D)	63,304	(48%)*
	Nixon (R)	57,712	(44%)
	Wallace (AIP)	10,061	(8%)

Representative

Hugh L. Carey (D) Elected 1960; b. April 11, 1919, Brooklyn; home, Brooklyn; St. John's Law School, LL.B., 1951; Army, WWII; Lt. Col. USAR; married, twelve children; Catholic.

Career Practicing atty., 1951– ; Bd. of Dir., Gallaudet Col.

Offices 106 CHOB, 202-225-4105. Also Suite 699A Fed. Ct. House, 225 Cadman Plaza East, Brooklyn 11201, 212-596-3839.

Committees

Ways and Means (14th).

Group Ratings

	ADA	COPE	NREP	NFU	LCV	CFA	NAB	NSI	ACA
1970	84	100	100	100	67	100	0	0	18
1969	73	—	—	83	—	—	—	—	10
1968	83	100	—	87	—	—	0	—	5

Key Votes

(1) ABM	AGN	(6) 18-Yr-Vote	ABS	(11) Clean Water $	ABS
(2) SST	AGN	(7) Farm Sub Lmt	FOR	(12) Mig Wrkrs Comp	FOR
(3) Phil Pln	ABS	(8) Coop-Church	ABS	(13) Jets to Chiang	AGN
(4) No-Knock	AGN	(9) Family Asst	FOR	(14) State OEO Veto	AGN
(5) Cmutr Tax	FOR	(10) Work Stamps	AGN	(15) Park Logging	AGN

* *These figures do not include votes Humphrey received on the Liberal line. His performance, therefore, is understated by one to five percent in each New York district.*

Election Results

1970 general:	Hugh L. Carey (D)	50,767	(65%)
	Frank C. Spinner (R)	17,931	(23%)
	Stephen P. Marion (C)	5,307	(7%)
	Carl Saks (L)	4,506	(5%)
1970 primary:	Hugh L. Carey (D), unopposed (Redistricted 1970)		

SIXTEENTH DISTRICT Political Background

New York 16 is Staten Island and the Bay Ridge section of Brooklyn. In area, Staten Island is as large as all of Brooklyn, but New York City's smallest borough casts just 60% of the votes in the 16th. Only the northern and eastern shores of Staten Island are thickly settled; the rest of it is almost rural in character, even though the Island's population has grown fairly rapidly since the 1965 opening of the Verrazano Narrows Bridge—its first direct link to the rest of New York City. The people here are mostly middle-class, Italian Catholics, many of whom were born and raised in the crowded streets of Brooklyn. Staten Island is the most conservative part of the City—the home of state Sen. John Marchi, the austere conservative intellectual who beat John Lindsay in the Republican Mayoral primary of 1969. In 1968 and 1970, the results here produced overwhelming majorities for Richard Nixon and James Buckley; in some races, the Republican and Conservative lines, taken separately, finished with more votes than the Democratic column.

Bay Ridge is a high-income area that has attracted many of Brooklyn's successful Catholics, including ex-Mayor William O'Dwyer. Bay Ridge has always been the most conservative part of Brooklyn, though not quite as conservative as Staten Island. For years, Republican legislators kept Bay Ridge in the 15th, hoping it would then elect a Republican congressman. But the 15th has been Democratic since 1960.

In 1970, the Republicans decided to concede the 15th and attached Bay Ridge to the 16th in an effort to defeat Democratic Congressman John M. Murphy. Murphy, a West Point graduate, has had hawkish views on the war, but has also supported gun control legislation. The Congressman lost Staten Island when he first won election to the House in 1962; since then, using the advantages of incumbency, he has been carrying it. In 1968, however, he lost the island again and won reelection only because of his margin in the non-contiguous areas of Brooklyn, then in his district. In 1970, as the legislators had hoped, Bay Ridge gave the Republican candidate a 6,700-margin, but Murphy regained his popularity on Staten Island and again won reelection.

The strong Republican showing in 1968 was due in large part to the presence of Richard Nixon at the top of the ticket. That factor was missing in 1970, but in 1972, regardless of what happens to Nixon's popularity in the rest of the country, his coattails will surely benefit the Republican candidate in the 16th. Those coattails, and the addition of Bay Ridge to the district, could spell the end of Murphy's House career.

Census Data 1970 pop. 470,130; deviation from current state average, +5.7%; change 1960–70, +15.3%. Metro. 100%, 100% central city.

1970 Share of Federal Outlays $565,470,000 (average outlay per district, New York 6–24)

DOD	$76,898,000	HEW	$154,742,000
AEC	$739,000	HUD	$2,744,000
NASA	$921,000	OEO	$2,012,000
DOT	$6,423,000	DOA	$42,872,000
		Other	$334,666,000

Federal Military-Industrial Commitments (See New York 17 for New York City listing.)

Economic Base Apparel and other finished products made from fabrics and similar materials, esp. women's, misses', and juniors' outerwear; chemicals and allied products, esp. soap, detergents, and cleaning preparations, perfumes and cosmetics, and other toilet preparations; ship and boat building and repairing.

The Voters

Registration 193,307 total. 111,782 D (58%); 61,335 R (32%); 2,071 L (1%); 7,765 C (4%); 10,354 other (5%).

Employment profile White collar, 53%. Blue collar, 47%.

Ethnic groups Black 4%. Puerto Rico, 1%. Total foreign stock, 43%. Italy, 14%; Ireland, 6%; Germany, UK, 4% each; Poland, 3%; Norway, 2%; Austria, Hungary, Sweden, Canada, 1% each; others, 4%.

Presidential vote

1968	Humphrey (D)	47,452	(34%)*
	Nixon (R)	83,380	(59%)
	Wallace (AIP)	10,130	(7%)

Representative

John Michael Murphy (D) Elected 1962; b. Aug. 3, 1926, Staten Island; home, Staten Island; Amherst Col., U.S. Military Academy, B.S., 1950; Army WWII and Korean War; married, three children; Catholic.

Career Mbr., Bd. of Dir., Empire State Highway Transportation Assoc., 1960–67; Pres., Cleveland Gen. Transport Co., Inc., 1957–65; Delegate, N.Y. Constitutional Convention, 1967; Delegate, Dem. Natl. Convention, 1964; Parliamentarian, 1968 Dem. Natl. Convention.

Offices 2445 RHOB, 202-225-3371. Also Gen. Post Office Bldg., 550 Manor Rd., Staten Island 10314, 212-981-9800.

Committees

Interstate and Foreign Commerce (10th); Sub. on Transportation and Aeronautics.

Merchant Marine and Fisheries (11th); Subs. (1) Chm., Panama Canal, (2) Merchant Marine, (3) Sp. on Maritime Education and Training.

Group Ratings

	ADA	COPE	NREP	NFU	LCV	CFA	NAB	NSI	ACA
1970	56	83	58	100	75	87	11	70	13
1969	43	—	—	93	—	—	—	—	13
1968	67	100	—	100	—	—	0	—	0

Key Votes

(1) ABM	FOR	(6) 18-Yr-Vote	FOR	(11) Clean Water $	FOR
(2) SST	FOR	(7) Farm Sub Lmt	FOR	(12) Mig Wrkrs Comp	FOR
(3) Phil Pln	FOR	(8) Coop-Church	AGN	(13) Jets to Chiang	ABS
(4) No-Knock	FOR	(9) Family Asst	FOR	(14) State OEO Veto	AGN
(5) Cmutr Tax	FOR	(10) Work Stamps	AGN	(15) Park Logging	AGN

Election Results

1970 general:	John M. Murphy (D and Ind. Alliance)	71,550	(52%)
	David D. Smith (R and C)	62,597	(45%)
	George D. McClain (L)	4,415	(3%)
1970 primary:	John M. Murphy (D)	13,426	(71%)
	Ronald Paul Fischetti (D)	5,390	(29%)
	(Redistricted 1970)		

SEVENTEENTH DISTRICT Political Background

New York 17 is the silk stocking district. It is dominated by the Upper East Side of Manhattan, which Theodore H. White once called the "Perfumed Stockade." The 17th also includes the skyscrapers of Midtown and much of Greenwich Village, which, in spite of its presumed bohemianism, is as fashionable and expensive an

** These figures do not include votes Humphrey received on the Liberal line. His performance, therefore, is understated by one to five percent in each New York district.*

address as any in New York. Not all of the 17th is wealthy; the Stuyvesant Town housing development to the south is middle-class, and there are a few blocks of Harlem to the north, and some middle-income areas off Central Park West. But the character and tone of the district is set by the affluent liberal intellectual community, which has had an extremely influential place in New York politics (see state write-up). The 17th probably has more writers, painters, theater people, and TV personalities, than any other district in the country. For these people, and for many New Yorkers who identify with them, politics sometimes becomes a question of personal style or lack of it, and political preference just one more fashionable accessory.

The current fashion is probably still best exemplified by the term "radical chic"—coined by writer Tom Wolfe to describe the atmosphere of several cocktail fund raisers held for the Black Panthers and the California grape strikers. The wealthy and chic people of the Upper East Side have genuine enthusiasm for liberal causes, but its intensity seems to grow as the objects of the sympathy grow more distant. There are no "radical chic" parties for the garbage collectors or doormen whose strikes make life on the Upper East Side more uncomfortable. At any rate, a politician disliked by the city's white middle class multitudes seems inevitably to be very popular on the Upper East Side. The 17th preferred Adlai Stevenson to John F. Kennedy in 1960 and Eugene McCarthy over Robert Kennedy in 1968. But the 17th's favorite politician is the one also most hated by the Queens truck driver, John Lindsay, ex-Republican, liberal, and ultra-stylish.

Like most high-income areas of the country, the 17th became increasingly liberal during the '60's, as the politics of Vietnam and of racial justice supplanted the economic issue politics of the post-New Deal era. Today, when most New Yorkers register Democratic and often vote Republican or Conservative, the residents of the 17th register Republican and often vote Democratic.

In the '50's, the 17th was still a stronghold of wealthy conservatives, the kind of people who, as once portrayed in an *Esquire* cartoon, would remark that little Mary used a dirty word when she wrote "Roosevelt" on the sidewalk. Perhaps the first sign of the liberalization of the upper classes came in 1958, when John Lindsay won the 17th's Republican congressional primary. Lindsay's margins increased as he moved to the left; he won 72% in 1964. He resigned from the House in 1965 to become mayor. By the time Lindsay won reelection in 1969, the district was the most liberal in New York City, giving its native son 80% of the votes. And by 1970, a Democrat represented the district in Congress and the 17th's last Republican assemblyman—from an assembly district along posh Fifth and Park Avenues—had been defeated.

In the close special election to fill the House seat vacated by Lindsay in 1965, the winner was liberal Republican Theodore R. Kupferman, a lawyer with many clients in the theater business. In 1966, Kupferman retained his seat by narrowly defeating a state senator, and in 1968, achieved the supreme goal of most New York City congressmen—a multi-party endorsement for a judgeship. And so, he did not seek re-relection.

The candidates for the seat in 1968 were Democratic City Councilman Edward I. Koch and Republican state Sen. Whitney North Seymour. Koch, a Greenwich Village lawyer, had once defeated Tammany boss Carmine deSapio for Democratic district leader. Seymour was a well-known Wall Street lawyer whose father was once president of the American Bar Association. Seymour lost, and he may have lost because the relatively liberal Republican was forced to run with Nixon at the top of the ticket. A more likely explanation is that the increasing conservatism of the Republican party turned many silk stocking residents into Democrats. Koch, moreover, was well-known and well-liked in the district and waged an energetic campaign. He became the first Democratic congressman from the 17th in 34 years, winning with 52% to Seymour's 43%. In 1970, Koch was reelected with 62% of the votes.

Koch is one of the strongest opponents of the Vietnam war and military spending in the House; and also, one of its most ardent supporters of procedural reform. As a freshman, he led the fight for a mass transit trust fund proposal and proposed a bill which would remove the Internal Revenue's tax bias against single people, of which his district has many.

The principal threat to Koch's reelection in 1972 will be redistricting. Since Manhattan lost 173,000 residents during the '60's, it will lose almost an entire congressional district. The Republican legislature might be able to force Koch into a primary contest with another outspoken liberal, Congresswoman Bella Abzug of the 19th.

Census Data 1970 pop. 408,933; deviation from current state average, –8.1%; change 1960–70, +0.5%. Metro. 100%, 100% central city.

1970 Share of Federal Outlays $565,470,000 (average outlay per district, New York 6–24)

DOD	$565,470,000	HEW	$154,742,000
AEC	$739,000	HUD	$2,744,000
NASA	$921,000	OEO	$2,012,000
DOT	$6,423,000	DOA	$42,872,000
		Other	$334,666,000

Federal Military-Industrial Commitments (New York 6–24, New York City listing.)

DOD Contractors Western Electric Div., AT&T (New York), $164.986m: Safeguard ABM development. States Marine Lines (New York), $98.765m: cargo transport services. Western Union Telegraph and Western Union International (New York), $67.829m: communication services. Moore McCormack Lines (New York), $57.391m: cargo transport services. Pan American World Airways (New York), $47.087m: cargo transport services. Seaboard World Airlines (Jamaica), $40.543m: cargo transport services. Waterman Steamship Co. (New York), $31.803m: cargo transport services. American Foreign Lines (New York), $27.516m: cargo transport services. Overseas National Airlines (Jamaica), $26.698m: cargo transport services. United States Lines (New York), $24.912m: cargo transport services. TWA (New York), $22.011m: cargo transport services. American Airlines (New York), $21.790m: cargo transport services. Sperry Rand (New York), $15.370m: unspecified. Eastern Airlines (New York), $14.476m: cargo transport services. IT&T Inc. (New York), $13.935m: unspecified Lockheed Aircraft (Jamaica), $13.779m: modification of C-121 aircraft. Long, Quinn, and Boylan Co. (New York), $13.305m: unspecified. Todd Shipyards (Brooklyn), $12.851m: ship repair and overhaul. Americargo Shipping (New York), $12.103m: cargo transport services. Hudson Waterway Co. (New York), $11.545m: cargo transport services. Cities Services Tankers (New York), $9.961m: cargo transport services. Mobil Oil (New York), $9.694m: petroleum products. EDO Corp. (College Point), $8.388m: modification of underwater mines. Overseas Carriers Corp. (New York), $7.808m: cargo transport services. Applied Devices Corp. (College Point), $7.264m: Hawk missile simulators. Victory Carriers (New York), $7.229m: cargo transport services. Trans Caribbean Airways (Jamaica), $7.206m: cargo transport services. Amman and Whitney (New York), $7.095m: design of Safeguard ABM radar sites. Shell Oil (New York), $6.238m: petroleum products. Gibbs and Cox (New York), $6.155m: design of amphibious assault landing craft. Automated Terminal Services Inc. (Jamaica), $6.069m: stevedoring. Gibraltar Fabrics Inc. (Brooklyn), $5.639m: camouflaged poncho liners. Loral Corp. (Bronx), $5.393m: aircraft electronic warfare equipment. American Brands Inc. (New York), $5.384m: unspecified. Columbia University (New York), $5.309m: unspecified research.

DOD Installations Fort Hamilton AB (Brooklyn). Naval Hospital (St. Albans). Naval Station (Brooklyn).

Economic Base Apparel and other finished products made from fabrics and similar materials, esp. women's, misses', and juniors' outerwear; textile mill products, esp. knitting mills; printing, publishing, and allied industries, esp. commercial printing and periodicals. Also, higher education (Hunter CUNY, and New York University); tourism (New York City); banking and stock brokerage.

The Voters

Registration 222,387 total. 110,692 D (50%); 70,846 R (32%); 7,765 L (3%); 2,117 C (1%); 30,967 other (14%).

Employment profile White collar, 67%. Blue collar, 33%.

Ethnic groups Black, 2%. Puerto Rico, 1%. Total foreign stock, 53%. USSR, 7%; Ireland, Germany, 6% each; Italy, 5%; UK, 4%; Austria, Poland, 3% each; Czech., Hungary, 2% each; Sweden, Canada, 1% each; others, 4%.

Presidential vote

1968	Humphrey (D)	97,623	(57%)*
	Nixon (R)	69,454	(41%)
	Wallace (AIP)	4,356	(3%)

** These figures do not include votes Humphrey received on the Liberal line. His performance, therefore, is understated by one to five percent in each New York district.*

Representative

Edward I. Koch (D-Lib.) Elected 1968; b. Dec. 12, 1924, New York City; home, New York City; City Col. of N.Y., 1949; N.Y.U., LL.B., 1948; Army, WWII; unmarried; Jewish.

Career Practicing atty., 1949–68; Dem. Dist. Leader, Greenwich Village, 1963–66; N.Y.C. Council, 1967–68.

Offices 1134 LHOB, 202-225-2436. Also Suite 3139, 26 Fed. Plaza, New York City, 212-264-1066.

Committees

Banking and Currency (20th); Subs. (1) Bank Supervision and Insurance, (2) Consumer Affairs, (3) International Trade.

Group Ratings

	ADA	COPE	NREP	NFU	LCV	CFA	NAB	NSI	ACA
1970	100	100	100	92	100	100	0	0	17
1969	100	—	—	73	—	—	—	—	18

Key Votes

(1) ABM	AGN	(6) 18-Yr-Vote	FOR	(11) Clean Water $	FOR
(2) SST	AGN	(7) Farm Sub Lmt	FOR	(12) Mig Wrkrs Comp	FOR
(3) Phil Pln	FOR	(8) Coop-Church	FOR	(13) Jets to Chiang	AGN
(4) No-Knock	AGN	(9) Family Asst	FOR	(14) State OEO Veto	AGN
(5) Cmutr Tax	FOR	(10) Work Stamps	AGN	(15) Park Logging	AGN

Election Results

1970 general:	Edward I. Koch (D and L)	98,300	(62%)
	Peter J. Sprague (R)	50,647	(32%)
	Richard J. Callahan (C)	9,586	(6%)
1970 primary:	Edward I. Koch (D)	29,804	(83%)
	Paul P. Rao, Jr. (D)	5,990	(17%)
	(Redistricted 1970)		

EIGHTEENTH DISTRICT Political Background

New York 18 is dominated by Harlem, the nation's most famous black ghetto. In the years following World War I, Harlem became the relatively prosperous center of American Negro culture. But the Depression of the '30's hit it hard; since then Harlem has become synonymous with poverty, racial injustice and all the attendant social ills. There are still a few comfortable middle-class pockets left, mostly in the apartments along the Harlem River. These were built by Metropolitan Life as an all-black counterpart to the then all-white Stuyvesant Town (see New York 17). But most of the 18th is very poor indeed, the kind of place people want to leave; the district's population was down some 20% in the '60's. Little of the antipoverty money that has been poured into Harlem seems to get to the people who need it. One project intended to stimulate the economy of Harlem—the construction of a state office building on 125th Street—was blocked for some time by militants protesting the lack of jobs in the building trades for blacks.

For years, Harlem had one of the best-known congressmen in the county, Adam Clayton Powell. Powell's career peaked in the early '60's, when he was chairman of the House Education and Labor Committee, a congressional unit with control over most important social legislation. Then, in 1966, Powell's trouble with the New York court system was regularly featured as the lead story in national TV news programs; he ran into more trouble when it was learned that he had been diverting committee salaries into his own ample bank account.

It was no more, Powell said in defense, than what many other congressmen were doing. He was probably right. But Powell, knowing that it enhanced his popularity in the 18th, loved to thumb his nose at white Middle America; by 1967, he had been doing it for too long. As the conservative 90th Congress convened that year, Middle America struck back. Against the wishes of the House leadership, Powell was not allowed to take the oath of office—an action which the Supreme Court later found unacceptable. But by that time, Powell had already returned to his district and won glorious reelection to replace himself in the seat he had been denied.

Powell, stripped of his seniority, returned to office in 1969. "Where's Adam?" became a common question, as he missed virtually every roll call. He was living on Bimini and even allowed himself to be photographed there on his boat. The romance between the minister of Harlem's largest church, the Abyssinian Baptist, and New York's 18th congressional district came to an end.

The 1970 Democratic primary attracted four challengers, and one of them, Assemblyman Charles Rangel, beat Powell by 150 votes. Rangel's victory was an unintended consequence of redistricting. A dozen or so blocks of the white liberal Upper West Side had been added to the 18th for the 1970 election; Rangel carried these by more than 1,500 votes—ten times his district-wide margin. But Powell could do only 40% in all-black election districts of central Harlem, where he was once simply unbeatable. Powell promised to run in the general election as an independent, but his once-vital organization could not obtain the 3,000 signatures necessary to put him on the ballot.

Congressman Rangel no doubt gets along better than his predecessor did with the rest of the City's liberal delegation and with the other members of the House's Black Caucus. Powell was becoming a lone wolf congressman. Rangel has won the big Democratic primary, his first one; in the future, he will probably encounter little serious opposition. Redistricting could hurt him, but the Republican legislature and Gov. Rockefeller would hesitate before depriving Harlem of black representation. Rangel should win reelection in 1972.

Census Data 1970 pop. 332,718; deviation from current state average, —25.2%; change 1960–70, —18.7%. Metro. 100%, 100% central city.

1970 Share of Federal Outlays $565,470,000 (average outlay per district, New York 6–24)

DOD	$76,898,000	HEW	$154,742,000
AEC	$739,000	HUD	$2,744,000
NASA	$921,000	OEO	$2,012,000
DOT	$6,423,000	DOA	$42,872,000
		Other	$334,666,000

Federal Military-Industrial Commitments (See New York 17 for New York City listing.)

Economic Base Apparel and other finished products made from fabrics and similar materials, esp. women's, misses', and juniors' outerwear; textile mill products, esp. knitting mills; printing, publishing, and allied industries, esp. commercial printing and periodicals.

The Voters

Registration 105,945 total. 84,928 D (80%); 11,973 R (11%); 3,014 L (3%); 313 C (0%); 5,717 other (5%).

Employment profile White collar, 24%. Blue collar, 76%.

Ethnic groups Black, 72%. Puerto Rico, 10%. Total foreign stock, 16%. Italy, 4%; Germany, Ireland, 1% each; others, 8%.

Presidential vote

1968	Humphrey (D)	68,644	(89%)*
	Nixon (R)	7,967	(10%)
	Wallace (AIP)	528	(1%)

* *These figures do not include votes Humphrey received on the Liberal line. His performance, therefore, is understated by one to five percent in each New York district.*

Representative

Charles B. Rangel (D) Elected 1970; b. June 11, 1930, New York City; home, New York City; N.Y.U., B.S., 1957; St. John's Law School, LL.B., 1960; Army, 1948–52; married, one child; Catholic.

Career Asst. U.S. Atty., Justice Dept., 1963–64; Asst. Counsel, Speaker Travia of N.Y. Assembly, 1965; Gen. Counsel, Natl. Advisory Commission on Selective Svc., 1966; Bd. Mbr., Harlem Neighborhood Assn.

Offices 226 CHOB, 202-225-4365. Also 144 W. 125th St., New York City 10027, 212-866-8600.

Committees

Public Works (21st); Subs. (1) Investigation and Oversight, (2) Public Buildings and Grounds, (3) Roads, (4) Sp. on Economic Development Programs.

Science and Astronautics (15th); Subs. (1) Advance Research and Technology, (2) NASA Oversight.

Sel. Com. on Crime (6th).

Group Ratings, Key Votes: Newly elected.

Election Results

1970 general:	Charles B. Rangel (R and D)	52,851	(88%)
	Charles Taylor (L)	6,385	(11%)
	Jose Stevens (Communist)	374	(1%)
1970 primary:	Charles B. Rangel (D)	8,032	(33%)
	Adam Clayton Powell (D)	7,882	(32%)
	Ramon A. Martinez (D)	4,510	(18%)
	Jesse Gray (D)	2,481	(10%)
	John H. Young (D)	1,584	(6%)
	(Redistricted 1970)		

NINETEENTH DISTRICT Political Background

New York 19 comprises all of lower and mid-Manhattan kept out of the 17th by Republican redistricters in 1970. These are the Democratic areas which might have jeopardized Republican hopes in the silk stocking district (see New York 17). The yeasty 19th is the most polyglot in New York. Here there are communities of Chinese, Jewish, Hungarian, Ukrainian, and Puerto Rican residents. Most of the votes in the 19th are cast in three places: the Lower East Side, which is an old world, predominantly Jewish neighborhood with other ethnic communities about, as well as the East Village hippies (who don't vote); Greenwich Village, which except for the more sedate, higher-income portion in the 17th, is an overwhelmingly liberal area, having many intellectual and theatrical people; and the Upper West Side, where writers, intellectuals and professionals—all mostly Jewish—live in Riverside Drive and West End Avenue apartments, and Puerto Ricans, blacks, and other poor people live on the side streets running east and west.

The congressional race in the 19th is usually decided in the Democratic primary, which since 1962 has been a close contest between incumbent Leonard Farbstein and one of a series of liberal, antiwar challengers. The challengers always carried Greenwich Village and the West Side by large margins, but Farbstein always squeaked through with still larger majorities in the Lower East Side, where the local Democratic organizations retained their ability to deliver votes.

The story in 1970 was different. Where the male reformers failed, Bella Abzug succeeded. Mrs. Abzug is a lawyer, long active in civil rights and peace groups; Bella is known for her powerful vocal chords and her not-so-conventional manner. Like Farbstein's other opponents, she campaigned hard in the streets of Greenwich Village and along the park benches of Upper Broadway. But she also took her efforts to the Lower East Side, where Farbstein was always strong. Accompanied by Barbra Streisand,

Bella campaigned around the housing projects occupied by Jewish retirees and in the nitty-gritty streets of the Lower East Side. When Bella spoke, people got out on their balconies and listened, and when the votes were counted later, she took 45% of them in the East Side assembly districts. Despite Farbstein's record, which became more liberal after every challenge, Mrs. Abzug carried the West Side districts nearly 2–1 and won the election by almost 4,000 votes.

But her strenuous campaigning was not finished; both the Republican and Liberal parties had nominated Barry Farber, a radio talk-show host. One of the enduring myths of New York politics is that the Liberal party is antiwar and pro-good-government. In fact, dominated as it is by aging union leaders, the Liberal party did not take a strong position against the Vietnam war until 1968, and the party still runs separate candidates against some antiwar New York congressmen. Moreover, the desire of its leadership to secure patronage posts for the party faithful is as great as those in the City's Democratic organization. Candidate Farber spent most of his time attacking what he considered Bella's lukewarm attitude towards Israel and also accusing her of being too strident and emotional. She denied the first charge, didn't attempt to refute the second, and continued to hit the streets as only she can.

Mrs. Abzug's margin in the general election was modest—8,000 votes out of nearly 90,000 cast. It was enough, however, to get her into the House, where her loud and sometimes profane use of the language draws pained expressions from aging regulars. Like most cheeky freshmen, Bella did not get the committee assignment she wanted. But it is unlikely that even the hallowed old ways of the House will keep battling Bella down for very long. Her major problem in 1972 is redistricting. Since Manhattan lost a seat in the 1970 census, the Republican legislature may split her district between Edward Koch's 17th and William Ryan's 20th. Both of the incumbents in those seats are also antiwar reformers. Details must await the redistricting plan adopted, but wherever Bella decides to run, there will be a lively campaign.

Census Data 1970 pop. 379,012; deviation from current state average, −14.8%; change 1960–70, −7.5%. Metro. 100%, 100% central city.

1970 Share of Federal Outlays $565,470,000 (average outlay per district, New York 6–24)

DOD	$76,898,000	HEW	$154,742,000
AEC	$739,000	HUD	$2,744,000
NASA	$921,000	OEO	$2,012,000
DOT	$6,423,000	DOA	$42,872,000
		Other	$334,666,000

Federal Military-Industrial Commitments (See New York 17 for New York City listing.)

Economic Base Apparel and other finished products made from fabrics and similar materials, esp. women's, misses', and juniors' outerwear; textile mill products, esp. knitting mills; printing, publishing, and allied industries, esp. commercial printing and periodicals. Also, banking, insurance, and stock brokerage.

The Voters

Registration 135,619 total. 94,545 D (70%); 20,164 R (15%); 5,655 L (4%); 1,023 C (1%); 14,323 other (10%).

Employment profile White collar, 44%. Blue collar, 56%.

Ethnic groups Black, 10%. Puerto Rico, 18%. Total foreign stock, 50%. Italy, 10%; USSR, 7%; Poland, 6%; Austria, Germany, 3% each; Ireland, UK, 2% each; Czech., Hungary, Canada, 1% each; others, 13%.

Presidential vote

1968	Humphrey (D)	64,240	(67%)*
	Nixon (R)	27,118	(28%)
	Wallace (AIP)	3,996	(4%)

* *These figures do not include votes Humphrey received on the Liberal line. His performance, therefore, is understated by one to five percent in each New York district.*

Representative

Bella S. Abzug (D) Elected 1970; b. July 24, 1920, New York City; home, New York City; Hunter Col., B.A., 1942; Columbia U., LL.B., 1945; married, two children; Jewish.

Career Practicing Atty., 1947–70; Natl. Legislative Rep. for Women's Strike for Peace Movement; Mbr., Mayor's Advisory Commission.

Offices 1506 LHOB, 202-225-5635. Also 252 7th Ave., New York City 10011, 212-269-8535.

Committees

Government Operations (23rd); Subs. (1) Conservation and Natural Resources, (2) Special Studies.

Public Works (23rd); Subs. (1) Investigation and Oversight, (2) Public Buildings and Grounds, (3) Rivers and Harbors, (4) Sp. on Economic Development Programs.

Group Ratings, Key Votes: Newly elected.

Election Results

1970 general:	Bella S. Abzug (D)	46,947	(52%)
	Barry Farber (R and L)	38,460	(43%)
	Salvatore Lodico (C)	4,426	(5%)
1970 primary:	Bella S. Abzug (D)	18,515	(55%)
	Leonard Farbstein (D)	14,856	(45%)
	(Redistricted 1970)		

TWENTIETH DISTRICT Political Background

New York 20 lies in the Upper West Side of Manhattan. Sandwiched between Harlem and the Hudson River, the district is only a few blocks wide and several miles long. Below 125th Street, where Morningside Heights dips into the Harlem valley, is liberal intellectual country: the site of Columbia University and, to the south, the high-rent apartments of Riverside and West End Avenues. Above 125th is a predominantly Jewish neighborhood that overlooks Harlem on one side and the river on the other. Beyond the George Washington Bridge is the Irish neighborhood of Inwood, a conservative stronghold in this otherwise overwhelmingly liberal district.

The congressman from the 20th is Willam Fitts Ryan, a product of the early years of Manhattan's reform Democrat movement. Ryan first won in 1960 by beating one machine-backed Democrat, and after redistricting in 1962, beat another. Ryan, an early critic of the Vietnam war, is an opponent of heavy military spending. Although the Congressman has ten years of seniority, his 12th ranking positions on both the Judiciary and the Interior and Insular Affairs committees is below that of some Democrats with less seniority. Ryan's plight is in part due to the House establishment, which is unsympathetic to the interests of an arch-liberal congressman. It is also due to the New York Democratic delegation, which has never possessed much clout. Today, liberals like Ryan are still not accepted in the inner councils of the House leadership. But because an increasing number of liberals have been sent to Congress, and because their parliamentary skills have been improving, they have started to win better committee assignments.

Like many other New York congressmen, Ryan has run for City office; his strong third in the 1965 Democratic mayoral primary allowed machine-backed Abraham Beame to beat Wagner protégé Paul Śrevane. Since his first two primaries, Ryan has had no trouble winning reelection, but he may face a difficult contest in 1972 if the Republican redistricting plan forces him into a race with another one of Manhattan's liberal Democrats.

Census Data 1970 pop. 361,337; deviation from current state average, –18.8%; change 1960–70, 11.7%. Metro. 100%, 100% central city.

1970 Share of Federal Outlays $565,470,000 (average outlay per district, New York 6–24)

DOD	$76,898,000	HEW	$154,742,000
AEC	$739,000	HUD	$2,744,000
NASA	$921,000	OEO	$2,012,000
DOT	$6,423,000	DOA	$42,872,000
		Other	$334,666,000

Federal Military-Industrial Commitments (See New York 17 for New York City listing.)

Economic Base Apparel and other finished products made from fabrics and similar materials, esp. women's, misses', and juniors' outerwear; textile mill products, esp. knitting mills; printing, publishing, and allied industries, esp. commercial printing and periodicals. Also, higher education (CUNY, City College, and Columbia University).

The Voters

Registration 93,352 total. 106,279 D (71%); 21,090 R (14%); 5,138 L (3%); 1,239 C (1%); 15,946 other (11%).

Employment profile White collar, 52%. Blue collar, 48%.

Ethnic groups Black, 20%. Puerto Rico, 13%. Total foreign stock, 51%. Germany, 8%; Ireland, 7%; USSR, 6%; Poland, 4%; Austria, UK, 3% each; Czech., Hungary, Canada, 1% each; others, 15%.

Presidential vote

1968	Humphrey (D)	78,209	(71%)*
	Nixon (R)	29,008	(26%)
	Wallace (AIP)	3,560	(3%)

Representative

William F. Ryan (D-Lib.) Elected 1960; b. June 28, 1922, Albion; home, New York City; Princeton U., B.A., 1944; Columbia U., LL.B., 1949; Army, WWII; married, four children; Catholic.

Career Practicing atty., 1949– ; Asst. Dist. Atty., N.Y. County, 1950–57.

Offices 303 CHOB, 202-225-6616. Also 1040 St. Nicholas Ave., New York City 10032, 212-234-6900.

Committees

Interior and Insular Affairs (12th); Subs. (1) Environment, (2) National Parks and Recreation, (3) Territorial and Insular Affairs.

Judiciary (12th); Subs. (1) No. 1, (2) No. 3.

Group Ratings

	ADA	COPE	NREP	NFU	LCV	CFA	NAB	NSI	ACA
1970	96	100	100	92	89	100	0	0	13
1969	100	—	—	80	—	—	—	—	12
1968	100	92	—	88	—	—	17	—	4

Key Votes

(1) ABM	AGN	(6) 18-Yr-Vote	FOR	(11) Clean Water $	FOR
(2) SST	AGN	(7) Farm Sub Lmt	FOR	(12) Mig Wrkrs Comp	FOR
(3) Phil Pln	FOR	(8) Coop-Church	FOR	(13) Jets to Chiang	AGN
(4) No-Knock	AGN	(9) Family Asst	FOR	(14) State OEO Veto	AGN
(5) Cmutr Tax	FOR	(10) Work Stamps	AGN	(15) Park Logging	AGN

Election Results

1970 general:	William F. Ryan (D and L)	73,779	(79%)
	William Goldstein (R)	13,527	(14%)
	Francis C. Saunders (C)	6,315	(7%)

* *These figures do not include votes Humphrey received on the Liberal line. His performance, therefore, is understated by one to five percent in each New York district.*

1970 primary: William F. Ryan (D and L), unopposed
(Redistricted 1970)

TWENTY-FIRST DISTRICT Political Background

New York 21 is the Triborough district: parts of Manhattan, the Bronx and Queens connected by the Triborough Bridge. The Manhattan portion of the district lies in East Harlem which used to be a predominantly Italian community; from 1938 to 1950, the people here sent Vito Marcantonio of the radical American Labor party to the House. There are still many Italians in the area, but today the majority of East Harlem's population is Puerto Rican. More than half of the district's people live in the south Bronx, which is predominantly Puerto Rican, with a large black minority. The south Bronx is as poverty-stricken an area as any in New York City. The Queens portion is very different; it consists of the Irish, Italian, and German working-class neighborhoods of Astoria and Steinway, site of the main plant of the piano company for which it was named. This area is traditionally Democratic, but lately has become increasingly conservative.

When the 21st was created in 1970, it was expected to be a Puerto Rican-majority district. But an analysis of the votes cast in the elections of that year indicates that this is not precisely the case: the homeowners in Queens register and vote with more regularity than either the Puerto Rican or black slum-dwellers. In 1970, the winner of the Democratic congressional primary would clearly win the November election. Six men entered that primary, and the early favorite, former Bronx Borough President Herman Badillo, wound up taking only 30% of the vote. The man who finished second trailed him by 587 votes. Two of the other candidates were of Puerto Rican descent, who polled 15% between them; this, of course, hurt Badillo. And a black former state senator siphoned off another 6%. Peter F. Vallone, a well-known community leader in Astoria, almost won the election. He took two out of every three of the votes cast in Queens, but showed no strength anywhere else in the district.

But this time Badillo was accustomed to close margins. In 1965, he was elected Bronx Borough president after winning two squeakers; first, over a machine-backed candidate in the Democratic primary, and then, over a popular conservative Republican incumbent in the general election. In 1969 he had the support of most of the city's peace groups when he ran for Mayor and finished a strong third. If one adds those votes cast for novelist Norman Mailer to Badillo's total, the figure is larger than the number received by the winner of the primary, conservative City Controller Mario Proccaccino.

Like most of New York City's growing number of liberal congressmen, Badillo will probably not accept the traditionally quiescent role of a freshman in the House. The leadership assigned the urban Congressman a seat on the Agriculture Committee; this, of course, struck Badillo as quite unacceptable and he persuaded them to give him the committee assignment of his choice, Education and Labor.

Rumors say that Badillo has his eyes on Gracie Mansion (the residence of New York's mayors), and will run for mayor again sometime in the near future. In the meantime, having won his initial primary, he should have no trouble winning reelection to the House. It is unlikely that the legislature's redistricting plan will threaten America's first Puerto Rican congressman.

Census Data 1970 pop. 386,554; deviation from current state average, —13.1%; change 1960–70, —5.5%. Metro. 100%, 100% central city.

1970 Share of Federal Outlays $565,470,000 (average outlay per district, New York 6–24)

DOD	$76,898,000	HEW	$154,742,000
AEC	$739,000	HUD	$2,744,000
NASA	$921,000	OEO	$2,012,000
DOT	$6,423,000	DOA	$42,872,000
		Other	$334,666,000

Federal Military-Industrial Commitments (See New York 17 for New York City listing.)

Economic Base Apparel and other finished products made from fabrics and similar materials, esp. women's, juniors', and misses' outerwear; food and kindred products, esp. bakery products; fabricated metal products, esp. fabricated structural metal products; electrical machinery, equipment, and supplies.

The Voters

Registration 93,352 total. 72,557 D (78%); 13,039 R (14%); 2,128 L (2%); 974 C (1%); 4,654 other (5%).

Employment profile White collar, 51%. Blue collar, 49%.

Ethnic groups Black, 34%. Puerto Rico, 30%. Total foreign stock, 51%. USSR, 9%; Ireland, 8%; Italy, Poland, 7% each; Austria, 4%; Germany, 3%; Hungary, UK, 2% each; Czech., Canada, 1% each; others, 8%.

Presidential vote

1968	Humphrey (D)	49,616	(68%)*
	Nixon (R)	20,008	(27%)
	Wallace (AIP)	3,406	(5%)

Representative

Herman Badillo (D) Elected 1970; b. Aug. 21, 1929, Caguas, P.R.; home, Bronx; City Col. of N.Y., B.A., 1951; Brooklyn Law School, LL.B., 1954; married, one child; Protestant.

Career Practicing atty., 1955– ; set up J. F. Kennedy Dem. Club, 1962; Deputy Commissioner for Relocation, N.Y.C., 1962, 1963–66; Bronx Borough Pres., 1966–70; Chm., Com. on Health, Housing and Social Security at State Constitutional Convention, 1967.

Offices 510 CHOB, 202-225-4361. Also 840 Grand Concourse, Bronx 10451, 212-665-9400; and 219 E. 116th St., New York City 10029; and 31-13 Ditmars Blvd., Astoria 11102, 212-626-6000.

Committees

Education and Labor (22nd); Subs. (1) Agricultural Labor, (2) Education, (3) Labor.

Group Ratings, Key Votes: Newly elected.

Election Results

1970 general:	Herman Badillo (D)	38,866	(84%)
	George B. Smaragdas (C)	7,561	(16%)
1970 primary:	Herman Badillo (D)	7,732	(30%)
	Peter F. Vallone (D)	7,145	(28%)
	Louis R. Gigante (D)	5,621	(22%)
	Ramon S. Velez (D)	2,844	(11%)
	Dennis R. Coleman (D)	1,508	(6%)
	Joseph A. Loubriel (D)	903	(4%)
	(Redistricted 1970)		

TWENTY-SECOND DISTRICT Political Background

New York 22 extends north from the East River into the middle of the Bronx. The Bronx River runs through the district and separates the south Bronx slums from some of the borough's uneasy middle-class communities; to the west are low-income black and Puerto Rican neighborhoods, to the east, an Italian community and, farther north, a middle-income Jewish neighborhood around the huge Parkchester apartment complex. The district as a whole is Democratic, but it has, like most of outer New York City, become increasingly conservative since John Lindsay has been mayor.

Redistricting drove two incumbent congressmen into the 22nd's 1970 Democratic primary. The primary, which in a district like this one determines the winner of the general election, featured a reform Democrat and a member of the Bronx's regular Democratic organization. James H. Scheuer had run for office in Manhattan before taking the 21st House seat in a bitter 1964 primary battle. He was forced to move again when the 21st was conceded to a non-incumbent, Herman Badillo. Scheuer, who comes from a wealthy real-estate family, had run for mayor in 1969 and finished last in the Democratic primary, behind Norman Mailer. The regular, Jacob H. Gilbert, had spent ten years in the state legislature before starting a ten-year career in the House.

** These figures do not include votes Humphrey received on the Liberal line. His performance, therefore, is understated by one to five percent in each New York district.*

The two candidates had virtually identical voting records. Gilbert, like many New York organization congressmen beleaguered by reformers, had long since earned ADA ratings around 90. Gilbert, who was the incumbent in most of the new district, depended on his clubhouse organization to get the regular vote out. He stressed his membership on the House Ways and Means Committee. Scheuer waged a more energetic and more expensive campaign, which featured his book, *To Walk the Streets Safely.* Both candidates avoided the carpetbagger issue; like many congressmen who represent lower- and lower-middle-income areas, neither occupied their district "residences" very often.

Scheuer's efforts paid off with a 57% victory. His position in the House, however, is hardly secure. The district lines will be redrawn again before the 1972 elections, and the regular Democratic organization, which today can consider just one of the four congressmen from the Bronx as one of its own, will be out for revenge.

Census Data 1970 pop. 431,704; deviation from current state average, —3.0%; change 1960–70, +6.2%. Metro. 100%, 100% central city.

1970 Share of Federal Outlays $565,470,000 (average outlay per district, New York 6–24)

DOD	$76,898,000	HEW	$154,742,000
AEC	$739,000	HUD	$2,744,000
NASA	$921,000	OEO	$2,012,000
DOT	$6,423,000	DOA	$42,872,000
		Other	$334,666,000

Federal Military-Industrial Commitments (See New York 17 for New York City listing.)

Economic Base Apparel and other finished products made from fabrics and similar materials, esp. women's, misses', and juniors' outerwear; food and kindred products, esp. bakery products; fabricated metal products, esp. fabricated structural metal products; electrical machinery, equipment, and supplies.

The Voters

Registration 122,972 total. 92,613 D (75%); 19,096 R (16%); 3,281 L (3%); 1,778 C (1%); 6,204 other (5%).

Employment profile White collar, 32%. Blue collar, 68%.

Ethnic groups Black, 28%. Puerto Rico, 26%. Total foreign stock, 33%. USSR, 6%; Italy, 5%; Poland, 4%; Austria, Germany, Ireland, 2% each; Hungary, UK, 1% each; others, 9%.

Presidential vote

1968	Humphrey (D)	61,650	(62%)*
	Nixon (R)	32,133	(32%)
	Wallace (AIP)	5,351	(6%)

Representative

James H. Scheuer (D-Lib.) Elected 1964; b. Feb. 6, 1920, New York City; home, Bronx; Swarthmore Col., B.A., 1946; Columbia U. Law School, LL.B., 1948; Harvard, Industrial Admin., 1943; USAAF, WWII; married, four children; Jewish.

Career Economist, U.S. Foreign Economic Admin., 1945–46; legal staff, Office of Price Stabilization, 1951–52; Chm., Housing Advisory Council, N.Y. State Commission against Discrimination, 1955–64; Consultant, Pres. Kennedy on housing and human rights problems, 1960–64; Pres., Citizens Housing and Planning Council of N.Y.C.; Bd. Mbr., Natl. Housing Conference.

Offices 431 CHOB, 202-225-3816. Also 2060 Cruger Ave., Bronx 10462, 212-931-3200.

* *These figures do not include votes Humphrey received on the Liberal line. His performance, therefore, is understated by one to five percent in each New York district.*

Committees

Education and Labor (12th); Subs. (1) Sel. on Education, (2) Sp. on Labor, (3) Sp. on Education.

Group Ratings

	ADA	COPE	NREP	NFU	LCV	CFA	NAB	NSI	ACA
1970	96	100	100	91	100	95	0	0	13
1969	100	—	—	85	—	—	—	—	14
1968	83	100	—	75	—	—	0	—	6

Key Votes

(1) ABM	AGN	(6) 18-Yr-Vote	FOR	(11) Clean Water $	FOR
(2) SST	AGN	(7) Farm Sub Lmt	FOR	(12) Mig Wrkrs Comp	FOR
(3) Phil Pln	FOR	(8) Coop-Church	FOR	(13) Jets to Chiang	ABS
(4) No-Knock	AGN	(9) Family Asst	FOR	(14) State OEO Veto	AGN
(5) Cmutr Tax	FOR	(10) Work Stamps	AGN	(15) Park Logging	ABS

Election Results

1970 general:	James H. Scheuer (D and L)	50,372	(72%)
	Robert M. Schneck (R and C)	19,994	(28%)
1970 primary:	James H. Scheuer (D)	11,733	(57%)
	Jacob H. Gilbert (D)	8,768	(43%)
	(Redistricted 1970)		

TWENTY-THIRD DISTRICT Political Background

New York 23, the western Bronx, spans the City's socio-economic and ethnic spectrums. The district runs north from Yankee Stadium to take in the blacks and Puerto Ricans of lower-income Morrisania, New York and Fordham universities in University Heights, and the middle-income Irish and Italian neighborhood of Kingsbridge. Apartment houses line the Grand Concourse, a boulevard that runs most of the length of the district. Most of the people living on the Concourse are Jewish, many of them elderly, and although they are worried about crime, they have remained staunchly Democratic. The northwest corner of the district is the upper-income neighborhood of Riverdale; here large houses and apartment buildings stand on the heights overlooking the Hudson River below.

Riverdale is the home of Jonathan Bingham, a liberal Democrat who has represented the 23rd in the House since 1964, when he beat Charles A. Buckley in the Democratic primary. Buckley was then the Bronx Democratic Chairman as well as the chairman of the House Public Works Committee. In 1964, Buckley apparently refused to take Bingham's candidacy seriously. He could not believe that the scion of an aristocratic WASP family could beat him in a predominantly Jewish and Irish district. Bingham's father, a Republican senator from Connecticut in the 1920's, was censured by the Senate for spending too much money on his campaigns.

Like most reform upstarts, Bingham had to wait a long time for his committee preference, Foreign Affairs—the assignment for which his background as a member of the American United Nations delegation, with the rank of ambassador, would seem to make him eminently suited. Since 1964, Bingham has been winning reelection easily, winning more than 70% of the vote in every general election. Redistricting poses the only threat to his tenure. He may be forced into a district with another incumbent congressman, perhaps James H. Scheuer of the 22nd.

Census Data 1970 pop. 422,499; deviation from current state average, −5.0%; change 1960–70, +3.2%. Metro. 100%, 100% central city.

1970 Share of Federal Outlays $565,470,000 (average outlay per district, New York 6–24)

DOD	$76,898,000	HEW	$154,742,000
AEC	$739,000	HUD	$2,744,000
NASA	$921,000	OEO	$2,012,000

DOT	$6,423,000	DOA	$42,872,000
		Other	$334,666,000

Federal Military-Industrial Commitments (See New York 17 for New York City listing.)

Economic Base Apparel and other finished products made from fabrics and similar materials; food and kindred products, esp. bakery products; fabricated metal products, esp. fabricated structural metal products; electrical machinery, equipment, and supplies. Also, higher education (NYU, and Fordham University).

The Voters

Registration 164,974 total. 121,598 D (74%); 21,849 R (13%); 5,548 L (3%); 2,648 C (2%); 13,331 other (8%).

Employment profile White collar, 55%. Blue collar, 45%.

Ethnic groups Black, 20%. Puerto Rico, 3%. Total foreign stock, 63%. USSR, 15%; Italy, 11%; Poland, 8%; Ireland, 7%; Austria, 5%; Germany, 4%; UK, 3%; Hungary, 2%; Czech., Canada, 1% each; others, 7%.

Presidential vote

1968	Humphrey (D)	85,523	(67%)*
	Nixon (R)	36,457	(29%)
	Wallace (AIP)	5,486	(4%)

Representative

Jonathan B. Bingham (D-Lib.) Elected 1964; b. April 24, 1914, New Haven, Conn.; home, Bronx and Manhattan; Yale U., B.A., 1936, LL.B., 1939; Army, WWII (Capt. Military Intelligence); married, four children; United Church of Christ.

Career Practicing atty., 1940–45, 1951–61; Correspondent, N.Y. *Herald Tribune,* 1935, 1938; Asst. Dir., Office Intl. Security Affairs, 1951; Deputy Admin., Technical Cooperation Admin., 1951–53; Secy., Governor Averell Harriman, 1955–58; U.S. Rep., UN Econ. and Social Council, Advisor to Ambassador Adlai E. Stevenson, 1961–63; U.S. Delegation to four UN Gen. Assemblies, 1961–63; U.S. Rep. on UN Trusteeship Council, 1961–62; Pres. of Council, 1962.

Offices 133 CHOB, 202-225-4411. Also 1 East Fordham, Bronx 10468, 212-933-2310.

Committees

Foreign Affairs (16th); Subs. (1) International Organizations, (2) National Security, (3) Policy and Scientific Development, (4) Near East.

House Administration (10th) Subs. (1) Library and Memorials, (2) Printing.

Group Ratings

	ADA	COPE	NREP	NFU	LCV	CFA	NAB	NSI	ACA
1970	100	100	100	92	100	100	0	0	16
1969	100	—	—	92	—	—	—	—	7
1968	100	100	—	100	—	—	0	—	0

Key Votes

(1) ABM	AGN	(6) 18-Yr-Vote	FOR	(11) Clean Water $	FOR
(2) SST	AGN	(7) Farm Sub Lmt	FOR	(12) Mig Wrkrs Comp	FOR
(3) Phil Pln	FOR	(8) Coop-Church	FOR	(13) Jets to Chiang	AGN
(4) No-Knock	AGN	(9) Family Asst	FOR	(14) State OEO Veto	AGN
(5) Cmutr Tax	FOR	(10) Work Stamps	AGN	(15) Park Logging	AGN

* *These figures do not include votes Humphrey received on the Liberal line. His performance, therefore, is understated by one to five percent in each New York district.*

Election Results

1970 general:	Jonathan B. Bingham (D)	78,723	(76%)
	George E. Sweeney (R)	16,172	(16%)
	Nora M. Kardian (C)	8,456	(8%)
1970 primary:	Jonathan B. Bingham (D and L), unopposed (Redistricted 1970)		

TWENTY-FOURTH DISTRICT Political Background

New York 24 is the northeast part of the Bronx and the southern portion of the city of Yonkers in suburban Westchester County. The Bronx neighborhoods—Throgs Neck, Baychester, Pelham, Williamsbridge—tend to be middle-class, Italian, and conservative; southern Yonkers is much the same. The northeast Bronx is the home of Mario Proccaccino, the peppery former city controller who almost beat John Lindsay for mayor in 1969. Proccaccino grew up in an Italian slum. He did well in college and then equally well in the Bronx Democratic organization. For a while he was a judge, but when the bosses needed an Italian candidate for the controller slot on their 1965 ticket, Proccaccino resigned the judgeship, ran, and won.

While serving as controller, Proccaccino was one of the many who recognized the growing dissatisfaction of New York City's predominantly Catholic, white middle-class majority with Mayor John Lindsay. That dissatisfaction was symbolized by the crime issue, and Proccaccino rode the issue to victory in the Democratic primary and then lost the mayor's job by only 5% of the vote. Only his uncontrolled outbursts of anger and self-pity kept him from winning. Lindsay, like Nelson Rockefeller, has been blessed with inept political opposition.

The 24th strongly supported Proccaccino's mayoral bid, of course; it also responded well to his endorsement of Conservative Senate candidate James Buckley in 1970. In local contests, the district is enthusiastic about Italian law-and-order candidates such as its present congressman, Mario Biaggi, a former New York City policeman. Biaggi was decorated 28 times in his 22 years on the force; he is also a lawyer, and at one time served as a community-relations specialist for the state Housing Division.

In 1968, when Republican Paul A. Fino resigned the 24th's House seat to take a judgeship—the traditional reward for veteran New York City congressmen—Biaggi succeeded him; he won the seat with an unusual alliance of the Democratic and Conservative parties. His record has not been entirely acceptable to either liberals or conservatives. He opposed the ABM and supported Cooper-Church, but opposed some urban spending bills and the Nixon family assistance plan. But this sort of urban populism with a law-and-order accent is probably more in line with the sentiments of his constituency than more conventional ideologies.

Biaggi is phenomenally popular in the 24th. In 1970, again running on both the Democratic and Conservative lines, he took 70% of the votes against ex-Borough President Joseph Periconi, a Republican who has carried the area many times. Biaggi should be able to stay in the House for a long time, no matter what redistricting plan is adopted.

Census Data 1970 pop. 435,400; deviation from current state average, –2.1%; change 1960–70, +6.5%. Metro. 100%, 82.2% central city.

1970 Share of Federal Outlays $565,470,000 (average outlay per district, New York 6–24)

DOD	$76,898,000	HEW	$154,742,000
AEC	$739,000	HUD	$2,744,000
NASA	$921,000	OEO	$2,012,000
DOT	$6,423,000	DOA	$42,872,000
		Other	$334,666,000

Federal Military-Industrial Commitments (See New York 17 for New York City listing.)

Economic Base Apparel and other finished products made from fabrics and similar materials, esp. women's, misses', and juniors' outerwear; electrical machinery, equipment, and supplies; food and kindred products, esp. bakery products; printing, publishing, and allied industries, esp. periodicals.

The Voters

Registration 201,400 total. 124,323 D (62%); 53,485 R (27%); 3,630 L (2%); 4,763 C (2%); 15,199 other (8%).

Employment profile White collar, 50%. Blue collar, 50%.

Ethnic groups Black, 12%. Puerto Rico, 1%. Total foreign stock, 57%. Italy, 25%; Ireland, 7%; Germany, 5%; USSR, 4%; Poland, UK, 3% each; Austria, 2%; Czech., Hungary, Canada, 1% each; others, 5%.

Presidential vote

1968	Humphrey (D)	72,979	(43%)*
	Nixon (R)	82,478	(49%)
	Wallace (AIP)	13,090	(8%)

Representative

Mario Biaggi (D-Cons.) Elected 1969; b. Oct. 26, 1917, New York City; home, Bronx; N.Y. Law School, LL.B., 1963; married, four children; Catholic.

Career N.Y. City Police Dept., 1942–65; Community Relations Specialist, N.Y. State Div. of Housing, 1961–63; Asst. to Secy. of State, N.Y., 1961–65; Pres., Natl. Police Officers Assn., 1967; Consultant, Pres., Grand Council of Columbia Assn. in Civil Service; practicing atty., 1969– .

Offices 1221 LHOB, 202-225-2464. Also 2010 Williamsbridge Rd., Bronx 10461, 212-931-0100.

Committees

Education and Labor (18th); Subs, (1) Gen. on Labor, (2) Gen. on Education, (3) Sel. on Labor.

Merchant Marine and Fisheries (16th); Subs. (1) Coast Guard, Coast and Geodetic Survey and Navigation, (2) Fisheries and Wildlife Conservation, (3) Oceanography.

Group Ratings

	ADA	COPE	NREP	NFU	LCV	CFA	NAB	NSI	ACA
1970	52	83	67	100	100	50	9	66	37
1969	80	—	—	86	—	—	—	—	40

Key Votes

(1) ABM	FOR	(6) 18-Yr-Vote	FOR	(11) Clean Water $	FOR
(2) SST	AGN	(7) Farm Sub Lmt	FOR	(12) Mig Wrkrs Comp	FOR
(3) Phil Pln	AGN	(8) Coop-Church	FOR	(13) Jets to Chiang	AGN
(4) No-Knock	FOR	(9) Family Asst	AGN	(14) State OEO Veto	AGN
(5) Cmutr Tax	FOR	(10) Work Stamps	AGN	(15) Park Logging	AGN

Election Results

1970 general:	Mario Biaggi (D and C)	106,942	(70%)
	Joseph F. Periconi (R and Silent Majority)	38,173	(25%)
	John Patrick Hagan (L)	7,970	(5%)
1970 primary:	Mario Biaggi (D and C), unopposed		

TWENTY-FIFTH DISTRICT Political Background

New York 25 lies on both sides of the Hudson River and takes in western Westchester County and eastern Rockland County. For the most part, Westchester lives up to its reputation as the classic wealthy American suburb: a paradise of Tudor homes, leafy trees, and gently sloping lawns. Most of this lies within a five mile radius of the Rockefeller family's huge estate in Pocantico Hills. Bronxville has traditionally been the home of New York's wealthiest Catholic families, at one time including the

** These figures do not include votes Humphrey received on the Liberal line. His performance, therefore, is understated by one to five percent in each New York district.*

Joseph P. Kennedys. But the 25th's portion of Westchester also contains a black ghetto, Elmsford, some lower-middle-class Italian and Irish neighborhoods in Yonkers, and huge Sing Sing state prison in up-the-river Ossining.

Rockland County, just north of the New Jersey line, is rather different. A newer suburban area, it lacks the tradition and the extremes of wealth and poverty found in Westchester. A large proportion of Rockland's population is Jewish, and it normally votes more Democratic than Westchester.

The district lines of the 25th were drawn in 1970, and those lines were in part responsible for Richard Ottinger's decision to run for the Senate in that year. Ottinger had represented the area for six years; he spent $200,000 in 1964 to win the seat from conservative Republican, Robert R. Barry. As congressman, Barry seemed to spend more time in California than New York; after losing in the 25th, he has run without success in the 11th and the 38th district of California. Ottinger, meanwhile, compiled a strong record in the House; the Congressman was particularly effective in protecting the scenery of the Hudson Valley. He won reelection by large margins. But Ottinger felt that the 1970 redistricting removed too many Democrats from south Yonkers and added too many Republicans elsewhere in the district, and so he decided the risks, if not the expense, of the Senate race would be more comfortable.

The contest to replace him was as hard fought as any New York election that year. William Dretzin, with the slogan "He can save Ottinger's seat," won an upset victory in the Democratic primary, but his principal opponent then ran in the general election as a Liberal party candidate and split the liberal, antiwar vote. Peter A. Peyser won the Republican primary with a vigorous campaign. Peyser, the mayor of Irvington, had won fame by starting an anti-drug effort in which police urged parents to inform on their children. His strongest opponent in the primary, Anthony J. DeVito ran as the Conservative party candidate in the general election.

By election day, Peyser had been campaigning for more than a year, and it paid off with a 43% victory. Dretzin got 37%, DeVito 17%, and Greenawalt 3%. The results are a fair reflection of the district's slight Republican leaning, and of the relative strength of the minor parties. DeVito's share of the votes indicates the strength of the Conservative line—James Buckley was running at the top of the ticket—even in an area like Westchester County, a presumed bastion of *noblesse oblige*. Of course, DeVito's name was an asset among the district's many Italian voters. Greenawalt's poor showing points up the general debility of the Liberal party and its weakness among antiwar voters.

Peyser ran as a supporter of the Nixon Administration, and the Republican legislature will do what it can to strengthen his chances for 1972. DeVito's showing has Peyser thinking twice before casting any liberal votes in the House. If he can compile a record which the Conservatives find acceptable, Peyser will probably get the Conservative as well as the Republican nomination in 1972. If the Congressman has both, reelection will be no problem at all.

Census Data 1970 pop. 489,605; deviation from current state average, +10.0%; change 1960–70, +19.5%. Metro. 100%, 0.0% central city.

1970 Share of Federal Outlays $347,668,000 (average outlay per district, New York 25 and 26)

DOD	$21,717,000	HEW	$106,608,000
AEC	$784,000	HUD	$4,812,000
NASA	$191,000	OEO	$727,000
DOT	$1,320,000	DOA	$1,468,000
		Other	$210,041,000

Federal Military-Industrial Commitments (See New York 26 for Westchester and Rockland counties listing.)

Economic Base Electrical machinery, equipment, and supplies, esp. electronic components and accessories; printing, publishing, and allied industries, esp. periodicals; transportation, esp. motor vehicles and motor vehicle equipment; apparel and other finished products made from fabrics and similar materials, esp. women's, misses' and juniors' dresses. Also, extensive commuting to New York 17, 19 (New York City).

The Voters

Registration 252,214 total. 88,799 D (25%); 118,839 R (47%); 2,156 L (1%); 3,676 C (1%); 38,744 other (15%).

Employment profile White collar, 54%. Blue collar, 46%.

Ethnic groups Black, 7%. Total foreign stock, 42%. Italy, 10%; Germany, 5%; Ireland, Poland, UK, USSR, 4% each; Austria, Canada, 2% each; Czech., Hungary, Sweden, 1% each; others, 5%.

Presidential vote

1968	Humphrey (D)	83,592	(39%)*
	Nixon (R)	114,492	(54%)
	Wallace (AIP)	13,616	(6%)

Representative

Peter A. Peyser (R) Elected 1970; b. Sept. 7, 1921, Cedarhurst; home, Irvington; Colgate U., B.A., 1943; Army, WWII; married, five children; Episcopalian.

Career Insurance; Mgr., Peter A. Peyser Agency of Mutual of N.Y., 1961–70; Mayor of Irvington, 1963–70.

Offices 1133 LHOB, 202-225-5536. Also 13–15 Neperan Rd., Tarrytown 10591, 914-631-8811; and P.O. Bldg., 48 S. Broadway, Nyack 10960, 914-358-1300.

Committees

Education and Labor (16th); Subs. (1) Education, (2) Sel. on Education, (3) Sel. on Labor.

Group Ratings, Key Votes: Newly elected.

Election Results

1970 general:	Peter A. Peyser (R)	76,611	(43%)
	William Dretzin (D)	66,688	(37%)
	Anthony J. DeVito (C)	31,250	(17%)
	William S. Greenawalt (L)	5,697	(3%)
1970 primary:	Peter A. Peyser (R)	7,261	(35%)
	Anthony J. DeVito (R)	5,180	(25%)
	Yale Rapkin (R)	5,127	(25%)
	Vincent F. Cerchiara (R)	3,181	(15%)
	(Redistricted 1970)		

TWENTY-SIXTH DISTRICT—Political Background

New York 26 comprises the eastern two-thirds of Westchester County. It includes the Italian middle-class neighborhoods of Mount Vernon and New Rochelle; the older, posh towns of Mamaroneck and Rye on Long Island Sound; wealthy Scarsdale, which has a large Jewish population; the commercial center of the county, White Plains, which has a few poor sections but is mostly wealthy; and to the north, the super-rich, woodsy towns of Bedford, Mount Kisco, and Chappaqua.

The 26th is one of the homes of liberal Republicanism; many of the wealthy residents here have forsaken their conservatism of the '40's and '50's, which was based on economic concerns, and have taken up with the liberalism of the '60's, with its concern for the social issues of peace and racial justice. For the voters of the district, liberalism is made more palatable by the Republican label and by one Republican in particular, Ogden Reid, an heir to the *Herald Tribune* fortune.

After his branch of the family lost control of the newspaper, Reid became ambassador to Israel for two years, a stint which did him no harm when he later decided to enter politics. First elected in 1962, Reid subsequently compiled a very liberal voting record

* *These figures do not include votes Humphrey received on the Liberal line. His performance, therefore, is understated by one to five percent in each New York district.*

(1970 ADA rating: 84) and huge majorities in bids for reelection (1970 share: 66%). His voting record and his success in general elections mark the success of the liberal Republican strategy. But his much more difficult primary contests in 1968 and 1970 testify to that strategy's serious weakness. Both times he won only small majorities over conservative candidates. Trouble in the primary is rare among ten-year incumbents.

Reid has trouble because only registered Republicans in New York can vote in the Republican primary. And even in white-collar and affluent Westchester County, many of these voters are more conservative than Reid. The satisfaction that comes from having a candidate labelled "Republican" palls when the conservatives realize that Reid shares few of their convictions. These people are therefore more willing to risk the chances of an occasional Democratic victory than put up with Reid's continued tenure.

The Conservatives will no doubt give the Congressman another stiff primary test in 1972. Whether he survives will depend on redistricting. The crucial votes in the Republican Caucuses of the state legislature are cast by members who owe their seats to the Conservative party, and as a price for their continued support, the Conservatives may demand the right to draw the boundaries of the new 26th. Reid's strength is concentrated in the Scarsdale-New Rochelle area, on the edge of the present district. Should he lose this area, Reid would have to go out and win votes in unfamiliar territory—a difficult task for any politician. The state's most liberal Republican congressman could lose his seat in 1972.

Census Data 1970 pop. 454,080; deviation from current state average, +2.1%; change 1960–70, +10.9%. Metro. 100%, 0.0% central city.

1970 Share of Federal Outlays $347,668,000 (average outlay per district, New York 26 and 25)

DOD	$21,717,000	HEW	$106,608,000
AEC	$784,000	HUD	$4,812,000
NASA	$191,000	OEO	$727,000
DOT	$1,320,000	DOA	$1,468,000
		Other	$210,041,000

Federal Military-Industrial Commitments (New York 25 and 26, Westchester and Rockland counties listing)

DOD Contractors Singer General Precision (Pleasantville), $7.819m: unspecified. General Foods (White Plains), $6.830m: packets of instant rice for South Vietnamese Army. Chromalloy American (West Nyack), $6.512m: unspecified.

Economic Base Electrical machinery, equipment, and supplies, esp. electronic components and accessories; printing, publishing, and allied industries, esp. periodicals; transportation equipment, esp. motor vehicles and motor vehicle equipment; apparel and other finished products made from fabrics and similar materials, esp. women's, misses', and juniors' dresses. Also, extensive commuting to New York 17, 19 (New York City) and banking.

The Voters

Registration 206,104 total. 60,620 D (29%); 106,437 R (52%); 1,746 L (1%); 2,181 C (1%); 35,120 other (17%).

Employment profile White collar, 55%. Blue collar, 45%.

Ethnic groups Black, 12%. Total foreign stock, 41%. Italy, 13%; Germany, UK, USSR, 4% each; Ireland, 3%; Austria, Poland, Canada, 2% each; Hungary, Sweden, 1% each; others, 6%.

Presidential vote

1968	Humphrey (D)	78,188	(42%)*
	Nixon (R)	97,911	(53%)
	Wallace (AIP)	8,516	(5%)

* *These figures do not include votes Humphrey received on the Liberal line. His performance, therefore, is understated by one to five percent in each New York district.*

Representative

Ogden Rogers Reid (R) Elected 1962; b. June 24, 1925, New York City; home, Purchase; Yale, B.A., 1949; Army, WWII; Capt. USAR; married, six children; Presbyterian.

Career Pres., N.Y. *Herald Tribune,* Societe Anonyme, 1953–58; Pres. and Editor, N.Y. *Herald Tribune,* Inc., 1955–59; Dir., Panama Canal Co., 1956–59; U.S. Ambassador to Israel, 1959–61; Governor Rockefeller's Cabinet, 1961–62; Chm., N.Y. State Commission for Human Rights, 1961–62; Dir., Atlantic Council of U.S.

Offices 240 CHOB, 202-225-6506. Also 371 Mamaroneck Ave., White Plains 10605, 914-428-3040.

Committees

Education and Labor (4th); Subs. (1) Sp. on Labor, (2) Sel. on Education.

Government Operations (2nd); Subs. (1) Foreign Operations and Government Information, (2) Government Activities.

Group Ratings

	ADA	COPE	NREP	NFU	LCV	CFA	NAB	NSI	ACA
1970	84	83	100	92	100	95	18	0	12
1969	87	—	—	73	—	—	—	—	12
1968	83	92	—	73	—	—	17	—	9

Key Votes

(1) ABM	AGN	(6) 18-Yr-Vote	FOR	(11) Clean Water $	FOR
(2) SST	AGN	(7) Farm Sub Lmt	FOR	(12) Mig Wrkrs Comp	FOR
(3) Phil Pln	FOR	(8) Coop-Church	FOR	(13) Jets to Chiang	AGN
(4) No-Knock	ABS	(9) Family Asst	FOR	(14) State OEO Veto	AGN
(5) Cmutr Tax	AGN	(10) Work Stamps	AGN	(15) Park Logging	AGN

Election Results

1970 general:	Ogden R. Reid (R and L)	109,783	(66%)
	Michael A. Coffey (C)	29,702	(18%)
	G. Russell James (D)	25,909	(16%)
1970 primary:	Ogden R. Reid (R)	18,501	(54%)
	Michael A. Coffey (R)	16,042	(46%)
	(Redistricted 1970)		

TWENTY-SEVENTH DISTRICT Political Background

New York 27 comprises Orange and Putnam counties, the southern parts of Dutchess and Sullivan counties, and a western portion of Rockland County. This is the borderland between metropolitan New York City and the vast Upstate empire. Fast-growing, suburban Rockland County is the only part of the district that lies within the City's sphere of influence; it has a large Jewish population, and tends to vote Democratic. Life in the rest of the 27th focuses on small Hudson River cities like Newburgh and Poughkeepsie. Except for these cities, the outer counties are heavily Republican, in part because of a traditional mistrust of the Democratic big City.

When Republican legislators redrew the 27th in 1970, they assumed that it would reelect Republican Congressman Martin McKneally. He had first won the office in 1968, ousting Democrat John Dow, a beneficiary of the 1964 Johnson landslide. The rematch in 1970 between these two men was, in the early phases of the campaign, a classic battle of ideological opposites. McKneally, former National Commander of the American Legion, is a staunch hawk and an outspoken advocate of law-and-order.

Dow, on the other hand, had been one of the first to oppose the Vietnam war, and his thoroughly liberal record included votes for a bill which would have lifted the penalty on those caught desecrating the flag, and against a bill raising the penalties for the possession of certain illegal drugs. Dow's position on these matters had done little to enhance his popularity in the aging small towns and the uptight suburbs of the 27th.

In usual circumstances, a confrontation like this would have produced an easy victory for McKneally. But in the early fall of 1970, the Internal Revenue Service disclosed that Congressman McKneally had not filed federal income tax returns for a number of years. The IRS reportedly claimed that he owed the government $60,000. McKneally replied that he had been over-withheld and owed the government nothing. Several weeks after the election, John Mitchell's Justice Department returned an indictment, and presumably the issue will be determined in court.

Even though the Justice Department did not act before election day, the charges completely transformed the character of the campaign, and the ideologies of the candidates were forgotten. Dow won the election with 52% of the vote. He carried every county in the district except Putnam, in spite of the fact that everyone of them returned substantial pluralities for Conservative party Senate candidate, James Buckley. Because the Republicans control the redistricting process and because the Republican candidate here in 1972 is unlikely to have tax problems, Dow will have trouble retaining his seat at the next election. He may not care about 1972, when he will be 67. His election in 1970 was really an accident, and he is obviously a man who enjoys the luxury of voting his conscience without regard to what may happen at the polls.

Census Data 1970 pop. 560,416; deviation from current state average, +25.9%; change 1960–70, +36.9%. Metro. 18.5%, 0.0% central city.

1970 Share of Federal Outlays $438,573,000 (average outlay per district, New York 27 and 28)

DOD	$60,841,000	HEW	$135,141,000
AEC	$69,000	HUD	$13,554,000
NASA	$334,000	OEO	$591,000
DOT	$5,923,000	DOA	$4,252,000
		Other	$222,869,000

Federal Military-Industrial Commitments (New York 27 and 28 listing)

DOD Contractors IBM (Kingston), $7.428m: data processing equipment.

DOD Installations West Point Military Reservation (West Point).

Economic Base Nonelectrical machinery; apparel and other finished products made from fabrics and similar materials, esp. women's, misses', and juniors' outerwear; womens' handbags and purses, and other leather and leather products; printing, publishing, and allied industries.

The Voters

Registration 223,228 total. 76,203 D (34%); 106,378 R (48%); 1,840 L (1%); 5,501 C (2%); 33,306 other (15%).

Employment profile White collar, 41%. Blue collar, 59%.

Ethnic groups Black, 6%. Puerto Rico, 1%. Total foreign stock, 28%. Italy, 5%; Germany, 4%; Poland, UK, USSR, 3% each; Ireland, 2%; Austria, Czech., Hungary, Canada, 1% each; others, 4%.

Presidential vote

1968	Humphrey (D)	78,398	(39%)*
	Nixon (R)	107,579	(53%)
	Wallace (AIP)	15,327	(8%)

* *These figures do not include votes Humphrey received on the Liberal line. His performance, therefore, is understated by one to five percent in each New York district.*

Representative

John Goodchild Dow (D) Elected 1970; b. May 6, 1905, New York City; home, Newburgh; Harvard Col., B.A., 1927; Columbia U., M.A., 1937; married, three children; Episcopalian.

Career Business systems analyst; U.S. House of Reps., 1965–69.

Offices 238 CHOB, 202-225-3776. Also P.O. Bldg., Newburgh 12550, 914-565-2250; and 20 Market St., Poughkeepsie 12601, 914-452-4466.

Committees

Agriculture (17th); Subs. (1) Dairy and Poultry, (2) Family Farms and Rural Development, (3) Forests.

Group Ratings, Key Votes: *Newly elected.*

Election Results

1970 general:	John G. Dow (D and L)	89,787	(52%)
	Martin McKneally (R and C)	82,191	(48%)
1970 primary:	John G. Dow (D and L), unopposed		
	(Redistricted 1970)		

TWENTY-EIGHTH DISTRICT Political Background

New York 28 contains the heart of the Hudson River Valley in the east and the Catskills in the west; the largest city in this rural district is Kingston, with 25,000 residents. On the banks of the polluted but still scenic Hudson River is the Hyde Park mansion of Franklin D. Roosevelt. The Catskills are famous for the huge Borscht Belt hotels, like Grossinger's and the Concord; for Dutch-descended Rip Van Winkle; and for the phenomenon of the Woodstock festival which was held in Bethel, fifty miles from Boy Dylan's home in Woodstock. To the west, the mountains subside into the hills of the Allegheny Plateau. In the north, the district takes in a bit of the Mohawk Valley, and the Baseball Hall of Fame at Cooperstown, a village founded on the New York frontier by Judge Cooper—James Fenimore Cooper's father.

Except for Democratic Sullivan County, which contains the sizeable Jewish population of the Borscht Belt, the 28th is traditionally Republican. Throughout the New Deal, one of Roosevelt's most vigorous opponents was his own congressman, conservative Hamilton Fish, a Republican isolationist. There have been socially prominent Hamilton Fishes in Congress on and off since 1842. FDR's opponent was ousted in 1944. He was replaced by a Republican named J. Ernest Wharton, who was best known for having attracted Gore Vidal for a Democratic challenger in 1960. Vidal lost, but Wharton was defeated in 1964 by Joseph Y. Resnick, a domestic liberal and Vietnam hawk. Resnick made an unsuccessful bid for the Democratic Senate nomination in 1968 and died shortly thereafter.

In 1968, the Fish dynasty regained control of the 28th in the person of Hamilton Fish, Jr. This Fish is also a Republican but considerably more liberal. Like his father, though, he is skeptical about intervening abroad and voted for the Cooper-Church Amendment to limit U.S. involvement in Cambodia and Laos. His victory in 1968 was based on 48% of the vote in a four-way race; the number two candidate took 46%. In 1970, Fish illustrated the advantages of incumbency by winning reelection with 71% of the district's votes. Fish has a good chance of bettering his father's record of 24 years of House service.

Census Data 1970 pop. 461,006; deviation from current state average, +3.6%; change 1960–70, +12.7%. Metro. 0.0%, 0.0% central city.

1970 Share of Federal Outlays $438,573,000 (average outlay per district, New York 27 and 28)

DOD	$60,841,000	HEW	$135,141,000
AEC	$69,000	HUD	$13,554,000
NASA	$334,000	OEO	$591,000
DOT	$5,923,000	DOA	$4,252,000
		Other	$222,869,000

Federal Military-Industrial Commitments (See New York 27 for New York 27 and 28 listing.)

Economic Base Nonelectrical machinery; dairy; apparel and other finished products made from fabrics and similar materials, esp. women's, misses', and juniors' outerwear.

The Voters

Registration 215,737 total. 56,842 D (26%); 115,276 R (53%); 1,184 L (1%); 2,475 C (1%); 39,960 other (19%).

Employment profile White collar, 40%. Blue collar, 60%.

Ethnic groups Black, 3%. Total foreign stock, 26%. Italy, 6%; Germany, 5%; Ireland, Poland, UK, USSR, 2% each; Austria, Czech., Hungary, Canada, 1% each; others, 3%.

Presidential vote

1968	Humphrey (D)	65,399	(33%)*
	Nixon (R)	117,884	(60%)
	Wallace (AIP)	12,812	(7%)

Representative

Hamilton Fish, Jr. (R) Elected 1968; b. June 3, 1926, Washington, D.C.; home, Millbrook; Harvard Col., B.A., 1949; N.Y.U., LL.B., 1957; USNR, WWII; widower, four children; Episcopalian.

Career Vice Counsel, U.S. Foreign Svc., Ireland, 1951–53; Counsel, N.Y. State Assembly Judicial Com., N.Y. Judiciary Com., 1961; Dir., Dutchess County Civil Defense, 1967–68.

Offices 1534 LHOB, 202-225-5441. Also 509 Warren St., Hudson 12534, 518-828-6960, and 292 Fair St., Kingston 12401, 914-331-4466.

Committees

Judiciary (11th); Sub. No. 3.

Group Ratings

	ADA	COPE	NREP	NFU	LCV	CFA	NAB	NSI	ACA
1970	48	42	67	62	100	86	83	89	68
1969	33	—	—	60	—	—	—	—	29

Key Votes

(1) ABM	FOR	(6) 18-Yr-Vote	FOR	(11) Clean Water $	FOR
(2) SST	AGN	(7) Farm Sub Lmt	FOR	(12) Mig Wrkrs Comp	AGN
(3) Phil Pln	FOR	(8) Coop-Church	FOR	(13) Jets to Chiang	AGN
(4) No-Knock	FOR	(9) Family Asst	FOR	(14) State OEO Veto	AGN
(5) Cmutr Tax	ABS	(10) Work Stamps	AGN	(15) Park Logging	AGN

Election Results

1970 general:	Hamilton Fish, Jr. (R)	119,954	(71%)
	John J. Greaney (D)	41,908	(25%)
	Harry S. Hoffman, Jr. (C)	7,606	(4%)
1970 primary:	Hamilton Fish, Jr. (R), unopposed (Redistricted 1970)		

TWENTY-NINTH DISTRICT Political Background

New York 29 is the Albany-Schenectady area, where the Mohawk River flows into the Hudson: all of Schenectady County; most of Albany County, including half of the city of Albany; and part of Montgomery County. The contorted outline of the district has, as usual, a political explanation. Albany is famous for its old-fashioned Democratic machine. Still headed by octogenarian Dan O'Connell, the machine con-

* *These figures do not include votes Humphrey received on the Liberal line. His performance, therefore, is understated by one to five percent in each New York district.*

sistently grinds out the largest Democratic majorities between New York City and Buffalo. The Republican legislature drew the 29th to split the Democratic stronghold. Lately, the O'Connell machine has shown some weakness; a few Republicans have actually carried Albany County. This may be due to the local enthusiasm for Governor Rockefeller's huge Albany Mall project, which has kept local construction workers employed for the past five years. Ten miles to the west is the General Electric town of Schenectady. General Electric used to employ Ronald Reagan to make speeches and boost the morale of its employees; the company's conservatism may explain why Schenectady is much more marginal politically than Albany. Montgomery County is an economically-depressed area which has been losing population.

The 1970 redistricting threw two incumbent congressmen into the 29th; Daniel Button, a liberal Republican from Albany, and Democrat Samuel S. Stratton from Schenectady and points west. Button had won the old 29th in 1966 with Republican and Liberal endorsement after machine-backed Rep. Leo W. O'Brien retired. Before that he was a newspaper man, TV commentator, and author of *Lindsay, a Man for Tomorrow*. Button made a liberal, antiwar record in the House, and was reelected easily in 1968.

Stratton had been in Washington longer. He was first elected from the 35th district in 1958; earlier, he had been a TV commentator and mayor of Schenectady. Stratton won reelection in 1960. Then the Republican legislature decided to take care of him; it moved Schenectady into the Albany district and drew a new 35th that stretched 200 miles across the rural and Republican hills of Upstate New York. Registered Republicans outnumbered Democrats here two to one. Stratton moved his residence to Amsterdam in Montgomery County and promptly won the congressional election in the 35th, two to one. The man had some kind of campaigning magic which defies description. Since then he has never gotten less than 64% of the vote.

All this time, Stratton kept creeping up the seniority ladder of the House Armed Services Committee, where he is now the 6th ranking member. Although he has a reputation as a maverick on military matters, he has supported the Johnson and Nixon Administration policies in Vietnam.

The 1970 Republican legislature may have thought that Button's popularity in Albany and his backing from peace groups would be enough to overcome Stratton's magic on the campaign circuit. Or, the Republicans may have disliked Button's liberal stance and figured they could never get rid of Stratton anyway. In any case, Stratton won his customary 66% of the district's votes; the best Button could do was 40% in Albany County.

Stratton will probably run even better in the '70's, especially if the legislature throws in the towel, and puts the other half of Albany back into the district. He has an outside chance of someday becoming chairman of Armed Services, since he is six years younger than the next youngest senior member. He has probably given up on any plans for statewide office; he is too conservative to win a New York state primary. It is to the Republicans' advantage to keep the phenomenally popular Stratton in the Albany area, which is going to elect a Democrat anyway.

Census Data 1970 pop. 444,289; deviation from current state average, —0.1%; change 1960–70, +8.5%. Metro. 91.0%, 33.5% central city.

1970 Share of Federal Outlays $716,327,000 (average outlay per district, New York 29 and 30)

DOD	$159,067,000	HEW	$204,514,000
AEC	$29,110,000	HUD	$5,275,000
NASA	$1,623,000	OEO	$2,413,000
DOT	$43,095,000	DOA	$5,785,000
		Other	$265,445,000

Federal Military-Industrial Commitments (See New York 30 for Albany area listing.)

Economic Base Electrical machinery, equipment, and supplies, esp. electrical industrial supplies apparatus; food and kindred products, esp. bakery products; stone, clay, glass, and concrete products, esp. abrasive, asbestos, and miscellaneous nonmetallic mineral products. Also, state government.

The Voters

Registration 218,040 total. 78,355 D (36%); 94,708 R (43%); 1,215 L (1%); 1,050 C (0%); 42,712 other (20%).

Employment profile White collar, 50%. Blue collar, 50%.

Ethnic groups Black, 2%. Total foreign stock, 29%. Italy, 7%; Poland, 4%; Germany, UK, Canada, 3% each; Ireland, USSR, 2% each; Austria, Czech., 1% each; others, 3%.

Presidential vote

1968	Humphrey (D)	105,758	(51%)*
	Nixon (R)	91,496	(44%)
	Wallace (AIP)	8,545	(4%)

Representative

Samuel S. Stratton (D) Elected 1958; b. Sept. 27, 1916, Yonkers; home, Amsterdam; U. of Rochester, B.A., 1937; Haverford Col., M.A., 1938; Harvard U., M.A., 1940; USNR, WWII and Korean War; Capt. USNR; married, four children; Presbyterian.

Career Secy., Rep. Thomas H. Eliot of Mass., 1940–42; Deputy Secy. Gen., Far Eastern Commission, 1946–48; City Councilman, 1950–56; Mayor of Schenectady, 1956–59.

Offices 2404 RHOB, 202-225-5076. Also Post Office Bldg., Schenectady 12304, 518-374-4547, and Post Office Bldg., Amsterdam 12010, 518-843-3400.

Committees

Armed Services (6th); Subs. (1) No. 3, (2) Armed Services Investigating.

Group Ratings

	ADA	COPE	NREP	NFU	LCV	CFA	NAB	NSI	ACA
1970	7	80	67	90	63	71	30	100	21
1969	40	—	—	79	—	—	—	—	24
1968	42	64	—	69	—	—	60	—	32

Key Votes

(1) ABM	FOR	(6) 18-Yr-Vote	FOR	(11) Clean Water $	FOR
(2) SST	FOR	(7) Farm Sub Lmt	FOR	(12) Mig Wrkrs Comp	ABS
(3) Phil Pln	FOR	(8) Coop-Church	AGN	(13) Jets to Chiang	FOR
(4) No-Knock	FOR	(9) Family Asst	FOR	(14) State OEO Veto	AGN
(5) Cmutr Tax	AGN	(10) Work Stamps	AGN	(15) Park Logging	ABS

Election Results

1970 general:	Samuel S. Stratton (D)	128,017	(66%)
	Daniel E. Button (R and L)	65,339	(34%)
1970 primary:	Samuel S. Stratton (D)	19,053	(82%)
	Edward A. Fox (D)	4,212	(18%)
	(Redistricted 1970)		

THIRTIETH DISTRICT Political Background

New York 30 takes in half of the city of Albany, the city of Troy, and four and a half counties to the east and north. Both Albany and nearby Troy are economically depressed industrial cities. The district extends north across the rolling hills of the upper Hudson River Valley into the Adirondacks around Lake George and Fort Ticonderoga. Saratoga Springs, near the center of the 30th, is the site of a fashionable race track and

* *These figures do not include votes Humphrey received on the Liberal line. His performance, therefore, is understated by one to five percent in each New York district.*

of Skidmore College. Many of the early settlers here came from adjacent Vermont and brought with them their Yankee Republicanism. Presently, the district has more residents than the entire state of Vermont. Although Albany, and to a lesser extent Troy, are Democratic strongholds, the 30th as a whole leans Republican.

Carleton J. King was first elected congressman from the district in 1960 after a long career as Saratoga County district attorney. He had the closest call of his political life in 1964, when he was reelected by a scant 1,109 votes. Since he would have lost in the district as presently constituted, his recent strong performances at the polls indicate that he has been working the district very hard indeed. His percentage dipped in 1970, but that can be attributed to redistricters who added half of heavily Democratic Albany to the 30th. He lost that part of the district by 10,000 votes, but still took 57% of the votes cast.

Congressman King is a conservative Republican—a breed that once dominated the Upstate New York congressional delegation. Just fifteen years ago, there were fourteen solidly-conservative Republican congressmen from Upstate; today there are no more than seven who fit that description. In Washington, King is a member of the House Armed Services Committee, where he is not known to dissent from its hawkish bipartisan consensus. Despite ten years of seniority, he is still a relatively low-ranking member of the Committee. Barring the unexpected, King can return to the House for as long as he likes; only his age (66 in 1970) suggests that he may not choose to do so.

Census Data 1970 pop. 446,634; deviation from current state average, +0.4%; change 1960–70, +9.2%. Metro. 71.4%, 24.1% central city.

1970 Share of Federal Outlays $716,327,000 (average outlay per district, New York 29 and 30)

DOD	$159,067,000	HEW	$204,514,000
AEC	$29,110,000	HUD	$5,275,000
NASA	$1,623,000	OEO	$2,413,000
DOT	$43,095,000	DOA	$5,785,000
		Other	$265,445,000

Federal Military-Industrial Commitments (New York 29 and 30, Albany area listing)

DOD Contractors General Electric (Schenectady), $225.621m: ship nuclear propulsion components.

DOD Installations Watervliet Arsenal (Watervliet). Plattsburgh AFB (Plattsburgh). Saratoga AF Station (Saratoga Springs).

AEC Operations General Electric (Schenectady), $52.169m: Knolls Atomic Power Laboratory.

Economic Base Paper and allied products, esp. paper mills other than building paper mills; dairy; chemicals and allied products. Also, higher education (CUNY, Albany); banking; tourism (Lake George).

The Voters

Registration 208,712 total. 56,915 D (27%); 109,895 R (53%); 983 L (0%); 1,271 C (1%); 39,648 other (19%).

Employment profile White collar, 40%. Blue collar, 60%.

Ethnic groups Black, 4%. Total foreign stock, 19%. Canada, 4%; Italy, 3%; Germany, UK, 2% each; Austria, Czech., Ireland, Poland, USSR, 1% each; others, 2%.

Presidential vote

1968	Humphrey (D)	79,800	(43%)*
	Nixon (R)	96,437	(52%)
	Wallace (AIP)	8,448	(5%)

* *These figures do not include votes Humphrey received on the Liberal line. His performance, therefore, is understated by one to five percent in each New York district.*

Representative

Carleton J. King (R) Elected 1960; b. June 15, 1904, Saratoga Springs; home, Saratoga Springs; Union U., LL.B., 1926; married, two children; Catholic.

Career Practicing atty., 1926–60; Acting City Judge, Saratoga Springs, 1936–41; Asst. Dist. Atty., Saratoga County, 1942–50; Dist. Atty., Saratoga County, 1950–61; Pres., N.Y. State Dist. Attys.' Assn., 1955.

Offices 2245 RHOB, 202-225-5615. Also Post Office Bldg., Troy 12180, 518-274-3121, and 444 Broadway, Saratoga Springs 12866, 518-584-2200.

Committees

Armed Services (10th); Subs. (1) No. 3, (2) Sp. on Real Estate.

Group Ratings

	ADA	COPE	NREP	NFU	LCV	CFA	NAB	NSI	ACA
1970	4	9	0	25	29	37	90	100	80
1969	0	—	—	33	—	—	—	—	82
1968	0	9	—	38	—	—	100	—	100

Key Votes

(1) ABM	FOR	(6) 18-Yr-Vote	AGN	(11) Clean Water $	AGN
(2) SST	AGN	(7) Farm Sub Lmt	AGN	(12) Mig Wrkrs Comp	AGN
(3) Phil Pln	AGN	(8) Coop-Church	AGN	(13) Jets to Chiang	FOR
(4) No-Knock	FOR	(9) Family Asst	AGN	(14) State OEO Veto	FOR
(5) Cmutr Tax	AGN	(10) Work Stamps	FOR	(15) Park Logging	AGN

Election Results

1970 general:	Carleton J. King (R and C)	95,470	(57%)
	Edward W. Pattison (D and L)	71,832	(43%)
1970 primary:	Carleton J. King (R and C), unopposed		
	(Redistricted 1970)		

THIRTY-FIRST DISTRICT Political Background

New York 31 is the northernmost part of New York. It contains three counties across the border from Canada along the St. Lawrence River and the eastern end of Lake Ontario. The large French-Canadian population of Franklin and Clinton counties, just a hundred miles south of Montreal, constitutes the only Democratic voting bloc in the district. As one moves west and south, there are fewer voters with French names and more Yankees. Here in the farm country between the St. Lawrence and the Adirondacks, where it gets bitterly cold in the winter time, the voting patterns are decidedly Republican. This region accounts for the Republican leanings of the district. Much of the 31st is covered by the Forest Preserve of the Adirondack Mountains, which the New York Constitution stipulates must remain "forever wild." Massena, in St. Lawrence County, contains the administrative headquarters of the St. Lawrence Seaway, and its poor financial performance has been a blow to this economically-depressed area.

In 1964 the congressman from the district, conservative Republican Clarence E. Kilburn, having just become 70, announced that he was retiring because of his age. This was a rather unusual move for a congressman with some seniority and with no reason to expect defeat at the polls. His successor was Robert C. McEwen, a like-minded Republican, who had been a state senator from the area ten years. McEwen has won reelection with solid majorities, even in the more Democratic portions of the 31st, and he is today the 5th-ranking Republican on the House Public Works Committee. He should have no trouble winning reelection for years to come.

Census Data 1970 pop. 424,272; deviation from current state average, —4.6%; change 1960–70, +3.6%. Metro. 23.0%, 0.0% central city.

1970 Share of Federal Outlays $387,055,000

DOD	$55,179,000	HEW	$116,728,000
AEC	$137,000	HUD	$5,655,000
NASA	$000	OEO	$555,000
DOT	$6,656,000	DOA	$6,282,000
		Other	$195,864,000

Federal Military-Industrial Commitments

DOD Contractors IBM (Owego), $36.788m: submarine sonar systems.

DOD Installations Watertown AF Station (Watertown).

Economic Base Dairy; paper and allied products; primary metal industries, esp. primary production of aluminum. Also, tourism (Adirondacks).

The Voters

Registration 169,528 total. 57,938 D (34%); 99,627 R (59%); 1,280 L (1%); 754 C (0%); 9,929 other (6%).

Employment profile White collar, 36%. Blue collar, 64%.

Ethnic groups Black, 1%. Total foreign stock, 20%. Canada, 11%; Italy, UK, 2% each; Hungary, Ireland, Poland, 1% each; others, 1%.

Presidential vote

1968	Humphrey (D)	52,832	(39%)*
	Nixon (R)	75,664	(56%)
	Wallace (AIP)	6,365	(5%)

Representative

Robert Cameron McEwen (R) Elected 1964; b. Jan. 5, 1920, Ogdensburg: home, Ogdensburg; U. of Vt.; U. of Pa., Wharton School of Finance and Commerce; Albany Law School, LL.B., 1947; Army Air Corps, WWII; married, two children; Presbyterian.

Career N.Y. Senate, 1954–64.

Offices 423 CHOB, 202-225-4611. Also 314 Ford St., Ogdensburg 13669, 315-393-0570.

Committees

Appropriations (21st); Subs. (1) District of Columbia, (2) Foreign Operations.

Group Ratings

	ADA	COPE	NREP	NFU	LCV	CFA	NAB	NSI	ACA
1970	12	18	17	46	0	42	82	90	65
1969	0	—	—	40	—	—	—	—	75
1968	8	0	—	57	—	—	83	—	84

Key Votes

(1) ABM	FOR	(6) 18-Yr-Vote	FOR	(11) Clean Water $	AGN
(2) SST	FOR	(7) Farm Sub Lmt	FOR	(12) Mig Wrkrs Comp	AGN
(3) Phil Pln	FOR	(8) Coop-Church	AGN	(13) Jets to Chiang	AGN
(4) No-Knock	FOR	(9) Family Asst	AGN	(14) State OEO Veto	FOR
(5) Cmutr Tax	FOR	(10) Work Stamps	ABS	(15) Park Logging	ABS

Election Results

1970 general:	Robert C. McEwen (R and C)	90,585	(72%)
	Erwin L. Bornstein (D)	34,568	(28%)

* *These figures do not include votes Humphrey received on the Liberal line. His performance, therefore, is understated by one to five percent in each New York district.*

1970 primary: Robert C. McEwen (R and C), unopposed
(Redistricted 1970)

THIRTY-SECOND DISTRICT Political Background

New York 32, in the middle of the state, comprises a portion of the Adirondack Mountains and part of the Mohawk River Valley. The Adirondacks are sparsely settled. Hamilton County, which lies entirely within the Forest Preserve that the State Constitution requires to be left "forever wild," has a population of 4,000. Most of the district's residents live within a few miles of the Mohawk River.

In the early years of the nineteenth century, the river valley was the main road west for migrating New England and New York Yankees. And when the Erie Canal, which runs parallel to the river, was opened in 1825, it became the main line of east-west commerce in the nation. The canal carried goods from the Northwest Territory (now the country's upper Midwest) to the Hudson River, and then, the goods went down that river to the port City of New York. The canal was in part responsible for the phenomenal growth of the City in the nineteenth century; Philadelphia and Boston were left far behind. The New York Central Line, which also runs through the Mohawk Valley, later replaced the canal as a mover of goods and also played a part in the City's growth.

These developments produced industrial cities in the Valley, like Utica and Rome. As these cities proposed, they attracted a new wave of immigration, and today a large proportion of the district's population is of Italian and Polish descent. In general, these Catholic voters have adopted the Republican bent of their Yankee predecessors. But Catholic Democrats run well here; Robert Kennedy, for example, took 56% of the district's votes in 1964.

Since 1958, however, the 32nd's congressional politics have been dominated by a Republican, Alexander Pirnie. As a member of the House Armed Services Committee, Pirnie is a conservative on matters relating to the military and foreign policy. At the same time, he is often liberal on domestic issues, and for the last three elections has been endorsed by the Liberal party. The middle-of-the-road Upstate Republican seems to have found the right formula for winning in the 32nd, and Pirnie, who was 67 in 1970, will go on winning until he retires.

Census Data 1970 pop. 421,665; deviation from current state average, —5.2%; change 1960–70, +2.9%. Metro. 72.3%, 53.0% central city.

1970 Share of Federal Outlays $507,748,825

DOD	$173,668,000	HEW	$119,417,416
AEC	$000	HUD	$6,042,116
NASA	$83,766	OEO	$565,441
DOT	$6,307,862	DOA	$6,338,148
		Other	$195,326,076

Federal Military-Industrial Commitments

DOD Contractors General Electric (Utica), $65.262m: Chaparral missile guidance systems; aircraft electronic warfare units.

DOD Installations Griffis AFB (Rome).

Economic Base Electrical machinery, equipment, and supplies; dairy; rolling, drawing, and extruding of nonferrous metals, and other primary metal industries; leather and other leather products, esp. leather gloves and mittens. Also, tourism (the Adirondacks).

The Voters

Registration 201,400 total. 124,323 D (62%); 53,485 R (27%); 3,630 L (2%); 4,763 C (2%); 15,199 other (8%).

Employment profile White collar, 42%. Blue collar, 58%.

Ethnic groups Black, 2%. Total foreign stock, 27%. Italy, 8%; Poland, 5%; UK, 3%; Germany, Canada, 2% each; Austria, Ireland, USSR, 1% each; others, 3%.

Presidential vote

1968	Humphrey (D)	66,934	(41%)*
	Nixon (R)	87,607	(54%)
	Wallace (AIP)	8,703	(5%)

Representative

Alexander Pirnie (R-Lib.) Elected 1958; b. April 10, 1903, Pulaski; home, Utica; Cornell U., B.A., 1924, LL.B., 1926; Army, WWII; married, two children; unspecified Protestant.

Career Practicing atty., 1926–59; V.P., Dir., Duofold, Inc., 1948– .

Offices 1434 LHOB, 202-225-3665. Also 19 Hopper St., Utica 13501, 315-724-9302.

Committees

Armed Services (6th); Subs. (1) No. 2, (2) Armed Services Investigating.

Group Ratings

	ADA	COPE	NREP	NFU	LCV	CFA	NAB	NSI	ACA
1970	24	60	50	85	14	47	64	100	47
1969	27	—	—	60	—	—	—	—	33
1968	33	31	—	60	—	—	80	—	59

Key Votes

(1) ABM	FOR	(6) 18-Yr-Vote	FOR	(11) Clean Water $	FOR
(2) SST	FOR	(7) Farm Sub Lmt	FOR	(12) Mig Wrkrs Comp	AGN
(3) Phil Pln	FOR	(8) Coop-Church	AGN	(13) Jets to Chiang	FOR
(4) No-Knock	FOR	(9) Family Asst	FOR	(14) State OEO Veto	AGN
(5) Cmutr Tax	FOR	(10) Work Stamps	FOR	(15) Park Logging	FOR

Election Results

1970 general:	Alexander Pirnie (R and L)	90,884	(66%)
	Joseph Simmons (D)	47,306	(34%)
1970 primary:	Alexander Pirnie (R and L), unopposed (Redistricted 1970)		

THIRTY-THIRD DISTRICT Political Background

New York 33 includes the three eastern counties of the state's Southern Tier, a group of counties that stretch across the hills and river valleys lying just north of the Pennsylvania line. The district also takes in part of Tompkins County, including Ithaca (pop. 26,000), home of Cornell University. Aside from Ithaca, there are two other population centers here: the manufacturing towns of Binghamton (pop. 64,000) and Elmira (pop. 40,000). The three cities are politically marginal; the surrounding countryside is heavily Republican.

The district's congressman, Howard W. Robison, was first elected to the House in a 1958 special election. Fifteen years ago the Upstate New York congressional delegation was dominated by conservative Republicans. During the Eisenhower years, John Taber (chairman of the House Appropriations Committee), Sterling Cole (chairman of the Joint Committee on Atomic Energy), and Daniel Reed (chairman of Ways and Means) were all leaders of the Taft wing of the party in Congress. Today, Robison is the dean of the New York Republican delegation, and his liberal voting record illustrates nicely the change which has occurred in Upstate representation. In the 92nd Congress, no more than seven Upstate Republicans have notably conservative voting records. The shift is due to the increasing numbers of Catholic working-class in urban areas here, and the growing liberalism among voters of Yankee stock. These developments were best summed up in 1964 when usually Republican Upstate emphatically rejected Barry Goldwater's candidacy.

** These figures do not include votes Humphrey received on the Liberal line. His performance, therefore, is understated by one to five percent in each New York district.*

The Johnson landslide made a dent in Robison's margin, but since then his record has secured 2–1 election victories. Moreover, the prospects of vehement opposition are unlikely; the Cornell antiwar community has been generally pleased with the Congressman's position on Vietnam. Robison is one of the few liberal Republicans on the Appropriations Committee. His position of 9th-ranking minority member gives him some influence, though he is unlikely to climb to the top levels of seniority within the committee.

Census Data 1970 pop. 440,401; deviation from current state average, −1.0%; change 1960–70, +7.6%. Metro. 60.9%, 14.6% central city.

1970 Share of Federal Outlays $408,308,000

DOD	$101,830,000	HEW	$102,175,000
AEC	$1,725,000	HUD	$7,718,000
NASA	$3,698,000	OEO	$632,000
DOT	$2,286,000	DOA	$6,872,000
		Other	$181,381,000

Federal Military-Industrial Commitments

DOD Contractors Singer General Precision (Binghamton), $35.865m: F-4 weapons system training sets; F-111 mission simulators. GAF Corp. (Binghamton), $6.028m: unspecified. General Electric (Binghamton), $5.887m: unspecified.

Economic Base Nonelectrical machinery, esp. office, computing, and accounting machines; dairy; photographic equipment and supplies, and other professional, scientific, and controlling instruments, photographic and optical goods, watches and clocks. Also, higher education (Cornell University).

The Voters

Registration 169,618 total. 55,732 D (33%); 104,237 R (61%); 1,155 L (1%); 975 D (1%); 7,519 other (4%).

Employment profile White collar, 43%. Blue collar, 57%.

Ethnic groups Black, 2%. Total foreign stock, 20%. Italy, 3%; Czech., Germany, Poland, UK, 2% each; Ireland, Austria, USSR, Canada, 1% each; others, 3%.

Presidential vote

1968	Humphrey (D)	65,829	(40%)*
	Nixon (R)	89,846	(54%)
	Wallace (AIP)	9,609	(6%)

Representative

Howard Winfield Robison (R) Elected Jan. 14, 1958; b. Oct. 30, 1915, Owego; home, Owego; Cornell U., B.A., 1937, LL.B., 1939; Army, WWII; married, two children; Methodist.

Career Practicing atty., 1939–57; County Atty., 1946–58.

Offices 2330 RHOB, 202-225-6335. Also 302 Fed. Bldg., Binghamton 13902, 607-723-4425.

Committees

Appropriations (9th); Subs (1) Public Works, (2) Treasury, Post Office, and General Government.

Group Ratings

	ADA	COPE	NREP	NFU	LCV	CFA	NAB	NSI	ACA
1970	64	60	75	80	38	47	67	80	56
1969	47	—	—	60	—	—	—	—	31
1968	33	31	—	56	—	—	80	—	59

* *These figures do not include votes Humphrey received on the Liberal line. His performance, therefore, is understated by one to five percent in each New York district.*

Key Votes

(1) ABM	FOR	(6) 18-Yr-Vote	FOR	(11) Clean Water $	AGN
(2) SST	AGN	(7) Farm Sub Lmt	FOR	(12) Mig Wrkrs Comp	FOR
(3) Phil Pln	FOR	(8) Coop-Church	FOR	(13) Jets to Chiang	AGN
(4) No-Knock	FOR	(9) Family Asst	FOR	(14) State OEO Veto	AGN
(5) Cmutr Tax	FOR	(10) Work Stamps	FOR	(15) Park Logging	AGN

Election Results

1970 general:	Howard W. Robison (R)	90,196	(66%)
	David Bernstein (D and L)	45,373	(34%)
1970 primary:	Howard W. Robison (R), unopposed (Redistricted 1970)		

THIRTY-FOURTH DISTRICT Political Background

New York 34 comprises the west side of Syracuse and some of its industrial suburbs, the nearby industrial city of Auburn in Cayuga County, and the Finger Lakes region. In the 1970 redistricting, the Republican legislature employed the strategy, long used in the Rochester area, of splitting the urban Democratic vote between heavily Republican districts; although the west side of Syracuse has a quarter of the district's population, it will never dominate the 34th politically. Auburn also leans Democratic. It has a large Catholic population which ousted a local assemblyman in the Democratic primary shortly after he cast the deciding vote in favor of New York's liberalized abortion law. The Republican majority in the 34th is supplied by the scenic Finger Lakes region. The region is dotted with small towns to which some early-nineteenth century Yankee, obviously devoted to his classics, gave names: Ovid, Scipio, Romulus, Camillus, and Pompey, among others.

The 1970 congressional race in the district was between Republican-Conservative John H. Terry and Democrat Neal P. McCurn. The candidates ran even in Syracuse and Onondaga County, but in the rest of the district, Terry won an almost 2–1 margin and finished with 59% overall. The results of the election show that Terry received a surprisingly large number of votes on the Conservative line in Syracuse and Auburn; it appears that the urban Catholics here, like those in New York City, are moving toward the party of the Buckleys. Terry is likely to establish himself as one of Upstate's more conservative congressmen, and he should have no trouble in 1972.

Census Data 1970 pop. 446,091; deviation from current state average, +0.3%; change 1960–70, +9.1%. Metro. 47.5%, 18.1% central city.

1970 Share of Federal Outlays $440,284,000 (average outlay per district, New York 34 and 35)

DOD	$62,182,000	HEW	$128,098,000
AEC	$108,000	HUD	$2,708,000
NASA	$621,000	OEO	$996,000
DOT	$5,769,000	DOA	$10,797,000
		Other	$229,005,000

Federal Military-Industrial Commitments (New York 34 and 35, Syracuse area listing)

DOD Contractors Western Electric Div., AT&T (Syracuse), $39.365m: Safeguard ABM radar components. General Electric (Syracuse), $16.382m: support of military space vehicle sensor sights.

DOD Installations Seneca Army Depot (Romulus).

Economic Base Electrical machinery, equipment, and supplies; dairy; nonelectrical machinery. Also, tourism (Finger Lakes).

The Voters

Registration 155,149 total. 48,438 D (31%); 93,923 R (61%); 913 L (1%); 1,682 C (1%); 15,193 other (10%).

Employment profile White collar, 49%. Blue collar, 51%.

Ethnic groups Black, 2%. Total foreign stock, 23%. Italy, 5%; Germany, Poland, UK, Canada, 3% each; Ireland, 2%; Austria, USSR, 1% each; others, 2%.

Presidential vote

1968	Humphrey (D)	72,174	(41%)*
	Nixon (R)	93,909	(54%)
	Wallace (AIP)	9,006	(5%)

Representative

John H. Terry (R-Cons.) Elected 1970; b. Nov. 14, 1924, Syracuse; home, Syracuse; U. of Notre Dame, B.A., 1945; Syracuse U., LL.B., 1949; Army, WWII; married, four children; Catholic.

Career Practicing atty., 1948– ; Onondaga County Bd. of Supervisors, 1948–58; Asst. Secy. to Gov. Nelson Rockefeller, 1959–61; N.Y. State Assembly, 1963–70; Chm., N.Y. State United Svcs. Organization.

Offices 1410 LHOB, 202-225-8090. Also 302 Fed. Bldg., Syracuse 13202, 315-472-2222; and 302 P.O. Bldg., Auburn 13021, 315-252-2222.

Committees

Interior and Insular Affairs (15th); Subs. (1) Environment, (2) Indian Affairs, (3) National Parks and Recreation.

Public Works (12th); Subs. (1) Investigation and Oversight, (2) Public Buildings and Grounds, (3) Rivers and Harbors, (4) Roads, (5) Sp. on Economic Development Programs.

Group Ratings, Key Votes: Newly elected.

Election Results

1970 general:	John H. Terry (R and C)	88,786	(59%)
	Neal P. McCurn (D)	60,452	(41%)
1970 primary:	John H. Terry (R)	15,203	(74%)
	Clarence Kadys (R)	5,364	(26%)
	(Redistricted 1970)		

THIRTY-FIFTH DISTRICT Political Background

New York 35 takes in the east side of Syracuse and most of surrounding Onondaga County, plus the rural and small-town Yankee counties of Madison, Cortland, and Chenango. The Syracuse portion of the district leans Democratic, but because the working-class suburbs of Syracuse lie in the 34th district, most of outer Onondaga County is Republican. The outer, Yankee-dominated counties are also, of course, Republican. This district, like the adjacent 34th, was the result of the 1970 Republican redistricting; Onondaga County used to comprise a single district.

That district was represented by James M. Hanley, a Syracuse Democrat who was first elected to the House in 1964. He won reelection in 1966 and 1968 against multi-party opposition. The redistricting was obviously an attempt to unseat Hanley—the plan and the hope being that the Republicans would amass majorities large enough in the outer counties and the suburbs to overcome the incumbent's edge in the city. Hanley's problems were compounded in 1970, when for the first time he was faced with a Republican opponent who also had the nomination of the Conservative party. He was John F. O'Conner, a former Syracuse police chief.

Like many attempted redistricting coups, this one did not quite work out. Hanley did lose the outer counties 3–2, but his visibility after six years of incumbency enabled him to run even in suburban Onondaga and to carry his portion of the county by a 58–42 margin. Since two-thirds of the district's votes are cast in Onondaga, Hanley won by a narrow 6,000-vote margin (52%).

Hanley's stance as a liberal to moderate Democrat is a fair reflection of his chief source of electoral strength, somewhat conservative, Catholic, blue-collar working-people. But he can expect another tough race in 1972, because the Republican legislators will undoubtedly do their best to whittle away at that strength in redistricting. The

* *These figures do not include votes Humphrey received on the Liberal line. His performance, therefore, is understated by one to five percent in each New York district.*

legislature, however, cannot move too much of Syracuse into the 34th without jeopardizing its Republican congressman, John Terry. Moreover, Hanley's 1970 performance bodes well for his chances in 1972. The outcome may depend on whether Richard Nixon, at the top of the Republican ticket, can match the popularity of James Buckley in Upstate New York.

Census Data 1970 pop. 469,711; deviation from current state average, +5.6%; change 1960–70, +14.5%. Metro. 80.4%, 24.7% central city.

1970 Share of Federal Outlays $440,284,000 (average outlay per district, New York 34 and 35)

DOD	$62,182,000	HEW	$128,098,000
AEC	$108,000	HUD	$2,708,000
NASA	$621,000	OEO	$996,000
DOT	$5,769,000	DOA	$10,797,000
		Other	$229,005,000

Federal Military-Industrial Commitments (See New York 34 for Syracuse area listing.)

Economic Base Electrical machinery, equipment, and supplies; nonelectrical machinery; dairy. Also, higher education (Syracuse University); banking.

The Voters

Registration 222,477 total. 58,973 D (27%); 137,899 R (62%); 1,457 L (1%); 2,276 C (1%); 21,872 other (10%).

Employment profile White collar, 36%. Blue collar, 64%.

Ethnic groups Black, 4%. Total foreign stock, 25%. Italy, 7%; Germany, UK, Canada, 3% each; Poland, 2%; Austria, Ireland, USSR, 1% each; others, 3%.

Presidential vote

1968	Humphrey (D)	69,186	(39%)*
	Nixon (R)	100,726	(56%)
	Wallace (AIP)	8,661	(5%)

Representative

James Michael Hanley (D) Elected 1964; b. July 19, 1920, Syracuse; home, Syracuse; Army, WWII; married, two children; Catholic.

Career Funeral Dir., Callahan-Hanley-Mooney Funeral Home, 1940–64.

Offices 109 CHOB, 202-225-3701. Also 509 Loew Bldg., Syracuse 13202, 315-422-2751.

Committees

Banking and Currency (17th); Subs. (1) Consumer Affairs, (2) Domestic Finance, (3) International Finance.

Post Office and Civil Service (6th); Subs. (1) Census and Statistics, (2) Postal Facilities and Mail.

Group Ratings

	ADA	COPE	NREP	NFU	LCV	CFA	NAB	NSI	ACA
1970	72	100	73	100	86	90	9	80	17
1969	67	—	—	86	—	—	—	—	13
1968	83	64	—	75	—	—	17	—	4

Key Votes

(1) ABM	FOR	(6) 18-Yr-Vote	FOR	(11) Clean Water $	FOR
(2) SST	AGN	(7) Farm Sub Lmt	ABS	(12) Mig Wrkrs Comp	FOR
(3) Phil Pln	FOR	(8) Coop-Church	FOR	(13) Jets to Chiang	AGN
(4) No-Knock	FOR	(9) Family Asst	FOR	(14) State OEO Veto	AGN
(5) Cmutr Tax	FOR	(10) Work Stamps	AGN	(15) Park Logging	AGN

* *These figures do not include votes Humphrey received on the Liberal line. His performance, therefore, is understated by one to five percent in each New York district.*

Election Results

1970 general:	James M. Hanley (D)	82,425	(52%)
	John F. O'Conner (R and C)	76,381	(48%)
1970 primary:	James M. Hanley (D)	10,557	(78%)
	Harvey H. Bates, Jr. (D)	2,948	(22%)
	(Redistricted 1970)		

THIRTY-SIXTH DISTRICT Political Background

New York 36, a district that lies along the southern shore of Lake Ontario, comprises the east side of the city of Rochester, eastern Monroe County, and rural Wayne County. Rochester's industries rely on highly-skilled, technical labor; these include Eastman Kodak and Xerox. Because the city of Rochester consistently goes Democratic, the Republican legislators have for years divided it between two districts. In both of these districts, the Republican voters of the surrounding suburbs and rural hinterlands of western New York overmatch the Democratic strength in the city; both districts, therefore, elect Republican congressmen. Profoundly conservative Wayne County is a Yankee Republican stronghold and birthplace of the Mormon religion (see Utah write-up).

Since 1962, the congressman from the 36th has been Frank Horton, Upstate New York's most liberal Republican. That particular political coloration is traditional in the district: for many years (1946–58) its representative was Kenneth B. Keating, U.S. senator from 1958 to 1964, later a judge on the state's highest court, and now ambassador to India. Congressman Horton, who serves as the 3rd-ranking Republican on the Government Operations Committee, is overwhelmingly popular among the district's voters. He regularly wins about 70% in general elections, and unlike other New York liberal Republican congressmen, he has never faced serious Conservative primary opposition. Unless such opposition develops, he should have no trouble winning reelection for many years to come.

Census Data 1970 pop. 492,782; deviation from current state average, +10.8%; change 1960–70, +20.4%. Metro. 100%, 34.2% central city.

1970 Share of Federal Outlays $408,221,000 (average outlay per district, New York 36 and 37)

DOD	$45,027,000	HEW	$118,401,000
AEC	$2,465,000	HUD	$11,989,000
NASA	$1,446,000	OEO	$1,541,000
DOT	$19,055,000	DOA	$5,020,000
		Other	$203,277,000

Federal Military-Industrial Commitments (See New York 37 for Rochester area listing.)

Economic Base Photographic equipment and supplies and other professional, scientific, and controlling instruments, photographic and optical goods, watches and clocks; electrical machinery, equipment, and supplies, esp. communication equipment; nonelectrical machinery, esp. metalworking machinery and equipment.

The Voters

Registration 305,956 total. 57,830 D (28%); 126,398 R (62%); 1,446 L (1%); 1,667 C (1%); 16,615 other (8%).

Employment profile White collar, 47%. Blue collar, 53%.

Ethnic groups Black, 6%. Total foreign stock, 33%. Italy, 9%; Germany, 5%; Canada, 4%; Poland, UK, USSR, 3% each; others, 5%.

Presidential vote

1968	Humphrey (D)	89,269	(45%)*
	Nixon (R)	102,524	(52%)
	Wallace (AIP)	7,184	(4%)

* *These figures do not include votes Humphrey received on the Liberal line. His performance, therefore, is understated by one to five percent in each New York district.*

Representative

Frank J. Horton (R) Elected 1962; b. Dec. 12, 1919, Cuero, Tex.; home, Rochester; La. State U., B.A., 1941; Cornell U., LL.B., 1947; Army, WWII; married, two children; Presbyterian.

Career Practicing atty., 1947–62; Rochester City Council, 1955–61.

Offices 407 CHOB, 202-225-4916. Also 107 Fed. Bldg., Rochester 14614, 716-546-4900, ext. 1380.

Committees

Government Operations (3rd); Subs. (1) Foreign Operations and Government Information, (2) Legislation and Military Operations.

Sel. Com. on Small Business (3rd); Subs. (1) Environment Problems Affecting Small Business, (2) Government Procurement, (3) Small Business Problems in Smaller Towns and Urban Areas.

Group Ratings

	ADA	COPE	NREP	NFU	LCV	CFA	NAB	NSI	ACA
1970	76	83	93	92	75	68	17	44	25
1969	80	—	—	73	—	—	—	—	29
1968	50	83	—	73	—	—	50	—	38

Key Votes

(1) ABM	AGN	(6) 18-Yr-Vote	FOR	(11) Clean Water $	FOR
(2) SST	AGN	(7) Farm Sub Lmt	FOR	(12) Mig Wrkrs Comp	FOR
(3) Phil Pln	FOR	(8) Coop-Church	FOR	(13) Jets to Chiang	AGN
(4) No-Knock	FOR	(9) Family Asst	FOR	(14) State OEO Veto	AGN
(5) Cmutr Tax	AGN	(10) Work Stamps	FOR	(15) Park Logging	AGN

Election Results

1970 general:	Frank J. Horton (R)	123,209	(71%)
	Jordan E. Pappas (D)	38,898	(22%)
	David F. Hampson (C)	10,442	(6%)
	Morley Schloss (L)	2,165	(1%)
1970 primary:	Frank J. Horton (R), unopposed (Redistricted 1970)		

THIRTY-SEVENTH DISTRICT Political Background

New York 37 comprises the western half of the city of Rochester and the surrounding countryside: suburban Monroe County, part of Erie County, and the whole counties of Orleans, Genesee, and Wyoming. Wyoming County contains the town of Attica, site of a September, 1971, prison tragedy. As is the case in the 36th district, Rochester's Democratic vote is nullified by the Republican residents of the countryside, who cast two-thirds of the vote in the district. Although the suburbs of Buffalo are beginning to encroach on the west, most of the district is rural. Batavia, the largest city outside Rochester, has 17,000 inhabitants. Out here, some 400 miles from New York City, Upstate New York has a Midwestern air to it; East Coast celebrities like Nelson Rockefeller, Jacob Javits, and the late Robert Kennedy seem as out of place here as they would in Indiana. But statewide politicians, like these men, do campaign in the district.

In 1964, Congressman Harold C. Ostertag retired, and his seat was won by Barber B. Conable, Jr., a wealthy state senator from Genesee County. Conable was expected to be a typical conservative Republican, but he has managed to distinguish himself. He was chosen a member of the powerful House Ways and Means Committee, and has been a leading proponent of procedural reform in the House. As the 92nd Congress convened, he helped to persuade the Republican Caucus to adopt certain reforms in its seniority system. This happened before the Democrats did anything, and it was a bit of a blow to those liberal Democrats who like to think of themselves as *the* reformers in the House. Conable's voting record is moderate to conservative; as a result, his popularity in the district is high. Because Conable has won reelection by 2–1 majorities every time out, he can look forward to a long, perhaps even notable, congressional career.

Census Data 1970 pop. 482,175; deviation from current state average, +8.4%; change 1960–70, +17.8%. Metro. 80.0%, 26.5% central city.

1970 Share of Federal Outlays $408,221,000 (average outlay per district, New York 36 and 37)

DOD	$45,027,000	HEW	$118,401,000
AEC	$2,465,000	HUD	$11,989,000
NASA	$1,446,000	OEO	$1,541,000
DOT	$19,055,000	DOA	$5,020,000
		Other	$203,277,000

Federal Military-Industrial Commitments (New York 36 and 37, Rochester area listing.)

DOD Contractors Eastman Kodak (Rochester), $29.460m: artillery fuze devices. Stromberg Carlson Div., General Dynamics (Rochester), $9.691m: operation of automatic telephone system in Southeast Asia. Rochester Independent Packer (Rochester), $9.379m: foodstuffs. University of Rochester (Rochester), $6.422m: studies of naval capabilities.

Economic Base Photographic equipment and supplies and other professional, scientific, and controlling instruments; photographic and optical goods, watches and clocks; electrical machinery, equipment, and supplies, esp. communication equipment; nonelectrical machinery, esp. metalworking equipment and machinery. Also, higher education (Rochester University); banking.

The Voters

Registration 219,792 total. 65,249 D (30%); 138,672 R (63%); 1,411 L (1%); 1,407 C (1%); 13,053 other (6%).

Employment profile White collar, 38%. Blue collar, 62%.

Ethnic groups Black, 6%. Total foreign stock, 26%. Italy, 8%; Germany, UK, Canada, 4% each; Ireland, 2%; Poland, 1%; others, 2%.

Presidential vote

1968	Humphrey (D)	84,791	(44%)*
	Nixon (R)	97,269	(51%)
	Wallace (AIP)	9,272	(5%)

Representative

Barber B. Conable, Jr. (R) Elected 1964; b. Nov. 2, 1922, Warsaw; home, Alexander; Cornell U., B.A., 1942, LL.B., 1948; USMC, WWII and Korean War; married, four children; Methodist.

Career Practicing atty., 1949– ; N.Y. State Senate, 1963, 1964.

Offices 230 CHOB, 202-225-3615. Also 105 Fed. Bldg., Rochester 14614, 716-232-5600.

Committees

Ways and Means (6th).

Jt. Economic Com. (2nd); Subs. (1) Fiscal Policy, (2) Foreign Economic Policy, (3) Inter-American Economic Relationships, (4) International Exchange and Payments, (5) Priorities and Economy.

Group Ratings

	ADA	COPE	NREP	NFU	LCV	CFA	NAB	NSI	ACA
1970	28	25	50	50	25	63	83	90	79
1969	27	—	—	54	—	—	—	—	56
1968	17	17	—	64	—	—	83	—	70

* *These figures do not include votes Humphrey received on the Liberal line. His performance, therefore, is understated by one to five percent in each New York district.*

Key Votes

(1) ABM	ABS	(6) 18-Yr-Vote	AGN	(11) Clean Water $	AGN
(2) SST	AGN	(7) Farm Sub Lmt	FOR	(12) Mig Wrkrs Comp	AGN
(3) Phil Pln	FOR	(8) Coop-Church	AGN	(13) Jets to Chiang	AGN
(4) No-Knock	FOR	(9) Family Asst	FOR	(14) State OEO Veto	AGN
(5) Cmutr Tax	FOR	(10) Work Stamps	FOR	(15) Park Logging	AGN

Election Results

1970 general:	Barber B. Conable, Jr. (R)	107,677	(66%)
	Richard N. Anderson (D)	48,061	(29%)
	Keith R. Wallis (C)	7,729	(5%)
1970 primary:	Barber B. Conable, Jr. (R), unopposed (Redistricted 1970)		

THIRTY-EIGHTH DISTRICT Political Background

New York 38 comprises the southern end of Erie County and the western half of the Southern Tier: four hilly counties that stretch from the Finger Lakes region to Lake Erie. The district contains the Corning Glass Works in Steuben County, two Indian Reservations, and a point on the state's western boundary, 496 miles from New York City via the Thomas E. Dewey Thruway. The small towns scattered through the district's valleys—Jamestown, Olean, Hornell, Corning—and along Lake Erie—Dunkirk, Fredonia—tend to be Democratic or marginal. This reflects the presence of Irish and Italian Catholics who came to this area after it had been settled originally by Yankee migrants. But outside the towns, the Yankee Republicans still predominate, and as in most of Upstate New York, control the district politically.

Before he was appointed to fill the late Robert Kennedy's seat in the Senate, Charles Goodell represented the 38th. In the House, Goodell was generally a conservative, if often innovative, Republican; he did not become an outspoken dove until he became a senator. Goodell was very popular here. In the Goldwater fiasco year of 1964, he ran better than any other New York Republican congressman, and he carried it again in his 1970 Senate race, even while running a poor third everywhere else in the state.

The 38th's present congressman, Republican James F. Hastings, is at least as conservative as Goodell himself ever was. In 1970, Hastings received the Conservative nomination, something that Goodell never got, and ran even better than his predecessor. Because the 38th had almost no population growth in the '60's, it will need adjustment in redistricting; but its position in the corner of the state secures it from any drastic modification. Hastings looks like a sure winner in the years ahead.

Census Data 1970 pop. 421,536; deviation from current state average, –5.3%; change 1960–70, +3.1%. Metro. 11.0%, 0.0% central city.

1970 Share of Federal Outlays $364,015,000

DOD	$9,904,000	HEW	$105,785,000
AEC	$2,577,000	HUD	$7,920,000
NASA	$82,000	OEO	$604,000
DOT	$43,951,000	DOA	$7,190,000
		Other	$186,002,000

Federal Military-Industrial Commitments

None.

Economic Base Nonelectrical machinery, esp. general industrial machinery and equipment; dairy; fabricated metal products, esp. cutlery, hand tools, and general hardware.

The Voters

Registration 175,080 total. 59,020 D (34%); 108,289 R (62%); 1,161 L (1%); 1,126 C (1%); 7,338 other (3%).

Employment profile White collar, 37%. Blue collar, 63%.

Ethnic groups Black, 1%. Total foreign stock, 19%. Italy, 4%; Sweden, 3%; Germany, Poland, UK, 2% each; Ireland, Canada, 1% each; others, 2%.

Presidential vote

1968	Humphrey (D)	62,269	(39%)*
	Nixon (R)	89,140	(55%)
	Wallace (AIP)	9,470	(6%)

Representative

James F. Hastings (R) Elected 1968; b. April 10, 1926, Olean; home, Allegany; Navy, WWII; married, five children; Methodist.

Career Allegany Town Bd., Allegany Police Justice; N.Y. State Assembly, 1962–65; Bd. of Advisors, N.Y.U. Center for Research and Advanced Training in Deafness Rehab.; Mgr., V.P., radio station WHDL, 1952–66; Natl. Advertising Mgr., The *Times Herald,* Olean, 1964–66; Hastings & Jewell, real estate and insurance, 1966–69.

Offices 118 CHOB, 202-225-3161. Also 63 W. Main St., Allegany 14706, 716-373-2234, and Rm. 122, P.O. Bldg., 300 E. 3rd St., Jamestown 14701, 716-484-0252.

Committees

Interstate and Foreign Commerce (12th); Sub. on Public Health and Environment.

Group Ratings

	ADA	COPE	NREP	NFU	LCV	CFA	NAB	NSI	ACA
1970	16	20	17	70	0	50	86	100	60
1969	7	—	—	27	—	—	—	—	57

Key Votes

(1) ABM	ABS	(6) 18-Yr-Vote	FOR	(11) Clean Water $	AGN
(2) SST	AGN	(7) Farm Sub Lmt	FOR	(12) Mig Wrkrs Comp	AGN
(3) Phil Pln	FOR	(8) Coop-Church	AGN	(13) Jets to Chiang	FOR
(4) No-Knock	ABS	(9) Family Asst	FOR	(14) State OEO Veto	FOR
(5) Cmutr Tax	AGN	(10) Work Stamps	FOR	(15) Park Logging	ABS

Election Results

1970 general:	James F. Hastings (R and C)	94,906	(71%)
	James G. Cretekos (D)	37,961	(29%)
1970 primary:	James F. Hastings (R and C), unopposed		
	(Redistricted 1970)		

THIRTY-NINTH DISTRICT Political Background

New York 39 comprises the greater part of suburban Erie County and a small part of northwest Buffalo. The district takes in the most prosperous portions of what is called the Niagara Frontier: the heavily industrial Buffalo-Niagara Falls metropolitan area along the Canadian border. The Buffalo area is the Democratic stronghold of Upstate New York. It is a place much more like Cleveland or Detroit than New York City, and its residents—Polish, Italian, and black working-class voters—give Democratic candidates huge majorities. Buffalo has few of those liberal intellectuals whose preferences are behind and responsible for so much of the complexity that structures the politics of New York City (see New York 17). As a result, in several recent statewide elections, Erie County, suburbs and all, produced larger Democratic percentages than four out of five of New York City's boroughs.

The 39th, as a suburban district, is usually the most Republican part of Erie County; most of Buffalo's rather small wealthy suburbs are found here. But much of the district's population is working-class Democratic, particularly in the town of Cheektowaga (pop. 113,000). The subdivisions of the town are occupied by the sons and daughters

* *These figures do not include votes Humphrey received on the Liberal line. His performance, therefore, is understated by one to five percent in each New York district.*

of Polish and Italian immigrants who have escaped from the central city. Overall, the 39th is as politically marginal as any in New York state.

From 1964 to 1970, the 39th's congressman was Richard D. (Max) McCarthy, the liberal Democrat who made national headlines when he exposed the Defense Department's stockpile of chemical and biological weapons. He would probably still represent the district if he had not decided to enter the Senate Democratic primary in 1970. His campaign was doomed from the beginning. McCarthy did attract some publicity for scuba-diving into the murky, polluted waters of the Hudson River, but when the votes were counted, he finished a poor fourth. He carried only the Buffalo area, and this he did with the help of Joe Crangle's Erie County organization, one of the few New York Democratic machines still capable of producing votes. After the defeat, McCarthy tried to get back into the race in the 39th district. There was talk that the Democratic nominee, Thomas P. Flaherty, would be slated for a judgeship, which would then permit the county Democratic organization to designate McCarthy as the candidate.

But Flaherty refused to budge. McCarthy then tried and failed to get on the ballot as an independent, and the attendant publicity among feuding Democratic politicians worked to the advantage of the Republican-Conservative nominee, Jack Kemp. Kemp was well-known, having been a successful quarterback for the Buffalo Bills, local AFL professional football team. Kemp's recognition among the voters, his campaigning ability, and his articulate support of the Nixon Administration won him a narrow 52% victory. Ordinarily, when a candidate like Kemp wins a close election, he can be expected, if he uses the advantages of incumbency diligently, to improve on his showing the next time out. Kemp will also be aided by a friendly state legislature when it draws district lines for 1972. But if McCarthy returns and challenges the former sports-hero, a close race is likely, and the seat could easily change partisan hands once again.

Census Data 1970 pop. 500,041; deviation from current state average, +12.4%; change 1960–70, +22.2%. Metro. 100%, 22.8% central city.

1970 Share of Federal Outlays $409,724,000 (average outlay per district, New York 39–41)

DOD	$57,472,000	HEW	$116,095,000
AEC	$240,000	HUD	$6,243,000
NASA	$1,378,000	OEO	$688,000
DOT	$2,148,000	DOA	$3,076,000
		Other	$223,285,000

Federal Military-Industrial Commitments (See New York 41 for greater Buffalo listing.)

Economic Base Primary metal industries; motor vehicles and motor vehicle equipment, and other transportation equipment; fabricated metal products, esp. metal stampings; nonelectrical machinery, esp. general industrial machinery and equipment. Also, extensive commuting to New York 41 (Buffalo).

The Voters

Registration 234,046 total. 97,531 D (42%); 122,469 R (52%); 2,350 L (1%); 1,358 C (1%); 7,338 other (3%).

Employment profile White collar, 47%. Blue collar, 53%.

Ethnic groups Black, 2%. Total foreign stock, 29%. Poland, 7%; Germany, 6%; Italy, Canada, 4% each; UK, 3%; Austria, Ireland, USSR, 1% each; others, 2%.

Presidential vote

1968	Humphrey (D)	100,276	(49%)*
	Nixon (R)	89,293	(44%)
	Wallace (AIP)	15,298	(7%)

* *These figures do not include votes Humphrey received on the Liberal line. His performance, therefore, is understated by one to five percent in each New York district.*

Representative

Jack F. Kemp (R-Cons.) Elected 1970; b. July 13, 1935, Los Angeles, Calif.; home, Hamburg; Occidental Col., B.A., 1957; USAR, 1958–62; married, three children; Presbyterian.

Career Quarterback for Buffalo Bills, professional football team; Player of the Year, 1965; Cofounder, Pres., American Football League Players Assn., 1965–70; Sp. Asst. to Gov. of Calif., 1967; Sp. Asst. to Chm. of Rep. Natl. Com., 1969; television and radio commentator, national networks and local stations; public relations officer, Marine Midland Bank of Buffalo.

Offices 1129 LHOB, 202-225-5265. Also 414 U.S. Ct. House, 68 Court Street, Buffalo 14202, 716-854-2155.

Committees

Education and Labor (15th); Subs. (1) Education, (2) Labor, (3) Sel. on Education.

Group Ratings, Key Votes: Newly elected.

Election Results

1970 general:	Jack F. Kemp (R and C)	96,989	(52%)
	Thomas P. Flaherty (D and L)	90,949	(48%)
1970 primary:	Jack F. Kemp (R and C), unopposed (Redistricted 1970)		

FORTIETH DISTRICT Political Background

New York 40 comprises Niagara County, site of the falls, and part of suburban Erie County. From the falls, power lines strung out on gigantic towers hum out to the urban Northeast, the Midwest, and southern Canada. The city of Niagara Falls is predominantly industrial, with many of its industries doing very poorly of late. The city has large Italian and Polish communities which lean Democratic, but the rest of Niagara County shares the staunch Republicanism common in Upstate New York. The county's population declined during the '60's. The Erie County portion of the district takes in the middle-class Buffalo suburbs of Tonawanda and Grand Island, as well as the predominantly industrial northwest corner of the city itself. The district as a whole is politically marginal or slightly Republican.

The district's marginal political character has not, however, shown itself in its congressional elections. From 1950 to 1964, the 40th was represented by William E. Miller, who was Republican National Chairman in the early '60's and Barry Goldwater's running mate in 1964. Miller, who barely won reelection in 1962, had already decided to retire from congressional politics when he was tapped for the vice-presidential nomination. His successor, Republican Henry P. Smith, III, has run much stronger in the district. After a 9,000-vote margin in 1964, Smith has since consistently won more the 60% of the vote. He looks entrenched in the 40th. Moreover, redistricting can only help the Congressman. Since Niagara County lost population during the past decade, the Republican legislature could easily attach heavily Republican Orleans County to the eastern end of his present district. Smith is now the 5th-ranking Republican on the House Judiciary Committee and will no doubt move up the seniority ladder in the years to come.

Census Data 1970 pop. 408,489; deviation from current state average, —8.2%; change 1960–70, —0.4%. Metro. 100%, 7.2% central city.

1970 Share of Federal Outlays $409,724,000 (average outlay per district, New York 39–41)

DOD	$57,472,000	HEW	$116,095,000
AEC	$240,000	HUD	$6,243,000
NASA	$1,378,000	OEO	$688,000
DOT	$2,148,000	DOA	$3,076,000
		Other	$223,285,000

Federal Military-Industrial Commitments (See New York 41 for greater Buffalo listing.)

Economic Base Primary metal industries; electrical machinery, equipment, and supplies, esp. electrical industrial apparatus; industrial inorganic and organic chemicals and other chemicals and allied products. Also, tourism (Niagara Falls).

The Voters

Registration 171,446 total. 66,867 D (39%); 96,613 R (56%); 1,493 L (1%); 1,066 C (1%); 5,407 other (3%).

Employment profile White collar, 44%. Blue collar, 56%.

Ethnic groups Black, 3%. Total foreign stock, 34%. Canada, 8%; Italy, 6%; Poland, 5%; Germany, UK, 4% each; Austria, Hungary, Ireland, USSR, 1% each; others, 3%.

Presidential vote

1968	Humphrey (D)	77,160	(48%)*
	Nixon (R)	72,072	(45%)
	Wallace (AIP)	11,480	(7%)

Representative

Henry P. Smith III (R) Elected 1964; b. Sept. 29, 1911, North Tonawanda; home, North Tonawanda; Dartmouth Col., B.A., 1933; Cornell U., LL.B., 1936; married, three children; Presbyterian.

Career Practicing atty., 1936–64; Mayor of N. Tonawanda, 1961–63; Judge, Niagara County, 1963.

Offices 422 CHOB, 202-225-3231. Also 4 Webster St., N. Tonawanda 14120, 716-695-1577.

Committees

District of Columbia (8th); Subs. (1) Education, (2) Housing and Youth Affairs, (3) Judiciary, (4) Public Health and Welfare.

Judiciary (5th); Sub. No. 2.

Group Ratings

	ADA	COPE	NREP	NFU	LCV	CFA	NAB	NSI	ACA
1970	20	25	64	42	25	53	91	89	78
1969	20	—	—	72	—	—	—	—	47
1968	25	25	—	56	—	—	100	—	68

Key Votes

(1) ABM	ABS	(6) 18-Yr-Vote	AGN	(11) Clean Water $	AGN
(2) SST	AGN	(7) Farm Sub Lmt	FOR	(12) Mig Wrkrs Comp	AGN
(3) Phil Pln	FOR	(8) Coop-Church	FOR	(13) Jets to Chiang	AGN
(4) No-Knock	FOR	(9) Family Asst	FOR	(14) State OEO Veto	AGN
(5) Cmutr Tax	ABS	(10) Work Stamps	FOR	(15) Park Logging	FOR

Election Results

1970 general:	Henry P. Smith III (R and C)	87,183	(63%)
	Edward Cuddy (D and L)	50,418	(37%)
1970 primary:	Henry P. Smith III (R and C), unopposed		
	(Redistricted 1970)		

FORTY-FIRST DISTRICT Political Background

New York 41 comprises most of the city of Buffalo and the city of Lackawanna, to the south; both are given over to heavy industry. Huge steel mills line the shore of Lake Erie, as the main east-west rail lines feed into downtown Buffalo and the industrial section to the south. The city is the easternmost U.S. port on the Great Lake;

** These figures do not include votes Humphrey received on the Liberal line. His performance, therefore, is understated by one to five percent in each New York district.*

and here, great ships unload iron ore from the Mesabi Range and grain from the western prairie. Because such activity defines Buffalo's economic base, this city, like its counterparts in the Midwest, is in decline. The newer, more sophisticated, high-value-added industries tend to locate on either coast, and the steel industry is hurting everywhere.

In the early years of this century, however, Buffalo attracted many immigrants eager to find work in its factories. Today the city has many ethnic groups, the largest being Polish and Italian; there is also an increasingly large black population. The mix has produced racial tensions, but on election day these groups all seem to pull the Democratic levers. Thanks in large part to a competent Democratic party organization, Buffalo currently produces larger Democratic percentages than New York City (see New York 39).

Among the beneficiaries of the party organization is the congressman from the 41st, Thaddeus J. Dulski. First elected in 1958, Dulski is now chairman of the Post Office and Civil Service Committee, which allows him to preside over matters like federal pay-increases and postal reform. The *Wall Street Journal* has criticized Dulski's performance as chairman, but that has had no effect on his standing in the district. Because the 41st lost population during the '60's, it will be altered considerably by redistricting. Chances are, however, that the Republican legislature will add Democratic territory now in the 39th. This will not only help the 39th's Republican congressman, Jack Kemp, it will also insure Dulski's reelection.

Census Data 1970 pop. 348,031; deviation from current state average, —21.8%; change 1960–70, 14.7%. Metro. 100%, 92.4% central city.

1970 Share of Federal Outlays $409,724,000 (average outlay per district, New York 39–41)

DOD	$57,472,000	HEW	$116,095,000
AEC	$240,000	HUD	$6,243,000
NASA	$1,378,000	OEO	$688,000
DOT	$2,148,000	DOA	$3,076,000
		Other	$223,285,000

Federal Military-Industrial Commitments (New York 39–41, greater Buffalo listing.)

DOD Contractors Bell Aerospace Corp. (Buffalo), $75.502m: propulsion subsystem for Minuteman III; aircraft carrier landing-control central trainers; amphibious assault landing craft development. Cornell Aeronautical Laboratories Inc. (Buffalo), $16.582m: Safeguard ABM terminal discrimination study; analysis of penetration aids for manned aircraft; variable stability aircraft development. Mid-State Packing Co. (Buffalo), $6.203m: foodstuffs. Sierra Research Corp. (Buffalo), $6.203m: unspecified research.

DOD Installations Lockport AF Station (Lockport). Niagara Falls Airport AF (Niagara Falls).

Economic Base Primary metal industries; motor vehicles and motor vehicle equipment, and other transportation equipment; fabricated metal products, esp. metal stampings; nonelectrical machinery, esp. general industrial machinery and equipment. Also, higher education (SUNY, Buffalo); banking.

The Voters

Registration 149,919 total. 100,754 D (67%); 43,403 R (29%); 1,944 L (1%); 534 C (0%); 3,284 other (2%).

Employment profile White collar, 34%. Blue collar, 66%.

Ethnic groups Black, 25%. Puerto Rico, 1%. Total foreign stock, 34%. Poland, 10%; Italy, 8%; Germany, 5%; Canada, 3%; UK, Ireland, 2% each; Austria, USSR, 1% each; others, 2%.

Presidential vote

1968	Humphrey (D)	91,837	(71%)*
	Nixon (R)	27,836	(21%)
	Wallace (AIP)	10,223	(8%)

** These figures do not include votes Humphrey received on the Liberal line. His performance, therefore, is understated by one to five percent in each New York district.*

Representative

Thaddeus J. Dulski (D-Lib.) Elected 1958; b. Sept. 27, 1915, Buffalo; home, Buffalo; Canisius Col., U. of Buffalo; Navy, WWII; married, five children; Catholic.

Career Accountant and tax consultant, Bureau of Internal Revenue, 1940–47; Sp. Agent, Price Stabilization Admin., 1951–53; Walden Dist. Councilman, 1954–57; Councilman-at-large, 1957.

Offices 205 CHOB, 202-225-3306. Also 212 U.S. Courthouse, Buffalo 14202, 716-853-4131.

Committees

Post Office and Civil Service (Chm.); Chm., Sub. on Investigations.

Veterans' Affairs (5th); Subs. (1) Education and Training, (2) Hospitals.

Group Ratings

	ADA	COPE	NREP	NFU	LCV	CFA	NAB	NSI	ACA
1970	80	100	67	100	78	100	8	70	22
1969	60	—	—	100	—	—	—	—	18
1968	75	100	—	93	—	—	0	—	5

Key Votes

(1) ABM	AGN	(6) 18-Yr-Vote	FOR	(11) Clean Water $	FOR
(2) SST	AGN	(7) Farm Sub Lmt	FOR	(12) Mig Wrkrs Comp	FOR
(3) Phil Pln	FOR	(8) Coop-Church	AGN	(13) Jets to Chiang	AGN
(4) No-Knock	FOR	(9) Family Asst	FOR	(14) State OEO Veto	AGN
(5) Cmutr Tax	FOR	(10) Work Stamps	AGN	(15) Park Logging	AGN

Election Results

1970 general:	Thaddeus J. Dulski (D and L)	79,151	(80%)
	William M. Johns (R and C)	20,108	(20%)
1970 primary:	Thaddeus J. Dulski (D and L), unopposed		

NORTH CAROLINA

Political Background

For more than two centuries, the differences between east and west have structured North Carolina politics. The Tidewater region in the east was pro-Tory in the Revolutionary War, while the Piedmont region to the west was a hotbed of anti-British radicalism. Likewise, during the Civil War, the east, which had most of the slaves in North Carolina, was strongly pro-Confederate, while to the west, particularly in the Appalachians, there was considerable Union sentiment. Today, each of the state's three major topographical regions has distinctive politics. The Tidewater still has a large black population and retains Democratic-segregationist voting habits; a bent similar to that of the Deep South. The residents of the Appalachians remain traditional, anti-planter Republicans, and also remain fiercely independent of the rest of the state. The central Piedmont, now with textile, tobacco, and furniture-manufacturing cities, has become increasingly Republican and conservative, as those two terms are commonly understood. Because of this regional mix, North Carolina's Republicans have always been a factor, though almost always a minority, in the politics of the state. And because of the relatively small black population in central and western North Carolina, the state has been relatively free of the racist demagoguery often heard in South Carolina, Georgia, Alabama, and other states of the Deep South.

Before the Civil War, North Carolina was an economic backwater, but for a full century after the conflict, industrial development within the state ran far ahead of the rest of the South. Recently, other Southern states have begun to catch up. This may be because the state has no one large metropolitan area to serve as a regional center; in short, North Carolina has no Atlanta. The urban population here is scattered; there are four metropolitan areas with between 200,000 and 350,000 residents—Charlotte, Greensboro, Winston-Salem, and Raleigh. There are, of course, a host of smaller cities of local importance, and a large part of the state is still rural, some 55% according to the 1970 census. The figure indicates that tobacco is still very important to the state, both as a crop and as an industry, and that not too many North Carolina politicians oppose cigarette smoking.

Moderate Republicans have long pointed to North Carolina's relatively calm attitude toward racial issues and then talked about the coming of the New South. There have been predictions of a Republican takeover of the state since it sent a member of the party, Charles R. Jonas, to Congress in 1952. In 1968, Nixon carried the state in a fairly close race, winning 40% to Wallace's 31%, and Humphrey's 29%. But in state races, the Republicans have been unable to make a breakthrough. In the late '50's and early '60's, they tried to be more moderate and more modern than the Democrats. The strategy did not win any statewide elections, though the Republicans gave Sen. B. Everett Jordan a scare in 1966. In 1968, they shifted abruptly to a Goldwater approach. When Republican James C. Gardner ran for governor, he tried to cut into the Democratic strength in the east by stressing his opposition to racial integration; but his militance had limited success in the Tidewater, and antagonized normally Republican voters in the Piedmont. Gardner improved on Goldwater's 1964 showing by 3%, but he was defeated by Lt. Governor Robert Scott, son of a governor and senator, who took 53% of the votes.

B. Everett Jordan was appointed senator from North Carolina in 1958, and won reelection in 1958, 1960, and 1966, the last time with a surprisingly weak 56%. Jordan, a conservative Democrat has a voting record pretty much in line with those of other Southern senators, though his ADA rating has moved from 0 in 1968, to 43 in 1970. He surprised observers in the summer of 1971 when he announced his opposition to the Vietnam war, and even went so far as to flash the "V" sign at the Democratic state convention. Jordan made his name in the Senate as chairman of the Rules and Administration Committee. In that capacity, he presided over the investigation of the Bobby Baker affair, but the results of that probe did not embarrass any senator, and Jordan seems today to be well-liked on Capitol Hill.

Jordan was 74 in 1970, but has given no indication that he will retire when his term expires in 1972. It is rumored that Nick Galifianakis, one of the state's most liberal congressmen, will challenge the incumbent in the primary. But Jordan's antiwar position may have undermined Galifianakis' position at the outset.

North Carolina was one of the last of the thirteen ex-colonies to ratify the Constitution. Members of the state legislature of that day balked because the document, as written, did not contain a section guaranteeing fundamental civil rights. That delay was in large part responsible for the first ten amendments to the Constitution known as the Bill of Rights. It is therefore fitting that North Carolina's senior senator, Sam Ervin, Jr., is a persistent and articulate opponent of federal legislation and administrative action that, in his opinion, violates fundamental constitutional freedoms. The Senator has opposed both civil rights legislation and the Nixon Administration's no-knock bill. In the latter case, Ervin was the floor leader for the civil libertarians while usually liberal, ex-Senator Joseph Tydings of Maryland was the bill's chief proponent. Ervin served on the North Carolina state Supreme Court before he was appointed to the Senate in 1954. He is now chairman of the Judiciary Committee's Subcommittee on Constitutional Rights, and has conducted hearings on government intrusions into personal privacy. The investigations revealed, among other things, that the Army conducted surveillance of several Illinois politicians, including Senator Adlai Stevenson, and that the Treasury Department kept track of persons who checked out certain "subversive books" from public libraries. Ervin is less concerned with encroachments on personal freedom by the states than he is with federal violations, and he has a conservative attitude on most policy questions. But it is a measure of his devotion to the Constitution, as he reads it, that the victims of many of the government practices he has denounced are people whose ideas he does not share.

Ervin has never had any trouble winning reelection. Like Senator Jordan, he turned 74 in 1970, but he will probably run again when his current term expires in 1974. If he does he will undoubtedly win.

Electoral Votes 13

Census Data 1970 pop. 5,082,059; 2.47% of U.S. total, 12th largest; change 1960–70, +11.5%. Metro. 37.3%, 18.8% central city. 1970 per capita income, $3,188; 40th highest. 12th in number of poor.

1970 Share of Federal Tax Burden $3,453,990,000; 1.77% of U.S. total, 17th largest.

1970 Share of Federal Outlays $3,459,530,024; 1.83% of U.S. total, 17th largest. Per capita federal spending, $681.

DOD	$1,192,177,000	17th (2.08%)	HEW	$1,059,658,970	14th (2.03%)
AEC	$2,132,823	32nd (0.08%)	HUD	$40,920,037	17th (2.10%)
NASA	$2,363,838	31st (0.06%)	OEO	$18,685,521	12th (2.46%)
DOT	$109,326,806	28th (1.53%)	DOA	$337,167,897	13th (2.62%)
DOC	$17,615,243	14th (1.52%)	POD	$116,440,648	18th (1.60%)
DOI	$16,892,303	37th (0.73%)	VA	$212,082,366	12th (2.87%)
DOJ	$7,463,055	23rd (1.30%)	CSC	$38,316,954	21st (0.95%)
			Other	$288,286,563	

Economic Base Tobacco, livestock, and poultry; textile mill products, esp. knitting mills and yarn and thread mills; apparel and other finished products made from fabrics and similar materials, esp. men's, boys', and youths' furnishings, work clothing, and allied garments; household furniture and other furniture and fixtures; electrical machinery, equipment, and supplies, esp. communication equipment; food and kindred products, esp. meat products; lumber and wood products other than furniture, esp. sawmills and planing mills; nonelectrical machinery, esp. metalworking machinery and equipment; chemicals and allied products, esp. plastics materials and synthetic resins, synthetic rubber, synthetic and other man-made fibers, other than glass; tobacco manufactures, esp. cigarettes.

Political Line-up Governor, Robert W. Scott (D); seat up, 1972. Senators, Sam J. Ervin, Jr. (D) and B. Everett Jordan (D). Representatives, 11 (7 D and 4 R). State Senate (43 D and 7 R); State House (97 D and 23 R).

The Voters

Registration 1,949,150 total. 1,464,005 D (75%); 430,258 R (22%); 54,887 other (3%).

Employment profile White collar, 30%. Blue collar, 70%.

Ethnic groups Black, 22%. Total foreign stock, 1%. All foreign groups less than 0.5% each.

Presidential vote

1968	Humphrey (D)	464,113	(29%)
	Nixon (R)	627,192	(40%)
	Wallace (AIP)	496,118	(31%)
1964	Johnson (D)	800,139	(56%)
	Goldwater (R)	624,844	(44%)
1960	Kennedy (D)	713,318	(52%)
	Nixon (R)	655,648	(48%)

Senator

Sam J. Ervin (D) Elected June 5, 1954, seat up 1974; b. Sept. 27, 1896, Morganton; home, Morganton; U. of N.C., B.A., 1917; Harvard U., LL.B., 1922; Army, WWI; married, three children; Presbyterian.

Career Practicing atty., 1922– ; N.C. General Assembly, 1923, 1925, 1931; Judge, Burke County Criminal Ct., 1935–37; Judge, N.C. Superior Ct., 1937–43; Assoc. Justice, N.C. Supreme Ct., 1948–54.

Offices 337 OSOB, 202-225-3154. Also Box 69, Morganton 28655, 704-437-5532.

Committees

Armed Services (4th); Subs. (1) Chm., Status of Forces, (2) Military Construction Authorization, (3) National Stockpile and Naval Petroleum Reserves.

Government Operations (3rd); Subs. (1) Intergovernmental Relations, (2) Permanent Investigations.

Judiciary (3rd); Subs. (1) Chm., Constitutional Rights, (2) Chm., Revision and Codification, (3) Chm., Separation of Powers, (4) Antitrust and Monopoly Legislation, (5) Constitutional Amendments, (6) Criminal Laws and Procedures, (7) Immigration and Naturalization, (8) Improvements in Judicial Machinery, (9) Internal Security.

Sel. Com. on Equal Educational Opportunity (9th).

Group Ratings

	ADA	COPE	NREP	NFU	LCV	NAB	NSI	ACA
1970	13	15	18	33	34	82	100	78
1969	6	—	—	63	—	—	—	86
1968	0	30	—	38	—	50	—	78

Key Votes

(1) ABM	FOR	(8) Phil Pln	AGN	(15) Coop-Church	AGN
(2) SST	AGN	(9) Vol Army	AGN	(16) Cut Oil Dpltn	AGN
(3) Busing	AGN	(10) Prison $	AGN	(17) Consumer Prot	FOR
(4) Tob Sub	FOR	(11) Cut Mil $	AGN	(18) Farm Sub Limit	AGN
(5) Carswell	FOR	(12) Defoliatn	FOR	(19) Comp Bid Sales	AGN
(6) No-Knock	AGN	(13) 18-Yr-Vote	AGN	(20) Pre-Prod Tests	AGN
(7) Seniorty	FOR	(14) Pentgn PR	FOR	(21) Cut Marjna Pen	AGN

Election Results

1968 general:	Sam J. Ervin, Jr. (D)	870,406	(61%)
	Robert Vance Somers (R)	566,934	(39%)
1968 primary:	Sam J. Ervin, Jr. (D)	499,392	(78%)
	Charles A. Pratt (D)	60,362	(9%)
	John T. Gathings, Sr. (D)	48,357	(8%)
	Fred G. Brummitt (D)	30,126	(5%)
1962 general:	Sam J. Ervin, Jr. (D)	491,520	(60%)
	Claude L. Greene, Jr. (R)	321,635	(40%)

Senator

B. Everett Jordan (D) Elected April 19, 1958, seat up 1972; b. Sept. 8, 1896, Ramseur; home, Saxapahaw; Trinity Col. (now Duke U.), 1914–15; Army, WWI; married, three children; Methodist.

Career Businessman, jewelry store; textile mfg., 1915–27; Gen. Mgr., Secy.-Treas., Dir., Sellers Mfg. Co., 1927– ; Gen. Mgr., Secy.-Treas., Dir., Jordan Spinning Co., 1939– ; Pres., Treas., Gen Mgr., Dir., Royal Cotton Mill Co., 1945– ; Secy.-Treas., Natl. Processing Co., 1945– ; Chm., N.C. Dem. Exec. Com., 1949–54; Mbr., N.C. Medical Care Commission, 1945–51.

Offices 3229 NSOB, 202-225-6342. Also 320 Fed. Office Bldg., Raleigh 27601, 919-755-4630, and 3302 Luther St., Winston-Salem 27107, 919-788-8095.

Committees

Agriculture and Forestry (4th); Subs. (1) Chm., Agricultural Production, Marketing, and Stabilization of Prices, (2) Agricultural Exports, (3) Agricultural Research and General Legislation, (4) Environment, Soil Conservation, Forestry.

Public Works (3rd); Subs. (1) Chm., Flood Control—Rivers and Harbors, (2) Public Buildings and Grounds, (3) Public Roads.

Rules and Administration (Chm.); Subs. (1) Chm., Computer Services, (2) Chm., Library, (3) Printing.

Jt. Com. on the Library (V. Chm.).

Jt. Com. on Printing (Chm.).

Group Ratings

	ADA	COPE	NREP	NFU	LCV	NAB	NSI	ACA
1970	43	17	9	22	23	67	80	74
1969	6	—	—	56	—	—	—	80
1968	0	11	—	30	—	40	—	67

Key Votes

(1) ABM	FOR	(8) Phil Pln	AGN	(15) Coop-Church	FOR
(2) SST	AGN	(9) Vol Army	AGN	(16) Cut Oil Dpltn	AGN
(3) Busing	AGN	(10) Prison $	AGN	(17) Consumer Prot	FOR
(4) Tob Sub	FOR	(11) Cut Mil $	AGN	(18) Farm Sub Limit	AGN
(5) Carswell	FOR	(12) Defoliatn	FOR	(19) Comp Bid Sales	ABS
(6) No-Knock	AGN	(13) 18-Yr-Vote	AGN	(20) Pre-Prod Tests	AGN
(7) Seniorty	ABS	(14) Pentgn PR	FOR	(21) Cut Marjna Pen	AGN

Election Results

1966 general:	B. Everett Jordan (D)	501,440	(56%)
	John S. Shalleross (R)	400,502	(44%)
1966 primary:	B. Everett Jordan (D)	445,454	(79%)
	Hubert E. Seymour, Jr. (D)	116,548	(21%)
1960 general:	B. Everett Jordan (D)	793,521	(61%)
	Kyle Hays (R)	497,964	(39%)

FIRST DISTRICT Political Background

North Carolina 1, in the northeast corner of the state, is part of the Tidewater area along the Atlantic Coast. Beyond the Pamlico and Albemarle Sounds are a series of thin coastal islands. These include Cape Hatteras, long feared by mariners; Kitty Hawk, where the Wright Brothers first flew their craft; and Roanoke Island, site of an abortive attempt at colonization in 1587. The islands are lonely resort areas, and virtually all of the people in the district live inland, near the sounds. Because this was the first part of North Carolina to be settled by British colonists, some of the state's colonial atmosphere still survives in towns like New Bern, once the colony's capital. Today, Greenville (pop. 29,000) is the largest city in the predominantly rural 1st district. Some 37% of the residents here are black, the second largest black population of any North Carolina district.

The white voters of the 1st retain from their slaveholding days a strong Democratic preference; they steadfastly supported Democratic presidential candidates until 1968. In that year, when it looked like the election might be thrown into the House of Representatives, the 1st's congressman, Walter B. Jones, was one of several Southern House members to announce that he would vote for whoever carried his district. That turned out to be George Wallace, as white voters abandoned the Democrats *en masse*. Wallace took 45%, while the 34% cast for Humphrey is a pretty accurate index of black voter participation. Nixon's 21% shows the district's continuing antipathy towards Republicans, even conservative ones, who make a determined effort to win Southern votes.

Walter Jones is a conservative Democratic congressman. He was a state senator before winning a 1966 special election to succeed the late Herbert C. Bonner. Bonner, who had served in the House since 1940, was chairman of the Merchant Marine and Fisheries Committee. Today, Jones is a member of that congressional unit as well as of the Agriculture Committee—appropriate assignments for a congressman from a rural, coastal district.

Jones has won the last three elections with spectacular majorities, and he will certainly represent the 1st for a long time. The district gained virtually no population during the '60's, but the legislature's redistricting plan guarantees Jones a safe seat.

Census Data 1970 pop. 412,973; deviation from current state average, −10.6%; change 1960–70, +0.1%. Metro. 0.0%, 0.0% central city.

1970 Share of Federal Outlays $311,875,785

DOD	$100,204,000	HEW	$87,726,028
AEC	$000	HUD	$1,169,397
NASA	$000	OEO	$3,446,329
DOT	$8,646,072	DOA	$56,645,327
		Other	$54,038,632

Federal Military-Industrial Commitments

DOD Installations Marine Corps Air Facility (New River). Naval Facility (Buston). Marine Corps Air Station (Cherry Point). Naval Air Rework Facility (Cherry Point).

Economic Base Tobacco and cash grain; apparel and other finished products made from fabrics and similar materials.

The Voters

Registration 155,683 total. 138,060 D (89%); 15,693 R (10%); 1,930 other (1%).

Employment profile White collar, 27%. Blue collar, 73%.

Ethnic groups Black, 37%. Total foreign stock, 1%. All foreign groups less than 0.5% each.

Presidential vote

1968	Humphrey (D)	43,458	(34%)
	Nixon (R)	25,900	(21%)
	Wallace (AIP)	56,357	(45%)

Representative

Walter B. Jones (D) Elected Feb. 5, 1966; b. Aug. 19, 1913, Fayetteville; home, Farmville; N.C. State U., B.S., 1934; married, two children; Baptist.

Career Businessman, office supplies, 1934–49; Mayor of Farmville, 1949–53; N.C. Gen. Assembly, 1955–59; N.C. Senate, 1965.

Offices 130 CHOB, 202-225-3101. Also Farmville 27828, 919-753-3082.

Committees

Agriculture (10th); Subs. (1) Chm., Oilseeds and Rice, (2) Livestock and Grains, (3) Tobacco.

Merchant Marine and Fisheries (13th); Subs. (1) Coast Guard, Coast and Geodetic Survey and Navigation, (2) Merchant Marine, (3) Oceanography, (4) Panama Canal.

Group Ratings

	ADA	COPE	NREP	NFU	LCV	CFA	NAB	NSI	ACA
1970	12	42	17	31	25	40	67	100	79
1969	7	—	—	54	—	—	—	—	76
1968	8	8	—	53	—	—	80	—	73

Key Votes

(1) ABM	FOR	(6) 18-Yr-Vote	AGN	(11) Clean Water $	AGN
(2) SST	FOR*	(7) Farm Sub Lmt	AGN	(12) Mig Wrkrs Comp	AGN
(3) Phil Pln	AGN	(8) Coop-Church	AGN	(13) Jets to Chiang	FOR
(4) No-Knock	FOR	(9) Family Asst	AGN	(14) State OEO Veto	FOR
(5) Cmutr Tax	AGN	(10) Work Stamps	FOR	(15) Park Logging	ABS

* *Voted "against" in previous vote on same issue.*

Election Results

1970 general:	Walter B. Jones (D)	41,674	(70%)
	R. Frank Everett (R)	16,217	(27%)
	Gene Leggett (AIP)	1,452	(2%)
1970 primary:	Walter B. Jones (D)	49,262	(87%)
	L. C. Nixon (D)	7,316	(13%)
1968 general:	Walter B. Jones (D)	75,796	(66%)
	Reece B. Gardner (R)	38,660	(34%)

SECOND DISTRICT Political Background

North Carolina 2 comprises the northwest portion of the state's coastal plain. It is a predominantly rural and agricultural area with few cities of any size; the largest is Rocky Mount with 34,000 residents. The 2nd has the largest black minority of any North Carolina district, some 43% of the population. Civil rights leader Floyd McKissick has announced plans for a black "newtown" in Warren County, in an effort to stem black outmigration and encourage black capitalism. Like much of central North Carolina, the 2nd's rural areas are comparatively thickly settled; there are still many family farms here. Inexpensive sites are attracting small factories that draw their labor from people who would rather stay on the farm than move north.

The 2nd is ancestrally Democratic, but in 1968 it produced the largest Wallace vote of any congressional district in the state, nearly 50%. The congressman from the 2nd is a reliably conservative member of the Southern Democrat bloc, L. H. Fountain, who has been in the House since 1952. Fountain has only been challenged twice, once in the 1966 general election and once in the 1968 primary, and defeated both opponents with ease. The only possible threat to his tenure would be a black or a black-supported candidate. But so far, the rural blacks have not chosen—or dared—to take an active part in the district's congressional politics.

Census Data 1970 pop. 395,806; deviation from current state average, −14.3%; change 1960–70, −4.7%. Metro. 0.0%, 0.0% central city.

1970 Share of Federal Outlays $249,387,972

DOD	$12,428,000	HEW	$81,554,398
AEC	$000	HUD	$2,126,405
NASA	$000	OEO	$580,331
DOT	$7,059,644	DOA	$104,793,282
		Other	$40,845,912

Federal Military-Industrial Commitments

DOD Installations Roanoke Rapids AF Station (Roanoke Rapids).

Economic Base Tobacco and other field crops; textile mill products; apparel and other finished products made from fabrics and similar materials.

The Voters

Registration 157,351 total. 143,927 D (92%); 11,584 R (7%); 1,840 other (1%).

Employment profile White collar, 26%. Blue collar, 74%.

Ethnic groups Black, 43%. Total foreign stock, 1%. All foreign groups less than 0.5% each.

Presidential vote

1968	Humphrey (D)	39,540	(33%)
	Nixon (R)	24,909	(21%)
	Wallace (AIP)	57,201	(47%)

Representative

L. H. Fountain (D) Elected 1952; b. April 23, 1913, Leggett; home, Tarboro; U. of N.C., B.A., 1934, LL.B., 1936; Army, WWII; married, one child; Presbyterian.

Career Practicing atty., 1936– ; Reading Clerk, N.C. Senate, 1936–41; N.C. Senate, 1947–52; V.P., Plains Broadcasting Co., WCPS Radio, Tarboro, 1949– .

Offices 2188 RHOB, 202-225-4531. Also Post Office, Tarboro 27886, 919-823-4200.

Committees

Foreign Affairs (4th); Subs. (1) International Organizations, (2) National Security Policy and Scientific Dev., (3)) Near East, (4) Sp. for Review of Foreign Aid Programs.

Government Operations (3rd); Chm., Intergovernmental Relations.

Group Ratings

	ADA	COPE	NREP	NFU	LCV	CFA	NAB	NSI	ACA
1970	4	17	0	23	30	46	75	100	79
1969	7	—	—	54	—	—	—	—	81
1968	0	0	—	44	—	—	83	—	91

Key Votes

(1) ABM	FOR	(6) 18-Yr-Vote	AGN	(11) Clean Water $	AGN
(2) SST	FOR	(7) Farm Sub Lmt	AGN	(12) Mig Wrkrs Comp	AGN
(3) Phil Pln	AGN	(8) Coop-Church	AGN	(13) Jets to Chiang	ABS
(4) No-Knock	FOR	(9) Family Asst	AGN	(14) State OEO Veto	FOR
(5) Cmutr Tax	AGN	(10) Work Stamps	FOR	(15) Park Logging	FOR

Election Results

1970 general: L. H. Fountain (D), unopposed
1970 primary: L. H. Fountain (D), unopposed
1968 general: L. H. Fountain (D), unopposed

THIRD DISTRICT Political Background

North Carolina 3, in the middle of the state's coastal plain, is a district of farms, small towns, and Atlantic shore seascape. The 3rd stretches from a point a few miles south of Raleigh and Durham all the way to the Cape Lookout National Seashore, near Cape Hatteras. The largest city here is Goldsboro (pop. 26,000), but the largest population concentration is Camp Lejeune (pop. 34,000), the Marine Corps' giant base at the estuary of the New River. The camp is an economic asset to the district, but the voters may have been disturbed by recent racial troubles there. The 3rd has fewer blacks than other coastal North Carolina districts, a fact which is reflected in the weak 1968 showing of the Democrat Humphrey (27%), and the relatively strong showing of the Republican Nixon (32%).

In 1960, Congressman Graham Barden of this district, then chairman of the House Education and Labor Committee, retired; when he left, Harlem's Adam Clayton Powell became chairman. Barden was succeeded by David N. Henderson, who had served briefly on the committee's staff while Barden was chairman. But like most Southern Democrats who have been elected to the House recently, Henderson did not obtain a seat on this increasingly liberal committee. Instead, he chose Post Office and Civil Service, where he is today the 2nd ranking Democrat; as a member of the committee, Henderson shares in such unpleasant tasks as raising postal rates and staving off civil service strikes.

Congressman Henderson has seldom had difficulty at the polls. But in 1968, his Republican opponent carried Johnston and Wayne counties in the western part of the district. That was the year in which Republican James Gardner made a bid for the Wallace votes in eastern North Carolina, and the 3rd was one of the state's eleven congressional districts he carried (see state write up). If North Carolina Republicans once again try using the Gardner strategy, Henderson might be in trouble; otherwise, he has little to worry about.

Census Data 1970 pop. 432,659; deviation from current state average, −6.4%; change 1960–70, +4.6%. Metro. 0.0%, 0.0% central city.

1970 Share of Federal Outlays $396,667,024

DOD	$237,528,000	HEW	$72,876,048
AEC	$135,050	HUD	$1,256,399
NASA	$000	OEO	$916,766
DOT	$3,743,175	DOA	$32,048,200
		Other	$48,163,486

Federal Military-Industrial Commitments

DOD Installations Marine Corps Base (Camp Lejeune). Naval Hospital (Camp Lejeune). Seymour-Johnson AFB (Goldsboro).

Economic Base Tobacco; apparel and other finished products made from fabrics and similar materials; electrical machinery, equipment, and supplies; textile mill products. Also, banking.

The Voters

Registration 140,182 total. 114,349 D (82%); 23,036 R (16%); 2,797 other (2%).

Employment profile White collar, 28%. Blue collar, 72%.

Ethnic groups Black, 25%. Total foreign stock, 2%. All foreign groups less than 0.5% each.

Presidential vote

1968	Humphrey (D)	31,070	(27%)
	Nixon (R)	35,991	(32%)
	Wallace (AIP)	46,384	(41%)

Representative

David Newton Henderson (D) Elected 1960; b. April 16, 1921, near Hubert; home, Wallace; Davidson Col., B.S., 1942; U. of N.C., LL.B., 1949; Army Air Corps, WWII; married, three children; Presbyterian.

Career Practicing atty., 1949–60; Asst. Gen. Counsel, House Ed. and Labor Com., 1951–52; Solicitor, Duplin County Gen. Ct., 1954–58; Judge, 1957–59.

Offices 217 CHOB, 202-225-3415. Also 110½ E. Main St., Wallace 28466, 919-285-2102, and Fed. Bldg., Goldsboro 27530, 919-736-1844.

Committees

Post Office and Civil Service (2nd); Subs. (1) Chm., Manpower and Civil Service, (2) Investigations, (3) Postal Facilities and Mail.

Public Works (10th); Subs. (1) Flood Control and Internal Development, (2) Rivers and Harbors, (3) Roads, (4) Sp. on Economic Development Programs.

Group Ratings

	ADA	COPE	NREP	NFU	LCV	CFA	NAB	NSI	ACA
1970	8	42	18	27	44	48	67	100	72
1969	7	—	—	54	—	—	—	—	81
1968	8	8	—	50	—	—	67	—	78

Key Votes

(1) ABM	ABS	(6) 18-Yr-Vote	AGN	(11) Clean Water $	AGN
(2) SST	FOR	(7) Farm Sub Lmt	AGN	(12) Mig Wrkrs Comp	AGN
(3) Phil Pln	AGN	(8) Coop-Church	AGN	(13) Jets to Chiang	FOR
(4) No-Knock	FOR	(9) Family Asst	AGN	(14) State OEO Veto	FOR
(5) Cmutr Tax	AGN	(10) Work Stamps	FOR	(15) Park Logging	FOR

Election Results

1970 general:	David N. Henderson (D)	41,065	(60%)
	Herbert H. Howell (R)	27,224	(40%)
1970 primary:	David N. Henderson (D), unopposed		
1968 general:	David N. Henderson (D)	57,244	(54%)
	Herbert H. Howell (R)	48,815	(46%)

FOURTH DISTRICT Political Background

North Carolina 4 comprises five counties in the middle of the state, where the Piedmont comes up out of the coastal plain of the Tidewater. Raleigh (pop. 121,000), the district's largest city, is the state capital, a tobacco center, and home of North Carolina State University. Durham (pop. 95,000), another tobacco center and site of Duke University, has one of the state's largest and most active black communities. Duke is where Richard Nixon went to law school. Chapel Hill, also in the district, contains the University of North Carolina and has a black mayor. The beginnings of a Boston Route 128-style electronic boom is developing in the Research Triangle area between Raleigh and Durham.

The 4th's strong black and academic communities make it North Carolina's most liberal district. Of the two rural counties in the district to the south and west, Chatham is generally Democratic while Randolph follows most of the Piedmont, of which it is a part, and votes Republican. But the politics of the 4th as a whole shares neither the Democratic conservatism of the Tidewater nor the Republican conservatism of the Piedmont. This is one of the two North Carolina districts which is more or less liberal and which has a more or less liberal congressman, a Democrat with the unlikely name of Nick Galifianakis.

Galifianakis, a native of the area, is a lawyer and an ex-Marine. He represented Durham in the state legislature from 1960 until 1966, when he ran for Congress in what was then the 5th district, following the retirement of Congressman Ralph J. Scott. At that time the 5th contained Durham and Winston-Salem, and he won both the primary and general elections by narrow margins. His victories were based on his strength in Durham County. In 1968, redistricting removed Winston-Salem and put Galifianakis in a redrawn 4th, which contained Raleigh as well as Durham. The Congressman ran in the district and defeated the Republican candidate with 52% of the votes.

The narrowness of his election margins and his liberal stands, including support for a fixed timetable for withdrawals from Vietnam, made Galifianakis a prime target for the Republicans in 1970. R. Jack Hawke, the Republican candidate, benefitted from strong financial support and a late-campaign visit from Vice-President Agnew—politics, in this case, being thicker than Greek-American blood. But Galifianakis won again with 52%; he ran even in Wake County (Raleigh), while winning 2,000-vote majorities in both Durham County (Durham) and Orange County (Chapel Hill).

The Democratic state legislature has seriously weakened Galifianakis with their redistricting plan, by removing liberal Orange County from the 4th. The Congressman was already, according to some reports, contemplating a primary race against Senator B. Everett Jordan, and the prospects of a difficult House race makes the run at statewide office more attractive. But whatever happens, the 4th will have another close race in 1972.

Census Data 1970 pop. 524,753; deviation from current state average, +27.3%; change 1960–70, +13.6%. Metro. 94.4%, 41.4% central city.

1970 Share of Federal Outlays $400,497,821

DOD	$36,351,000	HEW	$205,032,538
AEC	$1,938,769	HUD	$4,446,286
NASA	$2,118,433	OEO	$5,602,352
DOT	$14,329,627	DOA	$30,256,618
		Other	$100,422,198

Federal Military-Industrial Commitments

DOD Contractors Athey Products (Wake Forest), $8.959m: fork-lift trucks.

Economic Base Tobacco manufactures, esp. cigarettes; tobacco and poultry; textile mill products, esp. knitting mills. Also, higher education (University of North Carolina and UNC Raleigh).

The Voters

Registration 199,796 total. 152,911 D (77%); 40,928 R (21%); 5,957 other (3%).

Employment profile White collar, 35%. Blue collar, 65%.

Ethnic groups Black, 23%. Total foreign stock, 2%. All foreign groups less than 0.5% each.

Presidential vote

1968	Humphrey (D)	54,791	(33%)
	Nixon (R)	65,025	(40%)
	Wallace (AIP)	44,768	(27%)

Representative

Nick Galifianakis (D) Elected 1966; b. July 22, 1928, Durham; home, Durham; Duke U., B.A., 1951, LL.B., 1953; USMCR, 1953–56; Major USMCR; married, two children; Greek Orthodox.

Career Practicing atty., 1953– ; Commanding Officer, 41st Rifle Co., 1960–62; N.C. Assembly, 1961–66; Asst. Prof., Duke U., 1967.

Offices 225 CHOB, 202-225-2515. Also, 213 Post Office Bldg., Durham 27701, 919-688-8146, ext. 418, and 310 New Bern Ave., Raleigh 27601, 919-755-4120, ext. 557, and 101 Fed. Bldg., Sunset Ave., Asheboro 27203, 919-625-3060.

Committees

Appropriations (30th); Subs. (1) Foreign Operations, (2) Interior.

Group Ratings

	ADA	COPE	NREP	NFU	LCV	CFA	NAB	NSI	ACA
1970	40	50	42	62	50	65	50	90	37
1969	7	—	—	67	—	—	—	—	47
1968	17	39	—	73	—	—	67	—	64

Key Votes

(1) ABM	FOR	(6) 18-Yr-Vote	FOR	(11) Clean Water $	AGN
(2) SST	AGN	(7) Farm Sub Lmt	AGN	(12) Mig Wrkrs Comp	AGN
(3) Phil Pln	AGN	(8) Coop-Church	FOR	(13) Jets to Chiang	AGN
(4) No-Knock	FOR	(9) Family Asst	FOR	(14) State OEO Veto	FOR
(5) Cmutr Tax	AGN	(10) Work Stamps	FOR	(15) Park Logging	AGN

Election Results

1970 general:	Nick Galifianakis (D)	49,866	(52%)
	R. Jack Hawke (R)	45,386	(48%)
1970 primary:	Nick Galifianakis (D), unopposed		
1968 general:	Nick Galifianakis (D)	77,871	(52%)
	Fred Steele (R)	73,471	(48%)

FIFTH DISTRICT Political Background

North Carolina 5 comprises seven rural counties and Forsyth County, which contains the city of Winston-Salem. Winston-Salem (pop. 132,000), one of North Carolina's four large Piedmont cities, is heavily dependent on the tobacco industry. Each half of its name has been made famous by the huge R. J. Reynolds Company, which is based here. Forsyth County, which contains half of the district's population, is politically marginal; it votes for Republican presidential candidates, North Carolina Democratic favorites like Sam Ervin, and local and congressional candidates of both parties. Most of the rest of the district is heavily Republican, especially Davie and Davidson counties, in the heart of the Piedmont textile-mill area, and the mountain counties along the Tennessee border, which have been Republican since the Civil War.

This was clearly a marginal district when it was created in 1967, and in 1968, when the 5th had no incumbent running, there was a real fight for the House seat. The Democratic candidate was Smith Bagley, heir to the Reynolds tobacco fortune; he had been defeated in the primary two years earlier by Congressman Nick Galifianakis when the 5th included Durham (see North Carolina 4). Bagley was opposed by Republican Wilmer (Vinegar Bend) Mizell, who had been a pitcher for several major league baseball teams. Mizell settled here after retiring from the game probably because he had won many honors playing for Winston-Salem's minor club in the early '50's before being called up to the big leagues. These honors included "most popular player" and "Mr. Strike-Out King." Mizell campaigned as a conservative and a supporter of the Nixon Administration while Bagley took a somewhat more liberal stance. Bagley carried several northern counties and took Forsyth County by 2,000 votes, but it was not enough to overcome Mizell's large margins in Davidson (his wife's home county) and Davie. And so the former pitcher became yet another famous-athlete-turned-Republican congressman (see California 18 and New York 39).

In the North Carolina Republican tradition, the Congressman has compiled a steadfastly conservative record in Washington. He was reelected in 1970 with a solid 58%, a better figure than his won-lost percentage in the big leagues. This time he carried Forsyth County by a large majority. Because redistricting has not altered the 5th significantly, Mizell's recent performance suggests that he will enjoy a long career in the House.

Census Data 1970 pop. 456,331; deviation from current state average, −1.2%; change 1960–70, +12.3%. Metro. 52.4%, 29.1% central city.

1970 Share of Federal Outlays $220,736,507

DOD	$52,671,000	HEW	$89,854,265
AEC	$59,004	HUD	$2,517,213
NASA	$000	OEO	$1,356,166
DOT	$2,851,905	DOA	$17,560,058
		Other	$53,866,896

Federal Military-Industrial Commitments

DOD Contractors Western Electric Div., AT&T (Winston-Salem), $25.877m: Safeguard ABM development. R. J. Reynolds Industries (Winston-Salem), $14.273m: unspecified.

Economic Base Tobacco, livestock, and dairy; textile products, esp. knitting mills; household furniture and other furniture and fixtures; tobacco manufactures. Also, banking.

The Voters

Registration 169,557 total. 111,251 D (66%); 53,919 R (32%); 4,387 other (3%).
Employment profile White collar, 32%. Blue collar, 68%.

Ethnic groups Black, 14%. Total foreign stock, 1%. All foreign groups less than 0.5% each.

Presidential vote

1968	Humphrey (D)	42,810	(26%)
	Nixon (R)	79,060	(48%)
	Wallace (AIP)	41,442	(25%)

Representative

Wilmer David Mizell (R) Elected 1968; b. Aug. 13, 1930, Vinegar Bend, Ala.; home, Winston-Salem; Army, 1953–54; married, two children; Baptist.

Career Baseball pitcher, 1949–63; Natl. League All Star Team, 1959; sales management and public relations, Pepsi-Cola Co., 1963–67; Chm., Bd. of Davidson County Commissioners, 1966.

Offices 429 CHOB, 202-225-2071. Also 1819 Wachovia Bank Bldg., Winston-Salem 27101, 919-723-9211, ext. 348.

Committees

Agriculture (11th); Subs. (1) Cotton, (2) Oilseeds and Rice, (3) Tobacco.

Public Works (11th); Subs. (1) Flood Control and Internal Development, (2) Investigation and Oversight, (3) Public Buildings and Grounds, (4) Roads, (5) Sp. on Economic Development Programs.

Group Ratings

	ADA	COPE	NREP	NFU	LCV	CFA	NAB	NSI	ACA
1970	0	9	0	31	0	43	100	100	94
1969	0	—	—	33	—	—	—	—	69

Key Votes

(1) ABM	FOR	(6) 18-Yr-Vote	AGN	(11) Clean Water $	AGN
(2) SST	FOR	(7) Farm Sub Lmt	AGN	(12) Mig Wrkrs Comp	AGN
(3) Phil Pln	AGN	(8) Coop-Church	AGN	(13) Jets to Chiang	FOR
(4) No-Knock	FOR	(9) Family Asst	AGN	(14) State OEO Veto	FOR
(5) Cmutr Tax	AGN	(10) Work Stamps	FOR	(15) Park Logging	FOR

Election Results

1970 general:	Wilmer (Vinegar Bend) Mizell (R)	68,937	(58%)
	James G. (Jim) White (D)	49,663	(42%)
1970 primary:	Wilmer (Vinegar Bend) Mizell (R), unopposed		
1968 general:	Wilmer (Vinegar Bend) Mizell (R)	84,905	(52%)
	Smith Bagley (D)	77,112	(48%)

SIXTH DISTRICT Political Background

North Carolina 6 takes in the cities of Greensboro (pop. 144,000), High Point (pop. 63,000), and Burlington (pop. 35,000), all in the heart of the booming Piedmont region. One of the textile giants, Burlington Mills, is headquartered in the district. The area once contained only textile, furniture, and tobacco manufacturers, but it has recently achieved considerable economic diversification; Western Electric, for example. now operates out of both Greensboro and Burlington. The influx of Northern managerial talent is in part responsible for the growing Republican strength in Guilford County (Greensboro and High Point); the county has been trending Republican since the Eisenhower years. The other three counties in the district retain a Southern Democratic preference, and in

1968 went for George Wallace. But because there are fewer blacks here, 22%, than in some of the Tidewater districts to the east, there is less out-and-out racist politics. The voting patterns in the 6th, however, are more conservative than those in the 4th, which has strong black and academic communities.

In 1968, Congressman Horace Kornegay, a conservative Democrat, decided to retire from the House, perhaps because he had won reelection two years before by a scant 2,000 votes over a Republican challenger. In most Southern districts, the retirement would have triggered a riproaring Democratic primary fight. But in the 6th district of North Carolina, there was no primary; L. Richardson Preyer was nominated without opposition, as if by silent acclamation. This is made even more remarkable because Preyer is liberal by North Carolina standards. He does, however, have establishment credentials which are impeccable. A graduate of Princeton and the Harvard Law School, Preyer became a judge at 34 and served in city and state courts before President Kennedy appointed him to the federal district bench. Preyer resigned the judgeship in 1964 to run for governor; he conducted a campaign in the tradition of moderate Govs. Terry Sanford (now president of Duke University) and Luther Hodges (ex-secretary of Commerce). But with the conservative tide sweeping the South, Preyer lost a close primary to Dan K. Moore, and returned to legal and business circles in Greensboro.

In 1968 Preyer's local prominence made him the logical successor to Kornegay, and in spite of the strong Nixon-Wallace showing in the district that year, Preyer won the general election without difficulty. In 1970, he did even better, winning 66% in a three-man race. In the House, the Congressman has a moderate-to-liberal voting record. He was one of two North Carolina congressmen to vote for the Cooper-Church Amendment; Preyer did, however, vote for the ABM, perhaps because the Western Electric facilities in his district have done millions of dollars of work on the controversial project (see data below). Preyer does not yet have enough seniority in the House to be a real power. Chances are he will become one, since North Carolinians appreciate the benefits of seniority and vote accordingly. Preyer has already demonstrated he can win more than convincingly in the 6th district.

Census Data 1970 pop. 476,409; deviation from current state average, +3.1%; change 1960–70, +13.6%. Metro. 60.6%, 43.5% central city.

1970 Share of Federal Outlays $379,635,892

DOD	$198,054,000	HEW	$14,914,716
AEC	$000	HUD	$3,784,823
NASA	$39,170	OEO	$723,976
DOT	$11,867,945	DOA	$10,640,841
		Other	$139,610,521

Federal Military-Industrial Commitments

DOD Contractors Western Electric Div., AT&T (Burlington and Greensboro), $183.205m: Safeguard ABM development.

Economic Base Textile mill products, esp. knitting mills; household furniture and other furniture and fixtures; apparel and other finished products made from fabrics and similar materials; tobacco manufactures.

The Voters

Registration 176,057 total. 133,053 D (76%); 35,581 R (20%); 7,423 other (4%).

Employment profile White collar, 32%. Blue collar, 68%.

Ethnic groups Black, 22%. Total foreign stock, 1%. All foreign groups less than 0.5% each.

Presidential vote

1968	Humphrey (D)	42,756	(29%)
	Nixon (R)	60,437	(41%)
	Wallace (AIP)	45,065	(30%)

Representative

Lunsford Richardson Preyer (D) Elected 1968; b. Jan. 11, 1919, Greensboro; home, Greensboro; Princeton U., B.A., 1941; Harvard, LL.B., 1949; Navy, WWII; married, five children; Presbyterian.

Career Practicing atty., 1950–56; City Judge, 1953–54; Superior Ct. Judge, 1956–61; U.S. Dist. Judge, 1961–63; Candidate for Gov., 1964; Sr. V.P. Trust Officer, N.C. Natl. Bank, Greensboro, 1964–66.

Offices 501 CHOB, 202-225-3065. Also Fed. Bldg., 326 W. Market St., Greensboro 27401, 919-272-1161.

Committees

Internal Security (4th).
Interstate and Foreign Commerce (18th); Sub. on Public Health and Environment.

Group Ratings

	ADA	COPE	NREP	NFU	LCV	CFA	NAB	NSI	ACA
1970	40	50	45	85	100	86	42	90	37
1969	27	—	—	86	—	—	—	—	25

Key Votes

(1) ABM	FOR	(6) 18-Yr-Vote	FOR	(11) Clean Water $	FOR
(2) SST	AGN	(7) Farm Sub Lmt	AGN	(12) Mig Wrkrs Comp	AGN
(3) Phil Pln	AGN	(8) Coop-Church	FOR	(13) Jets to Chiang	AGN
(4) No-Knock	FOR	(9) Family Asst	FOR	(14) State OEO Veto	AGN
(5) Cmutr Tax	AGN	(10) Work Stamps	AGN	(15) Park Logging	AGN

Election Results

1970 general:	L. Richardson Preyer (D)	47,693	(66%)
	Clifton B. (Pete) Barham (R)	20,739	(29%)
	Lynwood (Lyn) Bullock (AIP)	3,849	(5%)
1970 primary:	L. Richardson Preyer (D), unopposed		
1968 general:	L. Richardson Preyer (D)	76,028	(54%)
	William L. Osteen (R)	65,703	(46%)

SEVENTH DISTRICT Political Background

North Carolina 7 takes in the southeast corner of the state, lying between South Carolina and the Atlantic Ocean. The district is part of the Deep South. Wilmington (pop. 46,000) is an old North Carolina coastal city that never became a major port, a failed-Charleston or Jacksonville. The other population center in the district lies to the west, across the rather sparsely-settled coastal plain around Fayetteville (pop. 53,000). The city's population is only slightly larger than that of adjacent Fort Bragg, the huge Army base to which Fayetteville owes its prosperity. The district has a large black population and a substantial number of Indians, including the Lumbees in Robeson County, some of whom oppose having their children go to school with blacks. The blacks and the Indians were responsible for Humphrey's plurality around Fayetteville in 1968. Although most of the coastal counties went for Wallace, Humphrey came closer to carrying this district than any other in North Carolina, winning 34% to Wallace's 37%. Nixon carried New Hanover (Wilmington) on the coast and finished with 29% district-wide.

A resident of New Hanover, Alton A. Lennon, has represented the 7th in the House since 1956. In local and congressional elections, the voters who backed Wallace and Nixon in 1968 seem to prefer conservative Democrats, while those who voted for Humphrey, mostly blacks and Indians, do not get a chance to vote for anybody who shares their views. Lennon, a conservative Democrat, has received no more than token opposition from the Republicans. He is one of two members of the House (Claude Pepper of Florida is the other) who were once U.S. senators; Lennon was appointed to the upper house in 1953 but failed to win another term in 1954. The Congressman is a member of the Merchant Marine and Fisheries Committee, which is important to the Wilmington area, and of the Armed Services Committee, which is important to the Fayetteville-Fort Bragg section of his district. Lennon is a reliable Southern conservative; in 1970, however, he joined the majority of the North Carolina delegation and voted against the SST. This position, of course, is not inconsistent with a conservative attitude toward government spending.

Lennon had no primary or general election opposition from 1962 through 1968. It was consequently a shock when Charles G. Rose, member of a locally prominent political family and an officeholder in Governor Sanford's relatively liberal administration, held him to 57% of the vote in the Democratic primary. Lennon actually lost the area around Fayetteville, and almost half of his district-wide majority was supplied by his home county. This relatively weak showing should attract another challenge, from Rose, and perhaps others, in 1972. Lennon will be 66 then, and it seems likely that retirement or defeat will end his House career fairly soon.

Census Data 1970 pop. 493,953; deviation from current state average, +6.9%; change 1960–70, +16.6%. Metro. 64.6%, 20.2% central city.

1970 Share of Federal Outlays $629,897,544

DOD	$439,006,000	HEW	$79,239,279
AEC	$000	HUD	$7,222,490
NASA	$000	OEO	$96,104
DOT	$17,934,901	DOA	$31,024,385
		Other	$55,374,386

Federal Military-Industrial Commitments

DOD Contractors Kings Point Mfg. (Fayetteville), $14.532m: men's flying coveralls; ammunition bandoliers. Burlington Industries (Raeford), $9.076m: unspecified. Ryan Stevedoring (Southport), $8.244m: services.

DOD Installations Fort Bragg AB (Fayetteville). Sunny Point Military Ocean Terminal (Southport). Pope AFB (Fayetteville). Fort Fisher AF Station (Kure Beach).

Economic Base Tobacco; textile mill products; apparel and other finished products made from fabrics and similar materials; lumber and wood products other than furniture.

The Voters

Registration 137,468 total. 119,806 D (87%); 15,039 R (11%); 2,623 other (2%).

Employment profile White collar, 31%. Blue collar, 69%.

Ethnic groups Black, 26%. Total foreign stock, 3%. Germany, 1%; all other groups less than 0.5% each.

Presidential vote

1968	Humphrey (D)	38,090	(34%)
	Nixon (R)	32,532	(29%)
	Wallace (AIP)	40,764	(37%)

Representative

Alton Asa Lennon (D) Elected 1956; b. Aug. 17, 1906, Wilmington; home, Wilmington; Wake Forest Col., LL.B., 1929; married, two children; Baptist.

Career Practicing atty., 1929–53; Judge, New Hanover Co., Recorder's Ct., 1934–42; N.C. Senate, 1947–53.

Offices 2437 RHOB, 202-225-2731. Also 315 Market St., Wilmington 28401, 919-762-4817.

Committees

Armed Services (10th); Subs. (1) No. 2, (2) Armed Services Investigating.

Merchant Marine and Fisheries (6th); Subs. (1) Chm., Oceanography, (2) Coast Guard, Coast and Geodetic Survey and Navigation, (3) Fisheries and Wildlife Conservation, (4) Merchant Marine.

Group Ratings

	ADA	COPE	NREP	NFU	LCV	CFA	NAB	NSI	ACA
1970	8	27	17	42	50	48	73	100	71
1969	7	—	—	47	—	—	—	—	82
1968	0	0	—	44	—	—	83	—	83

Key Votes

(1) ABM	FOR	(6) 18-Yr-Vote	AGN	(11) Clean Water $	AGN
(2) SST	FOR	(7) Farm Sub Lmt	AGN	(12) Mig Wrkrs Comp	AGN
(3) Phil Pln	AGN	(8) Coop-Church	AGN	(13) Jets to Chiang	FOR
(4) No-Knock	FOR	(9) Family Asst	AGN	(14) State OEO Veto	FOR
(5) Cmutr Tax	AGN	(10) Work Stamps	FOR	(15) Park Logging	ABS

Election Results

1970 general:	Alton A. Lennon (D)	37,377	(72%)
	Frederick R. Weber (R)	14,529	(28%)
1970 primary:	Alton A. Lennon (D)	32,675	(57%)
	Charles G. Rose (D)	24,942	(43%)
1968 general:	Alton A. Lennon (D), unopposed		

EIGHTH DISTRICT Political Background

North Carolina 8 consists of two distinct areas: a hunk out of the middle of the Piedmont textile country and the Sand Hills region on the coastal plain. The textile country in North Carolina lies on both sides of Interstate 85 between Charlotte and Greensboro; that roadway passes through Salisbury and Kannapolis (home of giant Cannon Mills), both of which lie within the district and which together comprise the most heavily Republican part of North Carolina. The three textile counties—Rowan, Cabarrus, and Stanly—cast a little more than half of the district's votes. The rest are cast in the less densely-populated Sand Hill counties to the east; here the traditional Southern allegiance to the Democratic party persists, except in presidential elections when George Wallace's newer American Independent party carries the day.

The Democratic state legislators created the 8th district in 1967. Because it had no incumbent, they presumably thought that the Democratic votes out of the Sand Hills area would exceed the Republican majorities coming out of Kannapolis. A Republican congressman from the 8th now sits in the House. In 1968, the Democrats put up Voit Gilmore, a liberal of sorts, who had been head of the U.S. Travel Service in the Johnson Administration. That affiliation, of course, did not produce much enthusiasm in most North Carolina voters. The Republican candidate was Earl B. Ruth who was a conservative ex-Democrat and former athletic director at a small college in the area. Ruth took 56% of the votes in the three textile counties, and Gilmore won 56% in the rest of the district. These percentages work out to a Ruth 3,199-vote victory, the closest congressional contest in the state that year. By 1970, Ruth had established himself as a conservative congressman on questions of fiscal, social, and foreign policy. As a result, the Democrats tried running a more conservative candidate in an effort to capture the seat from him. They chose H. Clifton Blue, the editor of a country newspaper; he was formerly Speaker of the North Carolina House and lost the Democratic nomination for governor in 1968 in a squeaker. The Democrats' strategy flopped—Blue doing worse than Gilmore two years before.

Ruth now looks entrenched in the district. Moreover, the Democratic legislators have not tampered appreciably with the 8th's boundary, which leaves Ruth the likely winner in 1972. But because this remains the most marginal North Carolina Republican seat, the Democrats may make major efforts to win it in the years ahead.

Census Data 1970 pop. 441,288; deviation from current state average, —4.5%; change 1960–70, +8.3%. Metro. 12.4%, 0.0% central city.

1970 Share of Federal Outlays $181,469,048

DOD	$9,707,000	HEW	$90,046,175
AEC	$000	HUD	$999,560
NASA	$000	OEO	$1,391,469

DOT	$1,988,615	DOA	$16,537,676
		Other	$60,798,553

Federal Military-Industrial Commitments

None.

Economic Base Textile mill products; apparel and other finished products made from fabrics and similar materials; tobacco, cotton, and poultry.

The Voters

Registration 172,920 total. 128,943 D (75%); 39,205 R (23%); 4,772 other (3%).
Employment profile White collar, 26%. Blue collar, 74%.
Ethnic groups Black, 21%. Total foreign stock, 1%. All foreign groups less than 0.5% each.

Presidential vote

1968	Humphrey (D)	39,399	(27%)
	Nixon (R)	60,185	(42%)
	Wallace (AIP)	45,502	(31%)

Representative

Earl B. Ruth (R) Elected 1968; b. Feb. 7, 1916, Spencer; home, Salisbury; U. of N.C., B.A., 1938, M.A., 1942, Ph.D., 1955; Navy, WWII; married, four children; Presbyterian.

Career Teacher-coach, 1938–40; Asst. Supt., N.C. State Parks, 1941; Graduate Asst. Phys. Ed. Dept., U. of N.C., 1941–42; Recreation Dir., Kings Mt., 1945; Athletic Dir., Dean of Students, Catawba Col., 1946–68; Mbr., Salisbury City Council, 1963–68; Mayor Pro Tem, 1967–68.

Offices 129 CHOB, 202-225-3715. Also 507 W. Innes St., Salisbury 28144, 704-633-6038.

Committees

Education and Labor (12th); Subs. (1) Gen. on Education, (2) Sp. on Education, (3) Sp. on Labor.
Veterans' Affairs (19th); Subs. (1) Education and Training, (2) Hospitals.

Group Ratings

	ADA	COPE	NREP	NFU	LCV	CFA	NAB	NSI	ACA
1970	0	9	8	38	50	57	92	100	89
1969	0	—	—	33	—	—	—	—	82

Key Votes

(1) ABM	FOR	(6) 18-Yr-Vote	AGN	(11) Clean Water $	AGN
(2) SST	FOR*	(7) Farm Sub Lmt	AGN	(12) Mig Wrkrs Comp	AGN
(3) Phil Pln	AGN	(8) Coop-Church	AGN	(13) Jets to Chiang	FOR
(4) No-Knock	FOR	(9) Family Asst	AGN	(14) State OEO Veto	FOR
(5) Cmutr Tax	AGN	(10) Work Stamps	FOR	(15) Park Logging	ABS

* *Voted "against" in previous vote on same issue.*

Election Results

1970 general:	Earl B. Ruth (R)	51,873	(56%)
	H. Clifton Blue (D)	40,563	(44%)
1970 primary:	Earl B. Ruth (R), unopposed		
1968 general:	Earl B. Ruth (R)	70,480	(51%)
	Voit Gilmore (D)	67,281	(49%)

NINTH DISTRICT Political Background

North Carolina 9 comprises the state's largest city, Charlotte (pop. 241,000), surrounding Mecklenburg County, and three other counties in western North Carolina. Charlotte is the state's leading financial and commercial center; it is a predominantly white-collar city with less manufacturing than other Piedmont metropolitan centers. Charlotte is the subject of the Supreme Court case that has decided the future course of school desegregation efforts in the South, and perhaps in the entire nation. A federal judge ordered a massive program of integration for Charlotte and Mecklenburg County, which together form one school district; the order required an extensive use of busing in both elementary and secondary grades. The outraged white population here had hopes that the Nixon Court would overturn the decision. But Chief Justice Warren Burger, writing for a unanimous Court, upheld the judge's plan. The decision soured Charlotte's white voters on the Administration; they had given Richard Nixon an overwhelming majority of their votes in 1968.

Some North Carolina political history accounts for the rather odd contours of the 9th district. The history begins in 1952, when Charles Raper Jonas, a conservative Republican, was elected congressman from a district that included Charlotte. Local Democrats made frantic efforts to oust him, but with no success. Jonas' assiduous use of the frank and attention to constituents' problems, combined with the popularity of the Eisenhower Administration in the Charlotte area, made the Republican congressman unbeatable. After the 1960 census, the Democratic legislators shifted the district's boundaries drastically; they put Mecklenburg and Jonas' home county of Lincoln in with the Sand Hill counties to the east. In 1962, this arrangement resulted in Jonas' toughest race, but a big majority in Charlotte pulled him through. Soon he was carrying the eastern counties as well. So in 1967 the Democrats gave up, and added heavily Republican Iredell and Wilkes counties to the current 9th.

Jonas is so strong in the district that the Democrats did not put up a candidate against him in 1968—the first time in memory that the party failed to contest a North Carolina House seat. In 1970, when Jonas did have opposition, he received 67% of the votes cast. It is certain that he can continue to win no matter how the state legislators draw the district lines. Jonas is currently the number two Republican on the House Appropriations Committee. He stands a fair chance of becoming ranking minority member, or even chairman, if the Republicans ever win control of the House.

Census Data 1970 pop. 509,059; deviation from current state average, +10.2%; change 1960–70, +24.5%. Metro. 69.7%, 47.4% central city.

1970 Share of Federal Outlays $246,646,282

DOD	$71,393,000	HEW	$78,977,609
AEC	$000	HUD	$11,743,577
NASA	$12,042	OEO	$1,075,032
DOT	$8,549,432	DOA	$8,860,175
		Other	$66,035,415

Federal Military-Industrial Commitments

DOD Contractors Condec Corp. (Charlotte), $45.525m: 1¼-ton cargo trucks. Union Carbide (Charlotte), $5.880m: battery development and production.

Economic Base Textile mill products; tobacco and cotton; food and kindred products, esp. bakery products. Also, banking.

The Voters

Registration 248,045 total. 165,153 D (67%); 74,537 R (30%); 8,355 other (3%).

Employment profile White collar, 37%. Blue collar, 63%.

Ethnic groups Black, 20%. Total foreign stock, 2%. All foreign groups less than 0.5% each.

Presidential vote

1968	Humphrey (D)	44,521	(27%)
	Nixon (R)	84,265	(51%)
	Wallace (AIP)	35,128	(21%)

Representative

Charles Raper Jonas (R) Elected 1952; b. Dec. 9, 1904, Lincolnton; home, Lincolnton; U. of N.C., B.A., 1925, J.D., 1928; Army, WWII; married, two children; Methodist.

Career Practicing atty., 1928– .

Offices 2133 RHOB, 202-225-3476. Also 239 Fed. Bldg., Charlotte 28202, 704-377-5151.

Committees

Appropriations (2nd); Subs. (1) HUD, Space, and Science, (2) Military Construction.

Group Ratings

	ADA	COPE	NREP	NFU	LCV	CFA	NAB	NSI	ACA
1970	0	0	0	31	10	65	100	100	95
1969	0	—	—	33	—	—	—	—	81
1968	0	0	—	33	—	—	100	—	96

Key Votes

(1) ABM	FOR	(6) 18-Yr-Vote	AGN	(11) Clean Water $	AGN
(2) SST	FOR	(7) Farm Sub Lmt	AGN	(12) Mig Wrkrs Comp	AGN
(3) Phil Pln	AGN	(8) Coop-Church	AGN	(13) Jets to Chiang	FOR
(4) No-Knock	FOR	(9) Family Asst	AGN	(14) State OEO Veto	FOR
(5) Cmutr Tax	AGN	(10) Work Stamps	FOR	(15) Park Logging	FOR

Election Results

1970 general:	Charles Raper Jonas (R)	57,525	(67%)
	Cy N. Bahakel (D)	28,801	(33%)
1970 primary:	Charles Raper Jonas (R), unopposed		
1968 general:	Charles Raper Jonas (R), unopposed		

TENTH DISTRICT Political Background

North Carolina 10 is a collection of eight counties in the western Piedmont and the Appalachian Mountains. The southern part of the district is dominated by Gastonia (pop. 47,000), an industrial town which ordinarily votes Democratic. But north of Gaston and Cleveland counties (see map in appendix), the district is as Republican as any part of North Carolina. The political preference reflects old Civil War allegiances, as well as present day satisfaction, which the people here take, in the policies of the Nixon Administration.

The current boundaries of the 10th took effect in the 1968 election. This featured a contest between two incumbents who had been thrown into the district to fight it out. Basil Whitener, a conservative Democrat, had 12 years' seniority in the House; he also represented most of the new district in his old district. The Republican, James T. Broyhill (whose brother represented the 10th district of Virginia) had only six years' seniority. But the political trends in the district were with the Republican candidate; Richard Nixon was going to carry the 10th easily in 1968.

The surprising thing about the result was not that Broyhill won, but that his margin was so large. Broyhill lost Gaston and Cleveland counties by a total of 9,000 votes, but he carried the rest of the district—most of it Whitener's old territory—by 25,000 votes. In 1970, Whitener tried again and ran even worse; he lost Gaston and carried Cleveland by just 1,300 votes, and was, of course, swamped in the rest of the district.

Like the other North Carolina Republicans in the House, Broyhill is a solid conservative. He has done well on the seniority ladder—5th ranking Republican on the Interstate and Foreign Commerce Committee. And it now appears that Broyhill will continue to sit in the House for some time to come.

Census Data 1970 pop. 484,432; deviation from current state average, +4.9%; change 1960–70, +17.1%. Metro. 0.0%, 0.0% central city.

1970 Share of Federal Outlays $167,406,121

DOD	$11,959,000	HEW	$84,445,977
AEC	$000	HUD	$3,166,707
NASA	$000	OEO	$971,517
DOT	$12,244,884	DOA	$12,244,884
		Other	$54,025,871

Federal Military-Industrial Commitments

None.

Economic Base Furniture and fixtures, esp. household furniture; textile mill products, esp. knitting mills; cotton.

The Voters

Registration 193,847 total. 127,218 D (66%); 57,017 R (29%); 9,612 other (5%).

Employment profile White collar, 26%. Blue collar, 74%.

Ethnic groups Black, 10%. Total foreign stock, 1%. All foreign groups less than 0.5% each.

Presidential vote

1968	Humphrey (D)	38,602	(24%)
	Nixon (R)	78,590	(48%)
	Wallace (AIP)	45,847	(28%)

Representative

James Thomas Broyhill (R) Elected 1962; b. Aug. 19, 1927, Lenoir; home, Lenoir; U. of N.C., B.S., 1950; married, three children; Baptist.

Career Sales and admin., Broyhill Furniture Industries, 1945–62.

Offices 2448 RHOB, 202-225-2576. Also 431 Pennton Ave., Lenoir 28645, 704-758-4247, and Rm. 304 Commercial Bldg., Gastonia 28052, 704-864-9922.

Committees

Interstate and Foreign Commerce (5th); Sub. on Commerce and Finance.

Sel. Com. on Small Business (2nd); Subs. (1) Business, Commerce, and Fiscal Affairs, (2) Housing and Youth Affairs, (3) Judiciary, (4) Public Health and Welfare.

Ways and Means (5th).

Group Ratings

	ADA	COPE	NREP	NFU	LCV	CFA	NAB	NSI	ACA
1970	8	17	0	42	0	40	83	90	87
1969	0	—	—	33	—	—	—	—	71
1968	0	0	—	38	—	—	100	—	91

Key Votes

(1) ABM	FOR	(6) 18-Yr-Vote	AGN	(11) Clean Water $	AGN
(2) SST	AGN	(7) Farm Sub Lmt	AGN	(12) Mig Wrkrs Comp	AGN
(3) Phil Pln	AGN	(8) Coop-Church	AGN	(13) Jets to Chiang	AGN
(4) No-Knock	FOR	(9) Family Asst	AGN	(14) State OEO Veto	FOR
(5) Cmutr Tax	AGN	(10) Work Stamps	FOR	(15) Park Logging	FOR

Election Results

1970 general:	James T. (Jim) Broyhill (R)	63,936	(57%)
	Basil L. Whitener (D)	48,113	(43%)
1970 primary:	James T. (Jim) Broyhill (R), unopposed		
1968 general:	James T. (Jim) Broyhill (R)	87,811	(55%)
	Basil L. Whitener (D)	72,295	(45%)

ELEVENTH DISTRICT Political Background

North Carolina 11 occupies the western end of the state. Its main features include Asheville (pop. 57,000), the town to which Thomas Wolfe could not go home again, and the Great Smoky Mountains National Park, which is the country's most heavily visited. Recently, there were so many vehicles on its roads that the Park Service was forced to install a traffic light—the first ever in a national park. Since before the Civil War, the foothills of the Appalachians have been Republican strongholds, but the areas farther east, including Asheville, have generally supported North Carolina Democrats. The 11th has the smallest black population of any district in the state—around 6%—and racial animosity, which is so important to the politics of the coastal districts, is not a major issue here.

Roy A. Taylor, a Democrat, has represented the district since the 1960 special election. He consistently runs ahead of other Democratic candidates here and usually wins reelection by comfortable margins. In 1970, for example, he took 67% of the votes cast. Taylor is one of the few Easterners on the House Interior and Insular Affairs Committee. His choice of this committee assignment, however, is hardly surprising; much of the land in his district is federally owned—there is a national forest and a Cherokee Indian reservation in addition to the national park.

Because of its geographical position in the state, redistricting cannot materially affect the boundaries of the district, and Taylor will probably be reelected as long as he chooses to run. But a Republican might be able to win the seat if Taylor retires, or is otherwise not the Democratic candidate.

Census Data 1970 pop. 454,396; deviation from current state average, –1.6%; change 1960–70, +8.2%. Metro. 31.9%, 12.7% central city.

1970 Share of Federal Outlays $275,292,028

DOD	$22,853,000	HEW	$102,453,053
AEC	$000	HUD	$2,487,180
NASA	$194,193	OEO	$1,660,537
DOT	$31,757,471	DOA	$16,565,379
		Other	$97,321,215

Federal Military-Industrial Commitments

DOD Contractors Northrop Carolina (Swannanoa), $5.702m: riot control agent; aircraft parachute flares.

Economic Base Textile mill products; tobacco; apparel and other finished products made from fabrics and similar materials. Also, tourism (Smokies).

The Voters

Registration 198,244 total. 129,334 D (65%); 63,719 R (32%); 5,191 other (3%).

Employment profile White collar, 30%. Blue collar, 70%.

Ethnic groups Black, 6%. Total foreign stock, 2%. All foreign groups less than 0.5% each.

Presidential vote

1968	Humphrey (D)	50,076	(30%)
	Nixon (R)	80,298	(48%)
	Wallace (AIP)	37,730	(22%)

Representative

Roy A. Taylor (D) Elected June 25, 1960; b. Jan. 31, 1910, Vader, Wash.; home, Black Mountain; Maryville Col., B.A., 1931; Asheville U. Law School, admitted to bar, 1936; Navy, WWII; married, two children; Baptist.

Career Practicing atty., 1949–60; N.C. Assembly, 1947–53.

Offices 2240 RHOB, 202-225-6401. Also 1204 Northwestern Bank Bldg., Asheville 28801, 704-254-6526.

Committees

Foreign Affairs (18th); Subs. (1) Europe, (2) Inter-American Affairs, (3) Near East.

Interior and Insular Affairs (5th); Subs. (1) Chm., National Parks and Recreation, (2) Environment, (3) Indian Affairs, (4) Territorial and Insular Affairs.

Group Ratings

	ADA	COPE	NREP	NFU	LCV	CFA	NAB	NSI	ACA
1970	20	50	17	54	55	48	55	100	63
1969	13	—	—	60	—	—	—	—	71
1968	8	8	—	69	—	—	83	—	70

Key Votes

(1) ABM	FOR	(6) 18-Yr-Vote	FOR	(11) Clean Water $	FOR
(2) SST	AGN	(7) Farm Sub Lmt	AGN	(12) Mig Wrkrs Comp	AGN
(3) Phil Pln	AGN	(8) Coop-Church	AGN	(13) Jets to Chiang	FOR
(4) No-Knock	FOR	(9) Family Asst	AGN	(14) State OEO Veto	FOR
(5) Cmutr Tax	AGN	(10) Work Stamps	FOR	(15) Park Logging	AGN

Election Results

1970 general:	Roy A. Taylor (D)	90,199	(67%)
	Luke Atkinson (R)	44,376	(33%)
1970 primary:	Roy A. Taylor (D), unopposed		
1968 general:	Roy A. Taylor (D)	91,477	(57%)
	W. Scott Harvey (R)	68,657	(43%)

NORTH DAKOTA

Political Background

North Dakota occupies a northern section of that vast agricultural plain, which extends from the Great Lakes and the Mississippi River on the east, to the Rocky Mountains on the west. North Dakota is mostly wheat country, but as the plains become more arid towards the west, ranchers and their livestock predominate. It is a hard, ungiving land, with the winters absorbing Arctic blasts from Canada, and the summers, short and often too dry. Some 50 years ago, 632,000 people lived in North Dakota; today the figure has dropped to 617,000. For every ten college graduates the state produces, seven leave it. Per capita, North Dakota residents are now poorer than those in many Southern states.

Because the North Dakota economy depends on its hard-pressed farmers and ranchers, and because they, in turn, have little control over fluctuations of the commodity and livestock market, there is usually a great deal of dissatisfaction here with the farm programs of the federal government. The most common topics, therefore, of the state's political discourse are the minutiae of wheat and feed grain legislation.

Agricultural discontent has been part of the state's radical political tradition, one that goes back to the years around World War I.

A large proportion of the people who settled in North Dakota were of immigrant stock; Norwegians in the east, Canadians along the border to the north, Volga Germans in the west, and native Germans throughout the state. Volga Germans were Germans who had immigrated to Russia, but were expelled in the wake of the Revolution in 1917. All of these people lived on lonely, marginal farms, cut off from the wider currents of American culture by language barriers. They were also at the mercy of the grain millers in Minneapolis, of the railroads, and of the banks.

Out of these circumstances, A. C. Townley and William Lemke formed North Dakota's Non-Partisan League in 1915. The League called for government ownership of the railroads and the grain elevators, and because of ethnic loyalities of many North Dakotans, opposed going to war with Germany. The positions of the League won it many supporters in North Dakota and neighboring states. For many years, the NPL was a power in the state's politics; it usually determined the outcome of the Republican primary and sometimes swung its support to the Democrats. A particular favorite of the NPL was "Wild Bill" Langer, who served intermittently as governor during the '30's, and who was elected senator in 1940. Langer was finally allowed to take his seat after an investigation of alleged campaign irregularities. His subsequent career was fully as controversial—Langer being the Senate's most unpredictable maverick until his death in 1959.

Another NPL favorite was Congressman Usher Burdick, who served from 1936 to 1946, and then from 1948 to 1958. Burdick, like Langer, was a nominal Republican, but usually voted with New Deal liberals on economic issues. Burdick's son, Quentin, a Democrat, was a member of the House when Langer died. Quentin Burdick won the special election to fill the seat after waging a campaign directed mainly at the allegedly iniquitous policies of Ezra Taft Benson, secretary of Agriculture in the Eisenhower Administration. The Non-Partisan League, of course, supported the younger Burdick; its name today, however, is misleading since the League consistently supports Democratic candidates.

North Dakota is ordinarily a Republican state; only a few counties along the Canadian border, or with Indian or Eastern European ethnic populations, regularly turn in Democratic majorities. But the Democrat Burdick demonstrated his popularity in 1964, winning reelection with 58% of the votes, which equalled LBJ's percentage in the state. In 1970, Burdick took 61%. His recent victory illustrates some of the problems faced by the Nixon Republicans in their efforts to unseat liberal Democrats in 1970. Burdick's opponent was Congressman Thomas Kleppe, a millionaire (Gold Seal wax) who ran against the Senator in 1964, and lost. He subsequently won two terms in the House. Kleppe's campaign was budgeted at $300,000: a huge sum in a state where $32.50 buys thirty seconds of prime time on its most powerful television station. The challenger bombarded the North Dakota voters with TV spots which reminded them that Burdick had not voted in line with their wishes on issues like school prayers, interstate travel to incite riots, and so on.

The feedback from the Kleppe media-campaign was bad. The voters were irritated by the novel tactic, and they simply couldn't believe that Quentin Burdick, Usher's son and their senator for ten years, was the awful man that Kleppe said he was. Herschel Lashkowitz, the mayor of Fargo, remarked, "People looked at those ads and then they thought of Quentin Burdick and they resented it." Affection and respect for an incumbent senator overcame whatever differences the voters may have had with him on the school prayer amendment and other such matters.

Besides, Burdick was on the right side of an issue much more important to North Dakotans than any of the issues of style that won conservative Republican votes in industrial cities. That issue was the Nixon Administration's wheat bill, and Burdick opposed it. Kleppe, on the other hand, worked out the compromise measure as a member of the House Agriculture Committee. The farmers feared that the legislation would produce a vast wheat surplus, the kind that killed the market for the commodity in the mid-'50's. So the more Kleppe talked about the wheat bill, and the more TV ads he bought, the worse things got for him. Even the support of the state's senior senator, Milton R. Young, could not save him from the worst defeat ever suffered by a North Dakota Republican.

Senator Young, meanwhile, has even less difficulty winning reelection than his Democratic colleague. He has held elective office continuously since 1924, and has been a member of the Senate since 1945. In 1968, he won 65% of the votes (against Mayor Lashkowitz), and if he runs in 1974, when he will be 77, he will probably do as well, no matter what objections North Dakotans may then have towards the Administration's farm policy. Young has more seniority than any other Senate Republican except George Aiken of Vermont; he is the ranking minority member of the Appropriations Committee and number two Republican on the Agriculture and Forestry Committee.

The state's two congressional districts will not be discussed separately. Because the 1970 census cost North Dakota one House seat, the state will elect just one congressman-at-large in 1972. The two present congressmen will probably fight it out for the job. Conservative Republican Mark Andrews of the 1st has served in the House since a 1963 special election. He is the ranking minority member of the Appropriations subcommittee which has jurisdiction over agriculture, as well as environmental and consumer protection programs. Democrat Arthur Link, of the 2nd, took the seat vacated by Senate candidate Kleppe in 1970, with just over 50%. He is a junior member of the House Agriculture Committee. Without question, farm policy will be the central issue of the campaign. Andrews has won solid majorities in the 1st, which contains just over half of the state's population, and in 1962 he ran the strongest race to date against Democrat William Guy, governor since 1960. Andrews, therefore, has to be the betting favorite. But Link will benefit from any discontent with Nixon's farm program. That and the advantages of incumbency would make him the favorite should Andrews make another try for the governorship.

Electoral Votes 3

Census Data 1970 pop. 617,761; 0.30% of U.S. total, 46th largest; change 1960–70, −1.3%. Metro. 11.9%, 8.6% central city. 1970 per capita income, $2,937; 46th highest. 44th in number of poor.

1970 Share of Federal Tax Burden $429,310,000; 0.22% of U.S. total, 48th largest.

1970 Share of Federal Outlays $1,061,422,842; 0.56% of U.S. total, 39th largest. Per capita federal spending, $1,718.

DOD	$309,168,000	35th (0.54%)	HEW	$156,453,193	46th (0.30%)
AEC	$67,098	48th (—)	HUD	$6,477,178	43rd (0.33%)
NASA	$000	(—)	OEO	$2,297,833	46th (0.30%)
DOT	$38,358,106	43rd (0.54%)	DOA	$396,908,136	10th (3.09%)
DOC	$4,858,485	34th (0.42%)	POD	$13,564,580	41st (0.19%)
DOI	$28,280,577	26th (1.22%)	VA	$25,198,638	46th (0.34%)
DOJ	$2,297,833	43rd (0.40%)	CSC	$5,747,549	48th (0.14%)
			Other	$71,893,741	

Economic Base Cash grain and livestock; food and kindred products, esp. dairy products; printing, publishing, and allied products, esp. newspapers; crude petroleum and natural gas; nonelectrical machinery.

Political Line-up

Governor, William L. Guy (D); seat up, 1972. Senators, Milton R. Young (R) and Quentin Burdick (D). Representatives, 2 (1 D and 1 R). State Senate (12 D and 37 R); State House (39 D and 58 R).

The Voters

Registration No statewide registration.

Employment profile White collar, 35%. Blue collar, 65%.

Ethnic groups Black, less than 0.5%. Total foreign stock, 30%. Norway, 9%; USSR, 7%; Germany, 4%; Canada, 3%; Sweden, 2%; UK, Czech., 1% each; others, 4%.

Presidential vote

1968	Humphrey (D)	94,769	(38%)
	Nixon (R)	138,669	(56%)
	Wallace (AIP)	14,244	(6%)

1964	Johnson (D)	149,784	(58%)
	Goldwater (R)	108,207	(42%)
1960	Kennedy (D)	123,963	(45%)
	Nixon (R)	154,310	(55%)

Senator

Milton R. Young (R) Elected March 12, 1945, seat up 1974; b. Dec. 6, 1897, Berlin; home, La Moure; N.D. Agricultural Col., Graceland Col.; married; Church of Latter Day Saints.

Career Farmer; N.D. State Legislature, 1932; N.D. Senate, 1943–45, Pres. Pro Tempore, 1941, Majority Floor Leader, 1943.

Offices 5205 NSOB, 202-225-2043. Also Box 241, La Moure 58102, 701-237-4000; and Fed. Bldg., Bismarck 58501, 701-255-2553.

Committees

Agriculture and Forestry (3rd); Subs. (1) Agricultural Production, Marketing, and Stabilization of Prices, (2) Agricultural Research and General Legislation.

Appropriations (Ranking Mbr.); Subs. (1) Agriculture, Environmental and Consumer Protection, (2) Defense and Intelligence, (3) Interior, (4) Public Works.

Group Ratings

	ADA	COPE	NREP	NFU	LCV	NAB	NSI	ACA
1970	3	23	0	43	14	75	100	75
1969	6	—	—	40	—	—	—	75
1968	0	10	—	54	—	67	—	80

Key Votes

(1) ABM	FOR	(8) Phil Pln	AGN	(15) Coop-Church	AGN
(2) SST	FOR	(9) Vol Army	AGN	(16) Cut Oil Dpltn	AGN
(3) Busing	AGN	(10) Prison $	AGN	(17) Consumer Prot	AGN
(4) Tob Sub	FOR	(11) Cut Mil $	AGN	(18) Farm Sub Limit	AGN
(5) Carswell	FOR	(12) Defoliatn	FOR	(19) Comp Bid Sales	AGN
(6) No-Knock	FOR	(13) 18-Yr-Vote	FOR	(20) Pre-Prod Tests	AGN
(7) Seniorty	FOR	(14) Pentgn PR	FOR	(21) Cut Marjna Pen	AGN

Election Results

1968 general:	Milton R. Young (R)	154,968	(65%)
	Herschel Lashkowitz (D)	80,815	(34%)
	Duane Mutch (Ind.)	3,393	(1%)
1968 primary:	Milton R. Young (R), unopposed		
1962 general:	Milton R. Young (R)	135,705	(61%)
	William Lanier (D)	88,032	(39%)

Senator

Quentin N. Burdick (D) Elected June 28, 1960, seat up 1974; b. June 19, 1908, Munich; home, Fargo; U. of Minn., B.A., 1931, LL.B., 1932; married; Congregationalist.

Career Practicing atty., 1932–58; Candidate for Gov., 1946.

Offices 110 OSOB, 202-225-2551. Also Fed. Bldg., Fargo 58102, 701-237-4000, and Fed. Bldg., Bismarck 58501, 701-255-2553.

Committees

Interior and Insular Affairs (6th); Subs. (1) Chm., Territories and Insular Affairs, (2) Indian Affairs, (3) Water and Power Resources.

Judiciary (7th); Subs. (1) Chm., Improvements in Judicial Machinery, (2) Chm., Penitentiaries, (3) Administrative Practice and Procedure, (4)

Constitutional Amendments, (5) Juvenile Delinquency, (6) Patents, Trademarks, and Copyrights.
Post Office and Civil Service (3rd); Subs. (1) Chm., Compensation and Employment Benefits, (2) Civil Services Policies and Practices.

Group Ratings

	ADA	COPE	NREP	NFU	LCV	NAB	NSI	ACA
1970	84	100	91	87	78	18	30	22
1969	83	—	—	75	—	—	—	20
1968	64	83	—	54	—	60	—	32

Key Votes

(1) ABM	AGN	(8) Phil Pln	AGN	(15) Coop-Church	FOR
(2) SST	AGN	(9) Vol Army	FOR	(16) Cut Oil Dpltn	AGN
(3) Busing	FOR	(10) Prison $	FOR	(17) Consumer Prot	FOR
(4) Tob Sub	FOR	(11) Cut Mil $	FOR	(18) Farm Sub Limit	AGN
(5) Carswell	AGN	(12) Defoliatn	FOR	(19) Comp Bid Sales	FOR
(6) No-Knock	AGN	(13) 18-Yr-Vote	FOR	(20) Pre-Prod Tests	AGN
(7) Seniorty	FOR	(14) Pentgn PR	AGN	(21) Cut Marjna Pen	AGN

Election Results

1970 general:	Quentin Burdick (D)	134,519	(61%)
	Thomas S. Kleppe (R)	82,996	(38%)
	Russell Kleppe (Ind.)	2,045	(1%)
1970 primary:	Quentin Burdick (D), unopposed		
1964 general:	Quentin Burdick (D)	149,264	(58%)
	Thomas S. Kleppe (R)	109,681	(42%)

Census Data 1970 pop. 329,279; deviation from current state average, +6.6%; change 1960–70, −1.2%. Metro. +22.3%, +16.2% central city.

1970 Share of Federal Outlays $631,587,063

DOD	$222,240,000	HEW	$88,872,057
AEC	$67,098	HUD	$1,977,178
NASA	$000	OEO	$508,622
DOT	$25,643,376	DOA	$215,142,010
		Other	$77,137,262

Federal Military-Industrial Commitments

DOD Contractors Morrison-Knudsen and Assoc. (Cavalier and Pembine counties), $137.859m: construction of Safeguard ABM sites. Needham Packing (West Fargo), $9.435m: foodstuffs. Woefel Corp. (La Moure), $5.993m: unspecified.

DOD Installations Finley AF Station (Finley). Grand Forks AFB (Grand Forks).

Economic Base Cash grain and livestock; food and kindred products; printing, publishing, and allied industries; nonelectrical machinery.

The Voters

Registration No district-wide registration.

Employment profile White collar, 36%. Blue collar, 64%.

Ethnic groups Black, less than 0.5%. Total foreign stock, 29%. Norway, 10%; Germany, 5%; Canada, 4%; USSR, 3%; Sweden, 2%; UK, Czech., Poland, 1% each; others, 3%.

Presidential vote

1968	Humphrey (D)	54,063	(41%)
	Nixon (R)	70,953	(54%)
	Wallace (AIP)	7,223	(6%)

Representative

Mark Andrews (R) Elected Oct. 23, 1963; b. May 19, 1926, Fargo; home, Mapleton; N.D. State U., B.S., 1949; U.S. Military Acad., 1944–46; Army, WWII; married, three children; Episcopalian.

Career Farmer, 1949– ; Exec. Commissioner, Garrison Conservancy Dist., admin. irrigation from Garrison Dam, 1955– ; Candidate for Gov., 1962.

Offices 409 CHOB, 202-225-2611. Also Fed. Bldg., Fargo 58102, 701-232-8030, and Fed. Bldg., Grand Forks 58201, 701-775-9601.

Committees

Appropriations (12th); Subs. (1) Agriculture, Environmental and Consumer Protection, (2) State, Justice, Commerce, and the Judiciary.

Group Ratings

	ADA	COPE	NREP	NFU	LCV	CFA	NAB	NSI	ACA
1970	24	36	50	54	22	61	50	100	36
1969	27	—	—	64	—	—	—	—	29
1968	17	31	—	81	—	—	67	—	59

Key Votes

(1) ABM	FOR	(6) 18-Yr-Vote	FOR	(11) Clean Water $	AGN
(2) SST	AGN	(7) Farm Sub Lmt	AGN	(12) Mig Wrkrs Comp	AGN
(3) Phil Pln	ABS	(8) Coop-Church	ABS	(13) Jets to Chiang	ABS
(4) No-Knock	ABS	(9) Family Asst	FOR	(14) State OEO Veto	AGN
(5) Cmutr Tax	AGN	(10) Work Stamps	AGN	(15) Park Logging	AGN

Election Results

1970 general:	Mark Andrews (R)	72,168	(66%)
	James E. Brooks (D)	37,688	(34%)
1970 primary:	Mark Andrews (R)	29,674	(90%)
	Rosemary M. Landsberger (R)	3,142	(10%)
1968 general:	Mark Andrews (R)	84,114	(72%)
	Bruce Hagen (D)	30,692	(26%)
	Rosemary M. Landsberger (Ind.)	2,166	(2%)

Census Data 1970 pop. 288,482; deviation from current state average, –6.6%; change 1960–70, –3.6%. Metro. 0.0%, 0.0% central city.

1970 Share of Federal Outlays $429,835,239

DOD	$86,928,000	HEW	$67,581,136
AEC	$000	HUD	$4,500,000
NASA	$000	OEO	$1,789,211
DOT	$12,714,730	DOA	$181,766,126
		Other	$74,556,036

Federal Military-Industrial Commitments

DOD Contractors Boeing Co. (Minot), $20.143m: Minuteman Wing force modernization.

DOD Installations Fortuna AF Station (Fortuna). Minot AFB (Minot).

Economic Base Cash grain and livestock; crude petroleum and natural gas; food and kindred products.

The Voters

Registration No district-wide registration.

Employment profile White collar, 33%. Blue collar, 67%.

Ethnic groups Black, 1%. Total foreign stock, 31%. USSR, 11%; Norway, 7%; Germany, 4%; Canada, Sweden, 2% each; Hungary, UK, 1% each; others, 4%.

Presidential vote

1968	Humphrey (D)	40,706	(35%)
	Nixon (R)	67,716	(59%)
	Wallace (AIP)	7,021	(6%)

Representative

Arthur A. Link (D) Elected 1970; b. May 24, 1914, McKenzie County; home, Alexander; N.D. Agricultural Col.; married, six children; Lutheran.

Career Farmer-rancher; N.D. House of Reps., 1947–70, Minority Leader, 14 years, Speaker of the House, 1965; Randolph Township Bd., 1943–70; McKenzie County Welfare Bd., 1950–70, Chm., N.D. Advisory Council for Vocational Ed.

Offices 1610 LHOB, 202-225-5736. Also 232 Fed. Bldg., Bismarck 58501, 701-255-4011, ext. 4344.

Committees

Agriculture (21st); Subs. (1) Domestic Marketing and Consumer Relations, (2) Livestock and Grains.

District of Columbia (13th); Subs. (1) Business, Commerce, and Fiscal Affairs, (2) Judiciary.

Group Ratings, Key Votes: Newly elected.

Election Results

1970 general:	Arthur A. Link (D)	50,416	(50%)
	Robert P. McCarney (R)	49,888	(50%)
1970 primary:	Arthur A. Link (D), unopposed		

OHIO

Political Background

Ohio epitomizes the twentieth century American Midwest: a land of well-tended farms, God-fearing small towns, and sprawling industrial cities. There are six metropolitan areas here with populations over 500,000 people. In 1803, Ohio was the first state out of the old Northwest Territory won from the British in the Revolutionary War to be admitted to the Union; within 25 years it was the fourth largest state in the country. Its migration patterns were somewhat unusual. The first settlers were attracted to the southwestern corner of Ohio around Cincinnati, and by the time of the Civil War, that heavily German and pro-Union city was the fourth largest in the nation. At that time, the northeast corner of Ohio was placid farmland inhabited by Yankee migrants from New England and Upstate New York. Not until the growth of the steel industry late in the nineteenth century did the huge industrial complexes of Cleveland, Akron, Youngstown, and Canton come into being. By 1910, Cleveland was larger than Cincinnati and the fourth largest city in the nation.

In politics, Ohio has a reputation for being profoundly Republican. One of the reasons commonly given for this is the decentralization of its urban population. Ohio has no one city like metropolitan New York, Chicago, or Detroit which dominate their respective states; moreover, some of its cities, particularly Cincinnati and Columbus, regularly vote Republican. But most of the credit for the state's political behavior belongs to the organization assembled by Ray Bliss, longtime Republican State Chairman. Bliss and his machine made fund-raising a science, pioneered the latest political techniques, and picked candidates with the kind of care and precision that cannot be simulated by a computer. After the dark days of the New Deal, the organization built solid control of the state's House delegation, which is still Republican by a 17-7 margin, the state legislature, and minor statewide offices.

A few statewide offices have eluded Bliss's Republicans. A major source of irritation was Democrat Frank J. Lausche, longtime governor from 1944 to 1946 and 1948 to 1956, and senator from 1956 to 1968. But happily for the Bliss men, Lausche was a reliably conservative politician. The Republicans made their only serious mistake in 1958, when they put on an all-out drive for a state right-to-work law. For once, organized labor was able to marshall its forces, and a Republican governor and senator were defeated in reelection bids. The Senate race defeat was particularly startling; veteran conservative John W. Bricker was beaten by Stephen M. Young, a 68-year-old maverick liberal. Young had previously served four terms as the state's congressman-at-large during the '30's and '40's. The Republicans confidently expected to get rid of Young in six years, but the Goldwater candidacy intervened, and the fiery 75-year-old Senator beat Robert Taft, Jr., son of the late Mr. Republican, by 16,000 votes in 1964.

The last two years have produced bad times for the Bliss organization. Bliss himself served as Republican National Chairman, from a year after the Goldwater debacle through the party's national triumph in 1968; but despite general agreement that he had done an excellent job, he was unceremoniously sacked by President Nixon. And in Ohio, things began to fall apart. Robert Taft, Jr., who had won a House seat in 1966, decided to run for the Senate against Republican Gov. James Rhodes, who was ineligible for a third term. The resulting primary was hard-fought and divisive. Moreover, several statewide officials, including State Auditor Roger Cloud—the organization's candidate for governor—had received campaign contributions from a Columbus firm which had earlier arranged several million dollars of illegal loans from the state treasury. Except for Cloud, who had returned the money, the Republican State Committee asked several of its nominees implicated in the scandal to step down. They refused to do so, and were defeated in the general election. John Gilligan scored the biggest Democratic victory; he had lost his House seat to Taft in 1966, and ran unsuccessfully for the Senate in 1968, but won the governorship in 1970. For the first time in memory, the Ohio Democrats now control the reapportionment of the state legislature and also have a veto on the redistricting of the state's congressional districts.

The Bliss organization can, however, take some comfort in having captured the state's two Senate seats, formerly held by Democrats, in 1968 and 1970. In the first of these election years, the Republicans got some help from an unexpected source. Organized labor backed then Congressman John Gilligan who defeated incumbent Sen. Frank Lausche in the Democratic primary. Lausche was unbeatable in general elections, where he received hundreds of thousands of normally Republican votes. The Democrats, however, didn't mind ousting the incumbent and risk losing the seat, because Lausche was only a nominal Democrat who voted the convictions of the party members only when it came time to organize the Senate. In the general election that followed, Gilligan lost to Atty. Gen. William Saxbe by a scant 114,000 votes out of nearly 4,000,000 cast; the Republican attributed his win to discontent with the war policies of the Johnson Administration. In the Senate, Saxbe has been fiercely independent and often liberal; he lines up on some issues as a staunch backer of the Nixon Administration and on others as a vigorous opponent.

The 1970 Senate race was one of the most exciting Ohio contests in a long time. In the Republican primary, Gov. James Rhodes had the support of most local organizations, but that was not quite enough to beat Congressman Robert Taft, Jr. Rhodes may have been hurt by the Kent State shootings, which occurred just a few days before the primary; Rhodes had sent the National Guard onto the campus. The Democratic primary produced a surprise winner, Howard Metzenbaum, a wealthy Cleveland businessman who was one of the masterminds of Sen. Young's campaigns. Metzenbaum won the support of most of the party professionals and also made himself a household word with an expensive television ad campaign. The combination was enough to beat John Glenn, the former astronaut, by 13,000 votes out of 900,000 cast.

Normally, in Ohio, it would be easy to pick the winner in a contest between a Taft and a Metzenbaum. But Taft had problems. Early on it was clear that the scandal was going to make losers out of the rest of the state Republican ticket. Moreover, the economic policies of the Nixon Administration were not popular in the industrial portions of the state; only Michigan had more men on the picket lines during the General Motors strike of that year. Taft and Metzenbaum agreed to limit their campaign expenditures to the amounts specified in the bill President Nixon vetoed; but Metzenbaum's name was already well-known from the primary. In addition, Metzenbaum continued to compaign well, stumping most of Ohio's rural areas as well as the cities, and assailing the Nixon Administration at every turn. In the end, Taft won, but by only 70,000 votes. County by county, the election was a near rematch of the 1964 Taft-Young race, with Metzenbaum falling behind in those areas where turnout sagged most—many rural counties and the city of Toledo. Both candidates ran well in what were thought to be the other's strongholds. Taft was given a boost in Cleveland when black leaders decided to support his cousin for county commissioner and split the local Democratic vote (see Ohio 21).

So after six years of waiting, Taft is finally in the Senate. He has already established himself as one of the Nixon Administration's more dependable backers. The Senator has announced that he will be a stand-in candidate for President Nixon in the state's 1972 presidential primary—a move designed to unify the badly splintered Republican party in the state as much as to help Nixon.

Both Saxbe and Taft will be strong favorites when they come up for reelection in 1974 and 1976, respectively. But the near successes of Gilligan and Metzenbaum suggest that counting on the form sheet may not be the wisest policy. The 1970 census cost the state one congressional seat; for a discussion of what may happen as a result, see Ohio 4.

Electoral Votes 25

Census Data 1970 pop. 10,652,017; 5.17% of U.S. total, 6th largest; change 1960–70, +9.7%. Metro. 77.7%, 32.2% central city. 1970 per capita income, $3,983; 15th highest. 7th in number of poor.

1970 Share of Federal Tax Burden $10,713,220,000; 5.49% of U.S. total, 5th largest.

1970 Share of Federal Outlays $6,757,932,449; 3.58% of U.S. total, 6th largest. Per capita federal spending, $634.

DOD	$1,871,595,000	8th (3.26%)	HEW	$2,370,697,915	5th (4.54%)
AEC	$100,930,408	11th (3.88%)	HUD	$66,670,734	10th (3.42%)
NASA	$118,038,920	8th (3.21%)	OEO	$22,395,761	8th (2.95%)
DOT	$257,260,231	8th (3.60%)	DOA	$202,103,366	25th (1.57%)
DOC	$12,600,563	18th (1.09%)	POD	$359,563,783	5th (4.93%)
DOI	$24,722,976	31st (1.07%)	VA	$417,023,970	5th (5.65%)
DOJ	$16,407,920	9th (2.86%)	CSC	$88,928,880	11th (2.21%)
			Other	$828,992,022	

Economic Base Nonelectrical machinery, esp. metalworking machinery and equipment, and office, computing, and accounting machines; motor vehicles and motor vehicle equipment, and other transportation equipment; primary metal industries, esp. blast furnaces, steel works, and rolling and finishing mills, and iron and steel foundries; fabricated metal products, esp. fabricated structural metal products; electrical machinery equipment and supplies, esp. electrical industrial apparatus and household appliances; livestock, dairy, and cash grain, food and kindred products; printing, publishing, and allied industries, esp. commercial printing and newspapers; stone, clay, glass, and concrete products.

Political Line-up Governor, John J. Gilligan (D); seat up, 1974. Senators, William B. Saxbe (R) and Robert Taft, Jr. (R). Representatives, 24 (7 D and 17 R), State Senate (13 D and 20 R); State House (45 D and 54 R).

The Voters

Registration No statewide registration.

Employment profile White collar, 40%. Blue collar, 60%.

Ethnic groups Black, 9%. Total foreign stock, 15%. Germany, 3%; Italy, 2%; Austria, Czech., Hungary, Ireland, Poland, UK, USSR, Canada, 1% each; others, 3%.

Presidential vote

1968	Humphrey (D)	1,700,586	(43%)
	Nixon (R)	1,791,014	(45%)
	Wallace (AIP)	467,495	(12%)
1964	Johnson (D)	2,498,331	(63%)
	Goldwater (R)	1,470,865	(37%)
1960	Kennedy (D)	1,944,248	(47%)
	Nixon (R)	2,217,611	(53%)

Senator

William B. Saxbe (R) Elected 1968, seat up 1974; b. June 24, 1916, Mechanicsburg; home, Mechanicsburg; Ohio State U., B.A., 1940, LL.B., 1948; Army Air Corps, WWII; Ohio Natl. Guard, 1940–45, 1951–52; married, three children; Episcopalian.

Career Ohio House of Reps., 1947–54, Majority Leader, 1951–52, Speaker, 1953–54; Ohio Atty. Gen., 1957–58, 1963–68.

Offices 1203 NSOB, 202-225-3353. Also 2956 Fed. Bldg., 1240 E. 9th St., Cleveland 44114, 216-522-4845, and Fed. Bldg., 85 Marconi Blvd., Columbus 43215, 614-469-6697.

Committees

Armed Services (7th); Subs. (1) General Legislation, (2) National Stockpile and Naval Petroleum Reserves, (3) Status of Forces, (4) Strategic Arms Limitation Talks.

Government Operations (6th); Sub. on Intergovernmental Relations.

Sel. Com. on Small Business (6th); Subs. (1) Financing and Investment, (2) Science and Technology.

Sp. Com. on Aging (7th); Subs. (1) Consumer Interests of the Elderly, (2) Health of the Elderly, (3) Housing for the Elderly, (4) Long-Term Care.

Group Ratings

	ADA	COPE	NREP	NFU	LCV	NAB	NSI	ACA
1970	47	56	75	64	47	50	22	47
1969	61	—	—	47	—	—	—	27

Key Votes

(1) ABM	AGN	(8) Phil Pln	ABS	(15) Coop-Church	FOR
(2) SST	FOR	(9) Vol Army	AGN	(16) Cut Oil Dpltn	AGN
(3) Busing	FOR	(10) Prison $	ABS	(17) Consumer Prot	FOR
(4) Tob Sub	FOR	(11) Cut Mil $	FOR	(18) Farm Sub Limit	FOR
(5) Carswell	FOR	(12) Defoliatn	ABS	(19) Comp Bid Sales	ABS
(6) No-Knock	FOR	(13) 18-Yr-Vote	ABS	(20) Pre-Prod Tests	AGN
(7) Seniorty	AGN	(14) Pentgn PR	AGN	(21) Cut Marjna Pen	AGN

Election Results

1968 general:	William B. Saxbe (R)	1,928,964	(52%)
	John J. Gilligan (D)	1,814,152	(48%)
1968 primary:	William B. Saxbe (R)	575,178	(82%)
	William L. White (R)	71,191	(10%)
	Albert E. Payne (R)	52,393	(7%)

Senator

Robert Taft, Jr. (R) Elected 1970, seat up 1976; b. Feb. 26, 1917, Cincinnati; home, Cincinnati; Yale U., B.A., 1939; Harvard U., LL.B., 1942; Navy, WWII; married, four children; Episcopalian.

Career Practicing atty., 1946–62, 1965–66; Ohio House of Reps., 1955–62, Majority Floor Leader, 1961–62; nominee for Senate, 1964; U.S. House of Reps., 1962–64, 1966–70.

Offices 3331 NSOB, 202-225-2315. Also 754 Post Office and Courthouse Bldg., Cincinnati 45202, 513-684-3284.

Committees

Banking, Housing, and Urban Affairs (7th); Subs. (1) Housing and Urban Affairs, (2) International Finance, (3) Production and Stabilization, (4) Small Business.

Labor and Public Welfare (6th); Subs. (1) Aging, (2) Children and Youth, (3) Employment, Manpower, and Poverty, (4) Labor, (5) Migratory Labor, (6) Railroad Retirement, (7) Sp. on Social Programs.

Sel. Com. on Nutrition and Human Needs (6th).

Sel. Com. on Small Business (8th); Subs. (1) Monopoly, (2) Sp. on Social Programs.

Note: The following ratings and votes cover Senator Taft's record in the House of Representatives, where he served prior to his election in 1970.

Group Ratings

	ADA	COPE	NREP	NFU	LCV	CFA	NAB	NSI	ACA
1970	20	30	40	55	67	33	80	86	61
1969	33	—	—	61	—	—	—	—	29
1968	33	39	—	47	—	—	100	—	60

Key Votes

(1) ABM	FOR	(6) 18-Yr-Vote	FOR	(11) Clean Water $	FOR
(2) SST	FOR*	(7) Farm Sub Lmt	FOR	(12) Mig Wrkrs Comp	AGN
(3) Phil Pln	FOR	(8) Coop-Church	AGN	(13) Jets to Chiang	AGN
(4) No-Knock	FOR	(9) Family Asst	FOR	(14) State OEO Veto	AGN
(5) Cmutr Tax	FOR	(10) Work Stamps	FOR	(15) Park Logging	ABS

* *As Senator.*

Election Results

1970 general:	Robert Taft, Jr. (R)	1,565,682	(50%)
	Howard H. Metzenbaum (D)	1,495,262	(47%)
	Richard B. Kay (AIP)	61,261	(2%)
	John O'Neill (SLP)	29,069	(1%)
1970 primary:	Robert Taft, Jr. (R)	472,202	(50%)
	James A. Rhodes (R)	466,932	(50%)

FIRST DISTRICT Political Background

Ohio 1 is the east side of Cincinnati and suburban Hamilton County. This is, by and large, the more prosperous half of the old river city, which was the cultural and commercial center of the Midwest even before the Tafts arrived. In the hills beyond the city-limits are the fashionable suburbs of the city's elite; among them, Indian Hill, home of Sen. Robert Taft, Jr. To the north is a mixture of shopping centers and high-income suburbs. Within the city itself are the formerly Jewish sections of Avondale and Walnut Hills, now predominately black. Many neighborhoods, like Norwood, a suburban enclave surrounded by Cincinnati, are inhabited by migrants from the hills of Kentucky and Tennessee. The 1st also has most of the city's Jewish population: from its early days as a heavily German Ohio River town, Cincinnati has had a prominent Jewish community. Hebrew Union College here is one of the nation's leading centers of Reform theology.

Cincinnati has a well-deserved reputation for being a Republican city. Of the country's 25 largest metropolitan areas, only Dallas and San Diego turn in Republican majorities with more regularity. This has been the case since before the Civil War, when the city was a German pro-Union island in a sea of Southern sentiment. Moreover, Cincinnati has never attracted large numbers of those ethnic groups which vote heavily Democratic; there are far fewer blacks here than in Cleveland, and very few people of Eastern European origin. Many of the city's Appalachians, from solidly Republican mountain counties, have carried their political preferences to the big city.

Out of Cincinnati have come some prominent Republican officials, including President William Howard Taft, Speaker of the House (1925–31) Nicholas Longworth (whose widow, the former Alice Roosevelt, still reigns as one of Washington's social arbiters), and of course Sen. Robert A. Taft, Mr. Republican. More recently, the 1st has elected a succession of prominent men to the House. In 1964, it unseated a conservative Republican in favor of John Gilligan, then a college professor and Cincinnati councilman, and now governor of Ohio. Two years later in a race that attracted national attention, Gilligan was challenged by none other than Robert Taft, Jr., who lost a bid for the U.S. Senate in 1964. Gilligan proved his vote-getting prowess even while losing; after all, a 7,000-vote loss in a heavily Republican district to the son of Mr. Republican was not a bad showing.

In 1968, Taft won reelection easily and then went on in 1970 to capture Stephen Young's seat in the Senate, though his margin of victory was surprisingly small (see state write-up). Taft's successor is William J. Keating, a popular Cincinnati councilman. His brother is Charles Keating, the Nixon appointee to the commission on obscenity, who filed a vehement dissent to its report. That, certainly, did not hurt candidate Keating's campaign. Against a black opponent, the Republican took a larger percentage of the vote than Taft two years before.

Congressman Keating now sits on the Judiciary Committee, where he will have the opportunity to draw up legislation on obscenity, civil rights, and other matters. Keating will win reelection in the foreseeable future. The Democrats would like to redesign the Cincinnati congressional districts, dividing them east and west rather than, as they are now, north and south. The Democrats do have the governorship, but the Republicans control both houses of the state legislature. Therefore, it seems likely that the present arrangement in Cincinnati will again determine the character of congressional elections here in 1972.

Census Data 1970 pop. 404,080; deviation from current state average, –8.7%; change 1960–70, –1.0%. Metro. 100.0%, 51.2% central city.

1970 Share of Federal Outlays $445,105,000 (average outlay per district, Ohio 1 and 2)

DOD	$153,742,000	HEW	$121,723,000
AEC	$8,779,000	HUD	$5,220,000
NASA	$7,716,000	OEO	$935,000
DOT	$41,294,000	DOA	$2,413,000
		Other	$103,283,000

Federal Military-Industrial Commitments (Ohio 1 and 2, greater Cincinnati listing.)

DOD Contractors General Electric (Cincinnati and Evendale), $235.634m: T-79, TF-39, and C5-A aircraft engines; other aircraft and shipboard engines. Procter and Gamble Distributing (Cincinnati), $11.418m: unspecified. Avco Corp. (Cincinnati), $7.259m: unspecified. KDI Precision Products (Cincinnati), $6.652m: metal parts for 2.75-inch rocket and 81-mm mortar fuzes.

NASA Contractors General Electric (Cincinnati), $9.401m: supersonic aircraft technology; Advance Superalloy protection system support.

AEC Operations National Lead Co. (Fernald), $16.656m: Feed Material Facility.

Economic Base Transportation equipment, esp. motor vehicles and motor vehicle equipment and aircraft engines and aircraft engine parts; detergents and cleaning agents: nonelectrical machinery, esp. metalworking machinery and equipment; food and kindred products, esp. bakery products and beverages; fabricated metal products. Also, banking and insurance.

The Voters

Registration No district-wide registration.
Employment profile White collar, 47%. Blue collar, 53%.
Ethnic groups Black, 21%. Total foreign stock, 12%. Germany 4%; Ireland, Italy, UK, USSR, 1% each; others, 2%.

Presidential vote

1968	Humphrey (D)	66,863	(40%)
	Nixon (R)	81,727	(49%)
	Wallace (AIP)	18,825	(11%)

Representative

William J. Keating (R) Elected 1970; b. March 30, 1927, Cincinnati; home, Cincinnati; U. of Cincinnati, B.B.A., 1950; U. of Cincinnati Law, J.D., 1950; Navy, WWII; USAFR; married, seven children; Catholic.

Career Practicing atty., 1954–58, 1967–70; Asst. Atty. Gen., 1957–58; Cincinnati Municipal Ct. Judge, 1958–63; Judge, Hamilton County Common Pleas Court, 1965–67; Cincinnati City Council, 1967–70.

Offices 1317 LHOB, 202-225-3164. Also 9407 Fed. Bldg., Cincinnati 45202.

Committees

Judiciary (15th); Sub. No. 4.
Sel. Com. on Crime (5th).

Group Ratings, Key Votes: Newly elected.

Election Results

1970 general:	William J. Keating (R)	89,169	(69%)
	Bailey W. Turner (D)	39,820	(31%)
1970 primary:	William J. Keating (R), unopposed		

SECOND DISTRICT Political Background

Ohio 2, except for a few townships which lie in the 24th district, comprises the western half of Cincinnati and Hamilton County. This is the less fashionable side of Cincinnati, though there are high-income areas here and there in the suburbs. For the most part, the 2nd is made up of white working-class and white-collar people living in neighborhoods spread out over the city's hills. The district includes the older and poorer black sections of Cincinnati, as well as some of its lower-income Appalachian and German communities. It also includes Cincinnati's industrial corridor along Mill Creek, a stream which passes through the northern suburbs and then bisects the city. Here lie the great Procter and Gamble soap factories, as well as the General Electric plant that was tooled up to produce engines for the SST.

Like the 1st, the 2nd district is heavily Republican; the only prominent Democrat it has supported in recent years was Lyndon Johnson in 1964. Its congressman is Donald D. Clancy, a former councilman who was first elected to the House in 1960. Clancy is a conservative Republican and a member of the House Armed Services Committee. He was, not surprisingly, one of the House's leading proponents of the SST.

Clancy has had little trouble winning reelection in the 2nd; in 1964, for example, he won with 61% of the votes, the 3rd best showing made among Ohio's then 18-member Republican House delegation. But in 1970, he had vigorous opposition from

Gerald Springer, a young antiwar attorney who enlisted many student volunteers in his cause. Springer cut Clancy's majority to 56%—quite an achievement in this heavily Republican district.

The results of the elections indicate that Clancy is vulnerable. But those same results may just spur Clancy on to greater efforts, sustaining and increasing his recognition in the district. This is something an incumbent congressman, armed with the franking privilege, has little difficulty doing. Before the 1972 elections, however, the district lines must be redrawn. The Republican legislature will probably try to add more conservative territory to the 2nd from the suburban townships now in the 24th. Gov. Gilligan, on the other hand, will probably try to pressure the legislators into adding more Democratic terrain from the 1st, since the outlook there for the Democrats is pretty hopeless anyway. The outcome of the bargaining will greatly influence how the district will go in 1972.

Census Data 1970 pop. 447,479; deviation from current state average, +1.2%; change 1960–70, +9.3%. Metro. 100.0%, 54.8% central city.

1970 Share of Federal Outlays $445,105,000 (average outlay per district, Ohio 1 and 2)

DOD	$153,742,000	HEW	$121,723,000
AEC	$8,779,000	HUD	$5,220,000
NASA	$7,716,000	OEO	$935,000
DOT	$41,294,000	DOA	$2,413,000
		Other	$103,283,000

Federal Military-Industrial Commitments (See Ohio 1 for greater Cincinnati listing.)

Economic Base Transportation equipment, esp. motor vehicles and motor vehicle equipment and aircraft engines and aircraft engine parts; soaps and detergents; nonelectrical machinery, esp. metalworking machinery and equipment; food and kindred products, esp. bakery products and beverages; fabricated metal products. Also, higher education (University of Cincinnati).

The Voters

Registration No district-wide registration.

Employment profile White collar, 44%. Blue collar, 56%.

Ethnic groups Black, 13%. Total foreign stock, 11%. Germany, 5%; Hungary, Ireland, Italy, UK, 1% each; others, 2%.

Presidential vote

1968	Humphrey (D)	61,387	(36%)
	Nixon (R)	88,208	(51%)
	Wallace (AIP)	23,052	(13%)

Representative

Donald D. Clancy (R) Elected 1960; b. July 24, 1921, Cincinnati; home, Cincinnati; Xavier U., 1939–43; U. of Cincinnati Law School, LL.B., 1948; married, three children; Presbyterian.

Career Practicing atty., 1948– ; Cincinnati Council, 1951–57; Mayor of Cincinnati, 1957–60.

Offices 2342 RHOB, 202-225-2216. Also Rm. 430, Post Office and Courthouse Bldg., Cincinnati 45202, 513-684-3738.

Committees

Armed Services (8th); Sub. No. 2.

Group Ratings

	ADA	COPE	NREP	NFU	LCV	CFA	NAB	NSI	ACA
1970	0	10	9	33	22	42	89	100	88
1969	7	—	—	20	—	—	—	—	100
1968	0	0	—	25	—	—	100	—	100

Key Votes

(1) ABM	FOR	(6) 18-Yr-Vote	FOR	(11) Clean Water $	AGN
(2) SST	FOR	(7) Farm Sub Lmt	FOR	(12) Mig Wrkrs Comp	AGN
(3) Phil Pln	AGN	(8) Coop-Church	AGN	(13) Jets to Chiang	FOR
(4) No-Knock	FOR	(9) Family Asst	AGN	(14) State OEO Veto	FOR
(5) Cmutr Tax	FOR	(10) Work Stamps	FOR	(15) Park Logging	AGN

Election Results

1970 general:	Donald D. Clancy (R)	77,071	(56%)
	Gerald N. Springer (D)	60,860	(44%)
1970 primary:	Donald D. Clancy (R), unopposed		
1968 general:	Donald D. Clancy (R)	108,157	(67%)
	Don Driehaus (D)	52,327	(33%)

THIRD DISTRICT Political Background

Ohio 3 is Dayton and adjacent suburbs, the home of Scammon and Wattenberg's typical Middle American voter. She is the now famous suburban housewife whose husband works in a factory, and whose brother-in-law is a policeman; usually a Democrat, she is worried about crime, lawlessness, and drugs, and is therefore tempted to vote Republican. Tempted or not, it seems that the housewife has stayed with the Democrats in the last two statewide elections: Montgomery County—which includes all of the 3rd district and small portions of the 7th and 24th—went for Humphrey in 1968 and also turned in good-sized majorities for John Gilligan and Howard Metzenbaum in 1970.

What kind of character does this presumed quintessential bit of Middle America possess? Dayton, Ohio, is a medium-sized industrial city (metropolitan pop. 600,000; central city pop. 243,000); while it has many of the usual urban problems, they are not as pressing here as they are in Cleveland. Dayton has a substantial black population, 30%, and even a black mayor, who occupies a largely ceremonial post. Beyond the city limits, there are some fast-growing middle-income suburbs. As in most of southern Ohio, the principal ethnic group here is German-American.

Because the Ohio Republican party has traditionally selected congressional candidates suited to their districts, the congressman from the Democratic-leaning 3rd is the most liberal member of the 17-man Ohio Republican delegation. Charles W. Whalen, Jr. was a 12-year veteran of the Ohio legislature when he challenged Rodney M. Love, a beneficiary of the Johnson landslide, in 1966. Whalen won with 52%, and has had no problems since.

Whalen's liberal record, an ADA rating of 88 in 1970, has won him the support of many other staunchly Democratic voters; he was the co-sponsor of the Nedzi-Whalen Amendment. Whalen is also a member of the dovish minority of the House Armed Services Committee. The Congressman's popularity is such—74% of the votes in 1970—that he is likely to win reelection as long as he cares to run. And it might be that the search for the nation's typical Middle American voter could be profitably moved somewhere outside Dayton and Montgomery County, Ohio.

Census Data 1970 pop. 455,018; deviation from current state average, +2.8%; change 1960–70, +12.9%. Metro. 100.0%, 53.4% central city.

1970 Share of Federal Outlays $818,973,000

DOD	$534,997,000	HEW	$117,183,000
AEC	$38,392,000	HUD	$6,588,000
NASA	$1,897,000	OEO	$1,429,000
DOT	$11,651,000	DOA	$3,413,000
		Other	$103,423,000

Federal Military-Industrial Commitments

DOD Installations Wright-Patterson AFB (Dayton). Gentile AF Station (Dayton).

AEC Operations Monsanto Chemical Co. (Miamisburg), $28.812m: Mound Laboratory.

Economic Base Nonelectrical machinery; electrical machinery, equipment, and supplies, esp. electrical industrial apparatus; rubber and miscellaneous plastics products; printing, publishing, and allied industries, esp. commercial printing. Also, banking.

The Voters

Registration No district-wide registration.

Employment profile White collar, 45%. Blue collar, 55%.

Ethnic groups Black, 16%. Total foreign stock, 8%. Germany, 2%; Hungary, Italy, UK, Canada, 1% each; others, 2%.

Presidential vote

1968	Humphrey (D)	74,485	(48%)
	Nixon (R)	62,206	(40%)
	Wallace (AIP)	17,288	(11%)

Representative

Charles W. Whalen, Jr. (R) Elected 1966; b. July 31, 1920, Dayton; home, Dayton; U. of Dayton, B.S., 1942; Harvard U., M.B.A., 1946; Army, WWII; married, five children; Catholic.

Career Businessman, V.P., Dayton Dress Co., 1946–52; Ohio House of Reps., 1955–60; Ohio Senate, 1961–66; Prof. and Head, Dept. of Econ., U. of Dayton, 1962–66.

Offices 1225 LHOB, 202-225-6465. Also 315 Old Post Office Bldg., 118 W. Third, Dayton 45402, 513-461-4830, ext. 5286.

Committees

Armed Services (12th); Sub. No. 1.

Group Ratings

	ADA	COPE	NREP	NFU	LCV	CFA	NAB	NSI	ACA
1970	88	75	83	100	25	65	27	10	26
1969	73	—	—	67	—	—	—	—	19
1968	67	83	—	69	—	—	50	—	27

Key Votes

(1) ABM	AGN	(6) 18-Yr-Vote	FOR	(11) Clean Water $	FOR
(2) SST	FOR	(7) Farm Sub Lmt	FOR	(12) Mig Wrkrs Comp	FOR
(3) Phil Pln	FOR	(8) Coop-Church	FOR	(13) Jets to Chiang	AGN
(4) No-Knock	FOR	(9) Family Asst	FOR	(14) State OEO Veto	AGN
(5) Cmutr Tax	FOR	(10) Work Stamps	AGN	(15) Park Logging	FOR

Election Results

1970 general:	Charles W. Whalen, Jr. (R)	86,973	(74%)
	Dempsey A. Kerr (D)	26,735	(23%)
	Russell G. Butcke (AIP)	3,545	(3%)
1970 primary:	Charles W. Whalen, Jr. (R), unopposed		
1968 general:	Charles W. Whalen, Jr. (R)	114,549	(78%)
	Paul Tipps (D)	32,012	(22%)

FOURTH DISTRICT Political Background

Ohio 4 is a series of counties in the western part of the state. The northern part of the district is one of the most Republican parts of Ohio. Allen County, which contains Lima, the 4th's largest city (pop. 53,000), was the largest county east of Chicago and north of Richmond, Virginia, to support the candidacy of Barry Goldwater in 1964. The southern part of the district, with rural German Catholic residents (Mercer County), and small industrial towns (Piqua and Troy in Miami County), is somewhat more marginal politically. The 4th also includes a Republican portion of Montgomery County (metropolitan Dayton).

Congressman William M. McCulloch has represented the district since he won a special election in 1947. He is currently the dean of the Ohio delegation. McCulloch is also the ranking Republican member of the House Judiciary Committee, which has jurisdiction over civil rights legislation. His support for the Civil Rights Act of 1964 was in large part responsible for its passage in the House. Because the Congressman usually votes with other Midwestern conservatives, many of whom were leery about the bill, McCulloch's advocacy was very important. He has supported subsequent civil rights legislation, and has also served on the Kerner Commission on Civil Disorders and on the Presidential Commission on the Causes and Prevention of Violence, which was chaired by Milton Eisenhower.

McCulloch is highly regarded by his colleagues in the House; that regard, judging from election returns in the 4th district, is shared by his constituents. In 1968, the Democrats didn't even put up a candidate against him. No one doubts that he could win reelection easily. But in 1971 he was injured in a fall in his Washington apartment and has decided to retire at the end of his current term. McCulloch's decision may ease the sticky Ohio redistricting situation. Under the 1970 census, the state lost one House seat, so the legislature may well choose to divide McCulloch's 4th among neighboring districts, and thereby avoid discomfiting any incumbents.

Census Data 1970 pop. 441,655; deviation from current state average, —0.2%; change 1960–70, +9.9%. Metro. 56.6%, 12.2% central city.

1970 Share of Federal Outlays $206,639,000

DOD	$37,142,000	HEW	$87,223,000
AEC	$199,000	HUD	$000
NASA	$527,000	OEO	$482,000
DOT	$1,240,000	DOA	$24,338,000
		Other	$55,489,000

Federal Military-Industrial Commitments

DOD Contractors Goodyear Tire (St. Marys), $14.308m: Track shoe assemblies for M48 and M60 tanks, M113 personnel carriers, and M108 and M109 howitzers.

Economic Base Cash grain, livestock, and dairy; nonelectrical machinery; transportation equipment.

The Voters

Registration No district-wide registration.

Employment profile White collar, 35%. Blue collar, 65%.

Ethnic groups Black, 3%. Total foreign stock, 5%. Germany, 2%; UK, 1%; others, 1%.

Presidential vote

1968	Humphrey (D)	60,681	(36%)
	Nixon (R)	90,751	(53%)
	Wallace (AIP)	18,766	(11%)

Representative

William M. McCulloch (R) Elected Nov. 4, 1947; b. Nov. 24, 1901, Holmes County; home, Piqua; Col. of Wooster, 1919–21; Ohio State U., LL.B., 1925; Army, WWII; married, two children; Presbyterian.

Career Practicing atty., 1925– ; Ohio House of Reps., 1933–45, Minority Leader, 1936–39, Speaker, 1939–44.

Offices 2186 RHOB, 202-225-2676. Also Piqua Natl. Bank Bldg., Piqua 45356, 513-773-2090.

Committees

Judiciary (Ranking Min. Mbr.); Sub. No. 5.

Jt. Com. on Atomic Energy (3rd); Subs. (1) Communities, (2) Raw Materials, (3) Security.

Group Ratings

	ADA	COPE	NREP	NFU	LCV	CFA	NAB	NSI	ACA
1970	28	50	45	67	14	50	89	100	53
1969	27	—	—	57	—	—	—	—	33
1968	42	34	—	71	—	—	33	—	61

Key Votes

(1) ABM	FOR	(6) 18-Yr-Vote	FOR	(11) Clean Water $	FOR
(2) SST	FOR*	(7) Farm Sub Lmt	FOR	(12) Mig Wrkrs Comp	AGN
(3) Phil Pln	FOR	(8) Coop-Church	AGN	(13) Jets to Chiang	ABS
(4) No-Knock	FOR	(9) Family Asst	FOR	(14) State OEO Veto	AGN
(5) Cmutr Tax	AGN	(10) Work Stamps	ABS	(15) Park Logging	FOR

* *Absent on previous vote on same issue.*

Election Results

1970 general:	William M. McCulloch (R)	82,521	(64%)
	Donald B. Laws (D)	45,619	(36%)
1970 primary:	William M. McCulloch (R)	32,213	(74%)
	James M. Carpenter (R)	6,414	(15%)
	Ralph Dull (R)	4,995	(11%)
1968 general:	William M. McCulloch (R), unopposed		

FIFTH DISTRICT Political Background

Ohio 5 takes in the flat farmlands of Ohio's northwest corner. The district's largest town is Bowling Green (pop. 21,000). The 5th, classic Republican territory, was first settled by New England Yankees, and the voters here today almost invariably support the party of their ancestors. The rare exception to the pattern occurred in the presidential contest of 1964. Unlike most of rural America, this is not an area of population decline. Small factories are going up in the district's small towns and countryside. This part of Ohio provides businessmen with a fine location—almost equidistant from the industrial giants of Chicago, Detroit, and Cleveland, and also near the smaller industrial centers of Toledo and Fort Wayne.

The 5th has been predictably steady in its support of its congressman, conservative Republican Delbert L. Latta. Latta is his party's most junior member of the House Rules Committee. An appointment to Rules is an indication of the Republican leadership's belief in the congressman's conservative orthodoxy, and in Latta's case, they were, as usual, right. (They did miscalculate, however, when they selected the increasingly liberal John Anderson of Illinois.) Latta's conservatism has won him reelection in the district by margins usually around 70%. Because his district occupies one of Ohio's corners, redistricting gives him little worry. Latta most likely will continue to represent the 5th for at least another ten years.

Census Data 1970 pop. 450,954; deviation from current state average, +1.9%; change 1960–70, +12.3%. Metro. 45.0%, 6.1% central city.

1970 Share of Federal Outlays $171,310,000

DOD	$11,310,000	HEW	$71,359,000
AEC	$000	HUD	$6,635,000
NASA	$000	OEO	$102,000
DOT	$1,967,000	DOA	$30,550,000
		Other	$49,386,000

Federal Military-Industrial Commitments

None.

Economic Base Cash grain, livestock, and dairy; stone, clay, glass, and concrete products; electrical machinery, equipment, and supplies; nonelectrical machinery. Also, higher education (Bowling Green State University).

The Voters

Registration No district-wide registration.
Employment profile White collar, 32%. Blue collar, 68%.
Ethnic groups Black, 1%. Total foreign stock, 9%. Germany, 4%; Czech., UK, Canada, Mexico, 1% each; others, 1%.

Presidential vote

1968	Humphrey (D)	62,510	(37%)
	Nixon (R)	89,569	(53%)
	Wallace (AIP)	15,876	(10%)

Representative

Delbert L. Latta (R) Elected 1958; b. March 5, 1920, Weston; home, Bowling Green; Ohio Northern U., B.A., LL.B.; married, two children; Church of Christ.
Career Practicing atty.; Ohio Senate.
Offices 2423 RHOB, 202-225-6405. Also 309 Wood County Bank Bldg., Bowling Green 43402, 419-353-8871.
Committees
Rules (5th).

Group Ratings

	ADA	COPE	NREP	NFU	LCV	CFA	NAB	NSI	ACA
1970	8	36	18	38	50	60	82	100	71
1969	13	—	—	27	—	—	—	—	69
1968	0	23	—	56	—	—	100	—	96

Key Votes

(1) ABM	FOR	(6) 18-Yr-Vote	FOR	(11) Clean Water $	FOR
(2) SST	FOR*	(7) Farm Sub Lmt	FOR	(12) Mig Wrkrs Comp	AGN
(3) Phil Pln	FOR	(8) Coop-Church	AGN	(13) Jets to Chiang	FOR
(4) No-Knock	FOR	(9) Family Asst	AGN	(14) State OEO Veto	FOR
(5) Cmutr Tax	AGN	(10) Work Stamps	FOR	(15) Park Logging	AGN

* *Voted "against" in previous vote on same issue.*

Election Results

1970 general:	Delbert L. Latta (R)	92,577	(71%)
	Carl G. Sherer (D)	37,545	(29%)
1970 primary:	Delbert L. Latta (R), unopposed		
1968 general:	Delbert L. Latta (R)	113,381	(71%)
	Louis Richard Batzler (D)	45,884	(29%)

SIXTH DISTRICT Political Background

Ohio 6 is a rural district in the southern part of the state. It touches the metropolitan areas of Cincinnati to the east, and Columbus to the north, and extends to the Ohio River boundary with Kentucky and West Virginia. The notable cities in the district are Portsmouth and Ironton, industrial centers on the River, and Chillicothe, which lies halfway between Portsmouth and Columbus. The rolling hill country in the valley of the Scioto River, which passes through Columbus, Chillicothe, and Portsmouth, is traditionally solid Democratic terrain. This fact reflects the Southern origin of the area's earliest settlers. Lately, like much of the rest of the South, it has been growing increasingly conservative and less Democratic; now only Pike County consistently delivers Democratic majorities here. In the western part of the 5th, in Clermont County, metropolitan growth from Republican Cincinnati has contributed to the Republican trend in the district.

Up through the '50's, the 6th sent a Democrat to the House. Upon his death in 1959, Ray Bliss's Republican organization carefully selected a Republican candidate, William H. Harsha, who won in the November, 1960 elections, and has been winning ever since. The former Scioto County (Portsmouth) prosecutor is a reliably conservative member of the reliably conservative Ohio Republican delegation.

When the 92nd Congress convened, Harsha became the ranking minority member of the House Public Works Committee—a post which gives him considerable say about who gets what in the federal pork barrel. Harsha, who regularly wins re-election by stunning majorities, probably will be left unaffected by redistricting.

Census Data 1970 pop. 419,615; deviation from current state average, −5.2%; change 1960–70, +2.8%. Metro. 38.7%, 0.0% central city.

1970 Share of Federal Outlays $257,497,000

DOD	$3,081,000	HEW	$100,086,000
AEC	$000	HUD	$670,000
NASA	$000	OEO	$1,147,000
DOT	$29,045,000	DOA	$16,922,000
		Other	$71,255,000

Federal Military-Industrial Commitments

None.

Economic Base Livestock, dairy, and cash grain; fabricated metal products; paper and allied products.

The Voters

Registration No district-wide registration.

Employment profile White collar, 32%. Blue collar, 68%.

Ethnic groups Black, 2%. Total foreign stock, 3%. Germany, 1%; others, 1%.

Presidential vote

1968	Humphrey (D)	55,649	(35%)
	Nixon (R)	77,496	(48%)
	Wallace (AIP)	26,975	(17%)

Representative

William H. Harsha (R) Elected 1960; b. Jan. 1, 1921, Portsmouth; home, Portsmouth; Kenyon Col., B.A., 1943; Western Reserve U., LL.B., 1947; USMCR, WWII; married, four children; Presbyterian.

Career Practicing atty., 1947–61; Asst. City Solicitor, Portsmouth, 1947–51; Scioto County Prosecutor, 1951–55.

Offices 2457 RHOB, 202-225-5705. Also 285 Main St., Batavia 45103, 513-732-2247, and Post Office Bldg., Hillsboro 45133, 513-393-4223.

Committees

District of Columbia (4th); Subs. (1) Business, Commerce, and Fiscal Affairs, (2) Judiciary.

Public Works (Ranking Min. Mbr.); Subs. (1) Investigation and Oversight, (2) Rivers and Harbors, (3) Roads, (4) Sp. on Economic Development Programs.

Group Ratings

	ADA	COPE	NREP	NFU	LCV	CFA	NAB	NSI	ACA
1970	8	17	9	31	40	48	92	100	84
1969	13	—	—	20	—	—	—	—	93
1968	8	9	—	56	—	—	100	—	87

Key Votes

(1) ABM	FOR	(6) 18-Yr-Vote	AGN	(11) Clean Water $	FOR
(2) SST	FOR	(7) Farm Sub Lmt	ABS	(12) Mig Wrkrs Comp	AGN
(3) Phil Pln	AGN	(8) Coop-Church	AGN	(13) Jets to Chiang	FOR
(4) No-Knock	FOR	(9) Family Asst	AGN	(14) State OEO Veto	FOR
(5) Cmutr Tax	FOR	(10) Work Stamps	FOR	(15) Park Logging	AGN

Election Results

1970 general:	William H. Harsha (R)	82,772	(68%)
	Raymond H. Stevens (D)	39,265	(32%)
1970 primary:	William H. Harsha (R), unopposed		
1968 general:	William H. Harsha (R)	107,289	(72%)
	Kenneth L. Kirbey (D)	40,964	(28%)

SEVENTH DISTRICT Political Background

Ohio 7 is a string of counties in west central Ohio, from Marion in the north, to the Dayton suburbs in the south. Marion was hometown to both President Warren G. Harding and socialist Norman Thomas. As a boy, Thomas delivered the paper of which Harding was the editor. This part of the 7th gives the district its Republican character; small towns here like Urbana and Bellefontaine, as well as Marion, are staunchly Republican. The southern end of the 7th is politically marginal. Scammon and Wattenberg's Dayton housewife may live in the blue-collar suburb of Fairborn in the 7th (see Ohio 3). Also here is Springfield, an industrial city of 81,000 which, like the Dayton suburbs, more often than not goes Democratic.

From 1938 to 1965, this district was represented by Clarence J. Brown of Blanchester, a conservative of the Taft school. He was the senior Republican on the House Rules Committee until his death in 1965. In that position, he often teamed with Chairman Howard Smith of Virginia to kill or delay liberal legislation. The late congressman's son, Clarence J. Brown, Jr., was chosen to replace him in a 1965 special election. The younger Brown now holds middle seniority seats on the House Government Operations and Interstate and Foreign Commerce committees. Brown has won reelection easily in the past; in 1966, he ran unopposed. Since redistricting will create no problems for him, he will continue to win in the foreseeable future.

Census Data 1970 pop. 475,634; deviation from current state average, +7.4%; change 1960–70, +16.8%. Metro. 67.6%, 17.4% central city.

1970 Share of Federal Outlays $207,398,000

DOD	$22,990,000	HEW	$79,922,000
AEC	$000	HUD	$964,000
NASA	$93,000	OEO	$364,000
DOT	$7,652,000	DOA	$17,671,000
		Other	$77,743,000

Federal Military-Industrial Commitments

DOD Contractors International Harvester (Springfield), $6.580m: stake, van, and trailer trucks.

Economic Base Livestock, dairy, and cash grain; nonelectrical machinery; fabricated metal products.

The Voters

Registration No district-wide registration.

Employment profile White collar, 38%. Blue collar, 62%.

Ethnic groups Black, 6%. Total foreign stock, 4%. Germany, UK, 1% each; others, 1%.

Presidential vote

1968	Humphrey (D)	63,362	(39%)
	Nixon (R)	78,637	(48%)
	Wallace (AIP)	21,868	(13%)

Representative

Clarence J. Brown (R) Elected Nov. 2, 1965; b. June 18, 1927, Columbus; home, Columbus; Duke U., B.A., 1947; Harvard, M.B.A., 1949; USNR, Korean War; married, three children; Presbyterian.

Career Editor, *Star Republican,* 1949–53; Editor, co-owner, *Franklin Chronicle,* 1953–57; Editor, *Urbana Daily Citizen,* 1957–65, Publisher, 1959– ; Mgr., WCOM-FM. 1965; Pres., Brown Publishing Co.; farm owner.

Offices 212 CHOB, 202-225-4324. Also 220 U.S. Post Office, 150 N. Limestone St., Springfield 45501, 513-325-0474.

Committees

Government Operations (6th); Subs. (1) Intergovernmental Relations, (2) Legal and Monetary Affairs, (3) Legislation and Military Operations, (4) Special Studies.

Interstate and Foreign Commerce (8th); Sub. on Communications and Power.

Jt. Economic Com. (3rd); Subs. (1) Economic Progress, (2) Economic Statistics, (3) Foreign Economic Policy, (4) Priorities and Economy in Government, (5) Urban Affairs.

Group Ratings

	ADA	COPE	NREP	NFU	LCV	CFA	NAB	NSI	ACA
1970	24	36	36	67	14	28	82	100	56
1969	13	—	—	57	—	—	—	—	53
1968	8	15	—	60	—	—	100	—	91

Key Votes

(1) ABM	FOR	(6) 18-Yr-Vote	FOR	(11) Clean Water $	AGN
(2) SST	FOR	(7) Farm Sub Lmt	ABS	(12) Mig Wrkrs Comp	AGN
(3) Phil Pln	FOR	(8) Coop-Church	AGN	(13) Jets to Chiang	ABS
(4) No-Knock	FOR	(9) Family Asst	FOR	(14) State OEO Veto	AGN
(5) Cmutr Tax	FOR	(10) Work Stamps	FOR	(15) Park Logging	FOR

Election Results

1970 general:	Clarence J. Brown, Jr. (R)	84,448	(69%)
	Joseph D. Lewis (D)	37,294	(31%)
1970 primary:	Clarence J. Brown, Jr. (R)	41,837	(92%)
	H. Quinn Licklider (R)	3,794	(8%)
1968 general:	Clarence J. Brown, Jr. (R)	97,581	(64%)
	Robert E. Cecile (D)	55,386	(36%)

EIGHTH DISTRICT Political Background

Ohio 8, lying between Columbus and Lake Erie, is a bloc of six counties and part of a seventh in northcentral Ohio. The district is anchored on three sides by three medium-sized cities: Findlay (pop. 35,000), a petroleum center of sorts; Mansfield (pop. 55,000), about halfway between Columbus and Cleveland; and Sandusky (pop. 32,000), a small port on Lake Erie. Between these cities, the 8th is primarily agricultural, with some small towns like Bucyrus, Tiffin, Fostoria, and Upper Sandusky (which is nowhere near Sandusky). This is the most Republican district in Ohio: the farmers here are reasonably prosperous and content, and, as is commonly the case throughout the Midwest, the cities and towns are Republican bastions.

Jackson E. Betts has represented the district since 1950. Betts, who is of course a conservative Republican, is currently the number two Republican on the powerful House Ways and Means Committee. He made some news recently when he led a fight against the inclusion of certain questions, which he considered invasions of privacy, in the 1970 census forms. Officials at the Census Bureau argued that without the questions not much could be learned about the country, and for the most part, their views on the issue prevailed. But the controversy did show that an increasing number of congressmen have become concerned about personal privacy in a computerized age. Betts also demonstrated that even a single congressman can irritate many, many Washington bureaucrats.

As might be expected, Betts has always won reelection easily. He took 71% in 1968, and faced no opposition in 1970. He will continue to win handsome percentages as long as redistricters don't slice up the 8th or force him into a district with another incumbent. There is only a slight possibility that either of these two things will occur; nonetheless, the Congressman has no doubt kept close tabs on the negotiations between the Republican legislature and Democratic Gov. Gilligan.

Census Data 1970 pop. 434,467; deviation from current state average, −1.9%; change 1960–70, +7.8%. Metro. 26.4%, 12.7% central city.

1970 Share of Federal Outlays $211,279,000

DOD	$37,407,000	HEW	$86,450,000
AEC	$3,000	HUD	$8,000
NASA	$2,637,000	OEO	$478,000
DOT	$2,639,000	DOA	$18,421,000
		Other	$63,237,000

Federal Military-Industrial Commitments

DOD Contractors North Electric Co. (Galion), $11.023m: switchboards for 407L tactical communication system.

Economic Base Electrical machinery, equipment, and supplies, esp. household appliances; nonelectrical machinery; cash grain, livestock, and dairy.

The Voters

Registration No district-wide registration.

Employment profile White collar, 35%. Blue collar, 65%.

Ethnic groups Black, 4%. Total foreign stock, 7%. Germany, 2%; Italy, UK, 1% each; others, 2%.

Presidential vote

1968	Humphrey (D)	57,022	(35%)
	Nixon (R)	87,364	(54%)
	Wallace (AIP)	16,657	(10%)

Representative

Jackson E. Betts (R) Elected 1950; b. May 26, 1904, Findlay; home, Findlay; Kenyon Col., B.A., 1926; Yale School of Law, LL.B., 1929; married, one child; Episcopalian.

Career Practicing atty., 1930– ; Prosecuting Atty., Hancock County, 1933–37; Ohio House of Reps., 1937–47.

Offices 2310 RHOB, 202-225-3865. Also 302 Niles Bldg., Findlay 45840, 419-422-5203, and 314 Richland Trust Bldg., Mansfield 44902, 419-525-3236.

Committees

Standards of Official Conduct (Ranking Mbr.).

Ways and Means (2nd).

Jt. Com. on Internal Revenue Taxation (2nd).

Group Ratings

	ADA	COPE	NREP	NFU	LCV	CFA	NAB	NSI	ACA
1970	12	0	18	23	13	40	100	100	89
1969	7	—	—	27	—	—	—	—	88
1968	8	8	—	38	—	—	100	—	95

Key Votes

(1) ABM	FOR	(6) 18-Yr-Vote	AGN	(11) Clean Water $	FOR
(2) SST	FOR	(7) Farm Sub Lmt	FOR	(12) Mig Wrkrs Comp	AGN
(3) Phil Pln	FOR	(8) Coop-Church	AGN	(13) Jets to Chiang	FOR
(4) No-Knock	FOR	(9) Family Asst	FOR	(14) State OEO Veto	FOR
(5) Cmutr Tax	FOR	(10) Work Stamps	FOR	(15) Park Logging	FOR

Election Results

1970 general:	Jackson E. Betts (R), unopposed		
1970 primary:	Jackson E. Betts (R), unopposed		
1968 general:	Jackson E. Betts (R)	101,974	(71%)
	Marie Baker (D)	40,898	(29%)

NINTH DISTRICT Political Background

Ohio 9 comprises the city of Toledo and most of its suburbs. Metropolitan Toledo is just about the right size for a single congressional district, currently having 484,000 residents or about 17,000 above the state district average. And it has always formed a single district with only slight variations in its boundaries. Toledo is an important industrial center and a major Great Lakes port; it handles far more tonnage than the much larger city of Detroit, 60 miles away. In most respects, Toledo is as different from the surrounding Yankee Republican countryside as one can imagine. The city has a large ethnic population, which is mostly Polish and German, while some 12% of the district's residents are black. These sociological contrasts manifest themselves in the politics of the 9th. In the midst of heavily Republican northwest Ohio, Toledo and Lucas County almost always turn in heavy Democratic majorities.

The district's congressman is Thomas Ludlow Ashley, a liberal Democrat, who was first elected in 1964. His great-grandfather was the Toledo congressman during the Civil War. The present day Ashley is currently the 4th ranking Democrat on the House Merchant Marine and Fisheries Committee, which is of obvious importance to this port city. The Congressman is also the 5th ranking Democrat on Banking and Currency, which handles housing legislation. That kind of legislation interests constituents living in urban Toledo. Within a decade, Ashley may well become chairman of one of these two committees. He will be only 49 in 1972, and redistricting and reelection pose no problems for him.

Census Data 1970 pop. 431,624; deviation from current state average, —2.5%; change 1960–70, +5.3%. Metro. 100.0%, 82.5% central city.

1970 Share of Federal Outlays $289,269,000

DOD	$45,730,000	HEW	$118,136,000
AEC	$33,000	HUD	$8,147,000
NASA	$122,000	OEO	$1,158,000
DOT	$28,083,000	DOA	$4,014,000
		Other	$83,845,000

Federal Military-Industrial Commitments

DOD Contractors Wheelar Bros. (Toledo), $37.419m: unspecified. Continental Aviation (Toledo), $17.341m: J-69 and T-29 aircraft engines. National Lead Co. (Toledo), $6.883m: bomb components. Jeep Div., American Motors (Toledo), $5.014m: unspecified.

Economic Base Nonelectrical machinery, esp. general industrial machinery and equipment; fabricated metal products, esp. metal stampings; primary metal industries, esp. nonferrous foundries; stone, clay, glass, and concrete products, esp. glass products made of purchased glass. Also, banking.

The Voters

Registration No district-wide registration.
Employment profile White collar, 43%. Blue collar, 57%.
Ethnic groups Black, 12%. Total foreign stock, 19%. Germany, 5%; Poland, 4%; Canada, 2%; Hungary, Ireland, Italy, UK, USSR, 1% each; others, 2%.

Presidential vote

1968	Humphrey (D)	81,932	(51%)
	Nixon (R)	64,081	(40%)
	Wallace (AIP)	15,082	(9%)

Representative

Thomas Ludlow Ashley (D) Elected 1964; b. Jan. 11, 1923, Toledo; home, Waterville; Yale U., B.A., 1948; Ohio State U., LL.B., 1951; Army, WWII; married, one child; Episcopalian.

Career Practicing atty., 1951–52; Gen. Counsel, Formed Steel Products, 1951–52; Co-Dir., Press Secy., Asst. Dir. Spec. Projects, Radio Free Europe, 1952–54.

Offices 2427 RHOB, 202-225-4146. Also 234 Summit St., Toledo 43604, 419-248-5325.

Committees

Banking and Currency (5th); Subs. (1) Chm., International Trade, (2) Housing, (3) International Finance.

Merchant Marine and Fisheries (4th); Subs. (1) Merchant Marine, (2) Oceanography.

Group Ratings

	ADA	COPE	NREP	NFU	LCV	CFA	NAB	NSI	ACA
1970	100	91	93	100	80	100	20	0	11
1969	73	—	—	75	—	—	—	—	6
1968	100	92	—	79	—	—	0	—	10

Key Votes

(1) ABM	AGN	(6) 18-Yr-Vote	FOR	(11) Clean Water $	FOR
(2) SST	AGN	(7) Farm Sub Lmt	FOR	(12) Mig Wrkrs Comp	FOR
(3) Phil Pln	FOR	(8) Coop-Church	FOR	(13) Jets to Chiang	AGN
(4) No-Knock	AGN	(9) Family Asst	FOR	(14) State OEO Veto	AGN
(5) Cmutr Tax	FOR	(10) Work Stamps	AGN	(15) Park Logging	FOR

Election Results

1970 general:	Thomas Ludlow Ashley (D)	82,777	(71%)
	Allen H. Shapiro (R)	33,947	(29%)
1970 primary:	Thomas Ludlow Ashley (D)	20,997	(87%)
	Henry Black (D)	3,008	(13%)
1968 general:	Thomas Ludlow Ashley (D)	85,280	(57%)
	Ben Marsh (R)	63,290	(43%)

TENTH DISTRICT Political Background

Ohio 10 occupies the southeast corner of the state. Like West Virginia across the Ohio River, this is an area of declining population and economic distress. Marietta, on the River, was the site of the first permanent American settlement (1788) in the Northwest Territory. In its Republican political leanings, the residents of the area around this small city (pop. 16,000) still show evidence of the Yankee origin of its first settlers. The rest of the 10th has a more Southern cast: people think of themselves as Democrats and vote conservative. Other population centers here include Zanesville, Lancaster, and Athens.

The 10th's Democratic-conservative tradition has produced rather frequent partisan changes in the district's congressional representation—an unusual phenomenon in rural

Ohio. In 1958, 1960, and 1964, conservative Democrat Walter H. Moeller was chosen to represent the 10th; in 1962, conservative Republican Homer E. Abele. The most recent change occurred in 1966, when Republican Clarence E. Miller defeated Moeller by some 4,000 votes (52%). Since then Miller, like most Ohio Republican congressmen, has worked hard to strengthen his position in the district. He has succeeded, even though the 1968 redistricting added some marginal counties to the 10th. Miller has won the last two elections with almost 70% of the vote.

Because the seniority system works in capricious ways, Miller has risen rapidly on the House Agriculture Committee. He is currently its 5th ranking Republican, but his chances of becoming the committee's top Republican are not good. One of the more senior Republicans is slightly younger. Because of the 10th's corner position, Miller is unlikely to face serious trouble in redistricting, despite the district's declining population. The Congressman's prospects for continued service in the House are excellent.

Census Data 1970 pop. 414,218; deviation from current state average, −6.4%; change 1960–70, +3.3%. Metro. 0.0%, 0.0% central city.

1970 Share of Federal Outlays $222,996,000

DOD	$27,723,000	HEW	$110,561,000
AEC	$190,000	HUD	$2,742,000
NASA	$15,000	OEO	$1,017,000
DOT	$6,165,000	DOA	$11,770,000
		Other	$62,813,000

Federal Military-Industrial Commitments

DOD Contractors Johnson and Massma Construction (Marietta), $9.450m: unspecified.

Economic Base Livestock and dairy; glass and glassware, pressed and blown, and other stone, clay, glass, and concrete products; primary metal industries. Also, higher education (Ohio University).

The Voters

Registration No district-wide registration.

Employment profile White collar, 33%. Blue collar, 67%.

Ethnic groups Black, 2%. Total foreign stock, 3%. Germany, UK, 1% each; all other groups, less than 0.5%.

Presidential vote

1968	Humphrey (D)	60,911	(39%)
	Nixon (R)	81,045	(51%)
	Wallace (AIP)	16,375	(10%)

Representative

Clarence E. Miller (R) Elected 1966; b. Nov. 1, 1917, Lancaster; home, Lancaster; professional schooling from Intl. Correspondence School, Scranton, Pa.; married, two children; Methodist.

Career Electrical engineer; Lancaster City Council, 1957–63; Mayor of Lancaster, 1964–66.

Offices 128 CHOB, 202-225-5131. Also 212 S. Broad St., Lancaster 43130, 614-654-5149.

Committees

Agriculture (5th); Subs. (1) Dairy and Poultry, (2) Family Farms and Rural Dev., (3) Tobacco.

Public Works (10th); Subs. (1) Flood Control and Internal Development, (2) Public Buildings and Grounds, (3) Watershed Development, (4) Sp. on Economic Development Programs.

Group Ratings

	ADA	COPE	NREP	NFU	LCV	CFA	NAB	NSI	ACA
1970	40	25	33	46	50	48	75	80	68
1969	7	—	—	33	—	—	—	—	71
1968	0	0	—	38	—	—	100	—	91

Key Votes

(1) ABM	FOR	(6) 18-Yr-Vote	FOR	(11) Clean Water $	FOR
(2) SST	AGN	(7) Farm Sub Lmt	AGN	(12) Mig Wrkrs Comp	AGN
(3) Phil Pln	FOR	(8) Coop-Church	FOR	(13) Jets to Chiang	FOR
(4) No-Knock	FOR	(9) Family Asst	FOR	(14) State OEO Veto	FOR
(5) Cmutr Tax	AGN	(10) Work Stamps	FOR	(15) Park Logging	FOR

Election Results

1970 general:	Clarence E. Miller (R)	80,838	(67%)
	Doug Arnett (D)	40,699	(33%)
1970 primary:	Clarence E. Miller (R), unopposed		
1968 general:	Clarence E. Miller (R)	102,890	(69%)
	Harry B. Crewson (D)	45,686	(31%)

ELEVENTH DISTRICT Political Background

Ohio 11 is the northeast corner of the state. The 11th is a varied district: Ashtabula is an industrial and Democratic city near Lake Erie and the Pennsylvania line; Lake County is a fast-growing part of the Cleveland metropolitan area, containing politically marginal suburbs like Wickliffe, Willowick, and Willoughby; Geauga County is a rural Republican enclave; Portage County is a politically marginal area whose largest town, Kent, is the home of Kent State University. According to registration figures, the district is politically marginal, but in most statewide elections, it produces a thin Republican majority.

The 11th has elected a Republican congressman since 1962 when Oliver P. Bolton won the seat and represented the district for a term. Bolton, whose mother represented the adjacent 22nd district (suburban Cleveland), is a member of the socially prominent Ohio family. He came to grief in 1964, when he attempted to become Ohio's congressman-at-large, a seat which was eliminated in 1966. When Bolton vacated the 11th, the district seemed ready for a Democratic takeover. But instead, the voters here elected conservative Republican J. William Stanton. The Lake County Commissioner ran almost 20% ahead of the Goldwater-Miller ticket, and won with 55% of the votes.

This was a considerable achievement for a Republican in that year. Stanton's vote-getting ability has been further demonstrated by landslide reelections in 1968 and 1970. Since his first election, Stanton has moved a little to the left; in 1970, for example, he voted for the Cooper-Church amendment and against the SST. He is now one of Ohio's most liberal Republican congressmen, with a 1970 ADA rating of 52. Stanton's voting record has made him less vulnerable in general elections, and probably reflects the feeling among his constituents in this increasingly suburban district. Because the 11th is one of the state's fastest-growing districts, Stanton faces little trouble in redistricting. He could be helped by the line-drawing if some of the Democratic-leaning suburbs in eastern Lake County are removed and added to Charles Vanik's 22nd.

Census Data 1970 pop. 510,253; deviation from current state average, +15.3%; change 1960–70, +26.3%. Metro. 80.7%, 0.0% central city.

1970 Share of Federal Outlays $167,745,000

DOD	$37,342,000	HEW	$65,669,000
AEC	$1,061,000	HUD	$280,000
NASA	$133,000	OEO	$387,000
DOT	$2,535,000	DOA	$3,120,000
		Other	$57,218,000

Federal Military-Industrial Commitments

DOD Contractors Firestone Tire and Rubber (Ravenna), $25.520m: 40-mm cartridges, and 8-inch and 175-mm projectiles, and operation of Ravenna Army Ammunition plant. General Motors (Hudson), $5.474m: rough terrain tractors.

Economic Base Rubber and miscellaneous plastics products; chemicals and allied products, esp. industrial inorganic and organic chemicals; nonelectrical machinery. Also, higher education (Kent State University).

The Voters

Registration No district-wide registration.

Employment profile White collar, 38%. Blue collar, 62%.

Ethnic groups Black, 2%. Total foreign stock, 20%. Italy, 3%; Czech., Germany, Hungary, UK, 2% each; Austria, Poland, Canada, 1% each; others, 4%.

Presidential vote

1968	Humphrey (D)	71,669	(42%)
	Nixon (R)	76,457	(45%)
	Wallace (AIP)	21,474	(13%)

Representative

John William Stanton (R) Elected 1964; b. Feb. 20, 1924, Painesville; home, Painesville; Georgetown U., B.S., 1949; Army, WWII; married, one child; Catholic.

Career Lake County Commissioner, 1956–64.

Offices 132 CHOB, 202-225-5306. Also 170 N. St. Clair St., Painesville 44077, 216-352-6167.

Committees

Merchant Marine and Fisheries (22nd); Subs. (1) Oceanography, (2) Panama Canal, (3) Sp. on Maritime Education and Training.

Public Works (22nd); Subs. (1) Investigation and Oversight, (2) Rivers and Harbors, (3) Roads, (4) Sp. on Economic Development Programs.

Group Ratings

	ADA	COPE	NREP	NFU	LCV	CFA	NAB	NSI	ACA
1970	52	50	67	77	43	45	83	80	41
1969	27	9	—	73	—	—	—	—	35
1968	42	25	—	69	—	—	83	—	45

Key Votes

(1) ABM	FOR	(6) 18-Yr-Vote	FOR	(11) Clean Water $	FOR
(2) SST	AGN	(7) Farm Sub Lmt	FOR	(12) Mig Wrkrs Comp	FOR
(3) Phil Pln	FOR	(8) Coop-Church	FOR	(13) Jets to Chiang	AGN
(4) No-Knock	ABS	(9) Family Asst	FOR	(14) State OEO Veto	AGN
(5) Cmutr Tax	FOR	(10) Work Stamps	FOR	(15) Park Logging	AGN

Election Results

1970 general:	J. William Stanton (R)	91,437	(68%)
	Ralph Rudd (D)	42,542	(32%)
1970 primary:	J. William Stanton (R), unopposed		
1968 general:	J. William Stanton (R)	116,323	(75%)
	Alan D. Wright (D)	38,063	(25%)

TWELFTH DISTRICT

Ohio 12 is one of two districts dominated by Columbus, the state capital. After the 1970 census, Columbus became Ohio's second largest city, having surpassed Cincinnati;

Cleveland is still the largest in the state. The 12th includes the east side of Columbus and adjacent Franklin County, plus rural and heavily Republican Delaware and Morrow counties to the north.

In the 1960 campaign, John F. Kennedy was greeted by a tumultuous crowd in Columbus; he later commented that it was the city where he got the largest crowds and the fewest votes. Columbus, like Cincinnati to the south, is a city stronghold of the Republican party. Of all the urban counties in the state, Barry Goldwater got his best vote here in 1964 (46%). The Republicanism is explained in part by the city's ethnic composition; though it does have a significant black population (18%), there are few residents of Eastern and Southern European stock. This is not the case in the state's Democratic and industrial cities to the north along Lake Erie. Moreover, Columbus is Ohio's most white-collar large city—leading industries include banking and insurance, state government, and higher education (Ohio State University).

The congressman from the 12th is former FBI agent, state legislator, and Franklin County prosecutor, Samuel L. Devine. In the 91st Congress, Devine helped to organize and lead a group called the Republican Regulars. The conservative organization was unhappy with some of the more liberal policies of the Nixon Administration, the family assistance program being one of them. At the beginning of the 92nd Congress, Devine challenged the increasingly liberal John Anderson of Illinois for the chairmanship of the House Republican Conference; Devine lost, but by only six votes, 88–82. Since some conservatives remained loyal to Anderson, the close vote indicates the continuing old-line conservative character of the Republican membership in the House.

Despite the loss, Devine is a powerful man in the Congress. First elected in 1958, he is now ranking minority member of the House Administration Committee and number two Republican on Interstate and Foreign Commerce. Since he was only 55 in 1970, it appears that he has many years of influence yet to come. But the 1970 election results indicate that he is having more trouble back in Columbus than he ever expected. In the election of that year, his Democratic opponent, liberal James Goodrich, waged a vigorous, but poorly financed, campaign and won 42% of the vote—a shockingly high percentage in Columbus where the local news media has no complaints about Spiro Agnew.

The Ohio Democrats would like very much to carve out a new 12th district in central Columbus; it would include all of the city's black population, which is currently split between the 12th and 15th districts. Such a new district could conceivably be won by a liberal like Goodrich, or by the city's conservative Democratic Mayor, Maynard E. Sensenbrenner. The problem is that the Democrats control the governorship but not the legislature, and the Republican legislators are not about to allow the creation of a Democratic Columbus district without a good fight. The Democrats, however, do control the five-man board that will redistrict the state legislative seats. So it is possible that they will control the legislature after the 1972 elections. In which case, the party will be perfectly free to draw the district lines any way they want—probably to the discomfiture of Devine and the 15th's Chalmers P. Wylie. The prospect of this has both Devine and Wylie busy cranking out franked mail to their constituents, and neither one will be easy to beat, even if all the Democrats' plans go through.

Census Data 1970 pop. 531,002; deviation from current state average, +19.9%; change 1960–70, +32.7%. Metro. 96.0%, 57.2% central city.

1970 Share of Federal Outlays $470,590,000 (average outlay per district, Ohio 12 and 15)

DOD	$192,408,000	HEW	$151,341,000
AEC	$2,196,000	HUD	$6,381,000
NASA	$1,715,000	OEO	$1,868,000
DOT	$10,689,000	DOA	$12,108,000
		Other	$91,883,000

Federal Military-Industrial Commitments (See Ohio 15 for Columbus area listing.)

Economic Base Nonelectrical machinery, esp. service industry equipment and general industrial machinery and equipment; electrical machinery, equipment, and supplies; fabricated metal products. Also, higher education, banking, insurance, and state government.

The Voters

Registration No district-wide registration.
Employment profile White collar, 51%. Blue collar, 49%.
Ethnic groups Black, 12%. Total foreign stock, 9%. Germany, Italy, 2% each; UK, USSR, Canada, 1% each; others, 2%.

Presidential vote

1968	Humphrey (D)	64,102	(35%)
	Nixon (R)	91,586	(50%)
	Wallace (AIP)	26,102	(14%)

Representative

Samuel L. Devine (R) Elected 1958; b. Dec. 21, 1915, South Bend, Ind.; home, Columbus; Colgate U., 1933–34; Ohio State U., 1934–37; U. of Notre Dame, LL.B., 1940; married, three children; Methodist.

Career Sp. Agent, FBI, 1940–45; practicing atty., 1945–55; Ohio House of Reps., 1951–55; Pros. Atty., Franklin County, 1955–58.

Offices 2262 RHOB, 202-225-5355. Also 408 New Fed. Bldg., 85 Narcibu Blvd., Columbus 43216, 614-221-3533.

Committees

House Administration (Ranking Mbr.).
Jt. Com. on Printing (Ranking Rep. House Mbr.).
Interstate and Foreign Commerce (2nd); Sub. on Transportation and Aeronautics.

Group Ratings

	ADA	COPE	NREP	NFU	LCV	CFA	NAB	NSI	ACA
1970	4	9	0	17	11	42	100	100	94
1969	0	—	—	20	—	—	—	—	91
1968	8	0	—	13	—	—	100	—	100

Key Votes

(1) ABM	FOR	(6) 18-Yr-Vote	AGN	(11) Clean Water $	AGN
(2) SST	FOR	(7) Farm Sub Lmt	AGN	(12) Mig Wrkrs Comp	AGN
(3) Phil Pln	AGN	(8) Coop-Church	AGN	(13) Jets to Chiang	ABS
(4) No-Knock	FOR	(9) Family Asst	AGN	(14) State OEO Veto	FOR
(5) Cmutr Tax	AGN	(10) Work Stamps	FOR	(15) Park Logging	AGN

Election Results

1970 general:	Samuel L. Devine (R)	82,486	(58%)
	James W. Goodrich (D)	60,538	(42%)
1970 primary:	Samuel L. Devine (R), unopposed		
1968 general:	Samuel L. Devine (R)	106,664	(68%)
	Herbert J. Pfeifer (D)	51,202	(32%)

THIRTEENTH DISTRICT Political Background

Ohio 13 is a portion of northcentral Ohio, a borderland area between the state's industrial, Democratic northeast and its rural, Republican northwest. The composition of the district changed substantially in the course of the successive redistrictings of 1964 and 1968. What has not changed is Lorain County, which contains about half of the 13th's population. Most of the county's residents live in and around the industrial cities of Lorain and Elyria, the latter, a nineteenth century small town and model for Sherwood Anderson's lament, *Winesburg, Ohio*. The county also includes the little town of Oberlin, home of Oberlin College. Before the 1964 redistricting, the 13th was a predominantly rural district containing those Republican counties now in the 5th and 8th districts (see map in appendix). The 13th presently has only one rural, Republican county (Medina). The rest of the population lives in the usually Republican southern townships of Cuyahoga County (the Cleveland suburbs of Brecksville, Strongsville, North Royalton, and Broadview Heights) and in the more marginal northern townships of Summit County (the Cleveland-Akron suburbs of Twinsburg, Hudson, Boston Heights, and Northfield).

The 13th regularly turns in Democratic majorities in statewide elections, but continues to reelect Republican Congressman Charles A. Mosher. He now receives margins about as large as those he used to receive when he represented the old, predominantly rural, 13th. Aside from Charles Whalen of Dayton, and the 3rd district, Mosher is Ohio's most liberal Republican congressman. His opposition to the Vietnam war has won him the support of peace groups, while he has also managed to sustain his popularity in the Democratic industrial sections of the district. Mosher has attained high committee rank for a congressman first elected in 1960; he is already the number three Repubican on the House Merchant Marine and Fisheries Committee and number two on Science and Astronautics. Redistricting should be no threat to Mosher, since he has proved he can win convincingly in a very marginal district.

Census Data 1970 pop. 503,342; deviation from current state average, +13.7%; change 1960–70, +25.8%. Metro. 100.0%, 26.1% central city.

1970 Share of Federal Outlays $107,891,000

DOD	$4,738,000	HEW	$51,483,000
AEC	$000	HUD	$3,971,000
NASA	$36,000	OEO	$14,000
DOT	$2,423,000	DOA	$3,939,000
		Other	$41,287,000

Federal Military-Industrial Commitments

None.

Economic Base Transportation equipment; fabricated metal products; primary metal industries.

The Voters

Registration No district-wide registration.

Employment profile White collar, 35%. Blue collar, 65%.

Ethnic groups Black, 4%. Puerto Rico, 1%. Total foreign stock, 18%. Germany, 3%; Hungary, Italy, Poland, UK, 2% each; Austria, Czech., USSR, Canada, 1% each; others, 3%.

Presidential vote

1968	Humphrey (D)	75,812	(44%)
	Nixon (R)	74,482	(44%)
	Wallace (AIP)	20,348	(12%)

Representative

Charles Adams Mosher (R) Elected 1960; b. May 7, 1906, Sandwich, Ill.; home, Oberlin; Oberlin Col., B.A., 1928; married, two children; United Church of Christ.

Career Newsman, Aurora, Ill., 1928–38, Janesville, Wisc., 1938–40; Pres., Oberlin Printing Co.; Editor-Publisher, Oberlin *News-Tribune,* 1940–62; Oberlin City Council, 1945–59; Ohio Senate, 1951–60.

Offices 2442 RHOB, 202-225-3401. Also 517 E. 28th St., Lorain 44055, 216-244-1572.

Committees

Merchant Marine and Fisheries (3rd); Subs. (1) Merchant Marine, (2) Oceanography, (3) Panama Canal.

Science and Astronautics (2nd); Subs. (1) International Cooperation in Science and Space, (2) Science, Research, and Development, (3) Space Sciences and Applications.

Group Ratings

	ADA	COPE	NREP	NFU	LCV	CFA	NAB	NSI	ACA
1970	88	67	8	92	67	64	64	10	42
1969	64	—	—	60	—	—	—	—	25
1968	42	50	—	69	—	—	83	—	38

Key Votes

(1) ABM	AGN	(6) 18-Yr-Vote	FOR	(11) Clean Water $	FOR
(2) SST	AGN	(7) Farm Sub Lmt	FOR	(12) Mig Wrkrs Comp	FOR
(3) Phil Pln	FOR	(8) Coop-Church	FOR	(13) Jets to Chiang	AGN
(4) No-Knock	FOR	(9) Family Asst	FOR	(14) State OEO Veto	AGN
(5) Cmutr Tax	FOR	(10) Work Stamps	AGN	(15) Park Logging	AGN

Election Results

1970 general:	Charles A. Mosher (R)	85,858	(62%)
	Joseph J. Bartolomeo (D)	53,271	(38%)
1970 primary:	Charles A. Mosher (R), unopposed		
1968 general:	Charles A. Mosher (R)	97,158	(62%)
	Adrian F. Betleski (D)	59,864	(38%)

FOURTEENTH DISTRICT Political Background

Ohio 14 is Akron and most of its suburbs. Akron is the rubber capital of the United States, the city where most of our millions of automobile and truck tires are produced. The rubber industry gives the city its peculiar odor and also gives its politics an old-time character. Political contests here are still very often what they were in the '30's and '40's—classic battles between labor and management. Since labor has the numbers, the district usually goes Democratic in statewide elections. But management has more money and entrepreneurial skill: Akron is the hometown of Ray Bliss, longtime Ohio Republican State Chairman and the man most responsible for the party's Ohio victories over the years.

The 1970 collapse of the Republican state ticket was paralleled in Akron by the defeat of Republican Congressman William H. Ayres, who was, of course, a man out of the Bliss organization. That organization always prided itself on matching its candidates to their districts, and for the 20 years Ayres served in the House, he was perfectly suited to Akron. A plumber by profession, the politician was an unabashed gladhander, always ready to show up at Rotary luncheons, rubber company picnics, the Soap Box Derby, or any other such gathering of 14th district voters to mingle among them, crack jokes, and press the flesh. Ayres helped many of Akron's ethnic residents with immigration problems and also won the favor of the pastors of the largest West Virginian evangelical churches. An extraordinary number of Akron voters have roots in West Virginia. Country and Western blues, which recall for us the green grass of home, are often written by homesick Appalachian people now living in places like Akron, Toledo, or Detroit. There is the story about a local judge who sentenced a prisoner to go to jail or West Virginia, whichever was worst; the judge was promptly defeated at the next election.

By 1970, Ayres had risen to become the ranking minority member of the House Education and Labor Committee. Here he usually steered a course between what the labor people in the district and the House Republican leadership wanted. He was also the number two Republican on the Veterans' Affairs Committee, a nice position for a congressman eager to do favors for his constituents. As the '60's went on, his voting record became more conservative, and his majorities quietly dwindled. Ayres had always been a prime Democratic target; in 1968, he won with only 55% of the vote in what was otherwise a pretty good year for Ohio Republicans.

The fact that five Democrats fought for the right to oppose him in 1970 was one sign of the incumbent's vulnerability. The winner of the primary was John F.

Seiberling, Jr., whose grandfather founded both the Seiberling and Goodyear rubber concerns. Seiberling was a staff lawyer for Goodyear, but his labor credentials were not bad. He had supported the United Rubber Workers' recent strike. He had also been an ecology buff and worked for years to keep power lines and highways out of the Cuyahoga River Valley. Ayres, on the other hand, was named one of the Dirty Dozen by the Washington-based Environmental Action group. Moreover, Seiberling was a longtime foe of the Vietnam war; Ayres supported the Nixon Administration position.

How did Seiberling succeed—he won a solid 56%—when Ayres' previous opponents, many of them well-known in the district, failed? The constellation of the peace-ecology issue was probably Seiberling's key. The *Akron Beacon Journal,* which had been endorsing Ayres for 20 years, supported Seiberling. The paper is owned by John S. Knight, who, on most issues, is a rather conservative Republican, but who has opposed the war throughout the '60's. The *Beacon Journal*'s endorsement symbolized Seiberling's respectability in upper-middle-class circles and also marked a breakdown of the old labor-vs.-management alignments. Ayres' other opponents usually had won the bulk of the union vote; but only Seiberling, whose name is as familiar in Akron as Henry Ford's is in Detroit, could win the additional 10% of the ballots necessary for victory.

Ayres, an old friend of Richard Nixon, will probably manage to find a job in Washington. There are rumors that he will be the next architect of the Capitol, a job that has belonged to more ex-congressmen than architects. As they say in Washington, they never go back to Pocatello. Seiberling, meanwhile, sits on the Judiciary and the Science and Astronautics committees. The Congressman is a member in good standing of the increasingly large antiwar bloc in the House. He probably will be helped to a degree by redistricting. Gov. Gilligan, as one price for his approval of the district lines drawn up by the legislature, probably will ask for a reshuffling of the Akron suburbs. This means moving to the 14th district the heavily Democratic Barberton, now in the 13th. Because of Seiberling's strong showing in 1970, and because of Ayres' unlikely return to the 14th, Seiberling seems assured of a long career in the House, and maybe even a shot at statewide office.

Census Data 1970 pop. 408,228; deviation from current state average, —7.8%; change 1960–70, +1.0%. Metro. 100.0%, 67.5% central city.

1970 Share of Federal Outlays $322,534,000

DOD	$105,480,000	HEW	$116,963,000
AEC	$676,000	HUD	$3,825,000
NASA	$1,505,000	OEO	$1,460,000
DOT	$3,412,000	DOA	$2,455,000
		Other	$86,757,000

Federal Military-Industrial Commitments

DOD Contractors Goodyear Aerospace Div., Goodyear Tire (Akron), $52.866m: production of SUBROC guided missiles; reconnaissance aircraft data interpretation. Goodyear Tire (Akron), $16.901m: tank and personnel carrier track shoes; half-ton truck tires; fuel cells for amphibious landing craft. B. F. Goodrich (Akron), $13.802m: sonar domes.

Economic Base Rubber and miscellaneous plastics products, esp. tires and inner tubes; fabricated metal products, esp. fabricated structural metal products and metal stampings; nonelectrical machinery, esp. metalworking machinery and equipment. Also, higher education (University of Akron).

The Voters

Registration No district-wide registration.

Employment profile White collar, 43%. Blue collar, 57%.

Ethnic groups Black, 12%. Total foreign stock, 18%. Germany, Hungary, Italy, UK, 2% each; Austria, Czech., Poland, USSR, Canada, 1% each; others, 4%.

Presidential vote

1968	Humphrey (D)	78,074	(49%)
	Nixon (R)	61,217	(39%)
	Wallace (AIP)	18,759	(12%)

Representative

John F. Seiberling (D) Elected 1970; b. Sept. 8, 1918, Akron; home, Akron; Harvard Col., B.A., 1941; Columbia U. Law School, LL.B., 1947; Army, WWII; married, three children; Protestant.

Career Practicing atty., 1949–54; legal staff, Goodyear Tire & Rubber Co., 1954–70; Mbr., Tri-County Regional Planning Commission, 1964–70.

Offices 1223 LHOB, 202-225-5231. Also 411 Wolf Ledges, Akron 44322, 216-762-9323.

Committees

Judiciary (19th); Sub. No. 1.

Science and Astronautics (13th); Subs. (1) Science, Research, and Development, (2) Space Sciences and Applications.

Group Ratings, Key Votes: Newly elected.

Election Results

1970 general:	John F. Seiberling, Jr. (D)	71,282	(56%)
	William H. Ayres (R)	55,038	(44%)
1970 primary:	John F. Seiberling, Jr. (D)	19,095	(38%)
	William B. Nye (D)	14,533	(29%)
	Thomas L. Thomas (D)	7,113	(14%)
	Ronald H. Weyandt (D)	5,459	(11%)
	Billy Robinson (D)	4,260	(8%)

FIFTEENTH DISTRICT Political Background

Ohio 15 comprises the west side of Columbus and Franklin County, plus rural Madison and Pickaway counties to the south and west. Columbus is, with Cincinnati, Ohio's most Republican city; Columbus, the state capital, is also the state's fastest-growing city (see Ohio 12). The 15th is, if anything, a little more Republican than the 12th, in large part because it includes Upper Arlington. This suburb is the city's largest (pop. 38,000) and most Republican (78% for Nixon in 1968).

The 15th was created in the 1964 redistricting and then altered in 1968 to take in the two rural counties. Its first and only congressman is Chalmers P. Wylie, a former state legislator and Columbus city attorney (an elective position). Wylie has compiled a solidly conservative record in Washington. Since his first victory, the Congressman has won by stunning majorities and seems likely to continue doing so; unlike his colleague Samuel Devine of the 12th, he has not attracted vigorous opposition. Redistricting will pose no problems for him for 1972, but if Ohio Democrats take control of the legislature in that election, they could redraw the lines in Columbus drastically. The Democrats could carve one of the city's two districts out of the central portion of Columbus with its large black population. Since neither Wylie nor Devine would want to run in such a district, a scramble could develop over who gets the safe Republican seat. But that is only a possibility of no immediate concern. Chances are, Wylie will continue to accumulate more seniority for at least another decade.

Census Data 1970 pop. 434,892; deviation from current state average, −1.8%; change 1960–70, +8.6%. Metro. 93.5%, 54.2% central city.

1970 Share of Federal Outlays $470,590,000 (average outlay per district, Ohio 12 and 15)

DOD	$192,408,000	HEW	$151,341,000
AEC	$2,196,000	HUD	$6,381,000
NASA	$1,715,000	OEO	$1,868,000

DOT	$10,689,000	DOA	$12,108,000
		Other	$91,883,000

Federal Military-Industrial Commitments (Ohio 12 and 15, Columbus area listing)

DOD Contractors North American Rockwell (Columbus), $127.008m: OV-10C aircraft; Condor missile system development; T-2C aircraft; electro-optical guided bomb kits; RA-5C aircraft parts. Battelle Memorial Institute (Columbus), $12.116m: unspecified research. Ashland Oil (Columbus), $5.932m: petroleum products.

DOD Installations Defense Army Construction Supply Center (Columbus). Lockbourne AFB (Columbus).

Economic Base Nonelectrical machinery, esp. service industry equipment and general industrial machinery and equipment; electrical machinery, equipment, and supplies; transportation equipment: fabricated metal products. Also, higher education (Ohio State University) and state government.

The Voters

Registration No district-wide registration.

Employment profile White collar, 47%. Blue collar, 53%.

Ethnic groups Black, 10%. Total foreign stock, 8%. Germany, 2%; Italy, UK, 1% each; others, 2%.

Presidential vote

1968	Humphrey (D)	49,915	(33%)
	Nixon (R)	83,846	(55%)
	Wallace (AIP)	19,320	(13%)

Representative

Chalmers Pangburn Wylie (R) Elected 1966; b. Nov. 23, 1920, Norwich; home, Columbus; Otterbein Col., Ohio State U., B.A.; Harvard Law School, LL.B.; Army, WWII; Lt. Col. USAR; married, two children; Methodist.

Career Asst. City Atty., Columbus, 1949–50; Asst. Atty. Gen. of Ohio, 1948, 1951–54; City Atty., 1953–56; Admin., Bureau of Workmen's Compensation, 1957; First Asst. to Governor, 1957–58; practicing atty., 1959–66; State Rep., 1961–67; Pres., Ohio Municipal League, 1957.

Offices 1331 LHOB, 202-225-2015. Also 404 Fed. Bldg., 85 Marconi Blvd., Columbus 43215, 614-469-5614.

Committees

Banking and Currency (8th); Subs. (1) Bank Supervision and Insurance, (2) Consumer Affairs, (3) Small Business.

Veterans' Affairs (7th); Subs. (1) Education and Training, (2) Hospitals, (3) Insurance.

Group Ratings

	ADA	COPE	NREP	NFU	LCV	CFA	NAB	NSI	ACA
1970	24	18	27	23	50	50	91	100	89
1969	7	—	—	46	—	—	—	—	73
1968	8	8	—	50	—	—	100	—	90

Key Votes

(1) ABM	FOR	(6) 18-Yr-Vote	AGN	(11) Clean Water $	AGN
(2) SST	AGN	(7) Farm Sub Lmt	AGN	(12) Mig Wrkrs Comp	AGN
(3) Phil Pln	FOR	(8) Coop-Church	AGN	(13) Jets to Chiang	ABS
(4) No-Knock	FOR	(9) Family Asst	ABS	(14) State OEO Veto	AGN
(5) Cmutr Tax	FOR	(10) Work Stamps	FOR	(15) Park Logging	AGN

Election Results

1970 general:	Chalmers P. Wylie (R)	81,536 (71%)
	Manley L. McGee (D)	34,018 (29%)
1970 primary:	Chalmers P. Wylie (R), unopposed	
1968 general:	Chalmers P. Wylie (R)	98,499 (73%)
	Russel H. Volkema (D)	35,861 (27%)

SIXTEENTH DISTRICT Political Background

Ohio 16, a portion of industrial northeast Ohio, centers on Canton and extends northeast to the Youngstown city limits. Canton (pop. 110,000) is an industrial city which casts about a quarter of the district's votes and usually goes Democratic, as do the smaller cities of Massillon (pop. 32,000), Alliance (pop. 26,000), and Boardman (pop. 30,000). The rest of the district—the suburban tracts around the cities and the rural hinterland first settled by Yankee farmers—is decidedly Republican, and it usually produces Republican margins that outweigh the Democrats' urban strength.

This pattern is particularly evident in the 16th's congressional elections. Representative Frank T. Bow, a conservative Republican, has been winning here with solid margins since 1950. In the House, he has risen to become the ranking minority member of the Appropriations Committee; his position enables him to wield an axe on those government expenditures he considers too generous. Because the congressman is the ranking member of the powerful committee, he is one of the most powerful conservatives in the House.

The continued reelection of conservative Republican congressmen from industrial districts is a political legacy of Ray Bliss, who led the Ohio Republican party for many years. But there are signs that Bow will soon encounter the same problems that eventually did in William Ayres of the neighboring 14th district. Advancing age (69 in 1970) suggests that Bow may not be able to campaign as vigorously in the future as he has in the past. In 1970, 36-year-old Virgil Musser waged a strong campaign and got 44% of the vote. Except for the unusual political year of 1964, this was the best anybody had done against the incumbent since 1956.

Redistricting may determine the outcome of the 1972 election. According to the 1970 census, the current 16th is about the proper size for an Ohio congressional district, but fluctuations in the size of neighboring areas probably will result in some redrawing of the lines. If the district expands to the west—rural countryside that is solidly Republican—Bow's reelection is insured. But if the 16th moves east, south, or north, into industrial Democratic areas, the Congressman may be in real trouble. The shape of the new 16th is no doubt a bone of contention between Gov. Gilligan and the Republican legislature. The outlines of the new district should be studied carefully before any predictions of the 1972 results are made.

Census Data 1970 pop. 453,853; deviation from current state average, +2.5%; change 1960–70, +11.3%. Metro. 100.0%, 24.2% central city.

1970 Share of Federal Outlays $184,450,000

DOD	$52,481,000	HEW	$78,221,000
AEC	$000	HUD	$45,000
NASA	$000	OEO	$543,000
DOT	$2,557,000	DOA	$2,139,000
		Other	$48,464,000

Federal Military-Industrial Commitments

DOD Contractors Hercules Engines (Canton), $44.505m: engines for 5- and 2½-ton Army trucks.

Economic Base Primary metal industries, esp. blast furnaces, steel works, and rolling and finishing mills; nonelectrical machinery, esp. metalworking machinery and equipment; fabricated metal products, esp. fabricated structural metal products.

The Voters

Registration No district-wide registration.

Employment profile White collar, 39%. Blue collar, 61%.

Ethnic groups Black, 5%. Total foreign stock, 16%. Italy, 3%; Germany, UK, 2% each; Austria, Czech., Hungary, Poland, 1% each; others, 4%.

Presidential vote

1968	Humphrey (D)	69,459	(40%)
	Nixon (R)	87,148	(50%)
	Wallace (AIP)	19,460	(11%)

Representative

Frank T. Bow (R) Elected 1950; b. Feb. 20, 1901, Canton; home, Canton; Ohio Northern U., 1919–21; admitted to the bar, 1923; WWII war correspondent; married, two children; Presbyterian.

Career Asst. Atty. Gen. of Ohio, 1929–32; Counsel, House Subcom. on Expenditures, 1947–48, Select Com. to Investigate FCC, 1948.

Offices 2182 RHOB, 202-225-3876. Also 452 Citizens Savings Bldg., 100 Central Plaza South, Canton 44702, 216-456-2869.

Committees

Appropriations (Ranking Mbr.); Subs. (1) State, Justice, Commerce, and the Judiciary, (2) Legislative.

Jt. Com. on Reduction of Federal Expenditures (Ranking Rep. House Mbr.).

Group Ratings

	ADA	COPE	NREP	NFU	LCV	CFA	NAB	NSI	ACA
1970	12	0	9	38	11	42	100	100	60
1969	0	—	—	36	—	—	—	—	60
1968	8	17	—	29	—	—	100	—	100

Key Votes

(1) ABM	FOR	(6) 18-Yr-Vote	FOR	(11) Clean Water $	AGN
(2) SST	FOR	(7) Farm Sub Lmt	AGN	(12) Mig Wrkrs Comp	AGN
(3) Phil Pln	FOR	(8) Coop-Church	AGN	(13) Jets to Chiang	FOR
(4) No-Knock	FOR	(9) Family Asst	FOR	(14) State OEO Veto	FOR
(5) Cmutr Tax	AGN	(10) Work Stamps	FOR	(15) Park Logging	FOR

Election Results

1970 general:	Frank T. Bow (R)	81,208	(56%)
	Virgil L. Musser (D)	63,187	(44%)
1970 primary:	Frank T. Bow (R)	45,588	(86%)
	Edward A. Mahoney, Jr. (R)	7,474	(14%)
1968 general:	Frank T. Bow (R)	101,495	(60%)
	Virgil L. Musser (D)	68,916	(40%)

SEVENTEENTH DISTRICT Political Background

Ohio 17 is a group of seven counties and parts of two others in east central Ohio, a land of rolling hills and carefully tended farms. The district contains only one city of any size, Newark (pop. 41,000), although there are several just outside the district's boundaries—among them, Columbus, Akron, and Canton. The countryside here, and to an even greater extent, the small county seat towns, are heavily Republican. This part of the state is almost as Republican as rural northwest Ohio (see Ohio 5). The 17th has not elected a Democratic congressman since 1958 and has backed the Republican nominee in every major statewide race since 1964.

The district's current congressman, John M. Ashbrook, is known as one of the most conservative members of the House. First elected in 1960, the Harvard man has amassed enough seniority to become number two Republican on the House Education and Labor Committee, and ranking minority member of the House Internal Security Committee (formerly the House Un-American Activities Committee). Like many Republicans now in Congress, Ashbrook was given a boost up the seniority ladder when many senior Republicans were slaughtered in the 1964 elections.

The Congressman's problem now is not winning reelection—of that he can be reasonably assured. The problem is to prevent his district from being sliced up among its neighbors. Since Ohio lost one House seat, one of the state's predominantly rural districts has to be eliminated. The situation once worried Ashbrook more than it does today. Veteran Republican Congressman William McCulloch of the 4th district has decided to retire; as a result, his district looks like the one which will go, and Ashbrook, barring the improbable, can look forward to another ten years in the House.

Census Data 1970 pop. 456,256; deviation from current state average, +3.1%; change 1960–70, +13.9%. Metro. 13.2%, 0.0% central city.

1970 Share of Federal Outlays $178,461,000

DOD	$40,089,000	HEW	$73,076,000
AEC	$48,000	HUD	$000
NASA	$000	OEO	$212,000
DOT	$4,848,000	DOA	$11,910,000
		Other	$48,278,000

Federal Military-Industrial Commitments

None.

Economic Base Dairy and livestock; stone, clay, glass, and concrete products; rubber and miscellaneous plastics products.

The Voters

Registration No district-wide registration.

Employment profile White collar, 34%. Blue collar, 66%.

Ethnic groups Black, 1%. Total foreign stock, 6%. Germany, USSR, 1% each; others, 1%.

Presidential vote

1968	Humphrey (D)	57,690	(36%)
	Nixon (R)	86,023	(53%)
	Wallace (AIP)	18,672	(12%)

Representative

John Milan Ashbrook (R) Elected 1960; b. Sept. 21, 1928, Johnstown; home, Johnstown; Harvard U., B.A., 1952; Ohio State U., J.D., 1955; Navy, 1946–48; married, three children; Baptist.

Career Publisher, Johnstown Independent, 1953– ; practicing atty., 1955– ; Young Repub. Chm., 1957–59; Ohio House of Reps., 1956–60.

Offices 206 CHOB, 202-225-6431. Also 53 S. Main St., Johnstown 43031, 614-967-5941, and 43 W. Main St., Ashland 44805, 419-322-1732, and 130½ E. Liberty St., Wooster 44691, 216-264-9779.

Committees

Education and Labor (2nd); Subs. (1) Agricultural Labor, (2) Education, (3) Labor.

Internal Security (Ranking Mbr.).

Group Ratings

	ADA	COPE	NREP	NFU	LCV	CFA	NAB	NSI	ACA
1970	4	25	17	15	40	33	75	100	93
1969	13	—	—	20	—	—	—	—	100
1968	0	8	—	14	—	—	100	—	100

Key Votes

(1) ABM	ABS	(6) 18-Yr-Vote	AGN	(11) Clean Water $	AGN
(2) SST	FOR	(7) Farm Sub Lmt	FOR	(12) Mig Wrkrs Comp	AGN
(3) Phil Pln	AGN	(8) Coop-Church	AGN	(13) Jets to Chiang	FOR
(4) No-Knock	FOR	(9) Family Asst	AGN	(14) State OEO Veto	FOR
(5) Cmutr Tax	AGN	(10) Work Stamps	FOR	(15) Park Logging	AGN

Election Results

1970 general:	John M. Ashbrook (R)	79,472	(62%)
	James C. Hood (D)	44,066	(34%)
	Clifford J. Simpson (AIP)	4,253	(3%)
1970 primary:	John M. Ashbrook (R), unopposed		
1968 general:	John M. Ashbrook (R)	100,148	(65%)
	Robert W. Levering (D)	54,127	(35%)

EIGHTEENTH DISTRICT Political Background

Ohio 18 is more like West Virginia and southwest Pennsylvania than the rest of Ohio: a rural and small town industrial district, complete with strip-mining of coal, heavy air pollution, economic distress, and declining population. Most of the district's residents are clustered in the small cities and the scarred countryside along the Ohio River, across from the West Virginia panhandle. One such city and the largest in the 18th is Steubenville (pop. 30,000), which has won a distinction from the National Air Pollution Control Administration. The pollution group said that the Ohio community had more particulate matter in its air (in layman's terms, soot) than any other American city. The 18th does have a significant foreign born population, especially Italians; Steubenville is Dean Martin's home town. But most of the people here are of Scots-Irish and WASP stock—sturdy steelworkers and coal miners who work hard, pay their taxes, send their sons dutifully off to Vietnam, and somehow miss out on all the good things that are supposed to be part of life in a rich country like ours. They also invariably vote Democratic, as they have since the days of Franklin D. Roosevelt.

Congressman Wayne L. Hays has represented this district since 1948, and is now the senior Democrat on the Ohio delegation. Hays has been a liberal on domestic issues and a staunch hawk on Vietnam. Very few members of the House have denounced student demonstrators as vehemently as Congressman Hays. And since he is the 3rd ranking Democrat on the House Foreign Affairs Committee, he has had a forum to air his feelings on the matter. But because the Constitution gave the Senate more say in foreign policy—power to approve treaties, among other things—the Foreign Affairs Committee is not as important as its dovish counterpart, the Senate Foreign Relations Committee. Consequently, Hays' views on Vietnam have had little impact. The Congressman's real power derives from chairing the House Administration Committee, a position he assumed after the involuntary retirement of Samuel Friedel of Baltimore in the 1970 Democratic primary. Hays ran for Majority Leader in the Democratic Caucus as the 92nd Congress convened. Although his candidacy was considered a joke by many, he received a respectable total of 28 votes, which is more than James O'Hara of Michigan got, and he had strong labor backing.

Hays has had no difficulty winning reelection; in 1970, for example, he had 68% of the votes. But he will have to watch the redistricting process carefully, and make sure that his population-losing district adds territory of suitable political inclination.

Census Data 1970 pop. 396,154; deviation from current state average, −10.5%; change 1960–70, −1.1%. Metro. 44.7%, 7.8% central city.

1970 Share of Federal Outlays $170,708,000

DOD	$5,959,000	HEW	$97,899,000
AEC	$139,000	HUD	$4,248,000
NASA	$000	OEO	$1,970,000
DOT	$460,000	DOA	$5,442,000
		Other	$54,591,000

Federal Military-Industrial Commitments
None.

Economic Base Primary metal industries, esp. blast furnaces, steel works, and rolling and finishing mills; fabricated metal products; dairy.

The Voters

Registration No district-wide registration.

Employment profile White collar, 32%. Blue collar, 68%.

Ethnic groups Black, 3%. Total foreign stock, 15%. Italy, 4%; Poland, UK, 2% each; Austria, Czech., Germany, Hungary, 1% each; others, 2%.

Presidential vote

1968	Humphrey (D)	84,870	(52%)
	Nixon (R)	65,713	(40%)
	Wallace (AIP)	14,204	(9%)

Representative

Wayne L. Hays (D) Elected 1948; b. May 13, 1911, Bannock; home, Flushing; Ohio State U., B.S., 1933; Duke U., 1935; USAR, WWII; married, one child; Presbyterian.

Career Belmont County Commissioner, 1945–49; owner, Red Gate Farms; Mayor of Flushing, 1939–45; Ohio State Senator, 1941–42; Chm. of Bd., Citizens Natl. Bank; Pres., NATO Parliamentarians' Conference, 1956–57; V.P. No. Atlantic Assembly, 1968–70.

Offices 2264 RHOB, 202-225-6265. Also Flushing 43977, 614-968-4114, and Columbia 44408, 216-482-3317.

Committees

Foreign Affairs (3rd); Subs. (1) Chm., State Department Organization and Foreign Operations, (2) Europe, (3) National Security Policy and Scientific Development, (4) Sp. for Review of Foreign Aid Programs.

House Administration (Chm.).

Jt. Com. on the Library (Chm.).

Jt. Com. on Printing (V. Chm.).

Group Ratings

	ADA	COPE	NREP	NFU	LCV	CFA	NAB	NSI	ACA
1970	32	82	36	91	57	71	10	75	17
1969	53	—	—	100	—	—	—	—	42
1968	50	91	—	14	—	—	20	—	35

Key Votes

(1) ABM	ABS	(6) 18-Yr-Vote	FOR	(11) Clean Water $	FOR
(2) SST	FOR	(7) Farm Sub Lmt	FOR	(12) Mig Wrkrs Comp	FOR
(3) Phil Pln	AGN	(8) Coop-Church	AGN	(13) Jets to Chiang	FOR
(4) No-Knock	ABS	(9) Family Asst	AGN	(14) State OEO Veto	AGN
(5) Cmutr Tax	AGN	(10) Work Stamps	AGN	(15) Park Logging	AGN

Election Results

1970 general:	Wayne L. Hays (D)	82,071	(68%)
	Robert Stewart (R)	38,104	(32%)
1970 primary:	Wayne L. Hays (D)	35,170	(82%)
	Joseph A. Pappano (D)	5,107	(12%)
	Nick B. Karnick (D)	2,370	(6%)

1968 general:	Wayne L. Hays (D)	96,711	(60%)
	James F. Sutherland (R)	63,747	(40%)

NINETEENTH DISTRICT Political Background

Ohio 19 takes in the cities of Youngstown (pop. 140,000) and Warren (pop. 63,000), and their immediate surroundings; these lie just west of the Pennsylvania line. Youngstown and Warren are the towns that steel built. About halfway between Cleveland and Pittsburgh, they are halfway between the docks that unload iron ore from the Great Lakes deposits and the coal fields of West Virginia and Pennsylvania. Recently, the two cities have been victims of the declining fortunes of the great steel firms; in the winter of 1969–70, Youngstown simply closed down its school system for a month. There was not enough money to keep it going, and the hard-pressed taxpayers, many of them laid off or deprived of overtime, would not vote for higher taxes.

Many of the voters in the 19th are of Italian and Czech descent. And since the days of the New Deal and the bloody steel strikes, they have had few doubts about who was and who was not a political friend. The district virtually always votes Democratic by large margins. From 1936 until 1970, Michael J. Kirwan represented the 19th in the House. Having a third grade education and a canny political sense, Kirwan became one of the powers in the House. He was number two Democrat on the Appropriations Committee and the shameless chairman of the pork-barreling Public Works Committee; Kirwan was also the longtime chairman of the House Democratic Campaign Committee, which dispenses rather meager funds for the reelection of Democratic congressmen. Kirwan ruthlessly pursued his pet projects. One was the proposed ten million dollar National Aquarium in Washington; and the other, the Ohio River-Lake Erie Canal, known affectionately as "Mike's Ditch." Kirwan died in the summer of 1970 at the age of 83. At that time, neither the canal, estimated to cost a billion dollars, nor the aquarium were as yet begun. With Kirwan gone, both projects never will be started.

Kirwan's successor, Democrat Charles J. Carney, is a 20-year veteran of the Ohio state senate and a former staffer with the United Steel Workers and United Rubber Workers unions. Carney won a 13-candidate Democratic primary and went on to beat Republican Margaret Dennison, whose husband represented the 11th district in the '50's, with 58% of the vote. Now that he is an incumbent, Carney will probably win with greater margins in elections to come; Kirwan seldom had less than 70%. In the 92nd Congress, Carney surprised many observers by coming out against the Vietnam war—another indication that the once hawkish blue-collar workers in areas like the 19th district of Ohio have changed their minds about that enterprise.

Census Data 1970 pop. 413,364; deviation from current state average, −6.6%; change 1960–70, +1.4%. Metro. 100.0%, 49.2% central city.

1970 Share of Federal Outlays $199,790,000

DOD	$8,618,000	HEW	$109,162,000
AEC	$000	HUD	$1,282,000
NASA	$34,000	OEO	$1,025,000
DOT	$5,415,000	DOA	$2,937,000
		Other	$71,316,000

Federal Military-Industrial Commitments

DOD Installations Youngstown Municipal Airport AF (Vienna).

Economic Base Blast furnaces, steel works, and rolling and finishing mills, and other primary metal industries; motor vehicles and motor vehicle equipment; fabricated metal products, esp. fabricated structural metal products. Also, higher education (Youngstown State University).

The Voters

Registration No district-wide registration.

Employment profile White collar, 34%. Blue collar, 66%.

Ethnic groups Black, 12%. Puerto Rico, 1%. Total foreign stock, 28%. Italy, 7%. Czech., 4%; UK, 3%; Hungary, Poland, 2% each; Austria, Ireland, Germany, USSR, Canada, 1% each; others, 5%.

Presidential vote

1968	Humphrey (D)	92,517	(58%)
	Nixon (R)	50,928	(32%)
	Wallace (AIP)	16,648	(10%)

Representative

Charles J. Carney (D) Elected 1970; b. April 17, 1913, Youngstown; home, Youngstown; Youngstown State U., three years; married, two children; Catholic.

Career Pres., V.P., United Rubber Workers Union, 1934; Pres. Dist. Council No. 1, United Rubber Workers Union, 1940–43, Staff Rep., Dist. Dir., 1942–50; Staff Rep., United Steelworkers of America, 1950–68; Ohio State Senate, 1951–70, Democratic Whip, 1959–69, Minority Leader, 1969–70.

Offices 1123 LHOB, 202-225-5261. Also 610 Stanbaugh Bldg., Youngstown 44501.

Committees

Interstate and Foreign Commerce (22nd); Sub. on Commerce and Finance.

Veterans' Affairs (12th); Subs. (1) Chm. Housing, (2) Hospitals.

Sel. Com. on Small Business (11th); Subs. (1) Environment Problems Affecting Small Business, (2) Small Business, Problems in Smaller Towns and Urban Areas.

Group Ratings, Key Votes: Newly elected.

Election Results

1970 general:	Charles J. Carney (D)	73,222	(58%)
	Margaret Dennison (R)	52,057	(42%)
1970 primary:	Charles J. Carney (D)	21,346	(30%)
	Richard P. McLaughlin (D)	15,262	(22%)
	Gary J. Thompson (D)	8,016	(11%)
	John M. Hudzik (D)	7,255	(10%)
	Joseph R. Lucas (D)	5,812	(8%)
	Thomas P. Gilmartin (D)	3,349	(5%)
	Violet Campana Whitman (D)	3,214	(5%)
	Frank R. Franko (D)	1,802	(3%)
	Eugene Lockett (D)	1,597	(2%)
	Frank X. Kryzan (D)	1,154	(2%)
	Romeo A. Latessa, Jr. (D)	442	(1%)
	John T. Dellick (D)	427	(1%)
	Paul J. Tobin (D)	400	(1%)

TWENTIETH DISTRICT Political Background

Ohio 20 comprises the west side of Cleveland and a couple of small suburbs. The Cuyahoga River, a waterway so polluted with industrial wastes that it recently caught fire, runs through the middle of this severely polarized city. To the east, most of the neighborhoods are all black; to the west, they are all white with no exceptions. Part of the 20th does extend into the destitute Hough ghetto in the East Side near the downtown area, but the heart of the district is the West Side. Here there are families of Germans, Czechs, Poles, Italians, and Hungarians living in a series of bedroom neighborhoods, which are here and there separated by industrial zones. Most of the people in the district depend on Cleveland's huge factories for their livelihoods.

The 20th is, of course, a traditionally Democratic district, but it has been unhappy with recent trends in the party. In 1967 and 1969, Cleveland's black mayor, Carl

Stokes, got very few votes here. The district went for Humphrey by a comfortable margin in 1968, but at the same time it gave George Wallace his second best percentage in an Ohio congressional district—16%.

For nearly 30 years, from 1942 to 1970, the 20th's congressman was Michael A. Feighan, a rather conservative Democrat. Feighan, as chairman of the House Judiciary Committee's Immigration and Nationality Subcommittee, blocked liberalization of the immigration laws for many years. By doing so, he insured that congressmen who wanted to help their constituents with immigration problems, and therefore often needed a private bill, were forced to come to him. Well along in years, Feighan began to encounter tough primary opposition in the late '60's, and was finally defeated in 1970 by James V. Stanton, the 38-year-old President of the Cleveland City Council. In 1968, Stanton was the Democratic nominee in the suburban 23rd district and nearly won there; he was so popular in the 20th that he beat Feighan by 11,000 votes, and then proceeded to win the general election with 81% of the vote, a percentage higher than Feighan ever enjoyed.

Stanton will stand with other liberal urban congressmen on most issues, though he will probably heed his constituency's conservatism on matters of law-and-order. Stanton is one of many Cleveland Democrats on bad political terms with Mayor Stokes and his brother, Congressman Louis Stokes of the 21st district (see Ohio 21). The West Side lost considerable population in the last ten years, but so long as a district is based there, Stanton is likely to remain in the House.

Census Data 1970 pop. 358,335; deviation from current state average, −19.1%; change 1960–70, −11.7%. Metro. 100.0%, 87.0% central city.

1970 Share of Federal Outlays $270,509,000 (average outlay per district, Ohio 20–23)

DOD	$46,674,000	HEW	$100,383,000
AEC	$272,000	HUD	$941,000
NASA	$23,042,000	OEO	$1,195,000
DOT	$10,694,000	DOA	$2,176,000
		Other	$85,132,000

Federal Military-Industrial Commitments (Ohio 20–23, greater Cleveland listing)

DOD Contractors General Motors (Cleveland), $54.985m: engineering services for Main Battle Tank and for M551 vehicle; production of 81-mm mortar shells. Clevite Corp. (Cleveland), $35.101m: production of Mark 48 torpedo. Weatherhead Co. (Cleveland), $6.864m: metal parts for 105-mm projectiles. Otis Elevator (Cleveland), $5.530m: forklift trucks.

NASA Installations Lewis Research Center (Cleveland).

Economic Base Nonelectrical machinery, esp. metalworking machinery and equipment; transportation equipment and aircraft and parts; fabricated metal products, bolts, nuts, screws, rivets, and washers; primary metal industries, esp. primary smelting and refining of nonferrous metals. Also, higher education (Cleveland State University); banking.

The Voters

Registration No district-wide registration.

Employment profile White collar, 32%. Blue collar, 68%.

Ethnic groups Black, 15%. Puerto Rico, 1%. Total foreign stock, 33%. Poland, 6%; Germany, 4%; Czech., Hungary, Italy, 3% each; Austria, UK, 2% each; Ireland, USSR, Canada, 1% each; others, 8%.

Presidential vote

1968	Humphrey (D)	66,428	(57%)
	Nixon (R)	31,726	(27%)
	Wallace (AIP)	18,122	(16%)

Representative

James Vincent Stanton (D) Elected 1970; b. Feb. 27, 1932, Cleveland; home, Cleveland; U. of Dayton, B.A., 1958; Cleveland-Marshall Col., J.D., 1961; USAF, Korean War; married, two children; Catholic.

Career Cleveland City Council, 1959–70; Pres., Cleveland City Council, 1964–70.

Offices 1107 LHOB, 202-225-5871. Also Rm. 203, Fed. Ct. House, Cleveland 44113, 216-522-4927.

Committees

Banking and Currency (4th); Subs. (1) Housing, (2) International Finance, (3) Small Business.

Sel. Com. on Small Business (4th); Subs. (1) Foundations: Their Impact on Small Business, (2) Small Business, Problems in Smaller Towns and Urban Areas, (3) Taxation, Oil Imports, and Marketing.

Group Ratings, Key Votes: Newly elected.

Election Results

1970 general:	James V. Stanton (D)	70,140	(81%)
	J. William Petro (R)	16,118	(19%)
1970 primary:	James V. Stanton (D)	25,383	(58%)
	Michael A. Feighan (D)	14,619	(33%)
	Warren Gilliam (D)	2,155	(5%)
	Anthony Pecyk (D)	1,158	(3%)
	John J. Lokos (D)	606	(1%)

TWENTY-FIRST DISTRICT Political Background

Ohio 21 comprises most of the East Side of Cleveland. This area was once made up of various Polish, Czech, and Italian neighborhoods, but it is today predominantly black. The central part of the district includes some of the poorest ghettos in the nation; the black neighborhoods to the north and south are more stable and middle-class. There are still a few ethnic enclaves left in the 21st, populated mostly by old people who cannot afford to move out of the city. The district also includes the Slavic working-class suburb of Garfield Heights, which, with one-tenth of the district's population, cast one-third of its Wallace votes in 1968.

Liberal Democrat Charles Vanik represented the 21st from 1954 to 1968. When the 1968 redistricting made it clear that the new 21st was to have a solid black majority, Vanik decided to run in the suburban 22nd, where he ousted a Republican incumbent. His successor in the 21st was Louis Stokes, brother of Cleveland Mayor Carl Stokes. Like his brother, Congressman Stokes grew up in poverty and was able to attend both college and law school only after service in the Army during World War II. His victory in the district was clearly a reflection of his brother's popularity on the East Side, but the Congressman in his own right has become one of the leading members of the Black Caucus in the House, and a leader of the 21st District Caucus in Cleveland. The District Caucus is the political arm of the Stokes brothers in Cleveland politics. In 1970, it supported a white Democrat in the primary for a county commissioner post against a black councilman who was a political enemy of the Mayor. The Caucus man was nominated, after which the Caucus decided to support Seth Taft, the Republican candidate; in 1967, Taft had nearly defeated Carl Stokes for mayor.

Seth Taft won the election with the help of some votes on the East Side, but the actions of the Caucus did not endear the Stokeses to other Democratic leaders in the city. They charged that the Taft endorsement hurt U.S. Senate candidate Howard Metzenbaum, who was running against Robert Taft Jr., Seth's cousin. Indeed, the figures show that Metzenbaum did not run as well in Cleveland as expected. Mayor Stokes' announced retirement will probably reduce the power of the Caucus and cool the feud among Cleveland Democrats. Meanwhile, there are rumors that the Democratic legislators and Gov. Gilligan will redesign the boundaries of the 21st in an effort to unseat Congressman Stokes. On paper, this is a simple task because Stokes has not run well in the "cosmo" (Eastern and Southern European ethnic) wards. If enough cosmo areas, either in the city or the suburbs, are placed in the 21st, Stokes could be defeated in a Democratic primary. But this is an unlikely possibility; few politicians want to be known these days for having deprived the black community of black representation.

Whatever his difficulties in the Byzantine world of Cleveland politics, Stokes has done well as a junior member of the House. In his first term he was assigned to the Education and Labor Committee, which handles most social legislation; he was also placed on Internal Security, which is often a dumping ground for liberal freshmen congressmen too eager for reform. In his second term, Stokes won a seat on the Appropriations Committee (giving up, of course, his other assignments) and became the first black congressman ever to serve on the legislative unit which oversees all government spending. The 1971 committee assignments, for the first time in memory, give domestic-issue liberals something approaching a majority on Appropriations—a fact which may be of more significance than some of the more publicized recent changes in the House.

Census Data 1970 pop. 354,891; deviation from current state average, −19.8%; change 1960–70, −12.6%. Metro. 100.0%, 87.4% central city.

1970 Share of Federal Outlays $270,509,000 (average outlay per district, Ohio 20–23)

DOD	$46,674,000	HEW	$100,383,000
AEC	$272,000	HUD	$941,000
NASA	$23,042,000	OEO	$1,195,000
DOT	$10,694,000	DOA	$2,176,000
		Other	$85,132,000

Federal Military-Industrial Commitments (See Ohio 20 for greater Cleveland listing.)

Economic Base Nonelectrical machinery, esp. metalworking machinery and equipment; transportation equipment, esp. motor vehicles and motor vehicle equipment, and aircraft and parts; fabricated metal products, esp. metal stampings and screw machine products, bolts, nuts, screws, rivets, and washers; primary metal industries, esp. primary smelting and refining of nonferrous metals.

The Voters

Registration No district-wide registration.

Employment profile White collar, 35%. Blue collar, 65%.

Ethnic groups Black, 61%. Total foreign stock, 23%. Czech., Poland, 4% each; Italy, 3%; Austria, Germany, 2% each; Hungary, Ireland, UK, USSR, Canada, 1% each; others, 3%.

Presidential vote

1968	Humphrey (D)	103,450	(80%)
	Nixon (R)	15,112	(12%)
	Wallace (AIP)	11,217	(9%)

Representative

Louis Stokes (D) Elected 1968; b. Feb. 23, 1925, Cleveland; home, Cleveland; Western Reserve U., 1946–48; Cleveland-Marshall Law School, J.D., 1953; Army, WWII; married, four children; Methodist.

Career Practicing atty., 1954–68.

Offices 315 CHOB, 202-225-7032. Also New Fed. Bldg., 1240 East 9th St., Cleveland 44199, 216-522-4900.

Committees

Appropriations (31st); Subs. (1) District of Columbia, (2) Treasury, Post Office, and General Government.

Group Ratings

	ADA	COPE	NREP	NFU	LCV	CFA	NAB	NSI	ACA
1970	96	100	100	83	100	100	0	0	18
1969	100	—	—	79	—	—	—	—	27

Key Votes

(1) ABM	AGN	(6) 18-Yr-Vote	FOR	(11) Clean Water $	FOR
(2) SST	AGN	(7) Farm Sub Lmt	FOR	(12) Mig Wrkrs Comp	FOR
(3) Phil Pln	FOR	(8) Coop-Church	FOR	(13) Jets to Chiang	AGN
(4) No-Knock	AGN	(9) Family Asst	FOR	(14) State OEO Veto	AGN
(5) Cmutr Tax	FOR	(10) Work Stamps	AGN	(15) Park Logging	AGN

Election Results

1970 general:	Louis Stokes (D)	74,340	(78%)
	Bill Mack (R)	21,440	(22%)
1970 primary:	Louis Stokes (D), unopposed		
1968 general:	Louis Stokes (D)	85,509	(75%)
	Charles P. Lucas (R)	28,931	(25%)

TWENTY-SECOND DISTRICT Political Background

Ohio 22 comprises the eastern suburbs of Cleveland and a small portion of the city itself. The city portion includes the "cosmo" (Eastern and Southern European), and black neighborhoods adjacent to suburban Shaker Heights, and the museum complex next to suburban Cleveland Heights. Some of the suburbs here are among Cleveland's most fashionable, particularly WASP Gates Mills and Pepper Pike. Shaker Heights is also a WASP suburb, but one with a large Jewish population and an increasing number of black residents; it has one of the highest per capita income levels in the nation. Because of the solidly all-white character of Cleveland's West Side (see Ohio 20), middle-class blacks have been moving east into suburbs like Shaker Heights and East Cleveland, which now has a black majority. Euclid, farther north on Lake Erie, has a substantial blue-collar population; there is also a large Italian-American community in the district, in some of the towns along Mayfield Road.

On balance, the 22nd is Democratic; it delivered majorities on the order of 10% to Senate candidates Stephen Young in 1964, John Gilligan in 1968, and Howard Metzenbaum, a resident of Shaker Heights, in 1970. But for 30 years, the district always went Republican in congressional elections, thanks to the vote-getting prowess of Mrs. Frances P. Bolton. Mrs. Bolton, a member of a socially prominent Cleveland family, became ranking member of the House Foreign Affairs Committee. But in 1968, her time was up; Congressman Charles Vanik moved from the 21st district, which had acquired a clear black majority in the 1968 redistricting, to the 22nd. Although Vanik had been in the House since 1954, he was almost 30 years younger than Mrs. Bolton, and his longtime support of Israel gave him a big edge in the Jewish suburbs.

Vanik had been one of the leading antiwar liberals in the House; he is also the 8th ranking Democrat on the Ways and Means Committee. Once over the 1968 hurdle, he won 72% of the vote in 1970, and he is now as entrenched in the 22nd as he used to be in the 21st. In his old district he won 90% of the vote in 1964—the best percentage of any opposed Democrat in the country that year. Redistricters will likely add the eastern part of suburban Lake County, now in the 11th district, to the 22nd; since this area is normally Democratic, the addition, if anything, should help Vanik in 1972.

Census Data 1970 pop. 440,536; deviation from current state average, —0.5%; change 1960–70, +9.5%. Metro. 100.0%, 22.4% central city.

1970 Share of Federal Outlays $270,509,000 (average outlay per district, Ohio 20–23)

DOD	$46,674,000	HEW	$100,383,000
AEC	$272,000	HUD	$941,000
NASA	$23,042,000	OEO	$1,195,000
DOT	$10,694,000	DOA	$2,176,000
		Other	$85,132,000

Federal Military-Industrial Commitments (See Ohio 20 for greater Cleveland listing.)

Economic Base Nonelectrical machinery, esp. metalworking machinery and equipment; transportation equipment, esp. motor vehicles and motor vehicle equipment and aircraft and parts; fabricated metal products, esp. metal stampings and screw machine products, bolts, nuts, screws, rivets, and washers; primary metal industries, esp. primary smelting and refining of nonferrous metals. Also, extensive commuting to Ohio 20 (Cleveland).

The Voters

Registration No district-wide registration.

Employment profile White collar, 56%. Blue collar, 44%.

Ethnic groups Black, 12%. Total foreign stock, 39%. Italy, 6%; Germany, Hungary, USSR, 4% each; Czech., Poland, UK, 3% each; Austria, Canada, 2% each; Ireland, Sweden, 1% each; others, 7%.

Presidential vote

1968	Humphrey (D)	98,780	(51%)
	Nixon (R)	79,014	(41%)
	Wallace (AIP)	16,817	(9%)

Representative

Charles A. Vanik (D) Elected 1954; b. April 7, 1913, Cleveland; home, Cleveland; Western Reserve U., B.A., 1933, LL.B., 1936; USNR, WWII; married, two children; Catholic.

Career Practicing atty., 1936– ; Cleveland City Council, 1938–39; Ohio Senate, 1940–41; Cleveland Bd. of Ed., 1941–42; Assoc. Judge, Cleveland Municipal Ct., 1947–54.

Offices 2463 RHOB, 202-225-6331. Also 107 Old Fed. Bldg., Cleveland 44114, 216-522-4253.

Committees

Ways and Means (8th).

Group Ratings

	ADA	COPE	NREP	NFU	LCV	CFA	NAB	NSI	ACA
1970	96	100	93	92	90	85	0	10	25
1969	87	—	—	72	—	—	—	—	25
1968	58	100	—	94	—	—	17	—	20

Key Votes

(1) ABM	AGN	(6) 18-Yr-Vote	FOR	(11) Clean Water $	FOR
(2) SST	AGN	(7) Farm Sub Lmt	FOR	(12) Mig Wrkrs Comp	FOR
(3) Phil Pln	FOR	(8) Coop-Church	FOR	(13) Jets to Chiang	AGN
(4) No-Knock	FOR	(9) Family Asst	FOR	(14) State OEO Veto	AGN
(5) Cmutr Tax	FOR	(10) Work Stamps	AGN	(15) Park Logging	AGN

Election Results

1970 general:	Charles A. Vanik (D)	114,790	(72%)
	Adrian Fink (R)	45,657	(28%)
1970 primary:	Charles A. Vanik (D)	47,280	(91%)
	Donald H. Tarantino (D)	4,457	(9%)
1968 general:	Charles A. Vanik (D)	102,656	(55%)
	Frances P. Bolton (R)	84,975	(45%)

TWENTY-THIRD DISTRICT Political Background

Ohio 23 is a half-circle of suburbs surrounding Cleveland and a small section of the West Side of the city itself. The western portion of the district is heavily Republican—middle- to high-income suburbs like Lakewood, Rocky River, and Bay Village along Lake Erie. The eastern portion, consisting of towns like Maple Heights, settled by Slavic residents who once lived in the West Side, leans Democratic. The largest city in the district is Parma (pop. 100,000), which lies in the middle of the 23rd and is a middle-income shopping center suburb filled with cosmo ex-residents of the West Side (see Ohio 22). This city is the Democratic stronghold of the district. The combination of Republican west and Democratic east and center makes the 23rd one of Ohio's most marginal districts in statewide elections.

In 1968, Cleveland City Council president, James V. Stanton, held the district's longtime incumbent Republican, William Minshall, down to 52%. Other than that, the 23rd has seldom been marginal in congressional races. In 1970, Stanton decided to run from the 20th district (Cleveland's West Side) and left Minshall with a somewhat easier race. The 1970 Democratic candidate here was Ronald Mottl of Parma. Mottl, a dovish, crew-cut state senator of Czech descent, ran a vigorous campaign, but he was handicapped because he had recently divorced his wife and married an 18-year-old runner-up in a local beauty contest. That pretty much determined the outcome of the election in which Minshall won a solid 60% of the votes; but it should be noted that the percentage was considerably below his winning majorities in 1966 and 1964 when Parma was not in the district.

Minshall is a conservative Republican who is the 5th ranking minority member on the powerful House Appropriations Committee. He is the ranking minority member of Appropriations' Defense Subcommittee, which, of course, has jurisdiction over the lion's share of the federal budget. Generally, Minshall has supported military budget requests and the Nixon Administration's policies on Vietnam and defense spending.

Recent election returns suggest that Minshall's positions on these issues are not as popular in the 23rd as they once were. Minshall no doubt has watched the redistricting process closely. His district will probably lose its portion of Cleveland and pick up four Republican cities in southern Cuyahoga County, which will strengthen the Congressman. But Minshall should be most concerned about what happens to the eastern portion of the district. If Garfield Heights, for example, should be added to the 23rd, the Democratic votes there could swing the district in a close election; on the other hand, the loss of Democratic suburbs like Maple Heights and Bedford will make Minshall's reelection prospects much better (see maps in appendix).

Census Data 1970 pop. 518,949; deviation from current state average, +17.2%; change 1960–70, +28.2%. Metro. 100.0%, 5.8% central city.

1970 Share of Federal Outlays $270,509,000 (average outlay per district, Ohio 20–23)

DOD	$46,674,000	HEW	$100,383,000
AEC	$272,000	HUD	$941,000
NASA	$23,042,000	OEO	$1,195,000
DOT	$10,694,000	DOA	$2,176,000
		Other	$85,132,000

Federal Military-Industrial Commitments (See Ohio 20 for greater Cleveland listing.)

Economic Base Nonelectrical machinery, esp. metalworking machinery and equipment; transportation equipment, esp. motor vehicles and motor vehicle equipment and aircraft and parts; fabricated metal products, esp. metal stampings and screw machine products, bolts, nuts, screws, rivets, and washers; primary metal industries, esp. primary smelting and refining of nonferrous metals. Also, extensive commuting to Ohio 20 (Cleveland).

The Voters

Registration No district-wide registration.

Employment profile White collar, 57%. Blue collar, 43%.

Ethnic groups Black, 1%. Total foreign stock, 38%. Czech., 7%; Germany, 6%; Poland, 5%; Italy, 4%; Hungary, UK, 3% each; Austria, Ireland, Canada, 2% each; USSR, 1%; others, 4%.

Presidential vote

1968	Humphrey (D)	88,303	(41%)
	Nixon (R)	103,569	(48%)
	Wallace (AIP)	22,674	(11%)

Representative

William E. Minshall (R) Elected 1954; b. Oct. 24, 1911, East Cleveland; home, Lakewood; U. of Va., 1932–34; Cleveland Law School, LL.B., 1940; Army, WWII; Lt. Col. USAR (Ret.); married, three children; Protestant.

Career Ohio House of Reps., 1939–40; Practicing atty., 1940– ; Gen. Counsel, Maritime Admin., 1953–54.

Offices 2243 RHOB, 202-225-5731. Also 2951 New Fed. Office Bldg., 1240 E. 9th St., Cleveland 44199, 216-522-4382.

Committees

Appropriations (5th); Subs. (1) Defense, (2) Transportation.

Group Ratings

	ADA	COPE	NREP	NFU	LCV	CFA	NAB	NSI	ACA
1970	12	27	18	50	55	40	75	100	71
1969	7	—	—	28	—	—	—	—	73
1968	3	15	—	46	—	—	—	—	67

Key Votes

(1) ABM	FOR	(6) 18-Yr-Vote	FOR	(11) Clean Water $	FOR
(2) SST	AGN	(7) Farm Sub Lmt	AGN	(12) Mig Wrkrs Comp	AGN
(3) Phil Pln	AGN	(8) Coop-Church	AGN	(13) Jets to Chiang	FOR
(4) No-Knock	ABS	(9) Family Asst	AGN	(14) State OEO Veto	ABS
(5) Cmutr Tax	AGN	(10) Work Stamps	ABS	(15) Park Logging	AGN

Election Results

1970 general:	William E. Minshall (R)	111,218	(60%)
	Ronald M. Mottl (D)	73,765	(40%)
1970 primary:	William E. Minshall (R), unopposed		
1968 general:	William E. Minshall (R)	106,852	(52%)
	James V. Stanton (D)	98,825	(48%)

TWENTY-FOURTH DISTRICT Political Background

Ohio 24 is a creation of the 1964 and 1968 redistricting plans; a group of counties and parts of counties sandwiched between Cincinnati and Dayton. The district includes the heavily Republican portions of Montgomery County (Dayton) and Hamilton County (Cincinnati), as well as arch-conservative Butler, Warren, and Clinton counties. Butler has about a quarter of the 24th's population, much of it in the conservative Republican cities of Hamilton (pop. 67,000) and Middletown (pop. 48,000). On paper, the district is heavily Republican, but the conservative politics of many of its residents derives from the Southern origins of the early settlers here. In 1968, the 24th cast Ohio's largest vote for George Wallace (20%). Outside of Oklahoma, this was his best showing in a state which was never a part of the old Confederacy.

For the first four years of existence, the 24th was represented by Donald E. (Buz) Lukens, a young (35 when first elected) arch-conservative. He was and remains today something of a maverick in Ohio's staid conservative Republican councils. Lukens decided to run for governor in 1970, and ran a fairly strong second to the Republican establishment's choice, Auditor Roger Cloud. His successor in the House, Republican state Sen. Walter Powell, is a conservative who won by a surprisingly small margin (52–45–3) over a rather conservative Democrat and an American Independent party candidate.

This left Powell's state Senate seat up for grabs, and it was won by none other than ex-Congressman Lukens, who will likely cause trouble for the Republican leadership in the legislature. The switch with Powell doubtless upsets Lukens; but most Ohio observers believe that he has his eye on a statewide office and now aims at maximum statewide publicity.

Meanwhile, Ohio must redistrict its congressional seats, and, because of the 1970 census, eliminate one district. The most likely for elimination is the 4th, whose congressman, veteran William McCulloch, will retire in 1972. This probably means that what is now the 24th will absorb several counties of the adjacent 4th. The move may affect the outcome of a Republican primary, but will not endanger Republican chances in the general election.

Census Data 1970 pop. 496,718; deviation from current state average, +12.2%; change 1960–70, +21.6%. Metro. 93.7%, 23.5% central city.

1970 Share of Federal Outlays $128,117,000

DOD	$17,437,000	HEW	$59,434,000
AEC	$000	HUD	$298,000
NASA	$000	OEO	$220,000
DOT	$119,000	DOA	$5,716,000
		Other	$44,893,000

Federal Military-Industrial Commitments

DOD Installations Clinton County AFB (Wilmington).

Economic Base Nonelectrical machinery; fabricated metal products; primary metal industries. Also, higher education (Miami University).

The Voters

Registration No district-wide registration.

Employment profile White collar, 35%. Blue collar, 65%.

Ethnic groups Black, 4%. Total foreign stock, 5%. Germany, 2%; UK, 1%; others, 1%.

Presidential vote

1968	Humphrey (D)	52,006	(32%)
	Nixon (R)	78,563	(48%)
	Wallace (AIP)	32,059	(20%)

Representative

Walter E. Powell (R) Elected 1970; b. April 25, 1931, Hamilton; home, Fairfield; Heidelberg Col., B.A., 1953; Miami U. (Ohio), M.Ed., 1961; married, two children; Presbyterian.

Career Teacher, Fairfield Jr. High School; Principal, Hopewell Elementary and Fairfield West Elementary; Fairfield City Clerk, 1956; Fairfield Councilman, 1957; Ohio Legislature, 1960–66; Ohio Senate, 1966–70.

Offices 1532 LHOB, 202-225-6205.

Committees

Government Operations (15th).

Post Office and Civil Service (10th); Subs. (1) Employee Benefits, (2) Retirement, Insurance, and Health Benefits.

Group Ratings, Key Votes: Newly elected.

Election Results

1970 general:	Walter E. Powell (R)	63,344	(52%)
	James D. Ruppert (D)	55,455	(45%)
	Joseph F. Payton (AIP)	4,179	(3%)
1970 primary:	Walter E. Powell (R)	24,864	(54%)
	Fred E. Jones (R)	21,380	(46%)

OKLAHOMA

OKLAHOMA Political Background

Oklahoma has a rather peculiar history, which was once distorted in a musical comedy produced for the Broadway stage. Throughout most of the nineteenth century, most of the area which is now Oklahoma was Indian reservations; the Indians had been driven off their ancestral lands in the South and Midwest, and forcibly resettled here. Then in 1889, the federal government decided to open up the Indian Territory, as it was then called, to white settlement. On the morning of the great land rush, thousands of would-be homesteaders, "boomer Sooners," drove their wagons across the territorial line in a moment that has been recaptured for us in numerous motion pictures.

But for many of the whites, the promise of Oklahoma turned out as sour as it was for the Indians. The depression and drought of the '30's drove thousands of Okies, as they were called, out to greener fields in California (see California 16). Currently, the population of Oklahoma is some two-and-a-half million; at statehood, the figure was not much lower at one-and-a-half million. Moreover, 42 of the state's 77 counties now have fewer people than in 1907. Almost all of Oklahoma's recent growth has occurred in the counties that contain its two large cities, Oklahoma City and Tulsa.

The state's changing demography has been reflected in recent election returns. Oklahoma has been, by tradition, a Democratic state, since most of it was settled by migrants from the South. Only the northcentral and northwest parts of the state, near the Kansas border, have consistently gone Republican; these areas were first occupied by Yankees who moved down from Kansas and by Republican Ozark people. But the fast-growing, oil-rich cities of Oklahoma City and especially Tulsa, are now strongholds of the same kind of hard-line Republican conservatism that dominates Dallas and other Texas metropolises. Taken together, the two cities cast a majority of their votes for Barry Goldwater in 1964, and, although they still contain only 35% of the voters of the state, the two cities were responsible for most of Oklahoma's statewide margins for Richard Nixon in 1960 and 1968.

The state's big cities have also provided the electoral basis for the Republican surge in recent state elections. In 1962, Oklahoma elected its first Republican governor; in that year, and again in 1966, the Republican candidates for the office—Henry Bellmon and Dewey Bartlett—won by fairly comfortable margins. In 1970, Democrat David Hall defeated Bartlett by a scant 3,000 votes; most of Hall's gains were made in the rural areas, where the farmers' chronic dissatisfaction with the farm programs of the incumbent national Administration worked against the Republicans.

Bellmon scored the most spectacular recent Republican victory in 1968, when he unseated three-term Democratic Sen. Mike Monroney. Monroney was elected to the House in 1938 and had served there before going to the Senate in 1950. During his 30 years in Washington, Monroney was an effective politician; he was responsible, for example, for the Federal Aviation Administration's huge Aeronautical Center in Oklahoma City. But Monroney somehow lost touch with the Oklahoma voters, and Bellmon swept the cities, and also succeeded in carrying the rural areas by a small margin. In the Senate, Bellmon, who has been one of Nixon's most fervent supporters, holds low-seniority seats on the Agriculture, the Interior and Insular Affairs, and the Post Office and Civil Service committees. His chances for reelection in 1974 are excellent.

From 1948 until his death in 1963, the state's other Senate seat belonged to Robert S. Kerr, who was for many years one of Washington's most powerful politicians. As Chairman of the Senate committee on the space program, Kerr made sure that valuable NASA contracts went to Oklahoma firms. As chairman of the Senate Finance Committee, he blocked passage of the Medicare program and jealously guarded the interests of the oil industry, including his own Kerr-McGee company, which is a major producer of oil and natural gas. As Kerr himself once put it, "I represent myself first, the state of Oklahoma second, and the people of the United States third—and don't you forget it." He was already a wealthy man when he entered the Senate; by the time he died, the Senator was worth something on the order of 40 million dollars.

After Kerr died, Governor J. Howard Edmondson, in the last days of his administration, had himself appointed to the seat. This move, of course, did not sit well among the voters, and they got rid of Edmondson the first chance they got, which was in the 1964 Democratic primary. The winner of that primary was a little-known state senator, Fred Harris. But he was not expected to have much of a chance against the Republican nominee, Bud Wilkinson, who had just resigned as football coach at the University of Oklahoma. Wilkinson produced some powerful teams at the university, and as a result, was well-known and well-liked throughout the state. But Harris had the support of the Kerr family and had another advantage which might have been decisive in the race; his wife LaDonna is a Comanche Indian, and Oklahoma has one of the largest Indian populations in the nation. If one compares a map showing the counties carried by Monroney in 1968, and those carried by Harris in 1964, it will show that virtually all the counties that Monroney lost and Harris won lie in the northeast corner of the state. This is where Oklahoma's largest Indian reservations were located, and where most of the Indians of the state still live. More generally, Harris did well enough in rural Oklahoma—55% outside Oklahoma and Tulsa counties—to overcome Wilkinson's lead in the cities.

In the Senate, Harris has compiled a surprisingly liberal voting record—a very different sort of record than the one compiled by his predecessor, Robert Kerr. Harris is, of course, one of the leading champions of Indian rights in Washington. The Senator also served on the Kerner Commission on Civil Disorders, and emphatically endorsed its conclusions. In 1968, Humphrey came close to naming the Oklahoma Senator his running-mate; that didn't pan out, but he did become chairman of the Democratic National Committee.

But as Harris' standing with national liberals went up, his popularity with Oklahoma voters declined. In 1968, only 32% of the votes in the state went to Humphrey. As the 1972 Senate race approached, the increasingly conservative Democratic congressman from the 2nd district, Ed Edmondson, announced that he might well challenge Harris. This represents something of a switch. In 1964, it was Harris who was the conservative and the congressman's brother, Howard Edmondson, who was the liberal; at least this is what the national press thought. In any case, Oklahoma polls showed that Senator Harris was in real trouble, and local politicians predicted that Edmondson would win easily.

Then in July of 1971, Harris suddenly decided to withdraw from the Senate race and run for President—the theory being, perhaps, that it is better to lose a presidential bid than lose a Senate seat. He announced a "new populism" based on economic issues; he wants to build, he says, a coalition of poor whites, blacks, Spanish-speaking people, and Indians. With new presidential primaries scheduled for states like Florida and Tennessee, Harris has a fair chance at amassing respectable delegate support. And he would be a logical vice-presidential nominee on a Muskie ticket.

Meanwhile, Edmondson can expect some Republican opposition, perhaps from ex-Gov. Dewey Bartlett. But most likely, the congressman's conservative stance will win over enough marginal votes for a victory, perhaps a convincing one, in the Senate race.

Electoral Votes 8

Census Data 1970 pop. 2,559,253; 1.24% of U.S. total, 28th largest; change 1960–70, +9.9%. Metro. 50.0%, 29.7% central city. 1970 per capita income, $3,269; 36th highest. 25th in number of poor.

1970 Share of Federal Tax Burden $1,931,890,000; 0.99% of U.S. total, 27th largest.

1970 Share of Federal Outlays $2,561,407,684; 1.36% of U.S. total, 25th largest. Per Capita federal spending, $1,001.

DOD	$852,211,000	21st (1.49%)	HEW	$672,182,867	27th (1.29%)
AEC	$134,988	43rd (0.02%)	HUD	$25,744,708	25th (1.32%)
NASA	$1,160,792	36th (0.32%)	OEO	$11,471,005	25th (1.51%)
DOT	$138,958,030	21st (1.95%)	DOA	$331,517,844	14th (2.58%)
DOC	$11,558,173	20th (1.00%)	POD	$85,882,100	26th (1.18%)
DOI	$49,420,670	14th (2.14%)	VA	$149,307,486	24th (2.02%)
DOJ	$7,274,532	25th (1.27%)	CSC	$40,506,951	19th (1.01%)
			Other	$184,076,538	

Economic Base Livestock and cash grain; crude petroleum and natural gas; nonelectrical machinery and equipment, esp. farm machinery and equipment; transportation equipment, esp. aircraft and parts; food and kindred products; fabricated metal products, esp. fabricated structural metal products; electrical machinery, equipment, and supplies, esp. communication equipment; apparel and other finished products made from fabrics and similar materials, esp. men's, youths', and boys' furnishings, work clothing, and allied garments; stone, clay, glass, and concrete products; printing, publishing, and allied industries, esp. newspapers.

Political Line-up Governor, David Hall (D); seat up, 1974. Senators, Fred R. Harris (D) and Henry Bellmon (R). Representatives, 6 (4 D and 2 R). State Senate (39 D and 9 R); State House (78 D and 21 R).

The Voters

Registration 1,205,202 total. 924,493 D (77%); 268,404 R (22%); 12,305 other (1%).

Employment profile White collar, 42%. Blue collar, 58%.

Ethnic groups Black, 7%. American Indian, 4%. Total foreign stock, 4%. Germany, 1%; all others less than 0.5%.

Presidential Vote

1968	Humphrey (D)	301,658	(32%)
	Nixon (R)	449,697	(48%)
	Wallace (AIP)	191,731	(20%)
1964	Johnson (D)	519,834	(56%)
	Goldwater (R)	412,655	(44%)
1960	Kennedy (D)	370,111	(41%)
	Nixon (R)	533,039	(59%)

Senator

Fred R. Harris (D) Elected Nov. 4, 1964, seat up 1972; b. Nov. 13, 1930, Walters; home, Lawton; U. of Okla., B.A., 1952, LL.B., 1954; married, three children; Baptist.

Career Practicing atty., 1954–64; Okla. State Senate, 1956–64; Chm., Dem. Natl. Com., 1968–69.

Offices 254 OSOB, 202-225-4721. Also Rm. 3-409 New Fed. Bldg., Tulsa 74103, 918-584-7151, ext. 7645, and Rm. 715, Old Post Office Bldg., Oklahoma City 73102, 405-231-4631.

Committees

Finance (7th).

Government Operations (6th); Subs. (1) Executive Reorganization, (2) National Security and Internal Operations.

Sel. Com. on Small Business (7th); Subs. (1) Chm., Retailing, Distribution, and Marketing, (2) Government Regulation, (3) Science and Technology.

Group Ratings

	ADA	COPE	NREP	NFU	LCV	NAB	NSI	ACA
1970	94	100	100	100	64	22	11	0
1969	83	—	—	81	—	—	—	8
1968	57	89	—	90	—	0	—	0

Key Votes

(1) ABM	AGN	(8) Phil Pln	FOR	(15) Coop-Church	FOR
(2) SST	AGN	(9) Vol Army	AGN	(16) Cut Oil Dpltn	AGN
(3) Busing	FOR	(10) Prison $	FOR	(17) Consumer Prot	FOR
(4) Tob Sub	ABS	(11) Cut Mil $	FOR	(18) Farm Sub Limit	ABS
(5) Carswell	AGN	(12) Defoliatn	AGN	(19) Comp Bid Sales	AGN
(6) No-Knock	AGN	(13) 18-Yr-Vote	FOR	(20) Pre-Prod Tests	FOR
(7) Seniorty	FOR	(14) Pentgn PR	AGN	(21) Cut Marjna Pen	FOR

Election Results

1966 general:	Fred R. Harris (D)	343,157	(54%)
	Pat J. Patterson (R)	295,585	(46%)
1966 primary:	Fred R. Harris (D)	359,747	(84%)
	Willard R. Owens (D)	41,580	(10%)
	Billy E. Brown (D)	29,184	(7%)
1964 special:	Fred R. Harris (D)	466,782	(51%)
	Bud Wilkinson (R)	445,392	(49%)

Senator

Henry L. Bellmon (R) Elected 1968, seat up 1974; b. Sept. 3, 1921, Tonakawa; home, Billings; Okla. State U., B.S., 1942; USMC, WWII; married, three children; Presbyterian.

Career Farming, wheat and cattle, 1946– ; Okla. House of Reps., 1946–48; Okla. Repub. Chm., 1960–62; First Repub. Governor of Okla., 1962–66; Natl. Chm., Nixon for Pres. Com., 1968.

Offices 4202 NSOB, 202-225-5754. Also 914 Fed. Bldg., Oklahoma City 73102, 405-231-4941, and 107 Wright Bldg., 113 W. Third St., Tulsa 74103, 918-584-7151.

Committees

Agriculture and Forestry (6th); Subs. (1) Agricultural Exports, (2) Agricultural Production, Marketing, and Stabilization of Prices, (3) Environment, Soil Conservation, Forestry, (4) Rural Development.

Interior and Insular Affairs (7th); Subs. (1) Indian Affairs, (2) Minerals, Materials, and Fuels, (3) Parks and Recreation, (4) Public Lands.

Post Office and Civil Service (4th); Sub. on Postal Operations.

Sel. Com. on Nutrition and Human Needs (2nd).

Group Ratings

	ADA	COPE	NREP	NFU	LCV	NAB	NSI	ACA
1970	19	13	9	40	0	83	100	85
1969	17	—	—	36	—	—	—	75

Key Votes

(1) ABM	FOR	(8) Phil Pln	FOR	(15) Coop-Church	AGN
(2) SST	FOR	(9) Vol Army	AGN	(16) Cut Oil Dpltn	AGN
(3) Busing	FOR	(10) Prison $	AGN	(17) Consumer Prot	AGN
(4) Tob Sub	FOR	(11) Cut Mil $	AGN	(18) Farm Sub Limit	AGN
(5) Carswell	FOR	(12) Defoliatn	FOR	(19) Comp Bid Sales	AGN
(6) No-Knock	FOR	(13) 18-Yr-Vote	FOR	(20) Pre-Prod Tests	ABS
(7) Seniorty	ABS	(14) Pentgn PR	FOR	(21) Cut Marjna Pen	AGN

Election Results

1968 general:	Henry Bellmon (R)	470,120	(52%)
	A. S. Mike Monroney (D)	419,658	(46%)
	George Washington (AIP)	19,341	(2%)
1968 primary:	Henry Bellmon (R), unopposed		

FIRST DISTRICT Political Background

Oklahoma 1 comprises Tulsa and Creek counties, which may be regarded as the city of Tulsa and its suburbs. The city's population was up from 261,000 in 1960, to 331,000 in 1970. It is one of those booming oil cities of the Southwest whose conservative politics is legendary. The new-rich, some observers have noted, are most resentful towards politicians whose programs are presumably designed to take from the rich and give to the poor. Tulsa is full of the new-rich. And they, therefore, seem to prefer a politics that is conservative; in 1968, for example, Nixon ran better in Tulsa than in any other part of Oklahoma. The Republican presidential nominee took 56% of the votes here, with 20% going to Wallace. This left a meager 24% for Humphrey, which is a good index of the city's feeling toward "liberals." In some local elections, however, Tulsa residents vote Democratic; many of them are migrants from the mountains and countryside of the South, and still think of themselves as Democrats. But in any election in which national issues are at stake, they plunk for the more conservative candidate.

Page Belcher, a conservative Republican, has been Tulsa's congressman since 1950. He is currently the ranking minority member of the House Agriculture Committee, which seems like a rather odd committee for an urban congressman. But Belcher chose the assignment when his district included all of rural northwest Oklahoma as well as Tulsa. Belcher was given the current 1st in the 1967 redistricting.

Belcher has not had a close reelection fight since 1958, when the farm revolt against the policies of the Republican secretary of Agriculture, Ezra Taft Benson, was at its height. In the election of that year, the Tulsa vote pulled Belcher through. Now that the district is basically urban, he is impervious to any rebellion among the farmers. But the 1970 election results show that he does not yet occupy a safe seat. His opponent in 1970 was 30-year-old James C. Jones, a former appointments secretary to President Johnson. Jones held the Congressman's vote down to 56%. That figure, and Belcher's advancing age (71 in 1970), suggest that the congressman may well have some trouble in the not so distant future. If the incumbent is not running in the 1st, a tough fight could easily develop in the district, though the form sheet would give the edge to the Republican candidate.

Redistricting is unlikely to affect the political character of the 1st. Creek County contains about 10% of the district's population and usually goes Democratic in congressional elections. Since it is now a little too large to remain in the district, the legislature will probably put Creek into the 2nd, and add to the 1st a somewhat smaller county adjacent to Tulsa. But if the Democratic governor and legislature wanted to get partisan about it, they could split Tulsa between two northeast Oklahoma districts. Belcher would then have a difficult time winning in either. Such a move, though, would endanger Democratic chances in the 2nd; besides, such tampering with the status quo is very rare.

Census Data 1970 pop. 446,241; deviation from current state average, +4.6%; change 1960–70, +15.4%. Metro. 100.0%, 73.2% central city.

1970 Share of Federal Outlays $288,279,890

DOD	$73,729,000	HEW	$93,225,280
AEC	$000	HUD	$6,268,585
NASA	$174,440	OEO	$2,692,607
DOT	$17,851,988	DOA	$14,083,282
		Other	$80,254,708

Federal Military-Industrial Commitments

DOD Contractors McDonnell Douglas (Tulsa), $28.014m: maintenance of Air Force Plant Number 3. North American Rockwell (Tulsa), $6.276m: inspection and repair of Hound Dog missile system on B-52 aircraft.

Economic Base Aircraft and parts, and other transportation equipment; fabricated metal products, esp. fabricated structural metal products; nonelectrical machinery, esp. construction, mining, and material handling machinery and equipment; crude petroleum and natural gas. Also, banking.

The Voters

Registration 202,690 total. 128,252 D (63%); 70,898 R (35%); 3,540 other (2%).

Employment profile White collar, 47%. Blue collar, 53%.

Ethnic groups Black, 9%. American Indians, 3%. Total foreign stock, 5%. Germany, UK, 1% each; others, 1%.

Presidential vote

1968	Humphrey (D)	37,899	(24%)
	Nixon (R)	88,410	(56%)
	Wallace (AIP)	32,356	(20%)

Representative

Page Belcher (R) Elected 1950; b. April 21, 1899, Jefferson; home, Tulsa; Friends U., U. of Okla.; married, two children; Methodist.

Career Court Clerk, Garfield County, 1934–38; practicing atty., 1935–50; Municipal Judge, 1938; Secy. to Rep. Ross Rizley, 1941.

Offices 2462 RHOB, 202-225-2211. Also 4536 Fed. Bldg., Tulsa 74103, 918-584-3614.

Committees

Agriculture (Ranking Mbr.).

Group Ratings

	ADA	COPE	NREP	NFU	LCV	CFA	NAB	NSI	ACA
1970	8	9	0	36	0	39	100	100	79
1969	0	—	—	33	—	—	—	—	60
1968	0	0	—	25	—	—	100	—	91

Key Votes

(1) ABM	FOR	(6) 18-Yr-Vote	AGN	(11) Clean Water $	AGN
(2) SST	FOR	(7) Farm Sub Lmt	AGN	(12) Mig Wrkrs Comp	AGN
(3) Phil Pln	FOR	(8) Coop-Church	AGN	(13) Jets to Chiang	ABS
(4) No-Knock	FOR	(9) Family Asst	AGN	(14) State OEO Veto	FOR
(5) Cmutr Tax	AGN	(10) Work Stamps	FOR	(15) Park Logging	FOR

Election Results

1970 general:	Page Belcher (R)	67,386	(56%)
	James R. Jones (D)	53,598	(44%)
1970 primary:	Page Belcher (R), unopposed		
1968 general:	Page Belcher (R)	92,513	(59%)
	John B. Jarboe (D)	63,451	(41%)

SECOND DISTRICT Political Background

Oklahoma 2 comprises the northeast corner of the state, except for the Tulsa area, which lies in the 1st district. This is the place where most of Oklahoma's Indians, removed from their ancestral lands in the Midwest and South, were resettled. The various tribes gave their names to some of the counties here: Cherokee, Delaware, Ottawa, Osage, among others. Beginning in 1889 (see state write-up), white settlers from the Democratic Deep South and the Republican Ozarks took up residence in this part of Oklahoma. The 2nd district, therefore, is something of a political borderland between Democratic and Republican territory. And because the 2nd has more Indians than any other district in the state, there is an Indian vote here as well.

Since 1952, the congressman from the 2nd has been Ed Edmondson, brother of ex-Gov. and Sen. J. Howard Edmondson. Congressman Edmondson has valuable seniority in the House. He is the number-three Democrat on the Interior and Insular Affairs Committee, and because both of the men who outrank him are at least 20 years older, Edmondson has a fair chance of becoming chairman of the committee. He is currently chairman of its Mines and Mining Subcommittee (although there are few mines in his district), and number two on the Indian Affairs Subcommittee. Edmondson also has a good deal of seniority on the Public Works Committee. His seat here is probably related to the presence of the Tulsa-Arkansas-Verdigris Navigation System in the 2nd district. The waterway, at $1.2 billion dollars, is the world's most expensive; it was one of the pet projects of the late Sen. Robert Kerr (see state write-up).

But in the summer of 1971, Edmondson decided to abandon all of his seniority and make a run at the Senate seat held by liberal Fred Harris. Harris' outspoken support of the Kerner Commission Report and of Indian rights undermined his popularity in

Oklahoma, and the county courthouse politicians quickly began lining up behind Edmondson. The courthouse people felt more comfortable with his kind of politics anyway. During the years of the New Frontier, Edmondson was a fairly dependable supporter of the programs of the Democratic Administration, but during the Johnson years, the Congressman became increasingly more conservative. The turning point seemed to come during the 89th Congress; during those sessions, LBJ could get his Great Society programs enacted by huge Democratic majorities. And so the President did not need to seek out the votes of border state congressmen like Ed Edmondson of Oklahoma. By 1967, the liberal majority had vanished, a wave of riots was sweeping the nation's major cities, and the Johnson Administration found itself preoccupied with a war. All these phenomena fortified the conservative instincts of congressmen like Ed Edmondson.

In 1971, therefore, Edmondson had a largely conservative record to bring before the increasingly conservative voters of Oklahoma. He was no doubt happy to embarrass the man who had beaten his brother in 1964 (see state write-up). In July, 1971, Edmondson's strength seemed so imposing Sen. Harris decided to withdraw from the Senate race and declare his candidacy for President. Oklahoma Democrats, spared from a nasty primary fight, were happy to support Harris' bid, and it appears at this writing that Edmondson will get the Senate nomination with no serious opposition. In Oklahoma, where the conservative Democratic tradition has made a comeback in recent years, Edmondson is the favorite to win the Senate seat in 1972.

Census Data 1970 pop. 409,057; deviation from current state average, —4.1%; change 1960–70, +7.0%. Metro. 13.0%, 0.8% central city.

1970 Share of Federal Outlays $286,759,393

DOD	$34,111,000	HEW	$120,929,027
AEC	$000	HUD	$271,673
NASA	$000	OEO	$2,414,411
DOT	$5,405,350	DOA	$24,999,832
		Other	$98,628,100

Federal Military-Industrial Commitments

None.

Economic Base Livestock, cash grain, and dairy; stone, clay, glass, and concrete products; food and kindred products; crude petroleum and natural gas.

The Voters

Registration 199,583 total. 155,276 D (78%); 43,106 R (22%); 1,291 other (0%).

Employment profile White collar, 39%. Blue collar, 61%.

Ethnic groups Black, 6%. American Indian, 9%. Total foreign stock, 2%. Germany, 1%; others, less than 0.5% each.

Presidential vote

1968	Humphrey (D)	53,690	(34%)
	Nixon (R)	72,075	(45%)
	Wallace (AIP)	34,037	(21%)

Representative

Ed Edmondson (D) Elected 1952; b. April 7, 1919, Muskogee; home, Muskogee; U. of Okla., B.A., 1940; Georgetown U., LL.B., 1947; Navy, WWII; married, five children; Presbyterian.

Career Newspaperman, 1936–40; Sp. Agent, FBI, 1941–43; Washington Correspondent, 1946–47; practicing atty., 1947–48; County Atty., Muskogee County, 1949–52.

Offices 2402 RHOB, 202-225-2701. Also P.O. Box 11, Muskogee 74401, 918-682-6230.

Committees

Interior and Insular Affairs (3rd); Subs. (1) Chm., Mines and Mining, (2) Environment, (3) Indian Affairs, (4) Irrigation and Reclamation, (5) Public Lands.

Public Works (7th); Subs. (1) Flood Control and Internal Development, (2) Investigation and Oversight, (3) Roads, (4) Watershed Development, (5) Sp. on Economic Development Programs.
Jt. Com. on Atomic Energy (5th); Subs. (1) Communities, (2) Raw Materials.

Group Ratings

	ADA	COPE	NREP	NFU	LCV	CFA	NAB	NSI	ACA
1970	28	67	33	92	44	74	22	100	37
1969	33	—	—	100	—	—	—	—	19
1968	42	77	—	94	—	—	33	—	13

Key Votes

(1) ABM	FOR	(6) 18-Yr-Vote	FOR	(11) Clean Water $	AGN
(2) SST	FOR	(7) Farm Sub Lmt	AGN	(12) Mig Wrkrs Comp	FOR
(3) Phil Pln	AGN	(8) Coop-Church	AGN	(13) Jets to Chiang	ABS
(4) No-Knock	FOR	(9) Family Asst	AGN	(14) State OEO Veto	AGN
(5) Cmutr Tax	AGN	(10) Work Stamps	AGN	(15) Park Logging	FOR

Election Results

1970 general:	Ed Edmondson (D)	87,131	(71%)
	Gene Humphries (R)	35,989	(29%)
1970 primary:	Ed Edmondson (D), unopposed		
1968 general:	Ed Edmondson (D)	77,192	(55%)
	Robert G. Smith (R)	63,437	(45%)

THIRD DISTRICT Political Background

Oklahoma 3, in the southeast corner of the state, is a region of red hills, coal mines, and rural poverty. The largest cities in the 3rd are Ardmore (pop. 21,000) and McAlester (pop. 18,000). The 3rd is also the most Democratic district in Oklahoma; the state's banner Democratic counties are found along the Red River (the Texas boundary) and in the coal-mining country to the north around McAlester. This area was settled by migrants from the Deep South and, to a lesser extent, from the Appalachians. The people were brought up Democrats, and hard conditions of life have turned them into rural populists. That populism showed itself in two ways in 1968. This was the only district that Humphrey carried in Oklahoma, winning 39%; but Wallace took 27%, which was his best showing outside the states of the old Confederacy. Nixon, who is by no means a rural populist, finished with 34%.

The 3rd district is the home of Carl Albert, the Speaker of the House. He was born here in the village of Bug Tussel, in 1908. Albert's father was a coal miner and a poor man. But young Carl was good at his books and won a scholarship to the University of Oklahoma. At the university, Albert showed nothing but excellence in his studies and on the debating team; his collegiate record won him a Rhodes scholarship. At Oxford, he took two law degrees and got to know another Rhodes from Georgia, Dean Rusk. After military service in World War II, the "little giant from little Dixie" (he is 5′4″) ran for Congress in 1946, and won the Democratic runoff primary by 330 votes out of 54,000 cast.

In Washington, Albert caught the eye of Speaker Sam Rayburn, whose Texas district adjoined the 3rd of Oklahoma. Albert became Majority Whip in 1955 and, on the elevation of John McCormack to the Speakership, Majority Leader in 1962. His attention to detail and his ability to marshal votes made him generally respected within the Democratic Caucus. So when McCormack retired, Albert became Speaker almost automatically; he did have token opposition from John Conyers of Michigan, who got only 20 votes in the Caucus while Albert took 220. Albert's own voting record in Congress has had something to please nearly everyone. He is a thoroughgoing liberal on domestic issues and has supported the foreign and military policies of the Johnson and Nixon Administrations. Presently, as Speaker, he votes only to break ties.

At this writing, Albert's performance as Speaker cannot be assessed; but he will, barring ill health (he had a heart attack a few years ago), serve in that post until his announced retirement date of 1978. Since 1946, reelection has been no problem for him. Carl Albert is a popular man in the 3rd; apart from his politics, citizens are quite proud that one of their own has done so well. The main street in McAlester has been renamed Carl Albert Parkway.

Census Data 1970 pop. 393,233; deviation from current state average, —7.8%; change 1960–70, —0.7%. Metro. 81.7%, 0.0% central city.

1970 Share of Federal Outlays $323,287,638

DOD	$57,689,000	HEW	$137,341,094
AEC	$000	HUD	$5,444,762
NASA	$130,360	OEO	$1,197,063
DOT	$7,293,289	DOA	$37,599,112
		Other	$76,592,958

Federal Military-Industrial Commitments

DOD Installations Naval Ammunition Depot (McAlester).

Economic Base Livestock; crude petroleum and natural gas; bituminus coal, apparel and other finished products made from fabrics and similar materials. Also, banking.

The Voters

Registration 204,649 total. 193,469 D (95%); 10,431 R (5%); 749 other (0%).

Employment profile White collar, 36%. Blue collar, 64%.

Ethnic groups Black, 5%. American Indians, 5%. Total foreign stock, 2%. All foreign groups less than 0.5% each.

Presidential vote

1968	Humphrey (D)	58,656	(39%)
	Nixon (R)	50,520	(34%)
	Wallace (AIP)	40,142	(27%)

Representative

Carl Bert Albert (D) Elected 1946; b. May 10, 1908, McAlester; home, McAlester; U. of Okla., B.A., 1931; Rhodes Scholar, Oxford U., B.A., 1933, B.C.L., 1934; Army, WWII; married, two children; Methodist.

Career Legal Clerk, FHA, 1934–37; Atty., Accountant, Sayre Oil Co., 1937–38; Legal Dept., Ohio Oil Co., 1939–40; practicing atty., 1938–39; Majority Whip, 1955–62; Dem. Majority Leader, 1962– .

Offices 2205 RHOB, 202-225-4565. Also Fed. Bldg., McAlester 74501, 918-423-7710.

Committees

Speaker of the House of Representatives.

Group Ratings

	ADA	COPE	NREP	NFU	LCV	CFA	NAB	NSI	ACA
1970	48	75	50	92	38	84	9	89	16
1969	33	—	—	93	—	—	—	—	6
1968	58	92	—	88	—	—	0	—	4

Key Votes

(1) ABM	FOR	(6) 18-Yr-Vote	FOR	(11) Clean Water $	AGN
(2) SST	FOR	(7) Farm Sub Lmt	AGN	(12) Mig Wrkrs Comp	AGN
(3) Phil Pln	FOR	(8) Coop-Church	AGN	(13) Jets to Chiang	ABS
(4) No-Knock	FOR	(9) Family Asst	FOR	(14) State OEO Veto	AGN
(5) Cmutr Tax	FOR	(10) Work Stamps	AGN	(15) Park Logging	FOR

Election Results

1970 general:	Carl Albert (D), unopposed		
1970 primary:	Carl Albert (D)	87,449	(80%)
	Marvin D. Andrews (D)	21,275	(20%)
1968 general:	Carl Albert (D)	85,981	(68%)
	Gerald Beasley, Jr. (R)	39,740	(32%)

FOURTH DISTRICT Political Background

Oklahoma 4 takes up the southwest portion of the state, including part of the Oklahoma City metropolitan area. The counties along the Red River are like the adjacent counties in Texas, cotton-growing Democratic strongholds. But as one proceeds north, the district becomes politically more marginal. The 4th's portion of Oklahoma City and its suburbs is definitely Republican, and so, more often than not, is Cleveland County, which contains Norman and the University of Oklahoma. The 4th was redrawn drastically in the 1967 redistricting, and its new boundaries reflect two decades of the state's changing demography. The only county it now has in common with the pre-1967 district is Pottawatomie, the home of Congressman Tom Steed.

Steed is a moderate-to-conservative Democrat who was first elected in 1948. Recently, he has been having problems at election time. In 1966, a good Republican year, he won reelection by only 364 votes. And in 1968, Steed was forced to run against another incumbent, Republican James V. Smith, whose home was also in the new 4th. That race had national significance which at the time went unnoticed. If Steed had lost, the Oklahoma delegation would have been deadlocked at three Democrats and three Republicans. Then, if the presidential election had gone into the House, where each state has one vote, the Democratic candidate quite possibly would not have had the 26 votes needed to win.

But Steed did win and the election was not thrown into the House. In 1968, the Congressman won with 54% of the votes, and the size of the margin against another incumbent suggested that he would have little trouble from then on. But that was not the conclusion reached by White House political strategists. They felt that Steed was too liberal for the district and that an attractive Republican could win it. And they had such a candidate in Jay Wilkinson, a 28-year-old White House assistant, all-American at Duke, and son of presidential advisor Bud Wilkinson (see state write-up). Wilkinson's campaign was an expensive and energetic one, with TV and radio ads, visits from Cabinet members, Sen. John Tower of Texas, and the President's daughter, Tricia. But in a year when the rural voters of the district were less than happy with the Administration's farm programs, Wilkinson's effort proved to be a waste of time and money. The young man got only 35% of the vote, and Steed now seems comfortably entrenched in his new district.

The Wilkinson campaign says something about Nixon's reputation for political genius. Congressman Steed is the 11th ranking Democrat on the House Appropriations Committee and chairman of its Subcommittee on the Treasury, Post Office, and General Government. The subcommittee handles appropriations for the operation of the White House. Chairman Steed announced that he was not pleased with some of the implications of Wilkinson's TV ads—one of them being, "There are men who give and men who take. Jay Wilkinson gives all he's got." Steed said that he would now take a very close look at the White House budget, which has been growing rapidly. So if the Nixon-Agnew strategists want to write up another bright idea and find themselves short of pencils, they can ponder the Wilkinson campaign in Oklahoma 4.

Census Data 1970 pop. 464,432; deviation from current state average, +8.9%; change 1960–70, +16.2%. Metro. 57.5%, 18.6% central city.

1970 Share of Federal Outlays $607,409,000 (average outlay per district, Oklahoma 4 and 5)

DOD	$311,484,000	HEW	$101,490,000
AEC	$31,000	HUD	$5,871,000
NASA	$36,109,000	OEO	$2,129,000
DOT	$51,911,000	DOA	$72,217,000
		Other	$92,847,000

Federal Military-Industrial Commitments (See Oklahoma 5 for Oklahoma City area listing.)

Economic Base Cash grain, livestock and cotton; petroleum and natural gas; food and kindred products. Also, higher education (University of Oklahoma).

The Voters

Registration 183,900 total. 158,766 D (86%); 23,242 R (13%); 1,822 other (1%).
Employment profile White collar, 38%. Blue collar, 62%.
Ethnic groups Black, 6%. American Indians, 4%. Total foreign stock, 3%. Germany, 1%; others, 1%.

Presidential vote

1968	Humphrey (D)	53,790	(37%)
	Nixon (R)	58,862	(41%)
	Wallace (AIP)	32,067	(22%)

Representative

Tom Steed (D) Elected, 1948; b. March 2, 1904, near Rising Star, Tex.; home, Shawnee; Army, WWII; married, one child; Methodist.

Career Office of War Information, 1944–45; newspaperman on Okla. dailies; Managing Editor, *Shawnee News and Star*.

Offices 2405 RHOB, 202-225-6165. Also P.O. Box 1265, 124 E. Main St., Norman 73069, 405-329-6500.

Committees

Appropriations (11th); Subs. (1) Chm., Treasury, Post Office, and General Government, (2) Transportation.

Sel. Com. on Small Business (3rd); Chm., Sub. on Taxation, Oil Imports, and Marketing.

Sel. Com. on House Restaurant (3rd).

Group Ratings

	ADA	COPE	NREP	NFU	LCV	CFA	NAB	NSI	ACA
1970	24	34	33	69	44	69	44	89	42
1969	13	—	—	67	—	—	—	—	31
1968	33	50	—	75	—	—	17	—	35

Key Votes

(1) ABM	FOR	(6) 18-Yr-Vote	FOR	(11) Clean Water $	AGN
(2) SST	FOR	(7) Farm Sub Lmt	AGN	(12) Mig Wrkrs Comp	AGN
(3) Phil Pln	AGN	(8) Coop-Church	AGN	(13) Jets to Chiang	FOR
(4) No-Knock	FOR	(9) Family Asst	FOR	(14) State OEO Veto	AGN
(5) Cmutr Tax	AGN	(10) Work Stamps	FOR	(15) Park Logging	AGN

Election Results

1970 general:	Tom Steed (D)	67,743	(64%)
	Jay G. Wilkinson (R)	37,081	(35%)
	Mary H. Rawls (AIP)	1,000	(1%)
	Kenneth A. Kottka (Ind.)	534	(0%)
1968 primary:	Tom Steed (D)	51,554	(75%)
	Keith Meyers (D)	14,003	(20%)
	Owen Trotter (D)	3,306	(5%)
1968 general:	Tom Steed (D)	67,352	(54%)
	James V. Smith (R)	58,253	(46%)

FIFTH DISTRICT Political Background

Oklahoma 5 is Oklahoma City and some of its suburbs. Oklahoma City (pop. 366,000) has annexed so much territory in the last decade that it spills over into five counties and three congressional districts. The economic health of the city is based largely on the oil industry; there are even a few wells on the grounds of the state capital here. It also benefits from federal spending: Tinker Air Force Base and the FAA Aeronautical Center are within the city limits. Politically, Oklahoma City is conservative, but it is less so than Tulsa; a Texas analogy is Houston and Dallas.

In the last 30 years, the 5th district has had only two congressmen, Mike Monroney (1938–50) and John Jarman (1950–). Of the two, Monroney was the more liberal —one of the reasons he was defeated in 1968 after 18 years in the Senate (see state write-up). Jarman has had no problems with the voters; he regularly wins with more than 70% of the vote. The Congressman is the 3rd ranking Democrat on the House Interstate and Foreign Commerce Committee and chairman of its Transportation and Aeronautics Subcommittee. Together with Monroney, who chaired a committee with similar jurisdiction in the Senate, Jarman has made Oklahoma City into one of the centers of the nation's aviation bureaucracy.

Census Data 1970 pop. 449,523; deviation from current state average, +5.4%; change 1960–70, +17.5%. Metro. 100.0%, 76.5% central city.

1970 Share of Federal Outlays $607,409,000 (average outlay per district, Oklahoma 4 and 5)

DOD	$311,484,000	HEW	$101,490,000
AEC	$31,000	HUD	$5,871,000
NASA	$36,109,000	OEO	$2,129,000
DOT	$51,911,000	DOA	$72,217,000
		Other	$92,847,000

Federal Military-Industrial Commitments (Oklahoma City area listing)

DOD Installations Fort Sill AB (Lawton). Altus AFB (Altus). Oklahoma City AF Station (Midwest City). Tinker AFB (Oklahoma City).

Economic Base Food and kindred products, esp. meat products; nonelectrical machinery, esp. construction, mining, and material handling machinery and equipment; fabricated metal products, esp. fabricated structural metal products; crude petroleum and natural gas. Also, banking.

The Voters

Registration 214,175 total. 157,898 D (74%); 52,785 R (25%); 3,492 other (2%).

Employment profile White collar, 48%. Blue collar, 52%.

Ethnic groups Black, 11%. American Indians, 2%. Total foreign stock, 4%. Germany, UK, 1% each; others, 1%.

Presidential vote

1968	Humphrey (D)	50,981	(32%)
	Nixon (R)	81,130	(51%)
	Wallace (AIP)	26,996	(17%)

Representative

John Jarman (D) Elected 1950; b. July 17, 1915, Sallisaw; home, Oklahoma City; Westminster Col., 1932–34; Yale U., B.A., 1937; Harvard, LL.B., 1941; Army, WWII; widowed, three children; Presbyterian.

Career Practicing atty; Okla. House of Reps., 1947; Okla. State Senate, 1948.

Offices 2416 RHOB, 202-225-2132. Also 619 Fed. Bldg., Oklahoma City 73102, 405-236-2311, ext. 543.

Committees

Interstate and Foreign Commerce (3rd); Chm., Transportation and Aeronautics.

Group Ratings

	ADA	COPE	NREP	NFU	LCV	CFA	NAB	NSI	ACA
1970	0	20	17	17	40	70	89	100	75
1969	13	—	—	40	—	—	—	—	88
1968	0	0	—	44	—	—	80	—	86

Key Votes

(1) ABM	FOR	(6) 18-Yr-Vote	AGN	(11) Clean Water $	AGN
(2) SST	FOR	(7) Farm Sub Lmt	FOR	(12) Mig Wrkrs Comp	AGN
(3) Phil Pln	AGN	(8) Coop-Church	AGN	(13) Jets to Chiang	FOR
(4) No-Knock	FOR	(9) Family Asst	AGN	(14) State OEO Veto	FOR
(5) Cmutr Tax	ABS	(10) Work Stamps	FOR	(15) Park Logging	FOR

Election Results

1970 general:	John Jarman (D)	62,034	(74%)
	Terry L. Campbell (R)	22,301	(26%)
1970 primary:	John Jarman (D), unopposed		
1968 general:	John Jarman (D)	86,420	(74%)
	Bob Leeper (R)	30,931	(26%)

SIXTH DISTRICT Political Background

Oklahoma 6 occupies the northwest corner of the state and includes the panhandle that abuts both the Colorado and New Mexico borders. Aside from Tulsa, this is the most conservative and Republican part of the state; it is more like western Kansas than southern Oklahoma. Most of the district is agricultural, with the plains growing more arid as one heads west. The country here was settled largely by Yankees from across the Kansas border, who thought that the land was more fertile than it actually was. In 1907, at the time of statehood, there were 411,000 people living within the current boundaries of the 6th district; according to the 1970 census, there are 397,000. And the number has probably dropped since the taking of the most recent census. A crippling drought struck the area—the worst since the dust storms of the '30's sent many Oklahoma residents to California.

In 1967, the legislature made radical changes in the boundaries of the state's congressional districts. Most of what is now the 6th was part of the old 1st district which then included Tulsa; the old 6th consisted of the panhandle and the western counties of the state all the way down to the Red River. This old 6th elected its first Republican congressman in 1966, one James V. Smith. After the redistricting, Smith decided to challenge Democrat Tom Steed in the new 4th district. That was a bad decision, because Steed won and the Republican candidate in the new 6th district also won.

The Republican was John N. (Happy) Camp, a staunch conservative with 20 years' experience in the Oklahoma legislature. Camp serves on the Interior and Insular Affairs and the Science and Astronautics committees. He won reelection easily in 1970 (64%), and will probably continue to win easily. His district must add about 30,000 people to come up to the state average. The most convenient way to do this would be to graft on the northern part of Oklahoma County (Oklahoma City). Because this area is heavily Republican, the move would please both John Camp and the man losing the territory, Democrat John Jarman of the 5th district.

Census Data 1970 pop. 396,767; deviation from current state average, —7.0%; change 1960–70, +4.2%. Metro. 8.1%, 0.1% central city.

1970 Share of Federal Outlays $448,263,665

DOD	$63,715,000	HEW	$117,707,775
AEC	$72,922	HUD	$2,018,168
NASA	$721,717	OEO	$908,589
DOT	$4,585,059	DOA	$171,676,983
		Other	$86,917,452

Federal Military-Industrial Commitments

DOD Contractors Serv Air (Enid), $12.201m: unspecified.

DOD Installations Vance AFB (Enid).

Economic Base Cash grain and livestock; crude petroleum and natural gas; nonelectrical machinery. Also, higher education (Oklahoma State University).

The Voters

Registration 200,205 total. 130,832 D (65%); 68,032 R (34%); 1,341 other (1%).
Employment profile White collar, 35%. Blue collar, 65%.
Ethnic groups Black, 3%. American Indians, 2%. Total foreign stock, 5%; Germany, USSR, 1% each; others, 1%.

Presidential vote

1968	Humphrey (D)	45,157	(27%)
	Nixon (R)	95,034	(58%)
	Wallace (AIP)	25,067	(15%)

Representative

John N. (Happy) Camp (R) Elected 1968; b. May 11, 1908, Enid; home, Waukomis; married, four children; Disciples of Christ.

Career Pres., Waukomis State Bank; Okla. House of Reps., 1943–62; Chm., Okla. Bd. of Public Affairs, 1967–68.

Offices 1406 LHOB, 202-225-5565. Also 231 Fed. Bldg., Enid 73701, 405-233-1969.

Committees

Interior and Insular Affairs (9th); Subs. (1) Indian Affairs, (2) Irrigation and Reclamation, (3) Mines and Mining, (4) Public Lands.

Science and Astronautics (12th); Sub. on NASA Oversight.

Group Ratings

	ADA	COPE	NREP	NFU	LCV	CFA	NAB	NSI	ACA
1970	12	9	0	25	0	43	100	100	88
1969	0	—	—	27	—	—	—	—	73

Key Votes

(1) ABM	FOR	(6) 18-Yr-Vote	AGN	(11) Clean Water $	AGN
(2) SST	FOR	(7) Farm Sub Lmt	AGN	(12) Mig Wrkrs Comp	AGN
(3) Phil Pln	FOR	(8) Coop-Church	AGN	(13) Jets to Chiang	ABS
(4) No-Knock	ABS	(9) Family Asst	AGN	(14) State OEO Veto	FOR
(5) Cmutr Tax	AGN	(10) Work Stamps	FOR	(15) Park Logging	AGN

Election Results

1970 general:	John (Happy) Camp (R)	81,959	(64%)
	R. O. (Joe) Cassity, Jr. (D)	45,742	(36%)
1970 primary:	John (Happy) Camp (R), unopposed		
1968 general:	John (Happy) Camp (R)	79,992	(55%)
	John W. Goodwin (D)	64,599	(45%)

OREGON

OREGON Political Background

Oregon is a bit of pre-industrial New England transplanted to the Pacific Coast. Many of the state's residents are descendants of the farmers who took the Oregon Trail west in 1847, and today the people here are almost all whites of Protestant stock

—the state, according to the campaign managers of one unsuccessful candidate, is "one big suburb." Oregon has not grown like California or Washington, and apparently does not want to. Gov. Tom McCall has cancelled the state's Chamber of Commerce-type promotions designed to attract industry to the state; he says that no industries are wanted unless they are non-polluters. Four-fifths of the state's current two million plus people live in the Willamette River Valley, which lies between the Coast Range and the Cascade mountains. And most of these people are found in and around the state's largest city, Portland (Metropolitan pop. 880,000).

While California and Washington are heavily dependent on defense industries, Oregon has virtually none. Its economic health depends on a nineteenth century crop, lumber—and, therefore, on the interest rates that determine the number of housing units built. Lately, of course, interest rates have been high and the production of lumber low. Still Oregon has not suffered from the heavy unemployment common in other states on the West Coast.

Unlike most other places, there are no long-standing sources of political division in Oregon. It is true that the coastal areas and the Columbia River Valley are marginally more Democratic than the rest of the state; and that Salem, the state capital, is usually more Republican than Eugene, the site of the University of Oregon; and that the low-lying, poorer sections of Portland near the Columbia and Willamette rivers are Democratic; and that the surrounding hills are Republican. But these kinds of differentiations do not constitute significant variations in political behavior. Oregon has no equivalent of a conservative Orange County and a liberal San Francisco.

It is, therefore, not too surprising that the state's two senators hold their seats by virtue of a combined total margin of just 27,000 votes. The closer of the two races was state Rep. Robert Packwood's 3,445-vote upset of veteran Sen. Wayne Morse. A University of Oregon law professor, Morse was elected to the Senate as a Republican in 1944; he then switched to independent status out of disgust with the Eisenhower Administration, and finally he won reelection as a Democrat in 1956 and 1962. Morse was one of the earliest and most vehement opponents of the Vietnam war, being one of the two senators who voted against the Gulf of Tonkin resolution in 1964. He was also chairman of the Labor and Public Welfare Committee. Morse's outspokenness won him many enemies, and in 1968, when he just barely defeated hawkish ex-Congressman Robert Duncan in the Democratic primary, it was clear that the Senator was in deep trouble.

Packwood's victory over Morse in the general election made him the youngest man in the Senate, and the Republican's previous political obscurity made his views on issues a bit of a mystery. As it turned out, Packwood is a rather liberal senator with an instinctive desire to hold fast to the orthodox Republican position whenever possible. Thus, he supported the Nixon Administration on several tight votes (Hatfield-McGovern, ABM, and Haynsworth) and opposed it on others (Carswell and the SST). Packwood is the Senate's leading proponent of the zero population growth idea—a position not unpopular in pollution-conscious, and heavily Protestant Oregon.

The state's senior senator is Mark Hatfield, a former professor of political science and dean of Willamette College. In 1958, he was elected governor of Oregon at age 36. Because Hatfield was a popular governor, it was a surprise when he won the 1966 Senate race with only 52% of the vote; he won that election against the same Congressman Duncan who was defeated by Wayne Morse in the Democratic primary two years later. Part of Hatfield's problem was his position on Vietnam; even as early as 1966, he was an outspoken dove. Hatfield did have Sen. Morse's support, but he undoubtedly lost some conservative Republican votes to Duncan, who, during the campaign, was one of the Johnson Administration's most vocal supporters.

Hatfield, who nominated Richard Nixon at the 1960 Republican convention, has not been a favorite at the White House. He has opposed the Nixon Administration on practically every important issue. The Senator was, of course, the co-sponsor of the unsuccessful Hatfield-McGovern amendment to set a definite time limit on U.S. involvement in Vietnam. There is now growing dissatisfaction with Hatfield among the state's Republicans. In an interview, he suggested that Nixon and Agnew might be dumped in 1972; the Republican State Chairman then said that the Senator, like Wayne Morse, might want to change his party identification.

It is unlikely, however, that Hatfield will do that. He has been active in the Republican party too long. But it seems likely that he will face a tough fight if he decides to run for reelection in 1972. There have been rumors that he will retire. If he decides to run, the popular governor, Tom McCall, will probably oppose him. McCall, who was reelected to a second four-year term in 1970, is a supporter of the Nixon Vietnam policies. In recent polls, he has run far ahead of Hatfield, and even in relatively liberal Oregon, the Republican primary is heavily weighted in favor of conservative candidates.

In the mid-'60's, Democrats held both of the state's Senate seats and then lost them both after bitter primaries in which Vietnam was the main issue. It now appears that the same thing might happen to the Republicans. The aftermath of a bruising Hatfield-McCall primary could produce a Democratic victory. Popular Congresswoman Edith Green of Portland is a Democratic possibility. And there is ex-Senator Wayne Morse, who could make a comeback. His reputation has risen since the publication of the Pentagon Papers.

According to the 1970 census, there is a wide variation in the populations of Oregon's congressional districts. Neither party has control of redistricting, with the Democrats holding the state Senate and the Republicans controlling the House and the governorship. Some compromise will have to be worked out. The plan mostly likely to emerge is one which would divide territory along the edges of the over-populated 1st district, in the northwest corner of the state, among the three other adjoining districts. This will not threaten any member of the well-entrenched congressional delegation.

Electoral Votes 6

Census Data 1970 pop. 2,091,385; 1.24% of U.S. total, 32nd largest; change 1960–70, +18.2%. Metro. 61.2%, 25.2% central city. 1970 per capita income, $3,700; 24th highest. 33rd in number of poor.

1970 Share of Federal Tax Burden $1,853,840,000; 0.95% of U.S. total, 29th largest.

1970 Share of Federal Outlays $1,723,642,600; 0.91% of U.S. total, 33rd largest. Per capita federal spending, $824.

DOD	$198,286,000	42nd (0.35%)	HEW	$554,000,915	28th (1.06%)
AEC	$1,132,086	36th (0.44%)	HUD	$18,316,120	31st (0.94%)
NASA	$578,415	39th (0.02%)	OEO	$7,551,295	32nd (0.99%)
DOT	$128,101,083	22nd (1.79%)	DOA	$269,841,045	18th (2.10%)
DOC	$2,995,081	41st (0.26%)	POD	$62,069,605	30th (0.85%)
DOI	$167,087,156	3rd (7.23%)	VA	$110,937,078	32nd (1.50%)
DOJ	$4,449,824	31st (0.77%)	CSC	$35,875,291	25th (0.89%)
			Other	$162,421,606	

Economic Base Lumber and wood products other than furniture, esp. sawmills and planing mills and logging camps and logging contractors; livestock, dairy, and wheat and other field crops; food and kindred products, esp. canned and preserved fruits, vegetables, and seafoods; transportation equipment, esp. ship and boat building and repairing and aircraft and parts; nonelectrical machinery, esp. construction, mining, and material handling machinery and equipment; paper and allied products, esp. paper mills other than building paper mills; fabricated metal products, esp. fabricated structural metal products; primary metal industries, esp. iron and steel foundries and primary smelling and refining of nonferrous metals.

Political Line-up Governor, Tom McCall (R); seat up, 1974. Senators, Mark Hatfield (R) and Robert W. Packwood (R). Representatives, 4 (2 D and 2 R). State Senate (16 D and 14 R); State House (26 D and 34 R).

The Voters

Registration 955,500 total. 521,684 D (55%); 410,712 R (43%); 23,104 other (2%).

Employment profile White collar, 42%. Blue collar, 58%.

Ethnic groups Black, 1%. Total foreign stock, 17%. Canada, Germany, 3% each; UK, 2%; Sweden, Norway, USSR, Italy, 1% each; others, 5%.

Presidential vote

1968	Humphrey (D)	358,866	(44%)
	Nixon (R)	408,433	(50%)
	Wallace (AIP)	49,683	(6%)
1964	Johnson (D)	501,017	(64%)
	Goldwater (R)	282,779	(36%)
1960	Kennedy (D)	367,402	(47%)
	Nixon (R)	408,060	(53%)

Senator

Mark O. Hatfield (R) Elected 1966, seat up 1972; b. July 12, 1922, Dallas; home, Salem; Willamette U., B.A., 1943; Stanford U., M.A., 1948; USNR, WWII; married, four children; Baptist.

Career Resident Asst., Stanford U., 1947–49; Instr., Willamette U., 1949, Dean of Students, Assoc. Prof., political science, 1950–56; Oreg. House of Reps., 1951–55; Oreg. Senate, 1955–57; Secy. of State, 1957–59; Governor, 1959–67.

Offices 463 OSOB, 202-225-3753. Also 475 Cottage St. NE, Salem 97301, 503-585-1793, ext. 228.

Committees

Commerce (7th); Subs. (1) Consumer, (2) Environment, (3) Merchant Marine, (4) Oceans and Atmosphere, (5) Surface Transportation, (6) Sp. to Study Transportation.

Interior and Insular Affairs (5th); Subs. (1) Parks and Recreation, (2) Public Lands, (3) Water and Power Resources.

Sel. Com. on Equal Educational Opportunity (5th).

Sel. Com. on Small Business (3rd); Subs. (1) Government Regulation, (2) Retailing, Distribution, Marketing Practices, (3) Science and Technology.

Group Ratings

	ADA	COPE	NREP	NFU	LCV	NAB	NSI	ACA
1970	84	92	83	94	44	18	0	17
1969	89	—	—	67	—	—	—	43
1968	71	73	—	46	—	75	—	50

Key Votes

(1) ABM	AGN	(8) Phil Pln	FOR	(15) Coop-Church	FOR
(2) SST	AGN	(9) Vol Army	FOR	(16) Cut Oil Dpltn	FOR
(3) Busing	FOR	(10) Prison $	FOR	(17) Consumer Prot	FOR
(4) Tob Sub	AGN	(11) Cut Mil $	FOR	(18) Farm Sub Limit	FOR
(5) Carswell	AGN	(12) Defoliatn	AGN	(19) Comp Bid Sales	AGN
(6) No-Knock	FOR	(13) 18-Yr-Vote	FOR	(20) Pre-Prod Tests	FOR
(7) Seniorty	AGN	(14) Pentgn PR	AGN	(21) Cut Marjna Pen	AGN

Election Results

1966 general:	Mark O. Hatfield (R)	354,391	(52%)
	Robert B. Duncan (D)	330,374	(48%)
1966 primary:	Mark O. Hatfield (R)	178,782	(76%)
	Walter Huss (R)	30,906	(13%)
	Jim Bacaloff (R)	19,699	(8%)
	George Altvater (R)	6,155	(3%)

Senator

Bob Packwood (R) Elected 1968, seat up 1974; b. Sept. 11, 1932, Portland; home, Portland; Willamette U., B.A., 1954; N.Y.U., LL.B., 1957; married, two children; Unitarian.

Career Practicing atty., 1958–68; Oreg. House of Reps., 1963–67.

Offices 6327 NSOB, 202-225-5244. Also 1002 N.E. Holladay St., Portland 97232, 503-233-4471.

Committees

Banking, Housing, and Urban Affairs (4th); Subs. (1) Financial Institutions, (2) Housing and Urban Affairs, (3) International Finance, (4) Production & Stabilization, (5) Securities.

Labor and Public Welfare (5th); Subs. (1) Aging, (2) Alcoholism and Narcotics, (3) Children and Youth, (4) Handicapped Workers, (5) Health, (6) Labor, (7) Sp. on Arts and Humanities, (8) Sp. on Human Resources, (9) Sp. on Natl. Science Foundation.

Group Ratings

	ADA	COPE	NREP	NFU	LCV	NAB	NSI	ACA
1970	50	69	70	71	47	82	60	50
1969	56	—	—	44	—	—	—	33

Key Votes

(1) ABM	FOR	(8) Phil Pln	FOR	(15) Coop-Church	FOR
(2) SST	AGN	(9) Vol Army	FOR	(16) Cut Oil Dpltn	AGN
(3) Busing	FOR	(10) Prison $	FOR	(17) Consumer Prot	AGN
(4) Tob Sub	AGN	(11) Cut Mil $	ABS	(18) Farm Sub Limit	FOR
(5) Carswell	AGN	(12) Defoliatn	ABS	(19) Comp Bid Sales	FOR
(6) No-Knock	ABS	(13) 18-Yr-Vote	FOR	(20) Pre-Prod Tests	FOR
(7) Seniorty	AGN	(14) Pentgn PR	FOR	(21) Cut Marjna Pen	ABS

Election Results

1968 general:	Robert W. Packwood (R)	408,825	(50%)
	Wayne Morse (D)	405,380	(50%)
1968 primary:	Robert W. Packwood (R)	241,464	(88%)
	John S. Boyd (R)	32,807	(12%)

FIRST DISTRICT Political Background

Oregon 1 comprises the northwest corner of the state. It takes in the Democratic Columbia River Valley and coastal counties of Lincoln, Tillamook, Clatsop, and Columbia. But most of the district's population is in the Portland metropolitan area. The 1st includes the eastern edge of the city itself—hilly, high-income neighborhoods that overlook the downtown area, as well as the Willamette and Columbia rivers. Here, as in most Western cities, the rich people live in the hills and the poor people live in the flat parts of town. About a quarter of the district's votes are cast in fast-growing Washington County, an affluent suburban area in the mountains west of Portland. The 1st also includes three Republican-leaning counties on the west bank of the Willamette River.

Since it was created in 1892, the 1st district has never elected a Democrat to Congress. In recent years, this has not been the result of the partisan leanings of the area; in 1968, for example, it gave Humphrey a respectable 42% of the vote, as against Nixon's 53%. Republicans win congressional elections mostly because of the popularity of the district's current congressman, Wendell Wyatt. Wyatt, a former FBI agent and state legislator, was first elected by a narrow margin in the Goldwater year of 1964, and he has won by phenomenal margins ever since. In 1968, he took 81% of the votes. Wyatt is a relatively low ranking member of the House Appropriations Committee, but he has still been able to claim credit for various navigational projects built in his district. The projects are important to the economic life of the 1st. The Congressman voted for the Cooper-Church amendment to limit American military action in Cambodia and Laos; otherwise, he has stayed fairly close to the policies of the Nixon Administration. Wyatt looks like a sure bet for reelection in the years to come.

Census Data 1970 pop. 633,941; deviation from current state average, +21.2%; change 1960–70, +35.2%. Metro. 69.2%, 11.4% central city.

1970 Share of Federal Outlays $323,353,546

DOD	$24,560,000	HEW	$115,712,173
AEC	$650,880	HUD	$1,330,000
NASA	$262,170	OEO	$439,937
DOT	$32,546,977	DOA	$37,255,527
		Other	$144,125,882

Federal Military-Industrial Commitments

DOD Contractors Tektronix (Beaverton), $5.984m: unspecified.

Economic Base Livestock and dairy; lumber and wood products other than furniture. Also, higher education (Oregon State University); tourism (coast).

The Voters

Registration 295,417 total. 148,670 D (50%); 139,214 R (47%); 7,533 other (3%).
Employment profile White collar, 45%. Blue collar, 55%.
Ethnic groups Black, less than 0.5%. Total foreign stock, 19%. Canada, 4%; Germany, 3%; UK, 2%; Sweden, Norway, USSR, 1% each; others, 7%.

Presidential Vote

1968	Humphrey (D)	105,214	(42%)
	Nixon (R)	132,575	(53%)
	Wallace (AIP)	12,053	(5%)

Representative

Wendell Wyatt (R) Elected Nov. 5, 1964; b. June 15, 1917, Eugene; home, Gearhart; U. of Oreg., LL.B., 1941; USMC, WWII; married, five children; Episcopalian.

Career Sp. Agent, FBI, 1941–42; practicing atty., 1946–64.

Offices 414 CHOB, 202-225-2206. Also 985 42nd St., Milwaukee 97222, 503-654-8408.

Committees

Appropriations (17th); Subs. (1) Interior, (2) Legislative.

Group Ratings

	ADA	COPE	NREP	NFU	LCV	CFA	NAB	NSI	ACA
1970	40	50	27	45	33	61	83	89	69
1969	13	—	—	54	—	—	—	—	50
1968	8	42	—	44	—	—	80	—	75

Key Votes

(1) ABM	FOR	(6) 18-Yr-Vote	AGN	(11) Clean Water $	AGN
(2) SST	FOR	(7) Farm Sub Lmt	AGN	(12) Mig Wrkrs Comp	FOR
(3) Phil Pln	FOR	(8) Coop-Church	FOR	(13) Jets to Chiang	AGN
(4) No-Knock	FOR	(9) Family Asst	ABS	(14) State OEO Veto	AGN
(5) Cmutr Tax	AGN	(10) Work Stamps	ABS	(15) Park Logging	FOR

Election Results

1970 general:	Wendell Wyatt (R)	147,239	(72%)
	Vern Cook (D)	57,837	(28%)
1970 primary:	Wendell Wyatt (R), unopposed		
1968 general:	Wendell Wyatt (R)	189,023	(81%)
	Thomas M. Baggs (D)	45,479	(19%)

SECOND DISTRICT Political Background

Oregon 2 is the sparsely populated eastern two-thirds of the state plus two counties in the Willamette Valley. Until 1965, the district included only the 18 counties east of the Cascades, which together have a population of only 270,000. The 1965 redistricting added Marion (Salem) and Linn (Albany) counties; both of them usually give Republican candidates a small edge. East Oregon is marginal political territory, where traditional Rocky Mountain populism on pocketbook issues—the area is particularly strong on public power development—has been overmatched lately by the mountain country's distaste for East Coast liberalism. Not that these people are hawkish: they gave Sen. Wayne Morse a majority over his pro-war opponent in the tight 1968 primary. Lumber is the big industry in East Oregon—and one which depends in large part on the actions of various federal agencies.

The 1965 redistricting was expected to cause problems for Democratic Congressman Al Ullman, but it did not. Ullman, who unseated a Republican in 1956, went on to win by bigger and bigger majorities in East Oregon. And when Marion and Linn counties were added to his district, he carried them too. Ullman, whose record has been increasingly conservative lately, lost just one county in 1968; otherwise, he has carried every county in the district in each of the last five elections. When Hale Boggs became the Majority Leader in 1971, Ullman became the 3rd ranking Democrat on the powerful House Ways and Means Committee. The Oregon Congressman is as likely as anyone to succeed Wilbur Mills someday as its chairman.

Census Data 1970 pop. 495,523; deviation from current state average, −5.2%; change 1960–70, +11.4%. Metro. 30.5%, 12.7% central city.

1970 Share of Federal Outlays $481,610,237

DOD	$50,422,000	HEW	$140,345,388
AEC	$30,500	HUD	$6,081,085
NASA	$16,244	OEO	$2,559,655
DOT	$44,714,467	DOA	$94,384,694
		Other	$143,056,254

Federal Military-Industrial Commitments

DOD Installations Umatilla Army Depot (Hermiston). Keno AF Station (Keno). Kingsley Field (Kalmath Falls).

Economic Base Livestock, cash grain, and other field crops; lumber and wood products other than furniture, esp. sawmills and planing mills; food and kindred products, esp. canned and preserved fruits, vegetables, and seafoods. Also, tourism (Crater Lake).

The Voters

Registration 214,469 total. 112,551 D (52%); 97,108 R (45%); 4,810 other (2%).

Employment profile White collar, 37%. Blue collar, 63%.

Ethnic groups Black, less than 0.5%. Total foreign stock, 13%. Germany, Canada, 2% each; UK, Norway, Sweden, USSR, Ireland, 1% each; others, 4%.

Presidential Vote

1968	Humphrey (D)	71,832	(39%)
	Nixon (R)	98,678	(54%)
	Wallace (AIP)	12,111	(7%)

Representative

Al Ullman (D) Elected 1956; b. March 9, 1914, Great Falls; home, Baker; Whitman Col., B.A., 1935; Columbia U., M.A., 1939; USNR, WWII; divorced, three children; Presbyterian.

Career Real estate broker, builder, 1945–56.

Offices 2410 RHOB, 202-225-5711. Also Box 247, P.O. Bldg., Salem 97308, 503-585-1793, ext. 220.

Committees

Ways and Means (3rd).

Jt. Com. on Internal Revenue Taxation (3rd).

Group Ratings

	ADA	COPE	NREP	NFU	LCV	CFA	NAB	NSI	ACA
1970	52	67	42	69	44	83	8	40	41
1969	40	—	—	73	—	—	—	—	35
1968	42	60	—	87	—	—	50	—	30

Key Votes

(1) ABM	FOR	(6) 18-Yr-Vote	AGN	(11) Clean Water $	FOR
(2) SST	FOR	(7) Farm Sub Lmt	AGN	(12) Mig Wrkrs Comp	AGN
(3) Phil Pln	AGN	(8) Coop-Church	FOR	(13) Jets to Chiang	AGN
(4) No-Knock	FOR	(9) Family Asst	AGN	(14) State OEO Veto	FOR
(5) Cmutr Tax	FOR	(10) Work Stamps	AGN	(15) Park Logging	FOR

Election Results

1970 general:	Al Ullman (D)	100,943	(71%)
	Everett Thoren (R)	40,620	(29%)
1970 primary:	Al Ullman (D), unopposed		
1968 general:	Al Ullman (D)	114,232	(64%)
	Marv Root (R)	64,478	(36%)

THIRD DISTRICT Political Background

Oregon 3 comprises most of the city of Portland and its eastern suburbs. Portland is Oregon's largest city; more than half of the people in the state live within 50 miles of its commercial and industrial center. The 3rd takes in most of the Democratic sections of town, the lower parts of town (see Oregon 1), along the Willamette River. These are lower- and middle-income neighborhoods. The suburbs that extend east from the city along the Columbia, toward Mount Hood, are also Democratic in most elections.

Since 1954, Edith Green, sometimes called "Mrs. Education," has been the representative from the 3rd. Mrs. Green, who spent 14 years as a schoolteacher, is now the 2nd ranking Democrat on the House Education and Labor Committee, and the chairman of its Subcommittee on Higher Education. Mrs. Green has had tremendous power to shape the nation's educational programs—power that she has used in an increasingly conservative fashion. When she first came to the House, the Congresswoman was considered a flaming liberal. But lately, she has been pushing state and local control of educational and poverty programs; she has supported, for example, the Whitten amendment to bar busing of school children to achieve racial balance. Generally, she lines up with the committee's Republicans and helps to form a conservative coalition that often carries the day.

Mrs. Green is a champion vote-getter in the 3rd district; in 1970, she had an astounding 74% of the vote. Now 60, she says she has no intention of remaining in the House for the rest of her life, but she has shown no inclination to retire. With the recent decline in the popularity of Sen. Mark Hatfield, rumors say that she might make the 1972 Senate race. But that would be politically risky and would require the kind of heavy campaigning that Mrs. Green has not had to do in recent years. If she remains in the House, she could become chairman of the full committee. But since current incumbent, Carl Perkins of Kentucky, is about the same age, her chances of becoming chairman are problematical. What is clear is that she will keep winning reelection in Portland as long as she cares to run.

Census Data 1970 pop. 777,020; deviation from current state average, —8.8%; change 1960–70, +5.8%. Metro. 100.0%, 66.2% central city.

1970 Share of Federal Outlays $593,612,559

DOD	$102,609,000	HEW	$179,743,279
AEC	$000	HUD	$8,625,317
NASA	$22,919	OEO	$2,931,078
DOT	$33,758,739	DOA	$93,127,578
		Other	$262,594,649

Federal Military-Industrial Commitments

DOD Contractors Columbia Steamship (Portland), $26.090m: cargo transport services. Northwest Marine Iron (Portland), $15.557m: ship repair and overhaul.

DOD Installations Portland International Airport (Portland).

Economic Base Transportation equipment, esp. ship and boat building and repairing and aircraft and parts; food and kindred products, esp. bakery goods and dairy products; fabricated metal products, esp. fabricated structural metal products; nonelectrical machinery, esp. construction, mining, and material handling machinery and equipment. Also, higher education (Portland State University); insurance.

The Voters

Registration 231,751 total. 142, 142 D (61%); 84,561 R (37%); 5,048 other (2%).

Employment profile White collar, 48%. Blue collar, 52%.

Ethnic groups Black, 5%. Total foreign stock, 24%. Canada, 4%; Germany, UK, 3% each; USSR, Sweden, Norway, 2% each; Italy, Ireland, Austria, 1% each; others, 6%.

Presidential Vote

1968	Humphrey (D)	108,230	(53%)
	Nixon (R)	85,621	(42%)
	Wallace (AIP)	9,807	(5%)

Representative

Edith Green (D) Elected 1954; b. Jan. 17, 1910, Trent, S.D.; home, Portland; Willamette U., 1927–29; U. of Oreg., B.S., 1939; Stanford U., 1944; married, two children; Disciples of Christ.

Career Teacher, 1930–41; Commentator, KALE Radio, 1944–45; free lance radio work, 1944–48; Dir., Public Relations, Oreg. Ed. Assn., 1952–55.

Offices 2441 RHOB, 202-225-4811. Also 344 U.S. Courthouse, Portland 97205, 503-226-3361, ext. 1028.

Committees

Education and Labor (2nd); Subs. (1) Chm., Sp. on Education, (2) Gen. on Education, (3) Sel. on Labor.

Group Ratings

	ADA	COPE	NREP	NFU	LCV	CFA	NAB	NSI	ACA
1970	40	55	25	64	71	83	10	63	41
1969	27	—	—	64	—	—	—	—	27
1968	58	75	—	73	—	—	0	—	24

Key Votes

(1) ABM	ABS	(6) 18-Yr-Vote	AGN	(11) Clean Water $	FOR
(2) SST	AGN	(7) Farm Sub Lmt	AGN	(12) Mig Wrkrs Comp	AGN
(3) Phil Pln	ABS	(8) Coop-Church	AGN	(13) Jets to Chiang	AGN
(4) No-Knock	FOR	(9) Family Asst	AGN	(14) State OEO Veto	FOR
(5) Cmutr Tax	AGN	(10) Work Stamps	AGN	(15) Park Logging	FOR

Election Results

1970 general:	Edith Green (D)	118,919	(74%)
	Robert E. Dugdale (R)	42,391	(26%)
1970 primary:	Edith Green (D)	59,992	(73%)
	John F. Callahan (D)	15,650	(19%)
	Elton J. Smith (D)	4,723	(6%)
	Bonnie Colton (D)	2,211	(3%)
1968 general:	Edith Green (D)	137,746	(70%)
	Douglas S. Warren (R)	59,447	(30%)

FOURTH DISTRICT Political Background

Oregon 4 comprises the southwest corner of the state. Most of the population lives along the Pacific Coast or in the valleys between the Cascades and the Coast Range. The terrain here is not especially rural, although there is some farming and livestock-raising; more than half of the residents of the district live in towns over 10,000—places like Medford, Grant's Pass, Roseburg, Coos Bay, and Springfield. The largest city here is Eugene (pop. 76,000), the home of the University of Oregon and the leading "peace vote" city in the 1966 and 1968 Democratic Senate primaries (see state write-up). Some have called the school "the University of California at Eugene." The Coast counties—Coos and Curry—are marginally Democratic, while the southern counties—Jackson and Josephine, along the California line—are marginally Republican.

The district, therefore, is rather closely balanced, and its congressional seat has changed parties several times in recent years, in 1956, 1960, 1962, and 1966. Between 1962 and 1966, the 4th's congressman was Democrat Robert Duncan, a strong campaigner who supported Johnson's Vietnam policies ardently (see state write-up). Duncan seems to have burned himself out in two tries for the Senate: in 1966, he lost to dovish Republican Gov. Mark Hatfield by 24,000 votes, and in the 1968 Democratic primary, Duncan lost to Sen. Wayne Morse by 11,000. In that election, the 4th gave Morse a 10,000-vote majority, but he went on to lose the general election. Duncan has not made any further attempts to win public office.

Duncan's successor is John R. Dellenback, a moderate-to-liberal Republican who has supported antiwar measures in the House. Dellenback, formerly a popular state legislator, has won the last three elections with about 60% of the vote. There have been rumors that Duncan—or even Morse, who spends much of his time tending his farm near Eugene—might return to contest the seat. But this is a rather unlikely event. Dellenback serves on the Education and Labor Committee, where he is already the 6th ranking Republican, and on Interior and Insular Affairs. If redistricting adds a county or two from the southern portion of the 1st district to the 4th, Dellenback's position would be strengthened somewhat. But in any case, he is likely to continue winning easily.

Census Data 1970 pop. 484,901; deviation from current state average, –7.3%; change 1960–70, +20.0%. Metro. 44.0%, 15.7% central city.

1970 Share of Federal Outlays $325,066,258

DOD	$20,695,000	HEW	$118,200,125
AEC	$450,706	HUD	$2,279,718
NASA	$277,082	OEO	$1,620,625
DOT	$17,080,900	DOA	$45,073,246
		Other	$113,388,856

Federal Military-Industrial Commitments

DOD Installations Naval Facility (Coos Head). North Bend AF Station (North Bend).

Economic Base Lumber and wood products other than furniture, esp. sawmills and planing mills, and millwork, veneer, plywood, and prefabricated structural wood products; livestock; food and kindred products. Also, higher education (University of Oregon); tourism (coast).

The Voters

Registration 213,849 total. 118,312 D (55%); 89,824 R (42%); 5,713 other (3%).
Employment profile White collar, 37%. Blue collar, 63%.
Ethnic groups Black, less than 0.5%. Total foreign stock, 12%. Canada, Germany, 2% each; UK, Norway, Sweden, 1% each; others, 4%.

Presidential Vote

1968	Humphrey (D)	73,590	(41%)
	Nixon (R)	91,559	(51%)
	Wallace (AIP)	15,712	(9%)

Representative

John Dellenback (R) Elected 1966; b. Nov. 6, 1918, Chicago, Ill.; home, Medford; Yale U., B.S., 1940; U. of Mich., J.D., 1949; USNR, WWII; Lt. Cdr. USNR; married, three children; Presbyterian.

Career Inst., Oreg. State U., 1949, Asst. Prof., 1950–51; practicing atty., 1951–66; Oreg. House of Reps., 1960–66.

Offices 1214 LHOB, 202-225-6416. Also 163 E. 12th, Eugene 97501, 503-342-5141.

Committees

Education and Labor (6th); Subs. (1) Sp. on Education, (2) Sp. on Labor.

Interior and Insular Affairs (12th); Subs. (1) Environment, (2) Irrigation and Reclamation, (3) Public Lands.

Group Ratings

	ADA	COPE	NREP	NFU	LCV	CFA	NAB	NSI	ACA
1970	32	50	58	62	25	44	82	80	47
1969	53	—	—	67	—	—	—	—	27
1968	25	31	—	63	—	—	83	—	57

Key Votes

(1) ABM	FOR	(6) 18-Yr-Vote	AGN	(11) Clean Water $	AGN
(2) SST	AGN	(7) Farm Sub Lmt	AGN	(12) Mig Wrkrs Comp	AGN
(3) Phil Pln	FOR	(8) Coop-Church	FOR	(13) Jets to Chiang	ABS
(4) No-Knock	ABS	(9) Family Asst	FOR	(14) State OEO Veto	AGN
(5) Cmutr Tax	AGN	(10) Work Stamps	FOR	(15) Park Logging	FOR

Election Results

1970 general:	John R. Dellenback (R)	84,474	(58%)
	James H. Weaver (D)	60,299	(42%)
1970 primary:	John R. Dellenback (R)	38,518	(73%)
	Ray Hannibal (R)	14,596	(27%)
1968 general:	John R. Dellenback (R)	104,159	(59%)
	Edward Fadeley (D)	72,579	(41%)

PENNSYLVANIA

PENNSYLVANIA Political Background

A look at a map of the country shows us how Pennsylvania got its nickname, the Keystone State. Pennsylvania lies between New York state and New England, and the rest of the country. But the nickname is not entirely appropriate. The state's position would seem to have made it the transportation and commercial hub of the nation. Things did not work out that way, however, because of the mountains that run north and south across the middle of the state. These mountains made the digging of any canal, like the Erie in Upstate New York, a very difficult business. As a result, the main routes of westward migration and trade passed to the north and south of Pennsylvania. In 1776, Philadelphia was the new nation's capital and largest city; it was soon eclipsed in the affairs of government by Washington, D.C., and in commerce by New York City. And those in New England will argue that Boston became the nation's center of culture, as that word pertains to excellence in the arts and sciences and in the application of the various social graces.

In the late nineteenth century, Pennsylvania boomed, as the state's steel mills and coal mines attracted large numbers of immigrants. But the Great Depression hit both industries hard, and some communities here have still not recovered from its effects. Moreover, the steel industry in Pennsylvania became complacent; it was left far behind by the technological advances made in the years following World War II. Today, Pennsylvania steel simply cannot match the product coming out of Japan and Germany. The state's lack of growth sums up the problems of the economy here; the population of Pennsylvania has increased by only a few percent in each of the last four decades.

In politics, Pennsylvania can be divided into two parts, east and west. East of the Appalachian ranges, the state leans slightly Republican, even though heavy Democratic margins come out of Philadelphia and the industrial towns like Reading, Scranton, and Wilkes-Barre. The main source of Republican strength lies in the Philadelphia suburbs and the Pennsylvania Dutch country around Lancaster and Harrisburg to the west. Some years ago, the Republican preference in the eastern half of the state was even more pronounced. That was because Philadelphia was the stronghold of an aging, old-time Republican city machine. The power of the machine was broken in 1951 when Joseph S. Clark was elected mayor; Clark later served as senator from the state from 1956 to 1968.

Western Pennsylvania leans Democratic. This area is economically quite separate from eastern Pennsylvania; it is part of a coal-and-steel empire that extends into northeast Ohio and northern West Virginia (see Ohio 18 and 19 and West Virginia 1). Pittsburgh, like Philadelphia, casts heavy Democratic margins, but most of Pittsburgh's suburbs, and the rural and small town areas beyond the city, also vote Democratic. Pittsburgh's Democratic organization, under Mayor Joseph Barr and David Lawrence (who was governor from 1958 to 1962), used to be the mainstay of the state's Democratic party. But in 1969, insurgent reform candidate Peter Flaherty won the Democratic primary and the mayor's office, and the power of the Pittsburgh machine is no more.

The same sort of thing happened to the governor's office. Millionaire manufacturer Milton Shapp, against the intentions of the party organization, won the Democratic primaries of 1966 and 1970 and the general election in 1970. The governor of Pennsylvania reputedly has 40,000 patronage jobs to distribute. But Shapp's campaign was based largely on the media, his personal campaign staff, and volunteers. So he probably doesn't have 40,000 people he wants or needs to reward, and he may, therefore, allow the jobs to become part of the civil service.

The state's Republican party was better organized and more tightly controlled, at least until it lost the governorship to Shapp. But before that, the Republicans were still unable to carry the state for their presidential candidate since the Eisenhower landslide of 1956. They have, however, managed to score successive victories in the Senate contests of 1968 and 1970, despite Democratic victories at the top of the ticket. The

1968 Senate victory of Richard Schweiker, then a congressman from suburban Philadelphia, was something of a surprise. He edged out incumbent liberal Democrat Joseph Clark for the seat. Clark was in trouble that year; he had never before won by big margins and meantime had antagonized many of the state's gun enthusiasts and Italian-American voters. Schweiker's record in the House was generally conservative, but in the Senate, he often joins other liberal Republicans in opposing Nixon Administration court appointments and military policy.

Pennsylvania's senior senator is Hugh Scott, Everett Dirksen's successor as Senate Minority Leader. Scott has had a great deal of experience in winning close elections. From 1942 to 1958, he was a congressman from Philadelphia, and during the 1948 Dewey campaign he served as Republican National Chairman. He chose the Democratic year of 1958 to run for the Senate; he may have done this figuring that his House seat would be wiped out by the 1960 census. At any rate, while the Democrats won the governorship by a large margin, Scott squeaked through. In 1964, his career looked doomed by the Goldwater candidacy, but the Senator again won a narrow 70,000-vote victory.

Scott's strength is based on a few carefully selected liberal votes and a shrewd cultivation of minority groups, especially blacks and Jews. He is a consummate politician, able to maintain an image of perfect consistency while taking inconsistent positions. The post of Minority Leader, which he won on another close vote, 24–19, has put him into some nasty binds. He antagonized the Administration and Senate conservaties by opposing the Haynsworth nomination and Nixon's changes in the Voting Rights Act. When Scott supported the Administration, backing the Carswell nomination, ABM, and SST, and opposing a fixed Vietnam withdrawal date, he antagonized many of his constituents. Typical of his strategy for dealing with such situations was his handling of the Carswell nomination. He supported Carswell in the Senate, throughout the most prolonged and searching debate over a Supreme Court nomination in recent history. Then, after the vote was taken, he called the judge a "racist" and told Pennsylvanians that he should never have voted for confirmation.

Because of Scott's stature in Washington, analysts of the 1970 national scene assumed that he would win reelection easily in Pennsylvania. The Democratic challenger, state Sen. William Sesler of Erie, was an unknown and had, at most, a quarter of the campaign funds available to Scott. The Democratic organization, such as it is, concentrated its efforts on the governor's race, as did organized labor, which is a much more potent political force, especially in western Pennsylvania. The smart money expected that the Senator's reelection margin would exceed that of Democratic gubernatorial candidate, Milton Shapp, who was running ahead in the polls. Scott, the betting people said, could very well sweep the Republican candidate into the governor's office. But they were wrong. Shapp won by 500,000; Scott's margin of 220,000, although the largest he ever received, was comparatively small.

Sesler ran almost as well as Sen. Clark, a much better known, if more controversial, candidate, two years before. By dint of years of cultivation, Scott ran better than most Republicans in Philadelphia, Pittsburgh, and the state's other industrial cities, though he did not do particularly well in the rural areas. Still, Scott's reelection was an achievement. Pennsylvania has a tradition of close Senate elections, and Scott is the first politician here to win a third full term since the popular election of senators was instituted.

In 1950, Pennsylvania had 32 House seats; after the reappointment based on the 1970 census, it will lose yet another two seats and send only 25 representatives to the House. For the first time since the days of James Buchanan, Democrats control the governorship and both houses of the legislature; redistricting, therefore, will be at the expense of the Republicans. It is possible that the Democrats will seek to augment their representation even further, but given the patterns of population decline and growth, and the patterns of political affiliation, the task will not be easy. Philadelphia, in particular, will be a problem. The city now has five congressmen, all Democrats; under the 1970 census, it is entitled to just slightly over four. To save all the incumbents' seats, the legislature might be able to extend some of the districts out into the relatively fast-growing suburbs. This would create city-surburban districts which Democratic city voters would continue to dominate. Pittsburgh will be easier. The city lost one seat, reducing its representation from four congressmen to three. Veteran Republican Congressman Robert Corbett died in the spring of 1971, and his district will probably be absorbed by the three others.

Electoral Votes 27

Census Data 1970 pop. 11,793,909; 5.73% of U.S. total, 3rd largest; change 1960–70, +4.2%. Metro. 79.4%, 28.6% central city. 1970 per capita income, $3,893; 17th highest. 6th in number of poor.

1970 Share of Federal Tax Burden $11,610,870,000; 5.95% of U.S. total, 4th largest.

1970 Share of Federal Outlays $8,452,089,786; 4.47% of U.S. total, 4th largest. Per capita federal spending, $717.

DOD	$2,395,050,000	4th (4.17%)	HEW	$3,112,114,991	3rd (5.95%)
AEC	$102,423,209	10th (1.20%)	HUD	$179,703,482	2nd (9.22%)
NASA	$44,068,043	15th (1.20%)	OEO	$33,047,720	5th (4.35%)
DOT	$309,728,594	5th (4.34%)	DOA	$129,302,687	35th (1.00%)
DOC	$28,077,119	10th (2.43%)	POD	$428,261,601	4th (5.87%)
DOI	$66,322,894	11th (2.87%)	VA	$518,935,257	4th (7.03%)
DOJ	$23,950,334	6th (4.17%)	CSC	$142,457,773	8th (3.54%)
			Other	$938,646,082	

Economic Base Primary metal industries, esp. blast furnaces, steel works, and rolling and finishing mills; apparel and other finished products made from fabrics and similar materials, esp. women's, misses', and juniors' outerwear; nonelectrical machinery, esp. general industrial apparatus, metalworking machinery and equipment, and special industrial machinery other than metalworking machinery; electrical machinery, equipment, and supplies, esp. electronic components and accessories and electric transmission and distribution equipment; fabricated metal products, esp. fabricated structural metal products; dairy, livestock, and poultry; food and kindred products, esp. bakery goods and dairy products; transportation equipment, esp. aircraft and parts and motor vehicles and motor vehicle equipment; textile mill products, esp. knitting mills.

Political Line-up Governor, Milton J. Shapp (D); seat up, 1974. Senators, Hugh Scott (R) and Richard S. Schweiker (R). Representatives, 27 (14 D and 13 R). State Senate (16 D and 14 R); State House (113 D and 90 R).

The Voters

Registration 5,367,719 total. 2,602,941 D (49%); 2,659,592 R (50%); 105,186 other (2%).

Employment profile White collar, 39%. Blue collar, 61%.

Ethnic groups Black, 9%. Total foreign stock, 22%. Italy, 5%; Poland, 3%; UK, Germany, USSR, Austria, 2% each; Ireland, Czech., Hungary, 1% each; others, 4%.

Presidential vote

1968	Humphrey (D)	2,259,403	(48%)
	Nixon (R)	2,090,017	(44%)
	Wallace (AIP)	378,582	(8%)
1964	Johnson (D)	3,130,954	(65%)
	Goldwater (R)	1,673,657	(35%)
1960	Kennedy (D)	2,556,282	(51%)
	Nixon (R)	2,439,956	(49%)

Senator

Hugh Scott (R) Elected 1958, seat up 1974; b. ca. 1900, Fredericksburg, Va.; home, Philadelphia; Randolph-Macon Col., B.A., 1919; U. of Va., LL.B., 1922; Army, WWII; USNR, WWII; married, one child; Episcopalian.

Career Practicing atty.; author; U.S. House of Reps., 1940–44, 1947–58; Natl. Chm., Rep. Party, 1948–49; Chm., Eisenhower Headquarters Com., 1952; Gen. Counsel, Rep. Natl. Com., 1955–60; V. Chm., Senatorial Campaign Com., 1964; Minority Whip, U.S. Senate, 1969; Senate Minority Leader, 1969– .

Offices 260 OSOB, 202-225-6324. Also 4004 U.S. Courthouse, Philadelphia 19107, 215-925-8181, and 434 Fed. Bldg., 1000 Liberty Ave., Pittsburgh 15222, 412-261-3230.

Committees

Foreign Relations (6th); Subs. (1) Far Eastern Affairs, (2) Near Eastern and South Asian Affairs, (3) Oceans and International Environment.

Judiciary (3rd); Subs. (1) Criminal Laws and Procedures, (2) Improvements in Judicial Machinery, (3) Internal Security, (4) Patents, Trademarks, and Copyrights, (5) Penitentiaries, (6) Revision and Codification.

Rules and Administration (3rd); Sub. on Library.

Jt. Com. on the Library (2nd).

Group Ratings

	ADA	COPE	NREP	NFU	LCV	NAB	NSI	ACA
1970	31	77	58	47	56	42	100	60
1969	56	—	—	50	—	—	—	25
1968	57	75	—	46	—	40	—	52

Key Votes

(1) ABM	FOR	(8) Phil Pln	FOR	(15) Coop-Church	AGN
(2) SST	FOR	(9) Vol Army	FOR	(16) Cut Oil Dpltn	AGN
(3) Busing	FOR	(10) Prison $	ABS	(17) Consumer Prot	AGN
(4) Tob Sub	FOR	(11) Cut Mil $	AGN	(18) Farm Sub Limit	FOR
(5) Carswell	FOR	(12) Defoliatn	FOR	(19) Comp Bid Sales	AGN
(6) No-Knock	AGN	(13) 18-Yr-Vote	AGN	(20) Pre-Prod Tests	AGN
(7) Seniorty	FOR	(14) Pentgn PR	FOR	(21) Cut Marjna Pen	AGN

Election Results

1970 general:	Hugh Scott (R)	1,874,106	(52%)
	William G. Sesler (D)	1,653,774	(46%)
	Frank W. Gaydosh (Const.)	85,813	(2%)
	W. H. MacFarland (AIP)	18,275	(0%)
1970 primary:	Hugh Scott (R), unopposed		
1964 general:	Hugh Scott (R)	2,429,858	(51%)
	Genevieve Blatt (D)	2,359,223	(49%)

Senator

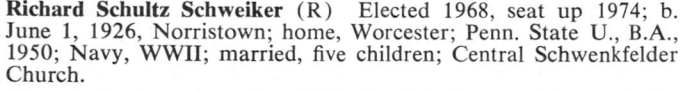

Richard Schultz Schweiker (R) Elected 1968, seat up 1974; b. June 1, 1926, Norristown; home, Worcester; Penn. State U., B.A., 1950; Navy, WWII; married, five children; Central Schwenkfelder Church.

Career Business executive, 1950–60; U.S. House of Reps., 1960–68.

Offices 6221 NSOB, 202-225-4254. Also 2001 Fed. Office Bldg., 1000 Liberty Ave., Pittsburgh 15222, 412-644-3400, and 4048 U.S. Courthouse, 9th and Chestnut, Philadelphia 19107, 215-597-7200.

Committees

Armed Services (6th); Subs. (1) General Legislation, (2) Preparedness Investigating, (3) Status of Forces, (4) Strategic Arms Limitation Talks.

Labor and Public Welfare (4th); Subs. (1) Aging, (2) Alcoholism and Narcotics, (3) Children and Youth, (4) Education, (5) Employment, Manpower, and Poverty, (6) Health, (7) Labor, (8) Railroad Retirement, (9) Sp. on Human Resources, (10) Sp. on International Health, Education, and Labor Programs.

Sel. Com. on Nutrition and Human Needs (3rd).

Jt. Com. on Congressional Operations (2nd).

Group Ratings

	ADA	COPE	NREP	NFU	LCV	NAB	NSI	ACA
1970	75	100	83	81	60	25	20	29
1969	78	—	—	75	—	—	—	19

Key Votes

(1) ABM	AGN	(8) Phil Pln	FOR	(15) Coop-Church	FOR
(2) SST	AGN	(9) Vol Army	FOR	(16) Cut Oil Dpltn	AGN
(3) Busing	FOR	(10) Prison $	FOR	(17) Consumer Prot	FOR
(4) Tob Sub	AGN	(11) Cut Mil $	AGN	(18) Farm Sub Limit	FOR
(5) Carswell	AGN	(12) Defoliatn	FOR	(19) Comp Bid Sales	AGN
(6) No-Knock	FOR	(13) 18-Yr-Vote	FOR	(20) Pre-Prod Tests	AGN
(7) Seniorty	AGN	(14) Pentgn PR	AGN	(21) Cut Marjna Pen	AGN

Election Results

1968 general:	Richard S. Schwieker (R)	2,399,762	(52%)
	Joseph S. Clark (D)	2,117,662	(46%)
	Frank W. Gaydosh (Const.)	96,742	(2%)
1968 primary:	Richard S. Schweiker (R), unopposed		

FIRST DISTRICT Political Background

Pennsylvania 1 comprises the southwestern portion of the city of Philadelphia. The district is separated into two parts by the Schuylkill River. On the west bank is the University of Pennsylvania, and beyond it, the large West Philadelphia black ghetto. On the east bank of the river are the predominantly Italian neighborhoods of South Philadelphia—a stronghold of ex-Police Commissioner Frank Rizzo, who is the 1971 Democratic nominee for mayor. Rizzo is as hated in the black community as he is adored in South Philly, and the two halves of the district have little in common except a preference to vote Democratic in national and congressional elections. Recently, however, the Italians have been giving an increasing percentage of their votes, though not yet a majority, to Republican conservatives. But because the blacks are approaching majority status in the district (48% in 1970), there is little chance the Democratic-leanings of the 1st will be overcome in any election in the foreseeable future.

William A. Barrett has represented the 1st district since 1948. One of the veterans of the Pennsylvania delegation, Congressman Barrett is now the 2nd ranking Democrat on the House Banking and Currency Committee. He will become chairman on the death or retirement of Wright Patman of Texas, who was 77 in 1970. If Barrett does become chairman of the congressional unit, Wall Street bankers will find him much more agreeable and pleasant than his predecessor, the crusading Patman. Barrett is an unobtrusive man in the House, though he does keep in close touch with his district. As a result, he has not encountered serious primary opposition, despite the increasing size of the 1st's black minority. In general elections, the Congressman is unbeatable; he usually wins with around 70%. Redistricting may cut into his margins to some degree if the boundaries of the 1st are extended to take in portions of suburban Delaware or Montgomery counties. But there is little doubt that Barrett will continue to win as long as he chooses to run.

Census Data 1970 pop. 376,427; deviation from current state average, —13.8%; change 1960–70, —5.8%. Metro. 100.0%, 100.0% central city.

1970 Share of Federal Outlays $472,901,000 (average outlay per district, Pennsylvania, 1–5)

DOD	$203,599,000	HEW	$139,248,000
AEC	$729,000	HUD	$11,798,000
NASA	$279,000	OEO	$3,469,000
DOT	$13,728,000	DOA	$2,624,000
		Other	$97,427,000

Federal Military-Industrial Commitments (See Pennsylvania 3 for Philadelphia listing.)

Economic Base Apparel and other finished products made from fabrics and similar materials, esp. men's, youths', and boys' suits, coats, and overcoats; printing, publishing, and allied industries, esp. commercial printing, and newspapers; electrical machinery, equipment, and supplies, esp. switchgear and switchboard apparatus; food and kindred products, esp. bakery products and meat products. Also, higher education (University of Pennsylvania and Drexel Institute of Technology).

The Voters

Registration 172,614 total. 114,643 D (66%); 57,971 R (34%).
Employment profile White collar, 41%. Blue collar, 59%.
Ethnic groups Black, 48%. Total foreign stock, 27%. Italy, 11%; Ireland, 4%; USSR, 3%; UK, 2%; Germany, Poland, Austria, 1% each; others, 4%.

Presidential vote

1968	Humphrey (D)	109,562	(69%)
	Nixon (R)	38,520	(24%)
	Wallace (AIP)	11,255	(7%)

Representative

William A. Barrett (D) Elected 1948; b. Aug. 14, ca. 1900, Philadelphia; home, Philadelphia; St. Joseph's Col.; married, three children; Catholic.

Career Real estate broker.

Offices 2304 RHOB, 202-225-4731. Also 2401 Wharton St., Philadelphia 19146, 215-389-2822.

Committees

Banking and Currency (2nd); Subs. (1) Chm., Housing, (2) Small Business.

Jt. Com. on Defense Production (2nd).

Group Ratings

	ADA	COPE	NREP	NFU	LCV	CFA	NAB	NSI	ACA
1970	80	100	82	100	50	89	8	40	6
1969	60	—	—	93	—	—	—	—	19
1968	92	100	—	93	—	—	0	—	5

Key Votes

(1) ABM	AGN	(6) 18-Yr-Vote	FOR	(11) Clean Water $	FOR
(2) SST	FOR	(7) Farm Sub Lmt	FOR	(12) Mig Wrkrs Comp	FOR
(3) Phil Pln	FOR	(8) Coop-Church	FOR	(13) Jets to Chiang	AGN
(4) No-Knock	AGN	(9) Family Asst	FOR	(14) State OEO Veto	AGN
(5) Cmutr Tax	FOR	(10) Work Stamps	AGN	(15) Park Logging	FOR

Election Results

1970 general:	William A. Barrett (D)	79,425	(69%)
	Joseph S. Ziccardi (R)	34,649	(30%)
	Paul K. Botts (AIP)	677	(1%)
1970 primary:	William A. Barrett (D)	28,580	(85%)
	W. Emanuel Barrett (D)	5,114	(15%)
1968 general:	William A. Barrett (D)	113,696	(75%)
	Leslie J. Carson (R)	38,432	(25%)

SECOND DISTRICT Political Background

Pennsylvania 2 is Philadelphia's black district. According to the 1960 census, just over 50% of its residents were black; today, the figure has risen to 59%. The black population of Philadelphia is spread about in several of its congressional districts, but the heart of the black community—North Philadelphia—is mostly here in the 2nd district. There are also significant black concentrations in that portion of the 2nd west of the Schuylkill River, and in the Germantown section far to the north. Beyond Germantown is plush, country-like Chestnut Hill, an area where some of Philadelphia's richest and most prominent families have lived for generations. Chestnut Hill usually goes Republican, but its votes are swamped by the huge Democratic majorities coming out of the black neighborhoods to the south and east. The 2nd is consistently Philadelphia's most Democratic district in statewide elections.

Robert N. C. Nix has represented the 2nd since a 1958 special election. Nix, Pennsylvania's first black congressman, is now the second most senior member of the Black Caucus in the House. But he is not one of the group's most active members. Despite his seniority, Nix holds relatively low ranking positions on Foreign Affairs and Post Office and Civil Service (see data section). The Congressman has no reelection problems; the Democratic legislature will no doubt provide him with a district to his liking for 1972.

Census Data 1970 pop. 374,420; deviation from current state average, —14.3%; change 1960–70, —7.8%. Metro. 100.0%, 100.0% central city.

1970 Share of Federal Outlays $472,901,000 (average outlay per district, Pennsylvania 1–5)

DOD	$203,599,000	HEW	$139,248,000
AEC	$729,000	HUD	$11,798,000
NASA	$279,000	OEO	$3,469,000
DOT	$13,728,000	DOA	$2,624,000
		Other	$97,427,000

Federal Military-Industrial Commitments (See Pennsylvania 3 for Philadelphia listing.)

Economic Base Apparel and other finished products made from fabrics and similar materials, esp. men's, youths', and boys' suits, coats, and overcoats; printing, publishing, and allied industries, esp. commercial printing and newspapers; electrical machinery, equipment, and supplies, esp. switchgear and switchboard apparatus; food and kindred products, esp. bakery products and meat products.

The Voters

Registration 256,338 total. 206,545 D (81%); 58,793 R (23%).

Employment profile White collar, 39%. Blue collar, 62%.

Ethnic groups Black, 59%. Total foreign stock, 21%. USSR, 6%; Italy, 3%; Ireland, UK, Poland, Germany, 2% each; Austria, 1%; others, 4%.

Presidential vote

1968	Humphrey (D)	111,175	(72%)
	Nixon (R)	36,759	(24%)
	Wallace (AIP)	5,523	(4%)

Representative

Robert N. C. Nix (D) Elected May 20, 1958; b. Aug. 9, 1905, Orangeburg, S.C.; home, Philadelphia; Lincoln U., B.A., 1921; U. of Pa., LL.B., 1924; married, one child; Baptist.

Career Practicing atty., 1925– ; Sp. Deputy Atty. Gen. of Pa., assigned to Escheats Div., State Dept. of Revenue, 1934–38; Ward Com. Chm., 1950–58.

Offices 2201 RHOB, 202-225-4001. Also 2139 N. 22nd St., Philadelphia 19121, 215-236-8341.

Committees

Foreign Affairs (8th); Subs. (1) Africa, (2) Foreign Economic Policy, (3) National Security Policy and Scientific Developments.

Post Office and Civil Service (5th); Subs. (1) Chm., Postal Facilities and Mail, (2) Postal Service.

Group Ratings

	ADA	COPE	NREP	NFU	LCV	CFA	NAB	NSI	ACA
1970	88	100	100	92	63	100	0	20	17
1969	80	—	—	93	—	—	—	—	6
1968	100	100	—	100	—	—	0	—	0

Key Votes

(1) ABM	AGN	(6) 18-Yr-Vote	FOR	(11) Clean Water $	FOR
(2) SST	FOR	(7) Farm Sub Lmt	FOR	(12) Mig Wrkrs Comp	FOR
(3) Phil Pln	FOR	(8) Coop-Church	FOR	(13) Jets to Chiang	AGN
(4) No-Knock	AGN	(9) Family Asst	FOR	(14) State OEO Veto	AGN
(5) Cmutr Tax	FOR	(10) Work Stamps	AGN	(15) Park Logging	FOR

Election Results

1970 general:	Robert N. C. Nix (D)	70,530	(68%)
	Edward L. Taylor (R)	32,858	(32%)
1970 primary:	Robert N. C. Nix (D)	11,965	(67%)
	Leroy E. Iverson (D)	5,794	(33%)
1968 general:	Robert N. C. Nix (D)	102,869	(70%)
	Herbert P. McMaster (R)	44,041	(30%)

THIRD DISTRICT Political Background

Pennsylvania 3 is Philadelphia's Center City and a number of disparate neighborhoods around it. Within walking distance of Center City's not-so-tall skyscrapers (by ordinance no building can be taller than the spire of Philadelphia's ornate City Hall) are fashionable Rittenhouse Square and Society Hill. Here, renovated eighteenth century townhouses lie in the shadow of ultra-modern high-rise apartment buildings. To the south is South Philadelphia, an Italian blue-collar neighborhood, about half of which is in the 3rd district (see Pennsylvania 1). On the other side of Center City is North Philadelphia, the city's largest black ghetto, a portion of which lies in the 3rd (see Pennsylvania 2). To the northeast, along the Delaware River, are a few old white ethnic neighborhoods, where the culture of poverty is as entrenched as it is in North Philly.

This combination of groups should make the 3rd an overwhelmingly Democratic district. But it has not been so in recent elections. The Italians of South Philly are particularly unhappy with what they—and the Nixon Administration—see as trends toward crime, drug use, and neglect of the older white neighborhoods. Such feelings have shown themselves in the increasing number of votes, though still not a majority, for Republican candidates in presidential and senatorial elections.

The same development is part of congressional politics in the 3rd. The district's representative, James A. Byrne, a veteran of the Philadelphia Democratic party, has been receiving smaller margins of late; 56% in 1970, down from 61% in 1968. This has occurred even though Byrne has a good deal of seniority, having served continuously in the House since 1952. In 1970, Byrne also had stiff competition from peace candidate Nicholas S. Lamont in the Democratic primary; the incumbent took only 58% of the votes.

In Washington, Byrne is the 5th ranking Democrat on the House Armed Services Committee, where he often finds himself agreeing with its pro-military majority. Apparently, this stance has not been popular with his constituents. Redistricting may add more territory hostile to the Congressman; more, for example, of black North Philadelphia. It is therefore possible that he will be defeated either in the primary or in the general election in 1972. Or it could develop that his seat will be eliminated completely by redistricting, which would force Byrne to run against William Barrett of the 1st or William Green of the 5th—or retire.

Census Data 1970 pop. 321,765; deviation from current state average, −26.3%; change 1960–70, −18.9%. Metro. 100.0%, 100.0% central city.

1970 Share of Federal Outlays $472,901,000 (average outlay per district, Pennsylvania 1–5)

DOD	$203,599,000	HEW	$139,248,000
AEC	$729,000	HUD	$11,798,000
NASA	$279,000	OEO	$3,469,000
DOT	$13,728,000	DOA	$2,624,000
		Other	$97,427,000

Federal Military-Industrial Commitments (Pennsylvania 1–5, Philadelphia listing)

DOD Contractors General Electric (Philadelphia), $175.755m: research and development on the Mark 12 reentry system. IBM (Philadelphia), $13.797m: unspecified. Philco-Ford (Philadelphia), $12.376m: shipboard computer systems. Action Mfg. (Philadelphia), $6.805m: rocket and bomb detonating fuze components. Kurz Charles Co. (Philadelphia), $6.741m: unspecified. Boeing Co. (Philadelphia), $6.400m: CH-47 helicopter support. ESB Inc. (Philadelphia), $5.987m: submarine batteries.

DOD Installations Frankford Army Arsenal (Philadelphia). Defense Personnel Support Center (Philadelphia). Naval Publications and Forms Center (Philadelphia). Marine Corps Supply Activity (Philadelphia). Naval Air Engineering Center (Philadelphia). Naval Aviation Supply Office (Philadelphia). Naval Hospital (Philadelphia). Naval Station (Philadelphia). Naval Shipyard (Philadelphia).

Economic Base Apparel and other finished products made from fabrics and similar materials, esp. men's, youths', and boys' suits, coats, and overcoats; printing, publishing, and allied industries, esp. commercial printing and newspapers; electrical machinery, equipment, and supplies, esp. switchgear and switchboard apparatus; food and kindred products, esp. bakery products and meat products. Also, banking and insurance.

The Voters

Registration 146,599 total. 83,593 D (57%); 62,996 R (43%).

Employment profile White collar, 30%. Blue collar, 70%.

Ethnic groups Black, 33%. Puerto Rico, 3%. Total foreign stock, 26%. Italy, 10%; USSR, 4%; Poland, Germany, Ireland, 2% each; UK, Austria, Hungary, 1% each; others, 4%.

Presidential vote

1968	Humphrey (D)	78,505	(60%)
	Nixon (R)	42,283	(32%)
	Wallace (AIP)	9,682	(7%)

Representative

James Aloysius Byrne (D) Elected 1952; b. June 22, 1906, Philadelphia; home, Philadelphia; St. Joseph's Col., married; Catholic.

Career Funeral Director, 1937–50; Chief U.S. Marshal Eastern Div., Pa., 1940–45; Sr. Disbursing Officer, Pa. Treas., 1945–50; Pa. Legislature, 1950–52; Lay Advisory Bd., St. Mary's Franciscan Hospital.

Offices 2412 RHOB, 202-225-2431. Also 114 U.S. Custom House Bldg., Philadelphia 19106, 215-922-3230.

Committees

Armed Services (5th); Subs. (1) Chm., No. 4, (2) Sp. on Real Estate.

Merchant Marine and Fisheries (8th); Subs. (1) Coast Guard, Coast and Geodetic Survey and Navigation, (2) Merchant Marine, (3) Panama Canal.

Group Ratings

	ADA	COPE	NREP	NFU	LCV	CFA	NAB	NSI	ACA
1970	84	100	93	100	80	95	8	38	6
1969	73	—	—	93	—	—	—	—	18
1968	100	100	—	100	—	—	0	—	4

Key Votes

(1) ABM	AGN	(6) 18-Yr-Vote	FOR	(11) Clean Water $	FOR
(2) SST	FOR	(7) Farm Sub Lmt	FOR	(12) Mig Wrkrs Comp	FOR
(3) Phil Pln	FOR	(8) Coop-Church	FOR	(13) Jets to Chiang	AGN
(4) No-Knock	AGN	(9) Family Asst	FOR	(14) State OEO Veto	AGN
(5) Cmutr Tax	FOR	(10) Work Stamps	AGN	(15) Park Logging	AGN

Election Results

1970 general:	James A. Byrne (D)	54,755	(56%)
	Gustine J. Pelagatti (R)	42,393	(44%)
1970 primary:	James A. Byrne (D)	18,303	(58%)
	Nicholas S. Lamont (D)	13,204	(42%)
1968 general:	James A. Byrne (D)	75,728	(61%)
	Richard R. Block (R)	47,813	(39%)

FOURTH DISTRICT Political Background

Pennsylvania 4 comprises northeast Philadelphia, the most middle-class and prosperous part of the city. This area has a suburban ambience; in fact, it is farther from Center City Philadelphia than the Main Line or Delaware County suburbs. It is the only part of Philadelphia that is still growing, as subdivisions go up near the city-limits. Much of the population here is Jewish, and there is a white working-class contingent in the neighborhoods along the Delaware River. The traditional Democratic allegiance of both groups is usually enough to tip this otherwise marginal district into the Democratic column.

The 4th is the only Philadelphia district which the Republicans have contested seriously in recent years. In 1966, after a redistricting that changed the shape of the 4th substantially, ailing Congressman Herman Toll retired. Republican candidate Robert B. Cohen then put up a strong effort to capture the seat, but fell about 7,000 votes short. The winner that year was Joshua Eilberg, then Majority Leader of the state House of Representatives. Eilberg has compiled a liberal, antiwar record in Washington and has won convincingly in succeeding elections. He should have little trouble in future elections even if the boundaries of the district are altered to bring in suburban areas across the city-limits. The adjacent suburbs are either Jewish or blue-collar—Democratic in either case.

Census Data 1970 pop. 471,271; deviation from current state average, +10.4%; change 1960–70, +23.0%. Metro. 100.0%, 100.0% central city.

1970 Share of Federal Outlays $472,901,000 (average outlay per district, Pennsylvania 1–5)

DOD	$203,599,000	HEW	$139,248,000
AEC	$729,000	HUD	$11,798,000
NASA	$279,000	OEO	$3,469,000
DOT	$13,728,000	DOA	$2,624,000
		Other	$97,427,000

Federal Military-Industrial Commitments (See Pennsylvania 3 for Philadelphia listing.)

Economic Base Apparel and other finished products made from fabrics and similar materials, esp. men's, youths', and boys' suits, coats, and overcoats; printing, publishing, and allied industries, esp. commercial printing and newspapers; electrical machinery, equipment, and supplies, esp. switchgear and switchboard apparatus; food and kindred products, esp. bakery products and meat products.

The Voters

Registration 253,970 total. 129,681 D (51%); 134,289 R (53%).

Employment profile White collar, 52%. Blue collar, 48%.

Ethnic groups Black, 1%. Total foreign stock, 37%. USSR, 9%; Germany, 5%; UK, Italy, Poland, 4% each; Ireland, 3%; Austria, Hungary, Canada, 1% each; others, 5%.

Presidential vote

1968	Humphrey (D)	123,040	(53%)
	Nixon (R)	88,325	(38%)
	Wallace (AIP)	22,112	(10%)

Representative

Joshua Eilberg (D) Elected 1966; b. Feb. 12, 1921, Philadelphia; home, Philadelphia; U. of Pa., B.S., 1941; Temple U., J.D., 1948; USNR, WWII; married, two children; Jewish.

Career Practicing atty., 1948– ; Asst. Dist. Atty., Philadelphia, 1952–54; Pa. Legislature, 1954–66, Majority Leader, 1965–66.

Offices 1130 LHOB, 202-225-4661. Also 216 First Fed. Savings & Loan Assn. Bldg., 1931 Cottman Ave., Philadelphia 19111, 215-722-1717.

Committees

Judiciary (11th); Sub. No. 1.

Group Ratings

	ADA	COPE	NREP	NFU	LCV	CFA	NAB	NSI	ACA
1970	84	100	93	100	67	100	0	38	11
1969	73	—	—	93	—	—	—	—	17
1968	75	100	—	100	—	—	0	—	0

Key Votes

(1) ABM	AGN	(6) 18-Yr-Vote	FOR	(11) Clean Water $	FOR
(2) SST	FOR	(7) Farm Sub Lmt	FOR	(12) Mig Wrkrs Comp	FOR
(3) Phil Pln	AGN	(8) Coop-Church	FOR	(13) Jets to Chiang	ABS
(4) No-Knock	AGN	(9) Family Asst	FOR	(14) State OEO Veto	AGN
(5) Cmutr Tax	FOR	(10) Work Stamps	AGN	(15) Park Logging	AGN

Election Results

1970 general:	Joshua Eilberg (D)	113,920	(59%)
	Charles F. Dougherty (R)	77,817	(41%)
1970 primary:	Joshua Eilberg (D), unopposed		
1968 general:	Joshua Eilberg (D)	131,810	(59%)
	Alexander Kaptik (R)	88,229	(40%)
	Paul D. Corbett (C)	2,214	(1%)

FIFTH DISTRICT Political Background

Pennsylvania 5 comprises a cross section of the city of Philadelphia. It includes portions of the North Philadelphia and Germantown black ghettos, as well as some predominantly Jewish areas near the northern city-limits. The bulk of the district, however, is white working-class. These are people who live in neighborhoods like Kensington, where the levels of education and income are nearly as low as they are in North Philly, and where the flimsy turn-of-the-century wooden houses are being abandoned as soon as their occupants or owners can afford to leave them. (Philadelphia is a home-owning city.) The 5th is a Democratic district, though not quite as Democratic as the predominantly black 2nd district. It is also an area—in the white neighborhoods at least—where the hard-line policies of ex-Police Commissioner and mayoral candidate Frank Rizzo are extremely popular.

Congressman William J. Green of the 5th first went to Washington after winning a special election in April of 1964. At that time, he was 25 and the youngest member of the House. The special election was called because his father, Congressman William J. Green, Jr., who was then only 53, died unexpectedly. The older Congressman Green was also head of Philadelphia's Democratic party, whose proudest moment came in 1960 when the city delivered a 331,000-vote margin to John F. Kennedy. The younger Congressman Green later succeeded to his father's position as head of the county party, with less happy results.

Since 1964, the Philadelphia Democratic party organization has been a parody of a successful party machine: bitter internecine feuds, squabbling over patronage and policies, but very little capacity to produce votes. Mayor James H. J. Tate beat the machine soundly in the 1967 mayoral primary—at which time Green was installed as chairman—but he just barely won reelection in November, with several city-wide offices picked up by Republicans. Then in 1968, Chairman Green wanted to support Robert Kennedy for President, but Mayor Tate and other old-line pols preferred Hubert Humphrey's politics of joy. After the 1968 elections, in which the machine failed to duplicate its 1960 showing, Green was removed as party chairman; he had proposed that the party be opened up to groups previously excluded from its workings.

In 1971, Green completed his apostasy by running for mayor against Frank Rizzo, who had the rousing support of Mayor Tate and his organization. Rizzo defeated Green in the Democratic primary. He swept the Italian wards of South Philadelphia with almost 90% of the vote and carried almost all of the white neighborhoods of the city by smaller margins. Rizzo finished with 50% of the vote; Green had 36%, mostly from blacks, white liberals, and Irish-Americans who remembered his father; Hardy Williams, a black candidate, won 13%. Even the familiarity of Green in his home district was not enough to overcome Rizzo's appeals to the fears of white voters: the Police Commissioner beat the Congressman there, 46–41.

Nevertheless, Green remains in an enviable position in the House. Only 33 in 1971, he is already the 12th ranking Democrat on the Ways and Means Committee—a full 11 years younger than the next youngest majority member. Under the current system, he could be the Wilbur Mills of the 1990's. But whether he becomes that depends entirely on redistricting. Even though Democrats control both houses of the legislature and the governorship, Green could still lose his seat. He is, of course, out of favor with the Philadelphia machine, which controls crucial votes in the legislature. And Mayor Tate has threatened to redistrict him out of office. The Congressman's fate will be sealed if he joins other Pennsylvania liberals, like Governor Shapp, and refuses to support Rizzo in the general election.

In the redistricting negotiations, Shapp will probably back Green's interests. But since Philadelphia stands to lose almost an entire congressional district by the 1970 census, the legislature could still choose to carve up his district among its neighbors. Green would then be forced into a primary with James Bryne of the 3rd or some other incumbent. Or the legislators may decide to create a second black district in Philadelphia, at Green's expense. Another black district in the city could be drawn rather easily. So at this writing, it appears that Green's congressional future depends on the intricate negotiation going on between hostile figures in Pennsylvania's byzantine politics.

Census Data 1970 pop. 404,726; deviation from current state average, —7.3%; change 1960–70, —3.0%. Metro. 100.0%, 100.0% central city.

1970 Share of Federal Outlays $472,901,000 (average outlay per district, Pennsylvania 1–5)

DOD	$203,599,000	HEW	$139,248,000
AEC	$729,000	HUD	$11,798,000
NASA	$279,000	OEO	$3,469,000
DOT	$13,728,000	DOA	$2,624,000
		Other	$97,427,000

Federal Military-Industrial Commitments (See Pennsylvania 3 for Philadelphia listing.)

Economic Base Apparel and other finished products made from fabrics and similar materials, esp. men's, youths', and boys' suit, coats, and overcoats; printing, publishing, and allied industries, esp. commercial printing and newspapers; electrical machinery, equipment, and supplies, esp. switchgear and switchboard apparatus; food and kindred products, esp. bakery products and meat products. Also, higher education (Temple University).

The Voters

Registration 180,304 total. 113,418 D (63%); 66,886 R (37%).

Employment profile White collar, 42%. Blue collar, 58%.

Ethnic groups Black, 34%. Total foreign stock, 35%. USSR, Poland, UK, 5% each; Italy, Germany, Ireland, 4% each; Austria, Hungary, Canada, 1% each; others, 4%.

Presidential vote

1968	Humphrey (D)	103,496	(62%)
	Nixon (R)	48,266	(29%)
	Wallace (AIP)	14,934	(9%)

Representative

William Joseph Green (D) Elected April 28, 1964; b. June 24, 1938, Philadelphia; home, Philadelphia; St. Joseph's Col., B.A., 1960; Villanova Law School, 1961–63; married, two children; Catholic.

Career Elected to fill the vacancy caused by the death of his father, William J. Green.

Offices 1128 LHOB, 202-225-6271. Also 3036 U.S. Courthouse, 9th and Chestnut St., Philadelphia 19107, 215-627-5548.

Committees

Ways and Means (12th).

Group Ratings

	ADA	COPE	NREP	NFU	LCV	CFA	NAB	NSI	ACA
1970	100	100	100	100	71	100	0	0	6
1969	100	—	—	93	—	—	—	—	6
1968	100	100	—	100	—	—	0	—	0

Key Votes

(1) ABM	AGN	(6) 18-Yr-Vote	FOR	(11) Clean Water $	FOR
(2) SST	AGN	(7) Farm Sub Lmt	FOR	(12) Mig Wrkrs Comp	FOR
(3) Phil Pln	FOR	(8) Coop-Church	FOR	(13) Jets to Chiang	AGN
(4) No-Knock	AGN	(9) Family Asst	FOR	(14) State OEO Veto	AGN
(5) Cmutr Tax	FOR	(10) Work Stamps	AGN	(15) Park Logging	ABS

Election Results

1970 general:	William J. Green (D)	80,142	(67%)
	James H. Ring (R)	38,955	(33%)
	John Donahue (AIP)	724	(1%)
1970 primary:	William J. Green (D), unopposed		
1968 general:	William J. Green (D)	108,234	(69%)
	Gregory J. Meade (R)	48,455	(31%)

SIXTH DISTRICT Political Background

Pennsylvania 6 is Berks and Schuylkill counties—an industrial and agricultural region northwest of Philadelphia. The 6th constitutes the borderland between the conservative Pennsylvania Dutch country and the industrial Lehigh and Lackawanna valleys. In politics, the district is more industrial than Dutch. The factory workers in Reading and the anthracite coal miners—or ex-coal miners—in Schuylkill County towns like Tamaqua and Mahanoy City vote Democratic in most elections. The blue-collar vote here usually overcomes the Republican margins cast in the southern, rural portions of the district. The 6th's Democratic tendency is accentuated by the hard-pressed economic conditions of local industries.

From 1948 to 1968, George M. Rhodes represented the district. The Congressman was a stalwart Democrat, labor leader, and one of the founders of the liberal Democratic Study Group. He retired in 1968 and was succeeded by Gus H. Yatron, a 12-year veteran of the state legislature and the owner of an ice cream business. Like Rhodes, Yatron usually votes with other House liberals; he has done so even on issues like Cooper-Church, which did not have the full support of labor. He also serves on the Foreign Affairs Committee, where he is a moderate.

Like his predecessor Rhodes, Yatron is a top vote-getter. In 1968, a Republican made a strong bid for the seat, but lost when Yatron took 51% of the vote; the Congressman ran 5% ahead of Humphrey in the district and 4% ahead of ex-Sen. Joseph Clark. Two years later, Yatron won in a breeze with 65%. He is unlikely to have any trouble in the future, and Democratic redistricters will no doubt be kind to him.

Census Data 1970 pop. 456,471; deviation from current state average, +4.5%; change 1960–70, +1.8%. Metro. 64.9%, 19.2% central city.

1970 Share of Federal Outlays $222,836,079

DOD	$24,898,000	HEW	$116,964,687
AEC	$000	HUD	$13,295,756
NASA	$149,438	OEO	$488,559
DOT	$467,964	DOA	$3,788,349
		Other	$62,783,326

Federal Military-Industrial Commitments

None.

Economic Base Apparel and other finished products made from fabrics and similar materials, esp. women's, misses', and juniors' outerwear; knitting mills and other textile mill products; primary metal industries, esp. iron and steel foundries. Also, banking.

The Voters

Registration 205,547 total. 102,706 D (50%); 102,841 R (50%).

Employment profile White collar, 31%. Blue collar, 69%.

Ethnic groups Black, 2%. Total foreign stock, 17%. Poland, Italy, 3% each; Germany, Austria, 2% each; UK, Czech., USSR, 1% each; others, 5%.

Presidential vote

1968	Humphrey (D)	84,859	(46%)
	Nixon (R)	87,817	(47%)
	Wallace (AIP)	12,474	(7%)

Representative

Gus Yatron (D) Elected 1968; b. Oct. 16, 1927, Reading; home, Reading; Kutztown State Teachers Col., 1950; married, two children; Greek Orthodox.

Career Businessman, Yatron's Ice Cream, 1950–68; Reading School Bd., 1955–60; Pa. Legislature, 1956–60; Pa. Senate, 1960-68.

Offices 313 CHOB, 202-225-5546. Also 203 P.O. Bldg., 5th and Washington Sts., Reading 19603, 215-375-4573, and 603 American Bank Bldg., Pottsville 17901, 717-622-4212.

Committees

Foreign Affairs (17th); Subs. (1) Africa, (2) Europe, (3) Foreign Economic Policy.

Group Ratings

	ADA	COPE	NREP	NFU	LCV	CFA	NAB	NSI	ACA
1970	68	92	92	92	100	86	9	66	26
1969	60	—	—	93	—	—	—	—	29

Key Votes

(1) ABM	AGN	(6) 18-Yr-Vote	FOR	(11) Clean Water $	FOR
(2) SST	AGN	(7) Farm Sub Lmt	FOR	(12) Mig Wrkrs Comp	FOR
(3) Phil Pln	AGN	(8) Coop-Church	FOR	(13) Jets to Chiang	AGN
(4) No-Knock	FOR	(9) Family Asst	AGN	(14) State OEO Veto	AGN
(5) Cmutr Tax	FOR	(10) Work Stamps	AGN	(15) Park Logging	AGN

Election Results

1970 general:	Gus Yatron (D)	96,453	(65%)
	Michael Kitsock (R)	48,397	(33%)
	George T. Atkins (C)	3,469	(2%)
1970 primary:	Gus Yatron (D), unopposed		
1968 general:	Gus Yatron (D)	94,247	(51%)
	Peter Yonavick (R)	87,090	(48%)
	Joseph G. Brewer (C)	1,914	(1%)

SEVENTH DISTRICT Political Background

Pennsylvania 7, a suburban area southwest of Philadelphia, contains the larger part of Delaware County. The county is adjacent to, and contains more people than, the state of Delaware. The northern portion of the district comprises part of the famous Main Line, the wealthy commuter suburbs that sprang up about 50 years ago along the then prosperous Pennsylvania Railroad. The district's boundary cuts through the middle of the Main Line and includes all or part of St. Davids, Radnor, Villanova, Bryn Mawr, and Haverford—all towns with colleges. To the south are similar, upper-middle-class suburbs like Springfield, Swarthmore (site of another famous college), and Drexel Hill. Nearer Philadelphia and the Delaware River are slightly less prosperous suburbs like Upper Darby, Yeadon, and Darby; all of these, nevertheless, have a well-settled, middle-class air about them. The district as a whole is Republican, though it does have a distinct Democratic minority.

The 7th was created by the 1966 redistricting. Its first and only congressman has been Republican Lawrence G. Williams. Williams is perhaps the most conservative member of the Pennsylvania delegation. He has run, if anything, slightly behind his party's usual showings in the district. With the Democrats now in complete control of the redistricting process, Williams, who got 59% of the vote in 1970, could have trouble in 1972. The legislature might put some of the more Republican parts of the 7th into the adjacent Philadelphia district, where they can do no harm, and then draw a new 7th which would run along the Delaware River. Such a district would include the industrial, low-income city of Chester—whose Democratic margins are now lost in the heavily Republican 9th district—and would exclude the heavily Republican Main Line suburbs. The aim, obviously, is the election of a Democratic congressman. And if the Democratic legislators fail in their design, it will be only because of the tremendous advantage enjoyed by any alert incumbent, armed with the franking privilege.

Census Data 1970 pop. 422,543; deviation from current state average, −3.3%; change 1960–70, +8.3%. Metro. 100.0%, 0.0% central city.

1970 Share of Federal Outlays $307,326,000 (average outlay per district, Pennsylvania 7 and 9)

DOD	$136,223,000	HEW	$81,311,000
AEC	$4,000	HUD	$619,000
NASA	$1,712,000	OEO	$1,043,000
DOT	$10,209,000	DOA	$3,412,000
		Other	$72,793,000

Federal Military-Industrial Commitments (Pennslyvania 7 and 9 listing)

DOD Contractors Boeing Co. (Morton), $142.254m: CH-47 helicopters. Sun Oil Co. (Marcus Hook), $18.408m: petroleum products. General Electric (Valley Forge), $12.288m: unspecified. Lasko Metal Products (West Chester), $11.239m: bomb dispensers and bomb fins. Burroughs Corp. (Paoli), $7.191m: data processing equipment and services.

Economic Base Transportation equipment, esp. aircraft and parts; nonelectrical machinery, esp. engines and turbines; converted paper and paperboard products other than containers and boxes, and other paper and allied products; printing, publishing, and allied industries. Also, extensive commuting to Pennsylvania 3 (Philadelphia).

The Voters

Registration 212,249 total. 47,348 D (22%); 164,901 R (78%).

Employment profile White collar, 58%. Blue collar, 42%.

Ethnic groups Black, 3%. Total foreign stock, 26%. Italy, 7%; UK, Ireland, 4% each; Germany, USSR, 2% each; Poland, Canada, Austria, 1% each; others, 4%.

Presidential vote

1968	Humphrey (D)	79,916	(41%)
	Nixon (R)	99,140	(51%)
	Wallace (AIP)	17,276	(9%)

Representative

Lawrence G. Williams (R) Elected 1966; b. Sept. 15, 1913, Pittsburgh; home, Springfield; Drexel Inst. of Tech.; Army, Air Corps, WWII; married, two children; Methodist.

Career Exec., Curtis Publishing Co., 1936–66; Rep., Del. County on Penn-Jersey Transportation Study, 1959–66; Del. Valley Reg. Planning Com., 1963–66.

Offices 1503 LHOB, 202-225-2011. Also Township Bldg., 50 Powell Rd., Springfield 19064, 215-543-2082.

Committees

Banking and Currency (7th); Subs. (1) Consumer Affairs, (2) Domestic Finance, (3) Small Business.

Standards of Official Conduct (4th).

Group Ratings

	ADA	COPE	NREP	NFU	LCV	CFA	NAB	NSI	ACA
1970	12	17	17	23	25	50	100	90	100
1969	0	—	—	20	—	—	—	—	88
1968	8	8	—	44	—	—	100	—	90

Key Votes

(1) ABM	FOR	(6) 18-Yr-Vote	AGN	(11) Clean Water $	AGN
(2) SST	FOR	(7) Farm Sub Lmt	FOR	(12) Mig Wrkrs Comp	AGN
(3) Phil Pln	AGN	(8) Coop-Church	AGN	(13) Jets to Chiang	AGN
(4) No-Knock	FOR	(9) Family Asst	AGN	(14) State OEO Veto	FOR
(5) Cmutr Tax	AGN	(10) Work Stamps	FOR	(15) Park Logging	FOR

Election Results

1970 general:	Lawrence G. Williams (R)	91,042	(59%)
	Joseph R. Breslin (D)	62,722	(41%)
1970 primary:	Lawrence G. Williams (R)	38,171	(65%)
	Bernard H. White (R)	20,410	(35%)
1968 general:	Lawrence G. Williams (R)	105,699	(57%)
	Edward J. O'Halloran (D)	79,782	(43%)
	John Phillips (C)	1,561	(1%)

EIGHTH DISTRICT Political Background

Pennsylvania 8 is another suburban Philadelphia district (see also Pennsylvania 7, 9, and 13). It includes two townships in Montgomery County that are heavily Republican; a small portion of Lehigh County, suburban Allentown, which is also Republican; and Bucks County. Three-quarters of the district's voters live in Bucks, whose politics have become familiar to some through the prose efforts of best-selling author James Michener. Michener has been active in the local Democratic party, but as a political man he has never been completely successful—Republicans win most elections in Bucks. Yet Michener has not labored in a suburban monolith. Bucks' image comes from the northern part of the county, which is a pastoral delight. This is where wealthy writers and rentiers live in stone Quaker farmhouses set in the rolling hills near places like Doylestown, Quakertown, and New Hope.

Almost half of Bucks' population, however, lives in surroundings which are quite different. These people can be found in the industrial and working-class suburbs built in the '50's along the Delaware River between Philadelphia and Trenton, New Jersey. Places like Levittown and Fairless Hills (site of U.S. Steel's huge Fairless Mill) usually go Democratic and make Bucks County marginal in its politics. In 1970, Democratic Gov. Milton Shapp got 56% of the vote here—his best showing in the Philadelphia suburbs—and Democratic state Sen. William Sesler, from Erie at the opposite end of the state, got 43% of the votes in Bucks against the well-known Sen. Hugh Scott.

The congressman from the district is Edward G. Biester, Jr. He is a member of the state's good-sized bloc of liberal Republicans in the House. Now the 8th ranking Republican on the Judiciary Committee, Biester has supported major civil rights legislation of the recent past. The Congressman's first race, in 1966, was expected to be a tough one, but he won 59% of the vote then and has been doing even better since. Since the Democrats control redistricting in the state, they could, as an academic exercise, draw some lines on the map which would give Biester trouble. But most likely the legislators will look other places for their gains and leave the 8th a marginal-to-Republican district, one which Biester has proved he can carry easily.

Census Data 1970 pop. 477,979; deviation from current state average, +9.4%; change 1960–70, +34.0%. Metro. 100.0%, 0.0% central city.

1970 Share of Federal Outlays $186,228,000

DOD	$66,865,000	HEW	$53,966,000
AEC	$000	HUD	$712,000
NASA	$275,000	OEO	$157,000
DOT	$13,491,000	DOA	$1,855,000
		Other	$48,905,000

Federal Military-Industrial Commitments

DOD Contractors Straightline Mfg. (Cornwells Heights), $8.002m: Mark 82 bomb fin assemblies. Philco-Ford (Willow Grove), $6.061m: computer card punch machines. American Electronic Labs (Colmar), $5.167m: electronic warfare assemblies.

DOD Installations Naval Air Station (Willow Grove).

Economic Base Primary metal industries; chemicals and allied products; professional, scientific, and controlling instruments, photographic and optical goods, watches and clocks. Also, extensive commuting to Pennsylvania 3 (Philadelphia).

The Voters

Registration 186,297 total. 75,334 D (40%); 110,963 R (60%).

Employment profile White collar, 43%. Blue collar, 57%.

Ethnic groups Black, 2%. Total foreign stock, 20%. Germany, UK, Italy, 3% each; Poland, 2%; USSR, Ireland, Austria, Canada, Czech., 1% each; others, 4%.

Presidential vote

1968	Humphrey (D)	66,257	(39%)
	Nixon (R)	84,963	(51%)
	Wallace (AIP)	16,890	(10%)

Representative

Edward G. Biester, Jr. (R) Elected 1966; b. Jan. 5, 1931, Trevose; home, Furlong; Wesleyan U., B.A., 1952; Temple U., LL.B., 1955; married, four children; United Church of Christ.

Career Practicing atty., 1956–66; Asst. Dist. Atty., Bucks County, 1958–64.

Offices 325 CHOB, 202-225-4276. Also 68 E. Court St., Doylestown 18901, 215-348-4005, and 7500 Bristol Pike, Rt. 13, P.O. Box 12, Levittown 19059, 215-348-2558.

Committees

Judiciary (8th); Sub. No. 3.

Group Ratings

	ADA	COPE	NREP	NFU	LCV	CFA	NAB	NSI	ACA
1970	76	75	75	100	75	79	58	90	32
1969	60	—	—	73	—	—	—	—	29
1968	33	31	—	75	—	—	83	—	50

Key Votes

(1) ABM	FOR	(6) 18-Yr-Vote	FOR	(11) Clean Water $	FOR
(2) SST	AGN	(7) Farm Sub Lmt	FOR	(12) Mig Wrkrs Comp	FOR
(3) Phil Pln	FOR	(8) Coop-Church	FOR	(13) Jets to Chiang	AGN
(4) No-Knock	FOR	(9) Family Asst	FOR	(14) State OEO Veto	AGN
(5) Cmutr Tax	AGN	(10) Work Stamps	AGN	(15) Park Logging	AGN

Election Results

1970 general:	Edward G. Biester, Jr. (R)	73,041	(56%)
	Arthur Leo Hennessy, Jr. (D)	51,464	(40%)
	Charles B. Moore (C)	5,118	(4%)
1970 primary:	Edward G. Biester, Jr. (R), unopposed		
1968 general:	Edward G. Biester, Jr. (R)	94,254	(58%)
	Richard M. Hepburn (D)	60,324	(27%)
	E. Stanley Rittenhouse (C)	8,064	(5%)

NINTH DISTRICT Political Background

Pennsylvania 9 comprises part of suburban Delaware County and all of exurban Chester County to the west. There are a few Democratic enclaves in the district, most notably the industrial city of Chester which has a large black population. But the 9th can be best characterized as a heavily Republican district; it almost gave Barry Goldwater a majority in 1960. From Valley Forge in the east, to the town of Oxford (site of black Lincoln University) in the west, the small towns and the picturesque countryside are all Republican. This political preference is particularly strong in the western half of Chester County, which is part of Pennsylvania Dutch country. The "Dutch" are actually descendants of German settlers who began farming this area in the eighteenth century, and to this day they have retained many of their customs (see Pennsylvania 16). Among the customs is a deep loyalty to the Republican party; the Republican margins in Dutch areas of the state are almost as large as Democratic margins in black ghettos.

The district's congressman, G. Robert Watkins, a conservative Republican died in the summer of 1970 after serving three terms in the House. His successor, John H. Ware, III, another Republican, campaigned as a strong backer of the Nixon Administration. Perhaps because of the antiwar sympathies of the district's many Quakers, Ware ran behind his party's usual showing in the district; he won 59% of the vote. Most likely, with the advantages of incumbency at hand, Ware will do better next time. Redistricting will probably shift the focus of the district to the west. That will decrease the number of Quaker voters in his constituency and increase the number of Dutch, which will work to Ware's advantage.

Census Data 1970 pop. 455,803; deviation from current state average, +4.3%; change 1960–70, +22.0%. Metro. 100.0%, 0.0% central city.

1970 Share of Federal Outlays $307,326,000 (average outlay per district, Pennsylvania 7 and 9)

DOD	$136,223,000	HEW	$81,311,000
AEC	$4,000	HUD	$619,000
NASA	$1,712,000	OEO	$1,043,000
DOT	$10,209,000	DOA	$3,412,000
		Other	$72,793,000

Federal Military-Industrial Commitments (See Pennsylvania 7 for listing.)

Economic Base Transportation equipment, esp. aircraft and parts; nonelectrical machinery, esp. engines and turbines; blast furnaces, esp. steel works, and rolling and finishing mills, and other primary metal industries; electrical machinery, equipment, and supplies. Also, extensive commuting to Pennsylvania 3 (Philadelphia).

The Voters

Registration 183,039 total. 40,994 D (22%); 142,045 R (78%).

Employment profile White collar, 40%. Blue collar, 60%.

Ethnic groups Black, 12%. Total foreign stock, 16%. Italy, 4%; UK, Poland, 2% each; Ireland, Germany, USSR, Austria, Canada, Czech., 1% each; others, 5%.

Presidential vote

1968	Humphrey (D)	52,218	(36%)
	Nixon (R)	90,487	(54%)
	Wallace (AIP)	16,902	(10%)

Representative

John H. Ware (R) Elected 1970; b. Aug. 29, 1908, Vineland, N.J.; home, Oxford; U. of Pa., B.S., 1930; married, four children; Presbyterian.

Career Chm. of Bd., North Penn Gas Co. and American Water Works Co.; Pres., Penn Fuel Gas Inc. and United Utilities Co.; Dir., Oxford Corp., Pa. Gas Assn.; Mayor, Borough of Oxford, 1956–60; Pa. Senate, 1961–70, Majority Caucus Chm., 1967–70; Chm., Rep. Finance Com. of Pa.

Offices 1021 LHOB, 202-225-5761. Also 323 West Front St., Media 19063, 215-566-1734, and 21 S. Church St., West Chester 19380.

Committees

House Administration (8th); Subs. (1) Elections, (2) Sp. on Police.

Interstate and Foreign Commerce (16th); Sub. on Commerce and Finance.

Group Ratings, Key Votes: Newly elected.

Election Results

1970 general:	John H. Ware, III (R)	76,535	(59%)
	Louis F. Waldmann (D)	52,852	(41%)
1970 primary:	Nominated by Republican caucus following the death of Congressman G. Robert Watkins.		

TENTH DISTRICT Political Background

Pennsylvania 10, in the northeast corner of the state, is made up of a group of rural counties and the city of Scranton in the Lackawanna River Valley. The rural areas, settled long ago by WASP and Scots-Irish farmers, are heavily Republican. Scranton is, or used to be, quite the opposite. Scranton is the home of Republican Congressman (1960–62), Governor (1962–66) and presidential candidate William Scranton, whose family gave its name to the city. Since the turn of the century, Scranton has been the center of the nation's anthracite (hard) coal industry; but about the time of the Great Depression, the veins began to give out. In 1940, the city had over 150,000 residents; today it has 105,000. Unemployment is a chronic problem; so is air and water pollution.

For a long time, the economic stagnation and unemployment produced steady Democratic margins in Scranton and Lackawanna County. But after a while, many of the ex-miners—most of them of Eastern European descent—moved out for good. As a result, Scranton today casts far fewer Democratic votes than it once did, and Republicans have been carrying the 10th district regularly. That regularity has been especially notable in the case of Congressman Joseph M. McDade, a liberal Republican who succeeded Scranton in the seat. After close shaves in 1962 and 1964, McDade has been winning with well over 60% of the vote. He has carried Scranton and Lackawanna, as well as the outlying counties.

McDade is one of the few liberal Republicans to win a seat on the House Appropriations Committee, where he is ranking minority member on its Interior Subcommittee. McDade is so entrenched in the district that the Democratic legislators will probably concede him the seat in redistricting. Nonetheless, the Democrats have a good chance in the 10th, if for some reason McDade does not run as the Republican incumbent.

Census Data 1970 pop. 432,546; deviation from current state average, −1.0%; change 1960–70, +3.1%. Metro. 62.1%, 23.9% central city.

1970 Share of Federal Outlays $304,806,793

DOD	$85,880,000	HEW	$120,154,995
AEC	$000	HUD	$5,731,466
NASA	$000	OEO	$184,741
DOT	$12,430,002	DOA	$7,723,152
		Other	$72,702,437

Federal Military-Industrial Commitments

DOD Contractors Chamberlain Mfg. (Scranton), $51.538m: components for 175-mm and 155-mm high explosive projectiles.

Economic Base Apparel and other finished products made from fabrics and similar materials, esp. womens', misses', and juniors' outerwear and men's, youths', and boys' furnishings, work clothing, and allied garments; dairy; fabricated metal products, esp. heating apparatus (except electric) and plumbing fixtures.

The Voters

Registration 217,638 total. 109,389 D (50%); 108,249 R (50%).

Employment profile White collar, 34%. Blue collar, 67%.

Ethnic groups Black, less than 0.5%. Total foreign stock, 26%. Italy, 6%; Poland, 5%; UK, 4%; Austria, Germany, Ireland, 2% each; USSR, Czech., 1% each; others, 5%.

Presidential vote

1968	Humphrey (D)	88,716	(46%)
	Nixon (R)	94,081	(49%)
	Wallace (AIP)	8,813	(5%)

Representative

Joseph Michael McDade (R) Elected 1962; b. Sept. 29, 1931, Scranton; home, Scranton; U. of Notre Dame, B.A., 1953; U. of Pa., LL.B., 1956; married, four children; Catholic.

Career Clerk to Fed. Judge, 1956–57 practicing atty., 1957– ; Scranton City Solicitor, 1962.

Offices 2438 RHOB, 202-225-3731. Also 1233 Northeastern Natl. Bank Bldg., Scranton 18503, 717-346-3834.

Committees

Appropriations (11th); Subs. (1) HUD, Space, and Science, (2) Interior.

Sel. Com. on Small Business (5th); Sub. on Special Small Business Problems.

Group Ratings

	ADA	COPE	NREP	NFU	LCV	CFA	NAB	NSI	ACA
1970	56	67	75	91	63	76	64	90	39
1969	47	—	—	73	—	—	—	—	29
1968	50	77	—	69	—	—	100	—	32

Key Votes

(1) ABM	FOR	(6) 18-Yr-Vote	FOR	(11) Clean Water $	AGN
(2) SST	FOR	(7) Farm Sub Lmt	FOR	(12) Mig Wrkrs Comp	AGN
(3) Phil Pln	FOR	(8) Coop-Church	FOR	(13) Jets to Chiang	AGN
(4) No-Knock	FOR	(9) Family Asst	FOR	(14) State OEO Veto	AGN
(5) Cmutr Tax	FOR	(10) Work Stamps	AGN	(15) Park Logging	AGN

Election Results

1970 general:	Joseph M. McDade (R)	102,716	(65%)
	Edward J. Smith (D)	51,506	(33%)
	Stephen P. Depue (C)	2,731	(2%)
1970 primary:	Joseph M. McDade (R), unopposed		
1968 general:	Joseph M. McDade (R)	125,916	(67%)
	Robert J. Landy (D)	61,960	(33%)
	Eugene Bancale (C)	1,073	(1%)

ELEVENTH DISTRICT Political Background

Pennsylvania 11 consists of three industrial counties—Luzerne, Carbon, and Columbia—in northeastern Pennsylvania. The largest of these is Luzerne and the county's largest city is Wilkes-Barre. The town was founded by settlers from the east in the late 1770's who wanted to commemorate two heroes of the Revolutionary War. Wilkes-Barre, like Scranton to the north, is a city dependent on the mining of anthracite coal, and because the anthracite veins have been worked out, the entire 11th is an economically-depressed area, with heavy unemployment and declining population. These circumstances have strengthened the Democratic voting habits of its residents, a large percentage of which are of Polish, Italian, and Czech ancestry. Outside of the Philadelphia and Pittsburgh metropolitan areas, the 11th is the most Democratic part of Pennsylvania in election after election.

Except for two terms following the Republican years of 1946 and 1952, Daniel J. Flood has represented the district in Congress since 1944. Flood is one of the most distinctive men in the House; he has a thin, neatly waxed mustache and is fond of quoting Shakespeare in speeches to his colleagues. He is also one of the more powerful men in that body: 10th ranking Democrat on the House Appropriations Committee and chairman of its Subcommittee on Labor and HEW. His chairmanship gives him a strong voice in the funding of most social programs. He also sits on the Defense Subcommittee, which, of course, has jurisdiction over about half of the federal budget.

Flood has always had strong labor support and he votes pretty much the way George Meany would have him: liberal on domestic issues, hawkish on foreign policy. The Congressman is unbeatable in the 11th district; in 1970 he did not even have a Republican opponent and took 97% of the vote against a candidate of the Constitution party, which is Wallaceite. Only advancing age endangers Flood's service in Congress; he was 67 in 1970.

Census Data 1970 pop. 447,988; deviation from current state average, +2.6%; change 1960–70, −1.2%. Metro. 76.4%, 19.9% central city.

1970 Share of Federal Outlays $265,998,548

DOD	$40,385,000	HEW	$133,231,902
AEC	$000	HUD	$8,083,464
NASA	$000	OEO	$692,759
DOT	$3,925,746	DOA	$2,962,433
		Other	$76,717,244

Federal Military-Industrial Commitments

DOD Contractors U.S. Steel (Berwick), $15.036m: 8-inch high explosive projectiles. Medico Industries (Wilkes-Barre), $7.694m: 2.75-inch rocket warhead components.

DOD Installations Benton AF Station (Red Rock).

Economic Base Apparel and other finished products made from fabrics and similar materials, esp. women's, misses', and juniors' outerwear; textile mill products; food and kindred products.

The Voters

Registration 220,176 total. 107,496 D (49%); 112,680 R (51%).
Employment profile White collar, 32%. Blue collar, 68%.
Ethnic groups Black, 1%. Total foreign stock, 32%. Poland, 8%; Italy, 5%; Austria, UK, 4% each; Czech., 3%; Germany, 2%; Ireland, USSR, 1% each; others, 5%.
Presidential vote

1968	Humphrey (D)	97,861	(52%)
	Nixon (R)	79,200	(42%)
	Wallace (AIP)	9,606	(5%)

Representative

Daniel J. Flood (D) elected 1954; b. Nov. 26, 1903, Hazleton; home, Wilkes-Barre; Syracuse U., B.A., 1924, M.A.; Harvard Law School, 1925–26; Dickinson School of Law, LL.B., 1929; married; Catholic.

Career Practicing atty., 1930– ; Deputy Atty. Gen., Pa., and Counsel for Pa. Liquor Control Bd., 1935–39; Dir., Bureau of Public Assistance Disbursements, State Treas., and Exec. Asst. to State Treas., 1941–44; Sp. Ambassador to Peru, 1945; U.S. House of Reps., 1944–46, 1948–52.

Offices 108 CHOB, 202-225-6511. Also Rm. 1015, United Penn Bank Bldg., Wilkes-Barre 18701, 717-822-2194.

Committees

Appropriations (10th); Subs. (1) Chm., Labor, Health, Education, and Welfare, (2) Defense.

Group Ratings

	ADA	COPE	NREP	NFU	LCV	CFA	NAB	NSI	ACA
1970	36	92	42	100	67	67	8	89	29
1969	47	—	—	100	—	—	—	—	12
1968	58	100	—	100	—	—	0	—	16

Key Votes

(1) ABM	FOR	(6) 18-Yr-Vote	FOR	(11) Clean Water $	FOR
(2) SST	FOR	(7) Farm Sub Lmt	AGN	(12) Mig Wrkrs Comp	FOR
(3) Phil Pln	AGN	(8) Coop-Church	AGN	(13) Jets to Chiang	FOR
(4) No-Knock	FOR	(9) Family Asst	FOR	(14) State OEO Veto	AGN
(5) Cmutr Tax	FOR	(10) Work Stamps	AGN	(15) Park Logging	AGN

Election Results

1970 general:	Daniel J. Flood (D-R)	146,789	(97%)
	Alvin J. Balschi (C)	5,123	(3%)
1970 primary:	Daniel J. Flood (D), unopposed		
1968 general:	Daniel J. Flood (D)	128,794	(70%)
	Stanley Bunn (R)	52,475	(29%)
	Dawn M. Baker (C)	2,822	(2%)

TWELFTH DISTRICT Political Background

Pennsylvania 12 spans the rugged Appalachian mountains from the Susquehanna River on the east to a point some 30 miles from Pittsburgh on the west. The mountain ridges in the district run from northeast to southwest, and most of the people here live in the narrow valleys between one chain and the next. There is relatively little industry or mining in this part of the Appalachians; the terrain is too wild and the rich seams of coal lie to the north and south. The 12th's largest city is Altoona (pop. 62,000), a longtime center of operation for the now bankrupt Penn Central Railroad. This part of

Pennsylvania, like West Virginia, is inhabited mostly by the descendants of Scots-Irish pioneers. The people in the 12th have retained their Protestantism, and unlike the West Virginia brethren, their Republicanism as well. This area does not suffer from poverty as grinding as that farther south.

J. Irving Whalley has served the district in the House since a special election in 1960. The Congressman, one of the state's more conservative Republicans, is a small town banker and a veteran of 12 years in the Pennsylvania legislature. In Washington, he sits on the Foreign Affairs Committee and in his district has proved to be a strong vote-getter. Redistricting could endanger his reelection chances, but a look at the 1970 census figures indicates the 12th is not the rural Pennsylvania district which may be absorbed by its neighbors (see Pennsylvania 17).

Census Data 1970 pop. 495,058; deviation from current state average, +13.3%; change 1960–70, +2.7%. Metro. 48.5%, 12.7% central city.

1970 Share of Federal Outlays $284,563,632

DOD	$64,573,000	HEW	$142,002,978
AEC	$000	HUD	$861,232
NASA	$43,862	OEO	$300,026
DOT	$3,666,127	DOA	$13,525,075
		Other	$59,591,332

Federal Military-Industrial Commitments

DOD Installations Letterkenny Army Depot (Chambersburg).

Economic Base Dairy; apparel and other finished products made from fabrics and similar materials; nonelectrical machinery, esp. metalworking machinery and equipment.

The Voters

Registration 203,948 total. 80,748 D (40%); 123,200 R (60%).

Employment profile White collar, 32%. Blue collar, 68%.

Ethnic groups Black, 4%. Total foreign stock, 7%. Italy, 2%; Germany, UK, Poland, Austria, Czech., 1% each; others, 2%.

Presidential vote

1968	Humphrey (D)	59,742	(33%)
	Nixon (R)	105,222	(58%)
	Wallace (AIP)	15,489	(9%)

Representative

J. Irving Whalley (R) Elected Nov. 8, 1960; b. Sept. 14, ca. 1900, Barnesboro; home, Windber; married, two children; Presbyterian.

Career Windber School Bd., 1935–47, Pres., 1938–44; Pres., Citizens Natl. Bank, 1944– ; Pa. Legislature, 1951–55; Pa. Senate, 1955–60; Chm., Somerset County Redevelopment Authority and Windber Planning Commission, 1957–69.

Offices 1235 LHOB, 202-225-4676. Also 1203 Graham Ave., Windber 15963, 814-467-4000.

Committees

Foreign Affairs (4th); Subs. (1) Africa, (2) Asian and Pacific Affairs, (3) Inter-American Affairs, (4) Sp. for Review of Foreign Aid Program.

Group Ratings

	ADA	COPE	NREP	NFU	LCV	CFA	NAB	NSI	ACA
1970	8	11	20	25	50	61	100	100	95
1969	0	—	—	33	—	—	—	—	45
1968	0	0	—	21	—	—	100	—	95

Key Votes

(1) ABM	FOR	(6) 18-Yr-Vote	AGN	(11) Clean Water $	ABS
(2) SST	FOR	(7) Farm Sub Lmt	FOR	(12) Mig Wrkrs Comp	AGN
(3) Phil Pln	FOR	(8) Coop-Church	AGN	(13) Jets to Chiang	ABS
(4) No-Knock	FOR	(9) Family Asst	AGN	(14) State OEO Veto	ABS
(5) Cmutr Tax	ABS	(10) Work Stamps	ABS	(15) Park Logging	AGN

Election Results

1970 general:	J. Irving Whalley (R)	93,385	(64%)
	Victor J. Karycki, Jr. (D)	48,738	(33%)
	Kenneth W. Ferry (AIP)	1,923	(1%)
	Lloyd G. Cope (C)	1,848	(1%)
1970 primary:	J. Irving Whalley (R)	35,754	(76%)
	Samuel E. Hayes (R)	11,243	(24%)
1968 general:	J. Irving Whalley (R)	119,522	(68%)
	H. Richard Hostetlet (D)	55,838	(32%)

THIRTEENTH DISTRICT Political Background

Pennsylvania 13 is all of suburban Montgomery County, except for two townships which lie in the 8th district. This is where most of the population growth in the Philadelphia area has occurred in the last ten years, and the 13th currently has more people than any other Pennsylvania congressional district. The most heavily populated areas here are the strongly Republican Main Line suburbs (see also Pennsylvania 7) near the west side of Philadelphia, and the politically marginal towns near northeast Philadelphia, which have a large Jewish population. Norristown and Pottstown along the Schuylkill River have some industry, but most of the district is definitely suburban, and as one goes north and west, even rural. Much of Philadelphia's large Quaker population, with its tradition of pacifism, lives in this district.

From 1960 to 1968, the 13th was represented in the House by the state's current senator, Richard Schweiker. His successor, R. Lawrence Coughlin, is a man very much like him. Coughlin, who was 41 in 1970, is a liberal Republican; he was one of the sponsors of the House resolution to end the war by a fixed date. Coughlin's showings at the polls, however, have not been quite as strong as Schweiker's; the Congressman received 58% of the vote in 1970. Still, he is in no danger of losing. Redistricting will pare off some of the district's territory; some of its suburbs may be placed in the population-losing Philadelphia districts. The move will not affect the political character of the 13th.

Census Data 1970 pop. 577,337; deviation from current state average, +32.2%; change 1960–70, +19.9%. Metro. 100.0%, 0.0% central city.

1970 Share of Federal Outlays $340,094,000

DOD	$78,721,000	HEW	$113,014,000
AEC	$2,000	HUD	$794,000
NASA	$27,937,000	OEO	$304,000
DOT	$18,743,000	DOA	$14,321,000
		Other	$86,258,000

Federal Military-Industrial Commitments

DOD Installations Naval Air Facility (Johnsville).

NASA Contractors General Electric (King of Prussia), $12.805m: Nimbus spacecraft; research in spectroscopy.

Economic Base Fabricated metal products, esp. fabricated structural metal products; chemicals and allied products, esp. drugs and plastics materials and synthetic resins, synthetic rubber, synthetic and other man-made fibers except glass; primary metal industries, esp. blast furnaces, steel works, and rolling and finishing mills; rubber and miscellaneous plastics products, esp. tires and innertubes. Also, banking.

The Voters

Registration 255,967 total. 67,412 D (26%); 188,555 R (74%).

Employment profile White collar, 51%. Blue collar, 49%.

Ethnic groups Black, 4%. Total foreign stock, 23%. Italy, 5%; UK, Germany, USSR, 3% each; Ireland, Poland, 2% each; Austria, Canada, Hungary, 1% each; others, 3%.

Presidential vote

1968	Humphrey (D)	95,947	(40%)
	Nixon (R)	128,536	(54%)
	Wallace (AIP)	14,183	(6%)

Representative

R. Lawrence Coughlin (R) Elected 1968; b. April 11, 1929, Wilkes-Barre; home, Villanova; Yale U., B.A., 1950; Harvard, M.B.A., 1954; Temple U. Evening Law School, LL.B., 1958; USMC, Korean War; married, four children; Episcopalian.

Career Practicing atty., 1958–1969; Pa. Legislature, 1965–66; Pa. Senate, 1967–68.

Offices 336 CHOB, 202-225-6111. Also 607 Swede St., Norristown 19401, 215-277-4040.

Committees

Judiciary (12th); Sub. No. 3.

Science and Astronautics (11th); Sub. on Science, Research, and Development.

Group Ratings

	ADA	COPE	NREP	NFU	LCV	CFA	NAB	NSI	ACA
1970	64	42	67	67	100	83	80	80	65
1969	47	—	—	60	—	—	—	—	47

Key Votes

(1) ABM	AGN	(6) 18-Yr-Vote	FOR	(11) Clean Water $	FOR
(2) SST	AGN	(7) Farm Sub Lmt	FOR	(12) Mig Wrkrs Comp	AGN
(3) Phil Pln	FOR	(8) Coop-Church	FOR	(13) Jets to Chiang	AGN
(4) No-Knock	FOR	(9) Family Asst	FOR	(14) State OEO Veto	AGN
(5) Cmutr Tax	AGN	(10) Work Stamps	FOR	(15) Park Logging	AGN

Election Results

1970 general:	R. Lawrence Coughlin (R)	101,953	(58%)
	Frank R. Romano (D)	68,743	(39%)
	John S. Matthews (C)	3,356	(2%)
	Anthony S. DeMeno (AIP)	718	(0%)
1970 primary:	R. Lawrence Coughlin (R)	35,392	(88%)
	John A. Capinski (R)	4,645	(12%)
1968 general:	R. Lawrence Coughlin (R)	141,764	(62%)
	Robert D. Gates (D)	84,137	(37%)
	John S. Matthews (C)	2,749	(1%)

FOURTEENTH DISTRICT Political Background

Pennsylvania 14 comprises most of Pittsburgh, the state's second largest city. Pittsburgh was one of the first urban centers in the American interior; it grew because the Allegheny and Monongahela meet here to form the Ohio River. Where that happens—the Golden Triangle—is still the city's focal point. It is now filled with impressive high-rise buildings, products of a downtown renaissance. Some of the buildings are occupied by the industry that built Pittsburgh, steel; that industry and the aluminum industry, later, were organized by that remarkable family of Pittsburgh Scots-Irishmen, the Mellons. Aside from U.S. Steel and Alcoa, the city is also headquarters for other major corporations, including Gulf Oil, Westinghouse, Koppers, and H. J. Heinz.

But in spite of the city's urban renewal program, and its relatively successful campaign against air pollution, Pittsburgh is not doing well. The population of the central city, which is now 520,000, is declining, as well as that of the entire metropolitan area. The steel industry is in sorry shape, and the city's location was good in the era of river and railroad transportation, but it is not so good in this day of trucks and air cargo.

The 14th contains most of the well-known features of Pittsburgh, including the Golden Triangle, the University of Pittsburgh and its skyscraper campus, and Carnegie Mellon University. The district also contains most of the city's black population and the numerous white ethnic neighborhoods that lie among Pittsburgh's many steep hills. The 14th is a heavily Democratic central city district and has not been known to go Republican in recent memory.

The congressman from the district is liberal Democrat William S. Moorhead. Moorhead is a middle-seniority member of the Banking and Currency and the Government Operations committees, and chairman of the latter's Subcommittee on Foreign Operations and Government Information. As chairman of that unit, he made some headlines when he uncovered government deception on foreign and military matters, including the tangled affairs of the Lockheed company. Moorhead has also been one of the House's leading advocates of legislation to protect the consumer. And finally, despite the presumed hawkish tendencies of his many labor union constituents, Moorhead has been a longtime critic of the war in its many phases.

Congressman Moorhead has had no difficulty winning reelection; in 1970, for example, he took 77% of the vote. He will have no trouble in the future. Because his district lost population, redistricting will add some suburban terrain. But Moorhead has had excellent press in white-collar areas as well as blue.

Census Data 1970 pop. 324,976; deviation from current state average, –25.6%; change 1960–70, –16.8%. Metro. 100.0%, 100.0% central city.

1970 Share of Federal Outlays $308,785,000 (average outlay per district, Pennsylvania 14, 18, 20, and 27)

DOD	$53,410,000	HEW	$111,378,000
AEC	$23,770,000	HUD	$9,216,000
NASA	$1,206,000	OEO	$1,348,000
DOT	$16,722,000	DOA	$1,558,000
		Other	$90,176,000

Federal Military-Industrial Commitments (Pennsylvania 14, 18, 20, and 27, greater Pittsburgh listing)

DOD Contractors Westinghouse Electric (Pittsburgh), $106.508m: ship nuclear propulsion reactors; radar equipment. U.S. Steel (McKeesport), $36.868m: unspecified. Levinson Steel (Pittsburgh), $11.153m: 105-mm projectiles.

DOD Installations Greater Pittsburgh Airport AF (Coraopolis).

AEC Operations Westinghouse Electric (Pittsburgh and West Miffiin), $64.863m: Bettis Atomic Power Laboratory and Astro Nuclear Laboratory. Aerojet General Corp. (Pittsburgh), $21.925m: unspecified.

Economic Base Primary metal industries, esp. blast furnaces, steel works, and rolling and finishing mills; fabricated metal products, esp. fabricated structural metal products; nonelectrical machinery, esp. metalworking machinery and equipment; food and kindred products; electrical machinery, equipment, and supplies. Also, higher education (University of Pittsburgh); banking.

The Voters

Registration 159,825 total. 121,540 D (76%); 38,285 R (24%).

Employment profile White collar, 44%. Blue collar, 56%.

Ethnic groups Black, 23%. Total foreign stock, 30%. Italy, 5%; Poland, Germany, 4% each; USSR, 3%; Ireland, UK, Austria, 2% each; Czech., Hungary, 1% each; others, 6%.

Presidential vote

1968	Humphrey (D)	91,248	(65%)
	Nixon (R)	35,277	(23%)
	Wallace (AIP)	13,083	(9%)

Representative

William S. Moorhead (D) Elected 1958; b. April 8, 1923, Pittsburgh; home, Pittsburgh; Yale U., B.A., 1944; Harvard Law School, J.D., 1949; Navy, WWII; married, four children; Episcopalian.

Career Practicing atty., 1949– ; Asst. City Solicitor, Pittsburgh, 1954–57; Allegheny County Housing Authority, 1956–58; Art Commission, Pittsburgh, 1958; Co-Chm., Pa. State Dem. Platform Com., 1966, 1970.

Offices 2418 RHOB, 202-225-2301. Also 2005 Fed. Bldg., Pittsburgh 15222, 412-644-2870.

Committees

Banking and Currency (6th); Subs. (1) Bank Supervision and Insurance, (2) Housing, (3) International Finance.

Government Operations (11th); Subs. (1) Chm., Foreign Operations and Government Information, (2) Legislation, (3) Legislation and Military Operations, (4) Sp. Studies.

Jt. Economic Com. (6th); Subs. (1) Economic Progress, (2) Fiscal Policy, (3) Foreign Economic Policy, (4) International Exchange and Payments, (5) Priorities and Economy in Government, (6) Urban Affairs.

Group Ratings

	ADA	COPE	NREP	NFU	LCV	CFA	NAB	NSI	ACA
1970	80	92	93	100	89	78	20	22	6
1969	87	—	—	80	—	—	—	—	13
1968	92	100	—	94	—	—	0	—	14

Key Votes

(1) ABM	AGN	(6) 18-Yr-Vote	FOR	(11) Clean Water $	FOR
(2) SST	AGN	(7) Farm Sub Lmt	FOR	(12) Mig Wrkrs Comp	FOR
(3) Phil Pln	FOR	(8) Coop-Church	FOR	(13) Jets to Chiang	ABS
(4) No-Knock	AGN	(9) Family Asst	FOR	(14) State OEO Veto	AGN
(5) Cmutr Tax	FOR	(10) Work Stamps	AGN	(15) Park Logging	AGN

Election Results

1970 general:	William S. Moorhead (D)	72,509	(77%)
	Barry Levine (R)	21,572	(23%)
	Reuben Francis Chaitin (AIP)	687	(1%)
1970 primary:	William S. Moorhead (D)	37,370	(70%)
	Byrd R. Brown (D)	14,251	(27%)
	Reuben Francis Chaitin (D)	1,942	(4%)
1968 general:	William S. Moorhead (D)	96,117	(69%)
	Algia Gary (R)	39,671	(29%)
	Harvey F. Johnston (C)	2,620	(2%)

FIFTEENTH DISTRICT Political Background

Pennsylvania 15 comprises the industrial Lehigh Valley in eastern Pennsylvania: Lehigh and Northampton counties, and Monroe County to the north. The heart of the district lies in the twin cities of Allentown and Bethlehem, the latter being the home of Bethlehem Steel, the nation's number-two producer of steel. Western Lehigh County shows some of the Republicanism of upper Bucks County (see Pennsylvania 8), as does Monroe, which includes much of the Pocono mountains resort region and the scenic Delaware Water Gap. But Bethlehem and Allentown, and the smaller town of Easton on the Delaware River, are solidly Democratic, and together they produce Democratic majorities in most elections. Neither of the state's two Republican senators has ever carried the 15th.

From 1932 to 1963, Francis E. Walter represented the district in Congress. Walter became a powerful man in the House; he was chairman of the Un-American Activities Committee and of the Judiciary Committee's Subcommittee on Immigration and Nationality. Because of the restrictive character of the nation's immigration laws, congressmen with ethnic constituencies constantly find themselves seeking private bills for the relief of their constituents' relatives and friends. As the chairman of the subcommittee, Walter controlled the flow of these private bills. In the early '60's, when the liberals began to seek an abolition of the Un-American Activities Committee, Walter reportedly got the word out that opponents of his committee would have no luck on any private bills. Therefore, most Northern Democrats with urban districts continued to support HUAC, as indeed most do to the present day. Its new name is the Committee on Internal Security. Walter also became famous for co-sponsoring the McCarran-Walter Act; a piece of anti-subversion legislation, much of which has turned out to be unconstitutional.

Congressman Walter's successor, Fred B. Rooney, is a very different kind of man. Rooney has shown very little interest in hunting out subversives in unlikely places; in fact, the Congressman usually lines up with other Northern liberal Democrats on the issues. In particular, Rooney, as a member of the Interstate and Foreign Commerce Committee, has championed the interests of the consumer. In the 15th district, Rooney has won reelection by solid margins, though he did slip to 52% in the Republican year of 1966. Redistricting will have only a minor effect on the shape of his district, and Rooney appears quite likely to continue winning.

Census Data 1970 pop. 498,633; deviation from current state average, +14.2%; change 1960–70, +9.5%. Metro. 90.9%, 42.6% central city.

1970 Share of Federal Outlays $276,573,000

DOD	$58,812,000	HEW	$115,043,000
AEC	$95,000	HUD	$16,371,000
NASA	$3,804,000	OEO	$190,000
DOT	$1,421,000	DOA	$3,263,000
		Other	$77,574,000

Federal Military-Industrial Commitments

DOD Installations Tobyhanna Army Depot (Tobyhanna).

Economic Base Apparel and other finished products made from fabrics and similar materials, esp. women's, misses', and juniors' outerwear; electrical machinery, equipment, and supplies; textile mill products, esp. knitting mills. Also, tourism (Poconos).

The Voters

Registration 180,464 total. 103,490 D (57%); 76,974 R (43%).

Employment profile White collar, 36%. Blue collar, 64%.

Ethnic groups Black, 1%. Total foreign stock, 22%. Austria, Italy, 4% each; Hungary, 3%; Germany, Czech., UK, Poland, 2% each; USSR, Ireland, 1% each; others, 4%.

Presidential vote

1968	Humphrey (D)	90,996	(49%)
	Nixon (R)	85,260	(46%)
	Wallace (AIP)	8,145	(4%)

Representative

Fred B. Rooney (D) Elected Aug. 6, 1963; b. Nov. 6, 1925, Bethlehem; home, Bethlehem; U. of Ga., B.S., 1950; Army, WWII; married, three children; Catholic.

Career Real estate and insurance business.

Offices 236 CHOB, 202-225-6411. Also 405 E. Fourth St., Bethlehem 18015, 215-866-0916, and P.O. Bldg., Allentown 18101, 215-437-4418.

Committees

Interstate and Foreign Commerce (9th); Sub. on Communications and Power.

Group Ratings

	ADA	COPE	NREP	NFU	LCV	CFA	NAB	NSI	ACA
1970	72	83	83	92	86	65	18	90	21
1969	47	—	—	86	—	—	—	—	27
1968	58	100	—	100	—	—	0	—	14

Key Votes

(1) ABM	AGN	(6) 18-Yr-Vote	FOR	(11) Clean Water $	FOR
(2) SST	AGN	(7) Farm Sub Lmt	FOR	(12) Mig Wrkrs Comp	FOR
(3) Phil Pln	AGN	(8) Coop-Church	FOR	(13) Jets to Chiang	FOR
(4) No-Knock	FOR	(9) Family Asst	FOR	(14) State OEO Veto	AGN
(5) Cmutr Tax	FOR	(10) Work Stamps	AGN	(15) Park Logging	AGN

Election Results

1970 general:	Fred B. Rooney (D)	93,169	(67%)
	Charles H. Roberts (R)	44,103	(32%)
	Chester R. Litz (C)	2,093	(2%)
1970 primary:	Fred B. Rooney (D), unopposed		
1968 general:	Fred B. Rooney (D)	106,877	(59%)
	Paul E. Henderson (R)	70,333	(39%)
	Peter G. Cohen (Common Sense)	2,749	(2%)
	Charles R. Litz (C)	1,683	(1%)

SIXTEENTH DISTRICT Political Background

Pennsylvania 16 lies in the heart of the Pennsylvania Dutch country: Lancaster and Lebanon counties and a small portion of Dauphin County. The word "Dutch," of course, is a misnomer, or at least a linguistic corruption of the word "Deutsch." The Dutch here are actually Germans; they are descended from the Amish, Mennonite, and members of other strict pietistic and fundamentalist sects who left principalities of eighteenth century Germany for the religious freedom of Quaker-dominated Pennsylvania. They settled in what was then almost the frontier, the rolling green hills around Lancaster and Lebanon and York. The land was naturally productive, and the careful farming techniques of the Dutch made it even more so. Today, farms in Lancaster County still sustain some of the highest per-acre yields of any land on earth. To a surprising extent, the Pennsylvania Dutch have kept to their traditions; and a tourist driving the back roads around Lancaster, near towns with names like Ephrata, Hessdale, and Strasburg, can see families, clad in black homespun, riding along in horse-drawn carriages.

The Pennsylvania Dutch are perhaps the most conservative people in America; conservative in the true sense of that word, not as it may be applied to describe the attitudes held by the frightened citizens of Orange County, California. Nevertheless, the conservative heritage of the Dutch does carry over into politics. Around the time of James Buchanan, who lived in Lancaster and who was Lincoln's Democratic predecessor, Pennsylvania Dutch country was Democratic in its politics; the Democrats at that time had the more conservative party. But before the Civil War began, the Dutch became

Republicans and they have remained that ever since. The 16th district ordinarily returns Republican majorities on the order of two and three to one—the highest in Pennsylvania and among the highest in the East.

It should come as no surprise, then, that the congressman from the 16th, Erwin D. Eshleman, is a conservative Republican. Eshleman has been in the House only since 1966 and has had little time to build up seniority. He is a member of the conservative bloc on the House Education and Labor Committee—a bloc that has become increasingly powerful lately with the help of Oregon's Edith Green, the committee's 2nd ranking Democrat. Eshleman will have no problem winning reelection in the 16th.

Census Data 1970 pop. 439,322; deviation from current state average, +0.6%; change 1960–70, +12.5%. Metro. 77.3%, 13.1% central city.

1970 Share of Federal Outlays $210,032,000

DOD	$50,906,000	HEW	$86,033,000
AEC	$127,000	HUD	$7,397,000
NASA	$219,000	OEO	$697,000
DOT	$5,711,000	DOA	$2,355,000
		Other	$56,588,000

Federal Military-Industrial Commitments

DOD Contractors Hamilton Watch Co. (Lancaster and East Petersburg), $23.653m: radio sets; artillery fuzes. American Flyers (Middletown), $6.111m: unspecified.

Economic Base Apparel and other finished products made from fabrics and similar materials; primary metal industries; fabricated metal products, esp. metal stampings; dairy and livestock.

The Voters

Registration 159,194 total. 45,456 D (29%); 113,738 R (71%).

Employment profile White collar, 33%. Blue collar, 67%.

Ethnic groups Black, 1%. Total foreign stock, 6%. Germany, 2%; Italy, UK, 1% each; others, 3%.

Presidential vote

1968	Humphrey (D)	40,999	(28%)
	Nixon (R)	95,239	(65%)
	Wallace (AIP)	11,472	(8%)

Representative

Edwin D. Eshleman (R) Elected 1966; b. Dec. 4, 1920, Lancaster County; home, Lancaster; Franklin and Marshall Col., B.S.; Temple U.; USCG, WWII; married, two children; Lutheran.

Career Public school teacher; Pa. Legislature, 12 years, Majority and Minority Whip; V. Chm., Pa. Higher Ed. Assistance Agency, 1964–67.

Offices 416 CHOB, 202-225-2411. Also Rm. 210, P.O. Bldg., Lancaster 17604, 717-393-0666.

Committees

Education and Labor (8th); Subs. (1) Agricultural Labor, (2) Sel. on Education, (3) Sel. on Labor.

Group Ratings

	ADA	COPE	NREP	NFU	LCV	CFA	NAB	NSI	ACA
1970	12	9	17	23	75	58	100	100	94
1969	0	—	—	20	—	—	—	—	71
1968	8	9	—	36	—	—	100	—	83

Key Votes

(1) ABM	FOR	(6) 18-Yr-Vote	AGN	(11) Clean Water $	AGN
(2) SST	AGN	(7) Farm Sub Lmt	FOR	(12) Mig Wrkrs Comp	AGN
(3) Phil Pln	FOR	(8) Coop-Church	AGN	(13) Jets to Chiang	FOR
(4) No-Knock	FOR	(9) Family Asst	AGN	(14) State OEO Veto	FOR
(5) Cmutr Tax	AGN	(10) Work Stamps	FOR	(15) Park Logging	AGN

Election Results

1970 general:	Edwin D. Eshleman (R)	74,006	(66%)
	John E. Pflum (D)	33,986	(31%)
	Walter B. Willard, III (C)	3,319	(3%)
1970 primary:	Edwin D. Eshleman (R), unopposed		
1968 general:	Edwin D. Eshleman (R)	98,877	(69%)
	Robert M. Going (D)	39,507	(28%)
	Lloyd G. Cope (C)	5,197	(4%)

SEVENTEENTH DISTRICT Political Background

Pennsylvania 17, in the eastcentral part of the state, takes in a collection of counties that lie along the Susquehanna River. The extreme southern end of the district in Dauphin County, around Harrisburg, contains nearly half of the people of the 17th. The main industry in Harrisburg, the state capital, is state government; the city has always been a rock-solid Republican town. Most of outlying Dauphin County is Pennsylvania Dutch and also Republican (see Pennsylvania 16). Farther up the Susquehanna, there is some Democratic territory in Northumberland County, where the tail-end of the anthracite seams once drew an ethnic population to towns like Sunbury and Shamokin. Right across the river are Union and Snyder counties, the banner Republican counties of Pennsylvania; they both went for Goldwater in 1964. The main point of interest in Union County is the Lewisburg Federal Prison, where James R. Hoffa has been in jail. To the north is Williamsport, a small manufacturing town on the upper Susquehanna. Its all-American character makes it an appropriate host for the annual Little League World Series. In 1970 and 1971, the event was won by a group of 11- and 12-year-old farm boys from the island of Formosa.

Despite Northumberland, the 17th is definitely a Republican district; it has not elected a Democratic congressman in the twentieth century. The current incumbent, Herman T. Schneebeli, first won the seat in a 1960 special election and has won reelection with little difficulty ever since. The Congressman, a middle-of-the-road Republican, has a good deal of power in the House as the 3rd ranking minority member of the Ways and Means Committee. His main worry at the moment is redistricting. The Democratic legislature and governor may decide that rural Pennsylvania, rather than Philadelphia, will absorb one of the two seats the state lost in the 1970 census (see state write-up). Schneebeli's district is so positioned geographically that adjoining districts can easily nibble away at its edges; the 17th has common boundaries with seven other districts—more than any other district in the state. Moreover, the various parts of the 17th have no traditional ties with other parts. Schneebeli, therefore, may be forced into retirement or into a primary with one of his Republican colleagues at a considerable disadvantage. The Congressman's prospects would now look much better if his party had won just a few more seats in the state legislature during the 1970 elections.

Census Data 1970 pop. 490,736; deviation from current state average, +12.3%; change 1960–70, +2.1%. Metro. 41.5%, 13.9% central city.

1970 Share of Federal Outlays $468,137,000

DOD	$54,873,000	HEW	$199,280,000
AEC	$000	HUD	$3,865,000
NASA	$159,000	OEO	$1,328,000
DOT	$51,746,000	DOA	$10,111,000
		Other	$146,774,000

Federal Military-Industrial Commitments

DOD Contractors Kennedy Van Saun Corp. (Danville), $7.096m: metal parts for 105-mm projectiles. Avco Corp. (Williamsport), $5.322m: unspecified.

Economic Base Apparel and other finished products made from fabrics and similar materials, esp. women's, misses', and juniors' outerwear; food and kindred products; dairy; fabricated metal products, esp. fabricated structural metal products. Also, banking and state government.

The Voters

Registration 209,204 total. 66,915 D (32%); 142,289 R (68%).

Employment profile White collar, 39%. Blue collar, 61%.

Ethnic groups Black, 6%. Total foreign stock, 11%. Italy, Poland, 2% each; Germany, UK, Austria, USSR, 1% each; others, 3%.

Presidential vote

1968	Humphrey (D)	64,123	(35%)
	Nixon (R)	107,510	(58%)
	Wallace (AIP)	13,945	(8%)

Representative

Herman T. Schneebeli (R) Elected April 26, 1960; b. July 7, 1907, Lancaster; home, Williamsport; Dartmouth, B.A., 1930; Amos Tuck School, M.C.S., 1961; Army, WWII; married, two children; Episcopalian.

Career Distributor, Gulf Oil Corp., 1939– ; Delegate, German-American Alliance Conference, West Geneva, 1961; U.S.-Japan Parliamentary Conference, Tokyo, Japan, April 1968.

Offices 1336 LHOB, 202-225-4315. Also Rm. 408 Fidelity Natl. Bank Bldg., Williamsport 17701, 717-326-2814, and 1146 Fed. Bldg., Harrisburg 17108, 717-238-0395.

Committees

Ways and Means (3rd).

Group Ratings

	ADA	COPE	NREP	NFU	LCV	CFA	NAB	NSI	ACA
1970	28	10	64	55	44	62	100	83	73
1969	20	—	—	60	—	—	—	—	53
1968	8	8	—	85	—	—	100	—	87

Key Votes

(1) ABM	FOR	(6) 18-Yr-Vote	FOR	(11) Clean Water $	AGN
(2) SST	ABS*	(7) Farm Sub Lmt	FOR	(12) Mig Wrkrs Comp	AGN
(3) Phil Pln	FOR	(8) Coop-Church	FOR	(13) Jets to Chiang	AGN
(4) No-Knock	ABS	(9) Family Asst	FOR	(14) State OEO Veto	AGN
(5) Cmutr Tax	FOR	(10) Work Stamps	FOR	(15) Park Logging	AGN

* *Voted "against" in previous vote on same issue.*

Election Results

1970 general:	Herman T. Schneebeli (R)	88,173	(58%)
	William P. Zurick (D)	60,714	(40%)
	Robert C. Weber (C)	3,342	(2%)
1970 primary:	Herman T. Schneebeli (R)	65,363	(73%)
	Robert F. Smith (R)	24,669	(27%)
1968 general:	Herman T. Schneebeli (R)	119,003	(66%)
	Donald J. Rippon (D)	57,093	(32%)
	Arnold J. Watson (C)	3,785	(2%)

EIGHTEENTH DISTRICT Political Background

Pennsylvania 18 takes in the most prosperous sections of the Pittsburgh metropolitan area. It includes all of Allegheny County north of the Ohio and Allegheny rivers, except for the city of Pittsburgh, and the suburbs directly east of Pittsburgh south of the Allegheny River (see maps in appendix). The latter portion of the 18th includes the middleclass suburbs of Wilkinsburg, Penn Hills, and Monroeville. In the Pittsburgh area, the general rule is that towns along the rivers are industrial, relatively poor, and Democratic, and the towns in the hills above are residential, relatively rich, and Republican. The epitome of the hill suburb is the town of Fox Chapel, a wealthy enclave inhabited by many of Pittsburgh's oldest and most affluent families.

The 18th, the most Republican of the Pittsburgh area districts, regularly returns Republican majorities in statewide elections. For years, even large majorities went to Congressman Robert J. Corbett. Corbett was first elected to the House in 1938 and was then defeated in the 1940 Roosevelt sweep; he made a political comeback in 1941 by winning the Allegheny County sheriff's office, and returned to Congress in 1944. Corbett won over the Democrat residents of his district and the support of organized labor by casting liberal votes on many economic issues. At the time of his death in the spring of 1971, he was the ranking Republican on the House Post Office and Civil Service Committee.

At this writing, Gov. Milton Shapp has not yet called a special election to fill the vacancy, perhaps because a Republican candidate would likely win the seat. But any special election now may have little significance for 1972. Because Pennsylvania lost two congressional districts in the 1970 census, it is quite possible that the 18th will be eliminated in the redistricting process controlled by the Democrats. Allegheny County, which now has 4 districts, is entitled to only 3.4 under the 1970 census figures. The 18th could be divided rather easily among the other districts in Allegheny and adjoining counties.

Census Data 1970 pop. 463,991; deviation from current state average, +6.2%; change 1960–70, +13.4%. Metro. 100.0%, 0.0% central city.

1970 Share of Federal Outlays $308,785,000 (average outlay per district, Pennsylvania 14, 18, 20, and 27)

DOD	$53,410,000	HEW	$111,378,000
AEC	$23,770,000	HUD	$9,216,000
NASA	$1,206,000	OEO	$1,348,000
DOT	$16,722,000	DOA	$1,558,000
		Other	$90,176,000

Federal Military-Industrial Commitments (See Pennsylvania 14 for greater Pittsburgh listings.)

Economic Base Primary metal industries, esp. blast furnaces, steel works, and rolling and finishing mills; fabricated metal products, esp. fabricated structural metal products; nonelectrical machinery, esp. metalworking machinery and equipment; food and kindred products; electrical machinery, equipment, and supplies. Also, extensive commuting to Pennsylvania 14 (Pittsburgh).

The Voters

Registration 227,694 total. 117,320 D (52%); 110,374 R (49%).

Employment profile White collar, 50%. Blue collar, 50%.

Ethnic groups Black, 3%. Total foreign stock, 25%. Italy, 5%; Germany, 4%; UK, Poland, 3% each; Czech., Austria, 2% each; Ireland, Hungary, USSR, Canada, 1% each; others, 4%.

Presidential vote

1968	Humphrey (D)	82,308	(42%)
	Nixon (R)	91,938	(47%)
	Wallace (AIP)	21,344	(11%)

Representative Seat Vacant

NINETEENTH DISTRICT **Political Background**

Pennsylvania 19 comprises three counties in the southcentral part of the state—Adams, Cumberland, and York. The district lies at the western edge of the deeply conservative Pennsylvania Dutch country (see Pennsylvania 16). The 19th is a land of rolling green farmland extending up to the base of the Appalachian ridges which begin at its western boundary. The most famous part of the 19th is Gettysburg, the tourist-thronged site of the Civil War's northernmost slaughter. Outside the town is the retirement home of the late President Dwight D. Eisenhower, who was descended out of Pennsylvania Dutch stock. His father had migrated with a group of Mennonite brethren out into Kansas and Texas in the late nineteenth century.

The largest city in the district is York (pop. 50,000), which was once, from September of 1777 until June of 1778, the capital of the young nation. It was moved out here when the British threatened Philadelphia during the Revolutionary War. While the Founding Fathers met in York, they passed the Articles of Confederation, received word from Ben Franklin in Paris that the French would help with men and ships, and issued the first proclamation calling for a national day of thanksgiving. Today, York is surprisingly Democratic for a city in the Pennsylvania Dutch area; it probably is so because of the influence of the *York Gazette,* which, until a recent change in ownership, was one of the most liberal and antiwar newspapers in the United States. The other large population center in the 19th is around the town of Camp Hill, across the Susquehanna River from the state capital of Harrisburg. Like Harrisburg, Camp Hill is heavily conservative.

The 19th is a Republican district which has on occasions elected Democratic congressmen; it did so, for example, in 1958 and 1964. The current incumbent is Republican George A. Goodling, one of the most conservative members of the Pennsylvania delegation. Goodling won the elections of 1960 and 1962, lost in 1964, and came back to win in 1966 and has won ever since. His margins of victory, however, have not been particularly impressive; in 1970 he had only 54% of the vote, as compared to Sen. Hugh Scott's 60% in the district.

This rather mediocre showing and the Congressman's age—he will be 76 in 1972—indicate that he may have some trouble in the immediate future. Redistricting adjustments will be minor. But the Democratic legislature will not doubt tack on some Democratic terrain and remove some Republican areas. The Democrats will do this because the 19th is the only district in this part of the state that they have a remote chance of carrying. Goodling, who is the 4th ranking Republican on the House Agriculture Committee, will be in real trouble if the farm policies of the Nixon Administration become unpopular among the normally prosperous farmers of the 19th district. Discontent with the policy is common in the Midwest, and in 1970 accounted for much of the Democratic success in the elections of that year.

Census Data 1970 pop. 487,717; deviation from current state average, +11.7%; change 1960–70, +17.5%. Metro. 100.0%, 10.3% central city.

1970 Share of Federal Outlays $437,411,981

DOD	$257,592,000	HEW	$100,175,374
AEC	$000	HUD	$2,297,000
NASA	$240,755	OEO	$859,778
DOT	$6,461,391	DOA	$7,077,838
		Other	$62,707,845

Federal Military-Industrial Commitments

DOD Contractors American Machine and Foundry Co. (York), $32.246m: Mark 82 bomb bodies. Harsco Corp. (York), $20.406m: unspecified. Gulf and Western Industries (Red Lion), $10.566m: unspecified.

DOD Installations Carlisle Army Barracks (Carlisle). Naval Ships Parts Control Center (Mechanicsburg).

Economic Base Nonelectrical machinery, esp. construction, mining, and material handling machinery and equipment; dairy and livestock; apparel and other finished products made from fabrics and similar materials; fabricated metal products.

The Voters

Registration 183,994 total. 80,948 D (44%); 103,046 R (56%).
Employment profile White collar, 37%. Blue collar, 63%.
Ethnic groups Black, 2%. Total foreign stock, 4%. Germany, UK, Italy, 1% each; others, 2%.

Presidential vote

1968	Humphrey (D)	54,788	(33%)
	Nixon (R)	95,842	(58%)
	Wallace (AIP)	14,526	(9%)

Representative

George A. Goodling (R) Elected 1960–64, 1966; b. Sept. 26, 1896, Loganville; home, Loganville; Penn. State U., B.S.; widowed, seven children; Methodist.
Career Fruit grower; Pa. Legislature, seven terms; Dir. of a bank, motor club, insurance co.; Exec. Secy., Pa. State Horticulture Assn.
Offices 1714 LHOB, 202-225-5836. Also Fed. Bldg., York 17403, 717-843-8887.

Committees

Agriculture (4th); Subs. (1) Conservation and Credit, (2) Domestic Marketing and Consumer Relations, (3) Family Farms and Rural Development.
Merchant Marine and Fisheries (7th); Subs. (1) Fisheries and Wildlife Conservation, (2) Oceanography.

Group Ratings

	ADA	COPE	NREP	NFU	LCV	CFA	NAB	NSI	ACA
1970	8	0	8	8	25	45	100	89	100
1969	0	—	—	31	—	—	—	—	81
1968	0	0	—	19	—	—	100	—	100

Key Votes

(1) ABM	FOR	(6) 18-Yr-Vote	AGN	(11) Clean Water $	AGN
(2) SST	AGN	(7) Farm Sub Lmt	AGN	(12) Mig Wrkrs Comp	AGN
(3) Phil Pln	FOR	(8) Coop-Church	AGN	(13) Jets to Chiang	AGN
(4) No-Knock	FOR	(9) Family Asst	AGN	(14) State OEO Veto	FOR
(5) Cmutr Tax	AGN	(10) Work Stamps	FOR	(15) Park Logging	FOR

Election Results

1970 general:	George A. Goodling (R)	71,497	(54%)
	Arthur I. Berger (D)	58,399	(44%)
	Joseph Paul (C)	2,704	(2%)
1970 primary:	George A. Goodling (R), unopposed		
1968 general:	George A. Goodling (R)	93,352	(58%)
	Robert L. Myers, III (D)	65,903	(41%)
	Carl M. Richter (C)	2,465	(2%)

TWENTIETH DISTRICT Political Background

Pennsylvania 20 is the Monongahela district. It comprises a string of industrial communities, beginning in southeast Pittsburgh, along this much polluted river, which a few miles downstream joins the Allegheny to form the Ohio. "Monongahela," Walt Whitman once wrote, "it rolls off the tongue like venison." The 20th district currently produces as much steel as any in the nation; the activity goes on in the huge and often technologically backward mills found in the valleys and hills that line the Monongahela. There are some black neighborhoods in the Pittsburgh portion of the district, but most of the 20th is white working-class country. The steel executives and white-collar employees live in the hills to the north and south (see Pennsylvania 18).

In the late nineteenth and early twentieth century, Czech, Italian, Polish, Welsh, and Scots immigrants thronged here to work in the mills. They soon found themselves engaged in the bloody and unsuccessful strikes of the period. Today many of their descendants remain in the same small frame houses clustered up and down the hills of towns like Braddock, Duquesne, McKeesport, and Clairton; these comprise an area of economic and environmental blight. The 20th's population is declining, as the steel industry finds itself increasingly unable to meet foreign competition.

The 20th is, of course, a heavily Democratic district. The residents here may on occasion take satisfaction in some of Spiro Agnew's fusillades, but on election day they usually vote their pocketbooks. George Wallace, however, took 14% of the vote in 1968, his highest percentage in any Pennsylvania district. Since the era of the New Deal, the 20th has sent only Democrats to Congress. The current incumbent is Joseph M. Gaydos, a former state senator and an attorney for the United Mine Workers District 5. Gaydos had Democratic party organization and union backing when he first won the seat in 1968; but he has subsequently proved to be a stronger critic of the Vietnam war than many of his friends at home. Otherwise, his record is what one might expect from a congressman representing a working-class district around Pittsburgh: liberal on most economic issues and conservative on some social issues.

In a district like the 20th, the initial Democratic primary is usually the congressman's toughest hurdle. Having cleared that obstacle rather easily, Gaydos appears headed for a long career in the House. In 1970, he won 77% of the district's votes; this is even more than his Democratic predecessor took in the Goldwater year of 1964. Redistricting will probably add some adjacent towns—higher in the hills and hence more Republican—to the 20th, but this should give Gaydos little to worry about.

Census Data 1970 pop. 356,034; deviation from current state average, −18.5%; change 1960–7, −12.1%. Metro. 100.0%, 27.9% central city.

1970 Share of Federal Outlays $308,785,000 (average outlay per district, Pennsylvania 14, 18, 20, and 27)

DOD	$53,410,000	HEW	$111,378,000
AEC	$23,770,000	HUD	$9,216,000
NASA	$1,206,000	OEO	$1,348,000
DOT	$16,722,000	DOA	$1,558,000
		Other	$90,176,000

Federal Military-Industrial Commitments (See Pennsylvania 14 for greater Pittsburgh listing.)

Economic Base Primary metal industries, esp. blast furnaces, steel works, and rolling and finishing mills; fabricated metal products, esp. fabricated structural metal products; nonelectrical machinery, esp. metalworking machinery and equipment; food and kindred products; electrical machinery, equipment, and supplies.

The Voters

Registration 187,679 total. 144,548 D (77%); 43,131 R (23%).

Employment profile White collar, 37%. Blue collar, 63%.

Ethnic groups Black, 10%. Total foreign stock, 34%. Czech., 6%; Italy, 5%; Poland, UK, 4% each; Germany, 3%; Hungary, Austria, Ireland, 2% each; USSR, Sweden, 1% each; others, 5%.

Presidential vote

1968	Humphrey (D)	96,127	(60%)
	Nixon (R)	40,745	(26%)
	Wallace (AIP)	22,475	(14%)

Representative

Joseph M. Gaydos (D) Elected Nov. 5, 1968; b. July 3, 1926, Braddock; home, McKeesport; Duquesne U., U. of Notre Dame, LL.B., 1951; USNR, WWII; married, five children; Catholic.

Career Deputy Atty. Gen., Asst. Solicitor, Allegheny County; Gen. Counsel, United Mine Workers of America, District 5; Pa. Senate, 1967–68.

Offices 1033 LHOB, 202-225-4631. Also Rm. 707, New Fed. Office Bldg., Pittsburgh 15222, 412-644-2860, and Rm. 207, 224 Fifth Ave. Bldg., McKeesport 15132, 412-673-3755.

Committees

Education and Labor (15th); Subs. (1) Gen. on Labor, (2) Sp. on Labor, (3) Sel. on Education, (4) Sel. on Labor.

House Administration (13th); Subs. (1) Library and Memorials, (2) Printing, (3) Sp. on Electrical and Mechanical Office Equipment, (4) Sp. on Police.

Group Ratings

	ADA	COPE	NREP	NFU	LCV	CFA	NAB	NSI	ACA
1970	72	100	82	75	100	83	22	60	21
1969	60	—	—	73	—	—	—	—	41

Key Votes

(1) ABM	AGN	(6) 18-Yr-Vote	FOR	(11) Clean Water $	FOR
(2) SST	AGN	(7) Farm Sub Lmt	FOR	(12) Mig Wrkrs Comp	FOR
(3) Phil Pln	AGN	(8) Coop-Church	FOR	(13) Jets to Chiang	AGN
(4) No-Knock	ABS	(9) Family Asst	FOR	(14) State OEO Veto	AGN
(5) Cmutr Tax	FOR	(10) Work Stamps	AGN	(15) Park Logging	AGN

Election Results

1970 general:	Joseph M. Gaydos (D)	84,911	(77%)
	Joseph Honeygosky (R)	22,553	(20%)
	Alan Staub (C)	2,840	(3%)
1970 primary:	Joseph M. Gaydos (D), unopposed		
1968 general:	Joseph M. Gaydos (D)	109,236	(70%)
	Joseph Sabol, Jr. (R)	44,037	(28%)
	Clayton Fox (C)	2,337	(2%)

TWENTY-FIRST DISTRICT Political Background

Pennsylvania 21 comprises Westmoreland County, just to the east of Pittsburgh, and a very small portion of Fayette County to the south. This is a mixed area. There are a few wealthy communities here, like Arnold Palmer's Latrobe; most of Westmoreland, however, is industrial—small factory towns that lie between the hills or along the Allegheny and Monongahela rivers at the extreme western edge of the county. There is a particularly large Italian-American population in the 21st, with other foreign stock groups in smaller numbers. The district is part of the state's "black country," so named from the coal deposits in the region. It is the most Democratic part of Pennsylvania outside of Philadelphia and Pittsburgh; even more Democratic than the anthracite region around Wilkes-Barre and Scranton (see Pennsylvania 10 and 11).

The Congressman from the 21st is John H. Dent, a Democrat who served in the state legislature from 1934 to 1958. For 17 years, Dent was his party's leader in the state Senate. Like many Democrats from safe districts, Dent has been winning reelection by overwhelming margins and has been accumulating seniority. He first won the seat in a 1958 special election. The Congressman is now the 4th ranking Democrat on the House Education and Labor Committee, and chairman of one of its labor subcommittees. He faces no problems at home in future elections.

In 1968, Dent, who like many of his constituents is of Itàlian descent, made a stab at running for statewide office. He challenged Sen. Joseph Clark in the Democratic primary. Dent did not expect to win; he merely wanted to focus opposition to Clark for many backers of the Vietnam war and opponents of gun registration. These same voters managed to bring about Clark's defeat in November of 1968 (see state write-up). It is unlikely that Dent, who was 62 in 1970, has any real interest in statewide office; he is probably content with his current office in which he has a great deal of job security.

Census Data 1970 pop. 384,634; deviation from current state average, −11.9%; change 1960–70, +6.9%. Metro. 98.0%, 0.0% central city.

1970 Share of Federal Outlays $153,141,000

DOD	$17,545,000	HEW	$82,485,000
AEC	$000	HUD	$1,769,000
NASA	$000	OEO	$130,000
DOT	$1,249,000	DOA	$2,015,000
		Other	$47,949,000

Federal Military-Industrial Commitments

DOD Contractors Alcoa (New Kensington), $10.306m: 2.75-inch rocket motor tubes; bridge erection boats.

Economic Base Primary metal industries, esp. blast furnaces, steel works, and rolling and finishing mills; nonelectrical machinery, esp. metalworking machinery and equipment; electrical machinery, equipment, and supplies; stone, clay, glass, and concrete products, esp. glass and glassware, pressed and blown.

The Voters

Registration 170,846 total. 113,688 D (67%); 57,158 R (34%).
Employment profile White collar, 36%. Blue collar, 64%.
Ethnic groups Black, 2%. Total foreign stock, 27%. Italy, 7%; Poland, Czech., Austria, UK, 3% each; Germany, 2%; Hungary, USSR, 1% each; others, 5%.

Presidential vote

1968	Humphrey (D)	82,842	(55%)
	Nixon (R)	53,200	(35%)
	Wallace (AIP)	14,722	(10%)

Representative

John H. Dent (D) Elected Jan. 21, 1958; b. March 10, 1908, Johnetta; home, Jeannette; Great Lakes Naval Aviation Acad., correspondence courses; U.S. Marine Air Corps., 1924–28; married, two children; Catholic.

Career Mbr., Natl. Council of United Rubber Workers, 1923–37, Pres., Local 1875; newspaperman; Pa. Legislature, 1934–36; Pa. Senate, 1936–58, Floor Leader, 1939–58; Exec. with coal and coke co. and building and transportation co.

Offices 2430 RHOB, 202-225-5631. Also 35 W. Pittsburgh St., Greensburg 15601, 412-837-6420.

Committees

Education and Labor (4th); Subs. (1) Chm., Gen. on Labor, (2) Sel. on Education.
House Administration (4th); Subs. (1) Chm., Sp. on Electrical and Mechanical Office Equipment, (2) Accounts, (3) Elections.

Group Ratings

	ADA	COPE	NREP	NFU	LCV	CFA	NAB	NSI	ACA
1970	60	89	45	88	63	69	0	63	22
1969	53	—	—	93	—	—	—	—	29
1968	92	100	—	85	—	—	0	—	6

Key Votes

(1) ABM	ABS	(6) 18-Yr-Vote	ABS	(11) Clean Water $	FOR
(2) SST	AGN	(7) Farm Sub Lmt	AGN	(12) Mig Wrkrs Comp	FOR
(3) Phil Pln	ABS	(8) Coop-Church	AGN	(13) Jets to Chiang	AGN
(4) No-Knock	ABS	(9) Family Asst	FOR	(14) State OEO Veto	AGN
(5) Cmutr Tax	FOR	(10) Work Stamps	AGN	(15) Park Logging	AGN

Election Results

1970 general:	John H. Dent (D)	76,915	(68%)
	Glenn G. Anderson (R)	33,396	(30%)
	Lloyd G. Cope (C)	1,979	(2%)
1970 primary:	John H. Dent (D), unopposed		
1968 general:	John H. Dent (D)	93,033	(63%)
	Thomas H. Young (R)	55,099	(37%)

TWENTY-SECOND DISTRICT Political Background

Pennsylvania 22 lies in the mountain fastness of western Pennsylvania. It is a predominantly rural district with just one city of any size, Johnstown (pop. 42,000); the city is known to some buffs of American history as a place that was ravaged by a great flood in the nineteenth century. The rest of the 22nd is dotted with small industrial towns like Kittanning and Punxsutawney. Politically, this is as evenly divided as any district in the state. Cambria County (Johnstown) usually produces a Democratic margin; the other four counties usually go Republican. In 1968, Richard Nixon carried the 22nd over Hubert Humphrey, 47–46; in 1970, it went for statewide winners Gov. Milton Shapp (Democrat) and Sen. Hugh Scott (Republican).

In congressional elections, however, the results are more one-sided, and the beneficiary of the pattern is Congressman John Saylor. Saylor, who has served in the House since a 1949 special election, is one of the state's more liberal Republican congressmen. He has become best known for his support of conservation and environmental protection generally. He pushed these concerns long before they became fashionable in the cities and universities of the East and West coasts. Saylor is the ranking Republican on the House Interior and Insular Affairs Committee. Here he has built up not only great expertise in matters pertaining to the environment, but also a good deal of legislative clout.

Because the small hill towns of his district are full of avid hunters and fishermen, Saylor's record in conservation has been popular. But lately, the Congressman has been receiving majorities not quite as large as those to which he had become accustomed; he took 58% in both 1968 and 1970. In 1970, he almost lost Cambria County, which contains almost half of the district's population. The results may have stemmed from the state's voters giving an unexpectedly large margin to the Democratic ticket in 1970. But it may also mean that Saylor's seat is a little less safe than is generally assumed.

Census Data 1970 pop. 423,935; deviation from current state average, –2.9%; change 1960–70, –4.2%. Metro. 44.1%, 10.0% central city.

1970 Share of Federal Outlays $219,819,439

DOD	$20,653,000	HEW	$118,954,768
AEC	$1,114,586	HUD	$3,678,696
NASA	$26,304	OEO	$1,598,268
DOT	$6,068,617	DOA	$7,249,218
		Other	$60,475,982

Federal Military-Industrial Commitments

DOD Contractors Stevens Mfg. (Ebensburg), $7.970m: portable water tank trailers.

Economic Base Dairy and livestock; stone, clay, glass, and concrete products; bituminous coal. Also, higher education (Indiana University of Pennsylvania).

The Voters

Registration 191,497 total. 93,516 D (49%); 97,981 R (51%).

Employment profile White collar, 33%. Blue collar, 67%.

Ethnic groups Black, 1%. Total foreign stock, 19%. Italy, 4%; Czech., 3%; Poland, Austria, UK, Germany, 2% each; Hungary, 1%; others, 4%.

Presidential vote

1968	Humphrey (D)	79,501	(46%)
	Nixon (R)	80,602	(47%)
	Wallace (AIP)	11,078	(7%)

Representative

John Phillips Saylor (R) Elected Sept. 13, 1949; b. July 23, 1908, Johnstown; home, Johnstown; Mercersburg Acad., Franklin and Marshall Col., B.A., 1929; Dickinson Law School, LL.B., 1933; Navy, WWII; Capt. USNR; married, two children; United Church of Christ.

Career Pres., Bd. of Dir., Johnstown Fed. Savings and Loan Assn.; V. Chm., Rep. Congressional Delegation.

Offices 2354 RHOB, 202-225-2065.

Committees

Interior and Insular Affairs (Ranking Mbr.); Sub. on Environment.

Veterans' Affairs (2nd); Subs. (1) Compensation and Pension, (2) Insurance.

Group Ratings

	ADA	COPE	NREP	NFU	LCV	CFA	NAB	NSI	ACA
1970	40	50	55	33	90	53	78	100	73
1969	33	—	—	43	—	—	—	—	63
1968	25	50	—	50	—	—	80	—	74

Key Votes

(1) ABM	ABS	(6) 18-Yr-Vote	AGN	(11) Clean Water $	FOR
(2) SST	AGN	(7) Farm Sub Lmt	FOR	(12) Mig Wrkrs Comp	AGN
(3) Phil Pln	FOR	(8) Coop-Church	ABS	(13) Jets to Chiang	FOR
(4) No-Knock	FOR	(9) Family Asst	FOR	(14) State OEO Veto	AGN
(5) Cmutr Tax	AGN	(10) Work Stamps	AGN	(15) Park Logging	AGN

Election Results

1970 general:	John P. Saylor (R)	81,675	(58%)
	Joseph F. O'Kicki (D)	58,720	(41%)
	Ellsworth L. Hahn (AIP)	1,213	(1%)
1970 primary:	John P. Saylor (R), unopposed		
1968 general:	John P. Saylor (R)	98,576	(58%)
	John P. Murtha (D)	71,297	(42%)

TWENTY-THIRD DISTRICT Political Background

Pennsylvania 23 is made up of rural northcentral Pennsylvania, the most sparsely populated region of the state. The district's terrain is mountainous and its valleys have only a few small towns here and there. The only significant concentrations of people are found in the Nittany Valley in the southern part of the district, and in the extreme western end around Oil City. The Nittany Valley is the home of Penn State University, which for some time has produced the East's best football teams. Another part of the University complex, the Ordnance Research Lab, has done a great deal of work on the Navy's controversial Mark 48 torpedo program. Oil City is the site of the nation's first oil well. Drilling operations began here in 1859, and the industry continues to prosper to this day.

With the recent opening of the Pennsylvania Shortway—a superhighway that has replaced the Pennsylvania Turnpike as the main highway between New York and Chicago—the isolation of this part of Pennsylvania has been ended. The Shortway could bring some light industrial development to the interchange towns. But the 23rd will no doubt remain a rural district, dominated by old-stock farmers. These people have lived apart from the movements of population and social change that have affected—and afflicted—their neighbors in the other parts of the East and Great Lakes region.

The 23rd is, of course, a solidly Republican district, and it has had a long, long tradition of electing Republican congressmen. The current incumbent is Albert W. Johnson, who won the seat in a 1963 special election. Johnson is the 3rd ranking Republican on the House Banking and Currency Committee (and its ranking conservative member), and the 4th ranking member on Post Office and Civil Service. Though his politics appear to sit well with the voters of the district, the 1970 statewide Democratic surge sent his share of the vote below 60% for the first time since 1964. But that is no cause for great alarm.

Redistricting will likely cause him little trouble, since districts to the west adjoining the 23rd do not need to acquire territory. A rural Republican district which the state's Democratic redistricters may eliminate lies farther east (see Pennsylvania 17).

Census Data 1970 pop. 439,744; deviation from current state average, —0.5%; change 1960–70, +2.5%. Metro. 0.0%, 0.0% central city.

1970 Share of Federal Outlays $244,617,961

DOD	$27,171,000	HEW	$110,643,302
AEC	$510,286	HUD	$3,855,256
NASA	$1,364,703	OEO	$632,669
DOT	$9,512,525	DOA	$55,843,158
		Other	$35,085,062

Federal Military-Industrial Commitments

DOD Contractors Pennsylvania State University (University Park), $8.949m: support for the Mark 48 torpedo program. HRB Singer (State College), $5.256m: unspecified.

Economic Base Electrical machinery, equipment, and supplies, esp. carbon and graphite products; dairy; stone, clay, glass, and concrete products; nonelectrical machinery. Also, higher education (Pennsylvania State University).

The Voters

Registration 168,931 total. 66,691 D (40%); 102,204 R (61%).

Employment profile White collar, 36%. Blue collar, 64%.

Ethnic groups Black, 1%. Total foreign stock, 14%. Italy, 3%; Sweden, UK, 2% each; Germany, Poland, Austria, Czech., Ireland, Canada, 1% each; others, 2%.

Presidential vote

1968	Humphrey (D)	61,365	(40%)
	Nixon (R)	81,823	(54%)
	Wallace (AIP)	8,633	(6%)

Representative

Albert W. Johnson (R) Elected Nov. 5, 1963; b. Apr. 17, 1906, Smethport; home, Smethport; U. of Pa., 1926–27; Stetson U., LL.B., 1938; married, four children; Protestant.

Career Practicing atty.; Pa. Legislature, 1946–62, Majority Whip, 1951, Minority Whip, 1955, Minority Leader, 1959, 1961, Majority Leader, 1953, 1957, 1963.

Offices 1424 LHOB, 202-225-5121. Also 205 Hamlin Bank Bldg., Smethport 16749, 814-887-2225.

Committees

Banking and Currency (3rd); Subs. (1) Bank Supervision and Insurance, (2) International Finance, (3) International Trade.

Post Office and Civil Service (4th); Subs. (1) Investigations, (2) Postal Facilities and Mail.

Group Ratings

	ADA	COPE	NREP	NFU	LCV	CFA	NAB	NSI	ACA
1970	4	9	8	20	57	47	100	100	89
1969	0	—	—	33	—	—	—	—	56
1968	0	0	—	33	—	—	83	83	90

Key Votes

(1) ABM	FOR	(6) 18-Yr-Vote	AGN	(11) Clean Water $	AGN
(2) SST	FOR	(7) Farm Sub Lmt	FOR	(12) Mig Wrkrs Comp	AGN
(3) Phil Pln	ABS	(8) Coop-Church	AGN	(13) Jets to Chiang	FOR
(4) No-Knock	FOR	(9) Family Asst	AGN	(14) State OEO Veto	FOR
(5) Cmutr Tax	AGN	(10) Work Stamps	ABS	(15) Park Logging	AGN

Election Results

1970 general:	Albert W. Johnson (R)	70,074	(58%)
	Cecil R. Harrington (D)	50,908	(42%)
1970 primary:	Albert W. Johnson (R), unopposed		
1968 general:	Albert W. Johnson (R)	87,968	(62%)
	Alan R. Cleeton (D)	54,453	(38%)
	Richard H. Buckle (C)	708	(1%)

TWENTY-FOURTH DISTRICT Political Background

Pennsylvania 24, in the northwest corner of the state, is part of the Great Lakes industrial region. It is a long way overland to the East Coast, and the district has none of metropolitan Philadelphia's seaboard ambience. The city of Erie (pop. 129,000), the state's third largest, dominates the 24th. Like most industrial cities on the nation's most polluted lake, Erie is a Democratic stronghold; as one goes inland, the country becomes more Republican. An exception to the pattern is the steel town of Sharon, which is just a few miles from Youngstown, Ohio; like most towns dominated by that industry, Sharon returns Democratic majorities. The political balance in the 24th makes it one of the state's most marginal districts; Humphrey edged out Nixon here in 1968, 49–46, with the rest going to Wallace. And it is one of only two districts in Pennsylvania in which the congressional seat has changed political parties in the last decade.

The turnabout came in 1964, when Democrat Joseph P. Vigorito, a political unknown, defeated Republican Congressman James B. Weaver by 2,784 votes. Weaver was expected to regain his seat in 1966; but Vigorito, despite having little experience, proved to be a strong campaigner and beat the Republican by a margin much larger than the one he got two years before. Since then, his performance at the polls has improved each time out; in 1970, he won 67% of the vote.

Vigorito is one of the few Northern Democrats on the House Agriculture Committee. Southerners, whose districts are usually more rural than those of Northern Democrats, occupy 13 of the committee's 21 Democratic seats and 8 of the 10 top seniority positions. Vigorito is also one of the few members (10 of 38) from a district east of the Mississippi on the Interior and Insular Affairs Committee. These assignments do not seem especially appropriate in Vigorito's case, although parts of the 24th district are given over to agriculture. But the Congressman's interest in the matters taken up by the committees seems genuine; he has urged, for example, a ban on throw-away bottles. Besides, it may not be a bad thing for a congressman to serve on committees not related to the economic interests of his constituents. Vigorito's prospects in upcoming elections are excellent, but the district could fall back into the marginal category if he is not the Democratic candidate.

Census Data 1970 pop. 472,171; deviation from current state average, +8.9%; change 1960–70, +3.5%. Metro. 55.8%, 27.4% central city.

1970 Share of Federal Outlays $233,054,130

DOD	$29,660,000	HEW	$110,839,130
AEC	$000	HUD	$9,720,185
NASA	$109,273	OEO	$348,547

DOT	$7,215,268	DOA	$6,497,053
		Other	$68,664,674

Federal Military-Industrial Commitments

DOD Contractors Bucyrun-Erie (Erie), $5.912m: unspecified.

Economic Base Primary metal industries, esp. blast furnaces, steel works and rolling and finishing mills; fabricated metal products, esp. fabricated structural metal products; nonelectrical machinery, esp. metalworking machinery and equipment; electrical machinery, equipment, and supplies.

The Voters

Registration 200,545 total. 99,891 D (50%); 100,240 R (50%).

Employment profile White collar, 38%. Blue collar, 62%.

Ethnic groups Black, 3%. Total foreign stock, 20%. Italy, Poland, 4% each; Germany, 3%; UK, Czech., 2% each; Austria, Canada, Hungary, Sweden, Ireland, USSR, 1% each; others, 2%.

Presidential vote

1968	Humphrey (D)	85,763	(49%)
	Nixon (R)	81,256	(46%)
	Wallace (AIP)	9,733	(6%)

Representative

Joseph Phillip Vigorito (D) Elected 1964; b. Nov. 10, 1918, Niles, Ohio; home, Erie; U. of Pa., B.S., 1947; U. of Denver, M.B.A., 1949; Army, WWII; married, three children; religion unspecified.

Career Certified Public Accountant; Asst. Professor, Penn. State U., 1949–64.

Offices 440 CHOB, 202-225-5406. Also Rm. 107, Court House Bldg., Erie 16501, 814-453-6071, ext. 2304, and U.S. P.O. Bldg., Meadville 16335, 814-336-3282, and 21 W. State St., Sharon 16146, 413-347-5424.

Committees

Agriculture (9th); Subs. (1) Chm., Family Farms and Rural Development, (2) Dairy and Poultry, (3) Forests.

Interior and Insular Affairs (19th); Subs. (1) Environment, (2) Mines and Mining, (3) Territorial and Insular Affairs.

Group Ratings

	ADA	COPE	NREP	NFU	LCV	CFA	NAB	NSI	ACA
1970	72	83	67	100	75	95	17	80	21
1969	60	—	—	93	—	—	—	—	18
1968	58	100	—	93	—	—	33	—	26

Key Votes

(1) ABM	FOR	(6) 18-Yr-Vote	FOR	(11) Clean Water $	FOR
(2) SST	AGN*	(7) Farm Sub Lmt	AGN	(12) Mig Wrkrs Comp	FOR
(3) Phil Pln	AGN	(8) Coop-Church	FOR	(13) Jets to Chiang	AGN
(4) No-Knock	FOR	(9) Family Asst	FOR	(14) State OEO Veto	AGN
(5) Cmutr Tax	FOR	(10) Work Stamps	AGN	(15) Park Logging	AGN

* *Voted "for" in previous vote on same issue.*

Election Results

1970 general:	Joseph P. Vigorito (D)	94,029	(67%)
	Wayne R. Merrick (R)	44,395	(32%)
	Robert Shilling (AIP-C)	2,424	(2%)
1970 primary:	Joseph P. Vigorito (D), unopposed		
1968 general:	Joseph P. Vigorito (D)	106,869	(62%)
	John V. Edwards (R)	66,429	(38%)

TWENTY-FIFTH DISTRICT Political Background

Pennsylvania 25 comprises part of western Pennsylvania's industrial region. The district adjoins both Ohio and West Virginia; the tip of the West Virginia panhandle abuts the Pennsylvania state line to the southwest of the district. About half the population in the 25th lives in Beaver County, whose industrial towns sit along the Ohio and Beaver rivers. The most famous of these towns is, of course, Beaver Falls, boyhood home of Joe Namath. Like all of the area west and south of Pittsburgh, Beaver County is rich in ethnic diversity, with especially large numbers of Italian-Americans. The county is also one of the Democratic bulwarks of the state; it has gone Republican in only one recent statewide election. That happened in 1968, when Sen. Joseph Clark, who was unpopular among many of the Italians in the state, was the Democratic candidate for reelection.

The other two counties in the district are more marginal. Lawrence, dominated by the manufacturing city of New Castle, is Pennsylvania's bellwether county, most reliable predictor of statewide winners. Butler County, separated by a few miles from the industrial concentration along the rivers, is less thickly-settled and tends to go Republican.

Since 1954, Frank M. Clark has represented the 25th district in Washington. Clark is a Northern Democrat who usually votes the AFL-CIO line: liberal on economic issues and conservative on matters of foreign policy and defense spending. The Congressman is a relatively high ranking member of the Merchant Marine and Fisheries and the Public Works committees. He is also a tireless advocate of the interests of the coal and steel industries, which are, of course, vital to his district. Clark wins reelection routinely by overwhelming majorities, and he has had no significant opposition in the Democratic primary. Only 55 in 1970, the Congressman can look forward to more seniority and power in the House in the years to come.

Census Data 1970 pop. 443,733; deviation from current state average, +1.6%; change 1960–70, +2.1%. Metro. 47.0%, 0.0% central city.

1970 Share of Federal Outlays $190,398,049

DOD	$9,320,000	HEW	$99,060,099
AEC	$1,842,802	HUD	$28,573,383
NASA	$91,515	OEO	$215,412
DOT	$7,580,033	DOA	$3,094,810
		Other	$40,619,995

Federal Military-Industrial Commitments

None.

Economic Base Primary metal industries, esp. blast furnaces, steel works, and rolling and finishing mills; fabricated metal products; nonelectrical machinery, esp. metalworking and equipment; stone, clay, glass, and concrete products.

The Voters

Registration 187,743 total. 97,523 D (52%); 90,220 R (48%).

Employment profile White collar, 34%. Blue collar, 66%.

Ethnic groups Black, 3%. Total foreign stock, 24%. Italy, 7%; Poland, 3%; UK, Germany, Czech., Austria, 2% each; USSR, Hungary, Ireland, 1% each; others, 5%.

Presidential vote

1968	Humphrey (D)	85,838	(51%)
	Nixon (R)	68,242	(40%)
	Wallace (AIP)	15,748	(9%)

Representative

Frank M. Clark (D) Elected 1954; b. Dec. 24, 1915, Bessemer; home, Bessemer; USAF, WWII; Major USAFR; married, two children; Presbyterian.

Career Chief of police, Bessemer, 1945–55; Delegate to NATO Conference 1965, 1960, 1964–70; Delegate, Interparliamentary Conference, 1957; International Christian Leadership Conference for Peace, The Hague, 1958.

Offices 2238 RHOB, 202-225-2565. Also Fed. Bldg., New Castle 16103, 412-654-9176, and Fed. Bldg., Beaver Falls 15010, 412-843-6840, and Fed. Bldg., Butler 16001, 412-287-1865.

Committees

Merchant Marine and Fisheries (3rd); Subs. (1) Chm., Coast Guard, Coast and Geodetic Survey and Navigation, (2) Merchant Marine, (3) Oceanography, (4) Panama Canal.

Public Works (6th); Subs. (1) Flood Control and Internal Development, (2) Investment and Oversight, (3) Rivers and Harbors, (4) Roads.

Group Ratings

	ADA	COPE	NREP	NFU	LCV	CFA	NAB	NSI	ACA
1970	32	83	33	100	88	63	8	100	31
1969	47	—	—	100	—	—	—	—	15
1968	50	92	—	92	—	—	20	—	20

Key Votes

(1) ABM	ABS	(6) 18-Yr-Vote	ABS	(11) Clean Water $	FOR
(2) SST	FOR	(7) Farm Sub Lmt	ABS	(12) Mig Wrkrs Comp	FOR
(3) Phil Pln	AGN	(8) Coop-Church	AGN	(13) Jets to Chiang	FOR
(4) No-Knock	FOR	(9) Family Asst	AGN	(14) State OEO Veto	AGN
(5) Cmutr Tax	FOR	(10) Work Stamps	AGN	(15) Park Logging	AGN

Election Results

1970 general:	Frank M. Clark (D)	92,638	(70%)
	John Loth (R)	37,355	(28%)
	Albert H. Thornton (C)	2,959	(2%)
1970 primary:	Frank M. Clark (D)	5,332	(70%)
	A. R. C. H. Snyder, Sr. (D)	1,387	(18%)
	Steve Zoccoli (D)	876	(12%)
1968 general:	Frank M. Clark (D)	105,048	(63%)
	Richard L. Doolittle (R)	59,576	(36%)
	Albert Thornton (C)	1,951	(1%)

TWENTY-SIXTH DISTRICT Political Background

Pennsylvania 26 comprises the northern tip of Appalachia, between Pittsburgh and the West Virginia line. It is a region of rugged hills and winding rivers, lined with industry. The poverty that is endemic in West Virginia is also common here; those of Italian, Polish, and Czech descent, who have filtered down from around Pittsburgh, share the poverty with the old-line Scots-Irish of the district. The great steel factories lie to the north of the 26th district, and this is where the rough, tough coal mining country begins. It was within the 26th that Joseph Yablonski, the insurgent leader of the United Mine Workers, was found shot to death with his wife and daughter.

The 26th, of course, is a safe Democrat district, and since 1944 it has sent Thomas E. Morgan to the House of Representatives. Morgan is a physician from tiny Fredericktown (pop. 1,067). Through the inexorable workings of the seniority system, "Doc" Morgan, as he is called, has become chairman of the House Foreign Affairs Committee. This committee has a disproportionate number (6 of 38) of members from Pennsylvania and the adjacent industrial areas of northeast Ohio (See Ohio 18). The chairman of Foreign Affairs is not a scholar in the field, and his congressional unit has regularly suffered adverse comparison with its counterpart, the Senate Foreign Relations Committee, chaired by J. William Fulbright. The criticism has been prompted by the support which Morgan and a majority of his committee's members have given to the war policies of the Johnson and Nixon administrations. Until the spring of 1971, the committee simply refused to hold hearings on the war.

But whatever journalists and academics may think of Congressman Morgan, it is quite clear that the voters of the 26th district are happy with his performance. Morgan wins reelection by huge margins, and barring retirement in 1972, when he will be 66, the Congressman will remain in the house and in the chairmanship for some time to come. Although the district lost population during the '60's, the Democratic legislature will doubtless be kind to Morgan and give him part of exurban Allegheny County (Pittsburgh) or part of rural Somerset County.

Census Data 1970 pop. 393,934; deviation from current state average, —9.8%; change 1960–70, —6.0%. Metro. 53.5%, 0.0% central city.

1970 Share of Federal Outlays $200,071,000

DOD	$5,861,000	HEW	$128,591,000
AEC	$000	HUD	$1,325,000
NASA	$000	OEO	$150,000
DOT	$4,090,000	DOA	$3,830,000
		Other	$56,225,000

Federal Military-Industrial Commitments

None.

Economic Base Bituminous coal; blast furnaces, steel works, and rolling and finishing mills, and other primary metal industries; stone, clay, glass, and concrete products, esp. glass and glassware, pressed and blown.

The Voters

Registration 180,432 total. 125,940 D (70%); 54,492 R (30%).

Employment profile White collar, 33%. Blue collar, 67%.

Ethnic groups Black, 4%. Total foreign stock, 25%. Italy, 6%; Czech., 5%; Poland, 4%; Austria, UK, 2%; Hungary, Germany, USSR, 1% each; others, 4%.

Presidential vote

1968	Humphrey (D)	89,334	(57%)
	Nixon (R)	51,049	(33%)
	Wallace (AIP)	15,808	(10%)

Representative

Thomas E. Morgan (D) Elected 1944; b. Oct. 13, 1906, Ellsworth; home, Fredericktown; Waynesburg Col., B.S., 1930; Detroit Col. of Medicine and Surgery, M.D., 1934; married, one child; Methodist.

Career Intern, Grace Hospital, Detroit, Mich., 1933–34; practice of medicine and surgery, 1934–

Offices 2183 RHOB, 202-225-4665. Also Fed. Bldg., Uniontown 15401, 412-438-9131.

Committees

Foreign Affairs (Chm.); Chm., Sp. Sub. for Review of Foreign Aid Programs.

Group Ratings

	ADA	COPE	NREP	NFU	LCV	CFA	NAB	NSI	ACA
1970	56	100	67	100	89	78	0	80	18
1969	60	—	—	86	—	—	—	—	25
1968	83	100	—	100	—	—	0	—	13

Key Votes

(1) ABM	FOR	(6) 18-Yr-Vote	FOR	(11) Clean Water $	FOR
(2) SST	FOR	(7) Farm Sub Lmt	FOR	(12) Mig Wrkrs Comp	FOR
(3) Phil Pln	AGN	(8) Coop-Church	AGN	(13) Jets to Chiang	FOR
(4) No-Knock	ABS	(9) Family Asst	FOR	(14) State OEO Veto	AGN
(5) Cmutr Tax	FOR	(10) Work Stamps	AGN	(15) Park Logging	AGN

Election Results

1970 general:	Thomas E. Morgan (D)	80,734	(68%)
	Domenick A. Cupelli (R)	35,038	(30%)
	Bernard M. Dae Check (C)	2,176	(2%)
1970 primary:	Thomas E. Morgan (D), unopposed		
1968 general:	Thomas E. Morgan (D)	95,898	(64%)
	Paul Riggle (R)	50,594	(34%)
	Arleign Cale (C)	4,273	(3%)

TWENTY-SEVENTH DISTRICT Political Background

Pennsylvania 27 comprises the southern portion of Allegheny County, including part of the city of Pittsburgh and many of its more prosperous suburbs. The Pittsburgh section of the district is working-class, but the suburbs—among them, Mount Lebanon, Bethel Park, and Carnegie—are inhabited by the city's white-collar executive and office workers. The outer parts of the district resemble the rural areas of the 25th and 26th districts: hills dotted with grimy industrial towns and smoke-belching factories. But the really heavy industrial areas of Pittsburgh and the Monongahela River are all found in the adjacent 14th and 20th districts.

On paper, the 27th is politically marginal; in 1968, it even went for Hubert Humphrey by a small margin. Since 1944, however, the district has been represented by a Republican, James G. Fulton. Fulton, who owns several area newspapers, long ago developed the knack of winning independent and Democratic votes; he consistently has majorities of better than 60%. In the House, he is the ranking minority member of the committee on Science and Astronautics, and is also the ranking minority member of its Manned Space Flight Subcommittee. The Congressman is an enthusiastic backer of the space program and of the U.S. Navy, in which he served during World War II.

Upon the death of Congressman Robert Corbett of the neighboring 18th district, Fulton became the 3rd most senior Republican member of the House, tied with John Byrnes of Wisconsin. With that much seniority to take back to his constituency, he has few worries for 1972. The Democratic legislature could very well eliminate Corbett's old seat (see Pennsylvania 18); if it does, the legislature will likely add Republican territory to Fulton's district, which would make reelection a virtual certainty.

Census Data 1970 pop. 460,015; deviation from current state average, +5.3%; change 1960–70, +8.5%. Metro. 100.0%, 20.8% central city.

1970 Share of Federal Outlays $308,785,000 (average outlay per district, Pennsylvania 14, 18, 20, and 27)

DOD	$53,410,000	HEW	$111,378,000
AEC	$23,770,000	HUD	$9,216,000
NASA	$1,206,000	OEO	$1,348,000
DOT	$16,722,000	DOA	$1,558,000
		Other	$90,176,000

Federal Military-Industrial Commitments (See Pennsylvania 14 for greater Pittsburgh listing.)

Economic Base Primary metal industries, esp. blast furnaces, steel works, and rolling and finishing mills; fabricated metal products, esp. fabricated structural metal products; nonelectrical machinery, esp. metalworking machinery and equipment; food and kindred products; electrical machinery, equipment, and supplies.

The Voters

Registration 223,974 total. 130,072 D (58%); 93,902 R (42%).

Employment profile White collar, 53%. Blue collar, 47%.

Ethnic groups Black, 2%. Total foreign stock, 28%. Italy, 6%; Germany, 4%; UK, Poland, 3% each; Austria, Czech., 2% each; Ireland, USSR, Hungary, Canada, 1% each; others, 5%.

Presidential vote

1968	Humphrey (D)	87,266	(45%)
	Nixon (R)	85,344	(44%)
	Wallace (AIP)	21,054	(11%)

Representative

James Grove Fulton (R) Elected 1944; b. March 1, 1903, Dormont; home, Dormont; Penn. State U., B.A., 1924; Harvard, LL.B., 1927; Carnegie Tech, 1939–41; USNR, WWII; unmarried; Presbyterian.

Career Practicing atty., Solictor Dormont Borough, 1942; Pa. Senate, 1939–40; U.S. Delegate, UN 14th Gen. Assembly, 1959; Founder, former owner, chain of seven Pittsburgh surburban weekly newspapers.

Offices 2161 RHOB, 202-225-2915. Also 2117 Fed. Bldg., Pittsburgh 15222, 412-644-2876.

Committees

Foreign Affairs (9th); Subs. (1) Europe, (2) Natl. Security Policy and Scientific Developments, (3) Near East.

Science and Astronautics (Ranking Mbr.); Subs. (1) International Cooperation in Science and Space, (2) Manned Space Flight.

Group Ratings

	ADA	COPE	NREP	NFU	LCV	CFA	NAB	NSI	ACA
1970	56	91	83	92	88	67	17	100	28
1969	60	—	—	73	—	—	—	—	41
1968	50	62	—	67	—	—	50	—	26

Key Votes

(1) ABM	FOR	(6) 18-Yr-Vote	FOR	(11) Clean Water $	FOR
(2) SST	FOR	(7) Farm Sub Lmt	FOR	(12) Mig Wrkrs Comp	FOR
(3) Phil Pln	AGN	(8) Coop-Church	FOR	(13) Jets to Chiang	FOR
(4) No-Knock	FOR	(9) Family Asst	ABS	(14) State OEO Veto	AGN
(5) Cmutr Tax	FOR	(10) Work Stamps	AGN	(15) Park Logging	AGN

Election Results

1970 general:	James G. Fulton (R)	86,932	(61%)
	Douglas Walgren (D)	55,050	(38%)
	Harvey F. Johnston (AIP)	1,618	(1%)
1970 primary:	James G. Fulton (R), unopposed		
1968 general:	James G. Fulton (R)	130,784	(67%)
	Joseph L. Cosetti (D)	62,638	(32%)
	Harvey F. Johnston (C)	2,668	(1%)

RHODE ISLAND

RHODE ISLAND Political Background

One of the first of many religious schisms within the Massachusetts Bay theocracy resulted in the separate existence of the colony of Rhode Island and Providence Plantations. Roger Williams, as most schoolchildren know, founded Providence in 1636 as a haven for dissident Calvinists fleeing the regime to the north. Williams, a very religious man, was what we would call today, a Baptist; but unlike the religious ministers who ran things in and around Boston, Williams had a profound belief in the theological validity of religious and political freedom. He was, in short, the New World's first civil libertarian; his colony was made up of a motley group of Baptists, Antinomians (later called Quakers), and even some Papists (Roman Catholics) and American natives, Indians. The learned Williams, unlike many contemporaries and other Americans to follow, felt kindly disposed toward the people who preceded him on this land and became a scholar of their language and customs.

Perhaps the most famous of Williams' fellow colonists was the Antinomian Anne Hutchinson, who presumed to know which of the male ministers in Boston preached the true word and which did not. She was banished to Rhode Island, but history has done well by her. Mistress Hutchinson became a martyr among Quakers and became also Hawthorne's model for Hester Prynne, heroine of *The Scarlet Letter.*

As time went on, Rhode Island continued to produce an idiosyncratic history. The descendants of Williams' group began to prosper and as they prospered they grew increasingly conservative. The "triangle trade" out of Newport—rum, slaves, and sugar—was especially lucrative. After the Revolutionary War, Rhode Island was the last of the 13 original colonies to ratify the Constitution. It did not send delegates to the Convention for fear that tariffs, which could be imposed by the Union, would work to its disadvantage. Only after the Union threatened to sever commercial relations with Rhode Island and blockade its ports did it agree to join. In 1840, long after most of the states had granted full voting privileges to all free white males, and some 12 years after they had elected a commoner, Andrew Jackson, to the presidency, Rhode Island still had severe property qualifications for the franchise. This situation produced the Dorr Rebellion which, among other things, provided Rhode Island with two separate state governments, each claiming sovereignty.

For our own time, the key event in the state's history occurred in 1793, when Samuel Slater, a British émigré, built the nation's first water-powered cotton mill in Pawtucket. The textile industry then boomed in the state, and in the century or so that followed Rhode Island attracted immigrants eager to work on the looms and assembly lines. Most of them came from French-Canada, Ireland, and in particular, from Italy. As a result, this colony of dissident Protestants became the most heavily Roman Catholic state in the nation; today, some 65% of its residents are members of that faith.

The Catholics and the Protestants, of course, didn't get along very well in politics; but by 1928, the Catholics succeeded in carrying the state for Al Smith, the first Catholic presidential candidate. And since that time the immigrants and their children have become the bulwark of the most successful Democratic machine in the United States. Only Hawaii produces more Democratic winners.

Nominations to public office in the state, both Democratic and Republican, are pretty much determined by party endorsements; in recent times, only two non-endorsed candidates, one of them being Sen. Claiborne Pell, have ever won major primaries in the state. Aside from organizational support, the endorsed candidate gets the first line on the primary ballot. The strength of the Democratic machine is also evident in the state's presidential elections. Since 1924, Eisenhower has been the only Republican to carry the state. And since 1938, Rhode Island has elected only Democratic candidates to either house of Congress. The Republicans have, however, done better in gubernatorial contests; perhaps because of Democratic overconfidence, they have captured the governor's office in four of the last eight elections, winning in 1958, 1962, 1964, and 1966.

Rhode Island's current congressional delegation has the kind of neat ethnic balance one expects from a state in which party organizations make most of the political decisions. One Senate seat is occupied by the son of Italian immigrants; the other, by a scion of an aristocratic WASP family. One congressman is of French-Canadian descent; the other, of Irish Catholic. The senior member of the delegation and Rhode Island's most powerful man in Washington is Sen. John Pastore. The career of John Pastore shows that the Horatio Alger stories were written for the benefit of many young men, not just for aspiring Yankee farm boys. After his father's death, Pastore, then in his teens, had to work in order to support his family. He kept at his books, however, and made a fine academic record and eventually won a degree in law. Then as a state assemblyman, he put in honest, hard work in the vineyards of local politics. Pastore was rewarded for this by being slated for lieutenant governor; upon the incumbent's resignation he became governor of the state. After two terms as governor, Pastore ran for the Senate in 1950. He won an overwhelming margin in that election and has continued to win them ever since. Pastore is the first, and so far the only, Italian-American to sit in the United States Senate.

Pastore's seniority gives him a great deal of influence. He is chairman of the Communications Subcommittee of the Senate Commerce Committee. In that capacity, he has a strong say in the regulation of television and other media. Pastore was the chief sponsor of the bill designed to limit campaign spending, which was vetoed by President Nixon in 1970. The Senator is also the chairman of the Joint Committee on Atomic Energy, a body whose expertise and close working relationship with the AEC gives it power far beyond that of other congressional committees. Pastore's chairmanship may explain why he has been less hostile to military spending than most other Northern Democratic senators; he supported, for example, Nixon's ABM program. He has also backed the Vietnam policies of Johnson and Nixon, though he has apparently begun to have some doubts. In 1970, perhaps because of the challenge of a Republican peace candidate, Pastore voted for the Hatfield-McGovern amendment.

Rhode Island's junior senator, Claiborne Pell, comes from a background quite different from Pastore's. Pell was born with a silver spoon lodged firmly in his mouth. He is out of the storied town of Newport, which, of course, contains the "cottages" built for the summer residence of the New York Vanderbilts and other nineteenth century barons. The Senator's father and several other forebearers served in Congress before him. In 1960, Sen. Theodore F. Green, then 93, decided to retire. In the race for succession, Pell entered the Democratic primary without the endorsement of the party, and won. Since then, he has had little worry about reelection. Pell took 68% of the vote in 1966 and will probably do as well in 1972, barring a challenge from Navy Secretary and ex-Gov. (1962–68) John Chafee.

The Rhode Island Senator has a keen interest in foreign policy. He is a member of the Foreign Relations Committee and chairman of its Subcommittee on Oceans and International Environment. The Senator has been a persistent critic of the war, such as it was and such as it has become. Pell also sits on the Labor and Public Welfare Committee and on the rather unimportant Senate Rules Committee. The inexorable workings of the seniority system will probably elevate the Senator to the chairmanship of one of these two committees during his next term.

Electoral Votes 4

Census Data 1970 pop. 949,723; 0.46% of U.S. total, 40th largest; change 1960–70, +10.5%. Metro. 84.7%, 35.9% central city. 1970 per capita income, $3,920; 16th highest. 42nd in number of poor.

1970 Share of Federal Tax Burden $936,670,000; 0.48% of U.S. total, 37th largest.

1970 Share of Federal Outlays $735,550,099; 0.39% of U.S. total, 44th largest. Per capita federal spending, $774.

DOD	$264,723,000	38th	(0.46%)	HEW	$269,510,373	38th	(0.52%)
AEC	$693,704	38th	(0.03%)	HUD	$20,914,022	30th	(1.07%)
NASA	$680,670	38th	(0.02%)	OEO	$2,999,561	44th	(0.39%)
DOT	$14,805,430	52nd	(0.21%)	DOA	$4,513,913	52nd	(0.04%)

DOC	$2,638,374	44th	(0.23%)	POD	$32,100,226	38th	(0.28%)
DOI	$4,676,673	50th	(0.20%)	VA	$47,040,276	41st	(0.64%)
DOJ	$1,787,912	45th	(0.31%)	CSC	$13,867,681	41st	(0.34%)
				Other	$54,598,284		

Economic Base Miscellaneous manufacturing industries, esp. jewelry, silverware, and plated ware, and costume jewelry, costume novelties, buttons, and miscellaneous notions, other than precious metal; textile mill products, esp. narrow fabrics and other small wares mills, cotton, wool, silk and man-made fiber; primary metal industries, esp. drawing and insulating of nonferrous wire; fabricated metal products; nonelectrical machinery, esp. metalworking machinery and equipment; electrical machinery, equipment, and supplies, esp. current-carrying wiring devices; rubber and miscellaneous plastics products; food and kindred products; professional, scientific, and controlling instruments, photographic and optical goods, watches and clocks.

Political Line-up Governor, Frank Licht (D); seat up, 1972. Senators, John O. Pastore (D) and Claiborne Pell (D). Represenatives, 2 (2 D and 0 R). State Senate (49 D and 9 R); State House (75 D, 24 R, and 1 Ind.).

The Voters

Registration 466,878 total. No party registration.

Employment profile White collar, 38%. Blue collar, 62%.

Ethnic groups Black, 3%. Total foreign stock, 40%. Italy, Canada, 9% each; UK, 6%; Ireland, 3%; Poland, USSR, 2% each; Germany, Sweden, 1% each; others, 7%.

Presidential Vote

1968	Humphrey (D)	246,518	(64%)
	Nixon (R)	122,359	(32%)
	Wallace (AIP)	15,678	(4%)
1964	Johnson (D)	315,463	(81%)
	Goldwater (R)	74,615	(19%)
1960	Kennedy (D)	258,032	(64%)
	Nixon (R)	147,502	(36%)

Senator

John O. Pastore (D) Elected Dec. 19, 1950, seat up 1974; b. March 17, 1907, Providence; home, Providence; Northeastern U., LL.B., 1931; married, three children; Catholic.

Career R.I. Legislature, 1935–38; Asst. Atty. Gen., 1940–44; Lt. Governor, 1944–45; Governor of R.I., 1945–50.

Offices 3215 NSOB, 202-225-2921. Also 301 Post Office Annex, Providence 02903, 401-421-4583.

Committees

Appropriations (5th); Subs. (1) Chm., HUD, Space, and Science, (2) Defense, (3) State, Justice, Commerce, the Judiciary, and Related Agencies, (4) Public Works, (5) Transportation.

Commerce (2nd); Subs. (1) Chm., Communications, (2) Consumer, (3) Environment, (4) Merchant Marine, (5) Oceans and Atmosphere.

Jt. Com. on Atomic Energy (Chm.); Subs. (1) Legislation, (2) Military Applications, (3) Research, Development, and Radiation, (4) Security.

Group Ratings

	ADA	COPE	NREP	NFU	LCV	NAB	NSI	ACA
1970	78	92	67	93	66	33	40	14
1969	89	—	—	94	—	—	—	25
1968	79	71	—	69	—	67	—	18

Key Votes

(1) ABM	FOR	(8) Phil Pln	FOR	(15) Coop-Church	FOR
(2) SST	AGN	(9) Vol Army	FOR	(16) Cut Oil Dpltn	FOR
(3) Busing	FOR	(10) Prison $	ABS	(17) Consumer Prot	FOR
(4) Tob Sub	AGN	(11) Cut Mil $	FOR	(18) Farm Sub Limit	FOR
(5) Carswell	AGN	(12) Defoliatn	FOR	(19) Comp Bid Sales	FOR
(6) No-Knock	AGN	(13) 18-Yr-Vote	FOR	(20) Pre-Prod Tests	FOR
(7) Seniorty	AGN	(14) Pentgn PR	FOR	(21) Cut Marjna Pen	FOR

Election Results

1970 general:	John O. Pastore (D)	230,469	(68%)
	John McLaughlin (R)	107,351	(32%)
1970 primary:	John O. Pastore (D)	54,090	(88%)
	John Quattrocchi, Jr. (D)	7,332	(12%)
1964 general:	John O. Pastore (D)	319,607	(83%)
	Ronald R. Lagueux (R)	66,715	(17%)

Senator

Claiborne Pell (D) Elected 1960, seat up 1972; b. Nov. 22, 1918, New York City; home, Newport; Princeton U., B.A., 1940; Columbia, M.A., 1946; USCG, WWII; Capt. USCGR; married, two children; Episcopalian.

Career Sp. Asst. at San Francisco UN Conference, 1945; State Dept., 1945–46; U.S. Embassy, Czechoslovakia, 1946–47; Consulate Gen., Bratislava, Czech., 1947–48; V. Consul, Genoa, Italy, 1949; State Dept., 1950–52; Intl. Rescue Com., Exec. Secy. to R.I. Dem. State Chm., 1952, 1954.

Offices 325 OSOB, 202-225-4642. Also 418 Fed. Bldg., Providence 02903, 401-528-4547.

Committees

Foreign Relations (6th); Subs. (1) Chm., Oceans and International Environment, (2) Arms Control, International Law and Organization, (3) European Affairs, (4) Genocide Convention.

Labor and Public Welfare (3rd); Subs. (1) Chm., Education, (2) Chm., Sp. on Arts and Humanities, (3) Health, (4) Labor, (5) Railroad Retirement, (6) Sp. on International Health, Education, and Labor Programs, (7) Sp. on National Science Foundation.

Rules and Administration (3rd); Subs. (1) Chm., Smithsonian Institution, (2) Library.

Jt. Com. on the Library (2nd).

Sp. Com. on Aging (10th); Subs. (1) Federal, State, and Community Services, (2) Health of the Elderly, (3) Housing for the Elderly, (4) Long-Term Care.

Group Ratings

	ADA	COPE	NREP	NFU	LCV	NAB	NSI	ACA
1970	84	100	100	92	55	17	10	5
1969	94	—	—	88	—	—	—	7
1968	79	100	—	69	—	33	—	14

Key Votes

(1) ABM	AGN	(8) Phil Pln	FOR	(15) Coop-Church	FOR
(2) SST	AGN	(9) Vol Army	AGN	(16) Cut Oil Dpltn	FOR
(3) Busing	FOR	(10) Prison $	AGN	(17) Consumer Prot	ABS
(4) Tob Sub	AGN	(11) Cut Mil $	FOR	(18) Farm Sub Limit	FOR
(5) Carswell	AGN	(12) Defoliatn	FOR	(19) Comp Bid Sales	FOR
(6) No-Knock	AGN	(13) 18-Yr-Vote	FOR	(20) Pre-Prod Tests	FOR
(7) Seniorty	ABS	(14) Pentgn PR	AGN	(21) Cut Marjna Pen	FOR

Election Results

1966 general:	Claiborne Pell (D)	219,331	(68%)
	Harriet Briggs (R)	104,838	(32%)
1966 primary:	Claiborne Pell (D), unopposed		
1960 general:	Claiborne Pell (D)	275,575	(69%)
	Raoul Archambault (R)	124,408	(31%)

FIRST DISTRICT Political Background

Rhode Island 1 comprises the eastern half of this tiny, densely-populated state. The district takes in the east side of Narragansett Bay, part of the city of Providence including Brown University, and the Seekonk River Valley, lined with textile mills, to the north. Most of the 1st's large French-Canadian population live in the valley mill towns of Pawtucket, Central Falls, and Woonsocket. And because the district is predominantly working-class bread-and-butter issues are the stuff of politics. There is strong sentiment here, for example, for import quotas on textiles and shoes. Already in the 1st, there is more federally-financed senior citizen housing than in any of the other 434 congressional districts. This fact is probably related to its congressman's membership on the House Banking and Currency Committee; Fernand J. St Germain serves on that body, which has jurisdiction over housing programs.

First elected when he was 32 in 1960, St Germain is now the 8th ranking Democrat on Banking and Currency. The Congressman is less distinguished by his ideological fervor than by scrupulous attention to the affairs of his district. He has combined a generally liberal and antiwar record with a specific opposition to the conclusions reached by the liberal members of the presidential commission on obscenity. St Germain routinely gets about 60% of the votes at election time, and will likely continue to serve in the House for some time to come.

Census Data 1970 pop. 426,532; deviation from current state average, —10.2%; change 1960–70, +7.2%. Metro. 81.5%, 30.8% central city.

1970 Share of Federal Outlays $367,775,000 (average outlay per district, Rhode Island 1 and 2)

DOD	$132,362,000	HEW	$134,755,000
AEC	$347,000	HUD	$10,457,000
NASA	$340,000	OEO	$1,500,000
DOT	$7,403,000	DOA	$2,257,000
		Other	$27,299,000

Federal Military-Industrial Commitments

DOD Contractors Raytheon (Portsmouth), $23.283m: submarine sonar equipment.

DOD Installations Naval Communication Station (Newport). Naval Hospital (Newport). Naval Schools Command (Newport). Naval Station (Newport). Naval Supply Center (Newport). Naval Underseas Research and Development Center (Newport). Naval Public Works Center (Newport).

Economic Base Miscellaneous manufacturing industries, esp. jewelry, silverware, and plated ware, and costume jewelry, costume novelties, buttons, and miscellaneous notions other than precious metal; textile mill products; fabricated metal products, esp. coatings, engravings, and allied services; rubber and miscellaneous plastics products, esp. rubber footwear. Also, banking.

The Voters

Registration 207,621 total. No party registration.

Employment profile White collar, 38%. Blue collar, 62%.

Ethnic groups Black, 3%. Total foreign stock, 42%. Canada, 12%; UK, Italy, 6% each; Ireland, 3%; Poland, USSR, 2% each; Germany, Sweden, 1% each; others, 9%.

Presidential Vote

1968	Humphrey (D)	112,101	(66%)
	Nixon (R)	51,891	(31%)
	Wallace (AIP)	5,833	(3%)

Representative

Fernand Joseph St Germain (D) Elected 1960; b. Jan. 9, 1928, Blackstone, Mass.; home, Woonsocket; Providence Col., Ph.B., 1948; Boston U., LL.B., 1955; Army, Korean War; married, two children; Catholic.

Career R.I. Legislature, 1952–60; practicing atty., 1956– .

Offices 2367 RHOB, 202-225-4911. Also 200 John Fogarty Bldg., Providence 02903, 401-272-7730.

Committees

Banking and Currency (8th); Subs. (1) Chm., Bank Supervision and Insurance, (2) Housing, (3) International Trade.

Government Operations (16th); Subs. (1) Legal and Monetary Affairs, (2) Legislation and Military Operations.

Sel. Com. on Small Business (10th); Subs. (1) Activities of Regulatory Agencies Relating to Small Business, (2) Foundations: Their Impact on Small Business.

Group Ratings

	ADA	COPE	NREP	NFU	LCV	CFA	NAB	NSI	ACA
1970	72	100	83	92	88	94	0	40	17
1969	80	—	—	77	—	—	—	—	27
1968	83	100	—	75	—	—	0	—	4

Key Votes

(1) ABM	AGN	(6) 18-Yr-Vote	FOR	(11) Clean Water $	FOR
(2) SST	AGN	(7) Farm Sub Lmt	FOR	(12) Mig Wrkrs Comp	FOR
(3) Phil Pln	AGN	(8) Coop-Church	FOR	(13) Jets to Chiang	AGN
(4) No-Knock	FOR	(9) Family Asst	FOR	(14) State OEO Veto	AGN
(5) Cmutr Tax	ABS	(10) Work Stamps	AGN	(15) Park Logging	ABS

Election Results

1970 general:	Fernand J. St Germain (D)	86,283	(61%)
	Walter J. Miska (R)	52,962	(37%)
	Stephen Bruce Murray (PF)	2,327	(2%)
1970 primary:	Fernand J. St Germain (D)	18,722	(82%)
	John E. Grant (D)	4,031	(18%)
1968 general:	Fernand J. St Germain (D)	97,945	(60%)
	Lincoln A. Almond (R)	62,394	(39%)
	Joseph O'Brien (Ind.)	1,684	(1%)

SECOND DISTRICT Political Background

Rhode Island 2, the western half of the state, includes most of the city of Providence and the large suburban cities of Cranston and Warwick. The district also takes in most of Rhode Island's small rural area. The 2nd is particularly notable for its large Italian-American population; very few other districts in the country have larger Italian communities. In the early part of the 20th century, these people lived mainly in the poorer parts of Providence. Today, most of the Italians have moved out and are living in the middle-class precincts of Cranston, Warwick, and other surburbs.

From 1940 to 1967, the 2nd was represented by John E. Fogarty, a high ranking member of the Appropriations Committee. Fogarty died of a heart attack at the age of 53 at the opening of the 90th Congress; had he lived longer, he very well might have become chairman of the full committee. The special election called to fill his seat took place in the spring of 1967, just when voters were beginning to tire of the Johnson Administration. Fogarty had always won easily, but the Republicans put on a strong campaign for his seat. They ran an Italian-American candidate and lost the election by a scant 313 votes.

The winner was Robert O. Tiernan, a state senator from Warwick. Tiernan has been a rather typical Eastern safe-district congressman: liberal on domestic issues, but inclined to support the war until the 1968 Tet offensive. Lately, Tiernan has expressed interest in statewide office. Apparently, he would like to succeed Sen. Pastore when he decides to step down. But that may not be too soon, since Pastore still is in his mid-sixties. And Rhode Island political buffs can recall that the late Senator Theodore Green was some 30 years older than Pastore is now when, at age 93 in 1960, he decided to retire. A full generation and more of Rhode Island politicians were eager to succeed the aging Sen. Green. Sen. Pastore is reported in good health and quite willing to go on performing his senatorial duties. It could be that Tiernan, like many other Rhode Island politicians who have aspired to the Senate, has a long wait.

Census Data 1970 pop. 523,191; deviation from current state average, +10.2%; change 1960–70, +13.3%. Metro. 87.3%, 40.1% central city.

1970 Share of Federal Outlays $367,775,000 (average outlay per district, Rhode Island, 1 and 2)

DOD	$132,362,000	HEW	$134,755,000
AEC	$347,000	HUD	$10,457,000
NASA	$340,000	OEO	$1,500,000
DOT	$7,403,000	DOA	$2,257,000
		Other	$27,299,000

Federal Military-Industrial Commitments

DOD Contractors Mine Safety Appliances Co. (Esmond), $18.709m: protective field masks. Bulova Watch Co. (Providence), $5.023m: artillery fuzes.

DOD Installations Naval Air Station (Quonset Point). Naval Construction Battalion Center (Davisville). Naval Air Rework Facility (Quonset Point).

Economic Base Miscellaneous manufacturing industries, esp. jewelry, silverware, and plated ware, and costume jewelry, costume novelties, buttons, and miscellaneous notions other than precious metal; textile mill products; fabricated metal products, esp. coatings, engravings, and allied services; primary metal industries, esp. drawing and insulating of nonferrous wire.

The Voters

Registration 259,257 total. No party registration.

Employment profile White collar, 38%. Blue collar, 62%.

Ethnic groups Black, 3%. Total foreign stock, 38%. Italy, 13%; Canada, 7%; UK, 5%; Ireland, 3%; USSR, 2%; Poland, Sweden, Germany, 1% each; others, 5%.

Presidential Vote

1968	Humphrey (D)	134,417	(63%)
	Nixon (R)	70,468	(33%)
	Wallace (AIP)	9,845	(5%)

Representative

Robert Owens Tiernan (D) Elected March 28, 1967; b. Feb. 24, 1929, Providence; home, Warwick; Providence Col., B.S., 1953; Catholic U., J.D., 1956; unmarried; Catholic.

Career Practicing atty., 1957–67; R.I. Legislature, 1961–67.

Offices 417 CHOB, 202-225-2735. Also 307 P.O. Annex, Providence 02903, 401-528-4561.

Committees

Interstate and Foreign Commerce (17th); Sub. on Communications and Power.

Merchant Marine and Fisheries (21st); Subs. (1) Coast Guard, Coast and Geodetic Survey and Navigation, (2) Fisheries and Wildlife Conservation, (3) Oceanography.

Group Ratings

	ADA	COPE	NREP	NFU	LCV	CFA	NAB	NSI	ACA
1970	80	100	83	100	100	100	0	50	13
1969	80	—	—	93	—	—	—	—	18
1968	83	100	—	81	—	—	0	—	4

Key Votes

(1) ABM	AGN	(6) 18-Yr-Vote	FOR	(11) Clean Water $	FOR
(2) SST	AGN	(7) Farm Sub Lmt	FOR	(12) Mig Wrkrs Comp	FOR
(3) Phil Pln	AGN	(8) Coop-Church	FOR	(13) Jets to Chiang	AGN
(4) No-Knock	FOR	(9) Family Asst	FOR	(14) State OEO Veto	AGN
(5) Cmutr Tax	ABS	(10) Work Stamps	AGN	(15) Park Logging	AGN

Election Results

1970 general:	Robert O. Tiernan (D)	121,704	(66%)
	William A. Dimitri, Jr. (R)	61,819	(34%)
	Louis Dona G. O'Hara (Ind)	518	(0%)
1970 primary:	Robert O. Tiernan (D), unopposed		
1968 general:	Robert O. Tiernan (D)	124,044	(61%)
	Howard E. Russell (R)	78,502	(39%)

SOUTH CAROLINA

SOUTH CAROLINA Political Background

Abraham Lincoln was, among other things, a very shrewd man. As President, he made certain that the first shots of the Civil War were fired by Southerners. Lincoln, a politician firmly committed to the idea of Union, knew that without this, the citizenry of the North—many of whom openly preferred secession to war—could not be galvanized into fighting. The scene was Fort Sumter in Charleston Harbor in the spring of 1861. South Carolina had already seceded, the first Southern state to do so, about six weeks after the election of the Republican Lincoln in 1860. Since it was no longer part of the Union, the state laid claim to the federal military installation in the harbor. Lincoln's advisors had it figured the way South Carolina did: he had to fight or quit the harbor. The President did neither. Lincoln announced that he would continue to supply Fort Sumter with non-military provisions. The prospects of a Union flag flying over Charleston Harbor day after day, business as usual, was too much for the citizens of the city to abide and they opened fire. Fort Sumter surrendered, but not before becoming the Pearl Harbor of the Civil War.

South Carolina was an uncompromising state, one which was led for some forty years by John C. Calhoun, an uncompromising man. In the years before the Civil War, it took leadership of the South away from the more moderate Virginia. The economy of South Carolina, still doing well at the time, was completely dependent on the labor-intensive crops of cotton, rice, and indigo; in short, dependent on slaves. So the South Carolina whites, rich planter and not-so-rich commoner alike, were heavily outnumbered by blacks. These black people were at once the economic mainstay of South Carolina and the source of apprehension. In 1822, Denmark Vesey led the nation's first black insurrection in Charleston; though it was quickly suppressed, Vesey frightened many South Carolinians and other Southerners as well. A heavy investment in black slaves and a desire to keep them in place could very easily lead a state or a region into war.

During Reconstruction, white people of the state actually saw what they considered to be a successful black revolt. Blacks won more political power here than in any other part of the old Confederacy; they controlled the state's legislature and its congressional delegation. In the years following Reconstruction, of course, blacks were shorn of the franchise and all other political rights. And also after Reconstruction, this once prosperous state, including the refined city of Charleston, settled into economic stagnation. For most of the twentieth century, South Carolina has been among the lowest ranking states in per capita income, education levels, and health services.

Like most other Southern states in the past twenty years, South Carolina has had many of its black citizens leave and many new white citizens move into the state. This pattern of migration set the stage for the resurgence of the local Republican party; most of its strength lies in the cities of the state, places like Greenville, Columbia, and Charleston. Meanwhile, since the beginning of the Civil Rights Revolution in the early '60's, the traditional strength of the Democratic party has been slipping. In 1960, Democrat John Kennedy carried the state by just 10,000 votes; four years later, Republican Barry Goldwater won the state easily. But by 1968, the Voting Rights Act of 1965 had made its impact, and South Carolina produced the nation's closest three-man contest for the presidency. Richard Nixon won with 38%, which was, despite the well-publicized boost from Sen. Strom Thurmond, his second lowest winning percentage in any of the 50 states. George Wallace finished second in South Carolina with 32%, and Hubert Humphrey won 30% of the state's votes. Since 24% of the state's voters are black, this means that 8% of the state's voters stayed with the party of John Calhoun and secession.

However close it might have been, the Nixon victory was touted as a triumph for Sen. Strom Thurmond. He served as the Democratic governor of the state from 1946 to 1950, and in 1948 received 39 electoral votes for President on the States' Rights Democratic ticket. Thurmond was elected to the Senate in 1954 as a Democrat, but before the 1964 elections he switched his party registration to Republican. In 1968, the Senator lobbied effectively among Southern delegates for Nixon at the Republican National Convention, thereby preventing any Reagan breakthrough. Thurmond later campaigned all over the South for the Nixon-Agnew ticket. On the stump, he proclaimed that Nixon would allow Southerners "freedom of choice schools" and would also support import quotas for textiles—the state's major industry. No doubt Thurmond's support kept many South Carolina votes from going to Wallace. There is, however, a revealing form of symmetry which exists between the 1968 white vote in South Carolina and the state's close Kennedy-Nixon race of 1960. Nixon did make some gains in the textile-mill towns and did lose some ground in the rural Wallace areas. But if the totals are analyzed by congressional district, Nixon, among white voters, ran no more than 5% above or 5% below his 1960 showings.

An analysis of the 1968 presidential returns indicates that whatever magic the name Thurmond has in South Carolina is something less than overpowering. In 1970, Thurmond influence demonstrated clear weakness. The major race in the state was for governor, which pitted Democratic Lt. Gov. John West against Republican Congressman Albert Watson. West, a moderate on racial matters, advised the voters that they would just have to get used to integration. Watson was a different kind of politician. The onetime Democrat supported Barry Goldwater in 1964; as a result, he was stripped of his congressional seniority. He then resigned, and won reelection as a Republican in a 1965 special election. In the 1970 campaign for governor, he urged a crowd of voters in Lamar to stand up against a desegregation order. A few days later, some Lamar citizens attacked three buses containing black schoolchildren.

The violence in Lamar was somewhat ironic. Watson's television ads called on the voters to restore discipline in the schools, as well as to resist rule by the "bloc vote" —which is, of course, a thinly disguised euphemism. Sen. Thurmond, Vice President Agnew, and David Eisenhower all campaigned enthusiastically for Watson. To counter their efforts, the Democrats showed a film called "Broken Promises," which featured clips of Thurmond campaigning in 1968. West won the election by a convincing 52–46 majority; and though he had the support of virtually all of the state's black voters, most of his votes came from whites.

The "Broken Promises" theme clearly nettled Thurmond, who, in 1970, pointedly criticized the Nixon Administration for some of its stands on integration. Moreover, the 1971 Supreme Court ruling in the Charlotte-Mecklenburg case (see North Carolina 9)—which authorizes busing to achieve integration—will give Thurmond more trouble. Integration continues apace, and now even Strom Thurmond High School in Edgefield has both black and white students in its classrooms. And, as of this writing, the Administration has been unable to impose import quotas on textiles.

In 1972, Thurmond may have trouble for the first time in years. Robert McNair, who was the state's governor from 1965 to 1970 and who is a racial moderate like West, is expected to be Thurmond's opponent. No doubt the Democratic theme will again be "Broken Promises." Each time Thurmond has run for the Senate he has carried virtually every county in the state. But in 1966, when he won reelection as a Republican, the Voting Rights Act had not yet taken full effect. In 1972, McNair will go into the race with 25% of the votes—those cast by South Carolina's blacks—already in his column. Add the 8% of the whites who voted for Humphrey in 1968, and McNair will need only another 27% of the white votes to win—not an impossible percentage, given West's showing in 1970. If, therefore, Thurmond loses any significant percentage of the white votes he won in 1966, he will lose the election. Also in 1966, the Senator ran against a political unknown.

South Carolina's junior senator, Ernest F. Hollings, Jr., appears to be in better political shape. Hollings was governor of the state from 1958 to 1962; in 1962, he made a run for the Senate, but was defeated by the incumbent Olin D. Johnston. After Johnston's death, then-Gov. Donald Russell had himself appointed to the seat, always an unpopular move everywhere. This set the stage for Hollings' victory in the 1966 Democratic primary. Hollings won the balance of the term in the general election with a narrow 51% victory, while at the same time Thurmond took 62% on the Republican side. But in 1968, against the same opponent, Hollings won easily, carrying every county. Because of Congressman Watson's defeat in the 1970 governor's race, the Senator is not expected to have serious opposition in the foreseeable future.

Hollings, like McNair and West, is a Southern moderate. The Senator votes against civil rights legislation, and, when it is enacted, he urges his constituents to comply with the law. Hollings rarely supports liberal social or antiwar initiatives; he did, however, stir the Senate with a speech concerning the severe forms of malnutrition common in South Carolina's poor rural counties. During his years in politics, he said, he had not known that such things existed in his state, and that as a South Carolina booster, he had not especially wanted to know. Hollings is now one of the major proponents of legislation to wipe out hunger and malnutrition in America.

Electoral Votes 8

Census Data 1970 pop. 2,590,516; 1.26% of U.S. total, 27th largest; change 1960–70, +8.7%. Metro. 39.3%, 9.3% central city. 1970 per capita income, $2,908; 48th highest. 20th in number of poor.

1970 Share of Federal Tax Burden $1,600,150,000; 0.82% of U.S. total, 30th largest.

1970 Share of Federal Outlays $1,920,782,486; 1.02% of U.S. total, 31st largest. Per capita federal spending, $741.

DOD	$698,644,000	26th (1.22%)	HEW	$494,621,588	34th (0.95%)
AEC	$119,910,884	8th (4.61%)	HUD	$16,222,119	33rd (0.83%)
NASA	$269,451	43rd (0.01%)	OEO	$11,095,863	26th (1.46%)
DOT	$66,143,998	36th (0.93%)	DOA	$178,077,257	28th (1.39%)
DOC	$9,797,318	25th (0.85%)	POD	$56,050,194	32nd (0.77%)
DOI	$12,829,853	38th (0.56%)	VA	$105,554,404	34th (1.43%)
DOJ	$4,407,062	33rd (0.77%)	CSC	$29,577,729	29th (0.73%)
			Other	$117,580,766	

Economic Base Textile mill products, esp. broad woven cotton fabric and broad woven man-made fiber and silk fabric, and dyeing and finishing textiles other than wool fabrics and knit goods; tobacco and cotton; apparel and other finished products made from fabrics and similar materials, esp. men's, youths', and boys' furnishings, work clothing, and allied garments; chemicals and allied products, esp. plastics and synthetic materials other than glass; nonelectrical machinery; lumber and wood products other than furniture; primary smelting and refining of nonferrous metals; food and kindred products; electrical machinery, equipment, and supplies, esp. electronic components and accessories; stone, clay, glass, and concrete products; paper and allied products, esp. paperboard mills.

Political Line-up Governor, John C. West (D); seat up, 1974. Senators, Strom Thurmond (R) and Ernest F. Hollings (D). Representatives 6 (5 D and 1 R). State Senate (11 D and 3 R); State House (113 D and 11 R).

The Voters

Registration 888,894 total. No party registration. 668,397 white (75%); 220,303 black (25%); 194 other (—).

Employment profile White collar, 30%. Blue collar, 70%.

Ethnic groups Black, 31%. Total foreign stock, 2%. All foreign groups less than 0.5% each.

Presidential Vote

1968	Humphrey (D)	197,486	(30%)
	Nixon (R)	254,062	(38%)
	Wallace (AIP)	215,430	(32%)
1964	Johnson (D)	215,700	(42%)
	Goldwater (R)	309,048	(59%)
1960	Kennedy (D)	198,129	(51%)
	Nixon (R)	188,588	(49%)

Senator

Strom Thurmond (R) Elected 1956, seat up 1972; b. Dec. 5, 1902, Edgefield; home, Aiken; Clemson U., B.S., 1923; admitted to S.C. bar in 1930 after studying law at night; Army, WWII; Major Gen. USAR; married; Baptist.

Career Farmer; teacher, 1923–29; Edgefield County Supt. of Ed., 1929–33; practicing atty., 1930–38, 1951–55; S.C. Senate, 1933–38; Circuit Judge, 1938–46; States Rights Candidate for Pres., 1948; U.S. Senate, Dec. 24, 1954–April 4, 1956; Governor of S.C., 1947–51; switched from Dem. to Rep., Sept. 16, 1964.

Offices 4241 NSOB 202-225-5972. Also Post Office Bldg., Aiken 29801, 803-649-2591, and Palmetto State Life Bldg., 1310 Lady St., Columbia 29201, 803-253-1636.

Committees

Armed Services (2nd); Subs. (1) Military Construction Authorization, (2) National Stockpile and Naval Petroleum, (3) Preparedness Investigating, (4) Sp. to Review Bomber Defense, (5) Ad Hoc on Tactical Air Power.

Judiciary (4th); Subs. (1) Administrative Practice and Procedure, (2) Antitrust and Monopoly Legislation, (3) Constitutional Amendments, (4) Constitutional Rights, (5) Criminal Laws and Procedures, (6) Immigration and Naturalization, (7) Internal Security.

Veterans' Affairs (Ranking Mbr.); Subs. (1) Compensation and Pension, (2) Health and Hospitals.

Group Ratings

	ADA	COPE	NREP	NFU	LCV	NAB	NSI	ACA
1970	0	0	0	13	27	91	100	96
1969	0	—	—	33	—	—	—	93
1968	0	0	—	15	—	60	—	92

Key Votes

(1) ABM	FOR	(8) Phil Pln	AGN	(15) Coop-Church	AGN
(2) SST	FOR	(9) Vol Army	AGN	(16) Cut Oil Dpltn	AGN
(3) Busing	AGN	(10) Prison $	AGN	(17) Consumer Prot	AGN
(4) Tob Sub	FOR	(11) Cut Mil $	AGN	(18) Farm Sub Limit	AGN
(5) Carswell	FOR	(12) Defoliatn	FOR	(19) Comp Bid Sales	FOR
(6) No-Knock	FOR	(13) 18-Yr-Vote	AGN	(20) Pre-Prod Tests	AGN
(7) Seniorty	FOR	(14) Pentgn PR	FOR	(21) Cut Marjna Pen	AGN

Election Results

1966 general:	Strom Thurmond (R)	271,297	(62%)
	Bradley Morrah, Jr. (D)	164,955	(38%)
1966 primary:	Strom Thurmond (R), unopposed		
1960 general:	Strom Thurmond (D), unopposed		

Senator

Ernest F. Hollings (D) Elected Nov. 8, 1966, seat up 1974; b. Jan. 1, 1922, Charleston; home, Charleston; The Citadel, B.A., 1942; U. of S.C., LL.B., 1947; Army, WWII; married, four children; Lutheran.

Career Practicing atty., 1947–58, 1962–66; S.C. Legislature, 1948–54, Speaker Pro Tem., 1950–54; Lt. Governor, 1955–59; Governor, 1959–63.

Offices 432 OSOB, 202-225-6121. Also 306 Fed. Bldg., Columbia 29201, 803-254-7636, and 323 Fed. Bldg., Spartanburg 29301, 803-585-8272, and 141 E. Bay St., Charleston 29402, 803-254-7636.

Committees

Appropriations (13th); Subs. (1) Chm., Legislative Branch, (2) Labor, HEW, and Related Agencies, (3) State, Justice, Commerce, the Judiciary, and Related Agencies, (4) District of Columbia, (5) Military Construction.

Commerce (8th); Subs. (1) Chm., Oceans and Atmosphere, (2) Aviation, (3) Merchant Marine, (4) Surface Transportation.

Post Office and Civil Service (4th); Subs. (1) Chm., Postal Operations, (2) Compensation and Employment Benefits.

Group Ratings

	ADA	COPE	NREP	NFU	LCV	NAB	NSI	ACA
1970	22	34	20	86	51	30	89	55
1969	22	—	—	69	—	—	—	55
1968	14	34	—	30	—	0	—	56

Key Votes

(1) ABM	FOR	(8) Phil Pln	AGN	(15) Coop-Church	FOR
(2) SST	FOR	(9) Vol Army	AGN	(16) Cut Oil Dpltn	ABS
(3) Busing	AGN	(10) Prison $	ABS	(17) Consumer Prot	FOR
(4) Tob Sub	FOR	(11) Cut Mil $	ABS	(18) Farm Sub Limit	AGN
(5) Carswell	FOR	(12) Defoliatn	FOR	(19) Comp Bid Sales	AGN
(6) No-Knock	AGN	(13) 18-Yr-Vote	FOR	(20) Pre-Prod Tests	AGN
(7) Seniorty	AGN	(14) Pentgn PR	AGN	(21) Cut Marjna Pen	AGN

Election Results

1968 general:	Ernest F. Hollings (D)	404,060	(62%)
	Marshall Parker (R)	248,780	(38%)
1968 primary:	Ernest F. Hollings (D)	308,016	(78%)
	John Bolt Culbertson (D)	84,913	(22%)
1966 special:	Ernest F. Hollings (D)	223,790	(51%)
	Marshall Parker (R)	212,032	(49%)

FIRST DISTRICT Political Background

South Carolina 1 lies in the heart of the South Carolina lowlands country, around and including the ancient city of Charleston, which was founded in 1670. Before the Civil War, this area was laced with plantations growing cotton, rice, and indigo—all crops which required vast numbers of slaves (see state write-up). Today, because many of the rural counties of the 1st are still black-majority, Humphrey was able to carry most of them in 1968. But Charleston, and the suburbs around it, are dominated by white people.

In the years after the Civil War, Charleston, once the nation's most prosperous South Atlantic port, became an economic backwater. But in the mid-twentieth century, the city was blessed with an economic benefactor who restored Charleston to some of its old majesty and much of its old power. That benefactor was L. Mendel Rivers, congressman from the 1st district for 30 years and chairman of the House Armed Services Committee from 1965 until his death in late 1970. Rivers was as unashamed of the Defense Department money he funneled into Charleston as he was of his unflinching superpatriotism. Both attitudes stemmed from his accomplishment: some 35% of the payrolls in the district depend on either military installations or defense industries (for Defense Department commitments, see data section below).

Rivers looked the part of a Southern congressman, with his long, flowing, white locks and his thick accent. He was bellicose, self-righteous, and, many said, too often drunk; though in his last few years, according to all reports, he quit drinking completely. Rivers compiled, of course, a heavily pro-Pentagon, conservative record in the House. But he sometimes supported dollars-and-cents social and economic measures; that perhaps came from Rivers having begun life as a very poor Southern boy. Rivers was invincible at the polls and won his last election in 1970 with no opposition in either the primary or general election.

The race to succeed the chairman illustrates the volatility of South Carolina politics these days. The heir apparent, and the eventual winner, was Mendel Davis—Rivers' godson who had served on the congressman's staff in Washington. Although Davis won the Democratic primary, the Republicans made a strong effort to capture the district, which, in 1968, had gone for Nixon in a close three-way race. There was even a Republican primary, where ultraconservative dentist James Edwards defeated Charleston businessman Arthur Ravenel, who tried to attract black support. And there was an independent candidate, civil rights activist Mrs. Victoria De Lee, who eventually took 10% of the vote.

Most of the black votes, however, went to Mendel Davis, as they had gone to Mendel Rivers before him. The Republicans sent in Vice President Agnew, Sen. James Buckley, Gov. Ronald Reagan, and Sen. Barry Goldwater to campaign for Edwards, which indicated quite clearly that the GOP was looking for white votes only. As it turned out, the black votes provided Davis' margin of victory, as the Democrat won by only 6,000 votes (49–41).

In his campaign, Davis stressed his age and argued that he would be able to accumulate more seniority than the other candidates. Southern voters are quite sophisticated in these matters. With the chairman gone, the economy of the district could be headed for trouble. Although no one thinks that the Charleston Shipyard can be moved somewhere else, it is at least possible that some of the military money will start to go other places—or no place at all. Davis promised his constituents that he would work hard to prevent this—no doubt he has already found that many of the aging Southern congressmen, who control military appropriations, sympathize with him. And since Mendel Davis is one young man respectful of his elders, he should get along quite well with members of the congressional establishment. Furthermore, it is likely that the election of 1971 has determined the representation from the 1st district for a long time to come; the Democratic primary of 1940 held up for some 30-odd years.

Census Data 1970 pop. 477,942; deviation from current state average, +13.4% change 1960–70, +10.7%. Metro. 63.6%, 14.0% central city.

1970 Share of Federal Outlays $582,220,745

DOD	$385,918,000	HEW	$76,968,912
AEC	$000	HUD	$1,189,000
NASA	$000	OEO	$4,151,661
DOT	$23,951,056	DOA	$31,625,848
		Other	$58,416,268

Federal Military-Industrial Commitments

DOD Contractors AVCO Corp. (Charleston), $23.955m: repair and overhaul of T-53 helicopter engines. Blair Algernon (Charleston), $14.801m: hospital construction at naval facilities.

DOD Installations Charleston Army Depot (North Charleston). Marine Corps Air Station (Beaufort). Marine Corps Recruit Depot (Parris Island). Charleston Naval Shipyard (Charleston). Naval Hospital (Charleston). Naval Hospital (Beaufort). Naval Station (Charleston). Naval Supply Center (Charleston). Naval Weapons Station (Charleston). Navy Fleet Ballistic Missile Submarine Training Center (Charleston). Polaris Missile Facility, Atlantic (Charleston). Charleston AFB (Charleston). North Charleston AF Station (North Charleston).

Economic Base Cotton and livestock; apparel and other finished products made from fabrics and similar materials; transportation equipment; stone, clay, glass, and concrete products. Also, tourism (Charleston, Hilton Head).

The Voters

Registration 154,284 total. No party registration. 101,826 white (66%); 52,405 black (34%); 53 other (—).

Employment profile White collar, 33%. Blue collar, 67%.

Ethnic groups Black, 36%. Total foreign stock, 3%. Germany, 1%; all other groups less than 0.5% each.

Presidential vote

1968	Humphrey (D)	42,331	(36%)
	Nixon (R)	42,966	(37%)
	Wallace (AIP)	31,220	(27%)

Representative

Mendel Davis (D) Elected Apr. 28, 1970; b. Oct. 23, 1942, Johnston; home, Johnston; College of Charleston, B.A., 1967; U. of S.C. Law School, LL.B., 1970; married, one child; Protestant.

Career Practicing atty., 1970–71.

Offices 1726 LHOB, 202-225-3176. Also 334 Meeting St., Charleston, 803-577-4171.

Committees

Science and Astronautics (18th).

Group Ratings, Key Votes: Newly elected.

Election Results

1971 special:	Mendel Davis (D)	38,012	(49%)
	James Edwards (R)	32,227	(41%)
	Victoria De Lee (Ind.)	7,965	(10%)
1971 primary:	Mendel Davis (D)	26,720	(55%)
	J. Palmer Gaillard, Jr. (D)	12,001	(25%)
	J. Mitchell Graham (D)	5,268	(10%)
	Thomas F. Harnett (D)	5,255	(10%)

SECOND DISTRICT Political Background

South Carolina 2 comprises most of the Midlands section of the state—the land which lies between the coastal plain to the south and the industrialized Piedmont to the north. The district also lies between the black-majority rural areas of lower South Carolina and the heavily white areas to the north. Here in the 2nd is Orangeburg, where nearly half the voters are black; in 1968, Orangeburg white highway patrolmen massacred some black students at predominantly black South Carolina State College. To the north is Lexington County, about half of which is suburban Columbia, where almost 90% of the voters are white.

A little more than half the voters of the 2nd live in Richland County, which contains Columbia, the state capital. Columbia is the state's fastest-growing major city and its only one with a population of more than 100,000. The increasingly prosperous white voters here have begun to feel at home in the Republican party of Strom Thurmond and Richard Nixon. George Wallace, on the other hand, smacks too much of the hayseed to do very well in the capital city. In 1968, the 25% the 2nd gave Wallace was the lowest percentage the AIP candidate got in any of the state's districts. The percentage was held down largely because of Columbia, where Wallace got only 12% of the votes—less than the Alabaman got in Flint, Michigan.

For eight years, from 1962 to 1970, the district was represented by Albert Watson, a flamboyant conservative. Watson won some national headlines in 1965 when he and John Bell Williams of Mississippi were stripped of their seniority by the Democratic Caucus. Both had supported Barry Goldwater in the 1964 presidential election. Watson, who had only one term of seniority anyway, resigned and won reelection as a Republican—the first to represent South Carolina in the House since the waning years of Reconstruction. His margins of victory steadily declined, however, as blacks registered to vote. In 1968, he won only 58% of the votes. In 1970, the strident Watson ran for governor, putting up a strong campaign, but losing to moderate Lt. Gov. John West. His defeat not only marked the end of rising Republican fortunes in South Carolina, but may also mean that Sen. Strom Thurmond will have trouble winning reelection in 1972 (see state write-up).

Watson's successor in the House is the man he beat in the 1962 Democratic primary, Floyd Spence, who, like Watson, is now a Republican. Spence's victory was a narrow one, more evidence of the declining appeal of Thurmond-Watson and the growing strength of moderates like West and McNair (see state write-up). The Democratic candidate, Heyward McDonald, managed to carry Richland County (Columbia) and all but one of the heavily black counties. Spence's margin of victory and then some came out of the all-white suburbs of Lexington County. The congressman's scat on the House Armed Services Committee may help him win reelection; the district includes huge Fort Jackson. But the Democrats will do the redistricting in South Carolina, and if they choose to detach Lexington County from the district, Spence could be defeated in 1972.

Census Data 1970 pop. 436,575; deviation from current state average, +1.1%; change 1960–70, +16.2%. Metro. 74.0%, 26.0% central city.

1970 Share of Federal Outlays $393,937,771

DOD	$161,054,000	HEW	$99,230,236
AEC	$74,910	HUD	$3,163,989
NASA	$139,501	OEO	$3,457,258
DOT	$14,100,813	DOA	$30,242,787
		Other	$82,375,277

Federal Military-Industrial Commitments

DOD Installations Fort Jackson (Columbia).

Economic Base Cotton and livestock; apparel and other finished products made from fabrics and similar materials; textile mill products; food and kindred products. Also, higher education (University of South Carolina).

The Voters

Registration 151,326 total. No party registration. 106,058 white (70%); 45,224 black (30%); 44 other (—).

Employment profile White collar, 38%. Blue collar, 62%.

Ethnic groups Black, 33%. Total foreign stock, 2%. Germany, 1%; all other groups less than 0.5% each.

Presidential vote

1968	Humphrey (D)	36,004	(32%)
	Nixon (R)	47,624	(43%)
	Wallace (AIP)	28,028	(25%)

Representative

Floyd D. Spence (R) Elected 1970; b. April 9, 1928, Columbia; home, Lexington; U. of S.C., B.A., 1952, LL.B., 1956; USNR, WWII; Cdr. USNR; married, four children; Lutheran.

Career Practicing atty., S.C. Legislature, 1956–62; S.C. Senate, 1966–68, Minority Leader, 1966–70; Chm., Jt. Senate-House Com. to Investigate Communist Activities in S.C., 1967–70; Sunday school teacher.

Offices 516 CHOB, 202-225-2452. Also 509 Fed. Bldg., Sumpter St., Columbia 29201, 803-254-6966.

Committees

Armed Services (15th); Sub. No. 3.

Group Ratings, Key Votes: Newly elected.

Election Results

1970 general:	Floyd Spence (R)	48,093	(53%)
	Heyward McDonald (D)	42,005	(46%)
	Donald R. Cole (Ind.)	486	(1%)
1970 primary:	Floyd Spence (R), unopposed		

THIRD DISTRICT Political Background

South Carolina 3 lies along the Savannah River, across from Georgia. It extends from the Midlands to the near mountainous Piedmont section of the state. The southern part of the 3rd is Strom Thurmond's home territory. The Senator was born in the town of Edgefield here and maintains his residence now in Aiken, a prosperous AEC city which lies halfway between Columbia and Augusta, Georgia. Aiken and Edgefield, like the Senator, are solidly Republican. The counties farther upriver are traditionally more Southern Democratic. Although relatively few blacks live in the 3rd, George Wallace carried the district in 1968; he ran especially well in Anderson (pop. 27,000), the district's largest city. Anderson has few blacks and cast proportionally more votes for Wallace than any other city in the state.

William Jennings Bryan Dorn has represented the district in Congress continuously since 1950. Very early on Dorn was a politician. He was 23 when he was elected to the state House of Representatives, 25 when he was chosen for the state Senate, and 30 when he was elected to Congress. Dorn first went to the House in 1946 and then tried and failed to win a Senate seat in 1948; since then, he has, in the Southern tradition, accumulated seniority in the lower legislative branch. Although he is now the 2nd ranking member of the Veterans' Affairs Committee, he remains a surprisingly low number-nine man on Public Works.

Dorn's generally conservative voting record, with a touch of populism on economic issues befitting his namesake, is popular with the voters of his district. He repulsed a strong Republican challenge in 1966, winning 58% of the vote, and has done better in subsequent elections. One reason for Dorn's increasing margins is the increasing number of black voters in the 3rd. The blacks, not as numerous here as they are in the lowlands, prefer to vote for Dorn over the even more conservative Thurmond-Republicans who run in the district. For a congressman with a great deal of seniority, Dorn is comparatively young, only 54 in 1970. He appears to have a long congressional career ahead of him.

Census Data 1970 pop. 434,427; deviation from current state average, +0.6%; change 1960–70, +8.6%. Metro. 34.5%, 0.0% central city.

1970 Share of Federal Outlays $309,892,295

DOD	$19,519,000	HEW	$85,224,062
AEC	$119,835,974	HUD	$3,667,000
NASA	$129,950	OEO	$424,920
DOT	$5,843,942	DOA	$26,672,072
		Other	$48,575,375

Federal Military-Industrial Commitments

AEC Operations E. E. Du Pont De Nemours (Aiken), $104.781m: Feed Material Facility, General Facilities, Heavy Water Production Facilities, Laboratory, and Production Reactor and Separation Facilities.

Economic Base Broad woven cotton fabric mills, broad woven man-made fiber and silk fabric mills and other textile mill products; apparel and other finished products made from fabrics and similar materials; cotton.

The Voters

Registration 148,540 total. No party registration. 125,732 white (85%); 22,796 black (30%); 12 other (—).

Employment profile White collar, 26%. Blue collar, 74%.

Ethnic groups Black, 23%. Total foreign stock, 1%. All foreign groups less than 0.5% each.

Presidential vote

1968	Humphrey (D)	26,585	(23%)
	Nixon (R)	41,678	(36%)
	Wallace (AIP)	47,223	(41%)

Representative

William Jennings Bryan Dorn (D) Elected 1950; b. April 14, 1916, Greenwood; home, Greenwood; Army Air Force, WWII; married, five children; Baptist.

Career S.C. Legislature, 1939–40; S.C. Senate, 1940–42; U.S. House of Reps., 1946–48; Staff of *U.S. News and World Report.*

Offices 2256 RHOB, 202-225-5301. Also 124 Fed. Bldg., Greenwood 29646, 803-223-8251.

Committees

Public Works (9th); Subs. (1) Flood Control and Internal Development, (2) Investment and Oversight, (3) Rivers and Harbors, (4) Roads, (5) Watershed Development.

Veterans' Affairs (2nd); Subs. (1) Chm., Compensation and Pension, (2) Education and Training, (3) Hospitals.

Group Ratings

	ADA	COPE	NREP	NFU	LCV	CFA	NAB	NSI	ACA
1970	16	34	17	38	13	60	58	100	56
1969	7	—	—	54	—	—	—	—	53
1968	17	0	—	29	—	—	83	—	71

Key Votes

(1) ABM	FOR	(6) 18-Yr-Vote	AGN	(11) Clean Water $	AGN
(2) SST	FOR	(7) Farm Sub Lmt	AGN	(12) Mig Wrkrs Comp	AGN
(3) Phil Pln	AGN	(8) Coop-Church	AGN	(13) Jets to Chiang	FOR
(4) No-Knock	FOR	(9) Family Asst	AGN	(14) State OEO Veto	FOR
(5) Cmutr Tax	AGN	(10) Work Stamps	AGN	(15) Park Logging	FOR

Election Results

1970 general:	Wm. Jennings Bryan Dorn (D)	60,708	(75%)
	H. Grady Ballard (R)	19,981	(25%)
1970 primary:	Wm. Jennings Bryan Dorn (D), unopposed		
1968 general:	Wm. Jennings Bryan Dorn (D)	74,104	(66%)
	John K. Grisso (R)	35,463	(32%)
	J. Harold Morton (Ind.)	2,489	(2%)

FOURTH DISTRICT Political Background

South Carolina 4 comprises the heart of South Carolina's Piedmont region. This is an area of rolling hills, which, at the time of secession, had relatively few people. In the years after Reconstruction, industry was attracted here, especially textile concerns, and the 4th is now the most densely populated part of South Carolina. There are fewer blacks up here—20% of the population and 13% of the registered voters—than around Charleston or Columbia. Accordingly, the district produces few votes for candidates put up by the national Democratic party; Humphrey got only 23% of the votes in the 4th, most of them cast by blacks.

Two cities, Greenville (pop. 61,000) and Spartanburg (pop. 44,000), dominate the district. Both of them lie along Interstate 85, the textile-mill highway, about halfway between Charlotte, North Carolina, and Atlanta, Georgia. Greenville and Spartanburg, however, have voting patterns that are quite dissimilar. Judge Clement Haynsworth is Greenville's most famous citizen and one who typifies the city. It is a prosperous, comfortable place, with large business, professional, and white-collar populations. In recent years, Greenville has been a stronghold of the state's Republicans, though the Republicans here are not fond of the kind of strident conservatism shown in 1970 by the party's gubernatorial candidate, Albert Watson (see state write-up). In fact, Greenville's Republican mayor flatly refused to endorse Watson's candidacy.

Spartanburg is a rough, tough factory town; this city's most famous resident and personification was the late Sen. Olin D. Johnson. The senator worked out of the old tradition of Southern populism, conservative on racial matters, sometimes a liberal on economic issues. Spartanburg usually votes Democratic; in 1968, however, it went for Nixon, with Wallace not far behind.

The Greenville establishment has produced men such as Judge Haynsworth and Donald S. Russell, former governor and senator and now federal judge. That establishment seems to have control of the 4th's congressional seat. The current incumbent is James R. Mann, a conservative Democrat who in any non-Southern state would be a Republican. Mann was elected in 1968 to succeed Robert T. Ashmore, whom he also succeeded as Greenville solicitor (prosecuting attorney). Mann is one of the conservative members of the House Judiciary Committee, though he may soon enough join or succeed his colleagues on the bench. Meanwhile, he is reasonably certain of reelection. Like all of South Carolina's Democratic congressmen, Mann should encounter no redistricting problems.

Census Data 1970 pop. 463,983; deviation from current state average, +7.5%; change 1960–70, +12.0%. Metro. 51.8%, 13.2% central city.

1970 Share of Federal Outlays $195,425,890

DOD	$33,745,000	HEW	$82,351,415
AEC	$000	HUD	$4,430,791
NASA	$000	OEO	$1,344,220
DOT	$3,122,802	DOA	$11,173,335
		Other	$59,258,327

Federal Military-Industrial Commitments

DOD Contractors LTV Electrosystems (Greenville), $7.716m: unspecified.

Economic Base Broad woven cotton fabric mills, broad woven man-made fabric mills and other textile mill products; apparel and other finished products made from fabrics and similar materials; special industry machinery, except metalworking machinery, and other nonelectrical machinery.

The Voters

Registration 155,885, total. No party registration. 134,082 white (86%); 21,789 black (14%); 14 other (—).

Employment profile White collar, 30%. Blue collar, 70%.

Ethnic groups Black, 20%. Total foreign stock, 1%. All foreign groups less than 0.5% each.

Presidential vote

1968	Humphrey (D)	27,411	(23%)
	Nixon (R)	54,648	(46%)
	Wallace (AIP)	36,866	(31%)

Representative

James Robert Mann (D) Elected 1968; b. April 27, 1920, Greenville; home, Greenville; The Citadel, B.A., 1941; U. of S.C., LL.B., 1947; Army, WWII; Col. USAR; married, four children; Baptist.

Career Practicing atty.; S.C. Legislature, 1949–52; Solicitor, 13th Judicial Circuit of S.C., 1953–63.

Offices 1109 LHOB, 202-225-6030. Also P.O. Box 10011, Fed. Station, Greenville 29603, 803-232-1141, and Spartanburg 29301, 803-582-6422.

Committees

Judiciary (16th); Sub. No. 2.

Sel. Com. on Crime (14th).

Group Ratings

	ADA	COPE	NREP	NFU	LCV	CFA	NAB	NSI	ACA
1970	4	9	0	36	0	71	67	100	75
1969	0	—	—	54	—	—	—	—	65

Key Votes

(1) ABM	FOR	(6) 18-Yr-Vote	AGN	(11) Clean Water $	AGN
(2) SST	FOR	(7) Farm Sub Lmt	AGN	(12) Mig Wrkrs Comp	AGN
(3) Phil Pln	AGN	(8) Coop-Church	AGN	(13) Jets to Chiang	FOR
(4) No-Knock	ABS	(9) Family Asst	AGN	(14) State OEO Veto	FOR
(5) Cmutr Tax	FOR	(10) Work Stamps	FOR	(15) Park Logging	FOR

Election Results

1970 general:	James R. Mann (D), unopposed		
1970 primary:	James R. Mann (D), unopposed		
1968 general:	James R. Mann (D)	68,437	(61%)
	Charles Bradshaw (R)	43,440	(39%)

FIFTH DISTRICT Political Background

South Carolina 5, in the northcentral part of the state, is a collection of industrial Piedmont and impoverished Black Belt counties. Rock Hill, Gaffney, and the other Piedmont industrial towns have been traditional strongholds of populistic Democrats. The white voters of these towns—who heavily outnumber the blacks—liked Wallace better than either Nixon or Humphrey, though Humphrey did manage 15% of the white vote in York County, which contains Rock Hill. Blacks are more numerous here than in the adjacent area around Greenville and Spartanburg in the 4th district to the west, but they are less numerous than in the coastal lowlands to the south. The 5th district, like the 4th and the rest of upper South Carolina, is a major textile producing region. Its voters, therefore, are vitally interested in the economic health of this currently troubled industry.

Thomas S. Gettys has been the congressman from the district since 1964. Gettys has had an interesting political career. In the late '40's, he served as an assistant to one of his congressional predecessors; then later became postmaster of Rock Hill. By day he saw that the mail went through and by night he studied law and eventually went into practice. In 1964, Gettys won the Democratic primary to succeed Congressman Robert Hemphill, who had been appointed a federal judge. Now that the postal service has been removed from politics, Gettys will get at least one footnote in history: the last postmaster to serve in Congress.

In his time there so far, Gettys has made a generally conservative record. He is a middle seniority member of the House Banking and Currency Committee. Since his first election, Gettys has not had serious opposition, and it seems unlikely that he will encounter any in the future.

Census Data 1970 pop. 392,194; deviation from current state average, —9.2%; change 1960–70, +4.0%. Metro. 0.0%, 0.0% central city.

1970 Share of Federal Outlays $215,442,825

DOD	$65,947,000	HEW	$72,669,611
AEC	$000	HUD	$3,173,339
NASA	$000	OEO	$940,831
DOT	$7,157,631	DOA	$26,083,545
		Other	$39,470,868

Federal Military-Industrial Commitments

DOD Installations Shaw AFB (Sumter).

Economic Base Broad woven cotton fabric mills and other textile mill products; apparel and other finished products made from fabrics and similar materials; food and kindred products; furniture and fixtures.

The Voters

Registration 139,481 total. No party registration. 105,871 white (76%); 33,569 black (24%); 41 other (—).

Employment profile White collar, 25%. Blue collar, 75%.

Ethnic groups Black, 32%. Total foreign stock, 1%. All foreign groups less than 0.5% each.

Presidential vote

1968	Humphrey (D)	30,689	(29%)
	Nixon (R)	34,909	(33%)
	Wallace (AIP)	39,356	(38%)

Representative

Thomas Smithwick Gettys (D) Elected Nov. 4, 1964; b. June 19, 1912, Rock Hill; home, Rock Hill; Clemson Col., Erskine Col., B.A., 1933; Duke U., Winthrop Col.; Navy WWII; married, two children; Presbyterian.

Career Teacher, coach, Rock Hill High School, 1933–35; Principal, Rock Hill, 1935–41; Secy. Rep. Richards, 1941–51; Postmaster, Rock Hill, 1951–54; practicing atty., 1954–64.

Offices 341 CHOB, 202-225-5501. Also Box 707 Fed. Bldg., Rock Hill 29730, 803-327-4729, and Fed. Bldg., Sumter 29150, 803-775-2943.

Committees

Banking and Currency (12th); Subs. (1) Domestic Finance, (2) International Trade, (3) Small Business.

House Administration (9th); Subs. (1) Accounts, (2) Printing, (3) Sp. on Police.

Group Ratings

	ADA	COPE	NREP	NFU	LCV	CFA	NAB	NSI	ACA
1970	8	27	8	25	38	69	44	88	62
1969	7	—	—	50	—	—	—	—	47
1968	8	15	—	38	—	—	50	—	53

Key Votes

(1) ABM	FOR	(6) 18-Yr-Vote	ABS	(11) Clean Water $	AGN
(2) SST	FOR	(7) Farm Sub Lmt	AGN	(12) Mig Wrkrs Comp	AGN
(3) Phil Pln	AGN	(8) Coop-Church	AGN	(13) Jets to Chiang	ABS
(4) No-Knock	FOR	(9) Family Asst	AGN	(14) State OEO Veto	FOR
(5) Cmutr Tax	AGN	(10) Work Stamps	FOR	(15) Park Logging	FOR

Election Results

1970 general:	Thomas S. Gettys (D)	43,742	(66%)
	B. Leonard Phillips (R)	21,911	(34%)
1970 primary:	Thomas S. Gettys (D), unopposed		
1968 general:	Thomas S. Gettys (D)	72,805	(75%)
	Hugh J. Boyd (R)	21,246	(22%)
	Bert Sumner (Ind.)	3,411	(4%)

SIXTH DISTRICT Political Background

South Carolina 6 is the Pee Dee district, so called from the river that winds its way through the coastal lowlands here. The 6th takes in some of the most heavily black portions of South Carolina, and since the 1965 Voting Rights Act, black registration has neared majority status in several counties. But the black-majority areas are rural, poor, and losing population, which is the case throughout the South. The bulk of the votes in the district are cast in white-majority cities like Florence and Darlington—both textile-mill towns—and Myrtle Beach, a motel-lined seaside resort. Darlington is the scene of the annual Southern 500 stock car race; this form of competition, it seems, has replaced the racing of horseflesh as the athletic event in the American South.

The 6th is a part of South Carolina dominated by Deep South attitudes on race and other issues. But because blacks now comprise a third of the district's registered voters, a minor revolution has been worked in the politics here. In 1968, the blacks carried the district for Humphrey (see data below). The influence of the newly enfranchised voters was also seen in the district's 1970 congressional primary.

Since 1938, John L. McMillan, an unreconstructed conservative, has represented the district in the House. McMillan, who has been chairman of the House District of Columbia Committee since 1948, has held life-and-death power over the governance of the nation's capital—a black-majority city. More important to the 6th district, McMillan is the 2nd ranking Democrat on the House Agriculture Committee. Here he uses his seniority defending the interests of the 6th's number-one crop, tobacco. Marlboro County lies in the district, while adjacent Chesterfield County is part of the 5th.

It was therefore a surprise when McMillan, one of Washington's most powerful congressmen, was forced into a runoff primary in 1970—the first in his political career. In the initial primary, the 72-year-old McMillan had three opponents, all of them younger, in their thirties, and more liberal—one being an antiwar college dean who attracted student volunteers. True, McMillan came only 431 votes short of an absolute majority in the initial primary. That, however, made little news. What was newsworthy was Dr. Claude Stephens' second place finish. Dr. Stephens was a black physician from Williamsburg County, who ran as a civil rights advocate and as an opponent of the Vietnam war. In the runoff, Stephens got all kinds of space in the New York and Washington papers and attracted volunteers from outside the district—which may have hurt more than it helped. In any case, he won just about all the black votes in the runoff and virtually none of the white votes. Stephens finished with 22% of the vote. But he did force McMillan, quite unaccustomed to such indignities, to go on television in his general election campaign.

In that appearance, the conservative congressman went looking for black votes. He surmised that Walter Washington, the black mayor of the nation's capitol, would campaign for John McMillan if asked. That nemesis of the city's black-majority had good reason to go on television. In the general election McMillan won 65% of the district's votes over a conservative Republican. And since the congressman won large majorities in black areas, somewhere between a third and a half of his support must have come from black voters. McMillan is not likely to change his conservative sentiments, but he is not about to go out of his way to antagonize voters who now constitute a significant portion of his electoral base.

When an old congressman in a Southern district begins to attract serious primary opposition, he is in trouble. As local Democrats—and Republicans—know, John McMillan is such a man. No one has yet put together a winning combination, but the chairman is getting on in years; in 1971 he listed the year of his birth as 1902, but all previous records have it as 1898. McMillan could very well lose his seat in 1972 or soon thereafter.

Census Data 1970 pop. 385,395; deviation from current state average, —10.7%; change 1960–70, —2.3%. Metro. 0.0%, 0.0% central city.

1970 Share of Federal Outlays $223,862,960

DOD	$32,461,000	HEW	$78,177,352
AEC	$000	HUD	$598,000
NASA	$000	OEO	$1,110,702
DOT	$11,868,754	DOA	$52,279,670
		Other	$47,367,482

Federal Military-Industrial Commitments

DOD Installations Myrtle Beach AFB (Myrtle Beach).

Economic Base Tobacco, cotton, and livestock; apparel and other finished products made from fabrics and similar materials, esp. women's, misses', and juniors' outerwear; textile mill products.

The Voters

Registration 128,782 total. No party registration. 87,535 white (68%); 41,218 black (25%); 194 other (—).

Employment profile White collar, 26%. Blue collar, 74%.

Ethnic groups Black, 41%. Total foreign stock, 1%. All foreign groups less than 0.5% each.

Presidential vote

1968	Humphrey (D)	34,466	(35%)
	Nixon (R)	32,237	(32%)
	Wallace (AIP)	32,737	(33%)

Representative

John L. McMillan (D) Elected 1938; b. April 12, 1902, Mullins; home, Florence; Mullins U. of N.C., U. of S.C. Law School, 1917–23; Navy, WWI; unmarried; Baptist.

Career Rep. Interparliamentary Union, London, 1960, Tokyo, 1961.

Offices 2208 RHOB, 202-225-3315. Also 308 Fed. Bldg., Florence 29501, 803-669-8110, and 210 Elm St., Conway 29526, 803-248-2604.

Committees

Agriculture (Vice Chm.); Subs. (1) Chm., Forests, (2) Tobacco.

District of Columbia (Chm.).

Group Ratings

	ADA	COPE	NREP	NFU	LCV	CFA	NAB	NSI	ACA
1970	4	20	9	17	40	35	43	100	67
1969	7	—	—	39	—	—	—	—	71
1968	17	17	—	36	—	—	0	—	73

Key Votes

(1) ABM	FOR	(6) 18-Yr-Vote	AGN	(11) Clean Water $	ABS
(2) SST	FOR	(7) Farm Sub Lmt	AGN	(12) Mig Wrkrs Comp	AGN
(3) Phil Pln	AGN	(8) Coop-Church	AGN	(13) Jets to Chiang	ABS
(4) No-Knock	FOR	(9) Family Asst	AGN	(14) State OEO Veto	FOR
(5) Cmutr Tax	ABS	(10) Work Stamps	FOR	(15) Park Logging	FOR

Election Results

1970 general:	John L. McMillan (D)	46,966	(65%)
	Edward B. Baskin (R)	25,546	(35%)
	Charles H. Smith (Ind.)	773	(1%)
1970 primary:	John L. McMillan (D)	26,192	(50%)
	Claude L. Stephens (D)	11,534	(22%)
	Bill R. Craig (D)	11,047	(21%)
	Olin Sansbury, Jr. (D)	4,042	(8%)
1968 general:	John L. McMillan (D)	58,304	(58%)
	Ray Harris (R)	39,876	(40%)
	Claude L. Harris (Ind.)	1,849	(2%)

SOUTH DAKOTA

Political Background

South Dakota was once the heartland of the Sioux Indians who roamed its plains hunting the buffalo. Then the white man came and exterminated the buffalo, and, in places like Wounded Knee, many of the Indians. Those that survived were herded on to reservations; today, the second largest Indian population of any state lives on South Dakota's several large reservations, mostly on the badlands west of the Missouri River.

The Black Hills gold rush brought the first white settlers to the state. Men like Wild Bill Hickock, America's first dime-novel hero, made legends in the mining towns of Deadwood, Lead, and Spearfish, and then, when the rich veins of ore were exhausted, moved on. At about the same time, land-hungry farmers staked out homesteads on the plains, only to find later that not much of the cheap land was workable: the sod busted many horse-drawn plows, and the rain, which was plentiful during the first years of settlement, suddenly stopped falling.

South Dakota, lying between the Midwest and the West, was settled by two separate streams of westward migration. The southern part of the state was occupied by Republican WASPs from Nebraska, Iowa, and points east. The northern and central sections were settled by people of Scandinavian and German descent, who brought with them the prairie radicalism of Wisconsin, Minnesota, and North Dakota. Subsequently, the more numerous WASPs have dominated South Dakota politics; between 1936 and 1970, the state sent only one Democrat, George McGovern, to Congress, while the governors were all Republicans.

But like other prairie states, the voters of South Dakota have been chronically dissatisfied with the farm programs of the national administrations, Republican and Democratic. Although he failed to carry the state, Adlai Stevenson did better here in 1956 than he had four years before, and in the same year McGovern won a House seat. In 1966, after six years of Kennedy and Johnson, the Republicans made their best recent showing in the state; in 1970, South Dakota reacted sharply to Nixon's departure from a policy of strict parity by electing its first Democratic governor since 1930, Richard Kneip, as well as a Democratic lieutenant governor. Although neither of the state's Senate seats were up, Democrats captured both House seats for the first time since the New Deal. This, perhaps the sternest rebuke Nixon received from any state in 1970, does not augur well for his chances in 1972.

That seems to be the analysis of George McGovern, now the state's Democratic senator, who announced his candidacy for President in January, 1971. Just ten years ago it was assumed that a presidential candidate had to come from a large state. But the 1968 campaign proved that television could make a national figure out of any presidential aspirant, and today no one demeans the chances of men like Muskie of Maine, Jackson of Washington, or McGovern of South Dakota.

McGovern began his political career in the mid-'50's as a professor at Dakota Wesleyan University in Mitchell, and leader by default of the moribund state Democratic party. In 1956, he ran for Congress against the advice of more experienced politicians and won, primarily because of the resentment generated by Ezra Taft Benson's farm policies. Two years later, McGovern won again, and then took on Sen. Karl Mundt in 1960. He gave the veteran conservative his toughest race ever, losing by a surprisingly close 52–48 margin. McGovern went on to become the director of the Food-for-Peace program in the Kennedy Administration. In 1962, after the death of Sen. Francis Case, McGovern returned to South Dakota for another Senate try. His Republican opponent was a governor who had had himself appointed to the vacancy (an unpopular move everywhere). The Democrat won the election by 597 votes.

McGovern has been one of the nation's leading opponents of the war. He spoke out against it as early as 1963, and sponsored the Hatfield-McGovern amendment in 1970 and 1971. After Robert Kennedy's assassination in 1968, the South Dakota Senator became a stand-in candidate for President on a peace platform. In his home state, however, McGovern is better known for his encyclopedic knowledge of the farm programs of the Department of Agriculture, and for his untiring advocacy of the traditional family farm. The Senator is the 5th ranking Democrat on the Agriculture Committee, and is chairman of the Select Committee on Nutrition and Human Needs. His work in Food-for-Peace, and his sponsorship of programs to assure a decent diet for the poor are related to his concern for the American farmer.

Although McGovern is criticized for being too soft-spoken his obvious sincerity has gone over well with South Dakota voters. In 1968, after his bid for the presidential nomination failed to work out, he had no trouble winning reelection to the Senate with 57% of the vote.

McGovern's stands on the issues are very different indeed from the ones taken by the state's other senator, Karl Mundt, presently one of the Senate's most conservative members. During his ten years in the House, Mundt was a personal friend of Congressman Richard Nixon, and their names appear together on a major piece of anti-subversive legislation passed during the '40's. Congressman Mundt was elected to the Senate in 1948, and since that time, except for McGovern's challenge in 1960, he has won reelection convincingly. Mundt was extremely ill in 1970, unable to attend the Senate session. But he seems to have regained his health to some extent, and may again campaign for reelection in 1972, when he will be 72. If he does run, the Senator may have trouble. Nixon's farm program will doubtless continue to be unpopular and many voters will be uncertain as to whether Mundt can serve out a full term.

There was speculation that Mundt would resign in December, 1970, which would have then allowed lame-duck Governor Frank Farrar to appoint a Republican successor. The Senator did not resign. But if the seat becomes vacant between now and 1972, Democratic Governor Richard Kneip would undoubtedly appoint a member of his party, perhaps one of South Dakota's two congressmen. That appointee, as the incumbent, would enjoy a slight advantage in the 1972 election.

Electoral Votes 4

Census Data 1970 pop. 666,257; 0.32% of U.S. total, 46th largest; change 1960–70, –2.1%. Metro. 14.3%, 10.9% central city. 1970 per capita income, $3,182; 41st highest. 41st in number of poor.

1970 Share of Federal Tax Burden $448,820,000; 0.23% of U.S. total, 47th largest.

1970 Share of Federal Outlays $724,124,474; 0.38% of U.S. total, 46th largest. Per capita federal spending, $1,087.

DOD	$76,051,000	51st (0.13%)	HEW	$201,349,176	42nd (0.39%)
AEC	$38,148	49th (0.00%)	HUD	$2,158,681	50th (0.11%)
NASA	$57,384	49th (0.00%)	OEO	$3,301,715	42nd (0.43%)

DOT	$38,014,966	45th (0.53%)	DOA	$214,147,949	23rd (1.67%)
DOC	$1,520,561	48th (0.13%)	POD	$26,532,524	40th (0.36%)
DOI	$35,709,217	21st (1.55%)	VA	$42,155,768	42nd (0.57%)
DOJ	$1,341,509	49th (0.23%)	CSC	$8,432,944	46th (0.21%)
			Other	$73,312,932	

Economic Base Livestock, cash grain, and dairy; food and kindred products, esp. meat products; printing, publishing, and allied industries, esp. newspapers; electrical machinery, equipment, and supplies, esp. electronic components and accessories; metal mining, esp. lode gold; nonelectrical machinery; stone, clay, glass, and concrete products, esp. concrete, gypsum, and plaster products; fabricated metal products; lumber and wood products other than furniture, esp. sawmills and planing mills.

Political Line-up Governor, Richard Kneip (D); seat up, 1972. Senators, Karl E. Mundt (R) and George S. McGovern (D). Representatives, 2 (2 D and 0 R). State Senate (11 D and 24 R); State House (30 D and 45 R).

The Voters

Registration 351,305 total. 134,123 D (38%); 182,505 R (52%); 34,691 other (10%).

Employment profile White collar, 34%. Blue collar, 66%.

Ethnic groups Black, less than 0.5%. Total foreign stock, 21%. Germany, 6%; Norway, 4%; USSR, 3%; Sweden, 2%; Canada, UK, Czech., 1% each; others, 4%.

Presidential vote

1968	Humphrey (D)	118,023	(42%)
	Nixon (R)	149,841	(53%)
	Wallace (AIP)	13,400	(5%)
1964	Johnson (D)	163,010	(56%)
	Goldwater (R)	130,108	(44%)
1960	Kennedy (D)	128,070	(42%)
	Nixon (R)	178,017	(58%)

Senator

Karl E. Mundt (R) Elected Dec. 31, 1948, seat up 1972; b. June 3, 1900, Humboldt; home, Madison; Carleton Col., B.A., 1923; Columbia U., M.A., 1927; married; Methodist.

Career Teacher, 1923–24; Supt. of Schools, 1924–27; Chm., Speech Dept. and Instructor in Soc. Sci., Gen. Beadle State Teachers Col., 1927–36; Secy.-Treas. Mundt Loan & Investment Co., 1936–48; Co-founder, Natl. Forensic League, Pres., 1933–71; author.

Offices 5241 NSOB, 202-225-5842. Also P.O. Bldg., Madison 57042, 605-256-3031.

Committees

Appropriations (2nd); Subs. (1) Agriculture, Environmental and Consumer Protection, (2) Interior, (3) Public Works, (4) Transportation.

Foreign Relations (2nd); Subs. (1) African Affairs, (2) Far Eastern Affairs, (3) Near Eastern and South Asian Affairs.

Government Operations (Ranking Mbr.); Subs. (1) National Security and International Operations, (2) Permanent Investigations.

Group Ratings

	ADA	COPE	NREP	NFU	LCV	NAB	NSI	ACA
1970	*	0	*	*	0	100	100	*
1969	6	—	—	50	—	—	—	70
1968	0	9	—	55	—	83	—	95

* *Sen. Mundt was hospitalized during this session, did not vote.*

Key Votes

(1) ABM	FOR	(8) Phil Pln	ABS	(15) Coop-Church	AGN
(2) SST	AGN	(9) Vol Army	AGN	(16) Cut Oil Dpltn	AGN
(3) Busing	AGN	(10) Prison $	AGN	(17) Consumer Prot	AGN
(4) Tob Sub	FOR	(11) Cut Mil $	AGN	(18) Farm Sub Limit	AGN
(5) Carswell	FOR	(12) Defoliatn	FOR	(19) Comp Bid Sales	FOR
(6) No-Knock	FOR	(13) 18-Yr-Vote	ABS	(20) Pre-Prod Tests	AGN
(7) Seniorty	AGN	(14) Pentgn PR	FOR	(21) Cut Marjna Pen	AGN

Election Results

1966 general:	Karl E. Mundt (R)	150,517	(66%)
	Donn H. Wright (D)	76,563	(34%)
1966 primary:	Karl E. Mundt (R)	66,758	(82%)
	Richard R. Murphy (R)	14,593	(18%)
1960 general:	Karl E. Mundt (R)	160,181	(52%)
	George S. McGovern (D)	145,261	(48%)

Senator

George McGovern (D) Elected 1962, seat up 1974; b. July 12, 1922, Avon; home, Mitchell; Dakota Wesleyan U., B.A., 1945; Northwestern U., M.A., 1949, Ph.D., 1953; Army Air Corps, WWII; married, five children; Methodist.

Career Professor, Dakota Wesleyan U., 1949–53; Exec. Secy., S.D. Dem. Party, 1953–56; Sp. Asst. to Pres. Kennedy and Dir. of Food for Peace, 1961–62.

Offices 362 OSOB, 202-225-2321. Also 108 E. Third, P.O. Box 1061, Mitchell 57301, 605-996-7563.

Committees

Agriculture and Forestry (5th); Subs. (1) Chm., Agricultural Credit and Rural Electrification, (2) Agricultural Exports, (3) Agricultural Production, Marketing, and Stabilization of Prices.

Interior and Insular Affairs, (7th); Subs. (1) Chm., Indian Affairs, (2) Minerals, Materials, and Fuels, (3) Territories and Insular Affairs.

Sel. Com. on Nutrition and Human Needs; (Chm.).

Group Ratings

	ADA	COPE	NREP	NFU	LCV	NAB	NSI	ACA
1970	84	100	91	100	79	8	0	5
1969	94	—	—	86	—	—	—	6
1968	43	92	—	89	—	80	—	39

Key Votes

(1) ABM	AGN	(8) Phil Pln	FOR	(15) Coop-Church	FOR
(2) SST	AGN	(9) Vol Army	FOR	(16) Cut Oil Dpltn	FOR
(3) Busing	FOR	(10) Prison $	ABS	(17) Consumer Prot	FOR
(4) Tob Sub	ABS	(11) Cut Mil $	FOR	(18) Farm Sub Limit	FOR
(5) Carswell	AGN	(12) Defoliatn	AGN	(19) Comp Bid Sales	AGN
(6) No-Knock	ABS	(13) 18-Yr-Vote	FOR	(20) Pre-Prod Tests	FOR
(7) Seniorty	AGN	(14) Pentgn PR	AGN	(21) Cut Marjna Pen	FOR

Election Results

1968 general:	George S. McGovern (D)	158,961	(57%)
	Archie Gubbrud (R)	120,951	(43%)
1968 primary:	George S. McGovern (D), unopposed		

1962 general:	George S. McGovern (D)	127,458 (50%)
	Joe Bottum (R)	126,861 (50%)

FIRST DISTRICT Political Background

South Dakota 1, along the eastern edge of the state, resembles the adjacent areas of western Minnesota and northwestern Iowa: treeless plains, large farms, and an occasional grain elevator town. But compared to the rest of the state, the 1st is densely populated. In it lies South Dakota's largest city, Sioux Falls (pop. 72,000), as well as the farm towns of Aberdeen (pop. 26,000), Brookings (pop. 13,000), and Watertown (pop. 13,000). Like most regions on the Great Plains dependent on agriculture, the district has been losing population during the past decade.

Easterners are accustomed to a Democratic city and a Republican countryside. But in many parts of the West, the city is the stronghold of the dominant Republican party. Here in the 1st, the residents of places like Sioux Falls and Aberdeen are very often owners of small businesses, salesmen, or bankers, who as a rule are more prosperous than the farmers they serve. They are also more likely to be of Yankee descent and hence more Republican. The Germans, Swedes, and Russians, who came to farm the vast plains, still live on their acres, if they haven't retired or given up and gone to California. These farmers constitute the strength of various forms of prairie radicalism and of the revolts against the farm programs of the Administration in Washington, whatever the party. Even here in rural South Dakota, ethnic origin is the strongest determinant of party affiliation: a predominantly Scandinavian county will be much more Democratic than an adjoining WASP county.

The 1st, which then included all of South Dakota east of the Missouri River, first sent George McGovern to Congress in 1956. The district reelected him in 1958, largely because he campaigned indefatigably and opposed the unpopular farm programs of Ezra Taft Benson. When McGovern stepped down to challenge Karl Mundt in 1960, conservative Republican Ben Reifel won the seat and held it without much trouble for 10 years. Reifel decided to retire in 1970, when he was 66; the move came at a bad time for the state's Republican party, since it coincided with the rising protest in the district over the farm programs of the Nixon Administration.

The Democratic candidate in the 1970 election was Frank Denholm, a former FBI agent who had won 42% of the vote against Reifel in 1968, while the Republicans ran Dexter Gunderson, Speaker of the state House of Representatives. The rhetoric of the campaign was on the conservative side, with attention focused mainly on the problems of the farmer. Although South Dakota political analysts expected a close race, Denholm won 56% of the vote and carried all but three small counties. The result was part of a pattern. Democratic gubernatorial candidate Richard Kneip carried the district by the same margin while Democrats also made solid gains in the state legislature.

In Washington, Denholm was awarded a seat on the House Agriculture Committee, where he will be able to show voters of the 1st just how much he disagrees with the programs of the Administration. Democratic congressmen who win surprise elections in a Republican farm state like South Dakota are usually unable to hang on to the seat for very long. McGovern is an exception. It remains to be seen whether Denholm can use the advantages of incumbency to create a personal constituency large enough to reelect him in the years to come.

Census Data 1970 pop. 349,919; deviation from current state average, +5.0%; change 1960–70, –0.6%. Metro. 27.2%, 20.7% central city.

1970 Share of Federal Outlays $328,231,091

DOD	$13,210,000	HEW	$108,440,167
AEC	$38,148	HUD	$1,304,187
NASA	$32,198	OEO	$1,012,927
DOT	$14,233,080	DOA	$103,014,881
		Other	$86,945,503

Federal Military-Industrial Commitments

None.

Economic Base Livestock, cash grain, and dairy; food and kindred products; primary metal industries.

The Voters

Registration 188,254 total. 71,000 D (38%); 96,956 R (52%); 20,298 other (11%).

Employment profile White collar, 34%. Blue collar, 66%.

Ethnic groups Black, less than 0.5%. Total foreign stock, 23%. Germany, Norway, 6% each; USSR, Sweden, 2% each; Canada, UK, Czech., 1% each; others, 5%.

Presidential vote

1968	Humphrey (D)	65,655	(43%)
	Nixon (R)	79,757	(53%)
	Wallace (AIP)	5,876	(4%)

Representative

Frank Edward Denholm (D) Elected 1970; b. Nov. 29, 1923, Andover; home, Brookings; S.D. State U., B.S., 1956; U. of S.D. Law School, J.D., 1962; U. of Minn.; married; Catholic.

Career Farmer; auctioneer; Interstate Truck Transportation business, 1945–53; Sheriff, Day County, 1950–52; FBI Agent, U.S. Dept. of Justice, 1956–61; practicing atty., 1962– ; Lecturer in economics, law, pol. sci., S.D. State U., 1962–66; Corporate Counsel for cities of Brookings, Volga, White, 1962–71.

Offices 1321 LHOB, 202-225-2801. Also 418 Fourth St., Brookings 57006, 605-692-2102.

Committees

Agriculture (21st); Subs. (1) Domestic Marketing and Consumer Relations, (2) Livestock and Grains.

Group Ratings, Key Votes: Newly elected.

Election Results

1970 general:	Frank E. Denholm (D)	71,636	(56%)
	Dexter H. Gunderson (R)	56,330	(44%)
1970 primary:	Frank E. Denholm (D), unopposed		
1968 general:	Ben Reifel (R)	85,232	(58%)
	Frank E. Denholm (D)	61,738	(42%)

SECOND DISTRICT Political Background

South Dakota 2, the state's western district, has half of South Dakota's population and three-quarters of its land area. Before 1965, the 2nd district comprised only that part of the state west of the Missouri River; as a result, it had the smallest population of any congressional district in the country, only 182,000 people. In 1965, its population was almost doubled when a substantial portion of central South Dakota was added to the district. The portion added includes Pierre (pop. 9,000), the state capital; Mitchell (pop. 13,000), where George McGovern taught at Dakota Wesleyan until 1956; and Huron (pop. 14,000), where Hubert Humphrey tended his father's drugstore in the '30's.

To the west is the district's largest town, Rapid City (pop. 43,000), the scenic Badlands, and the Black Hills, site of Mount Rushmore. The rest of the district is marginal ranch country, bleak dusty plains once inhabited by buffalo. The ranchers, unlike most South Dakota farmers, are stern, determined conservatives; some of the grazing counties here cast the state's largest Republican majorities. The district also contains most of the state's relatively large number of Indians, most of them sequestered on squalid reservations on the state's bleakest land. A group of them were once studied by social psychologist Erik Erickson, who, on the basis of his observations, formulated his now famous ideas of "identity," "identity crisis," and so on. The Indians, unlike the ranchers, vote heavily Democratic.

On balance, the 2nd is slightly more conservative than the 1st. For twenty years, the 2nd was represented by conservative Republican E. Y. Berry—from 1950 to 1970—when, at age 68, he decided to retire. One would have expected the Republicans to retain the seat without difficulty. But 1970 was an unusual year in South Dakota politics. The state's Democrats took advantage of the discontent among the voters with the farm policies of the Nixon Administration and had their best year since 1936. In the 2nd, the most debated issue of the campaign was a curious proposal advanced by the Republican candidate, Fred Brady, an engineer and former director of the state Water Development Association. Brady proposed that the government set up compulsory youth camps to teach "decency and respect for the law." The idea was not as odd as it might seem at first glance, coming in a year when the Vice-President of the United States made mention of "permissive" child-rearing techniques a cue for prolonged applause.

The Democratic candidate, James Abourezk, was an outspoken opponent of the Vietnam war. He denounced the youth camp proposal and found that most people in the district agreed with him. Abourezk, who is of Lebanese and American Indian descent, was the underdog and ran behind in preelection polls. But on election day, he won 52% of the votes. The Congressman's analysis of the youth camps was as follows, "Brady's theory was that government should reach down and regulate the private lives of the people. Well, the people rejected that."

Abourezk serves on the Interior and Insular Affairs and the Judiciary committees. Interior is especially important to his district since it contains a national park, a national monument, and four Indian reservations. He will be strengthened slightly by the redistricting plan approved by the Democratic governor and the Republican state legislature, which will transfer three Democratic-leaning counties from the 1st to the 2nd.

Census Data 1970 pop. 316,338; deviation from current state average, —5.0%; change 1960–70, —3.7%. Metro. 0.0%, 0.0% central city.

1970 Share of Federal Outlays $395,893,383

DOD	$62,841,000	HEW	$92,909,009
AEC	$000	HUD	$854,494
NASA	$25,186	OEO	$2,288,788
DOT	$23,781,886	DOA	$111,133,068
		Other	$102,059,952

Federal Military-Industrial Commitments

DOD Installations Ellsworth AFB (Rapid City).

Economic Base Livestock; food and kindred products; lode gold; lumber and wood products other than furniture.

The Voters

Registration 163,051 total. 63,123 D (39%); 85,546 R (53%); 14,393 other (9%).

Employment profile White collar, 34%. Blue collar, 66%.

Ethnic groups Black, less than 0.5%. Total foreign stock, 18%. Germany, 5%; USSR, 4%; Norway, 2%; UK, Canada, Czech., 1% each; others, 3%.

Presidential vote

1968	Humphrey (D)	52,368	(40%)
	Nixon (R)	70,084	(54%)
	Wallace (AIP)	7,524	(6%)

Representative

James G. Abourezk (D) Elected 1970; b. Feb. 24, 1931, Wood; home, Rapid City; S.D. School of Mines, B.S., 1961; U. of S.D. Law School, J.D., 1966; Navy, 1948–52; married, three children; Syrian Orthodox.

Career Practicing atty.

Offices 508 CHOB, 202-225-5165. Also 607½ Mt. Rushmore, Box 850, Rapid City 57701, 605-343-6011.

Committees

Interior and Insular Affairs (23rd); Subs. (1) Indian Affairs, (2) Irrigation and Reclamation, (3) National Parks and Recreation, (4) Public Lands.

Judiciary (20th).

Group Ratings, Key Votes: Newly elected.

Election Results

1970 general:	James Abourezk (D)	55,925	(52%)
	Fred D. Brady (R)	51,092	(48%)
1970 primary:	James Abourezk (D)	7,712	(37%)
	Donald V. Barnett (D)	7,055	(34%)
	Elvern Varilek (D)	5,994	(29%)

TENNESSEE

Political Background

Tennessee currently represents the number-one success story of the Nixon Administration's Southern strategy. For the first time in its history, the Volunteer State has two Republican senators, a Republican governor, and a near Republican majority in its House delegation, four out of nine. And Nixon, of course, carried the state in 1968. The story of how this came to be is one which shows how shrewd political strategists can capitalize on certain issues and then modify voting patterns that go back to the Civil War. But what is now happening in Tennessee also illustrates how ephemeral an emerging Republican majority, or any majority, can be in the turbulent politics of a border state.

Any study of Tennessee politics must begin with topography. Tennessee is divisible into three distinct sections, each with its own history and political inclination. East Tennessee is part of the Appalachian chain, an area populated almost entirely by white mountaineers. This part of the state produced Andrew Johnson, Lincoln's vice-presidential choice; it was against secession in 1861 and since that time has been one of the most solidly Republican parts of the entire nation. The mountaineer Republicanism has usually been matched by the Democratic leanings of middle Tennessee, a region of hilly farmland which lies roughly between the Tennessee River and the Appalachians. This was the home of Andrew Jackson, the first President who called himself a Democrat; middle Tennessee was strongly pro-Confederate during the Civil War. West Tennessee, the flat cotton lands along the Mississippi River, was the part of the state with the largest slave-tended plantations; like middle Tennessee, it has been traditionally Democratic. Lately, however, West Tennessee has voted much more like the rest of the Deep South: when middle Tennessee stayed with the national Democratic party in 1964, west Tennessee edged toward the Goldwater column.

Rural-urban differences in the state are not nearly as important as they are elsewhere. The four large Tennessee cities vote more like the regions in which they are found than like each other. Recently, Memphis, with its large black vote, has been less conservative than the rest of west Tennessee, while Chattanooga, along the Georgia border, is somewhat less Republican than the rest of east Tennessee. But the political behavior of Nashville and Knoxville is virtually indistinguishable from the rural counties that surround them.

So long as middle and west Tennessee remained solidly Democratic, the Republicans were unable to win a statewide election, no matter how many votes the GOP piled up in east Tennessee. The pattern was broken only twice, once in the 1920 Harding Republican landslide and in 1928 when Protestant Tennessee rejected Catholic Al Smith. Other than those two elections, no issue could dent the Civil War allegiances of Tennessee voters up through the '50's. But the civil rights issue, of course, changed things. As it happened, the state's two Democratic senators, Estes Kefauver (1948–63) and Albert Gore (1952–70), supported or at least refused to oppose very strenuously the civil rights legislation of the '50's and '60's. Both had come to the Senate as young, crusading liberal reformers, and both had defeated aging veterans supported by the Crump machine of Memphis.

Early in his Senate career Kefauver made a national name for himself. He chaired investigations of organized crime, which were the nation's first televised congressional hearings. And in 1952 and 1956, the Senator became a major presidential contender. In 1956, he became Adlai Stevenson's running mate, after edging out John F. Kennedy in a convention floor free-for-all. Gore, meanwhile, became widely recognized as the champion of the little man in the matters of tax and social security. Kefauver had to whip a segregationist in his 1960 primary, but he did so soundly, and it appeared that both senators would be reelected for life.

Then Kefauver died in 1963. There followed two spirited battles between Gov. Frank Clement and Rep. Ross Bass in the 1964 and 1966 Senate primaries. These races did little to maintain unity among the state's Democrats. Moreover, the civil rights revolution began to make conservatives out of many of the state's traditional Democrats—people who used to be much more concerned about the TVA and price of farm commodities than about race. As a result, normal Democratic majorities were cut; in 1964, Lyndon Johnson carried the state by just 125,000 votes (55%), while at the same time Albert Gore won by only 77,000 votes (54%). In the other senate race, Republican Howard Baker, Jr. almost upset Congressman Bass, coming within 50,000 votes.

In 1964, Baker was only 38-years-old. The candidate was a Knoxville lawyer with an impeccable Republican background; both his father (1950–1963) and his mother (1963–64) served as Republican congressmen. Moreover, his father-in-law was none other than Everett McKinley Dirksen, Republican senator from Illinois. For his 1966 campaign, Baker assembled an able, young organization, and, building on his east Tennessee power base, he campaigned vigorously all over the state. Frank Clement, governor of the state from 1952 to 1958, and 1962 to 1966, was Baker's Democratic opponent, having defeated Sen. Ross Bass in the primary. To many voters, especially to the young ones, the veteran Clement came over as a tarnished, old-line politician, while Baker was a new, fresh face on the scene. Baker won by almost 100,000 votes—the best Republican victory margin in modern Tennessee history.

In Washington, Baker soon established himself as one of the Senate's leading conservative Republicans. Moreover, he demonstrated to his colleagues that a Southern Republican need not be an outspoken foe of civil rights legislation. But no one claimed that he was as pro-civil rights as either Kefauver or Gore. When his father-in-law died in 1969, Baker emerged as the conservative candidate for the Minority Leadership. He had only three years of seniority, but he came within a few votes of defeating Hugh Scott of Pennsylvania, who had been in Congress since the '40's. The same scene was repeated in 1971, at the beginning of the 92nd Congress. It is therefore quite possible that when Scott, who was 70 in 1970, steps down, Baker will become the Republican Leader of the Senate.

Baker's victory inspired other Tennessee Republicans. In 1970, the state produced one of the nation's most interesting Senate elections: a classic battle between veteran Democratic Sen. Albert Gore and Republican Congressman William E. Brock III. It was a contest of opposites. Gore, "the old grey fox," as one Tennessee Republican called him, had served in the House from 1938 to 1952, and in the Senate since then. Brock, who was 40 in 1970, won a surprise victory in a House election in 1962. Gore is the son of a dirt farmer who came up through county politics and campaigned for Congress by playing the fiddle in country towns; Brock is the reserved heir to a candy fortune, a firm ideological conservative who, as a congressman, voted against Medicare and the Appalachia program.

Gore was vulnerable. The Senator had been a critic of the Vietnam war since the mid-'60's, a stand which was for some time not popular in Tennessee. He had openly proclaimed his support for civil rights measures, and voted against the Haynsworth and Carswell nominations. He had also said no to the ABM and the SST. Agnew called Gore the Nixon Administration's number-one target, something that Gore acknowledged with pride. And during the campaign, Republican orators referred to Gore as the third senator from Massachusetts—a reference perhaps to Ed Brooke, the black senator from the New England state.

It all looked pretty easy. In 1968, Humphrey took only 28% of the votes in Tennessee, as Wallace carried traditionally Democratic middle and west Tennessee. Brock's well-financed media campaign attacked Gore as a backer of school busing, an opponent of school prayer, and in general, a traitor to the South. The attempt to exploit racial prejudice was obvious in Brock's campaign, something which Baker's efforts in 1966 avoided. But the old grey fox fought back; he cited Brock's votes against Medicare and Appalachia and his own efforts to enact tax reform and increase Social Security benefits. It was a battle, as Tom Wicker put it, between attitudes and interests, and in the end, as usually happens, attitudes won out.

But not by much. Gore ran strong among the mountaineers of east Tennessee (38%, off 5% from his 1964 showing) and held his own in middle Tennessee (60%, off 2% from 1964). Where Gore lost was in the west. Here he won only 46% of the votes, down from 54% in 1964. In the rural counties along the Mississippi, Gore ran behind usual Democratic showings and he failed to carry Memphis, despite a large black turnout. The Republican candidate for governor, Dr. Winfield Dunn who won by a larger margin than Brock, is from Memphis and Memphis hasn't had a governor in 50 years. That hometown Republican tide, plus big inroads in segregationist areas, was enough to give Brock a 42,000-vote victory, 51% of the vote. Gore won back a majority of the 1968 Wallace voters, but not quite enough to win.

Baker and Brock now form the only all-Republican Senate delegation from the South. But as is often the case when both senators come from the same party, there are some signs of a rivalry between them. Baker's people reportedly supported one of Brock's primary opponents, and Brock presumably will show less than complete enthusiasm for Baker's reelection bid in 1972. Very often when a party just comes into the rewards of victory, uneasy allies become blood enemies and the resulting factional fights reduce the chances of future victories. This is precisely what happened within Florida's up-and-coming Republican party, a set of circumstances which produced Democratic victories there in 1970. It could easily happen in Tennessee.

It seems unlikely that Baker will face serious opposition in the 1972 primary, but he may have some trouble in the general election. Baker's opponent will probably be Congressman Ray Blanton, whose seat will be eliminated by redistricting. Blanton is a notably more conservative Democrat than either of the men Baker and Brock have defeated. The Congressman is from west Tennessee, where the Republicans picked up their biggest gains in 1970. Moreover, none of the winning Republican margins—not even Baker's in 1966—have been overwhelming. Baker, however, will have some notable advantages; national recognition as a leading Republican conservative, strong financial backing, and tested statewide organization. Nevertheless, by 1972, the Senator can be tagged as an "In," and to the extent that the voters here are dissatisfied with the drift of things, he will be vulnerable.

The defeat of Gore and Clement represent a repudiation of an old-fashioned, Southern oratorical style of politics in favor of smooth, well-organized, telegenic candidates. Few observers noted Brock's victory, which was narrower than expected, without relating it to another fact: the Republican share of the Tennessee vote in the House races declined sharply in 1970. And in 1968, Nixon won only 38% of the state's votes—his smallest victory percentage in the country. It is therefore quite possible that trends in the economy combined with younger, better-organized Democratic candidates can undermine the Republican's rather thin edge in Tennessee.

Electoral Votes 10

Census Data 1970 pop. 3,924,164; 1.91% of U.S. total, 17th largest; change 1960–70, +10.0%. Metro. 48.9%, 34.5% central city. 1970 per capita income, $3,051; 44th highest. 15th in number of poor.

1970 Share of Federal Tax Burden $2,770,100,000; 1.42% of U.S. total, 21st largest.

1970 Share of Federal Outlays $3,141,334,970; 1.66% of U.S. total, 20th largest. Per capita federal spending, $801.

DOD	$620,097,000	27th	(1.08%)	HEW	$883,107,989	20th	(1.69%)
AEC	$299,236,430	3rd	(11.51%)	HUD	$37,790,373	20th	(1.94%)
NASA	$1,626,348	33rd	(0.04%)	OEO	$14,427,932	17th	(1.90%)
DOT	$112,240,432	27th	(1.57%)	DOA	$324,043,559	15th	(2.52%)
DOC	$7,888,548	30th	(0.68%)	POD	$110,136,481	21st	(1.51%)
DOI	$21,240,612	34th	(0.92%)	VA	$201,527,757	15th	(2.73%)
DOJ	$5,942,893	29th	(1.03%)	CSC	$37,337,365	23rd	(0.93%)
				Other	$464,691,251		

Economic Base Cotton, livestock, tobacco, and dairy; apparel and other finished products made from fabrics and similar materials, esp. men's, youths', and boys' furnishings, work clothing and allied garments, and women's, misses', and juniors' outerwear; chemicals and allied products, esp. industrial inorganic and organic chemicals, plastics materials and synthetic resins, synthetic and other man-made fibers, except glass; textile mill products, esp. knitting mills; food and kindred products, esp. meat products, dairy products, grain mill products, and bakery goods; fabricated metal products, esp. fabricated structural metal products; household furniture and other furniture and fixtures; transportation equipment, esp. motor vehicles and motor vehicle equipment and aircraft and parts; electrical machinery, equipment, and supplies, esp. household appliances, radio and television receiving sets, except communication types, and communication equipment; printing, publishing, and allied industries, esp. newspapers; primary metal industries, esp. primary smelting and refining of nonferrous metals and secondary smelting and refining of nonferrous metals.

Political Line-up Governor, Winfield Dunn (R); seat up, 1974. Senators, Howard H. Baker, Jr. (R) and Bill Brock (R). Representatives, 9 (5 D and 4 R). State Senate (29 D and 13 R and 1 Ind.); State House (56 D and 43 R).

The Voters

Registration 1,709,433 total. No party registration.

Employment profile White collar, 35%. Blue collar, 65%.

Ethnic groups Black, 16%. Total foreign stock, 2%. All foreign groups less than 0.5% each.

Presidential vote

1968	Humphrey (D)	351,233	(28%)
	Nixon (R)	472,592	(38%)
	Wallace (AIP)	424,792	(34%)
1964	Johnson (D)	635,047	(55%)
	Goldwater (R)	508,965	(45%)
1960	Kennedy (D)	481,453	(46%)
	Nixon (R)	556,577	(53%)

Senator

Howard H. Baker, Jr. (R) Elected 1966, seat up 1972; b. Nov. 15, 1925, Huntsville; home, Huntsville and Knoxville; Tulane U., U. of the South; U. of Tenn. Law Col., LL.B., 1949; Navy, WWII; Lt. USNR; married, two children; Presbyterian.

Career Practicing atty., 1949–66.

Offices 2107 NSOB, 202-225-4944. Also 1002 Post Office Bldg., Memphis 38101, 901-534-3861, and 212 Fidelity Bankers Trust Bldg., Knoxville 37901, 615-546-5468, and U.S. Courthouse, 801 Broadway, Nashville 37201, 615-254-9426.

Committees

Commerce (5th); Subs. (1) Aviation, (2) Communications, (3) Environment, (4) Foreign Commerce and Tourism, (5) Surface Transportation.

Public Works (3rd); Subs. (1) Air and Water Pollution, (2) Economic Development, (3) Environmental Science and Technology, (4) Public Roads, (5) Sp. on Economic Development.

Jt. Com. on Atomic Energy (4th); Subs. (1) Agreements for Cooperation, (2) Communities, (3) Military Applications, (4) Research, Development, and Radiation.

Group Ratings

	ADA	COPE	NREP	NFU	LCV	NAB	NSI	ACA
1970	13	18	18	45	54	78	100	89
1969	11	—	—	44	—	—	—	36
1968	21	36	—	60	—	100	—	80

Key Votes

(1) ABM	FOR	(8) Phil Pln	AGN	(15) Coop-Church	AGN
(2) SST	FOR	(9) Vol Army	FOR	(16) Cut Oil Dpltn	AGN
(3) Busing	AGN	(10) Prison $	ABS	(17) Consumer Prot	AGN
(4) Tob Sub	ABS	(11) Cut Mil $	AGN	(18) Farm Sub Limit	AGN
(5) Carswell	FOR	(12) Defoliatn	FOR	(19) Comp Bid Sales	ABS
(6) No-Knock	FOR	(13) 18-Yr-Vote	ABS	(20) Pre-Prod Tests	ABS
(7) Seniorty	FOR	(14) Pentgn PR	FOR	(21) Cut Marjna Pen	AGN

Election Results

1966 general:	Howard Baker, Jr. (R)	483,063	(56%)
	Frank G. Clement (D)	383,843	(44%)
1966 primary:	Howard Baker, Jr. (R)	112,617	(76%)
	Kenneth Roberts (R)	36,043	(24%)

Senator

William Emerson Brock III (R) Elected 1970, seat up 1976; b. Nov. 23, 1930, Chattanooga; home, Chattanooga; Washington and Lee U., B.S., 1953; Navy, 1953–56; Lt. USNR; married, four children; Presbyterian.

Career V. P., Brock Candy Co., 1956–62; Chm., Natl. Teen Com., 1961.

Offices 456 OSOB, 202-225-3344. Also 230 Fed. Bldg., Chattanooga 37402, 615-266-3151; Fed. Bldg., Knoxville 37901, 615-524-4011; Fed. Bldg., Nashville 37201, 615-242-8321; 102 Jackson State Bank, Jackson, 901-424-8021; and Fed. Bldg., Memphis 38103, 901-534-3011.

Committees

Banking, Housing, and Urban Affairs, (6th); Subs. (1) Financial Institutions, (2) Housing and Urban Affairs, (3) Production and Stabilization, (4) Small Business.

Government Operations (8th); Subs. (1) Intergovernmental Relations, (2) National Security and International Operations.

Group Ratings Note: the following ratings and votes cover Sen. Brock's record in the House of Representatives where he served prior to his election in 1970.

	ADA	COPE	NREP	NFU	LCV	CFA	NAB	NSI	ACA
1970	4	0	8	18	0	33	78	100	80
1969	7	22	—	28	—	—	—	—	71
1968	0	9	—	33	—	—	83	—	87

Key Votes

(1) ABM	ABS	(6) 18-Yr-Vote	AGN	(11) Clean Water $	AGN
(2) SST	FOR*	(7) Farm Sub Lmt	AGN	(12) Mig Wrkrs Comp	ABS
(3) Phil Pln	ABS	(8) Coop-Church	AGN	(13) Jets to Chiang	FOR
(4) No-Knock	FOR	(9) Family Asst	FOR	(14) State OEO Veto	FOR
(5) Cmutr Tax	ABS	(10) Work Stamps	ABS	(15) Park Logging	FOR

* *as Senator.*

Election Results

1970 general:	William E. Brock III (R)	562,645	(51%)
	Albert Gore (D)	519,858	(47%)
	Cecil R. Pitard (AIP)	8,691	(1%)
	Dan R. East (Ind.)	5,845	(1%)
1970 primary:	William E. Brock III (R)	176,703	(75%)
	Tex Ritter (R)	54,401	(23%)
	James Durelle Boles (R)	4,942	(2%)

FIRST DISTRICT Political Background

Most of Tennessee 1, the far northeast corner of the state, is an extension of the Shenandoah Valley and the Blue Ridge Mountains of Virginia. The district is closer to Richmond than it is to Memphis. The 1st is better off than most of Appalachia—it is growing. In recent years, new industries have come into towns like Johnson City (pop. 33,000), Kingsport (pop. 31,000), and Bristol (pop. 20,000). They are attracted here by the region's low taxes and by the valleys of the 1st which provide the industries with reasonably level east-west transportation routes.

The changing economy of the district, however, has not produced any shift in its political inclinations. The 1st has been traditionally Republican, as solidly Republican as any district in Iowa or Nebraska. The ancestors of the current residents were ardently opposed to secession in 1861 and remained loyal to the Union and Mr. Lincoln during the Civil War. The people here have continued to support the party of the Union ever since; in 1964, for example, the 1st district of Tennessee produced the largest Republican percentage of any contested House race in the country.

For nearly 40 years, congressional politics in the 1st was dominated by B. Carroll Reece, a Republican who represented the district from 1920 to 1930, 1932 to 1946, and 1950 until his death in 1961. Reece also served as Republican National Chairman from 1946 to 1948. He was succeeded by James H. (Jimmy) Quillen, another conservative Republican. Quillen's seat on the Rules Committee attests to the utter security of his tenure and the orthodoxy of his conservatism.

In the past, the Democrats have often failed to put up a candidate in the 1st; when they do, he has had no chance of winning. But Quillen, like all but one of the state's Republican congressional candidates, received a lower percentage of the votes in 1970 than in 1968. This shows that despite Brock's Senate victory, Tennessee voters, like many Americans, are not entirely happy with the Nixon Administration.

In the 1st district, however, Quillen still received 68% of the votes, which means that he will stay in the House for as long as he wants to.

Census Data 1970 pop. 437,874; deviation from current state average, +0.4%; change 1960–70, +10.6%. Metro. 0.0%, 0.0% central city.

1970 Share of Federal Outlays $290,948,047

DOD	$92,935,000	HEW	$86,555,245
AEC	$000	HUD	$4,714,062
NASA	$000	OEO	$487,094
DOT	$9,867,690	DOA	$21,568,961
		Other	$74,819,995

Federal Military-Industrial Commitments

DOD Contractors Eastman Kodak (Kingsport), $51.633m: production of explosives and operation of Holston Army Ammunition plant. Raytheon (Bristol), $21.894m:

artillery proximity fuzes. Metals Engineering Co. (Greenville), $9.485m: 500-pound bomb fin assemblies.

Economic Base Tobacco and dairy; chemicals and allied products; household furniture and other furniture and fixtures. Also tourism (Smokies).

The Voters

Registration 194,212 total. No party registration.

Employment profile White collar, 30%. Blue collar, 70%.

Ethnic groups Black, 2%. Total foreign stock, 1%. All foreign groups less than 0.5% each.

Presidential vote

1968	Humphrey (D)	27,267	(20%)
	Nixon (R)	83,465	(60%)
	Wallace (AIP)	27,764	(20%)

Representative

James H. (Jimmy) Quillen (R) Elected 1962; b. Jan. 11, 1916, near Gate City, Va.; home, Kingsport; Navy, WWII; married; Methodist.

Career Former newspaper publisher; Pres., Chm. of Bd., real estate, mortgage loans and insurance business; Tenn. House of Reps., 1954–62, Minority Leader, 1959–60; Tenn. Legislative Council, 1957–59, 1961; Dir., Kingsport Natl. Bank.

Offices 102 CHOB, 202-225-6356. Also Rm. B-8, Fed. Bldg., Kingsport 37662, 615-247-8161.

Committees

Rules (4th).

Standards of Official Conduct (3rd).

Group Ratings

	ADA	COPE	NREP	NFU	LCV	CFA	NAB	NSI	ACA
1970	4	9	0	23	17	41	83	100	94
1969	7	—	—	20	—	—	—	—	75
1968	0	23	—	60	—	—	100	—	100

Key Votes

(1) ABM	ABS	(6) 18-Yr-Vote	AGN	(11) Clean Water $	FOR
(2) SST	FOR	(7) Farm Sub Lmt	AGN	(12) Mig Wrkrs Comp	AGN
(3) Phil Pln	AGN	(8) Coop-Church	AGN	(13) Jets to Chiang	FOR
(4) No-Knock	FOR	(9) Family Asst	AGN	(14) State OEO Veto	FOR
(5) Cmutr Tax	AGN	(10) Work Stamps	FOR	(15) Park Logging	FOR

Election Results

1970 general:	James H. Quillen (R)	78,896	(68%)
	David Bruce Shine (D)	37,348	(32%)
1970 primary:	James H. Quillen (R)	48,067	(84%)
	Dan W. Laws (R)	9,034	(16%)
1968 general:	James H. Quillen (R)	100,000	(85%)
	Arthur W. Bright (D)	17,441	(15%)

SECOND DISTRICT Political Background

Tennessee 2 is dominated by Knoxville, the largest city (pop. 174,000) in east Tennessee. Knoxville, which looks no different from dozens of other industrial cities that vote Democratic, is the most consistently Republican city in the state. Its conservatism is somewhat surprising since it has benefitted greatly from one of the New

Deal's most famous projects, the Tennessee Valley Authority. TVA, headquartered in Knoxville, has brought lower power costs, recreational lakes, and employment to east Tennessee. In 1970, the people here did cast more than the usual number of Democratic votes in Albert Gore's Senate race against free-market enthusiast, Congressman William Brock. But because most Tennessee Republicans believe in TVA as ardently as the state's Democrats, Knoxville and the rest of the 2nd have remained steadfastly Republican in virtually every contested election since the Civil War.

Knoxville is Sen. Howard Baker's political base: the 2nd had been represented by his father, Howard Baker, Sr., from 1950 to 1963, and after his death, by his mother, from 1963 to 1964. Sensing the potential for a Republican statewide victory, Howard Baker, Jr., ran for the Senate in 1964 and lost; but he ran again in 1966 and won. The successor to his parents' congressional seat was the former mayor of Knoxville, John J. Duncan, a quiet and restrained conservative in the Baker mold. In Washington, Duncan is a junior member of the House Ways and Means Committee. All indications are that he will continue to win reelection easily.

Census Data 1970 pop. 445,439; deviation from current state average, +2.2%; change 1960–70, +10.0%. Metro. 76.3%, 39.2% central city.

1970 Share of Federal Outlays $270,772,736

DOD	$21,055,000	HEW	$97,359,577
AEC	$334,514	HUD	$6,138,723
NASA	$407,750	OEO	$1,087,716
DOT	$13,609,363	DOA	$14,322,321
		Other	$116,457,760

Federal Military-Industrial Commitments

None.

Economic Base Apparel and other finished products made from fabrics and similar materials, esp. women's, misses', and juniors' outerwear; livestock and tobacco; food and kindred products; nonelectrical machinery. Also, higher education (University of Tennessee).

The Voters

Registration 182,291 total. No party registration.

Employment profile White collar, 40%. Blue collar, 60%.

Ethnic groups Black, 7%. Total foreign stock, 2%. All foreign groups less than 0.5% each.

Presidential vote

1968	Humphrey (D)	36,277	(25%)
	Nixon (R)	78,481	(55%)
	Wallace (AIP)	28,759	(20%)

Representative

John James Duncan (R) Elected 1964; b. March 24, 1919, Scott County; home, Knoxville; Army, WWII; married, four children; Presbyterian.

Career Asst. Atty. Gen., Tenn., 1947–56; Law Dir., Knoxville, 1956–59; Mayor, 1959–64; Pres., Knox Fed. Savings & Loan Assn.

Offices 117 CHOB, 202-225-5435. Also Rm. 314, Post Office Bldg., Knoxville 37902, 615-546-5686, and 111 East Main St., Morristown 37814, 615-581-8801.

Committees

Ways and Means (9th).

Group Ratings

	ADA	COPE	NREP	NFU	LCV	CFA	NAB	NSI	ACA
1970	12	25	8	54	38	48	83	100	74
1969	7	—	—	14	—	—	—	—	88
1968	0	23	—	38	—	—	100	—	96

Key Votes

(1) ABM	FOR	(6) 18-Yr-Vote	FOR	(11) Clean Water $	AGN
(2) SST	AGN	(7) Farm Sub Lmt	AGN	(12) Mig Wrkrs Comp	AGN
(3) Phil Pln	AGN	(8) Coop-Church	AGN	(13) Jets to Chiang	FOR
(4) No-Knock	FOR	(9) Family Asst	AGN	(14) State OEO Veto	FOR
(5) Cmutr Tax	AGN	(10) Work Stamps	FOR	(15) Park Logging	AGN

Election Results

1970 general:	John J. Duncan (R)	85,849	(73%)
	Roger Cowan (D)	30,146	(26%)
	William E. Butcher (Ind.)	1,116	(1%)
1970 primary:	John J. Duncan (R), unopposed		
1968 general:	John J. Duncan (R)	118,773	(85%)
	Lake Armstrong (D)	17,547	(15%)

THIRD DISTRICT Political Background

Tennessee 3, dominated by the city of Chattanooga (pop. 119,000), is the most marginal congressional district in east Tennessee. To the east of the city is rugged hill country, solidly Republican except for Polk County where the borders of Tennessee, Georgia, and North Carolina intersect. Polk is a Democratic county with a history of violence in its politics; three people lost their lives here during the 1948 campaign. The 3rd also has a few counties which lie west of the Tennessee River and which lean Democratic, like most of middle Tennessee.

Chattanooga itself has never been a consistently Republican city. Situated between the Tennessee River and the Georgia line, and flanked by steep ridges (one of which is Lookout Mountain), Chattanooga voted for many years like a city in the Deep South—somewhat populistic and Democratic. Even today the east Tennessee city shows signs of its maverick political past; in the 1971 municipal elections here, its residents elected a conservative mayor and a black health and education administrator.

But with the onset of the civil rights revolution and the growth of the state Republican party, Chattanooga's voting habits have been moving steadily to the right. The trend is nicely illustrated by comparing the district's last three congressmen. Estes Kefauver got his political start here, representing the 3rd from 1939 to 1948; he then went on to the Senate where he became famous fighting organized crime and the drug industry and campaigning in presidential primaries in a coonskin cap. Kefauver was succeeded by a much more conservative Democrat, James B. Frazier. In 1962, Frazier, who had a seat on Ways and Means, was upset in the Democratic primary, losing to liberal Wilkes Thrasher, Jr., by 269 votes out of 70,000 cast. Thrasher, in turn, lost the general election by 2,000 votes out of 93,000 cast to Republican William E. Brock III. Thrasher's mistake was allowing himself to be photographed with President Kennedy, who was never especially popular around Chattanooga.

Brock was the young (then 32) heir to candy millions, whose belief in the free enterprise system was so intense that he voted against the Appalachia bill. That vote did not go over well in the hill country of the 3rd, but his constituents were quite happy with the Congressman's other positions: he opposed the Civil Rights Act of 1964 as well as virtually all social legislation of the Kennedy and Johnson years. As a result, he was reelected by handsome margins. Today, of course, Bill Brock is the state's junior senator, having beaten Albert Gore in a classic contest between old-fashioned Southern liberalism and sleek, modern Southern conservatism.

Brock's departure set the stage for a close contest in the district in 1970. The contestants were Republican state Sen. LaMar Baker and Democratic Hamilton County Councilman Richard Winningham. Baker won, 51–46, carrying Hamilton County

(Chattanooga) by that margin and winning most of the rural counties. Barring a strong Democratic surge, chances are Baker will win again in 1972.

Census Data 1970 pop. 432,500; deviation from current state average, −0.8%; change 1960–70, +7.8%. Metro. 58.8%, 27.5% central city.

1970 Share of Federal Outlays $327,544,448

DOD	$77,815,000	HEW	$98,235,273
AEC	$000	HUD	$6,319,035
NASA	$000	OEO	$1,605,155
DOT	$18,524,027	DOA	$10,793,913
		Other	$114,252,045

Federal Military-Industrial Commitments

DOD Contractors Atlas Chemical Industries (Chattanooga), $36.384m: production of TNT and operation of the Volunteer Army Ammunition plant. Hoechst Uhde Co. (Chattanooga), $7.864m: unspecified. Monsanto Enviro-Chem Co. (Chattanooga), $5.270m: installation of an acid recovery system at the Volunteer Army Ammunition plant.

Economic Base Fabricated metal products, esp. fabricated structural metal products; chemical and allied products; livestock; textile mill products, esp. knitting mills. Also, insurance.

The Voters

Registration 190,956 total. No party registration.

Employment profile White collar, 34%. Blue collar, 66%.

Ethnic groups Black, 12%. Total foreign stock, 1%. All foreign groups less than 0.5% each.

Presidential vote

1968	Humphrey (D)	38,433	(27%)
	Nixon (R)	56,137	(39%)
	Wallace (AIP)	47,956	(34%)

Representative

LaMar Baker (R) Elected 1970; b. Dec. 29, 1915, Chattanooga; home, Chattanooga; Harding Col., B.A., 1940; Army Air Corps, 1941–46; married, two children; Church of Christ.

Career Owner, Commercial Janitors Inc. and Floormaster Rug Cleaning Co.; Tenn. House of Reps., 1966–68; Senate, 1968–70.

Offices 1116 LHOB, 202-225-3271. Also 230 Fed. Bldg., Chattanooga 37402, 615-266-3151.

Committees

Public Works (14th); Subs. (1) Flood Control and Internal Development, (2) Public Buildings and Grounds, (3) Rivers and Harbors, (4) Watershed Development, (5) Sp. on Economic Development Programs.

Group Ratings, Key Votes: Newly elected.

Election Results

1970 general:	LaMar Baker (R)	61,527	(51%)
	Richard Winningham (D)	54,662	(46%)
	Robert Shockey (Ind.)	2,124	(2%)
	Frank Massey (Ind.)	1,375	(1%)
1970 primary:	LaMar Baker (R)	18,967	(51%)
	Jack McDonald (R)	17,965	(49%)

FOURTH DISTRICT Political Background

Tennessee 4 stretches from the Appalachian ridges in the east across the fertile plains and hills of middle Tennessee to a point near Nashville. The district comprises an area of small and medium-sized farms and small, old county seat towns. It became thickly settled soon after the mountaineers found their way over the Smokies from North Carolina. The first local hero was Andrew Jackson, victor at the Battle of New Orleans and later President of the United States; most of middle Tennessee has remained loyal to his Democratic party since those days. Because there are fewer blacks here than in the west Tennesse cotton lands, the race issue has seldom been the issue that it is in the Deep South. Although most of the district's Democratic counties did go for George Wallace in 1968, they also went for Albert Gore in 1970. Gore is a native son, from Carthage in Smith County, who represented the district from 1938 to 1952.

Due to the requirements of redistricting in the '60's, the 4th acquired several traditionally Republican counties in and near the mountains in the east. The district also contains Oak Ridge (pop. 28,000), the largest city in the 4th. Oak Ridge is a town built totally by the AEC, and its voting behavior, like that of Los Alamos in New Mexico, is more typical of a Northern technocratic suburb than of the surrounding area.

Gore's successor in the House is a middle-of-the-road Democrat, Joe L. Evins. Evins has won reelection regularly with margins in excess of 75%, and has risen to a position of considerable influence in Congress. Evins is a senior Democratic member of the House Appropriations Committee and chairman of its Public Works Subcommittee. That post gives him power of the purse over all federal pork barrel projects and means that few congressmen care to cross him. Before 1969, Evins was chairman of the subcommittee handling housing appropriations, which might help to explain why his hometown of Smithville (pop. 2,997) was named one of the original Model Cities. Evins, who was 60 in 1970, can expect to serve another decade or two in the House, and with luck, might even succeed to the chairmanship of the full Appropriations Committee. Redistricting will change the boundaries of his district somewhat, but this has happened before without producing a visible effect on the election results.

Census Data 1970 pop. 415,239; deviation from current state average, —4.8%; change 1960–70, +5.0%. Metro. 23.4%, 0.0% central city.

1970 Share of Federal Outlays $588,633,405

DOD	$76,986,000	HEW	$95,532,011
AEC	$298,658,588	HUD	$8,927,397
NASA	$591,281	OEO	$1,082,673
DOT	$11,911,339	DOA	$17,814,354
		Other	$77,129,762

Federal Military-Industrial Commitments

DOD Contractors Aro Inc. (Tullahoma), $49.918m: laser research at the Arnold Engineering Development Center.

DOD Installations Arnold Engineering Development Center (Tullahoma).

AEC Operations Union Carbide (Oak Ridge), $209.031m: Oak Ridge National Laboratory, Feed Material Facility, Gaseous Diffusion Plant, Y-12 Plant. University of Tennessee (Oak Ridge), $5.248m: Agriculture Research Laboratory and Farm.

Economic Base Livestock, dairy, and tobacco; apparel and other finished products made from fabrics and similar materials, esp. men's, youths', and boys' furnishings, work clothing, and allied garments; electrical machinery.

The Voters

Registration 188,677 total. No party registration.

Employment profile White collar, 27%. Blue collar, 73%.

Ethnic groups Black, 3%. Total foreign stock, 1%. All foreign groups less than 0.5% each.

Presidential vote

1968	Humphrey (D)	38,383	(29%)
	Nixon (R)	50,662	(39%)
	Wallace (AIP)	42,400	(32%)

Representative

Joe L. Evins (D) Elected 1946; b. Oct. 24, 1910, DeKalb County; home, Smithville; Vanderbilt U., B.A., 1933; Cumberland U., LL.B., 1934; George Washington U., 1938–40; Army, WWII; married, three children; Church of Christ.

Career Asst. Secy., legal staff, Federal Trade Commission, 1935–41; Chm. of Bd., First Natl. Bank.

Offices 2300 RHOB, 202-225-4231. Also Fed. Bldg., Smithville 37166, 615-597-5475.

Committees

Appropriations (7th); Subs. (1) Chm., Public Works, (2) HUD, Space, and Science.

Sel. Com. on Small Business (Chm.).

Group Ratings

	ADA	COPE	NREP	NFU	LCV	CFA	NAB	NSI	ACA
1970	20	30	20	75	50	89	43	100	42
1969	20	—	—	73	—	—	—	—	22
1968	25	55	—	88	—	—	0	—	29

Key Votes

(1) ABM	FOR	(6) 18-Yr-Vote	FOR	(11) Clean Water $	AGN
(2) SST	AGN	(7) Farm Sub Lmt	AGN	(12) Mig Wrkrs Comp	AGN
(3) Phil Pln	ABS	(8) Coop-Church	AGN	(13) Jets to Chiang	ABS
(4) No-Knock	FOR	(9) Family Asst	AGN	(14) State OEO Veto	AGN
(5) Cmutr Tax	AGN	(10) Work Stamps	FOR	(15) Park Logging	AGN

Election Results

1970 general:	Joe L. Evins (D)	86,437	(83%)
	(Mrs.) J. Durelle Boles (R)	18,180	(17%)
1970 primary:	Joe L. Evins (D), unopposed		
1968 general:	Joe L. Evins (D)	74,041	(76%)
	(Mrs.) J. Durelle Boles (R)	25,553	(24%)

FIFTH DISTRICT Political Background

Tennessee 5 is Davidson County and the city of Nashville, which have recently been consolidated into one governmental unit. Together, county and city have a population of 447,000 people. Nashville is the state capital, and, after Memphis, the second largest city in Tennessee. It is, because of its location in the middle of the state, the dominant Tennessee city. Nashville is a major center for textiles and insurance, but the economic activity for which it is best known is music. Nashville, the country and western music capital of the nation, has been the home of the Grand Ole Opry since the '20's and, more recently, the site of several major recording studios. These days, music millionaires have moved into suburban mansions uncomfortably close to Nashville's older, more established upper-class.

Country music stars have even gone into politics—the most recent example being Tex Ritter's unsuccessful bid for the Republican Senate nomination in 1970. Country personalities have also had an important peripheral influence on Tennessee politics. Nashville attorney, John J. Hooker, promoted the Minnie Pearl Chicken franchise operation. Stockholders included some of the leading citizens of Tennessee, and its spectacular rise and resounding fall helped to defeat the lawyer in the 1970 governor's race.

Nashville's most famous local son is Andrew Jackson, whose home, the Hermitage, remains a local shrine. Jackson was, of course, a Democrat, and Nashville remains Tennessee's most Democratic city to this day. Like most of Tennessee, the city went for Wallace in 1968, but only by a narrow margin: 35% for Wallace, 33% for Humphrey, and 32% for Nixon. In the closely contested recent statewide races (see state write-up), Nashville has given Democratic candidates big margins. It has done the same in congressional elections; in fact, Nashville has not had a Republican congressman since 1872.

Richard M. Fulton currently represents the district in Washington. The Congressman is one of the two most liberal members of the Tennessee delegation; he and William Anderson of the 6th are the only ones from the state who have voted against controversial military spending programs and for measures to end the Vietnam war. Fulton was first elected in 1962, when he ousted conservative incumbent, J. Carlton Loser. In the primary of that year, Loser appeared to have won by 72 votes. There were charges of vote fraud, and neither candidate was given the Democratic nomination. Instead, in the general election, both ran as independents, with Fulton coming out on top by a surprisingly large 17,000-vote margin. After only one term in Congress, Fulton caught the eye of the party leadership and won a seat on the House Ways and Means Committee.

In 1968, Fulton had an unexpected close call, winning reelection by just 8,000 votes. Stung by the near defeat, he bounced back next time with 71% of the votes against the same opponent. Fulton looks like a good bet for continued reelection, but he could have trouble if challenged by a determined Republican in a good Republican year.

Census Data 1970 pop. 447,877; deviation from current state average, +2.7%; change 1960–70, +12.0%. Metro. 100.0%, 97.4% central city.

1970 Share of Federal Outlays $347,748,647

DOD	$50,758,000	HEW	$135,670,990
AEC	$169,659	HUD	$421,675
NASA	$243,640	OEO	$3,868,560
DOT	$6,883,062	DOA	$8,705,930
		Other	$141,027,131

Federal Military-Industrial Commitments

DOD Contractors Capitol Airways (Nashville), $12.474m: cargo transport services.

Economic Base Printing, publishing, and allied industries, esp. commercial printing; transportation equipment, esp. ship building and repairing; food and kindred products, esp. meat products; chemicals and allied products. Also, banking, insurance, and recorded music.

The Voters

Registration 203,004 total. No party registration.

Employment profile White collar, 46%. Blue collar, 54%.

Ethnic groups Black, 20%. Total foreign stock, 2%. All foreign groups less than 0.5% each.

Presidential vote

1968	Humphrey (D)	44,543	(33%)
	Nixon (R)	44,175	(32%)
	Wallace (AIP)	47,889	(35%)

Representative

Richard Harmon Fulton (D) Elected 1962; b. Jan. 27, 1927, Nashville; home, Nashville; U. of Tenn.; Navy, WWII; widowed, two children; Methodist.

Career Real estate broker; Tenn. Senate, 1959.

Offices 401 CHOB, 202-225-4311. Also 552 U.S. Court House, Nashville 37203, 615-242-8321, ext. 296.

Committees

Ways and Means (9th).

Group Ratings

	ADA	COPE	NREP	NFU	LCV	CFA	NAB	NSI	ACA
1970	44	82	70	100	44	84	0	86	21
1969	40	—	—	80	—	—	—	—	30
1968	50	92	—	82	—	—	33	—	33

Key Votes

(1) ABM	FOR	(6) 18-Yr-Vote	FOR	(11) Clean Water $	FOR
(2) SST	AGN	(7) Farm Sub Lmt	FOR	(12) Mig Wrkrs Comp	FOR
(3) Phil Pln	ABS	(8) Coop-Church	FOR	(13) Jets to Chiang	ABS
(4) No-Knock	FOR	(9) Family Asst	FOR	(14) State OEO Veto	AGN
(5) Cmutr Tax	ABS	(10) Work Stamps	FOR	(15) Park Logging	FOR

Election Results

1970 general:	Richard Fulton (D)	89,900	(71%)
	George Kelly (R)	37,522	(29%)
1970 primary:	Richard Fulton (D), unopposed		
1968 general:	Richard Fulton (D)	61,045	(54%)
	George Kelly (R)	52,836	(46%)

SIXTH DISTRICT Political Background

Tennessee 6 lies in the heart of middle Tennessee and consists of a group of counties, some of which have been represented in the House at various times by the heroes of the Tennessee Democracy: Andrew Jackson, James Knox Polk, Cordell Hull, and Albert Gore. The tortuous boundaries of the current 6th are the result of several redistrictings. But as it stands, virtually every county in the district is heavily Democratic, and the 6th is consistently the state's most Democratic district. In 1968, George Wallace did carry the 6th with 49%, but that election showed the continued weakness of one of the nation's major parties: although Richard Nixon carried Tennessee, he won only 23% of the votes in the 6th district. And in 1970, when conservative Republicans carried the state, the 6th still gave 64% of its votes to Albert Gore.

The Democratic character of the 6th cannot be explained by the presence here of large industrial cities or large numbers of black voters. Its largest city is Clarksville (pop. 31,000), and some 88% of its residents are white. Nor have the continuing Democratic majorities been dependent on the conservatism of local Democratic candidates. Ex-Rep. (1954–64) and Sen. (1964–66) Ross Bass had a generally liberal voting record and voted for the 1964 Civil Rights Act; his successor, William R. Anderson, is at least as far left on the political spectrum. The Democratic voting habits found here can only be explained as another of those continuing allegiances to Civil War party loyalties which are sustained by voters in rural America. These loyalties are strong among the small farmers and townspeople of the 6th who support liberal economic policies.

In the late '50's, Captain William R. Anderson, a native of Humphreys County, Tennessee, commanded the atomic submarine *Nautilus* on the first transpolar voyage under the ice. Later, Captain Anderson served as an aide to Admiral Hyman Rickover, several Navy secretaries, and President Kennedy. In 1963, Anderson left Washington and returned home to go into politics. When Congressman Ross Bass decided to run for the Senate in 1964, Anderson went after his House seat and won both the Democratic primary and the general election easily.

In the House, Anderson went about his business, compiling a generally liberal record on economic issues and rocking few boats. He won a seat on the Rules Committee, in large part because he was both a liberal and a Southerner—a combination that has become increasingly rare. Then in 1969, Anderson, along with two other congressmen, made an inspection trip in South Vietnam. There he discovered the Con San tiger cages in which the South Vietnamese government was confining political prisoners. Before that discovery, Anderson had usually gone along with the war policies of the Johnson and Nixon administrations; afterwards, he became a vehement critic. Later, Anderson came to know the Berrigan brothers, and when J. Edgar Hoover accused the two of plotting to kidnap Henry Kissinger, Anderson demanded that Hoover bring a case in court or retract the charges. The Justice Department responded by bringing the case, which at this writing has not come to trial.

Vice President Agnew got himself into the picture, charging that Anderson defended the Berrigans only for self-serving political reasons. Agnew thereby demonstrated his ignorance of the political realities in middle Tennessee. War protesters have never been especially popular among the voters of the 6th district and neither have Roman Catholics. Most of the people here are old-line white Protestants. Anderson's ideological fervor will surely cost him some votes, but he can afford to lose a few. In 1970, he won re-election by a vote of 87,000 to 19,000 (82%).

But Anderson could have problems in 1972. The 6th district is due to be merged with the 7th in the upcoming redistricting. Tennessee lost a congressional district in the 1970 census, with middle Tennessee showing the greatest population losses in the state. It is expected that Rep. Ray Blanton of the 7th will give up his House seat to run for the Senate; if he does not, Anderson will either face a difficult primary or an even more difficult try for the Senate against Howard Baker.

Census Data 1970 pop. 449,409; deviation from current state average, +3.1%; change 1960–70, +15.8%. Metro. 12.5%, 0.0% central city.

1970 Share of Federal Outlays $223,022,462

DOD	$24,140,000	HEW	$87,066,040
AEC	$000	HUD	$2,793,316
NASA	$378,715	OEO	$1,759,700
DOT	$14,130,801	DOA	$25,846,605
		Other	$66,907,285

Federal Military-Industrial Commitments

None.

Economic Base Tobacco, livestock, and dairy; apparel and other finished products made from fabrics and similar materials; nonelectrical machinery.

The Voters

Registration 191,262 total. No party registration.

Employment profile White collar, 27%. Blue collar, 73%.

Ethnic groups Black, 12%. Total foreign stock, 1%. All foreign groups less than 0.5% each.

Presidential vote

1968	Humphrey (D)	36,667	(28%)
	Nixon (R)	30,987	(23%)
	Wallace (AIP)	65,166	(49%)

Representative

William Robert Anderson (D) Elected 1964; b. June 17, 1921, Bakersville; home, Waverly; U.S. Naval Acad., B.S., 1942; Navy, 1942–62; married, two children; Protestant.

Career Commanding Officer of *Nautilus,* 1957–59, first transpolar voyage under ice; Asst. to V. Admiral H. G. Rickover; consultant to Pres. Kennedy for Natl. Service Corps, 1963.

Offices 316 CHOB, 202-225-2811. Also Box 400, Waverly 37185, 615-296-4557.

Committees

Rules (10th).

Group Ratings

	ADA	COPE	NREP	NFU	LCV	CFA	NAB	NSI	ACA
1970	40	56	27	57	80	100	13	88	47
1969	27	—	—	85	—	—	—	—	50
1968	42	82	—	92	—	—	20	—	22

Key Votes

(1) ABM	FOR	(6) 18-Yr-Vote	FOR	(11) Clean Water $	FOR
(2) SST	AGN	(7) Farm Sub Lmt	AGN	(12) Mig Wrkrs Comp	ABS
(3) Phil Pln	AGN	(8) Coop-Church	AGN	(13) Jets to Chiang	AGN
(4) No-Knock	FOR	(9) Family Asst	AGN	(14) State OEO Veto	AGN
(5) Cmutr Tax	ABS	(10) Work Stamps	AGN	(15) Park Logging	ABS

Election Results

1970 general:	William R. Anderson (D)	87,517	(82%)
	Elmer Davies, Jr. (R)	19,622	(18%)
1970 primary:	William R. Anderson (D)	54,867	(90%)
	Raymond Gibbs (D)	5,868	(10%)
1968 general:	William R. Anderson (D)	61,223	(59%)
	Ronnie Page (R)	41,923	(41%)

SEVENTH DISTRICT Political Background

Tennessee 7 comprises the southern half of west Tennessee, along with significant portions of middle Tennessee and the city of Memphis. Rural west Tennessee is very much like the adjoining state of Mississippi. There are substantial numbers of blacks here, far more than are found west of the Tennessee River, and during the '60's, the whites began to vote strictly along racial lines (see Mississippi state write-up). Jackson (pop. 40,000), the largest city in the district outside of Memphis, has had a bitter, protracted school desegregation suit. The white voters of the 7th, who used to bus their children to all-white schools, now respond positively to the anti-busing appeals of politicians like Sen. William Brock (see Tennessee state write-up). A belt of counties in the middle of the district have been traditionally Republican since the time of the Civil War; now the 7th as a whole has been trending Republican.

The district's few remaining Democratic areas lie in counties east of the Tennessee River and in its portion of the city of Memphis. The Tennessee legislature redrew the district lines after the 1964 election and made sure that the black voters would not dominate the new 9th; in the course of drawing a white 9th, they placed much of the large south side Memphis ghetto in the 7th.

The votes cast in the Memphis ghetto were enough to make the difference in the 1966 election. At that time, state Rep. Ray Blanton decided to take on veteran Congressman Tom Murray, who had been in the House since 1942. Blanton, who was somewhat less conservative than Murray, won by a razor-thin 384 votes. He won because of his showing in Shelby County (Memphis), where he beat Murray by 1,800 votes. The general election produced almost the same story. Republican State Chairman Julius Hurst put up a strong campaign and ran only 500 votes behind Blanton outside Shelby. But Blanton carried Memphis by almost 2,000 votes, for a narrow 51% victory. The Shelby total understates the contributions of the black voters to the Democratic cause, since the total figure includes some Republican suburbs.

Except for some liberal votes on bread-and-butter issues, Blanton has compiled a generally conservative record in the House. In the 7th district, meanwhile, he has become extremely popular, winning reelection in 1970 with 74% of the vote. Because the 1970 census cost Tennessee a congressional district, it is expected that the 7th and William Anderson's 6th will be merged. Blanton has reportedly decided to run for the Senate against Howard Baker. He could become a formidable candidate. Blanton, who will be 42 in 1972, is part of a younger generation of Tennessee politicians not in the old-fashioned oratorical tradition of Democrats Albert Gore and Frank Clement; these men lost Senate races in 1970 and 1966, respectively. And, unlike Gore, Blanton cannot be attacked as soft on civil rights or war protesters. At the same time, he will probably inherit near unanimous black support, running, as he will be, against the party of Richard Nixon. Blanton and Baker could easily produce another interesting Tennessee Senate race.

Census Data 1970 pop. 463,025; deviation from current state average, +6.2%; change 1960–70, +16.2%. Metro. 35.7%, 32.5% central city.

1970 Share of Federal Outlays $363,218,000 (average outlay per district, Tennessee 7–9)

DOD	$91,920,000	HEW	$93,717,000
AEC	$000	HUD	$2,825,000
NASA	$000	OEO	$1,512,000
DOT	$12,397,000	DOA	$75,937,000
		Other	$84,911,000

Federal Military-Industrial Commitments (See Tennessee 9 for Tennessee 7–9 listing.)

Economic Base Cotton and livestock; apparel and other finished products made from fabrics and similar materials. Also, some commuting to Tennessee 9 (Downtown Memphis).

The Voters

Registration 203,961 total. No party registration.

Employment profile White collar, 30%. Blue collar, 70%.

Ethnic groups Black, 29%. Total foreign stock, 1%. All foreign groups less than 0.5% each.

Presidential vote

1968	Humphrey (D)	46,218	(31%)
	Nixon (R)	45,001	(30%)
	Wallace (AIP)	57,647	(39%)

Representative

Leonard Ray Blanton (D) Elected 1966; b. April 10, 1930, Hardin County; home, Adamsville; U. of Tenn., B.S., 1951; married, three children; Methodist.

Career Organized B & B Construction Co., 1954–66; V. P., Tenn. Plant Mix Asphalt Assn., Tenn. House of Reps., 1964–66.

Offices 1005 LHOB, 202-225-7084. Also Post Office Bldg., Jackson 38301, 901-424-3067, and 5134 Mill Branch Rd., Memphis 38118, 901-397-2377.

Committees

District of Columbia (10th); Subs. (1) Business, Commerce, and Fiscal Affairs, (2) Education, (3) Public Health and Welfare.

Interstate and Foreign Commerce (13th); Sp. Sub. on Investigations.

Group Ratings

	ADA	COPE	NREP	NFU	LCV	CFA	NAB	NSI	ACA
1970	24	33	18	55	0	83	36	88	53
1969	13	—	—	77	—	—	—	—	40
1968	17	42	—	70	—	—	33	—	47

Key Votes

(1) ABM	FOR	(6) 18-Yr-Vote	AGN	(11) Clean Water $	AGN
(2) SST	FOR	(7) Farm Sub Lmt	AGN	(12) Mig Wrkrs Comp	AGN
(3) Phil Pln	ABS	(8) Coop-Church	AGN	(13) Jets to Chiang	AGN
(4) No-Knock	FOR	(9) Family Asst	AGN	(14) State OEO Veto	FOR
(5) Cmutr Tax	FOR	(10) Work Stamps	AGN	(15) Park Logging	FOR

Election Results

1970 general:	Ray Blanton (D)	83,904	(74%)
	W. G. Doss (R)	29,139	(26%)
1970 primary:	Ray Blanton (D), unopposed		
1968 general:	Ray Blanton (D)	80,893	(66%)
	John T. Williams (R)	41,457	(34%)

EIGHTH DISTRICT Political Background

Tennessee 8 comprises the northwest corner of the state. The district extends from the TVA lakes of the Tennessee and Cumberland rivers at the Kentucky state line to the city of Memphis. This area, physically and politically, resembles the Mississippi Delta country or eastern Arkansas: flat cotton lands, occasional small towns, and a black population running about 24%. The largest city in the district outside of the Memphis area is Dyersburg, with 14,000 residents. Most of the counties here are traditionally Democratic, but only those around the Tennessee River have given statewide Democratic candidates significant margins in recent years. Most of the rest of them have responded favorably to the thinly-disguised segregationist appeals of Republican candidates like Sen. William Brock. The Shelby County (Memphis) portion of the 8th, unlike that of the 7th, is heavily white and very conservative.

Perhaps because of its long-standing Democratic tradition, Tennessee Republicans did not strenuously contest congressional elections in the 8th for some time. From 1958 to 1969, the district was represented by conservative Democrat, Bob Everett, who faced Republican opposition only once during his tenure. In 1969, Everett died and a special election was called. George Wallace, who had carried the 8th with nearly 50% of the votes in 1968, came in to campaign for American party candidate William Davis, while Sen. Baker and other conservative Republicans stumped for the Republican, Leonard Dunavant. The race got some attention in the national press as a test of the Wallace and Nixon strategies in the South.

The result made both look rather bad. Davis won 25%, Dunavant took 24%, and the winner, conservative Democrat Ed Jones, won 51% and an absolute majority in the race. Jones, former commissioner of agriculture, had not asked outsiders to come in and campaign for him; he wisely relied on the traditional Democratic sentiments of the voters of his district. These people may plunk for Wallace in a presidential election, and they may applaud some of the policies of the Nixon Administration, but most of them preferred to stay with a Tennessee Democrat in what is, after all, a local election. Then too, against Wallace- and Nixon-backed candidates, Jones won the black vote with no effort at all.

In Congress, Jones received a seat on the House Agriculture Committee and on its Cotton Subcommittee. No doubt both assignments pleased him. Back home, the voters were apparently content with his conservative record; the new congressman had no opposition whatever in 1970. Most likely he will continue to represent the district for some time, barring an unanticipated redistricting plan that would throw him into a primary contest with another incumbent.

Census Data 1970 pop. 422,622; deviation from current state average, —3.1%; change 1960–70, +7.8%. Metro. 34.9%, 20.6% central city.

1970 Share of Federal Outlays $363,218,000 (average outlay per district, Tennessee 7–9)

DOD	$91,920,000	HEW	$93,717,000
AEC	$000	HUD	$2,825,000
NASA	$000	OEO	$1,512,000
DOT	$12,397,000	DOA	$75,937,000
		Other	$84,911,000

Federal Military-Industrial Commitments (See Tennessee 9 for Tennessee 7–9 listing.)

Economic Base Cotton; apparel and other finished products made from fabrics and similar materials; leather and leather products; textile mill products. Also, some commuting to Tennessee 9 (Downtown Memphis).

The Voters

Registration 175,694 total. No party registration.

Employment profile White collar, 28%. Blue collar, 72%.

Ethnic groups Black, 24%. Total foreign stock, 1%. All foreign groups less than 0.5% each.

Presidential vote

1968	Humphrey (D)	36,667	(28%)
	Nixon (R)	30,505	(24%)
	Wallace (AIP)	62,172	(48%)

Representative

Ed Jones (D) Elected March 25, 1969; b. April 20, 1912, Yorkville; home, Yorkville; U. of Tenn., B.S., 1934; married, two children; Presbyterian.

Career Inspector, Div. of Insect and Plant Diseases Control, 1934; Tenn. Dairy Products Assn., 1941–43; Agricultural Agent, Ill. Central Railroad, 1944–69; Tenn. Commissioner of Agriculture, 1949–52; Organizer, Pres., West Tenn. Artificial Breeding Assoc.; Assoc. Farm Dir., radio station WMC, Memphis.

Offices 1313 LHOB, 202-225-4714. Also 1758 Frayser Blvd., Memphis 38127, 901-358-4094, and Yorkville 38389, 901-643-6123.

Committees

Agriculture (15th); Subs. (1) Cotton, (2) Dairy and Poultry, (3) Department Operations.

House Administration (14th); Subs. (1) Elections, (2) Printing.

Group Ratings

	ADA	COPE	NREP	NFU	LCV	CFA	NAB	NSI	ACA
1970	24	42	27	50	50	80	27	88	60
1969	33	—	—	75	—	—	—	—	36

Key Votes

(1) ABM	ABS	(6) 18-Yr-Vote	AGN	(11) Clean Water $	FOR
(2) SST	AGN	(7) Farm Sub Lmt	AGN	(12) Mig Wrkrs Comp	AGN
(3) Phil Pln	AGN	(8) Coop-Church	AGN	(13) Jets to Chiang	ABS
(4) No-Knock	FOR	(9) Family Asst	AGN	(14) State OEO Veto	AGN
(5) Cmutr Tax	AGN	(10) Work Stamps	FOR	(15) Park Logging	FOR

Election Results

1970 general: Ed Jones (D), unopposed
1970 primary: Ed Jones (D), unopposed

NINTH DISTRICT Political Background

Tennessee 9 comprises most of the city of Memphis and the suburban areas of Raleigh, Bartlett, and Germantown in Shelby County. Memphis, the largest city in Tennessee (pop. 623,000), is the major commercial and financial center for much of the lower Mississippi Valley. In many respects, Memphis is a Deep South city, which looks south to Mississippi and west to Arkansas, as much as east and north to the rest of Tennessee. Nevertheless, it is the only city in the state with foreign-born populations of any size; Memphis is Abe Fortas' hometown. The city's history as a river port and railroad center gave it a touch of cosmopolitanism—and violence. Jazz was born in Memphis, and Martin Luther King, Jr., was murdered here.

Like the rural territory that surrounds it, Memphis is traditionally Democratic. But the shape of that tradition is a special one. During the '30's and '40's, Memphis basked under the rule of boss Ed Crump, who ran a machine much like Frank Hague's in Jersey City. Crump dominated Tennessee politics for nearly 20 years by delivering huge Shelby County majorities to his primary candidates. His power lapsed only when a Crump man was beaten by Estes Kefauver in the 1948 Senate race.

Crump also had a lock on the Memphis congressional district, which for years included all of Shelby County. Clifford Davis, a conservative Democrat and a Crump man, represented the district from 1940 to 1964. He managed to stay on long after the death of the boss in 1954. Davis was defeated in 1964 by liberal George Grider in the 1964 Democratic primary, and his defeat was a symbol of the changes that had occurred in the state's politics during the '60's. In Crump's day, blacks were allowed to vote, only because they voted the way they were told. By 1964, with the machine dead, the black voters got other ideas; Grider's victory was due in large part to solid black support. He won the 1964 general election, again with strong black support, with 52% of the vote.

But in that same year, it was apparent that the Tennessee congressional districts had to be redrawn. The 9th district, with a 1960 population of 627,000, was almost three times larger than the neighboring 8th. It therefore seemed appropriate to add portions of Shelby County to the under-populated 7th and 8th districts. If the Tennessee legislature had been so inclined, it could have drawn a near black-majority 9th district consisting of most of the city of Memphis. But, of course, it was not so inclined, and instead, the Democratic legislators decided to add a large part of the Memphis ghetto to the 8th and left the 9th politically marginal.

The result was a Republican victory in 1966. Dan Kuykendall, the Republican candidate, had come to Memphis 11 years before as a Procter and Gamble regional executive. In 1964, he made a political name for himself by running a strong race against Albert Gore, winning 46% against the Democrat. In 1966, candidate Kuykendall ran well in the growing white-collar precincts in Memphis, and beat Grider, 52–48. In subsequent elections, the growing dissatisfaction with the policies of liberal Democrats in blue-collar neighborhoods produced Kuykendall margins approaching 2–1. In 1970, he was the only Republican congressional candidate in Tennessee to improve on his 1968 showing.

Because Republicans now are occupying all the major statewide offices, Kuykendall will have to wait before making any move to seek higher office. In the meantime, he will probably continue to represent the Memphis area in the House. Redistricting will give Kuykendall some trouble. It will probably add the heavily black and Democratic south side to his district; the 7th, in which the black neighborhoods now lie, stands to be eliminated. This will make elections in the districts closer, but most likely Kuykendall will go on winning.

Census Data 1970 pop. 410,179; deviation from current state average, −5.9%; change 1960–70, +4.9%. Metro. 100.0%, 94.1% central city.

1970 Share of Federal Outlays $363,218,000 (average outlay per district, Tennessee 7–9)

DOD	$91,920,000	HEW	$93,717,000
AEC	$000	HUD	$2,825,000
NASA	$000	OEO	$1,512,000
DOT	$12,397,000	DOA	$75,937,000
		Other	$84,911,000

Federal Military-Industrial Commitments (Tennessee 7–9 listing)

DOD Contractors Pace Corp. (Memphis), $20.084m: parachute flare target markers. Delta Refining (Memphis), $10.035m: petroleum products. Airport Machining (Union City), $8.664m: metal parts for 2.75-inch rocket warheads. Heckethorn Mfg. (Dyersburg), $8.119m: metal parts for 40-mm projectiles. Kilgore Corp. (Toone), $7.787m: parachute flare target markers. Allen and O'Hara (Memphis), $6.150m: construction of a Naval hospital.

DOD Installations Memphis Army Defense Depot (Memphis). Naval Air Station (Memphis). Naval Hospital (Memphis). Naval Air Technical Training Command (Memphis).

Economic Base Food and kindred products; chemicals and allied products, esp. industrial organic and inorganic chemicals and soaps, detergents, and cleaning preparations, perfumes, cosmetics, and other toilet preparations; electrical machinery, equipment, and supplies; lumber and wood products other than furniture, esp. sawmills and planing mills. Also, higher education (Memphis State University); banking.

The Voters

Registration 179,376 total. No party registration.

Employment profile White collar, 47%. Blue collar, 53%.

Ethnic groups Black, 34%. Total foreign stock, 4%. Germany, Italy, 1% each; others, 1%.

Presidential vote

1968	Humphrey (D)	46,778	(32%)
	Nixon (R)	53,179	(37%)
	Wallace (AIP)	45,039	(31%)

Representative

Dan H. Kuykendall (R) Elected 1966; b. July 9, 1924, Cherokee, Tex.; home, Memphis; Tex. A & M U., B.S., 1947; Army Air Corps, WWII; married, four children; Methodist.

Career Mgr., Procter & Gamble Co., 1947–64; Equitable Life Insurance Society of U.S., 1964– ; Mbr., Bd. of Dir., group drafting charter for Memphis, 1965–66.

Offices 1526 LHOB, 202-225-3265. Also 369 Fed. Bldg., Memphis 38103, 901-534-3319.

Committees

Interstate and Foreign Commerce (9th); Sub. on Transportation and Aeronautics.

Group Ratings

	ADA	COPE	NREP	NFU	LCV	CFA	NAB	NSI	ACA
1970	12	9	8	33	0	43	100	100	60
1969	0	—	—	21	—	—	—	—	71
1968	0	15	—	50	—	—	100	—	94

Key Votes

(1) ABM	FOR	(6) 18-Yr-Vote	FOR	(11) Clean Water $	AGN
(2) SST	FOR	(7) Farm Sub Lmt	AGN	(12) Mig Wrkrs Comp	AGN
(3) Phil Pln	FOR	(8) Coop-Church	AGN	(13) Jets to Chiang	ABS
(4) No-Knock	FOR	(9) Family Asst	FOR	(14) State OEO Veto	FOR
(5) Cmutr Tax	AGN	(10) Work Stamps	FOR	(15) Park Logging	FOR

Election Results

1970 general:	Dan Kuykendall (R)	72,498	(62%)
	Michael Osborn (D)	43,279	(37%)
	Malley Byrd (Ind.)	744	(1%)
1970 primary:	Dan Kuykendall (R), unopposed		
1968 general:	Dan Kuykendall (R)	73,293	(62%)
	James E. Irwin (D)	45,434	(38%)

TEXAS

Political Background

Everybody's image of Texas is pretty much the same. Within the image there is the Alamo and sweet revenge; the old-time longhorns and the present-day King Ranch; the spouting gusher and men deliriously happy; the big money and the wheeler dealer—the Murchison brothers, H. L. Hunt, Jimmy Ling, Ross Perot, and Billy Sol Estes; and, of course, there is LBJ, the LBJ Ranch, the LBJ Library, and the LBJ war. Not many can conjure up the other Texans, not so rich and not so powerful. These are the beleaguered small farmers, the open-shop factory workers, and the Mexican field hands. These people, as a matter of fact, are much more common in Texas than the Stetson-hatted rich. In one respect, however, everybody's image of Texas is correct. It is vast. It is farther from El Paso to Texarkana—or from Amarillo to Brownsville—than from Chicago to New York. The farmlands of east Texas are reasonably fertile, but some of the ranches of west Texas lie in barren desert country. In the wintertime, blizzards move across the northern panhandle, while the climate in the southern Rio Grande Valley is semitropical.

This kind of diversity is also part of the politics of Texas. Conservative Democrats win most of the elections in the state, but their success is hard-won. Texas has some of the nation's most ardent Republicans of the Goldwater variety and some of the most tenacious liberals. The electoral clout of the liberals depends largely on the blacks and Mexican-Americans, who together cast more than a quarter of the state's votes. In general, Texas remains a Democratic state; in a recent poll, 55% of the respondents thought of themselves as Democrats and only 22% as Republicans. Nevertheless, Republicans can and do win elections in Texas. In 1972, Nixon stands a good chance of carrying the state, especially if John Connally, as the rumors have it, replaces Spiro Agnew on the ticket.

Texas began its history as part of the South, and today, to a great extent, it remains part of the South. The first bands of American settlers here, the men who set up the Texas Republic in 1836, were slaveholders. And in 1863, Sam Houston himself died out of office because he refused to swear an allegiance to the Confederacy. Rural east and central Texas were settled by farmers from Tennessee, Arkansas, and the Deep South; the farmers brought with them their Democratic politics and their views on race. Up through the 1920's, Texas remained a predominantly rural Southern state. Its turbulent politics were played out, consistent with Southern tradition, in the Democratic primary.

Today, rural Texas—which we will define as the 221 counties with fewer than 50,000 residents—still plays an important role in Texas politics. Although their percentage of the state's population is declining, these counties still cast almost 30% of the votes in the state, and most of them still go to Democratic candidates. In 1968, George Wallace carried many counties in east Texas, but most of the rural counties stuck with the Democratic party; they gave Hubert Humphrey a solid 42% to 35% margin over Richard Nixon. A kind of rural populism—as well as an undying allegiance to the Democratic party—is still alive in rural Texas.

The pivotal event in modern Texas was the east Texas oil strike of the 1930's. Fortunes were made, and what was a basically rural state was transformed by the infusion of people and money. Oil affects every aspect of Texas politics, but its influence can be seen most graphically in the state's smaller cities—these are found in the 17 counties with populations between 50,000 and 100,000. Most of these counties are dominated by glittering, air-conditioned enclaves out in the middle of scrubby farmland or the desert—Tyler, Longview, and Port Arthur in east Texas; Midland, Odessa, Abilene, San Angelo, and Amarillo in west Texas. Political attitudes in these places are usually set by a wealthy, and extremely conservative, white elite. In 1968, the voting patterns in the 17 counties were the near opposite of those found in rural Texas: 42% for Nixon, 34% for Humphrey, and 24% for Wallace. Residual Democratic allegiances are still apparent when the Democratic candidate is a conservative; but the small cities make up that part of Texas where the liberal tag carries the greatest political liability.

The oil boom brought new capital to Texas. With the money here, the more traditional industrialists discovered the development possible in this sunny, labor-rich state. The medium-sized cities of Texas—those in counties with populations between 100,000 and 500,000—have most enjoyed the fruits of the derivative boom. And in these same counties, organized labor, still quite weak statewide, has its greatest local clout. These counties, therefore, constitute the most liberal part of Texas and the most Democratic—at least when the Democratic candidate running is a liberal. These counties also include the cities with the largest proportions of Mexican-Americans: El Paso, Corpus Christi, and Cameron and Hidalgo counties in the lower Rio Grande Valley. Another city in this group is Austin, the state capital and home of the University of Texas. Austin has a vocal and well-organized liberal community which consistently defects to conservative Republicans whenever the Democrats put up a conservative candidate.

Texas' four large cities—Houston, Dallas, San Antonio, and Fort Worth—are the best-known and fastest-growing part of the state. In 1960, the four counties which include these cities had 36% of the state's population; in 1970, 41%. The demographic trend has been most responsible for the growth of Texas' Republican party. Many of the new residents of Houston and Dallas, especially, are conservative Northerners who have always voted Republican; moreover, many of the Southern-born, aspiring white-collar types prefer modern-day Republicanism to the old-style, heavily accented Texas Democracy. But these cities also have large black and Mexican-American minorities; San Antonio, in particular, has an especially large Mexican community. So, taken together, these cities are not as conservative as most people think. Organization by labor, black, and chicano leaders is approaching the level reached by the Republicans. In 1960, John Kennedy lost the four big counties by 82,000 votes; in 1968, Hubert Humphrey, though running somewhat weaker statewide, lost them by only 59,000.

Rural, small city, medium-sized city, and big metropolis Texas make up the structure of Texas politics upon which the various strategies have been played out in recent elections. The most successful strategy, of course, is the conservative-centrist one pioneered by Lyndon Johnson in the late '40's and '50's, and perfected by Gov. John Connally in the '60's. The Tory Democrats of the Johnson-Connally group, with heavy financial support from oil millionaires, usually win the state's Democratic primaries—the most recent one being the one between conservative ex-Rep. (1948–54) Lloyd Bentsen and liberal Sen. (1957–70) Ralph Yarborough.

But on occasion, the winner of the Democratic primary has been defeated by the unlikely combination of conservative Republicans and liberal Democrats. The coalition is, in fact, responsible for the senatorial career of John Tower. In 1960, Tower was a political unknown, a professor at Midwestern University in Wichita Falls (his wife had money); he was a free-market, conservative Republican living in a state with a preference for mildly populistic Democrats. Eisenhower did carry the state twice in the '50's, but this happened primarily because he had the support of conservative Democrats like ex-Gov. Allen Shivers and not so much because of any organized Republican party. In 1960, Tower decided to take on Lyndon Johnson for the Senate; the Texas legislature had passed a bill which allowed Johnson to run for either president or vice president and at the same time stand for reelection to the Senate. The Johnson ploy, combined with Tower's indefatigable campaigning, produced a respectable Tower vote. This made him the clear Republican choice in the race that followed Johnson's resignation in 1961. The Democrat temporarily appointed to the seat was William Blakely, a Dallas oil man generally considered even more conservative than Tower.

Blakely was too much for Texas liberals to stomach, and they decided to back Tower. After all, the liberals reasoned, a conservative Republican would have less power in the Senate than a conservative Democrat, and Tower, unlike a conservative Democrat, could not count on automatic reelection. Moreover, the only way the liberals—who lose most Texas primaries—could convince members of the conservative establishment to support men to their liking was to show them that outright conservatives could not win. The strategy worked. Tower won by a small margin, and the returns made it clear that liberal votes from places like Austin made the difference.

Tower became the first Texas Republican elected to the Senate since 1870. Tower assumed that he was fated to serve one term and be retired by the voters. But as time went on, it appeared that the same liberal-conservative coalition that elected him might come into play again. In 1966, the Democrats ran Waggoner Carr, a conservative who was then state attorney general. Carr was scarcely more acceptable to the liberals than Blakely. Again the liberals balked, and again Tower won—this time by almost 200,000 votes. He carried all the big cities heavily—including San Antonio, with its near-majority Mexican population—and won 57% of the votes in the medium-sized counties, the liberals' strongholds. By comparison, Yarborough had carried 59% of the votes in these counties two years before.

In the Senate, Tower serves on the Armed Services Committee, where he has little reason to differ with pro-military positions taken by its chairman, John Stennis of Mississippi. The Texas Senator is also the ranking minority member of the newly renamed Banking, Housing, and Urban Affairs Committee. Tower, one of the Senate's more articulate and ideological conservatives, has built a fairly solid personal following in Texas. This makes his chance for reelection in 1972 reasonably good. If the Democrats nominate a conservative, he may well pick up liberal votes for a third time; if the Democrats, in a surprise, nominate a liberal, Tower should make big gains in rural

Texas, which is Democratic, but conservative. With Lt. Gov. Ben Barnes, a talented Johnson-Connally protégé in his early thirties, slated for governor, it is unlikely that the Democrats can come up with a senatorial nominee acceptable to both wings of the party. Tower is the favorite, but the liberals might support a conservative Democrat if they thought a Tower defeat would embarrass the Nixon Administration.

The 1970 Senate race was a Texas classic. In the Democratic primary, an aging, 67-year-old, liberal veteran senator, Ralph Yarborough, was pitted against a younger and smoother, 49-year-old challenger, ex-Congressman Lloyd Bentsen. Yarborough first won his seat in a 1957 special election and he won again in 1958 after a wild Texas primary. Although he consistently supported liberal positions in the Senate, Yarborough could mesmerize home audiences with fiery east Texas oratory. In the early '60's, the Senator and Gov. John Connally were having a very bad feud, one which brought President Kennedy to Texas in 1963. And in 1964, only President Johnson's personal intervention spared Yarborough from serious primary opposition.

Perhaps Yarborough had been away from the stump too long. His 1970 campaign, off to a late start, was disorganized and badly underfinanced. Bentsen, a Houston insurance and banking millionaire, had no such problems; he had the support of Connally, and reportedly of Johnson, and the big Houston and Dallas money. Bentsen flooded the airwaves with scenes of disorder at the 1968 Democratic National Convention, implying that Yarborough, an opponent of the Vietnam war, was somehow responsible for the chaos. Because there is no party registration in Texas, conservative Republicans can and often do vote in Democratic primaries, and the result of this primary was close. Bentsen had 841,000 votes and Yarborough, 726,000. But the only places Yarborough could carry were the traditionally liberal, medium-sized cities. Organized labor was unable to produce the kind of margins it wanted, and the Mexican community, reportedly because of factional feuding, cast almost as many votes for Bentsen as for Yarborough.

With the liberals bitter over the results of the primary, it appeared that the general election would go to the Republican candidate, Congressman George Bush. The telegenic Bush was only three years younger than Bentsen, but the Republican projected a much more youthful image. The Bush campaign was never short of money. Nixon strategists apparently considered him their best bet; Bush received $72,000 from the Republican Senatorial Campaign Committee, which was twice as much as anybody else got that year. The candidate also received a visit from Vice President Agnew. Moreover, a liberal group, which called itself the Democratic Rebuilding Committee, campaigned for Bush, and he won the support, or the neutrality, of several important liberal leaders. The Republican and Democrat differed very little on the issues. Bentsen attacked Bush for backing the Nixon family assistance program, while Bush attacked Bentsen for being part of the old-fashioned Democratic power structure. The slogans were more revealing. The Bush ad men came up with "He can do more." The Bentsen people countered with "Texas needs a Democrat in the Senate."

After the primary, LBJ reportedly counseled Bentsen to move to the left on everything except, of course, the war. To some extent, Bentsen did that and picked up the support of black state Sen. Barbara Jordan of Houston, Congressman Henry Gonzalez of San Antonio, and the state AFL-CIO. But the factors which produced the Bentsen victory—with 53% of the vote—were fortuitous. Agnew's visit to the state brought more liberals into the Bentsen camp; the liberals realized that a Bush victory would be hailed as a Nixon-Agnew victory, even if the liberals were responsible for it. Moreover, some of the rural voters were discomforted by the well-circulated rumor that Bush, if elected, would replace Agnew on the 1972 Republican ticket. Finally, the ballot contained a proposal which would have allowed county option liquor-by-the-glass. The idea of that is anathema to voters in traditionally Democratic rural Texas and brought them out in unanticipated numbers.

The expectations were that about 1,800,000 Texans would vote in 1970, up sharply from the 1,500,000 who voted in the previous off-year election. Bush, who had some good organizations in the big cities, figured that he could bring out the bulk of the 900,000 voters he counted on. Turnout was higher in the big cities, where Bush was strong, but much of it represented increased participation by the minorities. And despite the demographic trends, the turnout increased almost as much in the rural areas as it did in the big cities; in the counties under 50,000 Bentsen took 63% of the votes. Bentsen's 174,000-margin in rural Texas far exceeded Bush's 73,000 cumulative margin in the four big cities. In the medium-sized cities, where conservative Carr had won only 43% of the votes in 1966, conservative Bentsen won 56% in this election—a clear indication that liberals did not defect in significant numbers.

Bentsen comes from the lower Rio Grande Valley, an area where wealthy Anglos (WASPs) have traditionally held benevolent sway over the chicano majority. In line with that tradition, Bentsen was a county judge at 25 and a congressman at 27. But unlike Lyndon Johnson, he gave up his congressional career to make more money, and he is presently as comfortably fixed as one expects a Texas senator to be. Since his election, he has denied Nixon Administration claims that he is, ideologically, one of their men. Bentsen opposed the Administration on the SST issue. And on occasion, he has even disagreed publicly with his political mentor, Treasury Secretary Connally. Bentsen's seat seems fairly safe so long as there is a Republican Administration in Washington; Texas liberals would rather swallow him than give Nixon or Agnew any kind of victory. But if the Democrats regain the White House, Bentsen will probably feel obliged to accelerate his slow movement to the left. Otherwise, he will be vulnerable to liberal defections.

The Texas House delegation is probably the most cohesive in Washington. Since the days of Sam Rayburn, Texas congressmen have had a habit of meeting weekly, and when possible, they have also had the habit of voting as a bloc, to increase their already considerable influence in the House. The membership presently includes the chairmen of Banking and Currency, Veterans' Affairs, Agriculture, and Appropriations committees, the chairman of the Democratic Caucus, and members of the Rules and the Ways and Means committees. The principal concern of the Texas delegation is, of course, maintaining the oil depletion allowance at the highest feasible figure. But the Texas congressmen have also been known for sometimes supplying the votes needed to enact liberal legislation.

Traditions crumble, and the cohesiveness of the Texas delegation is not what it once was. Speaker Sam Rayburn died in 1961, and other veteran practitioners of the Rayburn formula—"If you want to get along, go along"—have died or retired in the years since. Within the state, changing population patterns and Supreme Court decisions have reduced the number of rural districts, where congressmen seldom encounter any opposition. And the new urban districts have elected men more fixed to ideological positions; these include conservative Republicans like Jim Collins of Dallas and Bill Archer of Houston, and liberal Democrats like Bob Eckhardt of Houston and Henry Gonzalez of San Antonio.

The 1970 census seemed to require further changes in this direction, but the Texas legislature took care to protect the state's rural, senior congressmen. This was done by "fleshing out" the territory of the veterans with large hunks of urban territory. The Houston and the Dallas-Fort Worth area will each gain one seat for 1972, but since the state picked up one seat in the census, rural Texas lost only one rural district. That loss will produce a pitched battle between Republican Bob Price, now of the 18th, and Democrat Graham Purcell, now of the 13th. But none of the other 21 Texas incumbents should have any trouble in 1972.

Electoral Votes 26

Census Data 1970 pop. 11,196,730; 5.44% of U.S. total, 4th largest; change 1960–70, +16.9%. Metro. 73.5%, 48.2% central city. 1970 per capita income, $3.515; 31st highest. 2nd in number of poor.

1970 Share of Federal Tax Burden $9,327,720,000; 4.78% of U.S. total, 7th largest.

1970 Share of Federal Outlays $11,128,640,496; 5.89% of U.S. total, 3rd largest. Per capita federal spending, $994.

DOD	$5,044,027,000	2nd (8.81%)	HEW	$2,343,629,228	6th (4.48%)
AEC	$25,518,625	18th (0.98%)	HUD	$71,920,956	8th (3.69%)
NASA	$361,271,026	2nd (9.81%)	OEO	$32,822,933	6th (4.32%)
DOT	$336,806,716	4th (4.72%)	DOA	$1,054,852,131	1st (8.32%)
DOC	$37,187,981	8th (3.21%)	POD	$327,954,533	6th (4.50%)
DOI	$75,003,681	9th (3.08%)	VA	$536,141,175	3rd (7.26%)
DOJ	$44,840,006	4th (7.81%)	CSC	$122,029,471	9th (3.03%)
			Other	$714,635,034	

Economic Base Livestock, cotton, and cash grain; aircraft and parts, and other transportation equipment; food and kindred products; crude petroleum and natural gas; nonelectrical machinery, esp. construction, mining, and material handling machinery and equipment; apparel and other finished products made from fabrics and similar materials, esp. men's, youths', and boys' furnishings, work clothing, and allied garments; electrical machinery, equipment, and supplies, esp. communication equipment and electronic components and accessories; fabricated metal products, esp. fabricated structural metal products; chemicals and allied products, esp. industrial inorganic and organic chemicals; printing, publishing, and allied industries, esp. newspapers and commercial printing. Also, higher education, banking, and insurance.

Political Line-up Governor, Preston Smith (D); seat up, 1974. Senators, John G. Tower (R) and Lloyd M. Bentsen (D). Representatives, 23 (20 D and 3 R). State Senate (29 D and 2 R); State House (38 D and 31 R).

The Voters

Registration 4,149,250 total. No party registration.

Employment profile White collar, 41%. Blue collar, 59%.

Ethnic groups Black, 13%. Spanish surname, 15%. Total foreign stock, 11%. Mexico, 7%; Germany, 1%; others, 1%.

Presidential vote

1968	Humphrey (D)	1,266,804	(41%)
	Nixon (R)	1,227,844	(40%)
	Wallace (AIP)	584,269	(19%)
1964	Johnson (D)	1,663,185	(63%)
	Goldwater (R)	958,566	(37%)
1960	Kennedy (D)	1,167,932	(51%)
	Nixon (R)	1,121,699	(49%)

Senator

John Goodwin Tower (R) Elected May 27, 1961, seat up 1972; b. Sept. 29, 1925, Houston; home, Wichita Falls; Southwestern U., B.A., 1948; So. Methodist U., M.A., 1953; U. of London, 1952; Navy, WWII; USNR; married, three children; Methodist.

Career Faculty, Midwestern U., 1951–60; first Repub. to be elected to U.S. Senate from Tex. since 1870, elected to fill vacancy caused by resignation of Sen. Lyndon B. Johnson.

Offices 142 OSOB, 202-225-2934. Also 784 Fed. Office Bldg., 300 E. 8th St., Austin 78701, 512-475-5933, and 1814 Fed. Bldg., 1114 Commerce St., Dallas 75202, 214-749-3441.

Committees

Armed Services (3rd); Subs. (1) Military Construction Authorization, (2) Preparedness Investigating, (3) Strategic Arms Limitation Talks, (4) Ad Hoc on Tactical Air Power.

Banking, Housing, and Urban Affairs (Ranking Mbr.); Subs. (1) Financial Institutions, (2) Housing and Urban Affairs, (3) Production and Stabilization, (4) Securities, (5) Small Business.

Jt. Com. on Defense Production (2nd).

Group Ratings

	ADA	COPE	NREP	NFU	LCV	NAB	NSI	ACA
1970	3	0	0	13	8	90	100	94
1969	0	—	—	38	—	—	—	80
1968	0	0	—	46	—	50	—	94

Key Votes

(1) ABM	FOR	(8) Phil Pln	ABS	(15) Coop-Church	AGN
(2) SST	FOR	(9) Vol Army	AGN	(16) Cut Oil Dpltn	AGN
(3) Busing	AGN	(10) Prison $	AGN	(17) Consumer Prot	AGN
(4) Tob Sub	FOR	(11) Cut Mil $	AGN	(18) Farm Sub Limit	AGN
(5) Carswell	FOR	(12) Defoliatn	FOR	(19) Comp Bid Sales	AGN
(6) No-Knock	FOR	(13) 18-Yr-Vote	AGN	(20) Pre-Prod Tests	AGN
(7) Seniorty	FOR	(14) Pentgn PR	FOR	(21) Cut Marjna Pen	AGN

Election Results

1966 general:	John G. Tower (R)	841,501	(56%)
	Waggoner Carr (D)	643,855	(44%)
1966 primary:	John G. Tower (R), unopposed		
1961 special:	John G. Tower (R)	448,217	(51%)
	William A. Blakely (D)	437,874	(49%)

Senator

Lloyd Millard Bentsen, Jr. (D) Elected 1970, seat up 1976; b. Feb. 11, 1921, Mission; home, Houston; U. of Tex., LL.B., 1942; Army, WWII; married, three children; Presbyterian.

Career Atty., County Judge, Hidalgo County, 1946–48; U.S. House of Reps., Dec. 4, 1948–54.

Offices 115 OSOB, 202-225-5922. Also P.O. Box 61466, Fed. Bldg., Houston 77061, 713-226-5496, and Suite 769 Fed. Bldg., Austin 78731, 512-475-5834.

Committees

Armed Services (9th); Subs. (1) General Legislation, (2) National Stockpile and Naval Petroleum Reserves, (3) Ad Hoc on Research and Development.

Public Works (9th); Subs. (1) Air and Water Pollution, (2) Economic Development, (3) Environmental Science and Technology, (4) Flood Control—Rivers and Harbors.

Jt. Economic Com. (6th); Subs. (1) Economic Progress, (2) Foreign Economic Policy, (3) Inter-American Economic Relationships, (4) International Exchange and Payments.

Group Ratings, Key Votes: Newly elected.

Election Results

1970 general:	Lloyd Bentsen (D)	1,226,568	(53%)
	George Bush (R)	1,071,234	(47%)
1970 primary:	Lloyd Bentsen (D)	841,316	(53%)
	Ralph W. Yarborough (D)	726,477	(47%)

FIRST DISTRICT Political Background

Texas 1 comprises the northeast corner of the state, a part of Texas that is predominantly agricultural. The largest cities here are Marshall (pop. 30,000) and Texarkana (pop. 30,000); another 23,000 residents of Texarkana live over the line in Arkansas. The 1st is a Texas district still characterized by the rough-and-ready rural populism that used to dominate the politics of Texas. Like Jim Hogg, populist governor of Texas in the 1890's, the farmers and the townspeople of the 1st remain suspicious of bankers, insurance companies, oil men, and Republicans. They are also not particularly fond of race-mixers; in 1968, George Wallace almost carried the district.

Since 1929, the 1st has been represented by Wright Patman. He shares many of his constituents' prejudices, except the racial ones; Patman has voted for civil rights legislation. But he is especially suspicious about banks. Patman was born in 1893—the year of the nation's worst crash until 1929—and he combines the attitudes of the farmer who lost his savings in a failing bank and a shrewd lawyer's understanding of the workings of American financial institutions. In most congressmen, the existence of such attitudes would be worth only passing comment. But Wright Patman is chairman of the House Banking and Currency Committee, and has been for the past ten years.

Patman is known for his zealous attacks on the big New York banks and the Federal Reserve Board. He regularly took on former (1951–69) Fed. Chairman William McChesney Martin, who was otherwise something of an untouchable in Washington as well as on Wall Street. Patman has also attacked the big foundations and has helped to bring about significant changes in the legislation under which they exist. And chairman Patman was the man who balked at the Nixon Administration's plan to bail out the Penn Central Railroad. As a result, he can take much of the credit for the road's subsequent bankruptcy and for the revelation of the unsavory practices which followed.

Patman seldom gets all he wants, and his occasional lack of delicacy creates trouble for the programs he espouses. Despite his great seniority—42 years, second among all House members—he is not a part of the inner circle of the House establishment. Among financial people, of course, his ideas are treated with no more respect than those of William Jennings Bryan. Present-day liberals are bemused by the Texan, but tend to dismiss his concerns as dated.

But back home in the 1st district, Wright Patman is king. His constituents gladly forgive him his votes on civil rights and reelect him with overwhelming margins. Although the district gained virtually no population during the '60's, the legislature has been kind to Patman. It drew him a jagged district to keep the conservative cities of Tyler and Longview out of the 1st. Congressman John Dowdy's home county was placed in the district, but Dowdy, currently under indictment, poses no threat to the chairman's tenure. Patman, who will soon pass 80, shows no sign of slowing up. So he will no doubt remain the subject of outraged editorials in the *Wall Street Journal* for years to come. Should he die or retire, his successor will be his son, state Sen. William N. Patman.

Census Data 1970 pop. 404,850; deviation from current state average, −16.8%; change 1960–70, +1.7%. Metro. 16.8%, 7.5% central city.

1970 Share of Federal Outlays $384,087,863

DOD	$164,818,000	HEW	$133,657,745
AEC	$000	HUD	$4,658,775
NASA	$000	OEO	$1,160,100
DOT	$4,106,206	DOA	$19,310,863
		Other	$56,376,169

Federal Military-Industrial Commitments

DOD Contractors Day and Zimmerman (Texarkana), $64.963m: production of tracers, detonators, and boosters and operation of the Lone Star Ammunition plant. Thiokol Chemical Co. (Marshall), $21.629m: production of projectiles and illuminating signals and operation of Longhorn Army Ammunition plant. United Ammunition Container (Atlanta), $6.944m: unspecified.

DOD Installations Red River Army Depot (Texarkana).

Economic Base Livestock and cotton; lumber and wood products other than furniture; ordnance and accessories; fabricated metal products.

The Voters

Registration 161,238 total. No party registration.

Employment profile White collar, 33%. Blue collar, 67%.

Ethnic groups Black, 24%. Spanish surname, 1%. Total foreign stock, 1%. All foreign groups less than 0.5% each.

Presidential vote

1968	Humphrey (D)	48,345	(37%)
	Nixon (R)	35,395	(27%)
	Wallace (AIP)	47,344	(36%)

Representative

Wright Patman (D) Elected March 4, 1929; b. Aug. 6, 1893, Patman's Switch; home, Texarkana; Cumberland U., LL.B., 1916; Army, WWII; married, four children; Baptist.

Career Cotton farmer, 1913–14; Asst. County Atty., 1916–17; Tex. House of Reps., 1921–24; Dist. Atty. 5th Judicial Dist., 1924–29.

Offices 2328 RHOB, 202-225-3035. Also P.O. Box 1868, Texarkana 75501, 214-793-2471.

Committees

Banking and Currency (Chm.); Chm., Sub. on Domestic Finance.

Sel. Com. on Small Business; Chm., Sub. on Foundations: Their Impact on Small Business.

Jt. Com. on Defense Production (Chm.).

Jt. Economic Com. (Vice Chm.); Subs. (1) Chm., Economic Progress, (2) Priorities and Economy in Government.

Group Ratings

	ADA	COPE	NREP	NFU	LCV	CFA	NAB	NSI	ACA
1970	24	45	36	46	11	88	20	86	40
1969	33	—	—	86	—	—	—	—	19
1968	50	83	—	92	—	—	0	—	9

Key Votes

(1) ABM	FOR	(6) 18-Yr-Vote	AGN	(11) Clean Water $	AGN
(2) SST	AGN	(7) Farm Sub Lmt	AGN	(12) Mig Wrkrs Comp	AGN
(3) Phil Pln	AGN	(8) Coop-Church	AGN	(13) Jets to Chiang	ABS
(4) No-Knock	FOR	(9) Family Asst	ABS	(14) State OEO Veto	AGN
(5) Cmutr Tax	FOR	(10) Work Stamps	FOR	(15) Park Logging	FOR

Election Results

1970 general:	Wright Patman (D)	67,883	(78%)
	James Hogan (R)	18,614	(22%)
1970 primary:	Wright Patman (D)	59,479	(77%)
	Bill Russell (D)	17,845	(23%)
1968 general:	Wright Patman (D), unopposed		

SECOND DISTRICT Political Background

Texas 2 is the heart of east Texas. The district comprises a collection of predominantly rural counties that extend from the Louisiana line, almost all the way to Houston in the south, and Dallas in the north. This is the part of Texas most like the Deep South. It was the only Texas district which George Wallace won in 1968, with 37% of the vote. The richest of the east Texas oil fields were found within the boundaries of the 2nd, but for the most part, the money and the industry went elsewhere. The 2nd remains an area of increasingly marginal farms, small courthouse towns, and one significant industrial city, Orange (pop. 24,000)—a Wallace stronghold east of Beaumont on the Louisiana border.

The district's congressman, John Dowdy, was, until recently, a relatively obscure conservative Texas Democrat who had 19 years of seniority. He also had seats on the Judiciary and District of Columbia committees. Then in 1970, Dowdy was indicted on federal bribery, conspiracy, and perjury charges. The case has not yet come to trial; meanwhile, Dowdy has been hospitalized and has played a limited role in the affairs of the 92nd Congress.

Because the Texas Republican party was not clued in on the coming indictment, there was no Republican candidate in the 1970 general election. Nevertheless, a full

25% of the votes were cast for write-in candidates—a clear indication that, whatever the outcome of the trial, Congressman Dowdy is now serving his last term. Moreover, the Texas redistricting has sealed Dowdy's political fate. Only one county was removed from the 2nd; that was Henderson, Dowdy's home county. Since it is now a part of Wright Patman's 1st, Dowdy will have to choose between making a hopeless race against Patman or retire quietly. Most likely he will do the latter. The best bet for the seat in the new 2nd is state Sen. Charles Wilson of Lufkin. The state legislator helped to draw its new boundaries. Another possible candidate is Secretary of State Martin Dies, Jr., whose father once represented the area in the House and founded the House Un-American Activities Committee. There will probably be a spirited Democratic primary in the district, whose outcome cannot be predicted with certainty at this writing.

Census Data 1970 pop. 461,758; deviation from current state average, −5.1%; change 1960–70, +19.1%. Metro. 33.3%, 5.3% central city.

1970 Share of Federal Outlays $201,023,463

DOD	$10,820,000	HEW	$115,930,900
AEC	$000	HUD	$000
NASA	$200,000	OEO	$252,723
DOT	$5,188,464	DOA	$20,241,817
		Other	$48,389,550

Federal Military-Industrial Commitments

None.

Economic Base Livestock and cash grain; lumber and wood products other than furniture; chemicals and allied products; crude petroleum and natural gas.

The Voters

Registration 166,188 total. No party registration.

Employment profile White collar, 32%. Blue collar, 68%.

Ethnic groups Black, 20%. Spanish surname, 1%. Total foreign stock, 2%. All groups less than 0.5% each.

Presidential vote

1968	Humphrey (D)	48,466	(35%)
	Nixon (R)	37,836	(28%)
	Wallace (AIP)	50,961	(37%)

Representative

John Dowdy (D) Elected Sept. 23, 1952; b. Feb. 11, 1912, Waco; home, Athens; E. Tex. Baptist Col., 1929–31; married; Methodist.

Career Practicing atty., Dist. Atty., 3rd Judicial Dist., Tex., 1944–52.

Offices 2301 RHOB, 202-225-2401. Also P.O. Box 791, Athens 75751, 214-675-3022.

Committees

District of Columbia (3rd); Subs. (1) Chm., Education, (2) Business, Commerce, and Fiscal Affairs.

Judiciary (5th); Sub. No. 1.

Group Ratings

	ADA	COPE	NREP	NFU	LCV	CFA	NAB	NSI	ACA
1970	4	17	8	23	0	47	64	100	72
1969	7	—	—	33	—	—	—	—	94
1968	0	0	—	33	—	—	100	—	95

Key Votes

(1) ABM	FOR	(6) 18-Yr-Vote	AGN	(11) Clean Water $	AGN
(2) SST	FOR	(7) Farm Sub Lmt	AGN	(12) Mig Wrkrs Comp	AGN
(3) Phil Pln	AGN	(8) Coop-Church	AGN	(13) Jets to Chiang	FOR
(4) No-Knock	FOR	(9) Family Asst	AGN	(14) State OEO Veto	FOR
(5) Cmutr Tax	AGN	(10) Work Stamps	FOR	(15) Park Logging	FOR

Election Results

1970 general:	John Dowdy (D), unopposed
1970 primary:	John Dowdy (D), unopposed
1968 general:	John Dowdy (D), unopposed

THIRD DISTRICT Political Background

Texas 3 comprises the west side of Dallas, the state's second largest city (pop. 844,000). The district includes many of the city's wealthiest neighborhoods, as well as the fast-growing newer suburbs of Irving and Grand Prairie. Dallas is the most conservative large city in Texas (see state write-up). Houston's wealth is based on oil and heavy industry; Dallas' money, more on oil and high finance. Until recently, Dallas, though smaller, had larger bank deposits than Houston, and it still ranks as the Southwest's leading financial, banking, and insurance center. As a result, there are fewer blue-collar workers and fewer blacks and chicanos in Dallas than in Houston; accordingly, there are fewer liberal voters. Dallas' millionaires are more ostentatious (Neiman Marcus) and more ideological (H. L. Hunt). Dallas is also more Republican; it sent Bruce Alger to the House—the first Texas Republican congressman in recent times—and except for 1964, the city regularly casts huge majorities for Republican presidential candidates.

The 3rd district was created in 1965, when the one-man-one-vote ruling forced the Texas legislature to eliminate a rural district and cede it to Dallas. Its first congressman was Joe Pool, a conservative Democrat who had served the state as its congressman-at-large from 1962 to 1966. Pool, who occasionally made the papers as a member of the House Un-American Activities Committee, died in mid-term. He was succeeded by Republican James M. Collins.

Like all the Republicans who represented Texas in Congress during the '60's, Collins had lost an initial race before winning; he lost to Pool in 1966. And like most Texas congressmen, Collins is a wealthy man (insurance and other ventures). In 1970, he won some notoriety when he fired an assistant who was allegedly involved in a payroll kickback scheme. But for the most part, Collins has blended in well with other conservative Republicans in the House and on the Interstate and Foreign Commerce Committee. He has been increasing his margins of late and seems well on his way toward a long congressional career. The Texas legislature's redistricting plan, which adds heavily Republican Richardson, Highland Park, and north Dallas to the 3rd, gives Collins an utterly safe seat.

Census Data 1970 pop. 559,813; deviation from current state average, +15.0%; change 1960–70, +36.1%. Metro. 100.0%, 66.1% central city.

1970 Share of Federal Outlays $648,390,000 (average outlay per district, Texas 3 and 5)

DOD	$343,791,000	HEW	$110,502,000
AEC	$64,000	HUD	$847,000
NASA	$11,759,000	OEO	$1,176,000
DOT	$17,529,000	DOA	$44,115,000
		Other	$118,607,000

Federal Military-Industrial Commitments (Texas 3 and 5, greater Dallas listing)

DOD Contractors LTV Aerospace (Dallas), $278.364m: production of A-7 aircraft. Texas Instruments (Dallas), $162.308m: radar systems for F-4 aircraft; bomb guidance kits; airborne infrared detecting equipment; guidance for Bulldog missile system. Braniff Airways (Dallas), $34.007m: cargo transport service. Fischbach and Moore (Dallas), $20.462m: special Navy communication equipment. Collins Radio

(Dallas), $13.343m: installation of Naval line-of-sight communication system. Dallas Airmotive (Dallas), $5.547m: unspecified.

DOD Installations Naval Air Station (Dallas).

NASA Contractors LTV Aerospace (Dallas), $7.745m: Scout systems management.

Economic Base Electrical machinery, equipment, and supplies, esp. communication equipment; aircraft and parts, and other transportation equipment; crude petroleum and natural gas; nonelectrical machinery, esp. oil field machinery and equipment; food and kindred products; apparel and other finished products made from fabrics and similar materials.

The Voters

Registration 202,571 total. No party registration.

Employment profile White collar, 49%. Blue collar, 51%.

Ethnic groups Black, 14%. Spanish surname, 6%. Total foreign stock, 7%. Mexico, 3%; Germany, UK, 1% each; others, 1%.

Presidential vote

1968	Humphrey (D)	51,767	(33%)
	Nixon (R)	79,617	(51%)
	Wallace (AIP)	24,068	(16%)

Representative

James M. Collins (R) Elected Aug. 24, 1968; b. April 29, 1916, Hallsville; home, Irving; So. Methodist U., B.S.C., 1937; Northwestern U., M.B.A., 1938; American Col., C.L.U., 1940; Harvard, M.B.A., 1943; Army, WWII; married, three children; Baptist.

Career Pres., Consolidated Industries, Inc., and Intl. Industries, Inc.; Pres., Fidelity Union Life Insurance Co., 1954–65.

Offices 1512 LHOB, 202-225-4201. Also 1112 Fed. Bldg., 1114 Commerce St., Dallas 75202, 214-749-2453.

Committees

Interstate and Foreign Commerce (14th); Sub. on Communications and Power.

Group Ratings

	ADA	COPE	NREP	NFU	LCV	CFA	NAB	NSI	ACA
1970	0	9	0	23	0	40	91	90	84
1969	0	—	—	27	—	—	—	—	100

Key Votes

(1) ABM	FOR	(6) 18-Yr-Vote	AGN	(11) Clean Water $	AGN
(2) SST	FOR	(7) Farm Sub Lmt	ABS	(12) Mig Wrkrs Comp	AGN
(3) Phil Pln	AGN	(8) Coop-Church	AGN	(13) Jets to Chiang	AGN
(4) No-Knock	FOR	(9) Family Asst	AGN	(14) State OEO Veto	FOR
(5) Cmutr Tax	AGN	(10) Work Stamps	FOR	(15) Park Logging	FOR

Election Results

1970 general:	James M. Collins (R)	63,690	(61%)
	John Mead (D)	41,425	(39%)
1970 primary:	James M. Collins (R), unopposed		
1968 general:	James M. Collins (R)	81,696	(60%)
	Robert H. Hughes (D)	55,939	(40%)

FOURTH DISTRICT Political Background

Texas 4 is part of the Red River Valley, a place where a cowboy once found love and then lost it. In politics, the valley has remained staunchly Democratic since it was first settled by white men. This is where Deep South Texas blends into central

Texas; only 15% of the people here are black, as against 25% in the adjoining 1st district to the east. The district was once a land composed entirely of poor white farmers and small market center towns.

The Red River Valley can claim a number of famous sons. Speaker Carl Albert comes from Bug Tussle, just across the river in Oklahoma; President Dwight Eisenhower was born in Denison, in Grayson County (see Pennsylvania 19). But the valley's most fabled son is Mister Sam, Speaker Sam Rayburn, who represented the 4th district in the House of Representatives from 1912 to 1961. Rayburn's career spans almost all of our modern political history. He saw Washington grow from a provincial outpost disdained by Henry Adams to the most powerful city in the world. When the young Texan first came to the House, it had just freed itself from the iron rule of Speaker Joe Cannon; and he left it only a few months after he led, and won, a battle to increase the membership of the Rules Committee. That battle exposed all the fissure that had developed within the Democratic Caucus since Woodrow Wilson's days in the White House. At that time, Wilson and Speaker Champ Clark could enact their entire legislative program with automatic votes from the Democratic Caucus.

"You have to go along to get along," Mister Sam often said, and in saying so, he recognized that the Democratic party, split by civil rights and other social issues, could no longer operate as a cohesive unit. Members of the party, therefore, would just have to take account of the differences that existed among them. Sam Rayburn was Speaker for 17 years, longer than any man; except for the four years that the Republicans controlled the House, Rayburn served in the post, from 1940 until his death in 1961. Critics would say that he did not exert his power often enough or forcefully enough; he would say that he could and still could keep the Democratic party going.

Sam Rayburn also saw nearly all of the modern political history of Texas. In 1912, oil was not yet a major factor in the state's politics; fifty years later, oil dominated everything in the life of the state. Rayburn was most responsible for the cohesiveness of the Texas delegation, and he, as much as anyone, built the politics of oil into the congressional establishment. No anti-oil man, for example, could sit on the tax-writing Ways and Means Committee.

Not only has oil changed Rayburn's Texas, but also demographic shifts have as well. In 1912, towns like Rayburn's Bonham (1970 pop. 7,698) were typical of the state—small, dusty, agricultural market centers. In 1961, when Rayburn came home for the last time, Dallas and Houston had begun to dominate Texas politics. Dallas has even spread its influence into the 4th district; its metropolitan growth extends out into Collin County, which sometimes casts Republican majorities. And since Rayburn's death, the district has been enlarged to include the cities of Tyler and Longview, arch-conservative Republican strongholds, and to include a portion of Dallas County itself.

Rayburn's successor is Ray Roberts, a congressman who was born some three weeks after Mister Sam was first sworn in. Roberts was a state senator at the time of his first election in 1962, and before that, a staff assistant to the Speaker. He is a man out of the Rayburn mold. When Johnson was President, the Administration could usually count on him to deliver liberal votes when needed. But lately, Roberts' record has grown more conservative, reflecting the changing attitudes in his constituency. In 1960, Kennedy carried the 4th, but in 1968, in the redrawn district, Humphrey got only 36% of the vote.

Roberts has never been really tested in the district since it was enlarged. He beat ex-Congressman Lindley Beckworth, who was in the House from 1938 to 1952, and again from 1956 to 1966, in the 1966 primary. The primary, however, took place mainly on the old rural grounds of the 4th; and since 1964, the Republicans have not run anybody against him. Roberts will have to serve in the House until age 98, if he hopes to match Rayburn's tenure. Short of that, Roberts will no doubt win as long as he chooses to run.

Census Data 1970 pop. 492,608; deviation from current state average, +1.2%; change 1960–70, +20.0%. Metro. 65.0%, 22.7% central city.

1970 Share of Federal Outlays $337,568,354

DOD	$125,528,000	HEW	$118,446,801
AEC	$000	HUD	$556,507
NASA	$684,394	OEO	$000

DOT	$3,527,755	DOA	$27,995,504
		Other	$60,829,393

Federal Military-Industrial Commitments

DOD Contractors LTV Electrosystems (Greenville), $56.391m: modification of C-130, C-133, and RF-101 aircraft. R. G. LeTourneau Inc. (Longview), $25.530m: metal parts for 750-pound bombs.

DOD Installations Perrin AFB (Sherman).

Economic Base Livestock and poultry; nonelectrical machinery, esp. service industry machinery; apparel and other finished products made from fabrics and similar materials; crude petroleum and natural gas. Also, some commuting to Texas 3 (Dallas).

The Voters

Registration 185,685 total. No party registration.

Employment profile White collar, 35%. Blue collar, 65%.

Ethnic groups Black, 15%. Spanish surname, 1%. Total foreign stock, 2%. All foreign groups less than 0.5% each.

Presidential vote

1968	Humphrey (D)	48,779	(36%)
	Nixon (R)	49,925	(36%)
	Wallace (AIP)	38,472	(28%)

Representative

Ray Roberts (D) Elected Jan. 30, 1962; b. March 29, 1913, Collin County; home, McKinney; Tex. A & M, N. Tex. State, Tex. U.; Navy, WWII; Capt. USNR; married, one child; Methodist.

Career Staff of Speaker Sam Rayburn, 1940–42; Tex. Senate, 1955–62.

Offices 2455 RHOB, 202-225-6673. Also Rm. 225 Fed. Bldg., McKinney 75069, 214-542-2617, and 105 Smith County Court House, Tyler 75701, 214-597-3222.

Committees

Public Works (11th); Subs. (1) Chm., Rivers and Harbors, (2) Flood Control and Internal Development, (3) Public Buildings and Grounds, (4) Roads, (5) Sp. on Economic Development Programs.

Veterans' Affairs (6th); Subs. (1) Compensation and Pension, (2) Housing.

Group Ratings

	ADA	COPE	NREP	NFU	LCV	CFA	NAB	NSI	ACA
1970	12	34	20	36	38	53	55	100	61
1969	7	—	—	60	—	—	—	—	67
1968	17	23	—	50	—	—	33	—	53

Key Votes

(1) ABM	FOR	(6) 18-Yr-Vote	AGN	(11) Clean Water $	AGN
(2) SST	FOR	(7) Farm Sub Lmt	AGN	(12) Mig Wrkrs Comp	AGN
(3) Phil Pln	AGN	(8) Coop-Church	AGN	(13) Jets to Chiang	ABS
(4) No-Knock	FOR	(9) Family Asst	AGN	(14) State OEO Veto	FOR
(5) Cmutr Tax	AGN	(10) Work Stamps	FOR	(15) Park Logging	AGN

Election Results

1970 general:	Ray Roberts (D), unopposed
1970 primary:	Ray Roberts (D), unopposed
1968 general:	Ray Roberts (D), unopposed

FIFTH DISTRICT Political Background

Texas 5 is the east side of Dallas, the least conservative part of the very conservative city (see Texas 3). It is less conservative because most of the district's black population, which comes to 24%, lives on this side of Dallas. The district, however, is by no means liberal. The balance of power is held by middle-income Dallas homeowners, and these people usually find themselves agreeing with the city's conservative economic elite. The district also includes the high-income University Park and Highland Park enclaves around Southern Methodist University where much of that elite lives.

The political history of the 5th district has been shaped in a special way by an event that is perhaps central to the political history of the 1960's: the assassination here in Dallas of President Kennedy in 1963. For the ten years preceding the murder, Bruce Alger, a Republican, was the congressman from Dallas County; the whole county then formed the 5th district. Alger was a raucous, fiery ideological right-winger who, critics said, accomplished little in Congress except rant at liberals. His moment in American history came in 1960, when he was part of a pushing-and-shoving demonstration against Lyndon and Lady Bird Johnson in a Dallas hotel lobby.

The assassination of the President seemed to produce a politics of remorse among Texans generally, and among Dallas residents in particular. In 1964, LBJ carried the state by a huge majority and even carried Dallas County. The Dallas establishment was in a mood to atone for what seemed to be their city's violent predilections, and memories of the 1960 incident lingered. Bruce Alger was through in Dallas politics. He had won previous elections easily; in 1964, he managed only 43% of the vote—less than Barry Goldwater won in the district.

The winner was Earle Cabell, recently mayor of Dallas, and accordingly, a member in good standing with the city's business and financial elite. The elite, through the Citizens' Charter Association, has dominated Dallas city elections for the past twenty years. Cabell is usually considered a moderate-to-conservative Democrat, though in recent years, conservative would be a better description.

Despite repeated challenges, Cabell has won about 60% of the vote in the last three elections. He has had some problems, though, in the Democratic primary. In 1970, liberal state Sen. Mike McKool gave Cabell a stiff test, winning 46% of the vote. And with the defeat of the CCA in the 1971 mayor's race, it is possible he will run into opposition of this kind in the future. Close to half of the votes cast for Cabell in the general election come from blacks and chicanos. If, therefore, Texas primary laws did not permit conservative Republicans to vote in Democratic primaries, the Congressman might easily lose his seat. In 1971, however, the Texas legislature strengthened Cabell's position in the primary slightly by removing some black precincts from the 5th.

Census Data 1970 pop. 512,175; deviation from current state average, +5.2%; change 1960–70, +23.5%. Metro. 100.0%, 69.4% central city.

1970 Share of Federal Outlays $648,390,000 (average outlay per district, Texas 3 and 5)

DOD	$343,791,000	HEW	$110,502,000
AEC	$64,000	HUD	$847,000
NASA	$11,759,000	OEO	$1,176,000
DOT	$17,529,000	DOA	$44,115,000
		Other	$118,607,000

Federal Military-Industrial Commitments (See Texas 3 for greater Dallas listing.)

Economic Base Electrical machinery, equipment, and supplies, esp. communication equipment; aircraft and parts, and other transportation equipment; crude petroleum and natural gas; nonelectrical machinery, esp. oil field machinery and equipment; food and kindred products; apparel and other finished products made from fabrics and similar materials. Also, banking and insurance.

The Voters

Registration 195,729 total. No party registration.

Employment profile White collar, 51%. Blue collar, 49%.

Ethnic groups Black, 24%. Spanish surname, 2%. Total foreign stock, 5%. Germany, UK, Mexico, 1% each; others, 1%.

Presidential vote

1968	Humphrey (D)	54,664	(39%)
	Nixon (R)	64,402	(46%)
	Wallace (AIP)	21,050	(15%)

Representative

Earle Cabell (D) Elected 1964; b. Oct. 27, 1906, Dallas County; home, Dallas; Tex. A & M, 1925–26; So. Methodist U., 1926; Tex. State Guard, WWII; married, two children; Episcopalian.

Career Salesman, Morning Glory Creameries, Houston, 1926–28; Plant Supt., Mistletoe Creameries, Amarillo, 1928–30; owner Cabell's Dairy, Pine Bluff, Ark., 1930–32; Secy.-Treas., Exec. V.P., Pres., Chm. of Bd., Cabell's Inc., 1932–

Offices 418 CHOB, 202-225-2231. Also Rm. 716, 1114 Commerce St., Dallas 75202, 214-749-3571.

Committees

District of Columbia (9th); Subs. (1) Chm., Business, Commerce, and Fiscal Affairs, (2) Housing and Youth Affairs, (3) Public Health and Welfare.

Science and Astronautics (8th); Subs. (1) Manned Space Flight, (2) Science, Research, and Development.

Sel. Com. on House Restaurant (3rd).

Group Ratings

	ADA	COPE	NREP	NFU	LCV	CFA	NAB	NSI	ACA
1970	12	18	20	50	20	50	60	100	38
1969	0	—	—	54	—	—	—	—	73
1968	8	15	—	29	—	—	33	—	70

Key Votes

(1) ABM	FOR	(6) 18-Yr-Vote	FOR	(11) Clean Water $	AGN
(2) SST	FOR	(7) Farm Sub Lmt	AGN	(12) Mig Wrkrs Comp	AGN
(3) Phil Pln	AGN	(8) Coop-Church	AGN	(13) Jets to Chiang	ABS
(4) No-Knock	FOR	(9) Family Asst	ABS	(14) State OEO Veto	FOR
(5) Cmutr Tax	ABS	(10) Work Stamps	FOR	(15) Park Logging	AGN

Election Results

1970 general:	Earle Cabell (D)	57,058	(60%)
	Frank Crowley (R)	38,481	(40%)
1970 primary:	Earle Cabell (D)	29,787	(54%)
	Mike McKool (D)	25,742	(46%)
1968 general:	Earle Cabell (D)	79,317	(61%)
	Roy Wagoner (R)	49,821	(39%)

SIXTH DISTRICT Political Background

Texas 6 has one of the strangest shapes of any congressional district in the nation. It begins at the southern city limits of Houston, and cuts a tortuous path north to include the southern portions of the cities of Dallas and Fort Worth. Since no nonpolitical body could have devised the monstrosity, there is obviously a political story behind the shape of the 6th. The district is an outgrowth of a much smaller, almost entirely rural district represented by Congressman Olin E. Teague. When redistricting was forced on the Texas legislature, it simply extended the original district at its northern and southern ends as far as necessary to include the requisite number of people. And the 52,000 residents of Fort Bend County—fast becoming an exurban extension of Houston—find themselves joined with 159,000 residents of Tarrant County (Fort Worth), and 61,000 residents of Dallas County (Dallas), some 250 miles to the north. The district lines for 1972 perpetuate the pattern. Although the southern end of the new 6th is no longer so near Houston, its northern end cuts farther into Dallas County (131,000 residents). And the district retains a share of Tarrant County (100,000 residents). As it now stands and as it will stand for the 6th, the city dwellers and suburbanites almost outnumber the rural and small town people of the old core of the district.

In many states, demographic changes of this magnitude would spell trouble for the incumbent congressman—but not in Texas. Congressman Teague has been in the House since 1946, and he has not had a Republican opponent since 1964. In that year, Republicans, sensing a Goldwater landslide, ran a candidate in every district—but Johnson carried the state by a huge margin. Teague's primary opposition is desultory at best.

The virtually uncontested district has allowed "Tiger" Teague to build a strong power base in the House. When he first came to the House, Teague—a wounded and much-decorated World War II veteran—was assigned to the Veterans' Affairs Committee. The assignment is usually shunned because it means having the unpleasant task of turning down grandiose veterans' aid schemes. After the 1954 elections, Teague became chairman of the committee. Most House members seem to think that he has done an equitable job of balancing the claims of veterans with the needs of the Treasury Department. Teague is also the second ranking Democrat on the Science and Astronautics Committee, and chairman of its Manned Space Flight Subcommittee. The Congressman is an enthusiastic supporter of the manned flight program, which is currently in disfavor. But the program, of course, brings in a great deal of federal money to the Houston area; in fact, more NASA money is spent in Houston than at Cape Kennedy.

At the beginning of the 92nd Congress, Teague pulled off a coup and unseated Dan Rostenkowski of Chicago as chairman of the House Democratic Caucus. The Texan's victory was one more of personality than of ideology. Rostenkowski, who had thoughts about running for Majority Leader, did not know that he was going to be challenged for the chairmanship. Meanwhile, Teague—perhaps the premier back-slapper in the House—was able to assemble a coalition of Southerners, conservatives, and personal friends virtually unnoticed. The congressman, who was 60 in 1970, will probably remain in the House for many more years, and some time during those years, he will likely succeed George Miller of California, who was 79 in 1970, as chairman of Science and Astronautics.

Census Data 1970 pop. 563,595; deviation from current state average, +15.8%; change 1960–70, +24.9%. Metro. 75.1%, 32.4% central city.

1970 Share of Federal Outlays $197,883,000

DOD	$8,347,000	HEW	$90,608,000
AEC	$000	HUD	$1,029,000
NASA	$701,000	OEO	$441,000
DOT	$3,881,000	DOA	$47,587,000
		Other	$45,280,000

Federal Military-Industrial Commitments

None.

Economic Base Livestock and cotton; aircraft and parts, and other transportation equipment; food and kindred products, esp. meat products; nonelectrical machinery, esp. construction, mining, and material handling machinery and equipment and service industry machines. Also, higher education (Texas A & M).

The Voters

Registration 209,550 total. No party registration.
Employment profile White collar, 41%. Blue collar, 59%.

Ethnic groups Black, 14%. Spanish surname, 3%. Total foreign stock, 5%. Czech., Germany, Mexico, 1% each; others, 1%.

Presidential vote

1968	Humphrey (D)	60,560	(39%)
	Nixon (R)	60,284	(39%)
	Wallace (AIP)	35,115	(23%)

Representative

Olin E. Teague (D) Elected Aug. 24, 1946; b. April 6, 1910, Woodward, Okla.; home, College Station; Tex. A & M, 1928–32; Army, WWII; Tex. Natl. Guard; married, three children; Baptist.

Career Employed by Post Office, Animal Husbandry Dept., railroad; Supt. U.S. Post Office, College Station, 1932–40.

Offices 2311 RHOB, 202-225-2002.

Committees

Science and Astronautics (2nd); Subs. (1) Chm., Manned Space Flight, (2) NASA Oversight.

Standards of Official Conduct (2nd).

Veterans' Affairs (Chm.)

Group Ratings

	ADA	COPE	NREP	NFU	LCV	CFA	NAB	NSI	ACA
1970	8	0	9	40	14	46	50	100	42
1969	0	—	—	57	—	—	—	—	60
1968	25	18	—	45	—	—	40	—	59

Key Votes

(1) ABM	ABS	(6) 18-Yr-Vote	FOR	(11) Clean Water $	AGN
(2) SST	FOR	(7) Farm Sub Lmt	AGN	(12) Mig Wrkrs Comp	AGN
(3) Phil Pln	ABS	(8) Coop-Church	ABS	(13) Jets to Chiang	ABS
(4) No-Knock	FOR	(9) Family Asst	AGN	(14) State OEO Veto	FOR
(5) Cmutr Tax	AGN	(10) Work Stamps	FOR	(15) Park Logging	FOR

Election Results

1970 general:	Olin Teague (D), unopposed
1970 primary:	Olin Teague (D), unopposed
1968 general:	Olin Teague (D), unopposed

SEVENTH DISTRICT Political Background

Texas 7 comprises the northwest part of Harris County and includes about a third of the city of Houston. This city (pop. 1,232,000) is the largest in Texas and is also, of course, one of the major centers of the oil industry in the world. Houston is somewhat less conservative than Dallas (see Texas 3), but like Dallas, it has a large group of new-rich people, and the newest rich among them are usually the most conservative. Most of both groups live in the 7th district in the comfortable Sharpstown, Westheimer-Post Oak, and Memorial-Spring Branch areas, and in posh River Oaks along the Buffalo Bayou. There are few blacks or Mexican-Americans in this part of town.

So the 7th is Houston's most Republican congressional district. The district did not exist until 1965, when redistricting forced the legislature to create a third Harris County district. Its first congressman was George Bush, an oil millionaire who had been defeated for the Senate by Ralph Yarborough in 1964. Bush, now our ambassador to the United Nations, has an unusual background for a Texas politician. He was born in Connecticut, attended fashionable Eastern schools, and then, after World War II, moved to Texas and made (or added to) his fortune. His father, a prominent investment banker, was senator from Connecticut from 1952 to 1962.

Bush won 53% of the vote and grew so popular among the voters in the district that the Democrats did not even field a candidate in 1968. When he made another bid for the Senate (see state write-up), state Rep. Bill Archer won the Republican nomination, and hence, the election. Archer, a successful businessman, serves on the House Banking Committee, where he no doubt has difficulty comprehending the populist notions of his fellow Texan, chairman Wright Patman (see Texas 1). Archer, tabbed as a comer in the Republican Caucus, was elected to the Chowder and Marching Society, an unofficial rank from whose ranks spring most of the Republican leadership. The legislature's redistricting plan has given Archer an even safer district for 1972.

Census Data 1970 pop. 642,456; deviation from current state average, +32.0%; change 1960–70, +54.2%. Metro. 100.0%, 80.4% central city.

1970 Share of Federal Outlays $393,669,000 (average outlay per district, Texas 7, 8, and 22)

DOD	$58,245,000	HEW	$85,061,000
AEC	$348,000	HUD	$5,933,000
NASA	$110,631,000	OEO	$1,577,000
DOT	$15,350,000	DOA	$14,032,000
		Other	$102,492,000

Federal Military-Industrial Commitments (See Texas 22 for Houston listing.)

Economic Base Nonelectrical machinery, esp. woodworking machinery; fabricated structural metal products and valves and pipe fittings other than plumbers' brass goods; chemicals and allied products, esp. industrial inorganic and organic chemicals.

The Voters

Registration 245,171 total. No party registration.

Employment profile White collar, 51%. Blue collar, 49%.

Ethnic groups Black, 11%. Spanish surname, 6%. Total foreign stock, 10%. Mexico, 3%; Germany, 2%; Italy, UK, 1% each; others, 1%.

Presidential vote

1968	Humphrey (D)	48,329	(30%)
	Nixon (R)	85,546	(53%)
	Wallace (AIP)	28,308	(18%)

Representative

William R. Archer (R) Elected 1970; b. March 22, 1928, Houston; home, Houston; Rice U., 1945–46; U. of Tex., B.B.A., LL.B., 1946–51; USAF, Korean War; Capt. USAFR; married, five children; Catholic.

Career Practicing atty.; rancher; Pres. Uncle Johnny Mills, 1953–61; Councilman, Mayor Pro-Tem, Hunters Creek Village, 1955–62; Tex. House of Reps., 1966–70; V.P. Sierra Club of Houston.

Offices 1608 LHOB, 202-225-2571. Also 5607 Fed. Bldg., Houston 77002, 713-226-4941.

Committees

Banking and Currency (14th); Subs. (1) Bank Supervision and Insurance, (2) Consumer Affairs, (3) International Finance.

Group Ratings, Key Votes: Newly Elected.

Election Results

1970 general:	W. R. Archer (R)	93,457	(65%)
	Jim Greenwood (D)	50,750	(35%)

1970 primary:	W. R. Archer (R)	13,331	(54%)
	Ross Baker (R)	6,119	(25%)
	Dudley Sharp, Jr. (R)	5,381	(22%)

EIGHTH DISTRICT Political Background

Texas 8 comprises the northeast part of Harris County and Houston. It is a predominantly working-class area which contains most of the black and Mexican-American population of Houston. Together, these two groups cast almost a majority of the district's votes. Most of the rest are cast by white union members who usually support liberal candidates, though George Wallace did rather well among these voters in 1968. The 8th is the side of Houston seldom seen by the tourists. Huge oil refineries and chemical plants lie along the badly polluted Houston Ship Channel; and the small, often decrepit homes here contrast sharply with the houses in the air-conditioned sections of the city (see Texas 7).

For nearly 30 years, from 1936 to 1965, Albert Thomas represented the 8th district in Congress. A moderate-to-liberal Democrat, Thomas was a senior member of the Appropriations Committee. It was largely his efforts, and the clout enjoyed by the rest of the Texas delegation, that brought the massive NASA Space Center to Houston. But it was located in the adjoining 22nd district, not here in the 8th.

Thomas was a member in good standing of the get-along-go-along Texas delegation. When he died, his widow won the special election and then retired. And in 1966, Thomas was replaced by quite another kind of politician, Bob Eckhardt. Eckhardt made a name for himself as one of the leading liberal members of the Texas legislature. Texas liberals are a hardy breed of men. They have to be able to lose (since they seldom win anything), and still keep fighting. They have to be able to face down white working-class audiences not far removed from rural, Deep South origins, and at the same time, they must retain the trust of the black and chicano communities. Eckhardt is among the hardiest—and most successful—of Texas liberals. When Thomas died, it was assumed locally that Eckhardt would succeed him; he did, and has won reelection by stunning margins. In 1970, Eckhardt had no Republican opponent, probably because they knew he couldn't be beat, and because they knew a contest in the 8th would bring out many black and Mexican voters devoted to Eckhardt. That would have hurt Republican chances in statewide elections.

Congressman Eckhardt is clearly the most liberal and probably the most scholarly member of the Texas delegation. With Ralph Yarborough gone, Eckhardt has been its only member who has consistently opposed the war in all its phases. He has a middle-seniority seat on the Interstate and Foreign Commerce Committee, where he has fought for proconsumer and other types of liberal legislation. The Texas legislature's redistricting plan will not affect Eckhardt's reelection chances. Although he will lose many of his black constituents to the new 18th district, he has always run well among the Mexican-American and white blue-collar workers who will make up a solid majority of the new 8th.

The congressman from the new 18th is expected to be state Sen. Barbara Jordan, one of the state's leading liberal Democrats. The new district is about half black, and Miss Jordan, if elected, will become the first black representative since Reconstruction out of the old Confederacy.

Census Data 1970 pop. 493,684; deviation from current state average, +1.4%; change 1960–70, +20.4%. Metro. 100.0%, 61.9% central city.

1970 Share of Federal Outlays $393,669,000 (average outlay per district, Texas 7, 8, and 22)

DOD	$58,245,000	HEW	$85,061,000
AEC	$348,000	HUD	$5,933,000
NASA	$110,631,000	OEO	$1,577,000
DOT	$15,350,000	DOA	$14,032,000
		Other	$102,492,000

Federal Military-Industrial Commitments (See Texas 22 for Houston listing.)

Economic Base Nonelectrical machinery, esp. woodworking machinery; fabricated metal products, esp. fabricated structural metal products and valves and pipe fittings other than plumbers' brass goods; chemical and allied products, esp. industrial inorganic and organic chemicals.

The Voters

Registration 165,487 total. No party registration.

Employment profile White collar, 29%. Blue collar, 71%.

Ethnic groups Black, 29%. Spanish surname, 10%. Total foreign stock, 8%. Mexico, 5%; Germany, 1%; others, 1%.

Presidential vote

1968	Humphrey (D)	57,868	(54%)
	Nixon (R)	22,831	(21%)
	Wallace (AIP)	26,061	(24%)

Representative

Bob Eckhardt (D) Elected 1966; b. July 16, 1913, Austin; home, Houston; U. of Tex. B.A., 1935, LL.B., 1939; Army Air Corps, WWII; married, six children; Presbyterian.

Career Practicing atty., 1939–66; Tex. House of Reps., 1958–66.

Offices 1741 LHOB, 202-225-4901. Also Rm. 8632 Fed. Bldg., Houston 77002, 713-226-4931.

Committees

Interstate and Foreign Commerce (16th); Sub. on Commerce and Finance.

Group Ratings

	ADA	COPE	NREP	NFU	LCV	CFA	NAB	NSI	ACA
1970	92	100	93	91	100	95	0	10	0
1969	87	—	—	77	—	—	—	—	6
1968	100	100	—	100	—	—	0	—	0

Key Votes

(1) ABM	AGN	(6) 18-Yr-Vote	FOR	(11) Clean Water $	FOR
(2) SST	AGN	(7) Farm Sub Lmt	AGN	(12) Mig Wrkrs Comp	FOR
(3) Phil Pln	FOR	(8) Coop-Church	FOR	(13) Jets to Chiang	AGN
(4) No-Knock	ABS	(9) Family Asst	FOR	(14) State OEO Veto	AGN
(5) Cmutr Tax	FOR	(10) Work Stamps	AGN	(15) Park Logging	AGN

Election Results

1970 general:	Bob Eckhardt (D), unopposed		
1970 primary:	Bob Eckhardt (D)	31,279	(77%)
	Bobby A. Carley (D)	9,399	(23%)
1968 general:	Bob Eckhardt (D)	63,256	(71%)
	Joe Stevens (R)	26,402	(29%)

NINTH DISTRICT Political Background

Texas 9 comprises the eastern segment of the state's Gulf Coast. It is an area of heavy industry, and an extensive number of installations belonging to the oil industry. The district is dominated by two urban concentrations of roughly equal size. On Galveston Bay, which leads into the Houston Ship Channel, are the cities of Galveston (pop. 61,000) and Texas City (pop. 38,000). Galveston is one of the oldest cities in

Texas. Situated on a sand bar where the bay empties into the Gulf of Mexico, the city was the state's first port and still handles substantial tonnage. To the west, near the Louisiana border, are the cities of Beaumont (pop. 115,000) and Port Arthur (pop. 57,000). Like Galveston and Texas City, these are industrial towns dominated politically by white working-class migrants from the rural South. Because organized labor has as much influence here as anywhere in the state, the 9th district ordinarily gives heavy support to liberal Democrats. It is also one that defects to Republicans like John Tower whenever the Democrats nominate a conservative candidate (see state write-up). But on occasion, the Southern origin of the 9th's blue-collar voters shows itself. In 1968, the district gave George Wallace 25% of its votes, one of his best showings in Texas.

Before the 1965 redistricting, Galveston-Texas City and Beaumont-Port Arthur were in separate districts. Clark Thompson, who was congressman from 1933 to 1934, and then again from 1947 to 1966, was the older of the two incumbents thrown into the new 9th. He decided to retire, and left the seat to Congressman Jack Brooks, who still occupies it. Brooks is a Texas congressman in the Rayburn tradition; he often, but not always, takes liberal positions on the issues and stays close to the position of the leadership. Brooks' rather liberal voting record was quite noteworthy in the early '60's, when his district included some of the arch-segregationist counties of rural east Texas. Now that he has a somewhat more liberal constituency, he is voting more often with the conservatives. Congressman and constituency appear to be converging.

Only 30 when first elected to Congress in 1952, Brooks was considered a future House leader. But the surfeit of men from Texas, Oklahoma, and Louisiana in Democratic leadership positions has closed off this avenue of advancement for Brooks. And the seniority system has not yet rewarded him with a chairmanship. He is currently the 4th ranking Democrat on the House Judiciary Committee, where he voted for all the civil rights legislation of the '60's in spite of his constituency. The congressman also serves as the 2nd ranking member of Government Operations, whose chairman, Chet Holifield of California, shows no inclination to retire. All this probably annoys Brooks, but back home, reelection poses no problem for him. The redistricting plan does not significantly alter the shape of his district.

Census Data 1970 pop. 426,772; deviation from current state average, —12.3%; change 1960–70, +7.7%. Metro. 97.1%, 64.1% central city.

1970 Share of Federal Outlays $327,951,696

DOD	$127,929,000	HEW	$86,748,264
AEC	$000	HUD	$73,816
NASA	$185,323	OEO	$1,078,282
DOT	$12,303,843	DOA	$10,843,156
		Other	$88,790,012

Federal Military-Industrial Commitments

DOD Contractors Mobil Oil (Beaumont), $82.976m: petroleum products.

Economic Base Petroleum refining and related industries; chemicals and allied products, esp. industrial inorganic and organic chemicals; fabricated metal products; cotton, livestock, and cash grain. Also, insurance.

The Voters

Registration 187,939 total. No party registration.

Employment profile White collar, 38%. Blue collar, 62%.

Ethnic groups Black, 23%. Spanish surname, 7%. Total foreign stock, 9%. Mexico, 3%; Germany, Czech., Italy, UK, 1% each; others, 1%.

Presidential vote

1968	Humphrey (D)	57,290	(43%)
	Nixon (R)	43,297	(32%)
	Wallace (AIP)	33,475	(25%)

Representative

Jack Brooks (D) Elected 1952; b. Dec. 18, 1922, Crowley, La.; home, Beaumont; Lamar Jr. Col., 1939–41; U. of Tex., B.J., 1943, J.D., 1949; USMC, WWII; married, two children; Methodist.

Career Tex. House of Reps., 1946–50; atty., admitted to bar, 1949; elected by Tex. House Dem. Delegation as Majority Whip, 1964– .

Offices 2239 RHOB, 202-225-6565. Also 230 Fed. Bldg., Beaumont 77701, 713-832-8539, and Rm. 204, Fed. Bldg., Galveston 77550, 713-762-2733.

Committees

Government Operations (2nd); Chm., Sub. on Government Activities.

Judiciary (4th); Sub. No. 5.

Jt. Com. on Congressional Operations (Chm.).

Group Ratings

	ADA	COPE	NREP	NFU	LCV	CFA	NAB	NSI	ACA
1970	36	75	36	90	55	76	18	67	29
1969	33	—	—	93	—	—	—	—	13
1968	58	92	—	94	—	—	0	—	0

Key Votes

(1) ABM	ABS	(6) 18-Yr-Vote	FOR	(11) Clean Water $	AGN
(2) SST	AGN	(7) Farm Sub Lmt	AGN	(12) Mig Wrkrs Comp	FOR
(3) Phil Pln	AGN	(8) Coop-Church	AGN	(13) Jets to Chiang	AGN
(4) No-Knock	FOR	(9) Family Asst	AGN	(14) State OEO Veto	AGN
(5) Cmutr Tax	FOR	(10) Work Stamps	FOR	(15) Park Logging	ABS

Election Results

1970 general:	Jack Brooks (D)	57,180	(64%)
	Henry Pressler (R)	31,483	(36%)
1970 primary:	Jack Brooks (D), unopposed		
1968 general:	Jack Brooks (D)	71,937	(61%)
	Henry Pressler (R)	46,829	(39%)

TENTH DISTRICT Political Background

Texas 10 is the LBJ congressional district. Congressman Lyndon B. Johnson represented the 10th from 1937 to 1948. Since that time, redistricting has changed the shape of his old district, but in many respects it is the same kind of central Texas country that shaped the young Texan's career. As one moves west out of east Texas, the towns are farther apart, the trees become scarcer, and the raising of livestock becomes more important than farming. In short, it becomes drier.

Most of the counties in the 10th are still dominated politically by the staunchly Democratic descendants of the original migrants from the South. There are also traces of the Texas German settlements, which date back to the 1850's. The Germans have been Republican since the days before the Civil War; they considered it immoral to hold slaves and during the war, supported the cause of Union. Even today certain central Texas counties invariably cast heavy Republican margins. There was an exception, however, in 1964, when a native son was running for president.

The present 10th includes all the landmark's of Lyndon Johnson's life. These include the town of Johnson City, in Blanco County; the LBJ Ranch; Southwest Texas State Teachers College at San Marcos, in Hays County; and Austin, the state capital and the home of the Lyndon B. Johnson Library and of KTBC, the cornerstone of the Johnson family fortune.

Austin (pop. 251,000) has grown substantially since Johnson represented the 10th, and today it contains more than half of the district's residents. Unlike most of the state's cities, Austin is not an oil town, or an industrial town, or even a farm market town. Instead, it is dominated by growth industries: state government and, to an increasing extent, the University of Texas. An economic base like this, of course, attracts white-collar intellectual people. And so Austin has not only been the headquarters of LBJ's operations, but also of Texas liberalism. The capital city is the home of *The Texas Observer,* an irreverent periodical devoted to the shenanigans of Texas politicians.

Austin and Travis County always turn in large Democratic majorities for liberal candidates. But when the nominee is a conservative, they invariably go Republican. The strategy is to swing pivotal votes to punish the Democrats for nominating conservative candidates—and it often works. In 1966, for example, Travis County cast 62% of its votes for Republican Sen. John Tower; two years earlier it gave liberal Democratic Sen. Ralph Yarborough 57%. In 1970, Travis was one of the few Texas counties to go for Republican George Bush over conservative Democrat Lloyd Bentsen. But this time, fewer liberals defected, because many of them feared that a Bush win would be taken as a victory for Nixon and Agnew (see state write-up).

Although the Austin liberals have had some effect on statewide races—forcing conservative Democratic nominees a little to the left—they remain a negligible force in 10th district congressional politics. Johnson was succeeded in the House by Homer Thornberry, a moderate-to-liberal Democrat who was appointed to the federal bench in 1963. Judge Thornberry was Johnson's nominee to fill the Supreme Court seat that would have been vacated had Abe Fortas been confirmed as Chief Justice. No one took exception to Thornberry's performance as a judge, but his nomination smacked of cronyism and may have been one of the reasons Fortas was rejected by the Senate.

Thornberry's successor is a member of the Texas Democratic party establishment, J. J. (Jake) Pickle. Congressman Pickle, like ex-Gov. John Connally and many other Texas politicians, is a Johnson loyalist whose views on many domestic issues are decidedly more conservative than those of his mentor. Since Johnson left office, Pickle's liberal votes have become increasingly rare, both on roll call votes and in the Interstate and Foreign Commerce Committee. Pickle has never had to deal with serious opposition at home. His two predecessors could have been reelected for life if they had not gone on to bigger things. And Pickle, like most Texas congressmen, can look forward to indefinite reelection.

Census Data 1970 pop. 505,544; deviation from current state average, +3.8%; change 1960–70, +21.5%. Metro. 58.5%, 49.8% central city.

1970 Share of Federal Outlays $546,405,884

DOD	$121,541,000	HEW	$199,833,974
AEC	$973,985	HUD	$1,455,871
NASA	$1,470,013	OEO	$4,908,652
DOT	$27,166,842	DOA	$44,504,097
		Other	$144,551,450

Federal Military-Industrial Commitments

DOD Contractors Texas Instruments (Austin), $26.422m: photo interpretation equipment for evaluating aerial film. Tracor, Inc. (Austin), $5.852m: engineering services for submarine sonar systems. University of Texas (Austin), $5.005m: unspecified research.

DOD Installations Bergstrom AFB (Austin).

Economic Base Cotton and livestock; printing, publishing, and allied industries, esp. commercial printing; food and kindred products. Also, higher education (University of Texas); state government.

The Voters

Registration 225,636 total. No party registration.

Employment profile White collar, 40%. Blue collar, 60%.

Ethnic groups Black, 13%. Spanish surname, 12%. Total foreign stock, 13%. Mexico, 5%; Germany, 3%; Czech., 2%; Sweden, 1%; others, 1%.

Presidential vote

1968	Humphrey (D)	67,709	(48%)
	Nixon (R)	54,549	(38%)
	Wallace (AIP)	19,848	(14%)

Representative

J. J. (Jake) Pickle (D) Elected Dec. 24, 1963; b. Oct. 14, 1913, Roscoe; home, Austin; U. of Tex., B.A., 1938; Navy, WWII; married, three children; Methodist.

Career Area Dir., Natl. Youth Admin., 1939–41; Co-organizer, KVET Radio, Austin; public relations and advertising business; Dir., Texas Dem. Exec. Com., 1957–60; Texas Employment Commission, 1961–63.

Offices 231 CHOB, 202-225-4865. Also 774 Fed. Bldg., Austin 78701, 512-475-5921.

Committees

Interstate and Foreign Commerce (8th); Sub. on Transportation and Aeronautics.

Group Ratings

	ADA	COPE	NREP	NFU	LCV	CFA	NAB	NSI	ACA
1970	16	50	18	62	0	59	73	90	47
1969	20	—	—	73	—	—	—	—	35
1968	42	67	—	75	—	—	25	—	28

Key Votes

(1) ABM	ABS	(6) 18-Yr-Vote	FOR	(11) Clean Water $	AGN
(2) SST	FOR	(7) Farm Sub Lmt	AGN	(12) Mig Wrkrs Comp	AGN
(3) Phil Pln	AGN	(8) Coop-Church	AGN	(13) Jets to Chiang	FOR
(4) No-Knock	FOR	(9) Family Asst	AGN	(14) State OEO Veto	AGN
(5) Cmutr Tax	AGN	(10) Work Stamps	FOR	(15) Park Logging	FOR

Election Results

1970 general:	J. J. Pickle (D), unopposed		
1970 primary:	J. J. Pickle (D), unopposed		
1968 general:	J. J. Pickle (D)	85,037	(62%)
	Ray Gabler (R)	51,933	(38%)

ELEVENTH DISTRICT Political Background

Texas 11 lies in the heart of Texas. The district consists of 11 counties, slightly off the geographical center of the state, but just about at the center of its population. It includes two good-sized cities, Waco (pop. 95,000) and Temple (pop. 33,000), and a huge Army base, Fort Hood (pop. 33,000). The rest of the district is classic Texas agricultural country, given over to cotton, livestock, and occasional small towns. The political sentiment among the people here is solidly Democratic. They prefer conservative Democrats of the Connally stripe, but they are willing to go along with the ticket, no matter how liberal. In 1966, the 11th was the only congressional district that Republican John Tower could not carry. And in 1968, the 11th cast 51% of its votes for Hubert Humphrey; this was more than the Democrat got in all but four Texas congressional districts—two of them in liberal urban areas and the two others, heavily Mexican-American. Only 14% of the people here are black, a smaller percentage than is found in east Texas. Accordingly, there is less segregationist feeling in the 11th and continuing Democratic strength.

Since 1936, Texas newspapermen have had little trouble predicting the winner in the 11th district. That's when W. R. (Bob) Poage first ran. The last time the Republicans put up somebody in the 11th—that was 1964—Poage took 81% of the vote. The Republicans probably won't try again until he retires. Poage's career nicely illustrates the workings of the seniority system. He had an utterly safe district and was willing to wait 30 years. He became chairman of the House Agriculture Committee in 1966, when Harold Cooley of North Carolina failed to win reelection. A decisive victory in 1936 and a little patience have given chairman Poage as much authority over the nation's farm programs as any man in the country.

For the most part, Poage lines up with the conservative Southern Democrat-Republican majority which controls the Agriculture Committee. The chairman has been unsympathetic to liberals who want to extend surplus food distribution and food stamp programs to the poor; he has, at the same time, been quite content with the subsidy programs which give certain rich farmers and planters hundreds of thousands of dollars annually for not planting certain crops.

What the seniority system has given, it is unthinkable that the House—or the voters of the 11th district—will take away. Poage, who was 71 in 1970, will surely remain chairman of Agriculture for as long as he likes.

Census Data 1970 pop. 431,179; deviation from current state average, −11.4%; change 1960–70, +10.6%. Metro. 34.2%, 22.1% central city.

1970 Share of Federal Outlays $543,893,619

DOD	$290,605,000	HEW	$106,031,440
AEC	$454	HUD	$5,895,157
NASA	$000	OEO	$583,951
DOT	$72,339,998	DOA	$31,766,288
		Other	$36,671,331

Federal Military-Industrial Commitments

DOD Contractors Alcoa (Rockdale), $17.700m: aluminum powder bomb explosive.

DOD Installations Fort Hood AB (Killen).

Economic Base Cotton and livestock; apparel and other finished products made from fabrics and similar materials; food and kindred products.

The Voters

Registration 150,240 total. No party registration.

Employment profile White collar, 38%. Blue collar, 62%.

Ethnic groups Black, 14%. Spanish surname, 5%. Total foreign stock, 8%; Mexico, Germany, 2% each; Czech., 1%; others, 1%.

Presidential vote

1968	Humphrey (D)	56,813	(51%)
	Nixon (R)	34,121	(30%)
	Wallace (AIP)	21,498	(19%)

Representative

William Robert (Bob) Poage (D) Elected 1936; b. Dec. 28, 1899, Waco; home, Waco; U. of Tex.; U. of Colo., Baylor U., B.A., 1921, LL.B., 1924, LL.D., 1967; Navy, WWII; married; Unitarian.

Career Practicing atty., 1924–36; Tex. House of Reps., 1925–29; Tex. Senate, 1931–37.

Offices 2107 RHOB, 202-225-6105. Also 205 Fed. Bldg., Waco 76701, 817-752-7271.

Committees

Agriculture (Chm.); Chm., Sub. on Conservation and Credit.

Group Ratings

	ADA	COPE	NREP	NFU	LCV	CFA	NAB	NSI	ACA
1970	8	27	20	36	38	64	64	100	55
1969	0	—	—	55	—	—	—	—	62
1968	8	25	—	40	—	—	50	—	62

Key Votes

(1) ABM	ABS	(6) 18-Yr-Vote	AGN	(11) Clean Water $	AGN
(2) SST	FOR	(7) Farm Sub Lmt	AGN	(12) Mig Wrkrs Comp	AGN
(3) Phil Pln	ABS	(8) Coop-Church	AGN	(13) Jets to Chiang	ABS
(4) No-Knock	ABS	(9) Family Asst	AGN	(14) State OEO Veto	FOR
(5) Cmutr Tax	AGN	(10) Work Stamps	FOR	(15) Park Logging	AGN

Election Results

1970 general:	W. R. Poage (D), unopposed		
1970 primary:	W. R. Poage (D), unopposed		
1968 general:	W. R. Poage (D)	78,127	(97%)
	Laurel N. Dunn (Ind.)	2,807	(4%)

TWELFTH DISTRICT Political Background

Texas 12 comprises most of the city of Fort Worth and its northern suburbs in Tarrant County. Fort Worth and Dallas, only 30 miles apart, are often considered twin cities, but Dallas (pop. 844,000) long ago eclipsed Fort Worth (pop. 393,000) in size and wealth. Fort Worth is more blue-collar than Dallas: the smaller city has fewer blacks and more white working-class people. And because the Texas labor movement has a good deal of strength in Fort Worth, the city usually ends up in the Democratic column. Fort Worth is notable also for its defense plants, the most important of which are General Dynamics, which produced the F-111 (TFX), and Bell Helicopter, which produced many, if not most, of the helicopters used in the Vietnam war. Because of these two concerns, the 12th district of Texas received as much money from the federal government as any congressional district in the country. The outlay in fiscal 1970 for the Defense Department alone was nearly $1.4 billion, a figure not much below the amount spent for all federal operations in the entire state of Oregon.

James C. (Jim) Wright has been the congressman from the 12th since 1954. During his first years in the House, Wright was the foremost liberal in the Texas delegation, and he remains a staunch liberal on economic issues. On foreign policy, however, Wright lined up behind Johnson's moves in Vietnam, and in 1969 sponsored a resolution which was widely interpreted as an endorsement of the Nixon Administration's Vietnam policy.

For some time, Wright has had ambitions for statewide office. He was expected to challenge Sen. John Tower in 1966, but because he could not win the big money support necessary for a statewide campaign in Texas, he decided to remain in the House. Here, despite many years of service, Wright has been rather unlucky playing the seniority game. He is the 4th ranking Democrat on the Public Works Committee, where he has little chance of becoming chairman in the near future; the congressman also holds a comparatively low ranking seat on Government Operations. Back home in the 12th, Wright is comfortably ensconced, with no Republican opposition since 1964 and little threat of a strong primary challenge.

Census Data 1970 pop. 557,126; deviation from current state average, +14.4%; change 1960–70, +27.0%. Metro. 100.0%, 51.7% central city.

1970 Share of Federal Outlays $1,686,655,000

DOD	$1,374,198,000	HEW	$121,487,000
AEC	$662,000	HUD	$13,050,000
NASA	$1,036,000	OEO	$1,213,000
DOT	$39,018,000	DOA	$12,119,000
		Other	$123,873,000

Federal Military-Industrial Commitments

DOD Contractors General Dynamics (Fort Worth), $884.544m: production of F-111 aircraft. Bell Aerospace and Bell Helicopter Co. Divs., Textron (Fort Worth), $314.555m: production, maintenance, and modification of UH-1N helicopters and AH-1J helicopters. Taro Inc. (Arlington), $6.944m: unspecified.

DOD Installations Carswell AFB (Fort Worth).

Economic Base Livestock and cotton; aircraft and parts, and other transportation equipment; food and kindred products, esp. meat products; nonelectrical machinery, esp. construction, mining, and material handling machinery and equipment, and service industry machines. Also, higher education (University of Texas at Arlington); banking and insurance.

The Voters

Registration 184,468 total. No party registration.

Employment profile White collar, 44%. Blue collar, 56%.

Ethnic groups Black, 14%. Spanish surname, 4%. Total foreign stock, 5%. Mexico, 2%; Germany, UK, 1% each; others, 1%.

Presidential vote

1968	Humphrey (D)	61,672	(47%)
	Nixon (R)	53,349	(40%)
	Wallace (AIP)	16,950	(13%)

Representative

James C. Wright, Jr. (D) Elected 1954; b. Dec. 22, 1922, Fort Worth; home, Fort Worth; Weatherford Col., U. of Tex.; Army, WWII; married, four children; Presbyterian.

Career Partner in trade extension and advertising firm; Tex. House of Reps.; Mayor of Weatherford; Pres., League of Tex. Municipalities, 1953.

Offices 2459 RHOB, 202-225-5071. Also 9A-10 Lanham Fed. Office Bldg., Fort Worth 76102, 817-334-3212.

Committees

Government Operations (15th); Subs. (1) Foreign Operations and Government Information, (2) Legislation and Military Operations, (3)Legal and Monetary Affairs.

Public Works (4th); Subs. (1) Chm., Investigations and Oversight, (2) Flood Control and Internal Development, (3) Public Buildings and Grounds, (4) Rivers and Harbors, (5) Roads.

Group Ratings

	ADA	COPE	NREP	NFU	LCV	CFA	NAB	NSI	ACA
1970	32	67	36	92	86	83	18	80	35
1969	33	—	—	86	—	—	—	—	17
1968	25	69	—	88	—	—	0	—	48

Key Votes

(1) ABM	FOR	(6) 18-Yr-Vote	FOR	(11) Clean Water $	FOR
(2) SST	FOR	(7) Farm Sub Lmt	ABS	(12) Mig Wrkrs Comp	FOR
(3) Phil Pln	ABS	(8) Coop-Church	AGN	(13) Jets to Chiang	AGN
(4) No-Knock	FOR	(9) Family Asst	AGN	(14) State OEO Veto	AGN
(5) Cmutr Tax	ABS	(10) Work Stamps	FOR	(15) Park Logging	AGN

Election Results

1970 general:	James C. Wright (D), unopposed
1970 primary:	James C. Wright (D), unopposed
1968 general:	James C. Wright (D), unopposed

THIRTEENTH DISTRICT Political Background

Texas 13 is made up of two very different regions of the state. The larger portion—with about two-thirds of the population and the votes—consists of several tiers of counties along the Red River Valley. This area contains two major cities, Wichita Falls (pop. 97,000) and Denton (pop. 39,000), but it is otherwise rural and small town. The 100th parallel, which has traditionally been used to separate arable from desert land, passes through the district. And much of the land here is barren, suitable only for grazing livestock or drilling for oil. For much of 1970 and 1971, the 13th suffered a drought as severe as the one of the Dust Bowl years. The ranchers and farmers of the district, many of them operating marginal concerns, were driven deeply in debt or off the land. The drought was broken in mid-summer of 1971, but running cows and growing cotton have made few people much money of late, rain or no rain.

This part of the 13th, like the rest of the Red River Valley, is staunchly Democratic as a matter of long-standing tradition. In 1968, the Red River counties produced a surprising 45–37 plurality for Hubert Humphrey. The remaining third of the district presents a contrast. To meet population requirements, the northern part of Dallas County was appended to the 13th in 1965. This is an extremely wealthy, extremely conservative area where many of Dallas' nouveau-riche millionaires live, in what some in Boston or Philadelphia would call tasteless splendor. The Dallas portion of the 13th gave Richard Nixon a huge 68–23 margin over Humphrey in 1968, and this margin swung the district as a whole into the Republican column.

A situation like this obviously raises a potential threat to the tenure of Congressman Graham Purcell, a usually conservative Democrat from Wichita Falls. Purcell was first elected in 1962 to replace ex-Rep. (1951–61) Frank Ikard, who resigned to take a much higher-paying job lobbying for the American Petroleum Institute. In the old, predominantly rural 13th, Purcell had no problem winning reelection; in 1964, for example, he won 75% of the vote.

But in the current district, Purcell has had to face strong Republican challenges every time out—an uncommon lot for most Texas congressmen. The election in 1968 produced the closest race. Dallas County Commissioner Frank Crowley (who ran in the 5th district in 1970) took 66% of the Dallas County votes. Purcell won only because he had 67% of the votes in the rest of the district. The congressman did better in 1970—65% district-wide—but he has never carried Dallas County.

That county will not be a problem for Purcell in 1972, because the legislature has removed it from the district. But the congressman will run into even more trouble under the new arrangement. He has been thrown into the same district with Republican Bob Price of the 18th district. The new 13th extends from the Texas panhandle to a point near Dallas. If one takes the total congressional vote cast in 1968 (the last time both districts were contested), the Republicans come out with a 12,000-vote, 54–46 edge.

Purcell's strongest card will be his seniority on the House Agricultural Committee. He is currently the 6th ranking Democrat on the committee and chairman of its Livestock and Grains Subcommittee—one of vital importance to many of his constituents. Because the committee's senior Democrats are considerably older, Purcell has a reasonably good chance of some day becoming chairman of the full committee. Price, on the other hand, is a junior member of the Republican minority on Agriculture. Moreover, he is likely to be hurt by the discontent on the Great Plains with the farm programs of the Nixon Administration. The farm issue will probably decide the election, which should be close.

Census Data 1970 pop. 505,617; deviation from current state average, +3.9%; change 1960–70, +28.4%. Metro. 71.9%, 37.7% central city.

1970 Share of Federal Outlays $316,510,000

DOD	$132,141,000	HEW	$82,115,000
AEC	$31,000	HUD	$622,000
NASA	$31,000	OEO	$365,000
DOT	$12,184,000	DOA	$46,074,000
		Other	$42,946,000

Federal Military-Industrial Commitments

DOD Contractors Intercontinental Mfg. (Garland), $17.452m: Mark 82 500-pound bomb bodies. Collins Radio (Richardson), $16.057m: shipboard radar and communications systems. Crescent Precision (Garland), $11.724m: SUU-30 bomb dispensers. Space Corp. (Garland), $7.386m: jet engine test stands. Varo Inc. (Garland), $5.006m: electrical bomb fuzes; 40-mm image intensifier assemblies.

Economic Base Livestock and cotton; crude petroleum and natural gas; electrical machinery, equipment, and supplies; food and kindred products. Also, higher education (North Texas State College), and some commuting to Texas 3 (Dallas).

The Voters

Registration 197,122 total. No party registration.

Employment profile White collar, 45%. Blue collar, 55%.

Ethnic groups Black, 5%. Spanish surname, 2%. Total foreign stock, 5%. Germany, UK, 1% each; others, 1%.

Presidential vote

1968	Humphrey (D)	57,924	(38%)
	Nixon (R)	70,847	(46%)
	Wallace (AIP)	24,255	(16%)

Representative

Graham Purcell (D) Elected Jan. 27, 1962; b. May 5, 1919, Archer City; home, Wichita Falls; Tex. A & M, B.S., 1946; Baylor U., LL.B., 1949; Army, WWII; Lt. Col. USAR; married, four children; Presbyterian.

Career Practicing atty., 1949–55; Judge, 89th Judicial Dist. of Tex., 1955–62; Judge, Juvenile Ct., Wichita County, 1955–62.

Offices 120 CHOB, 202-225-3605. Also 206 Fed. Bldg., Wichita Falls 76301, 817-766-0286, and Rm. 2804, 6211 West Northwest Highway, Dallas 75225, 214-749-3889.

Committees

Agriculture (6th); Subs. (1) Chm., Livestock and Grains, (2) Department Operations, (3) Family Farms and Rural Development.

Post Office and Civil Service (13th); Subs. (1) Investigations, (2) Postal Facilities and Mail.

Group Ratings

	ADA	COPE	NREP	NFU	LCV	CFA	NAB	NSI	ACA
1970	12	27	18	30	0	63	50	79	61
1969	—	—	—	53	—	—	—	—	58
1968	—	27	—	64	—	—	—	—	—

Key Votes

(1) ABM	ABS	(6) 18-Yr-Vote	AGN	(11) Clean Water $	AGN
(2) SST	FOR	(7) Farm Sub Lmt	AGN	(12) Mig Wrkrs Comp	AGN
(3) Phil Pln	AGN	(8) Coop-Church	AGN	(13) Jets to Chiang	AGN
(4) No-Knock	FOR	(9) Family Asst	AGN	(14) State OEO Veto	FOR
(5) Cmutr Tax	AGN	(10) Work Stamps	ABS	(15) Park Logging	FOR

Election Results

1970 general:	Graham B. Purcell (D)	80,070	(65%)
	Joe Staley (R)	43,319	(35%)

1970 primary:	Graham B. Purcell (D), unopposed		
1968 general:	Graham B. Purcell (D)	83,839	(56%)
	Frank Crowley (R)	66,477	(44%)

FOURTEENTH DISTRICT Political Background

Texas 14 occupies most of the state's Gulf Coast. This area, like most of Texas, gets very hot in the summer time. Most of the residents live in port cities protected from the Gulf of Mexico by sandy barrier islands. There are a great number of oil refineries and chemical plants in the Brazosport area, due south of Houston, and around Victoria, Port Lavaca, and the district's largest city, Corpus Christi (pop. 204,000). The 14th is where south Texas begins; the district has relatively few blacks, only 7%, and, particularly towards the south in Corpus Christi, a large number of Mexican-Americans. Still, the chicano minority here is smaller and less important politically than in the neighboring 15th and 23rd districts. The black-white issue, which remains an important feature of politics in east Texas, has little influence here, and the district is one of the more liberal parts of Texas on economic issues.

The 14th's current congressman, John Young, has been in office since 1956. Young's vote was once firmly a part of the majorities fashioned by Speakers Sam Rayburn and John McCormack to support liberal legislation, and as a result, Young earned a seat on the House Rules Committee. Lately, he has voted less often with the liberals, a change perhaps due to his attitudes on the war. Congressman Young has given solid support to the Vietnam policies of both the Johnson and Nixon administrations. Like many of the dwindling band of economic liberals who share such views, he seems to have fallen away from the antiwar liberals on other issues as well. Young's voting record sits well in the 14th; he has not had any serious trouble at the polls for some time. He will surely be reelected for years to come, but it is unlikely, given the ages of men who outrank him on Rules, that he will ever become chairman of the committee.

Census Data 1970 pop. 511,050; deviation from current state average, +5.0%; change 1960–70, +13.7%. Metro. 76.9%, 40.0% central city.

1970 Share of Federal Outlays $377,640,768

DOD	$157,166,000	HEW	$82,400,223
AEC	$000	HUD	$143,000
NASA	$17,602	OEO	$1,054,960
DOT	$12,062,711	DOA	$38,715,589
		Other	$86,080,683

Federal Military-Industrial Commitments

DOD Contractors Coastal States Petrochemical (Corpus Christi), $24.784m: petroleum products. Amerada Hess (Corpus Christi), $8.314m: petroleum products. Southwestern Oil (Corpus Christi), $6.294m: petroleum products.

DOD Installations Naval Hospital (Corpus Christi). Naval Air Station (Corpus Christi).

Economic Base Livestock, cotton, and cash grain; chemicals and allied products, esp. industrial inorganic and organic chemicals; crude petroleum and natural gas.

The Voters

Registration 194,640, total. No party registration.

Employment profile White collar, 38%. Blue collar, 62%.

Ethnic groups Black, 7%. Spanish surname, 30%. Total foreign stock, 14%. Mexico, 10%; Czech., Germany, 1% each; others, 1%.

Presidential vote

1968	Humphrey (D)	72,452	(50%)
	Nixon (R)	48,963	(34%)
	Wallace (AIP)	23,142	(16%)

Representative

John Young (D) Elected 1956; b. Nov. 10, 1916, Corpus Christi; home, Corpus Christi; St. Edward's U., B.A., 1937; U. of Tex., 1937–40; married, five childern; Catholic.

Career Practicing atty., 1940– ; Asst. County Atty., Nueces County, 1947–50; County Atty., 1951–52; County Judge, 1953–56.

Offices 2419 RHOB, 202-225-2831. Also 311 Fed. Bldg., Corpus Christi 78401, 512-883-5511, ext. 348.

Committees

Rules (7th).

Jt. Com. on Atomic Energy (4th); Subs. (1) Chm., Communities, (2) Raw Materials, (3) Research, Development, and Radiation, (4) Security.

Group Ratings

	ADA	COPE	NREP	NFU	LCV	CFA	NAB	NSI	ACA
1970	24	64	27	69	50	78	18	89	38
1969	20	—	—	79	—	—	—	—	19
1968	50	92	—	94	—	—	20	—	5

Key Votes

(1) ABM	ABS	(6) 18-Yr-Vote	FOR	(11) Clean Water $	AGN
(2) SST	FOR	(7) Farm Sub Lmt	AGN	(12) Mig Wrkrs Comp	AGN
(3) Phil Pln	AGN	(8) Coop-Church	AGN	(13) Jets to Chiang	FOR
(4) No-Knock	FOR	(9) Family Asst	AGN	(14) State OEO Veto	AGN
(5) Cmutr Tax	AGN	(10) Work Stamps	AGN	(15) Park Logging	FOR

Election Results

1970 general:	John Young (D), unopposed
1970 primary:	John Young (D), unopposed
1968 general:	John Young (D), unopposed

FIFTEENTH DISTRICT Political Background

Texas 15 comprises the southernmost part of the state, the lower valley of the Rio Grande and the adjacent Gulf Coast. Most of the population of the district is concentrated in a narrow strip of land along the Mexican border. Here the near-desert land has been irrigated and the farms worked by Mexican-American field hands. Their standard of living can be considered decent only in comparison with what they remember of rural Mexico. The men who run the lower Rio Grande, the Anglo (WASP) bankers and lawyers and big landowners, operate out of the string of towns just north of the river—Brownsville, Harlingen, McAllen, Edinburg, and Mission. In the northern part of the district lies the King Ranch, still the largest such operation in the world.

The Mexican-American vote keeps the 15th Democratic in national elections. Some of the counties to the north of the district are heavily Mexican and heavily Democratic. But there is a substantial conservative, Anglo vote in the more thickly populated counties of Cameron and Hidalgo to the south. Mexican-Americans form a majority of the district's population, but until recently only men from the Anglo landowner class have represented the area in the House. Among them was Richard Kleberg, owner of the King Ranch, who was there from 1931 to 1944 and who hired young Lyndon Johnson as an assistant in the early '30's. Lloyd Bentsen, currently the U.S. senator from the state, was the district's congressman from 1948 to 1954. Bentsen, who as *patron* (boss man), was elected county judge at 25 and congressman at 27. Finally, there was Joe M. Kilgore, in the House from 1954 to 1964, and a political ally of Gov. John Connally and the ruling Texas Tory Democrat establishment.

In 1964, Kilgore retired from the House, eager to take on liberal Sen. Ralph Yarborough. He was dissuaded from doing so, it was reported, only by Lyndon Johnson himself. Kilgore's successor was the district's first Mexican-American congressman, Eligio de la Garza. De la Garza, who usually lines up with the moderate-to-conservative majority of the Texas delegation, is not a favorite among the militant younger generation of chicanos. Nevertheless, he wins in the 15th whenever he has opposition, and will probably remain in the House for some time. He is currently the 8th ranking Democrat on the House Agriculture Committee. His chances for the chairmanship are not too good, but he should become chairman of the important Cotton Subcommittee in a few years.

Census Data 1970 pop. 406,035; deviation from current state average, —16.6%; change 1960–70, —2.9%. Metro. 79.3%, 42.3% central city.

1970 Share of Federal Outlays $251,097,810

DOD	$31,138,000	HEW	$80,318,550
AEC	$2,102,684	HUD	$7,423,963
NASA	$000	OEO	$3,306,068
DOT	$830,932	DOA	$51,857,215
		Other	$105,227,260

Federal Military-Industrial Commitments

DOD Installations Naval Air Station (Kingsville).

Economic Base Cotton and livestock; canned and preserved fruits, vegetables, and seafood.

The Voters

Registration 143,646 total. No party registration.

Employment profile White collar, 33%. Blue collar, 67%.

Ethnic groups Black, 1%. Spanish surname, 67%. Total foreign stock, 40%. Mexico, 37%; Germany, 1%; others, 1%.

Presidential vote

1968	Humphrey (D)	50,487	(57%)
	Nixon (R)	32,628	(37%)
	Wallace (AIP)	6,095	(7%)

Representative

Eligio de la Garza (D) Elected 1964; b. Sept. 22, 1927, Mercedes; home, Mission; Edinburg Jr. Col.; St. Mary's U., LL.B., 1952; Navy, WWII, Korean War; married, three children; Catholic.

Career Practicing atty., 1952–64; Tex. House of Reps., 1952–64.

Offices 319 CHOB, 202-225-2531. Also 804 Quince, McAllen 78501, 512-682-5545.

Committees

Agriculture (8th); Subs. (1) Conservation and Credit, (2) Cotton.

Merchant Marine and Fisheries (19th); Subs. (1) Coast Guard, Coast and Geodetic Survey and Navigation, (2) Fisheries and Wildlife Conservation, (3) Oceanography, (4) Sp. on Maritime, (5) Education and Training.

Group Ratings

	ADA	COPE	NREP	NFU	LCV	CFA	NAB	NSI	ACA
1970	28	70	36	69	67	59	38	100	40
1969	40	—	—	80	—	—	—	—	23
1968	37	69	—	92	—	—	17	—	29

Key Votes

(1) ABM	FOR	(6) 18-Yr-Vote	FOR	(11) Clean Water $	AGN
(2) SST	AGN	(7) Farm Sub Lmt	AGN	(12) Mig Wrkrs Comp	FOR
(3) Phil Pln	AGN	(8) Coop-Church	AGN	(13) Jets to Chiang	ABS
(4) No-Knock	ABS	(9) Family Asst	FOR	(14) State OEO Veto	AGN
(5) Cmutr Tax	AGN	(10) Work Stamps	FOR	(15) Park Logging	AGN

Election Results

1970 general:	Eligio de la Garza (D)	54,498	(76%)
	Ben A. Martinez (R)	17,049	(24%)
1970 primary:	Eligio de la Garza (D), unopposed		
1968 general:	Eligio de la Garza (D), unopposed		

SIXTEENTH DISTRICT Political Background

Texas 16 is a district separated from the rest of Texas. The 16th comprises, in rough terms, Texas west of the Pecos River. The district is, for the most part, an unpopulated desert; one county here has 1,964 residents. Some 83% of the 16th's population lives in El Paso County (pop. 359,000). The city of El Paso is a long way from Austin, Texas; in fact, it is closer to the state capitals of Santa Fe, in New Mexico, and Phoenix, in Arizona. To the south lie the mountains of the Big Bend National Park.

El Paso is an American desert Sun Belt city that mushroomed during the years following World War II. It is filled with retirees, Mexican immigrants, and other people in one way or another dependent on military installations. Here in the district is the Biggs Air Force Base and the Fort Bliss Military Reservation, which stretches north into the New Mexico desert. The city, after Detroit, San Diego, and Buffalo, is the nation's largest border metropolitan area; Ciudad Juarez, Mexico, just south of the Rio Grande, is almost as large as El Paso itself.

In many ways, political alignments in El Paso resemble those of New Mexico more than those of Texas. Normally, the moderates of rural Texas descent and the large Mexican-American minority combine to produce Democratic majorities. The votes of these two groups are not significantly affected by the votes cast in the rest of the district. This was not so, however, before the 1965 redistricting; before that action by the legislature, the 16th included the intensely conservative oil oases of Midland and Odessa, which often tilted the district's balance to the Republicans.

The 16th is one of the few Texas districts that has changed partisan hands in recent years, and that can be explained entirely by the Billy Sol Estes scandal of 1962. Estes, a businessman from the small desert town of Pecos in the eastern part of the district, was caught defrauding the Department of Agriculture. Because he had been a liberal contributor to several prominent Texas Democrats, the Republicans smelled a political issue. One of the recipients of Estes' generosity was the 16th's then-congressman, J. T. Rutherford, who had been in the House since 1954. He was a moderate Democrat, who is perhaps best remembered as an employer of the former editor of *Harper's*, Larry L. King. Ed Foreman, meanwhile, trumpeted the Estes-Rutherford connection up and down the district, and the Goldwater Republican won the congressional seat here in 1962.

Foreman's tenure was short-lived. In 1964, the congressman was ousted by Democrat Richard C. White, the current incumbent. Foreman later left for New Mexico and made a name for himself in that state's 2nd district. White is a Texas moderate; he has a notably liberal record on civil rights (only 3% of the people here are black), and a conservative record on foreign and military policy (not surprising given the DOD money spent in the 16th). White currently holds middle seniority seats on the Armed Services and the Post Office and Civil Service committees. In a few years, he will probably move up to important subcommittee chairmanships. Since Foreman left for New Mexico, White's opposition has been negligible, and redistricting has not affected the political character of his district.

Census Data 1970 pop. 434,298; deviation from current state average, −10.8%; change 1960–70, +10.0%. Metro. 82.7%, 74.2% central city.

1970 Share of Federal Outlays $480,368,305

DOD	$242,760,000	HEW	$88,343,494
AEC	$000	HUD	$739,707
NASA	$209,457	OEO	$1,745,729
DOT	$39,485,327	DOA	$38,146,549
		Other	$68,938,042

Federal Military-Industrial Commitments

DOD Contractors McKee General Contractor (El Paso), $15.964m: hospital construction. Navaho Refining (El Paso), $6.755m: petroleum products. Standard Oil of California (El Paso), $6.730m: petroleum products. Continental Oil (El Paso), $5.917m: petroleum products.

DOD Installations Fort Bliss AB (El Paso). Biggs Air Force Base.

Economic Base Men's, youths', and boys' furnishings, work clothing, and allied garments; livestock and cotton; crude petroleum and natural gas. Also, higher education (University of Texas at El Paso).

The Voters

Registration 123,619 total. No party registration.

Employment profile White collar, 45%. Blue collar, 55%.

Ethnic groups Black, 3%. Spanish surname, 41%. Total foreign stock, 33%. Mexico, 27%; Germany, 1%; others, 2%.

Presidential vote

1968	Humphrey (D)	40,979	(46%)
	Nixon (R)	38,442	(43%)
	Wallace (AIP)	10,391	(12%)

Representative

Richard Crawford White (D) elected 1964; b. April 29, 1923, El Paso; home, El Paso; U. of Tex. at El Paso; U. of Tex. at Austin, B.A., 1946, LL.B., 1949; USMC, WWII; married, three children; Episcopalian.

Career Practicing atty., 1949–64; Tex. House of Reps., 1955–58; El Paso County Dem. Chm., 1962–63.

Offices 322 CHOB, 202-225-4831. Also 146 U.S. Courthouse, El Paso 79901, 915-533-9351, ext. 5330.

Committees

Armed Services (17th); Sub. No. 3.

Post Office and Civil Service (9th); Subs. (1) Employee Benefits, (2) Manpower and Civil Service, (3) Retirement, Insurance Health Benefits.

Group Ratings

	ADA	COPE	NREP	NFU	LCV	CFA	NAB	NSI	ACA
1970	32	64	42	75	38	70	42	90	47
1969	33	—	—	86	—	—	—	—	29
1968	25	39	—	75	—	—	40	—	47

Key Votes

(1) ABM	FOR	(6) 18-Yr-Vote	FOR	(11) Clean Water $	AGN
(2) SST	FOR	(7) Farm Sub Lmt	AGN	(12) Mig Wrkrs Comp	AGN
(3) Phil Pln	FOR	(8) Coop-Church	AGN	(13) Jets to Chiang	FOR
(4) No-Knock	FOR	(9) Family Asst	FOR	(14) State OEO Veto	AGN
(5) Cmutr Tax	AGN	(10) Work Stamps	FOR	(15) Park Logging	AGN

Election Results

1970 general:	Richard C. White (D)	54,617	(83%)
	J. R. Provencio (R)	11,420	(17%)

1970 primary:	Richard C. White (D)	41,142	(68%)
	Raymond Telles (D)	19,664	(32%)
1968 general:	Richard C. White (D)	62,491	(74%)
	Don Slaughter (R)	22,510	(27%)

SEVENTEENTH DISTRICT Political Background

Texas 17 comprises the geographical heart of the state: acres and acres of arid farming and grazing land west of Dallas and Fort Worth and north of San Antonio.The district has only two urban centers of any size, Abilene (pop. 89,000) and Big Spring (pop. 28,000). Both are rather conservative towns, whose economy is based on oil. The surrounding countryside is traditionally Democratic, and despite conservative trends, the district continues to turn in Democratic majorities in presidential elections, as well as statewide contests. In the Texas tradition, local and congressional elections are seldom contested; incumbents, once in, usually have only nominal opposition.

This has certainly been true of the district's congressman, Omar Burleson, an ex-FBI agent and congressional aide. Burleson, like so many veterans—among them John F. Kennedy and Richard M. Nixon—returned home after World War II and won a seat in Congress. Burleson has been there ever since, one of the more conservative members of the Texas delegation.

Burleson's career in the House exemplifies just how important the oil industry is in Texas politics. For several years, Burleson was a committee chairman (House Administration). Despite his rise to what most congressmen would consider the pinnacle of a political career, Burleson wanted another committee assignment, which would require him to give up the chairmanship. The Texas congressman wanted a seat on Ways and Means. This committee writes all tax legislation, which means that it determines the oil depletion allowance—set by tradition at 27½%. When Congressman Clark Thompson retired in 1966, the "Texas seat" on the committee became open, and Burleson was the Texas delegation's choice to fill it. House liberals had other ideas, and in an unusual election, the Democratic Caucus chose Congressman Jacob H. Gilbert of New York over Burleson by one vote.

So Burleson had to bide another two years as chairman. He finally won the seat after the 1968 elections. The former chairman now sits contentedly as the 10th ranking member of the Ways and Means Committee. Ironically, it was only after Burleson won back the Texas seat that the depletion allowance was finally reduced, to 25%, in the Tax Reform Act of 1969. Burleson will of course win reelection as a matter of routine, but at his age—he was 64 in 1970—he now has no hope of ever again becoming a chairman.

Census Data 1970 pop. 406,897; deviation from current state average, −16.4%; change 1960–70, −3.6%. Metro. 28.0%, 22.0% central city.

1970 Share of Federal Outlays $418,386,806

DOD	$154,113,000	HEW	$123,386,977
AEC	$000	HUD	$425,000
NASA	$000	OEO	$945,948
DOT	$13,784,865	DOA	$69,669,512
		Other	$56,061,509

Federal Military-Industrial Commitments

DOD Contractors Southern Airways (Fort Wolters), $34.701m: training of helicopter pilots and aircraft maintenance. American Petrofina (Big Spring), $5.902m: petroleum products.

DOD Installations Fort Wolters (Mineral Wells). Dyess AFB (Abilene). Webb AFB (Big Spring).

Economic Base Livestock and cotton; crude petroleum and natural gas; food and kindred products.

The Voters

Registration 131,890 total. No party registration.

Employment profile White collar, 37%. Blue collar, 63%.

Ethnic groups Black 4%. Spanish surname, 6%. Total foreign stock, 5%. Mexico, 2%; Germany, 1%; others, 1%.

Presidential vote

1968	Humphrey (D)	56,547	(44%)
	Nixon (R)	49,137	(38%)
	Wallace (AIP)	23,633	(18%)

Representative

Omar Burleson (D) Elected 1946; b. March 19, 1906, Anson; home, Anson; Abilene Christian Col., 1924–26; Hardin Simmons U., 1926–27; Cumberland U., 1927–29; Navy, WWII; married; Church of Christ.

Career Atty., Jones County, 1931–35; County Judge, 1935–41; Sp. Agent, FBI, 1940–41; Secy., Rep. Sam Russell, 1941–42; Gen. Counsel, Natl. Capital Housing Auth., 1942.

Offices 2369 RHOB, 202-225-6605. Also New Fed. Bldg., Rm. 2101, 3rd and N. Pine Sts., Abilene 79601, 915-673-7221.

Committees

Ways and Means (10th).

Group Ratings

	ADA	COPE	NREP	NFU	LCV	CFA	NAB	NSI	ACA
1970	0	17	0	42	22	28	83	100	72
1969	0	—	—	23	—	—	—	—	88
1968	8	9	—	33	—	—	100	—	86

Key Votes

(1) ABM	FOR	(6) 18-Yr-Vote	AGN	(11) Clean Water $	AGN
(2) SST	FOR	(7) Farm Sub Lmt	AGN	(12) Mig Wrkrs Comp	AGN
(3) Phil Pln	AGN	(8) Coop-Church	AGN	(13) Jets to Chiang	FOR
(4) No-Knock	FOR	(9) Family Asst	AGN	(14) State OEO Veto	FOR
(5) Cmutr Tax	ABS	(10) Work Stamps	FOR	(15) Park Logging	FOR

Election Results

1970 general:	Omar Burleson (D), unopposed
1970 primary:	Omar Burleson (D), unopposed
1968 general:	Omar Burleson (D), unopposed

EIGHTEENTH DISTRICT Political Background

Texas 18 comprises the Texas panhandle, the northernmost section of the state. It is the only part of Texas that will have a blizzard move across it in the winter time. The eastern boundary of the panhandle is the 100th parallel, traditionally taken as the line between arable and arid land. The 18th, therefore, is pretty dry country to start with. And for much of 1970 and 1971, there was a bad drought, which had the ranchers worried. No rain meant no grass for the white-faced Herefords they run out here; this breed of beef animal is a tough one, but it can only hold out so long. When the weather gets bad, the ranchers have to sell off their stock on a market not to their liking, or sell out completely. But in the summer of 1971, the dry spell broke. It rained nearly everyday for better than a month, and the people seemed happier about things.

The main city of the panhandle is Amarillo (pop. 127,000), which has a large air force base just out of town. The city, a conservative bastion, has had problems lately as the farming and ranching, drought or no drought, have become less and less profitable in this part of Texas.

The panhandle is the most Republican part of rural Texas. Its politics are much more like those found in northwest Oklahoma and western Kansas than with the diehard Democrats of central Texas (see Kansas 1 and Oklahoma 6). In 1964, the 18th was the Texas district that Barry Goldwater came closest to carrying. Its congressman from 1950 to 1966 was a conservative Democrat, Walter Rogers. Rogers faced several stiff Republican challenges in the early '60's and decided to retire in 1966. Bob Price, a Republican who had lost to Rogers in 1964, won the seat with a solid 59% over a Democrat named Dee D. Miller.

Price won reelection in 1968 by an even greater margin, and in 1970, the Democrats didn't run a candidate in the district—they didn't want to bring panhandle Republican votes out with a close Senate race on. Price sits on the Agriculture and the Science and Astronautics committees in the House, and he has compiled a very conservative voting record.

Redistricting has created problems for the Congressman. Population shifts in the state forced the legislature to eliminate one rural district. And it decided to combine Price's 18th with Democrat Graham Purcell's 13th. The portions of the district that are new to Price are staunchly Democratic counties in the Red River Valley. Price does have the edge on the basis of past performance (see Texas 13). But if the farm programs of the Nixon Administration remain unpopular among the rural residents, Price could have trouble.

Census Data 1970 pop. 390,710; deviation from current state average, −19.7%; change 1960–70, −6.1%. Metro. 37.0%, 32.5% central city.

1970 Share of Federal Outlays $439,488,917

DOD	$31,350,000	HEW	$74,495,274
AEC	$15,000,000	HUD	$1,400,000
NASA	$000	OEO	$1,340,674
DOT	$13,419,637	DOA	$218,892,705
		Other	$83,335,840

Federal Military-Industrial Commitments

DOD Contractors Bell Helicopter Div., Textron (Amarillo), $6.305m: repair of Vietnam crash-damaged UH-1 and AH-1G helicopters.

AEC Operations Mason and Hanger (Amarillo), $14.083m: Pantex Plant.

Economic Base Cash grain, cotton, and livestock; crude petroleum and natural gas; petroleum refining.

The Voters

Registration 154,670 total. No party registration.

Employment profile White collar, 38%. Blue collar, 62%.

Ethnic groups Black, 4%. Spanish surname, 5%. Total foreign stock, 4%. Germany, Mexico, 1% each; others, 1%.

Presidential vote

1968	Humphrey (D)	38,032	(29%)
	Nixon (R)	66,410	(50%)
	Wallace (AIP)	27,689	(21%)

Representative

Robert Dale (Bob) Price (R) Elected 1966; b. Sept. 7, 1927, Reading, Okla.; home, Pampa; Okla. State U., B.S., 1951; USAF, Korean War; married, three children; Baptist.

Career Rancher.

Offices 507 CHOB, 202-225-3706. Also Box 2476, Pampa 79065, 806-665-2351, and 310 Post Office Bldg., Amarillo 79105, 806-376-5151, ext. 381.

Committees

Agriculture (9th); Subs. (1) Cotton, (2) Livestock and Grains.

Science and Astronautics (7th); Subs. (1) Manned Space Flight, (2) NASA Oversight, (3) Space Sciences and Applications.

Group Ratings

	ADA	COPE	NREP	NFU	LCV	CFA	NAB	NSI	ACA
1970	4	0	0	8	0	32	89	100	86
1969	0	—	—	28	—	—	—	—	79
1968	0	0	—	19	—	—	100	—	95

Key Votes

(1) ABM	FOR	(6) 18-Yr-Vote	AGN	(11) Clean Water $	AGN
(2) SST	FOR	(7) Farm Sub Lmt	AGN	(12) Mig Wrkrs Comp	AGN
(3) Phil Pln	FOR	(8) Coop-Church	AGN	(13) Jets to Chiang	FOR
(4) No-Knock	FOR	(9) Family Asst	AGN	(14) State OEO Veto	FOR
(5) Cmutr Tax	AGN	(10) Work Stamps	FOR	(15) Park Logging	FOR

Election Results

1970 general:	Robert D. Price (R), unopposed		
1970 primary:	Robert D. Price (R), unopposed		
1968 general:	Robert D. Price (R)	81,715	(65%)
	J. R. Brown (D)	43,568	(35%)

NINETEENTH DISTRICT Political Background

Texas 19 takes in part of the flat, dusty plains and distant treeless skylines of west Texas. The small towns and ranching areas of the district, which never had many people, are now in general economic and population decline. Two oil cities, Lubbock (pop. 149,000) and Midland (pop. 59,000), dominate the district. Both grew rapidly in the years following World War II, but recently neither has grown at all. So the aura of boom, which not too long ago characterized the 19th, is gone. In 1971, a tornado devastated downtown Lubbock, as if the elements were part of the conspiracy of bad times, and as if the elements were reclaiming this air-conditioned town from the confident men who built it up.

The voters of the 19th district have the privilege of sending to the House of Representatives one of its most senior and most powerful members, George H. Mahon. Mahon was district attorney in Mitchell County (now no longer in the district) when he was first elected to Congress in 1934. Since the death of Clarence Cannon of Missouri in 1964, Mahon has been chairman of the House Appropriations Committee. He also serves as the chairman of its Defense Subcommittee. These two posts give him as much influence as any man in Congress over the federal budget.

Most observers consider Mahon, a tall, slender man who does not look his age (70 in 1970), a fair-minded, responsible chairman, and also a congressman who works hard and knows his field of specialty as well as anyone on the hill. Mahon's specialty, of course, is the defense budget. Mahon's general leaning is conservative—against high federal spending. Over the years, the chairman has been responsible for cuts in the defense budget, as well as in domestic programs. Liberals have complained that he cuts too deeply into domestic programs and not deeply enough into Pentagon requests. Mahon sometimes uses his influence to keep heavy spenders off the committee. Freshman are rarely appointed to Appropriations, and seats are a great prize among junior members.

Like Wilbur Mills of Ways and Means, Mahon has a fine sense of what the House will and will not accept. So he tailors his bills so that they will win acceptance on the floor. There is seldom a serious floor fight over an appropriations bill—the recent ones against the SST are a notable exception. The contents of a bill are determined in the Appropriations Committee and in conference committees, since the Senate usually votes for higher spending. Mahon has great influence in both forums. The Texas congressman is a nice example of the way power in the House works: outside of Washington, D.C., or the 19th district of Texas, the Congressman would look like just any other man in the street. But George Mahon has more to say about what this country will and will not do than dozens of better known political figures.

Mahon, of course, has absolutely no trouble winning elections in the 19th district. The last time the Republicans fielded a candidate—1964—the chairman took 78% of the vote. In recent years, the 19th has been voting more conservative, particularly since heavily Republican Midland was added to the 19th in the 1965 redistricting. The addition in 1971 of half of Odessa, Midland's twin city, to the district makes it even more conservative. So sometime in the future, when Mahon is not the Democratic candidate, the Republicans might well win the seat.

Census Data 1970 pop. 388,606; deviation from current state average, —20.2%; change 1960–70, —0.8%. Metro. 63.0%, 53.7% central city.

1970 Share of Federal Outlays $360,162,619

DOD	$51,530,000	HEW	$59,800,957
AEC	$55,586	HUD	$6,923,627
NASA	$152,702	OEO	$737,516
DOT	$4,145,977	DOA	$180,590,494
		Other	$56,225,760

Federal Military-Industrial Commitments

DOD Installations Reese AFB (Lubbock).

Economic Base Cotton; crude petroleum and natural gas; food and kindred products. Also, higher education (Texas Tech.).

The Voters

Registration 145,853 total. No party registration.

Employment profile White collar, 41%. Blue collar, 59%.

Ethnic groups Black, 7%. Spanish surname, 12%. Total foreign stock, 6%. Mexico, 4%; all other groups less than 0.5%.

Presidential vote

1968	Humphrey (D)	36,848	(31%)
	Nixon (R)	55,781	(47%)
	Wallace (AIP)	25,690	(22%)

Representative

George H. Mahon (D) Elected 1934; b. Sept. 22, 1900, Haynesville, La.; home, Lubbock; Simmons U., B.A., 1924; U. of Texas, LL.B., 1925, U. of Minn., 1925; married, one child; Methodist.

Career Practicing atty., 1925– ; County Atty., Mitchell County, 1926; Dist. Atty., 32nd Jud. Dist., 1927–34; Regent, Smithsonian Institution.

Offices 2314 RHOB, 202-225-4005. Also P.O. Bldg., Lubbock 79408, 806-763-1611.

Committees

Appropriations (Chm.); Chm., Sub. on Defense.

Jt. Com. on Reduction of Federal Expenditures (Chm.).

Group Ratings

	ADA	COPE	NREP	NFU	LCV	CFA	NAB	NSI	ACA
1970	8	18	9	62	20	67	67	90	58
1969	0	—	—	64	—	—	—	—	50
1968	33	39	—	63	—	—	33	—	43

Key Votes

(1) ABM	FOR	(6) 18-Yr-Vote	AGN	(11) Clean Water $	AGN
(2) SST	FOR	(7) Farm Sub Lmt	AGN	(12) Mig Wrkrs Comp	AGN
(3) Phil Pln	AGN	(8) Coop-Church	AGN	(13) Jets to Chiang	FOR
(4) No-Knock	FOR	(9) Family Asst	AGN	(14) State OEO Veto	ABS
(5) Cmutr Tax	AGN	(10) Work Stamps	FOR	(15) Park Logging	FOR

Election Results

1970 general:	George H. Mahon (D), unopposed
1970 primary:	George H. Mahon (D), unopposed
1968 general:	George H. Mahon (D), unopposed

TWENTIETH DISTRICT Political Background

Texas 20 comprises central San Antonio, the state's third largest city (pop. 654,000) and its most liberal large urban area. San Antonio's large community of Mexican-Americans account for the political leanings of the city. San Antonio, an important town when Texas was part of Mexico, was where Santa Ana wiped out Davy Crockett and his friends at the Alamo. Today, Mexican-Americans form nearly half of the city's population, and within the 20th district, they constitute a majority. Blacks, another 9% of the population, also cast liberal votes. The 20th, therefore, is the liberal bastion of Texas politics.

Aside from its large Mexican population, San Antonio is distinguished by its Defense Department operations. The city has no less than five major military installations: Fort Sam Houston, the Brooks Aero Medical Center, Kelly AFB, Lackland AFB, and, a few miles out of town, Randolph AFB. Why one city should have so many military facilities remains a mystery. Some local people figure that it might have had something to do with San Antonio's former congressman, Paul Kilday, who served from 1938 to 1961. Kilday was a prominent member of the House Armed Services Committee. He was the man who defeated the fabled Texas liberal, Maury Maverick, in the 1938 Democratic primary. Kilday, a staunch conservative, also headed a local political machine that dominated San Antonio during most of his years in the House.

The domination ended in 1961, when Kilday resigned to become a judge on the U.S. Court of Military Appeals. He was succeeded by a young Mexican-American lawyer and state senator, Henry Gonzalez. Gonzalez, then 35, was the first Mexican-American congressman from the district in more than 50 years. He campaigned as an outspoken liberal, and his victory reversed the result of the 1938 primary. Gonzalez is now a high-ranking member of the House Banking and Currency Committee and chairman of its International Finance Subcommittee.

In his first few terms, Gonzalez had a near perfect liberal voting record. But lately, he has been a little out of favor with liberal pundits, mostly because he did not take an early stand against the war. And at home, something of a generation gap has developed between the congressman and the rising young militants in the city's Mexican-American community. The militants stress the pride of La Raza, while Gonzalez would rather win power within the existing structure of things. Accordingly, Gonzalez is now more comfortable at the meetings held by the Texas delegation, where he was once, of course, a pariah.

But neither militants nor the Texas conservatives have had any effect on the congressman's electoral performance. He has not had serious opposition in the primary, and, when opposed, he wins general elections by huge majorities. The young militants have had little political success outside the small towns where Anglos have held all political power for years (see Texas 23). In San Antonio, they are unlikely to have much success against Gonzalez. Redistricting has added some Anglo votes to the congressman's district, but these will not hurt Gonzalez's chances for reelection.

Census Data 1970 pop. 408,573; deviation from current state average, –16.1%; change 1960–70, –8.5%. Metro. 100.0%, 92.0% central city.

1970 Share of Federal Outlays $757,243,000 (average outlay per district, Texas 20 and 21)

DOD	$538,174,000	HEW	$105,517,000
AEC	$367,000	HUD	$703,000
NASA	$434,000	OEO	$2,221,000
DOT	$17,997,000	DOA	$14,991,000
		Other	$76,388,000

Federal Military-Industrial Commitments (Texas 20 and 21, San Antonio listing)

DOD Contractors Chromalloy American (San Antonio), $9.987m: unspecified. Browning Construction (San Antonio), $7.979m: medical field service school at Brooks Army Medical Center.

DOD Installations Fort Sam Houston (San Antonio). Brooks Aero Medical Center (San Antonio). Kelly AFB (San Antonio). Lackland AFB (San Antonio). Randolph AFB (San Antonio). Laughlin AFB (Del Rio).

Economic Base Food and kindred products, esp. meat products and beverages; apparel and other finished products made from fabrics and similar materials; printing, publishing, and allied industries, esp. newspapers; fabricated metal products, esp. fabricated structural metal products. Also, banking.

The Voters

Registration 124,486 total. No party registration.

Employment profile White collar, 41%. Blue collar, 59%.

Ethnic groups Black, 9%. Spanish surname, 47%. Total foreign stock, 27%. Mexico, 21%; Germany, 2%; UK, 1%; others, 2%.

Presidential vote

1968	Humphrey (D)	54,810	(71%)
	Nixon (R)	18,062	(23%)
	Wallace (AIP)	4,676	(6%)

Representative

Henry B. Gonzalez (D) Elected Jan. 10, 1962; b. May 3, 1916, San Antonio; home, San Antonio; San Antonio Col., U. of Tex., St. Mary's U.; Army, WWII; married, eight children; Catholic.

Career Chief Probation Officer, Bexar County, 1946; San Antonio City Council, 1953–56; Mayor Pro Tem, 1955–56; Tex. Senate, 1956–61.

Offices 2446 RHOB, 202-225-3236. Also 203 Fed. Bldg., San Antonio 78205, 512-223-8851 or 512-225-5511, ext. 4389.

Committees

Banking and Currency (9th); Subs. (1) Chm., International Finance, (2) Consumer Affairs, (3) Housing.

Group Ratings

	ADA	COPE	NREP	NFU	LCV	CFA	NAB	NSI	ACA
1970	64	100	67	85	67	86	8	70	11
1969	67	—	—	100	—	—	—	—	12
1968	100	100	—	100	—	—	0	—	0

Key Votes

(1) ABM	FOR	(6) 18-Yr-Vote	FOR	(11) Clean Water $	FOR
(2) SST	FOR	(7) Farm Sub Lmt	AGN	(12) Mig Wrkrs Comp	FOR
(3) Phil Pln	FOR	(8) Coop-Church	FOR	(13) Jets to Chiang	FOR
(4) No-Knock	AGN	(9) Family Asst	FOR	(14) State OEO Veto	AGN
(5) Cmutr Tax	AGN	(10) Work Stamps	AGN	(15) Park Logging	AGN

Election Results

1970 general:	Henry B. Gonzalez (D), unopposed		
1970 primary:	Henry B. Gonzalez (D), unopposed		
1968 general:	Henry B. Gonzalez (D)	64,112	(82%)
	Robert A. Schneider (R)	14,569	(19%)

TWENTY-FIRST DISTRICT Political Background

Most of the physical expanse of Texas 21 is virtually unpopulated, a vast near-desert given over to raising cattle and pumping oil. In politics, the district is a rather peculiar combination of geographically disparate urban areas, most of which are quite conservative. Almost half of the district's population lives in Bexar County. This includes the north side of San Antonio, the heavily Anglo and Republican part of that predominantly Mexican-American city. At the far northern end of the district, some 350 miles away, is the city of Odessa (pop. 78,000). This is an air-conditioned desert oasis whose conservative citizens are mostly the beneficiaries of oil wealth. Both of these heavily Republican areas were added to the 21st in the 1965 redistricting. The smaller urban center, San Angelo (pop. 63,000), which used to dominate the district, leans toward Texas Democratic conservatism.

The most interesting rural parts of the district are the Texas German areas around San Antonio. Towns like New Braunfels and Fredericksburg (where Lyndon Johnson sometimes goes to church) were founded by '48ers. These people were liberal Germans who left their native land after the failure of the revolution of 1848 and settled in the then unpopulated region of southwestern Texas. The Germans, who considered slaveholding immoral, soon became attracted to the Republican party, which, in the years before the Civil War, was a new force in American politics. The Germans' resistance to secession solidified their Republican allegiances, and to this day, the counties in which the descendants of the '48ers still make a majority—Comal, Kendall, Gillespie, and Kerr—cast huge Republican margins in almost every election.

From the district's composition, it would appear that the 21st elects a Republican congressman. But so far, it has not. The politics here testifies to the power of incumbents and to the inertia that characterizes Texas congressional politics. Before the 1965 redistricting, the district was conservative and Democratic, and it therefore elected a conservative and Democratic congressman, O. C. Fisher. Despite the changes in the shape of the 21st, it still does. Fisher, who has been in office since 1942, bids fair to remain in Congress for at least a few more terms. He was 67 in 1970. His voting record—about as conservative as any in the Texas delegation—has commended him to the conservative Republicans in the newer parts of his constituency. In 1968, he lost Ector County (Odessa), but has otherwise carried the urban areas. Fisher is the 3rd ranking Democrat on the House Armed Services Committee, where he is a bulwark of its pro-Pentagon majority.

Census Data 1970 pop. 597,476; deviation from current state average, +22.7%; change 1960–70, +34.0%. Metro. 76.0%, 55.9% central city.

1970 Share of Federal Outlays $757,243,000 (average outlay per district, Texas 20 and 21)

DOD	$538,174,000	HEW	$105,517,000
AEC	$367,000	HUD	$703,000
NASA	$434,000	OEO	$2,221,000
DOT	$17,997,000	DOA	$14,991,000
		Other	$76,388,000

Federal Military-Industrial Commitments (See Texas 21 for San Antonio area listing.)

Economic Base Livestock and cotton; crude petroleum and natural gas; chemicals and allied products.

The Voters

Registration 228,326 total. No party registration.

Employment profile White collar, 47%. Blue collar, 53%.

Ethnic groups Black, 3%. Spanish surname, 15%. Total foreign stock, 12%; Mexico, 7%; Germany, 2%; UK, 1%; others, 1%.

Presidential vote

1968	Humphrey (D)	51,053	(33%)
	Nixon (R)	80,168	(51%)
	Wallace (AIP)	25,356	(16%)

Representative

O. Clark Fisher (D) Elected 1942; b. Nov. 22, ca. 1905, near Junction; home, San Angelo; U. of Tex.; Baylor U., LL.B., 1929; married, one child; Church of Christ.

Career County Atty., Green County, 1931–35; Tex. House of Reps., 1935–37; Dist. Atty., 51st Jud. Dist., 1937–43.

Offices 2407 RHOB, 202-225-4236. Also Fed. Bldg., P.O. Box 170, San Angelo 76901, 915-653-3971, and 602–03 South Texas Bldg., San Antonio 78205, 512-225-5511, ext. 4787.

Committees

Armed Services (3rd); Chm., Sub. No. 2.

Group Ratings

	ADA	COPE	NREP	NFU	LCV	CFA	NAB	NSI	ACA
1970	8	17	0	25	13	50	80	100	76
1969	0	—	—	50	—	—	—	—	67
1968	8	0	—	31	—	—	83	—	83

Key Votes

(1) ABM	FOR	(6) 18-Yr-Vote	AGN	(11) Clean Water $	AGN
(2) SST	FOR	(7) Farm Sub Lmt	AGN	(12) Mig Wrkrs Comp	AGN
(3) Phil Pln	AGN	(8) Coop-Church	AGN	(13) Jets to Chiang	FOR
(4) No-Knock	FOR	(9) Family Asst	AGN	(14) State OEO Veto	FOR
(5) Cmutr Tax	AGN	(10) Work Stamps	FOR	(15) Park Logging	AGN

Election Results

1970 general:	O. C. Fisher (D)	76,004	(61%)
	Richardson B. Gill (R)	47,868	(39%)
1970 primary:	O. C. Fisher (D), unopposed		
1968 general:	O. C. Fisher (D)	91,784	(61%)
	W. Jack Alexander (R)	59,082	(39%)

TWENTY-SECOND DISTRICT Political Background

Texas 22 comprises the southern portion of Harris County and the city of Houston (see also Texas 7 and 8). The district takes in a cross section of the state's largest city. In the northern part of the district, near Houston's gleaming modern downtown, is a substantial Negro ghetto. Almost a quarter of the district's residents are black. To the east and south are white working-class neighborhoods and suburbs, which include Pasadena and South Houston. West of downtown are the wealthy, conservative Republican communities of Bellaire and University Place. To the south is the Astrodome, and beyond that, the giant NASA center. Democratic Congressman Albert Thomas, who served from 1936 to 1965, brought NASA to Houston; the technicians who work at the facility vote Republican. In national elections, the district is evenly divided; in statewide contests, it leans or prefers, by a small margin, the state's urban-oriented Republicans over its rural-oriented Democrats.

The 22nd was created in 1957. At that time, the Texas legislature eliminated the state's at-large seat and gave a second district to the rapidly growing Houston area. The 22nd's first and only congressman has been Robert R. (Bob) Casey. Casey, a conservative Democrat, has survived numerous Republican attempts to unseat him. In Washington, Casey is currently a junior member of the Appropriations Committee. He is known as a hardline opponent of crime and a vocal conservative on most issues. Ironically, most of Casey's 1970 margin of 56% came from the black areas of the 22nd; here he received 84% of the vote, while he managed only 53% in the rest of the district.

For 1972, the Texas legislature has moved most of the 22nd's black areas into the new 18th district and it has added exurban Fort Bend and Brazoria counties. Because the new areas normally give Democratic candidates an edge, they should keep Casey in Congress for at least another decade.

Census Data 1970 pop. 605,772; deviation from current state average, +24.4%; change 1960–70, +45.4%. Metro. 100.0%, 67.5% central city.

1970 Share of Federal Outlays $393,669,000 (average outlay per district, Texas 7, 8, and 22)

DOD	$58,245,000	HEW	$85,061,000
AEC	$348,000	HUD	$5,933,000
NASA	$110,631,000	OEO	$1,577,000
DOT	$15,350,000	DOA	$14,032,000
		Other	$102,492,000

Federal Military-Industrial Commitments (Texas 7, 8, and 22, Houston listing)

DOD Contractors Gulf Oil (Houston), $17.432m: petroleum products. Humble Oil (Houston), $6.883m: petroleum products. Atlantic Richfield (Houston), $6.087m: petroleum products.

DOD Installations Ellington AFB (Houston).

NASA Contractors IBM (Houston), $31.945m: computer system at Mission Control; Gemini spacecraft support. Lockheed Aircraft (Houston), $29.436m: general electronics instrumentation support. TRW Inc. (Houston), $28.042m: Apollo spacecraft systems analysis program. Philco Ford (Houston), $20.866m: Mission Control integration support. General Electric (Houston), $20.524m: Apollo spacecraft checkout of reliability. Brown-Northrup, joint venture (Houston), $16.635m: operation of labs and test facilities. Services Technology (Houston), $13.843m: facilities support. Singer General Precision (Houston), $10.330m: support of the manned spacecraft simulator complex. Bludworth Shipyard (Houston), $7.114m: Apollo docking system study. Boeing (Houston), $5.400m: Apollo-Saturn V technical integration and evaluation.

NASA Installations Manned Spacecraft Center (Houston).

Economic Base Nonelectrical machinery, esp. woodworking machinery; fabricated metal products, esp. fabricated structural metal products and valves and pipe fittings other than plumbers' brass goods; chemicals and allied products, esp. industrial inorganic and organic chemicals. Also, higher education (University of Houston); banking and insurance.

The Voters

Registration 239,962 total. No party registration.

Employment profile White collar, 56%. Blue collar, 44%.

Ethnic groups Black, 22%. Spanish surname, 2%. Total foreign stock, 8%. Germany, Poland, UK, USSR, Canada, Mexico, 1% each; others, 2%.

Presidential vote

1968	Humphrey (D)	68,164	(40%)
	Nixon (R)	73,607	(44%)
	Wallace (AIP)	26,843	(16%)

Representative

Robert (Bob) Randolph Casey (D) Elected 1958; b. July 27, 1915, Joplin, Mo.; home, Houston; U. of Houston; South Tex. School of Law, 1934–40; married, ten children; First Christian Church.

Career Practicing atty., 1941–43, 1947–51; Asst. Dist. Atty., Harris County, 1943–47; County Judge, 1951–58; Texas House of Reps., 1949–50.

Offices 2353 RHOB, 202-225-5951. Also Rm. 12102, Fed. Bldg., 515 Rusk St., Houston 77002, 713-226-4486.

Committees

Appropriations (24th); Subs. (1) Labor and HEW, (2) Legislative.

Group Ratings

	ADA	COPE	NREP	NFU	LCV	CFA	NAB	NSI	ACA
1970	16	34	27	54	13	50	58	88	56
1969	7	—	—	60	—	—	—	—	63
1968	17	46	—	47	—	—	40	—	64

Key Votes

(1) ABM	ABS	(6) 18-Yr-Vote	AGN	(11) Clean Water $	AGN
(2) SST	FOR	(7) Farm Sub Lmt	AGN	(12) Mig Wrkrs Comp	AGN
(3) Phil Pln	AGN	(8) Coop-Church	AGN	(13) Jets to Chiang	FOR
(4) No-Knock	FOR	(9) Family Asst	AGN	(14) State OEO Veto	AGN
(5) Cmutr Tax	ABS	(10) Work Stamps	ABS	(15) Park Logging	FOR

Election Results

1970 general:	Bob Casey (D)	73,514	(56%)
	A. W. Busch (R)	58,598	(44%)
1970 primary:	Bob Casey (D)	39,679	(69%)
	Paul B. Haring (D)	17,530	(31%)
1968 general:	Bob Casey (D)	101,498	(62%)
	Walter Blaney (R)	61,278	(38%)

TWENTY-THIRD DISTRICT Political Background

Texas 23 comprises the southcentral part of the state and lies just south of LBJ country (see Texas 10). The district takes in a significant portion of Bexar County—the southern edges of the city of San Antonio—as well as several traditionally Republican counties in the Texas German area (see Texas 21). The 23rd without water looks like a desert, but much of the land here has been irrigated. The resulting farms are tended by chicano farm workers, who call this part of Texas home when they are not migrating north to work and pick other seasonal crops.

Almost half of the district's population is Mexican-American. Traditionally, the chicanos have left political decision-making to the local Anglo (WASP) landowners, bankers, and lawyers—with the Mexicans supplying only the votes. This pattern is most noticeable in rural areas; in Duval County, for example, the dominance of the Parr family is legend. The vote in Duval is always very one-sided: the county has been known to switch from one candidate to another between the initial primary and the runoff. Its most famous performance came in the Senate primary of 1948. Congressman Lyndon B. Johnson carried Duval in the runoff by a vote of 4,622 to 40—a margin which enabled him to carry the entire state of Texas by 87 votes. More recently, Duval gave Ralph Yarborough a 3,993 to 264 margin in the 1970 Democratic Senate primary, and then in the general election, it switched to the man who beat him, Lloyd Bentsen. Bentsen won, 3,435 to 269. Some folks say that the Parrs sell the county's vote to the highest bidder and then force the economically dependent Mexicans to vote right, using techniques like counting the ballots immediately after they are cast.

Nevertheless, other Duval County returns of late do manifest a growing Mexican-American solidarity. And Webb County, which adjoins Duval on the west and contains the city of Laredo, went for Humphrey over Nixon and Wallace by 9,419 to 2,103 to 304. There are more signs that the Mexicans are freeing themselves of Anglo domination. In little towns like Crystal City, Carrizo Springs, and Cotulla, in the eastern part of the district, "brown power" movements have developed. These movements, led by young chicano militants, have mobilized the formerly acquiescent Mexican voting majority and have begun to take over units of local government.

The 23rd's large Mexican population makes the district one of the state's most liberal in both national and congressional elections. The district was created in 1965 when the legislature eliminated Texas' at-large seat. Its first and only congressman has been Abraham Kazen, Jr., who had served in the state Senate for 14 years prior to his election. Kazen, of Lebanese descent, is an LBJ liberal; he has favored social and economic welfare programs, but has taken pro-Administration positions on the war. Kazen is also conservative on anticrime and other social legislation. In 1970, the congressman won a 75 rating from COPE but only a 28 from the ADA. Kazen won a tough primary in 1966, but since then he has had little trouble, and will surely be re-elected in the years to come.

Census Data 1970 pop. 790,136; deviation from current state average, +0.7%; change 1960–70, +10.4%. Metro. 48.3%, 31.7% central city.

1970 Share of Federal Outlays $266,228,000

DOD	$83,453,000	HEW	$83,825,000
AEC	$000	HUD	$3,356,000
NASA	$000	OEO	$1,885,000
DOT	$10,575,000	DOA	$30,527,000
		Other	$52,606,000

Federal Military-Industrial Commitments

DOD Installations Naval Air Station (Beeville). Laredo AFB (Laredo).

Economic Base Cotton and livestock; crude petroleum and natural gas; food and kindred products.

The Voters

Registration 178,198 total. No party registration.

Employment profile White collar, 31%. Blue collar, 69%.

Ethnic groups Black, 5%. Spanish surname, 43%. Total foreign stock, 24%. Mexico, 18%; Germany, 2%; Czech., 1%; others, 1%.

Presidential vote

1968	Humphrey (D)	61,524	(54%)
	Nixon (R)	37,197	(33%)
	Wallace (AIP)	14,295	(13%)

Representative

Abraham Kazen, Jr. (D) Elected 1966; b. Jan. 17, 1919, Laredo; home, Laredo; U. of Tex., 1937–40; Cumberland U. Law School, 1941; USAF, WWII; married, five children; Catholic.

Career Practicing atty., 1945–66; Tex. House of Reps., 1947–53; Tex. Senate, 1953–66, Pres., Pro Tem, 1959.

Offices 1514 LHOB, 202-225-4511. Also Rm. 201, Fed. Bldg., Laredo 78040, 512-723-4336, and 1818 Tower Life Bldg., San Antonio 78205, 512-225-6276.

Committees

Foreign Affairs (14th); Subs. (1) Asian and Pacific Affairs, (2) Inter-American Affairs, (3) International Organizations and Movements, (4) State Department Organization and Foreign Operations.

Interior and Insular Affairs (16th); Subs. (1) Irrigation and Reclamation, (2) Mines and Mining, (3) National Parks and Recreation.

Group Ratings

	ADA	COPE	NREP	NFU	LCV	CFA	NAB	NSI	ACA
1970	28	75	33	69	25	86	25	90	39
1969	33	—	—	100	—	—	—	—	24
1968	58	92	—	87	—	—	17	—	5

Key Votes

(1) ABM	FOR	(6) 18-Yr-Vote	FOR	(11) Clean Water $	AGN
(2) SST	FOR	(7) Farm Sub Lmt	AGN	(12) Mig Wrkrs Comp	AGN
(3) Phil Pln	AGN	(8) Coop-Church	AGN	(13) Jets to Chiang	AGN
(4) No-Knock	FOR	(9) Family Asst	AGN	(14) State OEO Veto	AGN
(5) Cmutr Tax	AGN	(10) Work Stamps	AGN	(15) Park Logging	AGN

Election Results

1970 general: Abraham Kazen, Jr. (D), unopposed
1970 primary: Abraham Kazen, Jr. (D), unopposed
1968 general: Abraham Kazen, Jr. (D), unopposed

UTAH

Political Background

In 1830, Joseph Smith, a young farmer in Palmyra, New York, published translations of writings that were inscribed on some golden plates. Smith had unearthed the plates at the direction of the Angel Moroni, who appeared to him in a vision. Moroni was, in about the year 400 A.D., a prophet among the lost tribe of Israel which had presumably found its way to the New World some thousand years earlier. What Smith published became the Book of Mormon, and the prophet founded a religious group called the Church of Jesus Christ of the Latter Day Saints.

In the first half of the nineteenth century, Upstate New York—Palmyra lies just east of Rochester—was repeatedly swept by waves of evangelical revivalism. And because of this, the Yankee migrants from New England who settled this part of New York came to live in what was called "The Burned-over District." Here in Upstate New York, the new church soon attracted hundreds of converts. Persecuted for their beliefs (which included polygamy), these Mormons, as they were called, moved west to Ohio, Missouri, and then to Illinois. In 1844, Smith was murdered in Nauvoo, Illinois. The Church's new president, Brigham Young, decided to move the faithful, "the saints," farther west into territory recently won from Mexico and beyond the pale of white settlement. Brigham Young led a great migration across the Great Plains. In 1847, he and his followers crossed the Wasatch Range, and as Brigham Young viewed the valley of the Great Salt Lake spread out below, he uttered the now famous words, "This is the place."

The place was Utah. From the beginning, of course, the society here was based on the teachings of the Church. Throughout the nineteenth century, "Zion" attracted thousands of converts from the Midwest and from Wales and Scandinavia. All of these people felt the sting of religious prejudice, and it was not until 1896, after the Church renounced polygamy, that Utah was granted statehood. Today, there are more than a million people in Utah, hundreds of miles from any other significant concentration of population; more than 70% of them are members of the LDS (Latter Day Saints) Church.

The distinctiveness of the LDS faith still dominates the state's politics. In the seventy-five years since statehood, Utah has rarely sent a Gentile (a non-Mormon) to Congress, and leaders of the Church have always been able to exert great political power. Today, the Church owns one of the two leading newspapers in the state and an influential television station. The body also has holdings in an insurance company, various banks, and real estate, among other things. And the Church often takes positions on important secular matters; it strongly supports, for example, Utah's right-to-work law. A specific religious doctrine of the Church has embarrassed many Mormons—one which denies Negroes the "priesthood." This means that a black cannot enjoy full-fledged membership in the Church; the Mormons are led by lay people and do not hire a regular priest or minister like other religious groups. Revision of the doctrine must await a theologically valid revelation to the president of the Church.

More generally, the LDS doctrine carries the virtues of nineteenth century Protestant Upstate New York to their logical end. Even today, Mormons are forbidden to consume alcohol, tobacco, caffeine, or other stimulants, though many so-called "jack-Mormons" do consume these things with no stern reprimands from the community at large. All of the Mormons, however, have a deserved reputation for their capacity for hard work. So in the '60's, when Eastern liberals appeared to be taking over the country, the media, and the moral standards of the nation, and when civil rights became a major national issue, people in Utah became notably more conservative in their voting habits. The economic issues, which had helped Democrats to win congressional elections in the '50's, became less important in the prosperous '60's. In 1964, Barry Goldwater won 45% of the state's votes. The trend was strengthened by the conservative political views of David O. McKay, the LDS president who died recently at the age of 91.

As in most western states, Utah's population is concentrated in urban areas. About 70% of its voters live in the so-called Wasatch Front. This is a string of cities north and south of Salt Lake City, lying between the Wasatch Range and the Great Salt Lake. There are pockets of long-standing Republican and Democratic strength in the little mining and crossroads towns in the central and southern parts of the state. But the outcome of elections in Utah is always determined in the Wasatch Front cities and suburbs. Here the usually conservative voters sometimes split their tickets with a frequency unknown in other parts of the country. These voters, for example, make up the principal source of strength for Democratic Governor Calvin Rampton. The governor's own kind of rather conservative politics helped him to buck the Republican tide and win reelection in 1968.

The Wasatch Front was therefore the main area of concern in the hotly contested Senate election of 1970. In 1958, Democrat Frank Moss won election to the Senate with just 38% of the vote. The vote was split three ways because the election featured the independent candidacy of J. Bracken Lee, now mayor of Salt Lake City. Lee, an ultraconservative, may have entered the 1958 election more interested in defeating Republican Sen. Arthur Watkins than in winning himself. Watkins was chairman of the committee which recommended censure of Sen. Joe McCarthy. Moss held on nicely in 1964, defeating the ultraconservative President of Brigham Young University, Ernest Wilkinson, 57–43.

But by 1968, the conservative trend in Utah had established itself firmly. In that year, Hubert Humphrey won only 37% of the state's votes. And by 1970, the Republicans felt that Moss' Senate seat was soon to be theirs. Moss had opposed the Church's position on right-to-work laws, and in the Senate, he voted with the liberals on the controversial military spending programs and Supreme Court appointments of the Nixon Administration. The Republican candidate, Congressman Laurence Burton, conducted a vigorous and well-financed campaign stressing these issues.

Moss, however, could fight back. As a two-term veteran, he had valuable seniority on a committee important to Utah. He was a member of the Senate Interior and Insular Affairs Committee and chairman of its Subcommittee on Minerals, Materials, and Fuels. His chairmanship is important in Utah, where copper mining is a major industry. As chairman of the Commerce Committee's Subcommittee on Consumer Affairs, he sponsored important pieces of consumer legislation. But perhaps most important in Utah, Senator Moss was the sponsor and driving force behind the bill that banned cigarette advertising on television. To devout Mormons, and to jack-Mormons as well, cigarette smoking is a sin. Moss prevailed over the tobacco lobby. And that probably impressed his constituents much more than his ability to defend Utah's interest in national parks, Hill Air Force base, and so on.

Although many thought the election was going to be close, Moss led in the polls all the way. Visits by President Nixon and Vice President Agnew didn't seem to help Burton much. Moss wound up with 56% of the vote, off 1% from 1964, mainly because Burton held down the Senator's margin in his old congressional district.

Although both men are devout members of the LDS Church, few states have senators with voting records as different as those from Utah. The state's senior senator is Wallace Bennett, a former president of the National Association of Manufacturers. He first won his seat in 1950. Bennett, one of the Senate's senior Republicans, seldom strays from the conservative ranks. Bennett is the ranking Republican on the tax-writing Senate Finance Committee and the 2nd ranking member of the Banking, Housing, and Urban Affairs Committee. The Senator was reelected in 1968 by a surprisingly narrow margin, 54–46, and he may choose to retire in 1974, when he will be 76.

Each of the state's two congressional districts contains a large portion of the relatively unpopulated mountain and desert areas of Utah. Both districts, therefore, are dominated by the Wasatch Front. In 1970, Burton's seat, the 1st, was picked up by a Democrat—only the second time in ten years that a Democrat won a Utah House seat. Redistricting has made only minor changes for 1972, and both incumbents will probably win reelection.

Electoral Votes 4

Census Data 1970 pop. 1,059,273; 0.51% of U.S. total, 37th largest; change 1960–70, +18.9%. Metro. 77.6%, 30.6% central city. 1970 per capita income, $3,210; 38th highest. 46th in number of poor.

1970 Share of Federal Tax Burden $741,530,000; 0.38% of U.S. total, 39th largest.

1970 Share of Federal Outlays $1,151,314,108; 0.61% of U.S. total, 38th largest. Per capita federal spending, $1,087.

DOD	$498,949,000	31st (0.87%)	HEW	$220,583,184	41st (0.42%)
AEC	$3,697,401	27th (0.14%)	HUD	$4,660,312	46th (0.17%)
NASA	$1,317,056	35th (0.04%)	OEO	$3,779,093	41st (0.50%)
DOT	$75,190,161	32nd (1.05%)	DOA	$68,007,684	40th (0.53%)
DOC	$4,385,266	35th (0.38%)	POD	$38,565,176	39th (0.53%)
DOI	$49,331,935	14th (2.14%)	VA	$51,783,464	40th (0.70%)
DOJ	$2,362,361	42nd (0.41%)	CSC	$22,566,133	36th (0.56%)
			Other	$106,135,882	

Economic Base Livestock and dairy; primary metal industries, esp. primary smelting and refining of nonferrous metals; metal mining, esp. copper, food and kindred products; electrical machinery, equipment, and supplies, esp. radio and television transmitting, signaling, and detection equipment and apparatus; transportation equipment, esp. aircraft and parts; apparel and other finished products made from fabrics and similar materials, esp. women's, misses', and juniors' outerwear; nonelectrical machinery, esp. contruction, mining, and material handling machinery and equipment; printing, publishing, and allied industries; fabricated metal products, esp. fabricated structural metal products.

Political Line-up Governor, Calvin L. Rampton (D); seat up, 1972. Senators, Wallace F. Bennett (R) and Frank E. Moss (D). Representatives, 2 (1 D and 1 R). State Senate (12 D and 16 R); State House (38 D and 31 R).

The Voters

Registration 560,650 total. No party registration.

Employment profile White collar, 45%. Blue collar, 55%.

Ethnic groups Black, 1%. Total foreign stock, 16%. UK, 5%; Germany, 2%; Sweden, Canada, Italy, Mexico, Norway, 1% each; others, 6%.

Presidential vote

1968	Humphrey (D)	156,665	(37%)
	Nixon (R)	238,728	(57%)
	Wallace (AIP)	26,906	(6%)
1964	Johnson (D)	219,628	(55%)
	Goldwater (R)	181,785	(45%)
1960	Kennedy (D)	169,248	(45%)
	Nixon (R)	205,361	(55%)

Senator

Wallace Foster Bennett (R) Elected 1950, seat up 1974; b. Nov. 13, 1898, Salt Lake City; home, Salt Lake City; U. of Utah, B.A., 1919; Army, WWI; married, five children; Church of Latter Day Saints.

Career Principal, San Luis Stake Acad., 1919–20; Bd. Chm., Bennett's; Bd. Chm., Bennett Motor Co., V.P., Natl. Paint, Varnish & Lacquer Assn., 1935–36; Pres., Natl. Glass Distributors Assn., 1937; Pres., Natl. Assn. of Manufacturers, 1949; author, "Faith and Freedom," 1950, "Why I Am a Mormon," 1958.

Offices 1121 NSOB, 202-225-5444. Also 4227 Fed. Bldg., Salt Lake City 84111, 801-524-5939, and 1010 Fed. Bldg., Ogden, 801-399-6208.

Committees

Banking, Housing, and Urban Affairs (2nd); Subs. (1) Financial Institutions, (2) Housing and Urban Affairs, (3) International Finance, (4) Production and Stabilization, (5) Securities.

Finance (ranking mbr.).

Joint Committee on Atomic Energy (2nd); Subs. (1) Agreements for Cooperation, (2) Raw Materials, (3) Research, Development, and Radiation.

Sel. Com. on Standards and Conduct (Vice Chm.).

Group Ratings

	ADA	COPE	NREP	NFU	LCV	NAB	NSI	ACA
1970	0	0	0	33	11	83	100	90
1969	6	—	—	38	—	—	—	69
1968	0	0	—	30	—	67	—	90

Key Votes

(1) ABM	FOR	(8) Phil Pln	FOR	(15) Coop-Church	AGN
(2) SST	FOR	(9) Vol Army	AGN	(16) Cut Oil Dpltn	AGN
(3) Busing	AGN	(10) Prison $	AGN	(17) Consumer Prot	AGN
(4) Tob Sub	FOR	(11) Cut Mil $	AGN	(18) Farm Sub Limit	AGN
(5) Carswell	FOR	(12) Defoliatn	FOR	(19) Comp Bid Sales	AGN
(6) No-Knock	FOR	(13) 18-Yr-Vote	AGN	(20) Pre-Prod Tests	AGN
(7) Seniorty	FOR	(14) Pentgn PR	FOR	(21) Cut Marjna Pen	AGN

General Election

1968 general:	Wallace F. Bennett (R)	225,075	(54%)
	Milton Weilenmann (D)	192,168	(46%)
1968 primary:	Wallace F. Bennett (R)	81,945	(61%)
	Mark E. Anderson (R)	52,689	(39%)
1962 general:	Wallace F. Bennett (R)	166,755	(52%)
	David S. King (D)	151,656	(48%)

Senator

Frank Edward Moss (D) Elected 1958, seat up 1976; b. Sept. 23, 1911, Holladay; home, Salt Lake City; U. of Utah, B.A., 1933; George Washington U., J.D., 1937; Army Air Corps, WWII; Col. USAFR; married, three children; Church of Latter Day Saints.

Career Practicing atty., Atty. for Securities and Exchange Commission, 1937–39; Judge, Salt Lake City, 1940–49; Salt Lake County Atty., 1950–54; Pres., Natl. Assn. of Dist. Attys.

Offices 6205 NSOB, 202-225-5251. Also 5430 New Fed. Bldg., Salt Lake City 84111, 801-524-5935.

Committees

Commerce (7th); Subs. (1) Chm., Consumer, (2) Vice Chm., Environment, (3) Aviation, (4) Communications, (5) Foreign Commerce and Tourism, (6) Surface Transportation, (7) Sp. on Freight Car Shortage.

Interior and Insular Affairs (5th); Subs. (1) Chm., Minerals, Materials, and Fuels, (2) Parks and Recreation, (3) Water and Power Resources.

Post Office and Civil Service (5th); Subs. (1) Civil Service Policies and Practices, (2) Compensation and Employment, (3) Postal Operations.

Sp. Com. on Aging (6th); Subs. (1) Chm., Long-Term Care, (2) Employment and Retirement Incomes, (3) Health of the Elderly.

Sel. Com. on Small Business; Subs. (1) Retailing, Distribution, and Marketing Practices, (2) Taxes.

Group Ratings

	ADA	COPE	NREP	NFU	LCV	NAB	NSI	ACA
1970	69	100	90	94	29	0	10	6
1969	83	—	—	88	—	—	—	7
1968	79	100	—	92	—	50	—	9

Key Votes

(1) ABM	AGN	(8) Phil Pln	FOR	(15) Coop-Church	FOR
(2) SST	FOR	(9) Vol Army	FOR	(16) Cut Oil Dpltn	AGN
(3) Busing	FOR	(10) Prison $	FOR	(17) Consumer Prot	FOR
(4) Tob Sub	AGN	(11) Cut Mil $	ABS	(18) Farm Sub Limit	ABS
(5) Carswell	AGN	(12) Defoliatn	AGN	(19) Comp Bid Sales	ABS
(6) No-Knock	AGN	(13) 18-Yr-Vote	FOR	(20) Pre-Prod Tests	ABS
(7) Seniorty	ABS	(14) Pentgn PR	AGN	(21) Cut Marjna Pen	ABS

Election Results

1970 general:	Frank Moss (D)	210,207	(56%)
	Laurence J. Burton (R)	159,004	(46%)
	Clyde B. Freeman (AIP)	5,092	(1%)
1970 primary:	Frank Moss (D), unopposed		
1964 general:	Frank Moss (D)	227,822	(57%)
	Ernest L. Wilkinson (R)	169,562	(43%)

FIRST DISTRICT Political Background

Utah 1 comprises the eastern half of the state. It includes Canyonlands National Park and Lake Powell, the large Uintah and Ouray Indian reservations, and the mountains in the east which were the site of the uranium boom of the '50's. The sparsely populated eastern counties take up nearly all of the district's land area, but 80% of the district's population—and its voters—live in the Wasatch Front towns (see state write-up). North of Salt Lake City are places like Ogden (pop. 69,000), Logan (pop. 22,000), and Bountiful (pop. 28,000); to the south, on the shores of Utah Lake, are Provo (pop. 53,000), and Orem (pop. 25,000).

Ordinarily, the 1st votes slightly more Republican than the state as a whole, but the differences have been minimal. Regional variations among Utah voters are overcome by the relatively homogeneous political performance of the Wasatch Front, which dominates both of the state's congressional districts. The Republicans, in the person of Congressman Laurence J. Burton, held the seat in very secure fashion between 1962 and 1970. Burton's convincing 68–32 victory in 1968 made him the natural Republican choice to oppose Sen. Frank Moss in 1970. Moss, however, was reelected.

In 1970, the Republican candidate, Richard Richards, was expected to win the seat. Richards was formerly his party's state chairman. But the Democrats, aided by high unemployment and unafflicted as they were in the late '60's by various social issues, did surprisingly well in Utah. They captured the control of the state House of Representatives and won here in the 1st district. The Democratic winner, K. Gunn McKay, was given a boost by his family name; he is a nephew of David O. McKay, who was for many years president of the LDS Church. K. Gunn McKay also benefited from his past association with the popular Democratic Gov. Calvin Rampton and from heavy unemployment around Ogden and some other cities in the district. McKay's margin in Weber County (Ogden) was larger than his margin district-wide.

In the House, McKay was granted a seat on the House Appropriations Committee, an unusual honor for a freshman. The Utah congressman will probably compile a record somewhat less liberal than most Northern congressmen on social issues. In 1972, he will probably have a difficult race. But the legislature did remove four small counties from his district, which, in 1970, he lost by a total of 1,000 votes. This should help him. If McKay makes a good showing, he may well run for Wallace Bennett's Senate seat in 1974. Or if Governor Rampton decides to retire, McKay may leave the House and run for the governorship in 1972.

Census Data 1970 pop. 537,913; deviation from current state average, +1.6%; change 1960–70, +19.0%. Metro. 67.5%, 27.6% central city.

1970 Share of Federal Outlays $575,657,000 (average outlay per district, Utah 1 and 2)

DOD	$249,475,000	HEW	$110,292,000
AEC	$1,849,000	HUD	$2,330,000
NASA	$659,000	OEO	$1,890,000
DOT	$37,595,000	DOA	$34,004,000
		Other	$133,133,000

Federal Military-Industrial Commitments

DOD Contractors Thiokol Chemical (Brigham City), $42.282m: stage one motors for Minuteman III missiles; rocket motors for Genie missile. Marquardt Co. (Ogden), $7.683m: nozzle and fin assemblies for 2.75-inch rocket; aerial tow target launchers. Boeing Co. (Hill AFB), $6.008m: force modernization of Engineering Test Facilities. U.S. Steel International (Provo), $5.009m: 72-inch fence posts.

DOD Installations Ogden Defense Depot (Ogden). Hill AFB (Ogden).

Economic Base Livestock and dairy; food and kindred products; apparel and other finished products made from fabrics and similar materials; bituminous coal. Also, higher education (Brigham Young University).

The Voters

Registration 309,487 total. No party registration.

Employment profile White collar, 45%. Blue collar, 55%.

Ethnic groups Black, 1%. Total foreign stock, 13%. UK, 4%; Canada, Germany, Sweden, Mexico, Italy, 1% each; others, 5%.

Presidential vote

1968	Humphrey (D)	70,363	(34%)
	Nixon (R)	122,293	(59%)
	Wallace (AIP)	15,185	(7%)

Representative

K. Gunn McKay (D) Elected 1970; b. Feb. 23, 1925, Ogden; home, Huntsville; Weber State Col., A.A., 1960; Utah State U., B.S., 1962; USCG, 1943–46; married, nine children; Church of Latter Day Saints.

Career Farmer; businessman; educator; Utah House of Reps., 1962–66; Legislative Council, 1963–66; Administrative Asst. to Gov. Calvin L. Rampton, 1968–70.

Offices 1427 LHOB, 202-225-3171. Also Suite 213, First Security Bank, Provo 84601, 801-373-4150, and Rm. 1424, Fed. Bldg., Ogden 84401, 801-399-6816.

Committees

Appropriations (33rd); Subs. (1) District of Columbia, (2) Military Construction.

Group Ratings, Key Votes: Newly elected.

Election Results

1970 general:	K. Gunn McKay (D)	95,499	(51%)
	Richard Richards (R)	89,269	(48%)
	Daniel L. Worthington (AIP)	1,489	(1%)
1970 primary:	K. Gunn McKay (D)	17,928	(55%)
	J. Keith Melville (D)	14,850	(45%)

SECOND DISTRICT Political Background

Utah 2 comprises the western half of the state. It extends from the Great Salt Lake and the Bonneville Salt Flats in the north to Bryce Canyon and Zion National parks in the south. Like the 1st, however, most of the district's population is concentrated in the Wasatch Front. Some 88% of the 2nd's population lives in Salt Lake County (Salt Lake City and suburbs). Salt Lake City is, of course, the headquarters of the LDS Church and the home of the famous Tabernacle and Tabernacle Choir. The city is also the state's capital and the only major mountain metropolis between Denver and the Pacific Coast. Mormons outnumber Gentiles (non-Mormons) by three to one in the district, and the Church's position on issues is extremely influential. Leaders of the Church enunciate their views in the *Deseret News* and on a local TV and radio station, all owned by the LDS.

The 2nd is usually the more Democratic of the state's two districts. Until 1970, it was the last to elect a Democratic congressman; he was David S. King, the son of an ex-U.S. senator, who served from 1958 to 1962 and then again from 1964 to 1966. The current congressman is Sherman P. Lloyd. In 1964, he stepped down to make an unsuccessful run for his party's Senate nomination, and returned to the House in 1966. Lloyd, who has compiled a fairly conservative record in the House, sits on the Foreign Affairs Committee and Interior and Insular Affairs. The latter, of course, is far more important to Utah.

Lloyd has been a strong, but not overpowering, vote-getter. In 1970, he encountered unexpected trouble from Democrat A. H. (Bob) Nance, a political novice, who took 47% of the vote. Nance stressed unemployment and pollution issues. The results indicate that Lloyd can expect more trouble in future elections and it also dampens whatever hopes he may have had for the governorship in 1972 or Sen. Wallace Bennett's seat in 1974.

Census Data 1970 pop. 521,360; deviation from current state average, −1.6%; change 1960–70, +18.8%. Metro. 88.0%, 33.7% central city.

1970 Share of Federal Outlays $575,657,000 (average outlay per district, Utah 1 and 2)

DOD	$249,457,000	HEW	$110,292,000
AEC	$1,849,000	HUD	$2,330,000
NASA	$659,000	OEO	$1,890,000
DOT	$37,595,000	DOA	$34,004,000
		Other	$133,133,000

Federal Military-Industrial Commitments

DOD Contractors Sperry Rand (Salt Lake City), $31.813m: guidance and control components for Shrike missiles; aircraft drones. Hercules, Inc. (Magna), $8.647m: stage three motors for Minuteman II missiles. American Oil (Salt Lake City), $7.599m: petroleum products.

DOD Installations Dugway Army Proving Ground (Dugway). Tooele Army Depot (Tooele).

Economic Base Metal mining, esp. copper; electrical machinery, equipment, and supplies, esp. radio and television transmitting, signaling, and detection equipment, and apparatus; food and kindred products, esp. dairy; livestock and dairy. Also, higher education (University of Utah).

The Voters

Registration 251,163 total. No party registration.

Employment profile White collar, 48%. Blue collar, 52%.

Ethnic groups Black, 1%. Total foreign stock, 18%. UK, 5%; Germany, 2%; Sweden, Canada, Italy, Norway, Mexico, 1% each; others, 7%.

Presidential vote

1968	Humphrey (D)	86,302	(40%)
	Nixon (R)	116,435	(54%)
	Wallace (AIP)	11,721	(6%)

Representative

Sherman Parkinson Lloyd (R) Elected 1966; b. Jan. 11, 1914, St. Anthony, Idaho; home, Salt Lake City; Utah State U., B.A.; George Washington U., LL.B.; married, four children; Church of Latter Day Saints.

Career Practicing atty.; Gen. Counsel, Utah Retail Grocers Assn.; Utah Senate, 1954–62, Majority Leader, 1957, Minority Leader, 1961, Pres., 1959; Utah Legislative Council, 1957–61, Chm., 1959–61; Utah Rep. on Bd. of Mgrs., Council of State Governments, 1959–61.

Offices 1114 LHOB, 202-225-3011. Also 2311 New Fed. Bldg., 125 S. State St., Salt Lake City 84111, 801-524-4141.

Committees

Foreign Affairs (12th); Subs. (1) Europe, (2) Near East, (3) State Department Organization and Foreign Operations.

Interior and Insular Affairs (11th); Subs. (1) Environment, (2) National Parks and Recreation, (3) Public Lands.

Group Ratings

	ADA	COPE	NREP	NFU	LCV	CFA	NAB	NSI	ACA
1970	16	18	9	73	0	50	100	89	60
1969	13	—	—	64	—	—	—	—	50
1968	0	8	—	27	—	—	67	—	74

Key Votes

(1) ABM	FOR	(6) 18-Yr-Vote	FOR	(11) Clean Water $	AGN
(2) SST	FOR	(7) Farm Sub Lmt	AGN	(12) Mig Wrkrs Comp	AGN
(3) Phil Pln	FOR	(8) Coop-Church	AGN	(13) Jets to Chiang	AGN
(4) No-Knock	FOR	(9) Family Asst	FOR	(14) State OEO Veto	FOR
(5) Cmutr Tax	AGN	(10) Work Stamps	FOR	(15) Park Logging	FOR

Election Results

1970 general:	Sherman P. Lloyd (R)	97,549	(52%)
	A. H. Nance (D)	87,000	(47%)
	Stephen D. Marsh (AIP)	2,094	(1%)
1970 primary:	Sherman P. Lloyd (R), unopposed		
1968 general:	Sherman P. Lloyd (R)	130,127	(62%)
	Galen J. Ross (D)	80,948	(38%)

VERMONT

Political Background

In many ways, Vermont is a state out of the nineteenth century. The classic New England town-squares still stand here; the cows still graze on the hillsides; the taciturn Yankee farmers still tap the sugar maple trees in the springtime; and in the fall, these same trees still produce the most beautiful blazing red foliage in the world. For a long time, Vermont was home to the nation's nineteenth century poet, Robert Frost. This man insisted, among other things, that "one had to be versed in country things." Poet and Census Bureau seem to have something in common on the matter, since Vermont is still the nation's most rural state—some 68% of the people here are rural, according to the definition used by the bureau.

The 1960's, however, did bring some changes to Vermont. There are now large IBM and GE complexes around Burlington (pop. 38,000), the state's largest city. The state's ski resort and summer home industries have been booming, and in some areas, old Yankee farms have been turned into hippie communes. In 1963, the number of people in Vermont for the first time exceeded the number of cows, and the state's population increase between 1960 and 1970 equalled the entire increase between 1890 and 1960. Today, the state has 444,000 people. Because residents here are concerned about these trends in the state's growth, Vermont probably has the nation's most progressive laws when it comes to protection of the environment.

For years, Vermont was known politically as the nation's number-one Republican stronghold. The only areas of Democratic strength lay in the small Irish and French-Canadian communities of Burlington and other towns in the northern part of the state. Recently, the Republicans' grip on Vermont politics has begun to loosen. In 1958, the state elected a Democratic congressman, and in 1962, a Democratic governor—the first in 109 years. That governor, Philip Hoff, was responsible for many of the changes that have occurred in the life of the state. Hoff attracted industry, built highways, and reversed the pattern of young people outmigration; the young had been leaving Vermont since before the Civil War. Hoff was reelected in 1964 and in 1966, and the governor appeared to be making Vermont into a two-party state. Lyndon Johnson carried it by a 2–1 margin in 1964.

All the polls indicated that the race would be close and that Hoff would cut heavily into the normally Republican Yankee vote. So when Hoff, who was only 46, decided to challenge incumbent Sen. Winston Prouty in 1970, it appeared that a fundamental shift in Vermont politics was about to take place. It was a classic contest of opposites. Prouty, a typically tight-lipped Vermonter, was a conservative who seldom bucked the Nixon Administration; Hoff an energetic campaigner who had angered Democratic regulars by supporting Robert Kennedy and, later, Eugene McCarthy in the 1968 Presidential campaign.

As it turned out, Prouty, with a low-key campaign and little organization, won 59% of the vote. Hoff took only 40%, with a splinter peace candidate taking the remaining 1%. Hoff had not scored quite as well as expected in the Yankee rural towns, but that did not account for the margin of his defeat.

What did is the same thing that happened in the larger Eastern states of New York and Connecticut. This was a split between two segments of Democratic party strength—the urban ethnics and the intellectual liberals. Many of the stands on issues which helped Hoff win Yankee votes also antagonized the conservative, patronage-oriented politicans who dominated the Democratic party before the Governor's rise. State Sen. Fiore Bove, for example, was a Democrat who resented Hoff's opposition to the war and his opposition of Lyndon Johnson in 1968. Bove entered the Senate primary and held Hoff down to 51% of the votes in Chittenden County (Burlington). In the general election, Bove supported Sen. Prouty, and Burlington, which had given Hoff large margins in his three gubernatorial races, gave Prouty a majority in 1970.

Sen. Prouty died after a short illness in September 1971, and Vermont Gov. Deane Davis, at the behest of White House political operatives, hastily appointed Republican Congressman-at-Large Robert T. Stafford to take his place. Stafford had served as Governor from 1958 to 1960, and in 1960 ran for the House and retained the Vermont seat for the Republicans who had lost it unexpectedly in 1958. In the House, Stafford was a member of the small coterie of liberal Republicans, but his standing was high enough among conservatives for him to be elected Vice-Chairman of the House Republican Conference, if only by 3 votes over Alabama's Jack Edwards. The Nixon Administration sought Stafford's appointment, because it needed his favorable vote on the draft extension issue, but he can be expected to oppose the Administration on other matters, much like his senior colleague, George Aiken.

Vermont's senior senator, George Aiken, is the senior Republican in the Senate and one of its most respected members. During the '30's, Aiken established a record as one of Vermont's most progressive governors. He was elected to the Senate in 1940, and has been reelected without difficulty ever since; in 1968, he had both the Republican and Democratic nominations. Aiken is currently the ranking Republican on the Senate

Foreign Relations Committee, and he is, like most members of that committee, a dove. His solution for the Vietnam war was enunciated some years ago—announce we won and withdraw. Many citizens have taken Aiken's idea on the matter as the most sensible yet proposed. The Vermont Senator is also a high-ranking member of the Agriculture Committee, where he has fought for tighter regulation of private utilities. New England pays more for its electricity than any other region in the country. Aiken, who was 78 in 1970, can remain in the Senate for as long as he likes.

At this writing, Stafford's House seat remains unfilled. (The new Senator will have to face the voters in 1972 for the unexpired portion of Sen. Prouty's term, but in light of Stafford's high majorities in previous House races, he should have no trouble winning.) Gov. Davis will probably call a special election for late 1971 or early 1972, and possible contenders could include the Governor himself (who will be just finishing his second and, in Vermont tradition, last term) and, for the Democrats, ex-Gov. Hoff. Quite possibly there will be a spirited Republican primary, and 100 years of Vermont history, as well as the 1970 election results, suggest that the new Republican nominee will be the next Congressman-at-Large.

Electoral Votes 3

Census Data 1970 pop. 444,732; 0.22% of U.S. total, 50th largest; change 1960–70, +14.1%. Metro. 0.0%, 0.0% central city. 1970 per capita income, $3,491; 32nd highest. 48th in number of poor.

1970 Share of Federal Tax Burden $351,250,000; 0.18% of U.S. total, 49th largest.

1970 Share of Federal Outlays $335,421,538; 0.18% of U.S. total, 51st largest. Per capita federal spending, $754.

DOD	$58,809,000	52nd (0.10%)	HEW	$125,627,846	48th (0.24%)
AEC	$99,523	45th (—)	HUD	$8,327,661	40th (0.43%)
NASA	$171,499	44th (—)	OEO	$2,019,173	47th (0.27%)
DOT	$32,510,491	48th (0.46%)	DOA	$14,367,781	50th (0.11%)
DOC	$738,495	52nd (0.06%)	POD	$18,117,136	49th (0.25%)
DOI	$4,451,831	51st (0.19%)	VA	$22,494,667	48th (0.30%)
DOJ	$3,708,959	35th (0.65%)	CSC	$5,390,915	49th (0.13%)
			Other	$38,586,561	

Federal Military-Industrial Commitments

DOD Contractors General Electric (Burlington), $34.864m: armament subsystems for 7.62-mm automatic guns. Union Carbide (Bennington), $5.016m: components for artillery fuzes.

DOD Installations St. Albans AF Station (St. Albans).

Economic Base Dairy and livestock; nonelectrical machinery, esp. metalworking machinery and equipment; electrical machinery, equipment, and supplies, esp. electronic components and accessories; printing, publishing, and allied industries, esp. book printing; lumber and wood products other than furniture, esp. sawmills and planing mills; stone, clay, glass, and concrete products, esp. cut stone and stone products; paper and allied products, esp. converted paper and paperboard products other than containers and boxes; household furniture; apparel and other finished products made from fabrics and similar materials; rubber and miscellaneous plastics products.

Political Line up Governor, Deane C. Davis (R); seat up, 1972. Senators, George D. Aiken (R) and Robert T. Stafford (R). Representatives, 1 R at large. State Senate (8 D and 22 R); State House (53 D, 96 R, and 1 Ind).

The Voters

Registration 230,148 total. No party registration.

Employment profile White collar, 38%. Blue collar, 62%.

Ethnic groups Black, less than 0.5%. Total foreign stock, 22%. Canada, 13%; UK, 2%; Italy, Ireland, Poland, Germany, 1% each; others, 3%.

Presidential vote

1968	Humphrey (D)	70,255	(44%)
	Nixon (R)	85,142	(53%)
	Wallace (AIP)	5,104	(3%)
1964	Johnson (D)	108,127	(66%)
	Goldwater (R)	54,942	(34%)
1960	Kennedy (D)	69,186	(41%)
	Nixon (R)	98,131	(59%)

Senator

George David Aiken (R) Elected 1940, seat up 1974; b. Aug. 20, 1892, Dummerston; home, Putney; married; Protestant.

Career Town Rep., 1931, 1933; School Dir., 1920–37; Vt. Legislature, 1930–33, Speaker, 1933–34; Lt. Gov. of Vt., 1935–37; Gov. of Vt., 1937–39.

Offices 358 OSOB, 202-225-4242.

Committees

Agricultural and Forestry (2nd); Subs. (1) Agricultural Credit and Rural Electrification, (2) Environment, Soil Conservation, Forestry.

Foreign Relations (Ranking Mbr.); Subs. (1) Far Eastern Affairs, (2) Near Eastern and South Asian Affairs, (3) U.S. Security Agreements and Commitments Abroad, (4) Western Hemisphere Affairs.

Jt. Com. on Atomic Energy (Ranking Rep. Sen. Mbr.); Subs. (1) Communities, (2) Legislation, (3) Research, Development, and Radiation.

Group Ratings

	ADA	COPE	NREP	NFU	LCV	NAB	NSI	ACA
1970	34	46	45	53	41	67	44	43
1969	56	—	—	73	—	—	—	40
1968	43	88	—	56	—	100	—	48

Key Votes

(1) ABM	AGN	(8) Phil Pln	FOR	(15) Coop-Church	FOR
(2) SST	AGN	(9) Vol Army	AGN	(16) Cut Oil Dpltn	FOR
(3) Busing	FOR	(10) Prison $	ABS	(17) Consumer Prot	AGN
(4) Tob Sub	FOR	(11) Cut Mil $	AGN	(18) Farm Sub Limit	AGN
(5) Carswell	FOR	(12) Defoliatn	FOR	(19) Comp Bid Sales	FOR
(6) No-Knock	FOR	(13) 18-Yr-Vote	FOR	(20) Pre-Prod Tests	FOR
(7) Seniorty	ABS	(14) Pentgn PR	FOR	(21) Cut Marjna Pen	AGN

Election Results

1968 general:	George D. Aiken (R and D), unopposed		
1968 primary:	George D. Aiken (R)	42,318	(73%)
	William K. Tufts (R)	15,786	(27%)
1962 general:	George D. Aiken (R)	81,242	(67%)
	W. Robert Johnson, Sr. (D)	40,134	(33%)

Senator

Robert Theodore Stafford (R) Appointed 1971; b. Aug. 8, 1913, Rutland; home, Rutland City; Middlebury Col., B.S., 1935; U. of Mich., Boston U., LL.B., 1938; Navy, WWII, Korean War; Capt. USNR; married, four children; Congregationalist.

Career Rutland City Grand Juror, 1938–42; Rutland County State Atty., 1947–51; Deputy Atty. Gen., 1953–55; Atty. Gen., 1955–57; Lt. Gov. of Vt., 1957–59; Gov. of Vt., 1959–61.

Offices 5215 NSOB, 202-225-5141. Also 27 S. Main St., Rutland 05701, 802-775-5446.

Committees

Labor and Public Welfare (7th); Subs. (1) Labor, (2) Education, (3) Aging, (4) Handicapped Workers, (5) Sp. Sub. on Evaluation and Planning of Social Programs.

Public Works (8th); Subs. (1) Flood Control—Rivers and Harbors, (2) Economic Development. (Subcommittee assignments tentative)

Veterans' Affairs (5th); Subs. (1) Housing and Insurance, (2) Readjustment, Education, and Employment. (Subcommittee assignments tentative)

Sp. Com. on Aging (9th); Subs. (1) Housing for the Elderly, (2) Employment and Retirement Incomes, (3) Health of the Elderly, (4) Retirement and the Individual. (Subcommittee assignments tentative)

Group Ratings*

	ADA	COPE	NREP	NFU	LCV	CFA	NAB	NSI	ACA
1970	60	60	75	77	43	89	67	80	28
1969	40	—	—	67	—	—	—	—	20
1968	42	39	—	69	—	—	83	—	35

Key Votes*

(1) ABM	FOR	(6) 18-Yr-Vote	FOR	(11) Clean Water $	AGN
(2) SST	AGN	(7) Farm Sub Lmt	FOR	(12) Mig Wrkrs Comp	AGN
(3) Phil Pln	FOR	(8) Coop-Church	FOR	(13) Jets to Chiang	AGN
(4) No-Knock	FOR	(9) Family Asst	FOR	(14) State OEO Veto	AGN
(5) Cmutr Tax	ABS	(10) Work Stamps	FOR	(15) Park Logging	AGN

Election Results†

1970 general:	Robert T. Stafford (R)	103,806	(68%)
	Bernard O'Shea (D)	44,415	(29%)
	Dennis J. Morrisseau (Liberty Union)	4,315	(3%)
1970 primary:	Robert T. Stafford (R)	33,678	(85%)
	Adelaide Knowles (R)	6,099	(15%)
1968 general:	Robert T. Stafford (D), unopposed		

VIRGINIA

Political Background

Ten years ago any analysis of Virginia politics was simply an analysis of the Byrd Machine, an organization that had dominated the state since 1925. That was the year in which Harry Flood Byrd was elected governor. When Byrd went to the Senate in 1933, Franklin Roosevelt had hopes that the Virginian, who was a relatively progressive governor, would support the New Deal. These hopes were dashed as Byrd's name soon became synonymous wih conservative opposition to government spending and deficit budgets. As chairman of the Senate Finance Committee and founder of the Joint Committee on Reduction of Federal Expenditures, Senator Byrd had at least two forums from which to promulgate his views. Despite his best efforts, however, the federal budget continued to rise year by year. At the same time, the voters of the Senator's home state continued to reelect Byrd with near automatic regularity, and he remained in the Senate until 1965—long enough to see most of Lyndon Johnson's Great Society programs enacted into law.

Senator Byrd controlled Virginia politics through an unusual and quite remarkable organization. This was the Byrd Machine. Most old-style political machines are run by

* As member of the House.

† Congressional races.

men who can make a living only in politics, and who do so by controlling large numbers of votes in large cities. By contrast, the men of the Byrd Machine were more often than not bankers, established lawyers, wealthy businessmen, and gentlemen farmers —men who dominated life in the small towns of the Shenandoah Valley, Byrd's home area, or Southside Virginia, an area of the state most like the Deep South. The key to the Machine's success was a small electorate; Virginia's voting laws, especially the poll tax, kept the turnout low and excluded most blacks and many poor whites from voting. The succession of Byrd Machine governors had personal friends who ran the Virginia Electric Power Company, the state's large banks, and the University of Virginia—rich, elderly, respected, reserved, and, of course, conservative.

The Byrd Machine made just one appeal to all of Virginia's voters. That came in the mid-'50's with the Massive Resistance program. For a few years, schools under orders to integrate were closed down and attempts were made to subsidize private, all-white schools. But the program of defiance collapsed and the governor agreed to comply with the law. During the period of Massive Resistance, the character of the oratory revealed the character of the Byrd Machine: the speech-making in Virginia was much more like that of John C. Calhoun and his stringent reading of the Constitution rather than that of Orval Faubus and George Wallace. During the same period, these two men preferred the standing-in-the-schoolhouse-door style of bombast.

Soon after Byrd's death in 1965, it became clear that the Byrd Machine was crumbling. His longtime senatorial colleague, A. Willis Robertson, chairman of the Senate Banking and Currency Committee, was defeated in the 1966 Democratic primary by state Sen. William B. Spong. By traditional Virginia standards, Spong was a flaming liberal. Harry F. Byrd, who spent almost 20 years in the state Senate as his father's heir apparent, had a close shave in the 1966 primary. The younger Byrd went on to win the general election with only 53% of the vote, which was 6% less than the more liberal Spong received in the same election. Moreover, Congressman Howard W. Smith, the 83-year-old autocratic and ultraconservative chairman of the House Rules Committee, was defeated that year in the Democratic primary. Smith had served in the House for 36 years.

During the Byrd years, Virginia had undergone a virtually unnoticed change. What was a predominantly rural state, which had a large urban voting bloc only in traditionally conservative Richmond, became a part of the East Coast megalopolis. By 1970, the Virginia suburbs of Washington made up nearly 20% of the state's population, and the industrialized Tidewater area around Norfolk and Newport News accounted for another 22%. The explosive growth of these places was due mostly to the operations of the federal government—particularly military installations. Arlington claims the Pentagon, while there are huge Naval bases and shipbuilding yards in and near Norfolk. The people living here, of course, do not share the Byrds' mistrust of Washington and of the money it spends. And when one adds the traditionally anti-Byrd mountain country in the far western part of the state, Byrd strongholds contain less than a majority of Virginia voters. The Senator's death coincided with the Voting Rights Act of 1965 and the abolition of the poll tax, both of which vastly increased the number of black, rural poor white, and industrial blue-collar white votes in the state.

The result is a politics in flux. The Byrds have tacitly supported Republican presidential candidates since 1952 and Richard Nixon did carry the state in 1968. But the race for governor clearly demonstrated the weakness of the Machine. In the Democratic primary, its candidate, Lt. Gov. Fred Pollard ran a poor third; Pollard finished behind moderate-to-liberal lawyer William Battle and ahead of populistic state Sen. Harry Howell of Norfolk. Howell has built a black and blue-collar white coalition based on opposition to the state's giant utilities and banks. In the general election, the form book again proved a false guide, as the governorship was won by Republican A. Linwood Holton. Holton did it by forging an alliance of blacks, labor, and white-collar suburbanites. By 1970, the situation looked so bleak for the Machine that Sen. Harry Byrd, Jr., who was up for reelection, announced that he would not enter the Democratic primary but run as an Independent. Many in the state figured Byrd would have lost had he run in that primary.

The primary turned out to be a replay of the Howell-Battle gubernatorial fight of 1969. The Howell-backed candidate, George Rawlings—the man who beat Chairman

Smith in 1966—won the election by a mere 700 votes. But the most notable fact about the primary was the low turnout. The supporters of the Machine simply didn't vote and left the result to the Tidewater area and to the Washington suburbs. For the general election, Nixon's key political advisors and Virginia Congressman Joel Broyhill wanted to endorse Byrd, or at least did not want to run any Republican against him. Gov. Holton, however, balked. Earlier, the governor made the front pages when he walked his daughter to a new, predominantly black school in Richmond. And Holton, for this election, engineered the nomination of state Delegate (state Representative) Ray Garland, a young moderate. Garland's plan was to occupy the middle ground between the conservative Byrd and the liberal, antiwar Rawlings.

At first, it appeared that Byrd was in trouble. But as the campaign wore on, federal court orders that required busing to achieve desegregation hit the newspapers, and Byrd took the lead. He used the slogan "You know what he stands for." The campaign then became not so much a contest between Byrd and his opponents but a struggle between Rawlings and Garland for the anti-Byrd vote. On election day, Byrd won 54% of the votes, leaving Rawlings with 31% and Garland just 15%.

Many conservative Republicans supported Byrd. These voters knew that Nixon strategists boycotted Garland's campaign, hoping (vainly as it turned out) that Byrd would vote with the Republicans to organize the Senate. Byrd, of course, also won what was left of the Machine votes in the Shenandoah Valley, Richmond, and Southside Virginia. Rawlings carried the western mountains, where Garland also did well, and almost carried the Tidewater area, where Garland got only about 10% of the vote. But the vote in the Washington suburbs—which Byrd carried by 20,000 votes over Rawlings—showed that there was one too many anti-Byrd candidates.

No candidate with similar views whose name was something other than Byrd could have done so well. Moreover, the thinness of the margin showed that the Machine was not the power that it once was. Still, the anti-Byrd people, whose sources of support are both geographically and demographically disparate, showed that they cannot defeat Byrd himself, even though they have pretty well dismantled the Machine.

The question now is whether Byrd's followers want back into the Democratic party. Part of the answer will be furnished by the 1972 congressional primaries. In 1970, the Machine left most of the slots in these elections to liberal candidates. And in the general elections that followed, the Republicans won six districts, which gave them a majority of the Virginia House delegation for the first time in history. Another part of the answer will be provided by the 1973 gubernatorial contest. Gov. Holton is ineligible for a second term, and the expected Democratic candidate—liberal Lt. Gov. J. Sergeant Reynolds, heir to the aluminum fortune—died of a brain tumor in 1971 at age 34. One likely candidate is Harry Howell, and if he looks like the sure nominee, the Machine might try another independent candidacy.

The 1972 Senate campaign will be a different sort of test. Virginians, as a matter of tradition, usually leave their incumbent senators alone. Only seven men, one of them an interim appointee, have represented the state in the Senate in the past fifty years. Sen. William Spong will probably win the Democratic nomination with little fuss. Spong has tread a middle course between the Nixon Administration and its opponents. He supported the Haynsworth nomination, but opposed Carswell; supported Nixon in foreign affairs and military policy, but voiced skepticism at times. His likely Republican opponent will be 8th district Congressman, William Scott; he is the man who beat George Rawlings in 1966 after Rawlings upset Chairman Smith. Scott, a hard-campaigning conservative, no doubt hopes to cut into Spong's strength in Southside Virginia, the conservative Shenandoah, and in his home district (which includes part of the Washington suburbs). A race between the two men will be the closest thing to a Northern style conservative-liberal contest that Virginia has ever seen. There could even be a Byrd-style Independent in the race to boot. One question in this race is whether Byrd will support Spong, his more liberal colleague; the other question is the extent to which Gov. Holton supports the more conservative Scott.

Electoral Votes 12

Census Data 1970 pop. 4,648,494; 2.26% of U.S. total, 14th largest; change 1960–70, +17.2%. Metro. 61.2%, 24.2% central city. 1970 per capita income, $3,586; 28th highest. 16th in number of poor.

1970 Share of Federal Tax Burden $3,863,780,000; 1.98% of U.S. total, 16th largest.

1970 Share of Federal Outlays $4,704,507,703; 2.48% of U.S. total, 12th largest. Per capita federal spending, $1,012.

DOD	$2,284,633,000	5th (3.98%)	HEW	$884,936,483	19th (1.69%)
AEC	$1,383,905	34th (0.53%)	HUD	$50,396,186	12th (2.59%)
NASA	$111,858,976	9th (3.04%)	OEO	$10,397,173	27th (1.37%)
DOT	$267,944,195	7th (3.75%)	DOA	$201,189,399	14th (1.56%)
DOC	$25,480,268	11th (2.20%)	POD	$130,551,393	17th (1.79%)
DOI	$41,267,220	17th (1.79%)	VA	$204,912,661	13th (2.78%)
DOJ	$11,165,487	16th (1.94%)	CSC	$171,176,993	6th (4.25%)
			Other	$307,214,364	

Economic Base Tobacco, livestock, and dairy; textile mill products, esp. broad woven cotton fabric mills; chemicals and allied products, esp. plastics materials and synthetic resins, synthetic rubber, synthetic and other man-made fibers except glass; apparel and other finished products made from fabrics and similar materials, esp. men's, youths', and boys' furnishings, work clothing, and allied garments; food and kindred products, esp. meat products; transportation equipment, esp. ship building and repairing; electrical machinery, equipment, and supplies, esp. communication equipment; furniture and fixtures, esp. household furniture; lumber and wood products other than furniture, esp. sawmills and planing mills.

Political Line-up Governor, Linwood Holton (R); seat up, 1973. Senators, Harry Flood Byrd, Jr. (Ind.) and William B. Spong, Jr. (D). Representatives, 10 (4 D and 6 R). State Senate (32 D, 7 R, and 1 Ind.); State House (76 D and 24 R).

The Voters

Registration 1,765,078 total. No party registration.

Employment profile White collar, 40%. Blue collar, 60%.

Ethnic groups Black, 19%. Total foreign stock, 5%. UK, Canada, 1% each; all other groups, less than 0.5% each.

Presidential vote

1968	Humphrey (D)	442,387	(33%)
	Nixon (R)	590,319	(44%)
	Wallace (AIP)	320,272	(24%)
1964	Johnson (D)	558,038	(54%)
	Goldwater (R)	481,334	(46%)
1960	Kennedy (D)	362,327	(47%)
	Nixon (R)	404,521	(53%)

Senator

Harry Flood Byrd, Jr. (Independent) Elected Nov. 12, 1965, seat up 1976; b. Dec. 20, 1914, Winchester; home, Winchester; Va. Military Inst., 1931–33; U. of Va., 1933–35; USNR, WWII; married, three children; Episcopalian.

Career Newspaper editor; orchardist; Chm., Va. Advisory Bd. on Industrial Dev., 1962–67; Va. Senate, 1948–65; second person in history of U.S. Senate to be elected as an Independent.

Offices 417 OSOB, 202-225-4024. Also Winchester 22601, 703-662-7745.

Committees

Armed Services (7th); Subs. (1) Chm., General Legislation, (2) Military Construction Authorization, (3) Preparedness Investigating, (4) Status of Forces, (5) Strategic Arms Limitation Talks, (6) Sp. to Review Bomber Defense, (7) Ad Hoc on Research and Development.

Finance (8th).

Group Ratings

	ADA	COPE	NREP	NFU	LCV	NAB	NSI	ACA
1970	22	8	17	47	33	75	90	87
1969	11	—	—	44	—	—	—	88
1968	0	17	—	30	—	67	—	83

Key Votes

(1) ABM	FOR	(8) Phil Pln	AGN	(15) Coop-Church	AGN
(2) SST	AGN	(9) Vol Army	AGN	(16) Cut Oil Dpltn	AGN
(3) Busing	AGN	(10) Prison $	AGN	(17) Consumer Prot	FOR
(4) Tob Sub	FOR	(11) Cut Mil $	AGN	(18) Farm Sub Limit	FOR
(5) Carswell	FOR	(12) Defoliatn	FOR	(19) Comp Bid Sales	FOR
(6) No-Knock	AGN	(13) 18-Yr-Vote	AGN	(20) Pre-Prod Tests	ABS
(7) Seniorty	FOR	(14) Pentgn PR	AGN	(21) Cut Marjna Pen	FOR

Election Results

1970 general:	Harry F. Byrd, Jr. (Ind.)	506,237	(54%)
	George C. Rawlings, Jr. (D)	294,582	(31%)
	Ray Garland (R)	144,765	(15%)
1970 primary:	Harry F. Byrd, Jr. (Ind.), unopposed		
1966 special:	Harry F. Byrd, Jr. (D)	389,028	(53%)
	Lawrence M. Traylor (R)	272,804	(37%)
	John W. Carter (Ind.)	57,692	(8%)
	J. B. Brayman (Ind.)	10,180	(1%)

Senator

William Belser Spong, Jr. (D) Elected 1966, seat up 1972; b. Sept. 29, 1920, Portsmouth; home, Portsmouth; Hampden-Sydney Col.; U. of Va., LL.B.; U. of Edinburgh, Scotland; Army Air Corps, WWII; married, two children; Methodist.

Career Practicing atty., 1947– ; Lecturer in law and gov., Col. of William and Mary, 1948–49; Va. state legislature, 1954–55; Va. Senate, 1956–66; Chm., Va. Commission on Pub. Ed., 1958–62.

Offices 5327 NSOB, 202-225-2023. Also 215 Fed. Bldg., Portsmouth 23704, 703-627-7471, ext. 7322.

Committees

Commerce (10th); Subs. (1) Aviation, (2) Consumer, (3) Environment, (4) Merchant Marine, (5) Oceans and Atmosphere.

Foreign Relations (9th); Subs. (1) European Affairs, (2) Oceans and International Environment, (3) Western Hemisphere Affairs.

Sel. Com. on Equal Educational Opportunity (7th).

Group Ratings

	ADA	COPE	NREP	NFU	LCV	NAB	NSI	ACA
1970	41	31	25	81	27	25	70	57
1969	50	—	—	75	—	—	—	63
1968	29	34	—	38	—	40	—	41

Key Votes

(1) ABM	FOR	(8) Phil Pln	AGN	(15) Coop-Church	FOR
(2) SST	AGN	(9) Vol Army	AGN	(16) Cut Oil Dpltn	FOR
(3) Busing	AGN	(10) Prison $	ABS	(17) Consumer Prot	FOR
(4) Tob Sub	FOR	(11) Cut Mil $	AGN	(18) Farm Sub Limit	FOR
(5) Carswell	AGN	(12) Defoliatn	FOR	(19) Comp Bid Sales	FOR
(6) No-Knock	AGN	(13) 18-Yr-Vote	FOR	(20) Pre-Prod Tests	FOR
(7) Seniorty	FOR	(14) Pentgn PR	AGN	(21) Cut Marjna Pen	AGN

Election Results

1966 general:	William B. Spong, Jr. (D)	429,855	(59%)
	James P. Ould, Jr. (R)	245,681	(34%)
	F. Lee Hawthorne (Ind.)	58,251	(8%)
1966 primary:	William B. Spong, Jr. (D)	216,885	(50%)
	A. Willis Robertson (D)	216,274	(50%)

FIRST DISTRICT Political Background

Virginia 1 is part of Tidewater Virginia, the lowlands lying along the Atlantic Coast and Chesapeake Bay. The district includes the tip of the Delmarva Peninsula, now connected with Norfolk by a bridge-and-tunnel complex, and several predominantly rural Tidewater counties which have changed little since George Washington's time. Almost 80% of the district's population, however, is concentrated in three Hampton Roads cities: Newport News (pop. 138,000), Hampton (pop. 120,000), and across the bay, Virginia Beach (pop. 172,000). All three are sustained in large part by the United States Navy and the National Aeronautics and Space Administration. The Navy has a large shipyard at Newport News and a giant training center at Virginia Beach; NASA has a large research facility in Hampton. There are substantial black communities in Newport News and Hampton, and the whole area, particularly Virginia Beach, has had substantial population growth in the last two decades.

Newport News and Hampton made up an area of strength for state Sen. Harry Howell of Norfolk. Howell has had some success forging an electoral alliance between blacks and blue-collar workers (see state write-up). His success, however, has been limited by the emergence of racial issues; the school busing controversy, for example, played an important part in the 1970 senatorial race. And because there has been little unemployment in the Navy-dominated Tidewater, conservative candidates have profited and populistic Howell-backed candidates have been hurt. Virginia Beach, which is somewhat higher income and more white than the cities across the bay, is usually Republican in statewide races.

The 1st is one of the few Virginia congressional districts which has not had a vigorous contest in recent years. The principal reason for this is Congressman Thomas N. Downing, a conservative-to-moderate Democrat who has represented the district since 1958. There is little in Downing's voting record to spur any potential opponent to action. Moreover, the congressman holds senior positions on two committees vital to the economy of the district: Merchant Marine and Fisheries, and Science and Astronautics. Downing has been unopposed in two of the last three general elections, and has won the other by a very large majority.

The state legislature's redistricting plan makes Downing's tenure even more secure. The plan removes Republican-leaning Virginia Beach from the district; this city is the only one which could have provided a base of support for a Republican challenge. The legislature added several Tidewater counties that ordinarily support conservative Democrats. If Downing should retire, the 1st could easily produce an interesting House race. But that is unlikely, and he will no doubt continue to represent the district for some time.

Census Data 1970 pop. 562,155; deviation from current state average, +20.9%; change 1960–70, +40.2%. Metro. 82.6%, 46.1% central city.

1970 Share of Federal Outlays $898,611,574

DOD	$604,201,000	HEW	$79,208,780
AEC	$55,000	HUD	$5,632,726
NASA	$104,046,029	OEO	$640,466
DOT	$11,480,405	DOA	$4,109,222
		Other	$89,237,946

Federal Military-Industrial Commitments

DOD Contractors Newport News Shipbuilding and Dry Dock Co. (Newport News), $242.375m: construction of two nuclear-powered submarines; long lead time appropriations for nuclear-powered guided missile frigate and nuclear-powered aircraft carrier programs; overhaul and refueling of various nuclear-powered submarines.

DOD Installations Fort Eustis AB (Newport News). Fort Monroe AB (Hampton). Naval Administrative Command, Armed Forces Staff College (Williamsburg). Fleet Anti-Air Warfare Training Center (Virginia Beach). Naval Air Station (Virginia Beach). Naval Weapons Station (Yorktown). Cape Charles AF Station (Kiptopeke). Langley AFB (Hampton).

NASA Installations Langley Research Center (Hampton). Wallops Station (Wallops).

Economic Base Cash grain; ship and boat building and repairing; food and kindred products. Also, tourism (Williamsburg).

The Voters

Registration 189,359 total. No party registration.

Employment profile White collar, 40%. Blue collar, 60%.

Ethnic groups Black, 22%. Total foreign stock, 5%. UK, Germany, Canada, 1% each; others, 2%.

Presidential vote

1968	Humphrey (D)	46,022	(32%)
	Nixon (R)	53,955	(37%)
	Wallace (AIP)	44,618	(31%)

Representative

Thomas N. Downing (D) Elected 1958; b. Feb. 1, 1919, Newport News; home, Newport News; Va. Military Inst., B.S., 1940; U. of Va., 1947; Army, WWII; married, one child; Episcopalian.

Career Practicing atty., 1958– ; Substitute Judge, Municipal Ct., City of Warwick (now Newport News), 1953–58.

Offices 2135 RHOB, 202-225-4261. Also 1 Court St., Hampton 23369, 703-723-1885, and City Hall, Princess Anne Station, Virginia Beach 23456, 703-427-5050, and P.O. Bldg., Cape Charles 23310, 703-331-3767.

Committees

Merchant Marine and Fisheries (7th); Subs. (1) Fisheries and Wildlife Conservation, (2) Merchant Marine, (3) Oceanography, (4) Sp. on Maritime Education and Training.

Science and Astronautics (6th); Subs. (1) Chm., NASA Oversight, (2) Space Sciences and Applications.

Group Ratings

	ADA	COPE	NREP	NFU	LCV	CFA	NAB	NSI	ACA
1970	8	25	8	46	22	52	67	100	61
1969	0	—	—	50	—	—	—	—	69
1968	0	34	—	44	—	—	40	—	67

Key Votes

(1) ABM	FOR	(6) 18-Yr-Vote	AGN	(11) Clean Water $	AGN
(2) SST	FOR	(7) Farm Sub Lmt	AGN	(12) Mig Wrkrs Comp	AGN
(3) Phil Pln	AGN	(8) Coop-Church	AGN	(13) Jets to Chiang	FOR
(4) No-Knock	FOR	(9) Family Asst	AGN	(14) State OEO Veto	FOR
(5) Cmutr Tax	ABS	(10) Work Stamps	FOR	(15) Park Logging	AGN

Election Results

1970 general:	Thomas N. Downing (D), unopposed		
1970 primary:	Thomas N. Downing (D), unopposed		
1968 general:	Thomas N. Downing (D)	96,265	(73%)
	James S. Stafford (R)	19,229	(15%)
	Rev. J. C. Fauntleroy, Jr. (Ind.)	16,456	(13%)

SECOND DISTRICT Political Background

Virginia 2 is made up of the cities of Norfolk and Portsmouth, two industrial ports with large Naval facilities. By all odds, this is the most liberal of Virginia's districts. It is the only one which gave a plurality to Hubert Humphrey in 1968. The 2nd is also the home of state Sen. Harry Howell, who ran a strong race for governor in 1969, and whose populistic kind of politics is now a major force in Virginia's Democratic party. Both Norfolk and Portsmouth are central cities, and both have large black populations—31% district-wide—which are well-organized politically. The blacks here usually function as part of Howell's coalition of Virginia blacks and working-class whites (see state write-up).

But despite the success of the coalition in statewide and local races, it has had no success in congressional contests. In 1968, Congressman Porter Hardy, Jr., a 22-year incumbent and high-ranking member of the House Armed Services Committee, decided to retire. Aspirants for the seat included Frederick T. Stant, a liberal Democrat backed by the Howell forces, and G. William Whitehurst, a college dean and for six years, a TV news analyst. It may have been the TV exposure that made the difference; Whitehurst won, 54–46, went to the House, and not surprisingly, to the Armed Services Committee. Here he has been a staunch supporter of the Pentagon and of Nixon's policies on the war.

Since his first election, Whitehurst has exhibited all the virtues needed by a freshman congressman to keep his seat. He flies home to speak before any gathering of 2nd district voters, including Sunday black church services. His seat on the Armed Services gives him some say on what happens to Norfolk's most important industry—the United States Navy. And he quite often reminds the voters of his seat on that committee. In 1970, the Congressman was challenged by Howell's 1969 campaign manager. But despite the challenger's local contacts, he fell far short of the 1968 Democratic showing. Whitehurst won a solid 62% of the vote and even cut into Democratic majorities in black areas.

The 1972 election should be no problem at all for Whitehurst. The legislature has removed working-class Portsmouth from the district and added high-income Virginia Beach, a city which usually produces substantial Republican majorities.

Census Data 1970 pop. 418,914; deviation from current state average, –9.9%; change 1960–70, –0.2%. Metro. 100.0%, 100.0% central city.

1970 Share of Federal Outlays $695,286,212

DOD	$468,632,000	HEW	$74,542,217
AEC	$4,553	HUD	$19,940,760
NASA	$1,241,038	OEO	$670,122
DOT	$40,219,820	DOA	$5,045,586
		Other	$84,990,113

Federal Military-Industrial Commitments

DOD Contractors Norfolk Shipbuilding Co. (Norfolk), $10.730m: overhaul of various ships.

DOD Installations Fort Story AB (Norfolk). Operational Control Office U.S. Atlantic Fleet (Norfolk). Naval Air Station (Norfolk). Naval Weapons Station (St. Juliens Creek). Naval Amphibious Base (Norfolk). Naval Communication Station (Norfolk). Naval Hospital (Portsmouth). Naval Air Rework Facility (Norfolk). Naval Supply Center (Norfolk). Naval Station (Norfolk). Public Works Center (Norfolk). Naval Degaussing Station (Norfolk).

Economic Base Ship building and repairing; food and kindred products; printing, publishing, and allied industries; stone, clay, glass, and concrete products. Also, banking.

The Voters

Registration 140,341 total. No party registration.

Employment profile White collar, 44%. Blue collar, 56%.

Ethnic groups Black, 31%. Total foreign stock, 7%. UK, Italy, Canada, USSR, Germany, 1% each; others, 3%.

Presidential vote

1968	Humphrey (D)	44,211	(43%)
	Nixon (R)	31,704	(31%)
	Wallace (AIP)	26,627	(26%)

Representative

G. William Whitehurst (R) Elected 1968; b. March 12, 1925, Norfolk; home, Norfolk; Washington and Lee U., B.A., 1950; U. of Va., M.A., 1951; W.Va. U., Ph.D., 1962; Navy, WWII; married, two children; Methodist.

Career Faculty, hist. dept., Old Dominion Col., 1950–68, Dean of Students, 1963–68; Bd. Chm., Norfolk Forum; Staff of pub. affairs and news dept., WTAR-TV, 1962–68.

Offices 424 CHOB, 202-225-4215. Also 201 Fed. Bldg., Norfolk 23510, 703-627-7471, ext. 7550, and Rm. 216, Fed. Bldg., Portsmouth 23704, 703-441-6763.

Committees

Armed Services (14th); Subs. (1) No. 4, (2) Sp. on Real Estate.

Group Ratings

	ADA	COPE	NREP	NFU	LCV	CFA	NAB	NSI	ACA
1970	16	42	45	67	50	80	58	100	50
1969	7	—	—	47	—	—	—	—	67

Key Votes

(1) ABM	FOR	(6) 18-Yr-Vote	FOR	(11) Clean Water $	AGN
(2) SST	FOR	(7) Farm Sub Lmt	ABS	(12) Mig Wrkrs Comp	AGN
(3) Phil Pln	AGN	(8) Coop-Church	AGN	(13) Jets to Chiang	FOR
(4) No-Knock	FOR	(9) Family Asst	FOR	(14) State OEO Veto	AGN
(5) Cmutr Tax	AGN	(10) Work Stamps	FOR	(15) Park Logging	ABS

Election Results

1970 general:	G. William Whitehurst (R)	44,099	(62%)
	Joseph T. Fitzpatrick (D)	27,362	(38%)
1970 primary:	G. William Whitehurst (R), unopposed		
1968 general:	G. William Whitehurst (R)	51,184	(54%)
	Frederick T. Stant, Jr. (D)	43,229	(46%)

THIRD DISTRICT Political Background

Virginia 3 comprises the city of Richmond and two surrounding suburban counties. Many of the white citizens of Richmond, the capital of the Confederacy, retain a conservatism not unlike the one espoused by Jefferson Davis. The city does have a large black minority, 42%, and these blacks, unlike those in many large cities, still show a willingness to support Republican candidates, if only because many Virginia Democrats are very conservative men. The black voters enabled Hubert Humphrey to carry the city in 1968. But in the district as a whole, their votes are overwhelmed once the returns for the rapidly-growing, nearly all-white suburban counties start coming in. As a result, the 3rd produced a solid margin for Richard Nixon in the last presidential election.

In recent years, the politics of this district nicely illustrates the kind of flux which characterizes Virginia politics generally. In 1969, the Republican gubernatorial candidate, Linwood Holton, received 65% of the district's votes. He compiled the margin through a coalition of city blacks and white suburbanites. The suburbanites have voted for Republican presidential candidates for years, but have usually stayed with the Byrd Machine in state races. The Crusade for Voters, a Richmond-based black organization, was unhappy enough with the state's Democrats to support the moderate Holton. The success of the governor inspired Holton Republicans to make a fight for the 3rd in 1970. Their candidate was J. Harvie Wilkinson III, a 26-year-old University of Virginia law student, whose father, a prominent banker, had many connections in Richmond's establishment. Wilkinson, the theory ran, was a candidate who could carry both the suburbs and the black community. The blacks, of course, were far from happy with incumbent Congressman David E. Satterfield III, a conservative Democrat.

Satterfield came to the seat more or less by inheritance. His father, David E. Satterfield, Jr., was congressman from 1937 to 1945, and was succeeded by another Byrd Democrat, J. Vaughn Gary. When Gary decided to retire, Satterfield III seemed the logical candidate. But Virginia House seats were not as easily passed along in the '60's as they were in the '40's and '50's. In 1964, Republican Barry Goldwater carried the district. And in the 1964 congressional campaign here, the Republican candidate waged a strong campaign. Moreover, a strong Independent candidate, liberal Edward Haddock, won most of the black vote. It was a rare political event, a close three-man House race. Satterfield won the election, but just barely; he beat the Republican by 654 votes and the independent by 4,657.

Once in office, Satterfield had less difficulty. And the 1970 Wilkinson challenge, which at first seemed so promising to Holton Republicans, fizzled. The failure stemmed from the Richmond school desegregation case. In it, a federal judge ordered into effect a plan that would require the busing of several thousand students. Satterfield came on strong against the idea, while Wilkinson, with his black support, of course seemed less vigorously opposed. As a result, Wilkinson's backing in the suburbs vanished. He ended up running nearly even with the total vote of the two anti-Byrd Senate candidates (see state write-up), which meant that Satterfield took 67% of the vote. Most of Wilkinson's votes came from blacks and the few white liberals who supported Humphrey in 1968. Virtually all of the 1968 Nixon voters—a majority in the district—switched to Byrd and Satterfield.

The defeat dealt a blow to Gov. Holton's brand of Republicanism and also demonstrated that the Byrd Machine, while no longer an irresistible force in statewide races, is still dominant in the Richmond area. And surely the results show that Satterfield is unbeatable in the 3rd district, one which will not be altered by redistricting.

Census Data 1970 pop. 480,840; deviation from current state average, +3.4%; change 1960–70, +17.7%. Metro. 100.0%, 52.0% central city.

1970 Share of Federal Outlays $501,995,081

DOD	$121,749,000	HEW	$150,185,207
AEC	$000	HUD	$11,684,234
NASA	$856,441	OEO	$1,231,754
DOT	$10,749,281	DOA	$70,710,957
		Other	$134,828,207

Federal Military-Industrial Commitments

DOD Installations Defense General Supply Center (Richmond).

Economic Base Tobacco manufactures, esp. cigarettes; chemicals and allied products, esp. plastics materials and synthetic resins, synthetic rubber, synthetic and other manmade fibers, except glass; food and kindred products, esp. bakery products; printing, publishing, and allied industries. Also, higher education (Virginia Commonwealth University); banking and insurance.

The Voters

Registration 201,663 total. No party registration.

Employment profile White collar, 48%. Blue collar, 52%.

Ethnic groups Black, 26%. Total foreign stock, 5%. Germany, UK, 1% each; others, 2%.

Presidential vote

1968	Humphrey (D)	47,172	(29%)
	Nixon (R)	82,607	(52%)
	Wallace (AIP)	30,697	(19%)

Representative

David Edward Satterfield, III (D) Elected 1964; b. Dec. 2, 1920, Richmond; home, Richmond; U. of Richmond; U. of Va.; Navy, WWII; Capt. USNAR; married, two children; Episcopalian.

Career Practicing atty., 1948–50, 1953–65; Asst. U.S. Atty., 1950–53; Richmond Councilman, 1954–56; Va. Legislature, 1960–64; Civilian Adviser to Natl. Health Svc.

Offices 324 CHOB, 202-225-2815. Also Fed. Office Bldg., Richmond 23240, 703-782-2519.

Committees

Interstate and Foreign Commerce (11th); Sub. on Public Health and Environment.

Veterans' Affairs (7th); Subs. (1) Chm., Hospitals, (2) Housing.

Group Ratings

	ADA	COPE	NREP	NFU	LCV	CFA	NAB	NSI	ACA
1970	4	17	0	15	13	45	82	100	79
1969	0	—	—	20	—	—	—	—	88
1968	0	8	—	25	—	—	100	—	100

Key Votes

(1) ABM	FOR	(6) 18-Yr-Vote	AGN	(11) Clean Water $	AGN
(2) SST	FOR	(7) Farm Sub Lmt	AGN	(12) Mig Wrkrs Comp	AGN
(3) Phil Pln	AGN	(8) Coop-Church	AGN	(13) Jets to Chiang	FOR
(4) No-Knock	FOR	(9) Family Asst	AGN	(14) State OEO Veto	FOR
(5) Cmutr Tax	AGN	(10) Work Stamps	FOR	(15) Park Logging	AGN

Election Results

1970 general:	David E. Satterfield III (D)	73,104	(67%)
	J. Harvie Wilkinson III (R)	35,229	(32%)
1970 primary:	David E. Satterfield III (D), unopposed		
1968 general:	David E. Satterfield III (D)	94,118	(60%)
	John S. Hansen (R)	62,082	(40%)

FOURTH DISTRICT Political Background

Virginia 4 comprises part of Southside Virginia—a region that is economically, socially, and politically part of the Deep South. Most of the district is made up of rural counties, where peanuts and tobacco continue to be farmed as they were a century ago. Before the Civil War, much of this area was, in effect, a breeding ground for slaves who were exported south and west (see Mississippi and West Virginia state write-ups). Today, the 4th district still has the largest percentage of blacks of any Virginia district, 38%. But only recently have any significant number of them been able to vote at all, and to a large extent, political decisions in the Southside are still made by a few men in the small courthouse towns. This is just as it was during the years in which the Byrd Machine held undisputed sway.

The current congressman from the district, Watkins M. Abbitt, from Appomattox, is a product of that era. He went to the House in 1948 after winning a special election, and until 1970, never had any serious competition. During that period, Abbitt has risen to become the 4th ranking Democrat on the House Agriculture Committee and chairman of its Tobacco Subcommittee—a post of no small importance to his district. He is also a senior member of the House Administration Committee, and one of the stalwarts of the conservative Southern Democratic bloc.

Abbitt opposed with some vigor the Voting Rights Act of 1965. He did so, of course, with good reason. That piece of legislation gave the rural Negroes of his district the effective right to vote; in short, it has created opposition to the congressman where none existed before. In 1966, the Rev. S. W. Tucker, a black, received 22% of the district's votes without a campaign. In 1970, Abbitt faced two opponents. The most dangerous, it seemed, was Ben Ragsdale, Jr., a 26-year-old native of the district who had served as an aide to liberal state Sen. Harry Howell of Norfolk. Ragsdale campaigned as an outspoken opponent of the war. That stand met little disapproval, but the district did polarize around the race issue. As it turned out, Ragsdale finished with 28% of the vote, most of which came from blacks. The Republican candidate got only 11%, a percentage which paralleled the weak Southside showing of Republican Senate candidate, Ray Garland, in his race against Harry Byrd, Jr. (see Virginia state write-up).

But Abbitt may face electoral problems once again in the near future. As the population of the rural Southside loses population relative to the rest of the state, the fulcrum of the district has been moving toward urban areas. The 4th already includes black-majority Petersburg (pop. 36,000), site of the famous Civil War battle, and the Norfolk-Portsmouth suburb of Chesapeake (pop. 89,000), a fast-growing, blue-collar area which borders the Dismal Swamp. Moreover, the 1971 redistricting plan removes several rural counties from the district and adds the industrial city of Portsmouth, which has a large and politically active black population.

In 1970, Abbitt ran almost even with Sen. Byrd in the old 4th district, about 61%. In the new district, Byrd's percentage moved down to 56%. This would put anti-Byrd and anti-Abbitt forces within striking distance of the incumbent congressman, if those forces could unite behind one candidate. But any change in representation will probably have to await Abbitt's retirement; he was 62 in 1970. The congressman's seniority and his views on race are formidable assets among the farmers and small town residents of the district. These people, despite the demographic changes, still make up a slight majority of the voters in the 4th.

Census Data 1970 pop. 421,584; deviation from current state average, —9.3%; change 1960–70, +9.2%. Metro. 51.8%, 12.1% central city.

1970 Share of Federal Outlays $288,899,860

DOD	$117,477,000	HEW	$79,111,577
AEC	$000	HUD	$1,095,412
NASA	$000	OEO	$176,902
DOT	$8,519,838	DOA	$25,281,159
		Other	$57,237,972

Federal Military-Industrial Commitments

DOD Installations Fort Lee AB (Petersburg). Fort Lee AF Station (Petersburg).

Economic Base Tobacco and livestock; food and kindred products; chemicals and allied products.

The Voters

Registration 157,012 total. No party registration.

Employment profile White collar, 30%. Blue collar, 70%.

Ethnic groups Black, 38%. Total foreign stock, 3%. Germany, 1%; all other groups, less than 0.5% each.

Presidential vote

1968	Humphrey (D)	40,712	(33%)
	Nixon (R)	38,455	(31%)
	Wallace (AIP)	44,678	(36%)

Representative

Watkins M. Abbitt (D) Elected Feb. 17, 1948; b. May 21, 1908, Appomattox; home, Appomattox; U. of Richmond, LL.B., 1931; married, three children; Baptist.

Career Practicing atty., 1931–48; Commonwealth Atty. for Appomattox, 1932–48; Dem. Elector, 4th Dist. of Va., 1944; Va. Constitutional Convention, 1945; State Dem. Chm., 1964; Dir., Farmers Natl. Bank.

Offices 2209 RHOB, 202-225-6365. Also Appomattox 24522, 703-352-2340, and Rm. 201, Post Office Bldg., Petersburg 23802, 703-732-2544, and Great Bridge Professional Bldg., 101 Mt. Pleasant Rd., Chesapeake 23320, 703-547-2151.

Committees

Agriculture (4th); Subs. (1) Chm., Tobacco, (2) Dairy and Poultry, (3) Livestock and Grains.
House Administration (3rd); Subs. (1) Chm., Elections, (2) Sp. on Contracts.
Standards of Official Conduct (3rd).

Group Ratings

	ADA	COPE	NREP	NFU	LCV	CFA	NAB	NSI	ACA
1970	0	20	0	31	25	36	70	100	76
1969	7	—	—	33	—	—	—	—	90
1968	0	0	—	29	—	—	100	—	95

Key Votes

(1) ABM	FOR	(6) 18-Yr-Vote	AGN	(11) Clean Water $	AGN
(2) SST	FOR	(7) Farm Sub Lmt	AGN	(12) Mig Wrkrs Comp	AGN
(3) Phil Pln	ABS	(8) Coop-Church	AGN	(13) Jets to Chiang	ABS
(4) No-Knock	FOR	(9) Family Asst	AGN	(14) State OEO Veto	ABS
(5) Cmutr Tax	AGN	(10) Work Stamps	FOR	(15) Park Logging	FOR

Election Results

1970 general:	Watkins M. Abbitt (D)	55,233	(61%)
	Ben Ragsdale (Ind.)	25,399	(28%)
	James M. Helms (R)	9,876	(11%)
1970 primary:	Watkins M. Abbitt (D), nominated by Convention		
1968 general:	Watkins M. Abbitt (D)	81,723	(72%)
	S. W. Tucker (R)	32,548	(29%)

FIFTH DISTRICT Political Background

Virginia 5 comprises the western part of Southside Virginia. The district extends from the Blue Ridge Mountains in the west to a point not too far from Norfolk in the east. Out in the mountain country, one place is especially notable, and that is Galax, Virginia—home of the Galax Old Time Fiddlers' Convention. The event, held every August, attracts fiddlers, guitar and banjo and mandolin pickers, and clear-throated vocal talent from four or five states. That fiddle here gets sawed damn near right half in two, and the pickers-and-grinners don't do so bad either. It's good old fashioned down to earth country music, as they say—no electronic circuitry and some of the most exhilarating and wonderful music anywhere, ever.

But most of the terrain of the 5th is taken up by the Piedmont. This is where most of the South's industry is located (see North Carolina 5, 6 and 9, and South Carolina 4). Here in the Virginia Piedmont are the principal cities of the 5th, Danville (pop. 46,000) and Martinsville (pop. 19,000). Both are important textile and furniture manufacturing centers. There are fewer blacks here—25% of the population district-wide—than in the Tidewater area to the east, and as is the pattern throughout the South, the traditional Democratic allegiance gives way to the traditional, pro-Union, anti-planter Republicanism as one approaches the mountain country. The 5th was one of two Virginia districts carried by Wallace in 1968, though Nixon was just a single percentage point behind the Alabaman.

For fifteen years, until his retirement in 1968, William M. Tuck represented the district in Congress. Tuck, an unreconstructed segregationist, served as governor of the state from 1945 to 1949. The current incumbent is a more up-to-date conservative Democrat, W. C. (Dan) Daniel, a former executive at Danville's Dan River Mills and former national commander of the American Legion. In his first election, Daniel had spirited competition from both Republican and Independent candidates, who held his share of the votes down to 55%. But in 1970, the congressman faced opposition from a Republican only, and he ran up a majority more typical of the Southside—73%. As befits a man interested in military matters, Daniel serves on the House Armed Services Committee, where he is a determined and unswerving member of its pro-Pentagon majority. Redistricting has not altered his excellent chances for reelection.

Census Data 1970 pop. 400,116; deviation from current state average, —13.9%; change 1960–70, +3.6%. Metro. 10.8%, 0.0% central city.

1970 Share of Federal Outlays $164,198,016

DOD	$6,167,000	HEW	$76,437,952
AEC	$000	HUD	$000
NASA	$000	OEO	$841,133
DOT	$2,277,495	DOA	$26,679,928
		Other	$51,794,508

Federal Military-Industrial Commitments

None.

Economic Base Tobacco, livestock and dairy; textile mill products; furniture and fixtures, esp. household furniture.

The Voters

Registration 172,735 total. No party registration.
Employment profile White collar, 25%. Blue collar, 75%.
Ethnic groups Black, 25%. Total foreign stock, 1%. All foreign groups less than 0.5% each.

Presidential vote

1968	Humphrey (D)	34,838	(27%)
	Nixon (R)	47,702	(36%)
	Wallace (AIP)	48,491	(37%)

Representative

W. C. (Dan) Daniel (D) Elected 1968; b. May 12, 1914, Chatham; home, Danville; Dan River Textile School; married, one child; Baptist.

Career Various positions including Asst. to Bd. Chm., Dan River Mills, Inc., 1939–68; Va. Legislature, 1959–68.

Offices 1705 LHOB, 202-225-4711. Also 202 Post Office Bldg., Danville 24541, 703-792-1280.

Committees

Armed Services (21st); Subs. (1) No. 2, (2) Sp. on Investigating, (3) Sp. on Real Estate.

Group Ratings

	ADA	COPE	NREP	NFU	LCV	CFA	NAB	NSI	ACA
1970	0	17	0	31	33	43	75	100	79
1969	7	—	—	27	—	—	—	—	94

Key Votes

(1) ABM	FOR	(6) 18-Yr-Vote	AGN	(11) Clean Water $	AGN
(2) SST	FOR	(7) Farm Sub Lmt	AGN	(12) Mig Wrkrs Comp	AGN
(3) Phil Pln	AGN	(8) Coop-Church	AGN	(13) Jets to Chiang	FOR
(4) No-Knock	FOR	(9) Family Asst	AGN	(14) State OEO Veto	FOR
(5) Cmutr Tax	AGN	(10) Work Stamps	FOR	(15) Park Logging	AGN

Election Results

1970 general:	W. C. Daniel (D)	54,261	(73%)
	Allen T. St. Clair, Jr. (R)	20,029	(37%)
1970 primary:	W. C. Daniel (D), unopposed		
1968 general:	W. C. Daniel (D)	70,681	(55%)
	Weldon W. Tuck (R)	34,608	(27%)
	Ruth L. Harvey (Ind.)	24,196	(19%)

SIXTH DISTRICT Political Background

Virginia 6 is part of mountainous western Virginia. The district spans both sides of the Blue Ridge and includes the major cities of Lynchburg (pop. 54,000) and Roanoke (pop. 92,000). Lynchburg, which lies east of the Blue Ridge on the James River, has been a reliable part of Byrd's Virginia—that is, conservative and Democratic; or, more recently, Republican and Independent. Roanoke, which lies between the Blue Ridge and the West Virginia border, is one of the largest urban centers within the Appalachian mountains. Like most mountain country, Roanoke was not particularly sympathetic to slaveholders and the Confederate cause, and since that time, it has been more Republican than most Virginia cities.

It was, therefore, not too surprising when the 6th elected a Republican congressman, Richard H. Poff, in 1952. In that year, the Byrd Machine quietly passed the word that an Eisenhower victory would be quite acceptable. No doubt because of this, the General carried Virginia in a big way and helped to elect three Republicans to the House. In the years that followed, Poff has usually won reelection by huge margins. Poff is now the 2nd ranking Republican on the House Judiciary Committee; in the 93rd Congress he should become the ranking minority member, since William McCulloch of Ohio is retiring.

Unlike McCulloch, Poff has not supported civil rights legislation, though he is highly respected on both sides of the aisle in the House for his knowledgeability and fairness. Poff, who was 47 in 1970, is comparatively young for a congressional veteran; was mentioned as a possible Nixon appointee to a federal judgeship—perhaps to the Supreme Court.

It is therefore likely that the Republican will continue to represent the 6th district. The Democratic legislature has, in a gratuitous move, placed Poff's home town of Radford in the far southwestern 9th district. But Poff, if he runs again, will no doubt change his residence to a place within the boundaries of the new 6th. Otherwise, he would face a primary fight against the 9th's Republican incumbent William Wampler.

Census Data 1970 pop. 424,209; deviation from current state average, —8.7%; change 1960–70, +11.2%. Metro. 61.6%, 34.5% central city.

1970 Share of Federal Outlays $333,025,837

DOD	$107,215,000	HEW	$90,556,096
AEC	$873,888	HUD	$3,171,385
NASA	$577,158	OEO	$2,210,804
DOT	$12,924,080	DOA	$10,197,098
		Other	$105,300,328

Federal Military-Industrial Commitments

DOD Contractors Hercules, Inc. (Radford), $73.681m: production of propellants and explosives and operation of the Army Ammunition plant. Monsanto Enviro-Chem (Radford), $6.102m: installation of an acid recovery system at the Radford Army Ammunition plant.

DOD Installations Bedford Air Force Station (Bedford).

Economic Base Livestock and dairy; electrical machinery, equipment, and supplies; apparel and other finished products made from fabrics and similar materials.

The Voters

Registration 163,086 total. No party registration.

Employment profile White collar, 39%. Blue collar, 61%.

Ethnic groups Black, 13%. Total foreign stock, 2%. UK, 1%; all other groups less than 0.5% each.

Presidential vote

1968	Humphrey (D)	32,892	(25%)
	Nixon (R)	68,099	(52%)
	Wallace (AIP)	29,471	(22%)

Representative

Richard H. Poff (R) Elected 1952; b. Oct. 19, 1923, Radford; home, Radford; Roanoke Col., U. of Va., LL.B., 1948; AAF, WWII; married, three children; Presbyterian.

Career Practicing atty., 1948–52; V. Chm., Natl. Commission on Reform of Fed. Criminal Law.

Offices 2408 RHOB, 202-225-5431. Also Fed. Bldg., Roanoke 24016, 703-345-1118.

Committees

Judiciary (2nd); Sub. No. 5.

Group Ratings

	ADA	COPE	NREP	NFU	LCV	CFA	NAB	NSI	ACA
1970	8	0	17	31	20	48	100	100	83
1969	0	—	—	33	—	—	—	—	88
1968	0	0	—	31	—	—	100	—	96

Key Votes

(1) ABM	FOR	(6) 18-Yr-Vote	AGN	(11) Clean Water $	AGN
(2) SST	ABS*	(7) Farm Sub Lmt	FOR	(12) Mig Wrkrs Comp	AGN
(3) Phil Pln	ABS	(8) Coop-Church	AGN	(13) Jets to Chiang	FOR
(4) No-Knock	FOR	(9) Family Asst	FOR	(14) State OEO Veto	FOR
(5) Cmutr Tax	AGN	(10) Work Stamps	FOR	(15) Park Logging	AGN

* *Voted "against" on previous vote on same issue.*

Election Results

1970 general:	Richard H. Poff (R)	62,311	(75%)
	Roy R. White (D)	21,219	(25%)
1970 primary:	Richard H. Poff (R), unopposed		
1968 general:	Richard H. Poff (R)	91,549	(93%)
	Tom Hufford (D)	7,221	(7%)

SEVENTH DISTRICT Political Background

Virginia 7 comprises the Shenandoah Valley and some adjacent territory east of the Blue Ridge Mountains. The valley, surrounded by mountains, is a scenic wonder; it contains acres of fertile farmland—which the Union forces took some pains to cut off from the rest of the Confederacy during the Civil War. Here also are small cities like Winchester, Front Royal, Harrisonburg, Staunton, and Waynesboro. East of the Blue Ridge is the city of Charlottesville (pop. 38,000), the home of the University of Virginia and Thomas Jefferson's Monticello.

The Shenandoah Valley is the homeland of the Harry Byrd dynasty. The late Senator developed one of the world's largest and most productive apple farms near Berryville, and also acquired newspapers in Winchester and Harrisonburg. His son, Sen. Harry Byrd, Jr., has sustained these interests. The valley today continues to be a Byrd stronghold—steadfastly, but never raucously, conservative. Out in the western part of the state, the race issue has never been as important as it has in Southside Virginia (see Virginia 4). But at the same time, because only 9% of the 7th's residents are black, any anti-Byrd candidate has a relatively small electoral base in the district. In the 1970 Senate race, the 7th was Harry Byrd, Jr.'s second best district; he won here with 61% of the vote. And in that same election, the voters chose a congressman very much like the Senator.

In the spring of 1970, when Sen. Byrd announced he would not seek the Democratic nomination for senator, Congressman John Marsh, a Byrd Democrat from the 7th, also announced that he was uninterested in the Democratic nomination for Congress. First elected in 1962 by a narrow margin, Marsh won only 54% in 1968. In 1970, there was speculation that he would run as an Independent or be drafted as the

Democratic candidate. For some reason, neither of these things happened, and the Democratic nomination went instead to liberal cattle farmer and former ambassador to El Salvador, Murat Williams. Most party officials seemed happier with Williams than Marsh—another indication of the decline of the Byrd forces within the Virginia Democratic party.

The Republican candidate was J. Kenneth Robinson, a Winchester lawyer. Robinson, Harry Byrd, Jr.'s successor in the state Senate, had nearly beaten Marsh in 1962. This candidate moved quickly to tag Williams a "liberal." So there was little question who would win. The interesting thing about Robinson's share of the vote, 62%, was that it nearly matched Sen. Byrd's 61% in the district. This means that virtually all of those in the 7th who voted against the Senator also voted for Williams. The performance is another example of the fluidity of party lines in post-Machine Virginia; the Byrd forces seem to be able to steer their votes to ideologically congenial candidates regardless of party identification.

Redistricting as altered the boundaries of the 7th considerably. The focus of the district has been shifted from the valley to the farmlands between Richmond and the Washington suburbs. The move will not change the electoral outlook here significantly, as the new portions of the district have already shown a willingness to support a conservative Republican congressman (see Virginia 8).

Census Data 1970 pop. 428,054; deviation from current state average, —7.9%; change 1960–70, +13.4%. Metro. 0.0%, 0.0% central city.

1970 Share of Federal Outlays $232,591,937

DOD	$24,934,000	HEW	$97,282,301
AEC	$352,867	HUD	$2,949,692
NASA	$1,014,644	OEO	$615,535
DOT	$17,211,530	DOA	$17,314,084
		Other	$70,917,284

Federal Military-Industrial Commitments

DOD Contractors Sperry Rand (Charlottesville), $7.867m: navigation and radar equipment for various naval craft.

Economic Base Livestock, poultry, and dairy; apparel and other finished products made from fabrics and similar materials; food and kindred products. Also, tourism (Shenandoah and Blue Ridge).

The Voters

Registration 164,607 total. No party registration.

Employment profile White collar, 33%. Blue collar, 67%.

Ethnic groups Black, 9%. Total foreign stock, 3%. UK, 1%; all other groups less than 0.5% each.

Presidential vote

1968	Humphrey (D)	30,026	(25%)
	Nixon (R)	67,004	(55%)
	Wallace (AIP)	24,250	(20%)

Representative

J. Kenneth Robinson (R) Elected 1970; b. May 14, 1916, Winchester; home, Winchester; Va. Polytechnic Inst., B.S., 1937; Army, WWII; married, seven children; Society of Friends.

Career Fruit grower; Pres., Winchester Cold Storage Co.; owner, J. K. Robinson's Orchard; Dir., Winchester Apple Growers Assn., Green Chemical Co., Shenandoah Apple Corp.; Secy., Treas., R & T Packing Corp., Inc.; Va. Senate, 1965–70; Chm., Repub. delegation to 1968, 1969 Gen. Assembly.

Offices 1723 LHOB, 202-225-6561. Also 36 Rouss Ave., Winchester 22601, 703-667-0990.

Committees

Agriculture (14th); Subs. (1) Domestic Marketing and Consumer Relations, (2) Forests.

Government Operations (14th); Subs. (1) Intergovernmental Relations, (2) Special Studies.

Group Ratings, Key Votes: Newly elected.

Election Results

1970 general:	J. Kenneth Robinson (R)	52,619	(62%)
	Murat Williams (D)	32,617	(38%)
1970 primary:	J. Kenneth Robinson (R), nominated by Convention		

EIGHTH DISTRICT Political Background

Virginia 8 comprises the rolling dairy and farm and fox hunting lands of northern Virginia. It is a green, fertile plain that stretches from Chesapeake Bay in the east to the Blue Ridge Mountains in the west. This part of Virginia was the northernmost extension of the Confederacy. Although most of the district lies north of Cincinnati, St. Louis, and San Francisco, the rural residents here have retained Southern accents and Southern political preferences. There are a couple of black-majority counties in the Tidewater area, but district-wide, blacks make up only 15% of the population. Most of the whites on the farms or in the small towns are strong supporters of whichever candidate the Byrd organization happens to be backing.

Recently, however, these rural areas of the district have been overmatched by the Washington suburbs. Prince William County, which contains Manassas—site of the Battle of Bull Run—more than doubled in population, to 111,000, during the '60's. Today, the 8th's portion of suburban Fairfax County, together with Prince William, has about 60% of the district's people.

The demographic trend was responsible for what was probably the most important election in the district's history: the 1966 Democratic primary. For 36 years, the 8th was represented by Howard W. Smith—known as Judge Smith, since he had once been a judge in Alexandria. Smith, who was 83 in 1966, was for many years chairman of the House Committee on Rules (as he insisted it be called). An unbending conservative, the Judge often used the committee's power to control the flow of legislation to his own ideological ends. His power to do so was reduced to some extent in 1961 when the Kennedy Administration and Speaker Sam Rayburn enlarged its membership. Whenever Smith wanted to block a piece of liberal legislation, he was known to repair to his prosperous dairy farm in northern Virginia and tend his cows. In the absence of the chairman, the committee could not meet, and if the committee did not meet, the bill would not reach the floor.

After the 1950 census, the Washington suburbs formerly in the 8th—Arlington, Alexandria, and Fairfax County—were made into a separate congressional district. The Judge then chose to run in the more agreeable confines of the predominantly rural 8th, where, he assumed, no doubt, that he would be reelected without fuss for the rest of his life.

Judge Smith, however, had not anticipated the sudden enfranchisement of blacks after the Voting Rights Act of 1965, or the abolition of the poll tax, or the one-man-one-vote rule which required a portion of Fairfax County to be returned to his district. These events did not escape the attention of liberal Delegate (state Representative) George Rawlings of Fredericksburg. Rawlings waged a spirited primary campaign in 1966, and to the surprise of official Washington—and the delight of most of it—the challenger soundly whipped the Judge.

But Rawlings' victory carried the seeds of his general election defeat. Most of the residents of the district, particularly the enraged courthouse politicians who revered the Judge, were not ready for a liberal congressman. And so the Republican nominee, William L. Scott, was elected in 1966. In any other year, the Republican would have lost quietly to Smith. Scott is an assiduous campaigner, a deeply religious teetotaler, and a conservative and sometimes fiery congressman. He has usually supported the Nixon Administration, though he balks at its family assistance legislation, which he says is "socialism," and therefore unacceptable. The Congressman is reportedly contemplating a 1972 Senate race against William B. Spong, a Democrat considered liberal by traditional Virginia standards. Scott can count on strong conservative Republican support, and he may get the support, or the neutrality, of Sen. Byrd (see state write-up).

Meanwhile, the explosive growth of the Washington suburbs has required a drastic reshaping of the 8th district. Judge Smith would probably fail to recognize it as his old terrain. For 1972, the 8th will consist of Prince William and Loudoun counties and about half of populous Fairfax County. Loudoun, still predominantly rural, is the home of many wealthy fox hunters. This new territory makes up the more conservative portion of the Virginia suburbs of Washington. It should by all odds elect a conservative Republican congressman, though not by an overwhelming margin. Scott would certainly be the favorite to win the new 8th, if for some reason he decides against the Senate race.

Census Data 1970 pop. 594,407; deviation from current state average, +27.9%; change 1960–70, +48.3%. Metro. 67.1%, 0.0% central city.

1970 Share of Federal Outlays $691,441,000 (average outlay per district, Virginia 8 and 10)

DOD	$410,411,000	HEW	$59,561,000
AEC	$22,000	HUD	$2,961,000
NASA	$2,058,000	OEO	$1,041,000
DOT	$74,160,000	DOA	$13,557,000
		Other	$127,670,000

Federal Military-Industrial Commitments (See Virginia 10 for Virginia 8 and 10 listing.)

Economic Base Livestock and dairy; lumber and wood products other than furniture; food and kindred products. Also, extensive commuting to Washington, D.C.

The Voters

Registration 63,081 total. No party registration.

Employment profile White collar, 39%. Blue collar, 61%.

Ethnic groups Black, 15%. Total foreign stock, 5%. UK, Germany, Canada, Italy, 1% each; others, 2%.

Presidential vote

1968	Humphrey (D)	50,200	(34%)
	Nixon (R)	63,769	(43%)
	Wallace (AIP)	33,683	(23%)

Representative

William Lloyd Scott (R) Elected 1966; b. July 1, 1915, Williamsburg; home, Fairfax; George Washington U., J.D., 1938; married, three children; Methodist.

Career Atty., employed by Fed. Gov., 1934–61; practicing atty., 1961–66.

Offices 1217 LHOB, 202-225-4376. Also P.O. Box 192, P.O., Fredericksburg 22401, 703-373-0536.

Committees

Post Office and Civil Service (5th); Subs. (1) Investigations, (2) Retirement, Insurance, and Health Benefits.

Veterans' Affairs (4th); Subs. (1) Compensation and Pension, (2) Hospitals.

Group Ratings

	ADA	COPE	NREP	NFU	LCV	CFA	NAB	NSI	ACA
1970	4	9	8	31	25	33	92	100	89
1969	7	—	—	27	—	—	—	—	100
1968	0	0	—	38	—	—	100	—	95

Key Votes

(1) ABM	FOR	(6) 18-Yr-Vote	AGN	(11) Clean Water $	AGN
(2) SST	FOR	(7) Farm Sub Lmt	FOR	(12) Mig Wrkrs Comp	AGN
(3) Phil Pln	AGN	(8) Coop-Church	AGN	(13) Jets to Chiang	FOR
(4) No-Knock	FOR	(9) Family Asst	AGN	(14) State OEO Veto	FOR
(5) Cmutr Tax	AGN	(10) Work Stamps	ABS	(15) Park Logging	FOR

Election Results

1970 general:	William Lloyd Scott (R)	68,167	(64%)
	Darrel H. Stearns (D)	38,680	(36%)
1970 primary:	William Lloyd Scott (R), unopposed		
1968 general:	William Lloyd Scott (R)	92,121	(65%)
	Andrew McCutcheon (D)	49,731	(35%)

NINTH DISTRICT Political Background

In Virginia political circles, the southwest corner of the state has long been known as the "Fighting 9th." The district has far more in common with neighboring West Virginia and eastern Kentucky than with most of the rest of Virginia. The 9th, a long way from the Tidewater, is really part of Appalachia, and only an accident of history prevented this part of the Old Dominion from becoming part of the new state of West Virginia in 1863 (see West Virginia state write-up). The 9th is a virtually all-white coal mining area, where the hills, scarred by strip miners, are dotted with the rude homes of the impoverished mountaineers who live here. Even today, the federal government means the hated revenuers raiding stills in the hollow.

The 9th, of course, had little sympathy with the Confederate cause up to and during the Civil War. And the Republican allegiances of many of its residents can be traced to those times. Other coal mining people here became Democrats under Franklin D. Roosevelt and John L. Lewis, and have since supported liberal Democrats. The district, as a whole, is an anti-Byrd stronghold in the state; in 1970, it was the only district that Sen. Harry Byrd could not carry. The Senator finished a poor third, with only 30% of the vote—a showing far below his performance anywhere else in the state.

For 12 years, from 1954 to 1966, the 9th elected Virginia's only liberal Democratic congressman, W. Pat Jennings. In 1966, however, given the sentiment that had developed against the Johnson Administration, Jennings was unseated by the man he had beaten in 1954 and 1956, Republican William C. Wampler. Jennings went on to become clerk of the House of Representatives. His appointment to the post was taken as a form of patronage to the liberal Democratic Study Group, and therefore something of a milestone in the progress that reform group had made in the House.

Wampler, who was first elected to Congress in 1952 at age 26, reentered the House at age 40. He went about making sure that he would not be defeated again. Because his previous service put him ahead of other members elected in 1966 in seniority, Wampler is now the 3rd ranking Republican on the House Agriculture Committee and ranking minority member on its Dairy and Poultry and its Tobacco subcommittees. The first subcommittee is important to his district; the second, to the state as a whole.

Congressman Wampler has succeeded in increasing his share of the district's votes in the two elections since 1966, and with Jennings safely ensconced in the clerk's post, Wampler appears entrenched in the 9th. Redistricting has added several counties to his terrain, including the independent city of Radford, home of 6th district congressman Richard Poff. But it is unlikely that Poff will challenge his fellow Republican Wampler in the new 9th (see Virginia 6).

Census Data 1970 pop. 358,050; deviation from current state average, —23.0%; change 1960–70, —7.5%. Metro. 0.0%, 0.0% central city.

1970 Share of Federal Outlays $205,911,320

DOD	$13,467,000	HEW	$99,691,667
AEC	$000	HUD	$000
NASA	$7,095	OEO	$1,928,705
DOT	$16,298,179	DOA	$14,736,419
		Other	$59,782,255

Federal Military-Industrial Commitments

None.

Economic Base Tobacco, livestock, and dairy; bituminous coal; apparel and other finished products made from fabrics and similar materials; household furniture.

The Voters

Registration 178,742 total. No party registration.

Employment profile White collar, 28%. Blue collar, 72%.

Ethnic groups Black, 2%. Total foreign stock, 1%. All foreign groups less than 0.5% each.

Presidential vote

1968	Humphrey (D)	44,664	(37%)
	Nixon (R)	56,296	(47%)
	Wallace (AIP)	19,516	(16%)

Representative

William Creed Wampler (R) Elected 1966; b. April 21, 1926, Pennington Gap; home, Bristol; Va. Polytechnic Inst., B.S., 1948; U. of Va., 1949–50; Navy, WWII; married, two children; Presbyterian.

Career Pres., Va. Young Repub.'s Fed., 1950–52; U.S. House of Reps., 1952–54; Chm., Va. 9th Dist. Repub. Com., 1965–66; furniture and carpet business; newspaperman; Sp. Asst. to Gen. Mgr., Atomic Energy Commission; Bristol Redev. and Housing Auth., 1965–66, Bristol Utilities Bd., 1966.

Offices 323 CHOB, 202-225-3861. Also 524 Cumberland St., P.O. Box 890, Bristol 24201, 703-669-9451.

Committees

Agriculture (3rd); Subs. (1) Dairy and Poultry, (2) Oilseeds and Rice, (3) Tobacco.

Group Ratings

	ADA	COPE	NREP	NFU	LCV	CFA	NAB	NSI	ACA
1970	16	0	17	31	25	55	92	100	84
1969	0	—	—	40	—	—	—	—	76
1968	8	31	—	56	—	—	100	—	83

Key Votes

(1) ABM	FOR	(6) 18-Yr-Vote	AGN	(11) Clean Water $	AGN
(2) SST	AGN	(7) Farm Sub Lmt	AGN	(12) Mig Wrkrs Comp	AGN
(3) Phil Pln	AGN	(8) Coop-Church	AGN	(13) Jets to Chiang	FOR
(4) No-Knock	FOR	(9) Family Asst	FOR	(14) State OEO Veto	FOR
(5) Cmutr Tax	AGN	(10) Work Stamps	FOR	(15) Park Logging	FOR

Election Results

1970 general:	William C. Wampler (R)	53,950	(61%)
	Tate C. Buchanan (D)	34,609	(39%)
1970 primary:	William C. Wamlper (R), nominated by Convention		
1968 general:	William C. Wampler (R)	71,531	(60%)
	Joseph P. Johnson (D)	47,906	(40%)

TENTH DISTRICT Political Background

Virginia 10 includes most of Virginia's share of metropolitan Washington. The district contains Arlington, the site of the Pentagon; Alexandria, another suburb, which has some quaint eighteenth century town-houses along the Potomac River; and much of sprawling Fairfax County. Fairfax consists of subdivisions of neat, prosperous homes; these radiate out from the freeways and old colonial pikes, which in George Washington's time, used to bear the traffic of ox carts and stately carriages. Almost all of the district's voters now depend directly or indirectly on government payrolls. Many of the voters here are prevented from participating actively (or at least openly) in congressional politics by the Hatch Act. In national elections, the 10th is pretty evenly split, with a slight edge usually going to the Republicans. Suburban Virginia is a little more conservative than suburban Montgomery County, Maryland—to which it is similar in most respects (see Maryland 8). That political inclination may be due to the large number of military and Defense Department personnel who choose to live on the Virginia side of the Potomac, near the Pentagon.

The 10th was created in 1952. Even then suburban Washington was undergoing explosive growth. In the twenty-odd years that have followed, the district has had only one congressman, conservative Republican Joel T. Broyhill. In the Eisenhower landslide of 1952, Broyhill, a real estate developer, won by 322 votes, and he has hung on since, despite spirited opposition; in 1964, he won by just 2,128 votes. Broyhill's prime source of political success has been constituent service; in a district where most working adults are government employees, the congressman estimates he has aided more than 100,000 10th district residents during his years in office. Broyhill's other source of strength has been an unwavering devotion to the interests of suburbanites as a member of the House District of Columbia Committee. Here the congressman, along with Lawrence J. Hogan of Maryland's suburban 5th district, is a hard line law-and-order man and a stern advocate of crackdowns on alleged welfare chiselers. But Broyhill, whose name appears constantly in the Washington papers, is the most controversial of Washington area congressmen: hated by thousands and loved, in the 10th district at least, by a few thousand more. His service on the Ways and Means Committee goes relatively unnoticed, though here, as elsewhere, he invariably lines up with House conservatives. Broyhill is the only member of Ways and Means with another committee assignment—an index of how important the District Committee is to a suburban Washington congressman.

Every two years, the liberal Democrats of northern Virginia put on a concerted drive to defeat Broyhill, and every two years to date, they have failed. The incumbent never wins by overwhelming margins. His best showing so far was 60% in 1968. So it must be assumed that his devotion to constituent requests has been the decisive factor in his electoral success. In 1970, his opponent was Harold Miller, a liberal, antiwar Democrat and 33-year-old vice-chairman of the Fairfax County Board of Supervisors. Miller held Broyhill down to 55%, a margin which indicates just how controversial Broyhill is. Most longtime incumbents are not affected by the normal partisan fluctuations that are part of national elections.

Redistricting has reduced the size of the 9th somewhat. For 1972, more of Fairfax County will lie in the 8th district. This should help the Democrats a little and they will no doubt wage another spirited campaign against the Congressman. But Broyhill's repeated successes show that he is one politician very hard to beat.

Census Data 1970 pop. 560,075; deviation from current state average, +20.5%; change 1960–70, +33.8%. Metro. 100.0%, 0.0% central city.

1970 Share of Federal Outlays $691,441,000 (average outlay per district, Virginia 8 and 10)

DOD	$410,411,000	HEW	$59,561,000
AEC	$22,000	HUD	$2,961,000
NASA	$2,058,000	OEO	$1,041,000
DOT	$74,160,000	DOA	$13,557,000
		Other	$127,670,000

Federal Military-Industrial Commitments (Virginia 8 and 10 listing)

DOD Contractors Institute for Defense Analysis (Arlington), $9.562m: basic and applied research for the Director of Defense Research and Engineering and for the Advanced Research Projects Agency. Research Analysis (McLean), $9.524m: studies of Army tactical operations. Communications and Systems (Falls Church), $8.337m: analysis of naval maintenance and material management. IBM (Arlington), $7.212m:

computer services for Naval air stations. Susquehanna Corp. (Alexandria), $6.941m: Mark 30 rocket motors. American Standard (Falls Church), $6.139m: unspecified electronic equipment.

DOD Installations The Pentagon (Arlington). Fort Belvoir (Alexandria). Vint Hills Farm Army Station (Warrenton). Cameron Army Station (Alexandria). Fort Meyer AB (Arlington). Marine Corps Air Station (Quantico). Marine Corps Development and Education Command (Quantico). Naval Hospital (Quantico). Naval Weapons Laboratory (Dahlgren).

Economic Base Electrical machinery, equipment, and supplies, esp. communication equipment; nonelectrical machinery, esp. office, computing, and accounting machines; aircraft engines and engine parts. Also, extensive commuting to Washington, D.C.

The Voters

Registration 131,960 total. No party registration.

Employment profile White collar, 71%. Blue collar, 30%.

Ethnic groups Black, 6%. Total foreign stock, 13%. UK, Germany, 2% each; Canada, Italy, Ireland, USSR, Poland, 1% each; others, 4%.

Presidential vote

1968	Humphrey (D)	71,600	(42%)
	Nixon (R)	80,728	(47%)
	Wallace (AIP)	19,802	(12%)

Representative

Joel T. Broyhill (R) Elected 1952; b. Nov. 4, 1919, Hopewell; home, Arlington; George Washington U., 1939–41; Army, WWII; married, three children; Lutheran.

Career Partner, Gen. Mgr., M. T. Broyhill & Sons, Real Estate, 1945–52.

Offices 2109 RHOB, 202-225-5136.

Committees

District of Columbia (5th); Subs. (1) Business, Commerce, and Fiscal Affairs, (2) Housing and Youth Affairs, (3) Judiciary, (4) Public Health and Welfare.

Ways and Means (5th).

Group Ratings

	ADA	COPE	NREP	NFU	LCV	CFA	NAB	NSI	ACA
1970	4	10	8	38	33	57	73	100	71
1969	0	—	—	33	—	—	—	—	82
1968	8	15	—	38	—	—	83	—	87

Key Votes

(1) ABM	FOR	(6) 18-Yr-Vote	AGN	(11) Clean Water $	AGN
(2) SST	AGN	(7) Farm Sub Lmt	AGN	(12) Mig Wrkrs Comp	AGN
(3) Phil Pln	AGN	(8) Coop-Church	AGN	(13) Jets to Chiang	FOR
(4) No-Knock	FOR	(9) Family Asst	FOR	(14) State OEO Veto	FOR
(5) Cmutr Tax	AGN	(10) Work Stamps	FOR	(15) Park Logging	FOR

Election Results

1970 general:	Joel T. Broyhill (R)	67,468	(55%)
	Harold O. Miller (D)	56,255	(45%)
1970 primary:	Joel T. Broyhill (R), unopposed		
1968 general:	Joel T. Broyhill (R)	97,465	(60%)
	David B. Kinney (D)	65,474	(40%)

WASHINGTON

Political Background

Washington is the nation's far Pacific Northwest. Topographically, the state can be divided into two distinct regions, which are separated by the massive Cascade Mountain Range. In the east is the so-called Inland Empire. The Columbia River winds its way through the relatively flat country here, and as it does, its water is backed up by a number of hydroelectric dams, the largest of which is the famous Grand Coulee. Except for the cities of Spokane and Yakima, and the complex around the AEC's Hanford Plant, the Inland Empire is predominantly rural, devoted mainly to wheat (see also Idaho 1). Like most rural areas in the United States, this part of Washington has not grown much in the last ten years.

The more populous region of the state comprises the urban complex around Puget Sound, a series of island-studded inlets in northwest Washington. The Olympia Mountains which lie to the west of the sound account for the surprisingly temperate, though rainy, climate of Seattle, Tacoma, Everett, and the other cities here. As Puget Sound became increasingly urban, its cities began to adjoin each other. Today, a continuous strip of development along the sound contains more than half of the state's population.

Scandinavian immigrants from Minnesota, Wisconsin, and the Dakotas were Washington's first settlers. These people came here largely because the great northern rail lines were laid from the Twin Cities to Puget Sound. The Scandinavians soon gave the new territory a radical political cast. In the years before World War I, Washington was the center of the IWW activities of the "Wobblies." Later, the Puget Sound cities gave Franklin Roosevelt some of his largest majorities in the nation. In recent years, Washington has lost some of its cultural and political distinctiveness, as management personnel from various parts of the country have moved in. What brought them here and what has shaped the state's politics since was the aircraft industry, mostly the Boeing concern. Since World War II, Boeing has been one of the state's major employers.

Building airplanes is anything but a stable enterprise. And in the late '60's it became clear that Boeing, and the state of Washington, was in trouble. The company lost out on a couple of major contracts; the TFX (F-111) went to General Dynamics of Lyndon Johnson's Texas and the NASA Apollo project went to California's North American. Moreover, the great demand for the 747 peaked rather early. In 1969, Boeing employed 101,000 people in Washington; for the end of 1971, the figure was projected at 30,000. Boom became depression, and thousands of white-collar executives and engineers, as well as production workers, found themselves collecting unemployment benefits.

Washington's two U.S. senators, Warren Magnuson and Henry Jackson, have been called by some Washington observers "the Senators from Boeing." In 1970 and 1971, these two Democrats allied themselves with the Nixon Administration in a major effort to sustain government support for Boeing's supersonic transport (SST). Few other states —none outside the South—could have called on a pair of senators with comparable seniority and clout. Magnuson had been in the Senate since 1944, and before that had spent eight years in the House; Jackson had been in the Senate since 1952, and before that had spent twelve years in the House. The two men possessed 66 years of collective service on Capitol Hill. Moreover, both were committee chairmen; Magnuson of Commerce and Jackson of Interior and Insular Affairs, and both men were highly respected experts in their committees' areas of jurisdiction and in others as well. Yet, despite all of these assets, they were unable to sell the SST to the Senate; a majority of their colleagues apparently found the environmental and economic objections raised against the project more compelling than the arguments advanced by the two senators and the Administration. The program has since folded; Boeing continues to lay off employees; and the Puget Sound area has settled into an economic depression.

Neither of the senators' failure in the SST fight is likely to affect his popularity at home. Sen. Jackson, who was up for reelection in 1970, won a phenomenal 82% of the vote—the best performance that year of any opposed Senate candidate except John Stennis of Mississippi. "Scoop" Jackson, as he is called, is one of that increasingly rare breed: a solid liberal on domestic issues and a supporter of the Vietnam and military spending policies of the Nixon Administration. Jackson, a member of the Senate Armed Services Committee, enjoys a reputation for expertise in defense matters; he was so well regarded that he was asked by the Nixon Administration to become Secretary of Defense. And as chairman of the Interior Committee, Jackson demonstrated a keen interest in ecological concerns long before they became a matter of popular interest. Although many current ecology activists find Jackson's record less than completely satisfactory, the senator is still undisputedly a leader in the field.

Jackson's political stance toward domestic and foreign affairs—and his vote-getting prowess in Washington—have made him into a dark-horse presidential candidate in 1972. His principal source of potential support are the Northern union members, led by labor leaders like George Meany of the AFL–CIO. Jackson's apparent strategy is to remain available in case a convention deadlock develops. If it does, Jackson hopes that power brokers from labor, the South, and the big cities can put together enough votes to give him the nomination. Jackson supporters figure that their man can beat Nixon on economic issues, on which he has consistently attacked the Administration. The idea behind the Jackson candidacy is to prevent any antiwar candidate from becoming president; in short, to deny the public the chance to vote for a clearly-defined antiwar candidate. As one business man supporting Jackson put it, "With Jackson and Nixon, we could take a walk during the election; we can't lose."

Washington's senior senator, Warren Magnuson, has quietly broken with the Administration war and defense policies, though he and Jackson still generally vote and work together on most issues. Magnuson is known as one of the canniest political operators in the Senate; he should be, because he has been in Congress longer than all but one senator and four congressmen. As chairman of the Commerce Committee, Magnuson fought for consumer rights long before Ralph Nader began to get headlines. The Senator continues to press his efforts in this often lonely area of concern.

For some reason, Magnuson is not as strong at the polls as Jackson. In 1962, he had an unexpectedly close call—probably the result of overconfidence—and in 1968, he won by 65% of the vote, which is a landslide by all standards except those used by Jackson. In the last 40 years, Washington has elected a Republican senator only once, that coming in the strong Republican year of 1946. It appears that the Republicans will have no better luck in the foreseeable future. Although Magnuson will be 69 when he comes up for reelection in 1974, he looks like a sure bet to win reelection; and Jackson, unless he becomes president, will be only 64 when he is up in 1976.

The voters in Washington have traditionally reelected their congressmen, regardless of party, except when one of the parties has an unusually good or bad year. So in 1964, four Republicans—three of them elected in strong Republican years—were defeated, and the four Democrats who beat them remain in the House today. The only other change in the House delegation since 1964 occurred in 1970 when Republican Catherine May of the 4th district lost in an upset. Her defeat was an index of Democratic sentiment in Washington during 1970. Both parties have a hand in the redistricting for the 1972 elections; the Democrats control the state Senate and the Republicans, the state House and the governorship. As a result of the split, there is unlikely to be any politically significant changes made in the boundaries of the state's seven congressional districts.

Electoral Votes 9

Census Data 1970 pop. 3,409,169; 1.66% of U.S. total, 22nd largest; change 1960–70, +19.5%. Metro. 66.0%, 26.7% central city. 1970 per capita income, $3,993; 14th highest. 30th in number of poor.

1970 Share of Federal Tax Burden $3,434,470,000; 1.76% of U.S. total, 18th largest.

1970 Share of Federal Outlays $3,415,188,946; 1.81% of U.S. total, 18th largest. Per capita federal spending, $1,002.

DOD	$1,121,849,000	18th (1.95%)	HEW	$833,879,809	22nd (1.60%)
AEC	$160,155,877	5th (6.16%)	HUD	$14,113,981	34th (0.72%)
NASA	$4,304,600	26th (0.12%)	OEO	$11,755,060	24th (1.55%)
DOT	$272,409,652	6th (3.82%)	DOA	$233,758,352	21st (1.82%)
DOC	$23,512,823	12th (2.03%)	POD	$112,041,477	13th (2.09%)
DOI	$109,263,038	6th (4.73%)	VA	$171,604,689	21st (2.32%)
DOJ	$11,992,047	13th (2.09%)	CSC	$81,533,836	13th (2.03%)
			Other	$253,014,705	

Economic Base Transportation equipment, esp. aircraft and parts; cash grain, livestock, and dairy; lumber and wood products other than furniture, esp. sawmills and planing mills; food and kindred products, esp. canned and preserved fruits, vegetables, and seafoods; paper and allied products, esp. paper mills other than building paper mills; primary metal industries, esp. primary smelting and refining of nonferrous metals; printing, publishing, and allied industries, esp. newspapers; nonelectrical machinery; fabricated metal products, esp. fabricated structural metal products; chemicals and allied products, esp. industrial inorganic and organic chemicals.

Political Line-up Governor, Daniel J. Evans (R); seat up, 1972. Senators, Warren G. Magnuson (D) and Henry M. Jackson (D). Representatives, 7 (6 D and 1 R). State Senate (29 D and 20 R); State House (51 D and 48 R).

The Voters

Registration 1,515,723 total. No party registration.

Employment profile White collar, 45%. Blue collar, 55%.

Ethnic groups Black, 2%. Total foreign stock, 23%. Canada, 5%; Germany, Norway, 3% each; Sweden, UK, 2% each; Ireland, Italy, USSR, 1% each; others, 4%.

Presidential vote

1968	Humphrey (D)	616,037	(47%)
	Nixon (R)	588,510	(45%)
	Wallace (AIP)	96,990	(7%)
1964	Johnson (D)	776,699	(62%)
	Goldwater (R)	470,366	(37%)
1960	Kennedy (D)	599,298	(48%)
	Nixon (R)	629,273	(51%)

Senator

Warren G. Magnuson (D) Elected Dec. 1944, seat up 1974; b. Apr. 12, 1905, Moorhead, Minn.; home, Seattle; U. of N.D., N.D. State, 1923–24; U. of Wash., LL.B., 1929; USNR, WWII; married; Lutheran.

Career Practicing atty.; sp. prosecutor, King Co., 1931; Wash. Legislature, 1933–34; Asst. U.S. Dist. Atty., 1934; Prosecuting Atty. King Co., 1934–36; U.S. House, 1936–44.

Offices 127 OSOB, 202-225-2621. Also 900 U.S. Courthouse, Seattle 98104, 206-583-5545.

Committees

Aeronautical and Space Sciences (2nd).

Appropriations (3rd); Subs. (1) Chm., Labor, HEW, and Related Agencies, (2) Defense, (3) HUD, Space, and Science, (4) Public Works, (5) Transportation.

Commerce (Chm.); (1) Aviation, (2) Sp. on Freight Car Shortage.

Sel. Com. on Equal Educational Opportunity (3rd).

Group Ratings

	ADA	COPE	NREP	NFU	LCV	NAB	NSI	ACA
1970	72	92	58	100	35	30	33	21
1969	78	—	—	81	—	—	—	15
1968	36	100	—	40	—	0	—	30

Key Votes

(1) ABM	AGN	(8) Phil Pln	FOR	(15) Coop-Church	FOR
(2) SST	FOR	(9) Vol Army	AGN	(16) Cut Oil Dpltn	FOR
(3) Busing	FOR	(10) Prison $	AGN	(17) Consumer Prot	FOR
(4) Tob Sub	AGN	(11) Cut Mil $	AGN	(18) Farm Sub Limit	FOR
(5) Carswell	AGN	(12) Defoliatn	AGN	(19) Comp Bid Sales	ABS
(6) No-Knock	FOR	(13) 18-Yr-Vote	FOR	(20) Pre-Prod Tests	AGN
(7) Seniorty	FOR	(14) Pentgn PR	FOR	(21) Cut Marjna Pen	FOR

Election Results

1968 general:	Warren G. Magnuson (D)	796,183	(65%)
	Jack Metcalf (R)	435,894	(35%)
1968 primary:	Warren G. Magnuson (D)	373,303	(93%)
	Arthur DeWitt (R)	28,683	(7%)
1962 general:	Warren G. Magnuson (D)	491,365	(52%)
	Richard G. Christensen (R)	446,204	(48%)

Senator

Henry M. Jackson (D) Elected 1952, seat up 1976; b. May 31, 1912, Everett; home, Everett; U. of Wash., LL.B., 1935; married, two children; Presbyterian.

Career Practicing atty., 1936–38; Prosecuting Atty. Snohomish County, 1938–40; U.S. House, 1940–52.

Offices 137 OSOB, 202-225-3441. Also Rm 802 U.S. Courthouse, Seattle 98104, 206-583-7476.

Committees

Armed Services (3rd); Subs. (1) Chm., Nuclear Test Ban Treaty Safeguards, (2) Chm., Strategic Arms Limitations Talks, (3) Military Construction Authorization, (4) CIA, (5) Ad Hoc on Tactical Air Power.

Government Operations (2nd); Subs. (1) Chm., National Security and International Operations, (2) Permanent Investigations.

Interior and Insular Affairs (Chm.); Subs. (1) Chm., Sp. on Legislative Oversight, (2) Indian Affairs, (3) Minerals, Materials, and Fuels, (4) Parks and Recreations, (5) Public Lands, (6) Territories and Insular Affairs, (7) Water and Power Resources.

Jt. Com. on Atomic Energy (3rd); Subs. (1) Chm., Military Applications, (2) Communities, (3) Legislation, (4) Research, Development, and Radiation, (5) Security.

Group Ratings

	ADA	COPE	NREP	NFU	LCV	NAB	NSI	ACA
1970	56	100	50	100	53	8	80	24
1969	78	—	—	88	—	—	—	14
1968	57	100	—	77	—	0	—	12

Key Votes

(1) ABM	FOR	(8) Phil Pln	FOR	(15) Coop-Church	FOR
(2) SST	FOR	(9) Vol Army	AGN	(16) Cut Oil Dpltn	FOR
(3) Busing	FOR	(10) Prison $	FOR	(17) Consumer Prot	FOR
(4) Tob Sub	AGN	(11) Cut Mil $	AGN	(18) Farm Sub Limit	FOR
(5) Carswell	AGN	(12) Defoliatn	FOR	(19) Comp Bid Sales	AGN
(6) No-Knock	FOR	(13) 18-Yr-Vote	FOR	(20) Pre-Prod Tests	AGN
(7) Seniorty	FOR	(14) Pentgn PR	FOR	(21) Cut Marjna Pen	FOR

Election Results

1970 general:	Henry M. Jackson (D)	879,385	(82%)
	Charles W. Elicker (R)	170,790	(16%)
	Bill Massey (SW)	9,255	(1%)
	Edison S. Fisk (Buffalo)	7,377	(1%)
1970 primary:	Henry M. Jackson (D)	497,309	(84%)
	Carl Maxey (D)	79,201	(13%)
	John Patric (D)	7,267	(1%)
	Clarice Privette (D)	6,240	(1%)

1964 general:	Henry M. Jackson (D)	875,950	(72%)
	Lloyd J. Andrews (R)	337,138	(28%)

FIRST DISTRICT Political Background

Washington 1 comprises the north side of Seattle and the adjacent suburbs. The most notable of these are the wealthy ones on the western side of Lake Washington; the lake is the eastern boundary of the city of Seattle. The district also includes Bainbridge Island, a wooded residential area across Puget Sound; it is connected to the city by a ferry, which the residents prefer to a bridge. The 1st takes in most of metropolitan Seattle's high income areas and the University of Washington. It is usually the most Republican district in the state, though the Democrats, in state legislative elections, have been making gains on the north side of Seattle, particularly around the university.

Since 1952, the congressman from this part of the state has been Thomas M. Pelly, a moderate Republican. Pelly is currently the ranking minority member of the House Merchant Marine and Fisheries Committee—a post of obvious importance to Seattle, a major port. Pelly also serves as a senior member of the Science and Astronautics Committee, where he was one of the leaders in the unsuccessful attempt to continue government funding of the SST.

Pelly is now the only Republican in Washington's congressional delegation, but he has had little difficulty in general elections, usually winning by margins in excess of 2–1. Lately, serious electoral problems have come in the Republican primary. In 1970, his former protégé, Joel Pritchard, waged a high-spending campaign and took 47% of the Republican votes. Pritchard was upset because the 68-year-old congressman has refused to retire. The strong showing indicates trouble ahead for Pelly, and he may well choose to retire in 1972.

Census Data 1970 pop. 501,185; deviation from current state average, +2.9%; change 1960–70, +17.3%. Metro. 98.3%, 62.9% central city.

1970 Share of Federal Outlays $620,135,000 (average outlay per district, Washington 1 and 7)

DOD	$201,183,000	HEW	$140,282,000
AEC	$1,270,000	HUD	$5,563,000
NASA	$2,024,000	OEO	$2,735,000
DOT	$101,282,000	DOA	$21,005,000
		Other	$144,791,000

Federal Military-Industrial Commitments (See Washington 7 for greater Seattle listing.)

Economic Base Transportation equipment, esp. aircraft and parts; food and kindred products, esp. bakery products; printing, publishing, and allied industries, esp. newspapers; fabricated metal products, esp. fabricated structural metal products; nonelectrical machinery. Also, higher education (University of Washington); banking.

The Voters

Registration 245,154 total. No party registration.

Employment profile White collar, 60%. Blue collar, 40%.

Ethnic groups Black, 1%. Total foreign stock, 29%. Canada, 7%; Norway, 5%; Germany, Sweden, UK, 3% each; USSR, 1%; others, 5%.

Presidential vote

1968	Humphrey (D)	92,510	(45%)
	Nixon (R)	102,918	(50%)
	Wallace (AIP)	10,579	(5%)

Representative

Thomas M. Pelly (R) Elected 1952; b. Aug. 22, 1902, Seattle; home, Seattle; married, two children; Episcopalian.

Career Trust Officer, Seattle Natl. Bank, 1921–30; V.P., Lowman & Hanford Co., 1930–35, Pres. and Gen. Mgr., 1937–55; Dir., Seattle Trust & Savings Bank and Northern Life Insurance Co.

Offices 2211 RHOB, 202-225-6311. Also 7004 Fed. Office Bldg., Seattle 98104, 206-623-8819.

Committees

Merchant Marine and Fisheries (Ranking Mbr.); Sub. on Fisheries and Wildlife.

Science and Astronautics (4th); Sub. on Advanced Research and Technology.

Group Ratings

	ADA	COPE	NREP	NFU	LCV	CFA	NAB	NSI	ACA
1970	24	45	40	58	50	71	82	100	50
1969	27	—	—	43	—	—	—	—	46
1968	18	34	—	43	—	—	100	—	70

Key Votes

(1) ABM	ABS	(6) 18-Yr-Vote	ABS	(11) Clean Water $	ABS
(2) SST	FOR	(7) Farm Sub Lmt	FOR	(12) Mig Wrkrs Comp	FOR
(3) Phil Pln	FOR	(8) Coop-Church	AGN	(13) Jets to Chiang	FOR
(4) No-Knock	FOR	(9) Family Asst	FOR	(14) State OEO Veto	AGN
(5) Cmutr Tax	ABS	(10) Work Stamps	FOR	(15) Park Logging	AGN

Election Results

1970 general:	Thomas M. Pelly (R)	107,072	(64%)
	David A. Hughes (D)	53,156	(32%)
	Stephanie Coontz (SW)	4,388	(3%)
	Stan Iverson (Buffalo)	1,724	(1%)
1970 primary:	Thomas M. Pelly (R)	55,967	(53%)
	Joel Pritchard (R)	48,724	(47%)
1968 general:	Thomas M. Pelly (R)	124,513	(61%)
	Don Cole (D)	76,456	(38%)
	Judith Shapiro (PF)	1,886	(1%)

SECOND DISTRICT Political Background

Washington 2 comprises the far northwest corner of the continental United States. The district is a region of mountains, of heavily wooded inlets, and of gentle rain and fog. The 2nd takes in the northern half of Olympic National Park, on the Olympic Peninsula between Puget Sound and the Pacific Ocean; the sparsely-populated islands in the sound and the Strait of Juan de Fuca; and the counties just east of Puget Sound between Seattle and the Canadian border. Most of the people here are concentrated on a narrow strip of land that runs between the sound and the Cascade Range—in cities like Bellingham, Everett (Sen. Jackson's hometown) and several northern suburbs of the city of Seattle. Politically, the district is marginal, with a slight advantage enjoyed by the Democrats in national elections.

The 2nd perhaps best demonstrates the Washington tradition in congressional politics. That is, a congressman first gets elected in a good year for his party, is reelected easily, and is turned out only if his party has a bad year. From 1940 to 1952, the 2nd was represented by Henry "Scoop" Jackson (see state write-up). Jackson may have anticipated an Eisenhower landslide in 1952, and so decided on a Senate try rather than face a House contest which would have been riskier than usual. His successor was Republican Jack Westland; he was reelected as a matter of routine until 1964 when the

Goldwater debacle apparently caught him napping. The winner that year was Democrat Lloyd Meeds, who was then Snohomish County (Everett) prosecutor, as was Jackson before his election to Congress. Meeds has been reelected with near automatic regularity ever since. As a member of the Education and Labor and the Interior and Insular Affairs committees, Meeds has usually voted with most other House liberals. Like many Democrats, the Congressman has become an opponent of the Vietnam war in recent years. Redistricting will not materially affect his chances for reelection in 1972.

Census Data 1970 pop. 562,371; deviation from current state average, +15.5%; change 1960–70, +39.6%. Metro. 62.9%, 9.5% central city.

1970 Share of Federal Outlays $243,709,316

DOD	$42,877,000	HEW	$100,641,651
AEC	$9,770	HUD	$286,656
NASA	$000	OEO	$1,376,669
DOT	$12,993,065	DOA	$12,993,065
		Other	$68,187,895

Federal Military-Industrial Commitments

DOD Installations Naval Air Station (Oak Harbor). Blaine AF Station (Blaine). Makah Air Force Station (Neah Bay). Naval Radio Station (Everett).

Economic Base Dairy and poultry; lumber and wood products other than furniture; paper and allied products; nonelectrical machinery.

The Voters

Registration 240,353 total. No party registration.

Employment profile White collar, 38%. Blue collar, 62%.

Ethnic groups Black, less than 0.5%. Total foreign stock, 25%. Canada, 7%; Norway, 4%; Sweden, 3%; Germany, UK, 2% each; USSR, 1%; others, 5%.

Presidential vote

1968	Humphrey (D)	93,506	(48%)
	Nixon (R)	87,466	(45%)
	Wallace (AIP)	15,728	(8%)

Representative

Lloyd Meeds (D) Elected 1964; b. Dec. 11, 1927, Dillon, Mont.; home, Everett; Everett Jr. Col., Gonzaga U., LL.B., 1958; USNR, WWII; married, four children; Episcopalian.

Career Deputy Prosecuting Atty., Spokane County, 1958–59, Snohomish County, 1959–61; practicing atty., 1961–62; Prosecuting Atty., Snohomish County, 1962–64.

Offices 308 CHOB, 202-225-2605. Also Fed. Bldg., 3002 Colby Ave., Everett 98201, 206-252-3188.

Committees

Education and Labor (21st); Subs. (1) Gen. on Education, (2) Sel. on Education, (3) Sel. on Labor.

Interior and Insular Affairs (15th); Subs. (1) Indian Affairs, (2) Irrigation and Reclamation, (3) National Parks and Recreation, (4) Territorial and Insular Affairs.

Group Ratings

	ADA	COPE	NREP	NFU	LCV	CFA	NAB	NSI	ACA
1970	84	100	75	92	63	95	0	40	0
1969	93	—	—	93	—	—	—	—	6
1968	75	92	—	94	—	—	17	—	4

Key Votes

(1) ABM	AGN	(6) 18-Yr-Vote	FOR	(11) Clean Water $	FOR
(2) SST	FOR	(7) Farm Sub Lmt	AGN	(12) Mig Wrkrs Comp	FOR
(3) Phil Pln	FOR	(8) Coop-Church	FOR	(13) Jets to Chiang	AGN
(4) No-Knock	AGN	(9) Family Asst	FOR	(14) State OEO Veto	AGN
(5) Cmutr Tax	FOR	(10) Work Stamps	AGN	(15) Park Logging	FOR

Election Results

1970 general:	Lloyd Meeds (D)	117,562	(73%)
	Edward A. McBride (R)	44,049	(27%)
1970 primary:	Lloyd Meeds (D), unopposed		
1968 general:	Lloyd Meeds (D)	102,522	(56%)
	Wally Turner (R)	79,800	(44%)

THIRD DISTRICT Political Background

Washington 3 comprises the southwest corner of the state. The district includes the mouth of the Columbia River, and the rocky, bay-indented shore of the Pacific to the north. The 3rd's largest urban concentration is around Vancouver, just across the Columbia from Portland, Oregon; the district also takes in Olympia (pop. 23,000), Washington's small capital city. Ordinarily, the 3rd goes Democratic, as the Democratic counties along the Columbia and the ocean outvote the Republican-leaning counties around Olympia. Most of the voters here live in sparsely-populated counties, with the few towns located in the sheltered river valleys, or along the coast, or Puget Sound to the northeast. In politics, the district still retains some of the rough-hewn lumbercamp atmosphere of an earlier day.

Since 1960, the 3rd has been represented by Julia Butler Hansen, a 22-year veteran of the state House of Representatives. Mrs. Hansen has risen to become chairman of the House Appropriations Committee's Interior Subcommittee; this unit controls the budget of the Interior Department and helps to determine policy on many ecological matters. During her first years in office, Mrs. Hansen was a champion vote-getter in the district; she took 70% in 1964. More recently, she has fallen behind her less senior Washington colleagues in this respect. In 1970, she received only 59% of the vote, running far below expectations in Clark County (Vancouver and suburbs). If she is faced with an energetic opponent in 1972, she may have to run hard to win. Otherwise, she could fall victim to what befell her fellow Washington congresswoman, Republican Catherine May of the 4th district in 1970—unexpected defeat.

Census Data 1970 pop. 435,137; deviation from current state average, −10.7%; change 1960–70, +23.2%. Metro. 29.5%, 0.0% central city.

1970 Share of Federal Outlays $314,083,920

DOD	$17,434,000	HEW	$128,219,969
AEC	$000	HUD	$922,521
NASA	$000	OEO	$1,327,189
DOT	$29,206,154	DOA	$23,715,237
		Other	$113,258,850

Federal Military-Industrial Commitments

DOD Installations Naval Facility (Pacific Beach).

Economic Base Lumber and wood products other than furniture, esp. sawmills and planing mills and logging camps and logging contractors; paper and allied products, esp. paper mills other than building paper mills; dairy, and livestock and poultry.

The Voters

Registration 195,806 total. No party registration.

Employment profile White collar, 37%. Blue collar, 63%.

Ethnic groups Black, less than 0.5%. Total foreign stock, 19%. Canada, 4%; Germany, 3%; Norway, Sweden, UK, 2% each; USSR, 1%; others, 4%.

Presidential vote

1968	Humphrey (D)	84,962	(52%)
	Nixon (R)	69,025	(42%)
	Wallace (AIP)	10,985	(7%)

Representative

Julia Butler Hansen (D) Elected Nov. 8, 1960; b. June 14, 1907, Portland, Oreg.; home, Cathlamet; U. of Wash., B.A., 1930; married, one child; Christian Scientist.

Career Wash. State Legislature, 1939–60, Minority Leader, 1953–55; Speaker Pro Tem, 1955–60.

Offices 201 CHOB, 202-225-3536. Also Fed. Bldg., Vancouver 98664, 206-695-8291, and P.O. Bldg., Longview 98632, 206-423-5652.

Committees

Appropriations (17th); Subs. (1) Chm., Interior, (2) Military Construction.

Group Ratings

	ADA	COPE	NREP	NFU	LCV	CFA	NAB	NSI	ACA
1970	68	91	70	100	44	80	0	56	0
1969	67	—	—	100	—	—	—	—	8
1968	67	100	—	100	—	—	0	—	5

Key Votes

(1) ABM	AGN	(6) 18-Yr-Vote	FOR	(11) Clean Water $	AGN
(2) SST	FOR	(7) Farm Sub Lmt	ABS	(12) Mig Wrkrs Comp	FOR
(3) Phil Pln	AGN	(8) Coop-Church	ABS	(13) Jets to Chiang	ABS
(4) No-Knock	AGN	(9) Family Asst	FOR	(14) State OEO Veto	AGN
(5) Cmutr Tax	ABS	(10) Work Stamps	AGN	(15) Park Logging	FOR

Election Results

1970 general:	Julia Butler Hansen (D)	81,892	(59%)
	R. C. McConkey (R)	56,566	(41%)
1970 primary:	Julia Butler Hansen (D), unopposed		
1968 general:	Julia Butler Hansen (D)	89,777	(57%)
	Wayne M. Adams (R)	68,387	(43%)

FOURTH DISTRICT Political Background

Washington 4 comprises the southeast quarter of the state—part of the agricultural Columbia River Valley east of the Cascade Range. The central portion of the district, in particular, is devoted to the cultivation of wheat, much like the land in Minnesota and the Dakotas. Many of the original settlers to this part of Washington came from those states; they were and are of Scandinavian descent. About a third of the residents of the district live in the Yakima Valley, which mountains isolate from the rest of the Columbia basin. This is a deeply conservative area politically, as is the region around Walla Walla and Pullman in the eastern part of the district. The normally Democratic sections of the 4th are those which have benefited from federal programs; these include the towns of Richland and Pasco near the AEC's giant Hanford Works, and the town of Clarkston, on the Snake River across from Lewiston, Idaho, and near the once-controversial Hell's Canyon Dam.

The 1970 election in the 4th produced that increasingly rare occurrence: the ouster of a veteran and seemingly well-entrenched congressman. The victim was Catherine May, a conservative Republican who had served in the House since 1956 and who, like most Washington congressmen, had been reelected with overwhelming pluralities ever since. The successful challenger was Mike McCormack, a research chemist at the Hanford Works and a 10-year veteran of the state Senate. Observers agreed that McCormack was the first well-known, well-financed candidate that the Democrats had put up against

Mrs. May in twelve years. But that does not really explain why he won, and won by running 20% ahead of the Democrat who ran here in 1968. Home town sentiment was one factor; during his years as a state legislator, McCormack built up a personal following in the Richland-Pasco area. But he won his biggest majority, numerically, in Mrs. May's home county of Yakima, which she had never lost before. Some writers credited Sen. Henry Jackson's coattails. But in 1964, when Jackson took 66% of the district's vote and LBJ won 57%, Mrs. May received 65%. Her margin indicates that at least 31% of the voters crossed over in order to cast a ballot for the congresswoman.

McCormack's campaign stressed the economy and Mrs. May's alleged neglect of it. The campaign issue seems the best explanation of the results, if it is applied selectively. An analysis of the returns indicates that McCormack made his greatest gains—up to 30% of the vote in some cases—in the most agricultural counties of the district. The farm rebellion, which shows up clearly in the 1970 election results in the wheat-growing counties of the Dakotas and elsewhere in the Midwest, is also evident in this part of Washington. In some wheat counties, McCormack ran about as well as Lyndon Johnson in 1964—an unusual feat for anyone challenging an incumbent congressman.

The normally conservative Republican farm areas show a very strong tendency to switch to the Democrats during periods that are perceived as bad economic times; in congressional elections at least, the farmers are far more switchable than urban voters. There was a bumper crop of wheat produced on the nation's farms during the 1971 season; this, of course, does little to improve the market for the commodity, which rarely shows strength anyway. These agricultural phenomena are produced by the success of the agricultural research operations in the country; the researchers, through genetic break-throughs and promulgating careful farming techniques, have boosted the per-acre yield of many crops, many fold.

So with a potential glut facing wheat farmers in the years to come and with the Nixon Administration departing from a policy of strict parity, the farmers are worried. In fact, an attempt to allay the fears of the American wheat farmer may have been one of the principal concerns behind the Administration's overtures toward mainland China, which has been buying Canadian wheat for years. Chances are, conservative Republican farmers would not object to selling their wheat to Chinese Communists if the price is right.

Congressman McCormack's committee assignments—Public Works and Science and Astronautics—both have direct implications for his district. And no doubt, he thinks of the farmers of his district many times before he begins his 1972 campaign. More generally, the farm revolt may become the surprise factor in the 1972 presidential elections, just as it was when it produced the surprise of 1948.

Census Data 1970 pop. 422,691; deviation from current state average, —13.2%; change 1960–70, +4.1%. Metro. 0.0%, 0.0% central city.

1970 Share of Federal Outlays $521,003,796

DOD	$56,601,000	HEW	$110,430,621
AEC	$157,587,371	HUD	$545,042
NASA	$255,922	OEO	$1,191,157
DOT	$6,378,666	DOA	$98,349,098
		Other	$89,664,919

Federal Military-Industrial Commitments

DOD Installations Yakima Army Firing Center (Yakima). Othello AF Station (Othello).

AEC Operations Battelle Memorial Institute (Richland), $52.336m: Pacific Northwest Laboratory. Douglas United Nuclear (Richland), $40.812m: Feed Material Facility; General Facilities; Production Reactor Facilities. Atlantic Richfield Hanford Company (Richland), $32.655m: Separation and Production Facilities.

Economic Base Wheat and livestock; food and kindred products, esp. canned and preserved fruits, vegetables, and fish; lumber and wood products other than furniture, esp. sawmills and planing mills. Also, higher education (Washington State University).

The Voters

Registration 186,391 total. No party registration.
Employment profile White collar, 38%. Blue collar, 62%.
Ethnic groups Black, 1%. Total foreign stock, 16%. Canada, 3%; Germany, USSR, Mexico, 2% each; Norway, Sweden, UK, 1% each; others, 3%.

Presidential vote

1968	Humphrey (D)	61,301	(39%)
	Nixon (R)	83,420	(53%)
	Wallace (AIP)	13,575	(9%)

Representative

Mike McCormack (D) Elected 1970; b. Dec. 14, 1921, Basil, Ohio; home, Richland; Wash. U., B.S., 1948, M.S., 1949; Army, WWII; married, three children; religion unspecified.

Career Research scientist; Wash. House, 1956–60, Senate, 1960– .

Offices 1205 LHOB, 202-225-5816. Also Richland 99352, 509-946-4672.

Committees

Public Works (20th); Subs. (1) Flood Control and Internal Development, (2) Investigation and Oversight, (3) Rivers and Harbors, (4) Roads, (5) Watershed Development.
Science and Astronautics (17th); Subs. (1) Advanced Research and Technology, (2) Science, Research, and Development.

Group Ratings, Key Votes: Newly elected.

Election Results

1970 general:	Mike McCormack (D)	70,119	(53%)
	Catherine May (R)	63,244	(47%)
1970 primary:	Mike McCormack (D), unopposed		

FIFTH DISTRICT Political Background

Washington 5 comprises the northeast corner of the state. The district is the heart of the "Inland Empire," which centers on Spokane (pop. 170,000). The 5th includes the Grand Coulee Dam, that engineering marvel built during the New Deal; since those days, the residents of the Columbia basin have remained among the staunchest backers of publicly-generated hydroelectric power in the United States. Most of the district's land—between the Cascade Range and the Idaho boundary—is given over to wheat farming.

North of Salt Lake City and Denver and east of the Pacific Coast, Spokane is the West's largest city. Spokane County, which contains the city and its suburbs, has 70% of the 5th's population and voters. Spokane is somewhat more conservative and Republican than the cities along Puget Sound, and as a result, the district more often than not ends up in the Republican column in close statewide races.

For the past 30 years, the district has had only two congressmen: conservative Republican Walt Horan, who served from 1942 to 1964, and liberal Democrat Thomas Foley. Foley upset Horan in 1964, and since that time has won reelection by convincing margins. The Congressman is currently the senior Northern Democrat on the House Agriculture Committee, and chairman of its Domestic Marketing and Consumer Relations Subcommittee. He is also a high-ranking member of the House Interior and Insular Affairs Committee, which is a congressional unit of great importance to Westerners generally, and Westerners dependent on reclamation projects specifically.

Foley appears to have built a personal following strong enough to repel any Republican attack, but if he were not the Democratic nominee, the Republicans would have an excellent chance to pick up the seat. Redistricting may add some territory west of the Cascades; this, however, will not affect the political make-up of the 5th in any significant way.

Census Data 1970 pop. 408,153; deviation from current state average, −16.2%; change 1960–70, +2.3%. Metro. 70.4%, 41.8% central city.

1970 Share of Federal Outlays $350,140,261

DOD	$66,291,000	HEW	$111,125,026
AEC	$18,073	HUD	$787,545
NASA	$000	OEO	$865,129
DOT	$9,707,350	DOA	$51,886,777
		Other	$109,459,361

Federal Military-Industrial Commitments

DOD Installations Mica Peak AF Station (Spokane). Fairchild AFB (Spokane).

Economic Base Wheat and livestock; primary metal industries; lumber and wood products other than furniture, esp. sawmills and planing mills; food and kindred products.

The Voters

Registration 180,809 total. No party registration.

Employment profile White collar, 44%. Blue collar, 56%.

Ethnic groups Black, 1%. Total foreign stock, 19%. Canada, 5%; Germany, 3%; Norway, Sweden, UK, 2% each; Ireland, Italy, USSR, 1% each; others, 3%.

Presidential vote

1968	Humphrey (D)	69,968	(44%)
	Nixon (R)	77,621	(48%)
	Wallace (AIP)	13,192	(8%)

Representative

Thomas Stephen Foley (D) Elected 1964; b. March 6, 1929, Spokane; home, Spokane; U. of Wash., B.A., 1951, J.D., 1957; married; Catholic.

Career Practicing atty., 1957; Dep. Prosecuting Atty., Spokane County, 1958–60; instructor, Gonzaga U. Law School, 1958–60; Asst. Atty. Gen., Wash., 1960–61; Asst. Chief Clerk and Counsel, Senate Interior and Insular Affairs Com., 1961–63.

Offices 1201 LHOB, 202-225-2006. Also U.S. Courthouse, Spokane, 99201, 509-456-4680.

Committees

Agriculture (7th); Subs. (1) Chm., Domestic Marketing and Consumer Relations, (2) Forests, (3) Livestock and Grains.

Interior and Insular Affairs (9th); Subs. (1) Irrigation and Reclamation, (2) Mines and Mining, (3) Territorial and Insular Affairs.

Group Ratings

	ADA	COPE	NREP	NFU	LCV	CFA	NAB	NSI	ACA
1970	88	83	82	92	67	100	25	44	22
1969	93	—	—	80	—	—	—	—	12
1968	92	83	—	94	—	—	0	—	4

Key Votes

(1) ABM	FOR	(6) 18-Yr-Vote	FOR	(11) Clean Water $	FOR
(2) SST	FOR	(7) Farm Sub Lmt	AGN	(12) Mig Wrkrs Comp	FOR
(3) Phil Pln	FOR	(8) Coop-Church	FOR	(13) Jets to Chiang	AGN
(4) No-Knock	AGN	(9) Family Asst	FOR	(14) State OEO Veto	AGN
(5) Cmutr Tax	FOR	(10) Work Stamps	AGN	(15) Park Logging	FOR

Election Results

1970 general:	Thomas S. Foley (D)	88,189	(67%)
	George Gamble (R)	43,376	(33%)
1970 primary:	Thomas S. Foley (D), unopposed		
1968 general:	Thomas S. Foley (D)	88,446	(57%)
	Dorothy R. Powers (R)	67,304	(43%)

SIXTH DISTRICT Political Background

Washington 6 comprises the lower part of the Puget Sound area, and includes all of Pierce County (Tacoma), most of Kitsap County, and a small part of King County. Tacoma (pop. 154,000) has always resented its larger neighbor, Seattle. Some years ago, the rivalry took the form of an attempt by the citizens of Tacoma to rename Mount Rainier—which is, after all, within the bounds of Pierce County—Mount Tacoma. The affair created a great fuss; petitions were circulated, specious historical arguments were advanced, and so on. Tacoma was unsuccessful in the renaming project. And as Seattle grew, Tacoma remained a lumber town (Weyerhaeuser), having only about a quarter of the people of its more famous neighbor. Because Tacoma never received the white-collar immigrants who flocked to Seattle, it remains more Democratic—in fact, the prime Democratic stronghold in the state.

Despite the Democratic leanings, the 6th elected a Republican congressman, Thor C. Tollefson for 20 years, from 1944 to 1964. In 1964, Tollefson was defeated by a small margin by Floyd V. Hicks, then a Pierce County Superior Court Judge. Hicks has won reelection rather easily since then. In Washington, the Congressman sits on the House Armed Services Committee; huge Fort Lewis lies just outside Tacoma and Bremerton has a large complex of Naval facilities. Despite the presence of the Defense Department activity, Hicks votes with the committee's beleaguered peace-minded minority. He also sits on the Government Operations Committee. Hicks won a solid 69% of the vote in 1970 and should continue to win for some time to come.

Census Data 1970 pop. 523,994; deviation from current state average, +7.6%; change 1960–70, +26.0%. Metro. 82.2%, 29.5% central city.

1970 Share of Federal Outlays $745,981,204

DOD	$537,281,000	HEW	$102,898,625
AEC	$000	HUD	$446,000
NASA	$000	OEO	$1,524,079
DOT	$7,341,601	DOA	$4,804,073
		Other	$91,685,826

Federal Military-Industrial Commitments

DOD Contractors American Mail Line (Tacoma), $5.570m: cargo transport services.

DOD Installations Fort Lewis AB (Tacoma). Polaris Missile Facility, Pacific (Bremerton). Naval Hospital (Bremerton). Naval Torpedo Station (Keyport). Naval Supply Center (Bremerton). Puget Sound Naval Shipyard (Bremerton). Naval Security Group Activity (Marietta). McChord AF Base (Tacoma).

Economic Base Lumber and wood products other than furniture, esp. millwork, veneer, plywood, and prefabricated structural wood products; food and kindred products; dairy and poultry. Also, tourism (Mount Rainier); banking.

The Voters

Registration 209,948 total. No party registration.

Employment profile White collar, 43%. Blue collar, 57%.

Ethnic groups Black, 4%. Total foreign stock, 24%. Canada, 4%; Germany, Norway, 3% each; Sweden, UK, 2% each; Austria, Ireland, Italy, USSR, 1% each; others, 4%.

Presidential vote

1968	Humphrey (D)	96,553	(54%)
	Nixon (R)	66,930	(38%)
	Wallace (AIP)	14,759	(8%)

Representative

Floyd V. Hicks (D) Elected 1964; b. May 29, 1915, Prosser; home, Tacoma; Cen. Wash. State Col., B.Ed., 1938; U. of Wash., LL.B., 1948; AAF, WWII; married, two children; religion unspecified.

Career Practicing atty., 1949–60, 63–64; judge, Pierce County Superior Ct., 1961–63.

Offices 1203 LHOB, 202-225-5916. Also 210 Broadway, Tacoma 98402, 206-383-1666.

Committees

Armed Services (15th); Sub. No. 1.

Government Operations (18th); Subs. (1) Conservation and Natural Resources, (2) Government Activities.

Group Ratings

	ADA	COPE	NREP	NFU	LCV	CFA	NAB	NSI	ACA
1970	68	92	65	85	60	86	8	70	24
1969	80	—	—	100	—	—	—	—	6
1968	83	92	—	81	—	—	0	—	9

Key Votes

(1) ABM	AGN	(6) 18-Yr-Vote	FOR	(11) Clean Water $	FOR
(2) SST	FOR	(7) Farm Sub Lmt	AGN	(12) Mig Wrkrs Comp	FOR
(3) Phil Pln	AGN	(8) Coop-Church	FOR	(13) Jets to Chiang	FOR
(4) No-Knock	FOR	(9) Family Asst	FOR	(14) State OEO Veto	AGN
(5) Cmutr Tax	FOR	(10) Work Stamps	AGN	(15) Park Logging	FOR

Election Results

1970 general:	Floyd V. Hicks (D)	98,282	(69%)
	John Jarstad (R)	42,213	(30%)
	Richard Congress (SW)	1,180	(1%)
1970 primary:	Floyd V. Hicks (D), unopposed		
1968 general:	Floyd V. Hicks (D)	93,399	(56%)
	Anthony Chase (R)	72,177	(43%)
	Betty Jane Hiegal (C)	1,736	(1%)

SEVENTH DISTRICT Political Background

Washington 7 comprises the south side of Seattle and its suburbs of Bryn Mawr, Burien, Kent, and Renton, which lie in the urbanized strip between Seattle and Tacoma. The south side is the working-class side of Seattle. The huge Boeing plants are here—now mostly quiet, having few commercial and military contracts. The 7th also includes Seattle's small black ghetto; blacks make up only 6% of the population district-wide. Here too are the even smaller Mexican-American and oriental communities.

In the late '60's, most of the 7th illustrated in fine fashion the prosperity of middle-class America. But the heavy layoffs at Boeing have created an atmosphere of depression in the district, not only among production workers, but also among engineers and middle management executives as well. All of a sudden, car and appliance payments could not be met; vacations had to be cancelled; and the once prosperous, confident men saw each other queued up at the unemployment office. The affluence of the 7th was based on brittle foundations—the inherently unstable and volatile aircraft industry. As in the '30's, the little people, who thought themselves masters of their fate, found themselves helpless.

But so far, the Boeing depression has not affected the political habits of the residents of the district. Henry Jackson, known around the Capitol as the Senator from Boeing, won 85% of the 7th's votes in 1970. But Jackson did nearly as well just about everywhere else in the state. Congressman Brock Adams, a liberal Democrat and a major proponent of the SST in the House, was reelected with 67% of the vote, which is about what he did in 1968. The 7th has always been a strongly Democratic district, and if hard times make Democrats out of Republicans in other places, not many more voters here can become Democrats. What remains to be seen is whether the SST's staunchest advocate, Richard Nixon, will pick up votes here in 1972. Some Republican strategists think that the opposition of leading Democrats to military and related spending will produce Republican votes in areas where that spending has been the basis of economic prosperity. The Seattle area will be a good test of that theory in 1972.

Meanwhile, it appears that Congressman Adams, a beneficiary of the Goldwater debacle of 1964, will continue to be reelected easily. Adams is probably the most liberal member of the Washington House delegation. He serves as a pro-consumer member of the House Interstate and Foreign Commerce Committee. Redistricting will shave off some portions of the 7th, which until 1969, was growing rapidly. This, however, will not affect Adams' political chances.

Census Data 1970 pop. 555,638; deviation from current state average, +14.1%; change 1960–70, +23.7%. Metro. 100.0%, 38.8% central city.

1970 Share of Federal Outlays $620,135,000 (average outlay per district, Washington 1 and 7)

DOD	$201,183,000	HEW	$140,282,000
AEC	$1,270,000	HUD	$5,563,000
NASA	$2,024,000	OEO	$2,735,000
DOT	$101,282,000	DOA	$21,005,000
		Other	$144,791,000

Federal Military-Industrial Commitments

DOD Contractors Boeing Co. (Seattle), $224.346m: production of Minuteman III missiles; Minuteman III trajectory prediction systems; hard rock silo development for Minuteman III; hydrofoil research. Alaska Barge and Transport (Seattle), $24.000m: cargo transport services. Lockheed Shipbuilding Div., Lockheed Aircraft (Seattle), $7.145m: unspecified.

DOD Installations Fort Lawton AB (Seattle). Naval Support Center (Seattle).

Economic Base Transportation equipment, esp. aircraft and parts; food and kindred products, esp. bakery products; printing, publishing, and allied industries, esp. newspapers; fabricated metal products, esp. fabricated structural metal products; nonelectrical machinery.

The Voters

Registration 257,262 total. No party registration.

Employment profile White collar, 47%. Blue collar, 53%.

Ethnic groups Black, 6%. Total foreign stock, 26%. Canada, 5%; UK, 3%; Germany, Norway, Sweden, 2% each; Austria, Ireland, Italy, Poland, USSR, 1% each; others, 7%.

Presidential vote

1968	Humphrey (D)	101,883	(52%)
	Nixon (R)	79,649	(40%)
	Wallace (AIP)	15,588	(8%)

Representative

Brock Adams (D) Elected 1964; b. Jan. 13, 1927, Atlanta, Ga.; home, Seattle; U. of Wash., B.A., 1949; Harvard, LL.B., 1952; Navy, WWII; married, four children; Episcopalian.

Career Practicing atty., 1952–61; U.S. Dist. Atty. for Western Wash., 1961–64.

Offices 436 CHOB, 202-225-3106. Also Rm. 1006, U.S. Courthouse, Seattle 98104, 206-583-7478.

Committees

Interstate and Foreign Commerce (12th); Sub. on Transportation and Aeronautics.

Group Ratings

	ADA	COPE	NREP	NFU	LCV	CFA	NAB	NSI	ACA
1970	88	100	93	92	86	94	0	40	6
1969	93	—	—	80	—	—	—	—	12
1968	92	100	—	81	—	—	0	—	4

Key Votes

(1) ABM	AGN	(6) 18-Yr-Vote	FOR	(11) Clean Water $	FOR
(2) SST	FOR	(7) Farm Sub Lmt	FOR	(12) Mig Wrkrs Comp	FOR
(3) Phil Pln	FOR	(8) Coop-Church	FOR	(13) Jets to Chiang	AGN
(4) No-Knock	AGN	(9) Family Asst	FOR	(14) State OEO Veto	AGN
(5) Cmutr Tax	FOR	(10) Work Stamps	AGN	(15) Park Logging	AGN

Election Results

1970 general:	Brock Adams (D)	99,308	(67%)
	Brian Lewis (R)	47,426	(32%)
	Russell Block (SW)	2,378	(1%)
1970 primary:	Brock Adams (D)	61,223	(86%)
	John McKee (D)	10,086	(14%)
1968 general:	Brock Adams (D)	123,429	(66%)
	Robert Eberle (R)	64,051	(34%)

WEST VIRGINIA

Political Background

West Virginia, the Mountain State, lies in the middle of the Appalachian chain that separates the East Coast from the vast trans-Mississippi Valley of mid-America. It is said here that if all the mountains of the state were smoothed out, West Virginia would extend from coast to coast. That may or may not be true, but the mountains—and the narrow, twisting roads that wind through them—do give the state a sense of isolation, a sense of distance from the rest of the country. West Virginia is the heart of Appalachia; and its residents do not think of themselves as Easterners, Midwesterners, or—especially—Southerners.

The mountain counties of old Virginia never had many slaves and always felt that they were treated unfairly by the aristocratic Tidewater plantation owners. In the late 1820's and the early 1830's, state legislators from the mountain counties and liberal aristocrats in the tradition of Thomas Jefferson teamed up and almost succeeded in abolishing slavery in Virginia. Since the tobacco lands in the state were by that time exhausted, even the plantation owners flagged in their enthusiasm for the peculiar institution. Soon, however, the market for slaves improved sharply as new cotton lands opened up in Alabama and Mississippi. The Virginia plantations became breeding grounds for slaves, and the golden time for abolition passed. But when the Civil War began, the western counties of old Virginia chose to remain loyal to Republican President Lincoln, and in 1863, these counties were admitted to the Union as the state of West Virginia.

The new state included about a quarter of the residents of old Virginia, but in the years that followed the Civil War, West Virginia was growing much faster than its parent. The reason was simple: coal. Under virtually all the mountains of the state are rich veins of bituminous coal, which was the essential fuel for the industries and homes of the late nineteenth and early twentieth centuries. Men from all over the Appalachian region, and in the northern counties, some immigrants from Eastern and Southern Europe, came to work in the booming mines. Even today, West Virginia still produces more than a quarter of the nation's bituminous, and the coal industry still dominates the state's economy.

The working conditions in the mines were never good—lovers of country music know something of life in the coal company towns and the practices of the company store. In the '30's, bloody strikes were common as John L. Lewis' United Mine Workers established itself as the bargaining agent for the miners. But even as unionization proceeded, the coal industry began to decline. Houses built in the '30's and the '40's were heated with oil, not coal, and the railroads switched from the steam locomotive to the oil-powered diesel. After World War II, Lewis and the UMW cooperated with the companies to encourage mechanization of the mines and reduce the number of men working in them. This program was outstandingly successful, but it resulted in hard times for West Virginia. The state's population was more than 2,000,000 in 1950; by 1970, it had declined to 1,744,000.

Today, the UMW and the coal companies continue their partnership in other ways. They join together to prevent enactment of anti-pollution legislation, although countless West Virginia towns, sandwiched between mountains, are fouled with dirty air and water. Neither companies nor union have been particularly interested in mine safety, or in diseases like black lung which ruin the lives of the men who work the long dark corridors. Recently, the Union was taken to court for abuses of its Welfare and Retirement Fund, from whose board UMW President Tony Boyle has been ordered to resign. There is some reason to believe that Boyle would not have beaten challenger Joseph Yablonski in the Union's 1969 election if the votes had been counted fairly. Yablonski, his wife, and daughter were murdered a few weeks after the result was announced.

Internal union dissent is bubbling up all over West Virginia; Yablonski forces are particularly strong in the northern part of the state near the slain man's base of power in western Pennsylvania. And though the UMW's troubles are a major issue in state politics, only a few officeholders—most notably Congressman Ken Hechler and Secretary of State John D. Rockefeller IV—have taken solid stands against the positions of the union hierarchy. Coincidentally, both men are from outside the state: Hechler was elected to the House a few years after he became a professor at Huntington's Marshall University, and Rockefeller decided to settle here after a year as a poverty program worker near Charleston. These men are exceptions to the clubby, patronage-oriented politicians who normally characterize West Virginia. Corruption is not uncommon. Gov. W. W. Barron, who served from 1960 to 1964, is now in jail for jury-tampering in a federal bribery case; and current Gov. Arch Moore, one of the state's few successful Republican politicians, has been dogged by charges that he owes the government income tax money.

West Virginia was a Republican state for some years after statehood. But with the rise of the coal industry and the UMW, it has become solidly Democratic and today sends an all-Democratic delegation to Washington. The state's best known senator is Robert C. Byrd, currently the Senate Majority Whip. Byrd upset Edward Kennedy for this post in 1971, and the way he did it is typical of the Senator's mode of operation. He did not announce his candidacy until he was sure of a one-vote majority, and that Byrd got by securing Richard Russell's death-bed proxy. Byrd's attention to detail, his elaborate courtesy to other senators, and all the little favors he has done over the years make him something of a natural for the Whip's post.

Byrd's ultraconservatism has also made him a favorite of the Southerners, who, as a group, still have considerable influence in the Upper Chamber. Not related to the aristocratic Byrds of Virginia, the Senator grew up in poverty. He only quit the Ku Klux Klan a year before he was elected to the West Virginia House of Delegates. Byrd is not known to talk much about the Klan now, but he has voted against civil rights legislation and has also conducted a vigorous campaign against what he considered welfare abuses in the District of Columbia. Byrd's record apparently sits well with the voters in West Virginia. He has whipped liberal primary challengers soundly, winning 89% of the vote in 1970; the Senator also wins a phenomenal number of usually Republican votes in general elections. In 1970, he was the first candidate to carry all of West Virginia's 55 counties—his lowest share of the vote in any of them being 61%. In October, 1971, the Democratic Senator was a leading candidate for a seat on the Supreme Court.

West Virginia's senior senator, Jennings Randolph, has not been quite as strong at the polls, but he has still won reelection rather easily. Randolph is one of the most experienced veterans in Congress. At age 30, he was first elected to the House in 1932; he remained there for 14 years until the Republican year of 1946. Then in 1958, he was elected to the Senate, where he has risen to become chairman of the Public Works Committee. This is the body with jurisdiction over the legendary pork barrel, and its work has many important implications for the environment—and for the coal industry. For the most part, Randolph has shown himself to be very mindful of the interests of West Virginia's largest business, and because of this, the coal industry usually gets what it wants in Washington.

There is some speculation that the Senator, who will be 70 when his term expires in 1972, will retire at that time. Secretary of State John D. Rockefeller is one man in the state who could succeed him with no trouble at all. But Rockefeller has indicated that he will run for governor against Arch Moore, who is the first West Virginia governor eligible to succeed himself. Randolph will be the favorite if he runs; if he chooses to retire, possible candidates for the job include Congressman Ken Hechler and Del. (state Rep.) Richard Neely, grandson of longtime Sen. Matthew M. Neely, who served intermittently from 1922 through 1958.

West Virginia lost a congressional district in the 1970 census. The state's districts have been redrawn to protect three of the five incumbents and to let two others—Ken Hechler and James Kee—fight it out for the fourth seat. At first, observers expected a rugged primary fight between these two Democrats whose records and bases of support are quite different (see West Virginia 4 and 5). But at this writing, Hechler has said that he will not make the race. He may change his mind or may run for the Senate instead, especially if Jennings Randolph decides to retire.

Electoral Votes 6

Census Data 1970 pop. 1,744,237; 0.85% of U.S. total, 35th largest; change 1960–70, −6.2%. Metro. 31.3%, 12.7% central city. 1970 per capita income, $2,929; 47th highest. 29th in number of poor.

1970 Share of Federal Tax Burden $1,190,360,000; 0.61% of U.S. total, 33rd largest.

1970 Share of Federal Outlays $1,182,741,550; 0.63% of U.S. total, 37th largest. Per capita federal spending, $678.

DOD	$89,912,000	49th	(0.16%)	HEW	$502,512,997	32nd	(0.96%)
AEC	$25,272	51st	(0.00%)	HUD	$8,046,161	41st	(0.41%)
NASA	$312,879	41st	(0.01%)	OEO	$8,178,706	31st	(1.08%)
DOT	$186,463,288	11th	(2.61%)	DOA	$46,807,672	42nd	(0.36%)
DOC	$7,394,558	32nd	(0.64%)	POD	$50,934,189	33rd	(0.69%)
DOI	$10,988,501	39th	(0.48%)	VA	$111,395,416	31st	(1.51%)
DOJ	$7,513,130	22nd	(1.31%)	CSC	$13,817,026	42nd	(0.34%)
				Other	$138,439,755		

Economic Base Bituminous coal; chemicals and allied products, esp. industrial inorganic and organic chemicals; primary metal industries, esp. blast furnaces, steel works, and rolling and finishing mills; livestock, dairy, and poultry; stone, clay, glass, and concrete products, esp. glass and glassware, pressed and blown; fabricated metal products, esp. cutlery, hand tools, and general hardware; food and kindred products, esp. bakery products; electrical machinery, equipment, and supplies, esp. electrical lighting and wiring equipment; lumber and wood products other than lumber, esp. sawmills and planing mills; apparel and other finished products made from fabrics and similar materials, esp. women's, misses', and juniors' outerwear.

Political Line-up Governor, Arch A. Moore (R); seat up, 1972. Senators, Jennings Randolph (D) and Robert C. Byrd (D). Representatives, 5 (5 D and 0 R). State Senate (23 D and 11 R); State House of Delegates (68 D and 32 R).

The Voters

Registration 932,702 total. 596,480 D (64%); 328,487 R (35%); 7,735 other (1%).
Employment profile White collar, 36%. Blue collar, 64%.
Ethnic groups Black, 4%. Total foreign stock, 5%; Italy, UK, 1% each; others, 1%.

Presidential vote

1968	Humphrey (D)	374,091	(50%)
	Nixon (R)	307,555	(41%)
	Wallace (AIP)	72,560	(10%)
1964	Johnson (D)	538,087	(68%)
	Goldwater (R)	253,953	(32%)
1960	Kennedy (D)	441,786	(53%)
	Nixon (R)	395,995	(47%)

Senator

Jennings Randolph (D) Elected 1958, seat up 1972; b. Mar. 8, 1902, Salem; home, Elkins; Salem Col., B.A., 1924; married, two children; Baptist.

Career U.S. House, 1933–47; newspaper and magazine editor; col. professor; university dean; airline executive.

Offices 5121 NSOB, 202-225-6472. Also 303 New P.O. Bldg., Clarksburg 26301, 304-623-2811.

Committees

Public Works (Chm.); Subs. (1) Air and Water Pollution, (2) Economic Development, (3) Public Roads.

Labor and Public Welfare (2nd); Subs. (1) Chm., Handicapped Workers, (2) Aging, (3) Alcoholism and Narcotics, (4) Children and Youth, (5) Education, (6) Employment, Manpower, and Poverty, (7) Labor, (8) Sp. on Human Resources.

Post Office and Civil Service (2nd); Subs. (1) Chm., Civil Service Policies and Practices, (2) Postal Operations.

Veterans' Affairs (3rd); Subs. (1) Compensation and Pension, (2) Health and Hospitals.

Sel. Com. on Equal Educational Opportunity (4th).

Sp. Com. on Aging (4th); Chm., Sub. on Employment and Retirement Incomes.

Group Ratings

	ADA	COPE	NREP	NFU	LCV	NAB	NSI	ACA
1970	59	69	50	93	21	25	40	26
1969	78	—	—	88	—	—	—	29
1968	64	91	—	69	—	40	—	32

Key Votes

(1) ABM	AGN	(8) Phil Pln	AGN	(15) Coop-Church	FOR
(2) SST	FOR	(9) Vol Army	AGN	(16) Cut Oil Dpltn	AGN
(3) Busing	AGN	(10) Prison $	AGN	(17) Consumer Prot	FOR
(4) Tob Sub	FOR	(11) Cut Mil $	FOR	(18) Farm Sub Limit	FOR
(5) Carswell	FOR	(12) Defoliatn	FOR	(19) Comp Bid Sales	AGN
(6) No-Knock	AGN	(13) 18-Yr-Vote	FOR	(20) Pre-Prod Tests	FOR
(7) Seniorty	AGN	(14) Pentgn PR	AGN	(21) Cut Marjna Pen	FOR

Election Results

1966 general:	Jennings Randolph (D)	292,325	(60%)
	Francis J. Love (R)	198,891	(40%)
1966 primary:	Jennings Randolph (D), unopposed		
1960 general:	Jennings Randolph (D)	458,355	(55%)
	Cecil H. Underwood (R)	369,935	(45%)

Senator

Robert C. Byrd (D) Elected 1958, seat up 1976; b. Jan. 15, 1918, N. Wilkesboro, N.C.; home, Sophia; Beckley Col., Concord Col., and Morris Harvey Col., 1950–51; American U., LL.B., 1963; married, three children; Baptist.

Career W. Va. Legislature, 1946–50, Senate 1950–52; U.S. House, 1952–58.

Offices 105 OSOB, 202-225-3954.

Committees

Appropriations (7th); Subs. (1) Chm., Transportation, (2) Interior, (3) Agriculture, Environmental and Consumer Protection, (4) Labor, HEW, and Related Agencies, (5) Public Works.

Judiciary (8th); Subs. (1) Constitutional Amendments, (2) Constitutional Rights, (3) Criminal Laws and Procedures, (4) Improvements in Judicial Machinery, (5) Internal Security, (6) Juvenile Delinquency.

Rules and Administration (4th); Subs. (1) Chm., Standing Rules of the Senate, (2) Privileges and Elections, (3) Restaurant, (4) Smithsonian Institution.

Group Ratings

	ADA	COPE	NREP	NFU	LCV	NAB	NSI	ACA
1970	3	46	33	87	30	27	90	50
1969	33	—	—	50	—	—	—	50
1968	21	25	—	46	—	50	—	63

Key Votes

(1) ABM	FOR	(8) Phil Pln	AGN	(15) Coop-Church	FOR
(2) SST	FOR	(9) Vol Army	AGN	(16) Cut Oil Dpltn	FOR
(3) Busing	AGN	(10) Prison $	AGN	(17) Consumer Prot	FOR
(4) Tob Sub	FOR	(11) Cut Mil $	FOR	(18) Farm Sub Limit	FOR
(5) Carswell	FOR	(12) Defoliatn	FOR	(19) Comp Bid Sales	FOR
(6) No-Knock	FOR	(13) 18-Yr-Vote	FOR	(20) Pre-Prod Tests	AGN
(7) Seniorty	FOR	(14) Pentgn PR	AGN	(21) Cut Marjna Pen	FOR

Election Results

1970 general:	Robert C. Byrd (D)	345,965	(78%)
	Elmer H. Dodson (R)	99,663	(22%)
1970 primary:	Robert C. Byrd (D)	195,725	(89%)
	John J. McOwen (D)	24,286	(11%)
1964 general:	Robert C. Byrd (D)	515,015	(68%)
	Cooper P. Benedict (R)	246,072	(32%)

FIRST DISTRICT Political Background

West Virginia 1 is a portion of northern West Virginia, including the state's panhandle that lies between the Ohio River and the Pennsylvania line. This is heavy industry country. The steel plants of Wheeling and Weirton have made the Ohio River Valley certainly one of the most polluted parts of the nation, while the air and water around Clarksburg and Fairmont, on the Monongahela south of Pittsburgh, is not much cleaner. Some of the district's rural counties have a Republican tradition going back to the Civil War, but in most elections, the 1st, as a whole, goes heavily Democratic.

In congressional elections, however, this has not always been the case—thanks to Arch A. Moore, Jr., formerly congressman from the district and now governor. Moore was first elected to Congress in 1956, as Eisenhower swept the state and the Republicans here won a Senate seat and the governorship. The years that followed were better for Democrats generally, but Moore, an unabashed booster of West Virginia, had by then developed great campaigning talents and won reelection by larger margins. His toughest test came in 1962, when he was placed in the same district with Democratic Congressman Cleveland Bailey. Moore won a solid 60% of the vote against Bailey, then 76, and he won four years later with 71%.

Electoral achievements of this magnitude are enough to make a man think of bigger things, and in 1968 Moore decided to make a run for governor. The experts figured his chances were slim at best, but relying heavily on home district strength, Moore defeated ex-Gov. (1956–60) Cecil Underwood in the Republican primary and edged Democratic State Chairman James Sprouse by 12,000 votes in the general election.

Moore's successor in the House is the Democrat he beat back in 1956, Robert H. Mollohan. Mollohan is a veteran of West Virginia political wars who serves on the House Armed Services Committee. Here he usually finds himself agreeing with its pro-Pentagon majority. Mollohan's prospects for reelection seem good; he clobbered ex-middle linebacker Sam Huff in the 1970 Democratic primary and won the general election with 62% of the votes. But for 1972, the West Virginia legislature has added the Republican city of Parkersburg to the district, and Mollohan could be in trouble if Gov. Moore comes back to the district and runs for his old House seat. In 1972, Moore will have a tough fight for reelection against Secretary of State John D. Rockefeller IV; if he loses, he may run for the House again in 1974. And if he does, his record in the 1st makes him the favorite against Mollohan or any other incumbent in the district.

Census Data 1970 pop. 357,073; deviation from current state average, +2.4%; change 1960–70, –3.2%. Metro. 48.0%, 21.1% central city.

1970 Share of Federal Outlays $188,152,819

DOD	$9,976,000	HEW	$93,797,461
AEC	$000	HUD	$1,194,687
NASA	$000	OEO	$411,114
DOT	$18,384,955	DOA	$6,851,443
		Other	$57,537,159

Federal Military-Industrial Commitments

DOD Contractors Rubber Fabricators, Inc. (Grantsville), $5.083m: pneumatic nylon mattress; collapsible water tanks.

Economic Base Stone, clay, glass, and concrete products, esp. glass and glassware, pressed and blown; bituminous coal; livestock and dairy; primary metal industries.

The Voters

Registration 199,689 total. 124,729 D (62%); 73,347 R (37%); 1,613 other (1%).
Employment profile White collar, 35%. Blue collar, 65%.
Ethnic groups Black, 2%. Total foreign stock, 11%. Italy, 3%; Czech., Germany, Poland, UK, 1% each; others, 2%.

Presidential vote

1968	Humphrey (D)	86,743	(52%)
	Nixon (R)	66,470	(40%)
	Wallace (AIP)	13,315	(8%)

Representative

Robert H. Mollohan (D) Elected 1952–56, 1968 to present; b, Sept. 18, 1909, Grantsville; home, Fairmont; Shepherd Col.; married, three children; Baptist.

Career Chief, tax div. and cashier, IRS in W. Va., 1933–36; Dist. Mgr. and State Pers. Dir., WPA, 1937–40; supt., W. Va. Industrial School for Boys, 1945–49; U.S. Marshal, 1949–51; clerk, U.S. Senate Com. on District of Columbia.

Offices 314 CHOB, 202-225-4172. Also Rm. 603, Deveny Bldg., Fairmont 26554, 304-363-3356.

Committees

Armed Services (20th); Subs. (1) No. 3, (2) Armed Services Investigating.

House Administration (15th); Subs. (1) Elections, (2) Electrical and Mechanical Equipment.

Group Ratings

	ADA	COPE	NREP	NFU	LCV	CFA	NAB	NSI	ACA
1970	36	100	60	82	67	67	0	88	18
1969	47	—	—	79	—	—	—	—	24

Key Votes

(1) ABM	FOR	(6) 18-Yr-Vote	FOR	(11) Clean Water $	FOR
(2) SST	FOR	(7) Farm Sub Lmt	FOR	(12) Mig Wrkrs Comp	FOR
(3) Phil Pln	AGN	(8) Coop-Church	AGN	(13) Jets to Chiang	FOR
(4) No-Knock	ABS	(9) Family Asst	ABS	(14) State OEO Veto	AGN
(5) Cmutr Tax	FOR	(10) Work Stamps	FOR	(15) Park Logging	AGN

Election Results

1970 general:	Robert H. Mollohan (D)	61,296	(62%)
	Ken Doll (R)	38,327	(38%)
1970 primary:	Robert H. Mollohan (D)	36,330	(68%)
	Robert L. (Sam) Huff (D)	17,011	(32%)
1968 general:	Robert H. Mollohan (D)	85,436	(54%)
	Tom Sweeney (R)	73,176	(46%)

SECOND DISTRICT Political Background

West Virginia 2 occupies the eastern part of the state, the most mountainous and most sparsely-settled counties of West Virginia. The district extends across the mountains from Harpers Ferry, not far from Washington, D.C., where John Brown's raiders seized the arsenal in 1859, south and west to Monroe County, not far from the Kentucky state line. In the northern part of the district is its largest city, Morgantown (pop. 29,000), which is the home of West Virginia University and part of the industrial Monongahela River Valley.

The problems of the 2nd district of West Virginia are shared by the entire Appalachian region. For one thing, there are virtually no four-lane highways in the district, and the roads, twisting around the mountains, effectively make the rural coal towns here more remote from the East Coast than the geographically more distant cities in the Great Lakes region. For another thing, the beauty of the West Virginia hills is often despoiled by the emissions from coal mines, chemical plants, and paper mills. And—even worse for its working people—many of the industries are leaving.

The political map of the 2nd is an odd looking patchwork of Democratic industrial areas and Republican mountain strongholds. In most statewide elections, the district is counted as marginal; but in congressional contests, it is solidly Democratic. Congressman Harley O. Staggers has been representing the 2nd in the House since 1949; in recent elections, he has grown accustomed to winning margins of 60% or better. For some five years, Staggers has been chairman of the House Interstate and Foreign Commerce Committee, which has jurisdiction over many consumer issues, transportation policy, and the communications industry, among other things. It was the committee's jurisdiction over the communications industry which brought Staggers before the public in the summer of 1971. At that time, he sought a contempt citation against CBS President Frank Stanton for his refusal to provide outtakes—edited pieces of film—from the controversial documentary "The Selling of the Pentagon." The committee dutifully voted for contempt, but the full House, under pressure from liberals and the usually conservative broadcasting lobby, voted it down—the first time in recent memory a committee chairman has been so repudiated.

The incident is another mark in the slow decline of the power of committee chairmen generally, and Staggers' lack of influence in particular. The CBS affair is unlikely, however, to affect his standing among the voters of the 2nd district. Redistricting has altered its boundaries less than those of any other West Virginia district, and Staggers, who was 63 in 1970, appears certain to remain congressman and chairman for some time to come.

Census Data 1970 pop. 373,595; deviation from current state average, +7.1%; change 1960–70, –0.6%. Metro. 0.0%, 0.0% central city.

1970 Share of Federal Outlays $258,586,283

DOD	$15,611,000	HEW	$99,443,172
AEC	$25,272	HUD	$000
NASA	$312,879	OEO	$463,221
DOT	$29,991,588	DOA	$19,983,979
		Other	$92,755,172

Federal Military-Industrial Commitments

None.

Economic Base Livestock, dairy and poultry; bituminous coal; lumber and wood products other than furniture. Also, higher education (West Virginia University).

The Voters

Registration 191,485 total. 113,212 D (59%); 76,324 R (40%); 1,949 other (1%).
Employment profile White collar, 32%. Blue collar, 68%.
Ethnic groups Black, 3%. Total foreign stock, 4%. Italy, UK, 1% each; others, 1%.

Presidential vote

1968	Humphrey (D)	68,663	(44%)
	Nixon (R)	72,571	(46%)
	Wallace (AIP)	15,124	(10%)

Representative

Harley O. Staggers (D) Elected 1949; b. Aug. 3, 1907, Keyser; home, Keyser; Emory and Henry Col., B.A., 1931; USN, WWII; married, six children; Methodist.

Career High school, col. coach; Sheriff, Mineral Co., 1937–41; Right-of-Way Agent, W.Va. Road Commission, 1941–42; Dir., W.Va. Office of Govt. Reports, 1942.

Offices 2366 RHOB, 202-225-4331. Also P.O. Box 906, Keyser 26726, 304-788-1298.

Committees

Interstate and Foreign Commerce (Chm.); Chm., Sp. on Investigations.

Group Ratings

	ADA	COPE	NREP	NFU	LCV	CFA	NAB	NSI	ACA
1970	52	92	64	83	80	88	0	88	26
1969	33	—	—	86	—	—	—	—	25
1968	67	100	—	92	—	—	0	—	5

Key Votes

(1) ABM	ABS	(6) 18-Yr-Vote	FOR	(11) Clean Water $	FOR
(2) SST	FOR	(7) Farm Sub Lmt	FOR	(12) Mig Wrkrs Comp	FOR
(3) Phil Pln	FOR	(8) Coop-Church	AGN	(13) Jets to Chiang	AGN
(4) No-Knock	FOR	(9) Family Asst	FOR	(14) State OEO Veto	AGN
(5) Cmutr Tax	FOR	(10) Work Stamps	AGN	(15) Park Logging	AGN

Election Results

1970 general:	Harley O. Staggers (D)	56,263	(63%)
	Richard M. Reddecliff (R)	33,509	(37%)
1970 primary:	Harley O. Staggers (D), unopposed		

1968 general:	Harley O. Staggers (D)	91,082	(62%)
	George L. Strader (R)	56,911	(38%)

THIRD DISTRICT Political Background

West Virginia 3 is the district around Charleston, the state capital. The city was the state's largest in 1960 but lost that status in 1970 to Huntington. Charleston lies in the narrow valley of the Kanawha River, hemmed in by mountains; into the valley, the steel and chemical plants pour their emissions and the resulting atmosphere here is one not unlike that of Gary, Indiana.

Beyond the Charleston area, the district is made up of rural towns and settlements in the Appalachian hills, places about as far removed from the neon-sign prosperity of the '60's as any in America. It was to one of these towns that John D. Rockefeller IV first came to West Virginia as a poverty program worker. Rockefeller found that he liked the area and decided to stay and enter politics—as a Democrat, despite the family tradition. He built a large house in the hills above Charleston, won a seat in the state legislature, and in 1968, became Secretary of State. Almost everyone here expects he will be elected governor in 1972. Rockefeller is one of the few West Virginia politicians who has taken on the coal companies and the leadership of the United Mine Workers (see state write-up). And he is one of the few public officials in scandal-ridden West Virginia who is not suspected to be in the business for personal gain.

Congressman John Slack of the 3rd district comes from a more traditional West Virginia background. A real estate man, he made his way up in politics as a Kanawha County official, and then, in 1958, won a seat in Congress. There Slack won a seat on the House Appropriations Committee and is now a member of its Public Works and State-Justice-Commerce-Judiciary subcommittees. The West Virginian is not yet a subcommittee chairman, but he probably will be within a few years. Slack has had negligible opposition in recent elections, and redistricting—which added some sparsely-populated, Republican counties along the Ohio River—will not affect his margins significantly.

Census Data 1970 pop. 340,917; deviation from current state average, —2.3%; change 1960–70, —8.7%. Metro. 67.3%, 21.0% central city.

1970 Share of Federal Outlays $321,410,258

DOD	$28,052,000	HEW	$107,207,903
AEC	$000	HUD	$4,768,260
NASA	$000	OEO	$1,547,919
DOT	$110,853,626	DOA	$6,214,562
		Other	$67,137,941

Federal Military-Industrial Commitments

DOD Contractors FMC Corp. (South Charleston), $18.578m: unspecified.

Economic Base Industrial inorganic and organic chemicals, and other chemicals and allied products; petroleum refining and related industries; bituminous coal.

The Voters

Registration 184,361 total. 115,843 D (63%); 66,893 R (36%); 1,625 other, (1%).

Employment profile White collar, 41%. Blue collar, 59%.

Registration 184,361 total. 115,843 D (63%); 66,893 R (36%); 1,625 other 1%.

Presidential vote

1968	Humphrey (D)	70,731	(48%)
	Nixon (R)	61,378	(42%)
	Wallace (AIP)	15,745	(11%)

Representative

John Slack (D) Elected 1958; b. Mar. 18, 1915, Charleston; home, Charleston; Virginia Mil. Institute; married, one child; Presbyterian.

Career Businessman; member Kanawha County Ct., 1948–52; assessor, Kanawha County, 1952–58.

Offices 2230 RHOB, 202-225-2711. Also 500 Quartier St., Charleston 25301, 304-343-8923.

Committees

Appropriations (13th); Subs. (1) Public Works, (2) State, Justice, Commerce, and the Judiciary.

Group Ratings

	ADA	COPE	NREP	NFU	LCV	CFA	NAB	NSI	ACA
1970	24	75	25	69	60	65	18	90	39
1969	27	—	—	80	—	—	—	—	29
1968	42	92	—	94	—	—	50	—	26

Key Votes

(1) ABM	FOR	(6) 18-Yr-Vote	FOR	(11) Clean Water $	AGN
(2) SST	FOR	(7) Farm Sub Lmt	AGN	(12) Mig Wrkrs Comp	AGN
(3) Phil Pln	AGN	(8) Coop-Church	AGN	(13) Jets to Chiang	FOR
(4) No-Knock	FOR	(9) Family Asst	AGN	(14) State OEO Veto	AGN
(5) Cmutr Tax	FOR	(10) Work Stamps	FOR	(15) Park Logging	AGN

General Elections

1970 general:	John Slack (D)	57,630	(65%)
	Neal A. Kinsolving (R)	30,525	(35%)
1970 primary:	John Slack (D)	30,204	(78%)
	Jack D. Huffman (D)	8,343	(22%)
1968 general:	John Slack (D)	82,911	(62%)
	Neal A. Kinsolving (R)	54,164	(38%)

FOURTH DISTRICT Political Background

West Virginia 4 lies in the western part of the state. The district, which has a rather odd shape, is made up of a group of counties that hug the Ohio River and the Kentucky border. The 4th is dominated by two medium-sized industrial cities, Huntington (pop. 74,000), which is the state's largest, and Parkersburg (pop. 44,000). Both are a little more prosperous than the coal mining towns up in the mountains, and both retain, especially Parkersburg, their traditional anti-planter Republicanism (see state write-up). The district also contains some classic West Virginia coal mining areas south of Huntington, but the population here is declining rapidly and the large Democratic margins produced by the miners sometimes do not equal the Republican votes cast in the counties along the river.

In 1956, Republican candidates swept statewide elections in West Virginia, and the state elected two Republican congressmen—the most the party has sent to Washington since the early years of the New Deal. One of two winners was William E. Neal, an 81-year-old physician and former mayor of Huntington; he was elected from the 4th district. Neal's chances for reelection were not regarded as particularly good—a fact which reportedly attracted the attention of Ken Hechler. At that time, Hechler was a political scientist who had written a bestseller on the World War II Remagen Bridge crossing; in 1956, he was a speechwriter for Adlai Stevenson. Hechler, who had no roots in West Virginia, had never before run for public office. In 1957, he moved to Huntington, got a professorship there at Marshall University, and became a commentator on the local TV station.

It is generally believed that Hechler moved to West Virginia solely to get himself elected to Congress. If so, he succeeded ably. In 1958, he beat Dr. Neal by 3,503 votes, and his margins have been improving ever since; in 1970, he got 67% of the votes in the district. Hechler has proved to be an untiring and resourceful campaigner; for an ex-professor, he shows little distaste for the campaign shenanigans that so many of his ex-colleagues find quite unattractive. Hechler is the most liberal member of West Virginia's congressional delegation, having battled the coal companies and the United Mine Workers for mine safety and black lung legislation. The Congressman has introduced a bill which would ban strip-mining everywhere in the nation.

West Virginia lost a congressional seat in the 1970 census; as a result, Hechler has been placed in a district with Congressman James Kee, now of the 5th. Kee has a record more in line with what the powers that be in the state like. And the new 4th dips far into the southern West Virginia coal counties, traditionally the strongholds of Tony Boyle's United Mine Workers. Some 56% of the new district's population—and about 60% of its registered Democrats—live in the portion that Kee now represents. On paper, that gives Kee the edge. At this writing, Hechler seems to be leaning against making the race. He has other alternatives: he could run in the new 3rd district, which includes some of his old counties, against Charleston's John Slack; or he could run for the Senate seat now held by Jennings Randolph. It seems a little hard to believe that an indefatigable campaigner and crusader like Hechler won't run for something. Whatever his prospects today, Hechler may still end up somewhere in the West Virginia delegation to the 93rd Congress.

Census Data 1970 pop. 363,280; deviation from current state average, +4.1%; change 1960–70, –2.5%. Metro. 39.8%, 20.5% central city.

1970 Share of Federal Outlays $212,267,718

DOD	$30,267,000	HEW	$92,135,299
AEC	$000	HUD	$1,067,214
NASA	$000	OEO	$1,525,012
DOT	$10,864,586	DOA	$6,434,897
		Other	$69,613,710

Federal Military-Industrial Commitments

None.

Economic Base Chemicals and allied products, esp. plastics materials and synthetic resins, synthetic rubber, synthetic and other man-made fibers, except glass; bituminous coal; stone, clay, glass, and concrete products, esp. glass and glassware, pressed and blown; livestock and dairy.

The Voters

Registration 190,449 total. 114,670 D (60%); 74,174 R (39%); 1,605 other (1%).

Employment profile White collar, 37%. Blue collar, 63%.

Ethnic groups Black, 2%. Total foreign stock, 2%. All foreign groups less than 0.5% each.

Presidential vote

1968	Humphrey (D)	71,244	(46%)
	Nixon (R)	68,870	(44%)
	Wallace (AIP)	15,031	(10%)

Representative

Ken Hechler (D) Elected 1958; b. Sept. 20, 1914, Roslyn, Long Island; home, Huntington; Swarthmore Col., B.A., 1935; Columbia U., M.A., 1936, Ph.D., 1940; Army WWII; unmarried; Episcopalian.

Career Section Chief, Census, 1940; Office of Emergency Mgmt., 1941; Analyst, Bureau of the Budget, 1941–42, 46–47; Asst. Prof., Princeton, 1947–49; Sp. Asst. to Pres. Truman, 1949–53; Research Dir., Stevenson-Kefauver campaign; radio-TV commentator, Huntington, 1957–58.

Offices 242 CHOB, 202-225-3457. Also Rm. 219, P.O. Bldg., Huntington 25701, 304-529-3350.

Committees

Science and Astronautics (4th); Subs. (1) Chm., Advanced Research and Technology, (2) NASA Oversight.

Group Ratings

	ADA	COPE	NREP	NFU	LCV	CFA	NAB	NSI	ACA
1970	88	83	93	77	80	95	8	10	37
1969	80	—	—	67	—	—	—	—	18
1968	83	92	—	88	—	—	0	—	9

Key Votes

(1) ABM	AGN	(6) 18-Yr-Vote	FOR	(11) Clean Water $	FOR
(2) SST	AGN	(7) Farm Sub Lmt	FOR	(12) Mig Wrkrs Comp	FOR
(3) Phil Pln	FOR	(8) Coop-Church	FOR	(13) Jets to Chiang	AGN
(4) No-Knock	FOR	(9) Family Asst	FOR	(14) State OEO Veto	AGN
(5) Cmutr Tax	FOR	(10) Work Stamps	AGN	(15) Park Logging	AGN

Election Results

1970 general:	Ken Hechler (D)	62,531	(67%)
	Ralph Shannon (R)	30,255	(33%)
1970 primary:	Ken Hechler (D)	32,033	(81%)
	James R. Burton (D)	7,778	(19%)
1968 general:	Ken Hechler (D)	94,507	(64%)
	Ralph Shannon (R)	52,636	(36%)

FIFTH DISTRICT Political Background

West Virginia 5 is most people's image of West Virginia: a group of desperately poor coal counties at the southern end of the state. The district's largest cities are Beckley (pop. 19,000) in Raleigh County and Bluefield (pop. 15,000) in Mercer County on the Virginia state line. Both of these cities—and the many smaller communities that are found throughout the hills—are heavily dependent on the coal industry. After John L. Lewis of the United Mine Workers and the coal company owners agreed to cut the mining work force, people began leaving this area; most have never returned (see, for example, Ohio 14, Akron). The recent boom in strip-mining has provided employment for a few, but a large majority of the people in the 5th remain near or below the poverty line. It could very well be that John F. Kennedy, while campaigning here in southern West Virginia, first felt the impulses that were to produce the antipoverty and Appalachia programs of the mid-'60's.

Unfortunately, the politics that develop in poverty-stricken areas is seldom as pure and altruistic as liberal reformers like to imagine. In a place like southern West Virginia, there is no way for a bright young man to make money except by owning a coal company—or winning public (or union) office. The 5th normally rolls up huge Democratic majorities at election time, with the help, some claim, of massive vote fraud. But recent federal indictments of top Democratic officeholders in Mingo County failed to produce convictions. The to-get-along-you-have-to-go-along atmosphere of local courthouses leaves little room for indignation about matters like unsafe mine conditions, black lung disease, and terrible air and water pollution—problems which are as much a part of life here as anywhere.

In this kind of context, it is not surprising to find that the 5th's congressional seat has remained in the hands of one family for nearly 40 years. In 1932, James Kee, a lawyer who had worked for a railroad and an oil company was swept into the House in the Roosevelt landslide; he remained there until his death in 1951. His widow, Elizabeth Kee, was elected to fill the vacancy and served until her retirement in 1964. That same year her son, James, won the Democratic primary without too much difficulty and remains in Congress today. James Kee serves on the Public Works and the Interior and Insular Affairs committees.

Congressman Kee is no doubt unhappy about his state's declining population. In 1970, the outmigration cost West Virginia a congressional seat and forced him into the same district with Ken Hechler, now of the 4th. Hechler (see West Virginia 4) has reportedly decided not to run in the new district; but if he does, he could give Kee a battle. Hechler is by far the more experienced campaigner, and local revolts against the UMW leadership might work in his favor. The general election will be no problem for whoever wins the primary, this being West Virginia's most Democratic district. It has provided most of the margins that have put the state in the Democratic column in nine of the last ten presidential elections.

Census Data 1970 pop. 309,372; deviation from current state average, −11.3%; change 1960–70, −16.2%. Metro. 0.0%, 0.0% central city.

1970 Share of Federal Outlays $196,671,263

DOD	$5,646,000	HEW	$109,929,162
AEC	$000	HUD	$1,018,000
NASA	$000	OEO	$4,231,440
DOT	$16,368,533	DOA	$7,322,661
		Other	$52,155,467

Federal Military-Industrial Commitments

None.

Economic Base Bituminous coal; food and kindred products; livestock.

The Voters

Registration 166,718 total. 128,026 D (77%); 37,749 R (23%); 943 other (1%).
Employment profile White collar, 34%. Blue collar, 66%.
Ethnic groups Black, 9%. Total foreign stock, 3%. Italy, 3%; others, 1%.

Presidential vote

1968	Humphrey (D)	76,710	(60%)
	Nixon (R)	38,266	(30%)
	Wallace (AIP)	13,345	(10%)

Representative

James Kee (D) Elected 1964; b. Apr. 15, 1917, Bluefield; home, Bluefield; Southeastern U. Law School, Georgetown University; AAF, WWII; married, three children; Episcopalian.

Career Asst. to Clerk of U.S. House; Adviser, U.S. Housing Authority; Adm. Asst. Rep. Elizabeth Kee, 1953–64.

Offices 215 CHOB, 202-225-2176. Also, Rm. 1005, Fed. Bldg., Bluefield 27401, 304-469-4661.

Committees

Interior and Insular Affairs (14th); Subs. (1) Environment, (2) Mines and Mining, (3) Public Lands.

Public Works (12th); Subs. (1) Chm., Watershed Development, (2) Flood Control and Internal Development, (3) Public Buildings and Grounds, (4) Sp. on Economic Development Programs.

Group Ratings

	ADA	COPE	NREP	NFU	LCV	CFA	NAB	NSI	ACA
1970	28	75	36	83	57	81	8	88	32
1969	27	—	—	93	—	—	—	—	18
1968	58	100	—	100	—	—	0	—	13

Key Votes

(1) ABM	FOR	(6) 18-Yr-Vote	FOR	(11) Clean Water $	FOR
(2) SST	FOR	(7) Farm Sub Lmt	AGN	(12) Mig Wrkrs Comp	AGN
(3) Phil Pln	AGN	(8) Coop-Church	AGN	(13) Jets to Chiang	FOR
(4) No-Knock	FOR	(9) Family Asst	FOR	(14) State OEO Veto	AGN
(5) Cmutr Tax	FOR	(10) Work Stamps	FOR	(15) Park Logging	AGN

Election Results

1970 general:	James Kee (D)	48,286	(71%)
	Mrs. Joe McQuade (R)	19,585	(29%)
1970 primary:	James Kee (D)	32,637	(64%)
	Hawey A. Wells, Jr. (D)	18,334	(36%)
1968 general:	James Kee (D)	80,204	(66%)
	J. Donald Clarke (R)	41,038	(34%)

WISCONSIN

Political Background

Wisconsin is dairy country, where the politics of milk and cheddar is still more important than those of Defense Department bases and contracts. This state, along with Minnesota and North Dakota, was settled in large part by German and Scandinavian immigrants. These people and their descendants have given Wisconsin a distinctive political stamp during the twentieth century; they combined an economic radicalism and an isolationist foreign policy. The state was the birthplace, in short, of American progressivism, whose finest incarnation was Robert LaFollette. "Fighting Bob" won the governorship in 1900 and put through a program of sweeping reform; he then went on to the Senate. While he was there, LaFollette rejected the appeals of Woodrow Wilson and voted against the country's intervention in World War I. As recriminations against our participation in the conflict that made nothing safe for democracy developed during the '20's, LaFollette ran for president as the candidate of the Progressive party in 1924. He made a respectable showing in that election, but most of the voters preferred Calvin Coolidge. LaFollette's sons carried on after their father. Robert M. LaFollette, Jr., served in the Senate from 1924 to 1946, and Philip LaFollette was governor of Wisconsin from 1934 to 1942. Both Midwest progressives, like another one in that same tradition today—Eugene McCarthy—dreamed of forming a third national party around their ideas. But when World War II broke out, all the strategies broke down, and after the war, the young Sen. LaFollette was defeated in a bid for renomination by one Joseph R. McCarthy.

Some political observers have wondered how one state could have produced the seemingly contrary movements of LaFollette Progressivism and McCarthyism. The answer, as is usually the case in American politics, lies in the ethnic alignments that form the basis of our political traditions. Since the Civil War, most Wisconsin voters have thought of themselves as Republicans, and most of the LaFollettes' epic battles were won—or lost—in Republican primaries. The same German-Americans—Wisconsin's largest ethnic group—who supported the LaFollettes' progressivism and isolationism also thronged to Joe McCarthy. McCarthy, who was not a thoroughgoing economic conservative, preached a kind of anti-communism that nicely exploited the unhappiness of the former isolationists over yet another war with Germany. Moreover, Joe McCarthy, an Irish Catholic, won big margins among the state's Irish and Polish voters. Roman Catholics make up about a third of the people of Wisconsin.

Joe McCarthy, censured by the Senate in 1954, died a broken man in 1957. His many detractors, however, have seldom noticed that the majorities which elected him—and the other Republicans who dominated the state's politics during the '40's and '50's—were not very large. But that fact became clearer after the special election to fill McCarthy's seat was held. The winner was Democrat William Proxmire, who, up to that time, enjoyed a reputation as a perennially unsuccessful candidate. The Wisconsin Democrats were never a major political force in the state's politics. The big fights of the '30's were between the orthodox Republicans and LaFollette's Progressives; meanwhile, city hall in Milwaukee was occupied by a series of Socialist mayors.

The new Democratic organization was able to weld together most of the disparate elements that had supported the Progressives, the Socialists, and the once hapless Democrats of the state. Key figures in that organization include Proxmire himself; Gaylord Nelson, who served as governor from 1958 to 1962, and since 1962 has been in the Senate; John Reynolds, who was governor from 1962 to 1964; and Patrick J. Lucey, who was elected governor in 1970 and currently holds the position. The main seat of the party is Milwaukee, which has large communities of German- and Polish-Americans, and which has about 30% of the state's population. The other concentration of support lies in Madison, the state capital and home of the University of Wisconsin. Madison, the LaFollettes' base of operation, became a Democratic stronghold during the '60's. Other elements of Democratic strength consists of the Irish Catholics of Green Bay; the blue-collar workers of Racine and Kenosha; the Scandinavians of the northern rural counties; and the men who work the paper mills and mines in the northern part of the state.

All this, however, was not enough to put Wisconsin in the Democratic column in the close presidential elections of 1960 and 1968. The Democratic coalition did prove its strength in the 1970 elections. The party swept the races for governor and senator, picked up one congressional seat, and won solid control of the state assembly. The party's biggest victory was Sen. Proxmire's 71–29 rout of John Erickson, the former general manager of the Milwaukee Bucks. When Proxmire entered the Senate in 1957, he soon incurred the wrath of then Majority Leader Lyndon Johnson. After that, Washington pundits wrote Proxmire off as an erratic maverick. The Senator did succeed, in time, to the chairmanship of the Joint Economic Committee and to seats on the Banking, Housing, and Urban Affairs and the Appropriations committees. Nevertheless, he was all too prone, according to many, to take on kooky, losing causes. That was the analysis, for example, of his campaign, which began in 1964, against Boeing's supersonic transport. But by the late '60's, the indicia of effectiveness used by the aficionados of the arcane ways of the Senate proved a little misleading. And in 1971, Proxmire, now the giant-killer, finished off the SST once and for all.

It could well be that the nation's general mood of revulsion at the Vietnam war accounts for Proxmire's recent successes. As late as 1964, when LBJ took Wisconsin by a landslide, Proxmire received only 53% of the votes; in 1964, none of the Senator's projects had yet borne any fruit. But in the years that followed, Proxmire used his subcommittee chairmanships to maximum advantage. His efforts have resulted in several pieces of pro-consumer legislation and in some rather interesting revelations of military waste. Proxmire found, for example, that Lockheed accumulated two billion dollars plus in cost overruns while building the C-5A transport aircraft. And now that the national press no longer regards him as Wisconsin's Quixote, it has celebrated his fabled energy: every day the man runs five miles from his home to Senate Chambers. Moreover, Proxmire hasn't missed a roll call in five years.

Republican candidate Erickson made a point of defending large Pentagon outlays, but the voters appeared to have preferred Proxmire's stand on the issue. The Senator carried all 72 counties of the state, and even managed to run up 2–1 margins in the Republican suburbs of Milwaukee.

Before Proxmire's victory in 1970, Gaylord Nelson was the state's top Democratic vote-getter. When Nelson became governor of Wisconsin in 1958, he launched an attack on industrial polluters and sponsored programs of environmental protection; this, of course, happened some ten years before the word ecology became fashionable among the academics and high-powered urban people. Nelson was reelected governor in 1960, and two years later, he beat the veteran Republican, Senator Alexander Wiley, who had been in the Senate since 1938.

In the Senate, Nelson, one of the first critics of the war, usually lines up with other liberal Democrats. In 1968, Nelson won reelection with 62% of the vote; no one doubts that he can remain in the Senate for as long as he likes. The only mystery about Nelson's career is why the national news media have mentioned him as a possible presidential candidate. The media people, who are rather bored by senators from the Midwest generally, may have him confused with Philip Hart of Michigan, or Vance Hartke of Indiana, or somebody else. Whatever the case, none of these men, including Nelson, have ever made any noises about the presidency.

The 1970 census reduced Wisconsin's House delegation from ten to nine members. Although it is not clear whose district will be eliminated, the most likely candidate is the 10th district, which is currently represented by ailing Republican Alvin O'Konski. Because control over redistricting is divided between the Democratic governor and House and the Republican Senate, it is unlikely that any major partisan advantages will come out of the process. In this context, eliminating O'Konski's seat would satisfy both sides. He is probably the only Republican who can carry the part of Wisconsin he now represents and will probably retire soon anyway. So as it will work out, both parties will in effect lose the seat that the state lost in the census.

Electoral Votes 11

Census Data 1970 pop. 4,417,933; 2.15% of U.S. total, 16th largest; change 1960–70, +11.8%. Metro. 57.6%, 30.4% central city. 1970 per capita income, $3,722; 22nd highest. 28th in number of poor.

1970 Share of Federal Tax Burden $3,980,870,000; 2.04% of U.S. total, 15th largest.

1970 Share of Federal Outlays $2,630,077,153; 1.39% of U.S. total, 23rd largest. Per capita federal spending, $595.

DOD	$459,228,000	33rd (0.80%)	HEW	$1,101,225,130	13th (2.11%)
AEC	$4,879,503	25th (0.19%)	HUD	$13,059,146	37th (0.67%)
NASA	$21,053,382	19th (0.57%)	OEO	$12,648,034	23rd (1.66%)
DOT	$11,576	38th (0.00%)	DOA	$171,207,001	30th (1.33%)
DOC	$3,304,744	39th (0.29%)	POD	$136,551,164	16th (1.87%)
DOI	$28,459,158	25th (1.23%)	VA	$192,010,222	18th (2.60%)
DOJ	$6,048,305	28th (1.05%)	CSC	$31,313,399	28th (0.78%)
			Other	$449,078,389	

Economic Base Dairy and livestock; nonelectrical machinery, esp. engines and turbines; food and kindred products, esp. beverages, dairy products, and meat products; electrical machinery, equipment, and supplies, esp. electrical industrial apparatus; fabricated metal products, esp. fabricated structural metal products and metal stampings; paper and allied products, esp. paper mills other than building paper mills; motor vehicles and motor vehicle equipment, and other transportation equipment; primary metal industries, esp. iron and steel foundries; lumber and wood products other than furniture, esp. millwork, veneer, plywood, and prefabricated structural wood products.

Political Line-up Governor, Patrick J. Lucey (D); seat up, 1974. Senators, William Proxmire (D) and Gaylord Nelson (D). Representatives, 10 (5 D and 5 R). State Senate (12 D, 20 R, and 1 Ind.); State Assembly (67 D and 33 R).

The Voters

Registration No statewide registration.

Employment profile White collar, 37%. Blue collar, 63%.

Ethnic groups Black, 3%. Total foreign stock, 23%. Germany, 8%; Poland, Norway, 2% each; Canada, UK, Sweden, Austria, Czech., Italy, USSR, 1% each; others, 5%.

Presidential vote

1968	Humphrey (D)	748,804	(44%)
	Nixon (R)	809,997	(48%)
	Wallace (AIP)	127,835	(8%)
1964	Johnson (D)	1,050,424	(62%)
	Goldwater (R)	638,495	(38%)
1960	Kennedy (D)	830,805	(48%)
	Nixon (R)	895,175	(52%)

Senator

William Proxmire (D) Elected Aug. 1957, seat up 1976; b. Nov. 11, 1915, Lake Forest, Illinois; home, Madison; Yale, B.A., 1938; Harvard, M.B.A., 1940, M.P.A., 1948; married; Episcopalian.

Career Pres., Artcraft Press, 1953–57; Wis. Legislature, 1951; nominee for Gov., 1952, 1954, 1956.

Offices 2311 NSOB, 202-225-5653. Also Rm. 235, Fed. Bldg., Madison 53701, 608-257-4654.

Committees

Appropriations (10th); Subs. (1) Chm., Foreign Operations, (2) Agriculture, Environmental and Consumer Protection, (3) Labor, HEW, and Related Agencies, (4) Military Construction, (5) Transportation.

Banking, Housing, and Urban Affairs (2nd); Subs. (1) Chm., Financial Institutions, (2) Housing and Urban Affairs, (3) Production and Stabilization, (4) Securities, (5) Small Business.

Jt. Com. on Defense Production (2nd).

Jt. Economic Com. (Chm.); Subs. (1) Chm., Priorities and Economy in the Government, (2) Economic Progress, (3) Fiscal Policy, (4) International Exchange and Payments, (5) Urban Affairs.

Group Ratings

	ADA	COPE	NREP	NFU	LCV	NAB	NSI	ACA
1970	78	92	75	93	94	33	0	25
1969	78	—	—	75	—	—	—	31
1968	64	75	—	62	—	83	—	32

Key Votes

(1) ABM	AGN	(8) Phil Pln	AGN	(15) Coop-Church	FOR
(2) SST	AGN	(9) Vol Army	FOR	(16) Cut Oil Dpltn	FOR
(3) Busing	FOR	(10) Prison $	AGN	(17) Consumer Prot	FOR
(4) Tob Sub	FOR	(11) Cut Mil $	FOR	(18) Farm Sub Limit	FOR
(5) Carswell	AGN	(12) Defoliatn	AGN	(19) Comp Bid Sales	FOR
(6) No-Knock	AGN	(13) 18-Yr-Vote	FOR	(20) Pre-Prod Tests	FOR
(7) Seniorty	FOR	(14) Pentgn PR	AGN	(21) Cut Marjna Pen	AGN

Election Results

1970 general:	William Proxmire (D)	948,445	(71%)
	John E. Erickson (R)	381,297	(29%)
1970 primary:	William Proxmire (D), unopposed		
1964 general:	William Proxmire (D)	892,013	(53%)
	Wilbur N. Renk (R)	780,116	(47%)

Senator

Gaylord Nelson (D) Elected 1962, seat up 1975; b. June 4, 1916, Clear Lake; home, Madison; San Jose State Col., B.A., 1939; U. of Wis., LL.B., 1942; Army, WWII; married; Methodist.

Career Practicing atty., 1946–58; Wis. Legislature, 1949–58.

Offices 404 OSOB, 202-225-5323. Also Rm. 570, Fed. Bldg., 517 E. Wisconsin Ave., Milwaukee 53202, 414-272-8600.

Committees

Finance (9th).

Labor and Public Welfare (5th); Subs. (1) Chm., Employment, Manpower, and Poverty, (2) Children and Youth, (3) Health, (4) Labor, (5) Railroad Retirement, (6) Sp. on Arts and Humanities, (7) Sp. on Human Resources, (8) Sp. on Social Programs.

Sel. Com. on Nutrition and Human Needs (5th).

Sel. Com. on Small Business (5th); Subs. (1) Chm., Monopoly, (2) Government Regulation, (3) Retailing, Distribution, Marketing Practices.

Group Ratings

	ADA	COPE	NREP	NFU	LCV	NAB	NSI	ACA
1970	97	100	93	100	83	10	0	6
1969	100	—	—	88	—	—	—	0
1968	71	100	—	77	—	40	—	21

Key Votes

(1) ABM	AGN	(8) Phil Pln	FOR	(15) Coop-Church	FOR
(2) SST	AGN	(9) Vol Army	FOR	(16) Cut Oil Dpltn	FOR
(3) Busing	FOR	(10) Prison $	FOR	(17) Consumer Prot	ABS
(4) Tob Sub	FOR	(11) Cut Mil $	FOR	(18) Farm Sub Limit	FOR
(5) Carswell	AGN	(12) Defoliatn	AGN	(19) Comp Bid Sales	FOR
(6) No-Knock	AGN	(13) 18-Yr-Vote	ABS	(20) Pre-Prod Tests	FOR
(7) Seniorty	AGN	(14) Pentgn PR	AGN	(21) Cut Marjna Pen	FOR

Election Results

1968 general:	Gaylord Nelson (D)	1,020,931	(62%)
	Jerris Leonard (R)	633,910	(38%)
1968 primary:	Gaylord Nelson (D), unopposed		
1962 general:	Gaylord Nelson (D)	662,342	(53%)
	Alexander Wiley (R)	594,846	(47%)

FIRST DISTRICT Political Background

Wisconsin 1, in the southeastern corner of the state, is a microcosm of Wisconsin at large. In the eastern part of the district, on Lake Michigan, are the industrial cities of Racine and Kenosha; during the 1970 elections, both of them had an unemployment figure running around 8%. Farther inland is the Republican stronghold of Walworth County, an area of small farms and the posh resort town of Lake Geneva. On the west are the cities of Janesville and Beloit; like Racine and Kenosha, these are predominantly industrial, but they are smaller and have much smaller ethnic communities. Here the blue-collar workers are usually Yankees or German-Americans out of the farm counties of southern Wisconsin. Janesville and Beloit ordinarily produce Republican majorities.

During the '60's, the 1st was the state's most marginal congressional district. In that decade, except for the two years following 1964, it was represented by Republican Henry C. Schadeberg. Schadeberg, a Congregationalist minister, voted against such measures as the Civil Rights Act of 1968, higher minimum wages, and the Peace Corps. The Congressman never won with more than 53% of the vote. Because of this and because of the rising unemployment in 1970, Schadeberg attracted several Democrats who wanted to challenge him. In the Democratic primary, the winner—by 20 votes—was Leslie Aspin, a 32-year-old Phi Beta Kappa, Rhodes Scholar, and Ph.D. in economics. He had served as a staff aide to the President's Council of Economic Advisors and to Defense Secretary Robert McNamara. Aspin also had some political experience; in 1964, he was Sen. Proxmire's campaign director, and in 1968, while serving under McNamara, he worked on the 1968 Wisconsin primary campaign for Lyndon Johnson. Aspin reportedly told the Administration that the situation was hopeless.

Aspin campaigned as an opponent of the Vietnam war and as a critic of Schadeberg's record on pollution issues. But Aspin spent most of his time talking about the economy, his field of expertise, and how badly off it was. In response, Congressman Schadeberg said, "I haven't noticed many people out of work." But the figures and the unemployment lines told another story. Aspin won with an astounding 61% of the votes, a figure which made Schadeberg the most soundly defeated incumbent in recent years.

Aspin's margin indicates that he should have little trouble in 1972. In the House, the new Congressman cited his experience working for McNamara and won a seat on the House Armed Services Committee. Here, he no doubt hopes someday to become a member of a dovish majority, rather than a clear minority, which is the case at present. Aspin looks like an excellent prospect for statewide office; the problem, though, is that all the top posts are now occupied by members of his own party. But because he will be only 42 in 1980, Aspin appears to have a long political career ahead of him.

Census Data 1970 pop. 484,169; deviation from current state average, +9.6%; change 1960–70, +18.5%. Metro. 59.6%, 35.9% central city.

1970 Share of Federal Outlays $219,954,449

DOD	$14,510,000	HEW	$106,536,578
AEC	$000	HUD	$918,000
NASA	$000	OEO	$439,354

DOT	$6,759,994	DOA	$9,429,334
		Other	$81,372,189

Federal Military-Industrial Commitments

DOD Contractors Fairbanks Morse (Beloit), $5.297m: unspecified.

Economic Base Nonelectrical machinery, esp. farm machinery and equipment; dairy; electrical machinery, equipment, and supplies.

The Voters

Registration No district-wide registration.

Employment profile White collar, 35%. Blue collar, 65%.

Ethnic groups Black, 3%. Total foreign stock, 25%. Germany, 7%; Italy, Poland, UK, Norway, 2% each; Czech., Sweden, Canada, USSR, Austria, 1% each; others, 7%.

Presidential vote

1968	Humphrey (D)	76,544	(43%)
	Nixon (R)	85,386	(48%)
	Wallace (AIP)	16,415	(9%)

Representative

Les Aspin (D) Elected 1970; b. Jul. 21, 1938, Milwaukee; home, Racine; Yale, B.A., 1960; Oxford U., M.A., 1962; M.I.T., Ph.D., 1965; Army, Vietnam, 1966–68; married; United Church of Christ.

Career Asst. Sen. Proxmire, 1960, Campaign Mgr., 1964; Asst. Walter Heller, Chm., Council of Economic Advisors, 1963; Econ. Adviser to Sec. of Def. Robert McNamara; prof. economics, Marquette.

Offices 515 CHOB, 202-225-3031. Also Rm. 200, 603 Main St., Racine 53403, 414-632-8194.

Committees

Armed Services (25th); Sub. No. 4.

Group Ratings, Key Votes: Newly elected.

Election Results

1970 general:	Les Aspin (D)	87,428	(61%)
	Henry C. Schadeberg (R)	56,067	(39%)
1970 primary:	Les Aspin (D)	15,185	(40%)
	Douglas LaFollette (D)	15,165	(40%)
	Gerald T. Flynn (D)	6,130	(16%)
	Perry Anderson (D)	1,644	(4%)

SECOND DISTRICT Political Background

Wisconsin 2 is the district centered on Madison, the state capital, the site of the University of Wisconsin, and the home of Wisconsin's progressive movement. Bob LaFollette, Sr., was a native of Madison. In 1900, when he was elected governor, LaFollette drew on academics from the University to set up the Wisconsin Tax Commission and to draw up its pioneering workmen's compensation law. Like most of Wisconsin, Madison was Republican in those days and the city stayed with the LaFollettes as their odyssey took them into the Progressive party and back to the Republicans again. In the '50's, Madison developed into the center of the state's nascent Democratic party (see state write-up). And when William Proxmire was reelected to the Senate and Gaylord Nelson was elected governor in 1958, Madison elected a Democratic congressman, Robert Kastenmeier.

From the first, Kastenmeier was one of the most liberal Democrats in the House. The Congressman assembled a talented staff, which included Marcus Raskin. Raskin was later an aide to President Kennedy, head of the Institute for Policy Studies, and a co-defendant in the Spock-Coffin trial. Kastenmeier took seats on the Judiciary and the Interior and Insular Affairs committees; he now has considerable seniority on both of them.

In 1960 and 1962, Kastenmeier won reelection by thin majorities. The dairy counties around Madison have always been conservative and Republican; moreover, the district then included Waukesha County, which contains many of Milwaukee's most affluent and most Republican suburbs. But the 1963 redistricting removed Waukesha from the 2nd and the 1964 Democratic landslide produced Kastenmeier's first big majority. By 1970, the Congressman had become well enough established in the rural counties to carry them; those margins added to the ones coming out of Madison gave Kastenmeier a 68% victory. He will go on winning reelection in the future.

Census Data 1970 pop. 486,200; deviation from current state average, +10.1%; change 1960–70, +22.2%. Metro. 59.7%, 35.6% central city.

1970 Share of Federal Outlays $349,307,010

DOD	$34,930,000	HEW	$154,218,655
AEC	$397,555	HUD	$992,283
NASA	$1,590,789	OEO	$5,561,923
DOT	$3,836,782	DOA	$30,086,757
		Other	$114,892,266

Federal Military-Industrial Commitments

DOD Contractors Oscar Mayer (Madison), $9.726m: twenty-ounce cans of pre-fried bacon.

Economic Base Dairy and livestock; food and kindred products; nonelectrical machinery. Also, higher education (University of Wisconsin).

The Voters

Registration No district-wide registration.

Employment profile White collar, 42%. Blue collar, 58%.

Ethnic groups Black, 1%. Total foreign stock, 19%. Germany, 7%; Norway, 3%; UK, Canada, Poland, Italy, 1% each; others, 6%.

Presidential vote

1968	Humphrey (D)	87,814	(49%)
	Nixon (R)	82,439	(46%)
	Wallace (AIP)	8,824	(5%)

Representative

Robert W. Kastenmeier (D) Elected 1958; b. Jan. 24, 1924, Beaver Dam; home, Watertown; U. of Wis., LL.B., 1952; Army, WWII; married, three children; religion unspecified.

Career Practicing atty., 1952–58.

Offices 2232 RHOB, 202-225-2906. Also 300 Main St., Watertown 54094, 414-261-6050.

Committees

Interior and Insular Affairs (10th); Subs. (1) Environment, (2) Mines and Mining, (3) National Parks and Recreation, (4) Public Lands.

Judiciary (6th); Chm., Sub. No. 3.

Group Ratings

	ADA	COPE	NREP	NFU	LCV	CFA	NAB	NSI	ACA
1970	92	100	100	85	100	100	0	0	11
1969	93	—	—	86	—	—	—	—	19
1968	100	92	—	94	—	—	17	—	0

Key Votes

(1) ABM	AGN	(6) 18-Yr-Vote	FOR	(11) Clean Water $	FOR
(2) SST	AGN	(7) Farm Sub Lmt	FOR	(12) Mig Wrkrs Comp	FOR
(3) Phil Pln	FOR	(8) Coop-Church	FOR	(13) Jets to Chiang	AGN
(4) No-Knock	AGN	(9) Family Asst	FOR	(14) State OEO Veto	AGN
(5) Cmutr Tax	FOR	(10) Work Stamps	AGN	(15) Park Logging	AGN

Election Results

1970 general:	Robert W. Kastenmeier (D)	102,879	(68%)
	Norman Anderson (R)	46,620	(32%)
1970 primary:	Robert W. Kastenmeier (D), unopposed		
1968 general:	Robert W. Kastenmeier (D)	107,804	(60%)
	Richard D. Murray (R)	72,229	(40%)

THIRD DISTRICT Political Background

Wisconsin 3 occupies the southwest corner of Wisconsin, historically the most Republican part of the state. The countryside here is much the way it was in the 1840's and 1850's, when the region first began to take white settlers. The present day 3rd stretches for some 150 miles along the rolling hills east of the Mississippi River; the district's only significant urban center is La Crosse (pop. 51,000). This is one of the nation's premier dairy districts, and its congressman inevitably finds himself concerned with the arcane matters of milk marketing programs and import restrictions on Dutch and Swiss cheese.

The current incumbent is Republican Vernon W. Thomson, who was governor of the state from 1956 to 1958. Thomson, who usually lines up with the Midwestern conservative bloc, has seats on the Foreign Relations and the District of Columbia committees. First elected in 1960, the Congressman is near the middle of the seniority ladder on both committees; but his age—he was 65 in 1970—suggests that he is unlikely to rise to the top levels of influence.

For a ten-year incumbent, Thomson had a relatively close time of it in 1970. He won only 55% of the vote, 6% less than he had in the Goldwater year. One of the reasons for the showing was the heavy unemployment which afflicted most of Wisconsin in 1970. Almost 10% of the labor force was out of work in La Crosse—the highest figure in the state; Thomson lost usually Republican La Crosse County.

The most likely redistricting plan will extend the boundaries of the district to the north and will take in the city of Eau Claire (pop. 44,000) and several other counties, all of which have been leaning Democratic in recent years. This would give Thomson a hard race in 1972, if present economic trends continue. Possible Democratic nominees include Walter Thoresen, who ran a strong race against 10th district veteran Alvin O'Konski in 1970, and Donald O. Peterson, an Eau Claire businessman. Peterson attracted national attention in 1968 as the leader of Wisconsin's McCarthy delegation to the Democratic National Convention; he also ran a strong, though losing race for the Democratic gubernatorial nomination in 1970. Either man could give Thomson trouble in 1972, and if the Congressman retires, the Democrats have a good chance to pick up the seat.

Census Data 1970 pop. 398,021; deviation from current state average, –9.9%; change 1960–70, +4.2%. Metro. 20.2%, 12.9% central city.

1970 Share of Federal Outlays $292,166,305

DOD	$81,267,000	HEW	$110,344,395
AEC	$1,534,344	HUD	$000
NASA	$000	OEO	$581,372
DOT	$11,119,639	DOA	$24,354,717
		Other	$62,964,838

Federal Military-Industrial Commitments

DOD Contractors Olin Corp. (Baraboo), $55.873m: production of artillery and small arms ammunition propellants and operation of the Badger Army Ammunition plant.

Economic Base Dairy and livestock; service industry machines and other nonelectrical machinery; food and kindred products.

The Voters

Registration No district-wide registration.

Employment profile White collar, 29%. Blue collar, 71%.

Ethnic groups Black, less than 0.5%. Total foreign stock, 17%. Germany, 6%; Norway, 4%; UK, Czech., Sweden, Canada, Poland, 1% each; others, 3%.

Presidential vote

1968	Humphrey (D)	58,514	(37%)
	Nixon (R)	86,474	(55%)
	Wallace (AIP)	11,373	(7%)

Representative

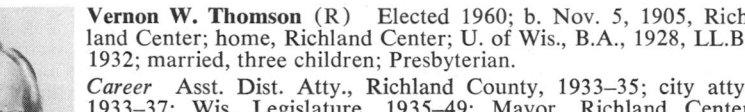

Vernon W. Thomson (R) Elected 1960; b. Nov. 5, 1905, Richland Center; home, Richland Center; U. of Wis., B.A., 1928, LL.B., 1932; married, three children; Presbyterian.

Career Asst. Dist. Atty., Richland County, 1933–35; city atty., 1933–37; Wis. Legislature, 1935–49; Mayor, Richland Center, 1944–50; Sec., Wis. Legislative Council, 1949–51; Wis. Atty. Gen., 1951–56; Wis. Gov., 1956–58; practicing atty., 1958–60.

Offices 2305 RHOB, 202-225-5506. Also Farmers & Mechanics Bank Bldg., Richland Center 53581.

Committees

District of Columbia (7th); Subs. (1) Business, Commerce, and Fiscal Affairs, (2) Housing and Youth Affairs, (3) Judiciary.

Foreign Affairs (8th); Subs. (1) Asian and Pacific Affairs, (2) National Security Policy and Scientific Development, (3) State Department Organization and Foreign Operations.

Sel. Com. on House Restaurant (2nd).

Group Ratings

	ADA	COPE	NREP	NFU	LCV	CFA	NAB	NSI	ACA
1970	24	17	25	46	22	45	100	100	79
1969	0	—	—	43	—	—	—	—	71
1968	0	0	—	50	—	—	100	—	96

Key Votes

(1) ABM	FOR	(6) 18-Yr-Vote	AGN	(11) Clean Water $	AGN
(2) SST	AGN	(7) Farm Sub Lmt	FOR	(12) Mig Wrkrs Comp	AGN
(3) Phil Pln	FOR	(8) Coop-Church	AGN	(13) Jets to Chiang	FOR
(4) No-Knock	FOR	(9) Family Asst	FOR	(14) State OEO Veto	FOR
(5) Cmutr Tax	AGN	(10) Work Stamps	FOR	(15) Park Logging	FOR

Election Results

1970 general:	Vernon W. Thomson (R)	64,891	(55%)
	Ray Short (D)	52,085	(45%)
1970 primary:	Vernon W. Thomson (R), unopposed		
1968 general:	Vernon W. Thomson (R)	95,606	(64%)
	Gunnar A. Gundersen (D)	54,517	(36%)

FOURTH DISTRICT Political Background

Wisconsin 4 comprises the south side of Milwaukee and the southern Milwaukee County suburbs. Milwaukee is split into two distinct sections by the Milwaukee River, which bisects the city. The north side has been traditionally German; the south side, ever since the days of industrial growth at the turn of the century, has been Polish. Today, the south side remains all white and heavily Polish, while the suburbs to the south are filled mainly with the newly prosperous blue-collar and white-collar descendants of the original Polish immigrants. In 1964, just as the word "backlash" entered the vocabulary, the south side surprised many observers when it gave George Wallace a near majority in the presidential primary of that year.

The fears and resentments that have affected many ethnic communities since that time are still apparent on the south side. In the late '60's, Father Groppi's marches in Milwaukee brought the south side's racial hostilities to the surface, and in 1968, Richard Nixon and George Wallace cut significantly into the district's usually heavy Democratic vote.

The 4th district's congressman, Clement J. Zablocki, reflects the attitudes of his constituency. Most Wisconsin Democratic officeholders are antiwar, crusading liberals like Senators Proxmire and Nelson. Zablocki's record, however, is more in line with representatives of other predominantly ethnic districts in cities like Chicago, Cleveland, and Buffalo. He is, for example, the only Wisconsin Democrat in Congress who has supported the Vietnam policies of the Johnson and Nixon administrations, and his position as the 2nd ranking Democrat on the House Foreign Affairs Committee has given him at least one forum for advancing his views on the war issue. Zablocki is also more likely than his home state colleagues to vote for anticrime measures, legislation which some have argued violates civil liberties. In 1970, the Congressman won a 100 rating from COPE of the AFL-CIO, though the ADA gave him a much lower mark of 44.

Zablocki's district, election by election, remains the most Democratic in Wisconsin. Ever since 1948, the Congressman has been reelected with large majorities; in 1970, he took 80% of the votes. And as long as he chooses to run, Zablocki will win. Redistricting may add the Republican suburb of Wauwatosa to the district, but that will reduce Zablocki's huge margins only slightly.

Census Data 1970 pop. 431,216; deviation from current state average, —2.4%; change 1960–70, +8.7%. Metro. 100.0%, 52.3% central city.

1970 Share of Federal Outlays $219,388,000 (average outlay per district, Wisconsin 4, 5, and 9)

DOD	$27,796,000	HEW	$84,455,000
AEC	$26,000	HUD	$1,371,000
NASA	$6,403,000	OEO	$1,228,000
DOT	$7,891,000	DOA	$7,407,000
		Other	$82,611,000

Federal Military-Industrial Commitments (See Wisconsin 5 for greater Milwaukee listing.)

Economic Base Nonelectrical machinery, esp. engines and turbines, and construction, mining, and material handling machinery and equipment; electrical machinery, equipment, and supplies, esp. electrical industrial apparatus; food and kindred products, esp. malt liquors; primary metal industries, esp. iron and steel foundries.

The Voters

Registration No district-wide registration.

Employment profile White collar, 39%. Blue collar, 61%.

Ethnic groups Black, less than 0.5%. Total foreign stock, 31%. Poland, 9%; Germany, 8%; Austria, Italy, Czech., Canada, Norway, UK, Hungary, USSR, Mexico, 1% each; others, 5%.

Presidential vote

1968	Humphrey (D)	91,625	(56%)
	Nixon (R)	55,976	(34%)
	Wallace (AIP)	17,389	(11%)

Representative

Clement J. Zablocki (D) Elected 1948; b. Nov. 18, 1912, Milwaukee; home, Milwaukee; Marquette U., Ph.B., 1936; married, two children; Catholic.

Career High school teacher, 1938–40; organist, choir dir., 1932–48; Wis. Senate, 1942–48.

Offices 2184 RHOB, 202-225-4572. Also 1401 W. Lincoln Ave., Milwaukee 53215, 414-383-4000.

Committees

Foreign Affairs (2nd); Subs. (1) Chm., National Security Policy and Scientific Developments (2) Foreign Economic Policy, (3) State Department Organization and Foreign Operations, (4) Sp. for Review of Foreign Aid Programs.

Group Ratings

	ADA	COPE	NREP	NFU	LCV	CFA	NAB	NSI	ACA
1970	44	100	58	100	80	85	0	90	26
1969	53	—	—	93	—	—	—	—	24
1968	83	100	—	93	—	—	20	—	13

Key Votes

(1) ABM	FOR	(6) 18-Yr-Vote	FOR	(11) Clean Water $	FOR
(2) SST	FOR	(7) Farm Sub Lmt	FOR	(12) Mig Wrkrs Comp	FOR
(3) Phil Pln	AGN	(8) Coop-Church	AGN	(13) Jets to Chiang	FOR
(4) No-Knock	FOR	(9) Family Asst	FOR	(14) State OEO Veto	AGN
(5) Cmutr Tax	FOR	(10) Work Stamps	AGN	(15) Park Logging	AGN

Election Results

1970 general:	Clement J. Zablocki (D)	102,464	(80%)
	Phillip D. Mrozinski (R)	23,081	(18%)
	John A. Zierhut (AIP)	1,985	(2%)
1970 primary:	Clement J. Zablocki (D)	32,201	(85%)
	Donald P. Lass (D)	5,529	(15%)
1968 general:	Clement J. Zablocki (D)	118,203	(73%)
	Walter McCullough (R)	44,558	(27%)

FIFTH DISTRICT Political Background

Wisconsin 5 comprises the north side of Milwaukee. This is, or was, the German side of town, and the gemütlichkeit atmosphere of old Milwaukee has since become part of the nation's legacy. Because many of the city's German-Americans went into brewing, Milwaukee is also well-known for its beer. These people, a highly intellectual group, developed their own kind of distinctive politics (see state write-up). During the days when Robert LaFollette and his progressives swept the rest of Wisconsin, Milwaukee elected a series of Socialist party mayors and congressmen. The most notable among them was Victor L. Berger, who served in the House from 1910 to 1912, and from 1922 to 1928. Berger was denied his seat after the 1918 and 1920 elections because of his opposition to American entry into World War I. During the years of the New Deal, Milwaukee's Germans, like the state's other disparate ethnic groups, tended to become Democrats.

Today, many of the descendants of the first German immigrants have left the north side for the suburbs, and they have been replaced here by blacks from the rural South. In 1960, 15% of the residents of the 5th were black; in 1970, 29% of the district, which lost some 13% of its people, was black. This is the only significant Negro concentration in Wisconsin, since there are virtually no blacks on the Polish south side (see Wisconsin 4). Milwaukee has been the scene of much racial turbulence in recent years. The most notable demonstrations were those led by Father James Groppi, which protested the City Council's refusal to enact an open housing ordinance.

Since 1954, the 5th's congressman has been Henry S. Reuss, whose name recalls the German origin of so many of the district's residents. Reuss is one of the most liberal members of the House and one of its few liberals with a great deal of seniority. For some years, he was chairman of the Banking and Currency Committee's Subcommittee on International Finance; he remains one of the leading congressional experts on such mysterious matters as the balance of payments, the gold market, and the ups and downs of various European and Asian currencies. He gave up that chairmanship to head the Government Operations' Subcommittee on Conservation and Natural Resources. Here Reuss is in a position to exercise oversight into the government's diverse activities in environmental regulation. Reuss' record in this area has made him one of the few congressional heroes of ecology activists.

The increasing number of black voters in the 5th has made this already safe Democratic district even more safe. Besides, Reuss usually runs ahead of his party's ticket anyway. The 5th's declining population will require the addition of more territory; if the legislators decide to append the outlaying portions of northwest Milwaukee to the district, the additional people would bring its population very close to the current statewide average. And even if these north shore Republican suburbs are added, the Congressman's reputation and vote-getting prowess should make his reelection automatic.

Census Data 1970 pop. 346,981; deviation from current state average, —21.5%; change 1960–70, —13.1%. Metro. 100.0%, 100.0% central city.

1970 Share of Federal Outlays $219,388,000 (average outlay per district, Wisconsin 4, 5, and 9)

DOD	$27,796,000	HEW	$84,455,000
AEC	$26,000	HUD	$1,371,000
NASA	$6,403,000	OEO	$1,228,000
DOT	$7,891,000	DOA	$7,407,000
		Other	$82,611,000

Federal Military-Industrial Commitments (Wisconsin 4, 5, and 9, greater Milwaukee listing)

DOD Contractors General Motors (Milwaukee), $34.838m: Titan III guidance systems; warhead exploder assemblies for Mk 48 torpedoes. Gulf and Western Industries (Waukesha), $21.248m: 20-mm and 40-mm cartridge cases. Amron (Waukesha), $12.754m: unspecified.

NASA Contractors General Motors (Milwaukee), $18.040m: spacecraft engine support services; guidance computer subsystem for Apollo command service module.

Economic Base Nonelectrical machinery, esp. engines and turbines, and construction, mining, and material handling machinery and equipment; electrical machinery, equipment, and supplies, esp. electrical industrial apparatus; food and kindred products, esp. malt liquors; primary metal industries, esp. iron and steel foundries. Also, higher education (University of Wisconsin at Milwaukee); banking and insurance.

The Voters

Registration No district-wide registration.

Employment profile White collar, 40%. Blue collar, 60%.

Ethnic groups Black, 29%. Total foreign stock, 30%. Germany, 11%; Poland, 3%; USSR, Italy, Austria, 2% each; Hungary, Czech., Canada, UK, Norway, Ireland, 1% each; others, 5%.

Presidential vote

1968	Humphrey (D)	67,361	(57%)
	Nixon (R)	40,750	(35%)
	Wallace (AIP)	9,151	(8%)

Representative

Henry S. Reuss (D) Elected 1954; b. Feb. 22, 1912, Milwaukee; home, Milwaukee; Cornell U., A.B., 1933; Harvard, LL.B., 1936; Army, WWII; married, four children; Episcopalian.

Career Practicing atty., 1936–55; lecturer, Wis. State Col., 1950–51; Asst. Counsel, Milwaukee County, 1939–40; Asst. Gen. Counsel, OPA, 1941–42; Chief, Price Control Branch, Mil. Govt. for Germany, 1945; Dep. Counsel, Marshall Plan, 1949; Milwaukee County Grand Jury Sp. Prosecutor, 1950.

Offices 2159 RHOB, 202-225-3571. Also 211 W. Wisconsin, 8th floor, Milwaukee 53203, 414-272-1226.

Committees

Banking and Currency (4th); Subs. (1) Housing, (2) International Finance.
Government Operations (8th); Subs. (1) Chm., Conservation and Natural Resources, (2) Special Studies.
Jt. Economic Com. (4th); Subs. (1) Chm., International Exchange and Payments, (2) Foreign Economic Policy, (3) Urban Affairs.

Group Ratings

	ADA	COPE	NREP	NFU	LCV	CFA	NAB	NSI	ACA
1970	88	100	100	92	90	100	0	0	17
1969	93	—	—	86	—	—	—	—	13
1968	100	100	—	94	—	—	0	—	9

Key Votes

(1) ABM	AGN	(6) 18-Yr-Vote	FOR	(11) Clean Water $	FOR
(2) SST	AGN	(7) Farm Sub Lmt	FOR	(12) Mig Wrkrs Comp	FOR
(3) Phil Pln	AGN	(8) Coop-Church	FOR	(13) Jets to Chiang	AGN
(4) No-Knock	ABS	(9) Family Asst	FOR	(14) State OEO Veto	AGN
(5) Cmutr Tax	FOR	(10) Work Stamps	AGN	(15) Park Logging	AGN

Election Results

1970 general:	Henry S. Reuss (D)	60,630	(76%)
	Robert J. Dwyer (R)	18,360	(23%)
	Earl R. Denny (AIP)	640	(1%)
1970 primary:	Henry S. Reuss (D), unopposed		
1968 general:	Henry S. Reuss (D)	76,607	(68%)
	Robert J. Dwyer (R)	35,536	(31%)
	Julian R. Chapman (AIP)	877	(1%)

SIXTH DISTRICT Political Background

Wisconsin 6 comprises a part of the state that lies just north of Milwaukee. The district consists mainly of a combination of small industrial cities and verdant dairy farm country. The Milwaukee metropolitan area has begun to protrude into the southern end of the district, and here the newly prosperous exurbanites have increased the Republican vote totals in Ozaukee and Washington counties. These people, however, have not worked any revolution in the political leanings of the 6th. With the exception of Sheboygan (pop. 48,000), which was the scene of a bitter, eight-year long UAW strike against the Kohler Company, the cities and townships of the 6th have been traditionally Republican. That political preference is especially strong in the district's two other large cities, Oshkosh (pop. 53,000) and Fond du Lac (pop. 35,000), both of which are quiet towns on Lake Winnebago.

The 6th also includes the small town of Ripon (pop. 7,053), where the Republican party is said to have been founded in 1854, though Jackson, Michigan, also claims this distinction. It is, therefore, appropriate that the district sends to the House one of the favorites of the liberal Republican Ripon Society, Congressman William Steiger.

When he was first elected in 1966, Steiger was the youngest man in Congress at age 28. In that year, he defeated an LBJ-landslide Democrat, who had earlier ousted conservative Republican William K. Van Pelt. Van Pelt served from 1950 to 1964.

Steiger's record in the House has been perceptibly more liberal than that compiled by other Midwestern Republicans, and as a skillful and well-informed speaker, the Congressman has built up a solid position among his constituents. In the otherwise heavily Democratic year of 1970, Steiger won 68% of the votes in the 6th district; he was the only Republican congressional candidate in Wisconsin to improve on his 1968 showing. Steiger, who is still quite young, is already the 9th ranking Republican on the House Education and Labor Committee. He will no doubt continue to win reelection easily and could be a very important member of future Congresses.

Census Data 1970 pop. 473,902; deviation from current state average, +7.3%; change 1960–70, +21.0%. Metro. 58.2%, 11.9% central city.

1970 Share of Federal Outlays $207,570,401

DOD	$22,227,000	HEW	$96,624,360
AEC	$000	HUD	$4,714,413
NASA	$85,944	OEO	$177,836
DOT	$3,405,643	DOA	$6,576,158
		Other	$73,699,047

Federal Military-Industrial Commitments

DOD Contractors Chrysler Outboard Div., Chrysler Motors (Hartford), $7.799m: 1.5-, 3-, and 6-horsepower engines.

Economic Base Dairy; nonelectrical machinery; paper and allied products, esp. paper mills other than building paper mills, and converted paper and paperboard products, other than containers and boxes. Also, higher education (Wisconsin State University at Oshkosh).

The Voters

Registration No district-wide registration.
Employment profile White collar, 34%. Blue collar, 66%.
Ethnic groups Black, less than 0.5%. Total foreign stock, 20%. Germany, 10%; USSR, Poland, Canada, Austria, UK, 1% each; others, 5%.

Presidential vote

1968	Humphrey (D)	72,596	(40%)
	Nixon (R)	96,588	(54%)
	Wallace (AIP)	11,421	(6%)

Representative

William A. Steiger (R) Elected 1966; b. May 15, 1938, Oshkosh; home, Oshkosh; U. of Wis., B.A., 1960; married, one child; Episcopalian.

Career Wis. Legislature, 1960–66.

Offices 1025 LHOB, 202-225-2476. Also 201 P.O. Bldg., Oshkosh 54901, 414-231-6333.

Committees

Education and Labor (9th); Subs. (1) Gen. on Labor, (2) Sp. on Education, (3) Sel. on Labor.

Group Ratings

	ADA	COPE	NREP	NFU	LCV	CFA	NAB	NSI	ACA
1970	24	33	33	46	50	53	75	100	58
1969	27	—	—	57	—	—	—	—	47
1968	25	31	—	69	—	—	100	—	70

Key Votes

(1) ABM	FOR	(6) 18-Yr-Vote	FOR	(11) Clean Water $	FOR
(2) SST	AGN	(7) Farm Sub Lmt	ABS	(12) Mig Wrkrs Comp	AGN
(3) Phil Pln	FOR	(8) Coop-Church	AGN	(13) Jets to Chiang	FOR
(4) No-Knock	FOR	(9) Family Asst	FOR	(14) State OEO Veto	AGN
(5) Cmutr Tax	FOR	(10) Work Stamps	FOR	(15) Park Logging	FOR

Election Results

1970 general:	William A. Steiger (R)	98,587	(68%)
	Franklin R. Utech (D)	44,794	(31%)
	Rani V. Davidson (AIP)	2,150	(1%)
1970 primary:	William A. Steiger (R), unopposed		
1968 general:	William A. Steiger (R)	111,934	(64%)
	John A. Race (D)	60,059	(34%)
	Albert Balthazar, Jr. (C)	2,944	(2%)

SEVENTH DISTRICT Political Background

Wisconsin 7 lies in the geographical heart of the state, where the gently rolling dairy farms of southern Wisconsin begin to give way to the northern forests and lakes. Up here the population is sparser and the winters colder than down around Milwaukee. The district's largest town is Wausau (pop. 32,000); its little towns include places like Marshfield (pop. 15,000), the home of Secretary of Defense Melvin Laird.

Laird represented the 7th for 18 years before he was named to Nixon's cabinet. While serving in the House, he was known as one of its most articulate exponents of conservative Republicanism and one of its shrewdest tacticians. Laird was not bad at winning votes either; in his last effort, which came in 1968, he won a solid 64%. Laird's margins, however, tended to overstate Republican strength in the district. He always ran ahead of the Republican ticket, and a large percentage of the 6th's many German- and Norwegian-American voters usually voted Democratic in other races. The cross-over voting was especially common in Marathon (Wausau) and Portage (Stevens Point) counties.

When Laird left the Hill for the Pentagon, most Republican strategists assumed they could hold the district, and most Democratic partisans considered the 7th a long shot. But the winner, by a 2% margin, was Democrat David Obey, a 30-year-old state representative. Obey, a member of the Wisconsin House since he was 24, made a liberal record in Madison on issues like education. In the campaign, however, he stressed economic matters. This was a wise course, because his Republican opponent was hurt by the unpopular sales tax of Republican Gov. Warren Knowles.

In 1970, elections showed that Obey had consolidated his hold on the district in record time. The Republicans, quite sensibly, figured that if they were ever going to win the district back, they would have to do it in 1970. The Republicans put up a major effort for their candidate, André Le Tendre, a former president of the National Jaycees. But because Obey had campaigned vigorously since 1969, he won an astonishing 67% of the vote, which was more than Laird had taken in his recent showings.

Obey's matter-of-fact style was no doubt a selling point among his Wisconsin constituents. The Democratic candidate did not stress issues like Vietnam or defense spending; this course might have made him appear to be running against Laird. Nevertheless, he has generally taken stands against the Nixon Administration on the issues. In Washington, Obey won a coveted seat on the House Appropriations Committee, where he is currently its youngest member.

If Obey continues to win reelection, the congressman has a good chance, under the seniority system, of becoming the chairman of Appropriations. This should happen somewhere around the year 2004. The 1970 results do show that reelection will be no problem; in fact, the legislature will probably add to the 7th some Democratic counties from the 10th district before the 1972 elections. Secretary Laird, however, has announced that he will retire from his current post at the beginning of 1973. And it has been said that he might run for something again in Wisconsin. Because Senators William Proxmire and Gaylord Nelson appear to have their seats locked up, that leaves the governorship and the House—and the intriguing possibility of a 1974 Obey-Laird confrontation.

Census Data 1970 pop. 417,318; deviation from current state average, −5.5%; change 1960–70, +7.8%. Metro. 0.0%, 0.0% central city.

1970 Share of Federal Outlays $224,644,085

DOD	$10,179,000	HEW	$113,300,625
AEC	$000	HUD	$1,586,000
NASA	$45,951	OEO	$635,179
DOT	$5,473,620	DOA	$33,211,323
		Other	$60,212,387

Federal Military-Industrial Commitments

DOD Installations Antigo Air Force Station (Antigo).

Economic Base Dairy and livestock; paper and allied products, esp. paper mills other than building paper mills; lumber and wood products other than furniture, esp. sawmills and planing mills, and millwork, veneer, plywood, and prefabricated structural wood products. Also, tourism (lakes).

The Voters

Registration No district-wide registration.

Employment profile White collar, 29%. Blue collar, 71%.

Ethnic groups Black, less than 0.5%. Total foreign stock, 23%. Germany, 11%; Poland, 3%; Norway, Canada, Sweden, Czech., Austria, UK, 1% each; others, 3%.

Presidential vote

1968	Humphrey (D)	68,224	(42%)
	Nixon (R)	82,321	(50%)
	Wallace (AIP)	13,683	(8%)

Representative

David R. Obey (D) Elected 1968; b. Oct. 3, 1938, Okmulgee, Okla.; home, Wausau; U. of Wis., M.A., 1960; married, one child; religion unspecified.

Career Wis. Legislature, 1962–68.

Offices 415 CHOB, 202-225-3365. Also Fed. Bldg., 317 First St., Wausau 54401, 715-842-5606.

Committees

Appropriations (27th); Subs. (1) District of Columbia, (2) Interior.

Group Ratings

	ADA	COPE	NREP	NFU	LCV	CFA	NAB	NSI	ACA
1970	84	92	83	77	100	100	9	55	33
1969	92	100	—	86	—	—	—	—	20

Key Votes

(1) ABM	AGN	(6) 18-Yr-Vote	FOR	(11) Clean Water $	FOR
(2) SST	AGN	(7) Farm Sub Lmt	FOR	(12) Mig Wrkrs Comp	FOR
(3) Phil Pln	FOR	(8) Coop-Church	FOR	(13) Jets to Chiang	AGN
(4) No-Knock	FOR	(9) Family Asst	FOR	(14) State OEO Veto	AGN
(5) Cmutr Tax	FOR	(10) Work Stamps	AGN	(15) Park Logging	AGN

Election Results

1970 general:	David R. Obey (D)	88,746	(67%)
	André E. Le Tendre (R)	41,330	(32%)
	Richard D. Wolfe (AIP)	1,189	(1%)
1970 primary:	David R. Obey (D), unopposed		

EIGHTH DISTRICT Political Background

Wisconsin 8 might be called the Packers' district. It is centered on the Midwest metropolis of Green Bay (pop. 87,000), small for a place with an NFL franchise. The Packers, under head coach Vince Lombardi, were an incredibly ferocious and stringently disciplined team. During the '60's, "the Pack" dominated both professional football and the fantasy life of millions of American men. The team is the most distinctive feature of the 8th district, which covers seven counties in the northeast corner of the state. Green Bay, the district's largest city, is a predominantly Irish and German Catholic town; it went for John F. Kennedy in 1960, and has since returned to its normal Republican voting habits.

Other urban concentrations include Manitowoc (pop. 33,000), a blue-collar, Democratic town on Lake Michigan, and Appleton (pop. 57,000), a conservative bastion just to the north of Lake Winnebago. Appleton is best known for being Sen. Joe McCarthy's home town. The Senator, of course, was a Republican who purged the State Department of people whose policies he did not find congenial. His later tilt with the Army and with President Eisenhower in 1954 led to his censure by the Senate and ultimately to his death in 1957.

Since 1944, the 8th has been represented by John W. Byrnes, a man who shares some of the late Senator's views, but very little of his temperament. Byrnes is currently the third most senior Republican in the House, and because he is the ranking minority member of the Ways and Means Committee, an important member of the House Republican leadership. One might expect the Republicans and Democrats on Ways and Means to be constant, hard-fighting adversaries. But this committee, which writes most of the nation's tax, welfare, and Social Security legislation, is a world unto itself. In its executive sessions, Chairman Wilbur Mills, Congressman Byrnes, and the other members iron out their differences, and then usually appear on the floor of the House as a united front. Because amendments are seldom permitted on the complex bills reported by Ways and Means, the committee's consensus usually becomes law, even if it is unlike anything the Nixon Administration or the Democratic leadership had in mind.

Byrnes shares with Wilbur Mills life and death power over such Nixon measures as the family assistance plan and revenue sharing. What Byrnes and Mills agree on, the Administration will probably have to take or get nothing (see also Arkansas 2). This may not be the kind of power that the home folks fully understand, but over the years, Byrnes has won reelection without much difficulty. The 1970 results, therefore, must have come as a surprise to the veteran Congressman. His opponent, a Roman Catholic priest and college teacher, held Byrnes down to 55%, which was less than he got in the bad Republican year of 1964.

Nevertheless, Byrnes' prospects for continued reelection look good. Political 1970 was an extremely good year for Wisconsin Democrats, and they cannot count on repeating that performance in the years to come. Moreover, redistricting should work out to Byrnes' advantage. The 8th may well lose Democratic Manitowoc and pick up at least one, if not more, of the heavily Republican counties at the eastern edge of the current 7th district. The addition should boost Byrnes' margin up towards more accustomed levels and should also please Democrat David Obey of the 7th.

Census Data 1970 pop. 460,324; deviation from current state average, +4.2%; change 1960–70, +14.9%. Metro. 60.3%, 30.8% central city.

1970 Share of Federal Outlays $210,820,858

DOD	$27,368,000	HEW	$96,630,551
AEC	$000	HUD	$000
NASA	$31,967	OEO	$117,724
DOT	$6,825,428	DOA	$18,138,469
		Other	$61,708,719

Federal Military-Industrial Commitments

DOD Contractors Peterson Builders (Sturgeon Bay), $6.325m: construction of harbor tugs. Marinette Marine (Marinette), $5.261m: unspecified.

Economic Base Dairy and livestock; paper and allied products, esp. paper mills other than building paper mills; nonelectrical machinery.

The Voters

Registration No district-wide registration.

Employment profile White collar, 34%. Blue collar, 66%.

Ethnic groups Black, less than 0.5%. Total foreign stock, 17%. Germany, 6%; Poland, 2%; Canada, Czech., Sweden, Norway, UK, 1% each; others, 5%.

Presidential vote

1968	Humphrey (D)	66,639	(39%)
	Nixon (R)	91,703	(54%)
	Wallace (AIP)	12,689	(7%)

Representative

John W. Byrnes (R) Elected 1944; b. June 12, 1913, Green Bay; home, Green Bay; U. of Wis., B.A., 1936, LL.B., 1938; married, six children; Catholic.

Career Sp. Dep. Commissioner of Banking, Wis., 1938–41; practicing atty., 1939–44; Wis. Senate, 1941–44; Majority Leader, 1944.

Offices 2206 RHOB, 202-225-5665. Also 207 Fed. Bldg., Green Bay 54301, 414-437-8168.

Committees

Ways and Means (Ranking Mbr.).

Jt. Com. on Internal Revenue Taxation (Ranking Rep. House Mbr.).

Jt. Com. on Reduction of Federal Expenditures (2nd).

Group Ratings

	ADA	COPE	NREP	NFU	LCV	CFA	NAB	NSI	ACA
1970	20	25	17	46	33	40	0	100	72
1969	7	—	—	43	—	—	—	—	53
1968	8	0	—	33	—	—	83	—	86

Key Votes

(1) ABM	FOR	(6) 18-Yr-Vote	AGN	(11) Clean Water $	AGN
(2) SST	AGN	(7) Farm Sub Lmt	AGN	(12) Mig Wrkrs Comp	AGN
(3) Phil Pln	FOR	(8) Coop-Church	AGN	(13) Jets to Chiang	ABS
(4) No-Knock	FOR	(9) Family Asst	FOR	(14) State OEO Veto	FOR
(5) Cmutr Tax	FOR	(10) Work Stamps	FOR	(15) Park Logging	AGN

Election Results

1970 general:	John W. Byrnes (R)	76,893	(55%)
	Robert J. Cornell (D)	60,345	(44%)
	Joseph W. Dery (AIP)	1,283	(1%)
1970 primary:	John W. Byrnes (R), unopposed		
1968 general:	John W. Byrnes (R)	111,859	(68%)
	John E. Nixon (D)	52,660	(32%)

NINTH DISTRICT Political Background

Wisconsin 9 is the state's only suburban congressional district. It was created in 1963 when population changes and Supreme Court decisions required the legislature to redraw the boundaries of Wisconsin's districts. The 9th includes fast-growing Waukesha

County, whose population jumped from 158,000 in 1960 to 231,000 in 1970; the northwest part of the city of Milwaukee; and the wealthy suburbs on the shore of Lake Michigan just north of the city. Except for the Milwaukee portion of the district, all of these areas are heavily Republican. When they were removed from neighboring districts in 1963, the Democratic congressmen Robert Kastenmeier, Henry Reuss, and Clement Zablocki were no doubt all quite happy to see them go. Most of Milwaukee's economic and social elite live here in the 9th, a land of country clubs, tree-shaded streets, shopping centers, and starkly new subdivisions.

The creation of the district set the stage for the political comeback of Glenn R. Davis. He is a Republican who had represented the old 2nd district from 1947 to 1956, and had also made two unsuccessful attempts to win the Republican senatorial nomination in 1956 and 1957. The election in 1957 was called to fill the vacancy created by the death of Joseph McCarthy. Davis' politics was—and is—a mixture of those of McCarthy and the young Richard Nixon—fierce anticommunism and general conservatism. In 1964, Davis carried the 9th despite the LBJ landslide. Given the Republican preferences of the district, he no doubt confidently expected automatic reelection and greater seniority on the House Appropriations Committee.

The 1970 election may have altered this expectation. For the first time, Davis ran into strenuous and well-financed opposition, in the person of Milwaukee County Supervisor Fred Tabak. According to Tabak, Davis was a "do nothing" congressman. Apparently some of the voters agreed with him—when the results came in, the challenger carried the usually Republican portion of Milwaukee County by 1,000 votes. Davis won reelection only because of his rather narrow 8,000-vote plurality in Waukesha, which got him a 52% victory.

What happens to Davis now depends mostly on redistricting. With control over the process split between the parties, Davis will probably get a district to his liking for 1972. Such a district would move north to take in the exurban dairy farm—and heavily Republican—Washington and Ozaukee counties. But if the Democrats repeat their strong 1970 showing in the 1972 elections, they could win control of the Wisconsin Senate. Because this would leave the Democrats free to change district lines once again, they could easily divide Davis' district between the Milwaukee- and Madison-based districts from which it sprang. Such a district would make things tough for the incumbent Republican.

Census Data 1970 pop. 507,431; deviation from current state average, +14.9%; change 1960–70, +27.4%. Metro. 100.0%, 28.5% central city.

1970 Share of Federal Outlays $219,388,000 (average outlay per district, Wisconsin 4, 5, and 9)

DOD	$27,796,000	HEW	$84,455,000
AEC	$26,000	HUD	$1,371,000
NASA	$6,403,000	OEO	$1,228,000
DOT	$7,891,000	DOA	$7,407,000
		Other	$82,611,000

Federal Military-Industrial Commitments (See Wisconsin 5 for greater Milwaukee listing.)

Economic Base Nonelectrical machinery; primary metal industries, esp. iron and steel foundries; fabricated metal products, esp. fabricated structural metal products. Also, extensive commuting to Wisconsin 4 and 5 (Milwaukee).

The Voters

Registration No district-wide registration.

Employment profile White collar, 53%. Blue collar, 47%.

Ethnic groups Black, 1%. Total foreign stock, 24%. Germany, 10%; Poland, 2%; USSR, Austria, UK, Italy, Canada, Czech., Norway, Hungary, Sweden, 1% each; others, 4%.

Presidential vote

1968	Humphrey (D)	78,988	(39%)
	Nixon (R)	110,853	(54%)
	Wallace (AIP)	15,437	(8%)

Representative

Glenn R. Davis (R) Elected 1946–56, 1964– ; b. Oct. 28, 1914, Vernon; home, Waukesha; Platteville State Teachers Col., B.Ed., 1934; U. Wis., J.D., 1940; USNR, WWII; married, five children; United Church of Christ.

Career Wis. Legislature, 1941–42; practicing atty., 1957–64; Pres. New Berlin State Bank, 1959–65.

Offices 2454 RHOB, 202-225-5101. Also 7746 Menomonee River Parkway, Wauwatosa 53213, 414-771-5780.

Committees

Appropriations (8th); Subs. (1) Defense, (2) District of Columbia, (3) Public Works.

Group Ratings

	ADA	COPE	NREP	NFU	LCV	CFA	NAB	NSI	ACA
1970	20	9	25	38	13	38	100	100	79
1969	0	—	—	43	—	—	—	—	71
1968	0	0	—	27	—	—	100	—	95

Key Votes

(1) ABM	ABS	(6) 18-Yr-Vote	AGN	(11) Clean Water $	AGN
(2) SST	AGN	(7) Farm Sub Lmt	AGN	(12) Mig Wrkrs Comp	AGN
(3) Phil Pln	FOR	(8) Coop-Church	AGN	(13) Jets to Chiang	FOR
(4) No-Knock	FOR	(9) Family Asst	AGN	(14) State OEO Veto	FOR
(5) Cmutr Tax	AGN	(10) Work Stamps	FOR	(15) Park Logging	FOR

Election Results

1970 general:	Glenn R. Davis (R)	84,732	(52%)
	Fred N. Tabak (D)	78,123	(48%)
1970 primary:	Glenn R. Davis (R), unopposed		
1968 general:	Glenn R. Davis (R)	126,392	(63%)
	Carol E. Baumann (D)	73,891	(37%)

TENTH DISTRICT Political Background

Wisconsin 10 comprises the northern tip of the state, a land of pine forest and blue, clear lakes—and of noxious paper mills and depleted iron mines. The 10th is largely a rural district; the largest cities here are Eau Claire (pop. 44,000), a river town about 100 miles east of Minneapolis and St. Paul, and Superior (pop. 35,000), a Great Lakes port city. Superior lies just across an inlet from Duluth, Minnesota, and both send huge iron ore freighters down the Great Lakes to Chicago, Gary, Detroit, Cleveland, and Buffalo. In addition to this, the 10th shares other characteristics with neighboring Minnesota. The district has large numbers of Norwegian, Swedish, and German descended residents. And it also has a near radical political tradition, born of the harsh environment and the grit of the district's pioneering lumbermen and miners.

The years after World War II have not been good ones for the north country. Although the tourist business continues to grow, the mines have nearly petered out, and lumber and paper industries are not the employers they once were. The 10th had only a small population gain during the '60's, and most of that occurred in the district's few urban centers. In situations like this, the local congressman is expected to do something to spur employment, and the 10th's congressman, Alvin E. O'Konski, has at least one plan: Project Sanguine.

Sanguine, a Navy program, would implant electronic sensors throughout northern Wisconsin in a geological formation, lying on or near the surface, called the shield.

These sensors would then convert all of northern Wisconsin into a gigantic radar screen, which would be capable, for example, of picking up the presence of a Soviet nuclear submarine in the South China Sea. In times like our own, such an idea was not greeted with universal enthusiasm, even among the residents of northern Wisconsin. Some here worried about the ecological effects, and others felt that Sanguine's circuitry might jam their own electronic gadgets.

The proposal is typical of Congressman O'Konski, a maverick Republican. First elected in 1942, the Congressman is now the 2nd most senior Republican in the House. Only the vagaries of the seniority system have kept him from being the ranking member on a standing committee. On Armed Services, he stands just behind Leslie C. Arends, the only House Republican who outranks him. On this committee, O'Konski almost always lines up with its hawkish, pro-Pentagon majority, but on domestic issues he votes more often than not with liberal Democrats. Because the Republican consistently gets high marks from labor, O'Konski survives politically. The 10th usually ends up in the Democratic column in statewide races; O'Konski, therefore, has had to run ahead of his party to stay in office.

But in 1970, running ahead of Wisconsin's weak statewide Republican ticket was just barely enough to win. O'Konski's opponent, a sociology professor at Eau Claire State College, ran a strong campaign and received a 5,500-vote margin in his home county of Eau Claire, at the southern end of the district. In the north, where the Congressman has been strong despite the area's Democratic traditions, O'Konski's margins were far below normal. Overall, he managed only a 3,000-vote, 51–48 victory over the professor —a poorer showing than he made in the Goldwater year of 1964.

Part of O'Konski's problem was his health, or rather, his lack of candor about it. The Congressman, who was 66 in 1970, announced in the fall of that year that he would not return to the district to campaign; he cited the press of business in Washington. Actually, as newspaper reporters found out, he was spending weekends at Bethesda Naval Hospital, being treated for hepatitis or jaundice or some such ailment. Reporters recalled that he had also tried to conceal his 1966 heart attack. So a credibility gap developed in the 10th district, which more than anything accounted for O'Konski's poor 1970 showing.

Because Wisconsin's population has not been increasing as rapidly as the national average, the state lost one of its ten congressional seats in the 1970 census. Current reports indicate that O'Konski's seat will be the one to be eliminated (see state write-up). The 10th could be divided rather neatly between Republican Vernon Thomson's 3rd and Democrat David Obey's 7th. Given the situation, O'Konski has indignantly denied reports that he will retire. And even if the 10th is carved up, he may be feisty enough to make a run at it in one of the new districts. Whatever happens, the outlook for O'Konski's continued service in the House looks gloomy for the first time in 30 years.

Census Data 1970 pop. 412,371; deviation from current state average, −6.7%; change 1960–70, +5.8%. Metro. 10.8%, 7.8% central city.

1970 Share of Federal Outlays $361,571,301

DOD	$147,039,000	HEW	$130,197,817
AEC	$20,000	HUD	$735,000
NASA	$90,000	OEO	$1,447,222
DOT	$1,748,130	DOA	$25,279,733
		Other	$55,014,399

Federal Military-Industrial Commitments

DOD Contractors National Presto Industries (Eau Claire), $132.629m: metal parts for 105-mm high explosive projectiles.

DOD Installations Osceola Air Force Station (Osceola).

Economic Base Dairy; food and kindred products. Also tourism (lakes).

The Voters

Registration No district-wide registration.

Employment profile White collar, 33%. Blue collar, 67%.

Ethnic groups Black, less than 0.5%. Total foreign stock, 26%. Germany, 6%; Norway, 5%; Sweden, 4%; Canada, Poland, 2% each; Czech., UK, Austria, Italy, 1% each; others, 5%.

Presidential vote

1968	Humphrey (D)	80,499	(48%)
	Nixon (R)	77,507	(46%)
	Wallace (AIP)	11,453	(7%)

Representative

Alvin E. O'Konski (R) Elected 1942; b. May 26, 1907, Kewaunee; home, Mercer; Wis. State Teachers Col., B.E., 1926; U. of Iowa, 1927–28; U. of Wis., 1932; married; Catholic.

Career Teacher, 1926–29; Instr., Ore. State Col., 1929–31; Supt. of Schools, Pulaski, 1932–35; Instr., Jr. Col., Coleraine, Minn., 1935–36; Chm., Speech Dept., U. of Detroit, 1936–38; Pub. Rel., Wis. Repub. Com., 1938–40; pres. WAEO-TV, Inc.

Offices 2406 RHOB, 202-225-3361. Also Box 558, Rhinelander 54501, 715-369-4700.

Committees

Armed Services (2nd); Sub. No. 1.

District of Columbia (3rd); Subs. (1) Business, Commerce, and Fiscal Affairs, (2) Education.

Group Ratings

	ADA	COPE	NREP	NFU	LCV	CFA	NAB	NSI	ACA
1970	40	70	75	54	33	76	40	55	44
1969	29	—	—	54	—	—	—	—	54
1968	33	64	—	75	—	—	80	—	67

Key Votes

(1) ABM	AGN	(6) 18-Yr-Vote	FOR	(11) Clean Water $	FOR
(2) SST	FOR	(7) Farm Sub Lmt	ABS	(12) Mig Wrkrs Comp	FOR
(3) Phil Pln	AGN	(8) Coop-Church	FOR	(13) Jets to Chiang	FOR
(4) No-Knock	AGN	(9) Family Asst	FOR	(14) State OEO Veto	AGN
(5) Cmutr Tax	AGN	(10) Work Stamps	ABS	(15) Park Logging	FOR

Election Results

1970 general:	Alvin E. O'Konski (R)	66,014	(51%)
	Walter Thorensen (D)	62,991	(48%)
	William Hable (AIP)	694	(1%)
1970 primary:	Alvin E. O'Konski (R), unopposed		
1968 general:	Alvin E. O'Konski (R)	106,266	(66%)
	Timothy J. Hirsch (D)	54,889	(34%)

WYOMING

Political Background

Wyoming began its history in the 1870's. Before that time, it was only a terrain to be explored by mountain men and trappers like Jim Coulter or traversed by Yankee farmers from the Midwest on their way to the Willamette Valley via the Oregon Trail. The famous roadway of migration was protected from the Indians by installations like Fort Laramie near the Nebraska state line. According to one story, this began to change when a man, eager to reach Oregon, set out in the fall of the year, and was caught in an early season blizzard. He cut loose his livestock and returned on foot to spend the winter in one of the territory's settlements. In the spring, he returned to collect his abandoned belongings and view his dead animals. Instead, he found his animals alive and flourishing. It was then discovered that livestock could not only do well on the summertime tuffets of grass hidden away amongst the sagebrush, but they could also survive the brutal winters of the Wyoming plains. The animals simply pawed through the covering of snow to get at the grass which was stored away like so much farm-grown hay.

Upon learning this, cattlemen from west Texas began to drive their herds north, as the "dogies knew that Wyoming would be their new home." Times were very good for a while, because the "open range" policy allowed the cattlemen to let their livestock roam over the land and then be rounded up during fall and sold. Expenses ran about a dollar a head per year and they were sold anywhere from five to fifteen dollars a head. Then, the sheepmen and a few homesteaders came and disrupted the operation. The sheep, the cattle farmers said, cropped the grass too close to the roots, and the cattle would not graze on land given the once-over by sheep. Sheep also used up the scarce supplies of water; besides, there was something undignified and smelly about sheep. The homesteaders, of course, fenced off the open range. This situation produced some interesting confrontations, the most famous of which was the Johnson County war, which featured shooting and killing.

During the state's territorial days, the Wyoming Cattlemen's Association pretty much had things its own way. When it had trouble with sheepmen, homesteaders, and particularly with rustlers, the association, which was a near de facto government, meted out quick and sometimes severe punishment. The rustlers often came from the ranks of the rancher's own bunch of cowboys, who, from time to time, would cut out a few head in order to start their own herd. Some were quite successful, and these would then join the Wyoming Cattlemen's Association. Things boomed until the blizzard of '88, which wiped out many herds; cattle froze and starved to death, as the snow reached depths of five, ten, and fifteen feet. After the catastrophe, things quieted down, and today most livestock men in the state run both sheep and cattle (sheep are now more important), and the ranchers often grow their own winter's supply of alfalfa and barley on irrigated farms.

Nevertheless, Wyoming, more than any place else in the country, is still the Wild West. It is one of the few states where livestock men and a railroad, the Union Pacific, are still major political forces. The UP earned alternate 30 mile sections of the state when it built the transcontinental railroad across southern Wyoming. The road still owns much of this land, upon which have been found deposits of coal and oil. In fact, outside of the federal government, the UP is the nation's largest land owner. The people who came to build and maintain the UP are the source of Democratic strength in Wyoming. The livestock men and the farmers working the irrigated lands along the Big Horn River, to the northwest, and along the North Platte, to the southeast, are usually conservative Republican in political preference.

Cheyenne, Laramie, Rock Springs, Sheridan, and Cody—all names exploited by network TV executives—are the state's urban concentrations. Rock Springs (pop. 12,000) is the state's fourth largest city, and Cheyenne, the state capital, has 40,000 residents. More common are tiny places like Ten Sleep (pop. 320) or Medicine Bow (pop. 455), which was where the now famous Virginian stepped off the train. Owen Wister, a fancy Philadelphia lawyer turned author, made him—a man of few words and many deeds—the West's equivalent of Horatio Alger or Frank Merriwell. Between the settlements, for stretches of 50 and 100 miles, lies the high, desolate, and serene plateau country of the Rocky Mountains to the south and east, and the mountains themselves to the north and west.

The wide open spaces here mean that Wyoming has not experienced the development that has come to the states around it. Some Wyomingites regard the growth of Denver, Colorado, and Billings, Montana with some jealousy. But many, except for those who hunt or poison the American Bald Eagle, take pride in the state's ecological purity. Wyoming, which grew very little during the '60's, does have an outmigration problem, but those who do leave come back on occasion and relish its communities which seem immune to the workings of time. Wyoming, which had 332,000 residents in the 1970 census, will by the next census be the nation's least populous state; Nevada has already passed it, and Alaska soon will. The only areas of significant growth recently lie in the Jackson

Hole area, near Grand Teton and Yellowstone National parks; in Laramie, home of the University of Wyoming; and in Campbell County (Gillette), site of an oil and natural gas boom. Nevertheless, Wyoming, along with California, New York, and Texas, will continue to send two men to the United States Senate.

Oil, which has always been important to the state's economy, plays a significant role in the state's politics. And the oilmen and livestock people have made Wyoming a Republican stronghold during its 80-odd years of statehood. It has never had a significant number of miners—always a source of Democratic strength in Western states, nor does it have many Indian or Spanish-speaking minorities. As in many Rocky Mountain states, the establishment in Wyoming is a stern foe of federal spending or intervention in the abstract. But, as is the case most everywhere, they support the activities of the federal government when it happens to sustain or protect their interests. People here do not object to the subsidy policies of the Department of Agriculture, or federal military commitments (of which the state has few), or the construction of a new post office building. And they are particularly keen on federal beef, oil, wool, and sugar import quotas.

One man who has defended these interests in Washington is the state's senior senator, Gale W. McGee. McGee, a Nebraska native, has an unlikely background for a Wyoming politician. He was a history professor at the University of Wyoming for 12 years before he first won the seat in 1958. For the first few years of service, McGee was a little known member of Democratic senators known as the class of '58. He was considered a liberal by many in the state and by some others as well.

After 1958, Wyoming began to swing toward candidates of the Goldwater stripe, and among the class of '58, McGee's seat was one of the most seriously threatened in 1964. But the professor pulled out a 54–46 victory over Republican State Chairman, John Wold of Casper. The Senator then went on to a considerably more distinctive term.

He became chairman of the Post Office and Civil Service Committee, one of the first '58er's to reach a chairmanship. But more notably, he became one of the leading defenders of Johnson's and then Nixon's Vietnam war policies. This put him in rather odd political company: most Senate liberals, even those who backed the war initially, were never so vigorous or enthusiastic about it. His campaign material asserts that he likes to be best known for "his vibrant, ringing defense of our Vietnam policy." Some peace-minded observers in the state figured that he had succumbed to the academic's occupational hazard, a preoccupation with toughness. Others thought he merely wanted to keep on the good side of Johnson for a reelection bid in 1970, when LBJ, it was presumed, would be in the middle of his second full term. Johnson, of course, was not around to help, but McGee won anyway in 1970. Still, McGee, who has written some diplomatic history, was, and is, convinced that Vietnam was the nation's best course.

Whatever the merits of that, McGee's politics have gone over pretty well in Wyoming. When the 1970 elections rolled around, the Senator had something to please everyone: liberal domestic policies for organized labor and traditional Democrats; a hawkish stance on the war for admirers of President Nixon; and 12 years of seniority for all of the residents of the state. And for some reason, probably not political, McGee can say that he is one of the Senate's staunchest supporters of Israel. So in 1970, he brushed aside a challenge from a peace candidate in the primary, talked a liberal, antiwar Casper lawyer out of an independent candidacy, and then beat the same man who opposed him in 1964, Republican Congressman John Wold. This time he won by an even larger margin, 56–44.

According to some reports, the Nixon Administration, grateful for McGee's support on foreign policy and military spending issues, did not provide much money or other support on Wold's behalf. However that may be, McGee's victory was a considerable achievement. In 1964, Wold was a political unknown, but by 1970, he had become a champion vote-getter, winning 63% of the vote for congressman in 1968. The size of McGee's 1970 victory seems to indicate that he has a life-time seat. He even beat Wold in his home county of Natrona (Casper), which is oil-dominated and a conservative bastion.

The state's junior senator, Clifford Hansen, is more in line with the traditions of Wyoming: cattle rancher and conservative Republican. He was governor from 1962 to 1966; during those days, he had a reputation for liberal Republicanism and made some noises about supporting Rockefeller at the convention in 1964. He was governor when aging Republican Milward Simpson of Cody decided to retire in 1966, which was a good Republican year. Hansen is a member of the Senate Interior and Insular Affairs Committee, which handles many matters vital to Wyoming, and also of the Senate Finance Committee, which concerns itself with the oil depletion allowance, among other things. Hansen usually lines up with the Senate's conservative block, but on occasion he does not. Despite a special plea from Nixon himself, Hansen voted against the SST program. That position is not inconsistent to a commitment to free enterprise. Moreover, Hansen said that he did not want to entertain any possibility that sonic booms would disrupt the expanses of his home state.

Hansen is up again in 1972, and his most likely opponent is the man he beat in 1966, Congressman Teno Roncalio. The state's congressman-at-large seat has been batted around between the parties for the last 30 years. Its most notable occupant was William Henry Harrison, a conservative Republican and descendent of the victor over the Indians at Tippecanoe, Indiana. Harrison served from 1952 to 1954, from 1960 to 1964, and from 1966 to 1968. The main reason for the alternation is the propensity of Wyoming congressmen to run for the Senate. After all, a politician has to run statewide either way, and if he wins a Senate race, he has more power and fewer campaign hassles. Congressman Frank Barrett tried in 1952; Harrison in 1954; Keith Thomson in 1960; Teno Roncalio in 1966; and John Wold in 1970. Only Barrett and Thomson won, and Thomson died a month after his successful bid.

Presently, Roncalio, a liberal Democrat out of the Union Pacific country to the south of the state, is back in the congressman-at-large seat by virtue of a 51–49 victory in 1970. Roncalio's win belies the theory that Sen. McGee's reelection was an endorsement among the voters of his Vietnam stance. Roncalio, who backed Robert Kennedy in 1968, is a dove who promised to vote against all Vietnam appropriations. In his primary against more hawkish candidates, he ran about as well as McGee, county by county—an indication that the voters were more interested in personal qualifications and seniority than about the war. More than likely, Roncalio will try for Hansen's seat again in 1972, rather than face another, and equally risky, reelection fight for the House.

Electoral Votes 3

Census Data 1970 pop. 332,416; 0.16% of U.S. total, 51st largest; change 1960–70, +0.7%. Metro. 0.0%, 0.0% central city. 1970 per capita income, $3,420; 33rd highest. 50th in number of poor.

1970 Share of Federal Tax Burden $273,200,000; 0.14% of U.S. total, 52nd largest.

1970 Share of Federal Outlays $324,533,370; 0.17% of U.S. total, 52nd largest. Per capita federal spending, $976.

DOD	$57,694,000	52nd (0.10%)	HEW	$69,437,998	51st (0.13%)
AEC	$6,741,432	22nd (0.26%)	HUD	$1,250,349	52nd (0.06%)
NASA	$116,726	46th (0.00%)	OEO	$756,479	52nd (0.10%)
DOT	$34,345,926	47th (0.48%)	DOA	$39,463,800	43rd (0.31%)
DOC	$1,109,212	50th (0.96%)	POD	$10,526,596	52nd (0.14%)
DOI	$45,773,030	15th (1.98%)	VA	$22,558,663	47th (0.31%)
DOJ	$1,015,749	52nd (0.18%)	CSC	$4,710,222	50th (0.12%)
			Other	$29,033,188	

Federal Military-Industrial Commitments

DOD Contractors Boeing (Cheyenne), $6.596m: alterations of Minuteman missile at site installation.

DOD Installations Francis E. Warren Air Force Base (Cheyenne).

Economic Base Livestock and cash grain; crude petroleum and natural gas; metal mining, esp. uranium-radium-vanadium ores; petroleum refining and related industries; mining and quarrying of nonmetallic minerals other than fuels, esp. chemical and fertilizer mineral mining; food and kindred products, esp. beet sugar; lumber and wood products other than furniture, esp. sawmills and planing mills; printing, publishing, and allied industries, esp. newspapers. Also, tourism (Yellowstone and Grand Tetons).

Political Line-up Governor, Stanley K. Hathaway (R); seat up, 1974. Senators, Gale W. McGee (D) and Clifford Hansen (R). Representatives, 1 D, at large. State Senate (11 D and 19 R); State House (20 D, 40 R, and 1 Ind.).

The Voters

Registration 134,875 total. 51,890 D; 61,170 R; other 21,815.
Employment profile White collar, 40%. Blue collar, 60%.
Ethnic groups Black, 1%. Total foreign stock, 15%. UK, 3%; Germany, 2%; USSR, Canada, Sweden, Mexico, Italy, Norway, 1% each; others, 5%.

Presidential vote

1968	Humphrey (D)	45,173	(36%)
	Nixon (R)	70,927	(56%)
	Wallace (AIP)	11,105	(9%)
1964	Johnson (R)	80,718	(57%)
	Goldwater (D)	61,998	(43%)
1960	Kennedy (D)	63,331	(45%)
	Nixon (R)	77,451	(55%)

Senator

Gale William McGee (D) Elected 1958, seat up 1976; b. Mar. 17, 1915, Lincoln, Neb.; home, Laramie; Neb. State Teachers Col., B.A., 1936; U. of Colo., M.A., 1939; U. of Chicago, Ph.D., 1947; married, four children; Presbyterian.

Career Teacher, 1936–40; prof., Neb. Wesleyan U., 1940–43, Iowa State, 1943–44, Notre Dame, 1944–45, U. of Chicago, 1945–46, U. of Wyoming, 1946– ; Legislative Asst. Sen. Joseph Mahoney, 1955–56.

Offices 344 OSOB, 202-225-6441. Also 150 N. Center, Casper 82601, 301-235-6218.

Committees

Appropriations (9th); Subs. (1) Chm., Agriculture, Environmental and Consumer Protection, (2) Interior, (3) Foreign Operations, (4) HUD, Space, and Science, (5) Public Works.
Foreign Relations (7th); Subs. (1) Chm., African Affairs, (2) Arms Control, International Law and Organizations, (3) Far Eastern Affairs.
Post Office and Civil Service (Chm.).

Group Ratings

	ADA	COPE	NREP	NFU	LCV	NAB	NSI	ACA
1970	47	83	55	100	60	25	90	32
1969	39	—	—	80	—	—	—	15
1968	57	90	—	100	—	0	—	5

Key Votes

(1) ABM	FOR	(8) Phil Pln	ABS	(15) Coop-Church	AGN
(2) SST	FOR	(9) Vol Army	AGN	(16) Cut Oil Dpltn	AGN
(3) Busing	FOR	(10) Prison $	FOR	(17) Consumer Prot	FOR
(4) Tob Sub	ABS	(11) Cut Mil $	AGN	(18) Farm Sub Limit	ABS
(5) Carswell	AGN	(12) Defoliatn	FOR	(19) Comp Bid Sales	AGN
(6) No-Knock	AGN	(13) 18-Yr-Vote	FOR	(20) Pre-Prod Tests	ABS
(7) Seniorty	ABS	(14) Pentgn PR	FOR	(21) Cut Marjna Pen	AGN

Election Results

1970 general:	Gale W. McGee (D)	67,207	(56%)
	John S. Wold (R)	53,279	(44%)
1970 primary:	Gale W. McGee (D)	32,956	(80%)
	D. P. Svilar (D)	8,448	(20%)

1964 general:	Gale W. McGee (D)	76,485	(54%)
	John S. Wold (R)	65,185	(46%)

Senator

Clifford P. Hansen (R) Elected 1966, seat up 1972; b. Oct. 16, 1912, Zenith; home, Jackson; U. of Wyo., B.S., 1934; married, two children; Episcopalian.

Career Cattle rancher; Gov. of Wyo., 1963–66.

Offices 3107 NSOB, 202-225-3424. Also Box 425, Cheyenne 82001, 307-634-7981.

Committees

Finance (6th).

Interior and Insular Affairs (4th); Subs. (1) Indian Affairs, (2) Parks and Recreation, (3) Territories and Insular Affairs, (4) Water and Power Resources.

Veterans' Affairs (2nd); Subs. (1) Compensation and Pension, (2) Health and Hospitals.

Sp. Com. on Aging (4th); Subs. (1) Consumer Interests of the Elderly, (2) Employment and Retirement Incomes, (3) Federal, State, and Community Services, (4) Health of the Elderly, (5) Housing for the Elderly, (6) Long-Term Care.

Group Ratings

	ADA	COPE	NREP	NFU	LCV	NAB	NSI	ACA
1970	3	0	0	27	26	100	100	87
1969	0	0	—	38	—	—	—	79
1968	7	18	—	25	—	100	—	89

Key Votes

(1) ABM	FOR	(8) Phil Pln	AGN	(15) Coop-Church	AGN
(2) SST	AGN	(9) Vol Army	AGN	(16) Cut Oil Dpltn	AGN
(3) Busing	AGN	(10) Prison $	AGN	(17) Consumer Prot	AGN
(4) Tob Sub	FOR	(11) Cut Mil $	AGN	(18) Farm Sub Limit	AGN
(5) Carswell	FOR	(12) Defoliatn	FOR	(19) Comp Bid Sales	FOR
(6) No-Knock	FOR	(13) 18-Yr-Vote	FOR	(20) Pre-Prod Tests	AGN
(7) Seniorty	FOR	(14) Pentgn PR	FOR	(21) Cut Marjna Pen	FOR

Election Results

1966 general:	Clifford P. Hansen (R)	63,548	(52%)
	Teno Roncalio (D)	59,141	(48%)
1966 primary:	Clifford P. Hansen (R)	40,102	(86%)
	I. Wayne Kinney (R)	6,468	(14%)

Representative

Teno Roncalio (D) Elected 1964–66, 1970; b. Mar. 23, 1916, Rock Springs; home, Cheyenne; U. of Wyo., LL.B., 1947; Army, WWII; married, four children; Episcopalian.

Career Asst., Sen. Joseph Mahoney, 1941; practicing atty., 1947– ; Dep. Prosecuting Atty., Laramie County, 1950–56; Chm., Wyo. Dem. Com., 1957–61; U.S. Senate candidate, 1966.

Offices 1314 LHOB, 202-225-2311.

Committees

Interior and Insular Affairs (21st); Subs. (1) Environment, (2) Irrigation and Reclamation, (3) National Parks and Recreation, (4) Public Lands, (5) Territorial and Insular Affairs.

Public Works (18th); Subs. (1) Public Buildings and Grounds, (2) Rivers and Harbors, (3) Roads, (4) Watershed Development, (5) Sp. on Economic Development Programs.

Group Ratings, Key Votes: Newly elected.

Election Results

1970 general:	Teno Roncalio (D)	58,456	(50%)
	Harry Roberts (R)	57,848	(50%)
1970 primary:	Teno Roncalio (D)	26,309	(66%)
	Ed Herschler (D)	11,238	(28%)
	George W. K. Posvar (D)	2,102	(5%)

APPENDIX

SENATE COMMITTEES

Committee on Aeronautical and Space Sciences

Senator Clinton Anderson, Chairman

Democratic Majority (6 D). Senators Anderson (N. Mex.), Magnuson (Wash.), Symington (Mo.), Stennis (Miss.), Cannon (Nev.), Gambrell (Ga.).

Republican Minority (5 R). Senators Curtis (Neb.), Smith (Maine), Goldwater (Ariz.), Weicker (Conn.), Buckley (N.Y.).

(NO SUBCOMMITTEES)

Committee on Agriculture and Forestry

Herman Talmadge, Chairman

The Chairman is an ex-officio member of all subcommittees.

Democratic Majority (8 D). Senators Talmadge (Ga.), Ellender (La.), Eastland (Miss.), Jordan (N.C.), McGovern (S. Dak.), Allen (Ala.), Humphrey (Minn.), and Chiles (Fla.).

Republican Minority (6 R). Senators Miller (Iowa), Aiken (Vt.), Young (N. Dak.), Curtis (Neb.), Dole (Kans.), and Bellmon (Okla.).

SUBCOMMITTEES

AGRICULTURAL CREDIT AND RURAL ELECTRIFICATION

George McGovern, Chairman

MAJORITY (4 D). Senators McGovern, Allen, Ellender, and Humphrey.
MINORITY (3 R). Senators Aiken, Miller, and Dole

AGRICULTURAL EXPORTS

Lawton Chiles, Chairman

MAJORITY (3 D). Senators Chiles, Jordan (N.C.), and McGovern.
MINORITY (2 R). Senators Miller and Bellmon.

AGRICULTURAL PRODUCTION, MARKETING, AND STABILIZATION OF PRICES

B. Everett Jordan, Chairman

MAJORITY (5 D). Senators Jordan (N.C.), McGovern, Eastland, Ellender, and Humphrey.
MINORITY (4 R). Senators Young, Miller, Curtis, and Bellmon.

AGRICULTURAL RESEARCH AND GENERAL LEGISLATION

James B. Allen, Chairman

MAJORITY (4 D). Senators Allen, Jordan (N.C.), Eastland, and Chiles.
MINORITY (3 R). Senators Dole, Young, and Curtis.
EX OFFICIO Senator Miller.

ENVIRONMENT, SOIL CONSERVATION AND FORESTRY

James O. Eastland, Chairman

MAJORITY (3 D). Senators Eastland, Jordan (N.C.), and Chiles.
MINORITY (2 R). Senators Bellmon and Aiken.
EX OFFICIO Senator Miller.

RURAL DEVELOPMENT

Hubert H. Humphrey, Chairman

MAJORITY (4 D). Senators Humphrey, Ellender, Eastland, and Allen.
MINORITY (3 R). Senators Curtis, Dole, and Bellmon.
The Food for Peace Program is taken up by the full committee.

Committee on Appropriations

Allen J. Ellender, Chairman

The Chairman and Ranking Minority Member are ex-officio members of all subcommittees of which they are not regular members.

Democratic Majority (13 D). Senators Ellender (La.), McClellan (Ark.), Magnuson (Wash.), Stennis (Miss.), Pastore (R.I.), Bible (Nev.), Byrd (W. Va.), McGee (Wyo.), Mansfield (Mont.), Proxmire (Wis.), Montoya (N. Mex.), Inouye (Hawaii), and Hollings (S.C.).

Republican Minority (11 R). Senators Young (N. Dak.), Mundt (S. Dak.), Smith (Maine), Hruska (Neb.), Allott (Colo.), Cotton (N.H.), Case (N.J.), Fong (Hawaii), Boggs (Del.), Percy (Ill.), and Brooke (Mass.).

SUBCOMMITTEES

AGRICULTURE, ENVIRONMENTAL AND CONSUMER PROTECTION

Gale W. McGee, Chairman

MAJORITY (6 D). Senators McGee, Stennis, Proxmire, Byrd (W. Va.), Mansfield, and Inouye.
MINORITY (5 R). Senators Hruska, Young, Mundt, Fong, and Boggs.
EX OFFICIO Senators Talmadge, Eastland, and Miller.

DEFENSE

Allen J. Ellender, Chairman

MAJORITY (7 D). Senators Ellender, McClellan, Stennis, Pastore, Magnuson, Mansfield, and Bible.
MINORITY (6 R). Senators Young, Smith, Allott, Hruska, Cotton, and Case.

INTELLIGENCE OPERATIONS Senators Ellender, McClellan, Stennis, Young, and Smith.

DISTRICT OF COLUMBIA

Daniel K. Inouye, Chairman

MAJORITY (3 D). Senators Inouye, Montoya, and Hollings.
MINORITY (2 R). Senators Percy, and Boggs.
EX OFFICIO Senators Eagleton, Stevenson, and Mathias.

FOREIGN OPERATIONS

William Proxmire, Chairman

MAJORITY (4 D). Senators Proxmire, McGee, Ellender, and McClellan.
MINORITY (3 R). Senators Fong, Cotton, and Brooke.

HOUSING AND URBAN DEVELOPMENT, SPACE, AND SCIENCE

John O. Pastore, Chairman

MAJORITY (6 D). Senators Pastore, Magnuson, Ellender, Stennis, Mansfield, and McGee.
MINORITY (5 R). Senators Allott, Smith, Hruska, Case, and Percy.

AERONAUTICAL AND SPACE ACTIVITIES Senators Anderson, Symington, and Curtis.

INTERIOR

Alan Bible, Chairman

MAJORITY (6 D). Senators Bible, McClellan, Byrd (W. Va.), McGee, Montoya, and Inouye.
MINORITY (5 R). Senators Percy, Mundt, Young, Boggs, and Fong.

LABOR AND HEALTH, EDUCATION AND WELFARE

Warren G. Magnuson, Chairman

MAJORITY (7 D). Senators Magnuson, Stennis, Bible, Byrd (W. Va.), Proxmire, Montoya, and Hollings.
MINORITY (6 R). Senators Cotton, Case, Fong, Boggs, Percy, and Brooke.

LEGISLATIVE

Ernest F. Hollings, Chairman

MAJORITY (3 D). Senators Mansfield, Ellender, and Inouye.
MINORITY (2 R). Senators Cotton and Brooke.

MILITARY CONSTRUCTION

Mike Mansfield, Chairman

MAJORITY (4 D). Senators Mansfield, Proxmire, Montoya, and Hollings.
MINORITY (3 R). Senators Brooke, Boggs, and Percy.
EX OFFICIO Senators Symington, Cannon, and Tower.

PUBLIC WORKS

John C. Stennis, Chairman

MAJORITY (8 D). Senators Stennis, Ellender, McClellan, Magnuson, Bible, Byrd (W. Va.), Pastore, and McGee.
MINORITY (7 R). Senators Mundt, Young, Hruska, Smith, Allott, Case, and Cotton.

RIVERS AND HARBORS ACTIVITIES Senators Randolph, Muskie, and Cooper.

ATOMIC ENERGY ITEMS Senators Anderson, Jackson, and Aiken.

STATE, JUSTICE, COMMERCE, THE JUDICIARY

John L. McClellan, Chairman

MAJORITY (5 D). Senators McClellan, Ellender, Pastore, Mansfield, and Hollings.
MINORITY (4 R). Senators Smith, Hruska, Fong, and Brooke.

DIPLOMATIC AND CONSULAR ITEMS Senators Fulbright, Sparkman, and Aiken.

TRANSPORTATION

Robert C. Byrd, Chairman

MAJORITY (6 D). Senators Byrd (W. Va.) Stennis, Magnuson, Pastore, Bible, and Proxmire.
MINORITY (5 R). Senators Case, Mundt, Smith, Allott, and Percy.

TREASURY, POST OFFICE, GENERAL GOVERNMENT

Joseph M. Montoya, Chairman

MAJORITY (3 D). Senators Montoya, Ellender, and Inouye.
MINORITY (2 R). Senators Boggs and Allott.

POST OFFICE ITEMS Senators McGee, Randolph, and Fong.

Committee on Armed Services

John Stennis, Chairman

Democratic Majority (9 D). Senators Stennis (Miss.), Symington (Mo.), Jackson (Wash.), Ervin (N.C.), Cannon (Nev.), McIntyre (N.H.), Byrd (Va.), Hughes (Iowa), and Bentsen (Tex.).
Republican Minority (7 R). Senators Smith (Maine), Thurmond (S.C.), Tower (Tex.), Dominick (Colo.), Goldwater (Ariz.), Schweiker (Pa.), and Saxbe (Ohio).

SUBCOMMITTEES

CENTRAL INTELLIGENCE

John C. Stennis, Chairman

MAJORITY (3 D). Senators Stennis, Symington, and Jackson.
MINORITY (2 R). Senators Dominick and Goldwater.

GENERAL LEGISLATION

Harry F. Byrd, Chairman

MAJORITY (4 D). Senators Byrd (Va.), McIntyre, Hughes, and Bentsen.
MINORITY (3 R). Senators Saxbe, Schweiker, and Dominick.

MILITARY CONSTRUCTION AUTHORIZATION

W. Stuart Symington, Chairman

MAJORITY (5 D). Senators Symington, Jackson, Ervin, Cannon, and Byrd (Va.).
MINORITY (3 R). Senators Tower, Thurmond, and Dominick.

NATIONAL STOCKPILE AND NAVAL PETROLEUM RESERVES

Howard W. Cannon, Chairman

MAJORITY (4 D). Senators Cannon, Symington, Ervin, and Bentsen.
MINORITY (3 R). Senators Goldwater, Thurmond, and Saxbe.

NUCLEAR TEST BAN TREATY SAFEGUARDS

Henry M. Jackson, Chairman

MAJORITY (2 D). Senators Jackson and Symington.
MINORITY (1 R). Senator Smith.

PREPAREDNESS INVESTIGATING

John C. Stennis, Chairman

MAJORITY (6 D). Senators Stennis, Symington, Jackson, Cannon, McIntyre, and Byrd (Va.).
MINORITY (5 R). Senators Thurmond, Tower, Goldwater, Schweiker, and Dominick.

STATUS OF FORCES

Samuel J. Ervin, Chairman

MAJORITY (3 D). Senators Ervin, McIntyre, and Byrd (Va.).
MINORITY (2 R). Senators Schweiker and Saxbe.

STRATEGIC ARMS LIMITATION TALKS

Henry M. Jackson, Chairman

MAJORITY (5 D). Senators Jackson, Stennis, Symington, Byrd (Va.), and Hughes.
MINORITY (3 R). Senators Tower, Schweiker, and Saxbe.

SPECIAL SUBCOMMITTEE TO REVIEW BOMBER DEFENSE

John C. Stennis, Chairman

MAJORITY (3 D). Senators Stennis, McIntyre, and Byrd (Va.).
MINORITY (2 R). Senators Thurmond and Dominick.

AD HOC SUBCOMMITTEE ON RESEARCH AND DEVELOPMENT

Thomas J. McIntyre, Chairman

MAJORITY (3 D). Senators McIntyre, Byrd (Va.), and Bentsen.
MINORITY (2 R). Senators Dominick and Goldwater.

AD HOC SUBCOMMITTEE ON TACTICAL AIR POWER

Howard W. Cannon, Chairman

MAJORITY (4 D). Senators Cannon, Symington, Jackson, and Hughes.
MINORITY (3 R). Senators Thurmond, Tower, and Goldwater.

Committee on Banking, Housing and Urban Affairs

John Sparkman, Chairman

Democratic Majority (8 D). Senators Sparkman (Ala.), Proxmire (Wis.), Williams (N.J.), McIntyre (N.H.), Mondale (Minn.), Cranston (Calif.), Stevenson III (Ill.), and Gambrell (Ga.).
Republican Minority (7 R). Senators Tower (Tex.), Bennett (Utah), Brooke (Mass.), Packwood (Oreg.), Roth (Del.), Brock (Tenn.), and Taft, Jr. (Ohio).

SUBCOMMITTEES

FINANCIAL INSTITUTIONS

William Proxmire, Chairman

MAJORITY (6 D). Senators Proxmire, Sparkman, Williams, McIntyre, Mondale, and Cranston.
MINORITY (5 R). Senators Bennett, Tower, Brooke, Packwood, and Brock.

HOUSING AND URBAN AFFAIRS

John Sparkman, Chairman

MAJORITY (8 D). Senators Sparkman, Proxmire, Williams, McIntyre, Mondale, Cranston, Stevenson, and Gambrell.

MINORITY (7 R). Senators Tower, Bennett, Brooke, Packwood, Roth, Brock, and Taft.

INTERNATIONAL FINANCE

Walter F. Mondale, Chairman

MAJORITY (6 D). Senators Mondale, Sparkman, Williams, Cranston, Stevenson, and Gambrell.

MINORITY (5 R). Senators Packwood, Bennett, Brooke, Roth, and Taft.

PRODUCTION AND STABILIZATION

Alan Cranston, Chairman

MAJORITY (6 D). Senators Cranston, Sparkman, Proxmire, McIntyre, Stevenson, and Gambrell.

MINORITY (5 R). Senators Brock, Tower, Bennett, Packwood, and Taft.

SECURITIES

Harrison A. Williams, Jr., Chairman

MAJORITY (6 D). Senators Williams, Proxmire, Mondale, McIntyre, Stevenson, and Gambrell.

MINORITY (5 R). Senators Brooke, Tower, Bennett, Packwood, and Roth.

SMALL BUSINESS

Thomas J. McIntyre, Chairman

MAJORITY (6 D). Senators McIntyre, Sparkman, Proxmire, Williams, Mondale, and Cranston.

MINORITY (5 R). Senators Roth, Tower, Brooke, Brock, and Taft.

Committee on Commerce

Warren Magnuson, Chairman

The Chairman and Ranking Minority Member are ex-officio members of all subcommittees.

Democratic Majority (10 D). Senators Magnuson (Wash.), Pastore (R.I.), Hartke (Ind.), Hart (Mich.), Cannon (Nev.), Long (La.), Moss (Utah), Hollings (S.C.), Inouye (Hawaii), and Spong (Va.).

Republican Minority (8 R). Senators Cotton (N.H.), Pearson (Kans.), Griffin (Mich.), Baker (Tenn.), Cook (Ky.), Hatfield (Oreg.), Stevens (Alaska), and one vacancy.

SUBCOMMITTEES

AVIATION

Howard W. Cannon, Chairman

MAJORITY (8 D). Senators Cannon, Magnuson, Hart, Hartke, Hollings, Inouye, Moss, and Spong.

MINORITY (6 R). Senators Pearson, Cotton, Baker, Griffin, Cook, and Stevens.

COMMUNICATIONS

John O. Pastore, Chairman

MAJORITY (6 D). Senators Pastore, Hartke, Hart, Long, Moss, and Cannon.
MINORITY (5 R). Senators Baker, Griffin, Cook, Pearson, and Stevens.

THE CONSUMER

Frank E. Moss, Chairman
Philip A. Hart, Vice Chairman

MAJORITY (6 D). Senators Moss, Hart, Pastore, Hartke, Inouye, and Spong.
MINORITY (5 R). Senators Cook, Pearson, Hatfield, Stevens, and Cotton.

ENVIRONMENT

Philip A. Hart, Chairman
Frank E. Moss, Vice Chairman

MAJORITY (5 D). Senators Hart, Moss, Pastore, Long, and Spong.
MINORITY (4 R). Senators Hatfield, Baker, Cook, and Pearson.

FOREIGN COMMERCE AND TOURISM

Daniel K. Inouye, Chairman

MAJORITY (5 D). Senators Inouye, Hartke, Cannon, Long, and Moss.
MINORITY (3 R). Senators Griffin, Baker, and Stevens.

MERCHANT MARINE

Russell B. Long, Chairman

MAJORITY (5 D). Senators Long, Pastore, Hollings, Inouye, and Spong.
MINORITY (3 R). Senators Griffin, Hatfield, and Stevens.

OCEANS AND ATMOSPHERE

Ernest F. Hollings, Chairman

MAJORITY (6 D). Senators Hollings, Pastore, Hart, Long, Inouye, and Spong.
MINORITY (4 R). Senators Stevens, Griffin, Cook, and Hatfield.

SURFACE TRANSPORTATION

Vance Hartke, Chairman

MAJORITY (5 D). Senators Hartke, Cannon, Moss, Hollings, and Long.
MINORITY (3 R). Senators Pearson, Baker, and Hatfield.

Committee on the District of Columbia

Thomas F. Eagleton, Chairman

Democratic Majority (4 D). Senators Eagleton (Mo.), Inouye (Hawaii), Stevenson III (Ill.), and Tunney (Calif.).

Republican Minority (3 R). Senators Mathias (Md.), Weicker (Conn.), and Buckley (N.Y.).

SUBCOMMITTEES

BUSINESS, COMMERCE, AND JUDICIARY

Adlai E. Stevenson III, Chairman

MAJORITY (2 D). Senators Stevenson and Tunney.
MINORITY (1 R). Senator Mathias.

FISCAL AFFAIRS

Thomas F. Eagleton, Chairman

MAJORITY (2 D). Senators Eagleton and Inouye.
MINORITY (1 R). Senator Weicker.

PUBLIC HEALTH, EDUCATION, WELFARE, AND SAFETY

John V. Tunney, Chairman

MAJORITY (2 D). Senators Tunney and Stevenson.
MINORITY (1 R). Senator Buckley.

Committee on Finance

Russell Long, Chairman

Democratic Majority (9 D). Senators Long (La.), Anderson (N. Mex.), Talmadge (Ga.), Hartke (Ind.), Fullbright (Ark.), Ribicoff (Conn.), Harris (Okla.), Byrd (Va.), and Nelson (Wis.).

Republican Minority (7 R). Senators Bennett (Utah), Curtis (Neb.), Miller (Iowa), Jordan (Idaho), Fannin (Ariz.), Hansen (Wyo.), and Griffin (Mich.).

(NO SUBCOMMITTEES)

Committee on Foreign Relations

J. W. Fulbright, Chairman

The Chairman is an ex-officio member of all subcommittees.

Democratic Majority (9 D). Senators Fulbright (Ark.), Sparkman (Ala.), Mansfield (Mont.), Church (Idaho), Symington (Mo.), Pell (R.I.), McGee (Wyo.), Muskie (Maine), and Spong (Va.).

Republican Minority (7 R). Senators Aiken (Vt.), Mundt (S. Dak.), Case (N.J.), Cooper (Ky.), Javits (N.Y.), Scott (Pa.), and Pearson (Kans.).

SUBCOMMITTEES

AFRICAN AFFAIRS

Gale W. McGee, Chairman

MAJORITY (1 D). Senator McGee.
MINORITY (2 R). Senators Mundt and Pearson.

ARMS CONTROL, INTERNATIONAL LAW AND ORGANIZATION

Edmund S. Muskie, Chairman

MAJORITY (4 D). Senators Muskie, Church, Pell, and McGee.
MINORITY (4 R). Senators Case, Cooper, Javits, and Pearson.

EUROPEAN AFFAIRS

John Sparkman, Chairman

MAJORITY (4 D). Senators Sparkman, Symington, Pell, and Spong.
MINORITY (4 R). Senators Case, Cooper, Javits, and Pearson.

FAR EASTERN AFFAIRS

Mike Mansfield, Chairman

MAJORITY (4 D). Senators Mansfield, Sparkman, McGee, and Muskie.
MINORITY (4 R). Senators Aiken, Mundt, Cooper, and Scott.

GENOCIDE CONVENTION

Frank Church, Chairman

MAJORITY (3 D). Senators Church, Symington, and Pell.
MINORITY (3 R). Senators Cooper and Javits.

NEAR EASTERN AND SOUTH ASIAN AFFAIRS

Stuart Symington, Chairman

MAJORITY (2 D). Senators Symington and Mansfield.
MINORITY (4 R). Senators Aiken, Mundt, Scott, and Pearson.

OCEANS AND INTERNATIONAL ENVIRONMENT

Claiborne Pell, Chairman

MAJORITY (3 D). Senators Pell, Church, and Spong.
MINORITY (2 R). Senators Case and Scott.

U.S. SECURITY AGREEMENTS AND COMMITMENTS ABROAD

Stuart Symington, Chairman

MAJORITY (4 D). Senators Symington, Fullbright, Sparkman, and Mansfield.
MINORITY (4 R). Senators Aiken, Case, Cooper, and Javits.

WESTERN HEMISPHERE AFFAIRS

Frank Church, Chairman

MAJORITY (5 D). Senators Church, Sparkman, Mansfield, Muskie, and Spong.
MINORITY (3 R). Senators Aiken, Case, and Javits.

Committee on Government Operations

John L. McClellan, Chairman

Democratic Majority (10 D). Senators McClellan (Ark.), Jackson (Wash.), Ervin (N.C.), Muskie (Maine), Ribicoff (Conn.), Harris (Okla.), Metcalf (Mont.), Allen (Ala.), Humphrey (Minn.), and Chiles (Fla.).

Republican Minority (8 R). Senators Mundt (S. Dak.), Javits (N.Y.), Percy (Ill.), Gurney (Fla.), Mathias (Md.), Saxbe (Ohio), Roth (Del.), and Brock (Tenn.).

SUBCOMMITTEES

PERMANENT SUBCOMMITTEE ON INVESTIGATIONS

John L. McClellan, Chairman

MAJORITY (5 D). Senators McClellan, Jackson, Ervin, Ribicoff, and Allen.
MINORITY (4 R). Senators Mundt, Percy, Javits, and Gurney.

EXECUTIVE REORGANIZATION

Abraham A. Ribicoff, Chairman

MAJORITY (5 D). Senators Ribicoff, Harris, Metcalf, Allen, and Humphrey.
MINORITY (4 R). Senators Javits, Percy, Mathias, and Saxbe.

INTERGOVERNMENTAL RELATIONS

Edmund S. Muskie, Chairman

MAJORITY (5 D). Senators Muskie, Ervin, Metcalf, McClellan, and Chiles.
MINORITY (4 R). Senators Burney, Saxbe, Roth, and Brock.

NATIONAL SECURITY AND INTERNATIONAL OPERATIONS

Henry M. Jackson, Chairman

MAJORITY (5 D). Senators Jackson, Muskie, Harris, Humphrey, and Chiles.
MINORITY (4 R). Senators Mathias, Mundt, Brock, and Roth.

Committee on Interior and Insular Affairs

Henry M. Jackson, Chairman

The Chairman is an ex-officio member of all subcommittees.

Democratic Majority (9 D). Senators Jackson (Wash.), Anderson (N. Mex.), Bible (Nev.), Church (Idaho), Moss (Utah), Burdick (N. Dak.), McGovern (S. Dak.), Metcalf (Mont.), and Gravel (Alaska).

Republican Minority (7 R). Senators Allott (Colo.), Jordan (Idaho), Fannin (Ariz.), Hansen (Wyo.), Hatfield (Oreg.), Stevens (Alaska), and Bellmon (Okla.).

SUBCOMMITTEES

INDIAN AFFAIRS

George McGovern, Chairman

MAJORITY (6 D). Senators McGovern, Jackson, Anderson, Burdick, Metcalf, and Gravel.
MINORITY (5 R). Senators Fannin, Hansen, Stevens, Bellmon, and Allott.

MINERALS, MATERIALS AND FUELS

Frank E. Moss, Chairman

MAJORITY (5 D). Senators Moss, Jackson, Bible, McGovern, and Gravel.
MINORITY (4 R). Senators Jordan (Idaho), Bellmon, Allott, and Stevens.

PARKS AND RECREATION

Alan Bible, Chairman

MAJORITY (5 D). Senators Bible, Jackson, Anderson, Church, and Moss.
MINORITY (4 R). Senators Hansen, Fannin, Hatfield, and Bellmon.

PUBLIC LANDS

Frank Church, Chairman

MAJORITY (5 D). Senators Church, Jackson, Bible, Metcalf, and Gravel.
MINORITY (4 R). Senators Hatfield, Allott, Fannin, and Bellmon.

TERRITORIES AND INSULAR AFFAIRS

Quentin N. Burdick, Chairman

MAJORITY (4 D). Senators Burdick, Jackson, McGovern, and Metcalf.
MINORITY (3 R). Senators Stevens, Jordan (Idaho), and Hansen.

WATER AND POWER RESOURCES

Clinton P. Anderson, Chairman

MAJORITY (6 D). Senators Anderson, Jackson, Church, Moss, Burdick, and Metcalf.
MINORITY (5 R). Senators Allott, Jordan (Idaho), Fannin, Hansen, and Hatfield.

SPECIAL SUBCOMMITTEE ON LEGISLATIVE OVERSIGHT

Henry M. Jackson, Chairman

MAJORITY (2 D). Senators Jackson and Anderson.
MINORITY (1 R). Senator Allott.

Committee on the Judiciary

James Eastland, Chairman

Democratic Majority (9 D). Senators Eastland (Miss.), McClellan (Ark.), Ervin (N.C.), Hart (Mich.), Kennedy (Mass.), Bayh (Ind.), Burdick (N. Dak.), Byrd (W. Va.), and Tunney (Calif.).

Republican Minority (7 R). Senators Hruska (Neb.), Fong (Hawaii), Scott (Pa.), Thurmond (S.C.), Cook (Ky.), Mathias (Md.), and Gurney (Fla.).

SUBCOMMITTEES

ADMINISTRATIVE PRACTICE AND PROCEDURE

Edward M. Kennedy, Chairman

MAJORITY (5 D). Senators Kennedy, Hart, Bayh, Burdick, and Tunney.
MINORITY (3 R). Senators Thurmond, Mathias, and Gurney.

ANTITRUST AND MONOPOLY LEGISLATION

Philip A. Hart, Chairman

MAJORITY (5 D). Senators Hart, McClellan, Ervin, Kennedy, and Tunney.
MINORITY (4 R). Senators Hruska, Fong, Thurmond, and Gurney.

CONSTITUTIONAL AMENDMENTS

Birch Bayh, Chairman

MAJORITY (6 D). Senators Bayh, Eastland, Ervin, Byrd (W. Va.), and two vacancies.
MINORITY (4 R). Senators Hruska, Fong, Thurmond, and Cook.

CONSTITUTIONAL RIGHTS

Sam J. Ervin, Chairman

MAJORITY (6 D). Senators Ervin, McClellan, Kennedy, Bayh, Byrd (W. Va.), and Tunney.
MINORITY (3 R). Senators Hruska, Fong, and Thurmond.

CRIMINAL LAWS AND PROCEDURES

John L. McClellan, Chairman

MAJORITY (6 D). Senators McClellan, Ervin, Hart, Eastland, Kennedy, and Byrd (W. Va.).
MINORITY (4 R). Senators Hruska, Scott, Thurmond, and Cook.

FEDERAL CHARTERS, HOLIDAYS AND CELEBRATIONS

Roman L. Hruska, Chairman

MAJORITY (1 D). Senator McClellan.
MINORITY (1 R). Senator Hruska.

IMMIGRATION AND NATURALIZATION

James O. Eastland, Chairman

MAJORITY (5 D). Senators Eastland, McClellan, Ervin, Kennedy, and Hart.
MINORITY (3 R). Senators Fong, Thurmond, and Cook.

IMPROVEMENTS IN JUDICIAL MACHINERY

Quentin N. Burdick, Chairman

MAJORITY (5 D). Senators Burdick, McClellan, Hart, Ervin, and Byrd (W. Va.).
MINORITY (3 R). Senators Hruska, Scott, and Gurney.

INTERNAL SECURITY

James O. Eastland, Chairman

MAJORITY (6 D). Senators Eastland, McClellan, Ervin, Bayh, Byrd (W. Va.), and one vacancy.
MINORITY (4 R). Senators Scott, Thurmond, Cook, and Gurney.

JUVENILE DELINQUENCY

Birch Bayh, Chairman

MAJORITY (5 D). Senators Bayh, Hart, Burdick, Kennedy, and Byrd (W. Va.).
MINORITY (4 R). Senators Cook, Hruska, Fong, and Mathias.

PATENTS, TRADEMARKS AND COPYRIGHTS

John L. McClellan, Chairman

MAJORITY (3 D). Senators McClellan, Hart, and Burdick.
MINORITY (2 R). Senators Scott and Fong.

PENITENTIARIES

Quentin N. Burdick, Chairman

MAJORITY (2 D). Senators Burdick and Hart.
MINORITY (2 R). Senators Hruska and Scott.

REFUGEES AND ESCAPEES

Edward M. Kennedy, Chairman

MAJORITY (3 D). Senators Kennedy, McClellan, and Hart.
MINORITY (2 R). Senators Fong and Mathias.

REVISION AND CODIFICATION

Sam J. Ervin, Chairman

MAJORITY (2 D). Senators Ervin and Hart.
MINORITY (1 R). Senator Scott.

SEPARATION OF POWERS

Sam J. Ervin, Chairman

MAJORITY (3 D). Senators Ervin, McClellan, and Burdick.
MINORITY (2 R). Senators Mathias and Gurney.

Committee on Labor and Public Welfare

Harrison A. Williams, Jr., Chairman

Democratic Majority (10 D). Senators Williams (N.J.), Randolph (W. Va.), Pell (R.I.), Kennedy (Mass.), Nelson (Wis.), Mondale (Minn.), Eagleton (Mo.), Cranston (Calif.), Hughes (Iowa), and Stevenson III (Ill.).

Republican Minority (7 R). Senators Javits (N.Y.), Dominick (Colo.), Schweiker (Pa.), Packwood (Oreg.), Taft (Ohio), Beall (Md.), and Stafford (Vt.).

SUBCOMMITTEES

AGING

Thomas F. Eagleton, Chairman

MAJORITY (7 D). Senators Eagleton, Cranston, Kennedy, Randolph, Williams, Hughes, and Stevenson.
MINORITY (5 R). Senators Beall, Schweiker, Taft, Packwood, and Stafford.

ALCOHOLISM AND NARCOTICS

Harold E. Hughes, Chairman

MAJORITY (6 D). Senators Hughes, Randolph, Williams, Kennedy, Mondale, and Cranston.
MINORITY (4 R). Senators Packwood, Javits, Dominick, and Schweiker.

CHILDREN AND YOUTH

Walter F. Mondale, Chairman

MAJORITY (7 D). Senators Mondale, Williams, Randolph, Kennedy, Nelson, Cranston, and Stevenson.
MINORITY (5 R). Senators Taft, Schweiker, Packwood, Beall, and Javits.

EDUCATION

Claiborne Pell, Chairman

MAJORITY (7 D). Senators Pell, Randolph, Williams, Kennedy, Mondale, Eagleton, and Cranston.
MINORITY (5 R). Senators Javits, Dominick, Schweiker, Beall, and Stafford.

EMPLOYMENT, MANPOWER, AND POVERTY

Gaylord Nelson, Chairman

MAJORITY (7 D). Senators Nelson, Kennedy, Mondale, Cranston, Hughes, Stevenson, and Randolph.
MINORITY (4 R). Senators Schweiker, Javits, Dominick, and Taft.

HANDICAPPED WORKERS

Jennings Randolph, Chairman

MAJORITY (3 D). Senators Randolph, Cranston, and Williams.
MINORITY (2 R). Senators Packwood and Stafford.

HEALTH

Edward M. Kennedy, Chairman

MAJORITY (8 D). Senators Kennedy, Williams, Nelson, Eagleton, Cranston, Hughes, Pell, and Mondale.
MINORITY (5 R). Senators Dominick, Javits, Schweiker, Packwood, and Beall.

LABOR

Harrison A. Williams, Jr., Chairman

MAJORITY (7 D). Senators Williams, Randolph, Pell, Nelson, Eagleton, Stevenson, and Hughes.
MINORITY (5 R). Senators Javits, Schweiker, Packwood, Taft, and Stafford.

MIGRATORY LABOR

Adlai E. Stevenson III, Chairman

MAJORITY (5 D). Senators Stevenson, Williams, Mondale, Kennedy, and Hughes.
MINORITY (3 R). Senators Taft, Beall, and Javits.

SPECIAL SUBCOMMITTEE ON ARTS AND HUMANITIES

Claiborne Pell, Chairman

MAJORITY (3 D). Senators Pell, Nelson, and Eagleton.
MINORITY (2 R). Senators Javits and Packwood.

SPECIAL SUBCOMMITTEE ON EVALUATION AND PLANNING OF SOCIAL PROGRAMS

Walter F. Mondale, Chairman

MAJORITY (4 D). Senators Mondale, Nelson, Eagleton, and Stevenson.
MINORITY (4 R). Senators Javits, Taft, Beall, and Stafford.

SPECIAL SUBCOMMITTEE ON HUMAN RESOURCES

Alan Cranston, Chairman

MAJORITY (3 D). Senators Cranston, Randolph, and Nelson.
MINORITY (2 R). Senators Packwood and Schweiker.

SPECIAL SUBCOMMITTEE ON INTERNATIONAL HEALTH, EDUCATION AND LABOR PROGRAMS

Harold E. Hughes, Chairman

MAJORITY (3 D). Senators Hughes, Williams, and Pell.
MINORITY (1 R). Senator Dominick.

SPECIAL SUBCOMMITTEE ON NATIONAL SCIENCE FOUNDATION

Edward M. Kennedy, Chairman

MAJORITY (4 D). Senators Kennedy, Pell, Eagleton, and Cranston.
MINORITY (3 R). Senators Dominick, Packwood, and Stafford.

Committee on Post Office and Civil Service

Gale McGee, Chairman

The Chairman is an ex-officio member of all subcommittees.

Democratic Majority (5 D). Senators McGee (Wyo.), Randolph (W. Va.), Burdick (N. Dak.), Hollings (S.C.), and Moss (Utah).

Republican Minority (4 R). Senators Fong (Hawaii), Boggs (Del.), Stevens (Alaska), and Bellmon (Okla.).

SUBCOMMITTEES

CIVIL SERVICE POLICIES AND PRACTICES

Jennings Randolph, Chairman

MAJORITY (3 D). Senators Randolph, Burdick, and Moss.
MINORITY (2 R). Senators Stevens and Boggs.

COMPENSATION AND EMPLOYMENT BENEFITS

Quentin N. Burdick, Chairman

MAJORITY (3 D). Senators Burdick, Hollings, and Moss.
MINORITY (2 R). Senators Boggs and Stevens.

POSTAL OPERATIONS

Ernest F. Hollings, Chairman

MAJORITY (3 D). Senators Hollings, Moss, and Randolph.
MINORITY (2 R). Senators Bellmon and Boggs.

Committee on Public Works

Jennings Randolph, Chairman

The Chairman is an ex-officio member of all subcommittees.

Democratic Majority (9 D). Senators Randolph (W. Va.), Muskie (Maine), Jordan (N.C.), Bayh (Ind.), Montoya (N. Mex.), Eagleton (Mo.), Gravel (Alaska), Tunney (Calif.), and Bentsen (Tex.).

Republican Minority (8 R). Senators Cooper (Ky.), Boggs (Del.), Baker (Tenn.), Dole (Kans.), Beall (Md.), Buckley (N.Y.), Weicker (Conn.), and Stafford (Vt.).

SUBCOMMITTEES

AIR AND WATER POLLUTION

Edmund S. Muskie, Chairman

MAJORITY (7 D). Senators Muskie, Randolph, Bayh, Montoya, Eagleton, Tunney, and Bentsen.
MINORITY (6 R). Senators Boggs, Cooper, Baker, Dole, Beall, and Buckley.

ECONOMIC DEVELOPMENT

Joseph M. Montoya, Chairman

MAJORITY (7 D). Senators Montoya, Randolph, Muskie, Eagleton, Gravel, Tunney, and Bentsen.
MINORITY (6 R). Senators Baker, Cooper, Dole, Beall, Buckley, and Stafford.

ENVIRONMENTAL SCIENCE AND TECHNOLOGY

Thomas F. Eagleton, Chairman

MAJORITY (3 D). Senators Eagleton, Tunney, and Bentsen.
MINORITY (2 R). Senators Baker and Buckley.

FLOOD CONTROLS, RIVERS AND HARBORS

B. Everett Jordan, Chairman

MAJORITY (5 D). Senators Jordan (N.C.), Bayh, Eagleton, Tunney, and Bentsen.
MINORITY (5 R). Senators Dole, Cooper, Beall, Weicker, and Stafford.

PUBLIC BUILDINGS AND GROUNDS

Mike Gravel, Chairman

MAJORITY (3 D). Senators Gravel, Jordan (N. C.), and Tunney.
MINORITY (2 R). Senators Weicker and Boggs.

ROADS

Birch Bayh, Chairman

MAJORITY (6 D). Senators Bayh, Randolph, Jordan (N.C.), Montoya, Gravel, and Muskie.
MINORITY (6 R). Senators Cooper, Boggs, Baker, Buckley, Weicker, and Stafford.

Committee on Rules and Administration

B. Everett Jordan, Chairman

Democratic Majority (5 D). Senators Jordan (N.C.), Cannon (Nev.), Pell (R.I.), Byrd (W. Va.), and Allen (Ala.).
Republican Minority (3 R). Senators Cooper (Ky.), Scott (Pa.), and Griffin (Mich.).

SUBCOMMITTEES

PRIVILEGES AND ELECTIONS

Howard W. Cannon, Chairman

MAJORITY (2 D). Senators Cannon and Byrd (W. Va.).
MINORITY (1 R). One vacancy.

STANDING RULES OF THE SENATE

Robert C. Byrd, Chairman

MAJORITY (2 D). Senators Byrd (W. Va.) and Cannon.
MINORITY (1 R). Senator Cooper.

COMPUTER SERVICES

B. Everett Jordan, Chairman

MAJORITY (2 D). Senators Jordan (N.C.) and Cannon.
MINORITY (1 R). One vacancy.

LIBRARY

B. Everett Jordan, Chairman

MAJORITY (2 D). Senators Jordan (N.C.) and Pell.
MINORITY (1 R). Senator Scott.

PRINTING

B. Everett Jordan, Chairman

MAJORITY (2 D). Senators Jordan (N.C.) and Allen.
MINORITY (1 R). Senator Griffin.

RESTAURANT

James B. Allen, Chairman

MAJORITY (2 D). Senators Allen and Byrd (W. Va.).
MINORITY (1 R). Senator Griffin.

SMITHSONIAN INSTITUTION

Claiborne Pell, Chairman

MAJORITY (2 D). Senators Jordan (N.C.) and Cannon.
MINORITY (1 R). Senator Cooper.

Committee on Veterans' Affairs

Vance Hartke, Chairman

Democratic Majority (5 D). Senators Hartke (Ind.), Talmadge (Ga.), Randolph (W. Va.), Hughes (Iowa), and Cranston (Calif.).
Republican Minority (5 R). Senators Thurmond (S.C.), Hansen (Wyo.), Cook (Ky.), Stevens (Alaska), and Stafford (Vt.).

SUBCOMMITTEES

HOUSING AND INSURANCE

Harold E. Hughes, Chairman

MAJORITY (3 D). Senators Hughes, Talmadge, and Cranston.
MINORITY (3 R). Senators Cook, Stevens, and Stafford.

READJUSTMENT EDUCATION AND EMPLOYMENT

Vance Hartke, Chairman

MAJORITY (3 D). Senators Hartke, Talmadge, and Cranston.
MINORITY (3 R). Senators Stevens, Cook, and Stafford.

HEALTH AND HOSPITALS

Alan Cranston, Chairman

MAJORITY (3 D). Senators Cranston, Randolph, and Hughes.
MINORITY (2 R). Senators Thurmond and Hansen.

COMPENSATION AND PENSION

Herman E. Talmadge, Chairman

MAJORITY (3 D). Senators Talmadge, Randolph, and Hughes.

MINORITY (2 R). Senators Hansen and Thurmond.

Special Committee on Aging

Frank Church, Chairman

Democratic Majority (10 D). Senators Church (Idaho), Williams (N.J.), Randolph (W. Va.), Muskie (Maine), Moss (Utah), Kennedy (Mass.), Mondale (Minn.), Hartke (Ind.), Pell (R.I.), and Eagleton (Mo.).

Republican Minority (9 R). Senators Fong (Hawaii), Miller (Iowa), Hansen (Wyo.), Fannin (Ariz.), Gurney (Fla.), Saxbe (Ohio), Brooke (Mass.), Percy (Ill.), and Stafford (Vt.).

Select Committee on Nutrition and Human Needs

George McGovern, Chairman

Democratic Majority (8 D). Senators McGovern (S. Dak.), Ellender (La.), Talmadge (Ga.), Hart (Mich.), Mondale (Minn.), Kennedy (Mass.), Nelson (Wis.), and Cranston (Calif.).

Republican Minority (6 R). Senators Percy (Ill.), Cook (Ky.), Dole (Kansas), Bellmon (Okla.), Schweiker (Pa.), and Taft (Ohio).

Select Committee on Small Business

Alan Bible, Chairman

Democratic Majority (9 D). Senators Bible (Nev.), Sparkman (Ala.), Long (La.), Williams (N.J.), Nelson (Wis.), Montoya (N. Mex.), Harris (Okla.), McIntyre (N.H.), and Gambrell (Ga.).

Republican Minority (8 R). Senators Javits (N.Y.), Dominick (Colo.), Hatfield (Oreg.), Dole (Kans.), Gurney (Fla.), Saxbe (Ohio), Beall (Md.), and Taft (Ohio).

Select Committee on Standards and Conduct

John Stennis, Chairman
Wallace Bennett, Vice Chairman

Democratic Majority (3 D). Senators Stennis (Miss.), Talmadge (Ga.), and one vacancy.

Republican Minority (3 R). Senators Bennett (Utah), Cooper (Ky.), and Jordan (Idaho).

Senate Democratic Policy Committee

Mike Mansfield, Chairman

Senators Mansfield (Mont.), Magnuson (Wash.), Pastore (R.I.), Symington (Mo.), Fulbright (Ark.), Hart (Mich.), and Talmadge (Ga.).

Ex-officio members. Senators Ellender (La.), Byrd (W. Va.), and Moss (Utah).

Legislative review committee members. Senators Muskie (Maine), Mansfield (Mont.), Inouye (Hawaii), Hollings (S.C.), and Hughes (Iowa).

Senate Republican Policy Committee

Gordon Allott, Chairman

Senators Allott (Colo.), Smith (Maine), Cotton (N.H.), Scott (Pa.), Griffin (Mich.), Bennett (Utah), Dominick (Colo.), Tower (Tex.), Hruska (Neb.), Boggs (Del.), Case (N.J.), Cooper (Ky.), Curtis (Neb.), Mundt (S. Dak.), and Thurmond (S.C.).

HOUSE COMMITTEES

Committee on Agriculture

W. R. Poage, Chairman

Democratic Majority (22 D). Congressmen Poage (Tex. 11), McMillan (S.C. 6), Abernethy (Miss. 1), Abbitt (Va. 4), Stubblefield (Ky. 1), Purcell (Tex. 13), Foley (Wash. 5), de la Garza (Tex. 15), Vigorito (Pa. 24), Jones (N.C. 1), Sisk (Calif. 16), Alexander (Ark. 1), Burlison (Mo. 10), Rarick (La. 6), Jones (Tenn. 8), Melcher (Mont. 2), Dow (N.Y. 27), Mathis (Ga. 2), Bergland (Minn. 7), Link (N. Dak. 2), Denholm (S. Dak. 1), and Matsunaga (Hawaii 1).

Republican Minority (14 R). Congressmen Blecher (Okla. 1), Teague (Calif. 13), Wampler (Va. 9), Goodling (Pa. 19), Miller (Ohio 10), Mathias (Calif. 18), Mayne (Iowa 6), Zwach (Minn. 6), Price (Texas 18), Sebelius (Kans. 1), Mizell (N.C. 5), Findley (Ill. 20), Kyl (Iowa 4), and Robinson (Va. 7).

SUBCOMMITTEES

COTTON

Thomas Abernethy, Chairman

MAJORITY (5 D). Congressmen Abernethy, de la Garza, Sisk, Burlison, and Jones (Tenn.).
MINORITY (3 R). Congressmen Mathias, Price, and Mizell.

DAIRY AND POULTRY

Frank Stubblefield, Chairman

MAJORITY (5 D). Congressmen Stubblefield, Vigorito, Jones (Tenn.), Dow, and Abbitt.
MINORITY (3 R). Congressmen Wampler, Miller (Ohio), and Zwach.

FORESTS

John McMillan, Chairman

MAJORITY (5 D). Congressmen McMillan, Foley, Burlison, Vigorito, and Dow.
MINORITY (3 R). Congressmen Teague (Calif.), Kyl, and Robinson.

LIVESTOCK AND GRAINS

Graham Purcell, Chairman

MAJORITY (10 D). Congressmen Purcell, Foley, Rarick, Abbitt, Jones (N.C.), Sisk, Melcher, Bergland, Link, and Denholm.
MINORITY (6 R). Congressmen Mayne, Zwach, Price (Tex.), Sebelius, Findley, and Kyl.

OILSEEDS AND RICE

Walter Jones, Chairman

MAJORITY (5 D). Congressmen Jones (N.C.), Rarick, Alexander, Burlison, and Mathis.
MINORITY (3 R). Congressmen Wampler, Mizell, and Findley.

TOBACCO

Watkins Abbitt, Chairman

MAJORITY (5 D). Congressmen Abbitt, McMillan, Stubblefield, Jones (N.C.), and Mathis.
MINORITY (3 R). Congressmen Wampler, Miller (Ohio), and Mizell.

CONSERVATION AND CREDIT

W. R. Poage, Chairman

MAJORITY (5 D). Congressmen Poage, Stubblefield, de la Garza, Alexander, and Bergland.
MINORITY (3 R). Congressmen Teague (Calif.), Goodling, and Mayne.

DOMESTIC MARKETING AND CONSUMER RELATIONS

Thomas S. Foley, Chairman

MAJORITY (5 D). Congressmen Foley, Sisk, Denholm, Link, and Matsunaga.
MINORITY (3 R). Congressmen Goodling, Zwach, and Robinson.

DEPARTMENT OPERATIONS

Eligio de la Garza, Chairman

MAJORITY (5 D). Congressmen de la Garza, Abernethy, Purcell, Jones (Tenn.), and Matsunaga.
MINORITY (3 R). Congressmen Mathias, Sebelius, and Mayne.

FAMILY FARMS AND RURAL DEVELOPMENT

Joseph P. Vigorito, Chairman

MAJORITY (5 D). Congressmen Vigorito, Purcell, Melcher, Mathis, and Dow.
MINORITY (3 R). Congressmen Goodling, Miller (Ohio), and Kyl.

Committee on Appropriations

George Mahon, Chairman

The Chairman is an ex-officio member of all subcommittees.

Democratic Majority (33 D). Congressmen Mahon (Tex. 19), Whitten (Miss. 2), Andrews (Ala. 3), Rooney (N.Y. 14), Sikes (Fla. 1), Passman (La. 5), Evine (Tenn. 4), Boland (Mass. 2), Natcher (Ky. 2), Flood (Pa. 11), Steed (Okla. 4), Shipley (Ill. 23), Slack (W. Va. 3), Flynt (Ga. 6), Smith (Iowa 5), Giaimo (Conn. 3), Hansen (Wash. 3), Addabbo (N.Y. 7), McFall (Calif. 15), Hull (Mo. 6), Patten (N.J. 15), Long (Md. 2), Yates (Ill. 9), Casey (Tex. 22), Pryor (Ark. 4), Evans (Colo. 3), Obey (Wis. 7), Roybal (Calif. 30), Hathaway (Maine 2), Galifianakis (N.C. 4), Stokes (Ohio 21), Roush (Ind. 4), and McKay (Utah 1).

Republican Minority (22 R). Congressmen Bow (Ohio 16), Jonas (N.C. 9), Cederberg (Mich. 10), Rhodes (Ariz. 1), Minshall (Ohio 23), Michel (Ill. 18), Conte (Mass. 1), Davis (Wis. 9), Robison (N.Y. 33), Shriver (Kans. 4), McDade (Pa. 10), Andrews (N. Dak. 1), Wyman (N.H. 1), Talcott (Calif. 12), Reid (Ill. 15), Riegle (Mich. 7), Wyatt (Oreg. 1), Edwards (Ala. 1), Clawson (Calif. 23), Scherle (Iowa 7), McEwen (N.Y. 31), and Myers (Ind. 7).

SUBCOMMITTEES

AGRICULTURE, ENVIRONMENTAL AND CONSUMER PROTECTION

Jamie L. Whitten, Chairman

MAJORITY (5 D). Congressmen Whitten, Natcher, Hull, Shipley, and Evans (Colo.).
MINORITY (3 R). Congressmen Andrews (N. Dak.), Michel, and Scherle.

DEFENSE

George H. Mahon, Chairman

MAJORITY (7 D). Congressmen Mahon, Sikes, Whitten, Andrews (Ala.), Flood, Addabbo, and McFall.
MINORITY (4 R). Congressmen Minshall, Rhodes, Davis (Wis.), and Wyman.

DISTRICT OF COLUMBIA

William H. Natcher, Chairman

MAJORITY (6 D). Congressmen Natcher, Giaimo, Pryor, Obey, Stokes, and McKay.
MINORITY (4 R). Congressmen Davis (Wis.), Scherle, McEwen, and Myers.

FOREIGN OPERATIONS

Otto E. Passman, Chairman

MAJORITY (6 D). Congressmen Passman, Rooney (N.Y.), Long (Md.), Roybal, Hathaway, and Galifianakis.
MINORITY (4 R). Congressmen Shriver, Reid (Ill.), Riegle, and McEwen.

HUD, SPACE, AND SCIENCE

Edward P. Boland, Chairman

MAJORITY (6 D). Congressmen Boland, Evins (Tenn.), Shipley, Giaimo, Pryor (Ark.), and Roush.
MINORITY (4 R). Congressmen Jonas, Talcott, McDade, and Clawson.

INTERIOR AND RELATED AGENCIES

Julia Butler Hansen, Chairman

MAJORITY (5 D). Congressmen Hansen (Wash.), Flynt, Obey, Yates, and Galifianakis.
MINORITY (3 R). Congressmen McDade, Wyatt, and Clawson.

LABOR, HEALTH, EDUCATION AND WELFARE

Daniel J. Flood, Chairman

MAJORITY (6 D). Congressmen Flood, Natcher, Smith (Iowa), Hull, Casey, and Patten.
MINORITY (4 R). Congressmen Michel, Shriver, Reid (Ill.), and Conte.

LEGISLATIVE

George W. Andrews, Chairman

MAJORITY (5 D). Congressmen Andrews (Ala.), Casey, Evans (Colo.), Hathaway, and Roush.
MINORITY (4 R). Congressmen Bow, Cederberg, Rhodes, and Wyatt.

MILITARY CONSTRUCTION

Robert L. F. Sikes, Chairman

MAJORITY (5 D). Congressmen Sikes, Patten, Long (Md.), Hansen (Wash.), and McKay.
MINORITY (3 R). Congressmen Cederberg, Jonas, and Talcott.

PUBLIC WORKS

Joe L. Evins, Chairman

MAJORITY (5 D). Congressmen Evins (Tenn.), Boland, Whitten, Andrews (Ala.), and Slack.
MINORITY (3 R). Congressmen Rhodes, Davis (Wis.), and Robison.

STATE, JUSTICE, COMMERCE, AND THE JUDICIARY

John J. Rooney, Chairman

MAJORITY (5 D). Congressmen Rooney (N.Y.), Sikes, Slack, Smith (Iowa), and Flynt.
MINORITY (3 R). Congressmen Bow, Cederberg, and Andrews (N. Dak.).

TRANSPORTATION

John J. McFall, Chairman

MAJORITY (4 D). Congressmen McFall, Boland, Yates, and Steed.
MINORITY (3 R). Congressmen Conte, Minshall, and Edwards (Ala.).

TREASURY, POST OFFICE AND GENERAL GOVERNMENT

Tom Steed, Chairman

MAJORITY (5 D). Congressmen Steed, Passman, Addabbo, Roybal, and Stokes.
MINORITY (4 R). Congressmen Robison, Edwards (Ala.), Riegle, and Myers.

Committee on Armed Services

F. Edward Hébert, Chairman

The Chairman and Ranking Minority Member are ex-officio members of all subcommittees.

Democratic Majority (25 D). Congressmen Hébert (La. 1), Price (Ill. 24), Fisher (Tex. 21), Bennett (Fla. 3), Byrne (Pa. 3), Stratton (N.Y. 29), Pike (N.Y. 1), Ichord (Mo. 8), Nedzi (Mich. 14), Lennon (N.C. 7), Randall (Mo. 4), Hagan (Ga. 1), Wilson (Calif. 31), Leggett (Calif. 4), Hicks (Wash. 6), Long (La. 8), White (Tex. 16), Nichols (Ala. 4), Brinkley (Ga. 3), Mollohan (W. Va. 1), Daniel (Va. 5), Montgomery (Miss. 4), Harrington (Mass. 6), Runnels (N. Mex. 2), and Aspin (Wis. 1).

Republican Minority (16 R). Congressmen Arends (Ill. 17), O'Konski (Wis. 10), Bray (Ind. 6), Wilson (Calif. 36), Gubser (Calif. 10), Pirnie (N.Y. 32), Hall (Mo. 7), Clancy (Ohio 2), King (N.Y. 30), Dickinson (Ala. 2), Whalen (Ohio 3), Hunt (N.J. 1), Whitehurst (Va. 2), Spence (S.C. 2), Young (Fla. 8), and one vacancy.

SUBCOMMITTEES

SUBCOMMITTEE NO. 1

Melvin Price, Chairman

MAJORITY (6 D). Congressmen Price (Ill.), Pike, Ichord, Leggett, Hicks, and Montgomery.
MINORITY (3 R). Congressmen O'Konski, Hall, and Whalen.

SUBCOMMITTEE NO. 2

O. C. Fisher, Chairman

MAJORITY (7 D). Congressmen Fisher, Nedzi, Lennon, Hagan, Long, Daniel, and Runnels.
MINORITY (4 R). Congressmen Bray, Pirnie, Clancy, and Young (Fla.).

SUBCOMMITTEE NO. 3

Charles E. Bennett, Chairman

MAJORITY (6 D). Congressmen Bennett, Stratton, Randall, White, Mollohan, and Harrington.
MINORITY (4 R). Congressmen Bob Wilson, King, Dickinson, and Spence.

SUBCOMMITTEE NO. 4

James A. Byrne, Chairman

MAJORITY (5 D). Congressmen Byrne, Charles Wilson, Nichols, Brinkley, and Aspin.
MINORITY (3 R). Congressmen Gubser, Hunt, and Whitehurst.

SPECIAL SUBCOMMITTEE ON ARMED SERVICES INVESTIGATING

F. Edward Hébert, Chairman

MAJORITY (7 D). Congressmen Hébert, Stratton, Pike, Lennon, Randall, Mollohan, and Daniel.
MINORITY (6 R). Congressmen Arends, Gubser, Pirnie, Hall, Dickinson, and Hunt.

SPECIAL SUBCOMMITTEE ON REAL ESTATE

Charles E. Bennett, Chairman

MAJORITY (4 D). Congressmen Bennett, Byrne, Stratton, and Daniel.
MINORITY (3 R). Congressmen Bray, King, and Whitehurst.

Committee on Banking and Currency

Wright Patman, Chairman

The Chairman and Ranking Minority Member are ex-officio members of all subcommittees.

Democratic Majority (22 D). Congressmen Patman (Tex. 1), Barrett (Pa. 1), Sullivan (Mo. 3), Reuss (Wis. 5), Ashley (Ohio 9), Moorhead (Pa. 14), Stephens (Ga. 10), St Germain (R.I. 1), Gonzalez (Tex. 20), Minish (N.J. 11), Hanna (Calif. 34), Gettys (S.C. 5), Annunzio (Ill. 7), Rees (Calif. 26), Bevill (Ala. 7), Griffin (Miss. 3), Hanley (N.Y. 35), Brasco (N.Y. 11), Chappell (Fla. 4), Koch (N.Y. 17), Cotter (Conn. 1), and Mitchell (Md. 7).

Republican Minority (15 R). Congressmen Widnall (N.J. 7), Dwyer (N.J. 12), Johnson (Pa. 23), Stanton (Ohio 11), Blackburn (Ga. 4), Brown (Mich. 3), Williams (Pa. 7), Wylie (Ohio 15), Heckler (Mass. 10), Crane (Ill. 13), Rousselot (Calif. 24), McKinney (Conn. 4), Lent (N.Y. 5), Archer (Tex. 7), and Frenzel (Minn. 3).

SUBCOMMITTEES

BANK SUPERVISION AND INSURANCE

Fernand J. St Germain, Chairman

MAJORITY (9 D). Congressmen St Germain, Moorhead, Annunzio, Bevill, Griffin, Brasco, Chappell, Koch, and Cotter.
MINORITY (6 R). Congressmen Johnson (Pa.), Wylie, Crane, Rousselot, Archer, and Lent.

CONSUMER AFFAIRS

Leonor K. Sullivan, Chairman

MAJORITY (9 D). Congressmen Sullivan, Stephens, Gonzalez, Minish, Hanna, Annunzio, Hanley, Chappell, and Koch.

MINORITY (6 R). Congressmen Dwyer, Wylie, Williams (Pa.), Heckler, Archer, and McKinney.

DOMESTIC FINANCE

Wright Patman, Chairman

MAJORITY (9 D). Congressmen Patman, Minish, Hanna, Gettys, Annunzio, Rees, Hanley, Brasco, and Mitchell.
MINORITY (6 R). Congressmen Widnall, Blackburn, Crane, Brown (Mich.), Williams, and Frenzel.

HOUSING

William A. Barrett, Chairman

MAJORITY (9 D). Congressmen Barrett, Sullivan, Ashley, Moorhead, Stephens, St Germain, Gonzalez, Reuss, and Minish.
MINORITY (6 R). Congressmen Widnall, Dwyer, Brown (Mich.), J. W. Stanton, Blackburn, and Heckler.

INTERNATIONAL FINANCE

Henry B. Gonzalez, Chairman

MAJORITY (9 D). Congressmen Gonzalez, Reuss, Ashley, Moorhead, Hanna, Rees, Hanley, Brasco, and Cotter.
MINORITY (6 R). Congressmen Johnson (Pa.), Stanton, Crane, Frenzel, Lent, and Archer.

INTERNATIONAL TRADE

Thomas L. Ashley, Chairman

MAJORITY (9 D). Congressmen Ashley, St Germain, Gettys, Rees, Bevill, Griffin, Hanna, Koch, and Mitchell.
MINORITY (6 R). Congressmen Blackburn, Brown (Mich.), Johnson (Pa.), Rousselot, McKinney, and Lent.

SMALL BUSINESS

Robert G. Stephens, Jr., Chairman

MAJORITY (9 D). Congressmen Stephens, Barrett, Sullivan, Gettys, Bevill, Griffin, Chappell, Cotter, and Mitchell.
MINORITY (6 R). Congressmen J. W. Stanton, Williams, Wylie, Heckler, Rousselot, and McKinney.

Committee on District of Columbia

John McMillan, Chairman

The Chairman and Ranking Minority Member are ex-officio members of all subcommittees.

Democratic Majority (15 D). Congressmen McMillan (S.C. 6), Abernethy (Miss. 1), Dowdy (Tex. 2), Diggs (Mich. 13), Hagan (Ga. 1), Fraser (Minn. 5), Jacobs (Ind. 11), Hungate (Mo. 9), Cabell (Tex. 5), Blanton (Tenn. 7), Stuckey (Ga. 8), Mikva (Ill. 2), Link (N. Dak. 2), Dellums (Calif. 7), and one vacancy.

Republican Minority (10 R). Congressmen Nelsen (Minn. 2), Springer (Ill. 22), O'Konski (Wis. 10), Harsha (Ohio 6), Broyhill (Va. 10), Gude (Md. 8), Thomson (Wis. 3), Smith III (N.Y. 40), Landgrebe (Ind. 2), and McKinney (Conn. 4).

SUBCOMMITTEES

BUSINESS, COMMERCE AND FISCAL AFFAIRS

Earle Cabell, Chairman

MAJORITY (7 D). Congressmen Cabell, Abernethy, Dowdy, Fraser, Blanton, Mikva, and Link.
MINORITY (5 R). Congressmen O'Konski, Harsha, Broyhill (Va.), Gude, and Thomson.

EDUCATION

John Dowdy, Chairman

MAJORITY (6 D). Congressmen Dowdy, Fraser, Hagan, Jacobs, Hungate, and Blanton.
MINORITY (5 R). Congressmen Springer, O'Konski, Gude, Smith (N.Y.), and McKinney.

THE JUDICIARY

William L. Hungate, Chairman

MAJORITY (6 D). Congressmen Hungate, Abernethy, Jacobs, Stuckey, Mikva, and Link.
MINORITY (5 R). Congressmen Harsha, Broyhill (Va.), Thomson, Smith (N.Y.), and Landgrebe.

HOUSING AND YOUTH AFFAIRS

W. S. Stuckey, Chairman

MAJORITY (6 D). Congressmen Stuckey, Diggs, Cabell, Jacobs, Mikva, and Dellums.
MINORITY (5 R). Congressmen Broyhill (Va.), Thomson, Smith (N.Y.), Landgrebe, and McKinney.

PUBLIC HEALTH AND WELFARE

G. Elliott Hagan, Chairman

MAJORITY (5 D). Congressmen Hagan, Cabell, Blanton, Stuckey, and Dellums.
MINORITY (5 R). Congressmen Broyhill (Va.), Gude, Smith (N.Y.), Landgrebe, and McKinney.

Committee on Education and Labor

Carl Perkins, Chairman

The Chairman and Ranking Minority Member are ex-officio members of all subcommittees.

Democratic Majority (22 D). Congressmen Perkins (Ky. 7), Green (Oreg. 3), Thompson (N.J. 4), Dent (Pa. 21), Pucinski (Ill. 11), Daniels (N.J. 14), Brademas (Ind. 3), O'Hara (Mich. 12), Hawkins (Calif. 21), Ford (Mich. 15), Mink (Hawaii 2), Scheuer (N.Y. 22), Meeds (Wash. 2), Burton (Calif. 5), Gaydos (Pa. 20), Clay (Mo. 1), Chisholm (N.Y. 12), Biaggi (N.Y. 24), Grasso (Conn. 6), Hicks (Mass. 9), Mazzoli (Ky. 3), and Badillo (N.Y. 21).

Republican Minority (16 R). Congressmen Quie (Minn. 1), Ashbrook (Ohio 17), Bell (Calif. 28), Reid (N.Y. 26), Erlenborn (Ill. 14), Dellenback (Oreg. 4), Esch (Mich. 2), Eshleman (Pa. 16), Steiger (Wis. 6), Landgrebe (Ind. 2), Hansen (Idaho 2), Ruth (N.C. 8), Forsythe (N.J. 6), Veysey (Calif. 38), Kemp (N.Y. 39), and Peyser (N.Y. 25).

SUBCOMMITTEES

AGRICULTURAL LABOR

James G. O'Hara, Chairman

MAJORITY (5 D). Congressmen O'Hara, Chisholm, Grasso, Badillo, and Thompson.
MINORITY (3 R). Congressmen Eshleman, Ashbrook, and Veysey.

SPECIAL SUBCOMMITTEE ON EDUCATION

Edith Green, Chairman

MAJORITY (8 D). Congressmen Green (Oreg.), Burton, Scheuer, Brademas, Daniels, Pucinski, Dent, and Thompson.
MINORITY (5 R). Congressmen Dellenback, Erlenborn, Esch, Steiger (Wis.), and Ruth.

SPECIAL SUBCOMMITTEE ON LABOR

Frank Thompson, Jr., Chairman

MAJORITY (5 D). Congressmen Thompson, Clay, Hicks (Mass.), Badillo, and O'Hara.
MINORITY (3 R). Congressmen Ashbrook, Reid (N.Y.), and Dellenback.

GENERAL SUBCOMMITTEE ON EDUCATION

Roman C. Pucinski, Chairman

MAJORITY (11 D). Congressmen Pucinski, Ford (Mich.), Meeds, Hawkins, Mink, Chisholm, Biaggi, Hicks (Mass.), Mazzoli, Badillo, and Green (Oreg.).
MINORITY (7 R). Congressmen Bell, Ashbrook, Ruth, Forsythe, Veysey, Kemp, and Peyser.

GENERAL SUBCOMMITTEE ON LABOR

John H. Dent, Chairman

MAJORITY (11 D). Congressmen Dent, Hawkins, Mink, Burton, Clay, Gaydos, Ford (Mich.), Biaggi, Mazzoli, Pucinski, and Brademas.
MINORITY (7 R). Congressmen Erlenborn, Bell, Esch, Landgrebe, Hansen, Steiger (Wis.), and Kemp.

SELECT SUBCOMMITTEE ON EDUCATION

John Brademas, Chairman

MAJORITY (11 D). Congressmen Brademas, Mink, Meeds, Scheuer, Gaydos, Clay, Chisholm, Grasso, Mazzoli, O'Hara, and Dent.
MINORITY (7 R). Congressmen Reid (N.Y.), Bell, Landgrebe, Hansen (Idaho), Eshleman, Kemp, and Peyser.

SELECT SUBCOMMITTEE ON LABOR

Dominick V. Daniels, Chairman

MAJORITY (11 D). Congressmen Daniels, Meeds, Ford (Mich.), Burton, Hawkins, Gaydos, Scheuer, Biaggi, Grasso, Hicks (Mass.), and Green (Oreg.).
MINORITY (7 R). Congressmen Esch, Steiger (Wis.), Eshleman, Ruth, Forsythe, Veysey, and Peyser.

Committee on Foreign Affairs

Thomas Morgan, Chairman

The Chairman and Ranking Minority Member are ex-officio members of all subcommittees.

Democratic Majority (21 D). Congressmen Morgan (Pa. 26), Zablocki (Wis. 4), Hays (Ohio 18), Fountain (N.C. 2), Fascell (Fla. 12), Diggs (Mich. 13), Gallagher (N.J. 13), Nix (Pa. 2), Monagan (Conn. 5), Fraser (Minn. 5), Rosenthal (N.Y. 8), Culver (Iowa 2), Hamilton (Ind. 9), Kazen (Tex. 23), Wolff (N.Y. 3), Bingham (N.Y. 23), Yatron (Pa. 6), Taylor (N.C. 11), Davis (Ga. 7), Murphy (Ill. 3), and Dellums (Calif. 7).

Republican Minority (17 R). Congressmen Mailliard (Calif. 6), Frelinghuysen (N.J. 5), Broomfield (Mich. 18), Whalley (Pa. 12), Gross (Iowa 3), Derwinski (Ill. 4), Morse (Mass. 5), Thomson (Wis. 3), Fulton (Pa. 27), Findley (Ill. 20), Buchanan (Ala. 6), Lloyd (Utah 2), Burke (Fla. 10), Halpern (N.Y. 6), Vander Jagt (Mich. 9), Steele (Conn. 2), and du Pont IV (Del. AL).

SUBCOMMITTEES

AFRICA

Charles C. Diggs, Chairman

MAJORITY (5 D). Congressmen Diggs, Nix, Culver, Yatron, and Dellums.
MINORITY (4 R). Congressmen Whalley, Broomfield, Derwinski, and Vander Jagt.

ASIAN AND PACIFIC AFFAIRS

Cornelius E. Gallagher, Chairman

MAJORITY (7 D). Congressmen Gallagher, Hamilton, Diggs, Wolff, Kazen, Davis (Ga.), and Murphy (Ill.).
MINORITY (6 R). Congressmen Broomfield, Whalley, Thomson, Burke (Fla.), Halpern and du Pont.

EUROPE

Benjamin S. Rosenthal, Chairman

MAJORITY (8 D). Congressmen Rosenthal, Hays, Gallagher, Monagan, Hamilton, Yatron, Taylor, and Murphy (Ill.).
MINORITY (7 R). Congressmen Frelinghuysen, Fulton, Findley, Burke (Fla.), Buchanan, Lloyd, and Vander Jagt.

FOREIGN ECONOMIC POLICY

John C. Culver, Chairman

MAJORITY (7 D). Congressmen Culver, Nix, Zablocki, Yatron, Wolff, Fraser, and Davis (Ga.).
MINORITY (4 R). Congressmen Derwinski, Burke (Fla.), Steele, and du Pont.

INTER-AMERICAN AFFAIRS

Dante B. Fascell, Chairman

MAJORITY (7 D). Congressmen Fascell, Monagan, Kazen, Rosenthal, Culver, Taylor, and Dellums.
MINORITY (5 R). Congressmen Morse, Whalley, Gross, Frelinghuysen, and Steele.

INTERNATIONAL ORGANIZATIONS AND MOVEMENTS
Donald M. Fraser, Chairman

MAJORITY (8 D). Congressmen Fraser, Fascell, Gallagher, Fountain, Rosenthal, Kazen, Bingham, and Dellums.
MINORITY (5 R). Congressmen Gross, Frelinghuysen, Derwinski, Findley, and Halpern.

NATIONAL SECURITY POLICY AND SCIENTIFIC DEVELOPMENTS
Clement J. Zablocki, Chairman

MAJORITY (7 D). Congressmen Zablocki, Hays, Nix, Fountain, Fraser, Bingham, and Davis (Ga).
MINORITY (5 R). Congressmen Findley, Broomfield, Thomson (Wis.), Fulton, and Morse.

NEAR EAST
Lee H. Hamilton, Chairman

MAJORITY (6 D), Congressmen Hamilton, Fountain, Monagan, Wolff, Bingham, and Taylor.
MINORITY (5 R). Congressmen Fulton (Pa.), Gross, Buchanan, Lloyd, and Halpern.

STATE DEPARTMENT ORGANIZATION AND FOREIGN OPERATIONS
Wayne L. Hays, Chairman

MAJORITY (7 D). Congressmen Hays, Zablocki, Fraser, Fascell, Kazen, Culver, and Murphy (Ill.).
MINORITY (5 R). Congressmen Thomson, Morse, Lloyd, Buchanan, and Vander Jagt.

SPECIAL SUBCOMMITTEE FOR REVIEW OF THE FOREIGN AID PROGRAMS
Thomas E. Morgan, Chairman

MAJORITY (5 D). Congressmen Morgan, Zablocki, Hays, Fountain, and Fascell.
MINORITY (4 R). Congressmen Mailliard, Frelinghuysen, Broomfield, and Whalley.

Committee on Government Operations
Chet Holifield, Chairman

The Chairman and Ranking Minority Member are ex-officio members of all subcommittees.

Democratic Majority (23 D). Congressmen Holifield (Calif. 19), Brooks (Tex. 9), Fountain (N.C. 2), Jones (Ala. 8), Garmatz (Md. 3), Moss (Calif. 3), Fascell (Fla. 12), Reuss (Wis. 5), Monagan (Conn. 5), Macdonald (Mass. 7), Moorhead (Pa. 14), Gallagher (N.J. 13), Randall (Mo. 4), Rosenthal (N.Y. 8), Wright (Tex. 12), St Germain (R.I. 1), Culver (Iowa 2), Hicks (Wash. 6), Collins (Ill. 6), Fuqua (Fla. 2), Conyers (Mich. 1), Alexander (Ark. 1), and Abzug (N.Y. 19).

Republican Minority (16 R). Congressmen Dwyer (N.J. 12), Reid (N.Y. 26), Horton (N.Y. 36), Erlenborn (Ill. 14), Wydler (N.Y. 4), Brown (Ohio 7), Vander Jagt (Mich. 9), Gude (Md. 8), McCloskey (Calif. 11), Buchanan (Ala. 6), Steiger (Ariz. 3), Brown (Mich. 3), Goldwater (Calif. 27), Robinson (Va. 7), Powell (Ohio 24), and Thone (Neb. 1).

SUBCOMMITTEES

CONSERVATION AND NATURAL RESOURCES

Henry Reuss, Chairman

MAJORITY (6 D). Congressmen Reuss, Moss, Fascell, Hicks (Wash.), Conyers, and Abzug.
MINORITY (4 R). Congressmen Vander Jagt, Gude, McCloskey, and Steiger (Ariz.).

FOREIGN OPERATIONS AND GOVERNMENT INFORMATION

William S. Moorhead, Chairman

MAJORITY (6 D). Congressmen Moorhead, Moss, Macdonald, Wright, Conyers, and Alexander.
MINORITY (4 R). Congressmen Reid (N.Y.), Horton, Erlenborn, and McCloskey.

GOVERNMENT ACTIVITIES

Jack Brooks, Chairman

MAJORITY (6 D). Congressmen Brooks, Jones (Ala.), Macdonald, Culver, Hicks (Wash.), and Monagan.
MINORITY (4 R). Congressmen Reid (N.Y.), Buchanan, Gude, and Goldwater.

INTERGOVERNMENTAL RELATIONS

L. H. Fountain, Chairman

MAJORITY (6 D). Congressmen Fountain, Jones (Ala.), Rosenthal, Culver, Fuqua, and Alexander.
MINORITY (5 R). Congressmen Dwyer, Brown (Ohio), Vander Jagt, Buchanan, and Robinson.

LEGAL AND MONETARY AFFAIRS

John S. Monagan, Chairman

MAJORITY (6 D). Congressmen Monagan, Fascell, Gallagher, St Germain, Collins, (Ill.), and Randall.
MINORITY (4 R). Congressmen Steiger (Ariz.), Brown (Ohio), Powell, and Thone.

LEGISLATION AND MILITARY OPERATIONS

Chet Holifield, Chairman

MAJORITY (7 D). Congressmen Holifield, Garmatz, Rosenthal, Wright, St Germain, Fuqua, and Moorhead.
MINORITY (4 R). Congressmen Horton, Erlenborn, Wydler, and Brown (Ohio).

SPECIAL STUDIES

William J. Randall, Chairman

MAJORITY (6 D). Congressmen Randall, Garmatz, Gallagher, Collins (Ill.), Abzug, and Reuss.
MINORITY (4 R). Congressmen Wydler, Brown (Ohio), Goldwater, and Robinson.

Committee on House Administration

Wayne Hays, Chairman

Democratic Majority (15 D). Congressmen Hays (Ohio 18), Thompson (N.J. 4), Abbitt (Va. 4), Dent (Pa. 21), Nedzi (Mich. 14), Brademas (Ind. 3), Gray (Ill. 21), Hawkins (Calif. 21), Gettys (S.C. 5), Bingham (N.Y. 23), Podell (N.Y. 13), Annunzio (Ill. 7), Gaydos (Pa. 20), Jones (Tenn. 8), and Mollohan (W. Va. 1).

Republican Minority (10 R). Congressmen Devine (Ohio 12), Dickinson (Ala. 2), Cleveland (N.H. 2), Schwengel (Iowa 1), Harvey (Mich. 8), Hansen (Idaho 2), Crane (Ill. 13), Ware (Pa. 9), Veysey (Calif. 38), and Frenzel (Minn. 3).

SUBCOMMITTEES

ACCOUNTS

Frank Thompson, Jr., Chairman

MAJORITY (6 D). Congressmen Thompson, Dent, Hawkins, Gettys, Podell, and Annunzio.

MINORITY (3 R). Congressmen Dickinson, Cleveland, and Crane.

ELECTIONS

Watkins M. Abbitt, Chairman

MAJORITY (5 D). Congressmen Abbitt, Gray, Dent, Jones (Tenn.), and Mollohan.

MINORITY (3 R). Congressmen Harvey, Ware, and Frenzel.

LIBRARY AND MEMORIALS

Lucien N. Nedzi, Chairman

MAJORITY (6 D). Congressmen Nedzi, Gray, Brademas, Bingham, Gaydos, and Thompson (N.J.).

MINORITY (3 R). Congressmen Schwengel, Harvey, and Frenzel.

PRINTING

John Brademas, Chairman

MAJORITY (5 D). Congressmen Brademas, Gettys, Bingham, Gaydos, and Jones (Tenn.).

MINORITY (3 R). Congressmen Cleveland, Hansen (Idaho), and Veysey.

SPECIAL SUBCOMMITTEE ON CONTRACTS

Augustus F. Hawkins, Chairman

MAJORITY (2 D). Congressmen Hawkins and Abbitt.

MINORITY (1 R). Congressman Cleveland.

SPECIAL SUBCOMMITTEE ON ELECTRICAL AND MECHANICAL OFFICE EQUIPMENT

John H. Dent, Chairman

MAJORITY (7 D). Congressmen Dent, Nedzi, Podell, Brademas, Gray, Gaydos, and Mollohan.

MINORITY (4 R). Congressmen Schwengel, Harvey, Dickinson, and Crane.

SPECIAL SUBCOMMITTEE ON POLICE

Kenneth J. Gray, Chairman

MAJORITY (5 D). Congressmen Gray, Hawkins, Gettys, Annunzio, and Gaydos.
MINORITY (3 R). Congressmen Dickinson, Ware, and Veysey.

Committee on Interior and Insular Affairs

Wayne Aspinall, Chairman

The Chairman and Ranking Minority Member are ex-officio members of all subcommittees.

Democratic Majority (23 D). Congressmen Aspinall (Colo. 4), Haley (Fla. 7), Edmondson (Okla. 2), Baring (Nev. AL), Taylor (N.C. 11), Johnson (Calif. 2), Udall (Ariz. 2), Burton (Calif. 5), Foley (Wash. 5), Kastenmeier (Wis. 2), O'Hara (Mich. 12), Ryan (N.Y. 20), Mink (Hawaii 2), Kee (W. Va. 5), Meeds (Wash. 2), Kazen (Tex. 23), Burlison (Mo. 10), Stephens (Ga. 10), Vigorito (Pa. 24), Melcher (Mont. 2), Roncalio (Wyo. AL), Begich (Alaska AL), and Abourezk (S. Dak. 2).

Republican Minority (15 R). Congressmen Saylor (Pa. 22), Hosmer (Calif. 32), Skubitz (Kans. 5), Kyl (Iowa 4), Steiger (Ariz. 3), McClure (Idaho 1), Clausen (Calif. 1), Ruppe (Mich. 11), Camp (Okla. 6), Lujan (N. Mex. 1), Lloyd (Utah 2), Dellenback (Oreg. 4), Sebelius (Kans. 1), McKevitt (Colo. 1), and Terry (N.Y. 34). Cordova, Resident Commissioner from Puerto Rico, is a non-voting Republican member of the committee.

SUBCOMMITTEES

ENVIRONMENT

Wayne N. Aspinall, Chairman

MAJORITY (15 D). Congressmen Aspinall, Haley, Edmondson, Baring, Taylor, Johnson (Calif.), Udall, Kastenmeier, O'Hara, Ryan, Kee, Burlison, Vigorito, Roncalio, and Melcher.
MINORITY (9 R). Congressmen Saylor, Hosmer, Kyl, Steiger (Ariz.), McClure, Lloyd, Dellenback, Sebelius, and Terry.

INDIAN AFFAIRS

James A. Haley, Chairman

MAJORITY (9 D). Congressmen Haley, Edmondson, Taylor, Mink, Meeds, Stephens, Melcher, Begich, and Abourezk.
MINORITY (6 R). Congressmen Steiger (Ariz.), Kyl, Camp, Lujan, Sebelius, and Terry.

IRRIGATION AND RECLAMATION

Harold T. Johnson, Chairman

MAJORITY (11 D). Congressmen Johnson (Calif.), Haley, Edmondson, Baring, Udall, Foley, Meeds, Kazen, Stephens, Roncalio, and Abourezk.
MINORITY (7 R). Congressmen Hosmer, McClure, Clausen, Camp, Lujan, Dellenback, and McKevitt.

MINES AND MINING

Ed Edmondson, Chairman

MAJORITY (10 D). Congressmen Edmondson, Baring, Burton, Foley, Kastenmeier, Kee, Kazen, Burlison, Vigorito, and Melcher.

MINORITY (7 R). Congressmen McClure, Hosmer, Skubitz, Steiger (Ariz.), Camp, McKevitt, and Cordova.

NATIONAL PARKS AND RECREATION

Roy A. Taylor, Chairman

MAJORITY (15 D). Congressmen Taylor, Johnson (Calif.), Udall, Kastenmeier, O'Hara, Ryan, Mink, Meeds, Kazen, Burlison, Stephens, Melcher, Roncalio, Begich, and Abourezk.

MINORITY (10 R). Congressmen Skubitz, Kyl, McClure, Clausen, Ruppe, Lloyd, Sebelius, McKevitt, Terry, and Cordova.

PUBLIC LANDS

Walter S. Baring, Chairman

MAJORITY (12 D). Congressmen Baring, Edmondson, Johnson (Calif.), Udall, Burton, Kastenmeier, O'Hara, Kee, Melcher, Roncalio, Begich, and Abourezk.

MINORITY (8 R). Congressmen Kyl, Steiger (Ariz.), Clausen, Ruppe, Camp, Lujan, Lloyd, and Dellenback.

TERRITORIAL AND INSULAR AFFAIRS

Phillip Burton, Chairman

MAJORITY (12 D). Congressmen Burton, Haley, Taylor, Foley, Ryan, Mink, Meeds, Burlison, Stephens, Vigorito, Roncalio, and Begich.

MINORITY (8 R). Congressmen Clausen, Hosmer, Skubitz, Ruppe, Lujan, Sebelius, McKevitt, and Cordova.

Committee on Internal Security

Richard Ichord, Chairman

Democratic Majority (5 D). Congressmen Ichord (Mo. 8), Pepper (Fla. 11), Edwards (La. 7), Preyer (N.C. 6), and Drinan (Mass. 3).

Republican Minority (4 R). Congressmen Ashbrook (Ohio 17), Zion (Ind. 8), Thompson (Ga. 5), and Schmitz (Calif. 35).

(NO SUBCOMMITTEES)

Committee on Interstate and Foreign Commerce

Harley Staggers, Chairman

The Chairman and Ranking Minority Member are ex-officio members of all subcommittees.

Democratic Majority (25 D). Congressmen Staggers (W. Va 2), Macdonald (Mass. 7), Jarman (Okla. 5), Moss (Calif. 3), Dingell (Mich. 16), Rogers (Fla. 9), Van Deerlin (Calif. 37), Pickle (Tex. 10), Rooney (Pa. 15), Murphy (N.Y. 16), Satterfield (Va. 3), Adams (Wash. 7), Blanton (Tenn. 7), Stuckey (Ga. 8), Kyros (Maine 1), Eckhardt (Tex. 8), Tiernan (R.I. 2), Preyer (N.C. 6), Podell (N.Y. 13), Helstoski (N.J. 9), Symington (Mo. 2), Carney (Ohio 19), Metcalfe (Ill. 1), Byron (Md. 6), and Roy (Kans. 2).

Republican Minority (18 R). Congressmen Springer (Ill. 22), Devine (Ohio 12), Nelsen (Minn. 2), Keith (Mass. 12), Broyhill (N.C. 10), Harvey (Mich. 8), Carter (Ky. 5), Brown (Ohio 7), Kuykendall (Tenn. 9), Skubitz (Kans. 5), Thompson (Ga. 5), Hastings (N.Y. 38), Schmitz (Calif. 35), Collins (Tex. 3), Frey (Fla. 5), Ware (Pa. 9), McCollister (Neb. 2), and Shoup (Mont. 1).

SUBCOMMITTEES

COMMERCE AND FINANCE

John E. Moss, Chairman

MAJORITY (4 D). Congressmen Moss, Stuckey, Eckhardt, and Carney.
MINORITY (3 R). Congressmen Broyhill (N.C.), Ware, and McCollister.

COMMUNICATIONS AND POWER

Torbert H. Macdonald, Chairman

MAJORITY (5 D). Congressmen Macdonald, Van Deerlin, Rooney (Pa.), Tiernan, and Byron.
MINORITY (4 R). Congressmen Keith, Brown (Ohio), Collins, and Frey.

PUBLIC HEALTH AND ENVIRONMENT

Paul G. Rogers Chairman

MAJORITY (6 D). Congressmen Rogers (Fla.), Satterfield, Kyros, Preyer, Symington, and Roy.
MINORITY (4 R). Congressmen Nelsen, Carter, Hastings, and Schmitz.

TRANSPORTATION AND AERONAUTICS

John Jarman, Chairman

MAJORITY (7 D). Congressmen Jarman, Dingell, Pickle, Murphy (N.Y.), Adams, Podell, and Metcalfe.
MINORITY (5 R). Congressmen Devine, Harvey, Kuykendall, Skubitz, and Thompson.

SPECIAL SUBCOMMITTEE ON INVESTIGATIONS

Harley O. Staggers, Chairman

MAJORITY (3 D). Congressmen Staggers, Blanton, and Helstoski.
MINORITY (2 R). Congressmen Springer and Shoup.

Committee on Judiciary

Emanuel Celler, Chairman

The Chairman and Ranking Minority Member are ex-officio members of all subcommittees.

Democratic Majority (22 D). Congressmen Celler (N.Y. 10), Rodino (N.J. 10), Donohue (Mass. 4), Brooks (Tex. 9), Dowdy (Tex. 2), Kastenmeier (Wis. 2), Edwards (Calif. 9), Hungate (Mo. 9), Conyers (Mich. 1), Jacobs (Ind. 11), Eilberg (Pa. 4), Ryan (N.Y. 20), Waldie (Calif. 14), Edwards (La. 7), Flowers (Ala. 5), Mann (S.C. 4), Mikva (Ill. 2), Sarbanes (Md. 4), Seiberling (Ohio 14), Abourezk (S. Dak. 2), Danielson (Calif. 29), and Drinan (Mass. 3).

Republican Minority (16 R). Congressmen McCulloch (Ohio 4), Poff (Va. 6), Hutchinson (Mich. 4), McClory (Ill. 12), Smith (N.Y. 40), Sandman (N.J. 2), Railsback (Ill. 19), Biester (Pa. 8), Wiggins (Calif. 25), Dennis (Ind. 10), Fish (N.Y. 28), Coughlin (Pa. 13), Mayne (Iowa 6), Hogan (Md. 5), Keating (Ohio 1), and McKevitt (Colo. 1).

SUBCOMMITTEES

SUBCOMMITTEE NO. 1

General jurisdiction over judiciary bills as assigned. Special jurisdiction over immigration and nationality.

Peter W. Rodino, Chairman

MAJORITY (5 D). Congressmen Rodino, Dowdy, Eilberg, Ryan, and Seiberling.
MINORITY (4 R). Congressmen Dennis, Mayne, Hogan, and McKevitt.

SUBCOMMITTEE NO. 2

General jurisdiction over judiciary bills as assigned. Special jurisdiction over claims.

Harold D. Donohue, Chairman

MAJORITY (5 D). Congressmen Donohue, Waldie, Flowers, Mann, and Danielson.
MINORITY (3 R). Congressmen Smith (N.Y.), Sandman, and Railsback.

SUBCOMMITTEE NO. 3

General jurisdiction over judiciary bills as assigned. Special jurisdiction over patents, trademarks, copyrights, and revision of the laws.

Robert W. Kastenmeier, Chairman

MAJORITY (5 D). Congressmen Kastenmeier, Conyers, Ryan, Mikva, and Drinan.
MINORITY (4 R). Congressmen Railsback, Biester, Fish, and Coughlin.

SUBCOMMITTEE NO. 4

General jurisdiction over judiciary bills as assigned. Special jurisdiction over bankruptcy and reorganization.

Don Edwards, Chairman

MAJORITY (6 D). Congressmen Edwards, Conyers, Jacobs, Waldie, Edwards (La.), and Sarbanes.
MINORITY (4 R). Congressmen Wiggins, Sandman, Keating, and McClory.

SUBCOMMITTEE NO. 5

General jurisdiction over judiciary bills as assigned. Special jurisdiction over antitrust matters.

Emanuel Celler, Chairman

MAJORITY (6 D). Congressmen Celler, Brooks, Hungate, Jacobs, Mikva, and Abourezk.
MINORITY (4 R). Congressmen McCulloch, Poff, Hutchinson, and McClory.

Committee on Merchant Marine and Fisheries

Edward A. Garmatz, Chairman

The Chairman and Ranking Minority Member are ex-officio members of all subcommittees.

Democratic Majority (22 D). Congressmen Garmatz (Md. 3), Sullivan (Mo. 3), Clark (Pa. 25), Ashley (Ohio 9), Dingell (Mich. 16), Lennon (N.C. 7), Downing (Va. 1), Byrne (Pa. 3), Rogers (Fla. 9), Stubblefield (Ky. 1), Murphy (N.Y. 16), Karth (Minn. 4), Jones (N.C. 1), Leggett (Calif. 4), Long (La. 8), Biaggi (N.Y. 24), Griffin (Miss. 3), Anderson (Calif. 17), de la Garza (Tex. 15), Kyros (Maine 1), Tiernan (R.I. 2), and Stanton (Ohio 20).

Republican Minority (15 R). Congressmen Pelly (Wash. 1), Mailliard (Calif. 6), Mosher (Ohio 13), Grover (N.Y. 2), Keith (Mass. 12), Ruppe (Mich. 11), Goodling (Pa. 19), Bray (Ind. 6), McCloskey (Calif. 11), McDonald (Mich. 19), Snyder (Ky. 4), Steele (Conn. 2), Forsythe (N.J. 6), du Pont IV (Del. AL), and Mills (Md. 1).

SUBCOMMITTEES

COAST GUARD, COAST & GEODETIC SURVEY & NAVIGATION

Frank M. Clark, Chairman

MAJORITY (12 D). Congressmen Clark, Lennon, Byrne (Pa.), Sullivan, Rogers (Fla.), Jones (N.C.), Stubblefield, Biaggi, Griffin, de la Garza, Kyros, and Tiernan.

MINORITY (8 R). Congressmen Keith, Grover, Ruppe, McDonald, Bray, Snyder, Steele, and du Pont.

FISHERIES AND WILDLIFE CONSERVATION

John D. Dingell, Chairman

MAJORITY (12 D). Congressmen Dingell, Lennon, Downing, Karth, Rogers (Fla.), Leggett, Long (La.), Biaggi, Anderson (Calif.), de la Garza, Kyros, and Tiernan.
MINORITY (8 R). Congressmen Pelly, Keith, Goodling, McCloskey, McDonald, Mailliard, Ruppe, and Forsythe.

MERCHANT MARINE

Edward A. Garmatz, Chairman

MAJORITY (14 D). Congressmen Garmatz, Ashley, Downing, Rogers (Fla.), Stubblefield, Murphy (N.Y.), Dingell, Byrne (Pa.), Sullivan, Clark, Lennon, Karth, Jones (N.C.), and Leggett.
MINORITY (9 R). Congressmen Mailliard, Mosher, Grover, Ruppe, Bray, McCloskey, Steele, du Pont, and Mills (Md.).

OCEANOGRAPHY

Alton Lennon, Chairman

MAJORITY (14 D). Congressmen Lennon, Rogers (Fla.), Ashley, Downing, Karth, Clark, Jones (N.C.), Leggett, Griffin, Anderson (Calif.), Biaggi, de la Garza, Tiernan, and James Stanton.
MINORITY (9 R). Congressmen Mosher, Keith, Goodling, Mailliard, Steele, Forsythe, du Pont, Mills (Md.), and one vacancy.

PANAMA CANAL

John M. Murphy, Chairman

MAJORITY (9 D). Congressmen Murphy (N.Y.), Sullivan, Clark, Byrne (Pa.), Stubblefield, Jones (N.C.), Karth, Long (La.), and James Stanton.
MINORITY (6 R). Congressmen Grover, Mosher, Bray, Snyder, McDonald (Mich.), and Forsythe.

SPECIAL SUBCOMMITTEE ON MARITIME EDUCATION AND TRAINING

Speedy O. Long, Chairman

MAJORITY (7 D). Congressmen Long, Downing, Murphy (N.Y.), Anderson (Calif.), de la Garza, Kyros, and James V. Stanton.
MINORITY (4 R). Congressmen McCloskey, Snyder, and two vacancies.

Committee on Post Office and Civil Service

Thaddeus Dulski, Chairman
David Henderson, Vice Chairman

The Chairman and Ranking Minority Member are ex-officio members of all subcommittees.

Democratic Majority (15 D). Congressmen Dulski (N.Y. 41), Henderson (N.C. 3), Udall (Ariz. 2), Daniels (N.J. 14), Nix (Pa. 2), Hanley (N.Y. 35), Wilson (Calif. 31), Waldie (Calif. 14), White (Tex. 16), Ford (Mich. 15), Hamilton (Ind. 9), Brasco (N.Y. 11), Purcell (Tex. 13), Bevill (Ala. 7), and Chappell (Fla. 4).

Republican Minority (11 R). Congressmen Gross (Iowa 3), Derwinski (Ill. 4), Johnson (Pa. 23), Scott (Va. 8), McClure (Idaho 1), Hogan (Md. 5), Rousselot (Calif. 24), Hillis (Ind. 5), Powell (Ohio 24), and Mills (Md. 1), and one vacancy.

SUBCOMMITTEES

CENSUS AND STATISTICS

Charles H. Wilson, Chairman

MAJORITY (5 D). Congressmen Wilson (Calif.), Bevill, Hanley, Chappell, and Udall.
MINORITY (3 R). Congressmen Rousselot, McClure, and Young (Fla.).

EMPLOYEE BENEFITS

James M. Hanley, Chairman

MAJORITY (5 D). Congressmen Hanley, Brasco, Udall, Wilson (Calif.), and White.
MINORITY (4 R). Congressmen Hogan, Hillis, Powell, and Mills (Md.).

INVESTIGATIONS

Thaddeus J. Dulski, Chairman

MAJORITY (5 D). Congressmen Dulski, Daniels, Hamilton, Purcell, and Henderson.
MINORITY (3 R). Congressmen Johnson (Pa.), Gross, and Scott.

MANPOWER AND CIVIL SERVICE

David N. Henderson, Chairman

MAJORITY (5 D). Congressmen Henderson, White, Ford (Mich.), Bevill, and Chappell.
MINORITY (4 R). Congressmen Derwinski, Gross, Rousselot, and Mills (Md.).

POSTAL FACILITIES AND MAIL

Robert N. C. Nix, Chairman

MAJORITY (5 D). Congressmen Nix, Purcell, Henderson, Hanley, and Bevill.
MINORITY (3 R). Congressmen McClure, Johnson (Pa.), and Young (Fla.).

POSTAL SERVICE

Morris K. Udall, Chairman

MAJORITY (5 D). Congressmen Udall, Ford (Mich.), Nix, Waldie, and Hamilton.
MINORITY (3 R). Congressmen Gross, Derwinski, and Hillis.

RETIREMENT, INSURANCE AND HEALTH BENEFITS

Jerome R. Waldie, Chairman

MAJORITY (5 D). Congressmen Waldie, Chappell, Daniels, White, and Brasco.
MINORITY (3 R). Congressmen Scott, Hogan, and Powell.

Committee on Public Works

John Blatnik, Chairman

The Chairman and Ranking Minority Member are ex-officio members of all subcommittees.

Democratic Majority (23 D). Congressmen Blatnik (Minn. 8), Jones (Ala. 8), Kluczynski (Ill. 5), Wright (Tex. 12), Gray (Ill. 21), Clark (Pa. 25), Edmondson (Okla. 2), Johnson (Calif. 2), Dorn (S.C. 3), Henderson (N.C. 3), Roberts (Tex. 4), Kee (W. Va. 5), Howard (N.J. 3), Anderson (Calif. 17), Caffery (La. 3), Roe (N.J. 8), Collins (Ill. 6), Roncalio (Wyo. AL), Begich (Alaska AL), McCormack (Wash. 4), Rangel (N.Y. 18), Stanton (Ohio 20), and Abzug (N.Y. 19).

Republican Minority (14 R). Congressmen Harsha (Ohio 6), Grover (N.Y. 2), Cleveland (N.H. 2), Clausen (Calif. 1), Schwengel (Iowa 1), Snyder (Ky. 4), Zion (Ind. 8), McDonald (Mich. 19), Hammerschmidt (Ark. 3), Miller (Ohio 10), Mizell (N.C. 5), Terry (N.Y. 34), Thone (Neb. 1), and Baker (Tenn. 3).

SUBCOMMITTEES

FLOOD CONTROL AND INTERNAL DEVELOPMENT

Robert E. Jones, Chairman

MAJORITY (15 D). Congressmen Jones (Ala.), Wright, Gray, Clark, Johnson (Calif.), Edmondson, Dorn, Henderson, Roberts, Kee, Anderson (Calif.), Roe, Caffery, Begich, and McCormack.

MINORITY (10 R). Congressmen Clausen (Calif.), Grover, Schwengel, Snyder, Zion, McDonald (Mich.), Hammerschmidt, Miller (Ohio), Mizell, and Baker.

INVESTIGATIONS AND OVERSIGHT

Jim Wright, Chairman

MAJORITY (16 D). Congressmen Wright, Jones (Ala.), Kluczynski, Gray, Clark, Edmondson, Johnson (Calif.), Dorn, Howard, Caffery, Roe, Collins (Ill.), McCormack, Rangel, Stanton (Ohio), and Abzug.

MINORITY (11 R). Congressmen Cleveland, Harsha, Grover, Clausen (Calif.), Snyder, Zion, McDonald (Mich.), Hammerschmidt, Mizell, Terry, and Thone.

PUBLIC BUILDINGS AND GROUNDS

Kenneth Gray, Chairman

MAJORITY (15 D). Congressmen Gray, Jones (Ala.), Kluczynski, Wright, Roberts, Kee, Johnson (Calif.), Howard, Anderson (Calif.), Caffery, Roe, Collins (Ill.), Roncalio, Rangel, and Abzug.

MINORITY (10 R). Congressmen Grover, Cleveland, Schwengel, Snyder, McDonald, Miller (Ohio), Mizell, Terry, Thone, and Baker.

RIVERS AND HARBORS

Ray Roberts, Chairman

MAJORITY (16 D). Congressmen Roberts, Johnson (Calif.), Gray, Wright, Henderson, Dorn, Howard, Anderson (Calif.), Caffery, Roe, Clark, Roncalio, Begich, McCormack, Stanton (Ohio), and Abzug.

MINORITY (11 R). Congressmen Snyder, Harsha, Grover, Cleveland, Clausen (Calif.), Zion, McDonald, Hammerschmidt, Terry, Thone, and Baker.

ROADS

John C. Kluczynski, Chairman

MAJORITY (15 D). Congressmen Kluczynski, Jones (Ala.), Clark, Edmondson, Wright, Howard, Dorn, Henderson, Roberts, Anderson (Calif.), Collins (Ill.), Roncalio, McCormack, Rangel, and Stanton (Ohio).

MINORITY (10 R). Congressmen Harsha, Cleveland, Clausen (Calif.), Schwengel, Zion, McDonald (Mich.), Hammerschmidt, Mizell, Terry, and Thone.

WATERSHED DEVELOPMENT

James Kee, Chairman

MAJORITY (9 D). Congressmen Kee, Kluczynski, Edmondson, Dorn, Anderson (Calif.), Caffery, Roncalio, Begich, and McCormack.
MINORITY (6 R). Congressmen Schwengel, Grover, Snyder, Zion, Miller (Ohio), and Baker.

SPECIAL SUBCOMMITTEE ON ECONOMIC DEVELOPMENT PROGRAMS

John A. Blatnik, Chairman

MAJORITY (15 D). Congressmen Blatnik, Edmondson, Henderson, Roberts, Kee, Howard, Roe, Gray, Johnson (Calif.), Collins (Ill.), Roncalio, Begich, Rangel, Stanton (Ohio), and Abzug.
MINORITY (10 R). Congressmen Hammerschmidt, Harsha, Cleveland, Clausen (Calif.), Schwengel, Miller (Ohio), Mizell, Terry, Thone, and Baker.

Committee on Rules

William Colmer, Chairman

Democratic Majority (10 D). Congressmen Colmer (Miss. 5), Madden (Ind. 1), Delaney (N.Y. 9), Bolling (Mo. 5), O'Neill (Mass. 8), Sisk (Calif. 16), Young (Tex. 14), Pepper (Fla. 11), Matsunaga (Hawaii 1), and Anderson (Tenn. 6).

Republican Minority (5 R). Congressmen Smith (Calif. 20), Anderson (Ill. 16), Martin (Neb. 3), Quillen (Tenn. 1), and Latta (Ohio 5).

(NO SUBCOMMITTEES)

Committee on Science and Astronautics

George Miller, Chairman

The Chairman and Ranking Minority Member are ex-officio members of all subcommittees.

Democratic Majority (18 D). Congressmen Miller (Calif. 8), Teague (Tex. 6), Karth (Minn. 4), Hechler (W. Va. 4), Davis (Ga. 7), Downing (Va. 1), Fuqua (Fla. 2), Cabell (Tex. 5), Symington (Mo. 2), Hanna (Calif. 34), Flowers (Ala. 5), Roe (N.J. 8), Seiberling (Ohio 14), Cotter (Conn. 1), Rangel (N.Y. 18), Murphy (Ill. 3), McCormack (Wash. 4), and Davis (S.C. 1).

Republican Minority (12 R). Congressmen Fulton (Pa. 27), Mosher (Ohio 13), Bell (Calif. 28), Pelly (Wash. 1), Wydler (N.Y. 4), Winn (Kans. 3), Price (Tex. 18), Frey (Fla. 5), Goldwater (Calif. 27), Esch (Mich. 2), Coughlin (Pa. 13), and Camp (Okla. 6).

SUBCOMMITTEES

ADVANCED RESEARCH AND TECHNOLOGY

Ken Hechler, Chairman

MAJORITY (5 D). Congressmen Hechler, Davis (Ga.), Cotter, Rangel, and McCormack.
MINORITY (4 R). Congressmen Pelly, Wydler, Goldwater, and Esch.

INTERNATIONAL COOPERATION IN SCIENCE AND SPACE

Don Fuqua, Chairman

MAJORITY (6 D). Congressmen Fuqua, Davis (Ga.), Roe, Cotter, Murphy (Ill.), and Davis (S.C.).
MINORITY (3 R). Congressmen Fulton (Pa.), Bell, and Winn.

MANNED SPACE FLIGHT

Olin E. Teague, Chairman

MAJORITY (6 D). Congressmen Teague (Tex.), Fuqua, Cabell, Hanna, Flowers, and Roe.
MINORITY (5 R). Congressmen Fulton (Pa.), Bell, Winn, Price (Tex.), and Frey.

NASA OVERSIGHT

Thomas N. Downing, Chairman

MAJORITY (5 D). Congressmen Downing, Teague (Tex.), Hechler, Flowers, and Rangel.
MINORITY (3 R). Congressmen Wydler, Goldwater, and Camp.

SCIENCE, RESEARCH AND DEVELOPMENT

John W. Davis, Chairman

MAJORITY (6 D). Congressmen Davis (Ga.), Cabell, Symington, Hanna, Seiberling, and McCormack.
MINORITY (5 R). Congressmen Bell, Mosher, Frey, Esch, and Coughlin.

SPACE SCIENCES AND APPLICATIONS

Joseph E. Karth, Chairman

MAJORITY (6 D). Congressmen Karth, Downing, Symington, Seiberling, Murphy (Ill.), and Davis (S.C.).
MINORITY (4 R). Congressmen Mosher, Winn, Price, and Goldwater.

Committee on Standards of Official Conduct

Melvin Price, Chairman

Democratic Majority (6 D). Congressmen Price (Ill. 24), Teague (Tex. 6), Abbitt (Va. 4), Aspinall (Colo. 4), Hébert (La. 1), and Holifield (Calif. 19).
Republican Minority (6 R). Congressmen Betts (Ohio 8), Stafford (Vt. AL), Quillen (Tenn. 1), Williams (Pa. 7), Hutchinson (Mich. 4), and Reid (Ill. 15).

(NO SUBCOMMITTEES)

Committee on Veterans' Affairs

Olin Teague, Chairman

The Chairman and Ranking Minority Member are ex-officio members of all subcommittees.

Democratic Majority (16 D). Congressmen Teague (Tex. 6), Dorn (S.C. 3), Haley (Fla. 7), Baring (Nev. AL), Dulski (N.Y. 41), Roberts (Tex. 4), Satterfield (Va. 3), Helstoski (N.J. 9), Pucinski (Ill. 11), Edwards (Calif. 9), Montgomery (Miss. 4), Carney (Ohio 19), Hicks (Mass. 9), Danielson (Calif. 29), Grasso (Conn. 6), and Wolff (N.Y. 3).

Republican Minority (10 R). Congressmen Teague (Calif. 13), Saylor (Pa. 22), Hammerschmidt (Ark. 3), Scott (Va. 8), Heckler (Mass. 10), Zwach (Minn. 6), Wylie (Ohio 15), Winn (Kans. 3), Ruth (N.C. 8), and Hillis (Ind. 5).

SUBCOMMITTEES

COMPENSATION AND PENSION

W. J. B. Dorn, Chairman

MAJORITY (3 D). Congressmen Dorn, Roberts, and Montgomery.
MINORITY (3 R). Congressmen Hammerschmidt, Saylor, and Scott.

EDUCATION AND TRAINING

Henry Helstoski, Chairman

MAJORITY (7 D). Congressmen Helstoski, Dulski, Baring, Dorn, Pucinski, Edwards, and Danielson.
MINORITY (6 R). Congressmen Scott, Heckler, Zwach, Wylie, Winn, and Ruth.

HOSPITALS

David Satterfield, Chairman

MAJORITY (14 D). Congressmen Satterfield, Haley, Baring, Dulski, Roberts, Dorn, Pucinski, Montgomery, Edwards, Carney, Danielson, Hicks (Mass.), Grasso, and Wolff.
MINORITY (9 R). Congressmen Saylor, Hammerschmidt, Scott, Heckler, Zwach, Wylie, Winn, Ruth, and Hillis.

HOUSING

Charles Carney, Chairman

MAJORITY (5 D). Congressmen Carney, Baring, Roberts, Satterfield, and Helstoski.
MINORITY (4 R). Congressmen Heckler, Hammerschmidt, Winn, and Hillis.

INSURANCE

G. V. Montgomery, Chairman

MAJORITY (4 D). Congressmen Montgomery, Hicks (Mass.), Grasso, and Wolff.
MINORITY (3 R). Congressmen Zwach, Saylor, and Wylie.

Committee on Ways and Means

Wilbur Mills, Chairman

Democratic Majority (15 D). Congressmen Mills (Ark. 2), Watts (Ky. 6), Ullman (Oreg. 2), Burke (Mass. 11), Griffiths (Mich. 17), Rostenkowski (Ill. 8), Landrum (Ga. 9), Vanik (Ohio 22), Fulton (Tenn. 5), Burleson (Tex. 17), Corman (Calif. 22), Green (Pa. 5), Gibbons (Fla. 6), Carey (N.Y. 15), and Waggonner (La. 4).

Republican Minority (10 R). Congressmen Byrnes (Wis. 8), Betts (Ohio 8), Schneebeli (Pa. 17), Collier (Ill. 10), Broyhill (Va. 10), Conable (N.Y. 37), Chamberlain (Mich. 6), Pettis (Calif. 33), Duncan (Tenn. 2), and Brotzman (Colo. 2).

(NO SUBCOMMITTEES)

Select Committee on Small Business

Joe Evins, Chairman

Democratic Majority (12 D). Congressmen Evins (Tenn. 4), Patman (Tex. 1), Steed (Okla. 4), Kluczynski (Ill. 5), Dingell (Mich. 16), Smith (Iowa 5), Corman (Calif.

22), Addabbo (N.Y. 7), Hungate (Mo. 9), St Germain (R.I. 1), Carney (Ohio 19), and Mitchell (Md. 7).

Republican Minority (7 R). Congressmen Conte (Mass. 1), Broyhill (N.C. 10), Horton (N.Y. 36), Stanton (Ohio 11), McDade (Pa. 10), Lujan (N. Mex. 1), and McKevitt (Colo. 1).

House Democratic Study Group

Phillip Burton (Calif. 5), Chairman

Vice Chairmen at Large. Sam Gibbons (Fla. 6), William Clay (Mo. 1), and John Culver (Iowa 2).

Secretary. William Ford (Mich. 15).

Program Chairman. Parren Mitchell (Md. 7).

Regional Vice Chairmen. Bob Eckhardt (Tex. 8), William Hathaway (Maine 2), Abner Mikva (Ill. 2), David Obey (Wis. 7), Thomas Rees (Calif. 26), and William Ryan (N.Y. 20).

Joint Committee on Atomic Energy

John Pastore, Chairman
Melvin Price, Vice Chairman

Congressmen. Price (D-Ill. 24), Holifield (D-Calif. 19), Aspinall (D-Colo. 4), Young (D-Tex. 14), Edmondson (D-Okla. 2), Hosmer (R-Calif. 32), Anderson (R-Ill. 16), McCulloch (R-Ohio 4), and Hansen (R-Idaho 2).

Senators. Pastore (R.I.), Anderson (N. Mex.), Jackson (Wash.), Symington (Mo.), Bible (Nev.), Aiken (Vt.), Bennett (Utah), Dominick (Colo.), and Baker (Tenn.).

Joint Economic Committee

William Proxmire, Chairman
Wright Patman, Vice Chairman

Congressmen. Patman, (D-Tex. 1), Bolling (D-Mo. 5), Boggs (D-La. 2), Reuss (D-Wis. 5), Griffiths (D-Mich. 17), Moorhead (D-Pa. 14), Widnall (R-N.J. 7), Conable (R-N.Y. 37), Brown (R-Ohio 7), and Blackburn (R-Ga. 4).

Senators. Proxmire (Wis.), Sparkman (Ala.), Fulbright (Ark.), Ribicoff (Conn.), Javits (N.Y.), Miller (Iowa), Percy (Ill.), Bentsen (Tex.), Humphrey (Minn.), and Pearson (Kans.).

ALABAMA

(8 districts)

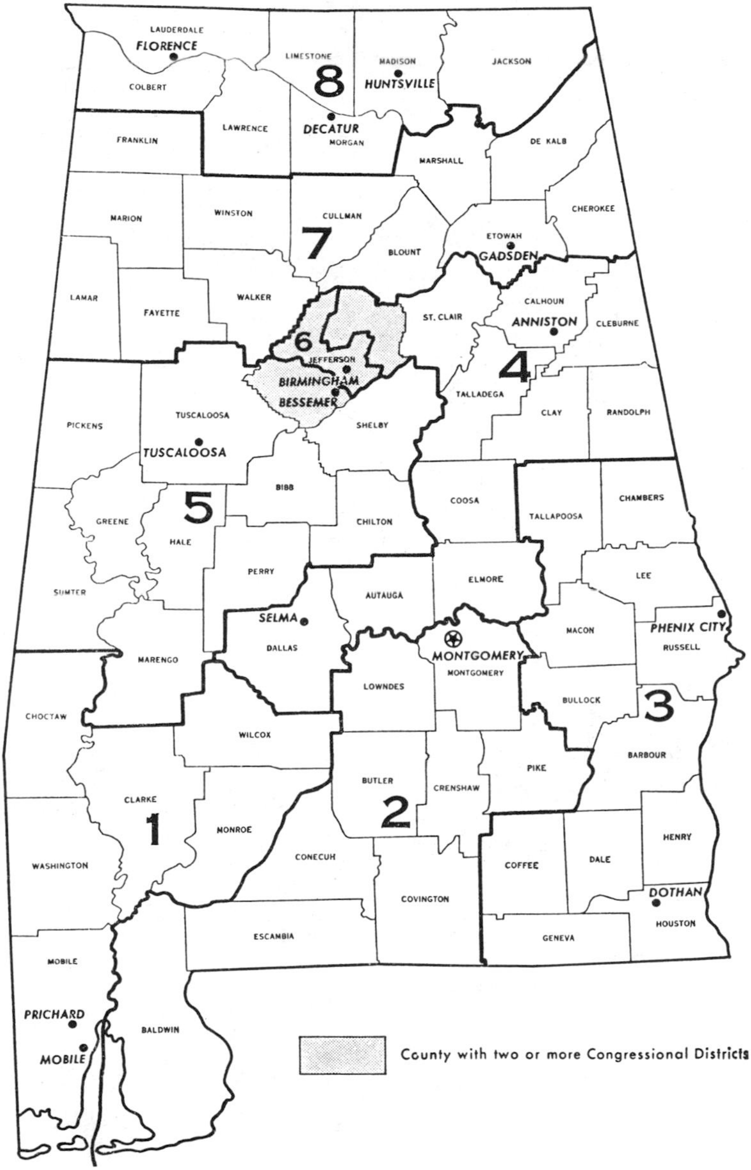

ALASKA

(1 at large)

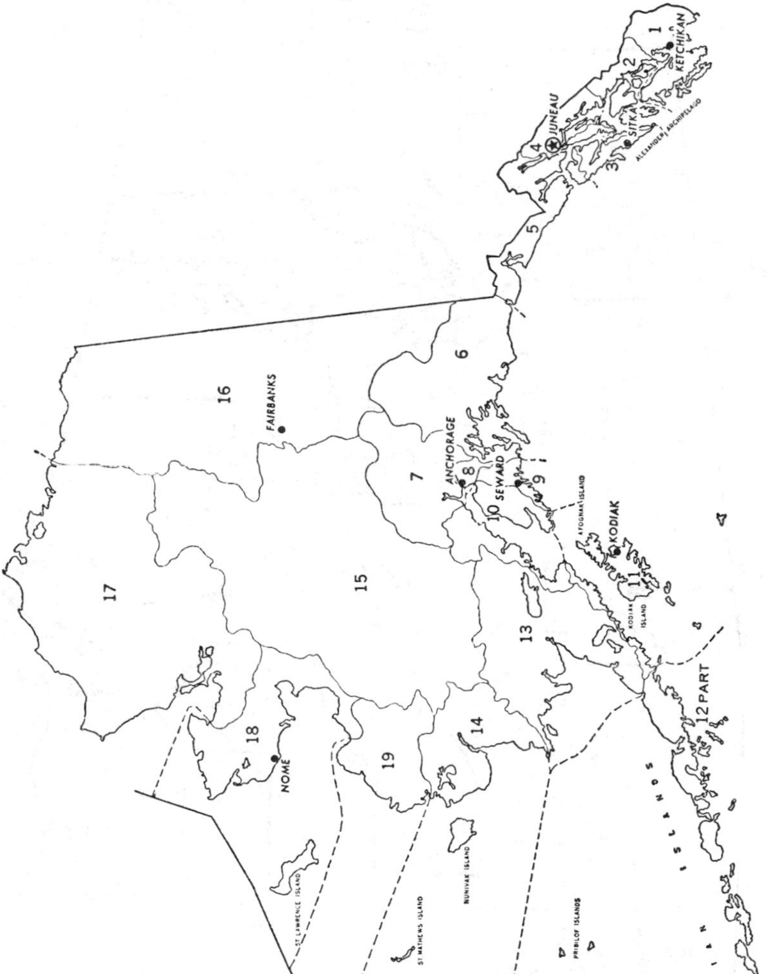

ARIZONA

(3 districts)

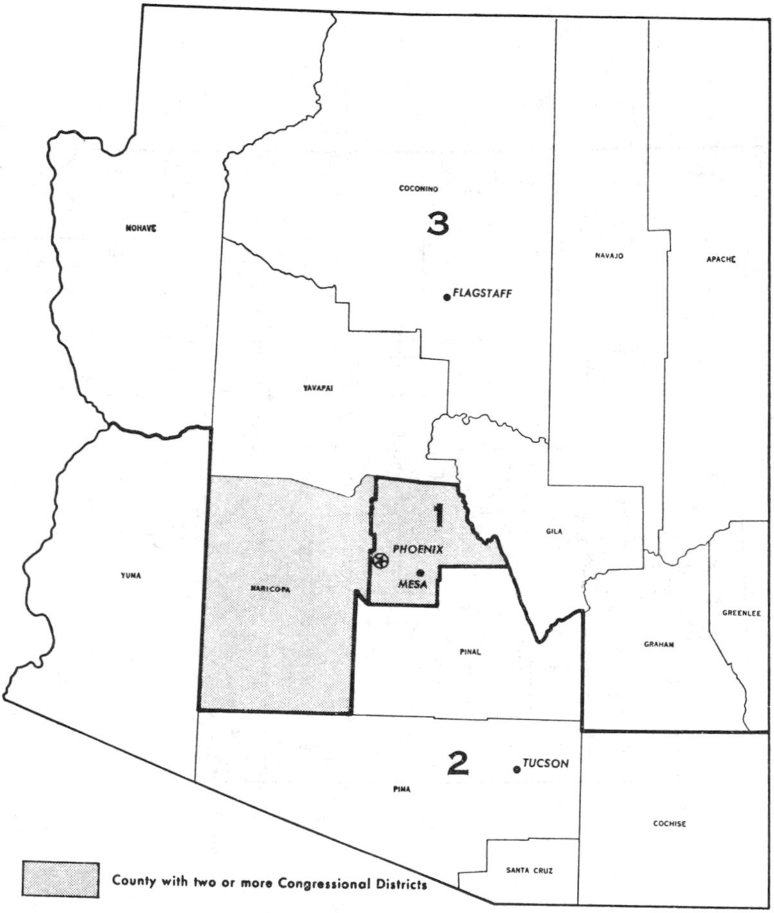

ARKANSAS

(4 districts)

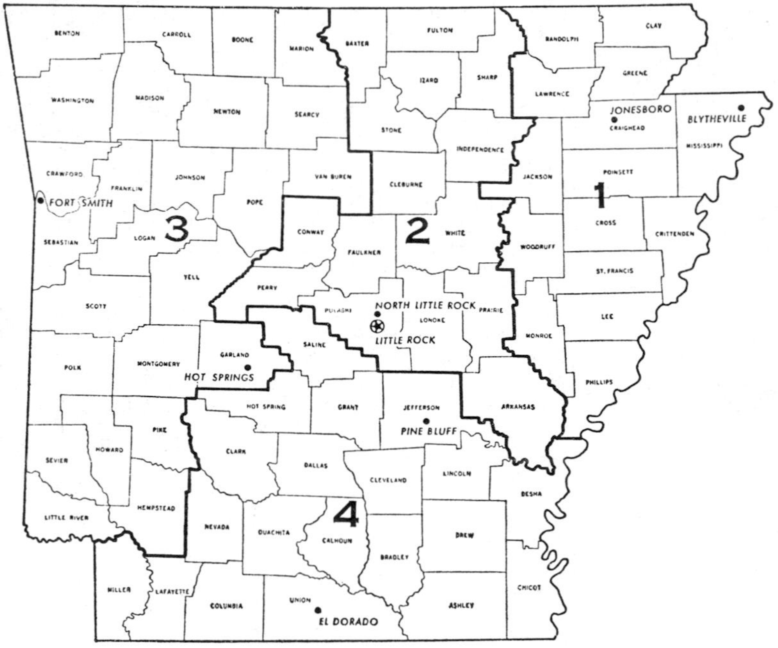

CALIFORNIA

(38 districts)

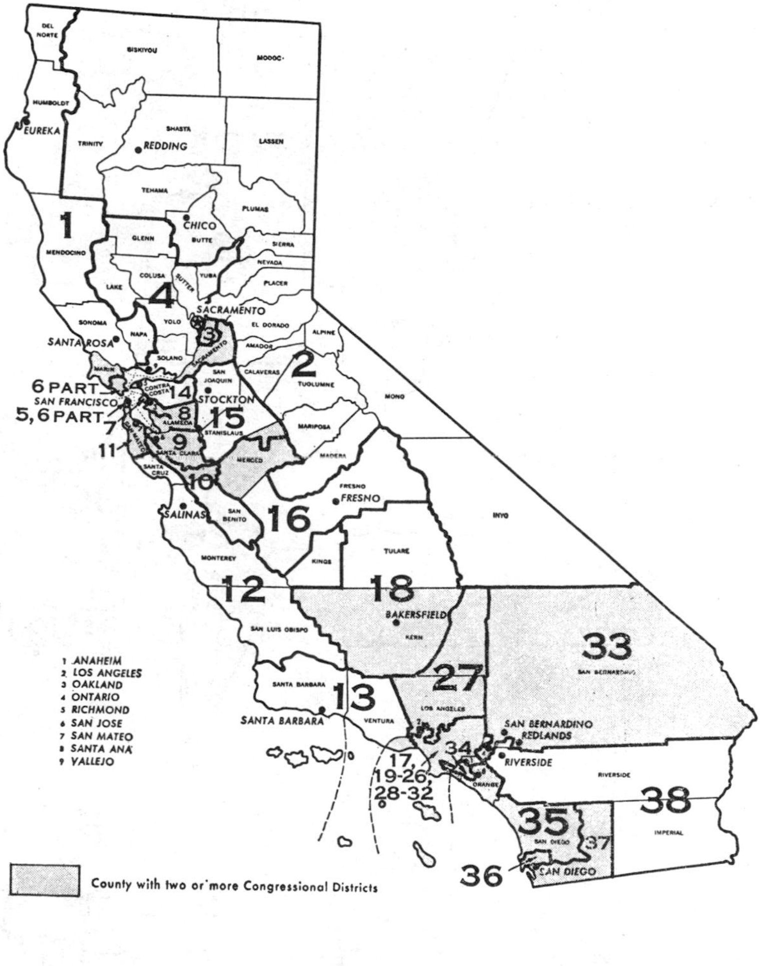

CALIFORNIA

Districts Established March 8, 1968

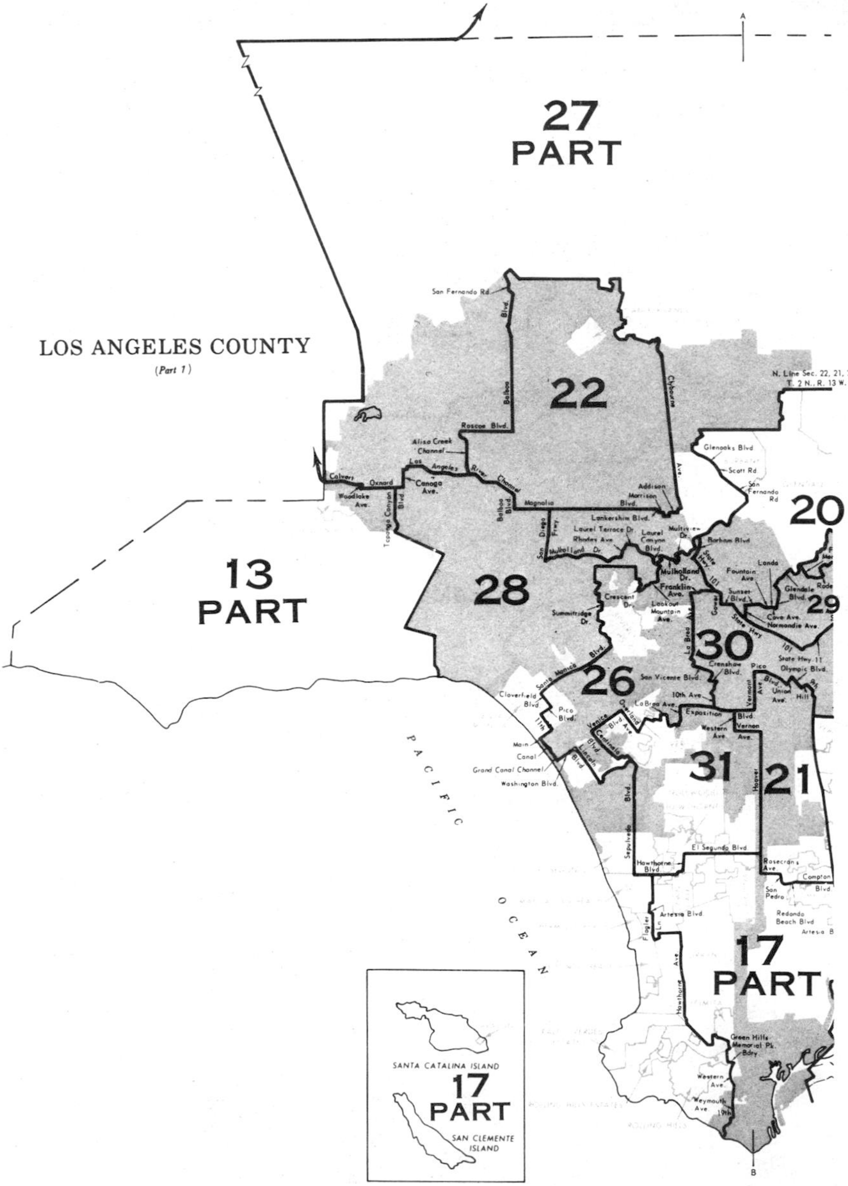

CALIFORNIA

Districts Established March 8, 1968

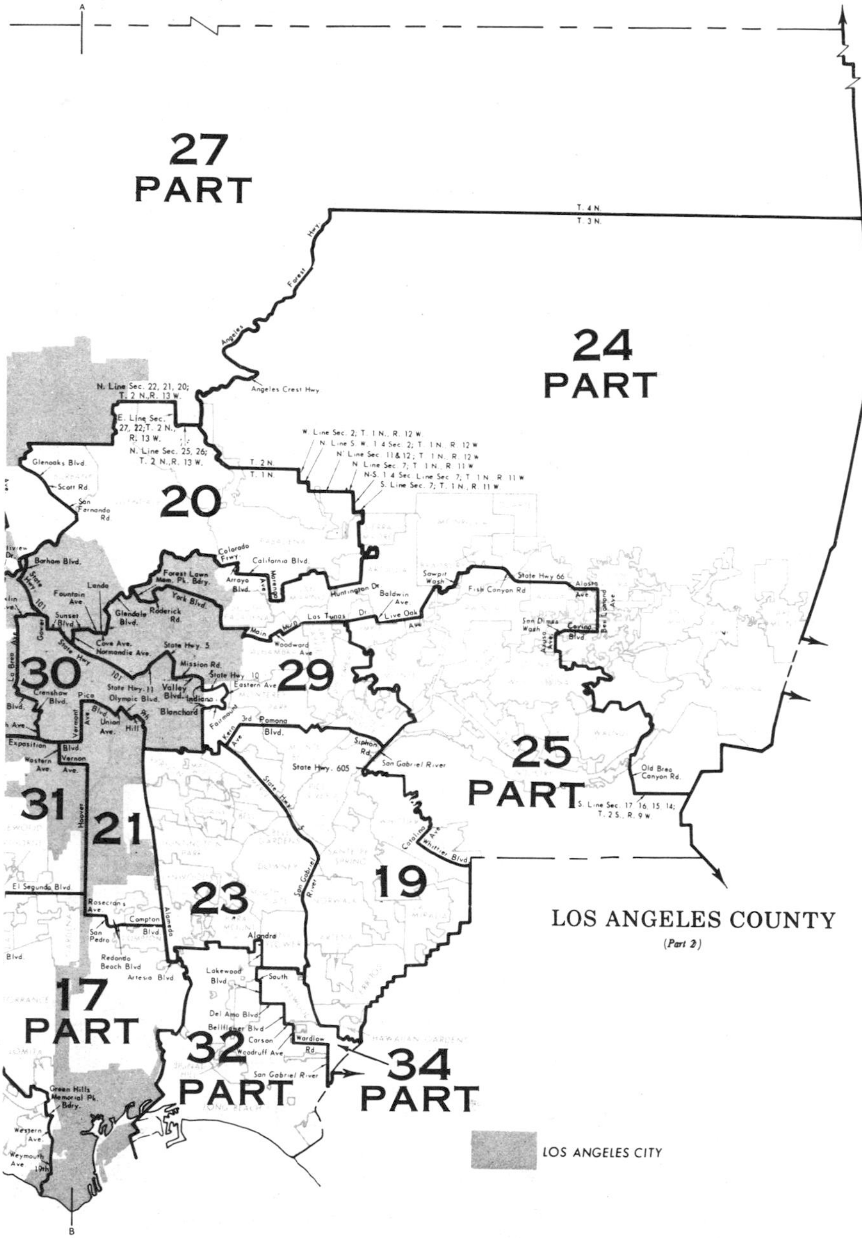

COLORADO

(4 districts)

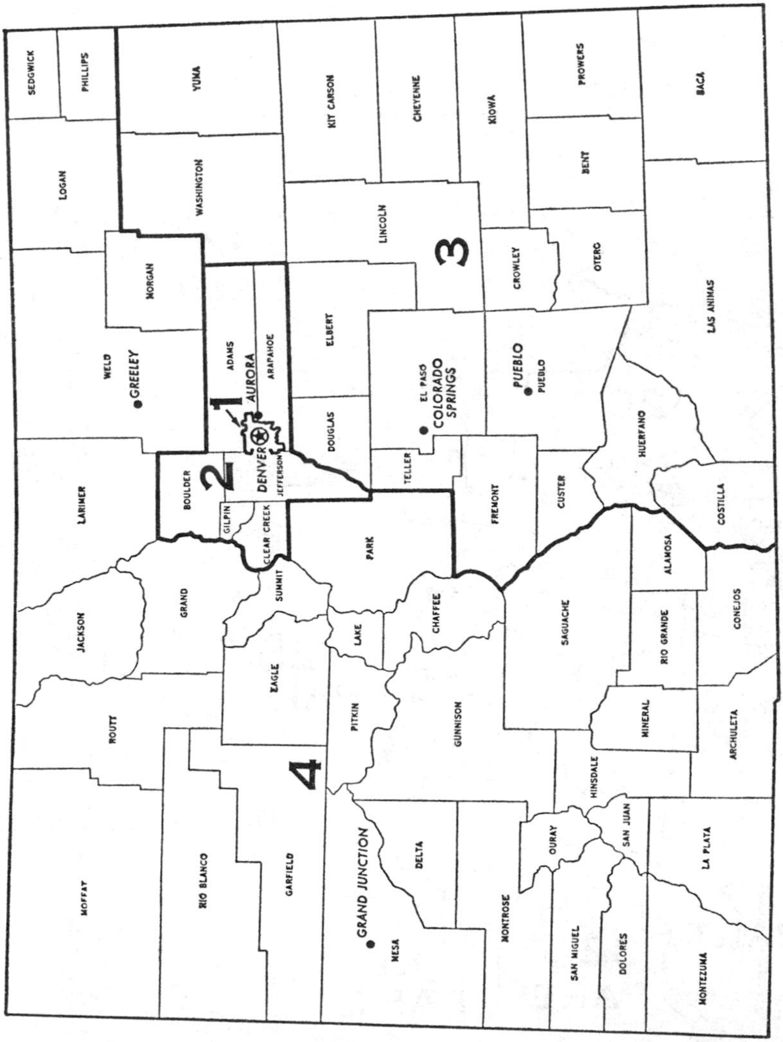

CONNECTICUT

(6 districts)

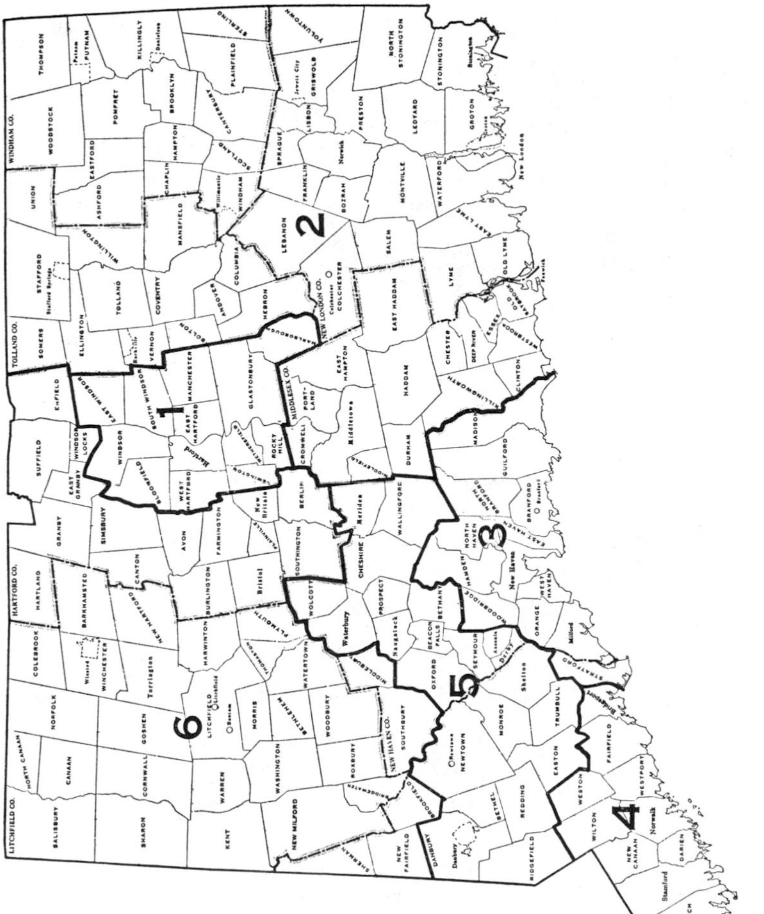

DELAWARE

(1 at large)

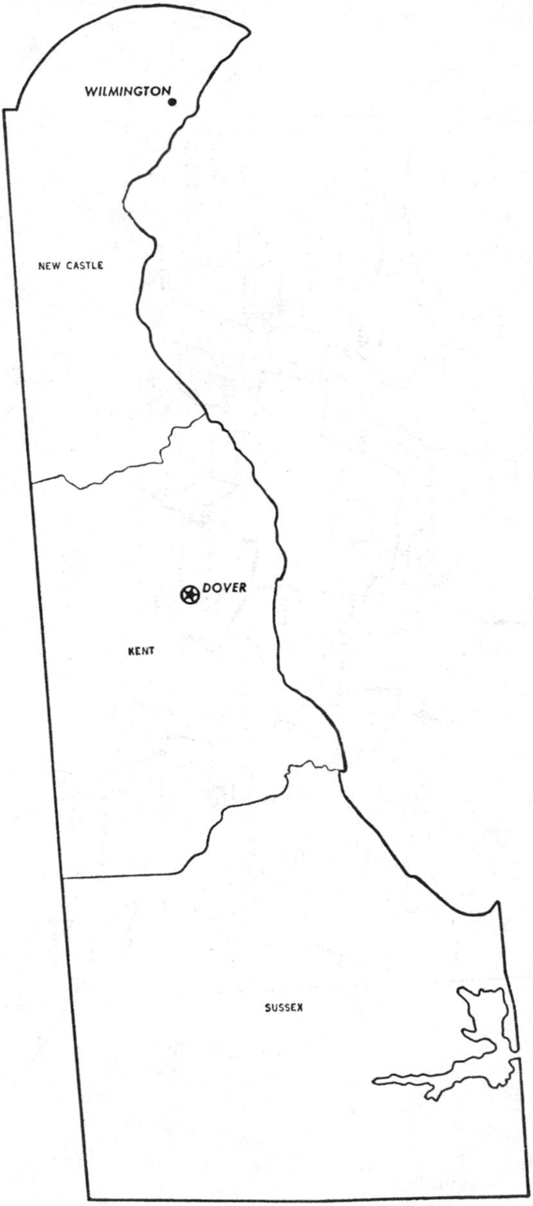

FLORIDA

(12 districts)

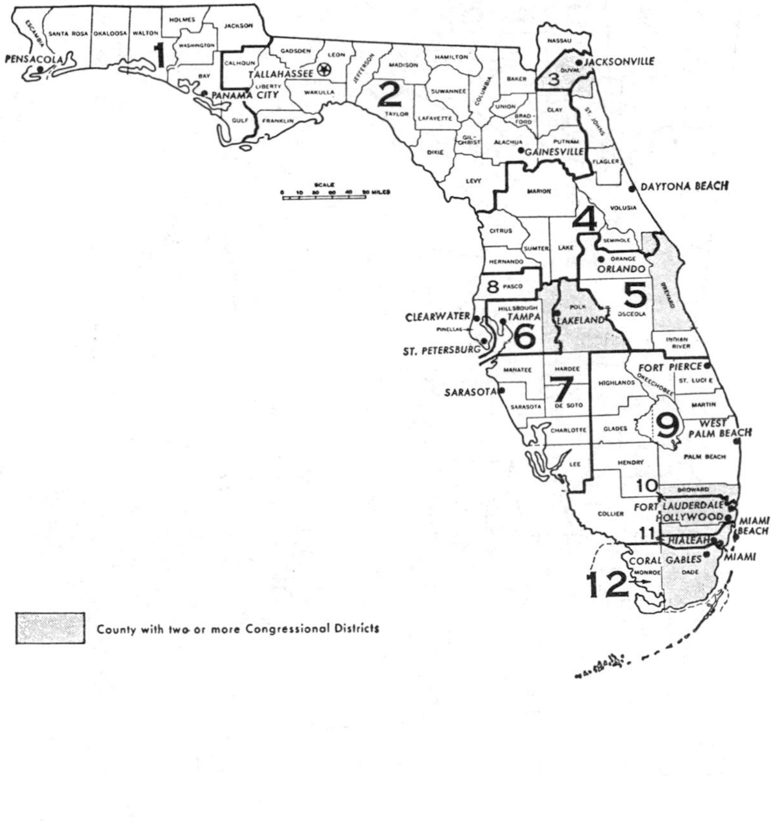

GEORGIA

(10 districts)

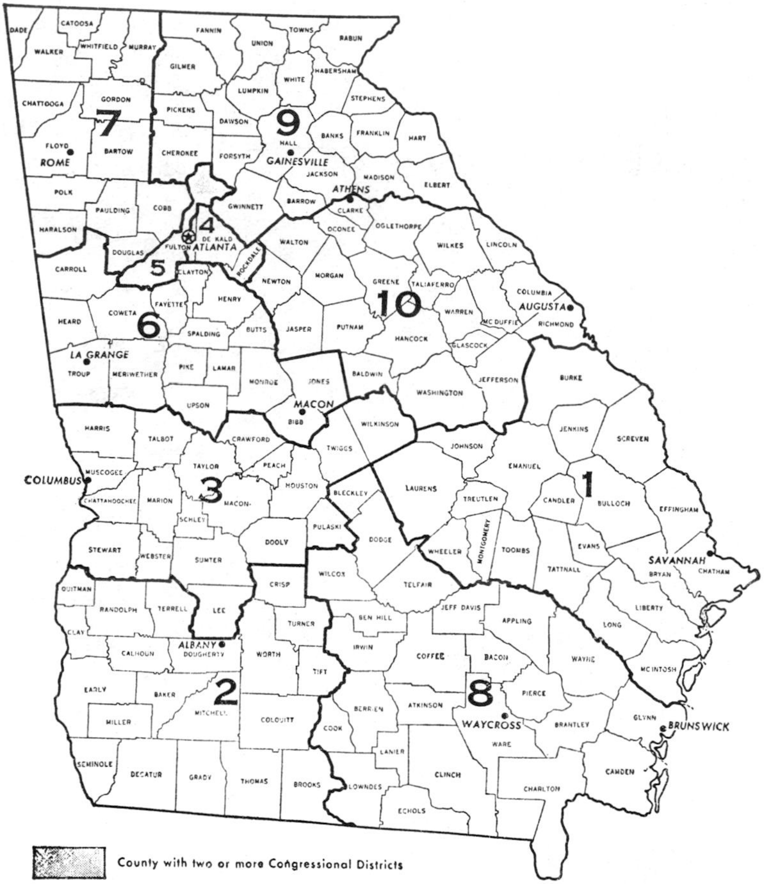

HAWAII

(2 districts)

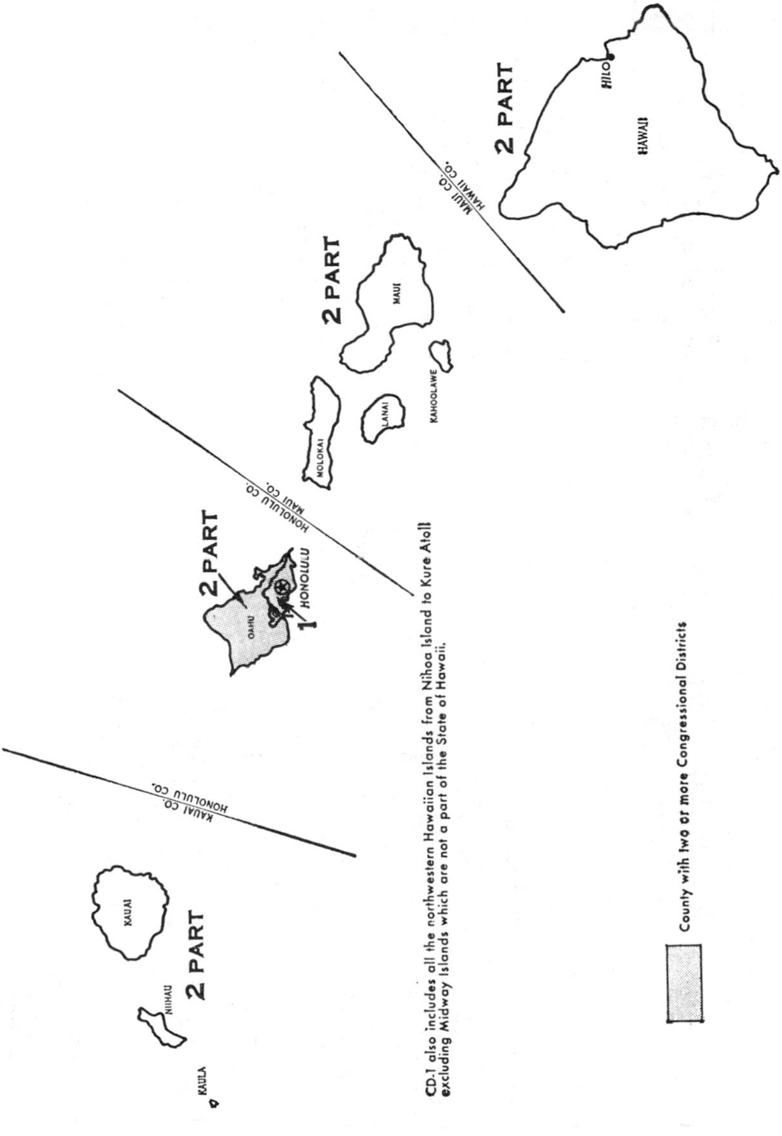
2 PART
HILO
HAWAII
HAWAII CO.
MAUI CO.
2 PART
MAUI
KAHOOLAWE
LANAI
MOLOKAI
MAUI CO.
HONOLULU CO.
2 PART
OAHU
HONOLULU
1
HONOLULU CO.
KAUAI CO.
KAUAI
2 PART
NIIHAU
KAULA
CD.1 also includes all the northwestern Hawaiian Islands from Nihoa Island to Kure Atoll excluding Midway Islands which are not a part of the State of Hawaii.
County with two or more Congressional Districts

IDAHO

(2 districts)

ILLINOIS

(24 districts)

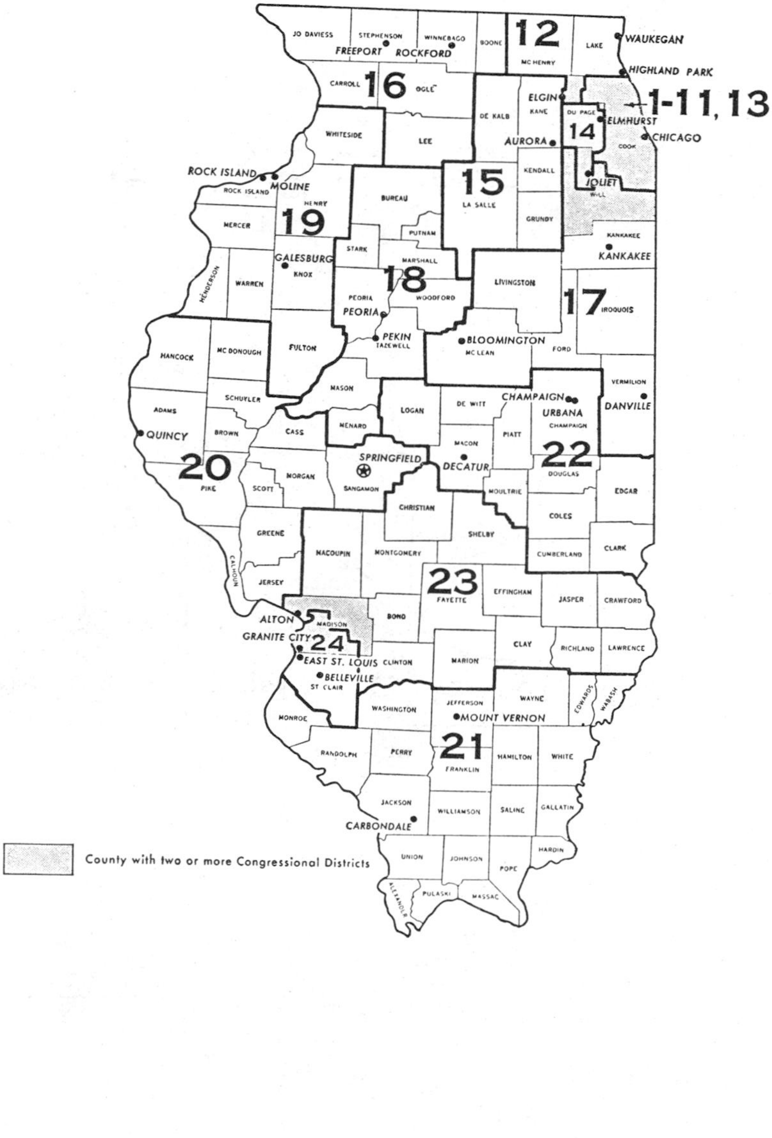

ILLINOIS

Districts Established November 24, 1965

COOK COUNTY AND PART OF DU PAGE COUNTY

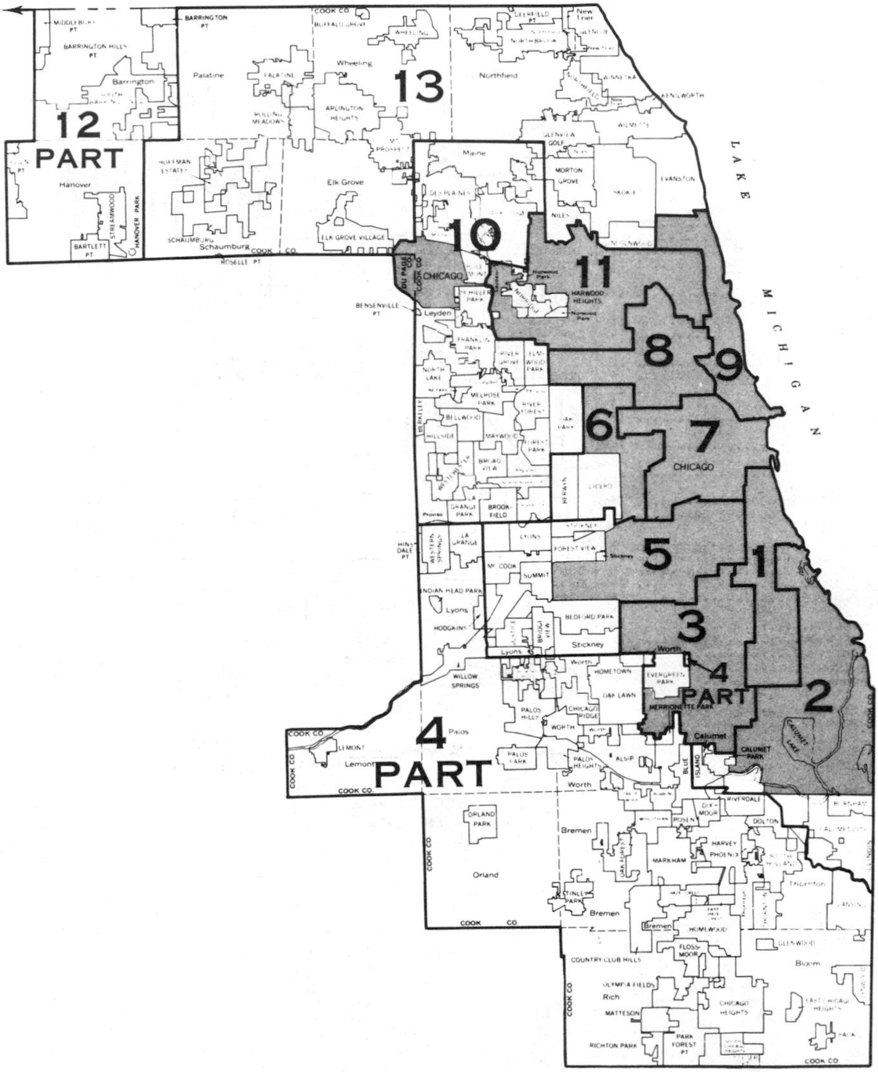

INDIANA

(11 districts)

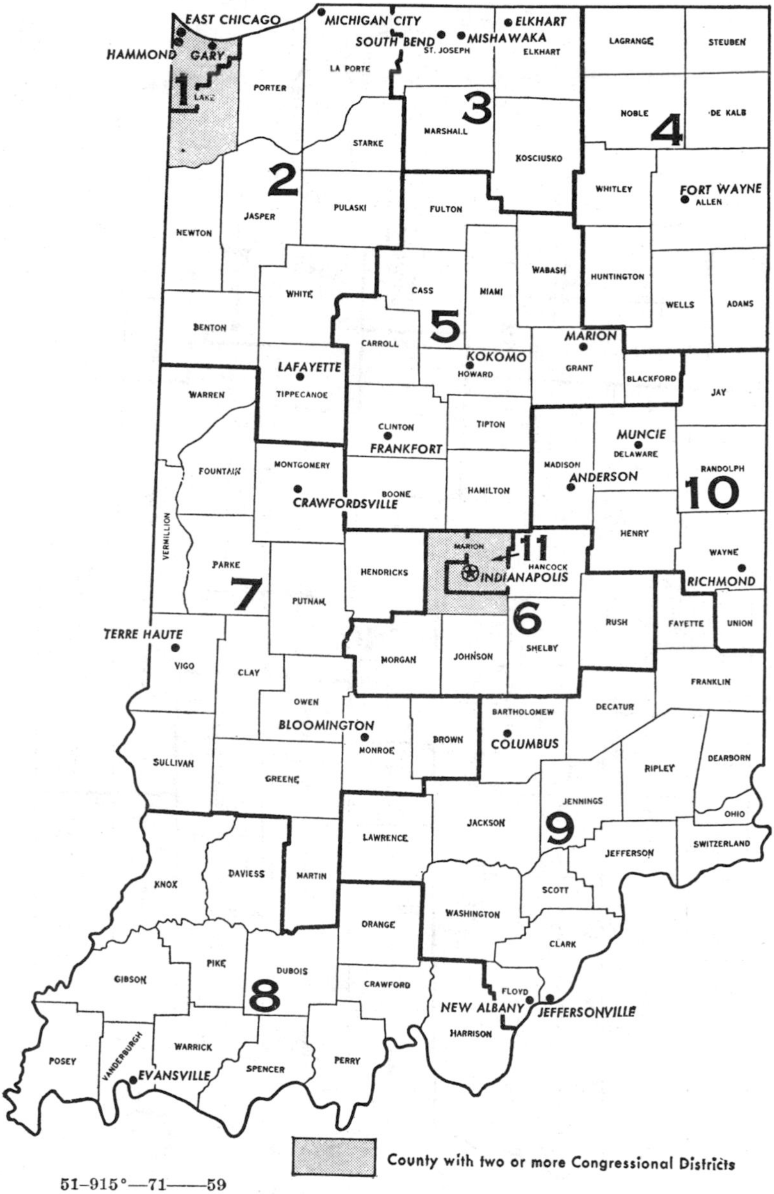

51-915°—71——59

IOWA

(7 districts)

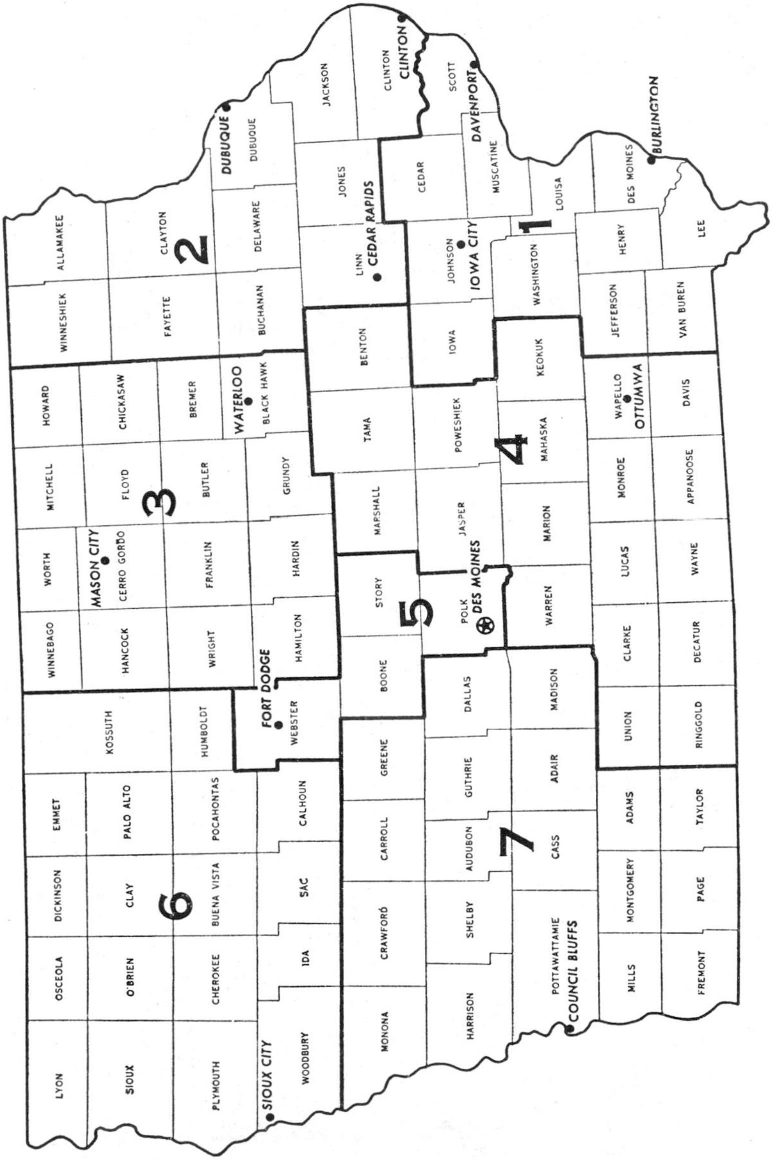

KANSAS

(5 districts)

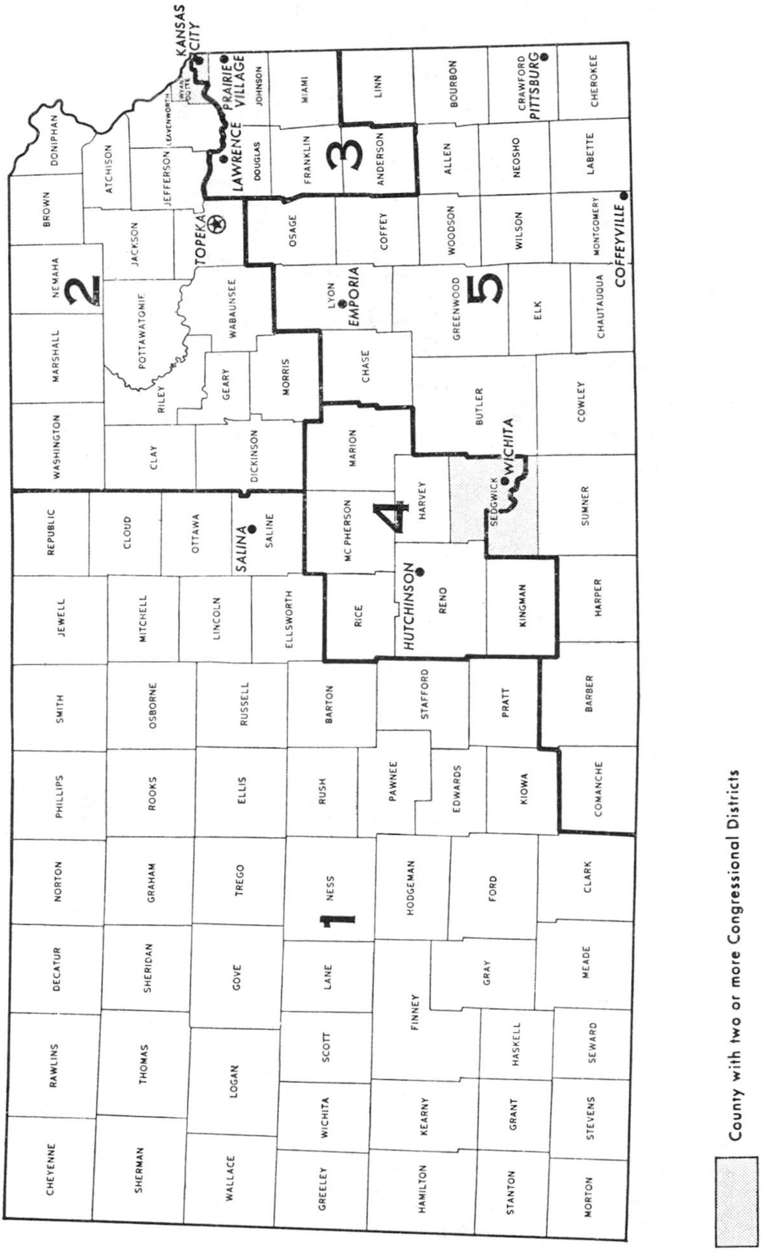

KENTUCKY

(7 districts)

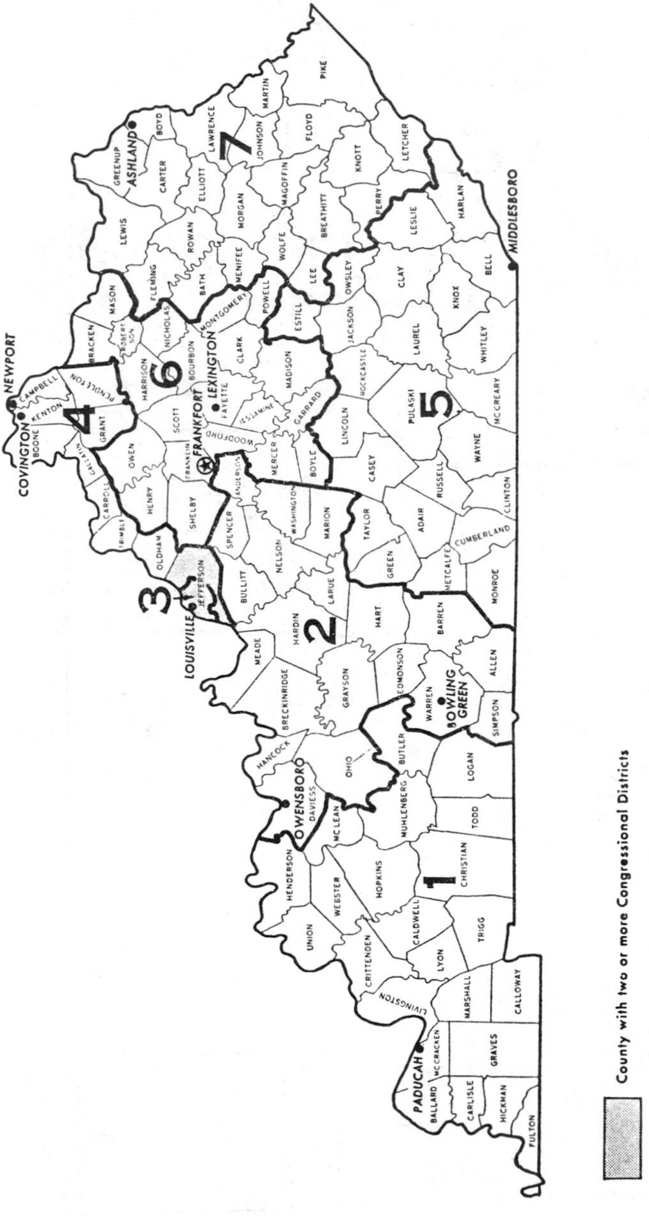

LOUISIANA

(8 districts)

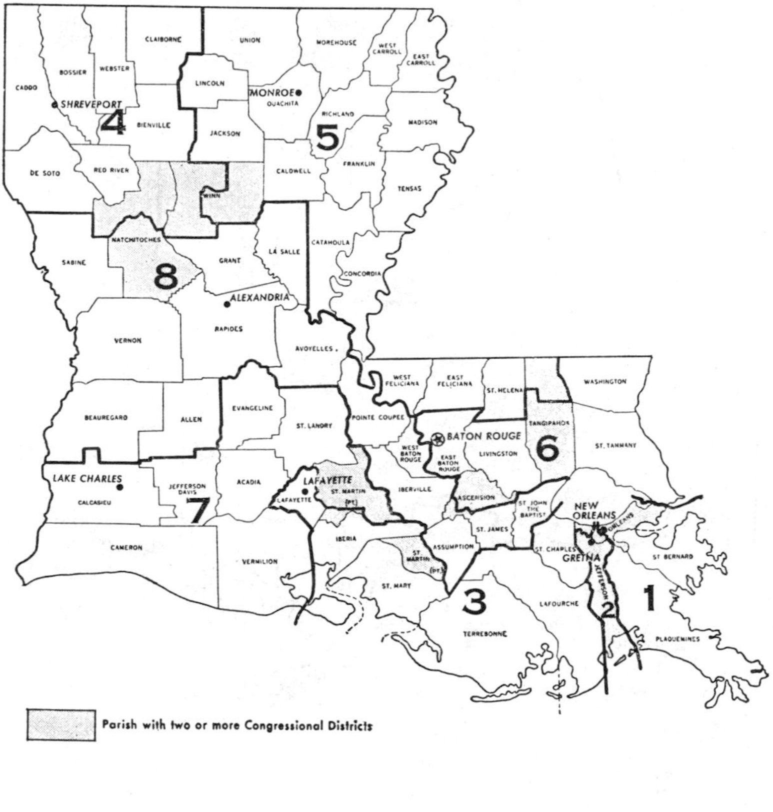

MAINE

(2 districts)

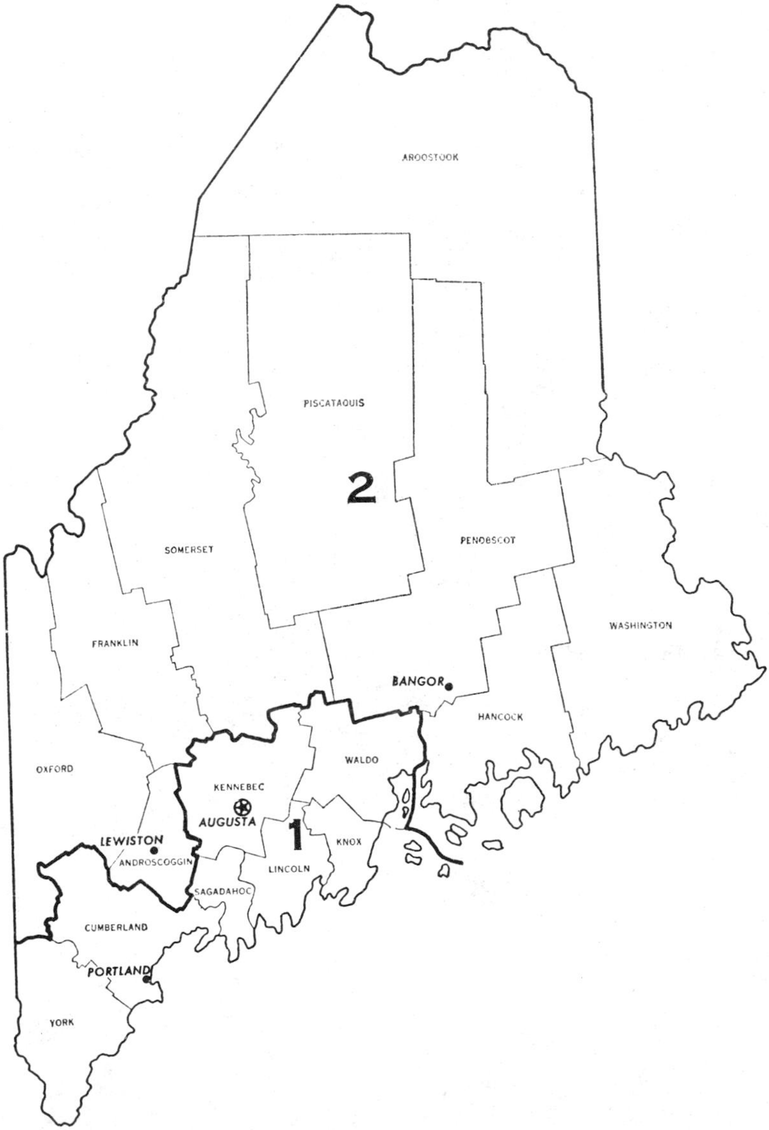

MARYLAND

(8 districts)

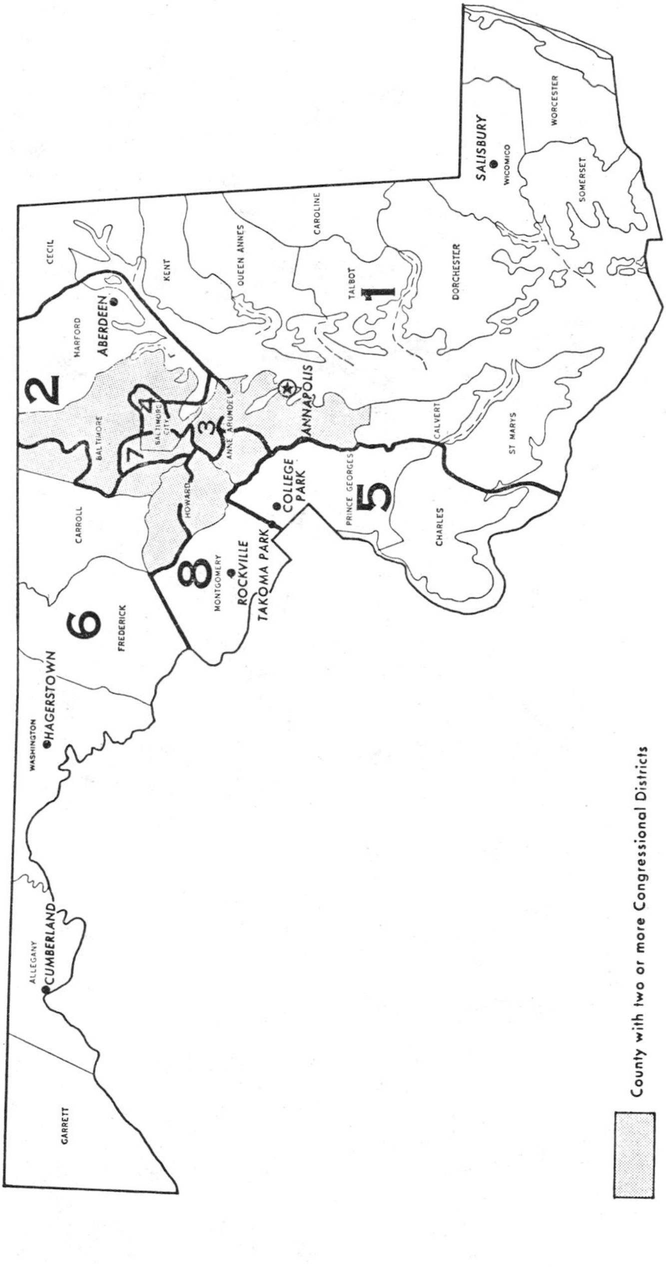

MASSACHUSETTS

(12 districts)

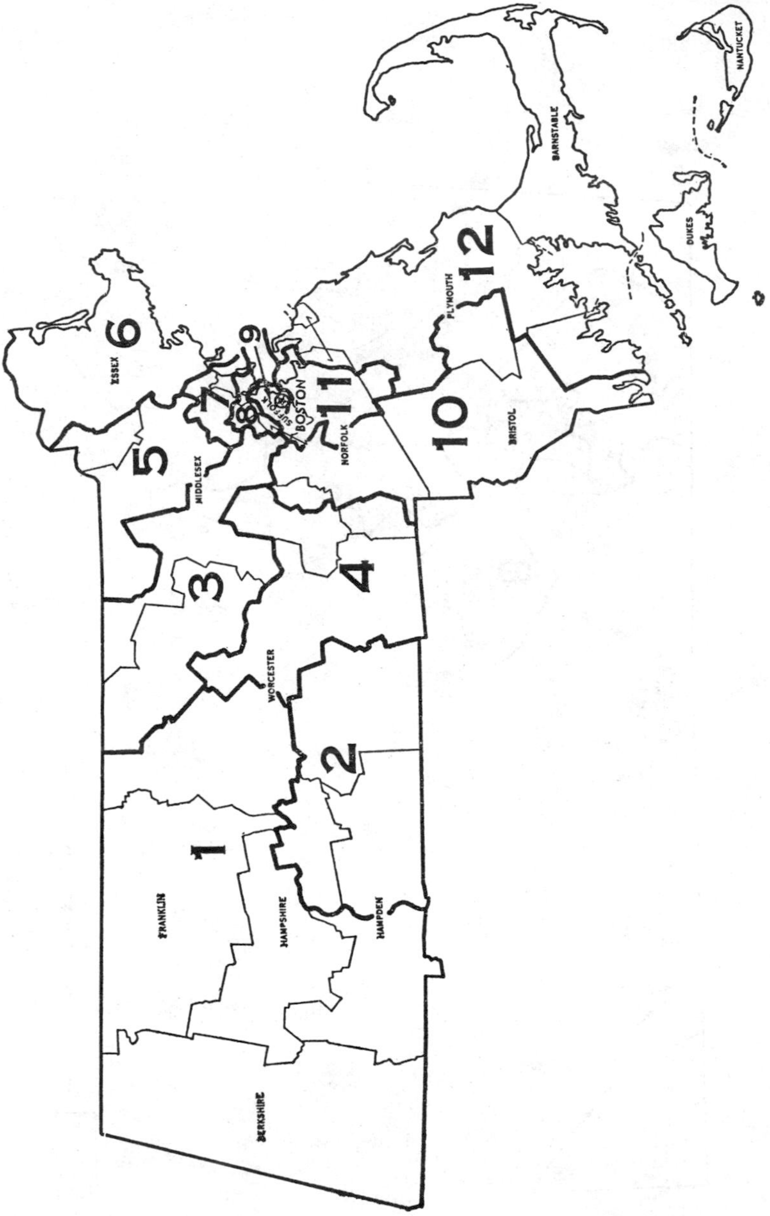

MICHIGAN

(19 districts)

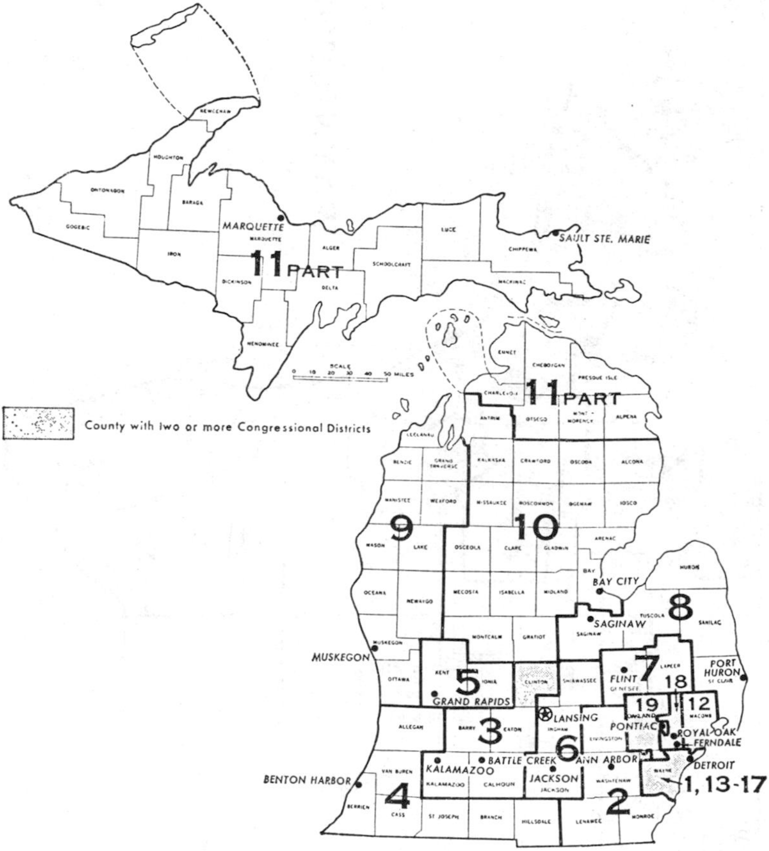

MICHIGAN

Districts Established August 28, 1964

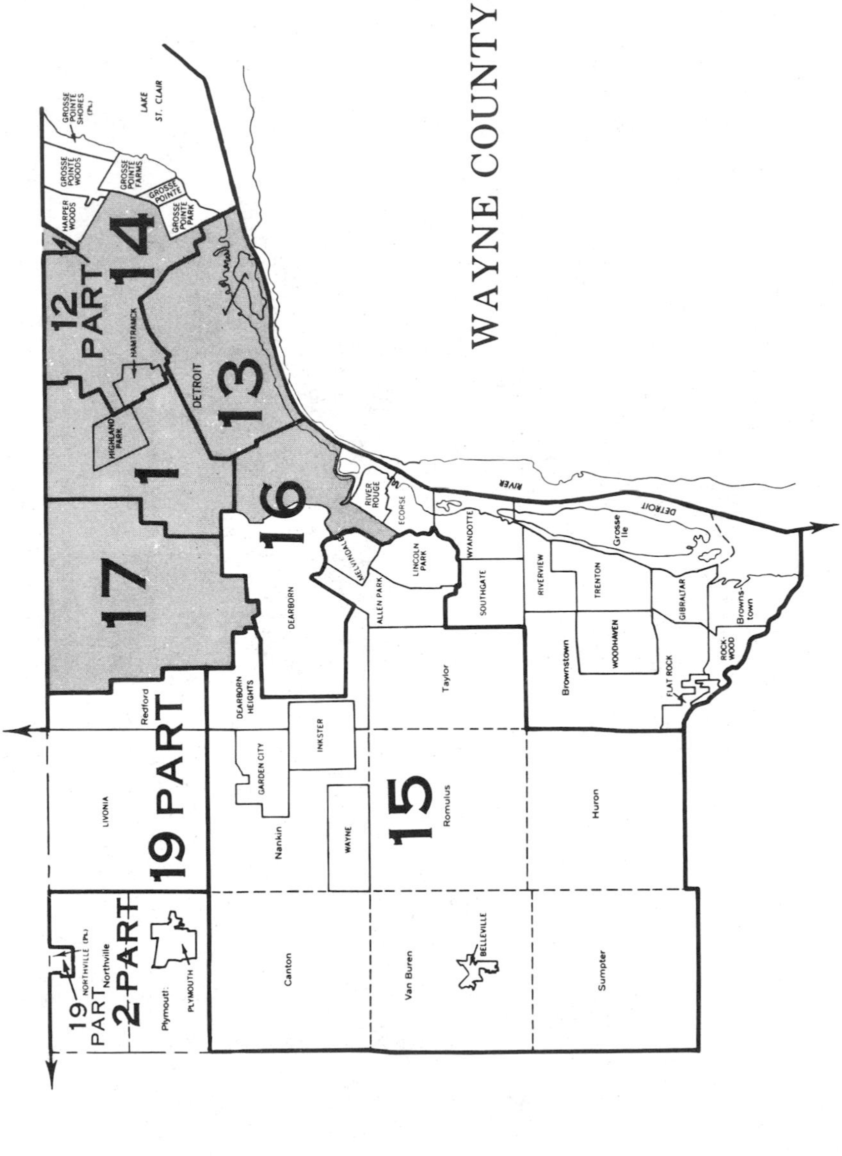

MINNESOTA

(8 districts)

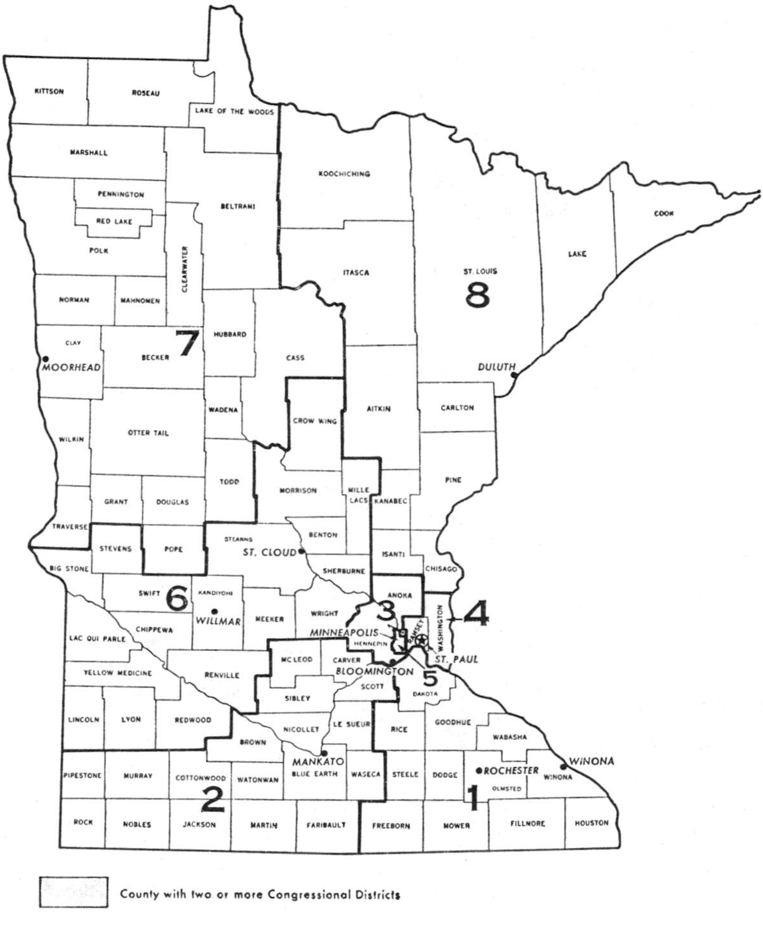

MISSISSIPPI

(5 districts)

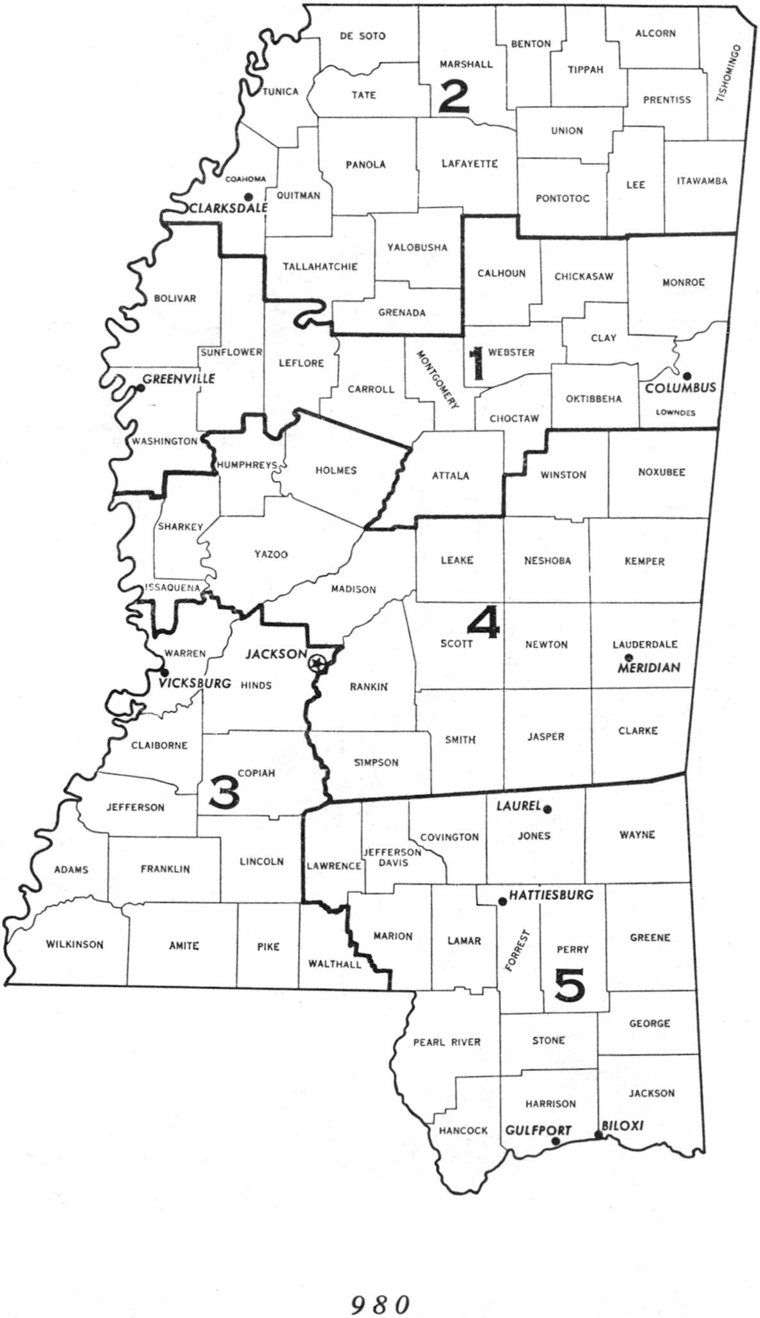

MISSOURI

(10 districts)

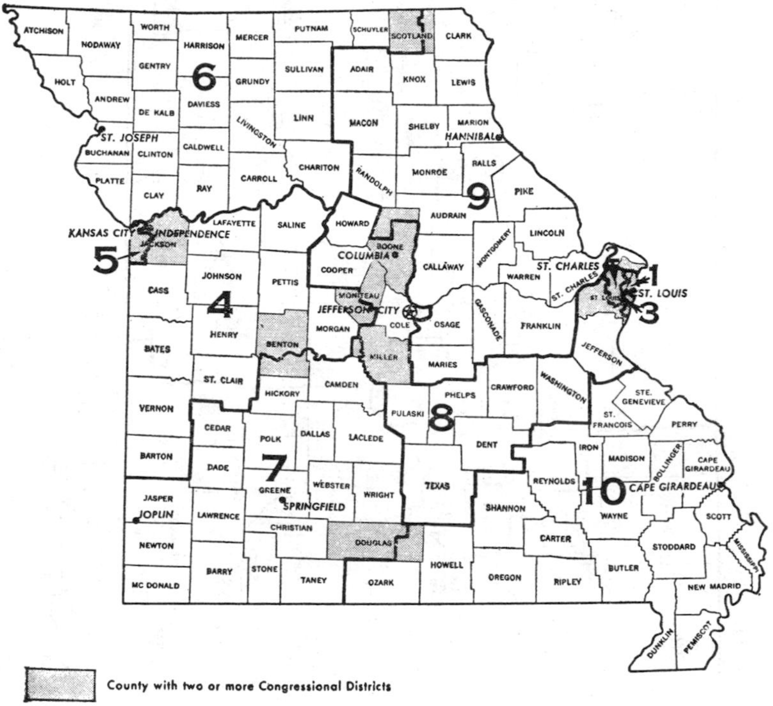

MONTANA

(2 districts)

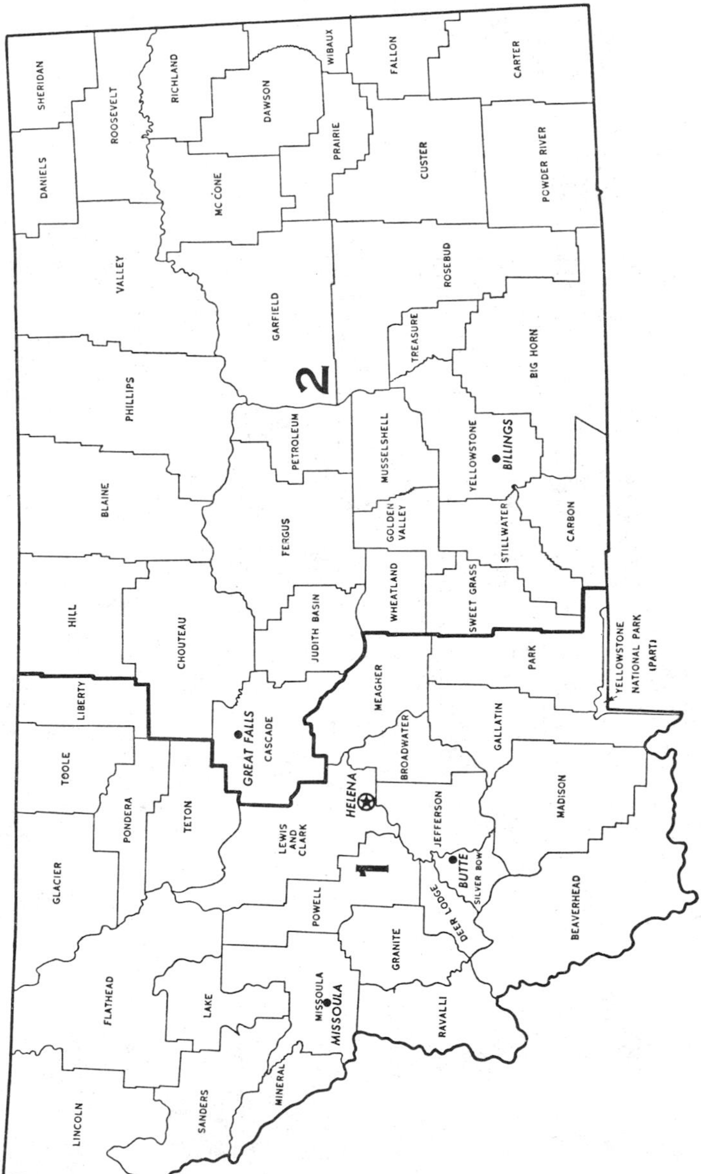

NEBRASKA

(3 districts)

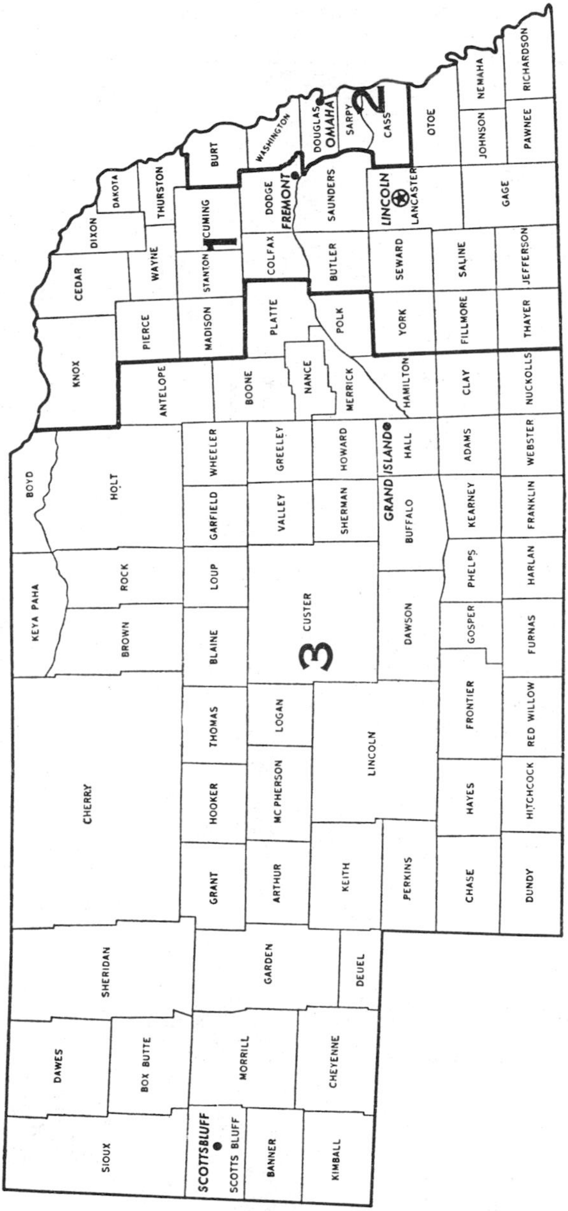

NEVADA

(1 at large)

NEW HAMPSHIRE

(2 districts)

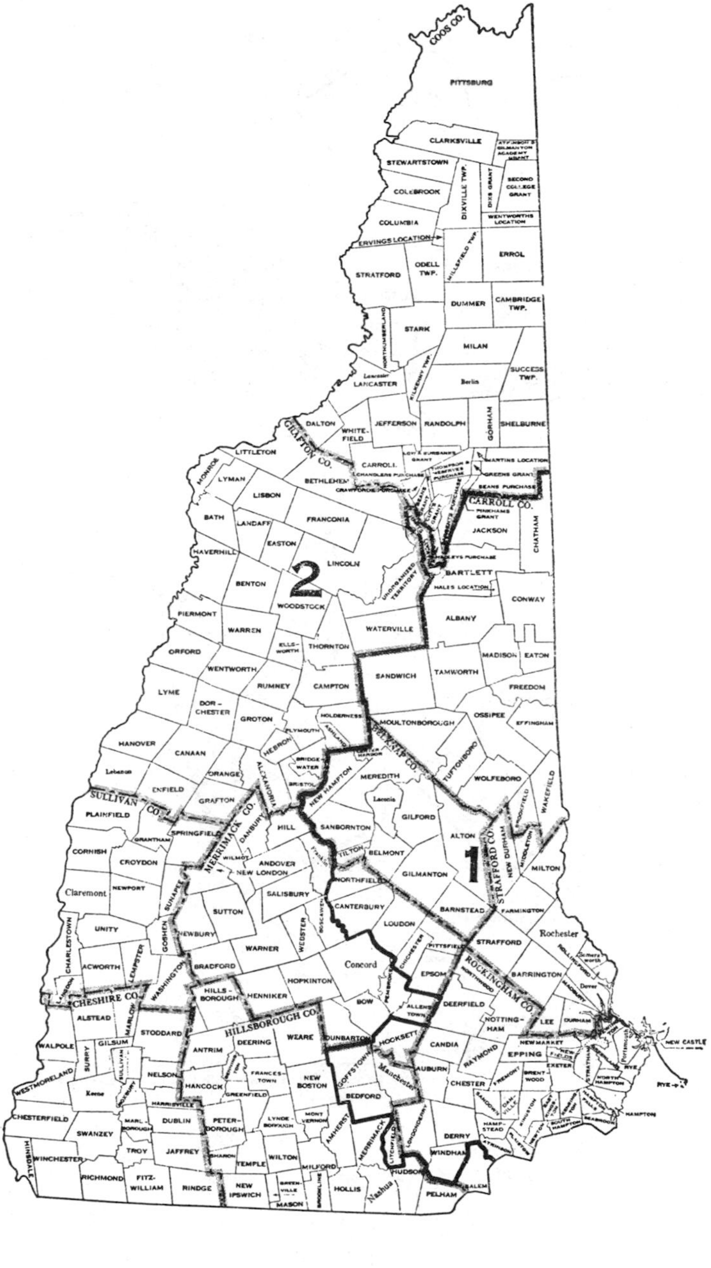

NEW JERSEY

(15 districts)

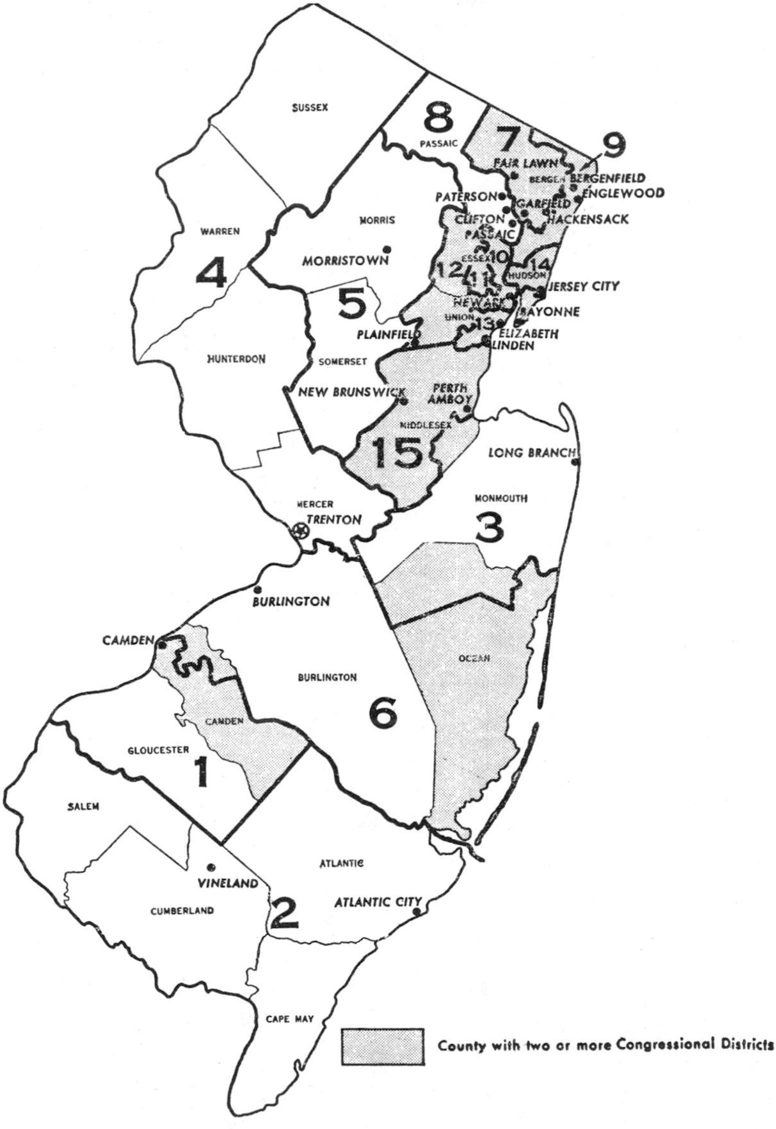

51-915°—71——60

NEW MEXICO

(2 districts)

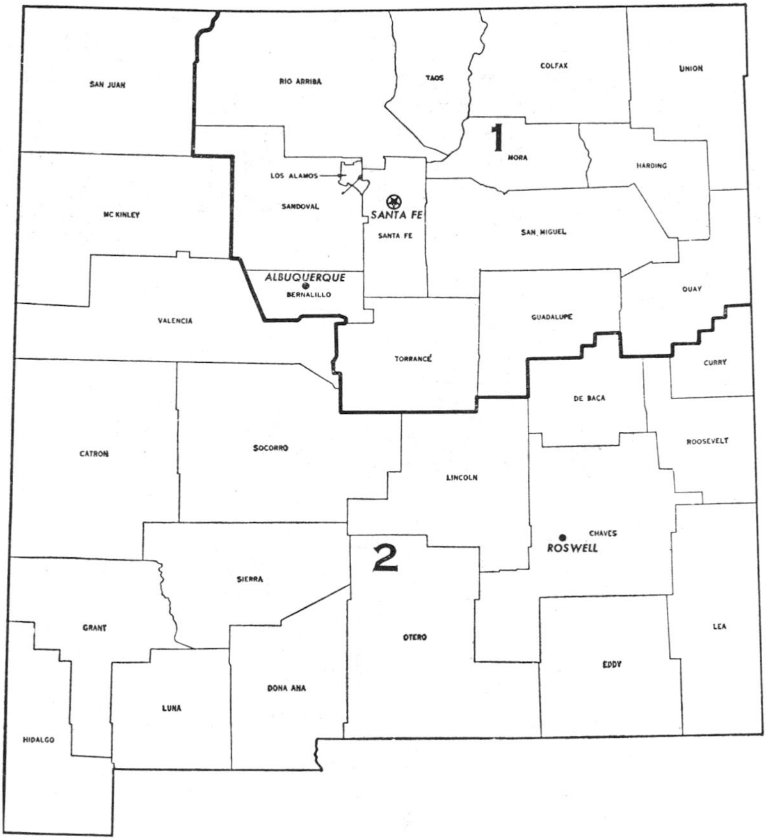

NEW YORK

(41 districts)

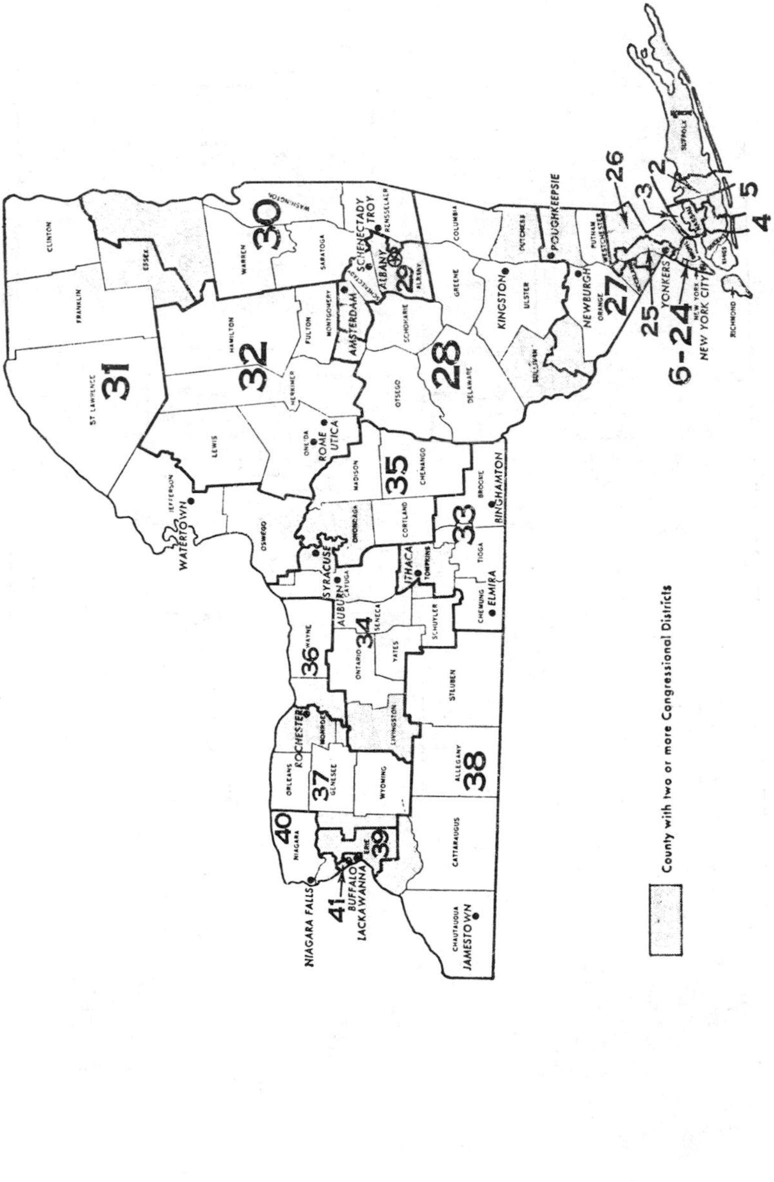

NEW YORK
Districts Established January 23, 1970

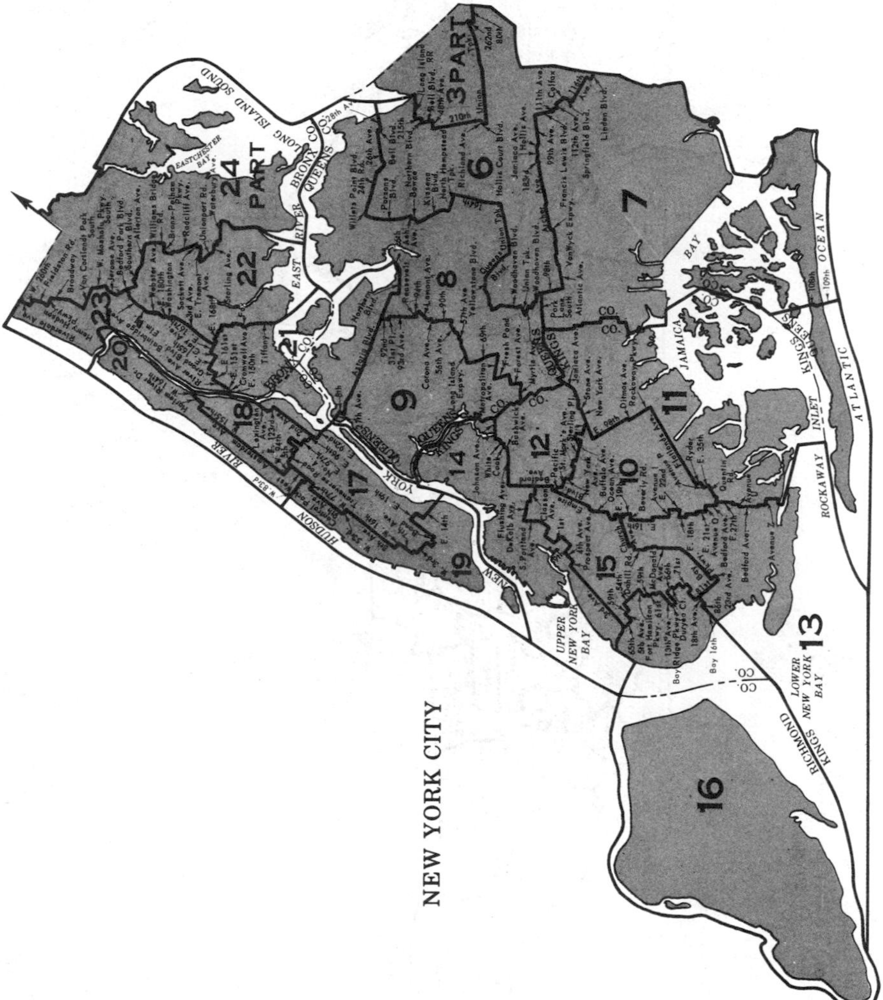

NORTH CAROLINA

(11 districts)

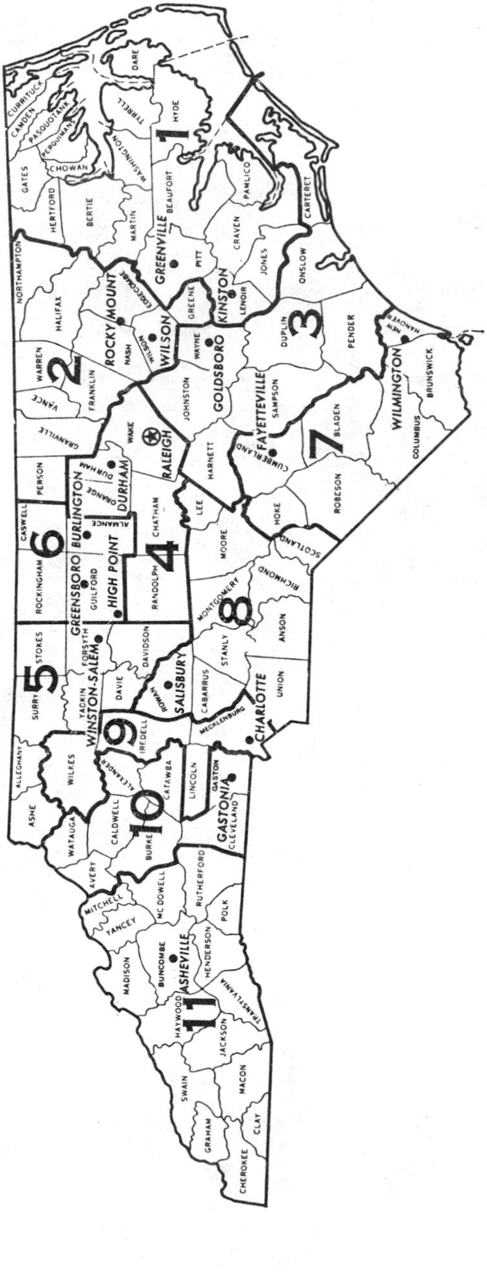

NORTH DAKOTA

(2 districts)

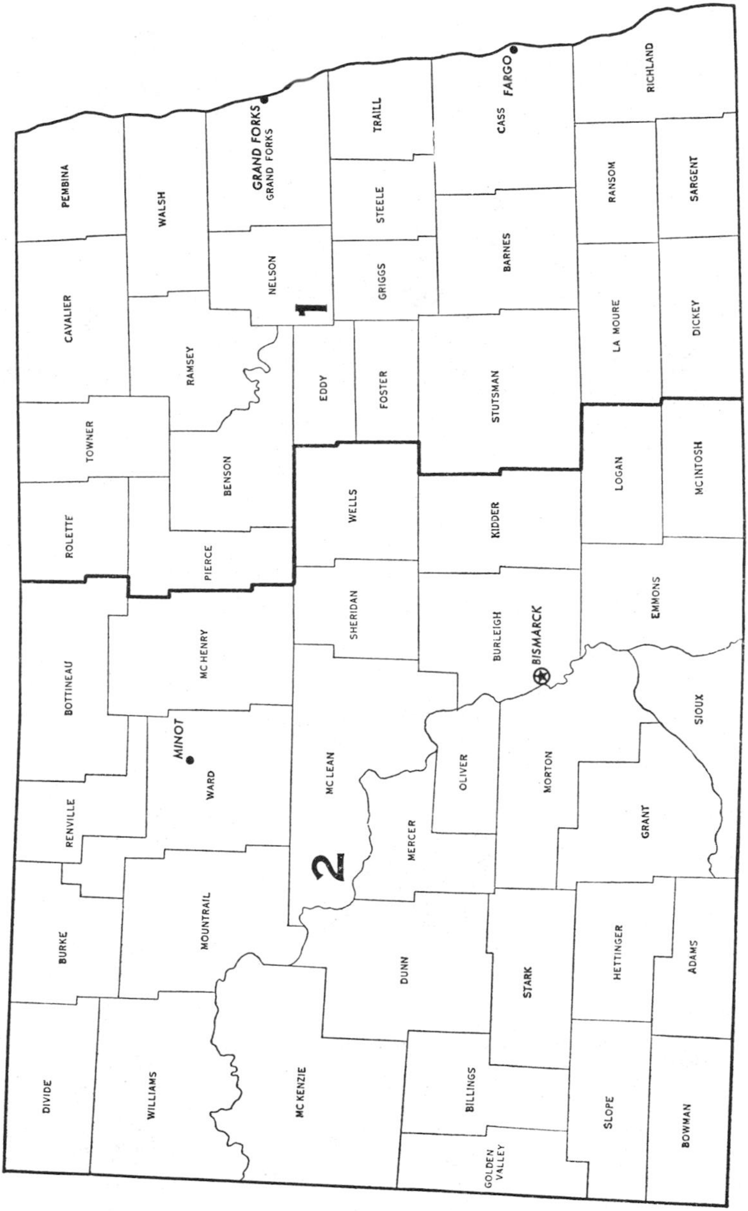

OHIO

(24 districts)

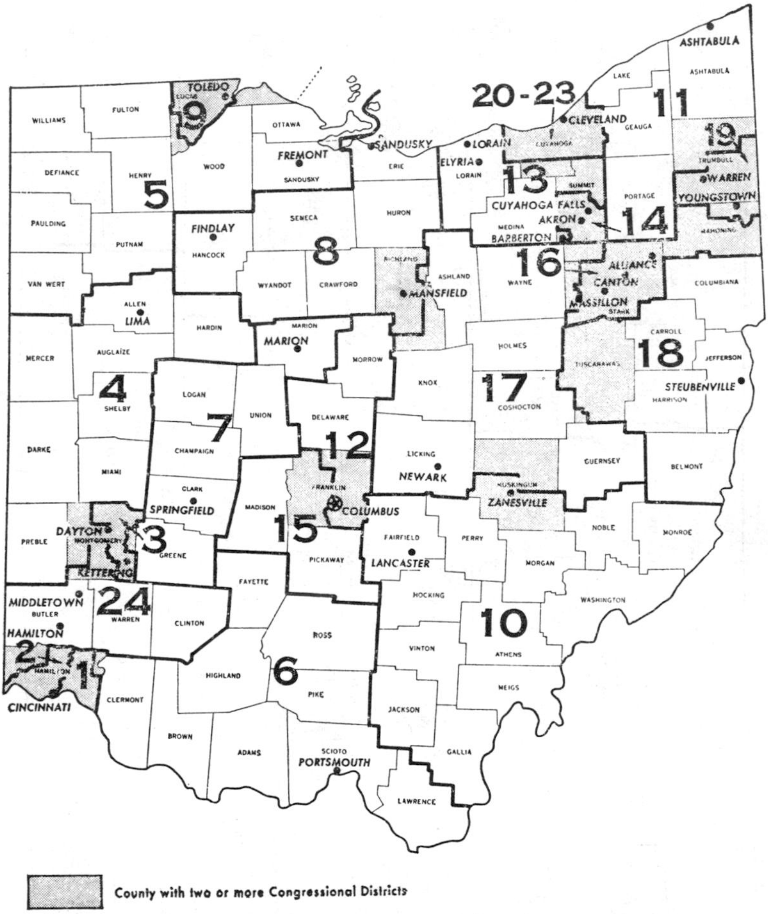

OHIO

Districts Established January 29, 1968

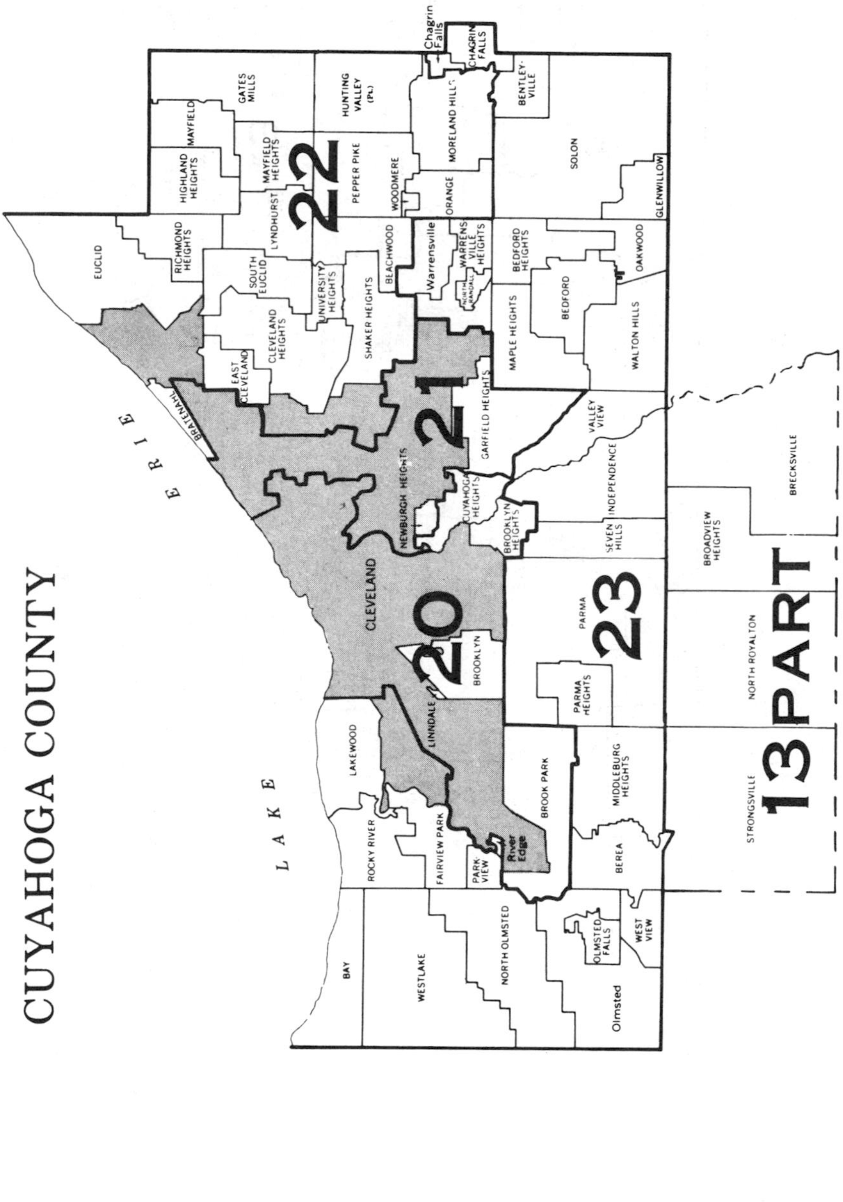

OKLAHOMA

(6 districts)

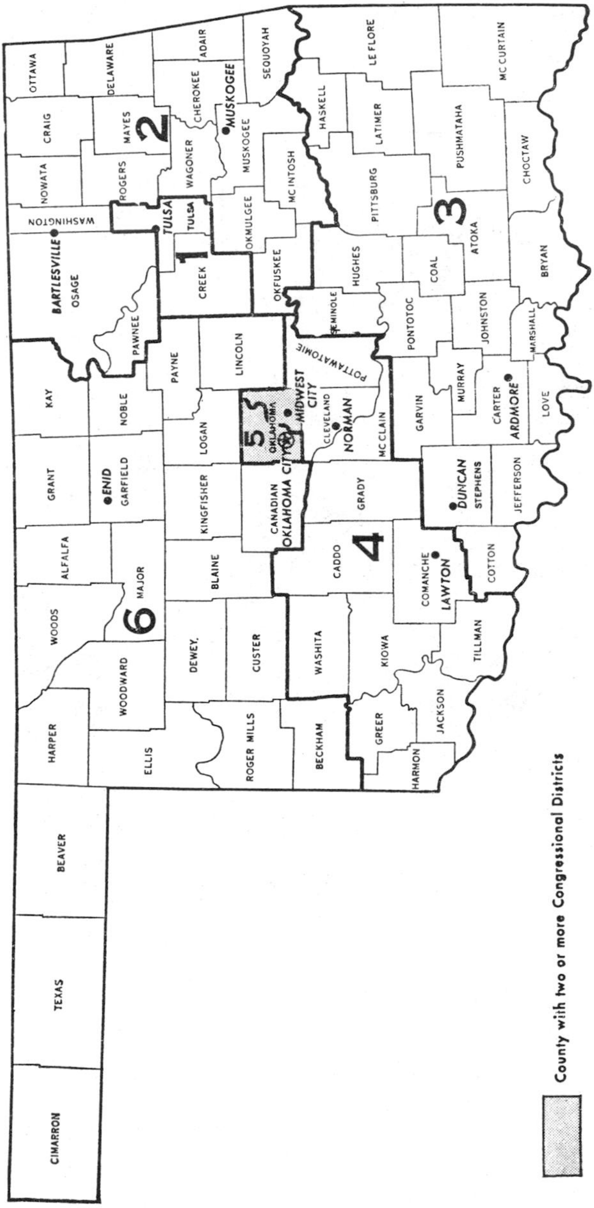

OREGON

(4 districts)

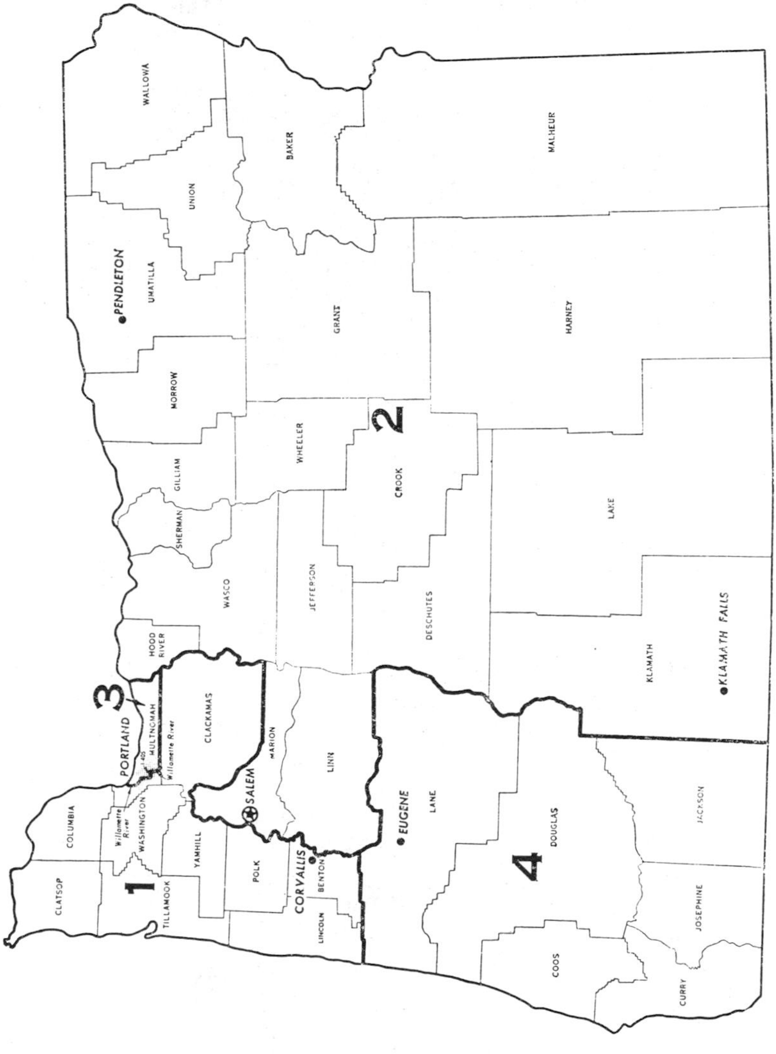

PENNSYLVANIA

(27 districts)

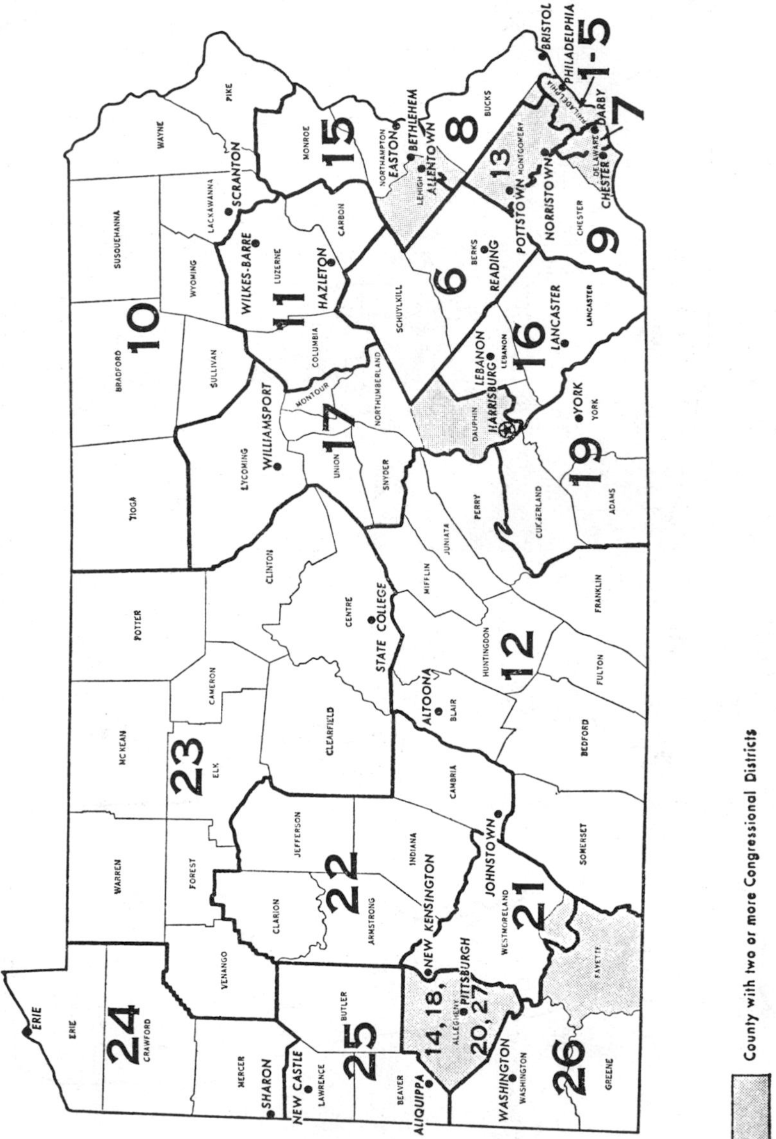

RHODE ISLAND

(2 districts)

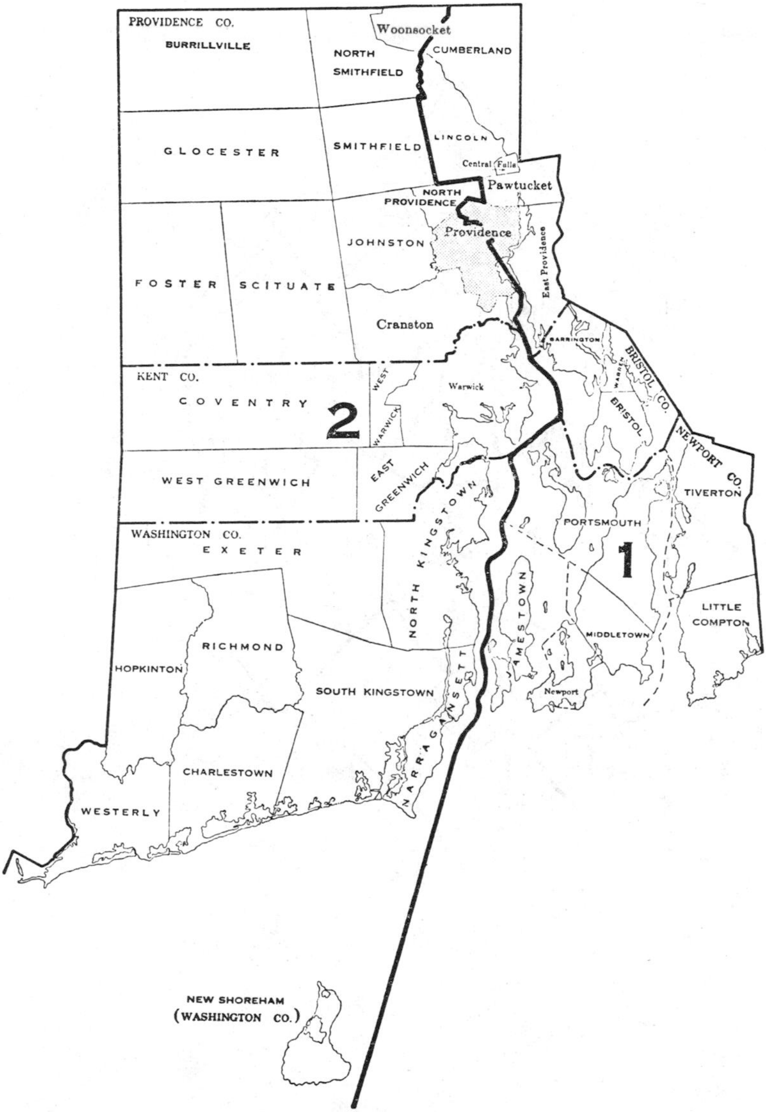

SOUTH CAROLINA

(6 districts)

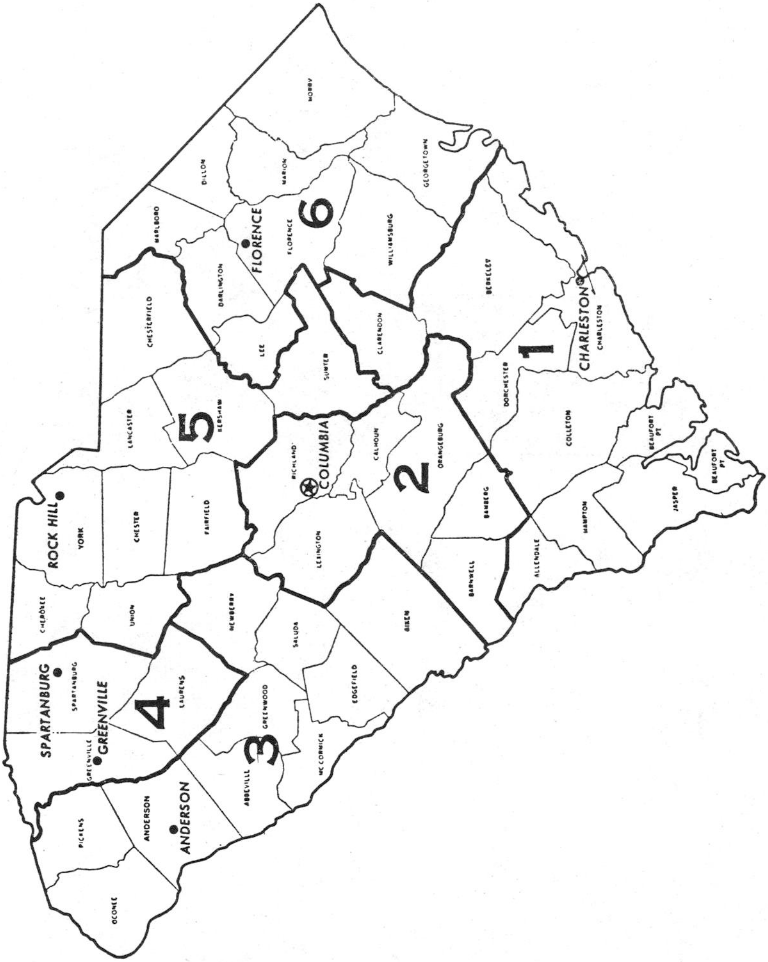

SOUTH DAKOTA

(2 districts)

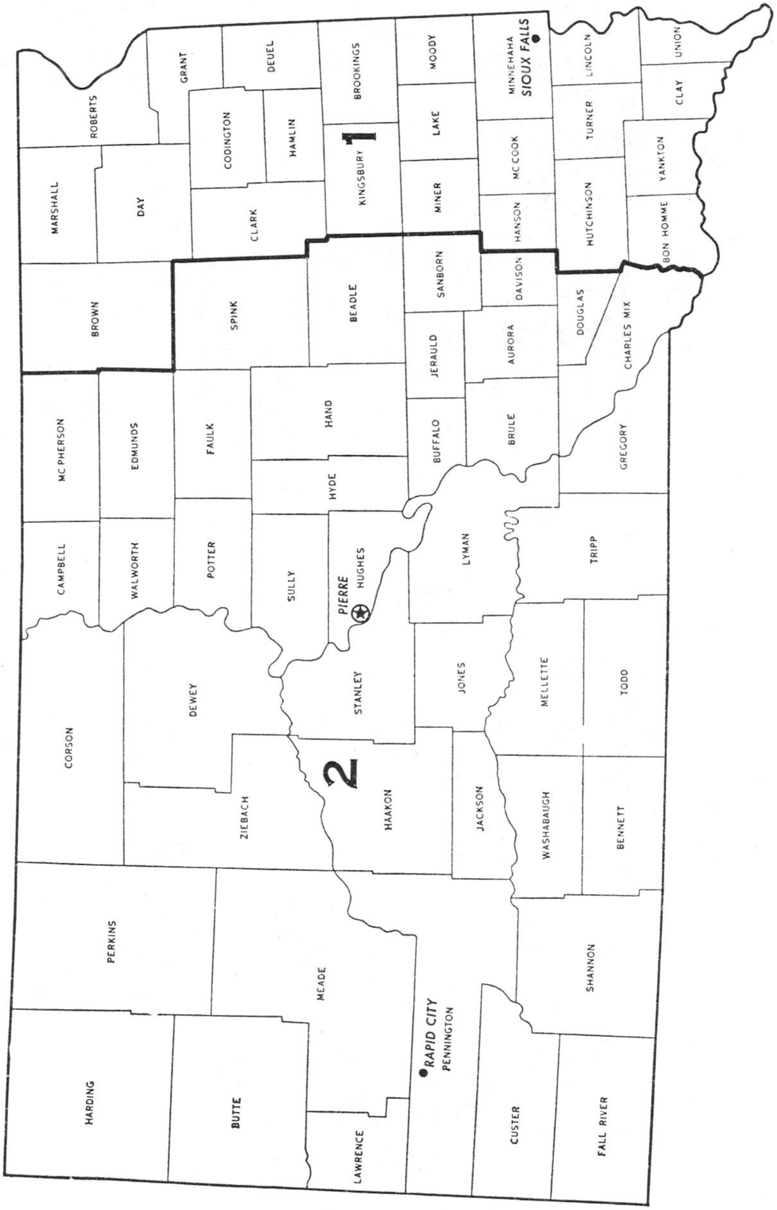

TENNESSEE

(9 districts)

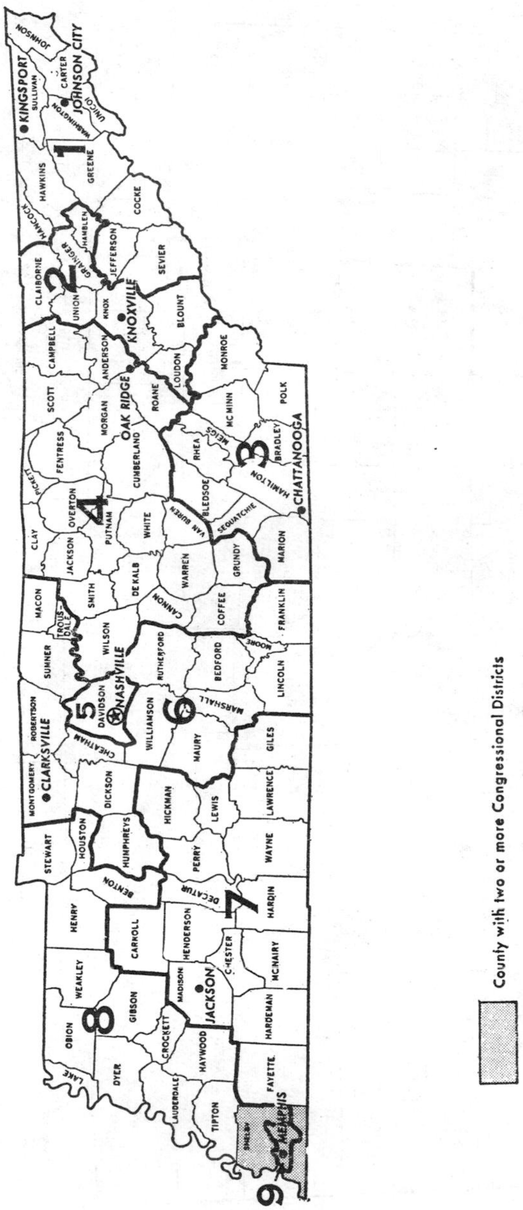

TEXAS

(23 districts)

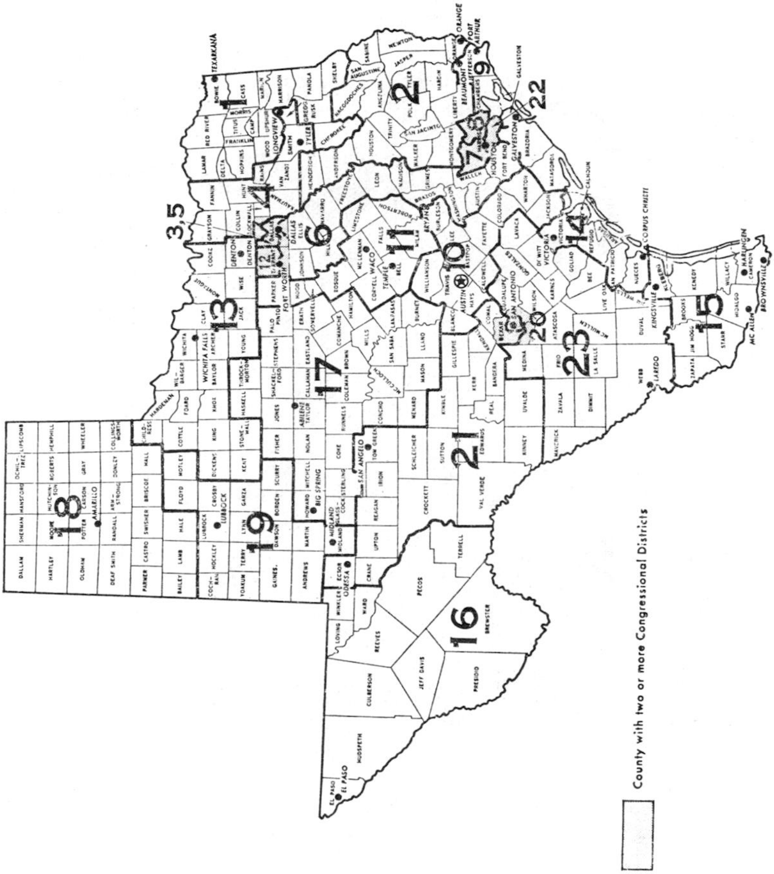

TEXAS
Districts Established August 28, 1967

DALLAS COUNTY

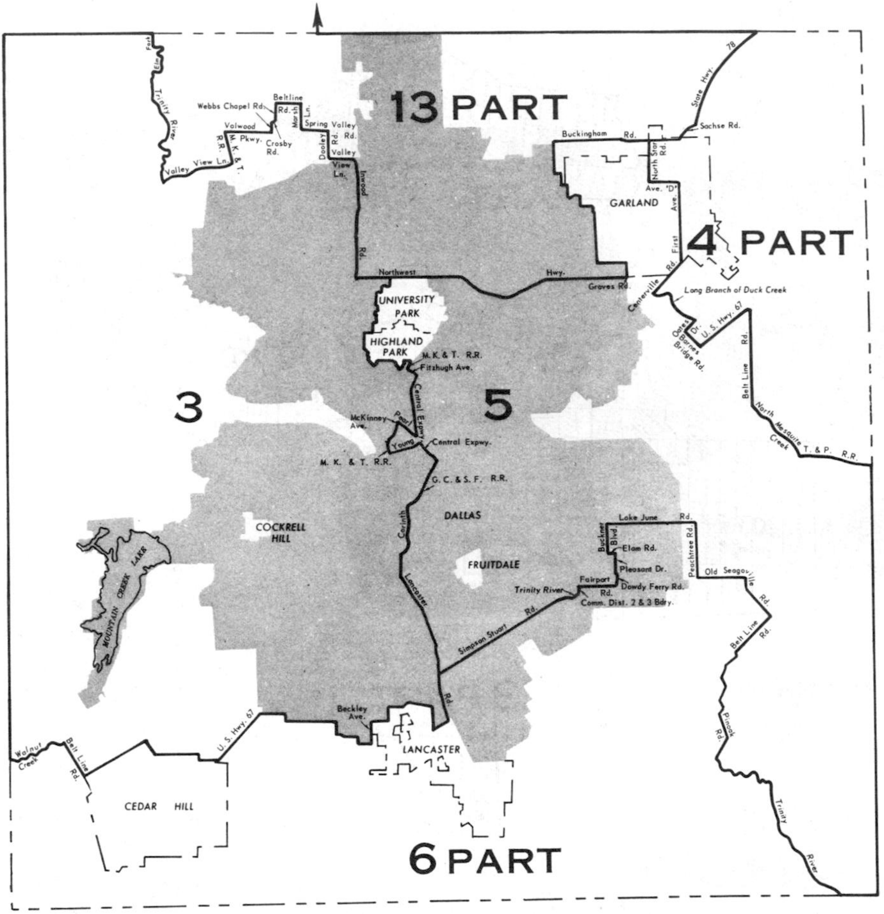

UTAH

(2 districts)

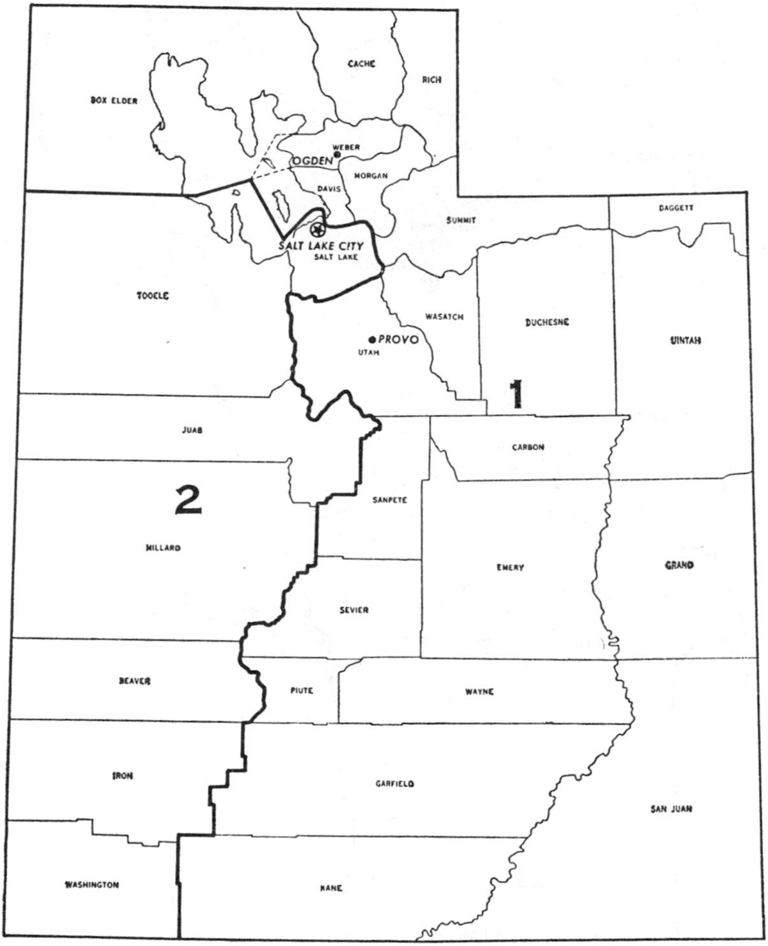

VERMONT

(1 at large)

VIRGINIA

(10 districts)

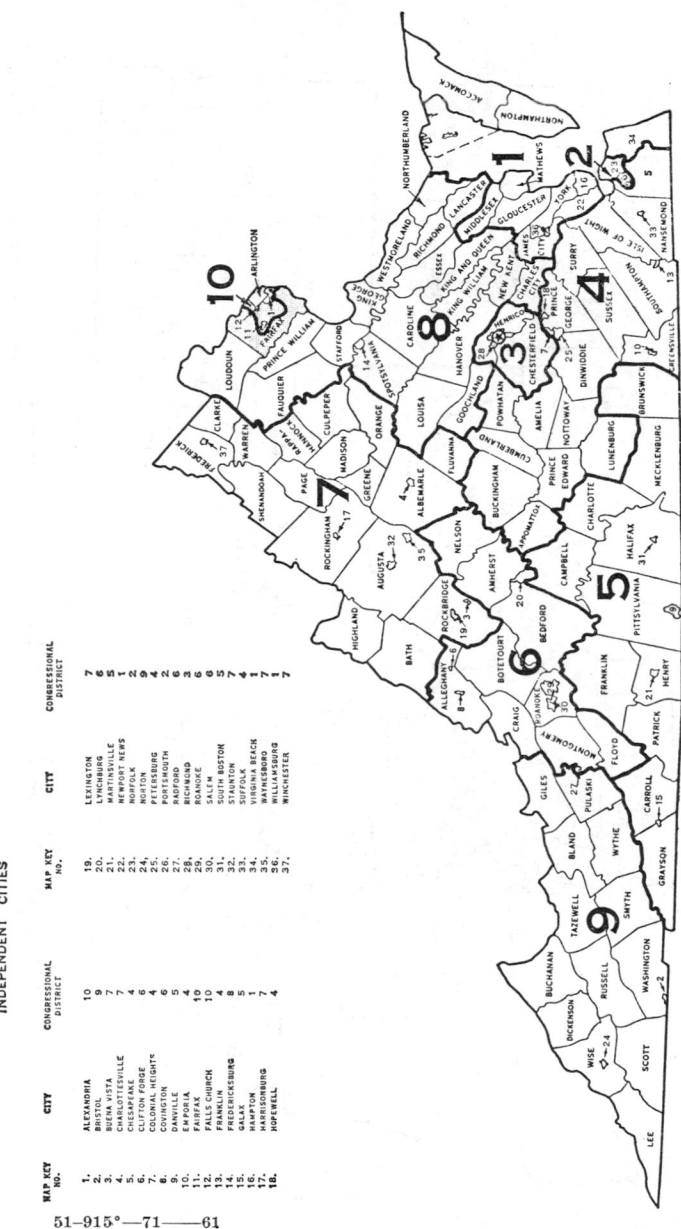

INDEPENDENT CITIES

MAP KEY NO.	CITY	CONGRESSIONAL DISTRICT	MAP KEY NO.	CITY	CONGRESSIONAL DISTRICT
1.	ALEXANDRIA	10	19.	LEXINGTON	7
2.	BRISTOL	9	20.	LYNCHBURG	6
3.	BUENA VISTA	7	21.	MARTINSVILLE	5
4.	CHARLOTTESVILLE	7	22.	NEWPORT NEWS	1
5.	CHESAPEAKE	4	23.	NORFOLK	2
6.	CLIFTON FORGE	6	24.	NORTON	9
7.	COLONIAL HEIGHTS	4	25.	PETERSBURG	4
8.	COVINGTON	6	26.	PORTSMOUTH	2
9.	DANVILLE	5	27.	RADFORD	6
10.	EMPORIA	4	28.	RICHMOND	3
11.	FAIRFAX	10	29.	ROANOKE	6
12.	FALLS CHURCH	10	30.	SALEM	6
13.	FRANKLIN	4	31.	SOUTH BOSTON	5
14.	FREDERICKSBURG	8	32.	STAUNTON	7
15.	GALAX	5	33.	SUFFOLK	4
16.	HAMPTON	1	34.	VIRGINIA BEACH	1
17.	HARRISONBURG	7	35.	WAYNESBORO	7
18.	HOPEWELL	4	36.	WILLIAMSBURG	1
			37.	WINCHESTER	7

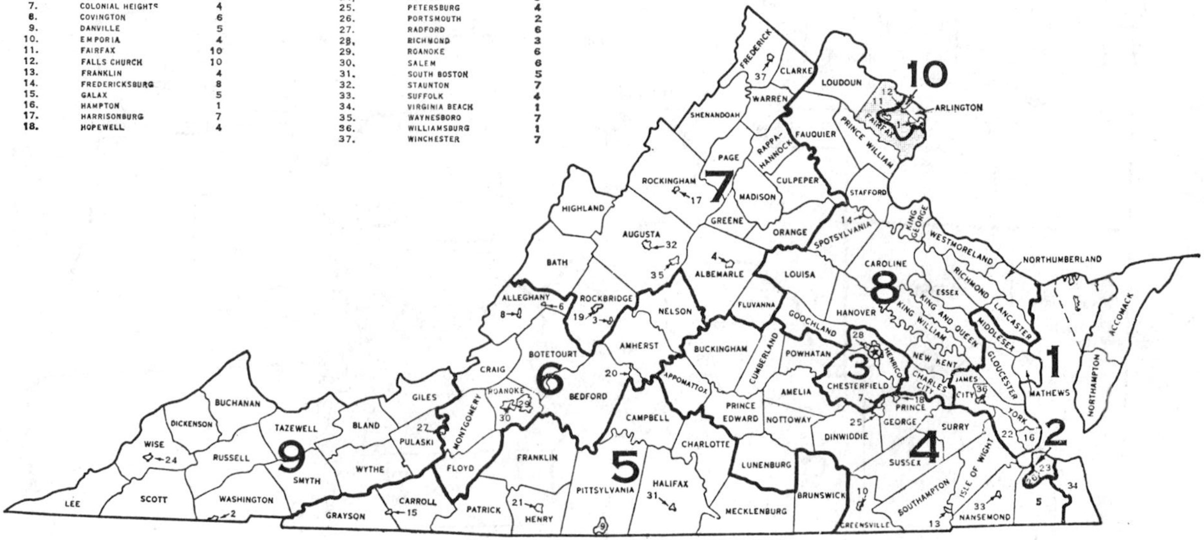

County with two or more Congressional Districts

WASHINGTON

(7 districts)

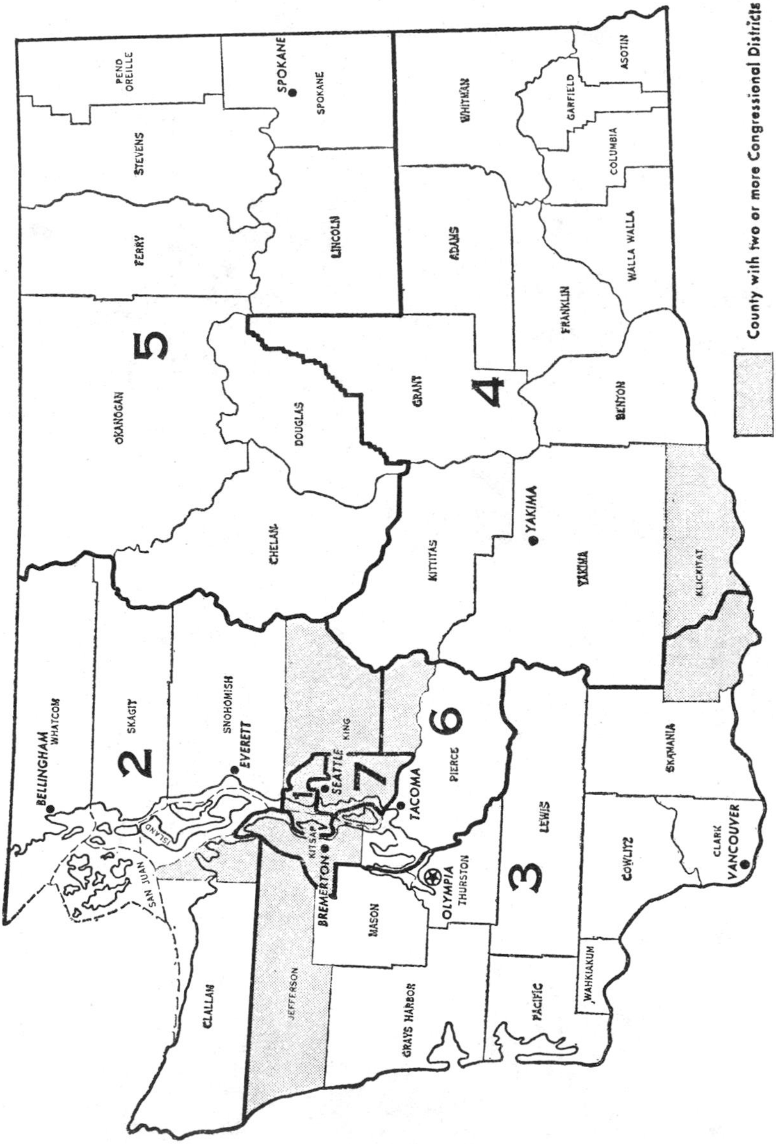

WEST VIRGINIA

(5 districts)

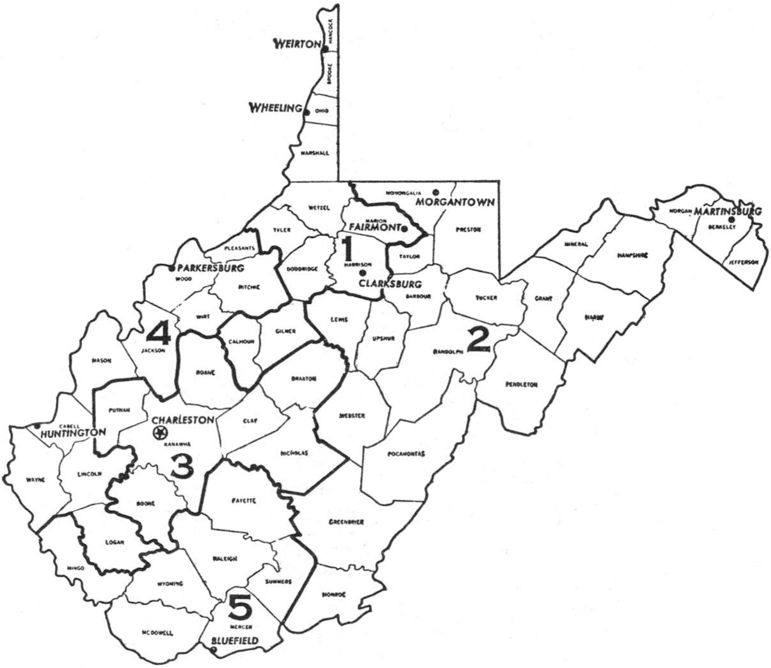

WISCONSIN

(10 districts)

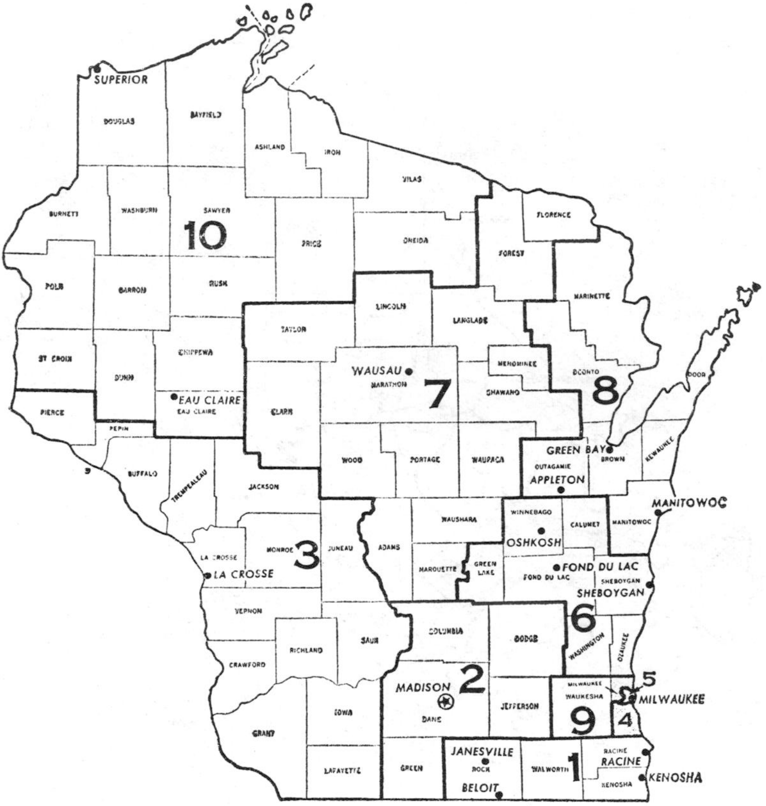

County with two or more Congressional Districts

WYOMING

(1 at large)

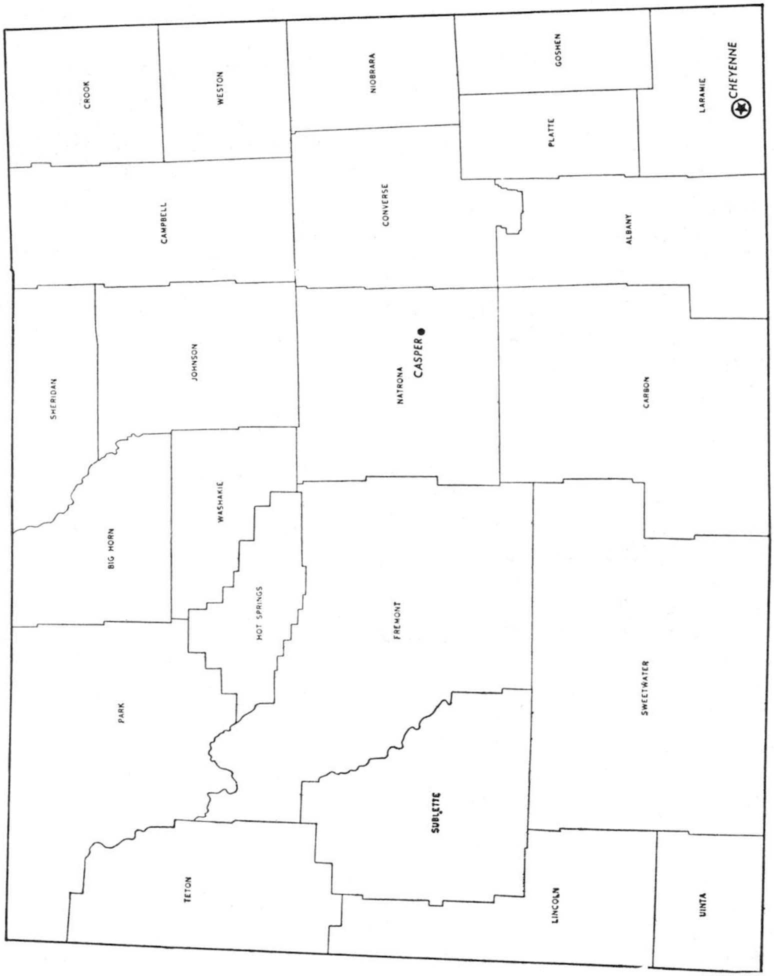

NATIONAL OUTLAYS

Federal Information Exchange System
National Summary, Outlays

DEPARTMENT OR AGENCY	FISCAL 1968	FISCAL 1969	FISCAL 1970
DEPARTMENT OF DEFENSE	$ 63,242,955,000*	$ 62,966,215,000*	$ 57,653,475,000*
ATOMIC ENERGY COMMISSION	2,654,376,261	2,640,891,269	2,603,856,927
NASA	4,297,660,089	3,847,351,174	3,681,179,846
DEPARTMENT OF TRANSPORTATION	5,882,740,153	6,675,256,941	7,172,212,141
DEPARTMENT OF COMMERCE	1,216,375,758	1,226,169,850	1,160,099,531
DEPARTMENT OF THE INTERIOR	1,808,079,354	1,973,736,716	2,397,794,908
DEPARTMENT OF JUSTICE	230,019,227	348,431,261	575,998,342
HEW	41,539,193,829	46,637,477,439	52,536,934,491
HOUSING AND URBAN DEV.	9,979,134,912	10,550,513,185	1,950,867,536
OEO	1,125,464,213	1,211,006,231	759,865,454
DEPARTMENT OF AGRICULTURE	11,864,038,009	13,702,923,633	12,858,526,390
POST OFFICE DEPARTMENT	6,120,314,956	6,664,165,282	7,311,471,999
VETERANS ADMINISTRATION	11,810,086,002	12,737,180,395	9,487,344,990
CIVIL SERVICE COMMISSION	3,119,369,162	3,493,646,569	4,049,168,209
TREASURY DEPARTMENT	12,583,235,474	14,486,865,642	15,972,748,090
DEPARTMENT OF LABOR	1,633,041,072	1,977,630,446	2,407,652,747
GENERAL SERVICES ADMIN.	1,820,458,835	2,053,487,527	1,738,775,003
RAILROAD RETIREMENT BOARD	1,499,912,254	1,653,982,730	1,710,065,344
AGENCY FOR INTERNAT. DEV.	1,223,282,914	1,304,459,084	1,322,496,969
NATIONAL SCIENCE FOUNDATION	488,050,575	425,180,189	449,349,237
TENNESSEE VALLEY AUTHORITY	516,599,663	590,836,967	690,697,726
DEPARTMENT OF STATE	404,904,605	410,884,221	406,585,952
OFFICE OF EMER. PREPAR.	46,516,350	34,569,203	191,445,860

DEPARTMENT OR AGENCY	FISCAL 1968	FISCAL 1969	FISCAL 1970
FED. HOME LOAN BANK	150,250,022	82,612,042	161,964,317
U.S. INFORMATION AGENCY	81,958,311	138,147,375	137,824,111
PANAMA CANAL	85,592,593	86,158,099	92,847,215
PEACE CORPS	90,647,594	80,593,039	77,600,962
SMALL BUSINESS ADMIN.	692,836,267	657,729,418	71,022,269
SELECTIVE SERVICE SYSTEM	54,994,000	58,602,000	68,816,000
CIVIL AERONAUTICS BOARD	62,988,281	51,689,714	45,031,418
NATIONAL LABOR REL. BOARD	30,287,861	33,062,043	37,354,422
SMITHSONIAN INSTITUTION	26,460,363	28,650,137	33,108,589
INTERSTATE COMMERCE COMM.	23,218,033	23,958,916	26,574,131
NATL. FOUND. ARTS, HUM.	14,411,843	13,110,142	24,990,965
SEC	17,270,932	18,173,434	21,243,871
FEDERAL TRADE COMMISSION	14,001,843	15,285,492	18,880,256
FEDERAL POWER COMMISSION	14,666,871	15,779,910	18,175,663
FEDERAL COMMUNICATIONS COMM.	19,689,773	20,932,448	13,035,095
BUREAU OF THE BUDGET	9,194,030	9,769,405	12,047,601
EQUAL EMPLOYMENT OPPORT.	5,560,495	7,874,480	11,951,687
FED. MEDIATION AND CONCIL.	7,378,423	8,067,593	8,977,092
U.S. SOLDIERS HOME	6,986,454	8,348,202	8,324,439
WATER RESOURCES COUNCIL	3,184,577	3,381,805	5,821,098
RENEGOTIATION BOARD	2,578,566	3,036,070	3,873,519
FARM CREDIT ADMINISTRATION	3,004,400	3,361,422	3,833,970
FEDERAL MARITIME COMM.	3,400,834	3,545,434	3,767,667
TAX COURT OF THE U.S.	2,296,967	2,514,483	3,020,810
AMERICAN BATTLE MONUMENTS	—	2,238,570	2,418,312

DEPARTMENT OR AGENCY	FISCAL 1968	FISCAL 1969	FISCAL 1970
COMMISSION ON CIVIL RIGHTS	2,299,040	2,193,140	2,393,250
NATIONAL MEDIATION BOARD	1,933,955	2,067,121	2,105,216
COUNCIL OF ECONOMIC ADVIS.	872,636	1,136,339	1,134,273
PUBLIC LAND LAW REVIEW	2,279,930	1,308,180	1,071,237
ADVISORY COMM. ON INGOV. REL.	446,854	549,139	748,844
NATL. COUNCIL, MARINE RES.	997,023	914,648	506,915
NASA COUNCIL	455,846	454,062	491,856
FEDERAL RADIATION COUNCIL	104,587	102,102	333,488
FED. COAL MINE SAFETY BOARD	90,975	101,747	76,396
APPALACHIAN REGIONAL COMM.	—	1,351,333	—
NATL. ADVIS. COMM. FOOD + FIB.	61,555	—	—
NATIONAL TOTALS	$186,541,508,803	$198,999,660,438	$190,009,979,646

** Department of Defense outlays include moneys distributed only to the various states of the Union, to territories, to trusts, and to possessions. The figures do not include amounts spent constructing and maintaining foreign military installations. Total fiscal 1968 budget: $78,227,000,000. Total fiscal 1969 budget: $78,666,000,000. Total fiscal 1970 budget: $77,880,000,000.*

Index of 50 parent companies which with their subsidiaries received the largest dollar volume of military prime contract awards in fiscal year 1970

Rank	Parent Company	Rank	Parent Company
21.	American Motors Corp.	36.	Mobil Oil Corp.
4.	American Tel. & Tel.	43.	Morrison-Knudsen Co. & Assoc. (joint venture)
46.	Asiatic Petroleum Corp.	44.	National Presto Industries, Inc.
20.	Avco Corp.	7.	North American Rockwell Corp.
35.	Bendix Corp.	33.	Northrop Corp.
12.	Boeing Co.	28.	Olin Corp.
39.	Collins Radio Co.	47.	Pacific Architects & Engrs., Inc.
37.	DuPont E. I. De Nemours & Co.	40.	Pan American World Airways, Inc.
41.	F M C Corp.	22.	R C A Corp.
19.	Ford Motor Co.	25.	Raymond, Morrison, Knudsen (joint venture)
2.	General Dynamics Corp.	18.	Raytheon Co.
3.	General Electric Co.	50.	R. J. Reynolds Industries, Inc.
17.	General Motors Corp.	38.	Singer Co.
49.	General Telephone & Electn. Corp.	15.	Sperry Rand Corp.
23.	General Tire & Rubber Co.	42.	Standard Oil of California
8.	Grumman Corp.	30.	Standard Oil of New Jersey
45.	Hercules, Inc.	34.	T R W, Inc.
16.	Honeywell, Inc.	29.	Teledyne, Inc.
10.	Hughes Aircraft Co.	27.	Tenneco, Inc.
24.	Intl. Business Machines Corp.	32.	Texas Instruments, Inc.
31.	International Tel. & Tel. Co.	13.	Textron, Inc.
11.	Ling Temco Vought, Inc.	48.	Uniroyal, Inc.
9.	Litton Industries, Inc.	6.	United Aircraft Corp.
1.	Lockheed Aircraft Corp.	14.	Westinghouse Electric Corp.
26.	Martin Marietta Corp.		
5.	McDonnell Douglas Corp.		

Rank	Companies	Dollars	Percent of U.S. total	Cumulative percent of U.S. total
	U.S. total military prime contract awards	$31,314,559,000	100.00	100.00
	Total, 50 top companies and their subsidiaries	$18,584,575,000	59.33	59.33
	All other companies and their subsidiaries	$12,729,984,000	40.67	40.67
1.	Lockheed Aircraft Corp.	$1,840,440,000		
	Lockheed Shipbuilding	$7,145,000		
	One other subsidiary	$153,000		
	Total	$1,847,738,000	5.90	5.90
2.	General Dynamics Corp.	$1,169,702,000		
	Stromberg Carlson Corp.	$6,293,000		
	Stromberg Datagraphics, Inc.	$6,956,000		
	Three other subsidiaries	$255,000		
	Total	$1,183,206,000	3.78	9.68

Rank	Companies	Dollars	Percent of U.S. total	Cumulative percent of U.S. total
3.	General Electric Co.	$998,737,000		
	General Electric Supply Co.	$1,715,000		
	Total	$1,000,452,000	3.19	12.87
4.	American Tel. and Tel. Co.	$178,581,000		
	Chesapeake & Potomac Tel. Co.	$12,726,000		
	Mountain States Tel. & Tel. Co.	$2,154,000		
	Southern Bell Tel. and Tel.	$2,477,000		
	Southwestern Bell Telephone	$1,774,000		
	Teletype Corp.	$12,350,000		
	Western Electric Co., Inc.	$719,029,000		
	Seven other subsidiaries	$2,142,000		
	Total	$931,233,000	2.97	15.84
5.	McDonnell Douglas Corp.	$856,764,000		
	Conductron Corp.	$21,534,000		
	Hycon Mfg. Co.	$3,297,000		
	Tridea Electronics, Inc.	$1,140,000		
	One other subsidiary	$10,000		
	Total	$882,745,000	2.82	18.66
6.	United Aircraft Corp.	$873,793,000	2.79	21.45
7.	North American Rockwell Corp.	$706,843,000		
	Three other subsidiaries	$287,000		
	Total	$707,130,000	2.26	23.71
8.	Grumman Corp.	$44,169,000		
	Grumman Aerospace Corp.	$616,603,000		
	Total	$660,772,000	2.11	25.82
9.	Litton Industries, Inc.	$9,314,000		
	Litton Precision Prods., Inc.	$4,837,000		
	Litton Systems, Inc.	$527,355,000		
	Ten other subsidiaries	$1,557,000		
	Total	$543,063,000	1.73	27.55
10.	Hughes Aircraft Co.	$496,685,000		
	One subsidiary	$188,000		
	Total	$496,873,000	1.59	29.14
11.	Ling Temco Vought, Inc.	$34,973,000		
	Braniff Airways, Inc.	$34,007,000		
	Kentron Hawaii Ltd.	$19,887,000		
	LTV Electrosystems	$86,067,000		
	LTV Aerospace Corp.	$295,491,000		
	Okonite Co.	$1,146,000		

Rank	Companies	Dollars	Percent of U.S. total	Cumulative percent of U.S. total
	Service Technology Corp.	$3,496,000		
	Wilson & Co., Inc.	$3,157,000		
	Seven other subsidiaries	$1,070,000		
	Total	$479,294,000	1.53	30.67
12.	Boeing Co.	$474,661,000	1.52	32.19
13.	Textron, Inc.	$161,995,000		
	Bell Aerospace Corp.	$266,351,000		
	Eight other subsidiaries	$2,563,000		
	Total	$430,909,000	1.38	33.57
14.	Westinghouse Electric Corp.	$409,970,000		
	Urban Systems Dev. Corp.	$5,990,000		
	Four other subsidiaries	$1,695,000		
	Total	$417,655,000	1.33	34.90
15.	Sperry Rand Corp.	$398,888,000	1.27	36.17
16.	Honeywell, Inc.	$397,938,000	1.27	37.44
17.	General Motors Corp.	$385,650,000		
	One subsidiary	$88,000		
	Total	$385,738,000	1.23	38.67
18.	Raytheon Co.	$375,579,000		
	Machlett Laboratories, Inc.	$3,520,000		
	Five other subsidiaries	$539,000		
	Total	$379,638,000	1.21	39.88
19.	Ford Motor Co.	$78,817,000		
	Philco Ford Corp.	$267,060,000		
	Total	$345,877,000	1.10	40.98
20.	Avco Corp.	$263,944,000		
	Avco Economic Systems Corp.	$5,761,000		
	Total	$269,705,000	0.86	41.84
21.	American Motors Corp.			
	Jeep Corp.	$266,212,000		
	Rambler Motors Ltd.	$88,000		
	Total	$266,300,000	0.85	42.69
22.	R C A Corp.	$244,413,000		
	R C A Global Communications, Inc.	$18,289,000		
	Three other subsidiaries	$103,000		
	Total	$262,805,000	0.84	43.53

Rank	Companies	Dollars	Percent of U.S. total	Cumulative percent of U.S. total
23.	General Tire & Rubber Co.	$4,978,000		
	Aerojet General Corp.	$239,047,000		
	Batesville Mfg. Corp.	$16,845,000		
	Six other subsidiaries	$969,000		
	Total	$261,839,000	0.84	44.37
24.	Intl. Business Machines Corp.	$255,875,000		
	Two subsidiaries	$177,000		
	Total	$256,052,000	0.82	45.19
25.	Raymond, Morrison, Knudsen (joint venture)	$256,000,000	0.82	46.01
26.	Martin Marietta Corp.	$188,403,000		
	Harvey Aluminum, Inc.	$7,512,000		
	Harvey Aluminum Sales	$54,924,000		
	One other subsidiary	$26,000		
	Total	$250,865,000	0.80	46.81
27.	Tenneco, Inc.			
	J. I. Case Co.	$5,520,000		
	Newport News Shipbld. & Dry Dock Co.	$242,804,000		
	Seven other subsidiaries	$620,000		
	Total	$248,944,000	0.79	47.60
28.	Olin Corp.	$247,654,000	0.79	48.39
29.	Teledyne, Inc.	$57,305,000		
	Amelco, Inc.	$1,706,000		
	Brown Engineering Co., Inc.	$2,976,000		
	Continental Aviation & Engr. Corp.	$24,339,000		
	Continental Motors Corp.	$33,699,000		
	Isotopes, Inc.	$1,830,000		
	Packard Bell Electronics Corp.	$9,632,000		
	Ryan Aeronautical Corp.	$98,356,000		
	Teledyne Industries, Inc.	$5,026,000		
	Fifteen other subsidiaries	$3,548,000		
	Total	$238,417,000	0.76	49.15
30.	Standard Oil Co. (New Jersey)			
	Esso A G	$4,115,000		
	Esso International Corp.	$121,980,000		
	Esso Standard Italiana	$2,169,000		
	Esso Standard Oil Co. S.A.	$2,157,000		
	Humble Oil & Refining Co.	$97,232,000		
	Seven other subsidiaries	$1,535,000		
	Total	$229,188,000	0.73	49.88

Rank	Companies	Dollars	Percent of U.S. total	Cumulative percent of U.S. total
31.	International Tel. & Tel. Corp.	$81,606,000		
	Federal Electric Corp.	$84,033,000		
	ITT Artic Services	$2,131,000		
	ITT Continental Baking Co.	$1,416,000		
	ITT Electro Physics Labs	$2,585,000		
	ITT Gilfillan, Inc.	$44,054,000		
	Twelve other subsidiaries	$1,500,000		
	Total	$217,325,000	0.69	50.57
32.	Texas Instruments, Inc.	$190,540,000	0.61	51.18
33.	Northrop Corp.	$137,136,000		
	Hallicrafters Co.	$19,256,000		
	Northrop Carolina, Inc.	$6,466,000		
	Page Communications, Inc.	$21,300,000		
	One other subsidiary	$35,000		
	Total	$184,193,000	0.59	51.77
34.	T R W, Inc.	$178,744,000		
	Three subsidiaries	$323,000		
	Total	$179,067,000	0.57	52.34
35.	Bendix Corp.	$163,299,000		
	Bendix Field Engineering Corp.	$4,019,000		
	Five other subsidiaries	$430,000		
	Total	$167,748,000	0.54	52.88
36.	Mobil Oil Corp.	$164,429,000		
	Two subsidiaries	$1,167,000		
	Total	$165,596,000	0.53	53.41
37.	DuPont E. I. De Nemours & Co.	$12,315,000		
	Remington Arms Co.	$149,356,000		
	Total	$161,671,000	0.52	53.93
38.	Singer Co.	$2,783,000		
	General Precision Decca Systems	$1,680,000		
	Graflex, Inc.	$1,094,000		
	HRB-Singer, Inc.	$6,710,000		
	Physical Sciences Corp.	$10,910,000		
	Singer General Precision, Inc.	$123,117,000		
	Tele-Signal Corp.	$3,663,000		
	Vapor Corp.	$2,782,000		
	Five other subsidiaries	$1,027,000		
	Total	$153,766,000	0.49	54.42
39.	Collins Radio Co.	$146,186,000	0.47	54.89

Rank	Companies	Dollars	Percent of U.S. total	Cumulative percent of U.S. total
40.	Pan American World Airways	$143,103,000	0.46	55.35
41.	F M C Corp.	$139,783,000		
	Kilby Steel Company, Inc.	$1,055,000		
	One other subsidiary	$73,000		
	Total	$140,911,000	0.45	55.80
42.	Standard Oil Co. of Calif.	$74,670,000		
	Caltex Asia Ltd.	$3,473,000		
	Caltex Oil Products Co.	$51,204,000		
	Caltex Oil Thailand Ltd.	$1,960,000		
	Chevron Oil Co.	$7,582,000		
	Eight other subsidiaries	$1,458,000		
	Total	$140,347,000	0.45	56.25
43.	Morrison-Knudsen Co. & Assocs. (joint venture)	$137,859,000	0.44	56.69
44.	National Presto Industries, Inc.	$132,629,000	0.42	57.11
45.	Hercules, Inc.	$125,521,000		
	Haveg Industries, Inc.	$1,033,000		
	Total	$126,554,000	0.40	57.51
46.	Asiatic Petroleum Corp.	$126,322,000	0.40	57.91
47.	Pacific Architects & Engineers, Inc.	$115,897,000	0.37	58.28
48.	Uniroyal, Inc.	$115,182,000		
	Uniroyal International Corp.	$71,000		
	Total	$115,253,000	0.37	58.65
49.	General Telephone & Electn. Corp.			
	Automatic Electric Co.	$2,941,000		
	Hawaiian Telephone Co.	$9,531,000		
	Lenkurt Electric Co., Inc.	$4,520,000		
	Sylvania Electric Products, Inc.	$81,946,000		
	Sylvania Electronic Systems	$7,557,000		
	Five other subsidiaries	$1,220,000		
	Total	$107,715,000	0.34	58.99
50.	R. J. Reynolds Industries, Inc.	$19,199,000		
	Sea Land Service, Inc.	$86,408,000		
	Two other subsidiaries	$924,000		
	Total	$106,531,000	0.34	59.33

CONGRESSMAN	Administrative Assistant	Page
LENNON (N.C. 7)	Mrs. John E. Campion	596
LENT (N.Y. 5)	Ralph J. Edsell, Jr.	520
LINK (N. Dak. 2)	Wallace Rustad	604
LLOYD (Utah 2)	Paul Winegar	827
LONG (La. 8)	D. Irvin Couvillion	312
LONG (Md. 2)	(none given)	326
LUJAN (N. Mex. 1)	Jack Crandall	504
McCLORY (Ill. 12)	Mrs. Barbara H. Ludden	214
McCLOSKEY (Calif. 11)	Robin Schmidt	62
McCLURE (Idaho 1)	Richard K. Thompson	188
McCOLLISTER (Nebr. 2)	Ronald C. Romans	456
McCORMACK (Wash. 4)	Ragnar F. Nowakowski	864
McCULLOCH (Ohio 4)	(none given)	619
McDADE (Pa. 10)	Francis E. O'Gorman	696
McDONALD (Mich. 19)	Laurence F. Fitzgerald	395
McEWEN (N.Y. 31)	John E. Mellon	565
McFALL (Calif. 15)	Raymond F. Barnes	69
McKAY (Utah 1)	Stan A. Taylor	826
McKEVITT (Colo. 1)	Edward A. Simons	115
McKINNEY (Conn. 4)	(none given)	130
McMILLAN (S.C. 6)	Major McGee	746
MACDONALD (Mass. 7)	Harry M. Shooshan III	351
MADDEN (Ind. 1)	Virginia P. Turner	239
MAHON (Tex. 19)	(none given)	813
MAILLIARD (Calif. 6)	(none given)	52
MANN (S.C. 4)	(none given)	743
MARTIN (Nebr. 3)	Jack Odgaard	458
MATHIAS (Calif. 18)	James Lake	74
MATHIS (Ga. 2)	John W. Ellis	165
MATSUNAGA (Hawaii 1)	Mrs. Cherry Katayama	179
MAYNE (Iowa 6)	Jack W. Watson	268
MAZZOLI (Ky. 3)	Robert J. Baughman	289
MEEDS (Wash. 2)	Leonard W. Saari	861
MELCHER (Mont. 2)	Benton J. Stong	449
METCALFE (Ill. 1)	Lawrence P. Redmond	195
MICHEL (Ill. 18)	Ralph Vinovich	224
MIKVA (Ill. 2)	Eugenie Ermoyan	197
MILLER (Calif. 8)	John A. Doyle	56
MILLER (Ohio 10)	Robert A. Reintsema	628
MILLS (Md. 1)	James Glover	324
MILLS (Ark. 2)	Gene Goss	35
MINISH (N.J. 11)	Margaret M. Sullivan	491
MINK (Hawaii 2)	Oscar Johnson	179
MINSHALL (Ohio 23)	(none given)	650
MITCHELL (Md. 7)	George Minor	334
MIZELL (N.C. 5)	Willard Phillips	593
MOLLOHAN (W. Va. 1)	Frances J. Munsey	875
MONAGAN (Conn. 5)	Joseph P. Donahue	131

CONGRESSMAN	Administrative Assistant	Page
REUSS (Wis. 5)	Donald L. Robinson	894
RHODES (Ariz. 1)	Alma A. Alkire	25
RIEGLE (Mich. 7)	Carl W. Blake	374
ROBERTS (Tex. 4)	(none given)	786
ROBINSON (Va. 7)	Chris Mathisen	848
ROBISON (N.Y. 33)	Charles O. Ingraham	568
RODINO (N.J. 10)	Merle Baumgart	489
ROE (N.J. 8)	(none given)	485
ROGERS (Fla. 9)	John A. Darlson	154
RONCALIO (Wyo. AL)	Mike Vinich	905
ROONEY (N.Y. 14)	Mrs. Jenalee D. Nivens	534
ROONEY (Pa. 15)	Ray A. Huber	704
ROSENTHAL (N.Y. 8)	Mary W. Davis	524
ROSTENKOWSKI (Ill. 8)	James C. Healey, Jr.	207
ROUSH (Ind. 4)	Thomas E. Coler	244
ROUSSELOT (Calif. 24)	H. Donald Harper	85
ROY (Kans. 2)	Paul Pendergast	276
ROYBAL (Calif. 30)	(none given)	95
RUNNELS (N. Mex. 2)	Richard D. Hapke	506
RUPPE (Mich. 11)	Ray B. Chambers	381
RUTH (N.C. 8)	J. B. Thayn	598
RYAN (N.Y. 20)	Erika Teutsch	546
ST GERMAIN (R.I. 1)	Joseph Scanlon	730
SANDMAN (N.J. 2)	Mrs. Dorothy Vagnozzi	476
SARBANES (Md. 4)	Frederick R. Millhiser	329
SATTERFIELD (Va. 3)	John D. Taylor	841
SAYLOR (Pa. 22)	O. Ann Dunbar	716
SCHERLE (Iowa 7)	Cal Hultman	269
SCHEUER (N.Y. 22)	David M. Cohen	549
SCHMITZ (Calif. 35)	Robert A. Geier	104
SCHNEEBELI (Pa. 17)	(none given)	708
SCHWENGEL (Iowa 1)	Allan Schimmel	260
SCOTT (Va. 8)	Henry B. Sweitzer	850
SEBELIUS (Kans. 1)	C. Patrick Roberts	274
SEIBERLING (Ohio 14)	Donald W. Mansfield	635
SHIPLEY (Ill. 23)	Goldie M. Eckl	231
SHOUP (Mont. 1)	Dr. Brad Hainsworth	447
SHRIVER (Kans. 4)	Lester Rosen	279
SIKES (Fla. 1)	Alma D. Butler	142
SISK (Calif. 16)	Anthony L. Coelho	71
SKUBITZ (Kans. 5)	(none given)	281
SLACK (W. Va. 3)	Paul H. Becker	879
SMITH (Calif. 20)	Mrs. Alice K. Andersen	78
SMITH (Iowa 5)	(none given)	266
SMITH (N.Y. 40)	Russel A. Rourke	579
SNYDER (Ky. 4)	William E. Tanner	290
SPENCE (S.C. 2)	Al Cook	739
SPRINGER (Ill. 22)	(none given)	230

CONGRESSMAN	Administrative Assistant	Page
STAGGERS (W. Va. 2)	Marguerite Furfari	877
STANTON, J.V. (Ohio 20)	(none given)	645
STANTON, J.W. (Ohio 11)	Shirlee Enders McGloon	630
STEED (Okla. 4)	Truman Richardson	663
STEELE (Conn. 2)	Russ Evans	127
STEIGER (Ariz. 3)	Paul G. Rosenblatt	28
STEIGER (Wis. 6)	Maureen Drummy	896
STEPHENS (Ga. 10)	D. Mayne Elder	178
STOKES (Ohio 21)	Owen Heggs	647
STRATTON (N.Y. 29)	Bill B. Holt	561
STUBBLEFIELD (Ky. 1)	Mrs. Marty Harding	286
STUCKEY (Ga. 8)	Wallace L. Jernigan	175
SULLIVAN (Mo. 3)	Irene M. Peterson	432
SYMINGTON (Mo. 2)	Charles G. Houghton III	430
TALCOTT (Calif. 12)	William J. MacNelis	64
TAYLOR (N.C. 11)	Luther W. Shaw	603
TEAGUE (Calif. 13)	Montgomery K. Winkler	65
TEAGUE (Tex. 6)	George W. Fisher	790
TERRY (N.Y. 34)	Frederic N. Smith	570
THOMPSON (Ga. 5)	Richard A. Ashworth	170
THOMPSON (N.J. 4)	William T. Deitz	479
THOMSON (Wis. 3)	Jean W. Gilligan	891
THONE (Nebr. 1)	(none given)	455
TIERNAN (R.I. 2)	William Hagan II	731
UDALL (Ariz. 2)	Roger K. Lewis	27
ULLMAN (Oreg. 2)	Don Barney	673
VAN DEERLIN (Calif. 37)	Siegmund W. Smith	108
VANDER JAGT (Mich. 9)	Bernard Nagelvoort	377
VANIK (Ohio 22)	Mark E. Talisman	649
VEYSEY (Calif. 38)	John A. Tucker, Jr.	109
VIGORITO (Pa. 24)	(none given)	719
WAGGONNER (La. 4)	David Kent	306
WALDIE (Calif. 14)	(none given)	67
WAMPLER (Va. 9)	J. Ray Dotson	852
WARE (Pa. 9)	Sallie K. Weaver	695
WATTS (Ky. 6)	Cora Bane	294
WHALEN (Ohio 3)	Alfred Swift Frank, Jr.	618
WHALLEY (Pa. 12)	(none given)	699
WHITE (Tex. 16)	Conrey Bryson	808
WHITEHURST (Va. 2)	R. Burnett Thompson	840
WHITTEN (Miss. 2)	Ann T. Watson	418
WIDNALL (N.J. 7)	(none given)	484
WIGGINS (Calif. 25)	Patrick Rowland	86
WILLIAMS (Pa. 7)	Robert Ryan Siegrist	692
WILSON, BOB (Calif. 36)	Paul Tsompanas	106
WILSON, C.H. (Calif. 31)	(none given)	97
WINN (Kans. 3)	(none given)	277
WOLFF (N.Y. 3)	Howard G. Paster	516